Ear	Radiology	Path/Lab
69000–69990	70010–79999	80048–89399

Medicine	Appendices	Index
90281–99569		

Category III

Fill in any of the blank tabs to mark the codes you use most often.

Tab Placement Instructions

Peel the first tab (Evaluation & Mgmt) from the backing and start at the top of the page of the first section (Evaluation & Management). Fold the tab in half and place it in the upper right-hand corner at the beginning of the Evaluation and Management Section.

The next tab (Anesthesia) should be placed immediately under the first tab at the beginning of the Anesthesia Section.

Place all subsequent tabs in the same manner.

Your book is now tabbed with all the major sections of CPT, enabling fast access to the codes you use.

Evaluation & Mgmt 99201–99499	Anesthesia 00100–01999	Integumentary 10021–19499	Musculoskeletal 20000–29909

Evaluation & Mgmt 99201–99499	Anesthesia 00100–01999	Integumentary 10021–19499	Musculoskeletal 20000–29909

Respiratory 30000–32999	Cardiovascular 33010–37799	Lymphatic 38100–38999	Mediastinum 39000–39599

Respiratory 30000–32999	Cardiovascular 33010–37799	Lymphatic 38100–38999	Mediastinum 39000–39599

Digestive System 40490–49999	Urinary 50010–53899	Male Genital 54000–55899	Intersex Surgery 55970–55980

Digestive System 40490–49999	Urinary 50010–53899	Male Genital 54000–55899	Intersex Surgery 55970–55980

Female Genital 56405–58999	Maternity 59000–59899	Endocrine/Nervous 60000–64999	Eye 65091–68899

Female Genital 56405–58999	Maternity 59000–59899	Endocrine/Nervous 60000–64999	Eye 65091–68899

American Medical Association

Physicians dedicated to the health of America

Current Procedural Terminology

cpt® 2002

Caryn A. Anderson, RHIT, CCS
Michael Beebe, MS
Joyce A. Dalton
Catherine Duffy, RHIT, BS
Desiree Evans, AD
Rejina L. Glenn

DeHandro Hayden, BS
Grace M. Kotowicz, RN, BS
Elizabeth Lumakovska, RHIT, BS
Marie L. Mindeman, RHIT
Karen E. O'Hara, BS, CCS-P
Mary R. O'Heron, RHIA, CCS-P

Dan Reyes, BA
Desiree Rozell, MPA
Lianne Stancik, RHIT
Ada Walker
Arletrice A. Watkins, RHIA
Joan Zacharias, RHIT

AMA press

Standard ISBN: 1-57947-220-6
ISSN: 0276-8283

For questions regarding the use of CPT codes, please contact the American Medical Association CPT
Information and Education Services at 800 634-6922.

To purchase additional CPT products, contact the American Medical Association Customer Service
at 800 621-8335.

To request a license for distribution of products containing or reprinting CPT, please see our Web site
at *www.ama-assn.org/cpt* or contact the American Medical Association CPT Intellectual Property
Services, 515 N. State Street, Chicago, Illinois 60610, 312 464-5022.

AC25:0098-01:10/01

Foreword

Current Procedural Terminology, Fourth Edition (*CPT*®) is a listing of descriptive terms and identifying codes for reporting medical services and procedures performed by physicians. The purpose of the terminology is to provide a uniform language that will accurately describe medical, surgical, and diagnostic services, and will thereby provide an effective means for reliable nationwide communication among physicians, patients, and third parties. *CPT 2002* is the most recent revision of a work that first appeared in 1966.

CPT descriptive terms and identifying codes currently serve a wide variety of important functions in the field of medical nomenclature. CPT is the most widely accepted nomenclature for the reporting of physician procedures and services under government and private health insurance programs. CPT is also useful for administrative management purposes such as claims processing and for the development of guidelines for medical care review. The uniform language is likewise applicable to medical education and research by providing a useful basis for local, regional, and national utilization comparisons.

The changes that appear in this revision have been prepared by the CPT Editorial Panel with the assistance of physicians representing all specialties of medicine, and with important contributions from many third party payors and governmental agencies.

The American Medical Association trusts that this revision will continue the usefulness of its predecessors in identifying, describing, and coding medical, surgical, and diagnostic services.

Acknowledgements

Publication of each annual *CPT* represents many challenges and opportunities. From reconciling the many differences of opinion about the best way to describe a procedure, to last details on the placement of a semicolon, many individuals and organizations devote their energies and expertise to the preparation of this revision.

The editorial staff wishes to express sincere thanks to the many national medical specialty societies, health insurance organizations and agencies, and to the many individual physicians and other health professionals who have made contributions.

Thanks are due to Robert A. Musacchio, PhD, Sr VP, American Medical Association; Claudia Bonnell, Blue Cross and Blue Shield Association; Nelly Leon-Chisen, American Hospital Association; Thomas Musco, Health Insurance Association of America; and Sue Prophet, RHIA, American Health Information Management Association, for their invaluable assistance in enhancing CPT.

And finally, our gratitude to AMA Press of the American Medical Association for their assistance in producing the books, diskettes, magnetic tapes, and CD-ROMs that contain CPT, including Rosalyn Carlton, Senior Production Coordinator, Erin Kalitowski, Marketing Manager, Pat Lee, Technical Developmental Editor, Jean Roberts, Director, Production and Manufacturing, Elise Schumacher, Senior Acquisition Editor, Ronnie Summers, Senior Print Coordinator, Boon Ai Tan, Senior Production Coordinator, and Todd Feinstein, Application Developer.

AMA CPT Editorial Panel

Chair
Tracy R. Gordy, MD*
Vice-Chair
Karen R. Borman, MD*
James Adamson, Jr, MD**
Simon Philip Cohn, MD
Lee D. Eisenberg, MD
Helene M. Fearon, PT
Laurie Feinberg, MD
Blair C. Filler, MD
Diller B. Groff, MD
Samuel Hassenbusch, MD
Lee Harold Hilborne, MD
Glenn D. Littenberg, MD
Allen J. McBride, MD*
Gerald E. Silverstein, MD*
Stanley W. Stead, MD
William T. Thorwarth, MD
James A. Zalla, MD
Secretary
Michael Beebe, MS
* Member of the CPT Executive Committee
** New Panel Member August 2001

AMA CPT Advisory Committee

Donald W. Aaronson, MD
American Academy of Allergy, Asthma and Immunology
H. Christopher Alexander III, MD
American College of Physicians-American Society of Internal Medicine
Freda Arlow, MD
American College of Gastroenterology
Michael Ashcraft, MD
The Endocrine Society
C. Robert Baisden, MD
Beverly P. Nelson, MD*
United States and Canadian Academy of Pathology
Stephen N. Bauer, MD
College of American Pathologists
David I. Berland, MD
American Academy of Child and Adolescent Psychiatry
Robert L. Bree, MD*
*Society of Radiologists in Ultrasound****
Joel Brill, MD
American Gastroenterological Association
Boyd Buser, DO
American Osteopathic Association
Neil A. Busis, MD
American Association of Electrodiagnostic Medicine
Jeffery B. Carter, MD, DMD
American Dental Association
Jean M. Colandrea, MD
David C. Hoak, MD*
American Society of Cytopathology
Mark V. Connelly, MD
American Academy of Facial Plastic and Reconstructive Surgery

John P. Crow, MD
American Pediatric Surgical Association
David O. Davis, MD
Radiology Society of North America
Robin K. Dore, MD
David A. Cooley MD*
American College of Rheumatology
Gary S. Dorfman, MD
Society of Cardiovascular and Interventional Radiology
Charles Drueck III, MD*
*American Society of General Surgeons****
Philip N. Eskew Jr, MD
American College of Obstetricians and Gynecologists
Tom Faciszewski, MD
Francis P. Lagattuta, MD*
North American Spine Society
Morton H. Field, MD
American Association of Clinical Endocrinologists
Robert H. Haralson III, MD
American Orthopaedic Association
David B. Flannery, MD
American College of Medical Genetics
P. Franco, MD
American Sleep Disorders Association
Gary F. Gates, MD
American College of Nuclear Physicians
Bob W. Gayler, MD
Association of University Radiologists
Elizabeth Genovese, MD*
American College of Occupational and Environmental Medicine
Dean Gesme, MD
American Society of Clinical Oncology
Thomas G. Goergen, MD
Jonathan Breslau, MD**
American Roentgen Ray Society
Arvind K. Goyal, MD, MPH
American Association of Public Health Physicians
Gary N. Gross, MD
American College of Allergy, Asthma and Immunology
Richard J. Hamburger, MD
Renal Physicians Association
Curtis Hawkins, MD
Society for Investigative Dermatology
Charles A. Hawtrey, MD
Jeffrey A. Dann, MD*
American Urological Association, Inc.
George A. Hill, MD
John T. Queenan, MD*
American Society for Reproductive Medicine
Raymond V. Janevicius, MD
American Society of Plastic and Reconstructive Surgeons
Blake A. Johnson, MD
Robert A. Murray, MD*
American Society of Neuroradiology

AMA Health Care Professionals Advisory Committee (HCPAC)

Tracy R. Gordy, MD, Co-Chair
AMA CPT Editorial Panel

Helene Fearon, PT, Co-Chair

Linda Botten, OTR, CHT
American Occupational Therapy Association

Patrick J. Cafferty, PA-C
American Academy of Physician Assistants

Rhea Cohn, PT
American Physical Therapy Association

R. Wayne Holland, EdD
American Speech-Language Hearing Association

K. Michael Larkin, OD (In Memoriam)
American Optometric Association

Craig S. Little, DC
American Chiropractic Association

Antonio Puente, PhD
American Psychological Association

Robert D. Sowell, DPM
American Podiatric Medical Association

Nelda Spyres, ACSW, LCSW
National Association of Social Workers

Ann M. Thrailkill, RN
American Nurses Association

Jane V. White, PhD, RD, FADA*
*American Dietetic Association**
*New Advisor June 2001
**New Specialty June 2001

Notes

Contents

Introduction . . . .**x**

   Section Numbers and Their Sequences x

   Instructions for Use of CPT x

      Format of the Terminology .x

      Requests to Update CPT .x

      Guidelines xi

      Starred Procedures xi

      Modifiers xi

      Unlisted Procedure or Service xii

      Special Report xii

      Code Changes xii

      Alphabetical Reference Index xii

      CPT in Electronic Formats xii

**Evaluation and Management (E/M) Services
Guidelines** **1**

Evaluation and Management **9**

   Office or Other Outpatient Services 9

   Hospital Observation Services 10

   Hospital Inpatient Services 11

   Consultations 14

   Emergency Department Services 17

   ▶Patient Transport . . . . .18◀

   Critical Care Services 18

   Neonatal Intensive Care .20

   Nursing Facility Services .21

   Domiciliary, Rest Home (eg, Boarding Home), or Custodial
   Care Services 23

   Home Services 24

   Prolonged Services 25

   Case Management Services 27

   Care Plan Oversight Services 27

   Preventive Medicine Services 28

   Newborn Care 29

   Special Evaluation and Management Services 29

   Other Evaluation and Management Services 30

Anesthesia Guidelines **31**

Anesthesia **33**

   Head 33

   Neck 33

   Thorax (Chest Wall and Shoulder Girdle) 33

   Intrathoracic 34

   Spine and Spinal Cord 34

   Upper Abdomen 34

   Lower Abdomen 34

   Perineum 35

   Pelvis (Except Hip) 35

   Upper Leg (Except Knee) 36

   Knee and Popliteal Area .36

   Lower Leg (Below Knee, Includes Ankle and Foot) 36

   Shoulder and Axilla 37

   Upper Arm and Elbow 37

   Forearm, Wrist, and Hand 37

   Radiological Procedures .37

   Burn Excisions or Debridement 38

   ▶Obstetric . . . . .38◀

   Other Procedures 38

Surgery Guidelines **39**

Surgery **45**

   ▶General . . . . .45◀

   Integumentary System 45

   Musculoskeletal System .57

   Respiratory System 99

   Cardiovascular System .107

   Hemic and Lymphatic Systems 124

   Mediastinum and Diaphragm 126

   Digestive System 127

   Urinary System 149

   Male Genital System 159

   Intersex Surgery 163

   Female Genital System .165

   Maternity Care and Delivery 170

   Endocrine System 173

   Nervous System 175

   Eye and Ocular Adnexa .189

Auditory System 199

Operating Microscope 201

Radiology Guidelines (Including Nuclear Medicine and Diagnostic Ultrasound) 203

Radiology 205

Diagnostic Radiology (Diagnostic Imaging) 205

Diagnostic Ultrasound 219

Radiation Oncology 221

Nuclear Medicine 225

Pathology and Laboratory Guidelines 231

Pathology and Laboratory 233

Organ or Disease Oriented Panels 233

Drug Testing 235

Therapeutic Drug Assays 235

Evocative/Suppression Testing 236

Consultations (Clinical Pathology) 237

Urinalysis 237

Chemistry 238

Hematology and Coagulation .250

Immunology 253

Transfusion Medicine 259

Microbiology 260

Anatomic Pathology 263

Cytopathology 264

Cytogenetic Studies 265

Surgical Pathology 265

Transcutaneous Procedures 269

Other Procedures 269

Medicine Guidelines 271

Medicine 273

Immune Globulins 273

Immunization Administration for Vaccines/Toxoids 273

Vaccines, Toxoids 274

Therapeutic or Diagnostic Infusions (Excludes Chemotherapy) 275

Therapeutic, Prophylactic or Diagnostic Injections 276

Psychiatry 276

Biofeedback 278

Dialysis 278

Gastroenterology 280

Ophthalmology 280

Special Otorhinolaryngologic Services 284

Cardiovascular 285

Non-Invasive Vascular Diagnostic Studies 292

Pulmonary 293

Allergy and Clinical Immunology 294

►Endocrinology . . . . .296◄

Neurology and Neuromuscular Procedures 296

Central Nervous System Assessments/Tests 299

►Health and Behavior Assessment/Intervention . . . . .300◄

Chemotherapy Administration .300

Photodynamic Therapy 301

Special Dermatological Procedures 301

Physical Medicine and Rehabilitation 302

Medical Nutrition Therapy 304

Osteopathic Manipulative Treatment 304

Chiropractic Manipulative Treatment 304

Special Services, Procedures and Reports 304

Qualifying Circumstances for Anesthesia 305

Sedation With or Without Analgesia (Conscious Sedation) 306

Other Services and Procedures 306

►Home Health Procedures/Services . . . . .306◄

►Home Infusion Procedures .307◄

Category III Codes 309

Appendix A—Modifiers 311

Appendix B—Summary of Additions, Deletions, and Revisions 316

Appendix C—Update to Short Descriptors 323

Appendix D—Clinical Examples 327

Appendix E—Summary of CPT Add-on Codes 347

Appendix F—Summary of CPT Codes Exempt from Modifier '-51' 348

Index 349

Introduction

Current Procedural Terminology, Fourth Edition (*CPT®*) is a systematic listing and coding of procedures and services performed by physicians. Each procedure or service is identified with a five-digit code. The use of CPT codes simplifies the reporting of services. With this coding and recording system, the procedure or service rendered by the physician is accurately identified.

Inclusion of a descriptor and its associated specific five-digit identifying code number in *CPT* is generally based upon the procedure being consistent with contemporary medical practice and being performed by many physicians in clinical practice in multiple locations. Inclusion in *CPT* does not represent endorsement by the American Medical Association of any particular diagnostic or therapeutic procedure. Inclusion or exclusion of a procedure does not imply any health insurance coverage or reimbursement policy.

The main body of the material is listed in six sections. Within each section are subsections with anatomic, procedural, condition, or descriptor subheadings. The procedures and services with their identifying codes are presented in numeric order with one exception—the entire **Evaluation and Management** section (99201-99499) has been placed at the beginning of the listed procedures. These items are used by most physicians in reporting a significant portion of their services. The **Medicine** (procedures) section now follows **Pathology and Laboratory.**

Section Numbers and Their Sequences

Evaluation and Management . . . . .99201 to 99499

Anesthesiology . . . . .00100 to 01999, 99100 to 99140

Surgery . . . . .10021 to 69990

Radiology (Including Nuclear Medicine and Diagnostic Ultrasound) . . . . .70010 to 79999

Pathology and Laboratory . . . . .80048 to 89399

Medicine (except Anesthesiology) . . .90281 to 99199, 99500-99569

The first and last code numbers and the subsection name of the items appear at the top of each page (eg, "11000-11313 Surgery/Integumentary System"). The continuous pagination of *CPT* is found on the lower, outer margin of each page along with the section name.

Instructions for Use of CPT

Select the name of the procedure or service that accurately identifies the service performed. ►Do not select a CPT code that merely approximates the service provided. If no such procedure or service exists, then report the service using the appropriate unlisted procedure or service code.◄ In surgery, it may be an operation; in medicine, a diagnostic or therapeutic procedure; in radiology, a radiograph. Other additional procedures performed or pertinent special services are also listed. When necessary, any modifying or extenuating circumstances are added. Any service or procedure should be adequately documented in the medical record.

It is important to recognize that the listing of a service or procedure and its code number in a specific section of this book does not restrict its use to a specific specialty group. Any procedure or service in any section of this book may be used to designate the services rendered by any qualified physician ►or other qualified health care professional.◄

Format of the Terminology

CPT procedure terminology has been developed as stand-alone descriptions of medical procedures. However, some of the procedures in *CPT* are not printed in their entirety but refer back to a common portion of the procedure listed in a preceding entry. This is evident when an entry is followed by one or more indentations. This is done in an effort to conserve space.

Example

25100   Arthrotomy, wrist joint; with biopsy

25105   with synovectomy

Note that the common part of code 25100 (that part before the semicolon) should be considered part of code 25105. Therefore the full procedure represented by code 25105 should read:

25105   Arthrotomy, wrist joint; for synovectomy

Requests to Update CPT

The effectiveness of *Current Procedural Terminology* (*CPT™*) is dependent upon constant updating to reflect changes in medical practice. This can only be accomplished through the interest and timely suggestions of practicing physicians, medical specialty societies, state medical associations, and other organizations and agencies. Accordingly, the American Medical Association welcomes correspondence, inquiries, and suggestions concerning old and new procedures, as well as other matters such as codes and indices.

For suggestions concerning the introduction of new procedures, or the coding, deleting, or revising of procedures contained in *CPT 2002*, correspondence requesting an application for coding change should be directed to:

CPT Editorial Research & Development
American Medical Association
515 North State Street
Chicago, Illinois 60610

▶Coding change request forms to introduce new procedures or to delete or revise procedures already in CPT are also available at the AMA/CPT website http://www.ama-assn.org/ama/pub/article/3866-3846.html.◀

All proposed additions to, or modifications of, *CPT 2002* will be by decision of the CPT Editorial Panel after consultation with appropriate medical specialty societies.

Guidelines

Specific "Guidelines" are presented at the beginning of each of the six sections. These guidelines define items that are necessary to appropriately interpret and report the procedures and services contained in that section. For example, in the **Medicine** section, specific instructions are provided for handling unlisted services or procedures, special reports, and supplies and materials provided. Guidelines also provide explanations regarding terms that apply only to a particular section. For instance, **Surgery Guidelines** provides an explanation of the use of the star, while in **Radiology**, the unique term, "radiological supervision and interpretation" is defined.

Starred Procedures

The star "*" is used to identify certain surgical procedures. A description of this reporting mechanism will be found in the **Surgery Guidelines**.

Modifiers

A modifier provides the means by which the reporting physician can indicate that a service or procedure that has been performed has been altered by some specific circumstance but not changed in its definition or code. The judicious application of modifiers obviates the necessity for separate procedure listings that may describe the modifying circumstance. Modifiers may be used to indicate to the recipient of a report that:

- A service or procedure has both a professional and technical component.

- A service or procedure was performed by more than one physician and/or in more than one location.

- A service or procedure has been increased or reduced.

- Only part of a service was performed.

- An adjunctive service was performed.

- A bilateral procedure was performed.

- A service or procedure was provided more than once.

- Unusual events occurred.

Example

A physician providing diagnostic or therapeutic radiology services, ultrasound or nuclear medicine services in a hospital would use either modifier '-26' or 09926 to report the professional component.

73090-26 = Professional component only for an x-ray of the forearm

or

73090 AND 09926 = Professional component only for an x-ray of the forearm

Example

Two surgeons may be required to manage a specific surgical problem. When two surgeons work together as primary surgeons performing distinct part(s) of a procedure, each surgeon should report his/her distinct operative work by adding the modifier '-62' to the procedure code ▶and any associated code(s) for that procedure as long as both surgeons continue to work together as primary surgeons◀. Each surgeon should report the co-surgery once using the same procedure code. The modifier '-62' or the alternative modifier five-digit code 09962 would be applicable. For instance, a neurological surgeon and an otolaryngologist are working as co-surgeons in performing transphenoidal excision of a pituitary neoplasm.

61548-62 = Hypophysectomy or excision of pituitary tumor, transnasal or transseptal approach, nonstereotactic + two surgeons modifier

or

61548 AND 09962 = Hypophysectomy or excision of pituitary tumor, transnasal or transseptal approach, nonstereotactic + two surgeons modifier

AND the second surgeon would report:

61548-62 = Hypophysectomy or excision of pituitary tumor, transnasal or transseptal approach, nonstereotactic + two surgeons modifier

or

61548 AND 09962 = Hypophysectomy or excision of pituitary tumor, transnasal or transseptal approach, nonstereotactic + two surgeons modifier

If additional procedure(s) (including add-on procedure(s)) are performed during the same surgical session, separate code(s) may ▶also◀ be reported with the modifier '-62' added. ▶Modifier code 09962 may be used as an alternative to modifier '-62'.◀ **Note:** If a co-surgeon acts as an assistant in the performance of additional procedure(s) during the same surgical session, those services may be reported using separate procedure code(s) with the modifier '-80' or modifier '-82' added, as appropriate. A complete listing of modifiers is found in Appendix A.

Unlisted Procedure or Service

It is recognized that there may be services or procedures performed by physicians that are not found in *CPT*. Therefore, a number of specific code numbers have been designated for reporting unlisted procedures. When an unlisted procedure number is used, the service or procedure should be described. Each of these unlisted procedural code numbers (with the appropriate accompanying topical entry) relates to a specific section of the book and is presented in the Guidelines of that section.

Special Report

A service that is rarely provided, unusual, variable, or new may require a special report in determining medical appropriateness of the service. Pertinent information should include an adequate definition or description of the nature, extent, and need for the procedure; and the time, effort, and equipment necessary to provide the service. Additional items which may be included are: complexity of symptoms, final diagnosis, pertinent physical findings, diagnostic and therapeutic procedures, concurrent problems, and follow-up care.

Code Changes

A summary listing of additions, deletions, and revisions applicable to *CPT 2002* is found in Appendix B. New procedure numbers added to *CPT* are identified throughout the text with the symbol "●" placed before the code number. In instances where a code revision has resulted in a substantially altered procedure descriptor, the symbol "▲" is placed before the code number. The symbols "► ◄" are used to indicate new and revised text other than the procedure descriptors. CPT add-on codes are annotated by a "✚" symbol and are listed in **Appendix E**. The "⊘" symbol is used to identify codes that are exempt from the use of modifier '-51', but have not been designated as CPT add-on procedures/services. A list of codes exempt from modifier '-51' usage is included in **Appendix F**.

Alphabetical Reference Index

A new, expanded alphabetical index is found in the back of the book. It includes listings by procedure and anatomic site. Procedures and services commonly known by their eponyms or other designations are also included.

CPT in Electronic Formats

CPT 2002 procedure codes and descriptors are also available on magnetic computer tapes, diskettes, and CD-ROM in various formats. For more information call 800 621-8335.

Visit CPT on the AMA Website
http://www.ama-assn.org/cpt

Evaluation and Management (E/M) Services Guidelines

In addition to the information presented in the **Introduction,** several other items unique to this section are defined or identified here.

Classification of Evaluation and Management (E/M) Services

The E/M section is divided into broad categories such as office visits, hospital visits, and consultations. Most of the categories are further divided into two or more subcategories of E/M services. For example, there are two subcategories of office visits (new patient and established patient) and there are two subcategories of hospital visits (initial and subsequent). The subcategories of E/M services are further classified into levels of E/M services that are identified by specific codes. This classification is important because the nature of physician work varies by type of service, place of service, and the patient's status.

The basic format of the levels of E/M services is the same for most categories. First, a unique code number is listed. Second, the place and/or type of service is specified, eg, office consultation. Third, the content of the service is defined, eg, comprehensive history and comprehensive examination. (See "Levels of E/M Services," page 2, for details on the content of E/M services.) Fourth, the nature of the presenting problem(s) usually associated with a given level is described. Fifth, the time typically required to provide the service is specified. (A detailed discussion of time is provided on page 3.)

Definitions of Commonly Used Terms

Certain key words and phrases are used throughout the E/M section. The following definitions are intended to reduce the potential for differing interpretations and to increase the consistency of reporting by physicians in differing specialties.

New and Established Patient

Solely for the purposes of distinguishing between new and established patients, **professional services** are those face-to-face services rendered by a physician and reported by a specific CPT code(s). A new patient is one who has not received any professional services from the physician or another physician of the same specialty who belongs to the same group practice, within the past three years.

An established patient is one who has received professional services from the physician or another physician of the same specialty who belongs to the same group practice, within the past three years.

In the instance where a physician is on call for or covering for another physician, the patient's encounter will be classified as it would have been by the physician who is not available.

No distinction is made between new and established patients in the emergency department. E/M services in the emergency department category may be reported for any new or established patient who presents for treatment in the emergency department.

Chief Complaint

A concise statement describing the symptom, problem, condition, diagnosis or other factor that is the reason for the encounter, usually stated in the patient's words.

Concurrent Care

Concurrent care is the provision of similar services, eg, hospital visits, to the same patient by more than one physician on the same day. When concurrent care is provided, no special reporting is required. Modifier '-75' has been deleted.

Counseling

Counseling is a discussion with a patient and/or family concerning one or more of the following areas:

- diagnostic results, impressions, and/or recommended diagnostic studies;
- prognosis;
- risks and benefits of management (treatment) options;
- instructions for management (treatment) and/or follow-up;

- importance of compliance with chosen management (treatment) options;
- risk factor reduction; and
- patient and family education.

(For psychotherapy, see 90804-90857)

Family History

A review of medical events in the patient's family that includes significant information about:

- the health status or cause of death of parents, siblings, and children;
- specific diseases related to problems identified in the Chief Complaint or History of the Present Illness, and/or System Review;
- diseases of family members which may be hereditary or place the patient at risk.

History of Present Illness

A chronological description of the development of the patient's present illness from the first sign and/or symptom to the present. This includes a description of location, quality, severity, timing, context, modifying factors and associated signs and symptoms significantly related to the presenting problem(s).

Levels of E/M Services

Within each category or subcategory of E/M service, there are three to five levels of E/M services available for reporting purposes. Levels of E/M services are **not** interchangeable among the different categories or subcategories of service. For example, the first level of E/M services in the subcategory of office visit, new patient, does not have the same definition as the first level of E/M services in the subcategory of office visit, established patient.

The levels of E/M services include examinations, evaluations, treatments, conferences with or concerning patients, preventive pediatric and adult health supervision, and similar medical services, such as the determination of the need and/or location for appropriate care. Medical screening includes the history, examination, and medical decision making required to determine the need and/or location for appropriate care and treatment of the patient (eg, office and other outpatient setting, emergency department, nursing facility, etc.). The levels of E/M services encompass the wide variations in skill, effort, time, responsibility and medical knowledge required for the prevention or diagnosis and treatment of illness or injury and the promotion of optimal health. Each level of E/M services may be used by all physicians.

The descriptors for the levels of E/M services recognize seven components, six of which are used in defining the levels of E/M services. These components are:

- history;
- examination;

- medical decision making;
- counseling;
- coordination of care;
- nature of presenting problem; and
- time.

The first three of these components (history, examination, and medical decision making) are considered the **key** components in selecting a level of E/M services. (See "Determine the Extent of History Obtained," page 5.)

The next three components (counseling, coordination of care, and the nature of the presenting problem) are considered **contributory** factors in the majority of encounters. Although the first two of these contributory factors are important E/M services, it is not required that these services be provided at every patient encounter.

Coordination of care with other providers or agencies without a patient encounter on that day is reported using the case management codes.

The final component, time, is discussed in detail (see page 3).

Any specifically identifiable procedure (ie, identified with a specific CPT code) performed on or subsequent to the date of initial or subsequent "E/M Services" should be reported separately.

The actual performance and/or interpretation of diagnostic tests/studies ordered during a patient encounter are not included in the levels of E/M services. Physician performance of diagnostic tests/studies for which specific CPT codes are available may be reported separately, in addition to the appropriate E/M code. The physician's interpretation of the results of diagnostic tests/studies (ie, professional component) with preparation of a separate distinctly identifiable signed written report may also be reported separately, using the appropriate CPT code with the modifier '-26' appended.

The physician may need to indicate that on the day a procedure or service identified by a CPT code was performed, the patient's condition required a significant separately identifiable E/M service above and beyond other services provided or beyond the usual preservice and postservice care associated with the procedure that was performed. The E/M service may be caused or prompted by the symptoms or condition for which the procedure and/or service was provided. This circumstance may be reported by adding the modifier '-25' to the appropriate level of E/M service. As such, different diagnoses are not required for reporting of the procedure and the E/M services on the same date.

Nature of Presenting Problem

A presenting problem is a disease, condition, illness, injury, symptom, sign, finding, complaint, or other reason for encounter, with or without a diagnosis being established at the time of the encounter. The E/M codes recognize five types of presenting problems that are defined as follows:

Minimal: A problem that may not require the presence of the physician, but service is provided under the physician's supervision.

Self-limited or minor: A problem that runs a definite and prescribed course, is transient in nature, and is not likely to permanently alter health status OR has a good prognosis with management/compliance.

Low severity: A problem where the risk of morbidity without treatment is low; there is little to no risk of mortality without treatment; full recovery without functional impairment is expected.

Moderate severity: A problem where the risk of morbidity without treatment is moderate; there is moderate risk of mortality without treatment; uncertain prognosis OR increased probability of prolonged functional impairment.

High severity: A problem where the risk of morbidity without treatment is high to extreme; there is a moderate to high risk of mortality without treatment OR high probability of severe, prolonged functional impairment.

Past History

A review of the patient's past experiences with illnesses, injuries, and treatments that includes significant information about:

- prior major illnesses and injuries;
- prior operations;
- prior hospitalizations;
- current medications;
- allergies (eg, drug, food);
- age appropriate immunization status;
- age appropriate feeding/dietary status.

Social History

An age appropriate review of past and current activities that includes significant information about:

- marital status and/or living arrangements;
- current employment;
- occupational history;
- use of drugs, alcohol, and tobacco;
- level of education;
- sexual history;
- other relevant social factors.

System Review (Review of Systems)

An inventory of body systems obtained through a series of questions seeking to identify signs and/or symptoms which the patient may be experiencing or has experienced. For the purposes of CPT the following elements of a system review have been identified:

- Constitutional symptoms (fever, weight loss, etc.)
- Eyes
- Ears, Nose, Mouth, Throat
- Cardiovascular
- Respiratory
- Gastrointestinal
- Genitourinary
- Musculoskeletal
- Integumentary (skin and/or breast)
- Neurological
- Psychiatric
- Endocrine
- Hematologic/Lymphatic
- Allergic/Immunologic

The review of systems helps define the problem, clarify the differential diagnosis, identify needed testing, or serves as baseline data on other systems that might be affected by any possible management options.

Time

The inclusion of time in the definitions of levels of E/M services has been implicit in prior editions of *CPT.* The inclusion of time as an explicit factor beginning in *CPT 1992* is done to assist physicians in selecting the most appropriate level of E/M services. It should be recognized that the specific times expressed in the visit code descriptors are averages, and therefore represent a range of times which may be higher or lower depending on actual clinical circumstances.

Time is **not** a descriptive component for the emergency department levels of E/M services because emergency department services are typically provided on a variable intensity basis, often involving multiple encounters with several patients over an extended period of time. Therefore, it is often difficult for physicians to provide accurate estimates of the time spent face-to-face with the patient.

Studies to establish levels of E/M services employed surveys of practicing physicians to obtain data on the amount of time and work associated with typical E/M services. Since "work" is not easily quantifiable, the codes must rely on other objective, verifiable measures that correlate with physicians' estimates of their "work". It has been demonstrated that physicians' estimations of **intraservice time** (as explained on the next page), both within and across specialties, is a variable that is predictive of the "work" of E/M services. This same research has shown there is a strong relationship between intra-service time and total time for E/M services. Intra-service time, rather than total time, was chosen for inclusion with the codes because of its relative ease of measurement and because of its direct correlation with measurements of the total amount of time and work associated with typical E/M services.

Intra-service times are defined as **face-to-face** time for office and other outpatient visits and as **unit/floor** time for hospital and other inpatient visits. This distinction is necessary because most of the work of typical office visits takes place during the face-to-face time with the patient, while most of the work of typical hospital visits takes place during the time spent on the patient's floor or unit.

Face-to-face time (office and other outpatient visits and office consultations): For coding purposes, face-to-face time for these services is defined as only that time that the physician spends face-to-face with the patient and/or family. This includes the time in which the physician performs such tasks as obtaining a history, performing an examination, and counseling the patient.

Physicians also spend time doing work before or after the face-to-face time with the patient, performing such tasks as reviewing records and tests, arranging for further services, and communicating further with other professionals and the patient through written reports and telephone contact.

This **non-face-to-face** time for office services—also called pre- and post-encounter time—is not included in the time component described in the E/M codes. However, the pre- and post-face-to-face work associated with an encounter was included in calculating the total work of typical services in physician surveys.

Thus, the face-to-face time associated with the services described by any E/M code is a valid proxy for the total work done before, during, and after the visit.

Unit/floor time (hospital observation services, inpatient hospital care, initial and follow-up hospital consultations, nursing facility): For reporting purposes, intra-service time for these services is defined as unit/floor time, which includes the time that the physician is present on the patient's hospital unit and at the bedside rendering services for that patient. This includes the time in which the physician establishes and/or reviews the patient's chart, examines the patient, writes notes and communicates with other professionals and the patient's family.

In the hospital, pre- and post-time includes time spent off the patient's floor performing such tasks as reviewing pathology and radiology findings in another part of the hospital.

This pre- and post-visit time is not included in the time component described in these codes. However, the pre- and post-work performed during the time spent off the floor or unit was included in calculating the total work of typical services in physician surveys.

Thus, the unit/floor time associated with the services described by any code is a valid proxy for the total work done before, during, and after the visit.

Unlisted Service

An E/M service may be provided that is not listed in this section of *CPT.* When reporting such a service, the appropriate "Unlisted" code may be used to indicate the service, identifying it by "Special Report", as discussed in the following paragraph. The "Unlisted Services" and accompanying codes for the E/M section are as follows:

99429   Unlisted preventive medicine service

99499   Unlisted evaluation and management service

99539   Unlisted home visit service or procedure

Special Report

An unlisted service or one that is unusual, variable, or new may require a special report demonstrating the medical appropriateness of the service. Pertinent information should include an adequate definition or description of the nature, extent, and need for the procedure; and the time, effort, and equipment necessary to provide the service. Additional items which may be included are complexity of symptoms, final diagnosis, pertinent physical findings, diagnostic and therapeutic procedures, concurrent problems, and follow-up care.

Clinical Examples

Clinical examples of the codes for E/M services are provided to assist physicians in understanding the meaning of the descriptors and selecting the correct code. The clinical examples are listed in Appendix D. Each example was developed by physicians in the specialties shown.

The same problem, when seen by physicians in different specialties, may involve different amounts of work. Therefore, the appropriate level of encounter should be reported using the descriptors rather than the examples.

The examples have been tested for validity and approved by the CPT Editorial Panel. Physicians were given the examples and asked to assign a code or assess the amount of time and work involved. Only those examples that were rated consistently have been included in Appendix D.

Table 1
Categories and Subcategories of Service

Category/Subcategory	Code Numbers	Category/Subcategory	Code Numbers
Office or Other Outpatient Services		Nursing Facility Discharge Services	99315-99316
New Patient	99201-99205	Domiciliary, Rest Home or	
Established Patient	99211-99215	Custodial Care Services	
Hospital Observation Discharge Services	99217	New Patient	99321-99323
Hospital Observation Services	99218-99220	Established Patient	99331-99333
Hospital Observation or Inpatient Care		Home Services	
Services (Including Admission and		New Patient	99341-99345
Discharge Services)	99234-99236	Established Patient	99347-99350
Hospital Inpatient Services		Prolonged Services	
Initial Hospital Care	99221-99223	With Direct Patient Contact	99354-99357
Subsequent Hospital Care	99231-99233	Without Direct Patient Contact	99358-99359
Hospital Discharge Services	99238-99239	Standby Services	99360
Consultations		Case Management Services	
Office Consultations	99241-99245	Team Conferences	99361-99362
Initial Inpatient Consultations	99251-99255	Telephone Calls	99371-99373
Follow-up Inpatient Consultations	99261-99263	Care Plan Oversight Services	99374-99380
Confirmatory Consultations	99271-99275	Preventive Medicine Services	
Emergency Department Services	99281-99288	New Patient	99381-99387
►Patient Transport◄	99289-99290	Established Patient	99391-99397
Critical Care Services	99291-99292	Individual Counseling	99401-99404
Neonatal Intensive Care	99295-99298	Group Counseling	99411-99412
Nursing Facility Services		Other	99420-99429
Comprehensive Nursing Facility		Newborn Care	99431-99440
Assessments	99301-99303	Special E/M Services	99450-99456
Subsequent Nursing Facility Care	99311-99313	Other E/M Services	99499

Instructions for Selecting a Level of E/M Service

Identify the Category and Subcategory of Service

The categories and subcategories of codes available for reporting E/M services are shown in Table 1.

Review the Reporting Instructions for the Selected Category or Subcategory

Most of the categories and many of the subcategories of service have special guidelines or instructions unique to that category or subcategory. Where these are indicated, eg, "Inpatient Hospital Care," special instructions will be presented preceding the levels of E/M services.

Review the Level of E/M Service Descriptors and Examples in the Selected Category or Subcategory

The descriptors for the levels of E/M services recognize seven components, six of which are used in defining the levels of E/M services. These components are:

- history;
- examination;
- medical decision making;
- counseling;
- coordination of care;
- nature of presenting problem; and
- time.

The first three of these components (ie, history, examination, and medical decision making) should be considered the **key** components in selecting the level of E/M services. An exception to this rule is in the case of visits which consist predominantly of counseling or coordination of care (See numbered paragraph 3, page 7.)

The nature of the presenting problem and time are provided in some levels to assist the physician in determining the appropriate level of E/M service.

Determine the Extent of History Obtained

The extent of the history is dependent upon clinical judgment and on the nature of the presenting problems(s). The levels of E/M services recognize four types of history that are defined as follows:

Problem focused: chief complaint; brief history of present illness or problem.

Expanded problem focused: chief complaint; brief history of present illness; problem pertinent system review.

Detailed: chief complaint; extended history of present illness; problem pertinent system review extended to include a review of a limited number of additional systems; **pertinent** past, family, and/or social history **directly related to the patient's problems.**

Comprehensive: chief complaint; extended history of present illness; review of systems which is directly related to the problem(s) identified in the history of the present illness plus a review of all additional body systems; **complete** past, family, and social history.

The comprehensive history obtained as part of the preventive medicine evaluation and management service is not problem-oriented and does not involve a chief complaint or present illness. It does, however, include a comprehensive system review and comprehensive or interval past, family, and social history as well as a comprehensive assessment/history of pertinent risk factors.

Determine the Extent of Examination Performed

The extent of the examination performed is dependent on clinical judgment and on the nature of the presenting problem(s). The levels of E/M services recognize four types of examination that are defined as follows:

Problem focused: a limited examination of the affected body area or organ system.

Expanded problem focused: a limited examination of the affected body area or organ system and other symptomatic or related organ system(s).

Detailed: an extended examination of the affected body area(s) and other symptomatic or related organ system(s).

Comprehensive: a general multi-system examination or a complete examination of a single organ system. **Note:** The comprehensive examination performed as part of the preventive medicine evaluation and management service is multisystem, but its extent is based on age and risk factors identified.

For the purposes of these CPT definitions, the following body areas are recognized:

- Head, including the face
- Neck
- Chest, including breasts and axilla
- Abdomen
- Genitalia, groin, buttocks
- Back
- Each extremity

For the purposes of these CPT definitions, the following organ systems are recognized:

- Eyes
- Ears, Nose, Mouth, and Throat
- Cardiovascular

- Respiratory
- Gastrointestinal
- Genitourinary
- Musculoskeletal
- Skin
- Neurologic
- Psychiatric
- Hematologic/Lymphatic/Immunologic

Determine the Complexity of Medical Decision Making

Medical decision making refers to the complexity of establishing a diagnosis and/or selecting a management option as measured by:

- the number of possible diagnoses and/or the number of management options that must be considered;
- the amount and/or complexity of medical records, diagnostic tests, and/or other information that must be obtained, reviewed, and analyzed; and
- the risk of significant complications, morbidity, and/or mortality, as well as comorbidities, associated with the patient's presenting problems(s), the diagnostic procedure(s) and/or the possible management options.

Four types of medical decision making are recognized: straightforward; low complexity; moderate complexity; and high complexity. To qualify for a given type of decision making, two of the three elements in Table 2 on the following page must be met or exceeded.

Comorbidities/underlying diseases, in and of themselves, are not considered in selecting a level of E/M services *unless* their presence significantly increases the complexity of the medical decision making.

Select the Appropriate Level of E/M Services Based on the Following

1. For the following categories/subcategories, **all of the key components,** ie, history, examination, and medical decision making, must meet or exceed the stated requirements to qualify for a particular level of E/M service: office, new patient; hospital observation services; initial hospital care; office consultations; initial inpatient consultations; confirmatory consultations; emergency department services; comprehensive nursing facility assessments; domiciliary care, new patient; and home, new patient.

2. For the following categories/subcategories, **two of the three key components** (ie, history, examination, and medical decision making) must meet or exceed the stated requirements to qualify for a particular level of E/M services: office, established patient; subsequent hospital care; follow-up inpatient consultations; subsequent nursing facility care; domiciliary care, established patient; and home, established patient.

Table 2
Complexity of Medical Decision Making

Number of Diagnoses or Management Options	Amount and/or Complexity of Data to be Reviewed	Risk of Complications and/or Morbidity or Mortality	Type of Decision Making
minimal	minimal or none	minimal	**straightforward**
limited	limited	low	**low complexity**
multiple	moderate	moderate	**moderate complexity**
extensive	extensive	high	**high complexity**

3. When counseling and/or coordination of care dominates (more than 50%) the physician/patient and/or family encounter (face-to-face time in the office or other outpatient setting or floor/unit time in the hospital or nursing facility), then **time** may be considered the key or controlling factor to qualify for a particular level of E/M services. This includes time spent with parties who have assumed responsibility for the care of the patient or decision making whether or not they are family members (eg, foster parents, person acting in locum parentis, legal guardian). The extent of counseling and/or coordination of care must be documented in the medical record.

Notes

Evaluation and Management

Office or Other Outpatient Services

The following codes are used to report evaluation and management services provided in the physician's office or in an outpatient or other ambulatory facility. A patient is considered an outpatient until inpatient admission to a health care facility occurs.

To report services provided to a patient who is admitted to a hospital or nursing facility in the course of an encounter in the office or other ambulatory facility, see the notes for initial hospital inpatient care (page 11) or comprehensive nursing facility assessments (page 21).

For services provided by physicians in the emergency department, see 99281-99285.

For observation care, see 99217-99220.

For observation or inpatient care services (including admission and discharge services), see 99234-99236.

New Patient

99201 **Office or other outpatient visit** for the evaluation and management of a new patient, which requires these three key components:

- **a problem focused history;**
- **a problem focused examination; and**
- **straightforward medical decision making.**

Counseling and/or coordination of care with other providers or agencies are provided consistent with the nature of the problem(s) and the patient's and/or family's needs.

Usually, the presenting problems are self limited or minor. Physicians typically spend 10 minutes face-to-face with the patient and/or family.

99202 **Office or other outpatient visit** for the evaluation and management of a new patient, which requires these three key components:

- **an expanded problem focused history;**
- **an expanded problem focused examination; and**
- **straightforward medical decision making.**

Counseling and/or coordination of care with other providers or agencies are provided consistent with the nature of the problem(s) and the patient's and/or family's needs.

Usually, the presenting problem(s) are of low to moderate severity. Physicians typically spend 20 minutes face-to-face with the patient and/or family.

99203 **Office or other outpatient visit** for the evaluation and management of a new patient, which requires these three key components:

- **a detailed history;**
- **a detailed examination; and**
- **medical decision making of low complexity.**

Counseling and/or coordination of care with other providers or agencies are provided consistent with the nature of the problem(s) and the patient's and/or family's needs.

Usually, the presenting problem(s) are of moderate severity. Physicians typically spend 30 minutes face-to-face with the patient and/or family.

99204 **Office or other outpatient visit** for the evaluation and management of a new patient, which requires these three key components:

- **a comprehensive history;**
- **a comprehensive examination; and**
- **medical decision making of moderate complexity.**

Counseling and/or coordination of care with other providers or agencies are provided consistent with the nature of the problem(s) and the patient's and/or family's needs.

Usually, the presenting problem(s) are of moderate to high severity. Physicians typically spend 45 minutes face-to-face with the patient and/or family.

99205 **Office or other outpatient visit** for the evaluation and management of a new patient, which requires these three key components:

- **a comprehensive history;**
- **a comprehensive examination; and**
- **medical decision making of high complexity.**

Counseling and/or coordination of care with other providers or agencies are provided consistent with the nature of the problem(s) and the patient's and/or family's needs.

Usually, the presenting problem(s) are of moderate to high severity. Physicians typically spend 60 minutes face-to-face with the patient and/or family.

Established Patient

99211 **Office or other outpatient visit** for the evaluation and management of an established patient, that may not require the presence of a physician. Usually, the presenting problem(s) are minimal. Typically, 5 minutes are spent performing or supervising these services.

99212 **Office or other outpatient visit** for the evaluation and management of an established patient, which requires at least two of these three key components:

- **a problem focused history;**
- **a problem focused examination;**
- **straightforward medical decision making.**

Counseling and/or coordination of care with other providers or agencies are provided consistent with the nature of the problem(s) and the patient's and/or family's needs.

Usually, the presenting problem(s) are self limited or minor. Physicians typically spend 10 minutes face-to-face with the patient and/or family.

99213 **Office or other outpatient visit** for the evaluation and management of an established patient, which requires at least two of these three key components:

- **an expanded problem focused history;**
- **an expanded problem focused examination;**
- **medical decision making of low complexity.**

Counseling and coordination of care with other providers or agencies are provided consistent with the nature of the problem(s) and the patient's and/or family's needs.

Usually, the presenting problem(s) are of low to moderate severity. Physicians typically spend 15 minutes face-to-face with the patient and/or family.

99214 **Office or other outpatient visit** for the evaluation and management of an established patient, which requires at least two of these three key components:

- **a detailed history;**
- **a detailed examination;**
- **medical decision making of moderate complexity.**

Counseling and/or coordination of care with other providers or agencies are provided consistent with the nature of the problem(s) and the patient's and/or family's needs.

Usually, the presenting problem(s) are of moderate to high severity. Physicians typically spend 25 minutes face-to-face with the patient and/or family.

99215 **Office or other outpatient visit** for the evaluation and management of an established patient, which requires at least two of these three key components:

- **a comprehensive history;**
- **a comprehensive examination;**
- **medical decision making of high complexity.**

Counseling and/or coordination of care with other providers or agencies are provided consistent with the nature of the problem(s) and the patient's and/or family's needs.

Usually, the presenting problem(s) are of moderate to high severity. Physicians typically spend 40 minutes face-to-face with the patient and/or family.

Hospital Observation Services

The following codes are used to report evaluation and management services provided to patients designated/admitted as "observation status" in a hospital. It is not necessary that the patient be located in an observation area designated by the hospital.

If such an area does exist in a hospital (as a separate unit in the hospital, in the emergency department, etc.), these codes are to be utilized if the patient is placed in such an area.

For definitions of key components and commonly used terms, please see **Evaluation and Management Services Guidelines.**

Typical times have not yet been established for this category of services.

Observation Care Discharge Services

Observation care discharge of a patient from "observation status" includes final examination of the patient, discussion of the hospital stay, instructions for continuing care, and preparation of discharge records. For observation or inpatient hospital care including the admission and discharge of the patient on the same date, see codes 99234-99236 as appropriate.

99217 **Observation care discharge** day management (This code is to be utilized by the physician to report all services provided to a patient on discharge from "observation status" if the discharge is on other than the initial date of "observation status." To report services to a patient designated as "observation status" or "inpatient status" and discharged on the same date, use the codes for Observation or Inpatient Care Services [including Admission and Discharge Services, 99234-99236 as appropriate.])

Initial Observation Care

New or Established Patient

The following codes are used to report the encounter(s) by the supervising physician with the patient when designated as "observation status." This refers to the initiation of observation status, supervision of the care plan for observation and performance of periodic reassessments. For observation encounters by other physicians, see Office or Other Outpatient Consultation codes (99241-99245).

To report services provided to a patient who is admitted to the hospital after receiving hospital observation care services on the same date, see the notes for initial hospital inpatient care (page 11). For a patient admitted to the hospital on a date subsequent to the date of observation status, the hospital admission would be reported with the appropriate Initial Hospital Care codes (99221-99223). For a patient admitted and discharged from observation or inpatient status on the same date, the services should be reported with codes 99234-99236 as appropriate. Do not report observation discharge (99217) in conjunction with a hospital admission.

When "observation status" is initiated in the course of an encounter in another site of service (eg, hospital emergency department, physician's office, nursing facility) all evaluation and management services provided by the supervising physician in conjunction with initiating "observation status" are considered part of the initial observation care when performed on the same date. The observation care level of service reported by the supervising physician should include the services related to initiating "observation status" provided in the other sites of service as well as in the observation setting.

Evaluation and management services on the same date provided in sites that are related to initiating "observation status" should NOT be reported separately.

These codes may not be utilized for post-operative recovery if the procedure is considered part of the surgical "package." These codes apply to all evaluation and management services that are provided on the same date of initiating "observation status."

99218   **Initial observation care,** per day, for the evaluation and management of a patient which requires these three key components:

- **a detailed or comprehensive history;**
- **a detailed or comprehensive examination; and**
- **medical decision making that is straightforward or of low complexity.**

Counseling and/or coordination of care with other providers or agencies are provided consistent with the nature of the problem(s) and the patient's and/or family's needs.

Usually, the problem(s) requiring admission to "observation status" are of low severity.

99219   **Initial observation care,** per day, for the evaluation and management of a patient, which requires these three key components:

- **a comprehensive history;**
- **a comprehensive examination; and**
- **medical decision making of moderate complexity.**

Counseling and/or coordination of care with other providers or agencies are provided consistent with the nature of the problem(s) and the patient's and/or family's needs.

Usually, the problem(s) requiring admission to "observation status" are of moderate severity.

99220   **Initial observation care,** per day, for the evaluation and management of a patient, which requires these three key components:

- **a comprehensive history;**
- **a comprehensive examination; and**
- **medical decision making of high complexity.**

Counseling and/or coordination of care with other providers or agencies are provided consistent with the nature of the problem(s) and the patient's and/or family's needs.

Usually, the problem(s) requiring admission to "observation status" are of high severity.

Hospital Inpatient Services

The following codes are used to report evaluation and management services provided to hospital inpatients. Hospital inpatient services include those services provided to patients in a "partial hospital" setting. These codes are to be used to report these partial hospitalization services. See also psychiatry notes in the full text of *CPT.*

For definitions of key components and commonly used terms, please see **Evaluation and Management Services Guidelines.** For Hospital Observation Services, see 99218-99220. For a patient admitted and discharged from observation or inpatient status on the same date, the services should be reported with codes 99234-99236 as appropriate.

Initial Hospital Care

New or Established Patient

The following codes are used to report the first hospital inpatient encounter with the patient by the admitting physician.

For initial inpatient encounters by physicians other than the admitting physician, see initial inpatient consultation codes (99251-99255) or subsequent hospital care codes (99231-99233) as appropriate.

When the patient is admitted to the hospital as an inpatient in the course of an encounter in another site of service (eg, hospital emergency department, observation status in a hospital, physician's office, nursing facility) all evaluation and management services provided by that physician in conjunction with that admission are considered part of the initial hospital care when performed on the same date as the admission. The inpatient care level of service reported by the admitting physician should include the services related to the admission he/she provided in the other sites of service as well as in the inpatient setting.

Evaluation and management services on the same date provided in sites that are related to the admission "observation status" should NOT be reported separately. For a patient admitted and discharged from observation or inpatient status on the same date, the services should be reported with codes 99234-99236 as appropriate.

99221 **Initial hospital care,** per day, for the evaluation and management of a patient which requires these three key components:

- **a detailed or comprehensive history;**
- **a detailed or comprehensive examination; and**
- **medical decision making that is straightforward or of low complexity.**

Counseling and/or coordination of care with other providers or agencies are provided consistent with the nature of the problem(s) and the patient's and/or family's needs.

Usually, the problem(s) requiring admission are of low severity. Physicians typically spend 30 minutes at the bedside and on the patient's hospital floor or unit.

99222 **Initial hospital care,** per day, for the evaluation and management of a patient, which requires these three key components:

- **a comprehensive history;**
- **a comprehensive examination; and**
- **medical decision making of moderate complexity.**

Counseling and/or coordination of care with other providers or agencies are provided consistent with the nature of the problem(s) and the patient's and/or family's needs.

Usually, the problem(s) requiring admission are of moderate severity. Physicians typically spend 50 minutes at the bedside and on the patient's hospital floor or unit.

99223 **Initial hospital care,** per day, for the evaluation and management of a patient, which requires these three key components:

- **a comprehensive history;**
- **a comprehensive examination; and**
- **medical decision making of high complexity.**

Counseling and/or coordination of care with other providers or agencies are provided consistent with the nature of the problem(s) and the patient's and/or family's needs.

Usually, the problem(s) requiring admission are of high severity. Physicians typically spend 70 minutes at the bedside and on the patient's hospital floor or unit.

Subsequent Hospital Care

All levels of subsequent hospital care include reviewing the medical record and reviewing the results of diagnostic studies and changes in the patient's status, (ie, changes in history, physical condition and response to management) since the last assessment by the physician.

99231 **Subsequent hospital care,** per day, for the evaluation and management of a patient, which requires at least two of these three key components:

- **a problem focused interval history;**
- **a problem focused examination;**
- **medical decision making that is straightforward or of low complexity.**

Counseling and/or coordination of care with other providers or agencies are provided consistent with the nature of the problem(s) and the patient's and/or family's needs.

Usually, the patient is stable, recovering or improving. Physicians typically spend 15 minutes at the bedside and on the patient's hospital floor or unit.

99232 **Subsequent hospital care,** per day, for the evaluation and management of a patient, which requires at least two of these three key components:

- **an expanded problem focused interval history;**
- **an expanded problem focused examination;**
- **medical decision making of moderate complexity.**

Counseling and/or coordination of care with other providers or agencies are provided consistent with the nature of the problem(s) and the patient's and/or family's needs.

Usually, the patient is responding inadequately to therapy or has developed a minor complication. Physicians typically spend 25 minutes at the bedside and on the patient's hospital floor or unit.

99233 **Subsequent hospital care,** per day, for the evaluation and management of a patient, which requires at least two of these three key components:

- **a detailed interval history;**
- **a detailed examination;**
- **medical decision making of high complexity.**

Counseling and/or coordination of care with other providers or agencies are provided consistent with the nature of the problem(s) and the patient's and/or family's needs.

Usually, the patient is unstable or has developed a significant complication or a significant new problem. Physicians typically spend 35 minutes at the bedside and on the patient's hospital floor or unit.

Observation or Inpatient Care Services (Including Admission and Discharge Services)

The following codes are used to report observation or inpatient hospital care services provided to patients admitted and discharged on the same date of service. When a patient is admitted to the hospital from observation status on the same date, the physician should report only the initial hospital care code. The initial hospital care code reported by the admitting physician should include the services related to the observation status services he/she provided on the same date of inpatient admission.

When "observation status" is initiated in the course of an encounter in another site of service (eg, hospital emergency department, physician's office, nursing facility) all evaluation and management services provided by the supervising physician in conjunction with initiating "observation status" are considered part of the initial observation care when performed on the same date. The observation care level of service should include the services related to initiating "observation status" provided in the other sites of service as well as in the observation setting when provided by the same physician.

For patients admitted to observation or inpatient care and discharged on a different date, see codes 99218-99220 and 99217, or 99221-99223 and 99238-99239.

99234 **Observation or inpatient hospital care,** for the evaluation and management of a patient including admission and discharge on the same date which requires these three key components:

- **a detailed or comprehensive history;**
- **a detailed or comprehensive examination; and**
- **medical decision making that is straightforward or of low complexity.**

Counseling and/or coordination of care with other providers or agencies are provided consistent with the nature of the problem(s) and the patient's and/or family's needs.

Usually the presenting problem(s) requiring admission are of low severity.

99235 **Observation or inpatient hospital care,** for the evaluation and management of a patient including admission and discharge on the same date which requires these three key components:

- **a comprehensive history;**
- **a comprehensive examination; and**
- **medical decision making of moderate complexity.**

Counseling and/or coordination of care with other providers or agencies are provided consistent with the nature of the problem(s) and the patient's and/or family's needs.

Usually the presenting problem(s) requiring admission are of moderate severity.

99236 **Observation or inpatient hospital care,** for the evaluation and management of a patient including admission and discharge on the same date which requires these three key components:

- **a comprehensive history;**
- **a comprehensive examination; and**
- **medical decision making of high complexity.**

Counseling and/or coordination of care with other providers or agencies are provided consistent with the nature of the problem(s) and the patient's and/or family's needs.

Usually the presenting problem(s) requiring admission are of high severity.

Hospital Discharge Services

The hospital discharge day management codes are to be used to report the total duration of time spent by a physician for final hospital discharge of a patient. The codes include, as appropriate, final examination of the patient, discussion of the hospital stay, even if the time spent by the physician on that date is not continuous, instructions for continuing care to all relevant caregivers, and preparation of discharge records, prescriptions and referral forms. For a patient admitted and discharged from observation or inpatient status on the same date, the services should be reported with codes 99234-99236 as appropriate.

99238 **Hospital discharge day management;** 30 minutes or less

99239 more than 30 minutes

(These codes are to be utilized by the physician to report all services provided to a patient on the date of discharge, if other than the initial date of inpatient status. To report services to a patient who is admitted as an inpatient, and discharged on the same date, see codes 99234-99236 for observation or inpatient hospital care including the admission and discharge of the patient on the same date. To report concurrent care services provided by a physician(s) other than the attending physician, use subsequent hospital care codes (99231-99233) on the day of discharge.)

(For Observation Care Discharge, use 99217)

(For observation or inpatient hospital care including the admission and discharge of the patient on the same date, see 99234-99236)

(For Nursing Facility Care Discharge, see 99315, 99316)

(For discharge services provided to newborns admitted and discharged on the same date, use 99435)

Consultations

A consultation is a type of service provided by a physician whose opinion or advice regarding evaluation and/or management of a specific problem is requested by another physician or other appropriate source.

A physician consultant may initiate diagnostic and/or therapeutic services at the same or subsequent visit.

The written or verbal request for a consult may be made by a physician or other appropriate source and documented in the patient's medical record. The consultant's opinion and any services that were ordered or performed must also be documented in the patient's medical record and communicated by written report to the requesting physician or other appropriate source.

A "consultation" initiated by a patient and/or family, and not requested by a physician, is not reported using the initial consultation codes but may be reported using the codes for confirmatory consultation or office visits, as appropriate.

If a confirmatory consultation is required, eg, by a third party payor, the modifier '-32', mandated services, should also be reported.

Any specifically identifiable procedure (ie, identified with a specific CPT code) performed on or subsequent to the date of the initial consultation should be reported separately.

If subsequent to the completion of a consultation, the consultant assumes responsibility for management of a portion or all of the patient's condition(s), the follow-up consultation codes should not be used. In the hospital setting, the consulting physician should use the appropriate inpatient hospital consultation code for the initial encounter and then subsequent hospital care codes (not follow-up consultation codes). In the office setting, the appropriate established patient code should be used.

There are four subcategories of consultations: office, initial inpatient, follow-up inpatient, and confirmatory. See each subcategory for specific reporting instructions.

For definitions of key components and commonly used terms, please see **Evaluation and Management Services Guidelines**.

Office or Other Outpatient Consultations

New or Established Patient

The following codes are used to report consultations provided in the physician's office or in an outpatient or other ambulatory facility, including hospital observation services, home services, domiciliary, rest home, custodial care, or emergency department (see consultation definition, above). Follow-up visits in the consultant's office or other outpatient facility that are initiated by the physician consultant are reported using office visit codes for established patients (99211-99215). If an additional request for an opinion or advice regarding the same or a new problem is received from the attending physician and documented in the medical record, the office consultation codes may be used again.

99241   **Office consultation** for a new or established patient, which requires these three key components:

- **a problem focused history;**
- **a problem focused examination; and**
- **straightforward medical decision making.**

Counseling and/or coordination of care with other providers or agencies are provided consistent with the nature of the problem(s) and the patient's and/or family's needs.

Usually, the presenting problem(s) are self limited or minor. Physicians typically spend 15 minutes face-to-face with the patient and/or family.

99242   **Office consultation** for a new or established patient, which requires these three key components:

- **an expanded problem focused history;**
- **an expanded problem focused examination; and**
- **straightforward medical decision making.**

Counseling and/or coordination of care with other providers or agencies are provided consistent with the nature of the problem(s) and the patient's and/or family's needs.

Usually, the presenting problem(s) are of low severity. Physicians typically spend 30 minutes face-to-face with the patient and/or family.

99243   **Office consultation** for a new or established patient, which requires these three key components:

- **a detailed history;**
- **a detailed examination; and**
- **medical decision making of low complexity.**

Counseling and/or coordination of care with other providers or agencies are provided consistent with the nature of the problem(s) and the patient's and/or family's needs.

Usually, the presenting problem(s) are of moderate severity. Physicians typically spend 40 minutes face-to-face with the patient and/or family.

99244   **Office consultation** for a new or established patient, which requires these three key components:

- **a comprehensive history;**
- **a comprehensive examination; and**
- **medical decision making of moderate complexity.**

Counseling and/or coordination of care with other providers or agencies are provided consistent with the nature of the problem(s) and the patient's and/or family's needs.

Usually, the presenting problem(s) are of moderate to high severity. Physicians typically spend 60 minutes face-to-face with the patient and/or family.

99245   Office consultation for a new or established patient, which requires these three key components:

- **a comprehensive history;**
- **a comprehensive examination; and**
- **medical decision making of high complexity.**

Counseling and/or coordination of care with other providers or agencies are provided consistent with the nature of the problem(s) and the patient's and/or family's needs.

Usually, the presenting problem(s) are of moderate to high severity. Physicians typically spend 80 minutes face-to-face with the patient and/or family.

Initial Inpatient Consultations

New or Established Patient

The following codes are used to report physician consultations provided to hospital inpatients, residents of nursing facilities, or patients in a partial hospital setting. Only one initial consultation should be reported by a consultant per admission.

99251   **Initial inpatient consultation** for a new or established patient, which requires these three key components:

- **a problem focused history;**
- **a problem focused examination; and**
- **straightforward medical decision making.**

Counseling and/or coordination of care with other providers or agencies are provided consistent with the nature of the problem(s) and the patient's and/or family's needs.

Usually, the presenting problem(s) are self limited or minor. Physicians typically spend 20 minutes at the bedside and on the patient's hospital floor or unit.

99252   **Initial inpatient consultation** for a new or established patient, which requires these three key components:

- **an expanded problem focused history;**
- **an expanded problem focused examination; and**
- **straightforward medical decision making.**

Counseling and/or coordination of care with other providers or agencies are provided consistent with the nature of the problem(s) and the patient's and/or family's needs.

Usually, the presenting problem(s) are of low severity. Physicians typically spend 40 minutes at the bedside and on the patient's hospital floor or unit.

99253   **Initial inpatient consultation** for a new or established patient, which requires these three key components:

- **a detailed history;**
- **a detailed examination; and**
- **medical decision making of low complexity.**

Counseling and/or coordination of care with other providers or agencies are provided consistent with the nature of the problem(s) and the patient's and/or family's needs.

Usually, the presenting problem(s) are of moderate severity. Physicians typically spend 55 minutes at the bedside and on the patient's hospital floor or unit.

99254   **Initial inpatient consultation** for a new or established patient, which requires three key components:

- **a comprehensive history;**
- **a comprehensive examination; and**
- **medical decision making of moderate complexity.**

Counseling and/or coordination of care with other providers or agencies are provided consistent with the nature of the problem(s) and the patient's and/or family's needs.

Usually, the presenting problem(s) are of moderate to high severity. Physicians typically spend 80 minutes at the bedside and on the patient's hospital floor or unit.

99255   **Initial inpatient consultation** for a new or established patient, which requires these three key components:

- **a comprehensive history;**
- **a comprehensive examination; and**
- **medical decision making of high complexity.**

Counseling and/or coordination of care with other providers or agencies are provided consistent with the nature of the problem(s) and the patient's and/or family's needs.

Usually, the presenting problem(s) are of moderate to high severity. Physicians typically spend 110 minutes at the bedside and on the patient's hospital floor or unit.

Follow-Up Inpatient Consultations

Established Patient

Follow-up consultations are visits to complete the initial consultation OR subsequent consultative visits requested by the attending physician.

A follow-up consultation includes monitoring progress, recommending management modifications or advising on a new plan of care in response to changes in the patient's status.

If the physician consultant has initiated treatment at the initial consultation, and participates thereafter in the patient's management, the codes for subsequent hospital care should be used (99231-99233).

The following codes are used to report follow-up consultations provided to hospital inpatients or nursing facility residents only. For consultative services provided in other settings, the codes for office or other outpatient consultations should be reported (99241-99245).

99261   **Follow-up inpatient consultation** for an established patient, which requires at least two of these three key components:

- **a problem focused interval history;**
- **a problem focused examination;**
- **medical decision making that is straightforward or of low complexity.**

Counseling and/or coordination of care with other providers or agencies are provided consistent with nature of the problem(s) and the patient's and/or family's needs.

Usually, the patient is stable, recovering or improving. Physicians typically spend 10 minutes at the bedside and on the patient's hospital floor or unit.

99262   **Follow-up inpatient consultation** for an established patient which requires at least two of these three key components:

- **an expanded problem focused interval history;**
- **an expanded problem focused examination;**
- **medical decision making of moderate complexity.**

Counseling and/or coordination of care with other providers or agencies are provided consistent with the nature of the problem(s) and the patient's and/or family's needs.

Usually, the patient is responding inadequately to therapy or has developed a minor complication. Physicians typically spend 20 minutes at the bedside and on the patient's hospital floor or unit.

99263   **Follow-up inpatient consultation** for an established patient which requires at least two of these three key components:

- **a detailed interval history;**
- **a detailed examination;**
- **medical decision making of high complexity.**

Counseling and/or coordination of care with other providers or agencies are provided consistent with the nature of the problem(s) and the patient's and/or family's needs.

Usually, the patient is unstable or has developed a significant complication or a significant new problem. Physicians typically spend 30 minutes at the bedside and on the patient's hospital floor or unit.

Confirmatory Consultations

New or Established Patient

The following codes are used to report the evaluation and management services provided to patients when the consulting physician is aware of the confirmatory nature of the opinion sought (eg, when a second/third opinion is requested or required on the necessity or appropriateness of a previously recommended medical treatment or surgical procedure).

Confirmatory consultations may be provided in any setting.

A physician consultant providing a confirmatory consultation is expected to provide an opinion and/or advice only. Any services subsequent to the opinion are coded at the appropriate level of office visit, established patient, or subsequent hospital care. If a confirmatory consultation is required, eg, by a third party payor, the modifier '-32', mandated services, should also be reported. (See also Consultation notes, page 14.) Typical times have not yet been established for this subcategory of services.

99271   **Confirmatory consultation** for a new or established patient, which requires these three key components:

- **a problem focused history;**
- **a problem focused examination; and**
- **straightforward medical decision making.**

Counseling and/or coordination of care with other providers or agencies are provided consistent with the nature of the problem(s) and the patient's and/or family's needs.

Usually, the presenting problem(s) are self limited or minor.

99272   **Confirmatory consultation** for a new or established patient, which requires these three key components:

- **an expanded problem focused history;**
- **an expanded problem focused examination; and**
- **straightforward medical decision making.**

Counseling and/or coordination of care with other providers or agencies are provided consistent with the nature of the problem(s) and the patient's and/or family's needs.

Usually, the presenting problem(s) are of low severity.

99273   **Confirmatory consultation** for a new or established patient, which requires these three key components:

- **a detailed history;**
- **a detailed examination; and**
- **medical decision making of low complexity.**

Counseling and/or coordination of care with other providers or agencies are provided consistent with the nature of the problem(s) and the patient's and/or family's needs.

Usually, the presenting problem(s) are of moderate severity.

99274   **Confirmatory consultation** for a new or established patient, which requires these three key components:

- **a comprehensive history;**
- **a comprehensive examination; and**
- **medical decision making of moderate complexity.**

Counseling and/or coordination of care with other providers or agencies are provided consistent with the nature of the problem(s) and the patient's and/or family's needs.

Usually, the presenting problem(s) are of moderate to high severity.

99275 **Confirmatory consultation** for a new or established patient, which requires these three key components:

- **a comprehensive history;**
- **a comprehensive examination; and**
- **medical decision making of high complexity.**

Counseling and/or coordination of care with other providers or agencies are provided consistent with |the nature of the problem(s) and the patient's and/or family's needs.

Usually, the presenting problem(s) are of moderate to high severity.

Emergency Department Services

New or Established Patient

The following codes are used to report evaluation and management services provided in the emergency department. No distinction is made between new and established patients in the emergency department.

An emergency department is defined as an organized hospital-based facility for the provision of unscheduled episodic services to patients who present for immediate medical attention. The facility must be available 24 hours a day.

For critical care services provided in the emergency department, see Critical Care notes and 99291, 99292.

For evaluation and management services provided to a patient in an observation area of a hospital, see 99217-99220.

For observation or inpatient care services (including admission and discharge services), see 99234-99236.

99281 **Emergency department visit** for the evaluation and management of a patient, which requires these three key components:

- **a problem focused history;**
- **a problem focused examination; and**
- **straightforward medical decision making.**

Counseling and/or coordination of care with other providers or agencies are provided consistent with the nature of the problem(s) and the patient's and/or family's needs.

Usually, the presenting problem(s) are self limited or minor.

99282 **Emergency department visit** for the evaluation and management of a patient, which requires these three key components:

- **an expanded problem focused history;**
- **an expanded problem focused examination; and**
- **medical decision making of low complexity.**

Counseling and/or coordination of care with other providers or agencies are provided consistent with the nature of the problem(s) and the patient's and/or family's needs.

Usually, the presenting problem(s) are of low to moderate severity.

99283 **Emergency department visit** for the evaluation and management of a patient, which requires these three key components:

- **an expanded problem focused history;**
- **an expanded problem focused examination; and**
- **medical decision making of moderate complexity.**

Counseling and/or coordination of care with other providers or agencies are provided consistent with the nature of the problem(s) and the patient's and/or family's needs.

Usually, the presenting problem(s) are of moderate severity.

99284 **Emergency department visit** for the evaluation and management of a patient, which requires these three key components:

- **a detailed history;**
- **a detailed examination; and**
- **medical decision making of moderate complexity.**

Counseling and/or coordination of care with other providers or agencies are provided consistent with the nature of the problem(s) and the patient's and/or family's needs.

Usually, the presenting problem(s) are of high severity, and require urgent evaluation by the physician but do not pose an immediate significant threat to life or physiologic function.

99285 **Emergency department visit** for the evaluation and management of a patient, which requires these three key components within the constraints imposed by the urgency of the patient's clinical condition and/or mental status:

- **a comprehensive history;**
- **a comprehensive examination; and**
- **medical decision making of high complexity.**

Counseling and/or coordination of care with other providers or agencies are provided consistent with the nature of the problem(s) and the patient's and/or family's needs.

Usually, the presenting problem(s) are of high severity and pose an immediate significant threat to life or physiologic function.

Other Emergency Services

In physician directed emergency care, advanced life support, the physician is located in a hospital emergency or critical care department, and is in two-way voice communication with ambulance or rescue personnel outside the hospital. The physician directs the performance of necessary medical procedures, including but not limited to: telemetry of cardiac rhythm; cardiac and/or pulmonary resuscitation; endotracheal or esophageal obturator airway intubation; administration of intravenous fluids and/or administration of intramuscular, intratracheal or subcutaneous drugs; and/or electrical conversion of arrhythmia.

99288 **Physician direction of** emergency medical systems (EMS) emergency care, advanced life support

▶Patient Transport◀

▶The following codes 99289 and 99290 are used to report the physical attendance and direct face-to-face care by a physician during the interfacility transport of a critically ill or injured patient. For the purpose of reporting codes 99289 and 99290, face-to-face care begins when the physician assumes the primary responsibility of the patient at the referring hospital/facility, and ends when the receiving hospital/facility accepts responsibility for the patient's care. Only the time the physician spends in direct face-to-face contact with the patient during the transport should be reported. Patient transport services involving less than 30 minutes of face-to-face physician care should not be reported using 99289, 99290. Procedure(s) or service(s) performed by other members of the transporting team may not be reported by the supervising physician. Any procedure(s) or service(s) performed by the physician before or during transport that are identified in *CPT* may be reported separately with the exception of routine monitoring evaluations (eg, heart rate, respiratory rate, blood pressure, and pulse oximetry) and the initiation of mechanical ventilation. Routine monitoring evaluations and initiation of mechanical ventilation performed by the physician are to be included in the face-to-face time reported by codes 99289, 99290 and should not be reported separately.

The time spent by the physician performing separately reportable services or procedures should not be included in the face-to-face time reported by codes 99289, 99290.

The direction of emergency care to transporting staff by a physician located in a hospital or other facility by two-way communication is not considered direct face-to-face care and should not be reported with codes 99289, 99290. Physician directed emergency care through outside voice communication to transporting staff personnel is reported with code 99288.

The emergency department services codes (99281-99285), initial hospital care codes (99221-99223), hourly critical care codes (99291, 99292), or initial date neonatal intensive care code (99295) are only reported after the patient has been admitted to the emergency department, the inpatient floor or the critical care unit of the receiving facility.

Code 99289 is used to report the first 30-74 minutes of direct face-to-face time with the transport patient and should be reported only once on a given date. Code 99290 is used to report each additional 30 minutes provided on a given date. Face-to-face services less than 30 minutes should not be reported with these codes.◀

● **99289** **Physician constant attention of** the critically ill or injured patient during an interfacility transport; first 30-74 minutes

✚ ● **99290** each additional 30 minutes (List separately in addition to code for primary service)

▶(Use 99290 in conjunction with 99289)◀

▶(Codes 99289, 99290 may be reported separately from any other procedure/service provided on the date of the transfer. The time spent by the physician performing separately reportable services or procedures should not be included in the face-to-face time reported by codes 99289, 99290)◀

Critical Care Services

Critical care is the direct delivery by a physician(s) of medical care for a critically ill or critically injured patient. A critical illness or injury acutely impairs one or more vital organ systems such that there is a high probability of imminent or life threatening deterioration in the patient's condition. Critical care involves high complexity decision making to assess, manipulate, and support vital system function(s) to treat single or multiple vital organ system failure and/or to prevent further life threatening deterioration of the patient's condition. Examples of vital organ system failure include, but are not limited to: central nervous system failure, circulatory failure, shock, renal, hepatic, metabolic, and/or respiratory failure. Although critical care typically requires interpretation of multiple physiologic parameters and/or application of advanced technology(s), critical care may be provided in life threatening situations when these elements are not present. Critical care may be provided on multiple days, even if no changes are made in the treatment rendered to the patient, provided that the patient's condition continues to require the level of physician attention described above.

Providing medical care to a critically ill, injured, or post-operative patient qualifies as a critical care service only if both the illness or injury and the treatment being provided meet the above requirements. Critical care is usually, but not always, given in a critical care area, such as the coronary care unit, intensive care unit, pediatric intensive care unit, respiratory care unit, or the emergency care facility.

Critical care services provided to infants older than one month of age at the time of admission to an intensive care unit are reported with critical care codes 99291 and 99292. Critical care services provided to neonates (30 days of age or less at the time of admission to an intensive care unit) are reported with the neonatal critical care codes 99295, 99296, 99297 and 99298. The neonatal critical care codes are reported as long as the neonate qualifies for critical care services during the hospital stay. The reporting of neonatal critical care services is not based on time, the type of unit (eg, pediatric or neonatal critical care unit) or the type of provider delivering the care. For additional instructions on reporting these services, see the Neonatal Intensive Care section and codes 99295-99298.

Services for a patient who is not critically ill but happens to be in a critical care unit are reported using other appropriate E/M codes.

Critical care and other E/M services may be provided to the same patient on the same date by the same physician.

The following services are included in reporting critical care when performed during the critical period by the physician(s) providing critical care: the interpretation of cardiac output measurements (93561, 93562), chest x-rays (71010, 71015, 71020), pulse oximetry (94760, 94761, 94762), blood gases, and information data stored in computers (eg, ECGs, blood pressures, hematologic data (99090)); gastric intubation (43752, 91105); temporary transcutaneous pacing (92953); ventilatory management (94656, 94657, 94660, 94662); and vascular access procedures (36000, 36410, 36415, 36540, 36600). Any services performed which are not listed above should be reported separately.

►Codes 99291-99292 should not be reported for the physician's attendance during the transport of critically ill or injured patients to or from a facility or hospital. Physician transport services of critically ill or injured patients are separately reportable, see 99289, 99290.◄

The critical care codes 99291 and 99292 are used to report the total duration of time spent by a physician providing critical care services to a critically ill or critically injured patient, even if the time spent by the physician on that date is not continuous. For any given period of time spent providing critical care services, the physician must devote his or her full attention to the patient and, therefore, cannot provide services to any other patient during the same period of time.

Time spent with the individual patient should be recorded in the patient's record. The time that can be reported as critical care is the time spent engaged in work directly related to the individual patient's care whether that time was spent at the immediate bedside or elsewhere on the floor or unit. For example, time spent on the unit or at the nursing station on the floor reviewing test results or imaging studies, discussing the critically ill patient's care with other medical staff or documenting critical care services in the medical record would be reported as critical care, even though it does not occur at the bedside. Also, when the patient is unable or clinically incompetent to participate in discussions, time spent on the floor or unit with family members or surrogate decision makers obtaining a medical history, reviewing the patient's condition or prognosis, or discussing treatment or limitation(s) of treatment may be reported as critical care, provided that the conversation bears directly on the management of the patient.

Time spent in activities that occur outside of the unit or off the floor (eg, telephone calls, whether taken at home, in the office, or elsewhere in the hospital) may not be reported as critical care since the physician is not immediately available to the patient. Time spent in activities that do not directly contribute to the treatment of the patient may not be reported as critical care, even if they are performed in the critical care unit (eg, participation in administrative meetings or telephone calls to discuss other patients). Time spent performing separately reportable procedures or services should not be included in the time reported as critical care time.

Code 99291 is used to report the first 30-74 minutes of critical care on a given date. It should be used only once per date even if the time spent by the physician is not continuous on that date. Critical care of less than 30 minutes total duration on a given date should be reported with the appropriate E/M code.

Code 99292 is used to report ►additional block(s) of time, of up to◄ 30 minutes ►each◄ beyond the first 74 minutes. ►(See table on following page.)◄

The following examples illustrate the correct reporting of critical care services:

Total Duration of Critical Care	Codes
less than 30 minutes (less than 1/2 hour)	appropriate E/M codes
30-74 minutes (1/2 hr. - 1 hr. 14 min.)	99291 X 1
75-104 minutes (1 hr. 15 min. - 1 hr. 44 min.)	99291 X 1 AND 99292 X 1
105-134 minutes (1 hr. 45 min. - 2 hr. 14 min.)	99291 X 1 AND 99292 X 2
135 - 164 minutes (2 hr. 15 min. - 2 hr. 44 min.)	99291 X 1 AND 99292 X 3
165 - 194 minutes (2 hr. 45 min. - 3 hr. 14 min.)	99291 X 1 AND 99292 X 4
▶194 minutes or longer (3 hr. 14 min. - etc.)◀	▶99291 and 99292 as appropriate (see illustrated reporting examples above)◀

99291   **Critical care, evaluation and management** of the critically ill or critically injured patient; first 30-74 minutes

+ 99292   each additional 30 minutes (List separately in addition to code for primary service)

(Use 99292 in conjunction with 99291)

Neonatal Intensive Care

The following codes (99295-99298) are used to report services provided by a physician directing the care of a critically ill newborn (or managing the continuing intensive care of the very low birth weight (VLBW) infant). They represent care starting with the date of admission and may be reported only once per day, per patient. Once the neonate is no longer considered to be critically ill and attains a body weight which exceeds 1500 grams, the codes for Subsequent Hospital Care (99231-99233) should be utilized.

These neonatal critical care codes are to be used in addition to codes 99360, 99436 or 99440 as appropriate, when the physician is present for the delivery and newborn resuscitation is required.

The same definitions for critical care services apply for the adult, child and neonate. The neonatal critical care codes, however, are global 24-hour codes and not reported as hourly services. Services for a patient who is not critically ill but happens to be in a critical care unit are reported using other appropriate E/M codes.

The neonatal critical care codes (99295, 99296, 99297, 99298) are applied to neonates (30 days of age or less) admitted to an intensive care unit. These codes will be applicable as long as the child qualifies for critical care services during this hospital stay. Infants admitted to an intensive care unit older than one month of age would be coded with hourly critical care codes (99291, 99292) if they qualify for critical care services. These neonatal codes are not applied based upon the type of unit (eg, pediatric or neonatal critical care unit) in which the child receives care nor the type of provider delivering the care.

Care rendered includes management, monitoring, and treatment of the patient including enteral and parenteral nutritional maintenance, metabolic and hematologic maintenance, pharmacologic control of the circulatory system, parent counseling, case management services, and personal direct supervision of the health care team in the performance of cognitive and procedural activities.

In addition to those services listed above for adult and pediatric hourly codes, the following procedures are also included in the bundled (global) neonatal codes (99295, 99296, 99297 and 99298): umbilical venous (36510) and umbilical arterial (36620) catheters, central (36488, 36490) or peripheral vessel catheterization (36000), other arterial catheters (36140, 36620), oral or nasogastric tube placement, endotracheal intubation (31500), lumbar puncture (62270), suprapubic bladder aspiration (51000), bladder catheterization (53670), initiation and management of mechanical ventilation (94656, 94657) or continuous positive airway pressure (CPAP) (94660), surfactant administration, intravascular fluid administration, transfusion of blood components (36430, 36440), vascular punctures (36420, 36600), invasive or non-invasive electronic monitoring of vital signs, bedside pulmonary function testing, and/or monitoring or interpretation of blood gases or oxygen saturation (94760-94762). Any services performed which are not listed above should be reported separately.

For additional instructions, see descriptions listed for 99295-99298.

99295   **Initial neonatal intensive care,** per day, for the evaluation and management of a critically ill neonate or infant

This code is reserved for the date of admission for neonates who are critically ill. Critically ill neonates require cardiac and/or respiratory support (including ventilator or nasal CPAP when indicated), continuous or frequent vital sign monitoring, laboratory and blood gas interpretations, follow-up physician reevaluations, and constant observation by the health care team under direct physician supervision. Immediate preoperative evaluation and stabilization of neonates with life threatening surgical or cardiac conditions are included under this code.

99296 **Subsequent neonatal intensive care,** per day, for the evaluation and management of a critically ill and unstable neonate or infant

A critically ill and unstable neonate will require cardiac and/or respiratory support (including ventilator or nasal CPAP when indicated), continuous or frequent vital sign monitoring, laboratory and blood gas interpretations, follow-up physician re-evaluations throughout a 24-hour period, and constant observation by the health care team under direct physician supervision. In addition, most will require frequent ventilator changes, intravenous fluid alterations, and/or early initiation of parenteral nutrition. Neonates in the immediate post-operative period or those who become critically ill and unstable during the hospital stay will commonly qualify for this level of care.

This code encompasses intensive care provided on dates subsequent to the admission date.

99297 **Subsequent neonatal intensive care,** per day, for the evaluation and management of a critically ill though stable neonate or infant

Critically ill though stable neonates require cardiac and/or respiratory support (including ventilator and nasal CPAP when indicated), continuous or frequent vital sign monitoring, laboratory and blood gas interpretations, follow-up physician re-evaluations throughout a 24-hour period, and constant observation by the health care team under direct physician supervision. Neonates at this level of care would be expected to require less frequent changes in respiratory, cardiovascular and fluid and electrolyte therapy as those included under code 99296.

This code encompasses intensive care provided on dates subsequent to the admission date.

99298 **Subsequent neonatal intensive care,** per day, for the evaluation and management of the recovering very low birth weight infant (less than 1500 grams)

Very low birth weight neonates who are no longer critically ill continue to require intensive cardiac and respiratory monitoring, continuous and/or frequent vital sign monitoring, heat maintenance, enteral and/or parenteral nutritional adjustments, laboratory and oxygen monitoring and constant observation by the health care team under direct physician supervision. Neonates of this level of care would be expected to require infrequent changes in respiratory, cardiovascular and/or fluid and electrolyte therapy as those induced under 99296 or 99297.

This code encompasses intensive care provided on days subsequent to the admission date.

Nursing Facility Services

The following codes are used to report evaluation and management services to patients in Nursing Facilities (formerly called Skilled Nursing Facilities (SNFs), Intermediate Care Facilities (ICFs) or Long Term Care Facilities (LTCFs)).

These codes should also be used to report evaluation and management services provided to a patient in a psychiatric residential treatment center (a facility or a distinct part of a facility for psychiatric care, which provides a 24-hour therapeutically planned and professionally staffed group living and learning environment). If procedures such as medical psychotherapy are provided in addition to evaluation and management services, these should be reported in addition to the evaluation and management services provided.

Nursing facilities that provide convalescent, rehabilitative, or long term care are required to conduct comprehensive, accurate, standardized, and reproducible assessments of each resident's functional capacity using a Resident Assessment Instrument (RAI). All RAIs include the Minimum Data Set (MDS), Resident Assessment Protocols (RAPs) and utilization guidelines. The MDS is the primary screening and assessment tool; the RAPs trigger the identification of potential problems and provide guidelines for follow-up assessments.

Physicians have a central role in assuring that all residents receive thorough assessments and that medical plans of care are instituted or revised to enhance or maintain the residents' physical and psychosocial functioning.

Two subcategories of nursing facility services are recognized: Comprehensive Nursing Facility Assessments and Subsequent Nursing Facility Care. Both subcategories apply to new or established patients. Comprehensive Assessments may be performed at one or more sites in the assessment process: the hospital, observation unit, office, nursing facility, domiciliary/non-nursing facility or patient's home.

For definitions of key components and commonly used terms, please see **Evaluation and Management Services Guidelines.**

Comprehensive Nursing Facility Assessments

New or Established Patient

When the patient is admitted to the nursing facility in the course of an encounter in another site of service (eg, hospital emergency department, physician's office), all evaluation and management services provided by that physician in conjunction with that admission are considered part of the initial nursing facility care when performed on the same date as the admission or readmission. The nursing facility care level of service reported by the admitting physician should include the services related to the admission he/she provided in the other sites of service as well as in the nursing facility setting.

Hospital discharge or observation discharge services performed on the same date of nursing facility admission or readmission may be reported separately. For a patient discharged from inpatient status on the same date of nursing facility admission or readmission, the hospital discharge services should be reported with codes 99238-99239 as appropriate. For a patient discharged from observation status on the same date of nursing facility admission or readmission, the observation care discharge services should be reported with code 99217. For a patient admitted and discharged from observation or inpatient status on the same date, see codes 99234-99236.

(For nursing facility care discharge, see 99315, 99316)

More than one comprehensive assessment may be necessary during an inpatient confinement.

99301   **Evaluation and management** of a new or established patient involving an annual nursing facility assessment which requires these three key components:

- **a detailed interval history;**
- **a comprehensive examination; and**
- **medical decision making that is straightforward or of low complexity.**

Counseling and/or coordination of care with other providers or agencies are provided consistent with the nature of the problem(s) and the patient's and/or family's needs.

Usually, the patient is stable, recovering or improving. The review and affirmation of the medical plan of care is required. Physicians typically spend 30 minutes at the bedside and on the patient's facility floor or unit.

99302   **Evaluation and management** of a new or established patient involving a nursing facility assessment which requires these three key components:

- **a detailed interval history;**
- **a comprehensive examination; and**
- **medical decision making of moderate to high complexity.**

Counseling and/or coordination of care with other providers or agencies are provided consistent with the nature of the problem(s) and the patient's and/or family's needs.

Usually, the patient has developed a significant complication or a significant new problem and has had a major permanent change in status.

The creation of a new medical plan of care is required. Physicians typically spend 40 minutes at the bedside and on the patient's facility floor or unit.

99303   **Evaluation and management** of a new or established patient involving a nursing facility assessment at the time of initial admission or readmission to the facility, which requires these three key components:

- **a comprehensive history;**
- **a comprehensive examination; and**
- **medical decision making of moderate to high complexity.**

Counseling and/or coordination of care with other providers or agencies are provided consistent with the nature of the problem(s) and the patient's and/or family's needs.

The creation of a medical plan of care is required. Physicians typically spend 50 minutes at the bedside and on the patient's facility floor or unit.

Subsequent Nursing Facility Care

New or Established Patient

The following codes are used to report the services provided to residents of nursing facilities who do not require a comprehensive assessment, and/or who have not had a major, permanent change of status.

All levels include reviewing the medical record, noting changes in the resident's status since the last visit, and reviewing and signing orders.

99311   **Subsequent nursing facility care,** per day, for the evaluation and management of a new or established patient, which requires at least two of these three key components:

- **a problem focused interval history;**
- **a problem focused examination;**
- **medical decision making that is straightforward or of low complexity.**

Counseling and/or coordination of care with other providers or agencies are provided consistent with the nature of the problem(s) and the patient's and/or family's needs.

Usually, the patient is stable, recovering or improving. Physicians typically spend 15 minutes at the bedside and on the patient's facility floor or unit.

99312   **Subsequent nursing facility care,** per day, for the evaluation and management of a new or established patient, which requires at least two of these three key components:

- **an expanded problem focused interval history;**
- **an expanded problem focused examination;**
- **medical decision making of moderate complexity.**

Counseling and/or coordination of care with other providers or agencies are provided consistent with the nature of the problem(s) and the patient's and/or family's needs.

Usually, the patient is responding inadequately to therapy or has developed a minor complication. Physicians typically spend 25 minutes at the bedside and on the patient's facility floor or unit.

99313 **Subsequent nursing facility care,** per day, for the evaluation and management of a new or established patient, which requires at least two of these three key components:

- **a detailed interval history;**
- **a detailed examination;**
- **medical decision making of moderate to high complexity.**

Counseling and/or coordination of care with other providers or agencies are provided consistent with the nature of the problem(s) and the patient's and/or family's needs.

Usually, the patient has developed a significant complication or a significant new problem. Physicians typically spend 35 minutes at the bedside and on the patient's facility floor or unit.

Nursing Facility Discharge Services

The nursing facility discharge day management codes are to be used to report the total duration of time spent by a physician for the final nursing facility discharge of a patient. The codes include, as appropriate, final examination of the patient, discussion of the nursing facility stay, even if the time spent by the physician on that date is not continuous. Instructions are given for continuing care to all relevant caregivers, and preparation of discharge records, prescriptions and referral forms.

99315 Nursing facility discharge day management; 30 minutes or less

99316 more than 30 minutes

Domiciliary, Rest Home (eg, Boarding Home), or Custodial Care Services

The following codes are used to report evaluation and management services in a facility which provides room, board and other personal assistance services, generally on a long-term basis. The facility's services do not include a medical component.

For definitions of key components and commonly used terms, please see **Evaluation and Management Services Guidelines.**

Typical times have not yet been established for this category of services.

New Patient

99321 **Domiciliary or rest home visit** for the evaluation and management of a new patient which requires these three key components:

- **a problem focused history;**
- **a problem focused examination; and**
- **medical decision making that is straightforward or of low complexity.**

Counseling and/or coordination of care with other providers or agencies are provided consistent with the nature of the problem(s) and the patient's and/or family's needs.

Usually, the presenting problem(s) are of low severity.

99322 **Domiciliary or rest home visit** for the evaluation and management of a new patient, which requires these three key components:

- **an expanded problem focused history;**
- **an expanded problem focused examination; and**
- **medical decision making of moderate complexity.**

Counseling and/or coordination of care with other providers or agencies are provided consistent with the nature of the problem(s) and the patient's and/or family's needs.

Usually, the presenting problem(s) are of moderate severity.

99323 **Domiciliary or rest home visit** for the evaluation and management of a new patient, which requires these three key components:

- **a detailed history;**
- **a detailed examination; and**
- **medical decision making of high complexity.**

Counseling and/or coordination of care with other providers or agencies are provided consistent with the nature of the problem(s) and the patient's and/or family's needs.

Usually, the presenting problem(s) are of high complexity.

Established Patient

99331 **Domiciliary or rest home visit** for the evaluation and management of an established patient, which requires at least two of these three key components:

- **a problem focused interval history;**
- **a problem focused examination;**
- **medical decision making that is straightforward or of low complexity.**

Counseling and/or coordination of care with other providers or agencies are provided consistent with the nature of the problem(s) and the patient's and/or family's needs.

Usually, the patient is stable, recovering or improving.

99332 **Domiciliary or rest home visit** for the evaluation and management of an established patient, which requires at least two of these three key components:

- **an expanded problem focused interval history;**
- **an expanded problem focused examination;**
- **medical decision making of moderate complexity.**

Counseling and/or coordination of care with other providers or agencies are provided consistent with the nature of the problem(s) and the patient's and/or family's needs.

Usually, the patient is responding inadequately to therapy or has developed a minor complication.

99333 **Domiciliary or rest home visit** for the evaluation and management of an established patient, which requires at least two of these three key components:

- **a detailed interval history;**
- **a detailed examination;**
- **medical decision making of high complexity.**

Counseling and/or coordination of care with other providers or agencies are provided consistent with the nature of the problem(s) and the patient's and/or family's needs.

Usually, the patient is unstable or has developed a significant complication or a significant new problem.

Home Services

The following codes are used to report evaluation and management services provided in a private residence.

For definitions of key components and commonly used terms, please see **Evaluation and Management Services Guidelines.**

New Patient

99341 **Home visit** for the evaluation and management of a new patient, which requires these three key components:

- **a problem focused history;**
- **a problem focused examination; and**
- **straightforward medical decision making.**

Counseling and/or coordination of care with other providers or agencies are provided consistent with the nature of the problem(s) and the patient's and/or family's needs.

Usually, the presenting problem(s) are of low severity. Physicians typically spend 20 minutes face-to-face with the patient and/or family.

99342 **Home visit** for the evaluation and management of a new patient, which requires these three key components:

- **an expanded problem focused history;**
- **an expanded problem focused examination; and**
- **medical decision making of low complexity.**

Counseling and/or coordination of care with other providers or agencies are provided consistent with the nature of the problem(s) and the patient's and/or family's needs.

Usually, the presenting problem(s) are of moderate severity. Physicians typically spend 30 minutes face-to-face with the patient and/or family.

99343 **Home visit** for the evaluation and management of a new patient, which requires these three key components:

- **a detailed history;**
- **a detailed examination; and**
- **medical decision making of moderate complexity.**

Counseling and/or coordination of care with other providers or agencies are provided consistent with the nature of the problem(s) and the patient's and/or family's needs.

Usually, the presenting problem(s) are of moderate to high severity. Physicians typically spend 45 minutes face-to-face with the patient and/or family.

99344 **Home visit** for the evaluation and management of a new patient, which requires these three components:

- **a comprehensive history;**
- **a comprehensive examination; and**
- **medical decision making of moderate complexity.**

Counseling and/or coordination of care with other providers or agencies are provided consistent with the nature of the problem(s) and the patient's and/or family's needs.

Usually, the presenting problem(s) are of high severity. Physicians typically spend 60 minutes face-to-face with the patient and/or family.

99345 **Home visit** for the evaluation and management of a new patient, which requires these three key components:

- **a comprehensive history;**
- **a comprehensive examination; and**
- **medical decision making of high complexity.**

Counseling and/or coordination of care with other providers or agencies are provided consistent with the nature of the problem(s) and the patient's and/or family's needs.

Usually, the patient is unstable or has developed a significant new problem requiring immediate physician attention. Physicians typically spend 75 minutes face-to-face with the patient and/or family.

Established Patient

99347   **Home visit** for the evaluation and management of an established patient, which requires at least two of these three key components:

- **a problem focused interval history;**
- **a problem focused examination;**
- **straightforward medical decision making.**

Counseling and/or coordination of care with other providers or agencies are provided consistent with the nature of the problem(s) and the patient's and/or family's needs.

Usually, the presenting problem(s) are self limited or minor. Physicians typically spend 15 minutes face-to-face with the patient and/or family.

99348   **Home visit** for the evaluation and management of an established patient, which requires at least two of these three key components:

- **an expanded problem focused interval history;**
- **an expanded problem focused examination;**
- **medical decision making of low complexity.**

Counseling and/or coordination of care with other providers or agencies are provided consistent with the nature of the problem(s) and the patient's and/or family's needs.

Usually, the presenting problem(s) are of low to moderate severity. Physicians typically spend 25 minutes face-to-face with the patient and/or family.

99349   **Home visit** for the evaluation and management of an established patient, which requires at least two of these three key components:

- **a detailed interval history;**
- **a detailed examination;**
- **medical decision making of moderate complexity.**

Counseling and/or coordination of care with other providers or agencies are provided consistent with the nature of the problem(s) and the patient's and/or family's needs.

Usually, the presenting problem(s) are moderate to high severity. Physicians typically spend 40 minutes face-to-face with the patient and/or family.

99350   **Home visit** for the evaluation and management of an established patient, which requires at least two of these three key components:

- **a comprehensive interval history;**
- **a comprehensive examination;**
- **medical decision making of moderate to high complexity.**

Counseling and/or coordination of care with other providers or agencies are provided consistent with the nature of the problem(s) and the patient's and/or family's needs.

Usually, the presenting problem(s) are of moderate to high severity. The patient may be unstable or may have developed a significant new problem requiring immediate physician attention. Physicians typically spend 60 minutes face-to-face with the patient and/or family.

(99351 has been deleted. To report, use 99347)

(99352 has been deleted. To report, use 99348)

(99353 has been deleted. To report, use 99349)

Prolonged Services

Prolonged Physician Service With Direct (Face-To-Face) Patient Contact

Codes 99354-99357 are used when a physician provides prolonged service involving direct (face-to-face) patient contact that is beyond the usual service in either the inpatient or outpatient setting. This service is reported in addition to other physician service, including evaluation and management services at any level. Appropriate codes should be selected for supplies provided or procedures performed in the care of the patient during this period.

Codes 99354-99357 are used to report the total duration of face-to-face time spent by a physician on a given date providing prolonged service, even if the time spent by the physician on that date is not continuous.

Code 99354 or 99356 is used to report the first hour of prolonged service on a given date, depending on the place of service.

Either code also may be used to report a total duration of prolonged service of 30-60 minutes on a given date. Either code should be used only once per date, even if the time spent by the physician is not continuous on that date. Prolonged service of less than 30 minutes total duration on a given date is not separately reported because the work involved is included in the total work of the evaluation and management codes.

Code 99355 or 99357 is used to report each additional 30 minutes beyond the first hour, depending on the place of service. Either code may also be used to report the final 15-30 minutes of prolonged service on a given date. Prolonged service of less than 15 minutes beyond the first hour or less than 15 minutes beyond the final 30 minutes is not reported separately.

The following examples illustrate the correct reporting of prolonged physician service with direct patient contact in the office setting:

Total Duration of Prolonged Services	Code(s)
less than 30 minutes (less than 1/2 hour)	Not reported separately
30-74 minutes (1/2 hr. - 1 hr. 14 min.)	99354 X 1
75-104 minutes (1 hr. 15 min. - 1 hr. 44 min.)	99354 X 1 AND 99355 X 1
105-134 minutes (1 hr. 45 min. - 2 hr. 14 min.)	99354 X 1 AND 99355 X 2
135-164 minutes (2 hr. 15 min. - 2 hr. 44 min.)	99354 X 1 AND 99355 X 3
165-194 minutes (2 hr. 45 min. - 3 hr. 14 min.)	99354 X 1 AND 99355 X 4

+ **99354**   Prolonged physician service in the office or other outpatient setting requiring direct (face-to-face) patient contact beyond the usual service (eg, prolonged care and treatment of an acute asthmatic patient in an outpatient setting); first hour (List separately in addition to code for office or other outpatient Evaluation and Management service)

(Use 99354 in conjunction with codes 99201-99215, 99241-99245, 99301-99350)

+ **99355**   each additional 30 minutes (List separately in addition to code for prolonged physician service)

(Use 99355 in conjunction with codes 99354)

+ **99356**   Prolonged physician service in the inpatient setting, requiring direct (face-to-face) patient contact beyond the usual service (eg, maternal fetal monitoring for high risk delivery or other physiological monitoring, prolonged care of an acutely ill inpatient); first hour (List separately in addition to code for inpatient Evaluation and Management service)

(Use 99356 in conjunction with codes 99221-99233, 99251-99255, 99261-99263)

+ **99357**   each additional 30 minutes (List separately in addition to code for prolonged physician service)

(Use 99357 in conjunction with code 99356)

Prolonged Physician Service Without Direct (Face-To-Face) Patient Contact

Codes 99358 and 99359 are used when a physician provides prolonged service not involving direct (face-to-face) care that is beyond the usual service in either the inpatient or outpatient setting.

This service is to be reported in addition to other physician service, including evaluation and management services at any level.

Codes 99358 and 99359 are used to report the total duration of non-face-to-face time spent by a physician on a given date providing prolonged service, even if the time spent by the physician on that date is not continuous. Code 99358 is used to report the first hour of prolonged service on a given date regardless of the place of service.

It may also be used to report a total duration of prolonged service of 30-60 minutes on a given date. It should be used only once per date even if the time spent by the physician is not continuous on that date.

Prolonged service of less than 30 minutes total duration on a given date is not separately reported.

Code 99359 is used to report each additional 30 minutes beyond the first hour regardless of the place of service. It may also be used to report the final 15-30 minutes of prolonged service on a given date.

Prolonged service of less than 15 minutes beyond the first hour or less than 15 minutes beyond the final 30 minutes is not reported separately.

+ **99358**   **Prolonged evaluation and management service** before and/or after direct (face-to-face) patient care (eg, review of extensive records and tests, communication with other professionals and/or the patient/family); first hour (List separately in addition to code(s) for other physician service(s) and/or inpatient or outpatient Evaluation and Management service)

+ **99359**   each additional 30 minutes (List separately in addition to code for prolonged physician service)

(Use 99359 in conjunction with code 99358)

(To report telephone calls, see 99371-99373)

Physician Standby Services

Code 99360 is used to report physician standby service that is requested by another physician and that involves prolonged physician attendance without direct (face-to-face) patient contact. The physician may not be providing care or services to other patients during this period. This code is not used to report time spent proctoring another physician. It is also not used if the period of standby ends with the performance of a procedure subject to a "surgical" package by the physician who was on standby.

Code 99360 is used to report the total duration of time spent by a physician on a given date on standby. Standby service of less than 30 minutes total duration on a given date is not reported separately.

Second and subsequent periods of standby beyond the first 30 minutes may be reported only if a full 30 minutes of standby was provided for each unit of service reported.

99360   **Physician standby service,** requiring prolonged physician attendance, each 30 minutes (eg, operative standby, standby for frozen section, for cesarean/high risk delivery, for monitoring EEG)

(99360 may be reported in addition to 99431, 99440 as appropriate)

(99360 may not be reported in addition to 99436)

Case Management Services

Physician case management is a process in which a physician is responsible for direct care of a patient, and for coordinating and controlling access to or initiating and/or supervising other health care services needed by the patient.

Team Conferences

99361   **Medical conference** by a physician with interdisciplinary team of health professionals or representatives of community agencies to coordinate activities of patient care (patient not present); approximately 30 minutes

99362   approximately 60 minutes

Telephone Calls

99371   **Telephone call** by a physician to patient or for consultation or medical management or for coordinating medical management with other health care professionals (eg, nurses, therapists, social workers, nutritionists, physicians, pharmacists); simple or brief (eg, to report on tests and/or laboratory results, to clarify or alter previous instructions, to integrate new information from other health professionals into the medical treatment plan, or to adjust therapy)

99372   intermediate (eg, to provide advice to an established patient on a new problem, to initiate therapy that can be handled by telephone, to discuss test results in detail, to coordinate medical management of a new problem in an established patient, to discuss and evaluate new information and details, or to initiate new plan of care)

99373   complex or lengthy (eg, lengthy counseling session with anxious or distraught patient, detailed or prolonged discussion with family members regarding seriously ill patient, lengthy communication necessary to coordinate complex services of several different health professionals working on different aspects of the total patient care plan)

Care Plan Oversight Services

Care Plan Oversight Services are reported separately from codes for office/outpatient, hospital, home, nursing facility or domiciliary services. The complexity and approximate physician time of the care plan oversight services provided within a 30-day period determine code selection. Only one physician may report services for a given period of time, to reflect that physician's sole or predominant supervisory role with a particular patient. These codes should not be reported for supervision of patients in nursing facilities or under the care of home health agencies unless they require recurrent supervision of therapy.

The work involved in providing very low intensity or infrequent supervision services is included in the pre- and post-encounter work for home, office/outpatient and nursing facility or domiciliary visit codes.

▲**99374**   **Physician supervision** of a patient under care of home health agency (patient not present) in home, domiciliary or equivalent environment (eg, Alzheimer's facility) requiring complex and multidisciplinary care modalities involving regular physician development and/or revision of care plans, review of subsequent reports of patient status, review of related laboratory and other studies, communication (including telephone calls) for purposes of assessment or care decisions with health care professional(s), family member(s), surrogate decision maker(s) (eg, legal guardian) and/or key caregiver(s) involved in patient's care, integration of new information into the medical treatment plan and/or adjustment of medical therapy, within a calendar month; 15-29 minutes

99375   30 minutes or more

(99376 has been deleted. To report, see 99375, 99378, 99380)

▲**99377**   **Physician supervision** of a hospice patient (patient not present) requiring complex and multidisciplinary care modalities involving regular physician development and/or revision of care plans, review of subsequent reports of patient status, review of related laboratory and other studies, communication (including telephone calls) for purposes of assessment or care decisions with health care professional(s), family member(s), surrogate decision maker(s) (eg, legal guardian) and/or key caregiver(s) involved in patient's care, integration of new information into the medical treatment plan and/or adjustment of medical therapy, within a calendar month; 15-29 minutes

99378   30 minutes or more

▲ **99379** **Physician supervision** of a nursing facility patient (patient not present) requiring complex and multidisciplinary care modalities involving regular physician development and/or revision of care plans, review of subsequent reports of patient status, review of related laboratory and other studies, communication (including telephone calls) for purposes of assessment or care decisions with health care professional(s), family member(s), surrogate decision maker(s) (eg, legal guardian) and/or key caregiver(s) involved in patient's care, integration of new information into the medical treatment plan and/or adjustment of medical therapy, within a calendar month; 15-29 minutes

99380 30 minutes or more

Preventive Medicine Services

The following codes are used to report the preventive medicine evaluation and management of infants, children, adolescents and adults.

The extent and focus of the services will largely depend on the age of the patient.

If an abnormality/ies is encountered or a preexisting problem is addressed in the process of performing this preventive medicine evaluation and management service, and if the problem/abnormality is significant enough to require additional work to perform the key components of a problem-oriented E/M service, then the appropriate Office/Outpatient code 99201-99215 should also be reported. Modifier '-25' should be added to the Office/Outpatient code to indicate that a significant, separately identifiable Evaluation and Management service was provided by the same physician on the same day as the preventive medicine service. The appropriate preventive medicine service is additionally reported.

An insignificant or trivial problem/abnormality that is encountered in the process of performing the preventive medicine evaluation and management service and which does not require additional work and the performance of the key components of a problem-oriented E/M service should not be reported.

The "comprehensive" ►nature◄ of the Preventive Medicine Services codes 99381-99397 ►reflects an age and gender appropriate history/exam and◄ is NOT synonymous with the "comprehensive" examination required in Evaluation and Management codes 99201-99350.

Codes 99381-99397 include counseling/anticipatory guidance/risk factor reduction interventions which are provided at the time of the initial or periodic comprehensive preventive medicine examination. (Refer

to codes 99401-99412 for reporting those counseling/anticipatory guidance/risk factor reduction interventions that are provided at an encounter separate from the preventive medicine examination.)

Immunizations and ancillary studies involving laboratory, radiology, other procedures, or screening tests identified with a specific CPT code are reported separately. For immunizations, see 90471-90474 and 90476-90749.

New Patient

▲ **99381** **Initial comprehensive preventive medicine** evaluation and management of an individual including an age and gender appropriate history, examination, counseling/anticipatory guidance/risk factor reduction interventions, and the ordering of appropriate immunization(s), laboratory/diagnostic procedures, new patient; infant (age under 1 year)

99382 early childhood (age 1 through 4 years)

99383 late childhood (age 5 through 11 years)

99384 adolescent (age 12 through 17 years)

99385 18-39 years

99386 40-64 years

99387 65 years and over

Established Patient

▲ **99391** **Periodic comprehensive preventive medicine** reevaluation and management of an individual including an age and gender appropriate history, examination, counseling/anticipatory guidance/risk factor reduction interventions, and the ordering of appropriate immunization(s), laboratory/diagnostic procedures, established patient; infant (age under 1 year)

99392 early childhood (age 1 through 4 years)

99393 late childhood (age 5 through 11 years)

99394 adolescent (age 12 through 17 years)

99395 18-39 years

99396 40-64 years

99397 65 years and over

Counseling and/or Risk Factor Reduction Intervention

New or Established Patient

These codes are used to report services provided to individuals at a separate encounter for the purpose of promoting health and preventing illness or injury.

Preventive medicine counseling and risk factor reduction interventions provided as a separate encounter will vary with age and should address such issues as family problems, diet and exercise, substance abuse, sexual practices, injury

⊘ =Modifier '-51' Exempt   ► ◄=New or Revised Text   ✦=Add-on Code   CPT 2002

prevention, dental health, and diagnostic and laboratory test results available at the time of the encounter.

These codes are not to be used to report counseling and risk factor reduction interventions provided to patients with symptoms or established illness. For counseling individual patients with symptoms or established illness, use the appropriate office, hospital or consultation or other evaluation and management codes. For counseling groups of patients with symptoms or established illness, use 99078.

Preventive Medicine, Individual Counseling

99401   **Preventive medicine counseling** and/or risk factor reduction intervention(s) provided to an individual (separate procedure); approximately 15 minutes

99402   approximately 30 minutes

99403   approximately 45 minutes

99404   approximately 60 minutes

Preventive Medicine, Group Counseling

99411   **Preventive medicine counseling** and/or risk factor reduction intervention(s) provided to individuals in a group setting (separate procedure); approximately 30 minutes

99412   approximately 60 minutes

Other Preventive Medicine Services

99420   **Administration and interpretation** of health risk assessment instrument (eg, health hazard appraisal)

99429   **Unlisted preventive** medicine service

Newborn Care

The following codes are used to report the services provided to newborns in several different settings.

For newborn hospital discharge services provided on a date subsequent to the admission date of the newborn, use 99238.

For discharge services provided to newborns admitted and discharged on the same date, use 99435.

99431   **History and examination** of the normal newborn infant, initiation of diagnostic and treatment programs and preparation of hospital records. (This code should also be used for birthing room deliveries.)

99432   **Normal newborn care** in other than hospital or birthing room setting, including physical examination of baby and conference(s) with parent(s)

99433   **Subsequent hospital care,** for the evaluation and management of a normal newborn, per day

99435   **History and examination** of the normal newborn infant, including the preparation of medical records. (This code should only be used for newborns assessed and discharged from the hospital or birthing room on the same date.)

99436   **Attendance** at delivery (when requested by delivering physician) and initial stabilization of newborn

(99436 may be reported in addition to 99431)

(99436 may not be reported in addition to 99440)

(99438 has been deleted)

99440   **Newborn resuscitation:** provision of positive pressure ventilation and/or chest compressions in the presence of acute inadequate ventilation and/or cardiac output

Special Evaluation and Management Services

The following codes are used to report evaluations performed to establish baseline information prior to life or disability insurance certificates being issued. This service is performed in the office or other setting, and applies to both new and established patients. When using these codes, no active management of the problem(s) is undertaken during the encounter.

If other evaluation and management services and/or procedures are performed on the same date, the appropriate E/M or procedure code(s) should be reported in addition to these codes.

Basic Life and/or Disability Evaluation Services

99450   **Basic life** and/or disability examination that includes:

- **measurement of height, weight and blood pressure;**
- **completion of a medical history following a life insurance pro forma;**
- **collection of blood sample and/or urinalysis complying with "chain of custody" protocols; and**
- **completion of necessary documentation/certificates.**

Work Related or Medical Disability Evaluation Services

99455 **Work related** or medical disability examination by the treating physician that includes:

- completion of a medical history commensurate with the patient's condition;
- performance of an examination commensurate with the patient's condition;
- formulation of a diagnosis, assessment of capabilities and stability, and calculation of impairment;
- development of future medical treatment plan; and
- completion of necessary documentation/certificates and report.

99456 **Work related** or medical disability examination by other than the treating physician that includes:

- completion of a medical history commensurate with the patient's condition;
- performance of an examination commensurate with the patient's condition;
- formulation of a diagnosis, assessment of capabilities and stability, and calculation of impairment;
- development of future medical treatment plan; and
- completion of necessary documentation/certificates and report.

Other Evaluation and Management Services

99499 **Unlisted evaluation and management** service

Anesthesia Guidelines

Services involving administration of anesthesia are reported by the use of the anesthesia five digit procedure code (00100-01999) plus modifier codes (defined under "Anesthesia Modifiers" later in these Guidelines).

The reporting of anesthesia services is appropriate by or under the responsible supervision of a physician. These services may include but are not limited to general, regional, supplementation of local anesthesia, or other supportive services in order to afford the patient the anesthesia care deemed optimal by the anesthesiologist during any procedure. These services include the usual preoperative and postoperative visits, the anesthesia care during the procedure, the administration of fluids and/or blood and the usual monitoring services (eg, ECG, temperature, blood pressure, oximetry, capnography, and mass spectrometry). Unusual forms of monitoring (eg, intra-arterial, central venous, and Swan-Ganz) are not included.

Items used by all physicians in reporting their services are presented in the **Introduction.** Some of the commonalities are repeated here for the convenience of those physicians referring to this section on **Anesthesia.** Other definitions and items unique to anesthesia are also listed.

To report sedation with or without analgesia (conscious sedation) provided by a physician also performing the service for which conscious sedation is being provided, see codes 99141, 99142.

To report regional or general anesthesia provided by a physician also performing the services for which the anesthesia is being provided, see modifier '-47,' Anesthesia by Surgeon, in Appendix A.

Time Reporting

Time for anesthesia procedures may be reported as is customary in the local area. Anesthesia time begins when the anesthesiologist begins to prepare the patient for the induction of anesthesia in the operating room or in an equivalent area and ends when the anesthesiologist is no longer in personal attendance, that is, when the patient may be safely placed under postoperative supervision.

Physician's Services

Physician's services rendered in the office, home, or hospital, consultation, and other medical services are listed in the section entitled **Evaluation and Management Services** (99200 series) found in the front of the book, beginning on page 1. "Special Services and Reporting" (99000 series) are presented in the **Medicine** section.

Materials Supplied by Physician

Supplies and materials provided by the physician (eg, sterile trays, drugs) over and above those usually included with the office visit or other services rendered may be listed separately. List drugs, tray supplies, and materials provided. Identify as 99070.

Separate or Multiple Procedures

It is appropriate to designate multiple procedures that are rendered on the same date by separate entries. This can be reported by using the multiple procedure modifier '-51'. See "Anesthesia Modifiers" for modifier definitions.

Special Report

A service that is rarely provided, unusual, variable, or new may require a special report in determining medical appropriateness of the service. Pertinent information should include an adequate definition or description of the nature, extent, and need for the procedure; and the time, effort, and equipment necessary to provide the service. Additional items which may be included are:

- complexity of symptoms;
- final diagnosis;
- pertinent physical findings;
- diagnostic and therapeutic procedures;
- concurrent problems;
- follow-up care.

Anesthesia Modifiers

All anesthesia services are reported by use of the anesthesia five digit procedure code (00100-01999) plus the addition of a physical status modifier. The use of other optional modifiers may be appropriate.

Physical Status Modifiers

Physical Status modifiers are represented by the initial letter 'P' followed by a single digit from 1 to 6 defined below.

P1-A normal healthy patient.

P2-A patient with mild systemic disease.

P3-A patient with severe systemic disease.

P4-A patient with severe systemic disease that is a constant threat to life.

P5-A moribund patient who is not expected to survive without the operation.

P6-A declared brain-dead patient whose organs are being removed for donor purposes.

The above six levels are consistent with the American Society of Anesthesiologists (ASA) ranking of patient physical status. Physical status is included in CPT to distinguish among various levels of complexity of the anesthesia service provided.

Example: 00100-P1

Qualifying Circumstances

More than one may be selected.

Many anesthesia services are provided under particularly difficult circumstances, depending on factors such as extraordinary condition of patient, notable operative conditions, and/or unusual risk factors. This section includes a list of important qualifying circumstances that significantly impact on the character of the anesthesia service provided. These procedures would not be reported alone but would be reported as additional procedure numbers qualifying an anesthesia procedure or service.

+ 99100   Anesthesia for patient of extreme age, under one year and over seventy (List separately in addition to code for primary anesthesia procedure)

+ 99116   Anesthesia complicated by utilization of total body hypothermia (List separately in addition to code for primary anesthesia procedure)

+ 99135   Anesthesia complicated by utilization of controlled hypotension (List separately in addition to code for primary anesthesia procedure)

+ 99140   Anesthesia complicated by emergency conditions (specify) (List separately in addition to code for primary anesthesia procedure)

(An emergency is defined as existing when delay in treatment of the patient would lead to a significant increase in the threat to life or body part.)

Anesthesia

Head

00100 Anesthesia for procedures on salivary glands, including biopsy

00102 Anesthesia for procedures on plastic repair of cleft lip

00103 Anesthesia for reconstructive procedures of eyelid (eg, blepharoplasty, ptosis surgery)

00104 Anesthesia for electroconvulsive therapy

00120 Anesthesia for procedures on external, middle, and inner ear including biopsy; not otherwise specified

(00122 has been deleted. To report, use 00120)

00124 otoscopy

00126 tympanotomy

00140 Anesthesia for procedures on eye; not otherwise specified

00142 lens surgery

00144 corneal transplant

00145 vitreoretinal surgery

(00146 has been deleted. To report, use 00140)

00147 iridectomy

00148 ophthalmoscopy

00160 Anesthesia for procedures on nose and accessory sinuses; not otherwise specified

00162 radical surgery

00164 biopsy, soft tissue

00170 Anesthesia for intraoral procedures, including biopsy; not otherwise specified

00172 repair of cleft palate

00174 excision of retropharyngeal tumor

00176 radical surgery

00190 Anesthesia for procedures on facial bones or skull; not otherwise specified

00192 radical surgery (including prognathism)

00210 Anesthesia for intracranial procedures; not otherwise specified

00212 subdural taps

00214 burr holes, including ventriculography

00215 cranioplasty or elevation of depressed skull fracture, extradural (simple or compound)

00216 vascular procedures

00218 procedures in sitting position

▲ 00220 cerebrospinal fluid shunting procedures

00222 electrocoagulation of intracranial nerve

Neck

00300 Anesthesia for all procedures on the integumentary system, muscles and nerves of head, neck, and posterior trunk, not otherwise specified

00320 Anesthesia for all procedures on esophagus, thyroid, larynx, trachea and lymphatic system of neck; not otherwise specified

00322 needle biopsy of thyroid

(For procedures on cervical spine and cord, see 00600, 00604, 00670)

00350 Anesthesia for procedures on major vessels of neck; not otherwise specified

00352 simple ligation

(For arteriography, use 01916)

Thorax (Chest Wall and Shoulder Girdle)

00400 Anesthesia for procedures on the integumentary system on the extremities, anterior trunk and perineum; not otherwise specified

00402 reconstructive procedures on breast (eg, reduction or augmentation mammoplasty, muscle flaps)

00404 radical or modified radical procedures on breast

00406 radical or modified radical procedures on breast with internal mammary node dissection

00410 electrical conversion of arrhythmias

(00420 has been deleted. To report, use 00300)

00450 Anesthesia for procedures on clavicle and scapula; not otherwise specified

00452 radical surgery

00454 biopsy of clavicle

00470 Anesthesia for partial rib resection; not otherwise specified

00472 thoracoplasty (any type)

00474 radical procedures (eg, pectus excavatum)

(00476 has been deleted. To report, use 00470)

Intrathoracic

00500 Anesthesia for all procedures on esophagus

00520 Anesthesia for closed chest procedures; (including bronchoscopy) not otherwise specified

00522 needle biopsy of pleura

00524 pneumocentesis

(00526 has been deleted. To report, use 00520)

00528 mediastinoscopy and diagnostic thoracoscopy

00530 Anesthesia for permanent transvenous pacemaker insertion

00532 Anesthesia for access to central venous circulation

00534 Anesthesia for transvenous insertion or replacement of pacing cardioverter-defibrillator

(For transthoracic approach, use 00560)

00537 Anesthesia for cardiac electrophysiologic procedures including radiofrequency ablation

00540 Anesthesia for thoracotomy procedures involving lungs, pleura, diaphragm, and mediastinum (including surgical thoracoscopy); not otherwise specified

00542 decortication

00544 pleurectomy

00546 pulmonary resection with thoracoplasty

00548 intrathoracic procedures on the trachea and bronchi

00550 Anesthesia for sternal debridement

▲ **00560** Anesthesia for procedures on heart, pericardial sac, and great vessels of chest; without pump oxygenator

00562 with pump oxygenator

00563 with pump oxygenator with hypothermic circulatory arrest

00566 Anesthesia for direct coronary artery bypass grafting without pump oxygenator

00580 Anesthesia for heart transplant or heart/lung transplant

Spine and Spinal Cord

00600 Anesthesia for procedures on cervical spine and cord; not otherwise specified

(For myelography and diskography, see radiological procedures ►01905◄)

00604 procedures with patient in the sitting position

00620 Anesthesia for procedures on thoracic spine and cord; not otherwise specified

00622 thoracolumbar sympathectomy

00630 Anesthesia for procedures in lumbar region; not otherwise specified

00632 lumbar sympathectomy

00634 chemonucleolysis

(00650 has been deleted. To report, use 00220)

00635 diagnostic or therapeutic lumbar puncture

00670 Anesthesia for extensive spine and spinal cord procedures (eg, spinal instrumentation or vascular procedures)

Upper Abdomen

00700 Anesthesia for procedures on upper anterior abdominal wall; not otherwise specified

00702 percutaneous liver biopsy

00730 Anesthesia for procedures on upper posterior abdominal wall

00740 Anesthesia for upper gastrointestinal endoscopic procedures, endoscope introduced proximal to duodenum

00750 Anesthesia for hernia repairs in upper abdomen; not otherwise specified

00752 lumbar and ventral (incisional) hernias and/or wound dehiscence

00754 omphalocele

00756 transabdominal repair of diaphragmatic hernia

00770 Anesthesia for all procedures on major abdominal blood vessels

00790 Anesthesia for intraperitoneal procedures in upper abdomen including laparoscopy; not otherwise specified

00792 partial hepatectomy or management of liver hemorrhage (excluding liver biopsy)

00794 pancreatectomy, partial or total (eg, Whipple procedure)

00796 liver transplant (recipient)

(For harvesting of liver, use 01990)

● **00797** gastric restrictive procedure for morbid obesity

Lower Abdomen

00800 Anesthesia for procedures on lower anterior abdominal wall; not otherwise specified

00802 panniculectomy

(00806 has been deleted. To report, see 00790, 00840)

00810 Anesthesia for lower intestinal endoscopic procedures, endoscope introduced distal to duodenum

⊘ =Modifier '-51' Exempt ► ◄=New or Revised Text ✚=Add-on Code CPT 2002

00820	Anesthesia for procedures on lower posterior abdominal wall
00830	Anesthesia for hernia repairs in lower abdomen; not otherwise specified
00832	ventral and incisional hernias
00840	Anesthesia for intraperitoneal procedures in lower abdomen including laparoscopy; not otherwise specified
00842	amniocentesis
00844	abdominoperineal resection
00846	radical hysterectomy
00848	pelvic exenteration

▶(00850 has been deleted. To report, use 01961)◀

● 00851 tubal ligation/transection

▶(00855 has been deleted. To report, use 01963)◀

▶(00857 has been deleted. To report, use 01968, 01969)◀

00860	Anesthesia for extraperitoneal procedures in lower abdomen, including urinary tract; not otherwise specified
00862	renal procedures, including upper 1/3 of ureter, or donor nephrectomy
00864	total cystectomy
00865	radical prostatectomy (suprapubic, retropubic)
00866	adrenalectomy
00868	renal transplant (recipient)

(For donor nephrectomy, use 00862)

(For harvesting kidney from brain-dead patient, use 01990)

● 00869 vasectomy, unilateral/bilateral

00870	cystolithotomy
00872	Anesthesia for lithotripsy, extracorporeal shock wave; with water bath
00873	without water bath
00880	Anesthesia for procedures on major lower abdominal vessels; not otherwise specified
00882	inferior vena cava ligation

▶(00884 has been deleted. To report, use 01930)◀

Perineum

(00900 has been deleted. To report, see 00300, 00400)

00902	Anesthesia for; anorectal procedure
00904	radical perineal procedure
00906	vulvectomy
00908	perineal prostatectomy

00910	Anesthesia for transurethral procedures (including urethrocystoscopy); not otherwise specified
00912	transurethral resection of bladder tumor(s)
00914	transurethral resection of prostate
00916	post-transurethral resection bleeding
00918	with fragmentation, manipulation and/or removal of ureteral calculus
00920	Anesthesia for procedures on male genitalia (including open urethral procedures); not otherwise specified
00922	seminal vesicles
00924	undescended testis, unilateral or bilateral
00926	radical orchiectomy, inguinal
00928	radical orchiectomy, abdominal
00930	orchiopexy, unilateral or bilateral
00932	complete amputation of penis
00934	radical amputation of penis with bilateral inguinal lymphadenectomy
00936	radical amputation of penis with bilateral inguinal and iliac lymphadenectomy
00938	insertion of penile prosthesis (perineal approach)
00940	Anesthesia for vaginal procedures (including biopsy of labia, vagina, cervix or endometrium); not otherwise specified

▲ 00942 colpotomy, vaginectomy, colporrhaphy, and open urethral procedures

00944 vaginal hysterectomy

▶(00946 has been deleted. To report, use 01960)◀

00948	cervical cerclage
00950	culdoscopy
00952	hysteroscopy and/or hysterosalpingography

▶(00955 has been deleted. To report, use 01967)◀

Pelvis (Except Hip)

(01000 has been deleted. To report, use 00400)

(01110 has been deleted. To report, use 00300)

01112	Anesthesia for bone marrow aspiration and/or biopsy, anterior or posterior iliac crest
01120	Anesthesia for procedures on bony pelvis

(01122 has been deleted. To report, use 01120)

01130	Anesthesia for body cast application or revision
01140	Anesthesia for interpelviabdominal (hindquarter) amputation
01150	Anesthesia for radical procedures for tumor of pelvis, except hindquarter amputation

---

▲=Revised Code   ●=New Code

01160   Anesthesia for closed procedures involving symphysis pubis or sacroiliac joint

01170   Anesthesia for open procedures involving symphysis pubis or sacroiliac joint

01180   Anesthesia for obturator neurectomy; extrapelvic

01190   intrapelvic

Upper Leg (Except Knee)

01200   Anesthesia for all closed procedures involving hip joint

01202   Anesthesia for arthroscopic procedures of hip joint

01210   Anesthesia for open procedures involving hip joint; not otherwise specified

01212   hip disarticulation

▲ 01214   total hip arthroplasty

01215   revision of total hip arthroplasty

01220   Anesthesia for all closed procedures involving upper 2/3 of femur

01230   Anesthesia for open procedures involving upper 2/3 of femur; not otherwise specified

01232   amputation

01234   radical resection

(01240 has been deleted. To report, use 00400)

01250   Anesthesia for all procedures on nerves, muscles, tendons, fascia, and bursae of upper leg

01260   Anesthesia for all procedures involving veins of upper leg, including exploration

01270   Anesthesia for procedures involving arteries of upper leg, including bypass graft; not otherwise specified

01272   femoral artery ligation

01274   femoral artery embolectomy

(01276 has been deleted. To report, use 00880)

Knee and Popliteal Area

(01300 has been deleted. To report, use 00400)

01320   Anesthesia for all procedures on nerves, muscles, tendons, fascia, and bursae of knee and/or popliteal area

01340   Anesthesia for all closed procedures on lower 1/3 of femur

01360   Anesthesia for all open procedures on lower 1/3 of femur

01380   Anesthesia for all closed procedures on knee joint

01382   Anesthesia for arthroscopic procedures of knee joint

01390   Anesthesia for all closed procedures on upper ends of tibia, fibula, and/or patella

01392   Anesthesia for all open procedures on upper ends of tibia, fibula, and/or patella

01400   Anesthesia for open procedures on knee joint; not otherwise specified

▲ 01402   total knee arthroplasty

01404   disarticulation at knee

01420   Anesthesia for all cast applications, removal, or repair involving knee joint

01430   Anesthesia for procedures on veins of knee and popliteal area; not otherwise specified

01432   arteriovenous fistula

01440   Anesthesia for procedures on arteries of knee and popliteal area; not otherwise specified

01442   popliteal thromboendarterectomy, with or without patch graft

01444   popliteal excision and graft or repair for occlusion or aneurysm

Lower Leg (Below Knee, Includes Ankle and Foot)

(01460 has been deleted. To report, use 00400)

01462   Anesthesia for all closed procedures on lower leg, ankle, and foot

01464   Anesthesia for arthroscopic procedures of ankle joint

01470   Anesthesia for procedures on nerves, muscles, tendons, and fascia of lower leg, ankle, and foot; not otherwise specified

01472   repair of ruptured Achilles tendon, with or without graft

01474   gastrocnemius recession (eg, Strayer procedure)

01480   Anesthesia for open procedures on bones of lower leg, ankle, and foot; not otherwise specified

01482   radical resection (including below knee amputation)

01484   osteotomy or osteoplasty of tibia and/or fibula

01486   total ankle replacement

01490   Anesthesia for lower leg cast application, removal, or repair

01500   Anesthesia for procedures on arteries of lower leg, including bypass graft; not otherwise specified

01502   embolectomy, direct or with catheter

01520   Anesthesia for procedures on veins of lower leg; not otherwise specified

01522   venous thrombectomy, direct or with catheter

Shoulder and Axilla

Includes humeral head and neck, sternoclavicular joint, acromioclavicular joint, and shoulder joint.

(01600 has been deleted. To report, use 00400)

01610   Anesthesia for all procedures on nerves, muscles, tendons, fascia, and bursae of shoulder and axilla

01620   Anesthesia for all closed procedures on humeral head and neck, sternoclavicular joint, acromioclavicular joint, and shoulder joint

01622   Anesthesia for arthroscopic procedures of shoulder joint

01630   Anesthesia for open procedures on humeral head and neck, sternoclavicular joint, acromioclavicular joint, and shoulder joint; not otherwise specified

01632   radical resection

01634   shoulder disarticulation

01636   interthoracoscapular (forequarter) amputation

01638   total shoulder replacement

01650   Anesthesia for procedures on arteries of shoulder and axilla; not otherwise specified

01652   axillary-brachial aneurysm

01654   bypass graft

01656   axillary-femoral bypass graft

01670   Anesthesia for all procedures on veins of shoulder and axilla

01680   Anesthesia for shoulder cast application, removal or repair; not otherwise specified

01682   shoulder spica

Upper Arm and Elbow

(01700 has been deleted. To report, use 00400)

01710   Anesthesia for procedures on nerves, muscles, tendons, fascia, and bursae of upper arm and elbow; not otherwise specified

01712   tenotomy, elbow to shoulder, open

01714   tenoplasty, elbow to shoulder

01716   tenodesis, rupture of long tendon of biceps

01730   Anesthesia for all closed procedures on humerus and elbow

01732   Anesthesia for arthroscopic procedures of elbow joint

01740   Anesthesia for open procedures on humerus and elbow; not otherwise specified

01742   osteotomy of humerus

01744   repair of nonunion or malunion of humerus

01756   radical procedures

01758   excision of cyst or tumor of humerus

01760   total elbow replacement

01770   Anesthesia for procedures on arteries of upper arm and elbow; not otherwise specified

01772   embolectomy

01780   Anesthesia for procedures on veins of upper arm and elbow; not otherwise specified

01782   phleborrhaphy

(01784 has been deleted. To report, see 01770, 01780)

Forearm, Wrist, and Hand

(01800 has been deleted. To report, use 00400)

01810   Anesthesia for all procedures on nerves, muscles, tendons, fascia, and bursae of forearm, wrist, and hand

01820   Anesthesia for all closed procedures on radius, ulna, wrist, or hand bones

01830   Anesthesia for open procedures on radius, ulna, wrist, or hand bones; not otherwise specified

01832   total wrist replacement

01840   Anesthesia for procedures on arteries of forearm, wrist, and hand; not otherwise specified

01842   embolectomy

01844   Anesthesia for vascular shunt, or shunt revision, any type (eg, dialysis)

01850   Anesthesia for procedures on veins of forearm, wrist, and hand; not otherwise specified

01852   phleborrhaphy

01860   Anesthesia for forearm, wrist, or hand cast application, removal, or repair

Radiological Procedures

(01900 has been deleted. To report, use 00952)

(01902 has been deleted. To report, use 00214)

►(01904 has been deleted. To report, use 01905)◄

●**01905**   Anesthesia for myelography, diskography, vertebroplasty

►(01906 has been deleted. To report, use 01905)◄

►(01908 has been deleted. To report, use 01905)◄

►(01910 has been deleted. To report, use 01905)◄

►(01912 has been deleted. To report, use 01905)◄

►(01914 has been deleted. To report, use 01905)◄

▲**01916**   Anesthesia for diagnostic arteriography/venography

---

▲=Revised Code   ●=New Code

►(Do not report 01916 in conjunction with therapeutic codes 01924-01926, 01930-01933)◄

►(01918 has been deleted. To report, use 01916)◄

▲ **01920** Anesthesia for cardiac catheterization including coronary angiography and ventriculography (not to include Swan-Ganz catheter)

►(01921 has been deleted. To report, see 01924-01926)◄

01922 Anesthesia for non-invasive imaging or radiation therapy

● **01924** Anesthesia for therapeutic interventional radiologic procedures involving the arterial system; not otherwise specified

● **01925** carotid or coronary

● **01926** intracranial, intracardiac, or aortic

● **01930** Anesthesia for therapeutic interventional radiologic procedures involving the venous/lymphatic system (not to include access to the central circulation); not otherwise specified

● **01931** intrahepatic or portal circulation (eg, transcutaneous porto-caval shunt (TIPS))

● **01932** intrathoracic or jugular

● **01933** intracranial

Burn Excisions or Debridement

▲ **01951** Anesthesia for second and third degree burn excision or debridement with or without skin grafting, any site, for total body surface area (TBSA) treated during anesthesia and surgery; less than four percent total body surface area

▲ **01952** between four and nine percent of total body surface area

+ **01953** each additional nine percent total body surface area or part thereof (List separately in addition to code for primary procedure)

(Use 01953 in conjunction with code 01952)

►Obstetric◄

● **01960** Anesthesia for; vaginal delivery only

● **01961** cesarean delivery only

● **01962** urgent hysterectomy following delivery

● **01963** cesarean hysterectomy without any labor analgesia/anesthesia care

● **01964** abortion procedures

● **01967** Neuraxial labor analgesia/anesthesia for planned vaginal delivery (this includes any repeat subarachnoid needle placement and drug injection and/or any necessary replacement of an epidural catheter during labor)

+ ● **01968** Cesarean delivery following neuraxial labor analgesia/anesthesia (List separately in addition to code for primary procedure)

►(Use 01968 in conjunction with code 01967)◄

+ ● **01969** Cesarean hysterectomy following neuraxial labor analgesia/anesthesia (List separately in addition to code for primary procedure)

►(Use 01969 in conjunction with code 01967)◄

Other Procedures

01990 Physiological support for harvesting of organ(s) from brain-dead patient

▲ **01995** Regional intravenous administration of local anesthetic agent or other medication (upper or lower extremity)

(For intra-arterial or intravenous therapy for pain management, see 90783, 90784)

01996 Daily management of epidural or subarachnoid drug administration

01999 Unlisted anesthesia procedure(s)

⊘ = Modifier '-51' Exempt ► ◄ = New or Revised Text + = Add-on Code CPT 2002

Surgery Guidelines

Items used by all physicians in reporting their services are presented in the **Introduction.** Some of the commonalities are repeated here for the convenience of those physicians referring to this section on **Surgery.** Other definitions and items unique to Surgery are also listed.

Physicians' Services

Physicians' services rendered in the office, home, or hospital, consultations, and other medical services are listed in the section entitled **Evaluation and Management Services** (99200 series) found in the front of the book, beginning on page 9. "Special Services and Reports" (99000 series) is presented in the **Medicine** section.

►CPT Surgical Package Definition◄

►The services provided by the physician to any patient by their very nature are variable. The CPT codes that represent a readily identifiable surgical procedure thereby include, on a procedure-by-procedure basis, a variety of services. In defining the specific services "included" in a given CPT surgical code, the following services are always included in addition to the operation per se:

- local infiltration, metacarpal/metatarsal/digital block or topical anesthesia;
- subsequent to the decision for surgery, one related E/M encounter on the date immediately prior to or on the date of procedure (including history and physical);
- immediate postoperative care, including dictating operative notes, talking with the family and other physicians;
- writing orders;
- evaluating the patient in the postanesthesia recovery area;
- typical postoperative follow-up care.◄

Follow-Up Care for Diagnostic Procedures

Follow-up care for diagnostic procedures (eg, endoscopy, arthroscopy, injection procedures for radiography) includes only that care related to recovery from the diagnostic procedure itself. Care of the condition for which the diagnostic procedure was performed or of other concomitant conditions is not included and may be listed separately.

Follow-Up Care for Therapeutic Surgical Procedures

Follow-up care for therapeutic surgical procedures includes only that care which is usually a part of the surgical service. Complications, exacerbations, recurrence, or the presence of other diseases or injuries requiring additional services should be ►separately◄ reported.

Materials Supplied by Physician

Supplies and materials provided by the physician (eg, sterile trays/drugs), over and above those usually included with the ►procedure(s)◄ rendered ►are reported◄ separately. List drugs, trays, supplies, and materials provided. Identify as 99070 ►or specific supply code.◄

Reporting More Than One Procedure/Service

When a physician performs more than one procedure/ service on the same date, same session or during a post-operative period (subject to the "surgical package" concept), several CPT modifiers may apply. (See Appendix A for definition.)

►-27 Multiple Outpatient Hospital E/M Encounters on the Same Date◄

►For hospital outpatient reporting purposes, utilization of hospital resources related to separate and distinct E/M encounters performed in multiple outpatient hospital settings on the same date may be reported by adding the modifier '-27' to each appropriate level outpatient and/or emergency department E/M code(s). This modifier provides a means of reporting circumstances involving evaluation and management services provided by physician(s) in more than one (multiple) outpatient hospital setting(s) (eg, hospital emergency department, clinic). **Note:** This modifier is not to be used for physician reporting of multiple E/M services performed by the same physician on the same date. For physician reporting of all outpatient evaluation and management services provided by the same physician on the same date and performed in multiple outpatient setting(s) (eg, hospital emergency department, clinic), see **Evaluation and Management, Emergency Department,** or **Preventive Medicine Services** codes.◄

-51 Multiple Procedures

When multiple procedures/services (other than evaluation and management) are performed at the same session, report the most significant procedure first, with all other procedures listed with the '-51' modifier appended. For a list of procedures exempt from the use of the '-51' modifier, see Appendices E and F.

-58 Staged or Related Procedure or Service by the Same Physician During the Postoperative Period

When a procedure(s) is prospectively planned as a staged procedure, or when the secondary and subsequent procedure(s) is more extensive, or to indicate therapy following a diagnostic surgical procedure, use the '-58' modifier with the staged procedure(s).

-59 Distinct Procedural Service

For procedure(s)/service(s) not ordinarily performed or encountered on the same day by the same physician, but appropriate under certain circumstances (eg, different site or organ system, separate excision or lesion), use the '-59' modifier.

-76 Repeat Procedure by Same Physician

When a procedure or service is repeated by the same physician subsequent to the original service, use the '-76' modifier.

-77 Repeat Procedure by Another Physician

When a procedure is repeated by another physician subsequent to the original service, use the '-77' modifier.

-78 Return to the Operating Room for a Related Procedure During the Postoperative Period

When a procedure, related to the initial procedure, requires a return to the operating room during the postoperative period of that initial procedure, use the '-78' modifier.

-79 Unrelated Procedure or Service by the Same Physician During the Postoperative Period

When a procedure, unrelated to the initial procedure, is performed by the same physician during the postoperative period of the initial procedure, use the '-79' modifier.

►-91 Repeat Clinical Diagnostic Laboratory Test◄

►In the course of treatment of the patient, it may be necessary to repeat the same laboratory test on the same day to obtain subsequent (multiple) test results. Under these circumstances, the laboratory test performed can be identified by its usual procedure number and the addition of the modifier '-91'. **Note:** This modifier may not be used when tests are rerun to confirm initial results; due to testing problems with specimens or equipment; or for any other reason when a normal, one-time, reportable result is all that is required. This modifier may not be used when other code(s) describe a series of test results (eg, glucose tolerance tests, evocative/suppression testing). This modifier may only be used for laboratory test(s) performed more than once on the same day on the same patient.◄

Add-on Codes

Some of the listed procedures are commonly carried out in addition to the primary procedure performed. These additional or supplemental procedures are designated as "add-on" codes with a "✚" symbol, and are listed in Appendix E of *CPT*. Add-on codes in *CPT* can be readily identified by specific descriptor nomenclature which includes phrases such as "each additional" or "(List separately in addition to primary procedure)".

The "add-on" code concept in *CPT* applies only to add-on procedures/services performed by the same physician. Add-on codes describe additional intra-service work associated with the primary procedure (eg, additional digit(s), lesion(s), neurorrhaphy(s), vertebral segment(s), tendon(s), joint(s)).

Add-on codes are always performed in addition to the primary service/procedure, and must never be reported as a stand-alone code. All add-on codes found in *CPT* are exempt from the multiple procedure concept (see modifier '-51' definition of Surgery Guidelines).

Separate Procedure

Some of the procedures or services listed in *CPT* that are commonly carried out as an integral component of a total service or procedure have been identified by the inclusion of the term "separate procedure." The codes designated as "separate procedure" should not be reported in addition to the code for the total procedure or service of which it is considered an integral component.

However, when a procedure or service that is designated as a "separate procedure" is carried out independently or considered to be unrelated or distinct from other procedures/services provided at that time, it may be reported by itself, or in addition to other procedures/services by appending the modifier '-59' to the specific "separate procedure" code to indicate that the procedure is not considered to be a component of another procedure, but is a distinct, independent procedure. This may represent a different session or patient encounter, different procedure or surgery, different site or organ system, separate incision/excision, separate lesion, or separate injury (or area of injury in extensive injuries).

Subsection Information

Several of the subheadings or subsections have special needs or instructions unique to that section. Where these are indicated (eg, "Maternity Care and Delivery"), special **"Notes"** will be presented preceding those procedural terminology listings, referring to that subsection specifically. If there is an "Unlisted Procedure" code number (see below) for the individual subsection, it will also be shown. Those subsections within the **Surgery** section that have **"Notes"** are as follows:

Removal of Skin Tags	11200-11201
Shaving of Lesions	11300-11313
Excision—Benign Lesions	11400-11471
Excision—Malignant Lesions	11600-11646
Repair (Closure)	12001-13160
Adjacent Tissue Transfer or Rearrangement	14000-14350
Free Skin Grafts	15000-15400
Flaps (Skin and/or Deep Tissue)	15570-15999
Burns, Local Treatment	16000-16042
Destruction, Benign Lesions	17000-17250
Destruction, Malignant Lesions	17260-17286
Mohs Micrographic Surgery	17304-17310
Musculoskeletal	20000-29909
Wound Exploration—Trauma	20100-20103
Grafts (or Implants)	20900-20999
Spine: Excision	22100-22116
Spine: Osteotomy	22210-22226
Spine: Fracture/Dislocation	22305-22328
Spine: Arthrodesis	22548-22812

Spinal Instrumentation	22840-22855
Casting and Strapping	29000-29750
Cardiovascular System	33010-37799
Pacing Cardioverter-Pacemaker or Defibrillator	33200-33249
Venous—CABG	33510-33516
Arterial—Venous—CABG	33517-33530
Arterial—CABG	33533-33545
►**Endovascular Repair of Abdominal Aortic Aneurysm**	34800-34826◄
Transluminal Angioplasty	35450-35476
Transluminal Atherectomy	35480-35495
Composite Grafts	35681-35683
Arteries and Veins	34001-35907
Vascular Injection Procedures:	
Intravenous	36000-36015
►**Intra-Arterial/Intra-Aortic**	36100-36299◄
Endoscopy	31505-31579, 32601-32665, 43200-43272, 44360-►44397◄, 45300-►45387◄, 46600-46615, ►47370-47371◄, 47550-47556
Herniotomy	►49491◄-49611
Urodynamics	51725-51797
Endoscopy	
►**Urinary**◄	►50945-50980, 51990-52400◄
►**Testis**◄	►54690-54699◄
►**Female Genital**◄	►58550-58579,◄ ►58660-58679◄
►**Endocrine**◄	►60650-60659◄
Ureter and Pelvis	52320-52339
Maternity Care and Delivery	59000-59899
Surgery of Skull Base	61580-61619
Neurostimulators (Intracranial)	61850-61888
Neurostimulators (Spinal)	63650-63688
Neurostimulators (Peripheral Nerve)	64553-64595
Secondary Implants(s)	65125-65175
Removal Cataract	66830-66999
Prophylaxis	67141-67145
Operating Microscope	69990

Unlisted Service or Procedure

A service or procedure may be provided that is not listed in this edition of *CPT*. When reporting such a service, the appropriate "Unlisted Procedure" code may be used to indicate the service, identifying it by "Special Report" as discussed in the section below. The "Unlisted Procedures" and accompanying codes for **Surgery** are as follows:

15999	Unlisted procedure, excision pressure ulcer
17999	Unlisted procedure, skin, mucous membrane and subcutaneous tissue
19499	Unlisted procedure, breast
20999	Unlisted procedure, musculoskeletal system, general
21089	Unlisted maxillofacial prosthetic procedure

21299	Unlisted craniofacial and maxillofacial procedure
21499	Unlisted musculoskeletal procedure, head
21899	Unlisted procedure, neck or thorax
22899	Unlisted procedure, spine
22999	Unlisted procedure, abdomen, musculoskeletal system
23929	Unlisted procedure, shoulder
24999	Unlisted procedure, humerus or elbow
25999	Unlisted procedure, forearm or wrist
26989	Unlisted procedure, hands or fingers
27299	Unlisted procedure, pelvis or hip joint
27599	Unlisted procedure, femur or knee
27899	Unlisted procedure, leg or ankle
28899	Unlisted procedure, foot or toes
29799	Unlisted procedure, casting or strapping
▶ **29999**	Unlisted procedure, arthroscopy ◀
30999	Unlisted procedure, nose
31299	Unlisted procedure, accessory sinuses
31599	Unlisted procedure, larynx
31899	Unlisted procedure, trachea, bronchi
32999	Unlisted procedure, lungs and pleura
33999	Unlisted procedure, cardiac surgery
36299	Unlisted procedure, vascular injection
37799	Unlisted procedure, vascular surgery
38129	Unlisted laparoscopy procedure, spleen
38589	Unlisted laparoscopy procedure, lymphatic system
38999	Unlisted procedure, hemic or lymphatic system
39499	Unlisted procedure, mediastinum
39599	Unlisted procedure, diaphragm
40799	Unlisted procedure, lips
40899	Unlisted procedure, vestibule of mouth
41599	Unlisted procedure, tongue, floor of mouth
41899	Unlisted procedure, dentoalveolar structures
42299	Unlisted procedure, palate, uvula
42699	Unlisted procedure, salivary glands or ducts
42999	Unlisted procedure, pharynx, adenoids, or tonsils
43289	Unlisted laparoscopy procedure, esophagus
43499	Unlisted procedure, esophagus
43659	Unlisted laparoscopy procedure, stomach
43999	Unlisted procedure, stomach
44209	Unlisted laparoscopy procedure, intestine (except rectum)
44799	Unlisted procedure, intestine
44899	Unlisted procedure, Meckels diverticulum and the mesentery
44979	Unlisted laparoscopy procedure, appendix
45999	Unlisted procedure, rectum
46999	Unlisted procedure, anus
47379	Unlisted laparoscopic procedure, liver
47399	Unlisted procedure, liver
47579	Unlisted laparoscopy procedure, biliary tract
47999	Unlisted procedure, biliary tract

48999	Unlisted procedure, pancreas
49329	Unlisted laparoscopy procedure, abdomen, peritoneum and omentum
49659	Unlisted laparoscopy procedure, hernioplasty, herniorrhaphy, herniotomy
49999	Unlisted procedure, abdomen, peritoneum and omentum
50549	Unlisted laparoscopy procedure, renal
50949	Unlisted laparoscopy procedure, ureter
53899	Unlisted procedure, urinary system
54699	Unlisted laparoscopy procedure, testis
55559	Unlisted laparoscopy procedure, spermatic cord
55899	Unlisted procedure, male genital system
58578	Unlisted laparoscopy procedure, uterus
58579	Unlisted hysteroscopy procedure, uterus
58679	Unlisted laparoscopy procedure, oviduct, ovary
58999	Unlisted procedure, female genital system (nonobstetrical)
59898	Unlisted laparoscopy procedure, maternity care and delivery
59899	Unlisted procedure, maternity care and delivery
60659	Unlisted laparoscopy procedure, endocrine system
60699	Unlisted procedure, endocrine system
64999	Unlisted procedure, nervous system
66999	Unlisted procedure, anterior segment of eye
67299	Unlisted procedure, posterior segment
67399	Unlisted procedure, ocular muscle
67599	Unlisted procedure, orbit
67999	Unlisted procedure, eyelids
68399	Unlisted procedure, conjunctiva
68899	Unlisted procedure, lacrimal system
69399	Unlisted procedure, external ear
69799	Unlisted procedure, middle ear
69949	Unlisted procedure, inner ear
69979	Unlisted procedure, temporal bone, middle fossa approach

Special Report

A service that is rarely provided, unusual, variable, or new may require a special report in determining medical appropriateness of the service. Pertinent information should include an adequate definition or description of the nature, extent, and need for the procedure, and the time, effort, and equipment necessary to provide the service. Additional items which may be included are:

- complexity of symptoms;
- final diagnosis;
- pertinent physical findings (such as size, locations, and number of lesion(s), if appropriate);

- diagnostic and therapeutic procedures (including major and supplementary surgical procedures, if appropriate);
- concurrent problems;
- follow-up care.

Starred (*) Procedures or Items

Certain relatively small surgical services involve a readily identifiable surgical procedure but include variable preoperative and postoperative services (eg, incision and drainage of an abscess, injection of a tendon sheath, manipulation of a joint under anesthesia, dilation of the urethra). Because of the indefinite pre- and postoperative services the usual "package" concept for surgical services (see above) cannot be applied. Such procedures are identified by a star (*) following the procedure code number.

When a star (*) follows a surgical procedure code number, the following rules apply:

1. *The service as listed includes the surgical procedure only.* Associated pre- and postoperative services are not included in the service as listed.

2. *Preoperative services are considered as one of the following:*

- When the starred (*) procedure is carried out at the time of an initial visit (new patient) and this procedure constitutes the major service at that visit, procedure number 99025 is listed in lieu of the usual initial visit as an additional service.

- When the starred (*) procedure is carried out at the time of an initial or established patient visit involving significant identifiable services, the appropriate visit is listed with the modifier '-25' appended in addition to the starred (*) procedure and its follow-up care.

- When the starred (*) procedure requires hospitalization, an appropriate hospital visit is listed in addition to the starred (*) procedure and its follow-up care.

3. *All postoperative care is added on a service-by-service basis (eg, office or hospital visit, cast change).*

4. *Complications are added on a service-by-service basis (as with all surgical procedures).*

Surgical Destruction

Surgical destruction is a part of a surgical procedure and different methods of destruction are not ordinarily listed separately unless the technique substantially alters the standard management of a problem or condition. Exceptions under special circumstances are provided for by separate code numbers.

Notes

Surgery

►General◄

(10000-10020 have been deleted. To report see 10060, 10061)

● **10021** Fine needle aspiration; without imaging guidance

● **10022**   with imaging guidance

    ►(For radiological supervision and interpretation, see 76003, 76360, 76942)◄

    ►(For percutaneous needle biopsy, see 32405 for lung, 47000, 47001 for liver, 48102 for pancreas, 49180 for abdominal or retroperitoneal mass)◄

    ►(For evaluation of fine needle aspirate, see 88172, 88173)◄

Integumentary System

Skin, Subcutaneous and Accessory Structures

Incision and Drainage

(For excision, see 11400, et seq)

10040* Acne surgery (eg, marsupialization, opening or removal of multiple milia, comedones, cysts, pustules)

10060* Incision and drainage of abscess (eg, carbuncle, suppurative hidradenitis, cutaneous or subcutaneous abscess, cyst, furuncle, or paronychia); simple or single

10061   complicated or multiple

10080* Incision and drainage of pilonidal cyst; simple

10081   complicated

(For excision of pilonidal cyst, see 11770-11772)

(10100, 10101 have been deleted. To report, see 10060, 10061)

10120* Incision and removal of foreign body, subcutaneous tissues; simple

10121   complicated

(To report wound exploration due to penetrating trauma without laparotomy or thoracotomy, see 20100-20103, as appropriate)

(To report debridement associated with open fracture(s) and/or dislocation(s), use 11010-11012, as appropriate)

10140* Incision and drainage of hematoma, seroma or fluid collection

    ►(If imaging guidance is performed, see 76360, 76393, 76942)◄

(10141 has been deleted. To report, use 10140)

10160* Puncture aspiration of abscess, hematoma, bulla, or cyst

    ►(If imaging guidance is performed, see 76360, 76393, 76942)◄

10180 Incision and drainage, complex, postoperative wound infection

(For secondary closure of surgical wound, see 12020, 12021, 13160)

Excision—Debridement

(For dermabrasions, see 15780-15783)

(For nail debridement, see 11720-11721)

(For burn(s), see 16000-16035)

11000* Debridement of extensive eczematous or infected skin; up to 10% of body surface

+ 11001   each additional 10% of the body surface (List separately in addition to code for primary procedure)

(Use 11001 in conjunction with code 11000)

11010 Debridement including removal of foreign material associated with open fracture(s) and/or dislocation(s); skin and subcutaneous tissues

11011   skin, subcutaneous tissue, muscle fascia, and muscle

11012   skin, subcutaneous tissue, muscle fascia, muscle, and bone

11040 Debridement; skin, partial thickness

11041   skin, full thickness

11042   skin, and subcutaneous tissue

11043   skin, subcutaneous tissue, and muscle

11044   skin, subcutaneous tissue, muscle, and bone

(Do not report 11040-11044 in addition to 97601, 97602)

Paring or Cutting

(11050-11052 have been deleted. To report paring, see 11055-11057, or to report destruction, see 17000-17004)

11055 Paring or cutting of benign hyperkeratotic lesion (eg, corn or callus); single lesion

11056   two to four lesions

11057 more than four lesions

(11060-11062 have been deleted. To report, see 11300-11313)

Biopsy

11100 Biopsy of skin, subcutaneous tissue and/or mucous membrane (including simple closure), unless otherwise listed (separate procedure); single lesion

+ 11101 each separate/additional lesion (List separately in addition to code for primary procedure)

(Use 11101 in conjunction with code 11100)

(For biopsy of conjunctiva, use 68100; eyelid, use 67810)

Removal of Skin Tags

Removal by scissoring or any sharp method, ligature strangulation, electrosurgical destruction or combination of treatment modalities including chemical or electrocauterization of wound, with or without local anesthesia.

11200* Removal of skin tags, multiple fibrocutaneous tags, any area; up to and including 15 lesions

+ 11201 each additional ten lesions (List separately in addition to code for primary procedure)

(Use 11201 in conjunction with code 11200)

Shaving of Epidermal or Dermal Lesions

Shaving is the sharp removal by transverse incision or horizontal slicing to remove epidermal and dermal lesions without a full-thickness dermal excision. This includes local anesthesia, chemical or electrocauterization of the wound. The wound does not require suture closure.

11300* Shaving of epidermal or dermal lesion, single lesion, trunk, arms or legs; lesion diameter 0.5 cm or less

11301 lesion diameter 0.6 to 1.0 cm

11302 lesion diameter 1.1 to 2.0 cm

11303 lesion diameter over 2.0 cm

11305* Shaving of epidermal or dermal lesion, single lesion, scalp, neck, hands, feet, genitalia; lesion diameter 0.5 cm or less

11306 lesion diameter 0.6 to 1.0 cm

11307 lesion diameter 1.1 to 2.0 cm

11308 lesion diameter over 2.0 cm

11310* Shaving of epidermal or dermal lesion, single lesion, face, ears, eyelids, nose, lips, mucous membrane; lesion diameter 0.5 cm or less

11311 lesion diameter 0.6 to 1.0 cm

11312 lesion diameter 1.1 to 2.0 cm

11313 lesion diameter over 2.0 cm

Excision—Benign Lesions

Excision (including simple closure) of benign lesions of skin or subcutaneous tissues (eg, cicatricial, fibrous, inflammatory, congenital, cystic lesions), including local anesthesia. See appropriate size and area below.

Excision is defined as full-thickness (through the dermis) removal of the following lesions and includes simple (non-layered) closure. The closure of defects created by incision, excision, or trauma may require intermediate or complex closure. Repair by intermediate or complex closure should be reported separately. See page 48 for definition of intermediate or complex closure.

(For excision of benign lesions requiring more than simple closure, ie, requiring intermediate or complex closure, report 11400-11446 in addition to appropriate intermediate (12031-12057) or complex closure (13100-13153) codes. For reconstructive closure, see 14000-14300, 15000-15261, 15570-15770)

(For electrosurgical and other methods, see 17000 et seq)

11400 Excision, benign lesion, except skin tag (unless listed elsewhere), trunk, arms or legs; lesion diameter 0.5 cm or less

11401 lesion diameter 0.6 to 1.0 cm

11402 lesion diameter 1.1 to 2.0 cm

11403 lesion diameter 2.1 to 3.0 cm

11404 lesion diameter 3.1 to 4.0 cm

11406 lesion diameter over 4.0 cm

(For unusual or complicated excision, add modifier '-22')

11420 Excision, benign lesion, except skin tag (unless listed elsewhere), scalp, neck, hands, feet, genitalia; lesion diameter 0.5 cm or less

11421 lesion diameter 0.6 to 1.0 cm

11422 lesion diameter 1.1 to 2.0 cm

11423 lesion diameter 2.1 to 3.0 cm

11424 lesion diameter 3.1 to 4.0 cm

11426 lesion diameter over 4.0 cm

(For unusual or complicated excision, add modifier '-22')

11440 Excision, other benign lesion (unless listed elsewhere), face, ears, eyelids, nose, lips, mucous membrane; lesion diameter 0.5 cm or less

11441 lesion diameter 0.6 to 1.0 cm

11442 lesion diameter 1.1 to 2.0 cm

11443 lesion diameter 2.1 to 3.0 cm

11444 lesion diameter 3.1 to 4.0 cm

11446   lesion diameter over 4.0 cm

(For unusual or complicated excision, add modifier '-22')

(For eyelids involving more than skin, see also 67800 et seq)

11450   Excision of skin and subcutaneous tissue for hidradenitis, axillary; with simple or intermediate repair

11451   with complex repair

11462   Excision of skin and subcutaneous tissue for hidradenitis, inguinal; with simple or intermediate repair

11463   with complex repair

11470   Excision of skin and subcutaneous tissue for hidradenitis, perianal, perineal, or umbilical; with simple or intermediate repair

11471   with complex repair

(When skin graft or flap is used for closure, use appropriate procedure code in addition)

(For bilateral procedure, add modifier '-50')

Excision—Malignant Lesions

Excision (including simple closure) of malignant lesion of skin or subcutaneous tissues including local anesthesia, each lesion. For removal of malignant lesions of skin by any method other than excision, as defined above, see destruction codes 17000-17999.

Excision is defined as full-thickness (through the dermis) removal of the following lesions and includes simple (non-layered) closure. The closure of defects created by incision, excision, or trauma may require intermediate or complex closure. Repair by intermediate or complex closure should be reported separately. See page 48 for definition of intermediate or complex closure.

(For excision of malignant lesions requiring more than simple closure, ie, requiring intermediate or complex closure, report 11600-11646 in addition to appropriate intermediate (12031-12057) or complex closure (13100-13153) codes. For reconstructive closure, see 14000-14300, 15000-15261, 15570-15770)

11600   Excision, malignant lesion, trunk, arms, or legs; lesion diameter 0.5 cm or less

11601   lesion diameter 0.6 to 1.0 cm

11602   lesion diameter 1.1 to 2.0 cm

11603   lesion diameter 2.1 to 3.0 cm

11604   lesion diameter 3.1 to 4.0 cm

11606   lesion diameter over 4.0 cm

11620   Excision, malignant lesion, scalp, neck, hands, feet, genitalia; lesion diameter 0.5 cm or less

11621   lesion diameter 0.6 to 1.0 cm

11622   lesion diameter 1.1 to 2.0 cm

11623   lesion diameter 2.1 to 3.0 cm

11624   lesion diameter 3.1 to 4.0 cm

11626   lesion diameter over 4.0 cm

11640   Excision, malignant lesion, face, ears, eyelids, nose, lips; lesion diameter 0.5 cm or less

11641   lesion diameter 0.6 to 1.0 cm

11642   lesion diameter 1.1 to 2.0 cm

11643   lesion diameter 2.1 to 3.0 cm

11644   lesion diameter 3.1 to 4.0 cm

11646   lesion diameter over 4.0 cm

(For eyelids involving more than skin, see also 67800 et seq)

Nails

(For drainage of paronychia or onychia, see 10060, 10061)

(11700, 11701 have been deleted. To report, use 11720, 11721)

(11710, 11711 have been deleted. To report, use 11720, 11721)

11719   Trimming of nondystrophic nails, any number

11720   Debridement of nail(s) by any method(s); one to five

11721   six or more

11730*   Avulsion of nail plate, partial or complete, simple; single

(11731 has been deleted. To report, use 11732)

+ 11732   each additional nail plate (List separately in addition to code for primary procedure)

(Use 11732 in conjunction with code 11730)

11740   Evacuation of subungual hematoma

11750   Excision of nail and nail matrix, partial or complete, (eg, ingrown or deformed nail) for permanent removal;

11752   with amputation of tuft of distal phalanx

(For skin graft, if used, use 15050)

▲11755   Biopsy of nail unit (eg, plate, bed, matrix, hyponychium, proximal and lateral nail folds) (separate procedure)

11760   Repair of nail bed

11762   Reconstruction of nail bed with graft

11765   Wedge excision of skin of nail fold (eg, for ingrown toenail)

(For incision of pilonidal cyst, see 10080, 10081)

11770   Excision of pilonidal cyst or sinus; simple

11771   extensive

11772   complicated

Introduction

11900* Injection, intralesional; up to and including seven lesions

11901* more than seven lesions

(11900, 11901 are not to be used for preoperative local anesthetic injection)

(For veins, see 36470, 36471)

(For intralesional chemotherapy administration, see 96405, 96406)

11920 Tattooing, intradermal introduction of insoluble opaque pigments to correct color defects of skin, including micropigmentation; 6.0 sq cm or less

11921 6.1 to 20.0 sq cm

+ 11922 each additional 20.0 sq cm (List separately in addition to code for primary procedure)

(Use 11922 in conjunction with code 11921)

11950 Subcutaneous injection of filling material (eg, collagen); 1 cc or less

11951 1.1 to 5.0 cc

11952 5.1 to 10.0 cc

11954 over 10.0 cc

11960 Insertion of tissue expander(s) for other than breast, including subsequent expansion

(For breast reconstruction with tissue expander(s), use 19357)

11970 Replacement of tissue expander with permanent prosthesis

11971 Removal of tissue expander(s) without insertion of prosthesis

11975 Insertion, implantable contraceptive capsules

11976 Removal, implantable contraceptive capsules

11977 Removal with reinsertion, implantable contraceptive capsules

11980 Subcutaneous hormone pellet implantation (implantation of estradiol and/or testosterone pellets beneath the skin)

● **11981** Insertion, non-biodegradable drug delivery implant

● **11982** Removal, non-biodegradable drug delivery implant

● **11983** Removal with reinsertion, non-biodegradable drug delivery implant

Repair (Closure)

Use the codes in this section to designate wound closure utilizing sutures, staples, or tissue adhesives (eg, 2-cyanoacrylate), either singly or in combination with each other, or in combination with adhesive strips. Wound closure utilizing adhesive strips as the sole repair material should be coded using the appropriate E/M code.

Definitions

The repair of wounds may be classified as Simple, Intermediate, or Complex.

Simple repair is used when the wound is superficial; eg, involving primarily epidermis or dermis, or subcutaneous tissues without significant involvement of deeper structures, and requires simple one layer closure. This includes local anesthesia and chemical or electrocauterization of wounds not closed.

Intermediate repair includes the repair of wounds that, in addition to the above, require layered closure of one or more of the deeper layers of subcutaneous tissue and superficial (non-muscle) fascia, in addition to the skin (epidermal and dermal) closure. Single-layer closure of heavily contaminated wounds that have required extensive cleaning or removal of particulate matter also constitutes intermediate repair.

Complex repair includes the repair of wounds requiring more than layered closure, viz., scar revision, debridement, (eg, traumatic lacerations or avulsions), extensive undermining, stents or retention sutures. Necessary preparation includes creation of a defect for repairs (eg, excision of a scar requiring a complex repair) or the debridement of complicated lacerations or avulsions. Complex repair does not include excision of benign (11400-11446) or malignant (11600-11646) lesions.

Instructions for listing services at time of wound repair:

1. The repaired wound(s) should be measured and recorded in centimeters, whether curved, angular, or stellate.

2. When multiple wounds are repaired, add together the lengths of those in the same classification (see above) and from all anatomic sites that are grouped together into the same code descriptor. For example, add together the lengths of intermediate repairs to the trunk and extremities. Do not add lengths of repairs from different groupings of anatomic sites (eg, face and extremities). Also, do not add together lengths of different classifications (eg, intermediate and complex repairs).

When more than one classification of wounds is repaired, list the more complicated as the primary procedure and the less complicated as the secondary procedure, using modifier '-51'.

3. Decontamination and/or debridement: Debridement is considered a separate procedure only when gross contamination requires prolonged cleansing, when appreciable amounts of devitalized or contaminated tissue are removed, or when debridement is carried out separately without immediate primary closure. (For extensive debridement of soft tissue and/or bone, see 11040-11044.)

(For extensive debridement of soft tissue and/or bone, not associated with open fracture(s) and/or dislocation(s) resulting from penetrating and/or blunt trauma, see 11040-11044.)

(For extensive debridement of subcutaneous tissue, muscle fascia, muscle, and/or bone associated with open fracture(s) and/or dislocation(s), see 11010-11012.)

4. Involvement of nerves, blood vessels and tendons: Report under appropriate system (Nervous, Cardiovascular, Musculoskeletal) for repair of these structures. The repair of these associated wounds is included in the primary procedure unless it qualifies as a complex wound, in which case modifier '-51' applies.

Simple ligation of vessels in an open wound is considered as part of any wound closure.

Simple "exploration" of nerves, blood vessels or tendons exposed in an open wound is also considered part of the essential treatment of the wound and is not a separate procedure unless appreciable dissection is required. If the wound requires enlargement, extension of dissection (to determine penetration), debridement, removal of foreign body(s), ligation or coagulation of minor subcutaneous and/or muscular blood vessel(s) of the subcutaneous tissue, muscle fascia, and/or muscle, not requiring thoracotomy or laparotomy, use codes 20100-20103, as appropriate.

Repair—Simple

Sum of lengths of repairs for each group of anatomic sites.

12001*	Simple repair of superficial wounds of scalp, neck, axillae, external genitalia, trunk and/or extremities (including hands and feet); 2.5 cm or less
12002*	2.6 cm to 7.5 cm
12004*	7.6 cm to 12.5 cm
12005	12.6 cm to 20.0 cm
12006	20.1 cm to 30.0 cm
12007	over 30.0 cm
12011*	Simple repair of superficial wounds of face, ears, eyelids, nose, lips and/or mucous membranes; 2.5 cm or less
12013*	2.6 cm to 5.0 cm
12014	5.1 cm to 7.5 cm
12015	7.6 cm to 12.5 cm
12016	12.6 cm to 20.0 cm
12017	20.1 cm to 30.0 cm
12018	over 30.0 cm
12020	Treatment of superficial wound dehiscence; simple closure
12021	with packing

(For extensive or complicated secondary wound closure, use 13160)

Repair—Intermediate

Sum of lengths of repairs for each group of anatomic sites.

12031*	Layer closure of wounds of scalp, axillae, trunk and/or extremities (excluding hands and feet); 2.5 cm or less
12032*	2.6 cm to 7.5 cm
12034	7.6 cm to 12.5 cm
12035	12.6 cm to 20.0 cm
12036	20.1 cm to 30.0 cm
12037	over 30.0 cm
12041*	Layer closure of wounds of neck, hands, feet and/or external genitalia; 2.5 cm or less
12042	2.6 cm to 7.5 cm
12044	7.6 cm to 12.5 cm
12045	12.6 cm to 20.0 cm
12046	20.1 cm to 30.0 cm
12047	over 30.0 cm
12051*	Layer closure of wounds of face, ears, eyelids, nose, lips and/or mucous membranes; 2.5 cm or less
12052	2.6 cm to 5.0 cm
12053	5.1 cm to 7.5 cm
12054	7.6 cm to 12.5 cm
12055	12.6 cm to 20.0 cm
12056	20.1 cm to 30.0 cm
12057	over 30.0 cm

Repair—Complex

Reconstructive procedures, complicated wound closure.

Sum of lengths of repairs for each group of anatomic sites.

	(For full thickness repair of lip or eyelid, see respective anatomical subsections)
13100	Repair, complex, trunk; 1.1 cm to 2.5 cm
	(For 1.0 cm or less, see simple or intermediate repairs)
13101	2.6 cm to 7.5 cm
+ 13102	each additional 5 cm or less (List separately in addition to code for primary procedure)
	(Use 13102 in conjunction with code 13101)
13120	Repair, complex, scalp, arms, and/or legs; 1.1 cm to 2.5 cm
	(For 1.0 cm or less, see simple or intermediate repairs)
13121	2.6 cm to 7.5 cm

+ 13122   each additional 5 cm or less (List separately in addition to code for primary procedure)

(Use 13122 in conjunction with code 13121)

13131   Repair, complex, forehead, cheeks, chin, mouth, neck, axillae, genitalia, hands and/or feet; 1.1 cm to 2.5 cm

(For 1.0 cm or less, see simple or intermediate repairs)

13132   2.6 cm to 7.5 cm

+ 13133   each additional 5 cm or less (List separately in addition to code for primary procedure)

(Use 13133 in conjunction with code 13132)

13150   Repair, complex, eyelids, nose, ears and/or lips; 1.0 cm or less

(See also 40650-40654, 67961-67975)

13151   1.1 cm to 2.5 cm

13152   2.6 cm to 7.5 cm

+ 13153   each additional 5 cm or less (List separately in addition to code for primary procedure)

(Use 13153 in conjunction with code 13152)

13160   Secondary closure of surgical wound or dehiscence, extensive or complicated

(For packing or simple secondary wound closure, see 12020, 12021)

(13300 has been deleted. To report, see 13102, 13122, 13133 and 13153)

Adjacent Tissue Transfer or Rearrangement

For full thickness repair of lip or eyelid, see respective anatomical subsections.

Excision (including lesion) and/or repair by adjacent tissue transfer or rearrangement (eg, Z-plasty, W-plasty, V-Y plasty, rotation flap, advancement flap, double pedicle flap). When applied in repairing lacerations, the procedures listed must be developed by the surgeon to accomplish the repair. They do not apply when direct closure or rearrangement of traumatic wounds incidentally result in these configurations.

Skin graft necessary to close secondary defect is considered an additional procedure.

14000   Adjacent tissue transfer or rearrangement, trunk; defect 10 sq cm or less

14001   defect 10.1 sq cm to 30.0 sq cm

14020   Adjacent tissue transfer or rearrangement, scalp, arms and/or legs; defect 10 sq cm or less

14021   defect 10.1 sq cm to 30.0 sq cm

14040   Adjacent tissue transfer or rearrangement, forehead, cheeks, chin, mouth, neck, axillae, genitalia, hands and/or feet; defect 10 sq cm or less

14041   defect 10.1 sq cm to 30.0 sq cm

14060   Adjacent tissue transfer or rearrangement, eyelids, nose, ears and/or lips; defect 10 sq cm or less

14061   defect 10.1 sq cm to 30.0 sq cm

(For eyelid, full thickness, see 67961 et seq)

14300   Adjacent tissue transfer or rearrangement, more than 30 sq cm, unusual or complicated, any area

14350   Filleted finger or toe flap, including preparation of recipient site

Free Skin Grafts

Identify by size and location of the defect (recipient area) and the type of graft; includes simple debridement of granulations or recent avulsion.

When a primary procedure such as orbitectomy, radical mastectomy, or deep tumor removal requires skin graft for definitive closure, see appropriate anatomical subsection for primary procedure and this section for skin graft.

►Use 15000 for initial wound preparation.◄

►Use 15100-15261 for autogenous skin grafts. For autogenous tissue-cultured skin grafts, use 15100-15121. These codes include harvesting of keratinocytes and their subsequent application. Procedures are coded by recipient site. Use codes 15342 and 15343 for application of skin substitute/neodermis. Use modifier '-58' for staged application procedure(s).◄

Repair of donor site requiring skin graft or local flaps is to be added as an additional procedure.

Codes 15000, 15001, 15350, 15351, 15400, 15401 describe burn and wound preparation and management procedures. The following definition should be applied to codes 15000, 15001, 15100, 15101, 15120, 15121 when determining the involvement of body size. The measurement of 100 sq cm is applicable to adults and children age 10 and over, percentages apply to infants and children under the age of 10.

(For microvascular flaps, see 15756-15758)

15000   Surgical preparation or creation of recipient site by excision of open wounds, burn eschar, or scar (including subcutaneous tissues); first 100 sq cm or one percent of body area of infants and children

(For appropriate skin grafts, see 15050-15261; list the free graft separately by its procedure number when the graft, immediate or delayed, is applied)

+ 15001   each additional 100 sq cm or each additional one percent of body area of infants and children (List separately in addition to code for primary procedure)

(Use code 15001 in conjunction with code 15000)

(For excision of benign lesions, see 11400-11471)

(For excision of malignant lesions, see 11600-11646)

(For excision with alloplastic dressing, use 15000 only)

(For excision with immediate skin grafting use 15050-15261 in addition to 15000)

(For excision with immediate allograft placement use 15350 in addition to 15000)

(For excision with immediate xenograft placement use 15400 in addition to 15000)

15050   Pinch graft, single or multiple, to cover small ulcer, tip of digit, or other minimal open area (except on face), up to defect size 2 cm diameter

15100   Split graft, trunk, arms, legs; first 100 sq cm or less, or one percent of body area of infants and children (except 15050)

+ 15101   each additional 100 sq cm, or each additional one percent of body area of infants and children, or part thereof (List separately in addition to code for primary procedure)

(Use 15101 in conjunction with code 15100)

15120   Split graft, face, scalp, eyelids, mouth, neck, ears, orbits, genitalia, hands, feet and/or multiple digits; first 100 sq cm or less, or one percent of body area of infants and children (except 15050)

+ 15121   each additional 100 sq cm, or each additional one percent of body area of infants and children, or part thereof (List separately in addition to code for primary procedure)

(Use 15121 in conjunction with code 15120)

(For eyelids, see also 67961 et seq)

15200   Full thickness graft, free, including direct closure of donor site, trunk; 20 sq cm or less

+ 15201   each additional 20 sq cm (List separately in addition to code for primary procedure)

(Use 15201 in conjunction with code 15200)

15220   Full thickness graft, free, including direct closure of donor site, scalp, arms, and/or legs; 20 sq cm or less

+ 15221   each additional 20 sq cm (List separately in addition to code for primary procedure)

(Use 15221 in conjunction with code 15220)

15240   Full thickness graft, free, including direct closure of donor site, forehead, cheeks, chin, mouth, neck, axillae, genitalia, hands, and/or feet; 20 sq cm or less

(For finger tip graft, use 15050)

(For repair of syndactyly, fingers, see 26560-26562)

+ 15241   each additional 20 sq cm (List separately in addition to code for primary procedure)

(Use 15241 in conjunction with code 15240)

15260   Full thickness graft, free, including direct closure of donor site, nose, ears, eyelids, and/or lips; 20 sq cm or less

+ 15261   each additional 20 sq cm (List separately in addition to code for primary procedure)

(Use 15261 in conjunction with code 15260)

(For eyelids, see also 67961 et seq)

(Repair of donor site requiring skin graft or local flaps, to be added as additional separate procedure)

15342   Application of bilaminate skin substitute/neodermis; 25 sq cm

+ 15343   each additional 25 sq cm (List separately in addition to code for primary procedure)

(Use 15343 in conjunction with code 15342)

15350   Application of allograft, skin; 100 sq cm or less

(For staged tissue graft implantation, use modifier '-58')

+ 15351   each additional 100 sq cm (List separately in addition to code for primary procedure)

(Use 15351 in conjunction with code 15350)

15400   Application of xenograft, skin; 100 sq cm or less

(15410-15416 have been deleted. To report, see 15756-15758)

+ 15401   each additional 100 sq cm (List separately in addition to code for primary procedure)

(Use 15401 in conjunction with code 15400)

Flaps (Skin and/or Deep Tissues)

Regions listed refer to recipient area (not donor site) when flap is being attached in transfer or to final site.

Regions listed refer to donor site when tube is formed for later or when "delay" of flap is prior to transfer.

Procedures 15570-15738 do not include extensive immobilization (eg, large plaster casts and other immobilizing devices are considered additional separate procedures).

Repair of donor site requiring skin graft or local flaps is considered an additional separate procedure.

(For microvascular flaps, see 15756-15758)

(15500-15515 have been deleted. To report, use 15000)

(15540-15555 have been deleted. To report, see 15570-15576)

15570   Formation of direct or tubed pedicle, with or without transfer; trunk

15572   scalp, arms, or legs

15574	forehead, cheeks, chin, mouth, neck, axillae, genitalia, hands or feet
15576	eyelids, nose, ears, lips, or intraoral

(15580 has been deleted. To report, use 15574)

15600	Delay of flap or sectioning of flap (division and inset); at trunk
15610	at scalp, arms, or legs
15620	at forehead, cheeks, chin, neck, axillae, genitalia, hands, or feet

(15625 has been deleted. To report, use 15620)

15630	at eyelids, nose, ears, or lips
15650	Transfer, intermediate, of any pedicle flap (eg, abdomen to wrist, Walking tube), any location

(15700-15730 have been deleted. To report, see 15570-15576)

(For eyelids, nose, ears, or lips, see also anatomical area)

(For revision, defatting or rearranging of transferred pedicle flap or skin graft, see 13100-14300)

(Procedures 15732-15738 are described by donor site of the muscle, myocutaneous, or fasciocutaneous flap)

▲ **15732**	Muscle, myocutaneous, or fasciocutaneous flap; head and neck (eg, temporalis, masseter muscle, sternocleidomastoid, levator scapulae)
15734	trunk
15736	upper extremity
15738	lower extremity

Other Flaps and Grafts

Repair of donor site requiring skin graft or local flaps should be reported as an additional procedure.

15740	Flap; island pedicle

(15745 has been deleted. To report, see 15732-15738)

15750	neurovascular pedicle

(15755 has been deleted. To report, see 15756-15758)

15756	Free muscle flap with or without skin with microvascular anastomosis

(Do not report code 69990 in addition to code 15756)

15757	Free skin flap with microvascular anastomosis

(Do not report code 69990 in addition to code 15757)

15758	Free fascial flap with microvascular anastomosis

(Do not report code 69990 in addition to code 15758)

15760	Graft; composite (eg, full thickness of external ear or nasal ala), including primary closure, donor area
15770	derma-fat-fascia

15775	Punch graft for hair transplant; 1 to 15 punch grafts
15776	more than 15 punch grafts

(For strip transplant, use 15220)

Other Procedures

15780	Dermabrasion; total face (eg, for acne scarring, fine wrinkling, rhytids, general keratosis)
15781	segmental, face
15782	regional, other than face
15783	superficial, any site, (eg, tattoo removal)

(15785 has been deleted. To report, see 15781, 15782)

15786✱	Abrasion; single lesion (eg, keratosis, scar)
+ 15787	each additional four lesions or less (List separately in addition to code for primary procedure)

(Use 15787 in conjunction with code 15786)

15788	Chemical peel, facial; epidermal
15789	dermal

(15790, 15791 have been deleted. To report, see 15788-15793)

15792	Chemical peel, nonfacial; epidermal
15793	dermal

(15800 has been deleted)

15810	Salabrasion; 20 sq cm or less
15811	over 20 sq cm
15819	Cervicoplasty
15820	Blepharoplasty, lower eyelid;
15821	with extensive herniated fat pad
15822	Blepharoplasty, upper eyelid;
15823	with excessive skin weighting down lid

(For bilateral blepharoplasty, add modifier '-50')

(See also 67916, 67917, 67923, 67924)

15824	Rhytidectomy; forehead

(For repair of brow ptosis, use 67900)

15825	neck with platysmal tightening (platysmal flap, P-flap)
15826	glabellar frown lines

(15827 has been deleted. To report, use 15838)

15828	cheek, chin, and neck
15829	superficial musculoaponeurotic system (SMAS) flap

(For bilateral rhytidectomy, add modifier '-50')

15831	Excision, excessive skin and subcutaneous tissue (including lipectomy); abdomen (abdominoplasty)
15832	thigh
15833	leg

15834	hip	**15937**	with ostectomy

15834   hip

15835   buttock

15836   arm

15837   forearm or hand

15838   submental fat pad

15839   other area

(For bilateral procedure, add modifier '-50')

15840   Graft for facial nerve paralysis; free fascia graft (including obtaining fascia)

(For bilateral procedure, add modifier '-50')

15841   free muscle graft (including obtaining graft)

15842   free muscle flap by microsurgical technique

(Do not report code 69990 in addition to code 15842)

15845   regional muscle transfer

(For intravenous fluorescein examination of blood flow in graft or flap, use 15860)

(For nerve transfers, decompression, or repair, see 64831-64876, 64905, 64907, 69720, 69725, 69740, 69745, 69955)

15850   Removal of sutures under anesthesia (other than local), same surgeon

15851   Removal of sutures under anesthesia (other than local), other surgeon

15852   Dressing change (for other than burns) under anesthesia (other than local)

▲ **15860**   Intravenous injection of agent (eg, fluorescein) to test vascular flow in flap or graft

(15875 has been deleted. To report, see 15876-15879)

15876   Suction assisted lipectomy; head and neck

15877   trunk

15878   upper extremity

15879   lower extremity

Pressure Ulcers (Decubitus Ulcers)

15920   Excision, coccygeal pressure ulcer, with coccygectomy; with primary suture

15922   with flap closure

(15930 has been deleted. To report, use 15934)

15931   Excision, sacral pressure ulcer, with primary suture;

(15932 has been deleted)

15933   with ostectomy

15934   Excision, sacral pressure ulcer, with skin flap closure;

15935   with ostectomy

15936   Excision, sacral pressure ulcer, in preparation for muscle or myocutaneous flap or skin graft closure;

15937   with ostectomy

(For repair of defect using muscle or myocutaneous flap, use code(s) 15734 and/or 15738 in addition to 15936, 15937. For repair of defect using split skin graft, use codes 15100 and/or 15101 in addition to 15936, 15937)

15940   Excision, ischial pressure ulcer, with primary suture;

15941   with ostectomy (ischiectomy)

(15942, 15943 have been deleted. To report, see 15944-15946)

15944   Excision, ischial pressure ulcer, with skin flap closure;

15945   with ostectomy

15946   Excision, ischial pressure ulcer, with ostectomy, in preparation for muscle or myocutaneous flap or skin graft closure

(For repair of defect using muscle or myocutaneous flap, use code(s) 15734 and/or 15738 in addition to 15946. For repair of defect using split skin graft, use codes 15100 and/or 15101 in addition to 15946)

15950   Excision, trochanteric pressure ulcer, with primary suture;

15951   with ostectomy

15952   Excision, trochanteric pressure ulcer, with skin flap closure;

15953   with ostectomy

(15954 and 15955 have been deleted. To report, use appropriate debridement, closure or flap codes)

15956   Excision, trochanteric pressure ulcer, in preparation for muscle or myocutaneous flap or skin graft closure;

15958   with ostectomy

(For repair of defect using muscle or myocutaneous flap, use code(s) 15734 and/or 15738 in addition to 15956, 15958. For repair of defect using split skin graft, use codes 15100 and/or 15101 in addition to 15956, 15958)

(15960-15983 have been deleted. To report, use appropriate debridement, closure or flap codes)

15999   Unlisted procedure, excision pressure ulcer

(For free skin graft to close ulcer or donor site, see 15000 et seq)

Burns, Local Treatment

Procedures 16000-16036 refer to local treatment of burned surface only.

List percentage of body surface involved and depth of burn.

For necessary related medical services (eg, hospital visits, detention) in management of burned patients, see appropriate services in **Evaluation and Management** and **Medicine** sections.

(For skin graft, see 15100-15650)

16000 Initial treatment, first degree burn, when no more than local treatment is required

16010 Dressings and/or debridement, initial or subsequent; under anesthesia, small

16015 under anesthesia, medium or large, or with major debridement

16020* without anesthesia, office or hospital, small

16025* without anesthesia, medium (eg, whole face or whole extremity)

16030 without anesthesia, large (eg, more than one extremity)

16035 Escharotomy; initial incision

+ 16036 each additional incision (List separately in addition to code for primary procedure)

(Use 16036 in conjunction with code 16035)

(For debridement, curettement of burn wound, see 16010-16030)

(16040-16042 have been deleted. To report, use 15000)

Destruction

Destruction means the ablation of benign, premalignant or malignant tissues by any method, with or without curettement, including local anesthesia, and not usually requiring closure.

Any method includes electrosurgery, cryosurgery, laser and chemical treatment. Lesions include condylomata, papillomata, molluscum contagiosum, herpetic lesions, warts (ie, common, plantar, flat), milia, or other benign, premalignant (eg, actinic keratoses), or malignant lesions.

(For destruction of lesion(s) in specific anatomic sites, see 40820, 46900-46917, 46924, 54050-54057, 54065, 56501, 56515, 57061, 57065, 67850, 68135)

(For paring or cutting of benign hyperkeratotic lesions (eg, corns or calluses), see 11055-11057)

(For sharp removal or electrosurgical destruction of skin tags and fibrocutaneous tags, see 11200, 11201)

(For cryotherapy of acne, use 17340)

(For initiation or follow-up care of topical chemotherapy (eg, 5-FU or similar agents), see appropriate office visits)

(For shaving of epidermal or dermal lesions, see 11300-11313)

Destruction, Benign or Premalignant Lesions

▲17000* Destruction (eg, laser surgery, electrosurgery, cryosurgery, chemosurgery, surgical curettement), all benign or premalignant lesions (eg, actinic keratoses) other than skin tags or cutaneous vascular proliferative lesions; first lesion

(17001, 17002 have been deleted. To report, see 17003, 17004)

+ 17003 second through 14 lesions, each (List separately in addition to code for first lesion)

(Use 17003 in conjunction with code 17000)

⊘ ▲ 17004 Destruction (eg, laser surgery, electrosurgery, cryosurgery, chemosurgery, surgical curettement), all benign or premalignant lesions (eg, actinic keratoses) other than skin tags or cutaneous vascular proliferative lesions; 15 or more lesions

(Do not report 17004 in conjunction with codes 17000-17003)

(17010 has been deleted. To report, see specific anatomic site code)

(17100-17105 have been deleted. To report, see 17000, 17003, 17004)

17106 Destruction of cutaneous vascular proliferative lesions (eg, laser technique); less than 10 sq cm

17107 10.0 - 50.0 sq cm

17108 over 50.0 sq cm

▲17110* Destruction (eg, laser surgery, electrosurgery, cryosurgery, chemosurgery, surgical curettement), of flat warts, molluscum contagiosum, or milia; up to 14 lesions

17111 15 or more lesions

(For destruction of common or plantar warts, see 17000, 17003, 17004)

(17200, 17201 have been deleted. To report, see 11200, 11201)

17250* Chemical cauterization of granulation tissue (proud flesh, sinus or fistula)

(17250 is not to be used with removal or excision codes for the same lesion)

Destruction, Malignant Lesions, Any Method

▲17260* Destruction, malignant lesion (eg, laser surgery, electrosurgery, cryosurgery, chemosurgery, surgical curettement), trunk, arms or legs; lesion diameter 0.5 cm or less

17261 lesion diameter 0.6 to 1.0 cm

17262 lesion diameter 1.1 to 2.0 cm

17263 lesion diameter 2.1 to 3.0 cm

17264 lesion diameter 3.1 to 4.0 cm

17266 lesion diameter over 4.0 cm

▲17270* Destruction, malignant lesion (eg, laser surgery, electrosurgery, cryosurgery, chemosurgery, surgical curettement), scalp, neck, hands, feet, genitalia; lesion diameter 0.5 cm or less

17271 lesion diameter 0.6 to 1.0 cm

17272 lesion diameter 1.1 to 2.0 cm

17273	lesion diameter 2.1 to 3.0 cm
17274	lesion diameter 3.1 to 4.0 cm
17276	lesion diameter over 4.0 cm
▲ **17280***	Destruction, malignant lesion (eg, laser surgery, electrosurgery, cryosurgery, chemosurgery, surgical curettement), face, ears, eyelids, nose, lips, mucous membrane; lesion diameter 0.5 cm or less
17281	lesion diameter 0.6 to 1.0 cm
17282	lesion diameter 1.1 to 2.0 cm
17283	lesion diameter 2.1 to 3.0 cm
17284	lesion diameter 3.1 to 4.0 cm
17286	lesion diameter over 4.0 cm

Mohs Micrographic Surgery

Mohs micrographic surgery, for the removal of complex or ill-defined skin cancer, requires a single physician to act in two integrated, but separate and distinct capacities: surgeon and pathologist. If either of these responsibilities are delegated to another physician who reports his services separately, these codes are not appropriate. If repair is performed, use separate repair, flap, or graft codes.

(17300-17302 have been deleted. To report, use 17304-17310)

(17303 has been deleted)

⊘ **17304**	Chemosurgery (Mohs micrographic technique), including removal of all gross tumor, surgical excision of tissue specimens, mapping, color coding of specimens, microscopic examination of specimens by the surgeon, and complete histopathologic preparation; first stage, fresh tissue technique, up to 5 specimens
⊘ **17305**	second stage, fixed or fresh tissue, up to 5 specimens
⊘ **17306**	third stage, fixed or fresh tissue, up to 5 specimens
⊘ **17307**	additional stage(s), up to 5 specimens, each stage
⊘ **17310**	more than 5 specimens, fixed or fresh tissue, any stage

Other Procedures

17340*	Cryotherapy (CO_2 slush, liquid N_2) for acne
17360*	Chemical exfoliation for acne (eg, acne paste, acid)
17380*	Electrolysis epilation, each 1/2 hour
	(For actinotherapy, use 96900)
17999	Unlisted procedure, skin, mucous membrane and subcutaneous tissue

Breast

Incision

19000*	Puncture aspiration of cyst of breast;
+ **19001**	each additional cyst (List separately in addition to code for primary procedure)
	(Use 19001 in conjunction with code 19000)
	▶(If imaging guidance is performed, see 76095, 76096, 76393, 76942)◀
19020	Mastotomy with exploration or drainage of abscess, deep
19030	Injection procedure only for mammary ductogram or galactogram
	(For radiological supervision and interpretation, see 76086, 76088)

Excision

(All codes for bilateral procedures have been deleted. To report, add modifier '-50')

19100*	Biopsy of breast; percutaneous, needle core, not using imaging guidance (separate procedure)
	(For fine needle aspiration, use ▶10021)◀
	(For image guided breast biopsy, see 19102, 19103, ▶10022)◀
19101	open, incisional
19102	percutaneous, needle core, using imaging guidance
	(For placement of percutaneous localization clip, use 19295)
19103	percutaneous, automated vacuum assisted or rotating biopsy device, using imaging guidance
	(For imaging guidance performed in conjunction with 19102, 19103, see 76095, ▶76096,◀ 76360, 76393, 76942)
	▶(For placement of percutaneous localization clip, use 19295)◀
19110	Nipple exploration, with or without excision of a solitary lactiferous duct or a papilloma lactiferous duct
19112	Excision of lactiferous duct fistula
19120	Excision of cyst, fibroadenoma, or other benign or malignant tumor, aberrant breast tissue, duct lesion, nipple or areolar lesion (except 19140), open, male or female, one or more lesions
19125	Excision of breast lesion identified by preoperative placement of radiological marker, open; single lesion
+ **19126**	each additional lesion separately identified by a preoperative radiological marker (List separately in addition to code for primary procedure)
	(Use 19126 in conjunction with code 19125)

19140	Mastectomy for gynecomastia
19160	Mastectomy, partial;
19162	with axillary lymphadenectomy
19180	Mastectomy, simple, complete

(For immediate or delayed insertion of implant, use 19340 or 19342)

(For gynecomastia, use 19140)

19182 Mastectomy, subcutaneous

(19184-19187 have been deleted. To report, use 19182 with 19340 or 19342)

19200 Mastectomy, radical, including pectoral muscles, axillary lymph nodes

(19211-19216 have been deleted. To report, use 19200 with 19340 or 19342)

19220 Mastectomy, radical, including pectoral muscles, axillary and internal mammary lymph nodes (Urban type operation)

(19224-19229 have been deleted. To report, use 19220 with 19340 or 19342)

19240 Mastectomy, modified radical, including axillary lymph nodes, with or without pectoralis minor muscle, but excluding pectoralis major muscle

(19250-19255 have been deleted. To report, use 19240 with 19340 or 19342)

19260 Excision of chest wall tumor including ribs

19271 Excision of chest wall tumor involving ribs, with plastic reconstruction; without mediastinal lymphadenectomy

19272   with mediastinal lymphadenectomy

Introduction

19290 Preoperative placement of needle localization wire, breast;

+ 19291   each additional lesion (List separately in addition to code for primary procedure)

(Use 19291 in conjunction with code 19290)

(For radiological supervision and interpretation, see ▶76095, 76096, 76942)◀

+ 19295 Image guided placement, metallic localization clip, percutaneous, during breast biopsy (List separately in addition to code for primary procedure)

(Use 19295 in conjunction with codes 19102, ▶19103)◀

Repair and/or Reconstruction

(19300-19304 have been deleted. To report, see 19316, 19318)

(19310, 19311 have been deleted. To report, use 19325)

(All codes for bilateral procedures have been deleted. To report, add modifier '-50')

19316	Mastopexy
19318	Reduction mammaplasty
19324	Mammaplasty, augmentation; without prosthetic implant
19325	with prosthetic implant

(For flap or graft, use also appropriate number)

19328 Removal of intact mammary implant

19330 Removal of mammary implant material

19340 Immediate insertion of breast prosthesis following mastopexy, mastectomy or in reconstruction

19342 Delayed insertion of breast prosthesis following mastopexy, mastectomy or in reconstruction

(For supply of implant, use 99070)

(For preparation of custom breast implant, use 19396)

19350 Nipple/areola reconstruction

19355 Correction of inverted nipples

19357 Breast reconstruction, immediate or delayed, with tissue expander, including subsequent expansion

(19360 has been deleted)

19361 Breast reconstruction with latissimus dorsi flap, with or without prosthetic implant

(19362 has been deleted. To report, see 19367-19369)

19364 Breast reconstruction with free flap

(Do not report code 69990 in addition to code 19364)

(19364 includes harvesting of the flap, microvascular transfer, closure of the donor site, and inset shaping the flap into a breast)

19366 Breast reconstruction with other technique

(For operating microscope, use 69990)

(For insertion of prosthesis, use also 19340 or 19342)

19367 Breast reconstruction with transverse rectus abdominis myocutaneous flap (TRAM), single pedicle, including closure of donor site;

19368   with microvascular anastomosis (supercharging)

(Do not report code 69990 in addition to code 19368)

19369 Breast reconstruction with transverse rectus abdominis myocutaneous flap (TRAM), double pedicle, including closure of donor site

19370 Open periprosthetic capsulotomy, breast

19371 Periprosthetic capsulectomy, breast

19380 Revision of reconstructed breast

19396 Preparation of moulage for custom breast implant

Other Procedures

19499 Unlisted procedure, breast

⊘ =Modifier '-51' Exempt   ▶ ◀=New or Revised Text   ✚ =Add-on Code   CPT 2002

Musculoskeletal System

Cast and strapping procedures appear at the end of this section.

The services listed below include the application and removal of the first cast or traction device only. Subsequent replacement of cast and/or traction device may require an additional listing.

Definitions

The terms "closed treatment," "open treatment," and "percutaneous skeletal fixation" have been carefully chosen to accurately reflect current orthopaedic procedural treatments.

Closed treatment specifically means that the fracture site is not surgically opened (exposed to the external environment and directly visualized). This terminology is used to describe procedures that treat fractures by three methods: 1) without manipulation 2) with manipulation 3) with or without traction.

Open treatment is used when the fracture is surgically opened (exposed to the external environment). In this instance, the fracture (bone ends) is visualized and internal fixation may be used.

Percutaneous skeletal fixation describes fracture treatment which is neither open nor closed. In this procedure, the fracture fragments are not visualized, but fixation (eg, pins) is placed across the fracture site, usually under x-ray imaging.

The type of fracture (eg, open, compound, closed) does not have any coding correlation with the type of treatment (eg, closed, open, or percutaneous) provided.

The codes for treatment of fractures and joint injuries (dislocations) are categorized by the type of manipulation (reduction) and stabilization (fixation or immobilization). These codes can apply to either open (compound) or closed fractures or joint injuries.

Skeletal traction is the application of a force (distracting or traction force) to a limb segment through a wire, pin, screw, or clamp that is attached (eg, penetrates) to bone.

Skin traction is the application of a force (longitudinal) to a limb using felt or strapping applied directly to skin only.

External fixation is the usage of skeletal pins plus an attaching mechanism/device used for temporary or definitive treatment of acute or chronic bony deformity.

Codes for obtaining autogenous bone grafts, cartilage, tendon, fascia lata grafts or other tissues through separate incisions are to be used only when the graft is not already listed as part of the basic procedure.

Re-reduction of a fracture and/or dislocation performed by the primary physician may be identified by the addition of the modifier '-76' to the usual procedure number to indicate "Repeat Procedure by Same Physician." (See guidelines.)

Codes for external fixation are to be used only when external fixation is not already listed as part of the basic procedure.

All codes for suction irrigation have been deleted. To report, list only the primary surgical procedure performed (eg, sequestrectomy, deep incision).

Manipulation is used throughout the musculoskeletal fracture and dislocation subsections to specifically mean the attempted reduction or restoration of a fracture or joint dislocation to its normal anatomic alignment by the application of manually applied forces.

General

Incision

20000*	Incision of soft tissue abscess (eg, secondary to osteomyelitis); superficial
20005	deep or complicated
	(20010 has been deleted)

Wound Exploration—Trauma (eg, Penetrating Gunshot, Stab Wound)

20100-20103 relate to wound(s) resulting from penetrating trauma. These codes describe surgical exploration and enlargement of the wound, extension of dissection (to determine penetration), debridement, removal of foreign body(s), ligation or coagulation of minor subcutaneous and/or muscular blood vessel(s), of the subcutaneous tissue, muscle fascia, and/or muscle, not requiring thoracotomy or laparotomy. If a repair is done to major structure(s) or major blood vessel(s) requiring thoracotomy or laparotomy, then those specific code(s) would supersede the use of codes 20100-20103.

To report Simple, Intermediate, or Complex repair of wound(s) that do not require enlargement of the wound, extension of dissection, etc., as stated above, use specific Repair code(s) in the Integumentary System section.

20100	Exploration of penetrating wound (separate procedure); neck
20101	chest
20102	abdomen/flank/back
20103	extremity

Excision

20150	Excision of epiphyseal bar, with or without autogenous soft tissue graft obtained through same fascial incision
	(For aspiration of bone marrow, use ▶38220)◀

20200	Biopsy, muscle; superficial
20205	deep
20206*	Biopsy, muscle, percutaneous needle

▶(If imaging guidance is performed,◀ see 76360, ▶76393,◀ 76942)

▶(For fine needle aspiration, use 10021 or 10022)◀

▶(For evaulation of fine needle aspirate, see 88172-88173)◀

(For excision of muscle tumor, deep, see specific anatomic section)

20220	Biopsy, bone, trocar, or needle; superficial (eg, ilium, sternum, spinous process, ribs)
▲ 20225	deep (eg, vertebral body, femur)

(For bone marrow biopsy, use ▶38221◀)

▶(For radiologic supervision and interpretation, see 76003, 76360, 76393)◀

20240	Biopsy, bone, excisional; superficial (eg, ilium, sternum, spinous process, ribs, trochanter of femur)
20245	deep (eg, humerus, ischium, femur)
20250	Biopsy, vertebral body, open; thoracic
20251	lumbar or cervical

(For sequestrectomy, osteomyelitis or drainage of bone abscess, see anatomical area)

Introduction or Removal

(For injection procedure for arthrography, see anatomical area)

20500*	Injection of sinus tract; therapeutic (separate procedure)
20501*	diagnostic (sinogram)

(For radiological supervision and interpretation, use 76080)

20520*	Removal of foreign body in muscle or tendon sheath; simple
20525	deep or complicated
● 20526	Injection, therapeutic (eg, local anesthetic, corticosteroid), carpal tunnel
▲ 20550*	Injection; tendon sheath, ligament, ganglion cyst

▶(If imaging guidance is performed, see 76003, 76393, 76942)◀

● 20551	tendon origin/insertion
● 20552	single or multiple trigger point(s), one or two muscle group(s)
● 20553	single or multiple trigger point(s), three or more muscle groups

20600*	Arthrocentesis, aspiration and/or injection; small joint, bursa or ganglion cyst (eg, fingers, toes)
20605*	intermediate joint, bursa or ganglion cyst (eg, temporomandibular, acromioclavicular, wrist, elbow or ankle, olecranon bursa)
20610*	major joint or bursa (eg, shoulder, hip, knee joint, subacromial bursa)

▶(If imaging guidance is performed, see 76003, 76360, 76393, 76942)◀

20615	Aspiration and injection for treatment of bone cyst
20650*	Insertion of wire or pin with application of skeletal traction, including removal (separate procedure)
⊘ 20660	Application of cranial tongs, caliper, or stereotactic frame, including removal (separate procedure)
20661	Application of halo, including removal; cranial
20662	pelvic
20663	femoral
20664	Application of halo, including removal, cranial, 6 or more pins placed, for thin skull osteology (eg, pediatric patients, hydrocephalus, osteogenesis imperfecta), requiring general anesthesia
20665*	Removal of tongs or halo applied by another physician
20670*	Removal of implant; superficial, (eg, buried wire, pin or rod) (separate procedure)
20680	deep (eg, buried wire, pin, screw, metal band, nail, rod or plate)
⊘ 20690	Application of a uniplane (pins or wires in one plane), unilateral, external fixation system

(20691 has been deleted. To report, use 20690)

⊘ 20692	Application of a multiplane (pins or wires in more than one plane), unilateral, external fixation system (eg, Ilizarov, Monticelli type)
20693	Adjustment or revision of external fixation system requiring anesthesia (eg, new pin(s) or wire(s) and/or new ring(s) or bar(s))
20694	Removal, under anesthesia, of external fixation system

Replantation

20802	Replantation, arm (includes surgical neck of humerus through elbow joint), complete amputation

(20804 has been deleted. To report, see specific code(s) for repair of bone(s), ligament(s), tendon(s), nerve(s), or blood vessel(s) with modifier '-52')

20805	Replantation, forearm (includes radius and ulna to radial carpal joint), complete amputation

(20806 has been deleted. To report, see specific code(s) for repair of bone(s), ligament(s), tendon(s), nerve(s), or blood vessel(s) with modifier '-52')

20808   Replantation, hand (includes hand through metacarpophalangeal joints), complete amputation

(20812 has been deleted. To report, see specific code(s) for repair of bone(s), ligament(s), tendon(s), nerve(s), or blood vessel(s) with modifier '-52')

20816   Replantation, digit, excluding thumb (includes metacarpophalangeal joint to insertion of flexor sublimis tendon), complete amputation

(20820 has been deleted. To report, see specific code(s) for repair of bone(s), ligament(s), tendon(s), nerve(s), or blood vessel(s) with modifier '-52')

20822   Replantation, digit, excluding thumb (includes distal tip to sublimis tendon insertion), complete amputation

(20823 has been deleted. To report, see specific code(s) for repair of bone(s), ligament(s), tendon(s), nerve(s), or blood vessel(s) with modifier '-52')

20824   Replantation, thumb (includes carpometacarpal joint to MP joint), complete amputation

(20826 has been deleted. To report, see specific code(s) for repair of bone(s), ligament(s), tendon(s), nerve(s), or blood vessel(s) with modifier '-52')

20827   Replantation, thumb (includes distal tip to MP joint), complete amputation

(20828 has been deleted. To report, see specific code(s) for repair of bone(s), ligament(s), tendon(s), nerve(s), or blood vessel(s) with modifier '-52')

(20832 has been deleted. To report, see specific code(s) for repair of bone(s), ligament(s), tendon(s), nerve(s), or blood vessel(s) with modifier '-52')

(20834 has been deleted. To report, see specific code(s) for repair of bone(s), ligament(s), tendon(s), nerve(s), or blood vessel(s) with modifier '-52')

20838   Replantation, foot, complete amputation

(20840 has been deleted. To report, see specific code(s) for repair of bone(s), ligament(s), tendon(s), nerve(s), or blood vessel(s) with modifier '-52')

Grafts (or Implants)

Codes for obtaining autogenous bone, cartilage, tendon, fascia lata grafts, or other tissues through separate incisions are to be used only when graft is not already listed as part of basic procedure.

▶Do not append modifier '-62' to bone graft codes 20900-20938.◀

(For spinal surgery bone graft(s) see codes 20930-20938)

⊘ **20900**   Bone graft, any donor area; minor or small (eg, dowel or button)

⊘ **20902**   major or large

⊘ **20910**   Cartilage graft; costochondral

⊘ **20912**   nasal septum

(For ear cartilage, use 21235)

⊘ **20920**   Fascia lata graft; by stripper

⊘ **20922**   by incision and area exposure, complex or sheet

⊘ **20924**   Tendon graft, from a distance (eg, palmaris, toe extensor, plantaris)

⊘ **20926**   Tissue grafts, other (eg, paratenon, fat, dermis)

(Codes 20930-20938 are reported in addition to codes for the definitive procedure(s) without modifier '-51')

⊘ **20930**   Allograft for spine surgery only; morselized

⊘ **20931**   structural

⊘ **20936**   Autograft for spine surgery only (includes harvesting the graft); local (eg, ribs, spinous process, or laminar fragments) obtained from same incision

⊘ **20937**   morselized (through separate skin or fascial incision)

⊘ **20938**   structural, bicortical or tricortical (through separate skin or fascial incision)

(For needle aspiration of bone marrow for the purpose of bone grafting, use ▶38220)◀

Other Procedures

20950   Monitoring of interstitial fluid pressure (includes insertion of device, eg, wick catheter technique, needle manometer technique) in detection of muscle compartment syndrome

20955   Bone graft with microvascular anastomosis; fibula

20956   iliac crest

20957   metatarsal

(20960 has been deleted. To report, use 20962)

20962   other than fibula, iliac crest, or metatarsal

(Do not report code 69990 in addition to codes 20955-20962)

20969   Free osteocutaneous flap with microvascular anastomosis; other than iliac crest, metatarsal, or great toe

20970   iliac crest

(20971 has been deleted. To report, use 20969)

20972   metatarsal

20973   great toe with web space

(Do not report code 69990 in addition to codes 20969-20973)

(For great toe, wrap-around procedure, use 26551)

⊘ **20974** Electrical stimulation to aid bone healing; noninvasive (nonoperative)

⊘ **20975** invasive (operative)

(20976 has been deleted)

20979 Low intensity ultrasound stimulation to aid bone healing, noninvasive (nonoperative)

20999 Unlisted procedure, musculoskeletal system, general

Head

Skull, facial bones and temporomandibular joint.

Incision

(For drainage of superficial abscess and hematoma, use 20000)

(For removal of embedded foreign body from dentoalveolar structure, see 41805, 41806)

21010 Arthrotomy, temporomandibular joint

(21011 has been deleted. To report, use 21010 with modifier '-50')

Excision

(For biopsy, see 20220, 20240)

21015 Radical resection of tumor (eg, malignant neoplasm), soft tissue of face or scalp

(21020 has been deleted. To report, use 61501)

21025 Excision of bone (eg, for osteomyelitis or bone abscess); mandible

21026 facial bone(s)

21029 Removal by contouring of benign tumor of facial bone (eg, fibrous dysplasia)

21030 Excision of benign tumor or cyst of facial bone other than mandible

21031 Excision of torus mandibularis

21032 Excision of maxillary torus palatinus

21034 Excision of malignant tumor of facial bone other than mandible

21040 Excision of benign cyst or tumor of mandible; simple

21041 complex

21044 Excision of malignant tumor of mandible;

21045 radical resection

(For bone graft, use 21215)

21050 Condylectomy, temporomandibular joint (separate procedure)

(21051 has been deleted. To report, use 21050 with modifier '-50')

21060 Meniscectomy, partial or complete, temporomandibular joint (separate procedure)

(21061 has been deleted. To report, use 21060 with modifier '-50')

21070 Coronoidectomy (separate procedure)

(21071 has been deleted. To report, use 21070 with modifier '-50')

Introduction or Removal

(For application or removal of caliper or tongs, see 20660, 20665.) Codes 21076-21089 describe professional services for the rehabilitation of patients with oral, facial or other anatomical deficiencies by means of prostheses such as an artificial eye, ear, or nose or intraoral obturator to close a cleft. Codes 21076-21089 should only be used when the physician actually designs and prepares the prosthesis (ie, not prepared by an outside laboratory).

21076 Impression and custom preparation; surgical obturator prosthesis

21077 orbital prosthesis

21079 interim obturator prosthesis

21080 definitive obturator prosthesis

21081 mandibular resection prosthesis

21082 palatal augmentation prosthesis

21083 palatal lift prosthesis

21084 speech aid prosthesis

21085 oral surgical splint

21086 auricular prosthesis

21087 nasal prosthesis

21088 facial prosthesis

21089 Unlisted maxillofacial prosthetic procedure

21100* Application of halo type appliance for maxillofacial fixation, includes removal (separate procedure)

21110 Application of interdental fixation device for conditions other than fracture or dislocation, includes removal

(For removal of interdental fixation by another physician, see 20670-20680)

21116 Injection procedure for temporomandibular joint arthrography

(For radiological supervision and interpretation, use 70332. ▶Do not report 76003 in addition to 70332)◀

⊘ =Modifier '-51' Exempt ▶ ◀=New or Revised Text ✚=Add-on Code CPT 2002

Repair, Revision, and/or Reconstruction

(For cranioplasty, see 21179, 21180 and 62116, 62120, 62140-62147)

21120   Genioplasty; augmentation (autograft, allograft, prosthetic material)

21121   sliding osteotomy, single piece

21122   sliding osteotomies, two or more osteotomies (eg, wedge excision or bone wedge reversal for asymmetrical chin)

21123   sliding, augmentation with interpositional bone grafts (includes obtaining autografts)

21125   Augmentation, mandibular body or angle; prosthetic material

21127   with bone graft, onlay or interpositional (includes obtaining autograft)

21137   Reduction forehead; contouring only

21138   contouring and application of prosthetic material or bone graft (includes obtaining autograft)

21139   contouring and setback of anterior frontal sinus wall

21141   Reconstruction midface, LeFort I; single piece, segment movement in any direction (eg, for Long Face Syndrome), without bone graft

21142   two pieces, segment movement in any direction, without bone graft

21143   three or more pieces, segment movement in any direction, without bone graft

(21144 has been deleted. To report, use 21141)

21145   single piece, segment movement in any direction, requiring bone grafts (includes obtaining autografts)

21146   two pieces, segment movement in any direction, requiring bone grafts (includes obtaining autografts) (eg, ungrafted unilateral alveolar cleft)

21147   three or more pieces, segment movement in any direction, requiring bone grafts (includes obtaining autografts) (eg, ungrafted bilateral alveolar cleft or multiple osteotomies)

21150   Reconstruction midface, LeFort II; anterior intrusion (eg, Treacher-Collins Syndrome)

21151   any direction, requiring bone grafts (includes obtaining autografts)

21154   Reconstruction midface, LeFort III (extracranial), any type, requiring bone grafts (includes obtaining autografts); without LeFort I

21155   with LeFort I

21159   Reconstruction midface, LeFort III (extra and intracranial) with forehead advancement (eg, mono bloc), requiring bone grafts (includes obtaining autografts); without LeFort I

21160   with LeFort I

21172   Reconstruction superior-lateral orbital rim and lower forehead, advancement or alteration, with or without grafts (includes obtaining autografts)

(For frontal or parietal craniotomy performed for craniosynostosis, use 61556)

21175   Reconstruction, bifrontal, superior-lateral orbital rims and lower forehead, advancement or alteration (eg, plagiocephaly, trigonocephaly, brachycephaly), with or without grafts (includes obtaining autografts)

(For bifrontal craniotomy performed for craniosynostosis, use 61557)

21179   Reconstruction, entire or majority of forehead and/or supraorbital rims; with grafts (allograft or prosthetic material)

21180   with autograft (includes obtaining grafts)

(For extensive craniectomy for multiple suture craniosynostosis, use only 61558 or 61559)

21181   Reconstruction by contouring of benign tumor of cranial bones (eg, fibrous dysplasia), extracranial

▲**21182**   Reconstruction of orbital walls, rims, forehead, nasoethmoid complex following intra- and extracranial excision of benign tumor of cranial bone (eg, fibrous dysplasia), with multiple autografts (includes obtaining grafts); total area of bone grafting less than 40 sq cm

▲**21183**   total area of bone grafting greater than 40 sq cm but less than 80 sq cm

▲**21184**   total area of bone grafting greater than 80 sq cm

(For excision of benign tumor of cranial bones, see 61563, 61564)

21188   Reconstruction midface, osteotomies (other than LeFort type) and bone grafts (includes obtaining autografts)

21193   Reconstruction of mandibular rami, horizontal, vertical, C, or L osteotomy; without bone graft

21194   with bone graft (includes obtaining graft)

21195   Reconstruction of mandibular rami and/or body, sagittal split; without internal rigid fixation

21196   with internal rigid fixation

21198   Osteotomy, mandible, segmental;

21199   with genioglossus advancement

(21200, 21202, 21203 have been deleted. To report, see 21193-21198)

(21204 has been deleted. To report, see 21141-21160)

21206   Osteotomy, maxilla, segmental (eg, Wassmund or Schuchard)

(21207 has been deleted. To report, use 21209)

21208   Osteoplasty, facial bones; augmentation (autograft, allograft, or prosthetic implant)

21209   reduction

21210   Graft, bone; nasal, maxillary or malar areas (includes obtaining graft)

(For cleft palate repair, see 42200-42225)

21215   mandible (includes obtaining graft)

21230   Graft; rib cartilage, autogenous, to face, chin, nose or ear (includes obtaining graft)

21235   ear cartilage, autogenous, to nose or ear (includes obtaining graft)

(21239 has been deleted. To report, use 21208)

21240   Arthroplasty, temporomandibular joint, with or without autograft (includes obtaining graft)

(21241 has been deleted. To report, use 21240)

21242   Arthroplasty, temporomandibular joint, with allograft

21243   Arthroplasty, temporomandibular joint, with prosthetic joint replacement

21244   Reconstruction of mandible, extraoral, with transosteal bone plate (eg, mandibular staple bone plate)

21245   Reconstruction of mandible or maxilla, subperiosteal implant; partial

21246   complete

21247   Reconstruction of mandibular condyle with bone and cartilage autografts (includes obtaining grafts) (eg, for hemifacial microsomia)

21248   Reconstruction of mandible or maxilla, endosteal implant (eg, blade, cylinder); partial

21249   complete

(21250, 21254 have been deleted. To report, see 21141-21160)

21255   Reconstruction of zygomatic arch and glenoid fossa with bone and cartilage (includes obtaining autografts)

21256   Reconstruction of orbit with osteotomies (extracranial) and with bone grafts (includes obtaining autografts) (eg, micro-ophthalmia)

21260   Periorbital osteotomies for orbital hypertelorism, with bone grafts; extracranial approach

21261   combined intra- and extracranial approach

21263   with forehead advancement

21267   Orbital repositioning, periorbital osteotomies, unilateral, with bone grafts; extracranial approach

21268   combined intra- and extracranial approach

21270   Malar augmentation, prosthetic material

(For malar augmentation with bone graft, use 21210)

21275   Secondary revision of orbitocraniofacial reconstruction

21280   Medial canthopexy (separate procedure)

(For medial canthoplasty, use 67950)

21282   Lateral canthopexy

21295   Reduction of masseter muscle and bone (eg, for treatment of benign masseteric hypertrophy); extraoral approach

21296   intraoral approach

Other Procedures

21299   Unlisted craniofacial and maxillofacial procedure

Fracture and/or Dislocation

21300   Closed treatment of skull fracture without operation

(For operative repair, see 62000-62010)

21310   Closed treatment of nasal bone fracture without manipulation

21315*   Closed treatment of nasal bone fracture; without stabilization

21320   with stabilization

21325   Open treatment of nasal fracture; uncomplicated

21330   complicated, with internal and/or external skeletal fixation

21335   with concomitant open treatment of fractured septum

21336   Open treatment of nasal septal fracture, with or without stabilization

21337   Closed treatment of nasal septal fracture, with or without stabilization

21338   Open treatment of nasoethmoid fracture; without external fixation

21339   with external fixation

21340   Percutaneous treatment of nasoethmoid complex fracture, with splint, wire or headcap fixation, including repair of canthal ligaments and/or the nasolacrimal apparatus

21343   Open treatment of depressed frontal sinus fracture

21344   Open treatment of complicated (eg, comminuted or involving posterior wall) frontal sinus fracture, via coronal or multiple approaches

21345   Closed treatment of nasomaxillary complex fracture (LeFort II type), with interdental wire fixation or fixation of denture or splint

21346   Open treatment of nasomaxillary complex fracture (LeFort II type); with wiring and/or local fixation

21347   requiring multiple open approaches

21348   with bone grafting (includes obtaining graft)

(21350 has been deleted. If necessary to report, use appropriate Evaluation and Management code)

21355*   Percutaneous treatment of fracture of malar area, including zygomatic arch and malar tripod, with manipulation

⊘=Modifier '-51' Exempt   ▶◀=New or Revised Text   ✚=Add-on Code   CPT 2002

21356 Open treatment of depressed zygomatic arch fracture (eg, Gillies approach)

21360 Open treatment of depressed malar fracture, including zygomatic arch and malar tripod

21365 Open treatment of complicated (eg, comminuted or involving cranial nerve foramina) fracture(s) of malar area, including zygomatic arch and malar tripod; with internal fixation and multiple surgical approaches

21366 with bone grafting (includes obtaining graft)

(21380 has been deleted. If necessary to report, use appropriate Evaluation and Management code)

21385 Open treatment of orbital floor blowout fracture; transantral approach (Caldwell-Luc type operation)

21386 periorbital approach

21387 combined approach

21390 periorbital approach, with alloplastic or other implant

21395 periorbital approach with bone graft (includes obtaining graft)

21400 Closed treatment of fracture of orbit, except blowout; without manipulation

21401 with manipulation

21406 Open treatment of fracture of orbit, except blowout; without implant

21407 with implant

21408 with bone grafting (includes obtaining graft)

(21420 has been deleted. If necessary to report, use appropriate Evaluation and Management code)

21421 Closed treatment of palatal or maxillary fracture (LeFort I type), with interdental wire fixation or fixation of denture or splint

21422 Open treatment of palatal or maxillary fracture (LeFort I type);

21423 complicated (comminuted or involving cranial nerve foramina), multiple approaches

21431 Closed treatment of craniofacial separation (LeFort III type) using interdental wire fixation of denture or splint

21432 Open treatment of craniofacial separation (LeFort III type); with wiring and/or internal fixation

21433 complicated (eg, comminuted or involving cranial nerve foramina), multiple surgical approaches

21435 complicated, utilizing internal and/or external fixation techniques (eg, head cap, halo device, and/or intermaxillary fixation)

(For removal of internal or external fixation device, use 20670)

21436 complicated, multiple surgical approaches, internal fixation, with bone grafting (includes obtaining graft)

21440 Closed treatment of mandibular or maxillary alveolar ridge fracture (separate procedure)

21445 Open treatment of mandibular or maxillary alveolar ridge fracture (separate procedure)

21450 Closed treatment of mandibular fracture; without manipulation

21451 with manipulation

21452 Percutaneous treatment of mandibular fracture, with external fixation

21453 Closed treatment of mandibular fracture with interdental fixation

21454 Open treatment of mandibular fracture with external fixation

(21455 has been deleted. To report, use 21453)

21461 Open treatment of mandibular fracture; without interdental fixation

21462 with interdental fixation

21465 Open treatment of mandibular condylar fracture

21470 Open treatment of complicated mandibular fracture by multiple surgical approaches including internal fixation, interdental fixation, and/or wiring of dentures or splints

21480 Closed treatment of temporomandibular dislocation; initial or subsequent

21485 complicated (eg, recurrent requiring intermaxillary fixation or splinting), initial or subsequent

21490 Open treatment of temporomandibular dislocation

(For interdental wire fixation, use 21497)

21493 Closed treatment of hyoid fracture; without manipulation

21494 with manipulation

21495 Open treatment of hyoid fracture

(For treatment of fracture of larynx, see 31584-31586)

21497 Interdental wiring, for condition other than fracture

Other Procedures

21499 Unlisted musculoskeletal procedure, head

(For unlisted craniofacial or maxillofacial procedure, use 21299)

Neck (Soft Tissues) and Thorax

(For cervical spine and back, see 21920 et seq)

(For injection of fracture site or trigger point, use 20550)

Incision

(For incision and drainage of abscess or hematoma, superficial, see 10060, 10140)

21501 Incision and drainage, deep abscess or hematoma, soft tissues of neck or thorax;

21502 with partial rib ostectomy

21510 Incision, deep, with opening of bone cortex (eg, for osteomyelitis or bone abscess), thorax

(21511 has been deleted)

Excision

(For bone biopsy, see 20220-20251)

21550 Biopsy, soft tissue of neck or thorax

(For needle biopsy of soft tissue, use 20206)

21555 Excision tumor, soft tissue of neck or thorax; subcutaneous

21556 deep, subfascial, intramuscular

21557 Radical resection of tumor (eg, malignant neoplasm), soft tissue of neck or thorax

21600 Excision of rib, partial

(For radical resection of chest wall and rib cage for tumor, use 19260)

(For radical debridement of chest wall and rib cage for injury, see 11040-11044)

21610 Costotransversectomy (separate procedure)

21615 Excision first and/or cervical rib;

21616 with sympathectomy

21620 Ostectomy of sternum, partial

21627 Sternal debridement

(For debridement and closure, use 21750)

21630 Radical resection of sternum;

21632 with mediastinal lymphadenectomy

(21633 has been deleted. To report, use 21630)

Repair, Revision, and/or Reconstruction

(For superficial wound, see **Integumentary System** section under Repair—Simple)

21700 Division of scalenus anticus; without resection of cervical rib

21705 with resection of cervical rib

21720 Division of sternocleidomastoid for torticollis, open operation; without cast application

(For transection of spinal accessory and cervical nerves, see 63191, 64722)

21725 with cast application

21740 Reconstructive repair of pectus excavatum or carinatum

(21741 has been deleted. To report, use 21899)

▲**21750** Closure of median sternotomy separation with or without debridement (separate procedure)

Fracture and/or Dislocation

21800 Closed treatment of rib fracture, uncomplicated, each

21805 Open treatment of rib fracture without fixation, each

21810 Treatment of rib fracture requiring external fixation (flail chest)

21820 Closed treatment of sternum fracture

21825 Open treatment of sternum fracture with or without skeletal fixation

(For sternoclavicular dislocation, see 23520-23532)

Other Procedures

21899 Unlisted procedure, neck or thorax

Back and Flank

Excision

21920 Biopsy, soft tissue of back or flank; superficial

21925 deep

(For needle biopsy of soft tissue, use 20206)

21930 Excision, tumor, soft tissue of back or flank

21935 Radical resection of tumor (eg, malignant neoplasm), soft tissue of back or flank

Spine (Vertebral Column)

Cervical, thoracic, and lumbar spine.

Within the SPINE section, bone grafting procedures are reported separately and in addition to arthrodesis. For bone grafts in other Musculoskeletal sections, see specific code(s) descriptor(s) and/or accompanying guidelines.

To report bone grafts performed after arthrodesis, see codes 20930-20938. Bone graft codes are reported without modifier '-51' (multiple procedure). ▶Do not append modifier '-62' to bone graft codes 20900-20938.◀

Example:

Posterior arthrodesis of L5-S1 for degenerative disc disease utilizing morselized autogenous iliac bone graft harvested through a separate fascial incision.

Report as 22612 and 20937.

Within the SPINE section, instrumentation is reported separately and in addition to arthrodesis. To report instrumentation procedures performed with definitive vertebral procedure(s), see codes 22840-22855. Instrumentation procedure codes 22840-22848 and 22851 are reported in addition to the definitive procedure(s) without modifier '-51'. ▶The modifier '-62' may not be appended to the definitive or add-on spinal instrumentation procedure code(s) 22840-22855.◀

Example:

Posterior arthrodesis of L4-S1, utilizing morselized autogenous iliac bone graft harvested through separate fascial incision, and pedicle screw fixation.

Report as 22612, 22614, 22842, and 20937.

Vertebral procedures are sometimes followed by arthrodesis and in addition may include bone grafts and instrumentation.

When arthrodesis is performed in addition to another procedure, the arthrodesis should be reported in addition to the original procedure with a modifier '-51' (multiple procedures). Examples are after osteotomy, fracture care, vertebral corpectomy and laminectomy. Since bone grafts and instrumentation are never performed without arthrodesis, modifier '-51' (multiple procedures) is not used.

Arthrodesis, however, may be performed in the absence of other procedures and therefore when it is combined with another definitive procedure, modifier '-51' (multiple procedure) is appropriate.

Example:

Treatment of a burst fracture of L2 by corpectomy followed by arthrodesis of L1-L3, utilizing anterior instrumentation L1-L3 and structural allograft.

Report as 63090, 22558-51, 22585, 22845, and 20931.

When two surgeons work together as primary surgeons performing distinct part(s) of a single reportable procedure, each surgeon should report his/her distinct operative work by appending the modifier '-62' to the single definitive procedure code. If additional procedure(s) (including add-on procedure(s)) are performed during the same surgical session, separate code(s) may be reported by each co-surgeon, without the modifier '-62' appended (see Appendix A).

Example:

A 42-year-old male with a history of posttraumatic degenerative disc disease at L3-4 and L4-5 (internal disc disruption) underwent surgical repair. Surgeon A performed an anterior exposure of the spine with mobilization of the great vessels. Surgeon B performed anterior (minimal) diskectomy and fusion at L3-4 and L4-5 using anterior interbody technique.

Report surgeon A: 22558-62, ▶22585-62◀
Report surgeon B: 22558-62, ▶22585-62◀, 20931

> ▶(Do not append modifier -62 to bone graft code 20931)◀

(For injection procedure for myelography, use 62284)

(For injection procedure for diskography, see 62290, 62291)

(For injection procedure, chemonucleolysis, single or multiple levels, use 62292)

(For injection procedure for facet joints, see 64470-64476, 64622-64627)

(For needle or trocar biopsy, see 20220-20225)

Excision

▶For the following codes, when two surgeons work together as primary surgeons performing distinct part(s) of partial vertebral body excision, each surgeon should report his/her distinct operative work by appending the modifier '-62' to the procedure code. In this situation, the modifier '-62' may be appended to the procedure code(s) 22100-22102, 22110-22114 and, as appropriate, to the associated additional vertebral segment add-on code(s) 22103, 22116 as long as both surgeons continue to work together as primary surgeons.◀

(For bone biopsy, see 20220-20251)

(22010 has been deleted. To report, use 21920)

(22011 has been deleted. To report, use 21925)

(22012 has been deleted. To report, use 20206)

(22030-22033 have been deleted. To report, use 21930)

22100 Partial excision of posterior vertebral component (eg, spinous process, lamina or facet) for intrinsic bony lesion, single vertebral segment; cervical

22101 thoracic

22102 lumbar

+ 22103 each additional segment (List separately in addition to code for primary procedure)

(Use 22103 in conjunction with codes 22100, 22101, 22102)

(22105 has been deleted. To report, use 22100)

(22106 has been deleted. To report, use 22101)

(22107 has been deleted. To report, use 22102)

22110 Partial excision of vertebral body, for intrinsic bony lesion, without decompression of spinal cord or nerve root(s), single vertebral segment; cervical

(22111 has been deleted)

22112 thoracic

(22113 has been deleted)

22114 lumbar

(22115 has been deleted)

+ 22116 each additional vertebral segment (List separately in addition to code for primary procedure)

(Use 22116 in conjunction with codes 22110, 22112, 22114)

(22120-22130 have been deleted. For complete or near complete resection of vertebral body, see vertebral corpectomy, 63081-63091)

(22140 has been deleted. To report, use 63081 and 22554 and 20931 or 20938)

(22141 has been deleted. To report, use 63085 or 63087 and 22556 and 20931 or 20938)

(22142 has been deleted. To report, use 63087 or 63090 and 22558 and 20931 or 20938)

(22145 has been deleted. To report, use 63082 or 63086 or 63088 or 63091, and 22585)

(22148 has been deleted. To report, see 20931 or 20938)

(22150 has been deleted. To report, use 63081 and 22554 and 20931 or 20938 and 22851)

(22151 has been deleted. To report, use 63085 or 63087 and 22556 and 20931 or 20938 and 22851)

(22152 has been deleted. To report, use 63087 or 63090 and 22558, and 20931 or 20938 and 22851)

(22200-22207 have been deleted. For osteotomy of spine, see 22210-22226)

Osteotomy

To report arthrodesis, see codes 22590-22632. (Report in addition to code(s) for the definitive procedure with modifier '-51'.)

To report instrumentation procedures, see codes 22840-22855. (Report in addition to code(s) for the definitive procedure(s) without modifier '-51'.) ▶Do not append modifier '-62' to spinal instrumentation codes 22840-22855.◀

To report bone graft procedures, see codes 20930-20938. (Report in addition to code(s) for the definitive procedure(s) without modifier '-51'.) ▶Do not append modifier '-62' to bone graft codes 20900-20938.◀

▶For the following codes, when two surgeons work together as primary surgeons performing distinct part(s) of an anterior spine osteotomy, each surgeon should report his/her distinct operative work by appending the modifier '-62' to the procedure code. In this situation, the modifier '-62' may be appended to the procedure code(s) 22210-22214, 22220-22224 and, as appropriate, to associated additional segment add-on code(s) 22216, 22226 as long as both surgeons continue to work together as primary surgeons.◀

22210	Osteotomy of spine, posterior or posterolateral approach, one vertebral segment; cervical
22212	thoracic
22214	lumbar
✛ 22216	each additional vertebral segment (List separately in addition to primary procedure)

(Use 22216 in conjunction with codes 22210, 22212, 22214)

22220	Osteotomy of spine, including diskectomy, anterior approach, single vertebral segment; cervical
22222	thoracic
22224	lumbar
✛ 22226	each additional vertebral segment (List separately in addition to code for primary procedure)

(Use 22226 in conjunction with codes 22220, 22222, 22224)

(22230 has been deleted. To report, use 22216 or 22226)

(22250, 22251 have been deleted. For vertebral corpectomy, see 63081-63091)

Fracture and/or Dislocation

To report arthrodesis, see codes 22590-22632. (Report in addition to code(s) for the definitive procedure with modifier '-51'.)

To report instrumentation procedures, see codes 22840-22855. (Report in addition to code(s) for the definitive procedure(s) without modifier '-51'.) ▶Do not append modifier '-62' to spinal instrumentation codes 22840-22855.◀

To report bone graft procedures, see codes 20930-20938. (Report in addition to code(s) for the definitive procedure(s) without modifier '-51'.) ▶Do not append modifier '-62' to bone graft codes 20900-20938.◀

▶For the following codes, when two surgeons work together as primary surgeons performing distinct part(s) of open fracture and/or dislocation procedure(s), each surgeon should report his/her distinct operative work by appending the modifier '-62' to the procedure code. In this situation, the modifier '-62' may be appended to the procedure code(s) 22318-22327 and, as appropriate, the associated additional fracture vertebrae or dislocated segment add-on code 22328 as long as both surgeons continue to work together as primary surgeons.◀

22305	Closed treatment of vertebral process fracture(s)
22310	Closed treatment of vertebral body fracture(s), without manipulation, requiring and including casting or bracing
22315	Closed treatment of vertebral fracture(s) and/or dislocation(s) requiring casting or bracing, with and including casting and/or bracing, with or without anesthesia, by manipulation or traction

(For spinal subluxation, use 97140)

22318	Open treatment and/or reduction of odontoid fracture(s) and or dislocation(s) (including os odontoideum), anterior approach, including placement of internal fixation; without grafting
22319	with grafting

⊘ =Modifier '-51' Exempt   ▶ ◀=New or Revised Text   ✛ =Add-on Code

22325 Open treatment and/or reduction of vertebral fracture(s) and/or dislocation(s), posterior approach, one fractured vertebrae or dislocated segment; lumbar

22326 cervical

22327 thoracic

+ 22328 each additional fractured vertebrae or dislocated segment (List separately in addition to code for primary procedure)

(Use 22328 in conjunction with codes 22325, 22326, 22327)

(For treatment of vertebral fracture by the anterior approach, see corpectomy 63081-63091, and appropriate arthrodesis, bone graft and instrument codes)

(22330-22379 have been deleted. For decompression of spine following fracture, see 63001-63091; for arthrodesis of spine following fracture, see 22548-22632)

Manipulation

(22500 has been deleted. To report, use 97140)

22505 Manipulation of spine requiring anesthesia, any region

Vertebral Body, Embolization or Injection

22520 Percutaneous vertebroplasty, one vertebral body, unilateral or bilateral injection; thoracic

22521 lumbar

+ 22522 each additional thoracic or lumbar vertebral body (List separately in addition to code for primary procedure)

(Use 22522 in conjunction with codes 22520, 22521 as appropriate)

(For radiological supervision and interpretation, see 76012, 76013)

Arthrodesis

Arthrodesis may be performed in the absence of other procedures and therefore when it is combined with another definitive procedure (eg, osteotomy, fracture care, vertebral corpectomy or laminectomy), modifier '-51' is appropriate. However, arthrodesis codes 22585, 22614, and 22632 are considered add-on procedure codes and should not be used with modifier '-51'.

To report instrumentation procedures, see codes 22840-22855. (Report in addition to code(s) for the definitive procedure(s) without modifier '-51'.) ►Do not append modifier '-62' to spinal instrumentation codes 22840-22855.◄

To report bone graft procedures, see codes 20930-20938. (Report in addition to code(s) for the definitive procedure(s) without modifier '-51'.) ►Do not append modifier '-62' to bone graft codes 20900-20938.◄

Anterior or Anterolateral Approach Technique

Procedure codes 22554-22558 are for SINGLE interspace; for additional interspaces, use 22585. A vertebral interspace is the non-bony compartment between two adjacent vertebral bodies, which contains the intervertebral disk, and includes the nucleus pulposus, annulus fibrosus, and two cartilagenous endplates.

►For the following codes, when two surgeons work together as primary surgeons performing distinct part(s) of an anterior interbody arthrodesis, each surgeon should report his/her distinct operative work by appending the modifier '-62' to the procedure code. In this situation, the modifier '-62' may be appended to the procedure code(s) 22548-22558 and, as appropriate, to the associated additional interspace add-on code 22585 as long as both surgeons continue to work together as primary surgeons.◄

22548 Arthrodesis, anterior transoral or extraoral technique, clivus-C1-C2 (atlas-axis), with or without excision of odontoid process

(22550, 22552, 22555, 22560, 22561, 22565 have been deleted. For intervertebral disk excision by laminotomy or laminectomy, see 63020-63042. For arthrodesis, see 22548-22632)

22554 Arthrodesis, anterior interbody technique, including minimal diskectomy to prepare interspace (other than for decompression); cervical below C2

22556 thoracic

22558 lumbar

+ 22585 each additional interspace (List separately in addition to code for primary procedure)

(Use 22585 in conjunction with codes 22554, 22556, 22558)

Posterior, Posterolateral or Lateral Transverse Process Technique

To report instrumentation procedures, see codes 22840-22855. (Report in addition to code(s) for the definitive procedure(s) without modifier '-51'.) ►Do not append modifier '-62' to spinal instrumentation codes 22840-22855.◄

To report bone graft procedures, see codes 20930-20938. (Report in addition to code(s) for the definitive procedure(s) without modifier '-51'.) ►Do not append modifier '-62' to bone graft codes 20900-20938.◄

A vertebral segment describes the basic constituent part into which the spine may be divided. It represents a single complete vertebral bone with its associated articular processes and laminae. A vertebral interspace is the non-bony compartment between two adjacent vertebral bodies which contains the intervertebral disk, and includes the nucleus pulposus, annulus fibrosus, and two cartilagenous endplates.

22590   Arthrodesis, posterior technique, craniocervical (occiput-C2)

22595   Arthrodesis, posterior technique, atlas-axis (C1-C2)

22600   Arthrodesis, posterior or posterolateral technique, single level; cervical below C2 segment

(22605 has been deleted. To report, use 22600)

22610   thoracic (with or without lateral transverse technique)

22612   lumbar (with or without lateral transverse technique)

+ 22614   each additional vertebral segment (List separately in addition to code for primary procedure)

(Use 22614 in conjunction with codes 22600, 22610, 22612)

(22615 has been deleted. To report, use 22554 and 20930-20938)

(22617 has been deleted. To report, use 22548 and 20930-20938)

(22620 has been deleted. To report, use 22590 and 20930-20938)

(22625 has been deleted. To report, use 22612 and 22840-22855, and 20930-20938)

22630   Arthrodesis, posterior interbody technique, including laminectomy and/or diskectomy to prepare interspace (other than for decompression), single interspace; lumbar

+ 22632   each additional interspace (List separately in addition to code for primary procedure)

(Use 22632 in conjunction with code 22630)

(22640-22645 have been deleted. To report, see 22610, 22612, and 20930-20938)

(22650 has been deleted. To report, use 22614)

(22655 has been deleted. To report, see 22630, 22632 and 20930-20938)

(22670 has been deleted. To report, see 22610 or 22612 and 22840-22855, and 20930-20938)

(22680 has been deleted. To report, see 22556-22585 and 20930-20938)

(22700 has been deleted. To report, see 22558 and 20930-20938)

(22720 has been deleted. To report, see 22612 and 20930-20938)

(22730 has been deleted. To report, see 22585, 22614)

(22735 has been deleted. To report, see 22585, 22614)

Spine Deformity (eg, Scoliosis, Kyphosis)

To report instrumentation procedures, see codes 22840-22855. (Report in addition to code(s) for the definitive procedure(s) without modifier '-51'.) ►Do not append modifier '-62' to spinal instrumentation codes 22840-22855.◄

To report bone graft procedures, see codes 20930-20938. (Report in addition to code(s) for the definitive procedure(s) without modifier '-51'.) ►Do not append modifier '-62' to bone graft codes 20900-20938.◄

A vertebral segment describes the basic constituent part into which the spine may be divided. It represents a single complete vertebral bone with its associated articular processes and laminae.

►For the following codes, when two surgeons work together as primary surgeons performing distinct part(s) of an arthrodesis for spinal deformity, each surgeon should report his/her distinct operative work by appending the modifier '-62' to the procedure code. In this situation, the modifier '-62' may be appended to the procedure code(s) 22800-22819 as long as both surgeons continue to work together as primary surgeons.◄

22800   Arthrodesis, posterior, for spinal deformity, with or without cast; up to 6 vertebral segments

(22801 has been deleted. To report, use 22800)

22802   7 to 12 vertebral segments

(22803 has been deleted. To report, use 22802)

22804   13 or more vertebral segments

22808   Arthrodesis, anterior, for spinal deformity, with or without cast; 2 to 3 vertebral segments

22810   4 to 7 vertebral segments

22812   8 or more vertebral segments

22818   Kyphectomy, circumferential exposure of spine and resection of vertebral segment(s) (including body and posterior elements); single or 2 segments

22819   3 or more segments

(To report arthrodesis, see 22800-22804 and add modifier '-51')

Exploration

(22820 has been deleted. To report, see 20930-20938)

22830   Exploration of spinal fusion

⊘ =Modifier '-51' Exempt   ► ◄=New or Revised Text   ✚=Add-on Code   CPT 2002

Spinal Instrumentation

Segmental instrumentation is defined as fixation at each end of the construct and at least one additional interposed bony attachment.

Non-segmental instrumentation is defined as fixation at each end of the construct and may span several vertebral segments without attachment to the intervening segments.

Insertion of spinal instrumentation is reported separately and in addition to arthrodesis. Instrumentation procedure codes 22840-22848, 22851 are reported in addition to the definitive procedure(s) without modifier '-51'. ▶Do not append modifier '-62' to spinal instrumentation codes 22840-22855.◀

To report bone graft procedures, see codes 20930-20938. (Report in addition to code(s) for definitive procedure(s) without modifier '-51'.) ▶Do not append modifier '-62' to bone graft codes 20900-20938.◀

A vertebral segment describes the basic constituent part into which the spine may be divided. It represents a single complete vertebral bone with its associated articular processes and laminae. A vertebral interspace is the non-bony compartment between two adjacent vertebral bodies, which contains the intervertebral disk, and includes the nucleus pulposus, annulus fibrosus, and two cartilagenous endplates.

(List codes 22840-22848, 22851 separately, in addition to code for fracture, dislocation, or arthrodesis of the spine, 22325, 22326, 22327, 22548-22812)

⊘ **22840** Posterior non-segmental instrumentation (eg, Harrington rod technique, pedicle fixation across one interspace, atlantoaxial transarticular screw fixation, sublaminar wiring at C1, facet screw fixation)

⊘ **22841** Internal spinal fixation by wiring of spinous processes

⊘ **22842** Posterior segmental instrumentation (eg, pedicle fixation, dual rods with multiple hooks and sublaminar wires); 3 to 6 vertebral segments

⊘ **22843** 7 to 12 vertebral segments

⊘ **22844** 13 or more vertebral segments

⊘ **22845** Anterior instrumentation; 2 to 3 vertebral segments

⊘ **22846** 4 to 7 vertebral segments

⊘ **22847** 8 or more vertebral segments

⊘ **22848** Pelvic fixation (attachment of caudal end of instrumentation to pelvic bony structures) other than sacrum

22849 Reinsertion of spinal fixation device

22850 Removal of posterior nonsegmental instrumentation (eg, Harrington rod)

⊘ **22851** Application of intervertebral biomechanical device(s) (eg, synthetic cage(s), threaded bone dowel(s), methylmethacrylate) to vertebral defect or interspace

22852 Removal of posterior segmental instrumentation

22855 Removal of anterior instrumentation

Other Procedures

22899 Unlisted procedure, spine

Abdomen

Excision

22900 Excision, abdominal wall tumor, subfascial (eg, desmoid)

(22910 has been deleted. To report, use 22999)

Other Procedures

22999 Unlisted procedure, abdomen, musculoskeletal system

Shoulder

Clavicle, scapula, humerus head and neck, sterno-clavicular joint, acromioclavicular joint and shoulder joint.

Incision

▲ **23000** Removal of subdeltoid calcareous deposits, open

23020 Capsular contracture release (eg, Sever type procedure)

(For incision and drainage procedures, superficial, see 10040-10160)

23030 Incision and drainage, shoulder area; deep abscess or hematoma

23031 infected bursa

23035 Incision, bone cortex (eg, osteomyelitis or bone abscess), shoulder area

(23036 has been deleted)

23040 Arthrotomy, glenohumeral joint, including exploration, drainage, or removal of foreign body

(23042 has been deleted)

23044 Arthrotomy, acromioclavicular, sternoclavicular joint, including exploration, drainage, or removal of foreign body

Excision

23065 Biopsy, soft tissue of shoulder area; superficial

23066 deep

(For needle biopsy of soft tissue, use 20206)

23075 Excision, soft tissue tumor, shoulder area; subcutaneous

23076 deep, subfascial, or intramuscular

23077 Radical resection of tumor (eg, malignant neoplasm), soft tissue of shoulder area

23100	Arthrotomy, glenohumeral joint, including biopsy
23101	Arthrotomy, acromioclavicular joint or sternoclavicular joint, including biopsy and/or excision of torn cartilage
23105	Arthrotomy; glenohumeral joint, with synovectomy, with or without biopsy
23106	sternoclavicular joint, with synovectomy, with or without biopsy
23107	Arthrotomy, glenohumeral joint, with joint exploration, with or without removal of loose or foreign body

(23110 has been deleted. To report, use 23929)

23120	Claviculectomy; partial

▶(For arthroscopic procedure, use 29824)◀

23125	total
23130	Acromioplasty or acromionectomy, partial, with or without coracoacromial ligament release
23140	Excision or curettage of bone cyst or benign tumor of clavicle or scapula;
23145	with autograft (includes obtaining graft)
23146	with allograft
23150	Excision or curettage of bone cyst or benign tumor of proximal humerus;
23155	with autograft (includes obtaining graft)
23156	with allograft
23170	Sequestrectomy (eg, for osteomyelitis or bone abscess), clavicle

(23171 has been deleted)

23172	Sequestrectomy (eg, for osteomyelitis or bone abscess), scapula

(23173 has been deleted)

23174	Sequestrectomy (eg, for osteomyelitis or bone abscess), humeral head to surgical neck

(23175 has been deleted)

23180	Partial excision (craterization, saucerization, or diaphysectomy) bone (eg, osteomyelitis), clavicle

(23181 has been deleted)

23182	Partial excision (craterization, saucerization, or diaphysectomy) bone (eg, osteomyelitis), scapula

(23183 has been deleted)

23184	Partial excision (craterization, saucerization, or diaphysectomy) bone (eg, osteomyelitis), proximal humerus

(23185 has been deleted)

23190	Ostectomy of scapula, partial (eg, superior medial angle)
23195	Resection, humeral head

(For replacement with implant, use 23470)

23200	Radical resection for tumor; clavicle
23210	scapula
23220	Radical resection of bone tumor, proximal humerus;
23221	with autograft (includes obtaining graft)
23222	with prosthetic replacement

Introduction or Removal

(For arthrocentesis or needling of bursa, use 20610)

(For K-wire or pin insertion or removal, see 20650, 20670, 20680)

23330	Removal of foreign body, shoulder; subcutaneous
23331	deep (eg, Neer hemiarthroplasty removal)
23332	complicated (eg, total shoulder)
▲ 23350	Injection procedure for shoulder arthrography or enhanced CT/MRI shoulder arthrography

(For radiological supervision and interpretation for arthrography, use 73040)

▶(For radiographic arthrography, radiological supervision and interpretation, use 73040. Fluoroscopy (76003) is inclusive of radiographic arthrography)◀

▶(When fluoroscopic guided injection is performed for enhanced CT arthrography, use codes 23350, 76003, and 73201 or 73202)◀

▶(When fluoroscopic guided injection is performed for enhanced MR arthrography, use codes 23350, 76003, and 73222 or 73223)◀

▶(For enhanced CT or enhanced MRI arthrography, use 76003 and either 73201, 73202, 73222 or 73223)◀

(23355-23358 have been deleted. To report, see ▶29805◀-29826)

Repair, Revision, and/or Reconstruction

23395	Muscle transfer, any type, shoulder or upper arm; single
23397	multiple
23400	Scapulopexy (eg, Sprengels deformity or for paralysis)
23405	Tenotomy, shoulder area; single tendon
23406	multiple tendons through same incision
23410	Repair of ruptured musculotendinous cuff (eg, rotator cuff); acute
23412	chronic
23415	Coracoacromial ligament release, with or without acromioplasty

▶(For arthroscopic procedure, use 29826)◀

23420	Reconstruction of complete shoulder (rotator) cuff avulsion, chronic (includes acromioplasty)
23430	Tenodesis of long tendon of biceps

⊘ =Modifier '-51' Exempt ▶ ◀=New or Revised Text ✚=Add-on Code CPT 2002

23440 Resection or transplantation of long tendon of biceps

23450 Capsulorrhaphy, anterior; Putti-Platt procedure or Magnuson type operation

►(To report arthroscopic thermal capsulorrhaphy, use 29999)◄

23455 with labral repair (eg, Bankart procedure)

►(For arthroscopic procedure, use 29807)◄

23460 Capsulorrhaphy, anterior, any type; with bone block

23462 with coracoid process transfer

►(To report open thermal capsulorrhaphy, use 23929)◄

23465 Capsulorrhaphy, glenohumeral joint, posterior, with or without bone block

(For sternoclavicular and acromioclavicular reconstruction, see 23530, 23550)

23466 Capsulorrhaphy, glenohumeral joint, any type multi-directional instability

23470 Arthroplasty, glenohumeral joint; hemiarthroplasty

23472 total shoulder (glenoid and proximal humeral replacement (eg, total shoulder))

(For removal of total shoulder implants, see 23331, 23332)

(For osteotomy, proximal humerus, use 24400)

23480 Osteotomy, clavicle, with or without internal fixation;

23485 with bone graft for nonunion or malunion (includes obtaining graft and/or necessary fixation)

23490 Prophylactic treatment (nailing, pinning, plating or wiring) with or without methylmethacrylate; clavicle

23491 proximal humerus

Fracture and/or Dislocation

23500 Closed treatment of clavicular fracture; without manipulation

23505 with manipulation

(23510 has been deleted. To report, see 23500, 23505, 23515)

23515 Open treatment of clavicular fracture, with or without internal or external fixation

23520 Closed treatment of sternoclavicular dislocation; without manipulation

23525 with manipulation

23530 Open treatment of sternoclavicular dislocation, acute or chronic;

23532 with fascial graft (includes obtaining graft)

23540 Closed treatment of acromioclavicular dislocation; without manipulation

23545 with manipulation

23550 Open treatment of acromioclavicular dislocation, acute or chronic;

23552 with fascial graft (includes obtaining graft)

23570 Closed treatment of scapular fracture; without manipulation

23575 with manipulation, with or without skeletal traction (with or without shoulder joint involvement)

(23580 has been deleted. To report, see 23570, 23575, 23585)

23585 Open treatment of scapular fracture (body, glenoid or acromion) with or without internal fixation

23600 Closed treatment of proximal humeral (surgical or anatomical neck) fracture; without manipulation

23605 with manipulation, with or without skeletal traction

(23610 has been deleted. To report, see 23600, 23605, 23615)

23615 Open treatment of proximal humeral (surgical or anatomical neck) fracture, with or without internal or external fixation, with or without repair of tuberosity(s);

23616 with proximal humeral prosthetic replacement

23620 Closed treatment of greater humeral tuberosity fracture; without manipulation

23625 with manipulation

23630 Open treatment of greater humeral tuberosity fracture, with or without internal or external fixation

23650 Closed treatment of shoulder dislocation, with manipulation; without anesthesia

23655 requiring anesthesia

(23658 has been deleted. To report, see 23650, 23655, 23660, 23665, 23670)

23660 Open treatment of acute shoulder dislocation

(Repairs for recurrent dislocations, see 23450-23466)

23665 Closed treatment of shoulder dislocation, with fracture of greater humeral tuberosity, with manipulation

23670 Open treatment of shoulder dislocation, with fracture of greater humeral tuberosity, with or without internal or external fixation

23675 Closed treatment of shoulder dislocation, with surgical or anatomical neck fracture, with manipulation

23680 Open treatment of shoulder dislocation, with surgical or anatomical neck fracture, with or without internal or external fixation

Manipulation

23700* Manipulation under anesthesia, shoulder joint, including application of fixation apparatus (dislocation excluded)

▲=Revised Code   ●=New Code   ✱=Service Includes Surgical Procedure Only

Arthrodesis

23800   Arthrodesis, glenohumeral joint;

23802   with autogenous graft (includes obtaining graft)

Amputation

23900   Interthoracoscapular amputation (forequarter)

23920   Disarticulation of shoulder;

23921   secondary closure or scar revision

Other Procedures

23929   Unlisted procedure, shoulder

Humerus (Upper Arm) and Elbow

Elbow area includes head and neck of radius and olecranon process.

Incision

(For incision and drainage procedures, superficial, see 10040-10160)

23930   Incision and drainage, upper arm or elbow area; deep abscess or hematoma

23931   bursa

23935   Incision, deep, with opening of bone cortex (eg, for osteomyelitis or bone abscess), humerus or elbow

(23936 has been deleted)

24000   Arthrotomy, elbow, including exploration, drainage, or removal of foreign body

(24001 has been deleted)

24006   Arthrotomy of the elbow, with capsular excision for capsular release (separate procedure)

Excision

24065   Biopsy, soft tissue of upper arm or elbow area; superficial

24066   deep (subfascial or intramuscular)

(For needle biopsy of soft tissue, use 20206)

▲ **24075**   Excision, tumor, soft tissue of upper arm or elbow area; subcutaneous

24076   deep (subfascial or intramuscular)

24077   Radical resection of tumor (eg, malignant neoplasm), soft tissue of upper arm or elbow area

24100   Arthrotomy, elbow; with synovial biopsy only

24101   with joint exploration, with or without biopsy, with or without removal of loose or foreign body

24102   with synovectomy

24105   Excision, olecranon bursa

24110   Excision or curettage of bone cyst or benign tumor, humerus;

24115   with autograft (includes obtaining graft)

24116   with allograft

24120   Excision or curettage of bone cyst or benign tumor of head or neck of radius or olecranon process;

24125   with autograft (includes obtaining graft)

24126   with allograft

24130   Excision, radial head

(For replacement with implant, use 24366)

24134   Sequestrectomy (eg, for osteomyelitis or bone abscess), shaft or distal humerus

(24135 has been deleted)

24136   Sequestrectomy (eg, for osteomyelitis or bone abscess), radial head or neck

(24137 has been deleted)

24138   Sequestrectomy (eg, for osteomyelitis or bone abscess), olecranon process

(24139 has been deleted)

24140   Partial excision (craterization, saucerization, or diaphysectomy) bone (eg, osteomyelitis), humerus

(24144 has been deleted)

24145   Partial excision (craterization, saucerization, or diaphysectomy) bone (eg, osteomyelitis), radial head or neck

(24146 has been deleted)

24147   Partial excision (craterization, saucerization, or diaphysectomy) bone (eg, osteomyelitis), olecranon process

(24148 has been deleted)

24149   Radical resection of capsule, soft tissue, and heterotopic bone, elbow, with contracture release (separate procedure)

(For capsular and soft tissue release only, use 24006)

24150   Radical resection for tumor, shaft or distal humerus;

24151   with autograft (includes obtaining graft)

24152   Radical resection for tumor, radial head or neck;

24153   with autograft (includes obtaining graft)

24155   Resection of elbow joint (arthrectomy)

     ⊘ =Modifier '-51' Exempt   ▶ ◀=New or Revised Text   ✚ =Add-on Code   CPT 2002

Introduction or Removal

(For K-wire or pin insertion or removal, see 20650, 20670, 20680)

(For arthrocentesis or needling of bursa or joint, use 20605)

24160   Implant removal; elbow joint

24164   radial head

24200   Removal of foreign body, upper arm or elbow area; subcutaneous

24201   deep (subfascial or intramuscular)

24220   Injection procedure for elbow arthrography

(For radiological supervision and interpretation, use 73085. ▶Do not report 76003 in addition to 73085)◀

(For injection of tennis elbow, use 20550)

Repair, Revision, and/or Reconstruction

● **24300**   Manipulation, elbow, under anesthesia

▶(For application of external fixation, see 20690 or 20692)◀

24301   Muscle or tendon transfer, any type, upper arm or elbow, single (excluding 24320-24331)

24305   Tendon lengthening, upper arm or elbow, each tendon

24310   Tenotomy, open, elbow to shoulder, each tendon

24320   Tenoplasty, with muscle transfer, with or without free graft, elbow to shoulder, single (Seddon-Brookes type procedure)

24330   Flexor-plasty, elbow (eg, Steindler type advancement);

24331   with extensor advancement

● **24332**   Tenolysis, triceps

24340   Tenodesis of biceps tendon at elbow (separate procedure)

24341   Repair, tendon or muscle, upper arm or elbow, each tendon or muscle, primary or secondary (excludes rotator cuff)

24342   Reinsertion of ruptured biceps or triceps tendon, distal, with or without tendon graft

● **24343**   Repair lateral collateral ligament, elbow, with local tissue

● **24344**   Reconstruction lateral collateral ligament, elbow, with tendon graft (includes harvesting of graft)

● **24345**   Repair medial collateral ligament, elbow, with local tissue

● **24346**   Reconstruction medial collateral ligament, elbow, with tendon graft (includes harvesting of graft)

24350   Fasciotomy, lateral or medial (eg, tennis elbow or epicondylitis);

24351   with extensor origin detachment

24352   with annular ligament resection

24354   with stripping

24356   with partial ostectomy

24360   Arthroplasty, elbow; with membrane (eg, fascial)

24361   with distal humeral prosthetic replacement

24362   with implant and fascia lata ligament reconstruction

24363   with distal humerus and proximal ulnar prosthetic replacement (eg, total elbow)

24365   Arthroplasty, radial head;

24366   with implant

24400   Osteotomy, humerus, with or without internal fixation

24410   Multiple osteotomies with realignment on intramedullary rod, humeral shaft (Sofield type procedure)

24420   Osteoplasty, humerus (eg, shortening or lengthening) (excluding 64876)

24430   Repair of nonunion or malunion, humerus; without graft (eg, compression technique)

24435   with iliac or other autograft (includes obtaining graft)

(For proximal radius and/or ulna, see 25400-25420)

24470   Hemiepiphyseal arrest (eg, cubitus varus or valgus, distal humerus)

24495   Decompression fasciotomy, forearm, with brachial artery exploration

24498   Prophylactic treatment (nailing, pinning, plating or wiring), with or without methylmethacrylate, humeral shaft

Fracture and/or Dislocation

24500   Closed treatment of humeral shaft fracture; without manipulation

24505   with manipulation, with or without skeletal traction

(24506 has been deleted. To report, use 24516)

(24510 has been deleted. To report, see 24500, 24505, 24515, 24516)

24515   Open treatment of humeral shaft fracture with plate/screws, with or without cerclage

24516   Open treatment of humeral shaft fracture, with insertion of intramedullary implant, with or without cerclage and/or locking screws

24530   Closed treatment of supracondylar or transcondylar humeral fracture, with or without intercondylar extension; without manipulation

(24531 has been deleted. To report, use 24535)

24535   with manipulation, with or without skin or skeletal traction

(24536 has been deleted. To report, use 24535)

24538   Percutaneous skeletal fixation of supracondylar or transcondylar humeral fracture, with or without intercondylar extension

(24540 and 24542 have been deleted. To report, see 24530, 24535, 24538, 24545, 24546)

24545   Open treatment of humeral supracondylar or transcondylar fracture, with or without internal or external fixation; without intercondylar extension

24546   with intercondylar extension

24560   Closed treatment of humeral epicondylar fracture, medial or lateral; without manipulation

24565   with manipulation

24566   Percutaneous skeletal fixation of humeral epicondylar fracture, medial or lateral, with manipulation

(24570 has been deleted. To report, see 24560, 24565, 24575)

24575   Open treatment of humeral epicondylar fracture, medial or lateral, with or without internal or external fixation

24576   Closed treatment of humeral condylar fracture, medial or lateral; without manipulation

24577   with manipulation

(24578 has been deleted. To report, see 24576, 24577, 24579)

24579   Open treatment of humeral condylar fracture, medial or lateral, with or without internal or external fixation

(24580 has been deleted. To report, see 24530, 24560, 24576, 24650, 24670)

(24581 has been deleted. To report, see 24535, 24565, 24577, 24675)

24582   Percutaneous skeletal fixation of humeral condylar fracture, medial or lateral, with manipulation

(24583 has been deleted. To report, see 24535, 24538, 24545, 24560, 24565, 24577)

(24585 has been deleted. To report, see 24538, 24545, 24575, 24579, 24665, 24666, 24685)

24586   Open treatment of periarticular fracture and/or dislocation of the elbow (fracture distal humerus and proximal ulna and/ or proximal radius);

24587   with implant arthroplasty

(See also 24361)

(24588 has been deleted. To report, see 24586, 24587)

24600   Treatment of closed elbow dislocation; without anesthesia

24605   requiring anesthesia

(24610 has been deleted. To report, see 24586, 24600, 24605, 24615)

24615   Open treatment of acute or chronic elbow dislocation

24620   Closed treatment of Monteggia type of fracture dislocation at elbow (fracture proximal end of ulna with dislocation of radial head), with manipulation

(24625 has been deleted. To report, see 24620, 24635)

24635   Open treatment of Monteggia type of fracture dislocation at elbow (fracture proximal end of ulna with dislocation of radial head), with or without internal or external fixation

24640*   Closed treatment of radial head subluxation in child, nursemaid elbow, with manipulation

24650   Closed treatment of radial head or neck fracture; without manipulation

24655   with manipulation

(24660 has been deleted. To report, see 24650, 24655, 24665, 24666)

24665   Open treatment of radial head or neck fracture, with or without internal fixation or radial head excision;

24666   with radial head prosthetic replacement

24670   Closed treatment of ulnar fracture, proximal end (olecranon process); without manipulation

24675   with manipulation

(24680 has been deleted. To report, see 24670, 24675, 24685)

24685   Open treatment of ulnar fracture proximal end (olecranon process), with or without internal or external fixation

(24700 has been deleted. To report, use 24999)

Arthrodesis

24800   Arthrodesis, elbow joint; local

24802   with autogenous graft (includes obtaining graft)

Amputation

24900   Amputation, arm through humerus; with primary closure

24920   open, circular (guillotine)

24925   secondary closure or scar revision

24930   re-amputation

24931   with implant

24935   Stump elongation, upper extremity

24940   Cineplasty, upper extremity, complete procedure

Other Procedures

24999   Unlisted procedure, humerus or elbow

⊘ =Modifier '-51' Exempt   ▶ ◀=New or Revised Text   ✛=Add-on Code   CPT 2002

Forearm and Wrist

Radius, ulna, carpal bones and joints.

Incision

25000   Incision, extensor tendon sheath, wrist (eg, deQuervains disease)

(For decompression median nerve or for carpal tunnel syndrome, use 64721)

(25005 has been deleted. To report, use 25000)

● **25001**   Incision, flexor tendon sheath, wrist (eg, flexor carpi radialis)

▲ **25020**   Decompression fasciotomy, forearm and/or wrist, flexor OR extensor compartment; without debridement of nonviable muscle and/or nerve

25023   with debridement of nonviable muscle and/or nerve

(For decompression fasciotomy with brachial artery exploration, use 24495)

(For incision and drainage procedures, superficial, see 10040-10160)

(For debridement, see also 11000-11044)

● **25024**   Decompression fasciotomy, forearm and/or wrist, flexor AND extensor compartment; without debridement of nonviable muscle and/or nerve

● **25025**   with debridement of nonviable muscle and/or nerve

25028   Incision and drainage, forearm and/or wrist; deep abscess or hematoma

25031   bursa

25035   Incision, deep, bone cortex, forearm and/or wrist (eg, osteomyelitis or bone abscess)

(25036 has been deleted)

25040   Arthrotomy, radiocarpal or midcarpal joint, with exploration, drainage, or removal of foreign body

(25041 has been deleted)

Excision

25065   Biopsy, soft tissue of forearm and/or wrist; superficial

25066   deep (subfascial or intramuscular)

(For needle biopsy of soft tissue, use 20206)

▲ **25075**   Excision, tumor, soft tissue of forearm and/or wrist area; subcutaneous

25076   deep (subfascial or intramuscular)

25077   Radical resection of tumor (eg, malignant neoplasm), soft tissue of forearm and/or wrist area

25085   Capsulotomy, wrist (eg, contracture)

25100   Arthrotomy, wrist joint; with biopsy

25101   with joint exploration, with or without biopsy, with or without removal of loose or foreign body

25105   with synovectomy

25107   Arthrotomy, distal radioulnar joint including repair of triangular cartilage, complex

25110   Excision, lesion of tendon sheath, forearm and/or wrist

25111   Excision of ganglion, wrist (dorsal or volar); primary

25112   recurrent

(For hand or finger, use 26160)

25115   Radical excision of bursa, synovia of wrist, or forearm tendon sheaths (eg, tenosynovitis, fungus, Tbc, or other granulomas, rheumatoid arthritis); flexors

25116   extensors, with or without transposition of dorsal retinaculum

(For finger synovectomies, use 26145)

25118   Synovectomy, extensor tendon sheath, wrist, single compartment;

25119   with resection of distal ulna

25120   Excision or curettage of bone cyst or benign tumor of radius or ulna (excluding head or neck of radius and olecranon process);

(For head or neck of radius or olecranon process, see 24120-24126)

25125   with autograft (includes obtaining graft)

25126   with allograft

25130   Excision or curettage of bone cyst or benign tumor of carpal bones;

25135   with autograft (includes obtaining graft)

25136   with allograft

25145   Sequestrectomy (eg, for osteomyelitis or bone abscess), forearm and/or wrist

(25146 has been deleted)

25150   Partial excision (craterization, saucerization, or diaphysectomy) of bone (eg, for osteomyelitis); ulna

25151   radius

(25153 has been deleted)

(For head or neck of radius or olecranon process, see 24145, 24147)

25170   Radical resection for tumor, radius or ulna

25210   Carpectomy; one bone

(For carpectomy with implant, see 25441-25445)

25215   all bones of proximal row

25230   Radial styloidectomy (separate procedure)

25240   Excision distal ulna partial or complete (eg, Darrach type or matched resection)

(For implant replacement, distal ulna, use 25442)

(For obtaining fascia for interposition, see 20920, 20922)

Introduction or Removal

(For K-wire, pin or rod insertion or removal, see 20650, 20670, 20680)

25246 Injection procedure for wrist arthrography

(For radiological supervision and interpretation, use 73115. ▶Do not report 76003 in addition to 73115)◄

(For foreign body removal, superficial use 20520)

25248 Exploration with removal of deep foreign body, forearm or wrist

25250 Removal of wrist prosthesis; (separate procedure)

25251 complicated, including total wrist

● **25259** Manipulation, wrist, under anesthesia

▶(For application of external fixation, see 20690 or 20692)◄

Repair, Revision, and/or Reconstruction

25260 Repair, tendon or muscle, flexor, forearm and/or wrist; primary, single, each tendon or muscle

25263 secondary, single, each tendon or muscle

25265 secondary, with free graft (includes obtaining graft), each tendon or muscle

25270 Repair, tendon or muscle, extensor, forearm and/or wrist; primary, single, each tendon or muscle

25272 secondary, single, each tendon or muscle

▲ **25274** secondary, with free graft (includes obtaining graft), each tendon or muscle

● **25275** Repair, tendon sheath, extensor, forearm and/or wrist, with free graft (includes obtaining graft) (eg, for extensor carpi ulnaris subluxation)

25280 Lengthening or shortening of flexor or extensor tendon, forearm and/or wrist, single, each tendon

25290 Tenotomy, open, flexor or extensor tendon, forearm and/or wrist, single, each tendon

25295 Tenolysis, flexor or extensor tendon, forearm and/or wrist, single, each tendon

25300 Tenodesis at wrist; flexors of fingers

25301 extensors of fingers

25310 Tendon transplantation or transfer, flexor or extensor, forearm and/or wrist, single; each tendon

25312 with tendon graft(s) (includes obtaining graft), each tendon

25315 Flexor origin slide (eg, for cerebral palsy, Volkmann contracture), forearm and/or wrist;

25316 with tendon(s) transfer

(25317, 25318 have been deleted. To report, see 25315, 25316)

25320 Capsulorrhaphy or reconstruction, wrist, any method (eg, capsulodesis, ligament repair, tendon transfer or graft) (includes synovectomy, capsulotomy and open reduction) for carpal instability

(25330, 25331 have been deleted. To report, see 25332 and 25441-25446)

25332 Arthroplasty, wrist, with or without interposition, with or without external or internal fixation

(For obtaining fascia for interposition, see 20920, 20922)

(For prosthetic replacement arthroplasty, see 25441-25446)

25335 Centralization of wrist on ulna (eg, radial club hand)

25337 Reconstruction for stabilization of unstable distal ulna or distal radioulnar joint, secondary by soft tissue stabilization (eg, tendon transfer, tendon graft or weave, or tenodesis) with or without open reduction of distal radioulnar joint

(For harvesting of fascia lata graft, see 20920, 20922)

25350 Osteotomy, radius; distal third

25355 middle or proximal third

25360 Osteotomy; ulna

25365 radius AND ulna

25370 Multiple osteotomies, with realignment on intramedullary rod (Sofield type procedure); radius OR ulna

25375 radius AND ulna

25390 Osteoplasty, radius OR ulna; shortening

25391 lengthening with autograft

25392 Osteoplasty, radius AND ulna; shortening (excluding 64876)

25393 lengthening with autograft

● **25394** Osteoplasty, carpal bone, shortening

25400 Repair of nonunion or malunion, radius OR ulna; without graft (eg, compression technique)

▲ **25405** with autograft (includes obtaining graft)

25415 Repair of nonunion or malunion, radius AND ulna; without graft (eg, compression technique)

▲ **25420** with autograft (includes obtaining graft)

25425 Repair of defect with autograft; radius OR ulna

25426 radius AND ulna

● **25430** Insertion of vascular pedicle into carpal bone (eg, Harii procedure)

● **25431** Repair of nonunion of carpal bone (excluding carpal scaphoid (navicular)) (includes obtaining graft and necessary fixation), each bone

▲ **25440** Repair of nonunion, scaphoid carpal (navicular) bone, with or without radial styloidectomy (includes obtaining graft and necessary fixation)

⊘ =Modifier '-51' Exempt ▶ ◄=New or Revised Text ✚ =Add-on Code CPT 2002

25441	Arthroplasty with prosthetic replacement; distal radius
25442	distal ulna
▲ **25443**	scaphoid carpal (navicular)
25444	lunate
25445	trapezium
25446	distal radius and partial or entire carpus (total wrist)
25447	Arthroplasty, interposition, intercarpal or carpometacarpal joints
	(For wrist arthroplasty, use 25332)
25449	Revision of arthroplasty, including removal of implant, wrist joint
25450	Epiphyseal arrest by epiphysiodesis or stapling; distal radius OR ulna
25455	distal radius AND ulna
25490	Prophylactic treatment (nailing, pinning, plating or wiring) with or without methylmethacrylate; radius
25491	ulna
25492	radius AND ulna

Fracture and/or Dislocation

25500 Closed treatment of radial shaft fracture; without manipulation

25505 with manipulation

(25510 has been deleted. To report, see 25500, 25505, 25515)

25515 Open treatment of radial shaft fracture, with or without internal or external fixation

▲ **25520** Closed treatment of radial shaft fracture and closed treatment of dislocation of distal radioulnar joint (Galeazzi fracture/dislocation)

25525 Open treatment of radial shaft fracture, with internal and/ or external fixation and closed treatment of dislocation of distal radioulnar joint (Galeazzi fracture/dislocation), with or without percutaneous skeletal fixation

▲ **25526** Open treatment of radial shaft fracture, with internal and/or external fixation and open treatment, with or without internal or external fixation of distal radioulnar joint (Galeazzi fracture/dislocation), includes repair of triangular fibrocartilage complex

25530 Closed treatment of ulnar shaft fracture; without manipulation

25535 with manipulation

(25540 has been deleted. To report, see 25530, 25535, 25545)

25545 Open treatment of ulnar shaft fracture, with or without internal or external fixation

25560 Closed treatment of radial and ulnar shaft fractures; without manipulation

25565 with manipulation

(25570 has been deleted. To report, see 25560, 25565, 25574, 25575)

25574 Open treatment of radial AND ulnar shaft fractures, with internal or external fixation; of radius OR ulna

25575 of radius AND ulna

25600 Closed treatment of distal radial fracture (eg, Colles or Smith type) or epiphyseal separation, with or without fracture of ulnar styloid; without manipulation

25605 with manipulation

(25610 has been deleted. To report, use 25605)

25611 Percutaneous skeletal fixation of distal radial fracture (eg, Colles or Smith type) or epiphyseal separation, with or without fracture of ulnar styloid, requiring manipulation, with or without external fixation

(25615 has been deleted. To report, see 25600, 25605, 25611, 25620)

25620 Open treatment of distal radial fracture (eg, Colles or Smith type) or epiphyseal separation, with or without fracture of ulnar styloid, with or without internal or external fixation

25622 Closed treatment of carpal scaphoid (navicular) fracture; without manipulation

25624 with manipulation

(25626 has been deleted. To report, see 25622, 25624, 25628)

25628 Open treatment of carpal scaphoid (navicular) fracture, with or without internal or external fixation

25630 Closed treatment of carpal bone fracture (excluding carpal scaphoid (navicular)); without manipulation, each bone

25635 with manipulation, each bone

(25640 has been deleted. To report, see 25630, 25635, 25645)

▲ **25645** Open treatment of carpal bone fracture (other than carpal scaphoid (navicular)), each bone

25650 Closed treatment of ulnar styloid fracture

● **25651** Percutaneous skeletal fixation of ulnar styloid fracture

● **25652** Open treatment of ulnar styloid fracture

25660 Closed treatment of radiocarpal or intercarpal dislocation, one or more bones, with manipulation

(25665 has been deleted. To report, see 25650, 25660, 25670)

25670 Open treatment of radiocarpal or intercarpal dislocation, one or more bones

---

● **25671** Percutaneous skeletal fixation of distal radioulnar dislocation

25675 Closed treatment of distal radioulnar dislocation with manipulation

25676 Open treatment of distal radioulnar dislocation, acute or chronic

25680 Closed treatment of trans-scaphoperilunar type of fracture dislocation, with manipulation

25685 Open treatment of trans-scaphoperilunar type of fracture dislocation

25690 Closed treatment of lunate dislocation, with manipulation

25695 Open treatment of lunate dislocation

(25700 has been deleted. To report, use 25999)

Arthrodesis

25800 Arthrodesis, wrist; complete, without bone graft (includes radiocarpal and/or intercarpal and/or carpometacarpal joints)

25805 with sliding graft

25810 with iliac or other autograft (includes obtaining graft)

(25815 has been deleted. To report, see 25820, 25825)

25820 Arthrodesis, wrist; limited, without bone graft (eg, intercarpal or radiocarpal)

25825 with autograft (includes obtaining graft)

25830 Arthrodesis, distal radioulnar joint with segmental resection of ulna, with or without bone graft (eg, Sauve-Kapandji procedure)

Amputation

25900 Amputation, forearm, through radius and ulna;

25905 open, circular (guillotine)

25907 secondary closure or scar revision

25909 re-amputation

25915 Krukenberg procedure

25920 Disarticulation through wrist;

25922 secondary closure or scar revision

25924 re-amputation

25927 Transmetacarpal amputation;

25929 secondary closure or scar revision

25931 re-amputation

Other Procedures

25999 Unlisted procedure, forearm or wrist

Hand and Fingers

Incision

26010* Drainage of finger abscess; simple

26011* complicated (eg, felon)

26020 Drainage of tendon sheath, digit and/or palm, each

26025 Drainage of palmar bursa; single, bursa

26030 multiple bursa

(26032 has been deleted)

26034 Incision, bone cortex, hand or finger (eg, osteomyelitis or bone abscess)

26035 Decompression fingers and/or hand, injection injury (eg, grease gun)

26037 Decompressive fasciotomy, hand (excludes 26035)

(For injection injury, use 26035)

26040 Fasciotomy, palmar (eg, Dupuytren's contracture); percutaneous

26045 open, partial

(For fasciectomy, see 26121-26125)

26055 Tendon sheath incision (eg, for trigger finger)

26060 Tenotomy, percutaneous, single, each digit

26070 Arthrotomy, with exploration, drainage, or removal of loose or foreign body; carpometacarpal joint

26075 metacarpophalangeal joint, each

26080 interphalangeal joint, each

Excision

26100 Arthrotomy with biopsy; carpometacarpal joint, each

26105 metacarpophalangeal joint, each

26110 interphalangeal joint, each

▲ **26115** Excision, tumor or vascular malformation, soft tissue of hand or finger; subcutaneous

▲ **26116** deep (subfascial or intramuscular)

26117 Radical resection of tumor (eg, malignant neoplasm), soft tissue of hand or finger

(26120 has been deleted. To report, see 26121-26125)

26121 Fasciectomy, palm only, with or without Z-plasty, other local tissue rearrangement, or skin grafting (includes obtaining graft)

(26122 has been deleted. To report, use 26121-26125)

26123 Fasciectomy, partial palmar with release of single digit including proximal interphalangeal joint, with or without Z-plasty, other local tissue rearrangement, or skin grafting (includes obtaining graft);

(26124 has been deleted. To report, use 26121-26125)

⊘ =Modifier '-51' Exempt   ▶ ◀ =New or Revised Text   ✛ =Add-on Code   CPT 2002

+ 26125   each additional digit (List separately in addition to code for primary procedure)

(Use 26125 in conjunction with code 26123)

(26126, 26128 have been deleted. To report, use 26121-26125)

(For fasciotomy, see 26040, 26045)

26130   Synovectomy, carpometacarpal joint

26135   Synovectomy, metacarpophalangeal joint including intrinsic release and extensor hood reconstruction, each digit

26140   Synovectomy, proximal interphalangeal joint, including extensor reconstruction, each interphalangeal joint

26145   Synovectomy, tendon sheath, radical (tenosynovectomy), flexor tendon, palm and/or finger, each tendon

(For tendon sheath synovectomies at wrist, see 25115, 25116)

▲ **26160**   Excision of lesion of tendon sheath or joint capsule (eg, cyst, mucous cyst, or ganglion), hand or finger

(For wrist ganglion, see 25111, 25112)

(For trigger digit, use 26055)

26170   Excision of tendon, palm, flexor, single (separate procedure), each

26180   Excision of tendon, finger, flexor (separate procedure), each tendon

26185   Sesamoidectomy, thumb or finger (separate procedure)

26200   Excision or curettage of bone cyst or benign tumor of metacarpal;

26205   with autograft (includes obtaining graft)

(26206 has been deleted. To report, use 26989)

26210   Excision or curettage of bone cyst or benign tumor of proximal, middle, or distal phalanx of finger;

26215   with autograft (includes obtaining graft)

(26216 has been deleted. To report, use 26989)

26230   Partial excision (craterization, saucerization, or diaphysectomy) bone (eg, osteomyelitis); metacarpal

26235   proximal or middle phalanx of finger

26236   distal phalanx of finger

26250   Radical resection, metacarpal (eg, tumor);

26255   with autograft (includes obtaining graft)

26260   Radical resection, proximal or middle phalanx of finger (eg, tumor);

26261   with autograft (includes obtaining graft)

26262   Radical resection, distal phalanx of finger (eg, tumor)

Introduction or Removal

26320   Removal of implant from finger or hand

(For removal of foreign body in hand or finger, see 20520, 20525)

Repair, Revision, and/or Reconstruction

● **26340**   Manipulation, finger joint, under anesthesia, each joint

▶(For application of external fixation, see 20690 or 20692)◀

▲ **26350**   Repair or advancement, flexor tendon, not in zone 2 digital flexor tendon sheath (eg, no man's land); primary or secondary without free graft, each tendon

26352   secondary with free graft (includes obtaining graft), each tendon

▲ **26356**   Repair or advancement, flexor tendon, in zone 2 digital flexor tendon sheath (eg, no man's land); primary or secondary without free graft, each tendon

26357   secondary, each tendon

26358   secondary with free graft (includes obtaining graft), each tendon

26370   Repair or advancement of profundus tendon, with intact superficialis tendon; primary, each tendon

26372   secondary with free graft (includes obtaining graft), each tendon

26373   secondary without free graft, each tendon

▲ **26390**   Excision flexor tendon, with implantation of synthetic rod for delayed tendon graft, hand or finger, each rod

▲ **26392**   Removal of synthetic rod and insertion of flexor tendon graft, hand or finger (includes obtaining graft), each rod

26410   Repair, extensor tendon, hand, primary or secondary; without free graft, each tendon

26412   with free graft (includes obtaining graft), each tendon

▲ **26415**   Excision of extensor tendon, with implantation of synthetic rod for delayed tendon graft, hand or finger, each rod

▲ **26416**   Removal of synthetic rod and insertion of extensor tendon graft (includes obtaining graft), hand or finger, each rod

26418   Repair, extensor tendon, finger, primary or secondary; without free graft, each tendon

26420   with free graft (includes obtaining graft) each tendon

▲ **26426**   Repair of extensor tendon, central slip, secondary (eg, boutonniere deformity); using local tissue(s), including lateral band(s), each finger

▲ **26428**   with free graft (includes obtaining graft), each finger

26432   Closed treatment of distal extensor tendon insertion, with or without percutaneous pinning (eg, mallet finger)

26433	Repair of extensor tendon, distal insertion, primary or secondary; without graft (eg, mallet finger)
26434	with free graft (includes obtaining graft)
	(For tenovaginotomy for trigger finger, use 26055)
26437	Realignment of extensor tendon, hand, each tendon
26440	Tenolysis, flexor tendon; palm OR finger; each tendon
26442	palm AND finger, each tendon
▲ 26445	Tenolysis, extensor tendon, hand OR finger; each tendon
26449	Tenolysis, complex, extensor tendon, finger, including forearm, each tendon
26450	Tenotomy, flexor, palm, open, each tendon
26455	Tenotomy, flexor, finger, open, each tendon
26460	Tenotomy, extensor, hand or finger, open, each tendon
26471	Tenodesis; of proximal interphalangeal joint, each joint
26474	of distal joint, each joint
26476	Lengthening of tendon, extensor, hand or finger, each tendon
26477	Shortening of tendon, extensor, hand or finger, each tendon
26478	Lengthening of tendon, flexor, hand or finger, each tendon
26479	Shortening of tendon, flexor, hand or finger, each tendon
26480	Transfer or transplant of tendon, carpometacarpal area or dorsum of hand; without free graft, each tendon
26483	with free tendon graft (includes obtaining graft), each tendon
26485	Transfer or transplant of tendon, palmar; without free tendon graft, each tendon
26489	with free tendon graft (includes obtaining graft), each tendon
26490	Opponensplasty; superficialis tendon transfer type, each tendon
26492	tendon transfer with graft (includes obtaining graft), each tendon
26494	hypothenar muscle transfer
26496	other methods
	(For thumb fusion in opposition, use 26820)
26497	Transfer of tendon to restore intrinsic function; ring and small finger
26498	all four fingers
26499	Correction claw finger, other methods
26500	Reconstruction of tendon pulley, each tendon; with local tissues (separate procedure)
26502	with tendon or fascial graft (includes obtaining graft) (separate procedure)
26504	with tendon prosthesis (separate procedure)

26508	Release of thenar muscle(s) (eg, thumb contracture)
▲ 26510	Cross intrinsic transfer, each tendon
26516	Capsulodesis, metacarpophalangeal joint; single digit
26517	two digits
26518	three or four digits
26520	Capsulectomy or capsulotomy; metacarpophalangeal joint, each joint
26525	interphalangeal joint, each joint
	(26527 has been deleted. To report, use 25447)
26530	Arthroplasty, metacarpophalangeal joint; each joint
26531	with prosthetic implant, each joint
26535	Arthroplasty, interphalangeal joint; each joint
26536	with prosthetic implant, each joint
26540	Repair of collateral ligament, metacarpophalangeal or interphalangeal joint
26541	Reconstruction, collateral ligament, metacarpophalangeal joint, single; with tendon or fascial graft (includes obtaining graft)
26542	with local tissue (eg, adductor advancement)
26545	Reconstruction, collateral ligament, interphalangeal joint, single, including graft, each joint
26546	Repair non-union, metacarpal or phalanx, (includes obtaining bone graft with or without external or internal fixation)
26548	Repair and reconstruction, finger, volar plate, interphalangeal joint
26550	Pollicization of a digit
26551	Transfer, toe-to-hand with microvascular anastomosis; great toe wrap-around with bone graft
	(For great toe with web space, use 20973)
	(26552 has been deleted. To report, see 20973 or 26551, 26553, 26554)
26553	other than great toe, single
26554	other than great toe, double
	(Do not report code 69990 in addition to codes 26551-26554)
26555	Transfer, finger to another position without microvascular anastomosis
26556	Transfer, free toe joint, with microvascular anastomosis
	(Do not report code 69990 in addition to code 26556)
	(26557-26559 have been deleted. To report, see 20973 or 26551, 26553, 26554)
26560	Repair of syndactyly (web finger) each web space; with skin flaps
26561	with skin flaps and grafts
26562	complex (eg, involving bone, nails)

⊘ =Modifier '-51' Exempt   ▶ ◀=New or Revised Text   ✦=Add-on Code   CPT 2002

26565 Osteotomy; metacarpal, each

26567 phalanx of finger, each

26568 Osteoplasty, lengthening, metacarpal or phalanx

(26570, 26574 have been deleted. To report, use 26989)

26580 Repair cleft hand

►(26585 has been deleted. To report, use 26587)◄

▲**26587** Reconstruction of polydactylous digit, soft tissue and bone

►(For excision of polydactylous digit, soft tissue only, use 11200)◄

▲**26590** Repair macrodactylia, each digit

26591 Repair, intrinsic muscles of hand, each muscle

26593 Release, intrinsic muscles of hand, each muscle

26596 Excision of constricting ring of finger, with multiple Z-plasties

►(26597 has been deleted. To report, see 11041-11042, 14040-14041, or 15120, 15240)◄

Fracture and/or Dislocation

26600 Closed treatment of metacarpal fracture, single; without manipulation, each bone

26605 with manipulation, each bone

▲**26607** Closed treatment of metacarpal fracture, with manipulation, with external fixation, each bone

26608 Percutaneous skeletal fixation of metacarpal fracture, each bone

(26610 has been deleted. To report, see 26605, 26607, 26608)

26615 Open treatment of metacarpal fracture, single, with or without internal or external fixation, each bone

26641 Closed treatment of carpometacarpal dislocation, thumb, with manipulation

26645 Closed treatment of carpometacarpal fracture dislocation, thumb (Bennett fracture), with manipulation

26650 Percutaneous skeletal fixation of carpometacarpal fracture dislocation, thumb (Bennett fracture), with manipulation, with or without external fixation

(26655 has been deleted. To report, see 26645, 26650, 26665)

(26660 has been deleted. To report, see 26650, 26665)

26665 Open treatment of carpometacarpal fracture dislocation, thumb (Bennett fracture), with or without internal or external fixation

▲**26670** Closed treatment of carpometacarpal dislocation, other than thumb, with manipulation, each joint; without anesthesia

26675 requiring anesthesia

▲**26676** Percutaneous skeletal fixation of carpometacarpal dislocation, other than thumb, with manipulation, each joint

(26680 has been deleted. To report, see 26670, 26675, 26676, 26685)

▲**26685** Open treatment of carpometacarpal dislocation, other than thumb; with or without internal or external fixation, each joint

26686 complex, multiple or delayed reduction

26700 Closed treatment of metacarpophalangeal dislocation, single, with manipulation; without anesthesia

26705 requiring anesthesia

26706 Percutaneous skeletal fixation of metacarpophalangeal dislocation, single, with manipulation

(26710 has been deleted. To report, see 26700, 26705, 26706, 26715)

26715 Open treatment of metacarpophalangeal dislocation, single, with or without internal or external fixation

26720 Closed treatment of phalangeal shaft fracture, proximal or middle phalanx, finger or thumb; without manipulation, each

26725 with manipulation, with or without skin or skeletal traction, each

26727 Percutaneous skeletal fixation of unstable phalangeal shaft fracture, proximal or middle phalanx, finger or thumb, with manipulation, each

(26730 has been deleted. To report, see 26720, 26725, 26727, 26735)

26735 Open treatment of phalangeal shaft fracture, proximal or middle phalanx, finger or thumb, with or without internal or external fixation, each

26740 Closed treatment of articular fracture, involving metacarpophalangeal or interphalangeal joint; without manipulation, each

26742 with manipulation, each

(26743 has been deleted. To report, use 26989)

(26744 has been deleted. To report, see 26740, 26742, 26746)

26746 Open treatment of articular fracture, involving metacarpophalangeal or interphalangeal joint, with or without internal or external fixation, each

26750 Closed treatment of distal phalangeal fracture, finger or thumb; without manipulation, each

26755 with manipulation, each

26756 Percutaneous skeletal fixation of distal phalangeal fracture, finger or thumb, each

(26760 has been deleted. To report, see 26750, 26755, 26756, 26765)

26765 Open treatment of distal phalangeal fracture, finger or thumb, with or without internal or external fixation, each

---

26770 Closed treatment of interphalangeal joint dislocation, single, with manipulation; without anesthesia

26775 requiring anesthesia

26776 Percutaneous skeletal fixation of interphalangeal joint dislocation, single, with manipulation

(26780 has been deleted. To report, see 26770, 26775, 26776, 26785)

26785 Open treatment of interphalangeal joint dislocation, with or without internal or external fixation, single

Arthrodesis

26820 Fusion in opposition, thumb, with autogenous graft (includes obtaining graft)

26841 Arthrodesis, carpometacarpal joint, thumb, with or without internal fixation;

26842 with autograft (includes obtaining graft)

▲ **26843** Arthrodesis, carpometacarpal joint, digit, other than thumb, each;

26844 with autograft (includes obtaining graft)

26850 Arthrodesis, metacarpophalangeal joint, with or without internal fixation;

26852 with autograft (includes obtaining graft)

26860 Arthrodesis, interphalangeal joint, with or without internal fixation;

+ **26861** each additional interphalangeal joint (List separately in addition to code for primary procedure)

(Use 26861 in conjunction with code 26860)

26862 with autograft (includes obtaining graft)

+ **26863** with autograft (includes obtaining graft), each additional joint (List separately in addition to code for primary procedure)

(Use 26863 in conjunction with code 26862)

Amputation

(For hand through metacarpal bones, use 25927)

26910 Amputation, metacarpal, with finger or thumb (ray amputation), single, with or without interosseous transfer

(For repositioning, see 26550, 26555)

26951 Amputation, finger or thumb, primary or secondary, any joint or phalanx, single, including neurectomies; with direct closure

26952 with local advancement flaps (V-Y, hood)

(For repair of soft tissue defect requiring split or full thickness graft or other pedicle flaps, see 15050-15758)

Other Procedures

26989 Unlisted procedure, hands or fingers

Pelvis and Hip Joint

Including head and neck of femur.

Incision

(For incision and drainage procedures, superficial, see 10040-10160)

26990 Incision and drainage, pelvis or hip joint area; deep abscess or hematoma

26991 infected bursa

26992 Incision, bone cortex, pelvis and/or hip joint (eg, osteomyelitis or bone abscess)

(26995 has been deleted)

27000 Tenotomy, adductor of hip, percutaneous (separate procedure)

27001 Tenotomy, adductor of hip, open

(27002 has been deleted. To report, use 27001 with modifier '-50')

27003 Tenotomy, adductor, subcutaneous, open, with obturator neurectomy

(27004 has been deleted. To report, use 27003 with modifier '-50')

27005 Tenotomy, hip flexor(s), open (separate procedure)

27006 Tenotomy, abductors and/or extensor(s) of hip, open (separate procedure)

(27010, 27015 have been deleted. To report, use 27025)

27025 Fasciotomy, hip or thigh, any type

(27026 has been deleted. To report, use 27025 with modifier '-50')

27030 Arthrotomy, hip, with drainage (eg, infection)

(27031 has been deleted)

27033 Arthrotomy, hip, including exploration or removal of loose or foreign body

27035 Denervation, hip joint, intrapelvic or extrapelvic intra-articular branches of sciatic, femoral, or obturator nerves

(For obturator neurectomy, see 64763, 64766)

27036 Capsulectomy or capsulotomy, hip, with or without excision of heterotopic bone, with release of hip flexor muscles (ie, gluteus medius, gluteus minimus, tensor fascia latae, rectus femoris, sartorius, iliopsoas)

Excision

27040 Biopsy, soft tissue of pelvis and hip area; superficial

27041 deep, subfascial or intramuscular

(For needle biopsy of soft tissue, use 20206)

27047 Excision, tumor, pelvis and hip area; subcutaneous tissue

27048 deep, subfascial, intramuscular

27049   Radical resection of tumor, soft tissue of pelvis and hip area (eg, malignant neoplasm)

27050   Arthrotomy, with biopsy; sacroiliac joint

27052   hip joint

27054   Arthrotomy with synovectomy, hip joint

27060   Excision; ischial bursa

27062   trochanteric bursa or calcification

(For arthrocentesis or needling of bursa, use 20610)

27065   Excision of bone cyst or benign tumor; superficial (wing of ilium, symphysis pubis, or greater trochanter of femur) with or without autograft

27066   deep, with or without autograft

27067   with autograft requiring separate incision

27070   Partial excision (craterization, saucerization) (eg, osteomyelitis or bone abscess); superficial (eg, wing of ilium, symphysis pubis, or greater trochanter of femur)

27071   deep (subfascial or intramuscular)

27075   Radical resection of tumor or infection; wing of ilium, one pubic or ischial ramus or symphysis pubis

27076   ilium, including acetabulum, both pubic rami, or ischium and acetabulum

27077   innominate bone, total

27078   ischial tuberosity and greater trochanter of femur

27079   ischial tuberosity and greater trochanter of femur, with skin flaps

27080   Coccygectomy, primary

(For pressure (decubitus) ulcer, see 15920, 15922 and 15931-15958)

Introduction or Removal

27086*   Removal of foreign body, pelvis or hip; subcutaneous tissue

27087   deep (subfascial or intramuscular)

(27088 has been deleted. To report, use 27087)

27090   Removal of hip prosthesis; (separate procedure)

27091   complicated, including total hip prosthesis, methylmethacrylate with or without insertion of spacer

27093   Injection procedure for hip arthrography; without anesthesia

(For radiological supervision and interpretation, use 73525. ►Do not report 76003 in addition to 73525)◄

27095   with anesthesia

(For radiological supervision and interpretation, use 73525. ►Do not report 76003 in addition to 73525)◄

27096   Injection procedure for sacroiliac joint, arthrography and/or anesthetic/steroid

►(27096 is to be used only with imaging confirmation of intra-articular needle positioning)◄

►(For radiological supervision and interpretation of sacroiliac joint arthrography, use 73542)◄

►(For fluoroscopic guidance without formal arthrography, use 76005)◄

►(Code 27096 is a unilateral procedure. For bilateral procedure, use modifier '-50')◄

Repair, Revision, and/or Reconstruction

27097   Release or recession, hamstring, proximal

27098   Transfer, adductor to ischium

27100   Transfer external oblique muscle to greater trochanter including fascial or tendon extension (graft)

27105   Transfer paraspinal muscle to hip (includes fascial or tendon extension graft)

▲**27110**   Transfer iliopsoas; to greater trochanter of femur

27111   to femoral neck

(27115 has been deleted. To report, use 27299)

27120   Acetabuloplasty; (eg, Whitman, Colonna, Haygroves, or cup type)

27122   resection, femoral head (eg, Girdlestone procedure)

27125   Hemiarthroplasty, hip, partial (eg, femoral stem prosthesis, bipolar arthroplasty)

(For prosthetic replacement following fracture of the hip, use 27236)

(27126, 27127 have been deleted. To report, use 27120)

▲**27130**   Arthroplasty, acetabular and proximal femoral prosthetic replacement (total hip arthroplasty), with or without autograft or allograft

(27131 has been deleted. To report, use 27132)

▲**27132**   Conversion of previous hip surgery to total hip arthroplasty, with or without autograft or allograft

27134   Revision of total hip arthroplasty; both components, with or without autograft or allograft

(27135 has been deleted. To report, see 27134, 27137, 27138)

27137   acetabular component only, with or without autograft or allograft

27138   femoral component only, with or without allograft

▲**27140**   Osteotomy and transfer of greater trochanter of femur (separate procedure)

27146   Osteotomy, iliac, acetabular or innominate bone;

27147   with open reduction of hip

27151   with femoral osteotomy

27156   with femoral osteotomy and with open reduction of hip

(27157 has been deleted)

27158   Osteotomy, pelvis, bilateral (eg, congenital malformation)

27161   Osteotomy, femoral neck (separate procedure)

27165   Osteotomy, intertrochanteric or subtrochanteric including internal or external fixation and/or cast

27170   Bone graft, femoral head, neck, intertrochanteric or subtrochanteric area (includes obtaining bone graft)

27175   Treatment of slipped femoral epiphysis; by traction, without reduction

27176   by single or multiple pinning, in situ

27177   Open treatment of slipped femoral epiphysis; single or multiple pinning or bone graft (includes obtaining graft)

27178   closed manipulation with single or multiple pinning

27179   osteoplasty of femoral neck (Heyman type procedure)

27181   osteotomy and internal fixation

▲ **27185**   Epiphyseal arrest by epiphysiodesis or stapling, greater trochanter of femur

27187   Prophylactic treatment (nailing, pinning, plating or wiring) with or without methylmethacrylate, femoral neck and proximal femur

Fracture and/or Dislocation

(27190, 27191 have been deleted. To report, see 27193, 27194)

(27192 has been deleted. To report, see 27215, 27216)

27193   Closed treatment of pelvic ring fracture, dislocation, diastasis or subluxation; without manipulation

27194   with manipulation, requiring more than local anesthesia

(27195 has been deleted. To report, use 27193)

(27196 has been deleted. To report, use 27194)

27200   Closed treatment of coccygeal fracture

(27201 has been deleted. To report, see 27200, 27202)

27202   Open treatment of coccygeal fracture

(27210, 27211, 27212 have been deleted. To report, see 27193, 27194, 27215, 27216, 27217, 27218)

(27214 has been deleted. To report, see 27215, 27216, 27217, 27218)

27215   Open treatment of iliac spine(s), tuberosity avulsion, or iliac wing fracture(s) (eg, pelvic fracture(s) which do not disrupt the pelvic ring), with internal fixation

27216   Percutaneous skeletal fixation of posterior pelvic ring fracture and/or dislocation (includes ilium, sacroiliac joint and/or sacrum)

27217   Open treatment of anterior ring fracture and/or dislocation with internal fixation (includes pubic symphysis and/or rami)

27218   Open treatment of posterior ring fracture and/or dislocation with internal fixation (includes ilium, sacroiliac joint and/or sacrum)

27220   Closed treatment of acetabulum (hip socket) fracture(s); without manipulation

27222   with manipulation, with or without skeletal traction

(27224 has been deleted. To report, see 27226, 27227)

(27225 has been deleted. To report, see 27227, 27228)

27226   Open treatment of posterior or anterior acetabular wall fracture, with internal fixation

27227   Open treatment of acetabular fracture(s) involving anterior or posterior (one) column, or a fracture running transversely across the acetabulum, with internal fixation

27228   Open treatment of acetabular fracture(s) involving anterior and posterior (two) columns, includes T-fracture and both column fracture with complete articular detachment, or single column or transverse fracture with associated acetabular wall fracture, with internal fixation

27230   Closed treatment of femoral fracture, proximal end, neck; without manipulation

27232   with manipulation, with or without skeletal traction

(27234 has been deleted. To report, see 27230, 27232, 27235, 27236)

27235   Percutaneous skeletal fixation of femoral fracture, proximal end, neck, undisplaced, mildly displaced, or impacted fracture

27236   Open treatment of femoral fracture, proximal end, neck, internal fixation or prosthetic replacement

27238   Closed treatment of intertrochanteric, pertrochanteric, or subtrochanteric femoral fracture; without manipulation

27240   with manipulation, with or without skin or skeletal traction

(27242 has been deleted. To report, see 27238, 27240, 27244, 27245)

27244   Open treatment of intertrochanteric, pertrochanteric, or subtrochanteric femoral fracture; with plate/screw type implant, with or without cerclage

27245   with intramedullary implant, with or without interlocking screws and/or cerclage

27246   Closed treatment of greater trochanteric fracture, without manipulation

27248   Open treatment of greater trochanteric fracture, with or without internal or external fixation

27250   Closed treatment of hip dislocation, traumatic; without anesthesia

27252   requiring anesthesia

27253   Open treatment of hip dislocation, traumatic, without internal fixation

27254   Open treatment of hip dislocation, traumatic, with acetabular wall and femoral head fracture, with or without internal or external fixation

(27255 has been deleted. To report, see 27226, 27227, 27253, 27254)

27256*   Treatment of spontaneous hip dislocation (developmental, including congenital or pathological), by abduction, splint or traction; without anesthesia, without manipulation

27257*   with manipulation, requiring anesthesia

27258   Open treatment of spontaneous hip dislocation (developmental, including congenital or pathological), replacement of femoral head in acetabulum (including tenotomy, etc);

27259   with femoral shaft shortening

27265   Closed treatment of post hip arthroplasty dislocation; without anesthesia

27266   requiring regional or general anesthesia

Manipulation

27275*   Manipulation, hip joint, requiring general anesthesia

Arthrodesis

27280   Arthrodesis, sacroiliac joint (including obtaining graft)

(27281 has been deleted. To report, use 27280 with modifier '-50')

27282   Arthrodesis, symphysis pubis (including obtaining graft)

27284   Arthrodesis, hip joint (including obtaining graft);

27286   with subtrochanteric osteotomy

Amputation

27290   Interpelviabdominal amputation (hindquarter amputation)

27295   Disarticulation of hip

Other Procedures

27299   Unlisted procedure, pelvis or hip joint

Femur (Thigh Region) and Knee Joint

Including tibial plateaus.

Incision

(For incision and drainage of abscess or hematoma, superficial, see 10040-10160)

27301   Incision and drainage, deep abscess, bursa, or hematoma, thigh or knee region

27303   Incision, deep, with opening of bone cortex, femur or knee (eg, osteomyelitis or bone abscess)

(27304 has been deleted)

27305   Fasciotomy, iliotibial (tenotomy), open

(For combined Ober-Yount fasciotomy, use 27025)

27306   Tenotomy, percutaneous, adductor or hamstring; single tendon (separate procedure)

27307   multiple tendons

27310   Arthrotomy, knee, with exploration, drainage, or removal of foreign body (eg, infection)

(27311 has been deleted)

27315   Neurectomy, hamstring muscle

27320   Neurectomy, popliteal (gastrocnemius)

Excision

27323   Biopsy, soft tissue of thigh or knee area; superficial

27324   deep (subfascial or intramuscular)

(For needle biopsy of soft tissue, use 20206)

27327   Excision, tumor, thigh or knee area; subcutaneous

27328   deep, subfascial, or intramuscular

27329   Radical resection of tumor (eg, malignant neoplasm), soft tissue of thigh or knee area

27330   Arthrotomy, knee; with synovial biopsy only

27331   including joint exploration, biopsy, or removal of loose or foreign bodies

27332   Arthrotomy, with excision of semilunar cartilage (meniscectomy) knee; medial OR lateral

27333   medial AND lateral

27334   Arthrotomy, with synovectomy, knee; anterior OR posterior

27335   anterior AND posterior including popliteal area

27340   Excision, prepatellar bursa

27345   Excision of synovial cyst of popliteal space (eg, Baker's cyst)

27347   Excision of lesion of meniscus or capsule (eg, cyst, ganglion), knee

27350   Patellectomy or hemipatellectomy

27355   Excision or curettage of bone cyst or benign tumor of femur;

27356   with allograft

27357   with autograft (includes obtaining graft)

+ 27358   with internal fixation (List in addition to code for primary procedure)

(Use 27358 in conjunction with codes 27355, 27356, or 27357)

▲=Revised Code   ●=New Code   *=Service Includes Surgical Procedure Only

27360 Partial excision (craterization, saucerization, or diaphysectomy) bone, femur, proximal tibia and/or fibula (eg, osteomyelitis or bone abscess)

(27361 has been deleted)

27365 Radical resection of tumor, bone, femur or knee

(For radical resection of tumor, soft tissue, use 27329)

Introduction or Removal

27370 Injection procedure for knee arthrography

(For radiological supervision and interpretation, use 73580. ►Do not report 76003 in addition to 73580)◄

27372 Removal of foreign body, deep, thigh region or knee area

(For removal of knee prosthesis including "total knee," use 27488)

(27373-27379 have been deleted. To report, see 29870-29887)

Repair, Revision, and/or Reconstruction

27380 Suture of infrapatellar tendon; primary

27381   secondary reconstruction, including fascial or tendon graft

27385 Suture of quadriceps or hamstring muscle rupture; primary

27386   secondary reconstruction, including fascial or tendon graft

27390 Tenotomy, open, hamstring, knee to hip; single tendon

27391   multiple tendons, one leg

27392   multiple tendons, bilateral

27393 Lengthening of hamstring tendon; single tendon

27394   multiple tendons, one leg

27395   multiple tendons, bilateral

27396 Transplant, hamstring tendon to patella; single tendon

27397   multiple tendons

27400 Transfer, tendon or muscle, hamstrings to femur (eg, Egger's type procedure)

27403 Arthrotomy with meniscus repair, knee

(For arthroscopic repair, use 29882)

27405 Repair, primary, torn ligament and/or capsule, knee; collateral

27407   cruciate

(27408 has been deleted. To report, use 27427)

27409   collateral and cruciate ligaments

(27410-27416 have been deleted. To report, see 27427-27429)

27418 Anterior tibial tubercleplasty (eg, Maquet type procedure)

27420 Reconstruction of dislocating patella; (eg, Hauser type procedure)

27422   with extensor realignment and/or muscle advancement or release (eg, Campbell, Goldwaite type procedure)

27424   with patellectomy

27425 Lateral retinacular release (any method)

27427 Ligamentous reconstruction (augmentation), knee; extra-articular

27428   intra-articular (open)

27429   intra-articular (open) and extra-articular

(For primary repair of ligament(s) performed in addition to reconstruction, report 27405, 27407 or 27409 in addition to code 27427, 27428 or 27429)

27430 Quadricepsplasty (eg, Bennett or Thompson type)

27435 Capsulotomy, posterior capsular release, knee

(27436 has been deleted. To report, use 29887)

27437 Arthroplasty, patella; without prosthesis

27438   with prosthesis

27440 Arthroplasty, knee, tibial plateau;

27441   with debridement and partial synovectomy

27442 Arthroplasty, femoral condyles or tibial plateau(s), knee;

27443   with debridement and partial synovectomy

(27444 has been deleted. To report, see 27445-27447)

27445 Arthroplasty, knee, hinge prosthesis (eg, Walldius type)

27446 Arthroplasty, knee, condyle and plateau; medial OR lateral compartment

▲ **27447**   medial AND lateral compartments with or without patella resurfacing (total knee arthroplasty)

(For revision of total knee arthroplasty, use 27487)

(For removal of total knee prosthesis, use 27488)

27448 Osteotomy, femur, shaft or supracondylar; without fixation

(27449 has been deleted. To report, use 27448 with modifier '-50')

27450   with fixation

(27452 has been deleted. To report, use 27450 with modifier '-50')

27454 Osteotomy, multiple, with realignment on intramedullary rod, femoral shaft (eg, Sofield type procedure)

27455 Osteotomy, proximal tibia, including fibular excision or osteotomy (includes correction of genu varus (bowleg) or genu valgus (knock-knee)); before epiphyseal closure

⊘=Modifier '-51' Exempt   ►◄=New or Revised Text   ✚=Add-on Code

27457   after epiphyseal closure

(27460 has been deleted. To report, use 27455 with modifier '-50')

(27462 has been deleted. To report, use 27457 with modifier '-50')

27465   Osteoplasty, femur; shortening (excluding 64876)

27466   lengthening

27468   combined, lengthening and shortening with femoral segment transfer

27470   Repair, nonunion or malunion, femur, distal to head and neck; without graft (eg, compression technique)

27472   with iliac or other autogenous bone graft (includes obtaining graft)

27475   Arrest, epiphyseal, any method (eg, epiphysiodesis); distal femur

27477   tibia and fibula, proximal

27479   combined distal femur, proximal tibia and fibula

27485   Arrest, hemiepiphyseal, distal femur or proximal tibia or fibula (eg, genu varus or valgus)

27486   Revision of total knee arthroplasty, with or without allograft; one component

27487   femoral and entire tibial component

27488   Removal of prosthesis, including total knee prosthesis, methylmethacrylate with or without insertion of spacer, knee

(27490 has been deleted. To report, use 29882)

27495   Prophylactic treatment (nailing, pinning, plating or wiring) with or without methylmethacrylate, femur

27496   Decompression fasciotomy, thigh and/or knee, one compartment (flexor or extensor or adductor);

27497   with debridement of nonviable muscle and/or nerve

27498   Decompression fasciotomy, thigh and/or knee, multiple compartments;

27499   with debridement of nonviable muscle and/or nerve

Fracture and/or Dislocation

(For arthroscopic treatment of intercondylar spine(s) and tuberosity fracture(s) of the knee, see 29850, 29851)

(For arthroscopic treatment of tibial fracture, see 29855, 29856)

27500   Closed treatment of femoral shaft fracture, without manipulation

27501   Closed treatment of supracondylar or transcondylar femoral fracture with or without intercondylar extension, without manipulation

27502   Closed treatment of femoral shaft fracture, with manipulation, with or without skin or skeletal traction

27503   Closed treatment of supracondylar or transcondylar femoral fracture with or without intercondylar extension, with manipulation, with or without skin or skeletal traction

(27504 has been deleted. To report, see 27500, 27501, 27502, 27503, 27506, 27507, 27509, 27511, 27513)

27506   Open treatment of femoral shaft fracture, with or without external fixation, with insertion of intramedullary implant, with or without cerclage and/or locking screws

27507   Open treatment of femoral shaft fracture with plate/screws, with or without cerclage

27508   Closed treatment of femoral fracture, distal end, medial or lateral condyle, without manipulation

27509   Percutaneous skeletal fixation of femoral fracture, distal end, medial or lateral condyle, or supracondylar or transcondylar, with or without intercondylar extension, or distal femoral epiphyseal separation

27510   Closed treatment of femoral fracture, distal end, medial or lateral condyle, with manipulation

27511   Open treatment of femoral supracondylar or transcondylar fracture without intercondylar extension, with or without internal or external fixation

(27512 has been deleted. To report, see 27508, 27510, 27514)

27513   Open treatment of femoral supracondylar or transcondylar fracture with intercondylar extension, with or without internal or external fixation

27514   Open treatment of femoral fracture, distal end, medial or lateral condyle, with or without internal or external fixation

27516   Closed treatment of distal femoral epiphyseal separation; without manipulation

27517   with manipulation, with or without skin or skeletal traction

(27518 has been deleted. To report, see 27516, 27517, 27519)

27519   Open treatment of distal femoral epiphyseal separation, with or without internal or external fixation

27520   Closed treatment of patellar fracture, without manipulation

(27522 has been deleted. To report, see 27520, 27524)

27524   Open treatment of patellar fracture, with internal fixation and/or partial or complete patellectomy and soft tissue repair

27530   Closed treatment of tibial fracture, proximal (plateau); without manipulation

27532   with or without manipulation, with skeletal traction

(27534 has been deleted. To report, see 27530, 27532, 27535, 27536)

(For arthroscopic treatment, see 29855, 29856)

27535 Open treatment of tibial fracture, proximal (plateau); unicondylar, with or without internal or external fixation

27536 bicondylar, with or without internal fixation

(For arthroscopic treatment, see 29855, 29856)

(27537 has been deleted. To report, see 27535, 27536)

27538 Closed treatment of intercondylar spine(s) and/or tuberosity fracture(s) of knee, with or without manipulation

(For arthroscopic treatment, see 29850, 29851)

27540 Open treatment of intercondylar spine(s) and/or tuberosity fracture(s) of the knee, with or without internal or external fixation

27550 Closed treatment of knee dislocation; without anesthesia

27552 requiring anesthesia

(27554 has been deleted. To report, see 27550, 27552, 27556, 27557, 27558)

27556 Open treatment of knee dislocation, with or without internal or external fixation; without primary ligamentous repair or augmentation/reconstruction

27557 with primary ligamentous repair

27558 with primary ligamentous repair, with augmentation/reconstruction

27560 Closed treatment of patellar dislocation; without anesthesia

(For recurrent dislocation, see 27420-27424)

27562 requiring anesthesia

(27564 has been deleted. To report, see 27560, 27562, 27566)

27566 Open treatment of patellar dislocation, with or without partial or total patellectomy

Manipulation

27570* Manipulation of knee joint under general anesthesia (includes application of traction or other fixation devices)

Arthrodesis

27580 Arthrodesis, knee, any technique

Amputation

27590 Amputation, thigh, through femur, any level;

27591 immediate fitting technique including first cast

27592 open, circular (guillotine)

27594 secondary closure or scar revision

27596 re-amputation

27598 Disarticulation at knee

Other Procedures

27599 Unlisted procedure, femur or knee

Leg (Tibia and Fibula) and Ankle Joint

Incision

27600 Decompression fasciotomy, leg; anterior and/or lateral compartments only

27601 posterior compartment(s) only

27602 anterior and/or lateral, and posterior compartment(s)

(For incision and drainage procedures, superficial, see 10040-10160)

(For decompression fasciotomy with debridement, see 27892-27894)

27603 Incision and drainage, leg or ankle; deep abscess or hematoma

27604 infected bursa

27605* Tenotomy, percutaneous, Achilles tendon (separate procedure); local anesthesia

27606 general anesthesia

27607 Incision (eg, osteomyelitis or bone abscess), leg or ankle

(27608 has been deleted)

27610 Arthrotomy, ankle, including exploration, drainage, or removal of foreign body

(27611 has been deleted)

27612 Arthrotomy, posterior capsular release, ankle, with or without Achilles tendon lengthening

(See also 27685)

Excision

27613 Biopsy, soft tissue of leg or ankle area; superficial

27614 deep (subfascial or intramuscular)

(For needle biopsy of soft tissue, use 20206)

27615 Radical resection of tumor (eg, malignant neoplasm), soft tissue of leg or ankle area

27618 Excision, tumor, leg or ankle area; subcutaneous tissue

27619 deep (subfascial or intramuscular)

27620 Arthrotomy, ankle, with joint exploration, with or without biopsy, with or without removal of loose or foreign body

27625 Arthrotomy, with synovectomy, ankle;

27626 including tenosynovectomy

27630 Excision of lesion of tendon sheath or capsule (eg, cyst or ganglion), leg and/or ankle

⊘ =Modifier '-51' Exempt   ▶◀=New or Revised Text   ✚=Add-on Code

27635 Excision or curettage of bone cyst or benign tumor, tibia or fibula;

27637 with autograft (includes obtaining graft)

27638 with allograft

27640 Partial excision (craterization, saucerization, or diaphysectomy) bone (eg, osteomyelitis or exostosis); tibia

27641 fibula

27645 Radical resection of tumor, bone; tibia

27646 fibula

27647 talus or calcaneus

Introduction or Removal

27648 Injection procedure for ankle arthrography

(For radiological supervision and interpretation, use 73615. ▶Do not report 76003 in addition to 73615)◀

(For ankle arthroscopy, see 29894-29898)

Repair, Revision, and/or Reconstruction

27650 Repair, primary, open or percutaneous, ruptured Achilles tendon;

27652 with graft (includes obtaining graft)

27654 Repair, secondary, Achilles tendon, with or without graft

27656 Repair, fascial defect of leg

27658 Repair, flexor tendon, leg; primary, without graft, each tendon

27659 secondary, with or without graft, each tendon

27664 Repair, extensor tendon, leg; primary, without graft, each tendon

27665 secondary, with or without graft, each tendon

27675 Repair, dislocating peroneal tendons; without fibular osteotomy

27676 with fibular osteotomy

27680 Tenolysis, flexor or extensor tendon, leg and/or ankle; single, each tendon

27681 multiple tendons (through separate incision(s))

27685 Lengthening or shortening of tendon, leg or ankle; single tendon (separate procedure)

27686 multiple tendons (through same incision), each

27687 Gastrocnemius recession (eg, Strayer procedure)

(Toe extensors are considered as a group to be a single tendon when transplanted into midfoot)

27690 Transfer or transplant of single tendon (with muscle redirection or rerouting); superficial (eg, anterior tibial extensors into midfoot)

27691 deep (eg, anterior tibial or posterior tibial through interosseous space, flexor digitorum longus, flexor hallucis longus, or peroneal tendon to midfoot or hindfoot)

+ 27692 each additional tendon (List separately in addition to code for primary procedure)

(Use 27692 in conjunction with codes 27690, 27691)

27695 Repair, primary, disrupted ligament, ankle; collateral

27696 both collateral ligaments

27698 Repair, secondary, disrupted ligament, ankle, collateral (eg, Watson-Jones procedure)

27700 Arthroplasty, ankle;

27702 with implant (total ankle)

27703 revision, total ankle

27704 Removal of ankle implant

27705 Osteotomy; tibia

27707 fibula

27709 tibia and fibula

27712 multiple, with realignment on intramedullary rod (eg, Sofield type procedure)

(For osteotomy to correct genu varus (bowleg) or genu valgus (knock-knee), see 27455-27457)

27715 Osteoplasty, tibia and fibula, lengthening or shortening

27720 Repair of nonunion or malunion, tibia; without graft, (eg, compression technique)

27722 with sliding graft

27724 with iliac or other autograft (includes obtaining graft)

27725 by synostosis, with fibula, any method

27727 Repair of congenital pseudarthrosis, tibia

27730 Arrest, epiphyseal (epiphysiodesis), any method; distal tibia

27732 distal fibula

27734 distal tibia and fibula

27740 Arrest, epiphyseal (epiphysiodesis), any method, combined, proximal and distal tibia and fibula;

27742 and distal femur

(For epiphyseal arrest of proximal tibia and fibula, use 27477)

27745 Prophylactic treatment (nailing, pinning, plating or wiring) with or without methylmethacrylate, tibia

---

Fracture and/or Dislocation

27750   Closed treatment of tibial shaft fracture (with or without fibular fracture); without manipulation

27752   with manipulation, with or without skeletal traction

(27754 has been deleted. To report, see 27750, 27752, 27756, 27758)

27756   Percutaneous skeletal fixation of tibial shaft fracture (with or without fibular fracture) (eg, pins or screws)

27758   Open treatment of tibial shaft fracture, (with or without fibular fracture) with plate/screws, with or without cerclage

27759   Open treatment of tibial shaft fracture (with or without fibular fracture) by intramedullary implant, with or without interlocking screws and/or cerclage

27760   Closed treatment of medial malleolus fracture; without manipulation

27762   with manipulation, with or without skin or skeletal traction

(27764 has been deleted. To report, see 27762, 27766)

27766   Open treatment of medial malleolus fracture, with or without internal or external fixation

27780   Closed treatment of proximal fibula or shaft fracture; without manipulation

27781   with manipulation

(27782 has been deleted. To report, see 27780, 27781, 27784)

27784   Open treatment of proximal fibula or shaft fracture, with or without internal or external fixation

27786   Closed treatment of distal fibular fracture (lateral malleolus); without manipulation

27788   with manipulation

(27790 has been deleted. To report, see 27786, 27788, 27792)

27792   Open treatment of distal fibular fracture (lateral malleolus), with or without internal or external fixation

(27800 has been deleted. To report, use 27750)

(27802 has been deleted. To report, use 27752)

(27804 has been deleted. To report, see 27750, 27752, 27756, 27758, 27759)

(27806 has been deleted. To report, see 27756, 27758, 27759)

27808   Closed treatment of bimalleolar ankle fracture, (including Potts); without manipulation

27810   with manipulation

(27812 has been deleted. To report, see 27808, 27810, 27814)

27814   Open treatment of bimalleolar ankle fracture, with or without internal or external fixation

27816   Closed treatment of trimalleolar ankle fracture; without manipulation

27818   with manipulation

(27820 has been deleted. To report, see 27816, 27818, 27822, 27823)

27822   Open treatment of trimalleolar ankle fracture, with or without internal or external fixation, medial and/or lateral malleolus; without fixation of posterior lip

27823   with fixation of posterior lip

27824   Closed treatment of fracture of weight bearing articular portion of distal tibia (eg, pilon or tibial plafond), with or without anesthesia; without manipulation

27825   with skeletal traction and/or requiring manipulation

27826   Open treatment of fracture of weight bearing articular surface/portion of distal tibia (eg, pilon or tibial plafond), with internal or external fixation; of fibula only

27827   of tibia only

27828   of both tibia and fibula

27829   Open treatment of distal tibiofibular joint (syndesmosis) disruption, with or without internal or external fixation

27830   Closed treatment of proximal tibiofibular joint dislocation; without anesthesia

27831   requiring anesthesia

27832   Open treatment of proximal tibiofibular joint dislocation, with or without internal or external fixation, or with excision of proximal fibula

27840   Closed treatment of ankle dislocation; without anesthesia

27842   requiring anesthesia, with or without percutaneous skeletal fixation

(27844 has been deleted. To report, see 27840, 27842, 27846, 27848)

27846   Open treatment of ankle dislocation, with or without percutaneous skeletal fixation; without repair or internal fixation

27848   with repair or internal or external fixation

(27850-27853 have been deleted. To report, see 29894-29898)

Manipulation

27860*   Manipulation of ankle under general anesthesia (includes application of traction or other fixation apparatus)

Arthrodesis

27870   Arthrodesis, ankle, any method

27871   Arthrodesis, tibiofibular joint, proximal or distal

Amputation

27880	Amputation, leg, through tibia and fibula;
27881	with immediate fitting technique including application of first cast
27882	open, circular (guillotine)
27884	secondary closure or scar revision
27886	re-amputation
27888	Amputation, ankle, through malleoli of tibia and fibula (eg, Syme, Pirogoff type procedures), with plastic closure and resection of nerves
27889	Ankle disarticulation

Other Procedures

27892	Decompression fasciotomy, leg; anterior and/or lateral compartments only, with debridement of nonviable muscle and/or nerve
	(For decompression fasciotomy of the leg without debridement, use 27600)
27893	posterior compartment(s) only, with debridement of nonviable muscle and/or nerve
	(For decompression fasciotomy of the leg without debridement, use 27601)
27894	anterior and/or lateral, and posterior compartment(s), with debridement of nonviable muscle and/or nerve
	(For decompression fasciotomy of the leg without debridement, use 27602)
27899	Unlisted procedure, leg or ankle

Foot and Toes

Incision

	(For incision and drainage procedures, superficial, see 10040-10160)
28001*	Incision and drainage, bursa, foot
28002*	Incision and drainage below fascia, with or without tendon sheath involvement, foot; single bursal space
28003	multiple areas
	(28004 has been deleted)
28005	Incision, bone cortex (eg, osteomyelitis or bone abscess), foot
	(28006 has been deleted)
28008	Fasciotomy, foot and/or toe
	(See also 28060, 28062, 28250)
28010	Tenotomy, percutaneous, toe; single tendon
28011	multiple tendons
	(For open tenotomy, see 28230-28234)

28020	Arthrotomy, including exploration, drainage, or removal of loose or foreign body; intertarsal or tarsometatarsal joint
28022	metatarsophalangeal joint
28024	interphalangeal joint
28030	Neurectomy, intrinsic musculature of foot
28035	Release, tarsal tunnel (posterior tibial nerve decompression)
	(For other nerve entrapments, see 64704, 64722)

Excision

28043	Excision, tumor, foot; subcutaneous tissue
28045	deep, subfascial, intramuscular
28046	Radical resection of tumor (eg, malignant neoplasm), soft tissue of foot
28050	Arthrotomy with biopsy; intertarsal or tarsometatarsal joint
28052	metatarsophalangeal joint
28054	interphalangeal joint
28060	Fasciectomy, plantar fascia; partial (separate procedure)
28062	radical (separate procedure)
	(For plantar fasciotomy, see 28008, 28250)
28070	Synovectomy; intertarsal or tarsometatarsal joint, each
28072	metatarsophalangeal joint, each
28080	Excision, interdigital (Morton) neuroma, single, each
28086	Synovectomy, tendon sheath, foot; flexor
28088	extensor
28090	Excision of lesion, tendon, tendon sheath, or capsule (including synovectomy) (eg, cyst or ganglion); foot
28092	toe(s), each
28100	Excision or curettage of bone cyst or benign tumor, talus or calcaneus;
28102	with iliac or other autograft (includes obtaining graft)
28103	with allograft
▲ **28104**	Excision or curettage of bone cyst or benign tumor, tarsal or metatarsal, except talus or calcaneus;
28106	with iliac or other autograft (includes obtaining graft)
28107	with allograft
28108	Excision or curettage of bone cyst or benign tumor, phalanges of foot
	(For ostectomy, partial (eg, hallux valgus, Silver type procedure), use 28290)
	(28109 has been deleted. To report, use 28899)
28110	Ostectomy, partial excision, fifth metatarsal head (bunionette) (separate procedure)

28111	Ostectomy, complete excision; first metatarsal head
28112	other metatarsal head (second, third or fourth)
28113	fifth metatarsal head
28114	all metatarsal heads, with partial proximal phalangectomy, excluding first metatarsal (eg, Clayton type procedure)
28116	Ostectomy, excision of tarsal coalition
28118	Ostectomy, calcaneus;
28119	for spur, with or without plantar fascial release
28120	Partial excision (craterization, saucerization, sequestrectomy, or diaphysectomy) bone (eg, osteomyelitis or bossing); talus or calcaneus
	(28121 has been deleted)
28122	tarsal or metatarsal bone, except talus or calcaneus
	(For partial excision of talus or calcaneus, use 28120)
	(For cheilectomy for hallux rigidus, use 28289)
	(28123 has been deleted)
28124	phalanx of toe
28126	Resection, partial or complete, phalangeal base, each toe
28130	Talectomy (astragalectomy)
	(28135 has been deleted. To report, use 28118)
28140	Metatarsectomy
28150	Phalangectomy, toe, each toe
28153	Resection, condyle(s), distal end of phalanx, each toe
28160	Hemiphalangectomy or interphalangeal joint excision, toe, proximal end of phalanx, each
28171	Radical resection of tumor, bone; tarsal (except talus or calcaneus)
28173	metatarsal
28175	phalanx of toe
	(For talus or calcaneus, use 27647)

Introduction or Removal

28190*	Removal of foreign body, foot; subcutaneous
28192	deep
28193	complicated

Repair, Revision, and/or Reconstruction

28200	Repair, tendon, flexor, foot; primary or secondary, without free graft, each tendon
28202	secondary with free graft, each tendon (includes obtaining graft)
28208	Repair, tendon, extensor, foot; primary or secondary, each tendon
28210	secondary with free graft, each tendon (includes obtaining graft)
28220	Tenolysis, flexor, foot; single tendon
28222	multiple tendons
28225	Tenolysis, extensor, foot; single tendon
28226	multiple tendons
28230	Tenotomy, open, tendon flexor; foot, single or multiple tendon(s) (separate procedure)
28232	toe, single tendon (separate procedure)
28234	Tenotomy, open, extensor, foot or toe, each tendon
	(28236 has been deleted. To report, see 27690, 27691)
▲ **28238**	Reconstruction (advancement), posterior tibial tendon with excision of accessory tarsal navicular bone (eg, Kidner type procedure)
	(For subcutaneous tenotomy, see 28010, 28011)
	(For transfer or transplant of tendon with muscle redirection or rerouting, see 27690-27692)
	(For extensor hallucis longus transfer with great toe IP fusion (Jones procedure), use 28760)
28240	Tenotomy, lengthening, or release, abductor hallucis muscle
28250	Division of plantar fascia and muscle (eg, Steindler stripping) (separate procedure)
28260	Capsulotomy, midfoot; medial release only (separate procedure)
28261	with tendon lengthening
28262	extensive, including posterior talotibial capsulotomy and tendon(s) lengthening (eg, resistant clubfoot deformity)
28264	Capsulotomy, midtarsal (eg, Heyman type procedure)
28270	Capsulotomy; metatarsophalangeal joint, with or without tenorrhaphy, each joint (separate procedure)
28272	interphalangeal joint, each joint (separate procedure)
28280	Syndactylization, toes (eg, webbing or Kelikian type procedure)
28285	Correction, hammertoe (eg, interphalangeal fusion, partial or total phalangectomy)
28286	Correction, cock-up fifth toe, with plastic skin closure (eg, Ruiz-Mora type procedure)
28288	Ostectomy, partial, exostectomy or condylectomy, metatarsal head, each metatarsal head
28289	Hallux rigidus correction with cheilectomy, debridement and capsular release of the first metatarsophalangeal joint

⊘ =Modifier '-51' Exempt   ▶ ◀ =New or Revised Text   ✚ =Add-on Code   CPT 2002

28290	Correction, hallux valgus (bunion), with or without sesamoidectomy; simple exostectomy (eg, Silver type procedure)
28292	Keller, McBride, or Mayo type procedure
28293	resection of joint with implant
28294	with tendon transplants (eg, Joplin type procedure)
28296	with metatarsal osteotomy (eg, Mitchell, Chevron, or concentric type procedures)
28297	Lapidus type procedure
28298	by phalanx osteotomy
▲ 28299	by double osteotomy
28300	Osteotomy; calcaneus (eg, Dwyer or Chambers type procedure), with or without internal fixation
28302	talus
28304	Osteotomy, tarsal bones, other than calcaneus or talus;
28305	with autograft (includes obtaining graft) (eg, Fowler type)
28306	Osteotomy, with or without lengthening, shortening or angular correction, metatarsal; first metatarsal
28307	first metatarsal with autograft (other than first toe)
28308	other than first metatarsal, each
28309	multiple (eg, Swanson type cavus foot procedure)
28310	Osteotomy, shortening, angular or rotational correction; proximal phalanx, first toe (separate procedure)
28312	other phalanges, any toe
28313	Reconstruction, angular deformity of toe, soft tissue procedures only (eg, overlapping second toe, fifth toe, curly toes)
28315	Sesamoidectomy, first toe (separate procedure)
28320	Repair, nonunion or malunion; tarsal bones
28322	metatarsal, with or without bone graft (includes obtaining graft)
28340	Reconstruction, toe, macrodactyly; soft tissue resection
28341	requiring bone resection
28344	Reconstruction, toe(s); polydactyly
28345	syndactyly, with or without skin graft(s), each web
28360	Reconstruction, cleft foot

Fracture and/or Dislocation

28400	Closed treatment of calcaneal fracture; without manipulation
28405	with manipulation
28406	Percutaneous skeletal fixation of calcaneal fracture, with manipulation
	(28410 has been deleted. To report, see 28400, 28405, 28406, 28415, 28420)

28415	Open treatment of calcaneal fracture, with or without internal or external fixation;
28420	with primary iliac or other autogenous bone graft (includes obtaining graft)
28430	Closed treatment of talus fracture; without manipulation
28435	with manipulation
28436	Percutaneous skeletal fixation of talus fracture, with manipulation
	(28440 has been deleted. To report, see 28430, 28435, 28436, 28445)
28445	Open treatment of talus fracture, with or without internal or external fixation
28450	Treatment of tarsal bone fracture (except talus and calcaneus); without manipulation, each
28455	with manipulation, each
28456	Percutaneous skeletal fixation of tarsal bone fracture (except talus and calcaneus), with manipulation, each
	(28460 has been deleted. To report, see 28450, 28455, 28456, 28465)
28465	Open treatment of tarsal bone fracture (except talus and calcaneus), with or without internal or external fixation, each
28470	Closed treatment of metatarsal fracture; without manipulation, each
28475	with manipulation, each
28476	Percutaneous skeletal fixation of metatarsal fracture, with manipulation, each
	(28480 has been deleted. To report, see 28470, 28475, 28476, 28485)
28485	Open treatment of metatarsal fracture, with or without internal or external fixation, each
28490	Closed treatment of fracture great toe, phalanx or phalanges; without manipulation
28495	with manipulation
28496	Percutaneous skeletal fixation of fracture great toe, phalanx or phalanges, with manipulation
	(28500 has been deleted. To report, see 28490, 28495, 28496, 28505)
28505	Open treatment of fracture great toe, phalanx or phalanges, with or without internal or external fixation
28510	Closed treatment of fracture, phalanx or phalanges, other than great toe; without manipulation, each
28515	with manipulation, each
	(28520 has been deleted. To report, see 28510, 28515, 28525)
28525	Open treatment of fracture, phalanx or phalanges, other than great toe, with or without internal or external fixation, each

28530   Closed treatment of sesamoid fracture

28531   Open treatment of sesamoid fracture, with or without internal fixation

28540   Closed treatment of tarsal bone dislocation, other than talotarsal; without anesthesia

28545   requiring anesthesia

28546   Percutaneous skeletal fixation of tarsal bone dislocation, other than talotarsal, with manipulation

(28550 has been deleted. To report, see 28540, 28545, 28546, 28555)

28555   Open treatment of tarsal bone dislocation, with or without internal or external fixation

28570   Closed treatment of talotarsal joint dislocation; without anesthesia

28575   requiring anesthesia

28576   Percutaneous skeletal fixation of talotarsal joint dislocation, with manipulation

(28580 has been deleted. To report, see 28570, 28575, 28576, 28585)

28585   Open treatment of talotarsal joint dislocation, with or without internal or external fixation

28600   Closed treatment of tarsometatarsal joint dislocation; without anesthesia

28605   requiring anesthesia

28606   Percutaneous skeletal fixation of tarsometatarsal joint dislocation, with manipulation

(28610 has been deleted. To report, see 28600, 28605, 28606, 28615)

28615   Open treatment of tarsometatarsal joint dislocation, with or without internal or external fixation

28630*   Closed treatment of metatarsophalangeal joint dislocation; without anesthesia

28635*   requiring anesthesia

28636   Percutaneous skeletal fixation of metatarsophalangeal joint dislocation, with manipulation

(28640 has been deleted. To report, see 28630, 28635, 28636, 28645)

28645   Open treatment of metatarsophalangeal joint dislocation, with or without internal or external fixation

28660*   Closed treatment of interphalangeal joint dislocation; without anesthesia

28665*   requiring anesthesia

28666   Percutaneous skeletal fixation of interphalangeal joint dislocation, with manipulation

(28670 has been deleted. To report, see 28660, 28665, 28666, 28675)

28675   Open treatment of interphalangeal joint dislocation, with or without internal or external fixation

Arthrodesis

28705   Arthrodesis; pantalar

28715   triple

28725   subtalar

28730   Arthrodesis, midtarsal or tarsometatarsal, multiple or transverse;

28735   with osteotomy (eg, flatfoot correction)

▲ **28737**   Arthrodesis, with tendon lengthening and advancement, midtarsal, tarsal navicular-cuneiform (eg, Miller type procedure)

28740   Arthrodesis, midtarsal or tarsometatarsal, single joint

28750   Arthrodesis, great toe; metatarsophalangeal joint

28755   interphalangeal joint

28760   Arthrodesis, with extensor hallucis longus transfer to first metatarsal neck, great toe, interphalangeal joint (eg, Jones type procedure)

(For hammertoe operation or interphalangeal fusion, use 28285)

Amputation

28800   Amputation, foot; midtarsal (eg, Chopart type procedure)

28805   transmetatarsal

28810   Amputation, metatarsal, with toe, single

28820   Amputation, toe; metatarsophalangeal joint

28825   interphalangeal joint

(For amputation of tuft of distal phalanx, use 11752)

Other Procedures

▶(For extracorporeal shock wave therapy involving musculoskeletal system, or plantar fascia, see Category III codes 0019T, 0020T)◀

28899   Unlisted procedure, foot or toes

Application of Casts and Strapping

The listed procedures apply when the cast application or strapping is a replacement procedure used during or after the period of follow-up care, or when the cast application or strapping is an initial service performed without a restorative treatment or procedure(s) to stabilize or protect a fracture, injury, or dislocation and/or to afford comfort to a patient. Restorative treatment or procedure(s) rendered by another physician following the application of the initial cast/splint/strap may be reported with a treatment of fracture and/or dislocation code.

A physician who applies the initial cast, strap or splint and also assumes all of the subsequent fracture, dislocation, or injury care cannot use the application of casts and strapping codes as an initial service, since the first cast/splint or strap application is included in the treatment of fracture and/or dislocation codes. (See notes under Musculoskeletal System, page 57). A temporary cast/splint/strap is not considered to be part of the preoperative care, and the use of the modifier '-56' is not applicable. Additional evaluation and management services are reportable only if significant identifiable further services are provided at the time of the cast application or strapping.

If cast application or strapping is provided as an initial service (eg, casting of a sprained ankle or knee) in which no other procedure or treatment (eg, surgical repair, reduction of a fracture or joint dislocation) is performed or is expected to be performed by a physician rendering the initial care only, use the casting, strapping and/or supply code (99070) in addition to an evaluation and management code as appropriate.

Listed procedures include removal of cast or strapping.

(For orthotics fitting and training, use 97504)

Body and Upper Extremity

Casts

29000	Application of halo type body cast (see 20661-20663 for insertion)
29010	Application of Risser jacket, localizer, body; only
29015	including head
29020	Application of turnbuckle jacket, body; only
29025	including head
29035	Application of body cast, shoulder to hips;
29040	including head, Minerva type
29044	including one thigh
29046	including both thighs
▲ 29049	Application, cast; figure-of-eight
29055	shoulder spica
29058	plaster Velpeau
29065	shoulder to hand (long arm)
29075	elbow to finger (short arm)
29085	hand and lower forearm (gauntlet)
● 29086	finger (eg, contracture)

Splints

29105	Application of long arm splint (shoulder to hand)
29125	Application of short arm splint (forearm to hand); static
29126	dynamic
29130	Application of finger splint; static
29131	dynamic

Strapping—Any Age

29200	Strapping; thorax
29220	low back
29240	shoulder (eg, Velpeau)
29260	elbow or wrist
29280	hand or finger

Lower Extremity

Casts

29305	Application of hip spica cast; one leg
29325	one and one-half spica or both legs
	(For hip spica (body) cast, including thighs only, use 29046)
29345	Application of long leg cast (thigh to toes);
29355	walker or ambulatory type
29358	Application of long leg cast brace
29365	Application of cylinder cast (thigh to ankle)
29405	Application of short leg cast (below knee to toes);
29425	walking or ambulatory type
29435	Application of patellar tendon bearing (PTB) cast
29440	Adding walker to previously applied cast
29445	Application of rigid total contact leg cast
29450	Application of clubfoot cast with molding or manipulation, long or short leg
	(29455 has been deleted. To report, use 29450 with modifier '-50')

Splints

29505	Application of long leg splint (thigh to ankle or toes)
29515	Application of short leg splint (calf to foot)

Strapping—Any Age

29520	Strapping; hip
29530	knee
29540	ankle
29550	toes
29580	Unna boot
29590	Denis-Browne splint strapping

Removal or Repair

Codes for cast removals should be employed only for casts applied by another physician.

29700   Removal or bivalving; gauntlet, boot or body cast

29705   full arm or full leg cast

29710   shoulder or hip spica, Minerva, or Risser jacket, etc.

29715   turnbuckle jacket

29720   Repair of spica, body cast or jacket

29730   Windowing of cast

29740   Wedging of cast (except clubfoot casts)

29750   Wedging of clubfoot cast

(29751 has been deleted. To report, use 29750 with modifier '-50')

Other Procedures

29799   Unlisted procedure, casting or strapping

Endoscopy/Arthroscopy

▶Surgical endoscopy/arthroscopy always includes a diagnostic endoscopy/arthroscopy.◀

When arthroscopy is performed in conjunction with arthrotomy, add modifier '-51'.

29800   Arthroscopy, temporomandibular joint, diagnostic, with or without synovial biopsy (separate procedure)

29804   Arthroscopy, temporomandibular joint, surgical

▶(For open procedure, use 21010)◀

● **29805**   Arthroscopy, shoulder, diagnostic, with or without synovial biopsy (separate procedure)

▶(For open procedure, see 23065-23066, 23100-23101)◀

● **29806**   Arthroscopy, shoulder, surgical; capsulorrhaphy

▶(For open procedure, see 23450-23466)◀

▶(To report thermal capsulorrhaphy, use 29999)◀

● **29807**   repair of slap lesion

▶(29815 has been deleted. To report, use 29805)◀

29819   with removal of loose body or foreign body

▶(For open procedure, see 23040-23044, 23107)◀

29820   synovectomy, partial

▶(For open procedure, see 23105)◀

29821   synovectomy, complete

▶(For open procedure, see 23105)◀

29822   debridement, limited

▶(For open procedure, see specific open shoulder procedure performed)◀

29823   debridement, extensive

▶(For open procedure, see specific open shoulder procedure performed)◀

● **29824**   distal claviculectomy including distal articular surface (Mumford procedure)

▶(For open procedure, use 23120)◀

29825   with lysis and resection of adhesions, with or without manipulation

▶(For open procedure, see specific open shoulder procedure performed)◀

29826   decompression of subacromial space with partial acromioplasty, with or without coracoacromial release

▶(For open procedure, use 23130 or 23415)◀

29830   Arthroscopy, elbow, diagnostic, with or without synovial biopsy (separate procedure)

29834   Arthroscopy, elbow, surgical; with removal of loose body or foreign body

29835   synovectomy, partial

29836   synovectomy, complete

29837   debridement, limited

29838   debridement, extensive

29840   Arthroscopy, wrist, diagnostic, with or without synovial biopsy (separate procedure)

29843   Arthroscopy, wrist, surgical; for infection, lavage and drainage

29844   synovectomy, partial

29845   synovectomy, complete

29846   excision and/or repair of triangular fibrocartilage and/or joint debridement

29847   internal fixation for fracture or instability

29848   Endoscopy, wrist, surgical, with release of transverse carpal ligament

(For open procedure, use 64721)

29850   Arthroscopically aided treatment of intercondylar spine(s) and/or tuberosity fracture(s) of the knee, with or without manipulation; without internal or external fixation (includes arthroscopy)

29851   with internal or external fixation (includes arthroscopy)

(For bone graft, use 20900, 20902)

29855   Arthroscopically aided treatment of tibial fracture, proximal (plateau); unicondylar, with or without internal or external fixation (includes arthroscopy)

29856   bicondylar, with or without internal or external fixation (includes arthroscopy)

(For bone graft, use 20900, 20902)

29860   Arthroscopy, hip, diagnostic with or without synovial biopsy (separate procedure)

29861   Arthroscopy, hip, surgical; with removal of loose body or foreign body

29862   with debridement/shaving of articular cartilage (chondroplasty), abrasion arthroplasty, and/or resection of labrum

29863   with synovectomy

29870   Arthroscopy, knee, diagnostic, with or without synovial biopsy (separate procedure)

►(For surgical arthroscopy of the knee with implantation of osteochondral graft for treatment of articular surface defect, see Category III codes 0012T, 0013T)◄

►(For meniscal transplantation, medial or lateral, knee, use Category III code 0014T)◄

29871   Arthroscopy, knee, surgical; for infection, lavage and drainage

(29872 has been deleted)

29874   for removal of loose body or foreign body (eg, osteochondritis dissecans fragmentation, chondral fragmentation)

29875   synovectomy, limited (eg, plica or shelf resection) (separate procedure)

29876   synovectomy, major, two or more compartments (eg, medial or lateral)

29877   debridement/shaving of articular cartilage (chondroplasty)

29879   abrasion arthroplasty (includes chondroplasty where necessary) or multiple drilling or microfracture

29880   with meniscectomy (medial AND lateral, including any meniscal shaving)

29881   with meniscectomy (medial OR lateral, including any meniscal shaving)

29882   with meniscus repair (medial OR lateral)

29883   with meniscus repair (medial AND lateral)

29884   with lysis of adhesions, with or without manipulation (separate procedure)

29885   drilling for osteochondritis dissecans with bone grafting, with or without internal fixation (including debridement of base of lesion)

29886   drilling for intact osteochondritis dissecans lesion

29887   drilling for intact osteochondritis dissecans lesion with internal fixation

29888   Arthroscopically aided anterior cruciate ligament repair/augmentation or reconstruction

29889   Arthroscopically aided posterior cruciate ligament repair/augmentation or reconstruction

(Procedures 29888 and 29889 should not be used with reconstruction procedures 27427-27429)

(29890 has been deleted)

29891   Arthroscopy, ankle, surgical; excision of osteochondral defect of talus and/or tibia, including drilling of the defect

29892   Arthroscopically aided repair of large osteochondritis dissecans lesion, talar dome fracture, or tibial plafond fracture, with or without internal fixation (includes arthroscopy)

29893   Endoscopic plantar fasciotomy

29894   Arthroscopy, ankle (tibiotalar and fibulotalar joints), surgical; with removal of loose body or foreign body

29895   synovectomy, partial

(29896 has been deleted)

29897   debridement, limited

29898   debridement, extensive

● **29900**   Arthroscopy, metacarpophalangeal joint, diagnostic, includes synovial biopsy

►(Do not report 29900 with 29901, 29902)◄

● **29901**   Arthroscopy, metacarpophalangeal joint, surgical; with debridement

● **29902**   with reduction of displaced ulnar collateral ligament (eg, Stenar lesion)

►(29909 has been deleted. To report, use 29999)◄

● **29999**   Unlisted procedure, arthroscopy

Notes

⊘ =Modifier '-51' Exempt ▶ ◀=New or Revised Text ✚=Add-on Code

Respiratory System

Nose

Incision

30000* Drainage abscess or hematoma, nasal, internal approach

(For external approach, see 10060, 10140)

30020* Drainage abscess or hematoma, nasal septum

(For lateral rhinotomy, see specific application (eg, 30118, 30320))

Excision

30100 Biopsy, intranasal

(For biopsy skin of nose, see 11100, 11101)

30110 Excision, nasal polyp(s), simple

(30110 would normally be completed in an office setting)

(30111 has been deleted. To report, use 30110 with modifier '-50')

30115 Excision, nasal polyp(s), extensive

(30115 would normally require the facilities available in a hospital setting)

(30116 has been deleted. To report, use 30115 with modifier '-50')

▲ **30117** Excision or destruction (eg, laser), intranasal lesion; internal approach

30118 external approach (lateral rhinotomy)

30120 Excision or surgical planing of skin of nose for rhinophyma

30124 Excision dermoid cyst, nose; simple, skin, subcutaneous

30125 complex, under bone or cartilage

30130 Excision turbinate, partial or complete, any method

30140 Submucous resection turbinate, partial or complete, any method

(For submucous resection of nasal septum, use 30520)

(For reduction of turbinates, use 30140 with modifier '-52')

30150 Rhinectomy; partial

30160 total

(For closure and/or reconstruction, primary or delayed, see **Integumentary System,** 13150-13160, 14060-14300, 15120, 15121, 15260, 15261, 15760, 20900-20912)

Introduction

30200* Injection into turbinate(s), therapeutic

30210* Displacement therapy (Proetz type)

30220 Insertion, nasal septal prosthesis (button)

Removal of Foreign Body

30300* Removal foreign body, intranasal; office type procedure

30310 requiring general anesthesia

30320 by lateral rhinotomy

Repair

(For obtaining tissues for graft, see 20900-20926, 21210)

30400 Rhinoplasty, primary; lateral and alar cartilages and/or elevation of nasal tip

(For columellar reconstruction, see 13150 et seq)

30410 complete, external parts including bony pyramid, lateral and alar cartilages, and/or elevation of nasal tip

30420 including major septal repair

30430 Rhinoplasty, secondary; minor revision (small amount of nasal tip work)

30435 intermediate revision (bony work with osteotomies)

30450 major revision (nasal tip work and osteotomies)

30460 Rhinoplasty for nasal deformity secondary to congenital cleft lip and/or palate, including columellar lengthening; tip only

30462 tip, septum, osteotomies

(30500 has been deleted. To report, use 30520)

30465 Repair of nasal vestibular stenosis (eg, spreader grafting, lateral nasal wall reconstruction)

(30465 excludes obtaining graft. For graft procedure, see 20900-20926, 21210)

(30465 is used to report a bilateral procedure. For unilateral procedure, use modifier '-52')

30520 Septoplasty or submucous resection, with or without cartilage scoring, contouring or replacement with graft

(For submucous resection of turbinates, use 30140)

30540 Repair choanal atresia; intranasal

30545 transpalatine

30560* Lysis intranasal synechia

30580 Repair fistula; oromaxillary (combine with 31030 if antrotomy is included)

30600 oronasal

30620   Septal or other intranasal dermatoplasty (does not include obtaining graft)

30630   Repair nasal septal perforations

Destruction

(30800 has been deleted. To report, see 30801 and 30802)

▲ **30801***   Cautery and/or ablation, mucosa of turbinates, unilateral or bilateral, any method, (separate procedure); superficial

30802   intramural

(30805, 30820 have been deleted. To report, see 30801 and 30802)

Other Procedures

(30900 has been deleted. To report, see 30901, 30903)

30901*   Control nasal hemorrhage, anterior, simple (limited cautery and/or packing) any method

(30902 has been deleted. To report, use 30901 with modifier '-50')

30903*   Control nasal hemorrhage, anterior, complex (extensive cautery and/or packing) any method

(30904 has been deleted. To report, use 30903 with modifier '-50')

▲ **30905***   Control nasal hemorrhage, posterior, with posterior nasal packs and/or cautery, any method; initial

30906*   subsequent

30915   Ligation arteries; ethmoidal

30920   internal maxillary artery, transantral

(For ligation external carotid artery, use 37600)

30930   Fracture nasal turbinate(s), therapeutic

30999   Unlisted procedure, nose

Accessory Sinuses

Incision

31000*   Lavage by cannulation; maxillary sinus (antrum puncture or natural ostium)

(31001 has been deleted. To report, use 31000 with modifier '-50')

31002*   sphenoid sinus

31020   Sinusotomy, maxillary (antrotomy); intranasal

(31021 has been deleted. To report, use 31020 with modifier '-50')

31030   radical (Caldwell-Luc) without removal of antrochoanal polyps

(31031 has been deleted. To report, use 31030 with modifier '-50')

31032   radical (Caldwell-Luc) with removal of antrochoanal polyps

(31033 has been deleted. To report, use 31032 with modifier '-50')

31040   Pterygomaxillary fossa surgery, any approach

(For transantral ligation of internal maxillary artery, use 30920)

31050   Sinusotomy, sphenoid, with or without biopsy;

31051   with mucosal stripping or removal of polyp(s)

31070   Sinusotomy frontal; external, simple (trephine operation)

(31071 has been deleted. To report, use 31276)

31075   transorbital, unilateral (for mucocele or osteoma, Lynch type)

31080   obliterative without osteoplastic flap, brow incision (includes ablation)

31081   obliterative, without osteoplastic flap, coronal incision (includes ablation)

31084   obliterative, with osteoplastic flap, brow incision

31085   obliterative, with osteoplastic flap, coronal incision

31086   nonobliterative, with osteoplastic flap, brow incision

31087   nonobliterative, with osteoplastic flap, coronal incision

31090   Sinusotomy, unilateral, three or more paranasal sinuses (frontal, maxillary, ethmoid, sphenoid)

Excision

31200   Ethmoidectomy; intranasal, anterior

31201   intranasal, total

31205   extranasal, total

31225   Maxillectomy; without orbital exenteration

31230   with orbital exenteration (en bloc)

(For orbital exenteration only, see 65110 et seq)

(For skin grafts, see 15120 et seq)

Endoscopy

A surgical sinus endoscopy includes a sinusotomy (when appropriate) and diagnostic endoscopy.

Codes 31231-31294 are used to report unilateral procedures unless otherwise specified.

The codes 31231-31235 for diagnostic evaluation refer to employing a nasal/sinus endoscope to inspect the interior of the nasal cavity and the middle and superior meatus, the turbinates, and the spheno-ethmoid recess. Any time a diagnostic evaluation is performed all these areas would be inspected and a separate code is not reported for each area.

31231 Nasal endoscopy, diagnostic, unilateral or bilateral (separate procedure)

31233 Nasal/sinus endoscopy, diagnostic with maxillary sinusoscopy (via inferior meatus or canine fossa puncture)

31235 Nasal/sinus endoscopy, diagnostic with sphenoid sinusoscopy (via puncture of sphenoidal face or cannulation of ostium)

31237 Nasal/sinus endoscopy, surgical; with biopsy, polypectomy or debridement (separate procedure)

▲ **31238**   with control of nasal hemorrhage

31239   with dacryocystorhinostomy

31240   with concha bullosa resection

(31245 has been deleted. To report, use 31254)

(31246 has been deleted. To report, use 31254 and 31256)

(31247 has been deleted. To report, use 31254 and 31267)

(31248 has been deleted. To report, use 31254 and 31276)

(31249 has been deleted. To report, use 31254, 31256, and 31276)

(31250 has been deleted. To report, see 31231-31235)

(31251 has been deleted. To report, use 31254, 31267, and 31276)

(31252 has been deleted. To report, use 31237)

31254 Nasal/sinus endoscopy, surgical; with ethmoidectomy, partial (anterior)

31255   with ethmoidectomy, total (anterior and posterior)

31256 Nasal/sinus endoscopy, surgical, with maxillary antrostomy;

(31258 has been deleted. To report, use 31237)

(31260 has been deleted. To report, use 31233)

(31261 has been deleted. To report, use 31255)

(31262 has been deleted. To report, use 31255 and 31256)

(31263 has been deleted. To report, use 31267)

(31264 has been deleted. To report, use 31255 and 31267)

(31265 has been deleted. To report, use 31267)

(31266 has been deleted. To report, use 31255 and 31276)

31267   with removal of tissue from maxillary sinus

(31268 has been deleted. To report, use 31267)

(31269 has been deleted. To report, use 31255, 31256, and 31276)

(31270 has been deleted. To report, use 31235)

(31271 has been deleted. To report, use 31255, 31267, and 31276)

(31275 has been deleted. To report, use 31287)

31276 Nasal/sinus endoscopy, surgical with frontal sinus exploration, with or without removal of tissue from frontal sinus

(31277 has been deleted. To report, use 31288)

(31280 has been deleted. To report, use 31255, and 31287 or 31288)

(31281 has been deleted. To report, use 31255, 31256, and 31287 or 31288)

(31282 has been deleted. To report, use 31255, 31267, and 31287 or 31288)

(31283 has been deleted. To report, use 31255, 31287 or 31288, and 31276)

(31284 has been deleted. To report, use 31255, 31256, 31287 or 31288, and 31276)

(31285 has been deleted. To report, see 31231-31235)

(31286 has been deleted. To report, use 31255, 31267, 31287 or 31288, and 31276)

31287 Nasal/sinus endoscopy, surgical, with sphenoidotomy;

31288   with removal of tissue from the sphenoid sinus

31290 Nasal/sinus endoscopy, surgical, with repair of cerebrospinal fluid leak; ethmoid region

31291   sphenoid region

31292 Nasal/sinus endoscopy, surgical; with medial or inferior orbital wall decompression

31293   with medial orbital wall and inferior orbital wall decompression

31294   with optic nerve decompression

Other Procedures

(For hypophysectomy, transantral or transeptal approach, use 61548)

(For transcranial hypophysectomy, use 61546)

31299 Unlisted procedure, accessory sinuses

Larynx

Excision

31300 Laryngotomy (thyrotomy, laryngofissure); with removal of tumor or laryngocele, cordectomy

31320   diagnostic

31360 Laryngectomy; total, without radical neck dissection

31365   total, with radical neck dissection

31367   subtotal supraglottic, without radical neck dissection

31368   subtotal supraglottic, with radical neck dissection

31370	Partial laryngectomy (hemilaryngectomy); horizontal
31375	laterovertical
31380	anterovertical
31382	antero-latero-vertical
31390	Pharyngolaryngectomy, with radical neck dissection; without reconstruction
31395	with reconstruction
31400	Arytenoidectomy or arytenoidopexy, external approach
	(For endoscopic arytenoidectomy, use 31560)
31420	Epiglottidectomy

Introduction

⊘ **31500**	Intubation, endotracheal, emergency procedure
	(For injection procedure for bronchography, see 31656, 31708, 31710)
31502	Tracheotomy tube change prior to establishment of fistula tract

Endoscopy

For endoscopic procedures, code appropriate endoscopy of each anatomic site examined.

31505	Laryngoscopy, indirect; diagnostic (separate procedure)
31510	with biopsy
31511	with removal of foreign body
31512	with removal of lesion
31513	with vocal cord injection
31515	Laryngoscopy direct, with or without tracheoscopy; for aspiration
31520	diagnostic, newborn
31525	diagnostic, except newborn
31526	diagnostic, with operating microscope
	(Do not report code 69990 in addition to code 31526)
31527	with insertion of obturator
▲ **31528**	with dilation, initial
▲ **31529**	with dilation, subsequent
31530	Laryngoscopy, direct, operative, with foreign body removal;
31531	with operating microscope
	(Do not report code 69990 in addition to code 31531)
31535	Laryngoscopy, direct, operative, with biopsy;
31536	with operating microscope
	(Do not report code 69990 in addition to code 31536)

31540	Laryngoscopy, direct, operative, with excision of tumor and/or stripping of vocal cords or epiglottis;
31541	with operating microscope
	(Do not report code 69990 in addition to code 31541)
31560	Laryngoscopy, direct, operative, with arytenoidectomy;
31561	with operating microscope
	(Do not report code 69990 in addition to code 31561)
31570	Laryngoscopy, direct, with injection into vocal cord(s), therapeutic;
31571	with operating microscope
	(Do not report code 69990 in addition to code 31571)
31575	Laryngoscopy, flexible fiberoptic; diagnostic
31576	with biopsy
31577	with removal of foreign body
31578	with removal of lesion
31579	Laryngoscopy, flexible or rigid fiberoptic, with stroboscopy

Repair

31580	Laryngoplasty; for laryngeal web, two stage, with keel insertion and removal
31582	for laryngeal stenosis, with graft or core mold, including tracheotomy
31584	with open reduction of fracture
31585	Treatment of closed laryngeal fracture; without manipulation
31586	with closed manipulative reduction
31587	Laryngoplasty, cricoid split
31588	Laryngoplasty, not otherwise specified (eg, for burns, reconstruction after partial laryngectomy)
31590	Laryngeal reinnervation by neuromuscular pedicle

Destruction

31595	Section recurrent laryngeal nerve, therapeutic (separate procedure), unilateral

Other Procedures

31599	Unlisted procedure, larynx

Trachea and Bronchi

Incision

31600	Tracheostomy, planned (separate procedure);
31601	under two years

⊘ =Modifier '-51' Exempt   ▶ ◀ =New or Revised Text   ✚ =Add-on Code   CPT 2002

31603	Tracheostomy, emergency procedure; transtracheal
31605	cricothyroid membrane
31610	Tracheostomy, fenestration procedure with skin flaps

(For endotracheal intubation, use 31500)

(For tracheal aspiration under direct vision, use 31515)

31611	Construction of tracheoesophageal fistula and subsequent insertion of an alaryngeal speech prosthesis (eg, voice button, Blom-Singer prosthesis)
31612	Tracheal puncture, percutaneous with transtracheal aspiration and/or injection
31613	Tracheostoma revision; simple, without flap rotation
31614	complex, with flap rotation

Endoscopy

For endoscopy procedures, code appropriate endoscopy of each anatomic site examined. Surgical bronchoscopy always includes diagnostic bronchoscopy when performed by the same physician. Codes 31622-31646 include fluoroscopic guidance, when performed.

(For tracheoscopy, see laryngoscopy codes 31515-31578)

31615	Tracheobronchoscopy through established tracheostomy incision

(31620, 31621 have been deleted. To report, use 31622)

31622	Bronchoscopy (rigid or flexible); diagnostic, with or without cell washing (separate procedure)
31623	with brushing or protected brushings
31624	with bronchial alveolar lavage
31625	with biopsy

(31626 has been deleted. To report, use 31625)

(31627 has been deleted. To report, use 31622)

31628	with transbronchial lung biopsy, with or without fluoroscopic guidance
31629	with transbronchial needle aspiration biopsy
31630	with tracheal or bronchial dilation or closed reduction of fracture
31631	with tracheal dilation and placement of tracheal stent
31635	with removal of foreign body
31640	with excision of tumor
▲ **31641**	Bronchoscopy, (rigid or flexible); with destruction of tumor or relief of stenosis by any method other than excision (eg, laser therapy, cryotherapy)

(For bronchoscopic photodynamic therapy, report 31641 in addition to 96570, 96571 as appropriate)

31643	with placement of catheter(s) for intracavitary radioelement application

(For intracavitary radioelement application, see 77761-77763, 77781-77784)

31645	with therapeutic aspiration of tracheobronchial tree, initial (eg, drainage of lung abscess)
31646	with therapeutic aspiration of tracheobronchial tree, subsequent

(For catheter aspiration of tracheobronchial tree at bedside, use 31725)

(31650, 31651 have been deleted. To report, see 31645, 31646)

31656	with injection of contrast material for segmental bronchography (fiberscope only)

(For radiological supervision and interpretation, see 71040, 71060)

(31659 has been deleted)

Introduction

(For endotracheal intubation, use 31500)

(For tracheal aspiration under direct vision, see 31515)

31700	Catheterization, transglottic (separate procedure)
31708	Instillation of contrast material for laryngography or bronchography, without catheterization

(For radiological supervision and interpretation, see 70373, 71040, 71060)

31710	Catheterization for bronchography, with or without instillation of contrast material

(For bronchoscopic catheterization for bronchography, fiberscope only, use 31656)

(For radiological supervision and interpretation, see 71040, 71060)

31715	Transtracheal injection for bronchography

(For radiological supervision and interpretation, see 71040, 71060)

(For prolonged services, see 99354-99360)

31717	Catheterization with bronchial brush biopsy

(31719 has been deleted. To report, use 31730)

31720	Catheter aspiration (separate procedure); nasotracheal
31725	tracheobronchial with fiberscope, bedside
31730	Transtracheal (percutaneous) introduction of needle wire dilator/stent or indwelling tube for oxygen therapy

Repair

31750	Tracheoplasty; cervical
31755	tracheopharyngeal fistulization, each stage
31760	intrathoracic
31766	Carinal reconstruction

31770	Bronchoplasty; graft repair
31775	excision stenosis and anastomosis
	(For lobectomy and bronchoplasty, use 32501)
31780	Excision tracheal stenosis and anastomosis; cervical
31781	cervicothoracic
31785	Excision of tracheal tumor or carcinoma; cervical
31786	thoracic
31800	Suture of tracheal wound or injury; cervical
31805	intrathoracic
31820	Surgical closure tracheostomy or fistula; without plastic repair
31825	with plastic repair
	(For repair tracheoesophageal fistula, see 43305, 43312)
31830	Revision of tracheostomy scar

Other Procedures

31899	Unlisted procedure, trachea, bronchi

Lungs and Pleura

Incision

⊘ 32000*	Thoracentesis, puncture of pleural cavity for aspiration, initial or subsequent
	(▶If imaging guidance is performed,◀ see 76003, 76360, ▶76942◀)
	(32001 has been deleted. To report, use 32997)
⊘ 32002	Thoracentesis with insertion of tube with or without water seal (eg, for pneumothorax) (separate procedure)
	(▶If imaging guidance is performed, see 76003, 76360, 76942)◀
32005	Chemical pleurodesis (eg, for recurrent or persistent pneumothorax)
⊘ 32020	Tube thoracostomy with or without water seal (eg, for abscess, hemothorax, empyema) (separate procedure)
	(If imaging guidance is performed, use 75989)
32035	Thoracostomy; with rib resection for empyema
32036	with open flap drainage for empyema
32095	Thoracotomy, limited, for biopsy of lung or pleura
	(To report wound exploration due to penetrating trauma without thoracotomy, use 20102)
32100	Thoracotomy, major; with exploration and biopsy
32110	with control of traumatic hemorrhage and/or repair of lung tear
32120	for postoperative complications
32124	with open intrapleural pneumonolysis

32140	with cyst(s) removal, with or without a pleural procedure
32141	with excision-plication of bullae, with or without any pleural procedure
	(For lung volume reduction, use 32491)
32150	with removal of intrapleural foreign body or fibrin deposit
32151	with removal of intrapulmonary foreign body
32160	with cardiac massage
	(For segmental or other resections of lung, see 32480-32525)
32200	Pneumonostomy; with open drainage of abscess or cyst
32201	with percutaneous drainage of abscess or cyst
	(For radiological supervision and interpretation, use 75989)
32215	Pleural scarification for repeat pneumothorax
32220	Decortication, pulmonary (separate procedure); total
32225	partial

Excision

32310	Pleurectomy, parietal (separate procedure)
	(32315 has been deleted. To report, use 32310)
32320	Decortication and parietal pleurectomy
32400*	Biopsy, pleura; percutaneous needle
	▶(If imaging guidance is performed, see 76003, 76360, 76393, 76942)◀
	▶(For fine needle aspiration, use 10021 or 10022)◀
	▶(For evaluation of fine needle aspirate, see 88172, 88173)◀
32402	open
32405	Biopsy, lung or mediastinum, percutaneous needle
	(For radiological supervision and interpretation, see ▶76003, 76360, 76393, 76942◀)
	(For fine needle aspiration, use ▶10022◀)
	▶(For evaluation of fine needle aspirate, see 88172, 88173)◀
▲ 32420*	Pneumocentesis, puncture of lung for aspiration
32440	Removal of lung, total pneumonectomy;
32442	with resection of segment of trachea followed by broncho-tracheal anastomosis (sleeve pneumonectomy)
32445	extrapleural
	(32450 has been deleted. To report, use 32445 and 32540)

32480	Removal of lung, other than total pneumonectomy; single lobe (lobectomy)	

32482   two lobes (bilobectomy)

32484   single segment (segmentectomy)

       (32485 has been deleted. To report, use 32501)

32486   with circumferential resection of segment of bronchus followed by broncho-bronchial anastomosis (sleeve lobectomy)

32488   all remaining lung following previous removal of a portion of lung (completion pneumonectomy)

       (32490 has been deleted. To report, use 32320 and the appropriate removal of lung code)

32491   excision-plication of emphysematous lung(s) (bullous or non-bullous) for lung volume reduction, sternal split or transthoracic approach, with or without any pleural procedure

32500   wedge resection, single or multiple

+ 32501 Resection and repair of portion of bronchus (bronchoplasty) when performed at time of lobectomy or segmentectomy (List separately in addition to code for primary procedure)

       (Use 32501 in conjunction with codes 32480, 32482, 32484)

       (32501 is to be used when a portion of the bronchus to preserved lung is removed and requires plastic closure to preserve function of that preserved lung. It is not to be used for closure for the proximal end of a resected bronchus.)

32520 Resection of lung; with resection of chest wall

32522   with reconstruction of chest wall, without prosthesis

32525   with major reconstruction of chest wall, with prosthesis

32540 Extrapleural enucleation of empyema (empyemectomy)

       (32545 has been deleted. To report, use 32540 and the appropriate removal of lung code)

Endoscopy

Surgical thoracoscopy always includes diagnostic thoracoscopy.

For endoscopic procedures, code appropriate endoscopy of each anatomic site examined.

32601 Thoracoscopy, diagnostic (separate procedure); lungs and pleural space, without biopsy

32602   lungs and pleural space, with biopsy

32603   pericardial sac, without biopsy

32604   pericardial sac, with biopsy

32605   mediastinal space, without biopsy

32606   mediastinal space, with biopsy

(Surgical thoracoscopy always includes diagnostic thoracoscopy)

▲ 32650 Thoracoscopy, surgical; with pleurodesis (eg, mechanical or chemical)

32651   with partial pulmonary decortication

32652   with total pulmonary decortication, including intrapleural pneumonolysis

32653   with removal of intrapleural foreign body or fibrin deposit

32654   with control of traumatic hemorrhage

32655   with excision-plication of bullae, including any pleural procedure

32656   with parietal pleurectomy

32657   with wedge resection of lung, single or multiple

32658   with removal of clot or foreign body from pericardial sac

32659   with creation of pericardial window or partial resection of pericardial sac for drainage

32660   with total pericardiectomy

32661   with excision of pericardial cyst, tumor, or mass

32662   with excision of mediastinal cyst, tumor, or mass

32663   with lobectomy, total or segmental

32664   with thoracic sympathectomy

32665   with esophagomyotomy (Heller type)

       (32700 and 32705 have been deleted. To report, see 32601-32606)

Repair

32800 Repair lung hernia through chest wall

32810 Closure of chest wall following open flap drainage for empyema (Clagett type procedure)

32815 Open closure of major bronchial fistula

32820 Major reconstruction, chest wall (posttraumatic)

Lung Transplantation

32850 Donor pneumonectomy(ies) with preparation and maintenance of allograft (cadaver)

32851 Lung transplant, single; without cardiopulmonary bypass

32852   with cardiopulmonary bypass

32853 Lung transplant, double (bilateral sequential or en bloc); without cardiopulmonary bypass

32854   with cardiopulmonary bypass

Surgical Collapse Therapy; Thoracoplasty

(See also 32520-32525)

32900   Resection of ribs, extrapleural, all stages

32905   Thoracoplasty, Schede type or extrapleural (all stages);

32906   with closure of bronchopleural fistula

(For open closure of major bronchial fistula, use 32815)

(For resection of first rib for thoracic outlet compression, see 21615, 21616)

32940   Pneumonolysis, extraperiosteal, including filling or packing procedures

32960*   Pneumothorax, therapeutic, intrapleural injection of air

Other Procedures

32997   Total lung lavage (unilateral)

(For bronchoscopic bronchial alveolar lavage, use 31624)

32999   Unlisted procedure, lungs and pleura

Cardiovascular System

Selective vascular catheterizations should be coded to include introduction and all lesser order selective catheterizations used in the approach (eg, the description for a selective right middle cerebral artery catheterization includes the introduction and placement catheterization of the right common and internal carotid arteries).

Additional second and/or third order arterial catheterizations within the same family of arteries supplied by a single first order artery should be expressed by 36218 or 36248. Additional first order or higher catheterizations in vascular families supplied by a first order vessel different from a previously selected and coded family should be separately coded using the conventions described above.

(For monitoring, operation of pump and other nonsurgical services, see 99190-99192, 99291, 99292, 99354-99360)

(For other medical or laboratory related services, see appropriate section)

(For radiological supervision and interpretation, see 75600-75978)

Heart and Pericardium

Pericardium

33010* Pericardiocentesis; initial

(For radiological supervision and interpretation, use 76930)

33011* subsequent

(For radiological supervision and interpretation, use 76930)

33015 Tube pericardiostomy

33020 Pericardiotomy for removal of clot or foreign body (primary procedure)

33025 Creation of pericardial window or partial resection for drainage

33030 Pericardiectomy, subtotal or complete; without cardiopulmonary bypass

33031 with cardiopulmonary bypass

(33035 has been deleted. To report, use 33031)

33050 Excision of pericardial cyst or tumor

(33100 has been deleted. To report, see 33030, 33031)

Cardiac Tumor

33120 Excision of intracardiac tumor, resection with cardiopulmonary bypass

33130 Resection of external cardiac tumor

Transmyocardial Revascularization

33140 Transmyocardial laser revascularization, by thoracotomy; (separate procedure)

+ 33141 performed at the time of other open cardiac procedure(s) (List separately in addition to code for primary procedure)

(Use 33141 in conjunction with codes ▶33400-33496,◀ 33510-33536)

Pacemaker or Pacing Cardioverter-Defibrillator

A pacemaker system includes a pulse generator containing electronics and a battery, and one or more electrodes (leads). Pulse generators are placed in a subcutaneous "pocket" created in either a subclavicular site or underneath the abdominal muscles just below the ribcage. Electrodes may be inserted through a vein (transvenous) or they may be placed on the surface of the heart (epicardial). The epicardial location of electrodes requires a thoracotomy for electrode insertion.

A single chamber pacemaker system includes a pulse generator and one electrode inserted in either the atrium or ventricle. A dual chamber pacemaker system includes a pulse generator and one electrode inserted in the atrium and one electrode inserted in the ventricle.

Like a pacemaker system, a pacing cardioverter-defibrillator system includes a pulse generator and electrodes, although pacing cardioverter-defibrillators may require multiple leads, even when only a single chamber is being paced. A pacing cardioverter-defibrillator system may be inserted in a single chamber (pacing in the ventricle) or in dual chambers (pacing in atrium and ventricle). These devices use a combination of antitachycardia pacing, low energy cardioversion or defibrillating shocks to treat ventricular tachycardia or ventricular fibrillation.

Pacing cardioverter-defibrillator pulse generators may be implanted in a subcutaneous infraclavicular pocket or in an abdominal pocket. Removal of a pacing cardioverter-defibrillator pulse generator requires opening of the existing subcutaneous pocket and disconnection of the pulse generator from its electrode(s). A thoracotomy (or laparotomy in the case of abdominally placed pulse generators) is not required to remove the pulse generator.

The electrodes (leads) of a pacing cardioverter-defibrillator system are positioned in the heart via the venous system (transvenously), in most circumstances. Electrode positioning on the epicardial surface of the heart requires a thoracotomy (codes 33245-33246). Removal of electrode(s) may first be attempted by transvenous extraction (code 33244). However, if transvenous extraction is unsuccessful, a thoracotomy may be required to remove the electrodes (code 33243).

When the "battery" of a pacemaker or pacing cardioverter-defibrillator is changed, it is actually the pulse generator that is changed. Replacement of a pulse generator should be reported with a code for removal of the pulse generator and another code for insertion of a pulse generator.

These procedures include repositioning or replacement in the first 14 days after the insertion (or replacement) of the device.

Modifiers '-76' and '-77' are not reported with pacemaker or pacing cardioverter-defibrillator codes after 14 days as these are considered new, not repeat, services.

(For electronic, telephonic analysis of internal pacemaker system, see 93731-93736)

(For radiological supervision and interpretation with insertion of pacemaker, use 71090)

33200 Insertion of permanent pacemaker with epicardial electrode(s); by thoracotomy

33201 by xiphoid approach

(33205 has been deleted. To report, see 33206-33208)

33206 Insertion or replacement of permanent pacemaker with transvenous electrode(s); atrial

33207 ventricular

33208 atrial and ventricular

(Codes 33206-33208 include subcutaneous insertion of the pulse generator and transvenous placement of electrode(s))

33210 Insertion or replacement of temporary transvenous single chamber cardiac electrode or pacemaker catheter (separate procedure)

33211 Insertion or replacement of temporary transvenous dual chamber pacing electrodes (separate procedure)

33212 Insertion or replacement of pacemaker pulse generator only; single chamber, atrial or ventricular

33213 dual chamber

33214 Upgrade of implanted pacemaker system, conversion of single chamber system to dual chamber system (includes removal of previously placed pulse generator, testing of existing lead, insertion of new lead, insertion of new pulse generator)

33216 Insertion or repositioning of a transvenous electrode (15 days or more after initial insertion); single chamber (one electrode) permanent pacemaker or single chamber pacing cardioverter-defibrillator

33217 dual chamber (two electrodes) permanent pacemaker or dual chamber pacing cardioverter-defibrillator

(Do not report 33216-33217 in conjunction with code 33214)

33218 Repair of single transvenous electrode for a single chamber, permanent pacemaker or single chamber pacing cardioverter-defibrillator

(33219 has been deleted. To report, see 33212 or 33213 and 33218 or 33220)

33220 Repair of two transvenous electrodes for a dual chamber permanent pacemaker or dual chamber pacing cardioverter-defibrillator

33222 Revision or relocation of skin pocket for pacemaker

33223 Revision of skin pocket for single or dual chamber pacing cardioverter-defibrillator

(33232 has been deleted. To report, see 33233, 33234, 33236)

33233 Removal of permanent pacemaker pulse generator

33234 Removal of transvenous pacemaker electrode(s); single lead system, atrial or ventricular

33235 dual lead system

33236 Removal of permanent epicardial pacemaker and electrodes by thoracotomy; single lead system, atrial or ventricular

33237 dual lead system

33238 Removal of permanent transvenous electrode(s) by thoracotomy

33240 Insertion of single or dual chamber pacing cardioverter-defibrillator pulse generator

33241 Subcutaneous removal of single or dual chamber pacing cardioverter-defibrillator pulse generator

(For removal of electrode(s) by thoracotomy, use 33243 in conjunction with code 33241)

(For removal of electrode(s) by transvenous extraction, use 33244 in conjunction with code 33241)

(For removal and reinsertion of a pacing cardioverter-defibrillator system (pulse generator and electrodes), report 33241 and 33243 or 33244 and 33249)

(33242 has been deleted. To report, see 33218, 33220)

33243 Removal of single or dual chamber pacing cardioverter-defibrillator electrode(s); by thoracotomy

33244 by transvenous extraction

(For subcutaneous removal of the pulse generator, use 33241 in conjunction with code 33243 or 33244)

33245 Insertion of epicardial single or dual chamber pacing cardioverter-defibrillator electrodes by thoracotomy;

33246 with insertion of pulse generator

(33247 has been deleted. To report, use 33216)

(33248 has been deleted. To report, see 33242, 33243, 33244)

33249   Insertion or repositioning of electrode lead(s) for single or dual chamber pacing cardioverter-defibrillator and insertion of pulse generator

(For removal and reinsertion of a pacing cardioverter-defibrillator system (pulse generator and electrodes), report 33241 and 33243 or 33244 and 33249)

Electrophysiologic Operative Procedures

▲ **33250**   Operative ablation of supraventricular arrhythmogenic focus or pathway (eg, Wolff-Parkinson-White, atrioventricular node re-entry), tract(s) and/or focus (foci); without cardiopulmonary bypass

33251   with cardiopulmonary bypass

33253   Operative incisions and reconstruction of atria for treatment of atrial fibrillation or atrial flutter (eg, maze procedure)

(33260 has been deleted. To report, use 33261)

33261   Operative ablation of ventricular arrhythmogenic focus with cardiopulmonary bypass

Patient-Activated Event Recorder

33282   Implantation of patient-activated cardiac event recorder

(Initial implantation includes programming. For subsequent electronic analysis and/or reprogramming, use 93727)

33284   Removal of an implantable, patient-activated cardiac event recorder

Wounds of the Heart and Great Vessels

33300   Repair of cardiac wound; without bypass

33305   with cardiopulmonary bypass

33310   Cardiotomy, exploratory (includes removal of foreign body); without bypass

33315   with cardiopulmonary bypass

33320   Suture repair of aorta or great vessels; without shunt or cardiopulmonary bypass

33321   with shunt bypass

33322   with cardiopulmonary bypass

33330   Insertion of graft, aorta or great vessels; without shunt, or cardiopulmonary bypass

33332   with shunt bypass

33335   with cardiopulmonary bypass

(33350 has been deleted)

Cardiac Valves

Aortic Valve

33400   Valvuloplasty, aortic valve; open, with cardiopulmonary bypass

33401   open, with inflow occlusion

33403   using transventricular dilation, with cardiopulmonary bypass

33404   Construction of apical-aortic conduit

33405   Replacement, aortic valve, with cardiopulmonary bypass; with prosthetic valve other than homograft or stentless valve

▲ **33406**   with allograft valve (freehand)

(33407 has been deleted. To report, use 33403)

(33408 has been deleted. To report, use 33401)

33410   with stentless tissue valve

33411   Replacement, aortic valve; with aortic annulus enlargement, noncoronary cusp

33412   with transventricular aortic annulus enlargement (Konno procedure)

▲ **33413**   by translocation of autologous pulmonary valve with allograft replacement of pulmonary valve (Ross procedure)

33414   Repair of left ventricular outflow tract obstruction by patch enlargement of the outflow tract

33415   Resection or incision of subvalvular tissue for discrete subvalvular aortic stenosis

33416   Ventriculomyotomy (-myectomy) for idiopathic hypertrophic subaortic stenosis (eg, asymmetric septal hypertrophy)

33417   Aortoplasty (gusset) for supravalvular stenosis

Mitral Valve

33420   Valvotomy, mitral valve; closed heart

33422   open heart, with cardiopulmonary bypass

33425   Valvuloplasty, mitral valve, with cardiopulmonary bypass;

33426   with prosthetic ring

33427   radical reconstruction, with or without ring

33430   Replacement, mitral valve, with cardiopulmonary bypass

Tricuspid Valve

(33450 has been deleted. To report, see 33463, 33464)

(33452 has been deleted. To report, see 33463, 33464)

33460   Valvectomy, tricuspid valve, with cardiopulmonary bypass

33463 Valvuloplasty, tricuspid valve; without ring insertion

33464 with ring insertion

33465 Replacement, tricuspid valve, with cardiopulmonary bypass

33468 Tricuspid valve repositioning and plication for Ebstein anomaly

Pulmonary Valve

33470 Valvotomy, pulmonary valve, closed heart; transventricular

33471 via pulmonary artery

(To report percutaneous valvuloplasty of pulmonary valve, use 92990)

33472 Valvotomy, pulmonary valve, open heart; with inflow occlusion

33474 with cardiopulmonary bypass

33475 Replacement, pulmonary valve

33476 Right ventricular resection for infundibular stenosis, with or without commissurotomy

33478 Outflow tract augmentation (gusset), with or without commissurotomy or infundibular resection

(33480-33492 have been deleted. To report, see 33400-33478 and add modifier '-51' to the secondary valve procedure code when multiple valve procedures are performed.)

Other Valvular Procedures

33496 Repair of non-structural prosthetic valve dysfunction with cardiopulmonary bypass (separate procedure)

(For reoperation, use 33530 in addition to 33496)

Coronary Artery Anomalies

Basic procedures include endarterectomy or angioplasty.

33500 Repair of coronary arteriovenous or arteriocardiac chamber fistula; with cardiopulmonary bypass

33501 without cardiopulmonary bypass

33502 Repair of anomalous coronary artery; by ligation

33503 by graft, without cardiopulmonary bypass

33504 by graft, with cardiopulmonary bypass

33505 with construction of intrapulmonary artery tunnel (Takeuchi procedure)

33506 by translocation from pulmonary artery to aorta

Venous Grafting Only for Coronary Artery Bypass

The following codes are used to report coronary artery bypass procedures using venous grafts only. These codes should NOT be used to report the performance of coronary artery bypass procedures using arterial grafts and venous grafts during the same procedure. See 33517-33523 and 33533-33536 for reporting combined arterial-venous grafts.

Procurement of the saphenous vein graft is included in the description of the work for 33510-33516 and should not be reported as a separate service or co-surgery. When graft procurement is performed by surgical assistant, add modifier '-80' to 33510-33516.

33510 Coronary artery bypass, vein only; single coronary venous graft

33511 two coronary venous grafts

33512 three coronary venous grafts

33513 four coronary venous grafts

33514 five coronary venous grafts

33516 six or more coronary venous grafts

Combined Arterial-Venous Grafting for Coronary Bypass

The following codes are used to report coronary artery bypass procedures using venous grafts and arterial grafts during the same procedure. These codes may NOT be used alone.

To report combined arterial-venous grafts it is necessary to report two codes: 1) the appropriate combined arterial-venous graft code (33517-33523); and 2) the appropriate arterial graft code (33533-33536).

Procurement of the saphenous vein graft is included in the description of the work for 33517-33523 and should not be reported as a separate service or co-surgery. Procurement of the artery for grafting is included in the description of the work for 33533-33536 and should not be reported as a separate service or co-surgery, except when an upper extremity artery (eg, radial artery) is procured. To report harvesting of an upper extremity artery, use 35600 in addition to the bypass procedure(s). When arterial and/or venous graft procurement is performed by surgical assistant, add modifier '-80' to 33517-33523, 33533-33536, as appropriate.

⊘ **33517** Coronary artery bypass, using venous graft(s) and arterial graft(s); single vein graft (List separately in addition to code for arterial graft)

⊘ **33518** two venous grafts (List separately in addition to code for arterial graft)

⊘ **33519**   three venous grafts (List separately in addition to code for arterial graft)

(33520 has been deleted)

⊘ **33521**   four venous grafts (List separately in addition to code for arterial graft)

⊘ **33522**   five venous grafts (List separately in addition to code for arterial graft)

⊘ **33523**   six or more venous grafts (List separately in addition to code for arterial graft)

(33525, 33528 have been deleted)

+ **33530**   Reoperation, coronary artery bypass procedure or valve procedure, more than one month after original operation (List separately in addition to code for primary procedure)

(Use 33530 in conjunction with codes 33400-33496; 33510-33536, 33863)

(33532 has been deleted. To report, use 33999)

Arterial Grafting for Coronary Artery Bypass

The following codes are used to report coronary artery bypass procedures using either arterial grafts only or a combination of arterial-venous grafts. The codes include the use of the internal mammary artery, gastroepiploic artery, epigastric artery, radial artery, and arterial conduits procured from other sites.

To report combined arterial-venous grafts it is necessary to report two codes: 1) the appropriate arterial graft code (33533-33536); and 2) the appropriate combined arterial-venous graft code (33517-33523).

Procurement of the artery for grafting is included in the description of the work for 33533-33536 and should not be reported as a separate service or co-surgery, except when an upper extremity artery (eg, radial artery) is procured. To report harvesting of an upper extremity artery, use 35600 in addition to the bypass procedure. Procurement of the saphenous vein graft is included in the description of the work for 33517-33523 and should not be reported as a separate service or co-surgery. When arterial and/or venous graft procurement is performed by surgical assistant, add modifier '-80' to 33517-33523, 33533-33536, as appropriate.

33533   Coronary artery bypass, using arterial graft(s); single arterial graft

33534   two coronary arterial grafts

33535   three coronary arterial grafts

33536   four or more coronary arterial grafts

33542   Myocardial resection (eg, ventricular aneurysmectomy)

33545   Repair of postinfarction ventricular septal defect, with or without myocardial resection

(33560 has been deleted)

Coronary Endarterectomy

(33570 has been deleted. To report, see 33510-33536 and 33572)

+ **33572**   Coronary endarterectomy, open, any method, of left anterior descending, circumflex, or right coronary artery performed in conjunction with coronary artery bypass graft procedure, each vessel (List separately in addition to primary procedure)

(Use 33572 in conjunction with 33510-33516, 33533-33536)

(33575 has been deleted. To report, see 33510-33536 and 33572)

Single Ventricle and Other Complex Cardiac Anomalies

33600   Closure of atrioventricular valve (mitral or tricuspid) by suture or patch

33602   Closure of semilunar valve (aortic or pulmonary) by suture or patch

33606   Anastomosis of pulmonary artery to aorta (Damus-Kaye-Stansel procedure)

33608   Repair of complex cardiac anomaly other than pulmonary atresia with ventricular septal defect by construction or replacement of conduit from right or left ventricle to pulmonary artery

(For repair of pulmonary atresia with ventricular septal defect, see 33918, 33919, 33920)

▲ **33610**   Repair of complex cardiac anomalies (eg, single ventricle with subaortic obstruction) by surgical enlargement of ventricular septal defect

33611   Repair of double outlet right ventricle with intraventricular tunnel repair;

33612   with repair of right ventricular outflow tract obstruction

33615   Repair of complex cardiac anomalies (eg, tricuspid atresia) by closure of atrial septal defect and anastomosis of atria or vena cava to pulmonary artery (simple Fontan procedure)

33617   Repair of complex cardiac anomalies (eg, single ventricle) by modified Fontan procedure

33619   Repair of single ventricle with aortic outflow obstruction and aortic arch hypoplasia (hypoplastic left heart syndrome) (eg, Norwood procedure)

Septal Defect

(33640 has been deleted. To report, use 33641)

33641   Repair atrial septal defect, secundum, with cardiopulmonary bypass, with or without patch

(33643 has been deleted. To report, use 33641)

33645 Direct or patch closure, sinus venosus, with or without anomalous pulmonary venous drainage

33647 Repair of atrial septal defect and ventricular septal defect, with direct or patch closure

(33649 has been deleted. To report, use 33615)

33660 Repair of incomplete or partial atrioventricular canal (ostium primum atrial septal defect), with or without atrioventricular valve repair

33665 Repair of intermediate or transitional atrioventricular canal, with or without atrioventricular valve repair

33670 Repair of complete atrioventricular canal, with or without prosthetic valve

33681 Closure of ventricular septal defect, with or without patch;

(33682 has been deleted. To report, use 33681)

33684 with pulmonary valvotomy or infundibular resection (acyanotic)

33688 with removal of pulmonary artery band, with or without gusset

33690 Banding of pulmonary artery

33692 Complete repair tetralogy of Fallot without pulmonary atresia;

33694 with transannular patch

(33696 has been deleted. To report, use 33924)

33697 Complete repair tetralogy of Fallot with pulmonary atresia including construction of conduit from right ventricle to pulmonary artery and closure of ventricular septal defect

(33698 has been deleted. To report, use 33924)

Sinus of Valsalva

33702 Repair sinus of Valsalva fistula, with cardiopulmonary bypass;

33710 with repair of ventricular septal defect

33720 Repair sinus of Valsalva aneurysm, with cardiopulmonary bypass

33722 Closure of aortico-left ventricular tunnel

Total Anomalous Pulmonary Venous Drainage

33730 Complete repair of anomalous venous return (supracardiac, intracardiac, or infracardiac types)

(For partial anomalous return, see atrial septal defect)

33732 Repair of cor triatriatum or supravalvular mitral ring by resection of left atrial membrane

Shunting Procedures

33735 Atrial septectomy or septostomy; closed heart (Blalock-Hanlon type operation)

33736 open heart with cardiopulmonary bypass

33737 open heart, with inflow occlusion

(33738 has been deleted. To report, use 92992)

(33739 has been deleted. To report, use 92993)

33750 Shunt; subclavian to pulmonary artery (Blalock-Taussig type operation)

33755 ascending aorta to pulmonary artery (Waterston type operation)

33762 descending aorta to pulmonary artery (Potts-Smith type operation)

33764 central, with prosthetic graft

33766 superior vena cava to pulmonary artery for flow to one lung (classical Glenn procedure)

33767 superior vena cava to pulmonary artery for flow to both lungs (bidirectional Glenn procedure)

Transposition of the Great Vessels

33770 Repair of transposition of the great arteries with ventricular septal defect and subpulmonary stenosis; without surgical enlargement of ventricular septal defect

33771 with surgical enlargement of ventricular septal defect

33774 Repair of transposition of the great arteries, atrial baffle procedure (eg, Mustard or Senning type) with cardiopulmonary bypass;

33775 with removal of pulmonary band

33776 with closure of ventricular septal defect

33777 with repair of subpulmonic obstruction

33778 Repair of transposition of the great arteries, aortic pulmonary artery reconstruction (eg, Jatene type);

33779 with removal of pulmonary band

33780 with closure of ventricular septal defect

33781 with repair of subpulmonic obstruction

(33782, 33783, 33784, 33785 have been deleted. To report, see 33774-33781)

Truncus Arteriosus

33786 Total repair, truncus arteriosus (Rastelli type operation)

33788 Reimplantation of an anomalous pulmonary artery

(For pulmonary artery band, use 33690)

Aortic Anomalies

33800   Aortic suspension (aortopexy) for tracheal decompression (eg, for tracheomalacia) (separate procedure)

33802   Division of aberrant vessel (vascular ring);

33803   with reanastomosis

(33810, 33812 have been deleted)

33813   Obliteration of aortopulmonary septal defect; without cardiopulmonary bypass

33814   with cardiopulmonary bypass

33820   Repair of patent ductus arteriosus; by ligation

33822   by division, under 18 years

33824   by division, 18 years and older

(33830 has been deleted. To report, see 33820-33824)

33840   Excision of coarctation of aorta, with or without associated patent ductus arteriosus; with direct anastomosis

33845   with graft

(33850 has been deleted. To report, use 33999)

33851   repair using either left subclavian artery or prosthetic material as gusset for enlargement

33852   Repair of hypoplastic or interrupted aortic arch using autogenous or prosthetic material; without cardiopulmonary bypass

33853   with cardiopulmonary bypass

(33855 has been deleted. To report, use 33619)

Thoracic Aortic Aneurysm

33860   Ascending aorta graft, with cardiopulmonary bypass, with or without valve suspension;

33861   with coronary reconstruction

33863   with aortic root replacement using composite prosthesis and coronary reconstruction

(33865 has been deleted. To report, see 33860 or 33861 and 33405 or 33406)

33870   Transverse arch graft, with cardiopulmonary bypass

33875   Descending thoracic aorta graft, with or without bypass

33877   Repair of thoracoabdominal aortic aneurysm with graft, with or without cardiopulmonary bypass

Pulmonary Artery

33910   Pulmonary artery embolectomy; with cardiopulmonary bypass

33915   without cardiopulmonary bypass

33916   Pulmonary endarterectomy, with or without embolectomy, with cardiopulmonary bypass

33917   Repair of pulmonary artery stenosis by reconstruction with patch or graft

33918   Repair of pulmonary atresia with ventricular septal defect, by unifocalization of pulmonary arteries; without cardiopulmonary bypass

33919   with cardiopulmonary bypass

33920   Repair of pulmonary atresia with ventricular septal defect, by construction or replacement of conduit from right or left ventricle to pulmonary artery

(For repair of other complex cardiac anomalies by construction or replacement of right or left ventricle to pulmonary artery conduit, use 33608)

33922   Transection of pulmonary artery with cardiopulmonary bypass

+ 33924   Ligation and takedown of a systemic-to-pulmonary artery shunt, performed in conjunction with a congenital heart procedure (List separately in addition to code for primary procedure)

(Use 33924 in conjunction with 33470-33475, 33600-33619, 33684-33688, 33692-33697, 33735-33767, 33770-33781, 33786, 33918-33922)

Heart/Lung Transplantation

33930   Donor cardiectomy-pneumonectomy, with preparation and maintenance of allograft

33935   Heart-lung transplant with recipient cardiectomy-pneumonectomy

33940   Donor cardiectomy, with preparation and maintenance of allograft

33945   Heart transplant, with or without recipient cardiectomy

(33950 has been deleted. To report, see 33940, 33945)

Cardiac Assist

33960   Prolonged extracorporeal circulation for cardiopulmonary insufficiency; initial 24 hours

+ 33961   each additional 24 hours (List separately in addition to code for primary procedure)

(Use 33961 in conjunction with code 33960)

(For insertion of cannula for prolonged extracorporeal circulation, use 36822)

● **33967**   Insertion of intra-aortic balloon assist device, percutaneous

33968   Removal of intra-aortic balloon assist device, percutaneous

33970   Insertion of intra-aortic balloon assist device through the femoral artery, open approach

33971   Removal of intra-aortic balloon assist device including repair of femoral artery, with or without graft

(33972 has been deleted. To report, use appropriate E/M code)

33973	Insertion of intra-aortic balloon assist device through the ascending aorta
33974	Removal of intra-aortic balloon assist device from the ascending aorta, including repair of the ascending aorta, with or without graft
▲ 33975	Insertion of ventricular assist device; extracorporeal, single ventricle
▲ 33976	extracorporeal, biventricular
▲ 33977	Removal of ventricular assist device; extracorporeal, single ventricle
▲ 33978	extracorporeal, biventricular
● 33979	Insertion of ventricular assist device, implantable intracorporeal, single ventricle
● 33980	Removal of ventricular assist device, implantable intracorporeal, single ventricle

Other Procedures

33999	Unlisted procedure, cardiac surgery

Arteries and Veins

Primary vascular procedure listings include establishing both inflow and outflow by whatever procedures necessary. Also included is that portion of the operative arteriogram performed by the surgeon, as indicated. Sympathectomy, when done, is included in the listed aortic procedures. For unlisted vascular procedure, use 37799.

Embolectomy/Thrombectomy

Arterial, With or Without Catheter

34001	Embolectomy or thrombectomy, with or without catheter; carotid, subclavian or innominate artery, by neck incision
34051	innominate, subclavian artery, by thoracic incision
34101	axillary, brachial, innominate, subclavian artery, by arm incision
34111	radial or ulnar artery, by arm incision
34151	renal, celiac, mesentery, aortoiliac artery, by abdominal incision
34201	femoropopliteal, aortoiliac artery, by leg incision
34203	popliteal-tibio-peroneal artery, by leg incision

Venous, Direct or With Catheter

34401	Thrombectomy, direct or with catheter; vena cava, iliac vein, by abdominal incision
34421	vena cava, iliac, femoropopliteal vein, by leg incision
34451	vena cava, iliac, femoropopliteal vein, by abdominal and leg incision
34471	subclavian vein, by neck incision
34490	axillary and subclavian vein, by arm incision

Venous Reconstruction

34501	Valvuloplasty, femoral vein
34502	Reconstruction of vena cava, any method
34510	Venous valve transposition, any vein donor
34520	Cross-over vein graft to venous system
34530	Saphenopopliteal vein anastomosis

Endovascular Repair of Abdominal Aortic Aneurysm

Codes 34800-34826 ▶represent a family of component procedures to report◀ placement of an endovascular graft for abdominal aortic aneurysm repair. ▶These codes describe open femoral or iliac artery exposure, device manipulation and deployment, and closure of the arteriotomy sites. Balloon angioplasty and/or stent deployment within the target treatment zone for the endoprosthesis, either before or after endograft deployment, are not separately reportable. Introduction of guidewires and catheters should be reported separately (eg, 36200, 36245-36248, 36140).◀ Extensive repair or replacement of an artery should be additionally reported (eg, 35226 or 35286).

For fluoroscopic guidance in conjunction with endovascular aneurysm repair, see code 75952 or 75953, as appropriate. Code 75952 includes angiography of the aorta and its branches for diagnostic imaging prior to deployment of the endovascular device (including all routine components of modular devices), fluoroscopic guidance in the delivery of the endovascular components, and intraprocedural arterial angiography (eg, confirm position, detect endoleak, evaluate runoff). Code 75953 includes the analogous services for placement of additional extension prostheses (not for routine components of modular devices).

Other interventional procedures performed at the time of endovascular abdominal aortic aneurysm repair should be additionally reported (eg, renal transluminal angioplasty, arterial embolization, intravascular ultrasound, balloon angioplasty or stenting of native artery(s) outside the ▶endoprosthesis target zone, when done◀ before ▶or after◀ deployment of graft).

34800	Endovascular repair of infrarenal abdominal aortic aneurysm or dissection; using aorto-aortic tube prosthesis

⊘ =Modifier '-51' Exempt   ▶ ◀=New or Revised Text   ✚ =Add-on Code   CPT 2002

34802   using modular bifurcated prosthesis (one docking limb)

▶(For endovascular repair of infrarenal abdominal aortic aneurysm or dissection using a modular bifurcated prosthesis (two docking limbs), use Category III code 0001T)◀

34804   using unibody bifurcated prosthesis

▶(For endovascular repair of infrarenal adbominal aortic aneurysm or dissection using an aorto-uniiliac or aorto-unifemoral prosthesis, use Category III code 0002T)◀

+ 34808   Endovascular placement of iliac artery occlusion device (List separately in addition to code for primary procedure)

(Use 34808 in conjunction with codes 34800, 34813, 34825, 34826)

(For radiological supervision and interpretation, use 75952 in conjunction with 34800, 34802, 34804, 34808)

(For open approach, report codes 34812-34820 in addition to codes 34800, 34802, 34804, 34808 as appropriate)

34812   Open femoral artery exposure for delivery of aortic endovascular prosthesis, by groin incision, unilateral

(For bilateral procedure, use modifier '-50')

+ 34813   Placement of femoral-femoral prosthetic graft during endovascular aortic aneurysm repair (List separately in addition to code for primary procedure)

(Use 34813 in conjunction with code 34812)

(For femoral artery grafting, see 35521, 35533, 35546, 35551-35558, 35566, 35621, 35646, 35651-35661, 35666, 35700)

34820   Open iliac artery exposure for delivery of endovascular prosthesis or iliac occlusion during endovascular therapy, by abdominal or retroperitoneal incision, unilateral

(For bilateral procedure, use modifier '-50')

34825   Placement of proximal or distal extension prosthesis for endovascular repair of infrarenal abdominal aortic aneurysm; initial vessel

+ 34826   each additional vessel (List separately in addition to code for primary procedure)

(Use 34826 in conjunction with code 34825)

(Use 34825, 34826 in addition to codes 34800-34808, as appropriate)

(For staged procedure, use modifier '-58')

(For radiological supervision and interpretation, use 75953)

34830   Open repair of infrarenal aortic aneurysm or dissection, plus repair of associated arterial trauma, following unsuccessful endovascular repair; tube prosthesis

34831   aorto-bi-iliac prosthesis

34832   aorto-bifemoral prosthesis

Direct Repair of Aneurysm or Excision (Partial or Total) and Graft Insertion for Aneurysm, False Aneurysm, Ruptured Aneurysm, and Associated Occlusive Disease

Procedures 35001-35162 include preparation of artery for anastomosis including endarterectomy.

(For direct repairs associated with occlusive disease only, see 35201-35286)

(For intracranial aneurysm, see 61700 et seq)

(For thoracic aortic aneurysm, see 33860-33875)

▲ **35001**   Direct repair of aneurysm, pseudoaneurysm, or excision (partial or total) and graft insertion, with or without patch graft; for aneurysm and associated occlusive disease, carotid, subclavian artery, by neck incision

35002   for ruptured aneurysm, carotid, subclavian artery, by neck incision

▲ **35005**   for aneurysm, pseudoaneurysm, and associated occlusive disease, vertebral artery

35011   for aneurysm and associated occlusive disease, axillary-brachial artery, by arm incision

35013   for ruptured aneurysm, axillary-brachial artery, by arm incision

▲ **35021**   for aneurysm, pseudoaneurysm, and associated occlusive disease, innominate, subclavian artery, by thoracic incision

35022   for ruptured aneurysm, innominate, subclavian artery, by thoracic incision

▲ **35045**   for aneurysm, pseudoaneurysm, and associated occlusive disease, radial or ulnar artery

▲ **35081**   for aneurysm, pseudoaneurysm, and associated occlusive disease, abdominal aorta

35082   for ruptured aneurysm, abdominal aorta

▲ **35091**   for aneurysm, pseudoaneurysm, and associated occlusive disease, abdominal aorta involving visceral vessels (mesenteric, celiac, renal)

35092   for ruptured aneurysm, abdominal aorta involving visceral vessels (mesenteric, celiac, renal)

▲ **35102**   for aneurysm, pseudoaneurysm, and associated occlusive disease, abdominal aorta involving iliac vessels (common, hypogastric, external)

35103   for ruptured aneurysm, abdominal aorta involving iliac vessels (common, hypogastric, external)

▲ **35111**   for aneurysm, pseudoaneurysm, and associated occlusive disease, splenic artery

35112   for ruptured aneurysm, splenic artery

▲ **35121**   for aneurysm, pseudoaneurysm, and associated occlusive disease, hepatic, celiac, renal, or mesenteric artery

35122   for ruptured aneurysm, hepatic, celiac, renal, or mesenteric artery

▲ 35131   for aneurysm, pseudoaneurysm, and associated occlusive disease, iliac artery (common, hypogastric, external)

35132   for ruptured aneurysm, iliac artery (common, hypogastric, external)

▲ 35141   for aneurysm, pseudoaneurysm, and associated occlusive disease, common femoral artery (profunda femoris, superficial femoral)

35142   for ruptured aneurysm, common femoral artery (profunda femoris, superficial femoral)

▲ 35151   for aneurysm, pseudoaneurysm, and associated occlusive disease, popliteal artery

35152   for ruptured aneurysm, popliteal artery

▲ 35161   for aneurysm, pseudoaneurysm, and associated occlusive disease, other arteries

35162   for ruptured aneurysm, other arteries

Repair Arteriovenous Fistula

35180   Repair, congenital arteriovenous fistula; head and neck

35182   thorax and abdomen

35184   extremities

35188   Repair, acquired or traumatic arteriovenous fistula; head and neck

35189   thorax and abdomen

35190   extremities

Repair Blood Vessel Other Than for Fistula, With or Without Patch Angioplasty

(For AV fistula repair, see 35180-35190)

35201   Repair blood vessel, direct; neck

35206   upper extremity

35207   hand, finger

35211   intrathoracic, with bypass

35216   intrathoracic, without bypass

35221   intra-abdominal

35226   lower extremity

35231   Repair blood vessel with vein graft; neck

35236   upper extremity

35241   intrathoracic, with bypass

35246   intrathoracic, without bypass

35251   intra-abdominal

35256   lower extremity

35261   Repair blood vessel with graft other than vein; neck

35266   upper extremity

35271   intrathoracic, with bypass

35276   intrathoracic, without bypass

35281   intra-abdominal

35286   lower extremity

Thromboendarterectomy

(For coronary artery, see 33510-33536 and 33572)

35301   Thromboendarterectomy, with or without patch graft; carotid, vertebral, subclavian, by neck incision

35311   subclavian, innominate, by thoracic incision

35321   axillary-brachial

35331   abdominal aorta

35341   mesenteric, celiac, or renal

35351   iliac

35355   iliofemoral

35361   combined aortoiliac

35363   combined aortoiliofemoral

35371   common femoral

35372   deep (profunda) femoral

35381   femoral and/or popliteal, and/or tibioperoneal

+ 35390   Reoperation, carotid, thromboendarterectomy, more than one month after original operation (List separately in addition to code for primary procedure)

(Use 35390 in conjunction with code 35301)

Angioscopy

+ 35400   Angioscopy (non-coronary vessels or grafts) during therapeutic intervention (List separately in addition to code for primary procedure)

Transluminal Angioplasty

If done as part of another operation, use modifier '-51' or use modifier '-52'.

(For radiological supervision and interpretation, see 75962-75968 and 75978)

Open

35450   Transluminal balloon angioplasty, open; renal or other visceral artery

35452   aortic

35454   iliac

35456   femoral-popliteal

⊘ =Modifier '-51' Exempt   ▶ ◀ =New or Revised Text   + =Add-on Code   CPT 2002

35458	brachiocephalic trunk or branches, each vessel
35459	tibioperoneal trunk and branches
35460	venous

Percutaneous

►Codes for catheter placement and the radiologic supervision and interpretation should also be reported, in addition to the code(s) for the therapeutic aspect of the procedure.◄

35470	Transluminal balloon angioplasty, percutaneous; tibioperoneal trunk or branches, each vessel
35471	renal or visceral artery
35472	aortic
35473	iliac
35474	femoral-popliteal
35475	brachiocephalic trunk or branches, each vessel
35476	venous
	(For radiological supervision and interpretation, use 75978)

Transluminal Atherectomy

If done as part of another operation, use modifier '-51' or use modifier '-52'.

(For radiological supervision and interpretation, see 75992-75996)

Open

35480	Transluminal peripheral atherectomy, open; renal or other visceral artery
35481	aortic
35482	iliac
35483	femoral-popliteal
35484	brachiocephalic trunk or branches, each vessel
35485	tibioperoneal trunk and branches

Percutaneous

►Codes for catheter placement and the radiologic supervision and interpretation should also be reported, in addition to the code(s) for the therapeutic aspect of the procedure.◄

35490	Transluminal peripheral atherectomy, percutaneous; renal or other visceral artery
35491	aortic
35492	iliac
35493	femoral-popliteal

35494	brachiocephalic trunk or branches, each vessel
35495	tibioperoneal trunk and branches

Bypass Graft

Vein

+ 35500	Harvest of upper extremity vein, one segment, for lower extremity or coronary artery bypass procedure (List separately in addition to code for primary procedure)
	►(Use 35500 in conjunction with codes 33510-33536, 35556, 35566, 35571, 35583-35587)◄
	(For harvest of more than one vein segment, see 35682, 35683)
35501	Bypass graft, with vein; carotid
35506	carotid-subclavian
35507	subclavian-carotid
35508	carotid-vertebral
35509	carotid-carotid
35511	subclavian-subclavian
35515	subclavian-vertebral
35516	subclavian-axillary
35518	axillary-axillary
35521	axillary-femoral
	(For bypass graft performed with synthetic graft, use 35621)
35526	aortosubclavian or carotid
	(For bypass graft performed with synthetic graft, use 35626)
35531	aortoceliac or aortomesenteric
35533	axillary-femoral-femoral
	(For bypass graft performed with synthetic graft, use 35654)
35536	splenorenal
35541	aortoiliac or bi-iliac
	(For bypass graft performed with synthetic graft, use 35641)
35546	aortofemoral or bifemoral
	(For bypass graft performed with synthetic graft, use 35646)
35548	aortoiliofemoral, unilateral
	(For bypass graft performed with synthetic graft, use 37799)
35549	aortoiliofemoral, bilateral
	(For bypass graft performed with synthetic graft, use 37799)

35551	aortofemoral-popliteal
35556	femoral-popliteal
35558	femoral-femoral
35560	aortorenal
35563	ilioiliac
35565	iliofemoral
35566	femoral-anterior tibial, posterior tibial, peroneal artery or other distal vessels
35571	popliteal-tibial, -peroneal artery or other distal vessels

In-Situ Vein

35582	In-situ vein bypass; aortofemoral-popliteal (only femoral-popliteal portion in-situ)
35583	femoral-popliteal
35585	femoral-anterior tibial, posterior tibial, or peroneal artery
35587	popliteal-tibial, peroneal

Other Than Vein

⊘ 35600	Harvest of upper extremity artery, one segment, for coronary artery bypass procedure
35601	Bypass graft, with other than vein; carotid
35606	carotid-subclavian
35612	subclavian-subclavian
35616	subclavian-axillary
35621	axillary-femoral
35623	axillary-popliteal or -tibial
35626	aortosubclavian or carotid
35631	aortoceliac, aortomesenteric, aortorenal
35636	splenorenal (splenic to renal arterial anastomosis)
	(35637 has been deleted. To report, use 35691)
	(35638 has been deleted. To report, use 35693)
35641	aortoiliac or bi-iliac
35642	carotid-vertebral
35645	subclavian-vertebral
▲ 35646	aortobifemoral
● 35647	aortofemoral
35650	axillary-axillary
35651	aortofemoral-popliteal
35654	axillary-femoral-femoral
35656	femoral-popliteal

35661	femoral-femoral
35663	ilioiliac
35665	iliofemoral
35666	femoral-anterior tibial, posterior tibial, or peroneal artery
35671	popliteal-tibial or -peroneal artery

Composite Grafts

Codes 35682-35683 are used to report harvest and anastomosis of multiple vein segments from distant sites for use as arterial bypass graft conduits. These codes are intended for use when the two or more vein segments are harvested from a limb other than that undergoing bypass. ►Add-on codes 35682 and 35683 may be reported in addition to codes 35556, 35566, 35571, 35583-35587, as appropriate.◄

✚ 35681	Bypass graft; composite, prosthetic and vein (List separately in addition to code for primary procedure)
	(Do not report 35681 in addition to 35682, 35683)
✚ 35682	autogenous composite, two segments of veins from two locations (List separately in addition to code for primary procedure)
	(Do not report 35682 in addition to 35681, 35683)
✚ 35683	autogenous composite, three or more segments of vein from two or more locations (List separately in addition to code for primary procedure)
	(Do not report 35683 in addition to 35681, 35682)

►Adjuvant Techniques◄

►Adjuvant (additional) technique(s) may be required at the time a bypass graft is created to improve patency of the lower extremity autogenous or synthetic bypass graft (eg, femoral-popliteal, femoral-tibial, or popliteal-tibial arteries). Code 35685 should be reported in addition to the primary synthetic bypass graft procedure, when an interposition of venous tissue (vein patch or cuff) is placed at the anastomosis between the synthetic bypass conduit and the involved artery (includes harvest).◄

►Code 35686 should be reported in addition to the primary bypass graft procedure, when autogenous vein is used to create a fistula between the tibial or peroneal artery and vein at or beyond the distal bypass anastomosis site of the involved artery.◄

►(For composite graft(s), see 35681-35683)◄

✚ ● 35685	Placement of vein patch or cuff at distal anastomosis of bypass graft, synthetic conduit (List separately in addition to code for primary procedure)
	►(Use 35685 in conjunction with codes 35656, 35666, or 35671)◄

+ ●**35686**   Creation of distal arteriovenous fistula during lower extremity bypass surgery (non-hemodialysis) (List separately in addition to code for primary procedure)

▶(Use 35686 in conjunction with codes 35556, 35566, 35571, 35583-35587, 35623, 35656, 35666, 35671)◀

Arterial Transposition

35691   Transposition and/or reimplantation; vertebral to carotid artery

35693   vertebral to subclavian artery

35694   subclavian to carotid artery

35695   carotid to subclavian artery

Exploration/Revision

+ **35700**   Reoperation, femoral-popliteal or femoral (popliteal)-anterior tibial, posterior tibial, peroneal artery or other distal vessels, more than one month after original operation (List separately in addition to code for primary procedure)

(Use 35700 in conjunction with codes 35556, 35566, 35571, 35583, 35585, 35587, 35656, 35666, 35671)

35701   Exploration (not followed by surgical repair), with or without lysis of artery; carotid artery

35721   femoral artery

35741   popliteal artery

35761   other vessels

35800   Exploration for postoperative hemorrhage, thrombosis or infection; neck

35820   chest

35840   abdomen

35860   extremity

35870   Repair of graft-enteric fistula

35875   Thrombectomy of arterial or venous graft (other than hemodialysis graft or fistula);

35876   with revision of arterial or venous graft

(For thrombectomy of hemodialysis graft or fistula, see 36831, 36833)

(35880 has been deleted. To report, use 35875)

(35900 has been deleted. To report, see 35901-35907 and appropriate revascularization code)

Codes 35879 and 35881 describe open revision of graft-threatening stenoses of lower extremity arterial bypass graft(s) (previously constructed with autogenous vein conduit) using vein patch angioplasty or segmental vein interposition techniques. For thrombectomy with revision of any non-coronary arterial or venous graft, including those of the lower extremity, (other than hemodialysis graft or fistula), use 35876. For direct repair

(other than for fistula) of a lower extremity blood vessel (with or without patch angioplasty), use 35226. For repair (other than for fistula) of a lower extremity blood vessel using a vein graft, use 35256.

35879   Revision, lower extremity arterial bypass, without thrombectomy, open; with vein patch angioplasty

35881   with segmental vein interposition

35901   Excision of infected graft; neck

35903   extremity

35905   thorax

35907   abdomen

(35910 has been deleted. To report, see 35901-35907 and appropriate revascularization code)

Vascular Injection Procedures

Listed services for injection procedures include necessary local anesthesia, introduction of needles or catheter, injection of contrast media with or without automatic power injection, and/or necessary pre- and postinjection care specifically related to the injection procedure.

Catheters, drugs, and contrast media are not included in the listed service for the injection procedures.

Selective vascular catheterization should be coded to include introduction and all lesser order selective catheterization used in the approach (eg, the description for a selective right middle cerebral artery catheterization includes the introduction and placement catheterization of the right common and internal carotid arteries).

Additional second and/or third order arterial catheterization within the same family of arteries or veins supplied by a single first order vessel should be expressed by 36012, 36218 or 36248.

Additional first order or higher catheterization in vascular families supplied by a first order vessel different from a previously selected and coded family should be separately coded using the conventions described above.

(For radiological supervision and interpretation, see **Radiology**)

(For injection procedures in conjunction with cardiac catheterization, see 93541-93545)

(For chemotherapy of malignant disease, see 96400-96549)

Intravenous

An intracatheter is a sheathed combination of needle and short catheter.

36000＊   Introduction of needle or intracatheter, vein

(36001 has been deleted. To report, use 36000 with modifier '-50')

● **36002** Injection procedures (eg, thrombin) for percutaneous treatment of extremity pseudoaneurysm

▶(For imaging guidance, see 76003, 76360, 76393, or 76942)◀

▶(For ultrasound guided compression repair of pseudoaneurysms, use 76936)◀

▶(Do not report 36002 for vascular sealant of an arteriotomy site)◀

▲ **36005** Injection procedure for extremity venography (including introduction of needle or intracatheter)

(For radiological supervision and interpretation, see 75820, 75822)

36010 Introduction of catheter, superior or inferior vena cava

36011 Selective catheter placement, venous system; first order branch (eg, renal vein, jugular vein)

36012 second order, or more selective, branch (eg, left adrenal vein, petrosal sinus)

36013 Introduction of catheter, right heart or main pulmonary artery

36014 Selective catheter placement, left or right pulmonary artery

36015 Selective catheter placement, segmental or subsegmental pulmonary artery

(For insertion of flow directed catheter (eg, Swan-Ganz), use 93503)

(For venous catheterization for selective organ blood sampling, use 36500)

Intra-Arterial—Intra-Aortic

(For radiological supervision and interpretation, see **Radiology**)

36100 Introduction of needle or intracatheter, carotid or vertebral artery

(36101 has been deleted. To report, use 36100 with modifier '-50')

36120 Introduction of needle or intracatheter; retrograde brachial artery

36140 extremity artery

36145 arteriovenous shunt created for dialysis (cannula, fistula, or graft)

(For insertion of arteriovenous cannula, see 36810-36821)

36160 Introduction of needle or intracatheter, aortic, translumbar

36200 Introduction of catheter, aorta

(36210 has been deleted. To report, see 36215-36218)

36215 Selective catheter placement, arterial system; each first order thoracic or brachiocephalic branch, within a vascular family

(For catheter placement for coronary angiography, use 93508)

36216 initial second order thoracic or brachiocephalic branch, within a vascular family

36217 initial third order or more selective thoracic or brachiocephalic branch, within a vascular family

+ **36218** additional second order, third order, and beyond, thoracic or brachiocephalic branch, within a vascular family (List in addition to code for initial second or third order vessel as appropriate)

(Use 36218 in conjunction with codes 36216, 36217)

(For angiography, see 75600-75790)

(For angioplasty, see 35470-35475)

(For transcatheter therapies, see 37200-37208, 61624, 61626)

(36220 has been deleted. To report, see 36215-36218)

(36230 has been deleted. When coronary artery, arterial conduit (eg, internal mammary, inferior epigastric or free radial artery) or venous bypass graft angiography is performed in conjunction with cardiac catheterization, see the appropriate cardiac catheterization code(s) (93501-93556) in the **Medicine** section of CPT. When coronary artery, arterial coronary conduit or venous bypass graft angiography is performed without concomitant left heart cardiac catheterization, use 93508. When internal mammary artery angiography only is performed without a concomitant left heart cardiac catheterization, use 36216 or 36217 as appropriate.)

(36240 has been deleted. To report, use 36248)

36245 Selective catheter placement, arterial system; each first order abdominal, pelvic, or lower extremity artery branch, within a vascular family

36246 initial second order abdominal, pelvic, or lower extremity artery branch, within a vascular family

36247 initial third order or more selective abdominal, pelvic, or lower extremity artery branch, within a vascular family

+ **36248** additional second order, third order, and beyond, abdominal, pelvic, or lower extremity artery branch, within a vascular family (List in addition to code for initial second or third order vessel as appropriate)

(Use 36248 in conjunction with codes 36246, 36247)

(36250 has been deleted. To report, use 36248)

36260 Insertion of implantable intra-arterial infusion pump (eg, for chemotherapy of liver)

36261 Revision of implanted intra-arterial infusion pump

36262 Removal of implanted intra-arterial infusion pump

36299 Unlisted procedure, vascular injection

Venous

Venipuncture, needle or catheter for diagnostic study or intravenous therapy, percutaneous.

▲ **36400**   Venipuncture, under age 3 years; femoral or jugular

36405*   scalp vein

36406   other vein

36410*   Venipuncture, child over age 3 years or adult, necessitating physician's skill (separate procedure), for diagnostic or therapeutic purposes. Not to be used for routine venipuncture.

36415*   Routine venipuncture or finger/heel/ear stick for collection of specimen(s)

36420   Venipuncture, cutdown; under age 1 year

36425   age 1 or over

36430   Transfusion, blood or blood components

(36431 has been deleted)

36440*   Push transfusion, blood, 2 years or under

36450   Exchange transfusion, blood; newborn

36455   other than newborn

36460   Transfusion, intrauterine, fetal

(For radiological supervision and interpretation, use 76941)

36468   Single or multiple injections of sclerosing solutions, spider veins (telangiectasia); limb or trunk

36469   face

36470*   Injection of sclerosing solution; single vein

36471*   multiple veins, same leg

(36480 has been deleted. To report, use 36488 or 36489)

36481   Percutaneous portal vein catheterization by any method

(For radiological supervision and interpretation, see 75885, 75887)

(36485 has been deleted. To report, use 36490 or 36491)

⊘ **36488***   Placement of central venous catheter (subclavian, jugular, or other vein) (eg, for central venous pressure, hyperalimentation, hemodialysis, or chemotherapy); percutaneous, age 2 years or under

⊘ **36489***   percutaneous, over age 2

▶(If imaging guidance is performed, see 76000, 76003, 76942)◀

⊘ **36490***   cutdown, age 2 years or under

⊘ **36491***   cutdown, over age 2

(For examination of patient and instruction to patient, review of prescription of fluids for long-term or permanent hyperalimentation, use **Evaluation and Management** codes for office or hospital inpatient category or follow-up inpatient consultation codes as appropriate)

36493   Repositioning of previously placed central venous catheter under fluoroscopic guidance

(For fluoroscopic guidance use 76000)

(36495-36497 have been deleted. To report, see 36530-36535)

36500   Venous catheterization for selective organ blood sampling

(For catheterization in superior or inferior vena cava, use 36010)

(For radiological supervision and interpretation, use 75893)

36510*   Catheterization of umbilical vein for diagnosis or therapy, newborn

36520   Therapeutic apheresis; plasma and/or cell exchange

36521   with extracorporeal affinity column adsorption and plasma reinfusion

36522   Photopheresis, extracorporeal

36530   Insertion of implantable intravenous infusion pump

▶(If imaging guidance is performed, see 76000, 76003, 76942)◀

36531   Revision of implantable intravenous infusion pump

36532   Removal of implantable intravenous infusion pump

▶(If imaging guidance is performed, use 76000)◀

36533   Insertion of implantable venous access device, with or without subcutaneous reservoir

(For removal, use 36535)

▶(If imaging guidance is performed, see 76000, 76003, 76942)◀

(For refilling and maintenance of an implantable venous access device reservoir, use 96530)

36534   Revision of implantable venous access device, and/or subcutaneous reservoir

(For removal, use 36535)

36535   Removal of implantable venous access device, and/or subcutaneous reservoir

(Use 36535 in conjunction with codes 36533, 36534, as appropriate)

(Do not use 36535 in conjunction with codes 36488-36491)

▶(If imaging guidance is performed, use 76000)◀

36540   Collection of blood specimen from a partially or completely implantable venous access device

36550   Declotting by thrombolytic agent of implanted vascular access device or catheter

---

Arterial

36600* Arterial puncture, withdrawal of blood for diagnosis

⊘ **36620** Arterial catheterization or cannulation for sampling, monitoring or transfusion (separate procedure); percutaneous

36625 cutdown

36640 Arterial catheterization for prolonged infusion therapy (chemotherapy), cutdown

(See also 96420-96425)

(For arterial catheterization for occlusion therapy, see 75894)

⊘ **36660*** Catheterization, umbilical artery, newborn, for diagnosis or therapy

Intraosseous

36680 Placement of needle for intraosseous infusion

►Hemodialysis Access, Intervascular Cannulation for Extracorporeal Circulation, or Shunt Insertion◄

36800 Insertion of cannula for hemodialysis, other purpose (separate procedure); vein to vein

36810 arteriovenous, external (Scribner type)

36815 arteriovenous, external revision, or closure

(36820 has been deleted. To report, use 36821)

▲ **36819** Arteriovenous anastomosis, open; by upper arm basilic vein transposition

● **36820** by forearm vein transposition

36821 direct, any site (eg, Cimino type) (separate procedure)

36822 Insertion of cannula(s) for prolonged extracorporeal circulation for cardiopulmonary insufficiency (ECMO) (separate procedure)

(For maintenance of prolonged extracorporeal circulation, use 33960)

▲ **36823** Insertion of arterial and venous cannula(s) for isolated extracorporeal circulation including regional chemotherapy perfusion to an extremity, with or without hyperthermia, with removal of cannula(s) and repair of arteriotomy and venotomy sites

►(36823 includes chemotherapy perfusion supported by a membrane oxygenator/perfusion pump. Do not report 96408-96425 in conjunction with 36823)◄

36825 Creation of arteriovenous fistula by other than direct arteriovenous anastomosis (separate procedure); autogenous graft

(For direct arteriovenous anastomosis, use 36821)

36830 nonautogenous graft

(For direct arteriovenous anastomosis, use 36821)

36831 Thrombectomy, open, arteriovenous fistula without revision, autogenous or nonautogenous dialysis graft (separate procedure)

36832 Revision, open, arteriovenous fistula; without thrombectomy, autogenous or nonautogenous dialysis graft (separate procedure)

36833 with thrombectomy, autogenous or nonautogenous dialysis graft (separate procedure)

36834 Plastic repair of arteriovenous aneurysm (separate procedure)

36835 Insertion of Thomas shunt (separate procedure)

(36840 has been deleted)

(36845 has been deleted)

36860 External cannula declotting (separate procedure); without balloon catheter

36861 with balloon catheter

►(If imaging guidance is performed, use 76000)◄

36870 Thrombectomy, percutaneous, arteriovenous fistula, autogenous or nonautogenous graft (includes mechanical thrombus extraction and intra-graft thrombolysis)

(Do not report 36550 in conjunction with code 36870)

(For catheterization, use 36145)

(For radiological supervision and interpretation, use 75790)

Portal Decompression Procedures

37140 Venous anastomosis; portocaval

(For peritoneal-venous shunt, use 49425)

37145 renoportal

37160 caval-mesenteric

37180 splenorenal, proximal

37181 splenorenal, distal (selective decompression of esophagogastric varices, any technique)

(37190 has been deleted. To report, use 36834)

Transcatheter Procedures

►Codes for catheter placement and the radiologic supervision and interpretation should also be reported, in addition to the code(s) for the therapeutic aspect of the procedure.◄

37195 Thrombolysis, cerebral, by intravenous infusion

37200 Transcatheter biopsy

(For radiological supervision and interpretation, use 75970)

37201 Transcatheter therapy, infusion for thrombolysis other than coronary

(For radiological supervision and interpretation, use 75896)

37202   Transcatheter therapy, infusion other than for thrombolysis, any type (eg, spasmolytic, vasoconstrictive)

(For thrombolysis of coronary vessels, see 92975, 92977)

(For radiological supervision and interpretation, use 75896)

37203   Transcatheter retrieval, percutaneous, of intravascular foreign body (eg, fractured venous or arterial catheter)

(For radiological supervision and interpretation, use 75961)

37204   Transcatheter occlusion or embolization (eg, for tumor destruction, to achieve hemostasis, to occlude a vascular malformation), percutaneous, any method, non-central nervous system, non-head or neck

(See also 61624, 61626)

(For radiological supervision and interpretation, use 75894)

37205   Transcatheter placement of an intravascular stent(s), (non-coronary vessel), percutaneous; initial vessel

(For radiological supervision and interpretation, use 75960)

+ 37206   each additional vessel (List separately in addition to code for primary procedure)

(Use 37206 in conjunction with code 37205)

▶(For transcatheter placement of extracranial cerebrovascular artery stent(s), see Category III codes 0005T, 0006T)◀

(For radiological supervision and interpretation, use 75960)

37207   Transcatheter placement of an intravascular stent(s), (non-coronary vessel), open; initial vessel

+ 37208   each additional vessel (List separately in addition to code for primary procedure)

(Use 37208 in conjunction with code 37207)

(For radiological supervision and interpretation, use 75960)

(For catheterizations, see 36215-36248)

(For transcatheter placement of intracoronary stent(s), see 92980, 92981)

37209   Exchange of a previously placed arterial catheter during thrombolytic therapy

(For radiological supervision and interpretation, use 75900)

Intravascular Ultrasound Services

Intravascular ultrasound services include all transducer manipulations and repositioning within the specific vessel being examined, both before and after therapeutic intervention (eg, stent placement).

Vascular access for intravascular ultrasound performed during a therapeutic intervention is not reported separately.

+ 37250   Intravascular ultrasound (non-coronary vessel) during diagnostic evaluation and/or therapeutic intervention; initial vessel (List separately in addition to code for primary procedure)

+ 37251   each additional vessel (List separately in addition to code for primary procedure)

(Use 37251 in conjunction with code 37250)

(For catheterizations, see 36215-36248)

(For transcatheter therapies, see 37200-37208, 61624, 61626)

(For radiological supervision and interpretation see 75945, 75946)

Ligation and Other Procedures

(37400-37560 have been deleted. To report, see 35201-35286)

37565   Ligation, internal jugular vein

37600   Ligation; external carotid artery

37605   internal or common carotid artery

37606   internal or common carotid artery, with gradual occlusion, as with Selverstone or Crutchfield clamp

(For ligation treatment of intracranial aneurysm, use 61703)

37607   Ligation or banding of angioaccess arteriovenous fistula

37609   Ligation or biopsy, temporal artery

37615   Ligation, major artery (eg, post-traumatic, rupture); neck

37616   chest

37617   abdomen

37618   extremity

37620   Interruption, partial or complete, of inferior vena cava by suture, ligation, plication, clip, extravascular, intravascular (umbrella device)

(For radiological supervision and interpretation, use 75940)

37650   Ligation of femoral vein

(37651 has been deleted. To report, use 37650 with modifier '-50')

37660   Ligation of common iliac vein

37700   Ligation and division of long saphenous vein at saphenofemoral junction, or distal interruptions

(37701 has been deleted. To report, use 37700 with modifier '-50')

37720 Ligation and division and complete stripping of long or short saphenous veins

(37721 has been deleted. To report, use 37720 with modifier '-50')

37730 Ligation and division and complete stripping of long and short saphenous veins

(37731 has been deleted. To report, use 37730 with modifier '-50')

37735 Ligation and division and complete stripping of long or short saphenous veins with radical excision of ulcer and skin graft and/or interruption of communicating veins of lower leg, with excision of deep fascia

(37737 has been deleted. To report, use 37735 with modifier '-50')

37760 Ligation of perforators, subfascial, radical (Linton type), with or without skin graft

37780 Ligation and division of short saphenous vein at saphenopopliteal junction (separate procedure)

(37781 has been deleted. To report, use 37780 with modifier '-50')

37785 Ligation, division, and/or excision of recurrent or secondary varicose veins (clusters), one leg

(37787 has been deleted. To report, use 37785 with modifier '-50')

37788 Penile revascularization, artery, with or without vein graft

37790 Penile venous occlusive procedure

37799 Unlisted procedure, vascular surgery

Hemic and Lymphatic Systems

Spleen

Excision

(38090 has been deleted. To report, use 38999)

38100 Splenectomy; total (separate procedure)

38101 partial (separate procedure)

+ 38102 total, en bloc for extensive disease, in conjunction with other procedure (List in addition to code for primary procedure)

Repair

38115 Repair of ruptured spleen (splenorrhaphy) with or without partial splenectomy

Laparoscopy

Surgical laparoscopy always includes diagnostic laparoscopy. To report a diagnostic laparoscopy (peritoneoscopy) (separate procedure), use 49320.

38120 Laparoscopy, surgical, splenectomy

38129 Unlisted laparoscopy procedure, spleen

Introduction

38200 Injection procedure for splenoportography

(For radiological supervision and interpretation, use 75810)

►General◄

Bone Marrow or Stem Cell Services/►Procedures◄

● **38220** Bone marrow aspiration

● **38221** Bone marrow biopsy, needle or trocar

►(For bone marrow biopsy interpretation, use 88305)◄

38230 Bone marrow harvesting for transplantation

38231 Blood-derived peripheral stem cell harvesting for transplantation, per collection

38240 Bone marrow or blood-derived peripheral stem cell transplantation; allogenic

38241 autologous

(For bone marrow aspiration, use ►38220◄)

(For modification, treatment, and processing of bone marrow or blood-derived stem cell specimens for transplantation, use 86915)

(For cryopreservation, freezing and storage of blood-derived stem cells for transplantation, use 88240)

(For thawing and expansion of blood-derived stem cells for transplantation, use 88241)

(For compatibility studies, see 86812-86822)

Lymph Nodes and Lymphatic Channels

Incision

38300* Drainage of lymph node abscess or lymphadenitis; simple

38305 extensive

38308 Lymphangiotomy or other operations on lymphatic channels

38380 Suture and/or ligation of thoracic duct; cervical approach

38381 thoracic approach

38382 abdominal approach

⊘ =Modifier '-51' Exempt   ► ◄=New or Revised Text   ✚ =Add-on Code   CPT 2002

Excision

(For injection for sentinel node identification, use 38792)

38500   Biopsy or excision of lymph node(s); open, superficial

(Do not report 38500 with 38700-38780)

38505   by needle, superficial (eg, cervical, inguinal, axillary)

►(If imaging guidance is performed, see 76360, 76393, 76942)◄

(For fine needle aspiration, use ►10021 or 10022◄)

►(For evaluation of fine needle aspirate, see 88172, 88173)◄

38510   open, deep cervical node(s)

38520   open, deep cervical node(s) with excision scalene fat pad

38525   open, deep axillary node(s)

38530   open, internal mammary node(s)

(Do not report 38530 with 38720-38746)

(For percutaneous needle biopsy, retroperitoneal lymph node or mass, use 49180. For fine needle aspiration, use ►10022)◄

(38540 has been deleted. To report, see 38510, 38520)

38542   Dissection, deep jugular node(s)

(For radical cervical neck dissection, use 38720)

38550   Excision of cystic hygroma, axillary or cervical; without deep neurovascular dissection

38555   with deep neurovascular dissection

Limited Lymphadenectomy for Staging

38562   Limited lymphadenectomy for staging (separate procedure); pelvic and para-aortic

(When combined with prostatectomy, use 55812 or 55842)

(When combined with insertion of radioactive substance into prostate, use 55862)

38564   retroperitoneal (aortic and/or splenic)

Laparoscopy

Surgical laparoscopy always includes diagnostic laparoscopy. To report a diagnostic laparoscopy (peritoneoscopy) (separate procedure), use 49320.

38570   Laparoscopy, surgical; with retroperitoneal lymph node sampling (biopsy), single or multiple

38571   with bilateral total pelvic lymphadenectomy

38572   with bilateral total pelvic lymphadenectomy and peri-aortic lymph node sampling (biopsy), single or multiple

(For drainage of lymphocele to peritoneal cavity, use 49323)

38589   Unlisted laparoscopy procedure, lymphatic system

Radical Lymphadenectomy (Radical Resection of Lymph Nodes)

(For limited pelvic and retroperitoneal lymphadenectomies, see 38562, 38564)

38700   Suprahyoid lymphadenectomy

(38701 has been deleted. To report, use 38700 with modifier '-50')

38720   Cervical lymphadenectomy (complete)

(38721 has been deleted. To report, use 38720 with modifier '-50')

38724   Cervical lymphadenectomy (modified radical neck dissection)

38740   Axillary lymphadenectomy; superficial

38745   complete

+ 38746   Thoracic lymphadenectomy, regional, including mediastinal and peritracheal nodes (List separately in addition to code for primary procedure)

+ 38747   Abdominal lymphadenectomy, regional, including celiac, gastric, portal, peripancreatic, with or without para-aortic and vena caval nodes (List separately in addition to code for primary procedure)

38760   Inguinofemoral lymphadenectomy, superficial, including Cloquets node (separate procedure)

(38761 has been deleted. To report, use 38760 with modifier '-50')

38765   Inguinofemoral lymphadenectomy, superficial, in continuity with pelvic lymphadenectomy, including external iliac, hypogastric, and obturator nodes (separate procedure)

(38766 has been deleted. To report, use 38765 with modifier '-50')

38770   Pelvic lymphadenectomy, including external iliac, hypogastric, and obturator nodes (separate procedure)

(38771 has been deleted. To report, use 38770 with modifier '-50')

38780   Retroperitoneal transabdominal lymphadenectomy, extensive, including pelvic, aortic, and renal nodes (separate procedure)

(For excision and repair of lymphedematous skin and subcutaneous tissue, see 15000, 15570-15650)

Introduction

38790   Injection procedure; lymphangiography

(For radiological supervision and interpretation, see 75801-75807)

(38791 has been deleted. To report, use 38790 with modifier '-50')

⊘ **38792**   for identification of sentinel node

(For excision of sentinel node, see 38500-38542)

(For nuclear medicine lymphatics and lymph gland imaging, use 78195)

38794   Cannulation, thoracic duct

Other Procedures

38999   Unlisted procedure, hemic or lymphatic system

Mediastinum and Diaphragm

Mediastinum

Incision

39000   Mediastinotomy with exploration, drainage, removal of foreign body, or biopsy; cervical approach

39010   transthoracic approach, including either transthoracic or median sternotomy

(39020 has been deleted. To report, use 39010)

(39050-39070 have been deleted. To report, see 39000-39010)

Excision

39200   Excision of mediastinal cyst

39220   Excision of mediastinal tumor

(For substernal thyroidectomy, use 60270)

(For thymectomy, use 60520)

Endoscopy

39400   Mediastinoscopy, with or without biopsy

Other Procedures

39499   Unlisted procedure, mediastinum

Diaphragm

Repair

(39500 has been deleted. To report, see 43324, 43325)

39501   Repair, laceration of diaphragm, any approach

39502   Repair, paraesophageal hiatus hernia, transabdominal, with or without fundoplasty, vagotomy, and/or pyloroplasty, except neonatal

39503   Repair, neonatal diaphragmatic hernia, with or without chest tube insertion and with or without creation of ventral hernia

(39510 has been deleted. To report, see 43324, 43325)

39520   Repair, diaphragmatic hernia (esophageal hiatal); transthoracic

39530   combined, thoracoabdominal

39531   combined, thoracoabdominal, with dilation of stricture (with or without gastroplasty)

39540   Repair, diaphragmatic hernia (other than neonatal), traumatic; acute

39541   chronic

39545   Imbrication of diaphragm for eventration, transthoracic or transabdominal, paralytic or nonparalytic

(39547 has been deleted. To report, use 39545)

39560   Resection, diaphragm; with simple repair (eg, primary suture)

39561   with complex repair (eg, prosthetic material, local muscle flap)

Other Procedures

39599   Unlisted procedure, diaphragm

⊘ =Modifier '-51' Exempt   ▶ ◀=New or Revised Text   ✚=Add-on Code   CPT 2002

Digestive System

Lips

(For procedures on skin of lips, see 10040 et seq)

Excision

40490   Biopsy of lip

40500   Vermilionectomy (lip shave), with mucosal advancement

40510   Excision of lip; transverse wedge excision with primary closure

40520   V-excision with primary direct linear closure

(For excision of mucous lesions, see 40810-40816)

40525   full thickness, reconstruction with local flap (eg, Estlander or fan)

40527   full thickness, reconstruction with cross lip flap (Abbe-Estlander)

40530   Resection of lip, more than one-fourth, without reconstruction

(For reconstruction, see 13131 et seq)

Repair (Cheiloplasty)

40650   Repair lip, full thickness; vermilion only

40652   up to half vertical height

40654   over one-half vertical height, or complex

40700   Plastic repair of cleft lip/nasal deformity; primary, partial or complete, unilateral

40701   primary bilateral, one stage procedure

40702   primary bilateral, one of two stages

40720   secondary, by recreation of defect and reclosure

(To report rhinoplasty only for nasal deformity secondary to congenital cleft lip, see 30460, 30462)

(40740 has been deleted. To report, use 40720 with modifier '-50')

(40760 has been deleted. To report, use 40527)

40761   with cross lip pedicle flap (Abbe-Estlander type), including sectioning and inserting of pedicle

(For repair cleft palate, see 42200 et seq)

(For other reconstructive procedures, see 14060, 14061, 15120-15261, 15574, 15576, 15630)

Other Procedures

40799   Unlisted procedure, lips

Vestibule of Mouth

The vestibule is the part of the oral cavity outside the dentoalveolar structures; it includes the mucosal and submucosal tissue of lips and cheeks.

Incision

40800*   Drainage of abscess, cyst, hematoma, vestibule of mouth; simple

40801   complicated

40804*   Removal of embedded foreign body, vestibule of mouth; simple

40805   complicated

40806   Incision of labial frenum (frenotomy)

Excision, Destruction

40808   Biopsy, vestibule of mouth

40810   Excision of lesion of mucosa and submucosa, vestibule of mouth; without repair

40812   with simple repair

40814   with complex repair

40816   complex, with excision of underlying muscle

40818   Excision of mucosa of vestibule of mouth as donor graft

40819   Excision of frenum, labial or buccal (frenumectomy, frenulectomy, frenectomy)

40820   Destruction of lesion or scar of vestibule of mouth by physical methods (eg, laser, thermal, cryo, chemical)

Repair

40830   Closure of laceration, vestibule of mouth; 2.5 cm or less

40831   over 2.5 cm or complex

40840   Vestibuloplasty; anterior

40842   posterior, unilateral

40843   posterior, bilateral

40844   entire arch

40845   complex (including ridge extension, muscle repositioning)

(For skin grafts, see 15000 et seq)

Other Procedures

40899   Unlisted procedure, vestibule of mouth

Tongue and Floor of Mouth

Incision

41000* Intraoral incision and drainage of abscess, cyst, or hematoma of tongue or floor of mouth; lingual

41005*   sublingual, superficial

41006   sublingual, deep, supramylohyoid

41007   submental space

41008   submandibular space

41009   masticator space

41010 Incision of lingual frenum (frenotomy)

41015 Extraoral incision and drainage of abscess, cyst, or hematoma of floor of mouth; sublingual

41016   submental

41017   submandibular

41018   masticator space

     (For frenoplasty, use 41520)

Excision

41100 Biopsy of tongue; anterior two-thirds

41105   posterior one-third

41108 Biopsy of floor of mouth

41110 Excision of lesion of tongue without closure

41112 Excision of lesion of tongue with closure; anterior two-thirds

41113   posterior one-third

41114   with local tongue flap

     (List 41114 in addition to code 41112 or 41113)

41115 Excision of lingual frenum (frenectomy)

41116 Excision, lesion of floor of mouth

41120 Glossectomy; less than one-half tongue

41130   hemiglossectomy

41135   partial, with unilateral radical neck dissection

41140   complete or total, with or without tracheostomy, without radical neck dissection

41145   complete or total, with or without tracheostomy, with unilateral radical neck dissection

41150   composite procedure with resection floor of mouth and mandibular resection, without radical neck dissection

41153   composite procedure with resection floor of mouth, with suprahyoid neck dissection

41155   composite procedure with resection floor of mouth, mandibular resection, and radical neck dissection (Commando type)

Repair

41250* Repair of laceration 2.5 cm or less; floor of mouth and/or anterior two-thirds of tongue

41251*   posterior one-third of tongue

41252* Repair of laceration of tongue, floor of mouth, over 2.6 cm or complex

Other Procedures

41500 Fixation of tongue, mechanical, other than suture (eg, K-wire)

41510 Suture of tongue to lip for micrognathia (Douglas type procedure)

41520 Frenoplasty (surgical revision of frenum, eg, with Z-plasty)

     (For frenotomy, see 40806, 41010)

41599 Unlisted procedure, tongue, floor of mouth

Dentoalveolar Structures

Incision

41800* Drainage of abscess, cyst, hematoma from dentoalveolar structures

41805 Removal of embedded foreign body from dentoalveolar structures; soft tissues

41806   bone

Excision, Destruction

41820 Gingivectomy, excision gingiva, each quadrant

41821 Operculectomy, excision pericoronal tissues

41822 Excision of fibrous tuberosities, dentoalveolar structures

41823 Excision of osseous tuberosities, dentoalveolar structures

41825 Excision of lesion or tumor (except listed above), dentoalveolar structures; without repair

41826   with simple repair

41827   with complex repair

     (For nonexcisional destruction, use 41850)

41828 Excision of hyperplastic alveolar mucosa, each quadrant (specify)

41830 Alveolectomy, including curettage of osteitis or sequestrectomy

41850 Destruction of lesion (except excision), dentoalveolar structures

Other Procedures

41870 Periodontal mucosal grafting

41872 Gingivoplasty, each quadrant (specify)

41874   Alveoloplasty, each quadrant (specify)

(For closure of lacerations, see 40830, 40831)

(For segmental osteotomy, use 21206)

(For reduction of fractures, see 21421-21490)

41899   Unlisted procedure, dentoalveolar structures

Palate and Uvula

Incision

42000*   Drainage of abscess of palate, uvula

Excision, Destruction

42100   Biopsy of palate, uvula

42104   Excision, lesion of palate, uvula; without closure

42106   with simple primary closure

42107   with local flap closure

(For skin graft, see 14040-14300)

(For mucosal graft, use 40818)

42120   Resection of palate or extensive resection of lesion

(For reconstruction of palate with extraoral tissue, see 14040-14300, 15050, 15120, 15240, 15576)

42140   Uvulectomy, excision of uvula

42145   Palatopharyngoplasty (eg, uvulopalatopharyngoplasty, uvulopharyngoplasty)

(42150 has been deleted. To report, see 21031, 21032)

42160   Destruction of lesion, palate or uvula (thermal, cryo or chemical)

Repair

42180   Repair, laceration of palate; up to 2 cm

42182   over 2 cm or complex

42200   Palatoplasty for cleft palate, soft and/or hard palate only

42205   Palatoplasty for cleft palate, with closure of alveolar ridge; soft tissue only

42210   with bone graft to alveolar ridge (includes obtaining graft)

42215   Palatoplasty for cleft palate; major revision

42220   secondary lengthening procedure

42225   attachment pharyngeal flap

42226   Lengthening of palate, and pharyngeal flap

42227   Lengthening of palate, with island flap

42235   Repair of anterior palate, including vomer flap

(42250 has been deleted. To report, use 30600)

42260   Repair of nasolabial fistula

(For repair of cleft lip, see 40700 et seq)

42280   Maxillary impression for palatal prosthesis

42281   Insertion of pin-retained palatal prosthesis

Other Procedures

42299   Unlisted procedure, palate, uvula

Salivary Gland and Ducts

Incision

42300*   Drainage of abscess; parotid, simple

42305   parotid, complicated

42310*   Drainage of abscess; submaxillary or sublingual, intraoral

42320*   submaxillary, external

42325   Fistulization of sublingual salivary cyst (ranula);

42326   with prosthesis

42330   Sialolithotomy; submandibular (submaxillary), sublingual or parotid, uncomplicated, intraoral

42335   submandibular (submaxillary), complicated, intraoral

42340   parotid, extraoral or complicated intraoral

Excision

42400*   Biopsy of salivary gland; needle

42405   incisional

▶(If imaging guidance is performed, see 76003, 76360, 76393, 76942)◀

42408   Excision of sublingual salivary cyst (ranula)

42409   Marsupialization of sublingual salivary cyst (ranula)

(For fistulization of sublingual salivary cyst, use 42325)

42410   Excision of parotid tumor or parotid gland; lateral lobe, without nerve dissection

42415   lateral lobe, with dissection and preservation of facial nerve

42420   total, with dissection and preservation of facial nerve

42425   total, en bloc removal with sacrifice of facial nerve

42426   total, with unilateral radical neck dissection

(For suture or grafting of facial nerve, see 64864, 64865, 69740, 69745)

42440   Excision of submandibular (submaxillary) gland

42450   Excision of sublingual gland

Repair

42500   Plastic repair of salivary duct, sialodochoplasty; primary or simple

42505   secondary or complicated

42507   Parotid duct diversion, bilateral (Wilke type procedure);

42508   with excision of one submandibular gland

42509   with excision of both submandibular glands

42510   with ligation of both submandibular (Wharton's) ducts

Other Procedures

42550   Injection procedure for sialography

(For radiological supervision and interpretation, use 70390)

42600   Closure salivary fistula

42650*   Dilation salivary duct

42660*   Dilation and catheterization of salivary duct, with or without injection

42665   Ligation salivary duct, intraoral

42699   Unlisted procedure, salivary glands or ducts

Pharynx, Adenoids, and Tonsils

Incision

42700*   Incision and drainage abscess; peritonsillar

42720   retropharyngeal or parapharyngeal, intraoral approach

42725   retropharyngeal or parapharyngeal, external approach

Excision, Destruction

42800   Biopsy; oropharynx

42802   hypopharynx

42804   nasopharynx, visible lesion, simple

42806   nasopharynx, survey for unknown primary lesion

(For laryngoscopic biopsy, see 31510, 31535, 31536)

42808   Excision or destruction of lesion of pharynx, any method

42809   Removal of foreign body from pharynx

42810   Excision branchial cleft cyst or vestige, confined to skin and subcutaneous tissues

42815   Excision branchial cleft cyst, vestige, or fistula, extending beneath subcutaneous tissues and/or into pharynx

42820   Tonsillectomy and adenoidectomy; under age 12

42821   age 12 or over

42825   Tonsillectomy, primary or secondary; under age 12

42826   age 12 or over

42830   Adenoidectomy, primary; under age 12

42831   age 12 or over

42835   Adenoidectomy, secondary; under age 12

42836   age 12 or over

42842   Radical resection of tonsil, tonsillar pillars, and/or retromolar trigone; without closure

42844   closure with local flap (eg, tongue, buccal)

42845   closure with other flap

(For closure with other flap(s), use appropriate number for flap(s))

(When combined with radical neck dissection, use also 38720)

42860   Excision of tonsil tags

42870   Excision or destruction lingual tonsil, any method (separate procedure)

(42880 has been deleted. For resection of the nasopharynx (eg, juvenile angiofibroma) by bicoronal and/or transzygomatic approach, see 61586 and 61600)

42890   Limited pharyngectomy

42892   Resection of lateral pharyngeal wall or pyriform sinus, direct closure by advancement of lateral and posterior pharyngeal walls

(When combined with radical neck dissection, use also 38720)

42894   Resection of pharyngeal wall requiring closure with myocutaneous flap

(When combined with radical neck dissection, use also 38720)

(42895 has been deleted. To report, use 38720 with 42890)

Repair

42900   Suture pharynx for wound or injury

42950   Pharyngoplasty (plastic or reconstructive operation on pharynx)

(For pharyngeal flap, use 42225)

42953   Pharyngoesophageal repair

(For closure with myocutaneous or other flap, use appropriate number in addition)

Other Procedures

42955   Pharyngostomy (fistulization of pharynx, external for feeding)

42960   Control oropharyngeal hemorrhage, primary or secondary (eg, post-tonsillectomy); simple

42961   complicated, requiring hospitalization

42962   with secondary surgical intervention

⊘ =Modifier '-51' Exempt   ▶ ◀ =New or Revised Text   ✚ =Add-on Code   CPT 2002

▲ **42970**   Control of nasopharyngeal hemorrhage, primary or secondary (eg, postadenoidectomy); simple, with posterior nasal packs, with or without anterior packs and/or cautery

42971   complicated, requiring hospitalization

42972   with secondary surgical intervention

42999   Unlisted procedure, pharynx, adenoids, or tonsils

Esophagus

Incision

(For esophageal intubation with laparotomy, use 43510)

(43000 has been deleted)

43020   Esophagotomy, cervical approach, with removal of foreign body

43030   Cricopharyngeal myotomy

(43040 has been deleted)

43045   Esophagotomy, thoracic approach, with removal of foreign body

Excision

(For gastrointestinal reconstruction for previous esophagectomy, see 43360, 43361)

43100   Excision of lesion, esophagus, with primary repair; cervical approach

43101   thoracic or abdominal approach

(43105 has been deleted. To report, see 43107, 43116, 43124, and 31360)

(43106 has been deleted. To report, see 43107, 43116, 43124, and 31365)

43107   Total or near total esophagectomy, without thoracotomy; with pharyngogastrostomy or cervical esophagogastrostomy, with or without pyloroplasty (transhiatal)

▲ **43108**   with colon interposition or small intestine reconstruction, including intestine mobilization, preparation and anastomosis(es)

(43110 has been deleted. To report, see 43107-43113)

(43111 has been deleted. To report, see 43107-43113)

43112   Total or near total esophagectomy, with thoracotomy; with pharyngogastrostomy or cervical esophagogastrostomy, with or without pyloroplasty

▲ **43113**   with colon interposition or small intestine reconstruction, including intestine mobilization, preparation, and anastomosis(es)

(43115 has been deleted. To report, see 43116-43118)

43116   Partial esophagectomy, cervical, with free intestinal graft, including microvascular anastomosis, obtaining the graft and intestinal reconstruction

(Do not report code 69990 in addition to code 43116)

(Report 43116 with the modifier '-52' appended if intestinal or free jejunal graft with microvascular anastomosis is performed by another physician)

(For free jejunal graft with microvascular anastomosis performed by another physician, use 43496)

43117   Partial esophagectomy, distal two-thirds, with thoracotomy and separate abdominal incision, with or without proximal gastrectomy; with thoracic esophagogastrostomy, with or without pyloroplasty (Ivor Lewis)

▲ **43118**   with colon interposition or small intestine reconstruction, including intestine mobilization, preparation, and anastomosis(es)

(43119 has been deleted. To report, see 43107, 43124)

(43120 has been deleted. To report, use 43122)

43121   Partial esophagectomy, distal two-thirds, with thoracotomy only, with or without proximal gastrectomy, with thoracic esophagogastrostomy, with or without pyloroplasty

43122   Partial esophagectomy, thoracoabdominal or abdominal approach, with or without proximal gastrectomy; with esophagogastrostomy, with or without pyloroplasty

▲ **43123**   with colon interposition or small intestine reconstruction, including intestine mobilization, preparation, and anastomosis(es)

43124   Total or partial esophagectomy, without reconstruction (any approach), with cervical esophagostomy

43130   Diverticulectomy of hypopharynx or esophagus, with or without myotomy; cervical approach

43135   thoracic approach

(43136 has been deleted. To report, use 43499)

Endoscopy

For endoscopic procedures, code appropriate endoscopy of each anatomic site examined.

Surgical endoscopy always includes diagnostic endoscopy.

43200   Esophagoscopy, rigid or flexible; diagnostic, with or without collection of specimen(s) by brushing or washing (separate procedure)

43202   with biopsy, single or multiple

43204   with injection sclerosis of esophageal varices

43205   with band ligation of esophageal varices

43215   with removal of foreign body

(For radiological supervision and interpretation, use 74235)

▲=Revised Code   ●=New Code   ✱=Service Includes Surgical Procedure Only

43216   with removal of tumor(s), polyp(s), or other lesion(s) by hot biopsy forceps or bipolar cautery

43217   with removal of tumor(s), polyp(s), or other lesion(s) by snare technique

(43218 has been deleted. To report, use 43499)

43219   with insertion of plastic tube or stent

43220   with balloon dilation (less than 30 mm diameter)

(If imaging guidance is performed, use 74360)

(For endoscopic dilation with balloon 30 mm diameter or larger, use 43458)

(For dilation without visualization, see 43450-43453)

(43221 has been deleted. To report, use 43200 or 43235)

(43222 has been deleted. To report, use 43200, 43202, 43235, or 43239)

(43223 has been deleted. To report, use 43215 or 43247)

(43224 has been deleted. To report, use 43217 or 43251)

(43225 has been deleted. To report, use 43499)

43226   with insertion of guide wire followed by dilation over guide wire

(For radiological supervision and interpretation, use 74360)

▲ **43227**   with control of bleeding (eg, injection, bipolar cautery, unipolar cautery, laser, heater probe, stapler, plasma coagulator)

43228   with ablation of tumor(s), polyp(s), or other lesion(s), not amenable to removal by hot biopsy forceps, bipolar cautery or snare technique

(For esophagoscopic photodynamic therapy, report 43228 in addition to 96570, 96571 as appropriate)

43231   with endoscopic ultrasound examination

43232   with transendoscopic ultrasound-guided intramural or transmural fine needle aspiration/biopsy(s)

(Do not report 76975 in conjunction with 43231, 43232)

(For interpretation of specimen, see 88172-88173)

43234   Upper gastrointestinal endoscopy, simple primary examination (eg, with small diameter flexible endoscope) (separate procedure)

43235   Upper gastrointestinal endoscopy including esophagus, stomach, and either the duodenum and/or jejunum as appropriate; diagnostic, with or without collection of specimen(s) by brushing or washing (separate procedure)

43239   with biopsy, single or multiple

▶(For upper gastrointestinal endoscopy with suturing of the esophagogastric junction, use Category III code 0008T)◀

43240   with transmural drainage of pseudocyst

43241   with transendoscopic intraluminal tube or catheter placement

43242   with transendoscopic ultrasound-guided intramural or transmural fine needle aspiration/biopsy(s)

(Do not report 76975 in conjunction with 43242)

(For interpretation of specimen, see 88172-88173)

43243   with injection sclerosis of esophageal and/or gastric varices

43244   with band ligation of esophageal and/or gastric varices

▲ **43245**   with dilation of gastric outlet for obstruction (eg, balloon, guide wire, bougie)

43246   with directed placement of percutaneous gastrostomy tube

(For radiological supervision and interpretation, use 74350)

43247   with removal of foreign body

(For radiological supervision and interpretation, use 74235)

43248   with insertion of guide wire followed by dilation of esophagus over guide wire

43249   with balloon dilation of esophagus (less than 30 mm diameter)

43250   with removal of tumor(s), polyp(s), or other lesion(s) by hot biopsy forceps or bipolar cautery

43251   with removal of tumor(s), polyp(s), or other lesion(s) by snare technique

43255   with control of bleeding, any method

43256   with transendoscopic stent placement (includes predilation)

43258   with ablation of tumor(s), polyp(s), or other lesion(s) not amenable to removal by hot biopsy forceps, bipolar cautery or snare technique

(For injection sclerosis of esophageal varices, use 43204 or 43243)

43259   with endoscopic ultrasound examination

(For radiological supervision and interpretation, use 76975)

43260   Endoscopic retrograde cholangiopancreatography (ERCP); diagnostic, with or without collection of specimen(s) by brushing or washing (separate procedure)

(For radiological supervision and interpretation, see 74328, 74329, 74330)

43261   with biopsy, single or multiple

43262   with sphincterotomy/papillotomy

(For radiological supervision and interpretation, see 74328, 74329, 74330)

43263   with pressure measurement of sphincter of Oddi (pancreatic duct or common bile duct)

(For radiological supervision and interpretation, see 74328, 74329, 74330)

⊘ =Modifier '-51' Exempt   ▶◀=New or Revised Text   ✚=Add-on Code   CPT 2002

▲ 43264   with endoscopic retrograde removal of calculus/ calculi from biliary and/or pancreatic ducts

(When done with sphincterotomy, also use 43262)

(For radiological supervision and interpretation, see 74328, 74329, 74330)

▲ 43265   with endoscopic retrograde destruction, lithotripsy of calculus/calculi, any method

(When done with sphincterotomy, also use 43262)

(For radiological supervision and interpretation, see 74328, 74329, 74330)

43267   with endoscopic retrograde insertion of nasobiliary or nasopancreatic drainage tube

(When done with sphincterotomy, also use 43262)

(For radiological supervision and interpretation, see 74328, 74329, 74330)

43268   with endoscopic retrograde insertion of tube or stent into bile or pancreatic duct

(When done with sphincterotomy, also use 43262)

(For radiological supervision and interpretation, see 74328, 74329, 74330)

43269   with endoscopic retrograde removal of foreign body and/or change of tube or stent

(When done with sphincterotomy, also use 43262)

(For radiological supervision and interpretation, see 74328, 74329, 74330)

43271   with endoscopic retrograde balloon dilation of ampulla, biliary and/or pancreatic duct(s)

(When done with sphincterotomy, also use 43262)

(For radiological supervision and interpretation, see 74328, 74329, 74330)

43272   with ablation of tumor(s), polyp(s), or other lesion(s) not amenable to removal by hot biopsy forceps, bipolar cautery or snare technique

(For radiological supervision and interpretation, see 74328, 74329, 74330)

Laparoscopy

Surgical laparoscopy always includes diagnostic laparoscopy. To report a diagnostic laparoscopy (peritoneoscopy) (separate procedure), use 49320.

43280   Laparoscopy, surgical, esophagogastric fundoplasty (eg, Nissen, Toupet procedures)

(For open approach, use 43324)

43289   Unlisted laparoscopy procedure, esophagus

Repair

43300   Esophagoplasty, (plastic repair or reconstruction), cervical approach; without repair of tracheoesophageal fistula

43305   with repair of tracheoesophageal fistula

43310   Esophagoplasty, (plastic repair or reconstruction), thoracic approach; without repair of tracheoesophageal fistula

43312   with repair of tracheoesophageal fistula

● 43313   Esophagoplasty for congenital defect, (plastic repair or reconstruction), thoracic approach; without repair of congenital tracheoesophageal fistula

● 43314   with repair of congenital tracheoesophageal fistula

43320   Esophagogastrostomy (cardioplasty), with or without vagotomy and pyloroplasty, transabdominal or transthoracic approach

(43321 has been deleted. To report, use 43320)

43324   Esophagogastric fundoplasty (eg, Nissen, Belsey IV, Hill procedures)

(For laparoscopic procedure, use 43280)

43325   Esophagogastric fundoplasty; with fundic patch (Thal-Nissen procedure)

(For cricopharyngeal myotomy, use 43030)

43326   with gastroplasty (eg, Collis)

43330   Esophagomyotomy (Heller type); abdominal approach

43331   thoracic approach

(For thoracoscopic esophagomyotomy, use 32665)

43340   Esophagojejunostomy (without total gastrectomy); abdominal approach

43341   thoracic approach

43350   Esophagostomy, fistulization of esophagus, external; abdominal approach

43351   thoracic approach

43352   cervical approach

43360   Gastrointestinal reconstruction for previous esophagectomy, for obstructing esophageal lesion or fistula, or for previous esophageal exclusion; with stomach, with or without pyloroplasty

▲ 43361   with colon interposition or small intestine reconstruction, including intestine mobilization, preparation, and anastomosis(es)

43400   Ligation, direct, esophageal varices

43401   Transection of esophagus with repair, for esophageal varices

43405	Ligation or stapling at gastroesophageal junction for pre-existing esophageal perforation
43410	Suture of esophageal wound or injury; cervical approach
43415	transthoracic or transabdominal approach
43420	Closure of esophagostomy or fistula; cervical approach
43425	transthoracic or transabdominal approach

(For repair of esophageal hiatal hernia, see 39520 et seq)

Manipulation

(For associated esophagogram, use 74220)

43450* Dilation of esophagus, by unguided sound or bougie, single or multiple passes

(43451 has been deleted. To report, use 43450)

43453 Dilation of esophagus, over guide wire

(For dilation with direct visualization, use 43220)

(43455 has been deleted. To report, see 43220, 43458, 74360)

43456 Dilation of esophagus, by balloon or dilator, retrograde

43458 Dilation of esophagus with balloon (30 mm diameter or larger) for achalasia

(For dilation with balloon less than 30 mm diameter, use 43220)

(For radiological supervision and interpretation, use 74360)

43460 Esophagogastric tamponade, with balloon (Sengstaaken type)

(For removal of esophageal foreign body by balloon catheter, see 43215, 43247, 74235)

Other Procedures

43496 Free jejunum transfer with microvascular anastomosis

(Do not report code 69990 in addition to code 43496)

43499 Unlisted procedure, esophagus

Stomach

Incision

43500 Gastrotomy; with exploration or foreign body removal

43501 with suture repair of bleeding ulcer

43502 with suture repair of pre-existing esophagogastric laceration (eg, Mallory-Weiss)

43510 with esophageal dilation and insertion of permanent intraluminal tube (eg, Celestin or Mousseaux-Barbin)

43520 Pyloromyotomy, cutting of pyloric muscle (Fredet-Ramstedt type operation)

Excision

43600 Biopsy of stomach; by capsule, tube, peroral (one or more specimens)

43605 by laparotomy

43610 Excision, local; ulcer or benign tumor of stomach

43611 malignant tumor of stomach

43620 Gastrectomy, total; with esophagoenterostomy

43621 with Roux-en-Y reconstruction

43622 with formation of intestinal pouch, any type

(43625 has been deleted. To report, use 43622)

(43630 has been deleted. To report, see 43631-43634)

43631 Gastrectomy, partial, distal; with gastroduodenostomy

43632 with gastrojejunostomy

43633 with Roux-en-Y reconstruction

43634 with formation of intestinal pouch

+ 43635 Vagotomy when performed with partial distal gastrectomy (List separately in addition to code(s) for primary procedure)

(Use 43635 in conjunction with codes 43631, 43632, 43633, 43634)

43638 Gastrectomy, partial, proximal, thoracic or abdominal approach including esophagogastrostomy, with vagotomy;

43639 with pyloroplasty or pyloromyotomy

(For regional thoracic lymphadenectomy, use 38746)

(For regional abdominal lymphadenectomy, use 38747)

43640 Vagotomy including pyloroplasty, with or without gastrostomy; truncal or selective

(For pyloroplasty, use 43800)

(For vagotomy, see 64752-64760)

43641 parietal cell (highly selective)

(For upper gastrointestinal endoscopy, see 43234-43259)

(43700 has been deleted. To report, use 43235)

(43702 has been deleted. To report, use 43239)

(43709 has been deleted. To report, use 43247)

(43711 has been deleted. To report, use 43251)

(43712 has been deleted. To report, use 43255)

(43714 has been deleted. To report, use 43258)

Laparoscopy

Surgical laparoscopy always includes diagnostic laparoscopy. To report a diagnostic laparoscopy (peritoneoscopy) (separate procedure), use 49320.

43651   Laparoscopy, surgical; transection of vagus nerves, truncal

43652   transection of vagus nerves, selective or highly selective

43653   gastrostomy, without construction of gastric tube (eg, Stamm procedure) (separate procedure)

43659   Unlisted laparoscopy procedure, stomach

Introduction

43750   Percutaneous placement of gastrostomy tube

(For radiological supervision and interpretation, use 74350)

43752   Naso- or oro-gastric tube placement, necessitating physician's skill

(If imaging guidance is performed, use 76000)

(For enteric tube placement, see 44500, 74340)

(Do not report 43752 in conjunction with critical care codes 99291-99292, or neonatal intensive care codes, 99295-99298)

43760*   Change of gastrostomy tube

(For endoscopic placement of gastrostomy tube, use 43246)

(For radiological supervision and interpretation, use 75984)

43761   Repositioning of the gastric feeding tube, any method, through the duodenum for enteric nutrition

▶(If imaging guidance is performed, use 75984)◀

(43765 has been deleted. To report, use 43760)

Other Procedures

43800   Pyloroplasty

(For pyloroplasty and vagotomy, use 43640)

43810   Gastroduodenostomy

43820   Gastrojejunostomy; without vagotomy

43825   with vagotomy, any type

43830   Gastrostomy, open; without construction of gastric tube (eg, Stamm procedure) (separate procedure)

43831   neonatal, for feeding

(For change of gastrostomy tube, use 43760)

43832   with construction of gastric tube (eg, Janeway procedure)

(43834 has been deleted. To report, use 43246)

43840   Gastrorrhaphy, suture of perforated duodenal or gastric ulcer, wound, or injury

43842   Gastric restrictive procedure, without gastric bypass, for morbid obesity; vertical-banded gastroplasty

43843   other than vertical-banded gastroplasty

(43844 has been deleted. To report, use 43847)

(43845 has been deleted. To report, see 43842, 43843)

43846   Gastric restrictive procedure, with gastric bypass for morbid obesity; with short limb (less than 100 cm) Roux-en-Y gastroenterostomy

▲**43847**   with small intestine reconstruction to limit absorption

43848   Revision of gastric restrictive procedure for morbid obesity (separate procedure)

43850   Revision of gastroduodenal anastomosis (gastroduodenostomy) with reconstruction; without vagotomy

43855   with vagotomy

▲**43860**   Revision of gastrojejunal anastomosis (gastrojejunostomy) with reconstruction, with or without partial gastrectomy or intestine resection; without vagotomy

43865   with vagotomy

43870   Closure of gastrostomy, surgical

43880   Closure of gastrocolic fistula

(43885 has been deleted)

43999   Unlisted procedure, stomach

Intestines (Except Rectum)

Incision

(44000 has been deleted)

44005   Enterolysis (freeing of intestinal adhesion) (separate procedure)

▶(Do not report 44005 in addition to 45136)◀

(For laparoscopic approach, use 44200)

44010   Duodenotomy, for exploration, biopsy(s), or foreign body removal

+ **44015**   Tube or needle catheter jejunostomy for enteral alimentation, intraoperative, any method (List separately in addition to primary procedure)

▲**44020**   Enterotomy, small intestine, other than duodenum; for exploration, biopsy(s), or foreign body removal

44021   for decompression (eg, Baker tube)

44025   Colotomy, for exploration, biopsy(s), or foreign body removal

(44040 has been deleted. To report, see 44602-44605)

44050 Reduction of volvulus, intussusception, internal hernia, by laparotomy

44055 Correction of malrotation by lysis of duodenal bands and/or reduction of midgut volvulus (eg, Ladd procedure)

(44060 has been deleted. To report, use 44799)

Excision

44100 Biopsy of intestine by capsule, tube, peroral (one or more specimens)

▲**44110** Excision of one or more lesions of small or large intestine not requiring anastomosis, exteriorization, or fistulization; single enterotomy

44111 multiple enterotomies

(44115 has been deleted. To report, use 44799)

44120 Enterectomy, resection of small intestine; single resection and anastomosis

▶(Do not report 44120 in addition to 45136)◀

✚ **44121** each additional resection and anastomosis (List separately in addition to code for primary procedure)

(Use 44121 in conjunction with code 44120)

44125 with enterostomy

● **44126** Enterectomy, resection of small intestine for congenital atresia, single resection and anastomosis of proximal segment of intestine; without tapering

● **44127** with tapering

✚ ● **44128** each additional resection and anastomosis (List separately in addition to code for primary procedure)

▶(Use 44128 in conjunction with codes 44126, 44127)◀

44130 Enteroenterostomy, anastomosis of intestine, with or without cutaneous enterostomy (separate procedure)

(44131 has been deleted)

44132 Donor enterectomy, open, with preparation and maintenance of allograft; from cadaver donor

44133 partial, from living donor

44135 Intestinal allotransplantation; from cadaver donor

44136 from living donor

✚ **44139** Mobilization (take-down) of splenic flexure performed in conjunction with partial colectomy (List separately in addition to primary procedure)

(Use 44139 in conjunction with codes 44140-44147)

44140 Colectomy, partial; with anastomosis

▶(For laparoscopic procedure, use 44204)◀

44141 with skin level cecostomy or colostomy

44143 with end colostomy and closure of distal segment (Hartmann type procedure)

44144 with resection, with colostomy or ileostomy and creation of mucofistula

44145 with coloproctostomy (low pelvic anastomosis)

44146 with coloproctostomy (low pelvic anastomosis), with colostomy

44147 abdominal and transanal approach

44150 Colectomy, total, abdominal, without proctectomy; with ileostomy or ileoproctostomy

44151 with continent ileostomy

44152 with rectal mucosectomy, ileoanal anastomosis, with or without loop ileostomy

44153 with rectal mucosectomy, ileoanal anastomosis, creation of ileal reservoir (S or J), with or without loop ileostomy

44155 Colectomy, total, abdominal, with proctectomy; with ileostomy

44156 with continent ileostomy

▲**44160** Colectomy, partial, with removal of terminal ileum with ileocolostomy

▶(For laparoscopic procedure, use 44205)◀

Laparoscopy

Surgical laparoscopy always includes diagnostic laparoscopy. To report a diagnostic laparoscopy (peritoneoscopy) (separate procedure), use 49320.

44200 Laparoscopy, surgical; enterolysis (freeing of intestinal adhesion) (separate procedure)

(For laparoscopy with salpingolysis, ovariolysis, use 58660)

44201 jejunostomy (eg, for decompression or feeding)

▲**44202** enterectomy, resection of small intestine, single resection and anastomosis

✚ ● **44203** each additional small intestine resection and anastomosis (List separately in addition to code for primary procedure)

▶(Use 44203 in conjunction with code 44202)◀

▶(For open procedure, see 44120, 44121)◀

● **44204** colectomy, partial, with anastomosis

▶(For open procedure, use 44140)◀

● **44205** colectomy, partial, with removal of terminal ileum with ileocolostomy

▶(For open procedure, use 44160)◀

44209 Unlisted laparoscopy procedure, intestine (except rectum)

⊘ =Modifier '-51' Exempt   ▶ ◀=New or Revised Text   ✚=Add-on Code   CPT 2002

Enterostomy—External Fistulization of Intestines

44300 Enterostomy or cecostomy, tube (eg, for decompression or feeding) (separate procedure)

(44305 has been deleted)

(44308 has been deleted. To report, use 44799)

44310 Ileostomy or jejunostomy, non-tube (separate procedure)

▶(Do not report 44310 in addition to 45136)◀

44312 Revision of ileostomy; simple (release of superficial scar) (separate procedure)

44314 complicated (reconstruction in-depth) (separate procedure)

44316 Continent ileostomy (Kock procedure) (separate procedure)

(For fiberoptic evaluation, use 44385)

44320 Colostomy or skin level cecostomy; (separate procedure)

▲ **44322** with multiple biopsies (eg, for congenital megacolon) (separate procedure)

44340 Revision of colostomy; simple (release of superficial scar) (separate procedure)

44345 complicated (reconstruction in-depth) (separate procedure)

44346 with repair of paracolostomy hernia (separate procedure)

Endoscopy, Small ▶Intestine◀ and Stomal

Surgical endoscopy always includes diagnostic endoscopy.

(For upper gastrointestinal endoscopy, see 43234-43258)

44360 Small intestinal endoscopy, enteroscopy beyond second portion of duodenum, not including ileum; diagnostic, with or without collection of specimen(s) by brushing or washing (separate procedure)

44361 with biopsy, single or multiple

44363 with removal of foreign body

44364 with removal of tumor(s), polyp(s), or other lesion(s) by snare technique

44365 with removal of tumor(s), polyp(s), or other lesion(s) by hot biopsy forceps or bipolar cautery

▲ **44366** with control of bleeding (eg, injection, bipolar cautery, unipolar cautery, laser, heater probe, stapler, plasma coagulator)

44369 with ablation of tumor(s), polyp(s), or other lesion(s) not amenable to removal by hot biopsy forceps, bipolar cautery or snare technique

44370 with transendoscopic stent placement (includes predilation)

44372 with placement of percutaneous jejunostomy tube

44373 with conversion of percutaneous gastrostomy tube to percutaneous jejunostomy tube

(44375 has been deleted. To report, use 43235)

44376 Small intestinal endoscopy, enteroscopy beyond second portion of duodenum, including ileum; diagnostic, with or without collection of specimen(s) by brushing or washing (separate procedure)

44377 with biopsy, single or multiple

▲ **44378** with control of bleeding (eg, injection, bipolar cautery, unipolar cautery, laser, heater probe, stapler, plasma coagulator)

44379 with transendoscopic stent placement (includes predilation)

44380 Ileoscopy, through stoma; diagnostic, with or without collection of specimen(s) by brushing or washing (separate procedure)

44382 with biopsy, single or multiple

44383 with transendoscopic stent placement (includes predilation)

44385 Endoscopic evaluation of small intestinal (abdominal or pelvic) pouch; diagnostic, with or without collection of specimen(s) by brushing or washing (separate procedure)

44386 with biopsy, single or multiple

44388 Colonoscopy through stoma; diagnostic, with or without collection of specimen(s) by brushing or washing (separate procedure)

44389 with biopsy, single or multiple

44390 with removal of foreign body

▲ **44391** with control of bleeding (eg, injection, bipolar cautery, unipolar cautery, laser, heater probe, stapler, plasma coagulator)

44392 with removal of tumor(s), polyp(s), or other lesion(s) by hot biopsy forceps or bipolar cautery

44393 with ablation of tumor(s), polyp(s), or other lesion(s) not amenable to removal by hot biopsy forceps, bipolar cautery or snare technique

44394 with removal of tumor(s), polyp(s), or other lesion(s) by snare technique

(For colonoscopy per rectum, see 45330-45385)

(44400, 44405 have been deleted. To report, use 44799)

44397 with transendoscopic stent placement (includes predilation)

Introduction

⊘ **44500** Introduction of long gastrointestinal tube (eg, Miller-Abbott) (separate procedure)

(For radiological supervision and interpretation, use 74340)

(For naso- or oro-gastric tube placement, use 43752)

Repair

(44600 has been deleted. To report, see 44602, 44604)

44602 Suture of small intestine (enterorrhaphy) for perforated ulcer, diverticulum, wound, injury or rupture; single perforation

44603 multiple perforations

44604 Suture of large intestine (colorrhaphy) for perforated ulcer, diverticulum, wound, injury or rupture (single or multiple perforations); without colostomy

44605 with colostomy

(44610 has been deleted. To report, see 44603, 44604)

44615 Intestinal stricturoplasty (enterotomy and enterorrhaphy) with or without dilation, for intestinal obstruction

44620 Closure of enterostomy, large or small intestine;

44625 with resection and anastomosis other than colorectal

44626 with resection and colorectal anastomosis (eg, closure of Hartmann type procedure)

44640 Closure of intestinal cutaneous fistula

44650 Closure of enteroenteric or enterocolic fistula

44660 Closure of enterovesical fistula; without intestinal or bladder resection

▲ **44661** with intestine and/or bladder resection

(For closure of renocolic fistula, see 50525, 50526)

(For closure of gastrocolic fistula, use 43880)

(For closure of rectovesical fistula, see 45800, 45805)

44680 Intestinal plication (separate procedure)

Other Procedures

▲ **44700** Exclusion of small intestine from pelvis by mesh or other prosthesis, or native tissue (eg, bladder or omentum)

(For therapeutic radiation clinical treatment, see **Radiation Oncology** section)

44799 Unlisted procedure, intestine

Meckel's Diverticulum and the Mesentery

Excision

44800 Excision of Meckel's diverticulum (diverticulectomy) or omphalomesenteric duct

44820 Excision of lesion of mesentery (separate procedure)

(With intestine resection, see 44120 or 44140 et seq)

Suture

44850 Suture of mesentery (separate procedure)

(For reduction and repair of internal hernia, use 44050)

Other Procedures

44899 Unlisted procedure, Meckels diverticulum and the mesentery

Appendix

Incision

44900 Incision and drainage of appendiceal abscess; open

44901 percutaneous

(For radiological supervision and interpretation, use 75989)

Excision

44950 Appendectomy;

(Incidental appendectomy during intra-abdominal surgery does not usually warrant a separate identification. If necessary to report, add modifier '-52')

✚ **44955** when done for indicated purpose at time of other major procedure (not as separate procedure) (List separately in addition to code for primary procedure)

44960 for ruptured appendix with abscess or generalized peritonitis

Laparoscopy

Surgical laparoscopy always includes diagnostic laparoscopy. To report a diagnostic laparoscopy (peritoneoscopy) (separate procedure), use 49320.

44970 Laparoscopy, surgical, appendectomy

44979 Unlisted laparoscopy procedure, appendix

⊘ =Modifier '-51' Exempt ▶ ◀ =New or Revised Text ✚ =Add-on Code CPT 2002

Rectum

Incision

45000   Transrectal drainage of pelvic abscess

45005   Incision and drainage of submucosal abscess, rectum

45020   Incision and drainage of deep supralevator, pelvirectal, or retrorectal abscess

(See also 46050, 46060)

Excision

45100   Biopsy of anorectal wall, anal approach (eg, congenital megacolon)

(45105 has been deleted. To report, use 45100)

(For endoscopic biopsy, use 45305)

45108   Anorectal myomectomy

45110   Proctectomy; complete, combined abdominoperineal, with colostomy

45111   partial resection of rectum, transabdominal approach

45112   Proctectomy, combined abdominoperineal, pull-through procedure (eg, colo-anal anastomosis)

(For colo-anal anastomosis with colonic reservoir or pouch, use 45119)

45113   Proctectomy, partial, with rectal mucosectomy, ileoanal anastomosis, creation of ileal reservoir (S or J), with or without loop ileostomy

45114   Proctectomy, partial, with anastomosis; abdominal and transsacral approach

45116   transsacral approach only (Kraske type)

45119   Proctectomy, combined abdominoperineal pull-through procedure (eg, colo-anal anastomosis), with creation of colonic reservoir (eg, J-pouch), with or without proximal diverting ostomy

45120   Proctectomy, complete (for congenital megacolon), abdominal and perineal approach; with pull-through procedure and anastomosis (eg, Swenson, Duhamel, or Soave type operation)

45121   with subtotal or total colectomy, with multiple biopsies

45123   Proctectomy, partial, without anastomosis, perineal approach

45126   Pelvic exenteration for colorectal malignancy, with proctectomy (with or without colostomy), with removal of bladder and ureteral transplantations, and/or hysterectomy, or cervicectomy, with or without removal of tube(s), with or without removal of ovary(s), or any combination thereof

45130   Excision of rectal procidentia, with anastomosis; perineal approach

45135   abdominal and perineal approach

● **45136**   Excision of ileoanal reservoir with ileostomy

▶(Do not report 45136 in addition to 44005, 44120, 44310)◀

45150   Division of stricture of rectum

45160   Excision of rectal tumor by proctotomy, transsacral or transcoccygeal approach

45170   Excision of rectal tumor, transanal approach

(45180, 45181 have been deleted. To report, see 45170, 45190)

Destruction

▲ **45190**   Destruction of rectal tumor (eg, electrodessication, electrosurgery, laser ablation, laser resection, cryosurgery) transanal approach

Endoscopy

Definitions

Proctosigmoidoscopy is the examination of the rectum and sigmoid colon.

Sigmoidoscopy is the examination of the entire rectum, sigmoid colon and may include examination of a portion of the descending colon.

Colonoscopy is the examination of the entire colon, from the rectum to the cecum, and may include the examination of the terminal ileum.

For an incomplete colonoscopy, with full preparation for a colonoscopy, use a colonoscopy code with the modifier '-52' and provide documentation.

Surgical endoscopy always includes diagnostic endoscopy.

45300   Proctosigmoidoscopy, rigid; diagnostic, with or without collection of specimen(s) by brushing or washing (separate procedure)

(45302 has been deleted. To report, use 45300)

▲ **45303**   with dilation (eg, balloon, guide wire, bougie)

(For radiological supervision and interpretation, use 74360)

45305   with biopsy, single or multiple

45307   with removal of foreign body

45308   with removal of single tumor, polyp, or other lesion by hot biopsy forceps or bipolar cautery

45309   with removal of single tumor, polyp, or other lesion by snare technique

(45310 has been deleted. To report, see 45308, 45309)

45315   with removal of multiple tumors, polyps, or other lesions by hot biopsy forceps, bipolar cautery or snare technique

▲ **45317**   with control of bleeding (eg, injection, bipolar cautery, unipolar cautery, laser, heater probe, stapler, plasma coagulator)

(45319 has been deleted. To report, use 45999)

45320   with ablation of tumor(s), polyp(s), or other lesion(s) not amenable to removal by hot biopsy forceps, bipolar cautery or snare technique (eg, laser)

45321   with decompression of volvulus

(45325 colonoscopy has been renumbered 45355 without change in terminology)

45327   with transendoscopic stent placement (includes predilation)

45330   Sigmoidoscopy, flexible; diagnostic, with or without collection of specimen(s) by brushing or washing (separate procedure)

45331   with biopsy, single or multiple

45332   with removal of foreign body

45333   with removal of tumor(s), polyp(s), or other lesion(s) by hot biopsy forceps or bipolar cautery

▲ **45334**   with control of bleeding (eg, injection, bipolar cautery, unipolar cautery, laser, heater probe, stapler, plasma coagulator)

(45336 has been deleted. To report, use 45339)

45337   with decompression of volvulus, any method

45338   with removal of tumor(s), polyp(s), or other lesion(s) by snare technique

45339   with ablation of tumor(s), polyp(s), or other lesion(s) not amenable to removal by hot biopsy forceps, bipolar cautery or snare technique

45341   with endoscopic ultrasound examination

45342   with transendoscopic ultrasound guided intramural or transmural fine needle aspiration/biopsy(s)

(Do not report 76975 in conjunction with codes 45341, 45342)

(For interpretation of specimen, see 88172-88173)

(For transrectal ultrasound utilizing rigid probe device, use 76872)

45345   with transendoscopic stent placement (includes predilation)

45355   Colonoscopy, rigid or flexible, transabdominal via colotomy, single or multiple

(45360-45372 have been deleted. To report, see 45330-45337)

45378   Colonoscopy, flexible, proximal to splenic flexure; diagnostic, with or without collection of specimen(s) by brushing or washing, with or without colon decompression (separate procedure)

45379   with removal of foreign body

45380   with biopsy, single or multiple

▲ **45382**   with control of bleeding (eg, injection, bipolar cautery, unipolar cautery, laser, heater probe, stapler, plasma coagulator)

45383   with ablation of tumor(s), polyp(s), or other lesion(s) not amenable to removal by hot biopsy forceps, bipolar cautery or snare technique

45384   with removal of tumor(s), polyp(s), or other lesion(s) by hot biopsy forceps or bipolar cautery

45385   with removal of tumor(s), polyp(s), or other lesion(s) by snare technique

(45386 has been deleted. To report, use 44799)

(For small ▶intestine◀ and stomal endoscopy, see 44360-44393)

45387   with transendoscopic stent placement (includes predilation)

Repair

45500   Proctoplasty; for stenosis

45505   for prolapse of mucous membrane

45520   Perirectal injection of sclerosing solution for prolapse

(45521 has been deleted)

45540   Proctopexy for prolapse; abdominal approach

45541   perineal approach

45550   Proctopexy combined with sigmoid resection, abdominal approach

45560   Repair of rectocele (separate procedure)

(For repair of rectocele with posterior colporrhaphy, use 57250)

45562   Exploration, repair, and presacral drainage for rectal injury;

45563   with colostomy

45800   Closure of rectovesical fistula;

45805   with colostomy

45820   Closure of rectourethral fistula;

45825   with colostomy

(For rectovaginal fistula closure, see 57300-57308)

Manipulation

45900* Reduction of procidentia (separate procedure) under anesthesia

45905* Dilation of anal sphincter (separate procedure) under anesthesia other than local

45910 Dilation of rectal stricture (separate procedure) under anesthesia other than local

45915* Removal of fecal impaction or foreign body (separate procedure) under anesthesia

Other Procedures

45999 Unlisted procedure, rectum

● **46020** Placement of seton

▶(Do not report 46020 in addition to 46060, 46280, 46600)◀

Anus

Incision

(46000 has been deleted. To report, use 46270)

46030* Removal of anal seton, other marker

(46032 has been deleted. To report, use 46999)

46040 Incision and drainage of ischiorectal and/or perirectal abscess (separate procedure)

46045 Incision and drainage of intramural, intramuscular, or submucosal abscess, transanal, under anesthesia

46050* Incision and drainage, perianal abscess, superficial

(See also 45020, 46060)

46060 Incision and drainage of ischiorectal or intramural abscess, with fistulectomy or fistulotomy, submuscular, with or without placement of seton

▶(Do not report 46060 in addition to 46020)◀

(See also 45020)

46070 Incision, anal septum (infant)

(For anoplasty, see 46700-46705)

46080* Sphincterotomy, anal, division of sphincter (separate procedure)

46083 Incision of thrombosed hemorrhoid, external

Excision

46200 Fissurectomy, with or without sphincterotomy

46210 Cryptectomy; single

46211 multiple (separate procedure)

46220 Papillectomy or excision of single tag, anus (separate procedure)

46221 Hemorrhoidectomy, by simple ligature (eg, rubber band)

46230 Excision of external hemorrhoid tags and/or multiple papillae

46250 Hemorrhoidectomy, external, complete

46255 Hemorrhoidectomy, internal and external, simple;

46257 with fissurectomy

46258 with fistulectomy, with or without fissurectomy

46260 Hemorrhoidectomy, internal and external, complex or extensive;

46261 with fissurectomy

46262 with fistulectomy, with or without fissurectomy

46270 Surgical treatment of anal fistula (fistulectomy/fistulotomy); subcutaneous

46275 submuscular

46280 complex or multiple, with or without placement of seton

▶(Do not report 46280 in addition to 46020)◀

(46281 has been renumbered to 46288 without change in terminology)

46285 second stage

46288 Closure of anal fistula with rectal advancement flap

46320* Enucleation or excision of external thrombotic hemorrhoid

Introduction

46500* Injection of sclerosing solution, hemorrhoids

(46510, 46530 have been deleted. To report, use 46999)

Endoscopy

Surgical endoscopy always includes diagnostic endoscopy.

46600 Anoscopy; diagnostic, with or without collection of specimen(s) by brushing or washing (separate procedure)

▶(Do not report 46600 in addition to 46020)◀

(46602 has been deleted. To report, use 46600)

▲ **46604** with dilation (eg, balloon, guide wire, bougie)

46606 with biopsy, single or multiple

46608 with removal of foreign body

46610 with removal of single tumor, polyp, or other lesion by hot biopsy forceps or bipolar cautery

46611 with removal of single tumor, polyp, or other lesion by snare technique

46612 with removal of multiple tumors, polyps, or other lesions by hot biopsy forceps, bipolar cautery or snare technique

▲ **46614**   with control of bleeding (eg, injection, bipolar cautery, unipolar cautery, laser, heater probe, stapler, plasma coagulator)

46615   with ablation of tumor(s), polyp(s), or other lesion(s) not amenable to removal by hot biopsy forceps, bipolar cautery or snare technique

Repair

46700   Anoplasty, plastic operation for stricture; adult

46705   infant

(For simple incision of anal septum, use 46070)

46715   Repair of low imperforate anus; with anoperineal fistula (cut-back procedure)

46716   with transposition of anoperineal or anovestibular fistula

46730   Repair of high imperforate anus without fistula; perineal or sacroperineal approach

46735   combined transabdominal and sacroperineal approaches

46740   Repair of high imperforate anus with rectourethral or rectovaginal fistula; perineal or sacroperineal approach

46742   combined transabdominal and sacroperineal approaches

46744   Repair of cloacal anomaly by anorectovaginoplasty and urethroplasty, sacroperineal approach

46746   Repair of cloacal anomaly by anorectovaginoplasty and urethroplasty, combined abdominal and sacroperineal approach;

46748   with vaginal lengthening by intestinal graft or pedicle flaps

46750   Sphincteroplasty, anal, for incontinence or prolapse; adult

46751   child

46753   Graft (Thiersch operation) for rectal incontinence and/or prolapse

46754   Removal of Thiersch wire or suture, anal canal

46760   Sphincteroplasty, anal, for incontinence, adult; muscle transplant

46761   levator muscle imbrication (Park posterior anal repair)

46762   implantation artificial sphincter

Destruction

46900*   Destruction of lesion(s), anus (eg, condyloma, papilloma, molluscum contagiosum, herpetic vesicle), simple; chemical

46910*   electrodesiccation

46916   cryosurgery

46917   laser surgery

(46920 has been deleted. To report, use 46922)

46922   surgical excision

▲ **46924**   Destruction of lesion(s), anus (eg, condyloma, papilloma, molluscum contagiosum, herpetic vesicle), extensive (eg, laser surgery, electrosurgery, cryosurgery, chemosurgery)

(46930 has been deleted. To report, use 46924)

(46932 has been deleted. To report, use 46916)

(46933 has been deleted. To report, use 46924)

46934   Destruction of hemorrhoids, any method; internal

46935   external

46936   internal and external

46937   Cryosurgery of rectal tumor; benign

46938   malignant

▲ **46940**   Curettage or cautery of anal fissure, including dilation of anal sphincter (separate procedure); initial

46942   subsequent

Suture

46945   Ligation of internal hemorrhoids; single procedure

46946   multiple procedures

Other Procedures

46999   Unlisted procedure, anus

Liver

Incision

47000*   Biopsy of liver, needle; percutaneous

►(If imaging guidance is performed,◄ see 76003, 76360, ►76393,◄ 76942)

✛ **47001**   when done for indicated purpose at time of other major procedure (List separately in addition to code for primary procedure)

►(If imaging guidance is performed,◄ see 76003, 76942)

►(For fine needle aspiration in conjunction with 47000, 47001, see 10021, 10022)◄

►(For evaluation of fine needle aspirate in conjunction with 47000, 47001, see 88172, 88173)◄

47010   Hepatotomy; for open drainage of abscess or cyst, one or two stages

47011   for percutaneous drainage of abscess or cyst, one or two stages

(For radiological supervision and interpretation, use 75989)

47015   Laparotomy, with aspiration and/or injection of hepatic parasitic (eg, amoebic or echinococcal) cyst(s) or abscess(es)

Excision

47100   Biopsy of liver, wedge

47120   Hepatectomy, resection of liver; partial lobectomy

47122   trisegmentectomy

47125   total left lobectomy

47130   total right lobectomy

47133   Donor hepatectomy, with preparation and maintenance of allograft; from cadaver donor

47134   partial, from living donor

47135   Liver allotransplantation; orthotopic, partial or whole, from cadaver or living donor, any age

47136   heterotopic, partial or whole, from cadaver or living donor, any age

Repair

47300   Marsupialization of cyst or abscess of liver

47350   Management of liver hemorrhage; simple suture of liver wound or injury

(47355 has been deleted)

47360   complex suture of liver wound or injury, with or without hepatic artery ligation

47361   exploration of hepatic wound, extensive debridement, coagulation and/or suture, with or without packing of liver

47362   re-exploration of hepatic wound for removal of packing

►Laparoscopy◄

►Surgical laparoscopy always includes diagnostic laparoscopy. To report a diagnostic laparoscopy (peritoneoscopy) (separate procedure), use 49320◄

● **47370**   Laparoscopy, surgical, ablation of one or more liver tumor(s); radiofrequency

►(For imaging guidance, use 76490)◄

● **47371**   cryosurgical

►(For imaging guidance, use 76490)◄

47379   Unlisted laparoscopic procedure, liver

Other Procedures

● **47380**   Ablation, open, of one or more liver tumor(s); radiofrequency

►(For imaging guidance, use 76490)◄

● **47381**   cryosurgical

►(For imaging guidance, use 76490)◄

● **47382**   Ablation, one or more liver tumor(s), percutaneous, radiofrequency

►(For imaging guidance and monitoring, see code 76362, 76394, or 76490)◄

47399   Unlisted procedure, liver

Biliary Tract

Incision

47400   Hepaticotomy or hepaticostomy with exploration, drainage, or removal of calculus

47420   Choledochotomy or choledochostomy with exploration, drainage, or removal of calculus, with or without cholecystotomy; without transduodenal sphincterotomy or sphincteroplasty

47425   with transduodenal sphincterotomy or sphincteroplasty

(47440 has been deleted)

47460   Transduodenal sphincterotomy or sphincteroplasty, with or without transduodenal extraction of calculus (separate procedure)

47480   Cholecystotomy or cholecystostomy with exploration, drainage, or removal of calculus (separate procedure)

47490   Percutaneous cholecystostomy

(For radiological supervision and interpretation, use 75989)

Introduction

47500   Injection procedure for percutaneous transhepatic cholangiography

(For radiological supervision and interpretation, use 74320)

47505   Injection procedure for cholangiography through an existing catheter (eg, percutaneous transhepatic or T-tube)

(For radiological supervision and interpretation, use 74305)

47510   Introduction of percutaneous transhepatic catheter for biliary drainage

(For radiological supervision and interpretation, use 75980)

47511   Introduction of percutaneous transhepatic stent for internal and external biliary drainage

(For radiological supervision and interpretation, use 75982)

47525   Change of percutaneous biliary drainage catheter

(For radiological supervision and interpretation, use 75984)

47530   Revision and/or reinsertion of transhepatic tube

(For radiological supervision and interpretation, use 75984)

Endoscopy

Surgical endoscopy always includes diagnostic endoscopy.

+ 47550   Biliary endoscopy, intraoperative (choledochoscopy) (List separately in addition to code for primary procedure)

47552   Biliary endoscopy, percutaneous via T-tube or other tract; diagnostic, with or without collection of specimen(s) by brushing and/or washing (separate procedure)

47553   with biopsy, single or multiple

▲47554   with removal of calculus/calculi

47555   with dilation of biliary duct stricture(s) without stent

(For ERCP, see 43260-43272, 74363)

(If imaging guidance is performed, see 74363, 75982)

47556   with dilation of biliary duct stricture(s) with stent

(If imaging guidance is performed, see 74363, 75982)

Laparoscopy

Surgical laparoscopy always includes diagnostic laparoscopy. To report a diagnostic laparoscopy (peritoneoscopy) (separate procedure), use 49320.

47560   Laparoscopy, surgical; with guided transhepatic cholangiography, without biopsy

47561   with guided transhepatic cholangiography with biopsy

47562   cholecystectomy

47563   cholecystectomy with cholangiography

47564   cholecystectomy with exploration of common duct

47570   cholecystoenterostomy

47579   Unlisted laparoscopy procedure, biliary tract

Excision

47600   Cholecystectomy;

47605   with cholangiography

(For laparoscopic approach, see 47562-47564)

47610   Cholecystectomy with exploration of common duct;

(47611 has been deleted. To report, use 47610 and 47550)

47612   with choledochoenterostomy

47620   with transduodenal sphincterotomy or sphincteroplasty, with or without cholangiography

47630   Biliary duct stone extraction, percutaneous via T-tube tract, basket, or snare (eg, Burhenne technique)

(For radiological supervision and interpretation, use 74327)

47700   Exploration for congenital atresia of bile ducts, without repair, with or without liver biopsy, with or without cholangiography

47701   Portoenterostomy (eg, Kasai procedure)

(47710 has been deleted. To report, see 47711, 47712)

47711   Excision of bile duct tumor, with or without primary repair of bile duct; extrahepatic

47712   intrahepatic

(For anastomosis, see 47760-47800)

47715   Excision of choledochal cyst

47716   Anastomosis, choledochal cyst, without excision

Repair

47720   Cholecystoenterostomy; direct

(For laparoscopic approach, use 47570)

47721   with gastroenterostomy

47740   Roux-en-Y

47741   Roux-en-Y with gastroenterostomy

47760   Anastomosis, of extrahepatic biliary ducts and gastrointestinal tract

47765   Anastomosis, of intrahepatic ducts and gastrointestinal tract

47780   Anastomosis, Roux-en-Y, of extrahepatic biliary ducts and gastrointestinal tract

47785   Anastomosis, Roux-en-Y, of intrahepatic biliary ducts and gastrointestinal tract

47800   Reconstruction, plastic, of extrahepatic biliary ducts with end-to-end anastomosis

47801   Placement of choledochal stent

47802   U-tube hepaticoenterostomy

(47810 has been deleted. To report, use 47999)

(47850, 47855 have been deleted. To report, use 47999)

47900   Suture of extrahepatic biliary duct for pre-existing injury (separate procedure)

Other Procedures

47999   Unlisted procedure, biliary tract

Pancreas

(For peroral pancreatic endoscopic procedures, see 43260-43272)

Incision

48000   Placement of drains, peripancreatic, for acute pancreatitis;

48001   with cholecystostomy, gastrostomy, and jejunostomy

48005   Resection or debridement of pancreas and peripancreatic tissue for acute necrotizing pancreatitis

48020   Removal of pancreatic calculus

Excision

▲ **48100**   Biopsy of pancreas, open (eg, fine needle aspiration, needle core biopsy, wedge biopsy)

48102*   Biopsy of pancreas, percutaneous needle

(For radiological supervision and interpretation, see 76003, 76360, ►76393,◄ 76942)

►(For fine needle aspiration, use 10022)◄

►(For evaluation of fine needle aspirate, see 88172, 88173)◄

48120   Excision of lesion of pancreas (eg, cyst, adenoma)

48140   Pancreatectomy, distal subtotal, with or without splenectomy; without pancreaticojejunostomy

48145   with pancreaticojejunostomy

48146   Pancreatectomy, distal, near-total with preservation of duodenum (Child-type procedure)

48148   Excision of ampulla of Vater

48150   Pancreatectomy, proximal subtotal with total duodenectomy, partial gastrectomy, choledochoenterostomy and gastrojejunostomy (Whipple-type procedure); with pancreatojejunostomy

(48151 has been deleted. To report, use 48146)

48152   without pancreatojejunostomy

48153   Pancreatectomy, proximal subtotal with near-total duodenectomy, choledochoenterostomy and duodenojejunostomy (pylorus-sparing, Whipple-type procedure); with pancreatojejunostomy

48154   without pancreatojejunostomy

48155   Pancreatectomy, total

▲ **48160**   Pancreatectomy, total or subtotal, with autologous transplantation of pancreas or pancreatic islet cells

48180   Pancreaticojejunostomy, side-to-side anastomosis (Puestow-type operation)

Introduction

✛ **48400**   Injection procedure for intraoperative pancreatography (List separately in addition to code for primary procedure)

(For radiological supervision and interpretation, see 74300-74305)

Repair

▲ **48500**   Marsupialization of pancreatic cyst

48510   External drainage, pseudocyst of pancreas; open

48511   percutaneous

(For radiological supervision and interpretation, use 75989)

48520   Internal anastomosis of pancreatic cyst to gastrointestinal tract; direct

48540   Roux-en-Y

▲ **48545**   Pancreatorrhaphy for injury

▲ **48547**   Duodenal exclusion with gastrojejunostomy for pancreatic injury

Pancreas Transplantation

48550   Donor pancreatectomy, with preparation and maintenance of allograft from cadaver donor, with or without duodenal segment for transplantation

48554   Transplantation of pancreatic allograft

48556   Removal of transplanted pancreatic allograft

Other Procedures

48999   Unlisted procedure, pancreas

Abdomen, Peritoneum, and Omentum

Incision

49000   Exploratory laparotomy, exploratory celiotomy with or without biopsy(s) (separate procedure)

(To report wound exploration due to penetrating trauma without laparotomy, use 20102)

49002   Reopening of recent laparotomy

(To report re-exploration of hepatic wound for removal of packing, use 47362)

49010   Exploration, retroperitoneal area with or without biopsy(s) (separate procedure)

(To report wound exploration due to penetrating trauma without laparotomy, use 20102)

49020 Drainage of peritoneal abscess or localized peritonitis, exclusive of appendiceal abscess; open

(For appendiceal abscess, use 44900)

49021 percutaneous

(For radiological supervision and interpretation, use 75989)

49040 Drainage of subdiaphragmatic or subphrenic abscess; open

49041 percutaneous

(For radiological supervision and interpretation, use 75989)

49060 Drainage of retroperitoneal abscess; open

49061 percutaneous

(For laparoscopic drainage, use 49323)

(For radiological supervision and interpretation, use 75989)

49062 Drainage of extraperitoneal lymphocele to peritoneal cavity, open

49080* Peritoneocentesis, abdominal paracentesis, or peritoneal lavage (diagnostic or therapeutic); initial

49081* subsequent

▶(If imaging guidance is performed, see 76360, 76942)◀

49085 Removal of peritoneal foreign body from peritoneal cavity

(For lysis of intestinal adhesions, use 44005)

Excision, Destruction

49180* Biopsy, abdominal or retroperitoneal mass, percutaneous needle

▶(If imaging guidance is performed,◀ see 76003, 76360, ▶76393,◀ 76942)

▶(For fine needle aspiration, use 10021 or 10022)◀

▶(For evaluation of fine needle aspirate, see 88172, 88173)◀

49200 Excision or destruction by any method of intra-abdominal or retroperitoneal tumors or cysts or endometriomas;

49201 extensive

49215 Excision of presacral or sacrococcygeal tumor

▲ **49220** Staging laparotomy for Hodgkins disease or lymphoma (includes splenectomy, needle or open biopsies of both liver lobes, possibly also removal of abdominal nodes, abdominal node and/or bone marrow biopsies, ovarian repositioning)

49250 Umbilectomy, omphalectomy, excision of umbilicus (separate procedure)

49255 Omentectomy, epiploectomy, resection of omentum (separate procedure)

(49300 has been deleted. To report, use 49320)

(49301 has been deleted. To report, use 49321)

(49302 has been deleted. To report, use 47560)

(49303 has been deleted. To report, use 47561)

(49310 has been deleted. To report, use 47562)

(49311 has been deleted. To report, use 47563)

(49315 has been deleted. To report, use 44970)

Laparoscopy

Surgical laparoscopy always includes diagnostic laparoscopy. To report a diagnostic laparoscopy (peritoneoscopy), (separate procedure), use 49320.

For laparoscopic fulguration or excision of lesions of the ovary, pelvic viscera, or peritoneal surface use 58662.

49320 Laparoscopy, abdomen, peritoneum, and omentum, diagnostic, with or without collection of specimen(s) by brushing or washing (separate procedure)

49321 Laparoscopy, surgical; with biopsy (single or multiple)

49322 with aspiration of cavity or cyst (eg, ovarian cyst) (single or multiple)

49323 with drainage of lymphocele to peritoneal cavity

(For percutaneous or open drainage, see 49060, 49061)

49329 Unlisted laparoscopy procedure, abdomen, peritoneum and omentum

Introduction, Revision, and/or Removal

49400* Injection of air or contrast into peritoneal cavity (separate procedure)

(For radiological supervision and interpretation, use 74190)

(49401 has been deleted. To report, use 49400)

49420* Insertion of intraperitoneal cannula or catheter for drainage or dialysis; temporary

49421 permanent

49422 Removal of permanent intraperitoneal cannula or catheter

(For removal of a temporary catheter/cannula, use appropriate E/M code)

49423 Exchange of previously placed abscess or cyst drainage catheter under radiological guidance (separate procedure)

(For radiological supervision and interpretation, use 75984)

▲ **49424** Contrast injection for assessment of abscess or cyst via previously placed drainage catheter or tube (separate procedure)

(For radiological supervision and interpretation, use 76080)

⊘ =Modifier '-51' Exempt ▶ ◀=New or Revised Text ✛ =Add-on Code CPT 2002

49425	Insertion of peritoneal-venous shunt
49426	Revision of peritoneal-venous shunt
	(For shunt patency test, use 78291)
49427	Injection procedure (eg, contrast media) for evaluation of previously placed peritoneal-venous shunt
	(For radiological supervision and interpretation, see 75809, 78291)
49428	Ligation of peritoneal-venous shunt
49429	Removal of peritoneal-venous shunt
	(49430, 49440 have been deleted. To report, use 49999)

Repair

Hernioplasty, Herniorrhaphy, Herniotomy

The hernia repair codes in this section are categorized primarily by the type of hernia (inguinal, femoral, incisional, etc).

Some types of hernias are further categorized as "initial" or "recurrent" based on whether or not the hernia has required previous repair(s).

Additional variables accounted for by some of the codes include patient age and clinical presentation (reducible vs. incarcerated or strangulated).

With the exception of the incisional hernia repairs (see 49560-49566) the use of mesh or other prostheses is not separately reported.

The excision/repair of strangulated organs or structures such as testicle(s), intestine, ovaries are reported by using the appropriate code for the excision/repair (eg, 44120, 54520, and 58940) in addition to the appropriate code for the repair of the strangulated hernia.

(For reduction and repair of intra-abdominal hernia, use 44050)

(For debridement of abdominal wall, see 11042, 11043)

(All codes for bilateral procedures in hernia repair have been deleted. To report, add modifier '-50')

● 49491 Repair, initial inguinal hernia, preterm infant (less than 37 weeks gestation at birth), performed from birth up to 50 weeks post-conceptual age, with or without hydrocelectomy; reducible

● 49492   incarcerated or strangulated

►(Post-conceptual age equals gestational age at birth plus age of infant in weeks at the time of the hernia repair. Initial inguinal hernia repairs that are performed on preterm infants who are over 50 weeks postconceptual age and under age 6 months at the time of surgery, should be reported using codes 49495, 49496)◄

▲ 49495 Repair, initial inguinal hernia, full term infant under age 6 months, or preterm infant over 50 weeks postconceptual age and under age 6 months at the time of surgery, with or without hydrocelectomy; reducible

49496   incarcerated or strangulated

►(Post-conceptual age equals gestational age at birth plus age in weeks at the time of the hernia repair. Initial inguinal hernia repairs that are performed on preterm infants who are under or up to 50 weeks postconceptual age but under 6 months of age since birth, should be reported using codes 49491, 49492. Inguinal hernia repairs on infants age 6 months to under 5 years should be reported using codes 49500-49501)◄

49500 Repair initial inguinal hernia, age 6 months to under 5 years, with or without hydrocelectomy; reducible

49501   incarcerated or strangulated

49505 Repair initial inguinal hernia, age 5 years or over; reducible

49507   incarcerated or strangulated

(49510 has been deleted. To report, see 49505 or 49507 and 54520)

(49515 has been deleted. To report, see 49505 or 49507 and 54840 or 55040)

49520 Repair recurrent inguinal hernia, any age; reducible

49521   incarcerated or strangulated

49525 Repair inguinal hernia, sliding, any age

(49530 has been deleted. To report, see 49496, 49501, 49507, 49521)

(49535 has been deleted. To report, see 49496, 49501, 49507, 49521)

49540 Repair lumbar hernia

49550 Repair initial femoral hernia, any age; reducible

(49552 has been deleted. To report, see 49550 or 49553)

49553   incarcerated or strangulated

49555 Repair recurrent femoral hernia; reducible

49557   incarcerated or strangulated

49560 Repair initial incisional or ventral hernia; reducible

49561   incarcerated or strangulated

49565 Repair recurrent incisional or ventral hernia; reducible

49566   incarcerated or strangulated

+ 49568 Implantation of mesh or other prosthesis for incisional or ventral hernia repair (List separately in addition to code for the incisional or ventral hernia repair)

49570 Repair epigastric hernia (eg, preperitoneal fat); reducible (separate procedure)

49572   incarcerated or strangulated

(49575 has been deleted. To report, use 49572)

49580	Repair umbilical hernia, under age 5 years; reducible

(49581 has been deleted. To report, see 49585 or 49587)

49582	incarcerated or strangulated
49585	Repair umbilical hernia, age 5 years or over; reducible
49587	incarcerated or strangulated
49590	Repair spigelian hernia
49600	Repair of small omphalocele, with primary closure
49605	Repair of large omphalocele or gastroschisis; with or without prosthesis
49606	with removal of prosthesis, final reduction and closure, in operating room
49610	Repair of omphalocele (Gross type operation); first stage
49611	second stage

(For diaphragmatic or hiatal hernia repair, see 39502-39541)

(49630-49640 have been deleted. For surgical repair of omentum, use 49999)

Laparoscopy

Surgical laparoscopy always includes diagnostic laparoscopy. To report a diagnostic laparoscopy (peritoneoscopy) (separate procedure), use 49320.

49650	Laparoscopy, surgical; repair initial inguinal hernia
49651	repair recurrent inguinal hernia
49659	Unlisted laparoscopy procedure, hernioplasty, herniorrhaphy, herniotomy

Suture

49900	Suture, secondary, of abdominal wall for evisceration or dehiscence

(For suture of ruptured diaphragm, see 39540, 39541)

(For debridement of abdominal wall, see 11042, 11043)

Other Procedures

+ 49905	Omental flap (eg, for reconstruction of sternal and chest wall defects) (List separately in addition to code for primary procedure)

(49910 has been deleted. To report, use 49999)

49906	Free omental flap with microvascular anastomosis

(Do not report code 69990 in addition to code 49906)

49999	Unlisted procedure, abdomen, peritoneum and omentum

Urinary System

(For provision of chemotherapeutic agents, use 96545 in addition to code for primary procedure)

Kidney

Incision

(For retroperitoneal exploration, abscess, tumor, or cyst, see 49010, 49060, 49200, 49201)

50010 Renal exploration, not necessitating other specific procedures

50020 Drainage of perirenal or renal abscess; open

50021 percutaneous

(For radiological supervision and interpretation, use 75989)

50040 Nephrostomy, nephrotomy with drainage

50045 Nephrotomy, with exploration

(For renal endoscopy performed in conjunction with this procedure, see 50570-50580)

50060 Nephrolithotomy; removal of calculus

50065 secondary surgical operation for calculus

50070 complicated by congenital kidney abnormality

50075 removal of large staghorn calculus filling renal pelvis and calyces (including anatrophic pyelolithotomy)

50080 Percutaneous nephrostolithotomy or pyelostolithotomy, with or without dilation, endoscopy, lithotripsy, stenting, or basket extraction; up to 2 cm

50081 over 2 cm

(For establishment of nephrostomy without nephrostolithotomy, see 50040, 50395, 52334)

(For fluoroscopic guidance, see 76000, 76001)

50100 Transection or repositioning of aberrant renal vessels (separate procedure)

50120 Pyelotomy; with exploration

(For renal endoscopy performed in conjunction with this procedure, see 50570-50580)

50125 with drainage, pyelostomy

50130 with removal of calculus (pyelolithotomy, pelviolithotomy, including coagulum pyelolithotomy)

50135 complicated (eg, secondary operation, congenital kidney abnormality)

(For supply of anticarcinogenic agents, use 99070 in addition to code for primary procedure)

Excision

(For excision of retroperitoneal tumor or cyst, see 49200, 49201)

50200* Renal biopsy; percutaneous, by trocar or needle

(For radiological supervision and interpretation, see 76003, 76360, ▶76393,◀ 76942)

▶(For fine needle aspiration, use 10022)◀

▶(For evaluation of fine needle aspirate, see 88172, 88173)◀

50205 by surgical exposure of kidney

▲**50220** Nephrectomy, including partial ureterectomy, any open approach including rib resection;

50225 complicated because of previous surgery on same kidney

50230 radical, with regional lymphadenectomy and/or vena caval thrombectomy

(When vena caval resection with reconstruction is necessary, use 37799)

50234 Nephrectomy with total ureterectomy and bladder cuff; through same incision

50236 through separate incision

50240 Nephrectomy, partial

50280 Excision or unroofing of cyst(s) of kidney

(For laparoscopic ablation of renal cysts, use 50541)

50290 Excision of perinephric cyst

Renal Transplantation

(For dialysis, see 90935-90999)

(For laparoscopic donor nephrectomy, use 50547)

(For laparoscopic drainage of lymphocele to peritoneal cavity, use 49323)

50300 Donor nephrectomy, with preparation and maintenance of allograft, from cadaver donor, unilateral or bilateral

50320 Donor nephrectomy, open from living donor (excluding preparation and maintenance of allograft)

50340 Recipient nephrectomy (separate procedure)

(50341 has been deleted. To report, use 50340 with modifier '-50')

50360 Renal allotransplantation, implantation of graft; excluding donor and recipient nephrectomy

50365 with recipient nephrectomy

(50366 has been deleted. To report, use 50365 with modifier '-50')

50370 Removal of transplanted renal allograft

50380 Renal autotransplantation, reimplantation of kidney

(For extra-corporeal "bench" surgery, use autotransplantation as the primary procedure and add the secondary procedure (eg, partial nephrectomy, nephrolithotomy), and use the modifier '-51')

Introduction

50390* Aspiration and/or injection of renal cyst or pelvis by needle, percutaneous

▶(For radiological supervision and interpretation, see 74425, 74470, 76003, 76360, ▶76393, 76942◀)

▶(For evaluation of fine needle aspirate, see 88172, 88173)◀

50392 Introduction of intracatheter or catheter into renal pelvis for drainage and/or injection, percutaneous

(For radiological supervision and interpretation, see 74475, 76360, ▶76942◀)

50393 Introduction of ureteral catheter or stent into ureter through renal pelvis for drainage and/or injection, percutaneous

(For radiological supervision and interpretation, see 74480, 76003, 76360, ▶76942◀)

50394 Injection procedure for pyelography (as nephrostogram, pyelostogram, antegrade pyeloureterograms) through nephrostomy or pyelostomy tube, or indwelling ureteral catheter

(For radiological supervision and interpretation, use 74425)

50395 Introduction of guide into renal pelvis and/or ureter with dilation to establish nephrostomy tract, percutaneous

(For radiological supervision and interpretation, see 74475, 74480, 74485)

(For nephrostolithotomy, see 50080, 50081)

(For retrograde percutaneous nephrostomy, use 52334)

(For endoscopic surgery, see 50551-50561)

50396 Manometric studies through nephrostomy or pyelostomy tube, or indwelling ureteral catheter

(For radiological supervision and interpretation, see 74425, 74475, 74480)

50398* Change of nephrostomy or pyelostomy tube

(For radiological supervision and interpretation, use 75984)

Repair

50400 Pyeloplasty (Foley Y-pyeloplasty), plastic operation on renal pelvis, with or without plastic operation on ureter, nephropexy, nephrostomy, pyelostomy, or ureteral splinting; simple

50405 complicated (congenital kidney abnormality, secondary pyeloplasty, solitary kidney, calycoplasty)

(For laparoscopic approach, use 50544)

(50420 has been deleted)

50500 Nephrorrhaphy, suture of kidney wound or injury

50520 Closure of nephrocutaneous or pyelocutaneous fistula

50525 Closure of nephrovisceral fistula (eg, renocolic), including visceral repair; abdominal approach

50526 thoracic approach

50540 Symphysiotomy for horseshoe kidney with or without pyeloplasty and/or other plastic procedure, unilateral or bilateral (one operation)

Laparoscopy

Surgical laparoscopy always includes diagnostic laparoscopy. To report a diagnostic laparoscopy (peritoneoscopy) (separate procedure), use 49320.

50541 Laparoscopy, surgical; ablation of renal cysts

50544 pyeloplasty

50545 radical nephrectomy (includes removal of Gerota's fascia and surrounding fatty tissue, removal of regional lymph nodes, and adrenalectomy)

(For open procedure, use 50230)

50546 nephrectomy, including partial ureterectomy

50547 donor nephrectomy from living donor (excluding preparation and maintenance of allograft)

(For open procedure, use 50320)

50548 nephrectomy with total ureterectomy

(For open procedure, see 50234, 50236)

50549 Unlisted laparoscopy procedure, renal

(For laparoscopic drainage of lymphocele to peritoneal cavity, use 49323)

Endoscopy

(For supplies and materials, use 99070)

(References to office and hospital have been deleted)

50551 Renal endoscopy through established nephrostomy or pyelostomy, with or without irrigation, instillation, or ureteropyelography, exclusive of radiologic service;

50553 with ureteral catheterization, with or without dilation of ureter

50555	with biopsy
50557	with fulguration and/or incision, with or without biopsy
50559	with insertion of radioactive substance with or without biopsy and/or fulguration
50561	with removal of foreign body or calculus

(When procedures 50570-50580 provide a significant identifiable service, they may be added to 50045 and 50120)

50570	Renal endoscopy through nephrotomy or pyelotomy, with or without irrigation, instillation, or ureteropyelography, exclusive of radiologic service;

(For nephrotomy, use 50045)

(For pyelotomy, use 50120)

50572	with ureteral catheterization, with or without dilation of ureter
50574	with biopsy
50575	with endopyelotomy (includes cystoscopy, ureteroscopy, dilation of ureter and ureteral pelvic junction, incision of ureteral pelvic junction and insertion of endopyelotomy stent)
50576	with fulguration and/or incision, with or without biopsy
50578	with insertion of radioactive substance, with or without biopsy and/or fulguration
50580	with removal of foreign body or calculus

Other Procedures

50590	Lithotripsy, extracorporeal shock wave

Ureter

Incision

50600	Ureterotomy with exploration or drainage (separate procedure)

(For ureteral endoscopy performed in conjunction with this procedure, see 50970-50980)

50605	Ureterotomy for insertion of indwelling stent, all types
50610	Ureterolithotomy; upper one-third of ureter
50620	middle one-third of ureter
50630	lower one-third of ureter

(For laparoscopic approach, use 50945)

(For transvesical ureterolithotomy, use 51060)

(For cystotomy with stone basket extraction of ureteral calculus, use 51065)

(For endoscopic extraction or manipulation of ureteral calculus, see 50080, 50081, 50561, 50961, 50980, 52320-52330, 52352, 52353)

Excision

(For ureterocele, see 51535, 52300)

50650	Ureterectomy, with bladder cuff (separate procedure)
50660	Ureterectomy, total, ectopic ureter, combination abdominal, vaginal and/or perineal approach

Introduction

50684	Injection procedure for ureterography or ureteropyelography through ureterostomy or indwelling ureteral catheter

(For radiological supervision and interpretation, use 74425)

50686	Manometric studies through ureterostomy or indwelling ureteral catheter
50688*	Change of ureterostomy tube

(If imaging guidance is performed, use 75984)

50690	Injection procedure for visualization of ileal conduit and/or ureteropyelography, exclusive of radiologic service

(For radiological supervision and interpretation, use 74425)

Repair

50700	Ureteroplasty, plastic operation on ureter (eg, stricture)
50715	Ureterolysis, with or without repositioning of ureter for retroperitoneal fibrosis

(50716 has been deleted. To report, use 50715 with modifier '-50')

50722	Ureterolysis for ovarian vein syndrome
50725	Ureterolysis for retrocaval ureter, with reanastomosis of upper urinary tract or vena cava
50727	Revision of urinary-cutaneous anastomosis (any type urostomy);
50728	with repair of fascial defect and hernia
50740	Ureteropyelostomy, anastomosis of ureter and renal pelvis
50750	Ureterocalycostomy, anastomosis of ureter to renal calyx
50760	Ureteroureterostomy
50770	Transureteroureterostomy, anastomosis of ureter to contralateral ureter

(Codes 50780-50785 include minor procedures to prevent vesicoureteral reflux)

50780	Ureteroneocystostomy; anastomosis of single ureter to bladder

(50781 has been deleted. To report, use 50780 with modifier '-50')

(When combined with cystourethroplasty or vesical neck revision, use 51820)

50782	anastomosis of duplicated ureter to bladder
50783	with extensive ureteral tailoring
50785	with vesico-psoas hitch or bladder flap

(50786 has been deleted. To report, use 50785 with modifier '-50')

50800 Ureteroenterostomy, direct anastomosis of ureter to intestine

(50801 has been deleted. To report, use 50800 with modifier '-50')

▲ **50810** Ureterosigmoidostomy, with creation of sigmoid bladder and establishment of abdominal or perineal colostomy, including intestine anastomosis

▲ **50815** Ureterocolon conduit, including intestine anastomosis

(50816 has been deleted. To report, use 50815 with modifier '-50')

▲ **50820** Ureteroileal conduit (ileal bladder), including intestine anastomosis (Bricker operation)

(50821 has been deleted. To report, use 50820 with modifier '-50')

(For combination of 50800-50820 with cystectomy, see 51580-51595)

▲ **50825** Continent diversion, including intestine anastomosis using any segment of small and/or large intestine (Kock pouch or Camey enterocystoplasty)

50830 Urinary undiversion (eg, taking down of ureteroileal conduit, ureterosigmoidostomy or ureteroenterostomy with ureteroureterostomy or ureteroneocystostomy)

▲ **50840** Replacement of all or part of ureter by intestine segment, including intestine anastomosis

(50841 has been deleted. To report, use 50840 with modifier '-50')

50845 Cutaneous appendico-vesicostomy

50860 Ureterostomy, transplantation of ureter to skin

(50861 has been deleted. To report, use 50860 with modifier '-50')

50900 Ureterorrhaphy, suture of ureter (separate procedure)

50920 Closure of ureterocutaneous fistula

50930 Closure of ureterovisceral fistula (including visceral repair)

50940 Deligation of ureter

(For ureteroplasty, ureterolysis, see 50700-50860)

Laparoscopy

Surgical laparoscopy always includes diagnostic laparoscopy. To report a diagnostic laparoscopy (peritoneoscopy) (separate procedure), use 49320.

50945 Laparoscopy, surgical; ureterolithotomy

50947 ureteroneocystostomy with cystoscopy and ureteral stent placement

50948 ureteroneocystostomy without cystoscopy and ureteral stent placement

(For open ureteroneocystostomy, see 50780-50785)

50949 Unlisted laparoscopy procedure, ureter

Endoscopy

(References to office and hospital have been deleted)

50951 Ureteral endoscopy through established ureterostomy, with or without irrigation, instillation, or ureteropyelography, exclusive of radiologic service;

50953 with ureteral catheterization, with or without dilation of ureter

50955 with biopsy

50957 with fulguration and/or incision, with or without biopsy

50959 with insertion of radioactive substance, with or without biopsy and/or fulguration (not including provision of material)

50961 with removal of foreign body or calculus

(When procedures 50970-50980 provide a significant identifiable service, they may be added to 50600)

50970 Ureteral endoscopy through ureterotomy, with or without irrigation, instillation, or ureteropyelography, exclusive of radiologic service;

(For ureterotomy, use 50600)

50972 with ureteral catheterization, with or without dilation of ureter

50974 with biopsy

50976 with fulguration and/or incision, with or without biopsy

50978 with insertion of radioactive substance, with or without biopsy and/or fulguration (not including provision of material)

50980 with removal of foreign body or calculus

⊘ = Modifier '-51' Exempt   ▶◀ = New or Revised Text   ✚ = Add-on Code

Bladder

Incision

51000*   Aspiration of bladder by needle

51005*   Aspiration of bladder; by trocar or intracatheter

51010   with insertion of suprapubic catheter

▶(If imaging guidance is performed, see 76003, 76360, 76942)◀

51020   Cystotomy or cystostomy; with fulguration and/or insertion of radioactive material

51030   with cryosurgical destruction of intravesical lesion

51040   Cystostomy, cystotomy with drainage

51045   Cystotomy, with insertion of ureteral catheter or stent (separate procedure)

51050   Cystolithotomy, cystotomy with removal of calculus, without vesical neck resection

51060   Transvesical ureterolithotomy

▲**51065**   Cystotomy, with calculus basket extraction and/or ultrasonic or electrohydraulic fragmentation of ureteral calculus

51080   Drainage of perivesical or prevesical space abscess

Excision

51500   Excision of urachal cyst or sinus, with or without umbilical hernia repair

51520   Cystotomy; for simple excision of vesical neck (separate procedure)

51525   for excision of bladder diverticulum, single or multiple (separate procedure)

51530   for excision of bladder tumor

(For transurethral resection, see 52234-52240, 52305)

51535   Cystotomy for excision, incision, or repair of ureterocele

(For transurethral excision, use 52300)

(51536 has been deleted. To report, use 51535 with modifier '-50')

51550   Cystectomy, partial; simple

51555   complicated (eg, postradiation, previous surgery, difficult location)

51565   Cystectomy, partial, with reimplantation of ureter(s) into bladder (ureteroneocystostomy)

51570   Cystectomy, complete; (separate procedure)

51575   with bilateral pelvic lymphadenectomy, including external iliac, hypogastric, and obturator nodes

51580   Cystectomy, complete, with ureterosigmoidostomy or ureterocutaneous transplantations;

51585   with bilateral pelvic lymphadenectomy, including external iliac, hypogastric, and obturator nodes

▲**51590**   Cystectomy, complete, with ureteroileal conduit or sigmoid bladder, including intestine anastomosis;

51595   with bilateral pelvic lymphadenectomy, including external iliac, hypogastric, and obturator nodes

▲**51596**   Cystectomy, complete, with continent diversion, any open technique, using any segment of small and/or large intestine to construct neobladder

51597   Pelvic exenteration, complete, for vesical, prostatic or urethral malignancy, with removal of bladder and ureteral transplantations, with or without hysterectomy and/or abdominoperineal resection of rectum and colon and colostomy, or any combination thereof

(For pelvic exenteration for gynecologic malignancy, use 58240)

Introduction

(For bladder catheterization, see 53670, 53675)

51600*   Injection procedure for cystography or voiding urethrocystography

(For radiological supervision and interpretation, see 74430, 74455)

51605   Injection procedure and placement of chain for contrast and/or chain urethrocystography

(For radiological supervision and interpretation, use 74430)

51610   Injection procedure for retrograde urethrocystography

(For radiological supervision and interpretation, use 74450)

51700*   Bladder irrigation, simple, lavage and/or instillation

51705*   Change of cystostomy tube; simple

51710*   complicated

(If imaging guidance is performed, use 75984)

51715   Endoscopic injection of implant material into the submucosal tissues of the urethra and/or bladder neck

51720   Bladder instillation of anticarcinogenic agent (including detention time)

Urodynamics

The following section (51725-51797) lists procedures that may be used separately or in many and varied combinations.

When multiple procedures are performed in the same investigative session, modifier '-51' should be employed.

All procedures in this section imply that these services are performed by, or are under the direct supervision of, a physician and that all instruments, equipment, fluids, gases, probes, catheters, technician's fees, medications, gloves, trays, tubing and other sterile supplies be provided by the physician. When the physician only interprets the

---

results and/or operates the equipment, a professional component, modifier '-26', should be used to identify physicians' services.

51725 Simple cystometrogram (CMG) (eg, spinal manometer)

51726 Complex cystometrogram (eg, calibrated electronic equipment)

(51727-51733 have been deleted. To report, use 51726)

51736 Simple uroflowmetry (UFR) (eg, stop-watch flow rate, mechanical uroflowmeter)

(51737, 51738 have been deleted. To report, use 51736)

(51739 has been deleted)

51741 Complex uroflowmetry (eg, calibrated electronic equipment)

(51742-51749 have been deleted. To report, use 51741)

(51751-51769 have been deleted. To report, use 53899)

51772 Urethral pressure profile studies (UPP) (urethral closure pressure profile), any technique

(51773-51783 have been deleted. To report, use 51772)

51784 Electromyography studies (EMG) of anal or urethral sphincter, other than needle, any technique

51785 Needle electromyography studies (EMG) of anal or urethral sphincter, any technique

(51786-51791 have been deleted. To report, use 51785)

51792 Stimulus evoked response (eg, measurement of bulbocavernosus reflex latency time)

51795 Voiding pressure studies (VP); bladder voiding pressure, any technique

(51796 has been deleted. To report, use 51795)

51797   intra-abdominal voiding pressure (AP) (rectal, gastric, intraperitoneal)

Repair

51800 Cystoplasty or cystourethroplasty, plastic operation on bladder and/or vesical neck (anterior Y-plasty, vesical fundus resection), any procedure, with or without wedge resection of posterior vesical neck

51820 Cystourethroplasty with unilateral or bilateral ureteroneocystostomy

51840 Anterior vesicourethropexy, or urethropexy (eg, Marshall-Marchetti-Krantz, Burch); simple

51841   complicated (eg, secondary repair)

(For urethropexy (Pereyra type), use 57289)

51845 Abdomino-vaginal vesical neck suspension, with or without endoscopic control (eg, Stamey, Raz, modified Pereyra)

51860 Cystorrhaphy, suture of bladder wound, injury or rupture; simple

51865   complicated

51880 Closure of cystostomy (separate procedure)

51900 Closure of vesicovaginal fistula, abdominal approach

(For vaginal approach, see 57320-57330)

51920 Closure of vesicouterine fistula;

51925   with hysterectomy

(For closure of vesicoenteric fistula, see 44660, 44661)

(For closure of rectovesical fistula, see 45800-45805)

▲ **51940** Closure, exstrophy of bladder

(See also 54390)

▲ **51960** Enterocystoplasty, including intestinal anastomosis

51980 Cutaneous vesicostomy

Laparoscopy

Surgical laparoscopy always includes diagnostic laparoscopy. To report a diagnostic laparoscopy (peritoneoscopy) (separate procedure), use 49320.

51990 Laparoscopy, surgical; urethral suspension for stress incontinence

51992   sling operation for stress incontinence (eg, fascia or synthetic)

(For open sling operation for stress incontinence, use 57288)

(For reversal or removal of sling operation for stress incontinence, use 57287)

Endoscopy—Cystoscopy, Urethroscopy, Cystourethroscopy

Endoscopic descriptions are listed so that the main procedure can be identified without having to list all the minor related functions performed at the same time. For example: meatotomy, urethral calibration and/or dilation, urethro-scopy, and cystoscopy prior to a transurethral resection of prostate; ureteral catheterization following extraction of ureteral calculus; internal urethrotomy and bladder neck fulguration when performing a cystourethroscopy for the female urethral syndrome. When the secondary procedure requires significant additional time and effort, it may be identified by the addition of modifier '-22'.

For example: urethrotomy performed for a documented pre-existing stricture or bladder neck contracture.

(References to office and hospital have been deleted)

52000 Cystourethroscopy (separate procedure)

● **52001** Cystourethroscopy with irrigation and evacuation of clots

▶(Do not report 52001 in addition to 52000)◀

52005   Cystourethroscopy, with ureteral catheterization, with or without irrigation, instillation, or ureteropyelography, exclusive of radiologic service;

52007   with brush biopsy of ureter and/or renal pelvis

52010   Cystourethroscopy, with ejaculatory duct catheterization, with or without irrigation, instillation, or duct radiography, exclusive of radiologic service

(For radiological supervision and interpretation, use 74440)

(52190 has been deleted)

Transurethral Surgery

Urethra and Bladder

(References to office and hospital have been deleted)

52204   Cystourethroscopy, with biopsy

52214   Cystourethroscopy, with fulguration (including cryosurgery or laser surgery) of trigone, bladder neck, prostatic fossa, urethra, or periurethral glands

52224   Cystourethroscopy, with fulguration (including cryosurgery or laser surgery) or treatment of MINOR (less than 0.5 cm) lesion(s) with or without biopsy

52234   Cystourethroscopy, with fulguration (including cryosurgery or laser surgery) and/or resection of; SMALL bladder tumor(s) (0.5 to 2.0 cm)

52235   MEDIUM bladder tumor(s) (2.0 to 5.0 cm)

52240   LARGE bladder tumor(s)

52250   Cystourethroscopy with insertion of radioactive substance, with or without biopsy or fulguration

52260   Cystourethroscopy, with dilation of bladder for interstitial cystitis; general or conduction (spinal) anesthesia

52265   local anesthesia

52270   Cystourethroscopy, with internal urethrotomy; female

52275   male

52276   Cystourethroscopy with direct vision internal urethrotomy

52277   Cystourethroscopy, with resection of external sphincter (sphincterotomy)

52281   Cystourethroscopy, with calibration and/or dilation of urethral stricture or stenosis, with or without meatotomy, with or without injection procedure for cystography, male or female

52282   Cystourethroscopy, with insertion of urethral stent

52283   Cystourethroscopy, with steroid injection into stricture

52285   Cystourethroscopy for treatment of the female urethral syndrome with any or all of the following: urethral meatotomy, urethral dilation, internal urethrotomy, lysis of urethrovaginal septal fibrosis, lateral incisions of the bladder neck, and fulguration of polyp(s) of urethra, bladder neck, and/or trigone

52290   Cystourethroscopy; with ureteral meatotomy, unilateral or bilateral

52300   with resection or fulguration of orthotopic ureterocele(s), unilateral or bilateral

52301   with resection or fulguration of ectopic ureterocele(s), unilateral or bilateral

52305   with incision or resection of orifice of bladder diverticulum, single or multiple

52310   Cystourethroscopy, with removal of foreign body, calculus, or ureteral stent from urethra or bladder (separate procedure); simple

52315   complicated

52317   Litholapaxy: crushing or fragmentation of calculus by any means in bladder and removal of fragments; simple or small (less than 2.5 cm)

52318   complicated or large (over 2.5 cm)

Ureter and Pelvis

Surgical cystourethroscopy always includes diagnostic cystourethroscopy. To report a diagnostic cystourethroscopy, use 52351.

Do not report 52351 in conjunction with 52341-52346, 52352-52355.

The insertion and removal of a temporary stent during diagnostic or therapeutic cystourethroscopic intervention(s) is included in 52320-52355 and should not be reported separately.

To report insertion of a self-retaining, indwelling stent performed during cystourethroscopic diagnostic or therapeutic intervention(s), use code 52332, in addition to primary procedure(s) performed, and append the modifier '-51'. Code 52332 is used to report a unilateral procedure unless otherwise specified.

For bilateral insertion of self-retaining, indwelling ureteral stents, use code 52332, and append the modifier '-50'.

To report cystourethroscopic removal of a self-retaining, indwelling ureteral stent, see codes 52310, 52315, and append the modifier '-58'.

52320   Cystourethroscopy (including ureteral catheterization); with removal of ureteral calculus

52325   with fragmentation of ureteral calculus (eg, ultrasonic or electro-hydraulic technique)

52327   with subureteric injection of implant material

52330   with manipulation, without removal of ureteral calculus

52332   Cystourethroscopy, with insertion of indwelling ureteral stent (eg, Gibbons or double-J type)

52334   Cystourethroscopy with insertion of ureteral guide wire through kidney to establish a percutaneous nephrostomy, retrograde

(For percutaneous nephrostolithotomy, see 50080, 50081; for establishment of nephrostomy tract only, use 50395)

(52335 has been deleted. To report, use 52351)

(52336 has been deleted. To report, use 52352)

(52337 has been deleted. To report, use 52353)

(52338 has been deleted. To report, use 52354)

(52339 has been deleted. To report, use 52355)

(52340 has been deleted. To report, use 52400)

52341   Cystourethroscopy; with treatment of ureteral stricture (eg, balloon dilation, laser, electrocautery, and incision)

52342   with treatment of ureteropelvic junction stricture (eg, balloon dilation, laser, electrocautery, and incision)

52343   with treatment of intra-renal stricture (eg, balloon dilation, laser, electrocautery, and incision)

52344   Cystourethroscopy with ureteroscopy; with treatment of ureteral stricture (eg, balloon dilation, laser, electrocautery, and incision)

52345   with treatment of ureteropelvic junction stricture (eg, balloon dilation, laser, electrocautery, and incision)

52346   with treatment of intra-renal stricture (eg, balloon dilation, laser, electrocautery, and incision)

● **52347**   Cystourethroscopy with transurethral resection or incision of ejaculatory ducts

52351   Cystourethroscopy, with ureteroscopy and/or pyeloscopy; diagnostic

(For radiological supervision and interpretation, use 74485)

(Do not report 52351 in conjunction with 52341-52346, 52352-52355)

52352   with removal or manipulation of calculus (ureteral catheterization is included)

52353   with lithotripsy (ureteral catheterization is included)

52354   with biopsy and/or fulguration of lesion

52355   with resection of tumor

Vesical Neck and Prostate

52400   Cystourethroscopy with incision, fulguration, or resection of congenital posterior urethral valves, or congenital obstructive hypertrophic mucosal folds

52450   Transurethral incision of prostate

52500   Transurethral resection of bladder neck (separate procedure)

▲ **52510**   Transurethral balloon dilation of the prostatic urethra

52601   Transurethral electrosurgical resection of prostate, including control of postoperative bleeding, complete (vasectomy, meatotomy, cystourethroscopy, urethral calibration and/or dilation, and internal urethrotomy are included)

(For other approaches, see 55801-55845)

(52605 has been deleted. To report, use 52606)

52606   Transurethral fulguration for postoperative bleeding occurring after the usual follow-up time

52612   Transurethral resection of prostate; first stage of two-stage resection (partial resection)

52614   second stage of two-stage resection (resection completed)

52620   Transurethral resection; of residual obstructive tissue after 90 days postoperative

52630   of regrowth of obstructive tissue longer than one year postoperative

52640   of postoperative bladder neck contracture

52647   Non-contact laser coagulation of prostate, including control of postoperative bleeding, complete (vasectomy, meatotomy, cystourethroscopy, urethral calibration and/or dilation, and internal urethrotomy are included)

52648   Contact laser vaporization with or without transurethral resection of prostate, including control of postoperative bleeding, complete (vasectomy, meatotomy, cystourethroscopy, urethral calibration and/or dilation, and internal urethrotomy are included)

(52650 has been deleted)

52700   Transurethral drainage of prostatic abscess

(52800, 52805 have been deleted. To report, see 52317, 52318)

Urethra

(For endoscopy, see cystoscopy, urethroscopy, cystourethroscopy, 52000-52700)

(For injection procedure for urethrocystography, see 51600-51610)

Incision

53000   Urethrotomy or urethrostomy, external (separate procedure); pendulous urethra

53010   perineal urethra, external

53020   Meatotomy, cutting of meatus (separate procedure); except infant

(53021 has been deleted. To report, use 53020)

53025   infant

53040   Drainage of deep periurethral abscess

(For subcutaneous abscess, see 10060, 10061)

53060 Drainage of Skene's gland abscess or cyst

53080 Drainage of perineal urinary extravasation; uncomplicated (separate procedure)

53085   complicated

Excision

53200 Biopsy of urethra

53210 Urethrectomy, total, including cystostomy; female

53215   male

53220 Excision or fulguration of carcinoma of urethra

53230 Excision of urethral diverticulum (separate procedure); female

53235   male

53240 Marsupialization of urethral diverticulum, male or female

53250 Excision of bulbourethral gland (Cowper's gland)

53260 Excision or fulguration; urethral polyp(s), distal urethra

    (For endoscopic approach, see 52214, 52224)

53265   urethral caruncle

53270   Skene's glands

53275   urethral prolapse

Repair

    (For hypospadias, see 54300-54352)

53400 Urethroplasty; first stage, for fistula, diverticulum, or stricture (eg, Johannsen type)

53405   second stage (formation of urethra), including urinary diversion

53410 Urethroplasty, one-stage reconstruction of male anterior urethra

53415 Urethroplasty, transpubic or perineal, one stage, for reconstruction or repair of prostatic or membranous urethra

53420 Urethroplasty, two-stage reconstruction or repair of prostatic or membranous urethra; first stage

53425   second stage

53430 Urethroplasty, reconstruction of female urethra

● **53431** Urethroplasty with tubularization of posterior urethra and/or lower bladder for incontinence (eg, Tenago, Leadbetter procedure)

53440 Operation for correction of male urinary incontinence, with or without introduction of prosthesis

53442 Removal of perineal prosthesis introduced for continence

    ►(53443 has been deleted. To report, use 53431)◄

● **53444** Insertion of tandem cuff (dual cuff)

▲ **53445** Insertion of inflatable urethral/bladder neck sphincter, including placement of pump, reservoir, and cuff

● **53446** Removal of inflatable urethral/bladder neck sphincter, including pump, reservoir, and cuff

▲ **53447** Removal and replacement of inflatable urethral/bladder neck sphincter including pump, reservoir, and cuff at the same operative session

● **53448** Removal and replacement of inflatable urethral/bladder neck sphincter including pump, reservoir, and cuff through an infected field at the same operative session including irrigation and debridement of infected tissue

    ►(Do not report 11040-11043 in addition to 53448)◄

▲ **53449** Repair of inflatable urethral/bladder neck sphincter, including pump, reservoir, and cuff

53450 Urethromeatoplasty, with mucosal advancement

    (For meatotomy, see 53020, 53025)

53460 Urethromeatoplasty, with partial excision of distal urethral segment (Richardson type procedure)

53502 Urethrorrhaphy, suture of urethral wound or injury, female

53505 Urethrorrhaphy, suture of urethral wound or injury; penile

53510   perineal

53515   prostatomembranous

53520 Closure of urethrostomy or urethrocutaneous fistula, male (separate procedure)

    (For closure of urethrovaginal fistula, use 57310)

    (For closure of urethrorectal fistula, see 45820, 45825)

Manipulation

    (For radiological supervision and interpretation, use 74485)

53600* Dilation of urethral stricture by passage of sound or urethral dilator, male; initial

53601*   subsequent

53605 Dilation of urethral stricture or vesical neck by passage of sound or urethral dilator, male, general or conduction (spinal) anesthesia

53620* Dilation of urethral stricture by passage of filiform and follower, male; initial

53621*   subsequent

    (53640 has been deleted. To report, use 53620)

53660* Dilation of female urethra including suppository and/or instillation; initial

53661*   subsequent

53665 Dilation of female urethra, general or conduction (spinal) anesthesia

---

▲=Revised Code   ●=New Code   ✱=Service Includes Surgical Procedure Only

53670*   Catheterization, urethra; simple

53675*   complicated (may include difficult removal of balloon catheter)

Other Procedures

(53800 has been deleted. To report, use 81020)

53850   Transurethral destruction of prostate tissue; by microwave thermotherapy

53852   by radiofrequency thermotherapy

● **53853**   by water-induced thermotherapy

53899   Unlisted procedure, urinary system

Male Genital System

Penis

Incision

54000   Slitting of prepuce, dorsal or lateral (separate procedure); newborn

54001   except newborn

54015   Incision and drainage of penis, deep

(For skin and subcutaneous abscess, see 10060-10160)

Destruction

54050*   Destruction of lesion(s), penis (eg, condyloma, papilloma, molluscum contagiosum, herpetic vesicle), simple; chemical

54055*   electrodesiccation

54056   cryosurgery

54057   laser surgery

54060   surgical excision

▲**54065**   Destruction of lesion(s), penis (eg, condyloma, papilloma, molluscum contagiosum, herpetic vesicle), extensive (eg, laser surgery, electrosurgery, cryosurgery, chemosurgery)

(For destruction or excision of other lesions, see **Integumentary System**)

Excision

54100   Biopsy of penis; (separate procedure)

54105   deep structures

54110   Excision of penile plaque (Peyronie disease);

54111   with graft to 5 cm in length

54112   with graft greater than 5 cm in length

54115   Removal foreign body from deep penile tissue (eg, plastic implant)

54120   Amputation of penis; partial

54125   complete

54130   Amputation of penis, radical; with bilateral inguinofemoral lymphadenectomy

54135   in continuity with bilateral pelvic lymphadenectomy, including external iliac, hypogastric and obturator nodes

(For lymphadenectomy (separate procedure), see 38760-38770)

54150   Circumcision, using clamp or other device; newborn

54152   except newborn

(54154 has been deleted. To report, use 54152)

54160   Circumcision, surgical excision other than clamp, device or dorsal slit; newborn

54161   except newborn

● **54162**   Lysis or excision of penile post-circumcision adhesions

● **54163**   Repair incomplete circumcision

● **54164**   Frenulotomy of penis

►(Do not report with circumcision codes 54150-54161, 54162, 54163)◄

Introduction

54200*   Injection procedure for Peyronie disease;

54205   with surgical exposure of plaque

54220   Irrigation of corpora cavernosa for priapism

54230   Injection procedure for corpora cavernosography

(For radiological supervision and interpretation, use 74445)

54231   Dynamic cavernosometry, including intracavernosal injection of vasoactive drugs (eg, papaverine, phentolamine)

54235   Injection of corpora cavernosa with pharmacologic agent(s) (eg, papaverine, phentolamine)

54240   Penile plethysmography

54250   Nocturnal penile tumescence and/or rigidity test

Repair

(For other urethroplasties, see 53400-53430)

(For penile revascularization, use 37788)

54300   Plastic operation of penis for straightening of chordee (eg, hypospadias), with or without mobilization of urethra

54304   Plastic operation on penis for correction of chordee or for first stage hypospadias repair with or without transplantation of prepuce and/or skin flaps

(54305 has been deleted. To report, see 54304 et seq)

54308   Urethroplasty for second stage hypospadias repair (including urinary diversion); less than 3 cm

54312   greater than 3 cm

54316   Urethroplasty for second stage hypospadias repair (including urinary diversion) with free skin graft obtained from site other than genitalia

54318   Urethroplasty for third stage hypospadias repair to release penis from scrotum (eg, third stage Cecil repair)

(54320 has been deleted. To report, see 54308 et seq)

54322   One stage distal hypospadias repair (with or without chordee or circumcision); with simple meatal advancement (eg, Magpi, V-flap)

54324   with urethroplasty by local skin flaps (eg, flip-flap, prepucial flap)

(54325 has been deleted. To report, see 54308 et seq)

54326   with urethroplasty by local skin flaps and mobilization of urethra

54328   with extensive dissection to correct chordee and urethroplasty with local skin flaps, skin graft patch, and/or island flap

(54330 has been deleted. To report, use 54308)

54332   One stage proximal penile or penoscrotal hypospadias repair requiring extensive dissection to correct chordee and urethroplasty by use of skin graft tube and/or island flap

54336   One stage perineal hypospadias repair requiring extensive dissection to correct chordee and urethroplasty by use of skin graft tube and/or island flap

54340   Repair of hypospadias complications (ie, fistula, stricture, diverticula); by closure, incision, or excision, simple

54344   requiring mobilization of skin flaps and urethroplasty with flap or patch graft

54348   requiring extensive dissection and urethroplasty with flap, patch or tubed graft (includes urinary diversion)

54352   Repair of hypospadias cripple requiring extensive dissection and excision of previously constructed structures including re-release of chordee and reconstruction of urethra and penis by use of local skin as grafts and island flaps and skin brought in as flaps or grafts

54360   Plastic operation on penis to correct angulation

54380   Plastic operation on penis for epispadias distal to external sphincter;

54385   with incontinence

54390   with exstrophy of bladder

54400   Insertion of penile prosthesis; non-inflatable (semi-rigid)

54401   inflatable (self-contained)

►(54402 has been deleted. To report, see 54415, 54416)◄

▲**54405**   Insertion of multi-component, inflatable penile prosthesis, including placement of pump, cylinders, and reservoir

►(For reduced services, report 54405 with modifier '-52')◄

●**54406**   Removal of all components of a multi-component, inflatable penile prosthesis without replacement of prosthesis

►(For reduced services, report 54406 with modifier '-52')◄

►(54407 has been deleted. To report, see 54406, 54408, 54410)◄

●**54408**   Repair of component(s) of a multi-component, inflatable penile prosthesis

►(54409 has been deleted. To report, use 54408)◄

●**54410**   Removal and replacement of all component(s) of a multi-component, inflatable penile prosthesis at the same operative session

●**54411**   Removal and replacement of all components of a multi-component inflatable penile prosthesis through an infected field at the same operative session, including irrigation and debridement of infected tissue

►(For reduced services, report 54411 with modifier '-52')◄

►(Do not report 11040-11043 in addition to 54411)◄

●**54415**   Removal of non-inflatable (semi-rigid) or inflatable (self-contained) penile prosthesis, without replacement of prosthesis

●**54416**   Removal and replacement of non-inflatable (semi-rigid) or inflatable (self-contained) penile prosthesis at the same operative session

●**54417**   Removal and replacement of non-inflatable (semi-rigid) or inflatable (self-contained) penile prosthesis through an infected field at the same operative session, including irrigation and debridement of infected tissue

►(Do not report 11040-11043 in addition to 54417)◄

54420   Corpora cavernosa-saphenous vein shunt (priapism operation), unilateral or bilateral

54430   Corpora cavernosa-corpus spongiosum shunt (priapism operation), unilateral or bilateral

54435   Corpora cavernosa-glans penis fistulization (eg, biopsy needle, Winter procedure, rongeur, or punch) for priapism

54440   Plastic operation of penis for injury

Manipulation

54450   Foreskin manipulation including lysis of preputial adhesions and stretching

Testis

Excision

54500   Biopsy of testis, needle (separate procedure)

►(For fine needle aspiration, see 10021, 10022)◄

►(For evaluation of fine needle aspirate, see 88172, 88173)◄

54505   Biopsy of testis, incisional (separate procedure)

(When combined with vasogram, seminal vesiculogram, or epididymogram, use 55300)

⊘ =Modifier '-51' Exempt   ► ◄=New or Revised Text   ✚ =Add-on Code   CPT 2002

(54506 has been deleted. To report, use 54505 with modifier '-50')

▶(54510 has been deleted. To report, use 54512)◄

54512   Excision of extraparenchymal lesion of testis

54520   Orchiectomy, simple (including subcapsular), with or without testicular prosthesis, scrotal or inguinal approach

(54521 has been deleted. To report, use 54520 with modifier '-50')

54522   Orchiectomy, partial

54530   Orchiectomy, radical, for tumor; inguinal approach

54535   with abdominal exploration

(For orchiectomy with repair of hernia, see 49505 or 49507 and 54520)

(For radical retroperitoneal lymphadenectomy, use 38780)

54550   Exploration for undescended testis (inguinal or scrotal area)

(54555 has been deleted. To report, use 54550 with modifier '-50')

54560   Exploration for undescended testis with abdominal exploration

(54565 has been deleted. To report, use 54560 with modifier '-50')

Repair

54600   Reduction of torsion of testis, surgical, with or without fixation of contralateral testis

54620   Fixation of contralateral testis (separate procedure)

54640   Orchiopexy, inguinal approach, with or without hernia repair

(For inguinal hernia repair performed in conjunction with inguinal orchiopexy, see 49495-49525)

(54641 has been deleted. To report, use 54640 with modifier '-50')

(54645 has been deleted)

54650   Orchiopexy, abdominal approach, for intra-abdominal testis (eg, Fowler-Stephens)

(For laparoscopic approach, use 54692)

54660   Insertion of testicular prosthesis (separate procedure)

(54661 has been deleted. To report, use 54660 with modifier '-50')

54670   Suture or repair of testicular injury

54680   Transplantation of testis(es) to thigh (because of scrotal destruction)

Laparoscopy

Surgical laparoscopy always includes diagnostic laparoscopy. To report a diagnostic laparoscopy (peritoneoscopy) (separate procedure), use 49320.

54690   Laparoscopy, surgical; orchiectomy

54692   orchiopexy for intra-abdominal testis

54699   Unlisted laparoscopy procedure, testis

Epididymis

Incision

54700   Incision and drainage of epididymis, testis and/or scrotal space (eg, abscess or hematoma)

Excision

54800   Biopsy of epididymis, needle

▶(For fine needle aspiration, see 10021, 10022)◄

▶(For evaluation of fine needle aspirate, see 88172, 88173)◄

54820   Exploration of epididymis, with or without biopsy

54830   Excision of local lesion of epididymis

54840   Excision of spermatocele, with or without epididymectomy

54860   Epididymectomy; unilateral

54861   bilateral

Repair

54900   Epididymovasostomy, anastomosis of epididymis to vas deferens; unilateral

54901   bilateral

(For operating microscope, use 69990)

Tunica Vaginalis

Incision

55000＊   Puncture aspiration of hydrocele, tunica vaginalis, with or without injection of medication

Excision

55040   Excision of hydrocele; unilateral

55041   bilateral

(With hernia repair, see 49495-49501)

▲=Revised Code   ●=New Code   ＊=Service Includes Surgical Procedure Only

Repair

55060   Repair of tunica vaginalis hydrocele (Bottle type)

Scrotum

Incision

55100*   Drainage of scrotal wall abscess

(See also 54700)

55110   Scrotal exploration

55120   Removal of foreign body in scrotum

Excision

(For excision of local lesion of skin of scrotum, see **Integumentary System**)

55150   Resection of scrotum

Repair

(55170 has been deleted. To report, see 55175, 55180)

55175   Scrotoplasty; simple

55180   complicated

Vas Deferens

Incision

55200   Vasotomy, cannulization with or without incision of vas, unilateral or bilateral (separate procedure)

Excision

55250   Vasectomy, unilateral or bilateral (separate procedure), including postoperative semen examination(s)

Introduction

55300   Vasotomy for vasograms, seminal vesiculograms, or epididymograms, unilateral or bilateral

(For radiological supervision and interpretation, use 74440)

(When combined with biopsy of testis, see 54505 and use modifier '-51')

Repair

55400   Vasovasostomy, vasovasorrhaphy

(For operating microscope, use 69990)

(55401 has been deleted. To report, use 55400 with modifier '-50')

Suture

55450   Ligation (percutaneous) of vas deferens, unilateral or bilateral (separate procedure)

Spermatic Cord

Excision

55500   Excision of hydrocele of spermatic cord, unilateral (separate procedure)

55520   Excision of lesion of spermatic cord (separate procedure)

55530   Excision of varicocele or ligation of spermatic veins for varicocele; (separate procedure)

55535   abdominal approach

55540   with hernia repair

Laparoscopy

Surgical laparoscopy always includes diagnostic laparoscopy. To report a diagnostic laparoscopy (peritoneoscopy) (separate procedure), use 49320.

55550   Laparoscopy, surgical, with ligation of spermatic veins for varicocele

55559   Unlisted laparoscopy procedure, spermatic cord

Seminal Vesicles

Incision

55600   Vesiculotomy;

(55601 has been deleted. To report, use 55600 with modifier '-50')

55605   complicated

Excision

55650   Vesiculectomy, any approach

(55651 has been deleted. To report, use 55650 with modifier '-50')

55680   Excision of Mullerian duct cyst

(For injection procedure, see 52010, 55300)

Prostate

Incision

55700   Biopsy, prostate; needle or punch, single or multiple, any approach

▶(If imaging guidance is performed, use 76942)◀

⊘ =Modifier '-51' Exempt   ▶ ◀=New or Revised Text   ✚=Add-on Code   CPT 2002

▶(For fine needle aspiration, see 10021, 10022)◀

▶(For evaluation of fine needle aspirate, see 88172, 88173)◀

55705   incisional, any approach

55720   Prostatotomy, external drainage of prostatic abscess, any approach; simple

55725   complicated

(For transurethral drainage, use 52700)

(55740 has been deleted. To report, use 55899)

Excision

(For transurethral removal of prostate, see 52601-52640)

(For transurethral destruction of prostate, see 53850-53852)

(For limited pelvic lymphadenectomy for staging (separate procedure), use 38562)

(For independent node dissection, see 38770-38780)

55801   Prostatectomy, perineal, subtotal (including control of postoperative bleeding, vasectomy, meatotomy, urethral calibration and/or dilation, and internal urethrotomy)

55810   Prostatectomy, perineal radical;

55812   with lymph node biopsy(s) (limited pelvic lymphadenectomy)

55815   with bilateral pelvic lymphadenectomy, including external iliac, hypogastric and obturator nodes

(If 55815 is carried out on separate days, use 38770 with modifier '-50' and 55810)

55821   Prostatectomy (including control of postoperative bleeding, vasectomy, meatotomy, urethral calibration and/or dilation, and internal urethrotomy); suprapubic, subtotal, one or two stages

55831   retropubic, subtotal

55840   Prostatectomy, retropubic radical, with or without nerve sparing;

55842   with lymph node biopsy(s) (limited pelvic lymphadenectomy)

55845   with bilateral pelvic lymphadenectomy, including external iliac, hypogastric, and obturator nodes

(If 55845 is carried out on separate days, use 38770 with modifier '-50' and 55840)

55859   Transperineal placement of needles or catheters into prostate for interstitial radioelement application, with or without cystoscopy

(For interstitial radioelement application, see 77776-77778)

(For ultrasonic guidance for interstitial radioelement application, use 76965)

55860   Exposure of prostate, any approach, for insertion of radioactive substance;

(For application of interstitial radioelement, see 77776-77778)

55862   with lymph node biopsy(s) (limited pelvic lymphadenectomy)

55865   with bilateral pelvic lymphadenectomy, including external iliac, hypogastric and obturator nodes

Other Procedures

(For artificial insemination, see 58321, 58322)

55870   Electroejaculation

55873   Cryosurgical ablation of the prostate (includes ultrasonic guidance for interstitial cryosurgical probe placement)

55899   Unlisted procedure, male genital system

Intersex Surgery

55970   Intersex surgery; male to female

55980   female to male

(56300 has been deleted. To report, use 49320)

(56301 has been deleted. To report, use 58670)

(56302 has been deleted. To report, use 58671)

(56303 has been deleted. To report, use 58662)

(56304 has been deleted. To report, use 58660)

(56305 has been deleted. To report, use 49321)

(56306 has been deleted. To report, use 49322)

(56307 has been deleted. To report, use 58661)

(56308 has been deleted. To report, use 58550)

(56309 has been deleted. To report, use 58551)

(56310 has been deleted. To report, use 44200)

(56311 has been deleted. To report, use 38570)

(56312 has been deleted. To report, use 38571)

(56313 has been deleted. To report, use 38572)

(56314 has been deleted. To report, use 49323)

(56315 has been deleted. To report, use 44970)

(56316 has been deleted. To report, use 49650)

(56317 has been deleted. To report, use 49651)

(56318 has been deleted. To report, use 54690)

(56320 has been deleted. To report, use 55550)

(56321 has been deleted. To report, use 60650)

(56322 has been deleted. To report, use 43651)

(56323 has been deleted. To report, use 43652)

(56324 has been deleted. To report, use 47570)

(56340 has been deleted. To report, use 47562)

(56341 has been deleted. To report, use 47563)

(56342 has been deleted. To report, use 47564)

(56343 has been deleted. To report, use 58673)

(56344 has been deleted. To report, use 58672)

(56345 has been deleted. To report, use 38120)

(56346 has been deleted. To report, use 43653)

(56347 has been deleted. To report, use 44201)

(56348 has been deleted. To report, use 44202)

(56349 has been deleted. To report, use 43280)

(56350 has been deleted. To report, use 58555)

(56351 has been deleted. To report, use 58558)

(56352 has been deleted. To report, use 58559)

(56353 has been deleted. To report, use 58560)

(56354 has been deleted. To report, use 58561)

(56355 has been deleted. To report, use 58562)

(56356 has been deleted. To report, use 58563)

(56360 has been deleted. To report, use 49320)

(56361 has been deleted. To report, use 49321)

(56362 has been deleted. To report, use 47560)

(56363 has been deleted. To report, use 47561)

(56399 has been deleted. To report, see site-specific unlisted laparoscopy/hysteroscopy procedure codes)

Female Genital System

(For pelvic laparotomy, use 49000)

(For excision or destruction of endometriomas, open method, see 49200, 49201)

(For paracentesis, see 49080, 49081)

(For secondary closure of abdominal wall evisceration or disruption, use 49900)

(For fulguration or excision of lesions, laparoscopic approach, use 58662)

(For chemotherapy, see 96400-96549)

(56000 has been deleted. To report, use 56405)

(56100 has been deleted. To report, use 56605)

(56200 has been deleted. To report, use 56810)

Vulva, Perineum and Introitus

Definitions

The following definitions apply to the vulvectomy codes (56620-56640).

A *simple* procedure is the removal of skin and superficial subcutaneous tissues.

A *radical* procedure is the removal of skin and deep subcutaneous tissue.

A *partial* procedure is the removal of less than 80% of the vulvar area.

A *complete* procedure is the removal of greater than 80% of the vulvar area.

Incision

(For incision and drainage of sebaceous cyst, furuncle, or abscess, see 10040, 10060, 10061)

(56400 has been deleted. To report, use 56405)

56405*   Incision and drainage of vulva or perineal abscess

56420*   Incision and drainage of Bartholin's gland abscess

(For incision and drainage of Skene's gland abscess or cyst, use 53060)

56440   Marsupialization of Bartholin's gland cyst

56441   Lysis of labial adhesions

Destruction

(56500 has been deleted. To report, use 56501)

▲**56501**   Destruction of lesion(s), vulva; simple (eg, laser surgery, electrosurgery, cryosurgery, chemosurgery)

(56505-56507, 56510 have been deleted. To report, use 56501)

▲**56515**   extensive (eg, laser surgery, electrosurgery, cryosurgery, chemosurgery)

(56520, 56521 have been deleted. To report, use 56501 or 56515)

(For destruction of Skene's gland cyst or abscess, use 53270)

(For cautery destruction of urethral caruncle, use 53265)

Excision

(56600 has been deleted. To report, use 56605)

56605*   Biopsy of vulva or perineum (separate procedure); one lesion

+ **56606***   each separate additional lesion (List separately in addition to code for primary procedure)

(Use 56606 in conjunction with code 56605)

(For excision of local lesion, see 11420-11426, 11620-11626)

56620   Vulvectomy simple; partial

56625   complete

(For skin graft, see 15000 et seq)

56630   Vulvectomy, radical, partial;

(For skin graft, if used, see 15000, 15120, 15121, 15240, 15241)

56631   with unilateral inguinofemoral lymphadenectomy

56632   with bilateral inguinofemoral lymphadenectomy

56633   Vulvectomy, radical, complete;

56634   with unilateral inguinofemoral lymphadenectomy

(56635 has been deleted. To report, see 56634, 56637)

(56636 has been deleted. To report, see 56634, 56637)

56637   with bilateral inguinofemoral lymphadenectomy

56640   Vulvectomy, radical, complete, with inguinofemoral, iliac, and pelvic lymphadenectomy

(56641 has been deleted. To report, use 56640 with modifier '-50')

(For lymphadenectomy, see 38760-38780)

(56680, 56685 have been deleted)

56700   Partial hymenectomy or revision of hymenal ring

(56710 has been deleted. To report, use 56700)

56720*   Hymenotomy, simple incision

56740   Excision of Bartholin's gland or cyst

(For excision of Skene's gland, use 53270)

(For excision of urethral caruncle, use 53265)

(For excision or fulguration of urethral carcinoma, use 53220)

(For excision or marsupialization of urethral diverticulum, see 53230, 53240)

Repair

(For repair of urethra for mucosal prolapse, use 53275)

56800   Plastic repair of introitus

56805   Clitoroplasty for intersex state

56810   Perineoplasty, repair of perineum, nonobstetrical (separate procedure)

(See also 56800)

(For repair of wounds to genitalia, see 12001-12007, 12041-12047, 13131-13133)

(For repair of recent injury of vagina and perineum, nonobstetrical, use 57210)

(For anal sphincteroplasty, see 46750, 46751)

(For episiorrhaphy, episioperineorrhaphy for recent injury of vulva and/or perineum, nonobstetrical, use 57210)

Vagina

Incision

57000   Colpotomy; with exploration

57010   with drainage of pelvic abscess

57020*   Colpocentesis (separate procedure)

▲ **57022**   Incision and drainage of vaginal hematoma; obstetrical/postpartum

57023   non-obstetrical (eg, post-trauma, spontaneous bleeding)

Destruction

(57050, 57057, 57060 have been deleted. To report, use 57061 or 57065)

▲ **57061**   Destruction of vaginal lesion(s); simple (eg, laser surgery, electrosurgery, cryosurgery, chemosurgery)

(57063 has been deleted. To report, use 57061 or 57065)

▲ **57065**   extensive (eg, laser surgery, electrosurgery, cryosurgery, chemosurgery)

Excision

57100*   Biopsy of vaginal mucosa; simple (separate procedure)

57105   extensive, requiring suture (including cysts)

57106   Vaginectomy, partial removal of vaginal wall;

57107   with removal of paravaginal tissue (radical vaginectomy)

(57108 has been deleted. To report, use 57106)

57109   with removal of paravaginal tissue (radical vaginectomy) with bilateral total pelvic lymphadenectomy and para-aortic lymph node sampling (biopsy)

57110   Vaginectomy, complete removal of vaginal wall;

57111   with removal of paravaginal tissue (radical vaginectomy)

57112   with removal of paravaginal tissue (radical vaginectomy) with bilateral total pelvic lymphadenectomy and para-aortic lymph node sampling (biopsy)

57120   Colpocleisis (Le Fort type)

57130   Excision of vaginal septum

57135   Excision of vaginal cyst or tumor

Introduction

57150*   Irrigation of vagina and/or application of medicament for treatment of bacterial, parasitic, or fungoid disease

● **57155**   Insertion of uterine tandems and/or vaginal ovoids for clinical brachytherapy

►(For insertion of radioelement sources or ribbons, see 77761-77763, 77781-77784)◄

57160*   Fitting and insertion of pessary or other intravaginal support device

57170   Diaphragm or cervical cap fitting with instructions

57180   Introduction of any hemostatic agent or pack for spontaneous or traumatic nonobstetrical vaginal hemorrhage (separate procedure)

Repair

(For urethral suspension, Marshall-Marchetti-Krantz type, abdominal approach, see 51840, 51841)

(For laparoscopic suspension, use 51990)

57200   Colporrhaphy, suture of injury of vagina (nonobstetrical)

57210   Colpoperineorrhaphy, suture of injury of vagina and/or perineum (nonobstetrical)

57220   Plastic operation on urethral sphincter, vaginal approach (eg, Kelly urethral plication)

57230   Plastic repair of urethrocele

57240   Anterior colporrhaphy, repair of cystocele with or without repair of urethrocele

57250   Posterior colporrhaphy, repair of rectocele with or without perineorrhaphy

(For repair of rectocele (separate procedure) without posterior colporrhaphy, use 45560)

57260   Combined anteroposterior colporrhaphy;

57265   with enterocele repair

57268   Repair of enterocele, vaginal approach (separate procedure)

57270   Repair of enterocele, abdominal approach (separate procedure)

⊘ =Modifier '-51' Exempt   ► ◄=New or Revised Text   ✚ =Add-on Code   CPT 2002

57280	Colpopexy, abdominal approach
57282	Sacrospinous ligament fixation for prolapse of vagina
57284	Paravaginal defect repair (including repair of cystocele, stress urinary incontinence, and/or incomplete vaginal prolapse)
57287	Removal or revision of sling for stress incontinence (eg, fascia or synthetic)
57288	Sling operation for stress incontinence (eg, fascia or synthetic)

(For laparoscopic approach, use 51992)

57289	Pereyra procedure, including anterior colporrhaphy

(57290 has been deleted. To report, use 57291 or 57292)

57291	Construction of artificial vagina; without graft
57292	with graft
57300	Closure of rectovaginal fistula; vaginal or transanal approach
57305	abdominal approach
57307	abdominal approach, with concomitant colostomy
57308	transperineal approach, with perineal body reconstruction, with or without levator plication
57310	Closure of urethrovaginal fistula;
57311	with bulbocavernosus transplant
57320	Closure of vesicovaginal fistula; vaginal approach

(For concomitant cystostomy, see 51005-51040)

57330	transvesical and vaginal approach

(For abdominal approach, use 51900)

57335	Vaginoplasty for intersex state

Manipulation

57400*	Dilation of vagina under anesthesia
57410*	Pelvic examination under anesthesia
57415	Removal of impacted vaginal foreign body (separate procedure) under anesthesia

(For removal without anesthesia of an impacted vaginal foreign body, use the appropriate E/M code)

Endoscopy

(57450, 57451 have been deleted)

57452*	Colposcopy (vaginoscopy); (separate procedure)
57454*	with biopsy(s) of the cervix and/or endocervical curettage
57460	with loop electrode excision procedure of the cervix

Cervix Uteri

Excision

(For radical surgical procedures, see 58200-58240)

57500*	Biopsy, single or multiple, or local excision of lesion, with or without fulguration (separate procedure)
57505	Endocervical curettage (not done as part of a dilation and curettage)
▲ **57510**	Cautery of cervix; electro or thermal
57511*	cryocautery, initial or repeat
57513	laser ablation
57520	Conization of cervix, with or without fulguration, with or without dilation and curettage, with or without repair; cold knife or laser

(See also 58120)

57522	loop electrode excision
57530	Trachelectomy (cervicectomy), amputation of cervix (separate procedure)
57531	Radical trachelectomy, with bilateral total pelvic lymphadenectomy and para-aortic lymph node sampling biopsy, with or without removal of tube(s), with or without removal of ovary(s)

(For radical abdominal hysterectomy, use 58210)

57540	Excision of cervical stump, abdominal approach;
57545	with pelvic floor repair
57550	Excision of cervical stump, vaginal approach;
57555	with anterior and/or posterior repair
57556	with repair of enterocele

(For insertion of intrauterine device, use 58300)

(57600-57620 have been deleted. For insertion of any hemostatic agent or pack for control of spontaneous non-obstetrical hemorrhage, use 57180)

Repair

57700	Cerclage of uterine cervix, nonobstetrical
57720	Trachelorrhaphy, plastic repair of uterine cervix, vaginal approach

Manipulation

57800*	Dilation of cervical canal, instrumental (separate procedure)
57820	Dilation and curettage of cervical stump

Corpus Uteri

Excision

58100*   Endometrial sampling (biopsy) with or without endocervical sampling (biopsy), without cervical dilation, any method (separate procedure)

(For endocervical curettage only, use 57505)

(58101, 58102, 58103 have been deleted)

58120   Dilation and curettage, diagnostic and/or therapeutic (nonobstetrical)

(For postpartum hemorrhage, use 59160)

▲ **58140**   Myomectomy, excision of leiomyomata of uterus, single or multiple (separate procedure); abdominal approach

58145   vaginal approach

58150   Total abdominal hysterectomy (corpus and cervix), with or without removal of tube(s), with or without removal of ovary(s);

58152   with colpo-urethrocystopexy (eg, Marshall-Marchetti-Krantz, Burch)

(For urethrocystopexy without hysterectomy, see 51840, 51841)

58180   Supracervical abdominal hysterectomy (subtotal hysterectomy), with or without removal of tube(s), with or without removal of ovary(s)

58200   Total abdominal hysterectomy, including partial vaginectomy, with para-aortic and pelvic lymph node sampling, with or without removal of tube(s), with or without removal of ovary(s)

(58205 has been deleted. For hysterectomy with pelvic lymphadenectomy, use 58210)

58210   Radical abdominal hysterectomy, with bilateral total pelvic lymphadenectomy and para-aortic lymph node sampling (biopsy), with or without removal of tube(s), with or without removal of ovary(s)

(For radical hysterectomy with ovarian transposition, use also 58825)

58240   Pelvic exenteration for gynecologic malignancy, with total abdominal hysterectomy or cervicectomy, with or without removal of tube(s), with or without removal of ovary(s), with removal of bladder and ureteral transplantations, and/or abdominoperineal resection of rectum and colon and colostomy, or any combination thereof

(For pelvic exenteration for lower urinary tract or male genital malignancy, use 51597)

58260   Vaginal hysterectomy;

58262   with removal of tube(s), and/or ovary(s)

58263   with removal of tube(s), and/or ovary(s), with repair of enterocele

(58265 has been deleted. To report, see 57240, 57250, 57260, 57265)

58267   with colpo-urethrocystopexy (Marshall-Marchetti-Krantz type, Pereyra type, with or without endoscopic control)

58270   with repair of enterocele

(For repair of enterocele with removal of tubes and/or ovaries, use 58263)

▲ **58275**   Vaginal hysterectomy, with total or partial vaginectomy;

58280   with repair of enterocele

58285   Vaginal hysterectomy, radical (Schauta type operation)

Introduction

(For insertion/removal of implantable contraceptive capsules, see 11975, 11976, 11977)

58300*   Insertion of intrauterine device (IUD)

58301   Removal of intrauterine device (IUD)

(58310 has been deleted. To report, see 58321, 58322)

(58311 has been deleted. To report, use 58323)

(58320 has been deleted)

58321   Artificial insemination; intra-cervical

58322   intra-uterine

58323   Sperm washing for artificial insemination

58340*   Catheterization and introduction of saline or contrast material for hysterosonography or hysterosalpingography

(For radiological supervision and interpretation of hysterosonography, use 76831)

(For radiological supervision and interpretation of hysterosalpingography, use 74740)

▶(For endometrial cryoablation with ultrasonic guidance, use Category III code 0009T)◀

58345   Transcervical introduction of fallopian tube catheter for diagnosis and/or re-establishing patency (any method), with or without hysterosalpingography

(For radiological supervision and interpretation, use 74742)

● **58346**   Insertion of Heyman capsules for clinical brachytherapy

▶(For insertion of radioelement sources or ribbons, see 77761-77763, 77781-77784)◀

58350*   Chromotubation of oviduct, including materials

(For materials supplied by physician, use 99070)

58353   Endometrial ablation, thermal, without hysteroscopic guidance

(For hysteroscopic procedure, use 58563)

Repair

58400   Uterine suspension, with or without shortening of round ligaments, with or without shortening of sacrouterine ligaments; (separate procedure)

58410   with presacral sympathectomy

(58430 has been deleted. To report, use 58999)

(58500 has been deleted. To report, use 58752)

58520   Hysterorrhaphy, repair of ruptured uterus (nonobstetrical)

58540   Hysteroplasty, repair of uterine anomaly (Strassman type)

(For closure of vesicouterine fistula, use 51920)

Laparoscopy/Hysteroscopy

Surgical laparoscopy always includes diagnostic laparoscopy. To report a diagnostic laparoscopy (peritoneoscopy) (separate procedure), use 49320. To report a diagnostic hysteroscopy (separate procedure), use 58555.

58550   Laparoscopy, surgical; with vaginal hysterectomy with or without removal of tube(s), with or without removal of ovary(s) (laparoscopic assisted vaginal hysterectomy)

58551   with removal of leiomyomata (single or multiple)

58555   Hysteroscopy, diagnostic (separate procedure)

58558   Hysteroscopy, surgical; with sampling (biopsy) of endometrium and/or polypectomy, with or without D & C

58559   with lysis of intrauterine adhesions (any method)

58560   with division or resection of intrauterine septum (any method)

58561   with removal of leiomyomata

58562   with removal of impacted foreign body

▲ **58563**   with endometrial ablation (eg, endometrial resection, electrosurgical ablation, thermoablation)

58578   Unlisted laparoscopy procedure, uterus

58579   Unlisted hysteroscopy procedure, uterus

Oviduct/Ovary

Incision

58600   Ligation or transection of fallopian tube(s), abdominal or vaginal approach, unilateral or bilateral

58605   Ligation or transection of fallopian tube(s), abdominal or vaginal approach, postpartum, unilateral or bilateral, during same hospitalization (separate procedure)

(For laparoscopic procedures, use 58670, 58671)

(58610 has been deleted. To report, see 58600-58611)

+ ▲ **58611**   Ligation or transection of fallopian tube(s) when done at the time of cesarean delivery or intra-abdominal surgery (not a separate procedure) (List separately in addition to code for primary procedure)

58615   Occlusion of fallopian tube(s) by device (eg, band, clip, Falope ring) vaginal or suprapubic approach

(For laparoscopic approach, use 58671)

(58618 has been deleted. To report, use 58740)

Laparoscopy

Surgical laparoscopy always includes diagnostic laparoscopy. To report a diagnostic laparoscopy (peritoneoscopy) (separate procedure), use 49320.

(For laparoscopic biopsy of the ovary or fallopian tube, use 49321)

58660   Laparoscopy, surgical; with lysis of adhesions (salpingolysis, ovariolysis) (separate procedure)

58661   with removal of adnexal structures (partial or total oophorectomy and/or salpingectomy)

58662   with fulguration or excision of lesions of the ovary, pelvic viscera, or peritoneal surface by any method

58670   with fulguration of oviducts (with or without transection)

58671   with occlusion of oviducts by device (eg, band, clip, or Falope ring)

58672   with fimbrioplasty

58673   with salpingostomy (salpingoneostomy)

(Codes 58672 and 58673 are used to report unilateral procedures. For bilateral procedure, use modifier '-50')

58679   Unlisted laparoscopy procedure, oviduct, ovary

Excision

58700   Salpingectomy, complete or partial, unilateral or bilateral (separate procedure)

58720   Salpingo-oophorectomy, complete or partial, unilateral or bilateral (separate procedure)

Repair

58740   Lysis of adhesions (salpingolysis, ovariolysis)

(For laparoscopic approach, use 58660)

(For excision or destruction of endometriomas, open method, see 49200, 49201)

(For fulguration or excision of lesions, laparoscopic approach, use 58662)

58750   Tubotubal anastomosis

58752   Tubouterine implantation

58760   Fimbrioplasty

(For laparoscopic approach, use 58672)

58770   Salpingostomy (salpingoneostomy)

(For laparoscopic approach, use 58673)

Ovary

Incision

58800 Drainage of ovarian cyst(s), unilateral or bilateral, (separate procedure); vaginal approach

58805   abdominal approach

58820 Drainage of ovarian abscess; vaginal approach, open

58822   abdominal approach

58823 Drainage of pelvic abscess, transvaginal or transrectal approach, percutaneous (eg, ovarian, pericolic)

    (For radiological supervision and interpretation, use 75989)

58825 Transposition, ovary(s)

Excision

58900 Biopsy of ovary, unilateral or bilateral (separate procedure)

    (For laparoscopic biopsy of the ovary or fallopian tube, use 49321)

58920 Wedge resection or bisection of ovary, unilateral or bilateral

58925 Ovarian cystectomy, unilateral or bilateral

58940 Oophorectomy, partial or total, unilateral or bilateral;

    (58942 has been deleted. To report, use 58952)

58943   for ovarian, tubal or primary peritoneal malignancy, with para-aortic and pelvic lymph node biopsies, peritoneal washings, peritoneal biopsies, diaphragmatic assessments, with or without salpingectomy(s), with or without omentectomy

    (58945 has been deleted. To report, use 58950)

58950 Resection of ovarian, tubal or primary peritoneal malignancy with bilateral salpingo-oophorectomy and omentectomy;

58951   with total abdominal hysterectomy, pelvic and limited para-aortic lymphadenectomy

58952   with radical dissection for debulking (ie, radical excision or destruction, intra-abdominal or retroperitoneal tumors)

● **58953** Bilateral salpingo-oophorectomy with omentectomy, total abdominal hysterectomy and radical dissection for debulking;

● **58954**   with pelvic lymphadenectomy and limited para-aortic lymphadenectomy

58960 Laparotomy, for staging or restaging of ovarian, tubal or primary peritoneal malignancy (second look), with or without omentectomy, peritoneal washing, biopsy of abdominal and pelvic peritoneum, diaphragmatic assessment with pelvic and limited para-aortic lymphadenectomy

In Vitro Fertilization

58970 Follicle puncture for oocyte retrieval, any method

    (For radiological supervision and interpretation, use 76948)

    (58972 has been deleted. To report, use 89250)

58974 Embryo transfer, intrauterine

58976 Gamete, zygote, or embryo intrafallopian transfer, any method

    (58980 has been deleted. To report, use 49320)

    (58982 has been deleted. To report, use 58670)

    (58983 has been deleted. To report, use 58671)

    (58984 has been deleted. To report, use 58662)

    (58985 has been deleted. To report, use 58660)

    (58986 has been deleted. To report, use 49321)

    (58987 has been deleted. To report, use 49322)

    (58988 has been deleted. To report, use 58661)

    (58990 has been deleted. To report, use 58555)

    (58992 has been deleted. To report, see 58559, 58560)

    (58994 has been deleted. To report, use 58561)

    (58995 has been deleted. To report, see 58559, 58561, 58563)

    (58996 has been deleted. To report, use 58563)

Other Procedures

58999 Unlisted procedure, female genital system (nonobstetrical)

Maternity Care and Delivery

The services normally provided in uncomplicated maternity cases include antepartum care, delivery, and postpartum care.

Antepartum care includes the initial and subsequent history, physical examinations, recording of weight, blood pressures, fetal heart tones, routine chemical urinalysis, and monthly visits up to 28 weeks gestation, biweekly visits to 36 weeks gestation, and weekly visits until delivery. Any other visits or services within this time period should be coded separately.

Delivery services include admission to the hospital, the admission history and physical examination, management of uncomplicated labor, vaginal delivery (with or without episiotomy, with or without forceps), or cesarean delivery. Medical problems complicating labor and delivery management may require additional resources and should be identified by utilizing the codes in the **Medicine** and **Evaluation and Management Services** section in addition to codes for maternity care.

Postpartum care includes hospital and office visits following vaginal or cesarean section delivery.

For medical complications of pregnancy (eg, cardiac problems, neurological problems, diabetes, hypertension, toxemia, hyperemesis, pre-term labor, premature rupture of membranes), see services in the **Medicine** and **Evaluation and Management Services** section.

For surgical complications of pregnancy (eg, appendectomy, hernia, ovarian cyst, Bartholin cyst), see services in the **Surgery** section.

If a physician provides all or part of the antepartum and/or postpartum patient care but does not perform delivery due to termination of pregnancy by abortion or referral to another physician for delivery, see the antepartum and postpartum care codes 59425-59426 and 59430.

(For circumcision of newborn, see 54150, 54160)

Antepartum Services

▶(For insertion of transcervical or transvaginal fetal oximetry sensor, use Category III code 0021T)◀

▲ **59000*** Amniocentesis; diagnostic

(For radiological supervision and interpretation, use 76946)

● **59001** therapeutic amniotic fluid reduction (includes ultrasound guidance)

(59010, 59011 have been deleted)

59012 Cordocentesis (intrauterine), any method

(For radiological supervision and interpretation, use 76941)

59015 Chorionic villus sampling, any method

(For radiological supervision and interpretation, use 76945)

59020* Fetal contraction stress test

59025 Fetal non-stress test

59030* Fetal scalp blood sampling

(59031 has been deleted. To report, use 59030 and see modifiers '-76' and '-77')

59050 Fetal monitoring during labor by consulting physician (ie, non-attending physician) with written report; supervision and interpretation

59051 interpretation only

Excision

59100 Hysterotomy, abdominal (eg, for hydatidiform mole, abortion)

(When tubal ligation is performed at the same time as hysterotomy, use 58611 in addition to 59100)

(59101, 59105, 59106 have been deleted. To report, see 59100, 58611)

59120 Surgical treatment of ectopic pregnancy; tubal or ovarian, requiring salpingectomy and/or oophorectomy, abdominal or vaginal approach

59121 tubal or ovarian, without salpingectomy and/or oophorectomy

(59125, 59126 have been deleted. To report, see 59120, 59121)

59130 abdominal pregnancy

59135 interstitial, uterine pregnancy requiring total hysterectomy

59136 interstitial, uterine pregnancy with partial resection of uterus

59140 cervical, with evacuation

59150 Laparoscopic treatment of ectopic pregnancy; without salpingectomy and/or oophorectomy

59151 with salpingectomy and/or oophorectomy

59160 Curettage, postpartum

Introduction

(For intrauterine fetal transfusion, use 36460)

(For introduction of hypertonic solution and/or prostaglandins to initiate labor, see 59850-59857)

59200 Insertion of cervical dilator (eg, laminaria, prostaglandin) (separate procedure)

Repair

(For tracheloplasty, use 57700)

59300 Episiotomy or vaginal repair, by other than attending physician

(59305 has been deleted)

59320 Cerclage of cervix, during pregnancy; vaginal

59325 abdominal

59350 Hysterorrhaphy of ruptured uterus

(59351 has been deleted)

Vaginal Delivery, Antepartum and Postpartum Care

▶(For insertion of transcervical or transvaginal fetal oximetry sensor, use Category III code 0021T)◀

59400 Routine obstetric care including antepartum care, vaginal delivery (with or without episiotomy, and/or forceps) and postpartum care

59409 Vaginal delivery only (with or without episiotomy and/or forceps);

59410 including postpartum care

▲=Revised Code ●=New Code *=Service Includes Surgical Procedure Only

59412 External cephalic version, with or without tocolysis

(Use 59412 in addition to code(s) for delivery)

59414 Delivery of placenta (separate procedure)

(59420 has been deleted. To report, see 59425, 59426 or appropriate E/M code(s))

(For 1-3 antepartum care visits, see appropriate E/M code(s))

59425 Antepartum care only; 4-6 visits

59426 7 or more visits

59430 Postpartum care only (separate procedure)

Cesarean Delivery

(For standby attendance for infant, use 99360)

►(For insertion of transcervical or transvaginal fetal oximetry sensor, use Category III code 0021T)◄

(59500, 59501 have been deleted. To report, see 59510, 59515, 59525)

59510 Routine obstetric care including antepartum care, cesarean delivery, and postpartum care

59514 Cesarean delivery only;

59515 including postpartum care

(59520, 59521 have been deleted. To report, see 59510, 59515, 59525)

✚ 59525 Subtotal or total hysterectomy after cesarean delivery (List separately in addition to code for primary procedure)

(Use 59525 in conjunction with codes 59510, 59514, 59515, 59618, 59620, 59622)

(59540, 59541, 59560, 59561, 59580, 59581 have been deleted. To report, see 59510, 59515, 59525)

Delivery After Previous Cesarean Delivery

Patients who have had a previous cesarean delivery and now present with the expectation of a vaginal delivery are coded using codes 59610-59622. If the patient has a successful vaginal delivery after a previous cesarean delivery (VBAC), use codes 59610-59614. If the attempt is unsuccessful and another cesarean delivery is carried out, use codes 59618-59622. To report elective cesarean deliveries use code 59510, 59514 or 59515.

►(For insertion of transcervical or transvaginal fetal oximetry sensor, use Category III code 0021T)◄

59610 Routine obstetric care including antepartum care, vaginal delivery (with or without episiotomy, and/or forceps) and postpartum care, after previous cesarean delivery

59612 Vaginal delivery only, after previous cesarean delivery (with or without episiotomy and/or forceps);

59614 including postpartum care

59618 Routine obstetric care including antepartum care, cesarean delivery, and postpartum care, following attempted vaginal delivery after previous cesarean delivery

59620 Cesarean delivery only, following attempted vaginal delivery after previous cesarean delivery;

59622 including postpartum care

Abortion

(For medical treatment of spontaneous complete abortion, any trimester, use E/M codes 99201-99233)

(59800, 59810 have been deleted. To report, see 99201-99233)

(59801, 59811 have been deleted. To report, use 59812)

59812 Treatment of incomplete abortion, any trimester, completed surgically

59820 Treatment of missed abortion, completed surgically; first trimester

59821 second trimester

59830 Treatment of septic abortion, completed surgically

59840 Induced abortion, by dilation and curettage

59841 Induced abortion, by dilation and evacuation

59850 Induced abortion, by one or more intra-amniotic injections (amniocentesis-injections), including hospital admission and visits, delivery of fetus and secundines;

59851 with dilation and curettage and/or evacuation

59852 with hysterotomy (failed intra-amniotic injection)

(For insertion of cervical dilator, use 59200)

59855 Induced abortion, by one or more vaginal suppositories (eg, prostaglandin) with or without cervical dilation (eg, laminaria), including hospital admission and visits, delivery of fetus and secundines;

59856 with dilation and curettage and/or evacuation

59857 with hysterotomy (failed medical evacuation)

Other Procedures

59866 Multifetal pregnancy reduction(s) (MPR)

59870 Uterine evacuation and curettage for hydatidiform mole

59871 Removal of cerclage suture under anesthesia (other than local)

59898 Unlisted laparoscopy procedure, maternity care and delivery

59899 Unlisted procedure, maternity care and delivery

Endocrine System

(For pituitary and pineal surgery, see **Nervous System**)

Thyroid Gland

Incision

▲ **60000***　Incision and drainage of thyroglossal duct cyst, infected

Excision

60001　Aspiration and/or injection, thyroid cyst

(For fine needle aspiration, see ▶10021, 10022◀)

▶(If imaging guidance is performed, see 76360, 76942)◀

60100*　Biopsy thyroid, percutaneous core needle

▶(If imaging guidance is performed,◀ see ▶76003◀, 76360, ▶76393◀, 76942)

▶(For fine needle aspiration, use 10021 or 10022)◀

▶(For evaluation of fine needle aspirate, see 88172, 88173)◀

60200　Excision of cyst or adenoma of thyroid, or transection of isthmus

60210　Partial thyroid lobectomy, unilateral; with or without isthmusectomy

60212　　with contralateral subtotal lobectomy, including isthmusectomy

60220　Total thyroid lobectomy, unilateral; with or without isthmusectomy

60225　　with contralateral subtotal lobectomy, including isthmusectomy

60240　Thyroidectomy, total or complete

(60242 has been deleted. To report, see 60210-60225)

(60245 has been deleted. To report, see 60210-60225)

(60246 has been deleted. To report, use 60271)

60252　Thyroidectomy, total or subtotal for malignancy; with limited neck dissection

60254　　with radical neck dissection

60260　Thyroidectomy, removal of all remaining thyroid tissue following previous removal of a portion of thyroid

(60261 has been deleted. To report, use 60260 with modifier '-50')

▲ **60270**　Thyroidectomy, including substernal thyroid; sternal split or transthoracic approach

60271　　cervical approach

60280　Excision of thyroglossal duct cyst or sinus;

60281　　recurrent

(For thyroid ultrasonography, use 76536)

Parathyroid, Thymus, Adrenal Glands, and Carotid Body

Excision

(For pituitary and pineal surgery, see **Nervous System**)

60500　Parathyroidectomy or exploration of parathyroid(s);

60502　　re-exploration

60505　　with mediastinal exploration, sternal split or transthoracic approach

(60510 has been deleted)

+ **60512**　Parathyroid autotransplantation (List separately in addition to code for primary procedure)

(Use 60512 in conjunction with codes 60500, 60502, 60505, 60212, 60225, 60240, 60252, 60254, 60260, 60270, 60271)

60520　Thymectomy, partial or total; transcervical approach (separate procedure)

60521　　sternal split or transthoracic approach, without radical mediastinal dissection (separate procedure)

60522　　sternal split or transthoracic approach, with radical mediastinal dissection (separate procedure)

60540　Adrenalectomy, partial or complete, or exploration of adrenal gland with or without biopsy, transabdominal, lumbar or dorsal (separate procedure);

60545　　with excision of adjacent retroperitoneal tumor

(For excision of remote or disseminated pheochromocytoma, see 49200, 49201)

(For laparoscopic approach, use 56321)

(60550, 60555 have been deleted. To report, use 60540 with modifier '-50')

60600　Excision of carotid body tumor; without excision of carotid artery

60605　　with excision of carotid artery

Laparoscopy

Surgical laparoscopy always includes diagnostic laparoscopy. To report a diagnostic laparoscopy (peritoneoscopy) (separate procedure), use 49320.

60650　Laparoscopy, surgical, with adrenalectomy, partial or complete, or exploration of adrenal gland with or without biopsy, transabdominal, lumbar or dorsal

60659　Unlisted laparoscopy procedure, endocrine system

Other Procedures

60699　Unlisted procedure, endocrine system

▲=Revised Code　　●=New Code　　*=Service Includes Surgical Procedure Only

Notes

Nervous System

Skull, Meninges, and Brain

(For injection procedure for cerebral angiography, see 36100-36218)

(For injection procedure for ventriculography, see 61026, 61120, 61130)

(For injection procedure for pneumoencephalography, use 61055)

Injection, Drainage, or Aspiration

61000* Subdural tap through fontanelle, or suture, infant, unilateral or bilateral; initial

61001* subsequent taps

61020* Ventricular puncture through previous burr hole, fontanelle, suture, or implanted ventricular catheter/reservoir; without injection

(61025 has been deleted. To report, use 61026)

▲**61026*** with injection of medication or other substance for diagnosis or treatment

(61030, 61045 have been deleted. To report, use 61026)

61050* Cisternal or lateral cervical (C1-C2) puncture; without injection (separate procedure)

(61051, 61052, 61053 have been deleted. To report, use 61055)

▲**61055*** with injection of medication or other substance for diagnosis or treatment (eg, C1-C2)

(For radiological supervision and interpretation, see **Radiology**)

61070* Puncture of shunt tubing or reservoir for aspiration or injection procedure

(For radiological supervision and interpretation, use 75809)

Twist Drill, Burr Hole(s), or Trephine

61105* Twist drill hole for subdural or ventricular puncture;

(61106 has been deleted)

⊘**61107*** for implanting ventricular catheter or pressure recording device

61108 for evacuation and/or drainage of subdural hematoma

61120 Burr hole(s) for ventricular puncture (including injection of gas, contrast media, dye, or radioactive material)

(61130 has been deleted)

61140 Burr hole(s) or trephine; with biopsy of brain or intracranial lesion

61150 with drainage of brain abscess or cyst

61151 with subsequent tapping (aspiration) of intracranial abscess or cyst

61154 Burr hole(s) with evacuation and/or drainage of hematoma, extradural or subdural

(61155 has been deleted. To report, use 61154 with modifier '-50')

61156 Burr hole(s); with aspiration of hematoma or cyst, intracerebral

⊘**61210*** for implanting ventricular catheter, reservoir, EEG electrode(s) or pressure recording device (separate procedure)

61215 Insertion of subcutaneous reservoir, pump or continuous infusion system for connection to ventricular catheter

(For chemotherapy, use 96450)

61250 Burr hole(s) or trephine, supratentorial, exploratory, not followed by other surgery

(61251 has been deleted. To report, use 61250 with modifier '-50')

61253 Burr hole(s) or trephine, infratentorial, unilateral or bilateral

(If burr hole(s) or trephine are followed by craniotomy at same operative session, use 61304-61321; do not use 61250 or 61253)

Craniectomy or Craniotomy

61304 Craniectomy or craniotomy, exploratory; supratentorial

61305 infratentorial (posterior fossa)

(61310, 61311 have been deleted. To report, see 61312-61315)

61312 Craniectomy or craniotomy for evacuation of hematoma, supratentorial; extradural or subdural

61313 intracerebral

61314 Craniectomy or craniotomy for evacuation of hematoma, infratentorial; extradural or subdural

61315 intracerebellar

61320 Craniectomy or craniotomy, drainage of intracranial abscess; supratentorial

61321 infratentorial

61330 Decompression of orbit only, transcranial approach

(61331 has been deleted. To report, use 61330 with modifier '-50')

61332 Exploration of orbit (transcranial approach); with biopsy

61333 with removal of lesion

61334 with removal of foreign body

61340 Other cranial decompression (eg, subtemporal), supratentorial

(61341 has been deleted. To report, use 61340 with modifier '-50')

61343 Craniectomy, suboccipital with cervical laminectomy for decompression of medulla and spinal cord, with or without dural graft (eg, Arnold-Chiari malformation)

61345 Other cranial decompression, posterior fossa

(For orbital decompression by lateral wall approach, Kroenlein type, use 67445)

61440 Craniotomy for section of tentorium cerebelli (separate procedure)

61450 Craniectomy, subtemporal, for section, compression, or decompression of sensory root of gasserian ganglion

61458 Craniectomy, suboccipital; for exploration or decompression of cranial nerves

61460 for section of one or more cranial nerves

61470 for medullary tractotomy

61480 for mesencephalic tractotomy or pedunculotomy

61490 Craniotomy for lobotomy, including cingulotomy

(61491 has been deleted. To report, use 61490 with modifier '-50')

61500 Craniectomy; with excision of tumor or other bone lesion of skull

61501 for osteomyelitis

61510 Craniectomy, trephination, bone flap craniotomy; for excision of brain tumor, supratentorial, except meningioma

61512 for excision of meningioma, supratentorial

61514 for excision of brain abscess, supratentorial

61516 for excision or fenestration of cyst, supratentorial

(For excision of pituitary tumor or craniopharyngioma, see 61545, 61546, 61548)

61518 Craniectomy for excision of brain tumor, infratentorial or posterior fossa; except meningioma, cerebellopontine angle tumor, or midline tumor at base of skull

61519 meningioma

61520 cerebellopontine angle tumor

61521 midline tumor at base of skull

61522 Craniectomy, infratentorial or posterior fossa; for excision of brain abscess

61524 for excision or fenestration of cyst

61526 Craniectomy, bone flap craniotomy, transtemporal (mastoid) for excision of cerebellopontine angle tumor;

61530 combined with middle/posterior fossa craniotomy/craniectomy

61531 Subdural implantation of strip electrodes through one or more burr or trephine hole(s) for long term seizure monitoring

(For stereotactic implantation of electrodes, use 61760)

(61532 has been deleted. To report, see 61680-61692)

61533 Craniotomy with elevation of bone flap; for subdural implantation of an electrode array, for long term seizure monitoring

(For continuous EEG monitoring, see 95950-95954)

61534 for excision of epileptogenic focus without electrocorticography during surgery

61535 for removal of epidural or subdural electrode array, without excision of cerebral tissue (separate procedure)

61536 for excision of cerebral epileptogenic focus, with electrocorticography during surgery (includes removal of electrode array)

61538 for lobectomy with electrocorticography during surgery, temporal lobe

61539 for lobectomy with electrocorticography during surgery, other than temporal lobe, partial or total

61541 for transection of corpus callosum

61542 for total hemispherectomy

61543 for partial or subtotal hemispherectomy

61544 for excision or coagulation of choroid plexus

61545 for excision of craniopharyngioma

61546 Craniotomy for hypophysectomy or excision of pituitary tumor, intracranial approach

61548 Hypophysectomy or excision of pituitary tumor, transnasal or transseptal approach, nonstereotactic

(Do not report code 69990 in addition to code 61548)

61550 Craniectomy for craniosynostosis; single cranial suture

61552 multiple cranial sutures

(61553 has been deleted. To report, see 61552, 61558, 61559)

(61555 has been deleted. To report, see 21172-21180, 61552, 61558, 61559)

(For cranial reconstruction for orbital hypertelorism, see 21260-21263)

61556 Craniotomy for craniosynostosis; frontal or parietal bone flap

61557 bifrontal bone flap

61558 Extensive craniectomy for multiple cranial suture craniosynostosis (eg, cloverleaf skull); not requiring bone grafts

61559 recontouring with multiple osteotomies and bone autografts (eg, barrel-stave procedure) (includes obtaining grafts)

(61561 has been deleted. To report, see 21172-21180)

61563 Excision, intra and extracranial, benign tumor of cranial bone (eg, fibrous dysplasia); without optic nerve decompression

61564 with optic nerve decompression

(For reconstruction, see 21181-21183)

⊘ =Modifier '-51' Exempt ▶ ◀=New or Revised Text ✚=Add-on Code CPT 2002

61570 Craniectomy or craniotomy; with excision of foreign body from brain

61571 with treatment of penetrating wound of brain

(For sequestrectomy for osteomyelitis, use 61501)

61575 Transoral approach to skull base, brain stem or upper spinal cord for biopsy, decompression or excision of lesion;

61576 requiring splitting of tongue and/or mandible (including tracheostomy)

(For arthrodesis, use 22548)

Surgery of Skull Base

The surgical management of lesions involving the skull base (base of anterior, middle, and posterior cranial fossae) often requires the skills of several surgeons of different surgical specialties working together or in tandem during the operative session. These operations are usually not staged because of the need for definitive closure of dura, subcutaneous tissues, and skin to avoid serious infections such as osteomyelitis and/or meningitis.

The procedures are categorized according to: 1) *approach procedure* necessary to obtain adequate exposure to the lesion (pathologic entity), 2) *definitive procedure(s)* necessary to biopsy, excise or otherwise treat the lesion, and 3) *repair/reconstruction* of the defect present following the definitive procedure(s).

The *approach procedure* is described according to anatomical area involved, ie, anterior cranial fossa, middle cranial fossa, posterior cranial fossa, and brain stem or upper spinal cord.

The *definitive procedure(s)* describes the repair, biopsy, resection, or excision of various lesions of the skull base and, when appropriate, primary closure of the dura, mucous membranes, and skin.

The *repair/reconstruction procedure(s)* is reported separately if extensive dural grafting, cranioplasty, local or regional myocutaneous pedicle flaps, or extensive skin grafts are required.

For primary closure, see the appropriate codes, ie, 15732, 15755.

When one surgeon performs the approach procedure, another surgeon performs the definitive procedure, and another surgeon performs the repair/reconstruction procedure, each surgeon reports only the code for the specific procedure performed.

If one surgeon performs more than one procedure (ie, approach procedure and definitive procedure), then both codes are reported, adding modifier '-51' to the secondary, additional procedure(s).

Approach Procedures

Anterior Cranial Fossa

61580 Craniofacial approach to anterior cranial fossa; extradural, including lateral rhinotomy, ethmoidectomy, sphenoidectomy, without maxillectomy or orbital exenteration

61581 extradural, including lateral rhinotomy, orbital exenteration, ethmoidectomy, sphenoidectomy and/or maxillectomy

61582 extradural, including unilateral or bifrontal craniotomy, elevation of frontal lobe(s), osteotomy of base of anterior cranial fossa

61583 intradural, including unilateral or bifrontal craniotomy, elevation or resection of frontal lobe, osteotomy of base of anterior cranial fossa

61584 Orbitocranial approach to anterior cranial fossa, extradural, including supraorbital ridge osteotomy and elevation of frontal and/or temporal lobe(s); without orbital exenteration

61585 with orbital exenteration

61586 Bicoronal, transzygomatic and/or LeFort I osteotomy approach to anterior cranial fossa with or without internal fixation, without bone graft

Middle Cranial Fossa

61590 Infratemporal pre-auricular approach to middle cranial fossa (parapharyngeal space, infratemporal and midline skull base, nasopharynx), with or without disarticulation of the mandible, including parotidectomy, craniotomy, decompression and/or mobilization of the facial nerve and/or petrous carotid artery

61591 Infratemporal post-auricular approach to middle cranial fossa (internal auditory meatus, petrous apex, tentorium, cavernous sinus, parasellar area, infratemporal fossa) including mastoidectomy, resection of sigmoid sinus, with or without decompression and/or mobilization of contents of auditory canal or petrous carotid artery

61592 Orbitocranial zygomatic approach to middle cranial fossa (cavernous sinus and carotid artery, clivus, basilar artery or petrous apex) including osteotomy of zygoma, craniotomy, extra- or intradural elevation of temporal lobe

Posterior Cranial Fossa

61595 Transtemporal approach to posterior cranial fossa, jugular foramen or midline skull base, including mastoidectomy, decompression of sigmoid sinus and/or facial nerve, with or without mobilization

61596 Transcochlear approach to posterior cranial fossa, jugular foramen or midline skull base, including labyrinthectomy, decompression, with or without mobilization of facial nerve and/or petrous carotid artery

61597 Transcondylar (far lateral) approach to posterior cranial fossa, jugular foramen or midline skull base, including occipital condylectomy, mastoidectomy, resection of C1-C3 vertebral body(s), decompression of vertebral artery, with or without mobilization

61598 Transpetrosal approach to posterior cranial fossa, clivus or foramen magnum, including ligation of superior petrosal sinus and/or sigmoid sinus

Definitive Procedures

Base of Anterior Cranial Fossa

61600 Resection or excision of neoplastic, vascular or infectious lesion of base of anterior cranial fossa; extradural

61601 intradural, including dural repair, with or without graft

Base of Middle Cranial Fossa

61605 Resection or excision of neoplastic, vascular or infectious lesion of infratemporal fossa, parapharyngeal space, petrous apex; extradural

61606 intradural, including dural repair, with or without graft

61607 Resection or excision of neoplastic, vascular or infectious lesion of parasellar area, cavernous sinus, clivus or midline skull base; extradural

61608 intradural, including dural repair, with or without graft

Codes 61609-61612 are reported in addition to code(s) for primary procedure(s) 61605-61608. Report only one transection or ligation of carotid artery code per operative session.

+ 61609 Transection or ligation, carotid artery in cavernous sinus; without repair (List separately in addition to code for primary procedure)

+ 61610 with repair by anastomosis or graft (List separately in addition to code for primary procedure)

+ 61611 Transection or ligation, carotid artery in petrous canal; without repair (List separately in addition to code for primary procedure)

+ 61612 with repair by anastomosis or graft (List separately in addition to code for primary procedure)

61613 Obliteration of carotid aneurysm, arteriovenous malformation, or carotid-cavernous fistula by dissection within cavernous sinus

Base of Posterior Cranial Fossa

61615 Resection or excision of neoplastic, vascular or infectious lesion of base of posterior cranial fossa, jugular foramen, foramen magnum, or C1-C3 vertebral bodies; extradural

61616 intradural, including dural repair, with or without graft

Repair and/or Reconstruction of Surgical Defects of Skull Base

▲ 61618 Secondary repair of dura for cerebrospinal fluid leak, anterior, middle or posterior cranial fossa following surgery of the skull base; by free tissue graft (eg, pericranium, fascia, tensor fascia lata, adipose tissue, homologous or synthetic grafts)

61619 by local or regionalized vascularized pedicle flap or myocutaneous flap (including galea, temporalis, frontalis or occipitalis muscle)

Endovascular Therapy

61624 Transcatheter occlusion or embolization (eg, for tumor destruction, to achieve hemostasis, to occlude a vascular malformation), percutaneous, any method; central nervous system (intracranial, spinal cord)

(See also 37204)

(For radiological supervision and interpretation, use 75894)

61626 non-central nervous system, head or neck (extracranial, brachiocephalic branch)

(See also 37204)

(For radiological supervision and interpretation, use 75894)

Surgery for Aneurysm, Arteriovenous Malformation or Vascular Disease

Includes craniotomy when appropriate for procedure.

61680 Surgery of intracranial arteriovenous malformation; supratentorial, simple

61682 supratentorial, complex

61684 infratentorial, simple

61686 infratentorial, complex

61690 dural, simple

61692 dural, complex

61697 Surgery of complex intracranial aneurysm, intracranial approach; carotid circulation

61698 vertebrobasilar circulation

(61697, 61698 involve aneurysms that are larger than 15 mm or with calcification of the aneurysm neck, or with incorporation of normal vessels into the aneurysm neck, or a procedure requiring temporary vessel occlusion, trapping or cardiopulmonary bypass to successfully treat the aneurysm)

61700 Surgery of simple intracranial aneurysm, intracranial approach; carotid circulation

61702 vertebrobasilar circulation

61703 Surgery of intracranial aneurysm, cervical approach by application of occluding clamp to cervical carotid artery (Selverstone-Crutchfield type)

(For cervical approach for direct ligation of carotid artery, see 37600-37606)

61705 Surgery of aneurysm, vascular malformation or carotid-cavernous fistula; by intracranial and cervical occlusion of carotid artery

61708 by intracranial electrothrombosis

(For ligation or gradual occlusion of internal/common carotid artery, see 37605, 37606)

61710 by intra-arterial embolization, injection procedure, or balloon catheter

61711 Anastomosis, arterial, extracranial-intracranial (eg, middle cerebral/cortical) arteries

(For carotid or vertebral thromboendarterectomy, use 35301)

(61712 has been deleted. Use 69990 when the surgical microscope is employed for the microsurgical procedure. Do not use 69990 for visualization with magnifying loupes or corrected vision.)

Stereotaxis

61720 Creation of lesion by stereotactic method, including burr hole(s) and localizing and recording techniques, single or multiple stages; globus pallidus or thalamus

61735 subcortical structure(s) other than globus pallidus or thalamus

61750 Stereotactic biopsy, aspiration, or excision, including burr hole(s), for intracranial lesion;

61751 with computerized axial tomography and/or magnetic resonance guidance

(For radiological supervision and interpretation of computerized tomography, see 70450, 70460, or 70470 as appropriate)

(For radiological supervision and interpretation of magnetic resonance imaging, see 70551, 70552, or 70553 as appropriate)

61760 Stereotactic implantation of depth electrodes into the cerebrum for long term seizure monitoring

61770 Stereotactic localization, including burr hole(s), with insertion of catheter(s) or probe(s) for placement of radiation source

(61780 has been deleted. To report, use 61760)

61790 Creation of lesion by stereotactic method, percutaneous, by neurolytic agent (eg, alcohol, thermal, electrical, radiofrequency); gasserian ganglion

61791 trigeminal medullary tract

61793 Stereotactic radiosurgery (particle beam, gamma ray or linear accelerator), one or more sessions

▶(For intensity modulated beam delivery plan and treatment, see 77301, 77418)◀

+ 61795 Stereotactic computer assisted volumetric (navigational) procedure, intracranial, extracranial, or spinal (List separately in addition to code for primary procedure)

Neurostimulators (Intracranial)

Codes 61850-61888 apply to both simple and complex neurostimulators. For initial or subsequent electronic analysis and programming of neurostimulator pulse generators, see codes 95970-95975.

61850 Twist drill or burr hole(s) for implantation of neurostimulator electrodes, cortical

(61855 has been deleted. To report, use 61862)

61860 Craniectomy or craniotomy for implantation of neurostimulator electrodes, cerebral, cortical

61862 Twist drill, burr hole, craniotomy, or craniectomy for stereotactic implantation of one neurostimulator array in subcortical site (eg, thalamus, globus pallidus, subthalamic nucleus, periventricular, periaqueductal gray)

(61865 has been deleted. To report, use 61862)

61870 Craniectomy for implantation of neurostimulator electrodes, cerebellar; cortical

61875 subcortical

61880 Revision or removal of intracranial neurostimulator electrodes

61885 Incision and subcutaneous placement of cranial neurostimulator pulse generator or receiver, direct or inductive coupling; with connection to a single electrode array

61886 with connection to two or more electrode arrays

(For open placement of cranial nerve (eg, vagal, trigeminal) neurostimulator electrode(s), use 64573)

(For percutaneous placement of cranial nerve (eg, vagal, trigeminal) neurostimulator electrode(s), use 64553)

(For revision or removal of cranial nerve (eg, vagal, trigeminal) neurostimulator electrode(s), use 64585)

61888 Revision or removal of cranial neurostimulator pulse generator or receiver

Repair

62000 Elevation of depressed skull fracture; simple, extradural

62005 compound or comminuted, extradural

62010 with repair of dura and/or debridement of brain

▲ **62100** Craniotomy for repair of dural/cerebrospinal fluid leak, including surgery for rhinorrhea/otorrhea

(For repair of spinal dural/CSF leak, see 63707, 63709)

62115   Reduction of craniomegalic skull (eg, treated hydrocephalus); not requiring bone grafts or cranioplasty

62116   with simple cranioplasty

62117   requiring craniotomy and reconstruction with or without bone graft (includes obtaining grafts)

62120   Repair of encephalocele, skull vault, including cranioplasty

62121   Craniotomy for repair of encephalocele, skull base

62140   Cranioplasty for skull defect; up to 5 cm diameter

62141   larger than 5 cm diameter

62142   Removal of bone flap or prosthetic plate of skull

62143   Replacement of bone flap or prosthetic plate of skull

62145   Cranioplasty for skull defect with reparative brain surgery

62146   Cranioplasty with autograft (includes obtaining bone grafts); up to 5 cm diameter

62147   larger than 5 cm diameter

Cerebrospinal Fluid (CSF) Shunt

62180   Ventriculocisternostomy (Torkildsen type operation)

62190   Creation of shunt; subarachnoid/subdural-atrial, -jugular, -auricular

62192   subarachnoid/subdural-peritoneal, -pleural, other terminus

62194   Replacement or irrigation, subarachnoid/subdural catheter

62200   Ventriculocisternostomy, third ventricle;

62201   stereotactic method

62220   Creation of shunt; ventriculo-atrial, -jugular, -auricular

62223   ventriculo-peritoneal, -pleural, other terminus

62225   Replacement or irrigation, ventricular catheter

▲ **62230**   Replacement or revision of cerebrospinal fluid shunt, obstructed valve, or distal catheter in shunt system

▲ **62252**   Reprogramming of programmable cerebrospinal shunt

▲ **62256**   Removal of complete cerebrospinal fluid shunt system; without replacement

62258   with replacement by similar or other shunt at same operation

(For percutaneous irrigation or aspiration of shunt reservoir, use 61070)

(For reprogramming of programmable CSF shunt, use 62252)

Spine and Spinal Cord

(For application of caliper or tongs, use 20660)

(For treatment of fracture or dislocation of spine, see 22305-22327)

Injection, Drainage, or Aspiration

Injection of contrast during fluoroscopic guidance and localization is an inclusive component of codes 62270-62273, 62280-62282, 62310-62319. Fluoroscopic guidance and localization is reported by code 76005, unless a formal contrast study (myelography, epidurography, or arthrography) is performed, in which case the use of fluoroscopy is included in the supervision and interpretation codes.

For radiologic supervision and interpretation of epidurography, use 72275. Code 72275 is only to be used when an epidurogram is performed, recorded, and a formal radiologic report is issued.

For codes 62318 and 62319, use code 01996 for subsequent daily management of epidural or subarachnoid catheter drug administration.

62263   Percutaneous lysis of epidural adhesions using solution injection (eg, hypertonic saline, enzyme) or mechanical means (eg, spring-wound catheter) including radiologic localization (includes contrast when administered)

62268*   Percutaneous aspiration, spinal cord cyst or syrinx

(For radiological supervision and interpretation, see 76003, 76360, ▶76942◀)

62269*   Biopsy of spinal cord, percutaneous needle

(For radiological supervision and interpretation, see 76003, 76360, 76942)

62270*   Spinal puncture, lumbar, diagnostic

▲ **62272***   Spinal puncture, therapeutic, for drainage of cerebrospinal fluid (by needle or catheter)

62273*   Injection, epidural, of blood or clot patch

(62274 has been deleted. To report, see 62310, 62311)

(62275 has been deleted. To report, use 62310)

(62276 has been deleted. To report, see 62318, 62319)

(62277 has been deleted. To report, see 62318, 62319)

(62278 has been deleted. To report, use 62311)

(62279 has been deleted. To report, use 62319)

62280*   Injection/infusion of neurolytic substance (eg, alcohol, phenol, iced saline solutions), with or without other therapeutic substance; subarachnoid

62281*   epidural, cervical or thoracic

62282*   epidural, lumbar, sacral (caudal)

⊘ **62284*** Injection procedure for myelography and/or computerized axial tomography, spinal (other than C1-C2 and posterior fossa)

(For injection procedure at C1-C2, use 61055)

(For radiological supervision and interpretation, see **Radiology**)

(62286 has been deleted. To report, use 64999)

62287 Aspiration or decompression procedure, percutaneous, of nucleus pulposus of intervertebral disk, any method, single or multiple levels, lumbar (eg, manual or automated percutaneous diskectomy, percutaneous laser diskectomy)

(For fluoroscopic guidance, use 76003)

(62288 has been deleted. To report, see 62310, 62311)

(62289 has been deleted. To report, use 62311)

62290* Injection procedure for diskography, each level; lumbar

62291* cervical or thoracic

(For radiological supervision and interpretation, see 72285, 72295)

62292 Injection procedure for chemonucleolysis, including diskography, intervertebral disk, single or multiple levels, lumbar

(62293 has been deleted)

62294 Injection procedure, arterial, for occlusion of arteriovenous malformation, spinal

(62295-62297 have been deleted. To report, see 63001-63017)

(62298 has been deleted. To report, use 62310)

62310 Injection, single (not via indwelling catheter), not including neurolytic substances, with or without contrast (for either localization or epidurography), of diagnostic or therapeutic substance(s) (including anesthetic, antispasmodic, opioid, steroid, other solution), epidural or subarachnoid; cervical or thoracic

62311 lumbar, sacral (caudal)

62318 Injection, including catheter placement, continuous infusion or intermittent bolus, not including neurolytic substances, with or without contrast (for either localization or epidurography), of diagnostic or therapeutic substance(s) (including anesthetic, antispasmodic, opioid, steroid, other solution), epidural or subarachnoid; cervical or thoracic

62319 lumbar, sacral (caudal)

(For transforaminal epidural injection, see 64479-64484)

Catheter Implantation

(For percutaneous placement of intrathecal or epidural catheter, see codes 62270-62273, 62280-62284, 62310-62319)

(62301-62303 have been deleted. To report, see 63001-63017)

62350 Implantation, revision or repositioning of tunneled intrathecal or epidural catheter, for long-term medication administration via an external pump or implantable reservoir/infusion pump; without laminectomy

62351 with laminectomy

(For refilling and maintenance of an implantable reservoir or infusion pump, use 96530)

62355 Removal of previously implanted intrathecal or epidural catheter

Reservoir/Pump Implantation

62360 Implantation or replacement of device for intrathecal or epidural drug infusion; subcutaneous reservoir

62361 non-programmable pump

62362 programmable pump, including preparation of pump, with or without programming

62365 Removal of subcutaneous reservoir or pump, previously implanted for intrathecal or epidural infusion

62367 Electronic analysis of programmable, implanted pump for intrathecal or epidural drug infusion (includes evaluation of reservoir status, alarm status, drug prescription status); without reprogramming

62368 with reprogramming

(To report implantable pump or reservoir refill, use 96530)

Posterior Extradural Laminotomy or Laminectomy for Exploration/ Decompression of Neural Elements or Excision of Herniated Intervertebral Disks

(When 63001-63048 are followed by arthrodesis, see 22590-22614)

63001 Laminectomy with exploration and/or decompression of spinal cord and/or cauda equina, without facetectomy, foraminotomy or diskectomy, (eg, spinal stenosis), one or two vertebral segments; cervical

63003 thoracic

63005 lumbar, except for spondylolisthesis

(63010 has been deleted. To report, use 63012)

63011 sacral

63012   Laminectomy with removal of abnormal facets and/or pars inter-articularis with decompression of cauda equina and nerve roots for spondylolisthesis, lumbar (Gill type procedure)

63015   Laminectomy with exploration and/or decompression of spinal cord and/or cauda equina, without facetectomy, foraminotomy or diskectomy, (eg, spinal stenosis), more than 2 vertebral segments; cervical

63016   thoracic

63017   lumbar

63020   Laminotomy (hemilaminectomy), with decompression of nerve root(s), including partial facetectomy, foraminotomy and/or excision of herniated intervertebral disk; one interspace, cervical

(63021 has been deleted. To report, use 63020 with modifier '-50')

63030   one interspace, lumbar (including open or endoscopically-assisted approach)

(63031 has been deleted. To report, use 63030 with modifier '-50')

+ 63035   each additional interspace, cervical or lumbar (List separately in addition to code for primary procedure)

(Use 63035 in conjunction with codes 63020-63030)

63040   Laminotomy (hemilaminectomy), with decompression of nerve root(s), including partial facetectomy, foraminotomy and/or excision of herniated intervertebral disk, reexploration, single interspace; cervical

(63041 has been deleted)

63042   lumbar

(Codes 63040-►63044◄ are unilateral procedures. For bilateral procedures, use modifier '-50')

+ 63043   each additional cervical interspace (List separately in addition to code for primary procedure)

(Use 63043 in conjunction with code 63040)

+ 63044   each additional lumbar interspace (List separately in addition to code for primary procedure)

(Use 63044 in conjunction with code 63042)

63045   Laminectomy, facetectomy and foraminotomy (unilateral or bilateral with decompression of spinal cord, cauda equina and/or nerve root(s), (eg, spinal or lateral recess stenosis)), single vertebral segment; cervical

63046   thoracic

63047   lumbar

+ 63048   each additional segment, cervical, thoracic, or lumbar (List separately in addition to code for primary procedure)

(Use 63048 in conjunction with codes 63045-63047)

Transpedicular or Costovertebral Approach for Posterolateral Extradural Exploration/Decompression

63055   Transpedicular approach with decompression of spinal cord, equina and/or nerve root(s) (eg, herniated intervertebral disk), single segment; thoracic

63056   lumbar (including transfacet, or lateral extraforaminal approach) (eg, far lateral herniated intervertebral disk)

+ 63057   each additional segment, thoracic or lumbar (List separately in addition to code for primary procedure)

(Use 63057 in conjunction with codes 63055, 63056)

(63060 has been deleted)

63064   Costovertebral approach with decompression of spinal cord or nerve root(s), (eg, herniated intervertebral disk), thoracic; single segment

(63065 has been deleted)

+ 63066   each additional segment (List separately in addition to code for primary procedure)

(Use 63066 in conjunction with code 63064)

(For excision of thoracic intraspinal lesions by laminectomy, see 63266, 63271, 63276, 63281, 63286)

Anterior or Anterolateral Approach for Extradural Exploration/Decompression

►For the following codes, when two surgeons work together as primary surgeons performing distinct part(s) of spinal cord exploration/decompression operation, each surgeon should report his/her distinct operative work by appending the modifier '-62' to the procedure code (and any associated add-on codes for that procedure code as long as both surgeons continue to work together as primary surgeons). In this situation, the modifier '-62' may be appended to the definitive procedure code(s) 63075, 63077, 63081, 63085, 63087, 63090 and, as appropriate, to associated additional interspace add-on code(s) 63076, 63078 or additional segment add-on code(s) 63082, 63086, 63088, 63091 as long as both surgeons continue to work together as primary surgeons.◄

63075   Diskectomy, anterior, with decompression of spinal cord and/or nerve root(s), including osteophytectomy; cervical, single interspace

+ 63076   cervical, each additional interspace (List separately in addition to code for primary procedure)

(Use 63076 in conjunction with code 63075)

63077   thoracic, single interspace

+ 63078   thoracic, each additional interspace (List separately in addition to code for primary procedure)

(Use 63078 in conjunction with code 63077)

(Do not report code 69990 in addition to codes 63075-63078)

63081   Vertebral corpectomy (vertebral body resection), partial or complete, anterior approach with decompression of spinal cord and/or nerve root(s); cervical, single segment

+ 63082   cervical, each additional segment (List separately in addition to code for primary procedure)

(Use 63082 in conjunction with code 63081)

(For transoral approach, see 61575, 61576)

63085   Vertebral corpectomy (vertebral body resection), partial or complete, transthoracic approach with decompression of spinal cord and/or nerve root(s); thoracic, single segment

+ 63086   thoracic, each additional segment (List separately in addition to code for primary procedure)

(Use 63086 in conjunction with code 63085)

63087   Vertebral corpectomy (vertebral body resection), partial or complete, combined thoracolumbar approach with decompression of spinal cord, cauda equina or nerve root(s), lower thoracic or lumbar; single segment

+ 63088   each additional segment (List separately in addition to code for primary procedure)

(Use 63088 in conjunction with code 63087)

63090   Vertebral corpectomy (vertebral body resection), partial or complete, transperitoneal or retroperitoneal approach with decompression of spinal cord, cauda equina or nerve root(s), lower thoracic, lumbar, or sacral; single segment

+ 63091   each additional segment (List separately in addition to code for primary procedure)

(Use 63091 in conjunction with code 63090)

(Procedures 63081-63091 include diskectomy above and/or below vertebral segment)

(If followed by arthrodesis, see 22548-22812)

(For reconstruction of spine, use appropriate vertebral corpectomy codes 63081-63091, bone graft codes 20930-20938, arthrodesis codes 22548-22812, and spinal instrumentation codes 22840-22855)

Incision

63170   Laminectomy with myelotomy (eg, Bischof or DREZ type), cervical, thoracic, or thoracolumbar

63172   Laminectomy with drainage of intramedullary cyst/syrinx; to subarachnoid space

63173   to peritoneal space

63180   Laminectomy and section of dentate ligaments, with or without dural graft, cervical; one or two segments

63182   more than two segments

63185   Laminectomy with rhizotomy; one or two segments

63190   more than two segments

63191   Laminectomy with section of spinal accessory nerve

(63192 has been deleted. To report, use 63191 with modifier '-50')

(For resection of sternocleidomastoid muscle, use 21720)

63194   Laminectomy with cordotomy, with section of one spinothalamic tract, one stage; cervical

63195   thoracic

63196   Laminectomy with cordotomy, with section of both spinothalamic tracts, one stage; cervical

63197   thoracic

63198   Laminectomy with cordotomy with section of both spinothalamic tracts, two stages within 14 days; cervical

63199   thoracic

63200   Laminectomy, with release of tethered spinal cord, lumbar

Excision by Laminectomy of Lesion Other Than Herniated Disk

(63210-63242 have been deleted. To report, see 63265-63290)

63250   Laminectomy for excision or occlusion of arteriovenous malformation of spinal cord; cervical

63251   thoracic

63252   thoracolumbar

63265   Laminectomy for excision or evacuation of intraspinal lesion other than neoplasm, extradural; cervical

63266   thoracic

63267   lumbar

63268   sacral

63270   Laminectomy for excision of intraspinal lesion other than neoplasm, intradural; cervical

63271   thoracic

63272   lumbar

63273   sacral

63275   Laminectomy for biopsy/excision of intraspinal neoplasm; extradural, cervical

63276   extradural, thoracic

63277   extradural, lumbar

63278   extradural, sacral

63280   intradural, extramedullary, cervical

63281   intradural, extramedullary, thoracic

63282   intradural, extramedullary, lumbar

63283   intradural, sacral

63285	intradural, intramedullary, cervical
63286	intradural, intramedullary, thoracic
63287	intradural, intramedullary, thoracolumbar
63290	combined extradural-intradural lesion, any level

(For drainage of intramedullary cyst/syrinx, use 63172, 63173)

Excision, Anterior or Anterolateral Approach, Intraspinal Lesion

►For the following codes, when two surgeons work together as primary surgeons performing distinct part(s) of an anterior approach for an intraspinal excision, each surgeon should report his/her distinct operative work by appending the modifier '-62' to the single definitive procedure code. In this situation, the modifier '-62' may be appended to the definitive procedure code(s) 63300-63307 and, as appropriate, to the associated additional segment add-on code 63308 as long as both surgeons continue to work together as primary surgeons.◄

(For arthrodesis, see 22548-22585)

(For reconstruction of spine, see 20930-20938)

63300	Vertebral corpectomy (vertebral body resection), partial or complete, for excision of intraspinal lesion, single segment; extradural, cervical
63301	extradural, thoracic by transthoracic approach
63302	extradural, thoracic by thoracolumbar approach
63303	extradural, lumbar or sacral by transperitoneal or retroperitoneal approach
63304	intradural, cervical
63305	intradural, thoracic by transthoracic approach
63306	intradural, thoracic by thoracolumbar approach
63307	intradural, lumbar or sacral by transperitoneal or retroperitoneal approach
+ 63308	each additional segment (List separately in addition to codes for single segment)

(Use 63308 in conjunction with codes 63300-63307)

Stereotaxis

63600	Creation of lesion of spinal cord by stereotactic method, percutaneous, any modality (including stimulation and/or recording)
63610	Stereotactic stimulation of spinal cord, percutaneous, separate procedure not followed by other surgery
63615	Stereotactic biopsy, aspiration, or excision of lesion, spinal cord

Neurostimulators (Spinal)

Codes 63650-63688 apply to both simple and complex neurostimulators. For initial or subsequent electronic analysis and programming of neurostimulator pulse generators, see codes 95970-95975.

Codes 63650, 63655, and 63660 describe the operative placement, revision, or removal of the spinal neurostimulator system components to provide spinal electrical stimulation. A neurostimulator system includes an implanted neurostimulator, external controller, extension, and collection of contacts. Multiple contacts or electrodes (4 or more) provide the actual electrical stimulation in the epidural space.

For percutaneously placed neurostimulator systems (63650, 63660), the contacts are on a catheter-like lead. An array defines the collection of contacts that are on one catheter.

For systems placed via an open surgical exposure (63655, 63660), the contacts are on a plate or paddle-shaped surface.

63650	Percutaneous implantation of neurostimulator electrode array, epidural

(63652 has been deleted)

63655	Laminectomy for implantation of neurostimulator electrodes, plate/paddle, epidural

(63656 has been deleted)

(63657 and 63658 have been deleted)

63660	Revision or removal of spinal neurostimulator electrode percutaneous array(s) or plate/paddle(s)
63685	Incision and subcutaneous placement of spinal neurostimulator pulse generator or receiver, direct or inductive coupling
63688	Revision or removal of implanted spinal neurostimulator pulse generator or receiver

(63690, 63691 have been deleted. To report, see 95970-95975)

Repair

63700	Repair of meningocele; less than 5 cm diameter
63702	larger than 5 cm diameter
63704	Repair of myelomeningocele; less than 5 cm diameter
63706	larger than 5 cm diameter

(For complex skin closure, see **Integumentary System**)

▲ 63707	Repair of dural/cerebrospinal fluid leak, not requiring laminectomy

(63708 has been deleted. To report, see 63707, 63709)

⊘ =Modifier '-51' Exempt   ► ◄ =New or Revised Text   ✛ =Add-on Code   CPT 2002

▲ **63709** Repair of dural/cerebrospinal fluid leak or pseudomeningocele, with laminectomy

63710 Dural graft, spinal

(For laminectomy and section of dentate ligaments, with or without dural graft, cervical, see 63180, 63182)

Shunt, Spinal CSF

63740 Creation of shunt, lumbar, subarachnoid-peritoneal, -pleural, or other; including laminectomy

63741 percutaneous, not requiring laminectomy

63744 Replacement, irrigation or revision of lumbosubarachnoid shunt

63746 Removal of entire lumbosubarachnoid shunt system without replacement

(63750 has been deleted. To report, see 62351 and 62360, 62361 or 62362)

(63780 has been deleted. To report, see 62350 and 62360, 62361 or 62362)

Extracranial Nerves, Peripheral Nerves, and Autonomic Nervous System

(For intracranial surgery on cranial nerves, see 61450, 61460, 61790)

Introduction/Injection of Anesthetic Agent (Nerve Block), Diagnostic or Therapeutic

Somatic Nerves

64400* Injection, anesthetic agent; trigeminal nerve, any division or branch

64402* facial nerve

64405* greater occipital nerve

64408* vagus nerve

64410* phrenic nerve

64412* spinal accessory nerve

64413* cervical plexus

64415* brachial plexus

64417* axillary nerve

64418* suprascapular nerve

64420* intercostal nerve, single

64421* intercostal nerves, multiple, regional block

64425* ilioinguinal, iliohypogastric nerves

64430* pudendal nerve

64435* paracervical (uterine) nerve

(64440 has been deleted. To report, see 64479, 64483)

(64441 has been deleted. To report, see 64480, 64484)

(64442 has been deleted. To report, use 64475)

(64443 has been deleted. To report, use 64476)

64445* sciatic nerve

64450* other peripheral nerve or branch

(For phenol destruction, see 64622-64627)

(For subarachnoid or subdural injection, see 62280, 62310-62319)

(For epidural or caudal injection, see 62273, 62281-62282, 62310-62319)

(Codes 64470-64484 are unilateral procedures. For bilateral procedures, use modifier '-50')

(For fluoroscopic guidance and localization for needle placement and injection in conjunction with codes 64470-64484, use code 76005)

64470 Injection, anesthetic agent and/or steroid, paravertebral facet joint or facet joint nerve; cervical or thoracic, single level

+ **64472** cervical or thoracic, each additional level (List separately in addition to code for primary procedure)

(Use code 64472 in conjunction with code 64470)

64475 lumbar or sacral, single level

+ **64476** lumbar or sacral, each additional level (List separately in addition to code for primary procedure)

(Use code 64476 in conjunction with code 64475)

64479 Injection, anesthetic agent and/or steroid, transforaminal epidural; cervical or thoracic, single level

+ **64480** cervical or thoracic, each additional level (List separately in addition to code for primary procedure)

(Use code 64480 in conjunction with code 64479)

64483 lumbar or sacral, single level

+ **64484** lumbar or sacral, each additional level (List separately in addition to code for primary procedure)

(Use code 64484 in conjunction with code 64483)

Sympathetic Nerves

64505* Injection, anesthetic agent; sphenopalatine ganglion

64508* carotid sinus (separate procedure)

64510* stellate ganglion (cervical sympathetic)

64520* lumbar or thoracic (paravertebral sympathetic)

64530* celiac plexus, with or without radiologic monitoring

Neurostimulators (Peripheral Nerve)

Codes 64553-64595 apply to both simple and complex neurostimulators. For initial or subsequent electronic analysis and programming of neurostimulator pulse generators, see codes 95970-95975.

64550 Application of surface (transcutaneous) neurostimulator

64553 Percutaneous implantation of neurostimulator electrodes; cranial nerve

(For open placement of cranial nerve (eg, vagal, trigeminal) neurostimulator pulse generator or receiver, see 61885, 61886, as appropriate)

▲ **64555** peripheral nerve (excludes sacral nerve)

64560 autonomic nerve

● **64561** sacral nerve (transforaminal placement)

64565 neuromuscular

64573 Incision for implantation of neurostimulator electrodes; cranial nerve

(For open placement of cranial nerve (eg, vagal, trigeminal) neurostimulator pulse generator or receiver, see 61885, 61886, as appropriate)

(For revision or removal of cranial nerve (eg, vagal, trigeminal) neurostimulator pulse generator or receiver, use 61888)

▲ **64575** peripheral nerve (excludes sacral nerve)

64577 autonomic nerve

64580 neuromuscular

● **64581** sacral nerve (transforaminal placement)

64585 Revision or removal of peripheral neurostimulator electrodes

64590 Incision and subcutaneous placement of peripheral neurostimulator pulse generator or receiver, direct or inductive coupling

64595 Revision or removal of peripheral neurostimulator pulse generator or receiver

Destruction by Neurolytic Agent (eg, Chemical, Thermal, Electrical, Radiofrequency or Chemodenervation)

Somatic Nerves

64600 Destruction by neurolytic agent, trigeminal nerve; supraorbital, infraorbital, mental, or inferior alveolar branch

64605 second and third division branches at foramen ovale

64610 second and third division branches at foramen ovale under radiologic monitoring

64612 Chemodenervation of muscle(s); muscle(s) innervated by facial nerve (eg, for blepharospasm, hemifacial spasm)

64613 cervical spinal muscle(s) (eg, for spasmodic torticollis)

64614 extremity(s) and/or trunk muscle(s) (eg, for dystonia, cerebral palsy, multiple sclerosis)

(For chemodenervation for strabismus involving the extraocular muscles, use 67345)

64620 Destruction by neurolytic agent, intercostal nerve

(Codes 64622-64627 are unilateral procedures. For bilateral procedures, use modifier '-50')

(For fluoroscopic guidance and localization for needle placement and neurolysis in conjunction with codes 64622-64627, use 76005)

64622 Destruction by neurolytic agent, paravertebral facet joint nerve; lumbar or sacral, single level

➕ **64623** lumbar or sacral, each additional level (List separately in addition to code for primary procedure)

(Use 64623 in conjunction with code 64622)

64626 cervical or thoracic, single level

➕ **64627** cervical or thoracic, each additional level (List separately in addition to code for primary procedure)

(Use 64627 in conjunction with code 64626)

64630 Destruction by neurolytic agent; pudendal nerve

64640 other peripheral nerve or branch

Sympathetic Nerves

64680 Destruction by neurolytic agent, celiac plexus, with or without radiologic monitoring

Neuroplasty (Exploration, Neurolysis or Nerve Decompression)

Neuroplasty is the decompression or freeing of intact nerve from scar tissue, including external neurolysis and/or transposition.

(For internal neurolysis requiring use of operating microscope, use 64727)

(For facial nerve decompression, use 69720)

64702 Neuroplasty; digital, one or both, same digit

64704 nerve of hand or foot

64708 Neuroplasty, major peripheral nerve, arm or leg; other than specified

64712 sciatic nerve

64713 brachial plexus

64714 lumbar plexus

64716 Neuroplasty and/or transposition; cranial nerve (specify)

64718   ulnar nerve at elbow

64719   ulnar nerve at wrist

64721   median nerve at carpal tunnel

(For arthroscopic procedure, use 29848)

64722 Decompression; unspecified nerve(s) (specify)

64726   plantar digital nerve

+ 64727 Internal neurolysis, requiring use of operating microscope (List separately in addition to code for neuroplasty) (Neuroplasty includes external neurolysis)

(Do not report code 69990 in addition to code 64727)

Transection or Avulsion

(For stereotactic lesion of gasserian ganglion, use 61790)

64732 Transection or avulsion of; supraorbital nerve

64734   infraorbital nerve

64736   mental nerve

64738   inferior alveolar nerve by osteotomy

64740   lingual nerve

64742   facial nerve, differential or complete

64744   greater occipital nerve

64746   phrenic nerve

(For section of recurrent laryngeal nerve, use 31595)

64752   vagus nerve (vagotomy), transthoracic

▲ 64755   vagus nerves limited to proximal stomach (selective proximal vagotomy, proximal gastric vagotomy, parietal cell vagotomy, supra- or highly selective vagotomy)

(For laparoscopic approach, use 43652)

64760   vagus nerve (vagotomy), abdominal

(For laparoscopic approach, use 43651)

64761   pudendal nerve

(64762 has been deleted. To report, use 64761 with modifier '-50')

64763 Transection or avulsion of obturator nerve, extrapelvic, with or without adductor tenotomy

(64764 has been deleted. To report, use 64763 with modifier '-50')

64766 Transection or avulsion of obturator nerve, intrapelvic, with or without adductor tenotomy

(64768 has been deleted. To report, use 64766 with modifier '-50')

64771 Transection or avulsion of other cranial nerve, extradural

64772 Transection or avulsion of other spinal nerve, extradural

(For excision of tender scar, skin and subcutaneous tissue, with or without tiny neuroma, see 11400-11446, 13100-13153)

Excision

Somatic Nerves

(For Morton neurectomy, use 28080)

64774 Excision of neuroma; cutaneous nerve, surgically identifiable

64776   digital nerve, one or both, same digit

+ 64778   digital nerve, each additional digit (List separately in addition to code for primary procedure)

(Use 64778 in conjunction with code 64776)

64782   hand or foot, except digital nerve

+ 64783   hand or foot, each additional nerve, except same digit (List separately in addition to code for primary procedure)

(Use 64783 in conjunction with code 64782)

64784   major peripheral nerve, except sciatic

64786   sciatic nerve

+ 64787 Implantation of nerve end into bone or muscle (List separately in addition to neuroma excision)

(Use 64787 in conjunction with codes 64774-64786)

64788 Excision of neurofibroma or neurolemmoma; cutaneous nerve

64790   major peripheral nerve

64792   extensive (including malignant type)

64795 Biopsy of nerve

Sympathetic Nerves

64802 Sympathectomy, cervical

(64803 has been deleted. To report, use 64802 with modifier '-50')

64804 Sympathectomy, cervicothoracic

(64806 has been deleted. To report, use 64804 with modifier '-50')

64809 Sympathectomy, thoracolumbar

(64811 has been deleted. To report, use 64809 with modifier '-50')

(64814 has been deleted. To report, use 64999)

64818 Sympathectomy, lumbar

(64819 has been deleted. To report, use 64818 with modifier '-50')

▲ **64820**   Sympathectomy; digital arteries, each digit

►(Do not report 69990 in addition to code 64820)◄

(64824 has been deleted. To report, use 64999)

● **64821**   radial artery

►(Do not report 69990 in addition to code 64821)◄

● **64822**   ulnar artery

►(Do not report 69990 in addition to code 64822)◄

● **64823**   superficial palmar arch

►(Do not report 69990 in addition to code 64823)◄

Neurorrhaphy

(64830 has been deleted. Use 69990 when the surgical microscope is employed for the microsurgical procedure. Do not use 69990 for visualization with magnifying loupes or corrected vision)

64831   Suture of digital nerve, hand or foot; one nerve

+ **64832**   each additional digital nerve (List separately in addition to code for primary procedure)

(Use 64832 in conjunction with code 64831)

64834   Suture of one nerve, hand or foot; common sensory nerve

64835   median motor thenar

64836   ulnar motor

+ **64837**   Suture of each additional nerve, hand or foot (List separately in addition to code for primary procedure)

(Use 64837 in conjunction with codes 64834-64836)

64840   Suture of posterior tibial nerve

64856   Suture of major peripheral nerve, arm or leg, except sciatic; including transposition

64857   without transposition

64858   Suture of sciatic nerve

+ **64859**   Suture of each additional major peripheral nerve (List separately in addition to code for primary procedure)

(Use 64859 in conjunction with codes 64856, 64857)

64861   Suture of; brachial plexus

64862   lumbar plexus

64864   Suture of facial nerve; extracranial

64865   infratemporal, with or without grafting

64866   Anastomosis; facial-spinal accessory

64868   facial-hypoglossal

64870   facial-phrenic

+ **64872**   Suture of nerve; requiring secondary or delayed suture (List separately in addition to code for primary neurorrhaphy)

(Use 64872 in conjunction with codes 64831-64865)

+ **64874**   requiring extensive mobilization, or transposition of nerve (List separately in addition to code for nerve suture)

(Use 64874 in conjunction with codes 64831-64865)

+ **64876**   requiring shortening of bone of extremity (List separately in addition to code for nerve suture)

(Use 64876 in conjunction with codes 64831-64865)

Neurorrhaphy With Nerve Graft

64885   Nerve graft (includes obtaining graft), head or neck; up to 4 cm in length

64886   more than 4 cm length

64890   Nerve graft (includes obtaining graft), single strand, hand or foot; up to 4 cm length

64891   more than 4 cm length

64892   Nerve graft (includes obtaining graft), single strand, arm or leg; up to 4 cm length

64893   more than 4 cm length

64895   Nerve graft (includes obtaining graft), multiple strands (cable), hand or foot; up to 4 cm length

64896   more than 4 cm length

64897   Nerve graft (includes obtaining graft), multiple strands (cable), arm or leg; up to 4 cm length

64898   more than 4 cm length

+ **64901**   Nerve graft, each additional nerve; single strand (List separately in addition to code for primary procedure)

(Use 64901 in conjunction with codes 64885-64893)

+ **64902**   multiple strands (cable) (List separately in addition to code for primary procedure)

(Use 64902 in conjunction with codes 64885, 64886, 64895-64898)

64905   Nerve pedicle transfer; first stage

64907   second stage

Other Procedures

64999   Unlisted procedure, nervous system

Eye and Ocular Adnexa

(For diagnostic and treatment ophthalmological services, see **Medicine, Ophthalmology,** and 92002 et seq)

(Do not report code 69990 in addition to codes 65091-68850)

Eyeball

Removal of Eye

65091 Evisceration of ocular contents; without implant

65093 with implant

65101 Enucleation of eye; without implant

65103 with implant, muscles not attached to implant

65105 with implant, muscles attached to implant

(For conjunctivoplasty after enucleation, see 68320 et seq)

65110 Exenteration of orbit (does not include skin graft), removal of orbital contents; only

65112 with therapeutic removal of bone

65114 with muscle or myocutaneous flap

(For skin graft to orbit (split skin), see 15120, 15121; free, full thickness, see 15260, 15261)

(For eyelid repair involving more than skin, see 67930 et seq)

Secondary Implant(s) Procedures

An ocular implant is an implant inside muscular cone; an orbital implant is an implant outside muscular cone.

65125 Modification of ocular implant with placement or replacement of pegs (eg, drilling receptacle for prosthesis appendage) (separate procedure)

65130 Insertion of ocular implant secondary; after evisceration, in scleral shell

65135 after enucleation, muscles not attached to implant

65140 after enucleation, muscles attached to implant

65150 Reinsertion of ocular implant; with or without conjunctival graft

65155 with use of foreign material for reinforcement and/or attachment of muscles to implant

65175 Removal of ocular implant

(For orbital implant (implant outside muscle cone) insertion, use 67550; removal, use 67560)

Removal of Foreign Body

(For removal of implanted material: ocular implant, use 65175; anterior segment implant, use 65920; posterior segment implant, use 67120; orbital implant, use 67560)

(For diagnostic x-ray for foreign body, use 70030)

(For diagnostic echography for foreign body, use 76529)

(For removal of foreign body from orbit: frontal approach, use 67413; lateral approach, use 67430; transcranial approach, use 61334)

(For removal of foreign body from eyelid, embedded, use 67938)

(For removal of foreign body from lacrimal system, use 68530)

65205* Removal of foreign body, external eye; conjunctival superficial

65210* conjunctival embedded (includes concretions), subconjunctival, or scleral nonperforating

65220* corneal, without slit lamp

65222* corneal, with slit lamp

(For repair of corneal laceration with foreign body, use 65275)

(65230 has been deleted. To report, use 65235)

▲ **65235** Removal of foreign body, intraocular; from anterior chamber of eye or lens

(65240, 65245 have been deleted. To report, use 65235)

(For removal of implanted material from anterior segment, use 65920)

65260 from posterior segment, magnetic extraction, anterior or posterior route

65265 from posterior segment, nonmagnetic extraction

(For removal of implanted material from posterior segment, use 67120)

Repair of Laceration

(For fracture of orbit, see 21385 et seq)

(For repair of wound of eyelid, skin, linear, simple, see 12011-12018; intermediate, layered closure, see 12051-12057; linear, complex, see 13150-13160; other, see 67930, 67935)

(For repair of wound of lacrimal system, use 68700)

(For repair of operative wound, use 66250)

65270* Repair of laceration; conjunctiva, with or without nonperforating laceration sclera, direct closure

65272 conjunctiva, by mobilization and rearrangement, without hospitalization

65273 conjunctiva, by mobilization and rearrangement, with hospitalization

65275   cornea, nonperforating, with or without removal foreign body

65280   cornea and/or sclera, perforating, not involving uveal tissue

65285   cornea and/or sclera, perforating, with reposition or resection of uveal tissue

65286   application of tissue glue, wounds of cornea and/or sclera

(Repair of laceration includes use of conjunctival flap and restoration of anterior chamber, by air or saline injection when indicated)

(For repair of iris or ciliary body, use 66680)

65290   Repair of wound, extraocular muscle, tendon and/or Tenon's capsule

Anterior Segment

Cornea

Excision

(65300 has been deleted)

65400   Excision of lesion, cornea (keratectomy, lamellar, partial), except pterygium

65410*   Biopsy of cornea

65420   Excision or transposition of pterygium; without graft

65426   with graft

Removal or Destruction

65430*   Scraping of cornea, diagnostic, for smear and/or culture

65435*   Removal of corneal epithelium; with or without chemocauterization (abrasion, curettage)

65436   with application of chelating agent (eg, EDTA)

(65445 has been deleted. To report, use 65450)

65450   Destruction of lesion of cornea by cryotherapy, photocoagulation or thermocauterization

(65455 has been deleted. To report, use 65450)

65600   Multiple punctures of anterior cornea (eg, for corneal erosion, tattoo)

Keratoplasty

Corneal transplant includes use of fresh or preserved grafts, and preparation of donor material.

(Keratoplasty excludes refractive keratoplasty procedures, 65760, 65765, and 65767)

65710   Keratoplasty (corneal transplant); lamellar

(65720, 65725 have been deleted. To report, use 65710)

65730   penetrating (except in aphakia)

(65740, 65745 have been deleted. To report, use 65730)

65750   penetrating (in aphakia)

65755   penetrating (in pseudophakia)

Other Procedures

65760   Keratomileusis

65765   Keratophakia

65767   Epikeratoplasty

65770   Keratoprosthesis

65771   Radial keratotomy

65772   Corneal relaxing incision for correction of surgically induced astigmatism

65775   Corneal wedge resection for correction of surgically induced astigmatism

(For fitting of contact lens for treatment of disease, use 92070)

(For unlisted procedures on cornea, use 66999)

Anterior Chamber

Incision

65800*   Paracentesis of anterior chamber of eye (separate procedure); with diagnostic aspiration of aqueous

65805*   with therapeutic release of aqueous

65810   with removal of vitreous and/or discission of anterior hyaloid membrane, with or without air injection

65815   with removal of blood, with or without irrigation and/or air injection

(For injection, see 66020-66030)

(For removal of blood clot, use 65930)

65820   Goniotomy

(65825, 65830 have been deleted)

65850   Trabeculotomy ab externo

65855   Trabeculoplasty by laser surgery, one or more sessions (defined treatment series)

(If re-treatment is necessary after several months because of disease progression, a new treatment or treatment series should be reported with a modifier, if necessary, to indicate lesser or greater complexity)

(For trabeculectomy, use 66170)

65860   Severing adhesions of anterior segment, laser technique (separate procedure)

⊘ =Modifier '-51' Exempt   ▶ ◀ =New or Revised Text   ✚ =Add-on Code   CPT 2002

Other Procedures

65865 Severing adhesions of anterior segment of eye, incisional technique (with or without injection of air or liquid) (separate procedure); goniosynechiae

(For trabeculoplasty by laser surgery, use 65855)

65870 anterior synechiae, except goniosynechiae

65875 posterior synechiae

65880 corneovitreal adhesions

(For laser surgery, use 66821)

▲ **65900** Removal of epithelial downgrowth, anterior chamber of eye

▲ **65920** Removal of implanted material, anterior segment of eye

▲ **65930** Removal of blood clot, anterior segment of eye

▲ **66020** Injection, anterior chamber of eye (separate procedure); air or liquid

66030* medication

(For unlisted procedures on anterior segment, use 66999)

Anterior Sclera

Excision

(For removal of intraocular foreign body, use 65235)

(For operations on posterior sclera, use 67250, 67255)

66130 Excision of lesion, sclera

66150 Fistulization of sclera for glaucoma; trephination with iridectomy

66155 thermocauterization with iridectomy

66160 sclerectomy with punch or scissors, with iridectomy

66165 iridencleisis or iridotasis

66170 trabeculectomy ab externo in absence of previous surgery

(For trabeculotomy ab externo, use 65850)

(For repair of operative wound, use 66250)

66172 trabeculectomy ab externo with scarring from previous ocular surgery or trauma (includes injection of antifibrotic agents)

66180 Aqueous shunt to extraocular reservoir (eg, Molteno, Schocket, Denver-Krupin)

66185 Revision of aqueous shunt to extraocular reservoir

(For removal of implanted shunt, use 67120)

Repair or Revision

(For scleral procedures in retinal surgery, see 67101 et seq)

66220 Repair of scleral staphyloma; without graft

66225 with graft

(For scleral reinforcement, see 67250, 67255)

66250 Revision or repair of operative wound of anterior segment, any type, early or late, major or minor procedure

(For unlisted procedures on anterior sclera, use 66999)

Iris, Ciliary Body

Incision

66500 Iridotomy by stab incision (separate procedure); except transfixion

66505 with transfixion as for iris bombe

(For iridotomy by photocoagulation, use 66761)

Excision

66600 Iridectomy, with corneoscleral or corneal section; for removal of lesion

66605 with cyclectomy

66625 peripheral for glaucoma (separate procedure)

66630 sector for glaucoma (separate procedure)

66635 optical (separate procedure)

(For coreoplasty by photocoagulation, use 66762)

Repair

66680 Repair of iris, ciliary body (as for iridodialysis)

(For reposition or resection of uveal tissue with perforating wound of cornea or sclera, use 65285)

66682 Suture of iris, ciliary body (separate procedure) with retrieval of suture through small incision (eg, McCannel suture)

Destruction

66700 Ciliary body destruction; diathermy

(66701, 66702 have been deleted. To report, see 66700, 66710, 66720, 66740)

66710 cyclophotocoagulation

66720 cryotherapy

(66721 has been deleted. To report, see 66700, 66710, 66720, 66740)

66740   cyclodialysis

(66741 has been deleted. To report, see 66700, 66710, 66720, 66740)

66761   Iridotomy/iridectomy by laser surgery (eg, for glaucoma) (one or more sessions)

66762   Iridoplasty by photocoagulation (one or more sessions) (eg, for improvement of vision, for widening of anterior chamber angle)

66770   Destruction of cyst or lesion iris or ciliary body (nonexcisional procedure)

(For excision lesion iris, ciliary body, see 66600, 66605; for removal of epithelial downgrowth, use 65900)

(For unlisted procedures on iris, ciliary body, use 66999)

Lens

Incision

(66800, 66801 have been deleted. To report, use 66999)

(66802 has been deleted)

66820   Discission of secondary membranous cataract (opacified posterior lens capsule and/or anterior hyaloid); stab incision technique (Ziegler or Wheeler knife)

66821   laser surgery (eg, YAG laser) (one or more stages)

66825   Repositioning of intraocular lens prosthesis, requiring an incision (separate procedure)

Removal Cataract

Lateral canthotomy, iridectomy, iridotomy, anterior capsulotomy, posterior capsulotomy, the use of viscoelastic agents, enzymatic zonulysis, use of other pharmacologic agents, and subconjunctival or sub-tenon injections are included as part of the code for the extraction of lens.

66830   Removal of secondary membranous cataract (opacified posterior lens capsule and/or anterior hyaloid) with corneo-scleral section, with or without iridectomy (iridocapsulotomy, iridocapsulectomy)

66840   Removal of lens material; aspiration technique, one or more stages

66850   phacofragmentation technique (mechanical or ultrasonic) (eg, phacoemulsification), with aspiration

66852   pars plana approach, with or without vitrectomy

(66915 has been deleted)

66920   intracapsular

66930   intracapsular, for dislocated lens

66940   extracapsular (other than 66840, 66850, 66852)

(66945 has been deleted. To report, see 66920-66940)

(For removal of intralenticular foreign body without lens extraction, use 65235)

(For repair of operative wound, use 66250)

(66980 has been deleted. To report, see 66983, 66984)

▲ **66982**   Extracapsular cataract removal with insertion of intraocular lens prosthesis (one stage procedure), manual or mechanical technique (eg, irrigation and aspiration or phacoemulsification), complex, requiring devices or techniques not generally used in routine cataract surgery (eg, iris expansion device, suture support for intraocular lens, or primary posterior capsulorrhexis) or performed on patients in the amblyogenic developmental stage

66983   Intracapsular cataract extraction with insertion of intraocular lens prosthesis (one stage procedure)

66984   Extracapsular cataract removal with insertion of intraocular lens prosthesis (one stage procedure), manual or mechanical technique (eg, irrigation and aspiration or phacoemulsification)

(For complex extracapsular cataract removal, use 66982)

66985   Insertion of intraocular lens prosthesis (secondary implant), not associated with concurrent cataract removal

(To code implant at time of concurrent cataract surgery, see 66982, 66983, 66984)

(For intraocular lens prosthesis supplied by physician, use 99070)

(For ultrasonic determination of intraocular lens power, use 76519)

(For removal of implanted material from anterior segment, use 65920)

(For secondary fixation (separate procedure), use 66682)

66986   Exchange of intraocular lens

Other Procedures

66999   Unlisted procedure, anterior segment of eye

Posterior Segment

Vitreous

67005   Removal of vitreous, anterior approach (open sky technique or limbal incision); partial removal

67010   subtotal removal with mechanical vitrectomy

(For removal of vitreous by paracentesis of anterior chamber, use 65810)

(For removal of corneovitreal adhesions, use 65880)

67015   Aspiration or release of vitreous, subretinal or choroidal fluid, pars plana approach (posterior sclerotomy)

67025   Injection of vitreous substitute, pars plana or limbal approach, (fluid-gas exchange), with or without aspiration (separate procedure)

67027 Implantation of intravitreal drug delivery system (eg, ganciclovir implant), includes concomitant removal of vitreous

(For removal, use 67121)

67028 Intravitreal injection of a pharmacologic agent (separate procedure)

67030 Discission of vitreous strands (without removal), pars plana approach

67031 Severing of vitreous strands, vitreous face adhesions, sheets, membranes or opacities, laser surgery (one or more stages)

(67035 has been deleted. To report, use 67036)

67036 Vitrectomy, mechanical, pars plana approach;

67038 with epiretinal membrane stripping

67039 with focal endolaser photocoagulation

67040 with endolaser panretinal photocoagulation

(For associated lensectomy, use 66850)

(For use of vitrectomy in retinal detachment surgery, use 67108)

(For associated removal of foreign body, see 65260, 65265)

(For unlisted procedures on vitreous, use 67299)

Retina or Choroid

Repair

(If diathermy, cryotherapy and/or photocoagulation are combined, report under principal modality used)

67101 Repair of retinal detachment, one or more sessions; cryotherapy or diathermy, with or without drainage of subretinal fluid

(67102, 67103 have been deleted. To report, use 67101)

(67104 has been deleted. To report, use 67105)

67105 photocoagulation, with or without drainage of subretinal fluid

(67106 has been deleted. To report, use 67105)

67107 Repair of retinal detachment; scleral buckling (such as lamellar scleral dissection, imbrication or encircling procedure), with or without implant, with or without cryotherapy, photocoagulation, and drainage of subretinal fluid

67108 with vitrectomy, any method, with or without air or gas tamponade, focal endolaser photocoagulation, cryotherapy, drainage of subretinal fluid, scleral buckling, and/or removal of lens by same technique

(67109 has been deleted. To report, use 67299)

67110 by injection of air or other gas (eg, pneumatic retinopexy)

67112 by scleral buckling or vitrectomy, on patient having previous ipsilateral retinal detachment repair(s) using scleral buckling or vitrectomy techniques

(For aspiration or drainage of subretinal or subchoroidal fluid, use 67015)

67115 Release of encircling material (posterior segment)

67120 Removal of implanted material, posterior segment; extraocular

67121 intraocular

(For removal from anterior segment, use 65920)

(For removal of foreign body, see 65260, 65265)

Prophylaxis

Repetitive services. The services listed below are often performed in multiple sessions or groups of sessions. The methods of reporting vary.

The following descriptors are intended to include all sessions in a defined treatment period.

67141 Prophylaxis of retinal detachment (eg, retinal break, lattice degeneration) without drainage, one or more sessions; cryotherapy, diathermy

(67142, 67143 have been deleted. To report, use 67141)

(67144 has been deleted. To report, use 67145)

67145 photocoagulation (laser or xenon arc)

(67146 has been deleted. To report, use 67145)

Destruction

67208 Destruction of localized lesion of retina (eg, macular edema, tumors), one or more sessions; cryotherapy, diathermy

67210 photocoagulation

(67212, 67213 have been deleted. To report, use 67208)

(67214, 67216 have been deleted. To report, use 67210)

67218 radiation by implantation of source (includes removal of source)

67220 Destruction of localized lesion of choroid (eg, choroidal neovascularization); photocoagulation (eg, laser), one or more sessions

►(For destruction of macular drusen, photocoagulation, use Category III code 0017T)◄

►(For destruction of localized lesion of choroid by transpupillary thermotherapy, use Category III code 0016T)◄

67221 photodynamic therapy (includes intravenous infusion)

(67222, 67223 have been deleted. To report, use 67227)

►(67224 has been deleted. To report, use 67228)◄

+ ● **67225**   photodynamic therapy, second eye, at single session (List separately in addition to code for primary eye treatment)

▶(Use 67225 in conjunction with code 67221)◀

▶(67226 has been deleted. To report, use 67228)◀

67227   Destruction of extensive or progressive retinopathy (eg, diabetic retinopathy), one or more sessions; cryotherapy, diathermy

67228   photocoagulation (laser or xenon arc)

(For unlisted procedures on retina, use 67299)

Sclera

Repair

(For excision lesion sclera, use 66130)

67250   Scleral reinforcement (separate procedure); without graft

67255   with graft

(For repair scleral staphyloma, see 66220, 66225)

Other Procedures

67299   Unlisted procedure, posterior segment

Ocular Adnexa

Extraocular Muscles

67311   Strabismus surgery, recession or resection procedure; one horizontal muscle

67312   two horizontal muscles

(67313 has been deleted)

67314   one vertical muscle (excluding superior oblique)

67316   two or more vertical muscles (excluding superior oblique)

(For adjustable sutures, use 67335 in addition to codes 67311-67334 for primary procedure reflecting number of muscles operated on)

67318   Strabismus surgery, any procedure, superior oblique muscle

+ **67320**   Transposition procedure (eg, for paretic extraocular muscle), any extraocular muscle (specify) (List separately in addition to code for primary procedure)

(Use 67320 in conjunction with codes 67311-67318)

+ **67331**   Strabismus surgery on patient with previous eye surgery or injury that did not involve the extraocular muscles (List separately in addition to code for primary procedure)

(Use 67331 in conjunction with codes 67311-67318)

+ **67332**   Strabismus surgery on patient with scarring of extraocular muscles (eg, prior ocular injury, strabismus or retinal detachment surgery) or restrictive myopathy (eg, dysthyroid ophthalmopathy) (List separately in addition to code for primary procedure)

(Use 67332 in conjunction with codes 67311-67318)

+ **67334**   Strabismus surgery by posterior fixation suture technique, with or without muscle recession (List separately in addition to code for primary procedure)

(Use 67334 in conjunction with codes 67311-67318)

+ **67335**   Placement of adjustable suture(s) during strabismus surgery, including postoperative adjustment(s) of suture(s) (List separately in addition to code for specific strabismus surgery)

(Use 67335 in conjunction with codes 67311-67334)

+ **67340**   Strabismus surgery involving exploration and/or repair of detached extraocular muscle(s) (List separately in addition to code for primary procedure)

(Use 67340 in conjunction with codes 67311-67334)

67343   Release of extensive scar tissue without detaching extraocular muscle (separate procedure)

(Use 67343 in conjunction with codes 67311-67340, when such procedures are performed other than on the affected muscle)

67345   Chemodenervation of extraocular muscle

(For chemodenervation for blepharospasm and other neurological disorders, see 64612 and 64613)

Other Procedures

67350   Biopsy of extraocular muscle

(For repair of wound, extraocular muscle, tendon or Tenon's capsule, use 65290)

67399   Unlisted procedure, ocular muscle

Orbit

Exploration, Excision, Decompression

67400   Orbitotomy without bone flap (frontal or transconjunctival approach); for exploration, with or without biopsy

67405   with drainage only

67412   with removal of lesion

67413   with removal of foreign body

67414   with removal of bone for decompression

67415   Fine needle aspiration of orbital contents

(For exenteration, enucleation, and repair, see 65101 et seq; for optic nerve decompression, use 67570)

67420 Orbitotomy with bone flap or window, lateral approach (eg, Kroenlein); with removal of lesion

67430   with removal of foreign body

67440   with drainage

67445   with removal of bone for decompression

(For optic nerve sheath decompression, use 67570)

67450   for exploration, with or without biopsy

(For orbitotomy, transcranial approach, see 61330-61334)

(For orbital implant, see 67550, 67560)

(For removal of eyeball or for repair after removal, see 65091-65175)

Other Procedures

67500* Retrobulbar injection; medication (separate procedure, does not include supply of medication)

67505   alcohol

(67510 has been deleted. To report, use 67599)

▲ **67515*** Injection of medication or other substance into Tenon's capsule

(For subconjunctival injection, use 68200)

67550 Orbital implant (implant outside muscle cone); insertion

67560   removal or revision

(For ocular implant (implant inside muscle cone), see 65093-65105, 65130-65175)

(For treatment of fractures of malar area, orbit, see 21355 et seq)

67570 Optic nerve decompression (eg, incision or fenestration of optic nerve sheath)

67599 Unlisted procedure, orbit

Eyelids

Incision

67700* Blepharotomy, drainage of abscess, eyelid

67710* Severing of tarsorrhaphy

67715* Canthotomy (separate procedure)

(For canthoplasty, use 67950)

(For division of symblepharon, use 68340)

Excision

Codes for removal of lesion include more than skin (ie, involving lid margin, tarsus, and/or palpebral conjunctiva).

(For removal of lesion, involving mainly skin of eyelid, see 11310-11313; 11440-11446; 11640-11646; 17000-17004)

(For repair of wounds, blepharoplasty, grafts, reconstructive surgery, see 67930-67975)

67800 Excision of chalazion; single

67801   multiple, same lid

67805   multiple, different lids

67808   under general anesthesia and/or requiring hospitalization, single or multiple

67810* Biopsy of eyelid

67820* Correction of trichiasis; epilation, by forceps only

67825*   epilation by other than forceps (eg, by electrosurgery, cryotherapy, laser surgery)

67830   incision of lid margin

67835   incision of lid margin, with free mucous membrane graft

67840* Excision of lesion of eyelid (except chalazion) without closure or with simple direct closure

(For excision and repair of eyelid by reconstructive surgery, see 67961, 67966)

67850* Destruction of lesion of lid margin (up to 1 cm)

(For Mohs micrographic surgery, see 17304-17310)

(For initiation or follow-up care of topical chemotherapy (eg, 5-FU or similar agents), see appropriate office visits)

Tarsorrhaphy

67875 Temporary closure of eyelids by suture (eg, Frost suture)

67880 Construction of intermarginal adhesions, median tarsorrhaphy, or canthorrhaphy;

67882   with transposition of tarsal plate

(For severing of tarsorrhaphy, use 67710)

(For canthoplasty, reconstruction canthus, use 67950)

(For canthotomy, use 67715)

Repair (Brow Ptosis, Blepharoptosis, Lid Retraction, Ectropion, Entropion)

67900 Repair of brow ptosis (supraciliary, mid-forehead or coronal approach)

(For forehead rhytidectomy, use 15824)

67901   Repair of blepharoptosis; frontalis muscle technique with suture or other material

67902   frontalis muscle technique with fascial sling (includes obtaining fascia)

67903   (tarso) levator resection or advancement, internal approach

67904   (tarso) levator resection or advancement, external approach

67906   superior rectus technique with fascial sling (includes obtaining fascia)

(67907 has been deleted. To report, use 67999)

67908   conjunctivo-tarso-Muller's muscle-levator resection (eg, Fasanella-Servat type)

67909   Reduction of overcorrection of ptosis

67911   Correction of lid retraction

(For obtaining autogenous graft materials, see 20920, 20922 or 20926)

(For correction of trichiasis by mucous membrane graft, use 67835)

67914   Repair of ectropion; suture

67915   thermocauterization

67916   blepharoplasty, excision tarsal wedge

67917   blepharoplasty, extensive (eg, Kuhnt-Szymanowski or tarsal strip operations)

(For correction of everted punctum, use 68705)

67921   Repair of entropion; suture

67922   thermocauterization

67923   blepharoplasty, excision tarsal wedge

67924   blepharoplasty, extensive (eg, Wheeler operation)

(For repair of cicatricial ectropion or entropion requiring scar excision or skin graft, see also 67961 et seq)

Reconstruction

Codes for blepharoplasty involve more than skin (ie, involving lid margin, tarsus, and/or palpebral conjunctiva).

67930   Suture of recent wound, eyelid, involving lid margin, tarsus, and/or palpebral conjunctiva direct closure; partial thickness

67935   full thickness

67938   Removal of embedded foreign body, eyelid

(For repair of skin of eyelid, see 12011-12018; 12051-12057; 13150-13153)

(For tarsorrhaphy, canthorrhaphy, see 67880, 67882)

(For repair of blepharoptosis and lid retraction, see 67901-67911)

(For blepharoplasty for entropion, ectropion, see 67916, 67917, 67923, 67924)

(For correction of blepharochalasis (blepharorhytidectomy), see 15820-15823)

(For repair of skin of eyelid, adjacent tissue transfer, see 14060, 14061; preparation for graft, use 15000; free graft, see 15120, 15121, 15260, 15261)

(For excision of lesion of eyelid, use 67800 et seq)

(For repair of lacrimal canaliculi, use 68700)

67950   Canthoplasty (reconstruction of canthus)

67961   Excision and repair of eyelid, involving lid margin, tarsus, conjunctiva, canthus, or full thickness, may include preparation for skin graft or pedicle flap with adjacent tissue transfer or rearrangement; up to one-fourth of lid margin

67966   over one-fourth of lid margin

(For canthoplasty, use 67950)

(For free skin grafts, see 15120, 15121, 15260, 15261)

(For tubed pedicle flap preparation, use 15576; for delay, use 15630; for attachment, use 15650)

67971   Reconstruction of eyelid, full thickness by transfer of tarsoconjunctival flap from opposing eyelid; up to two-thirds of eyelid, one stage or first stage

67973   total eyelid, lower, one stage or first stage

67974   total eyelid, upper, one stage or first stage

67975   second stage

Other Procedures

67999   Unlisted procedure, eyelids

Conjunctiva

(For removal of foreign body, see 65205 et seq)

Incision and Drainage

68020   Incision of conjunctiva, drainage of cyst

68040   Expression of conjunctival follicles (eg, for trachoma)

Excision and/or Destruction

68100   Biopsy of conjunctiva

68110   Excision of lesion, conjunctiva; up to 1 cm

68115   over 1 cm

68130   with adjacent sclera

68135*   Destruction of lesion, conjunctiva

⊘ =Modifier '-51' Exempt   ▶ ◀=New or Revised Text   ✚ =Add-on Code   CPT 2002

Injection

(For injection into Tenon's capsule or retrobulbar injection, see 67500-67515)

68200＊ Subconjunctival injection

Conjunctivoplasty

(For wound repair, see 65270-65273)

68320 Conjunctivoplasty; with conjunctival graft or extensive rearrangement

68325 with buccal mucous membrane graft (includes obtaining graft)

68326 Conjunctivoplasty, reconstruction cul-de-sac; with conjunctival graft or extensive rearrangement

68328 with buccal mucous membrane graft (includes obtaining graft)

68330 Repair of symblepharon; conjunctivoplasty, without graft

68335 with free graft conjunctiva or buccal mucous membrane (includes obtaining graft)

68340 division of symblepharon, with or without insertion of conformer or contact lens

Other Procedures

68360 Conjunctival flap; bridge or partial (separate procedure)

68362 total (such as Gunderson thin flap or purse string flap)

(For conjunctival flap for perforating injury, see 65280, 65285)

(For repair of operative wound, use 66250)

(For removal of conjunctival foreign body, see 65205, 65210)

68399 Unlisted procedure, conjunctiva

Lacrimal System

Incision

68400 Incision, drainage of lacrimal gland

68420 Incision, drainage of lacrimal sac (dacryocystotomy or dacryocystostomy)

68440＊ Snip incision of lacrimal punctum

Excision

68500 Excision of lacrimal gland (dacryoadenectomy), except for tumor; total

68505 partial

68510 Biopsy of lacrimal gland

68520 Excision of lacrimal sac (dacryocystectomy)

68525 Biopsy of lacrimal sac

68530 Removal of foreign body or dacryolith, lacrimal passages

68540 Excision of lacrimal gland tumor; frontal approach

68550 involving osteotomy

Repair

68700 Plastic repair of canaliculi

68705 Correction of everted punctum, cautery

68720 Dacryocystorhinostomy (fistulization of lacrimal sac to nasal cavity)

68745 Conjunctivorhinostomy (fistulization of conjunctiva to nasal cavity); without tube

68750 with insertion of tube or stent

68760 Closure of the lacrimal punctum; by thermocauterization, ligation, or laser surgery

68761 by plug, each

68770 Closure of lacrimal fistula (separate procedure)

Probing and/or Related Procedures

(68800 has been deleted. To report, use 68801)

68801＊ Dilation of lacrimal punctum, with or without irrigation

(To report a bilateral procedure, use 68801 with modifier '-50')

68810＊ Probing of nasolacrimal duct, with or without irrigation;

68811 requiring general anesthesia

68815 with insertion of tube or stent

(See also 92018)

(To report a bilateral procedure, use 68810, 68811, or 68815 with modifier '-50')

(68820, 68825, 68830 have been deleted. To report, see 68810, 68811, or 68815)

68840＊ Probing of lacrimal canaliculi, with or without irrigation

68850＊ Injection of contrast medium for dacryocystography

(For radiological supervision and interpretation, see 70170, 78660)

Other Procedures

68899 Unlisted procedure, lacrimal system

Notes

Auditory System

(For diagnostic services (eg, audiometry, vestibular tests), see 92502 et seq)

External Ear

Incision

69000*   Drainage external ear, abscess or hematoma; simple

69005   complicated

69020*   Drainage external auditory canal, abscess

69090   Ear piercing

Excision

69100   Biopsy external ear

69105   Biopsy external auditory canal

69110   Excision external ear; partial, simple repair

69120   complete amputation

(For reconstruction of ear, see 15120 et seq)

69140   Excision exostosis(es), external auditory canal

69145   Excision soft tissue lesion, external auditory canal

69150   Radical excision external auditory canal lesion; without neck dissection

69155   with neck dissection

(For resection of temporal bone, use 69535)

(For skin grafting, see 15000-15261)

Removal of Foreign Body

69200   Removal foreign body from external auditory canal; without general anesthesia

69205   with general anesthesia

69210   Removal impacted cerumen (separate procedure), one or both ears

69220   Debridement, mastoidectomy cavity, simple (eg, routine cleaning)

(69221 has been deleted. To report, use 69220 with modifier '-50')

69222   Debridement, mastoidectomy cavity, complex (eg, with anesthesia or more than routine cleaning)

(69223 has been deleted. To report, use 69222 with modifier '-50')

Repair

(For suture of wound or injury of external ear, see 12011-14300)

69300   Otoplasty, protruding ear, with or without size reduction

(69301 has been deleted. To report, use 69300 with modifier '-50')

▲ **69310**   Reconstruction of external auditory canal (meatoplasty) (eg, for stenosis due to injury, infection) (separate procedure)

69320   Reconstruction external auditory canal for congenital atresia, single stage

(For combination with middle ear reconstruction, see 69631, 69641)

(For other reconstructive procedures with grafts (eg, skin, cartilage, bone), see 13150-15760, 21230-21235)

Other Procedures

(For otoscopy under general anesthesia, use 92502)

69399   Unlisted procedure, external ear

Middle Ear

Introduction

69400   Eustachian tube inflation, transnasal; with catheterization

69401   without catheterization

69405   Eustachian tube catheterization, transtympanic

69410   Focal application of phase control substance, middle ear (baffle technique)

Incision

69420*   Myringotomy including aspiration and/or eustachian tube inflation

69421*   Myringotomy including aspiration and/or eustachian tube inflation requiring general anesthesia

69424   Ventilating tube removal when originally inserted by another physician

(69425 has been deleted. To report, use 69424 with modifier '-50')

(Tympanostomy 69431-69435 has been revised as 69433, 69436)

69433*   Tympanostomy (requiring insertion of ventilating tube), local or topical anesthesia

(69434 has been deleted. To report, use 69433 with modifier '-50')

69436 Tympanostomy (requiring insertion of ventilating tube), general anesthesia

(69437 has been deleted. To report, use 69436 with modifier '-50')

69440 Middle ear exploration through postauricular or ear canal incision

(For atticotomy, see 69601 et seq)

69450 Tympanolysis, transcanal

Excision

69501 Transmastoid antrotomy (simple mastoidectomy)

69502 Mastoidectomy; complete

69505　　modified radical

69511　　radical

(For skin graft, see 15000 et seq)

(For mastoidectomy cavity debridement, see 69220, 69222)

69530 Petrous apicectomy including radical mastoidectomy

69535 Resection temporal bone, external approach

(For middle fossa approach, see 69950-69970)

69540 Excision aural polyp

69550 Excision aural glomus tumor; transcanal

69552　　transmastoid

69554　　extended (extratemporal)

Repair

69601 Revision mastoidectomy; resulting in complete mastoidectomy

69602　　resulting in modified radical mastoidectomy

69603　　resulting in radical mastoidectomy

69604　　resulting in tympanoplasty

(For planned secondary tympanoplasty after mastoidectomy, see 69631, 69632)

69605　　with apicectomy

(For skin graft, see 15120, 15121, 15260, 15261)

69610 Tympanic membrane repair, with or without site preparation or perforation for closure, with or without patch

(69611 has been deleted. To report, use 69610)

69620 Myringoplasty (surgery confined to drumhead and donor area)

69631 Tympanoplasty without mastoidectomy (including canalplasty, atticotomy and/or middle ear surgery), initial or revision; without ossicular chain reconstruction

69632　　with ossicular chain reconstruction (eg, postfenestration)

69633　　with ossicular chain reconstruction and synthetic prosthesis (eg, partial ossicular replacement prosthesis (PORP), total ossicular replacement prosthesis (TORP))

69635 Tympanoplasty with antrotomy or mastoidotomy (including canalplasty, atticotomy, middle ear surgery, and/or tympanic membrane repair); without ossicular chain reconstruction

69636　　with ossicular chain reconstruction

69637　　with ossicular chain reconstruction and synthetic prosthesis (eg, partial ossicular replacement prosthesis (PORP), total ossicular replacement prosthesis (TORP))

69641 Tympanoplasty with mastoidectomy (including canalplasty, middle ear surgery, tympanic membrane repair); without ossicular chain reconstruction

69642　　with ossicular chain reconstruction

69643　　with intact or reconstructed wall, without ossicular chain reconstruction

69644　　with intact or reconstructed canal wall, with ossicular chain reconstruction

69645　　radical or complete, without ossicular chain reconstruction

69646　　radical or complete, with ossicular chain reconstruction

69650　　Stapes mobilization

69660 Stapedectomy or stapedotomy with reestablishment of ossicular continuity, with or without use of foreign material;

69661　　with footplate drill out

69662 Revision of stapedectomy or stapedotomy

69666 Repair oval window fistula

69667 Repair round window fistula

69670 Mastoid obliteration (separate procedure)

(69675 Tympanic neurectomy has been revised as 69676)

69676 Tympanic neurectomy

(69677 has been deleted. To report, use 69676 with modifier '-50')

⊘ =Modifier '-51' Exempt　▶ ◀=New or Revised Text　✚=Add-on Code　CPT 2002

Other Procedures

69700   Closure postauricular fistula, mastoid (separate procedure)

69710   Implantation or replacement of electromagnetic bone conduction hearing device in temporal bone

(Replacement procedure includes removal of old device)

69711   Removal or repair of electromagnetic bone conduction hearing device in temporal bone

69714   Implantation, osseointegrated implant, temporal bone, with percutaneous attachment to external speech processor/cochlear stimulator; without mastoidectomy

69715   with mastoidectomy

69717   Replacement (including removal of existing device), osseointegrated implant, temporal bone, with percutaneous attachment to external speech processor/cochlear stimulator; without mastoidectomy

69718   with mastoidectomy

69720   Decompression facial nerve, intratemporal; lateral to geniculate ganglion

69725   including medial to geniculate ganglion

69740   Suture facial nerve, intratemporal, with or without graft or decompression; lateral to geniculate ganglion

69745   including medial to geniculate ganglion

(For extracranial suture of facial nerve, use 64864)

69799   Unlisted procedure, middle ear

Inner Ear

Incision and/or Destruction

69801   Labyrinthotomy, with or without cryosurgery including other nonexcisional destructive procedures or perfusion of vestibuloactive drugs (single or multiple perfusions); transcanal

(69801 includes all required infusions performed on initial and subsequent days of treatment)

69802   with mastoidectomy

69805   Endolymphatic sac operation; without shunt

69806   with shunt

69820   Fenestration semicircular canal

69840   Revision fenestration operation

Excision

69905   Labyrinthectomy; transcanal

69910   with mastoidectomy

69915   Vestibular nerve section, translabyrinthine approach

(For transcranial approach, use 69950)

Introduction

69930   Cochlear device implantation, with or without mastoidectomy

Other Procedures

69949   Unlisted procedure, inner ear

Temporal Bone, Middle Fossa Approach

(For external approach, use 69535)

69950   Vestibular nerve section, transcranial approach

69955   Total facial nerve decompression and/or repair (may include graft)

69960   Decompression internal auditory canal

(69965 has been deleted. To report, use 69979)

69970   Removal of tumor, temporal bone

Other Procedures

69979   Unlisted procedure, temporal bone, middle fossa approach

Operating Microscope

The surgical microscope is employed when the surgical services are performed using the techniques of microsurgery. Code 69990 should be reported (without the modifier '-51' appended) in addition to the code for the primary procedure performed. Do not use 69990 for visualization with magnifying loupes or corrected vision. Do not report code 69990 in addition to procedures where use of the operating microscope is an inclusive component (15756-15758, 15842, 19364, 19368, 20955-20962, 20969-20973, 26551-26554, 26556, 31526, 31531, 31536, 31541, 31561, 31571, 43116, 43496, 49906, 61548, 63075-63078, 64727, ▶64820–64823◀, 65091-68850).

+ ▲ **69990**   Microsurgical techniques, requiring use of operating microscope (List separately in addition to code for primary procedure)

Notes

⊘ =Modifier '-51' Exempt ▶ ◀=New or Revised Text ✚=Add-on Code CPT 2002

Radiology Guidelines (Including Nuclear Medicine and Diagnostic Ultrasound)

Items used by all physicians in reporting their services are presented in the **Introduction.** Some of the commonalities are repeated here for the convenience of those physicians referring to this section on **Radiology (Including Nuclear Medicine and Diagnostic Ultrasound).** Other definitions and items unique to Radiology are also listed.

Subject Listings

Subject listings apply when radiological services are performed by or under the responsible supervision of a physician.

Multiple Procedures

It is appropriate to designate multiple procedures that are rendered on the same date by separate entries. This can be reported by using the multiple procedure modifier '-51'. See Appendix A for modifier definitions.

Separate Procedures

Some of the procedures or services listed in *CPT* that are commonly carried out as an integral component of a total service or procedure have been identified by the inclusion of the term "separate procedure." The codes designated as "separate procedure" should not be reported in addition to the code for the total procedure or service of which it is considered an integral component.

However, when a procedure or service that is designated as a "separate procedure" is carried out independently or considered to be unrelated or distinct from other procedures/services provided at that time, it may be reported by itself, or in addition to other procedures/ services by appending the modifier '-59' to the specific "separate procedure" code to indicate that the procedure is not considered to be a component of another procedure, but is a distinct, independent procedure. This may represent a different session or patient encounter, different procedure or surgery, different site or organ system, separate incision/excision, separate lesion, or separate injury (or area of injury in extensive injuries).

Subsection Information

Several of the subheadings or subsections have special needs or instructions unique to that section. Where these are indicated (eg, "Radiation Oncology") special **"Notes"** will be presented preceding those procedural terminology listings, referring to that subsection specifically. If there is an "Unlisted Procedure" code number (see section below) for the individual subsection, it will be shown. Those subsections with **"Notes"** are as follows:

Diagnostic Radiology (Diagnostic Imaging)	70010-76499
Aorta and Arteries	75600-75790
Diagnostic Ultrasound	76506-76999
Radiation Oncology	77261-77799
Clinical Treatment Planning	77261-77299
Radiation Treatment Management	77427-77499
Proton Beam Treatment Delivery	77520-77523
Hyperthermia	77600-77620
Clinical Brachytherapy	77750-77799
Nuclear Medicine	78000-78299
Musculoskeletal System	78300-78399
Cardiovascular System	78414-78499

Unlisted Service or Procedure

A service or procedure may be provided that is not listed in this edition of *CPT*. When reporting such a service, the appropriate "Unlisted Procedure" code may be used to indicate the service, identifying it by "Special Report" as discussed below. The "Unlisted Procedures" and accompanying codes for **Radiology (Including Nuclear Medicine and Diagnostic Ultrasound)** are as follows:

76499	Unlisted diagnostic radiologic procedure
76999	Unlisted ultrasound procedure
77299	Unlisted procedure, therapeutic radiology clinical treatment planning
77399	Unlisted procedure, medical radiation physics, dosimetry and treatment devices, and special services
77499	Unlisted procedure, therapeutic radiology treatment management

77799 Unlisted procedure, clinical brachytherapy

78099 Unlisted endocrine procedure, diagnostic nuclear medicine

78199 Unlisted hematopoietic, reticuloendothelial and lymphatic procedure, diagnostic nuclear medicine

78299 Unlisted gastrointestinal procedure, diagnostic nuclear medicine

78399 Unlisted musculoskeletal procedure, diagnostic nuclear medicine

78499 Unlisted cardiovascular procedure, diagnostic nuclear medicine

78599 Unlisted respiratory procedure, diagnostic nuclear medicine

78699 Unlisted nervous system procedure, diagnostic nuclear medicine

78799 Unlisted genitourinary procedure, diagnostic nuclear medicine

78999 Unlisted miscellaneous procedure, diagnostic nuclear medicine

79999 Unlisted radiopharmaceutical therapeutic procedure

Special Report

A service that is rarely provided, unusual, variable, or new may require a special report in determining medical appropriateness of the service. Pertinent information should include an adequate definition or description of the nature, extent, and need for the procedure; and the time, effort, and equipment necessary to provide the service. Additional items which may be included are:

- complexity of symptoms;
- final diagnosis;
- pertinent physical findings;
- diagnostic and therapeutic procedures;
- concurrent problems;
- follow-up care.

Supervision and Interpretation

When a procedure is performed by two physicians, the radiologic portion of the procedure is designated as "radiological supervision and interpretation." When a physician performs both the procedure and provides imaging supervision and interpretation, a combination of procedure codes outside the 70000 series and imaging supervision and interpretation codes are to be used.

(The Radiological Supervision and Interpretation codes are not applicable to the Radiation Oncology subsection.)

Administration of Contrast Material(s)

Some of the listed procedures are commonly carried out without the use of contrast material for imaging enhancement. For those codes that may or may not be performed using contrast material for imaging enhancement, the phrase "with contrast" represents contrast material administered intravascularly or intra-articularly (for intra-articular injection use appropriate joint injection code and, if used, appropriate imaging guidance code).

For spine examinations using computerized tomography, magnetic resonance imaging, magnetic resonance angiography, "with contrast" includes intrathecal or intravascular injection. For intrathecal injection, use also 61055 or 62284.

Injection of contrast material is part of the "with contrast" CT, MRI, MRA procedure.

Oral and /or rectal contrast administration alone does not qualify as a study "with contrast."

Written Report(s)

A written report, signed by the interpreting physician, should be considered an integral part of a radiologic procedure or interpretation.

Radiology

Diagnostic Radiology (Diagnostic Imaging)

Head and Neck

(70002, 70003 have been deleted. To report, use 76499)

70010 Myelography, posterior fossa, radiological supervision and interpretation

(70011 (complete procedure) has been deleted, see 61055, 62284, 70010)

70015 Cisternography, positive contrast, radiological supervision and interpretation

(70016 (complete procedure) has been deleted, see 61055, 62284, 70015)

(70020, 70021 have been deleted. To report, use 76499)

(70022 has been deleted. To report CT guidance for stereotactic localization, use 76355)

70030 Radiologic examination, eye, for detection of foreign body

(70040, 70050 have been deleted)

70100 Radiologic examination, mandible; partial, less than four views

70110 complete, minimum of four views

70120 Radiologic examination, mastoids; less than three views per side

70130 complete, minimum of three views per side

70134 Radiologic examination, internal auditory meati, complete

70140 Radiologic examination, facial bones; less than three views

70150 complete, minimum of three views

70160 Radiologic examination, nasal bones, complete, minimum of three views

70170 Dacryocystography, nasolacrimal duct, radiological supervision and interpretation

(70171 (complete procedure) has been deleted, see 68850, 70170)

70190 Radiologic examination; optic foramina

70200 orbits, complete, minimum of four views

70210 Radiologic examination, sinuses, paranasal, less than three views

70220 Radiologic examination, sinuses, paranasal, complete, minimum of three views

(70230, 70231 have been deleted. To report, use 76499)

70240 Radiologic examination, sella turcica

70250 Radiologic examination, skull; less than four views, with or without stereo

70260 complete, minimum of four views, with or without stereo

70300 Radiologic examination, teeth; single view

70310 partial examination, less than full mouth

70320 complete, full mouth

70328 Radiologic examination, temporomandibular joint, open and closed mouth; unilateral

70330 bilateral

70332 Temporomandibular joint arthrography, radiological supervision and interpretation

►(Do not report 76003 in addition to 70332)◄

(70333 (complete procedure) has been deleted, see 21116, 70332)

70336 Magnetic resonance (eg, proton) imaging, temporomandibular joint(s)

70350 Cephalogram, orthodontic

70355 Orthopantogram

70360 Radiologic examination; neck, soft tissue

70370 pharynx or larynx, including fluoroscopy and/or magnification technique

70371 Complex dynamic pharyngeal and speech evaluation by cine or video recording

70373 Laryngography, contrast, radiological supervision and interpretation

(70374 (complete procedure) has been deleted, see 31708, 70373)

70380 Radiologic examination, salivary gland for calculus

70390 Sialography, radiological supervision and interpretation

(70391 (complete procedure) has been deleted, see 42550, 70390)

(70400, 70401 have been deleted. To report, use 76499)

70450 Computerized axial tomography, head or brain; without contrast material

70460 with contrast material(s)

70470 without contrast material, followed by contrast material(s) and further sections

(For coronal, sagittal, and/or oblique sections, use 76375)

70480 Computerized axial tomography, orbit, sella, or posterior fossa or outer, middle, or inner ear; without contrast material

70481   with contrast material(s)

70482   without contrast material, followed by contrast material(s) and further sections

(For coronal, sagittal, and/or oblique sections, use 76375)

70486 Computerized axial tomography, maxillofacial area; without contrast material

70487   with contrast material(s)

70488   without contrast material, followed by contrast material(s) and further sections

(For coronal, sagittal, and/or oblique sections, use 76375)

70490 Computerized axial tomography, soft tissue neck; without contrast material

70491   with contrast material(s)

70492   without contrast material followed by contrast material(s) and further sections

(For coronal, sagittal, and/or oblique sections, use 76375)

(For cervical spine, see 72125, 72126)

70496 Computed tomographic angiography, head, without contrast material(s), followed by contrast material(s) and further sections, including image post-processing

70498 Computed tomographic angiography, neck, without contrast material(s), followed by contrast material(s) and further sections, including image post-processing

70540 Magnetic resonance (eg, proton) imaging, orbit, face, and neck; without contrast material(s)

(70541 has been deleted. To report head or neck magnetic resonance angiography studies, see 70544-70546, 70547-70549)

70542   with contrast material(s)

70543   without contrast material(s), followed by contrast material(s) and further sequences

70544 Magnetic resonance angiography, head; without contrast material(s)

70545   with contrast material(s)

70546   without contrast material(s), followed by contrast material(s) and further sequences

70547 Magnetic resonance angiography, neck; without contrast material(s)

70548   with contrast material(s)

70549   without contrast material(s), followed by contrast material(s) and further sequences

(70550 has been deleted. To report, use 70551)

70551 Magnetic resonance (eg, proton) imaging, brain (including brain stem); without contrast material

70552   with contrast material(s)

70553   without contrast material, followed by contrast material(s) and further sequences

(For magnetic spectroscopy, use 76390)

Chest

(71000 has been deleted)

71010 Radiologic examination, chest; single view, frontal

71015   stereo, frontal

71020 Radiologic examination, chest, two views, frontal and lateral;

71021   with apical lordotic procedure

71022   with oblique projections

71023   with fluoroscopy

71030 Radiologic examination, chest, complete, minimum of four views;

71034   with fluoroscopy

(For separate chest fluoroscopy, use 76000)

71035 Radiologic examination, chest, special views (eg, lateral decubitus, Bucky studies)

(71036 has been deleted. To report, use 76003)

(71037 (complete procedure) has been deleted, see 32400, 32405, 76003)

(71038 has been deleted. To report, use 31628)

71040 Bronchography, unilateral, radiological supervision and interpretation

(71041 (complete procedure) has been deleted, see 31656, 31708, 31710, 31715, 71040)

71060 Bronchography, bilateral, radiological supervision and interpretation

(71061 (complete procedure) has been deleted, see 31656, 31708, 31710, 31715, 71060)

71090 Insertion pacemaker, fluoroscopy and radiography, radiological supervision and interpretation

►(For procedure, see appropriate organ or site)◄

71100 Radiologic examination, ribs, unilateral; two views

71101   including posteroanterior chest, minimum of three views

71110 Radiologic examination, ribs, bilateral; three views

71111   including posteroanterior chest, minimum of four views

71120 Radiologic examination; sternum, minimum of two views

71130   sternoclavicular joint or joints, minimum of three views

71250 Computerized axial tomography, thorax; without contrast material

71260   with contrast material(s)

⊘ =Modifier '-51' Exempt ► ◄ =New or Revised Text ✦ =Add-on Code CPT 2002

71270   without contrast material, followed by contrast material(s) and further sections

(For coronal, sagittal, and/or oblique sections, use 76375)

71275   Computed tomographic angiography, chest, without contrast material(s), followed by contrast material(s) and further sections, including image post-processing

71550   Magnetic resonance (eg, proton) imaging, chest (eg, for evaluation of hilar and mediastinal lymphadenopathy); without contrast material(s)

71551   with contrast material(s)

71552   without contrast material(s), followed by contrast material(s) and further sequences

(For breast MRI, see 76093 and 76094)

71555   Magnetic resonance angiography, chest (excluding myocardium), with or without contrast material(s)

Spine and Pelvis

72010   Radiologic examination, spine, entire, survey study, anteroposterior and lateral

72020   Radiologic examination, spine, single view, specify level

72040   Radiologic examination, spine, cervical; two or three views

72050   minimum of four views

72052   complete, including oblique and flexion and/or extension studies

72069   Radiologic examination, spine, thoracolumbar, standing (scoliosis)

72070   Radiologic examination, spine; thoracic, two views

72072   thoracic, three views

72074   thoracic, minimum of four views

72080   thoracolumbar, two views

72090   scoliosis study, including supine and erect studies

72100   Radiologic examination, spine, lumbosacral; two or three views

72110   minimum of four views

72114   complete, including bending views

72120   Radiologic examination, spine, lumbosacral, bending views only, minimum of four views

(Contrast material in CT of spine is either by intrathecal or intravenous injection. For intrathecal injection, use also 61055 or 62284. IV injection of contrast material is part of the CT procedure)

72125   Computerized axial tomography, cervical spine; without contrast material

72126   with contrast material

72127   without contrast material, followed by contrast material(s) and further sections

(For intrathecal injection procedure, see 61055, 62284)

72128   Computerized axial tomography, thoracic spine; without contrast material

72129   with contrast material

(For intrathecal injection procedure, see 61055, 62284)

72130   without contrast material, followed by contrast material(s) and further sections

(For intrathecal injection procedure, see 61055, 62284)

72131   Computerized axial tomography, lumbar spine; without contrast material

72132   with contrast material

72133   without contrast material, followed by contrast material(s) and further sections

(For intrathecal injection procedure, see 61055, 62284)

(For coronal, sagittal, and/or oblique sections, use 76375)

(72140 has been deleted. To report, see 72141-72149)

72141   Magnetic resonance (eg, proton) imaging, spinal canal and contents, cervical; without contrast material

72142   with contrast material(s)

(For cervical spinal canal imaging without contrast material followed by contrast material, use 72156)

(72143 has been deleted. To report, see 72146, 72147)

(72144 has been deleted. To report, see 72148, 72149)

(72145 has been deleted. To report, see 72125-72133)

72146   Magnetic resonance (eg, proton) imaging, spinal canal and contents, thoracic; without contrast material

72147   with contrast material(s)

(For thoracic spinal canal imaging without contrast material followed by contrast material, use 72157)

72148   Magnetic resonance (eg, proton) imaging, spinal canal and contents, lumbar; without contrast material

72149   with contrast material(s)

(For lumbar spinal canal imaging without contrast material followed by contrast material, use 72158)

72156   Magnetic resonance (eg, proton) imaging, spinal canal and contents, without contrast material, followed by contrast material(s) and further sequences; cervical

72157   thoracic

72158   lumbar

72159   Magnetic resonance angiography, spinal canal and contents, with or without contrast material(s)

72170   Radiologic examination, pelvis; one or two views

(72180 has been deleted. To report, use 72170)

72190   complete, minimum of three views

(For pelvimetry, use 74710)

72191 Computed tomographic angiography, pelvis, without contrast material(s), followed by contrast material(s) and further sections, including image post-processing

(For CTA aorto-iliofemoral runoff, use 75635)

72192 Computerized axial tomography, pelvis; without contrast material

72193 with contrast material(s)

72194 without contrast material, followed by contrast material(s) and further sections

(For coronal, sagittal, and/or oblique sections, use 76375)

72195 Magnetic resonance (eg, proton) imaging, pelvis; without contrast material(s)

72196 with contrast material(s)

72197 without contrast material(s), followed by contrast material(s) and further sequences

72198 Magnetic resonance angiography, pelvis, with or without contrast material(s)

72200 Radiologic examination, sacroiliac joints; less than three views

72202 three or more views

72220 Radiologic examination, sacrum and coccyx, minimum of two views

72240 Myelography, cervical, radiological supervision and interpretation

(72241 (complete procedure) has been deleted, see 61055, 62284, 72240)

72255 Myelography, thoracic, radiological supervision and interpretation

(72256 (complete procedure) has been deleted, see 61055, 62284, 72255)

72265 Myelography, lumbosacral, radiological supervision and interpretation

(72266 (complete procedure) has been deleted, see 61055, 62284, 72265)

72270 Myelography, entire spinal canal, radiological supervision and interpretation

(72271 (complete procedure) has been deleted, see 61055, 62284, 72270)

72275 Epidurography, radiological supervision and interpretation

(For injection procedure, see 62280-62282, 62310-62319, 64479-64484)

72285 Diskography, cervical or thoracic, radiological supervision and interpretation

(72286 (complete procedure) has been deleted, see 62291, 72285)

72295 Diskography, lumbar, radiological supervision and interpretation

(72296 (complete procedure) has been deleted, see 62290, 72295)

Upper Extremities

(For stress views, any joint, use 76006)

73000 Radiologic examination; clavicle, complete

73010 scapula, complete

73020 Radiologic examination, shoulder; one view

73030 complete, minimum of two views

73040 Radiologic examination, shoulder, arthrography, radiological supervision and interpretation

►(Do not report 76003 in addition to 73040)◄

(73041 (complete procedure) has been deleted, see 23350, 73040)

73050 Radiologic examination; acromioclavicular joints, bilateral, with or without weighted distraction

73060 humerus, minimum of two views

73070 Radiologic examination, elbow; two views

73080 complete, minimum of three views

73085 Radiologic examination, elbow, arthrography, radiological supervision and interpretation

►(Do not report 76003 in addition to 73085)◄

(73086 (complete procedure) has been deleted, see 24220, 73085)

73090 Radiologic examination; forearm, two views

73092 upper extremity, infant, minimum of two views

73100 Radiologic examination, wrist; two views

73110 complete, minimum of three views

73115 Radiologic examination, wrist, arthrography, radiological supervision and interpretation

►(Do not report 76003 in addition to 73115)◄

(73116 (complete procedure) has been deleted, see 25246, 73115)

73120 Radiologic examination, hand; two views

73130 minimum of three views

73140 Radiologic examination, finger(s), minimum of two views

73200 Computerized axial tomography, upper extremity; without contrast material

73201 with contrast material(s)

73202 without contrast material, followed by contrast material(s) and further sections

(For coronal, sagittal, and/or oblique sections, use 76375)

73206 Computed tomographic angiography, upper extremity, without contrast material(s), followed by contrast material(s) and further sections, including image post-processing

73218 Magnetic resonance (eg, proton) imaging, upper extremity, other than joint; without contrast material(s)

73219 with contrast material(s)

○=Modifier '-51' Exempt ►◄=New or Revised Text ✛=Add-on Code CPT 2002

73220	without contrast material(s), followed by contrast material(s) and further sequences
73221	Magnetic resonance (eg, proton) imaging, any joint of upper extremity; without contrast material(s)
73222	with contrast material(s)
73223	without contrast material(s), followed by contrast material(s) and further sequences
73225	Magnetic resonance angiography, upper extremity, with or without contrast material(s)

Lower Extremities

(For stress views, any joint, use 76006)

73500	Radiologic examination, hip, unilateral; one view
73510	complete, minimum of two views
73520	Radiologic examination, hips, bilateral, minimum of two views of each hip, including anteroposterior view of pelvis
73525	Radiologic examination, hip, arthrography, radiological supervision and interpretation

▶(Do not report 76003 in addition to 73525)◀

(73526 (complete procedure) has been deleted, see 27093, 27095, 73525)

73530	Radiologic examination, hip, during operative procedure

(73531 has been deleted. To report, use 73530)

73540	Radiologic examination, pelvis and hips, infant or child, minimum of two views
73542	Radiological examination, sacroiliac joint arthrography, radiological supervision and interpretation

▶(Do not report 76003 in addition to 73542)◀

(For procedure, use 27096. If formal arthrography is not performed, recorded, and a formal radiologic report is not issued, use 76005 for fluoroscopic guidance for sacroiliac joint injections)

73550	Radiologic examination, femur, two views
73560	Radiologic examination, knee; one or two views
73562	three views
73564	complete, four or more views
73565	both knees, standing, anteroposterior

(73570 has been deleted. To report, see 73562, 73564)

73580	Radiologic examination, knee, arthrography, radiological supervision and interpretation

▶(Do not report 76003 in addition to 73580)◀

(73581 (complete procedure) has been deleted, see 27370, 73580)

73590	Radiologic examination; tibia and fibula, two views
73592	lower extremity, infant, minimum of two views

73600	Radiologic examination, ankle; two views
73610	complete, minimum of three views
73615	Radiologic examination, ankle, arthrography, radiological supervision and interpretation

▶(Do not report 76003 in addition to 73615)◀

(73616 (complete procedure) has been deleted, see 27648, 73615)

73620	Radiologic examination, foot; two views
73630	complete, minimum of three views
73650	Radiologic examination; calcaneus, minimum of two views
73660	toe(s), minimum of two views
73700	Computerized axial tomography, lower extremity; without contrast material
73701	with contrast material(s)
73702	without contrast material, followed by contrast material(s) and further sections

(For coronal, sagittal, and/or oblique sections, use 76375)

73706	Computed tomographic angiography, lower extremity, without contrast material(s), followed by contrast material(s) and further sections, including image post-processing

(For CTA aorto-iliofemoral runoff, use 75635)

73718	Magnetic resonance (eg, proton) imaging, lower extremity other than joint; without contrast material(s)
73719	with contrast material(s)
73720	without contrast material(s), followed by contrast material(s) and further sequences
73721	Magnetic resonance (eg, proton) imaging, any joint of lower extremity; without contrast material
73722	with contrast material(s)
73723	without contrast material(s), followed by contrast material(s) and further sequences
73725	Magnetic resonance angiography, lower extremity, with or without contrast material(s)

Abdomen

74000	Radiologic examination, abdomen; single anteroposterior view
74010	anteroposterior and additional oblique and cone views
74020	complete, including decubitus and/or erect views
74022	complete acute abdomen series, including supine, erect, and/or decubitus views, upright PA chest
74150	Computerized axial tomography, abdomen; without contrast material
74160	with contrast material(s)

74170 without contrast material, followed by contrast material(s) and further sections

(For coronal, sagittal, and/or oblique sections, use 76375)

74175 Computed tomographic angiography, abdomen, without contrast material(s), followed by contrast material(s) and further sections, including image post-processing

(For CTA aorto-iliofemoral runoff, use 75635)

74181 Magnetic resonance (eg, proton) imaging, abdomen; without contrast material(s)

74182 with contrast material(s)

74183 without contrast material(s), followed by with contrast material(s) and further sequences

74185 Magnetic resonance angiography, abdomen, with or without contrast material(s)

74190 Peritoneogram (eg, after injection of air or contrast), radiological supervision and interpretation

(For procedure, use 49400)

(For computerized axial tomography, see 72192 or 74150)

Gastrointestinal Tract

(For percutaneous placement of gastrostomy tube, use 43750)

74210 Radiologic examination; pharynx and/or cervical esophagus

74220 esophagus

▲**74230** Swallowing function, with cineradiography/videoradiography

74235 Removal of foreign body(s), esophageal, with use of balloon catheter, radiological supervision and interpretation

(For procedure, see 43215, 43247)

74240 Radiologic examination, gastrointestinal tract, upper; with or without delayed films, without KUB

74241 with or without delayed films, with KUB

▲**74245** with small intestine, includes multiple serial films

74246 Radiological examination, gastrointestinal tract, upper, air contrast, with specific high density barium, effervescent agent, with or without glucagon; with or without delayed films, without KUB

74247 with or without delayed films, with KUB

▲**74249** with small intestine follow-through

▲**74250** Radiologic examination, small intestine, includes multiple serial films;

74251 via enteroclysis tube

74260 Duodenography, hypotonic

74270 Radiologic examination, colon; barium enema, with or without KUB

(74275 has been deleted. To report, use 76499)

74280 air contrast with specific high density barium, with or without glucagon

74283 Therapeutic enema, contrast or air, for reduction of intussusception or other intraluminal obstruction (eg, meconium ileus)

(74285 has been deleted. To report, see 74270, 74280)

74290 Cholecystography, oral contrast;

74291 additional or repeat examination or multiple day examination

74300 Cholangiography and/or pancreatography; intraoperative, radiological supervision and interpretation

+ **74301** additional set intraoperative, radiological supervision and interpretation (List separately in addition to code for primary procedure)

(Use 74301 in conjunction with code 74300)

▲**74305** through existing catheter, radiological supervision and interpretation

(For procedure, see 47505, 48400, 47560-47561, 47563)

(For biliary duct stone extraction, percutaneous, see 47630, 74327)

(74310, 74315 have been deleted. To report, use 76499)

74320 Cholangiography, percutaneous, transhepatic, radiological supervision and interpretation

(74321 (complete procedure) has been deleted, see 47500, 74320)

(74325, 74326 have been deleted. To report, use 76499)

▲**74327** Postoperative biliary duct calculus removal, percutaneous via T-tube tract, basket, or snare (eg, Burhenne technique), radiological supervision and interpretation

(For procedure, use 47630)

74328 Endoscopic catheterization of the biliary ductal system, radiological supervision and interpretation

(For procedure, see 43260-43272 as appropriate)

74329 Endoscopic catheterization of the pancreatic ductal system, radiological supervision and interpretation

(For procedure, see 43260-43272 as appropriate)

74330 Combined endoscopic catheterization of the biliary and pancreatic ductal systems, radiological supervision and interpretation

(For procedure, see 43260-43272 as appropriate)

(74331 has been deleted. To report, use 43262)

74340 Introduction of long gastrointestinal tube (eg, Miller-Abbott), including multiple fluoroscopies and films, radiological supervision and interpretation

(For tube placement, use 44500)

74350 Percutaneous placement of gastrostomy tube, radiological supervision and interpretation

⊘ =Modifier '-51' Exempt   ▶ ◀=New or Revised Text   ✦ =Add-on Code   CPT 2002

74355   Percutaneous placement of enteroclysis tube, radiological supervision and interpretation

(74356 (complete procedure) has been deleted, see 44015, 74355)

74360   Intraluminal dilation of strictures and/or obstructions (eg, esophagus), radiological supervision and interpretation

(74361 (complete procedure) has been deleted, see 43220, 43458, 74360)

▲ **74363**   Percutaneous transhepatic dilation of biliary duct stricture with or without placement of stent, radiological supervision and interpretation

(For procedure, see 47510, 47511, 47555, 47556)

Urinary Tract

74400   Urography (pyelography), intravenous, with or without KUB, with or without tomography

(74405 has been deleted. To report, see 74400, 74410 or 74415)

74410   Urography, infusion, drip technique and/or bolus technique;

74415   with nephrotomography

74420   Urography, retrograde, with or without KUB

74425   Urography, antegrade, (pyelostogram, nephrostogram, loopogram), radiological supervision and interpretation

(74426 (complete procedure) has been deleted, see 50394, 50684, 50690, 74425)

74430   Cystography, minimum of three views, radiological supervision and interpretation

(74431 (complete procedure) has been deleted, see 51600, 51605, 74430)

74440   Vasography, vesiculography, or epididymography, radiological supervision and interpretation

(74441 (complete procedure) has been deleted, see 52010, 55300, 74440)

74445   Corpora cavernosography, radiological supervision and interpretation

(74446 (complete procedure) has been deleted, see 54230, 74445)

74450   Urethrocystography, retrograde, radiological supervision and interpretation

(74451 (complete procedure) has been deleted, see 51610, 74450)

74455   Urethrocystography, voiding, radiological supervision and interpretation

(74456 (complete procedure) has been deleted, see 51600, 74455)

(74460, 74461 have been deleted. To report, use 76499)

74470   Radiologic examination, renal cyst study, translumbar, contrast visualization, radiological supervision and interpretation

(74471 (complete procedure) has been deleted, see 50390, 74470)

74475   Introduction of intracatheter or catheter into renal pelvis for drainage and/or injection, percutaneous, radiological supervision and interpretation

(74476 (complete procedure) has been deleted, see 50392-50398, 74475)

74480   Introduction of ureteral catheter or stent into ureter through renal pelvis for drainage and/or injection, percutaneous, radiological supervision and interpretation

(74481 (complete procedure) has been deleted, see 50392-50398, 74480)

(For transurethral surgery (ureter and pelvis), see 52320-52355)

74485   Dilation of nephrostomy, ureters, or urethra, radiological supervision and interpretation

(74486 (complete procedure) has been deleted, see 50395, 53600-53621, 74485)

(For dilation of ureter without radiologic guidance, use ▶52341, 52344◀)

(For change of nephrostomy or pyelostomy tube, use 50398)

Gynecological and Obstetrical

(For abdomen and pelvis, see 72170-72190, 74000-74170)

74710   Pelvimetry, with or without placental localization

(74720, 74725 have been deleted. To report, use 74000)

(74730, 74731 have been deleted. To report, use 76499)

74740   Hysterosalpingography, radiological supervision and interpretation

(For introduction of saline or contrast for hysterosalpingography, see 58340)

(74741 (complete procedure) has been deleted, see 58340, 74740)

74742   Transcervical catheterization of fallopian tube, radiological supervision and interpretation

(For procedure, use 58345)

(74760, 74761, 74770, 74771 have been deleted. To report, use 76499)

74775   Perineogram (eg, vaginogram, for sex determination or extent of anomalies)

Heart

(For separate injection procedures for vascular radiology, see **Surgery** section, 36000-36299)

(For cardiac catheterization procedures, see 93501-93556)

(75500 has been deleted. To report, use 93555)

(75501 (complete procedure) has been deleted, see 93501-▶93533◀, 93542, 93543, 93555)

(75505 has been deleted. To report, use 93555)

(75506 (complete procedure) has been deleted, see 36400-36425 for intravenous procedure, 36100-36248 for intra-arterial procedure and 93501-▶93533◀, 93542, 93543, 93555)

(75507 has been deleted. To report, use 93555)

(75509 (complete procedure) has been deleted. To report, see 36400-36425 for intravenous procedure, 36100-36248 for intra-arterial procedure and 93501-▶93533◀, 93542, 93543)

(75510, 75511 have been deleted. To report, use 76499)

(75519 has been deleted. To report, use 93555)

(75520 (complete procedure) has been deleted, see 36400-36425 for intravenous procedure, 36100-36248 for intra-arterial procedure, and 93501, 93542)

(75523 has been deleted. To report, use 93555)

(75524 has been deleted, see 36400-36425 for intravenous procedure, 36100-36248 for intra-arterial procedure, and 93510-93514, 93524, 93543)

(75527 has been deleted. To report, use 93555)

(75528 has been deleted, see 36400-36425 for intravenous procedure, 36100-36248 for intra-arterial procedure, and 93526-93529, 93543, and 93555)

75552 Cardiac magnetic resonance imaging for morphology; without contrast material

75553   with contrast material

75554 Cardiac magnetic resonance imaging for function, with or without morphology; complete study

75555   limited study

75556 Cardiac magnetic resonance imaging for velocity flow mapping

Aorta and Arteries

Selective vascular catheterizations should be coded to include introduction and all lesser order selective catheterizations used in the approach (eg, the description for a selective right middle cerebral artery catheterization includes the introduction and placement catheterization of the right common and internal carotid arteries).

Additional second and/or third order arterial catheterizations within the same family of arteries supplied by a single first order artery should be expressed by 36218 or 36248. Additional first order or higher catheterizations in vascular families supplied by a first order vessel different from a previously selected and coded family should be separately coded using the conventions described above.

(For intravenous procedure, see 36000-36013, 36400-36425 and 36100-36248 for intra-arterial procedure)

(For radiological supervision and interpretation, see 75600-75978)

75600 Aortography, thoracic, without serialography, radiological supervision and interpretation

(For injection procedure, use 93544)

(75601 (complete procedure) has been deleted, see 36000-36013, 36400-36425 for intravenous procedure, and 36100-36200 for intra-arterial procedure and 75600)

75605 Aortography, thoracic, by serialography, radiological supervision and interpretation

(For injection procedure, use 93544)

(75606 (complete procedure) has been deleted, see 36000-36013, 36400-36425 for intravenous procedure, and 36100-36200 for intra-arterial procedure and 75605)

(75620, 75621, 75622, 75623 have been deleted. To report, use 76499)

75625 Aortography, abdominal, by serialography, radiological supervision and interpretation

(For injection procedure, use 93544)

(75626, 75627 and 75628 have been deleted, see 36000-36013, 36400-36425 for intravenous procedure, and 36100-36200 for intra-arterial procedure and 75625)

75630 Aortography, abdominal plus bilateral iliofemoral lower extremity, catheter, by serialography, radiological supervision and interpretation

(75631 (complete procedure) has been deleted, see 36000-36013, 36400-36425 for intravenous procedure, and 36100-36200 and 36245-36248 for intra-arterial procedure and 75630)

75635 Computed tomographic angiography, abdominal aorta and bilateral iliofemoral lower extremity runoff, radiological supervision and interpretation, without contrast material(s), followed by contrast material(s) and further sections, including image post-processing

75650 Angiography, cervicocerebral, catheter, including vessel origin, radiological supervision and interpretation

(75651-75657 (complete procedure) have been deleted, see 36000-36013, 36400-36425 for intravenous procedure, and 36100-36218 for intra-arterial procedure and 75650, 75660-75685 as appropriate)

75658 Angiography, brachial, retrograde, radiological supervision and interpretation

(75659 (complete procedure) has been deleted, see 36000-36013, 36400-36425 for intravenous procedure, and 36100-36218 for intra-arterial procedure and 75658)

⊘ =Modifier '-51' Exempt   ▶ ◀=New or Revised Text   ✚=Add-on Code   CPT 2002

75660   Angiography, external carotid, unilateral, selective, radiological supervision and interpretation

(75661 (complete procedure) has been deleted, see 36000-36013, 36400-36425 for intravenous procedure, and 36100-36218 and 75660)

75662   Angiography, external carotid, bilateral, selective, radiological supervision and interpretation

(75663 (complete procedure) has been deleted, see 36000-36013, 36400-36425 for intravenous procedure, and 36100-36218 for intra-arterial procedure and 75662)

75665   Angiography, carotid, cerebral, unilateral, radiological supervision and interpretation

(75667, 75669 (complete procedure) have been deleted, see 36000-36013, 36400-36425 for intravenous procedure, and 36100-36218 for intra-arterial procedure and 75665)

75671   Angiography, carotid, cerebral, bilateral, radiological supervision and interpretation

(75672, 75673 (complete procedure) have been deleted, see 36000-36013, 36400-36425 for intravenous procedure, and 36100-36218 for intra-arterial procedure and 75671)

75676   Angiography, carotid, cervical, unilateral, radiological supervision and interpretation

(75677, 75678 (complete procedure) have been deleted, see 36000-36013, 36400-36425 for intravenous procedure, and 36100-36218 for intra-arterial procedure and 75676)

75680   Angiography, carotid, cervical, bilateral, radiological supervision and interpretation

(75681, 75682 (complete procedure) have been deleted, see 36000-36013, 36400-36425 for intravenous procedure, and 36100-36218 for intra-arterial procedure and 75680)

75685   Angiography, vertebral, cervical, and/or intracranial, radiological supervision and interpretation

(75686 has been deleted)

(75687 (complete procedure) has been deleted, see 36000-36013, 36400-36425 for intravenous procedure, and 36100-36218 for intra-arterial procedure and 75685)

(75690 (complete procedure) has been deleted, see 36000-36013, 36400-36425 for intravenous procedure, and 36100-36218 for intra-arterial procedure and 75685)

(75691 has been deleted)

(75692 (complete procedure) has been deleted, see 36000-36013, 36400-36425 for intravenous procedure, and 36100-36218 for intra-arterial procedure and 75685)

(75695 (complete procedure) has been deleted, see 36000-36013, 36400-36425 for intravenous procedure, and 36100-36218 for intra-arterial procedure and 75685)

(75696 has been deleted)

(75697 (complete procedure) has been deleted, see 36000-36013, 36400-36425 for intravenous procedure, and 36100-36218 for intra-arterial procedure and 75685)

75705   Angiography, spinal, selective, radiological supervision and interpretation

(75706 (complete procedure) has been deleted, see 36000-36013, 36400-36425 for intravenous procedure, and 36100-36248 for intra-arterial procedure and 75705)

75710   Angiography, extremity, unilateral, radiological supervision and interpretation

(75711, 75712 (complete procedure) have been deleted, see 36000-36013, 36400-36425 for intravenous procedure, and 36100-36248 for intra-arterial procedure and 75710)

75716   Angiography, extremity, bilateral, radiological supervision and interpretation

(75717, 75718 (complete procedure) have been deleted, see 36000-36013, 36400-36425 for intravenous procedure, and 36100-36248 for intra-arterial procedure and 75716)

75722   Angiography, renal, unilateral, selective (including flush aortogram), radiological supervision and interpretation

(75723 (complete procedure) has been deleted, see 36000-36013, 36400-36425 for intravenous procedure, and 36100-36200 and 36245-36248 for intra-arterial procedure and 75722)

75724   Angiography, renal, bilateral, selective (including flush aortogram), radiological supervision and interpretation

(75725 (complete procedure) has been deleted, see 36000-36013, 36400-36425 for intravenous procedure, and 36100-36200 and 36245-36248 for intra-arterial procedure and 75724)

75726   Angiography, visceral, selective or supraselective, (with or without flush aortogram), radiological supervision and interpretation

(For selective angiography, each additional visceral vessel studied after basic examination, use 75774)

(75727, 75728 (complete procedure) have been deleted, see 36000-36013, 36400-36425 for intravenous procedure, and 36100-36248 for intra-arterial procedure and 75726)

75731   Angiography, adrenal, unilateral, selective, radiological supervision and interpretation

(75732 (complete procedure) has been deleted, see 36000-36013, 36400-36425 for intravenous procedure, and 36100-36200 and 36245-36248 for intra-arterial procedure and 75731)

75733   Angiography, adrenal, bilateral, selective, radiological supervision and interpretation

(75734 (complete procedure) has been deleted, see 36000-36013, 36400-36425 for intravenous procedure, and 36100-36200 and 36245-36248 for intra-arterial procedure and 75733)

75736 Angiography, pelvic, selective or supraselective, radiological supervision and interpretation

(75737, 75738 (complete procedure) have been deleted, see 36000-36013, 36400-36425 for intravenous procedure, and 36100-36200 and 36245-36248 for intra-arterial procedure and 75736)

75741 Angiography, pulmonary, unilateral, selective, radiological supervision and interpretation

(For injection procedure, use 93541)

(75742 (complete procedure) has been deleted, see 36000-36015, 36400-36425 for intravenous procedure and 75741)

75743 Angiography, pulmonary, bilateral, selective, radiological supervision and interpretation

(For injection procedure, use 93541)

(75744 (complete procedure) has been deleted, see 36000-36015, 36400-36425 for intravenous procedure and 75743)

75746 Angiography, pulmonary, by nonselective catheter or venous injection, radiological supervision and interpretation

(75747, 75748 (complete procedure) have been deleted, see 36000-36013, 36400-36425 for intravenous procedure, and 36100-36200 for intra-arterial procedure and 75746)

(For injection procedure, use 93541)

(75750 has been deleted. To report, use 93556)

(75751 (complete procedure) has been deleted, see 36000-36013, 36400-36425 for intravenous procedure, and 36100-36200 for intra-arterial procedure and 93556)

(For introduction of catheter, injection procedure, see 93501-►93533◄, 93539, 93540, 93545, 93556)

(75752 has been deleted. To report, use 93556)

(75753 (complete procedure) has been deleted, see 36100-36218 for intra-arterial procedure and 93556)

(For introduction of catheter, injection procedure, see 93501-►93533◄, 93545, 93556)

(75754 has been deleted. To report, use 93556)

(75755 (complete procedure) has been deleted, see 36100-36218 for intra-arterial procedure and 93556)

(For introduction of catheter, injection procedure, see 93501-►93533◄, 93539, 93540, 93545, 93556)

75756 Angiography, internal mammary, radiological supervision and interpretation

(For introduction of catheter, injection procedure, see 93501-►93533◄, 93545, 93556)

(75757 (complete procedure) has been deleted, see 36000-36013, 36400-36425 for intravenous procedure, and 36100-36218 for intra-arterial procedure and 93556)

(75762 has been deleted. To report, use 93556)

(75764 (complete procedure) has been deleted, see 36000-36013, 36400-36425 for intravenous procedure, and 36100-36218 for intra-arterial procedure and 93556)

(75766 has been deleted. To report, use 93556)

(75767 has been deleted. To report, see 36000-36013, 36400-36425 for intravenous procedure, and 36100-36218 for intra-arterial procedure and 93556)

(75772, 75773 have been deleted. To report, use 75774)

+ 75774 Angiography, selective, each additional vessel studied after basic examination, radiological supervision and interpretation (List separately in addition to code for primary procedure)

(Use 75774 in addition to code for specific initial vessel studied)

(For angiography, see codes 75600-75790)

(For catheterizations, see codes 36215-36248)

(For introduction of catheter, injection procedure, see 93501-►93533◄, 93545, 93555, 93556)

(75775 (complete procedure) has been deleted, see 36000-36015, 36400-36425 for intravenous procedure, and 36100-36248 for intra-arterial procedure and 75774)

75790 Angiography, arteriovenous shunt (eg, dialysis patient), radiological supervision and interpretation

(For introduction of catheter, use 36140, 36145, 36215-36217, 36245-36247)

Veins and Lymphatics

(For injection procedure for venous system, see 36000-36015, 36400-36510)

(For injection procedure for lymphatic system, use 38790)

75801 Lymphangiography, extremity only, unilateral, radiological supervision and interpretation

(75802 (complete procedure) has been deleted, see 38790, 75801)

75803 Lymphangiography, extremity only, bilateral, radiological supervision and interpretation

(75804 (complete procedure) has been deleted, see 38790, 75803)

75805 Lymphangiography, pelvic/abdominal, unilateral, radiological supervision and interpretation

(75806 (complete procedure) has been deleted, see 38790, 75805)

75807 Lymphangiography, pelvic/abdominal, bilateral, radiological supervision and interpretation

(75808 (complete procedure) has been deleted, see 38790, 75807)

75809 Shuntogram for investigation of previously placed indwelling nonvascular shunt (eg, LeVeen shunt, ventriculoperitoneal shunt, indwelling infusion pump), radiological supervision and interpretation

(For procedure, see 49427 or 61070)

75810 Splenoportography, radiological supervision and interpretation

(75811 (complete procedure) has been deleted, see 38200, 75810)

75820 Venography, extremity, unilateral, radiological supervision and interpretation

(75821 (complete procedure) has been deleted, see 36000, 36005, 36406, 36410, 36420, 36425, 75820)

75822 Venography, extremity, bilateral, radiological supervision and interpretation

(75823 (complete procedure) has been deleted, see 36000, 36005, 36406, 36410, 36420, 36425, 75822)

75825 Venography, caval, inferior, with serialography, radiological supervision and interpretation

(75826 (complete procedure) has been deleted, see 36010, 75825)

75827 Venography, caval, superior, with serialography, radiological supervision and interpretation

(75828 (complete procedure) has been deleted, see 36010, 75827)

75831 Venography, renal, unilateral, selective, radiological supervision and interpretation

(75832 (complete procedure) has been deleted, see 36000-36012, 75831)

75833 Venography, renal, bilateral, selective, radiological supervision and interpretation

(75834 (complete procedure) has been deleted, see 36000-36012, 75833)

75840 Venography, adrenal, unilateral, selective, radiological supervision and interpretation

(75841 (complete procedure) has been deleted, see 36000-36012, 75840)

75842 Venography, adrenal, bilateral, selective, radiological supervision and interpretation

(75843 (complete procedure) has been deleted, see 36000-36012, 75842)

(75845, 75846, 75847, 75850, 75851 have been deleted)

75860 Venography, sinus or jugular, catheter, radiological supervision and interpretation

(75861 (complete procedure) has been deleted, see 36000-36012 for intravenous procedure and 36100-36218 for intra-arterial procedure, 75860)

75870 Venography, superior sagittal sinus, radiological supervision and interpretation

(75871 (complete procedure) has been deleted, see 36000-36012 for intravenous procedure and 36100-36218 for intra-arterial procedure, 75870)

75872 Venography, epidural, radiological supervision and interpretation

(75873 (complete procedure) has been deleted, see 36000-36012 for intravenous procedure and 36100-36218 for intra-arterial procedure, 75872)

75880 Venography, orbital, radiological supervision and interpretation

(75881 (complete procedure) has been deleted, see 36000-36012 for intravenous procedure and 36100-36218 for intra-arterial procedure, 75880)

75885 Percutaneous transhepatic portography with hemodynamic evaluation, radiological supervision and interpretation

(75886 (complete procedure) has been deleted, see 36011, 36012, 36481, 75885)

75887 Percutaneous transhepatic portography without hemodynamic evaluation, radiological supervision and interpretation

(75888 (complete procedure) has been deleted, see 36011, 36012, 36481, 75887)

75889 Hepatic venography, wedged or free, with hemodynamic evaluation, radiological supervision and interpretation

(75890 (complete procedure) has been deleted, see 36000-36012, 75889)

75891 Hepatic venography, wedged or free, without hemodynamic evaluation, radiological supervision and interpretation

(75892 (complete procedure) has been deleted, see 36000-36012, 75891)

75893 Venous sampling through catheter, with or without angiography (eg, for parathyroid hormone, renin), radiological supervision and interpretation

(For procedure, use 36500)

Transcatheter Procedures

75894 Transcatheter therapy, embolization, any method, radiological supervision and interpretation

(75895 (complete procedure) has been deleted, see 37204, 61624, 61626, 75894)

75896 Transcatheter therapy, infusion, any method (eg, thrombolysis other than coronary), radiological supervision and interpretation

(75897 (complete procedure) has been deleted, see 37201, 37202, 75896)

(For infusion for coronary disease, see 92975, 92977)

▲ **75898**   Angiography through existing catheter for follow-up study for transcatheter therapy, embolization or infusion

75900   Exchange of a previously placed arterial catheter during thrombolytic therapy with contrast monitoring, radiological supervision and interpretation

(For procedure, use 37209)

75940   Percutaneous placement of IVC filter, radiological supervision and interpretation

(75941 (complete procedure) has been deleted, see 37620, 75940)

75945   Intravascular ultrasound (non-coronary vessel), radiological supervision and interpretation; initial vessel

+ **75946**   each additional non-coronary vessel (List separately in addition to code for primary procedure)

(Use 75946 in conjunction with code 75945)

(For catheterizations, see codes 36215-36248)

(For transcatheter therapies, see codes 37200-37208, 61624, 61626)

(For procedure, see 37250, 37251)

(75950, 75951, 75955, 75956 (complete procedure) have been deleted, see 37204, 61624, 61626, 75894)

75952   Endovascular repair of infrarenal abdominal aortic aneurysm or dissection, radiological supervision and interpretation

(For implantation of endovascular grafts, see 34800-34808)

75953   Placement of proximal or distal extension prosthesis for endovascular repair of infrarenal abdominal aortic aneurysm, radiological supervision and interpretation

(For implantation of endovascular extension prostheses, see 34825, 34826)

75960   Transcatheter introduction of intravascular stent(s), (non-coronary vessel), percutaneous and/or open, radiological supervision and interpretation, each vessel

(For procedure, see 37205-37208)

▶(For radiologic supervision and interpretation for transcatheter placement of extracranial cerebrovascular artery stent(s), use Category III code 0007T)◀

75961   Transcatheter retrieval, percutaneous, of intravascular foreign body (eg, fractured venous or arterial catheter), radiological supervision and interpretation

(For procedure, use 37203)

75962   Transluminal balloon angioplasty, peripheral artery, radiological supervision and interpretation

(75963 (complete procedure) has been deleted, see 35450-35460 or 35470-35476 and 75962)

+ **75964**   Transluminal balloon angioplasty, each additional peripheral artery, radiological supervision and interpretation (List separately in addition to code for primary procedure)

(Use 75964 in conjunction with code 75962)

(75965 (complete procedure) has been deleted, see 35450-35460 or 35470-35476 and 75964)

75966   Transluminal balloon angioplasty, renal or other visceral artery, radiological supervision and interpretation

(75967 (complete procedure) has been deleted, see 35450-35460 or 35470-35476 and 75966)

+ **75968**   Transluminal balloon angioplasty, each additional visceral artery, radiological supervision and interpretation (List separately in addition to code for primary procedure)

(Use 75968 in conjunction with code 75966)

(75969 (complete procedure) has been deleted, see 35450-35460 or 35470-35476 and 75968)

(For percutaneous transluminal coronary angioplasty, see 92982-92984)

75970   Transcatheter biopsy, radiological supervision and interpretation

(For injection procedure only for transcatheter therapy or biopsy, see 36100-36299)

(For transcatheter renal and ureteral biopsy, use 52007)

(For percutaneous needle biopsy of pancreas, use 48102; of retroperitoneal lymph node or mass, use 49180)

(75971 (complete procedure) has been deleted, see 37200, 75970)

(75972-75977 have been deleted. To report, see 75962-75968)

75978   Transluminal balloon angioplasty, venous (eg, subclavian stenosis), radiological supervision and interpretation

(75979 (complete procedure) has been deleted, see 35460, 35476, 75978)

75980   Percutaneous transhepatic biliary drainage with contrast monitoring, radiological supervision and interpretation

(75981 (complete procedure) has been deleted, see 47510, 75980)

75982   Percutaneous placement of drainage catheter for combined internal and external biliary drainage or of a drainage stent for internal biliary drainage in patients with an inoperable mechanical biliary obstruction, radiological supervision and interpretation

(75983 (complete procedure) has been deleted, see 47511, 47556, 75982)

75984   Change of percutaneous tube or drainage catheter with contrast monitoring (eg, gastrointestinal system, genitourinary system, abscess), radiological supervision and interpretation

(75985 (complete procedure) has been deleted, see 43760, 47525, 47530, 50398, 50688, 51705, 51710, 75984)

(For change of nephrostomy or pyelostomy tube only, use 50398)

(For introduction procedure only for percutaneous biliary drainage, see 47510, 47511)

(For percutaneous cholecystostomy, use 47490)

(For change of percutaneous biliary drainage catheter only, use 47525)

(For percutaneous nephrostolithotomy or pyelostolithotomy, see 50080, 50081)

▲ **75989**   Radiological guidance for percutaneous drainage of abscess, or specimen collection (ie, fluoroscopy, ultrasound, or computed axial tomography), with placement of indwelling catheter, radiological supervision and interpretation

(75990 (complete procedure) has been deleted, see appropriate organ or site and 75989)

Transluminal Atherectomy

75992   Transluminal atherectomy, peripheral artery, radiological supervision and interpretation

(For procedure, see 35481-35485, 35491-35495)

+ **75993**   Transluminal atherectomy, each additional peripheral artery, radiological supervision and interpretation (List separately in addition to code for primary procedure)

(Use 75993 in conjunction with code 75992)

(For procedure, see 35481-35485, 35491-35495)

75994   Transluminal atherectomy, renal, radiological supervision and interpretation

(For procedure, see 35480, 35490)

75995   Transluminal atherectomy, visceral, radiological supervision and interpretation

(For procedure, see 35480, 35490)

+ **75996**   Transluminal atherectomy, each additional visceral artery, radiological supervision and interpretation (List separately in addition to code for primary procedure)

(Use 75996 in conjunction with code 75995)

(For procedure, see 35480, 35490)

Other Procedures

(For arthrography of shoulder, use 73040; elbow, use 73085; wrist, use 73115; hip, use 73525; knee, use 73580; ankle, use 73615)

76000   Fluoroscopy (separate procedure), up to one hour physician time, other than 71023 or 71034 (eg, cardiac fluoroscopy)

76001   Fluoroscopy, physician time more than one hour, assisting a non-radiologic physician (eg, nephrostolithotomy, ERCP, bronchoscopy, transbronchial biopsy)

76003   Fluoroscopic guidance for needle placement (eg, biopsy, aspiration, injection, localization device)

▶(See appropriate surgical code for procedure and anatomic location)◀

▶(Fluoroscopy 76003 is considered inclusive of all radiographic arthrography with the exception of supervision and interpretation for CT and MR arthrography)◀

▶Do not report 76003 in addition to 70332, 73040, 73085, 73115, 73525, 73580, 73615)◀

▶(Fluoroscopy 76003 is considered inclusive of organ/anatomic specific radiological supervision and interpretation procedures 74320, 74350, 74355, 74445, 74470, 74475, 75809, 75810, 75885, 75887, 75980, 75982, 75989)◀

76005   Fluoroscopic guidance and localization of needle or catheter tip for spine or paraspinous diagnostic or therapeutic injection procedures (epidural, transforaminal epidural, subarachnoid, paravertebral facet joint, paravertebral facet joint nerve or sacroiliac joint), including neurolytic agent destruction

(Injection of contrast during fluoroscopic guidance and localization is an inclusive component of codes 62270-62273, 62280-62282, 62310-62319)

(Fluoroscopic guidance for subarachnoid puncture for diagnostic radiographic myelography is included in supervision and interpretation codes 72240, 72255, 72265, 72270)

(For epidural or subarachnoid needle or catheter placement and injection, see codes 62270-62273, 62280-62282, 62310-62319)

(For sacroiliac joint arthrography, see 27096, 73542. If formal arthrography is not performed, recorded, and a formal radiographic report is not issued, use 76005 for fluoroscopic guidance for sacroiliac joint injections)

(For paravertebral facet joint injection, see 64470-64476. For transforaminal epidural needle placement and injection, see 64479-64484)

(For destruction by neurolytic agent, see 64600-64680)

76006   Radiologic examination, stress view(s), any joint, stress applied by a physician (includes comparison views)

76010 Radiologic examination from nose to rectum for foreign body, single view, child

76012 Radiological supervision and interpretation, percutaneous vertebroplasty, per vertebral body; under fluoroscopic guidance

76013 under CT guidance

(For procedure, see 22520-22522)

76020 Bone age studies

76040 Bone length studies (orthoroentgenogram, scanogram)

(76060 has been deleted. See 76061, 76062)

76061 Radiologic examination, osseous survey; limited (eg, for metastases)

76062 complete (axial and appendicular skeleton)

76065 Radiologic examination, osseous survey, infant

▲ **76066** Joint survey, single view, two or more joints (specify)

▲ **76070** Computerized axial tomography bone density study, one or more sites

76075 Dual energy x-ray absorptiometry (DEXA), bone density study, one or more sites; axial skeleton (eg, hips, pelvis, spine)

76076 appendicular skeleton (peripheral) (eg, radius, wrist, heel)

▲ **76078** Radiographic absorptiometry (eg, photodensitometry, radiogrammetry), one or more sites

76080 Radiologic examination, abscess, fistula or sinus tract study, radiological supervision and interpretation

(76081 (complete procedure) has been deleted, see 20501, 49424, 76080)

✚ ● **76085** Digitization of film radiographic images with computer analysis for lesion detection and further physician review for interpretation, screening mammography (List separately in addition to code for primary procedure)

►(Use 76085 in conjunction with code 76092)◄

76086 Mammary ductogram or galactogram, single duct, radiological supervision and interpretation

(76087 (complete procedure) has been deleted, see 19030, 76086)

76088 Mammary ductogram or galactogram, multiple ducts, radiological supervision and interpretation

(76089 (complete procedure) has been deleted, see 19030, 76088)

76090 Mammography; unilateral

76091 bilateral

76092 Screening mammography, bilateral (two view film study of each breast)

►(For computer aided detection applied to a screening mammogram, use 76085)◄

76093 Magnetic resonance imaging, breast, without and/or with contrast material(s); unilateral

76094 bilateral

76095 Stereotactic localization guidance for breast biopsy or needle placement (eg, for wire localization or for injection), each lesion, radiological supervision and interpretation

(For procedure, see ►10022, 19000, 19001,◄ 19102, 19103, ►19290, 19291◄)

(For injection for sentinel node localization without lymphoscintigraphy, use 38792)

76096 Mammographic guidance for needle placement, breast (eg, for wire localization or for injection), each lesion, radiological supervision and interpretation

(For procedure, see ►10022,◄ 19000, 19102, 19103, ►19290, 19291◄)

(For injection for sentinel node localization without lymphoscintigraphy, use 38792)

(76097 has been deleted. To report, see 19291, 76096)

76098 Radiological examination, surgical specimen

76100 Radiologic examination, single plane body section (eg, tomography), other than with urography

76101 Radiologic examination, complex motion (ie, hypercycloidal) body section (eg, mastoid polytomography), other than with urography; unilateral

76102 bilateral

(For nephrotomography, use 74415)

▲ **76120** Cineradiography/videoradiography, except where specifically included

✚ ▲ **76125** Cineradiography/videoradiography to complement routine examination (List separately in addition to code for primary procedure)

(76127 has been deleted. The use of photographic media is not reported separately but is considered to be a component of the basic procedure)

(76130-76137 have been deleted. To report, use code for specific radiologic examination)

76140 Consultation on x-ray examination made elsewhere, written report

76150 Xeroradiography

(76150 is to be used for non-mammographic studies only)

(76300 has been deleted. To report, use 76499)

76350 Subtraction in conjunction with contrast studies

▲ **76355** Computerized axial tomographic guidance for stereotactic localization

⊘ =Modifier '-51' Exempt   ► ◄=New or Revised Text   ✚ =Add-on Code   CPT 2002

▲ 76360   Computerized axial tomographic guidance for needle biopsy, radiological supervision and interpretation

(76361 (complete procedure) has been deleted, see appropriate organ or site and 76360)

● 76362   Computerized axial tomographic guidance for, and monitoring of, tissue ablation

►(For percutaneous radiofrequency ablation, use 47382)◄

(76365 has been deleted. For computed tomographic guidance for cyst aspiration, see appropriate organ or site and 76360)

(76366 (complete procedure) has been deleted, see appropriate organ or site and 76360)

▲ 76370   Computerized axial tomographic guidance for placement of radiation therapy fields

▲ 76375   Coronal, sagittal, multiplanar, oblique, 3-dimensional and/or holographic reconstruction of computerized axial tomography, magnetic resonance imaging, or other tomographic modality

(Use 76375 in addition to code for imaging procedure)

▲ 76380   Computerized axial tomography, limited or localized follow-up study

76390   Magnetic resonance spectroscopy

(For magnetic resonance imaging, use appropriate MRI body site code)

76393   Magnetic resonance guidance for needle placement (eg, for biopsy, needle aspiration, injection, or placement of localization device) radiological supervision and interpretation

►(For procedure see appropriate organ or site)◄

● 76394   Magnetic resonance guidance for, and monitoring of, tissue ablation

►(For percutaneous radiofrequency ablation, use 47382)◄

76400   Magnetic resonance (eg, proton) imaging, bone marrow blood supply

● 76490   Ultrasound guidance for, and monitoring of, tissue ablation

►(Do not report 76490 in addition to 76986)◄

►(For ablation, see codes 47370-47382)◄

76499   Unlisted diagnostic radiologic procedure

Diagnostic Ultrasound

Definitions

A-mode implies a one-dimensional ultrasonic measurement procedure.

M-mode implies a one-dimensional ultrasonic measurement procedure with movement of the trace to record amplitude and velocity of moving echo-producing structures.

B-scan implies a two-dimensional ultrasonic scanning procedure with a two-dimensional display.

Real-time scan implies a two-dimensional ultrasonic scanning procedure with display of both two-dimensional structure and motion with time.

Head and Neck

►(For determination of corneal thickness (eg, pachymetry) with interpretation and report, bilateral, use Category III code 0025T)◄

(76500, 76505 have been deleted. To report, use 76999)

76506   Echoencephalography, B-scan and/or real time with image documentation (gray scale) (for determination of ventricular size, delineation of cerebral contents and detection of fluid masses or other intracranial abnormalities), including A-mode encephalography as secondary component where indicated

76511   Ophthalmic ultrasound, echography, diagnostic; A-scan only, with amplitude quantification

76512   contact B-scan (with or without simultaneous A-scan)

76513   anterior segment ultrasound, immersion (water bath) B-scan or high resolution biomicroscopy

(76515 has been deleted. To report, use 76999)

76516   Ophthalmic biometry by ultrasound echography, A-scan;

(76517 has been deleted. To report, use 76999)

76519   with intraocular lens power calculation

►(For partial coherence interferometry, use 92136)◄

76529   Ophthalmic ultrasonic foreign body localization

(76530 has been deleted. To report, use 76999)

(76535 has been deleted. To report, use 76536)

▲ 76536   Ultrasound, soft tissues of head and neck (eg, thyroid, parathyroid, parotid), B-scan and/or real time with image documentation

(76550 has been deleted. To report, see 93880-93888)

Chest

(76601 has been deleted. To report, use 76999)

▲ **76604** Ultrasound, chest, B-scan (includes mediastinum) and/or real time with image documentation

(76620, 76625 have been deleted)

(76627, 76628 have been deleted. To report, see 93307, 93308)

(76629 has been deleted)

(76632 has been deleted. To report, see 93320, 93321)

(76640 has been deleted. To report, use 76999)

▲ **76645** Ultrasound, breast(s) (unilateral or bilateral), B-scan and/or real time with image documentation

Abdomen and Retroperitoneum

▲ **76700** Ultrasound, abdominal, B-scan and/or real time with image documentation; complete

76705 limited (eg, single organ, quadrant, follow-up)

▲ **76770** Ultrasound, retroperitoneal (eg, renal, aorta, nodes), B-scan and/or real time with image documentation; complete

76775 limited

▲ **76778** Ultrasound, transplanted kidney, B-scan and/or real time with image documentation, with or without duplex Doppler study

Spinal Canal

▲ **76800** Ultrasound, spinal canal and contents

Pelvis

▲ **76805** Ultrasound, pregnant uterus, B-scan and/or real time with image documentation; complete (complete fetal and maternal evaluation)

76810 complete (complete fetal and maternal evaluation), multiple gestation, after the first trimester

76815 limited (fetal size, heart beat, placental location, fetal position, or emergency in the delivery room)

76816 follow-up or repeat

76818 Fetal biophysical profile; with non-stress testing

▲ **76819** without non-stress testing

►(Fetal biophysical profile assessments for the second and any additional fetuses, should be reported separately by code 76818 or 76819 with the modifier '-51' appended)◄

(For amniotic fluid index without non-stress test, use 76815)

76825 Echocardiography, fetal, cardiovascular system, real time with image documentation (2D), with or without M-mode recording;

76826 follow-up or repeat study

76827 Doppler echocardiography, fetal, cardiovascular system, pulsed wave and/or continuous wave with spectral display; complete

76828 follow-up or repeat study

(To report the use of color mapping, use 93325)

▲ **76830** Ultrasound, transvaginal

76831 Hysterosonography, with or without color flow Doppler

(For introduction of saline or contrast for hysterosonography, use 58340)

(76855 has been deleted. To report, see 93975-93979)

▲ **76856** Ultrasound, pelvic (nonobstetric), B-scan and/or real time with image documentation; complete

76857 limited or follow-up (eg, for follicles)

Genitalia

▲ **76870** Ultrasound, scrotum and contents

76872 Echography, transrectal;

76873 prostate volume study for brachytherapy treatment planning (separate procedure)

Extremities

▲ **76880** Ultrasound, extremity, non-vascular, B-scan and/or real time with image documentation

▲ **76885** Ultrasound, infant hips, real time with imaging documentation; dynamic (requiring physician manipulation)

▲ **76886** limited, static (not requiring physician manipulation)

Vascular Studies

(76900-76920 have been deleted. To report, see 93922-93971; for cerebrovascular studies, see 93875-93888)

(76925 has been deleted. To report, see 93922-93931 or 93965-93971)

(76926 has been deleted. To report, see 93875-93888 or 93975-93979)

Ultrasonic Guidance Procedures

76930 Ultrasonic guidance for pericardiocentesis, imaging supervision and interpretation

(76931 (complete procedure) has been deleted, see 33010, 33011, 76930)

76932 Ultrasonic guidance for endomyocardial biopsy, imaging supervision and interpretation

(76933 (complete procedure) has been deleted, see 93505, 76932)

(76934 has been deleted. For ultrasound guidance for thoracentesis or abdominal paracentesis, see 32000 and 76942)

(76935 (complete procedure) has been deleted, see 32000, 76942)

⊘ = Modifier '-51' Exempt ▶◀ = New or Revised Text ✚ = Add-on Code CPT 2002

76936   Ultrasound guided compression repair of arterial pseudoaneurysm or arteriovenous fistulae (includes diagnostic ultrasound evaluation, compression of lesion and imaging)

(76938 has been deleted. For ultrasound guidance for cyst or renal pelvis aspiration, see appropriate organ or site and 76942)

(76939 (complete procedure) has been deleted, see appropriate organ or site and 76942)

76941   Ultrasonic guidance for intrauterine fetal transfusion or cordocentesis, imaging supervision and interpretation

(For procedure, see 36460, 59012)

76942   Ultrasonic guidance for needle placement (eg, biopsy, aspiration, injection, localization device), imaging supervision and interpretation

(76943 (complete procedure) has been deleted, see appropriate organ or site and 76942)

(76944 has been deleted. To report, use 75989)

76945   Ultrasonic guidance for chorionic villus sampling, imaging supervision and interpretation

(For procedure, use 59015)

76946   Ultrasonic guidance for amniocentesis, imaging supervision and interpretation

(76947 (complete procedure) has been deleted, see 59000, 76946)

76948   Ultrasonic guidance for aspiration of ova, imaging supervision and interpretation

(76949 (complete procedure) has been deleted, see 58970, 76948)

76950   Ultrasonic guidance for placement of radiation therapy fields

(76960 has been deleted. To report, use 76950)

76965   Ultrasonic guidance for interstitial radioelement application

Other Procedures

76970   Ultrasound study follow-up (specify)

76975   Gastrointestinal endoscopic ultrasound, supervision and interpretation

(For procedure, use 43259)

(Do not report 76975 in conjunction with 43231, 43232, 43242, 45341, 45342)

76977   Ultrasound bone density measurement and interpretation, peripheral site(s), any method

(76980 has been deleted. To report, use code for specific ultrasound examination)

(76985 has been deleted. To report, use 76986)

76986   Ultrasonic guidance, intraoperative

▶(Do not report 76986 in addition to 47370-47382)◀

▶(For ultrasound guidance for open and laparoscopic radiofrequency tissue ablation, use 76490)◀

(76990 has been deleted. To report, use 76999)

(76991 has been deleted. To report, see 76830, 76872)

76999   Unlisted ultrasound procedure

Radiation Oncology

Listings for Radiation Oncology provide for teletherapy and brachytherapy to include initial consultation, clinical treatment planning, simulation, medical radiation physics, dosimetry, treatment devices, special services, and clinical treatment management procedures. They include normal follow-up care during course of treatment and for three months following its completion.

When a service or procedure is provided that is not listed in this edition of *CPT* it should be identified by a Special Report (see page 204) and one of the unlisted procedure codes listed below:

77299 Unlisted procedure, therapeutic radiology clinical treatment planning
77399 Unlisted procedure, medical radiation physics, dosimetry and treatment devices, and special services
77499 Unlisted procedure, therapeutic radiology treatment management
77799 Unlisted procedure, clinical brachytherapy

For treatment by injectable or ingestible isotopes, see subsection **Nuclear Medicine**.

Consultation: Clinical Management

Preliminary consultation, evaluation of patient prior to decision to treat, or full medical care (in addition to treatment management) when provided by the therapeutic radiologist may be identified by the appropriate procedure codes from **Evaluation and Management, Medicine,** or **Surgery** sections.

Clinical Treatment Planning (External and Internal Sources)

The clinical treatment planning process is a complex service including interpretation of special testing, tumor localization, treatment volume determination, treatment time/dosage determination, choice of treatment modality, determination of number and size of treatment ports, selection of appropriate treatment devices, and other procedures.

Definitions

Simple planning requires a single treatment area of interest encompassed in a single port or simple parallel opposed ports with simple or no blocking.

Intermediate planning requires three or more converging ports, two separate treatment areas, multiple blocks, or special time dose constraints.

Complex planning requires highly complex blocking, custom shielding blocks, tangential ports, special wedges or compensators, three or more separate treatment areas, rotational or special beam considerations, combination of therapeutic modalities.

> (77260, 77265, 77270, 77275 have been deleted. To report, see 77261-77263)

77261 Therapeutic radiology treatment planning; simple

77262 intermediate

77263 complex

Definitions

Simple simulation of a single treatment area with either a single port or parallel opposed ports. Simple or no blocking.

Intermediate simulation of three or more converging ports, two separate treatment areas, multiple blocks.

Complex simulation of tangential portals, three or more treatment areas, rotation or arc therapy, complex blocking, custom shielding blocks, brachytherapy source verification, hyperthermia probe verification, any use of contrast materials.

Three-dimensional computer-generated three dimensional reconstruction of tumor volume and surrounding critical normal tissue structures from direct CT scans and/or MRI data in preparation for non-coplanar or coplanar therapy. The simulation utilizes documented three-dimensional beam's eye view volume-dose displays of multiple or moving beams. Documentation with three-dimensional volume reconstruction and dose distribution is required.

Simulation may be carried out on a dedicated simulator, a radiation therapy treatment unit, or diagnostic x-ray machine.

77280 Therapeutic radiology simulation-aided field setting; simple

77285 intermediate

77290 complex

77295 three-dimensional

77299 Unlisted procedure, therapeutic radiology clinical treatment planning

Medical Radiation Physics, Dosimetry, Treatment Devices, and Special Services

▲ **77300** Basic radiation dosimetry calculation, central axis depth dose calculation, TDF, NSD, gap calculation, off axis factor, tissue inhomogeneity factors, calculation of non-ionizing radiation surface and depth dose, as required during course of treatment, only when prescribed by the treating physician

● **77301** Intensity modulated radiotherapy plan, including dose-volume histograms for target and critical structure partial tolerance specifications

> ▶(Dose plan is optimized using inverse or forward planning technique for modulated beam delivery (eg, binary, dynamic MLC) to create highly conformal dose distribution. Computer plan distribution must be verified for positional accuracy based on dosimetric verification of the intensity map with verification of treatment set up and interpretation of verification methodology)◀

77305 Teletherapy, isodose plan (whether hand or computer calculated); simple (one or two parallel opposed unmodified ports directed to a single area of interest)

77310 intermediate (three or more treatment ports directed to a single area of interest)

77315 complex (mantle or inverted Y, tangential ports, the use of wedges, compensators, complex blocking, rotational beam, or special beam considerations)

> (Only one teletherapy isodose plan may be reported for a given course of therapy to a specific treatment area)

> (77320 has been deleted. To report, see 77300-77399)

77321 Special teletherapy port plan, particles, hemibody, total body

> (77325 has been deleted. To report, see 77300-77399)

77326 Brachytherapy isodose calculation; simple (calculation made from single plane, one to four sources/ribbon application, remote afterloading brachytherapy, 1 to 8 sources)

> (For definition of source/ribbon, see page 224)

77327 intermediate (multiplane dosage calculations, application involving 5 to 10 sources/ribbons, remote afterloading brachytherapy, 9 to 12 sources)

77328 complex (multiplane isodose plan, volume implant calculations, over 10 sources/ribbons used, special spatial reconstruction, remote afterloading brachytherapy, over 12 sources)

> (77330 has been deleted. To report, see 77300-77399)

77331 Special dosimetry (eg, TLD, microdosimetry) (specify), only when prescribed by the treating physician

⊘ =Modifier '-51' Exempt   ▶◀=New or Revised Text   ✚=Add-on Code   CPT 2002

77332   Treatment devices, design and construction; simple (simple block, simple bolus)

77333   intermediate (multiple blocks, stents, bite blocks, special bolus)

77334   complex (irregular blocks, special shields, compensators, wedges, molds or casts)

(77335 has been deleted. To report, see 77300-77399)

77336   Continuing medical physics consultation, including assessment of treatment parameters, quality assurance of dose delivery, and review of patient treatment documentation in support of the radiation oncologist, reported per week of therapy

(77340 has been deleted. To report, see 77300-77399)

(77345-77360 have been deleted. To report, see 77300-77399)

77370   Special medical radiation physics consultation

(77380 has been deleted. To report, use 77520)

(77381 has been deleted. To report, use 77523)

77399   Unlisted procedure, medical radiation physics, dosimetry and treatment devices, and special services

Radiation Treatment Delivery

(Radiation treatment delivery (77401-77416) recognizes the technical component and the various energy levels.)

(77400 has been deleted)

77401   Radiation treatment delivery, superficial and/or ortho voltage

77402   Radiation treatment delivery, single treatment area, single port or parallel opposed ports, simple blocks or no blocks; up to 5 MeV

77403   6-10 MeV

77404   11-19 MeV

(77405 has been deleted)

77406   20 MeV or greater

77407   Radiation treatment delivery, two separate treatment areas, three or more ports on a single treatment area, use of multiple blocks; up to 5 MeV

77408   6-10 MeV

77409   11-19 MeV

(77410 has been deleted)

77411   20 MeV or greater

77412   Radiation treatment delivery, three or more separate treatment areas, custom blocking, tangential ports, wedges, rotational beam, compensators, special particle beam (eg, electron or neutrons); up to 5 MeV

77413   6-10 MeV

77414   11-19 MeV

(77415 has been deleted. To report, use 77417)

77416   20 MeV or greater

77417   Therapeutic radiology port film(s)

● **77418**   Intensity modulated treatment delivery, single or multiple fields/arcs, via narrow spatially and temporally modulated beams (eg, binary, dynamic MLC), per treatment session

▶(For intensity modulated treatment planning, use 77301)◀

Radiation Treatment Management

Radiation treatment management is reported in units of five fractions or treatment sessions, regardless of the actual time period in which the services are furnished. The services need not be furnished on consecutive days. Multiple fractions representing two or more treatment sessions furnished on the same day may be counted separately as long as there has been a distinct break in therapy sessions, and the fractions are of the character usually furnished on different days. Code 77427 is also reported if there are three or four fractions beyond a multiple of five at the end of a course of treatment; one or two fractions beyond a multiple of five at the end of a course of treatment are not reported separately. The professional services furnished during treatment management typically consists of:

■ Review of port films;

■ Review of dosimetry, dose delivery, and treatment parameters;

■ Review of patient treatment set-up;

■ Examination of patient for medical evaluation and management (eg, assessment of the patient's response to treatment, coordination of care and treatment, review of imaging and/or lab test results).

(77419, 77420, 77425, and 77430 have been deleted. To report radiation treatment management, use 77427)

77427   Radiation treatment management, five treatments

77431   Radiation therapy management with complete course of therapy consisting of one or two fractions only

(77431 is not to be used to fill in the last week of a long course of therapy)

77432   Stereotactic radiation treatment management of cerebral lesion(s) (complete course of treatment consisting of one session)

(77435-77460 have been deleted. To report, see 77401-77499)

(77465 has been deleted)

77470 Special treatment procedure (eg, total body irradiation, hemibody radiation, per oral, endocavitary or intraoperative cone irradiation)

(77470 assumes that the procedure is performed one or more times during the course of therapy, in addition to daily or weekly patient management)

77499 Unlisted procedure, therapeutic radiology treatment management

Proton Beam Treatment Delivery

Definitions

Simple proton treatment delivery to a single treatment area utilizing a single non-tangential/oblique port, custom block with compensation (77522) and without compensation (77520).

Intermediate proton treatment delivery to one or more treatment areas utilizing two or more ports or one or more tangential/oblique ports, with custom blocks and compensators.

Complex proton treatment delivery to one or more treatment areas utilizing two or more ports per treatment area with matching or patching fields and/or multiple isocenters, with custom blocks and compensators.

77520 Proton treatment delivery; simple, without compensation

77522 simple, with compensation

77523 intermediate

77525 complex

Hyperthermia

Hyperthermia treatments as listed in this section include external (superficial and deep), interstitial, and intracavitary.

Radiation therapy when given concurrently is listed separately.

Hyperthermia is used only as an adjunct to radiation therapy or chemotherapy. It may be induced by a variety of sources (eg, microwave, ultrasound, low energy radio-frequency conduction, or by probes).

The listed treatments include management during the course of therapy and follow-up care for three months after completion.

Preliminary consultation is not included (see **Medicine** 99241-99263).

Physics planning and interstitial insertion of temperature sensors, and use of external or interstitial heat generating sources are included.

The following descriptors are included in the treatment schedule:

77600 Hyperthermia, externally generated; superficial (ie, heating to a depth of 4 cm or less)

77605 deep (ie, heating to depths greater than 4 cm)

77610 Hyperthermia generated by interstitial probe(s); 5 or fewer interstitial applicators

77615 more than 5 interstitial applicators

Clinical Intracavitary Hyperthermia

77620 Hyperthermia generated by intracavitary probe(s)

Clinical Brachytherapy

Clinical brachytherapy requires the use of either natural or man-made radioelements applied into or around a treatment field of interest. The supervision of radioelements and dose interpretation are performed solely by the therapeutic radiologist.

Services 77750-77799 include admission to the hospital and daily visits.

►For insertion of ovoids and tandems, use 57155.◄

►For insertion of Heyman capsules, use 58346.◄

Definitions

(Sources refer to intracavitary placement or permanent interstitial placement; ribbons refer to temporary interstitial placement)

A simple application has one to four sources/ribbons.

An intermediate application has five to ten sources/ribbons.

A complex application has greater than ten sources/ribbons.

(77700-77749 have been deleted. To report, see 77761-77799)

77750 Infusion or instillation of radioelement solution

(77755, 77760 have been deleted. To report, see 77761-77799)

77761 Intracavitary radiation source application; simple

77762 intermediate

77763 complex

(77765, 77770, 77775 have been deleted. To report, see 77761-77799)

77776 Interstitial radiation source application; simple

77777 intermediate

77778 complex

(77780 has been deleted. To report, see 77761-77799)

77781 Remote afterloading high intensity brachytherapy; 1-4 source positions or catheters

77782 5-8 source positions or catheters

77783 9-12 source positions or catheters

77784 over 12 source positions or catheters

(77785 has been deleted. To report, see 77761-77799)

77789	Surface application of radiation source
77790	Supervision, handling, loading of radiation source
77799	Unlisted procedure, clinical brachytherapy

(77800 has been deleted. To report, use 77331)

(77805-77810 have been deleted. To report, see 77305-77321 or 77326-77328)

(77850 has been deleted. To report, see 77300, 77336, 77370)

(77860 has been deleted. To report, use 77336)

(77999 has been deleted. To report, use 77399)

Nuclear Medicine

Listed procedures may be performed independently or in the course of overall medical care. If the physician providing these services is also responsible for diagnostic work-up and/or follow-up care of patient, see appropriate sections also.

Radioimmunoassay tests are found in the **Clinical Pathology** section (codes 82000-84999). These codes can be appropriately used by any specialist performing such tests in a laboratory licensed and/or certified for radioimmunoassays. The reporting of these tests is not confined to clinical pathology laboratories alone.

The services listed do not include the provision of radium or other radioelements. Those materials supplied by the physician should be listed separately and identified by the code 78990 for diagnostic radiopharmaceutical and 79900 for therapeutic radiopharmaceutical.

Diagnostic

Endocrine System

78000	Thyroid uptake; single determination
78001	multiple determinations
78003	stimulation, suppression or discharge (not including initial uptake studies)
78006	Thyroid imaging, with uptake; single determination
78007	multiple determinations
78010	Thyroid imaging; only
78011	with vascular flow
78015	Thyroid carcinoma metastases imaging; limited area (eg, neck and chest only)
78016	with additional studies (eg, urinary recovery)

(78017 has been deleted. To report, use 78018)

78018	whole body

(For calcitonin, use 82308)

(For triiodothyronine (true TT-3), use 84480)

(For triiodothyronine, free (FT-3), (unbound T-3 only), use 84481)

(For TT-4 thyroxine, use 84436)

(For T-4 thyroxine, neonatal, use 84437)

(For FT-4 thyroxine, free, (unbound T-4 only), use 84439)

+ 78020	Thyroid carcinoma metastases uptake (List separately in addition to code for primary procedure)

(Use 78020 in conjunction with code 78018 only)

78070	Parathyroid imaging

(For parathormone (parathyroid hormone), use 83970)

78075	Adrenal imaging, cortex and/or medulla

(For cortisol, plasma, use 82533)

(For cortisol, urine, use 82533)

(For aldosterone, double isotope technique, use 82088)

(For aldosterone, blood, use 82088)

(For aldosterone, urine, use 82088)

(For 17-ketosteroids, use 83586)

(For 17-OH ketosteroids, use 83586)

(For 17-hydroxycorticosteroids, use 83491)

(For insulin, use 83525)

(For insulin antibodies, use 86337)

(For proinsulin, use 84206)

(For glucagon, use 82943)

(For adrenocorticotropic hormone (ACTH), use 82024)

(For human growth hormone (HGH), (somatotropin), use 83003)

(For human growth antibody, use 86277)

(For thyroglobulin antibody, use 86800)

(For thyroid microsomal antibody, use 86376)

(For thyroid stimulating hormone (TSH), use 84443)

(For thyrotropin releasing factor, see 80438, 80439)

(For plus long-acting thyroid stimulator (LATS), use 84445)

(For follicle stimulating hormone (FSH component of pituitary gonadotropin), use 83001)

(For luteinizing hormone (LH component of pituitary gonadotropin), (ICSH), use 83002)

(For luteinizing releasing factor (LRH), use 83727)

(For prolactin level (mammotropin), use 84146)

(For vasopressin level (antidiuretic hormone), use 84588)

(For estradiol, use 82670)

(For progesterone, use 84144)

(For testosterone, blood, use 84403)

(For testosterone, urine, use 84403)

(For etiocholanolone, use 82696)

78099   Unlisted endocrine procedure, diagnostic nuclear medicine

(For chemical analysis, see **Chemistry** section)

Hematopoietic, Reticuloendothelial and Lymphatic System

78102   Bone marrow imaging; limited area

78103   multiple areas

78104   whole body

78110   Plasma volume, radiopharmaceutical volume-dilution technique (separate procedure); single sampling

78111   multiple samplings

78120   Red cell volume determination (separate procedure); single sampling

78121   multiple samplings

78122   Whole blood volume determination, including separate measurement of plasma volume and red cell volume (radiopharmaceutical volume-dilution technique)

78130   Red cell survival study;

78135   differential organ/tissue kinetics, (eg, splenic and/or hepatic sequestration)

78140   Labeled red cell sequestration, differential organ/tissue, (eg, splenic and/or hepatic)

78160   Plasma radioiron disappearance (turnover) rate

78162   Radioiron oral absorption

78170   Radioiron red cell utilization

78172   Chelatable iron for estimation of total body iron

(78180 has been deleted. To report, use 78199)

(For hemosiderin, use 83071)

(For intrinsic factor antibodies, use 86340)

(For cyanocobalamin (vitamin B-12), use 82607)

(For folic acid (folate) serum, use 82746)

(For hepatitis B antigen, see 87340, 87350)

(For hepatitis A antibody (HAAb), see 86708, 86709)

(For hepatitis B core antibody (HBcAb), see 86704, 86705)

(For hepatitis B surface antigen (HBsAb), use 87340)

(For hepatitis B surface antibody (HBsAb), use 86706)

(For hepatitis Be antigen (HBeAg), use 87350)

(For hepatitis Be antibody (HBeAb), use 86707)

78185   Spleen imaging only, with or without vascular flow

(If combined with liver study, use procedures 78215 and 78216)

(78186 has been deleted)

78190   Kinetics, study of platelet survival, with or without differential organ/tissue localization

78191   Platelet survival study

(78192 has been deleted. To report, use 78805)

(78193 has been deleted. To report, use 78806)

▲ **78195**   Lymphatics and lymph nodes imaging

(For sentinel node identification without scintigraphy imaging, use 38792)

(For sentinal node excision, see 38500-38542)

78199   Unlisted hematopoietic, reticuloendothelial and lymphatic procedure, diagnostic nuclear medicine

(For chemical analysis, see **Chemistry** section)

Gastrointestinal System

78201   Liver imaging; static only

78202   with vascular flow

(For spleen imaging only, use 78185)

78205   Liver imaging (SPECT);

78206   with vascular flow

78215   Liver and spleen imaging; static only

78216   with vascular flow

78220   Liver function study with hepatobiliary agents, with serial images

(78221 has been deleted. To report, use 78299)

78223   Hepatobiliary ductal system imaging, including gallbladder, with or without pharmacologic intervention, with or without quantitative measurement of gallbladder function

(78225 has been deleted)

78230   Salivary gland imaging;

78231   with serial images

78232   Salivary gland function study

(78240 has been deleted. To report pancreas imaging, use 78299)

78258   Esophageal motility

78261   Gastric mucosa imaging

78262   Gastroesophageal reflux study

78264   Gastric emptying study

78267	Urea breath test, C-14; acquisition for analysis
78268	analysis
78270	Vitamin B-12 absorption study (eg, Schilling test); without intrinsic factor
78271	with intrinsic factor
78272	Vitamin B-12 absorption studies combined, with and without intrinsic factor

(78276 has been deleted)

78278	Acute gastrointestinal blood loss imaging

(78280 has been deleted)

78282	Gastrointestinal protein loss

(78285, 78286 have been deleted. To report, use 78299)

(For gastrin, use 82941)

(For intrinsic factor level, use 83528)

(For carcinoembryonic antigen level (CEA), use 82378)

▲ **78290**	Intestine imaging (eg, ectopic gastric mucosa, Meckels localization, volvulus)
78291	Peritoneal-venous shunt patency test (eg, for LeVeen, Denver shunt)

(For injection procedure, use 49427)

78299	Unlisted gastrointestinal procedure, diagnostic nuclear medicine

(For chemical analysis, see **Chemistry** section)

Musculoskeletal System

Bone and joint imaging can be used in the diagnosis of a variety of inflammatory processes (eg, osteomyelitis), as well as for localization of primary and/or metastatic neoplasms.

78300	Bone and/or joint imaging; limited area
78305	multiple areas
78306	whole body

(78310 has been deleted. To report, use 78445)

78315	three phase study
78320	tomographic (SPECT)
78350	Bone density (bone mineral content) study, one or more sites; single photon absorptiometry
78351	dual photon absorptiometry, one or more sites

(78380, 78381 have been deleted. To report, see 78300, 78305)

(For radiographic bone density (photodensitometry), use 76078)

78399	Unlisted musculoskeletal procedure, diagnostic nuclear medicine

Cardiovascular System

Myocardial perfusion and cardiac blood pool imaging studies may be performed at rest and/or during stress. When performed during exercise and/or pharmacologic stress, the appropriate stress testing code from the 93015-93018 series should be reported in addition to code(s) 78460-78465, 78472, 78473, 78478, 78480, 78481, 78483, 78491, and 78492.

(78401-78412 have been deleted. To report, see 78472-78483)

78414	Determination of central c-v hemodynamics (non-imaging) (eg, ejection fraction with probe technique) with or without pharmacologic intervention or exercise, single or multiple determinations

(78415 has been deleted. To report, use 78472)

(78418-78424 have been deleted. To report, see 78460-78469)

(78425 has been deleted. To report, use 78472)

78428	Cardiac shunt detection

(78435 has been deleted. To report, use 78481)

78445	Non-cardiac vascular flow imaging (ie, angiography, venography)
78455	Venous thrombosis study (eg, radioactive fibrinogen)
78456	Acute venous thrombosis imaging, peptide
78457	Venous thrombosis imaging, venogram; unilateral
78458	bilateral
78459	Myocardial imaging, positron emission tomography (PET), metabolic evaluation

(For myocardial perfusion study, see 78491-78492)

78460	Myocardial perfusion imaging; (planar) single study, at rest or stress (exercise and/or pharmacologic), with or without quantification
78461	multiple studies, (planar) at rest and/or stress (exercise and/or pharmacologic), and redistribution and/or rest injection, with or without quantification

(78462, 78463 have been deleted. To report, see 78460, 78461)

78464	tomographic (SPECT), single study at rest or stress (exercise and/or pharmacologic), with or without quantification
78465	tomographic (SPECT), multiple studies, at rest and/or stress (exercise and/or pharmacologic) and redistribution and/or rest injection, with or without quantification

78466 Myocardial imaging, infarct avid, planar; qualitative or quantitative

(78467 has been deleted. To report, use 78466)

78468 with ejection fraction by first pass technique

78469 tomographic SPECT with or without quantification

(78470 has been deleted. To report, see 78472, 78473, or 78481)

(78471 has been deleted. To report, use 78472)

78472 Cardiac blood pool imaging, gated equilibrium; planar, single study at rest or stress (exercise and/or pharmacologic), wall motion study plus ejection fraction, with or without additional quantitative processing

(For assessment of cardiac function by first pass technique, use 78496)

78473 multiple studies, wall motion study plus ejection fraction, at rest and stress (exercise and/or pharmacologic), with or without additional quantification

(78474 has been deleted. To report, use 78472)

(78475-78477 have been deleted. To report, use 78473)

+ 78478 Myocardial perfusion study with wall motion, qualitative or quantitative study (List separately in addition to code for primary procedure)

(Use 78478 in conjunction with codes 78460, 78461, 78464, 78465)

(78479 has been deleted)

+ 78480 Myocardial perfusion study with ejection fraction (List separately in addition to code for primary procedure)

(Use 78480 in conjunction with codes 78460, 78461, 78464, 78465)

78481 Cardiac blood pool imaging, (planar), first pass technique; single study, at rest or with stress (exercise and/or pharmacologic), wall motion study plus ejection fraction, with or without quantification

78483 multiple studies, at rest and with stress (exercise and/ or pharmacologic), wall motion study plus ejection fraction, with or without quantification

(78484 has been deleted. To report, use 78481)

(78485, 78486 have been deleted. To report, use 78483)

(78487 and 78489 have been deleted. To report, use 78483)

(78490 has been deleted. To report, use 78499)

(For digoxin, use 80162)

(For cerebral blood flow study, use 78615)

78491 Myocardial imaging, positron emission tomography (PET), perfusion; single study at rest or stress

78492 multiple studies at rest and/or stress

78494 Cardiac blood pool imaging, gated equilibrium, SPECT, at rest, wall motion study plus ejection fraction, with or without quantitative processing

+ 78496 Cardiac blood pool imaging, gated equilibrium, single study, at rest, with right ventricular ejection fraction by first pass technique (List separately in addition to code for primary procedure)

(Use 78496 in conjunction with code 78472)

78499 Unlisted cardiovascular procedure, diagnostic nuclear medicine

(For chemical analysis, see **Chemistry** section)

Respiratory System

78580 Pulmonary perfusion imaging, particulate

(78581 and 78582 have been deleted)

78584 Pulmonary perfusion imaging, particulate, with ventilation; single breath

78585 rebreathing and washout, with or without single breath

78586 Pulmonary ventilation imaging, aerosol; single projection

78587 multiple projections (eg, anterior, posterior, lateral views)

78588 Pulmonary perfusion imaging, particulate, with ventilation imaging, aerosol, one or multiple projections

78591 Pulmonary ventilation imaging, gaseous, single breath, single projection

78593 Pulmonary ventilation imaging, gaseous, with rebreathing and washout with or without single breath; single projection

78594 multiple projections (eg, anterior, posterior, lateral views)

78596 Pulmonary quantitative differential function (ventilation/perfusion) study

78599 Unlisted respiratory procedure, diagnostic nuclear medicine

Nervous System

78600 Brain imaging, limited procedure; static

78601 with vascular flow

78605 Brain imaging, complete study; static

78606 with vascular flow

78607 tomographic (SPECT)

78608 Brain imaging, positron emission tomography (PET); metabolic evaluation

78609 perfusion evaluation

⊘ =Modifier '-51' Exempt ▶ ◀=New or Revised Text ✚=Add-on Code CPT 2002

78610	Brain imaging, vascular flow only
▲ **78615**	Cerebral vascular flow
78630	Cerebrospinal fluid flow, imaging (not including introduction of material); cisternography

(For injection procedure, see 61000-61070, 62270-62319)

78635	ventriculography

(For injection procedure, see 61000-61070, 62270-62294)

(78640 has been deleted. To report, use 78699)

78645	shunt evaluation

(For injection procedure, see 61000-61070, 62270-62294)

78647	tomographic (SPECT)
▲ **78650**	Cerebrospinal fluid leakage detection and localization

(For injection procedure, see 61000-61070, 62270-62294)

(For myelin basic protein, CSF, use 83873)

(78652 has been deleted. To report, use 78647)

(78655 has been deleted. To report, use 78800)

78660	Radiopharmaceutical dacryocystography
78699	Unlisted nervous system procedure, diagnostic nuclear medicine

Genitourinary System

78700	Kidney imaging; static only
78701	with vascular flow
78704	with function study (ie, imaging renogram)
78707	Kidney imaging with vascular flow and function; single study without pharmacological intervention
78708	single study, with pharmacological intervention (eg, angiotensin converting enzyme inhibitor and/or diuretic)
78709	multiple studies, with and without pharmacological intervention (eg, angiotensin converting enzyme inhibitor and/or diuretic)

(For introduction of radioactive substance in association with renal endoscopy, see 50559, 50578)

78710	Kidney imaging, tomographic (SPECT)
78715	Kidney vascular flow only

(78720 has been deleted. To report, use 78704)

78725	Kidney function study, non-imaging radioisotopic study

(78726 has been deleted. To report, use 78799)

(78727 has been deleted. To report, see 78700-78707)

(For renin (angiotensin I), use 84244)

(For angiotensin II, use 82163)

(For beta-2 microglobulin, use 82232)

78730	Urinary bladder residual study

(For introduction of radioactive substance in association with cystotomy or cystostomy, use 51020; in association with cystourethroscopy, use 52250)

78740	Ureteral reflux study (radiopharmaceutical voiding cystogram)

(For catheterization, see 53670, 53675)

(For estradiol, use 82670)

(For estriol, use 82677)

(For progesterone, use 84144)

(For prostatic acid phosphatase, use 84066)

78760	Testicular imaging;
78761	with vascular flow

(For testosterone, blood or urine, use 84403)

(For introduction of radioactive substance in association with ureteral endoscopy, see 50959, 50978)

(For lactogen, human placental (HPL) chorionic somatomammotropin, use 83632)

(For chorionic gonadotropin, beta subunit, see 84702, 84703)

(For pregnanediol, use 84135)

(For pregnanetriol, use 84138)

(78770, 78775 have been deleted. To report, use 78799)

78799	Unlisted genitourinary procedure, diagnostic nuclear medicine

(For chemical analysis, see **Chemistry** section)

Other Procedures

(For specific organ, see appropriate heading)

(For radiophosphorus tumor identification, ocular, see 78800)

78800	Radiopharmaceutical localization of tumor; limited area

(For specific organ, see appropriate heading)

78801	multiple areas
78802	whole body
78803	tomographic (SPECT)
78805	Radiopharmaceutical localization of inflammatory process; limited area
78806	whole body

78807   tomographic (SPECT)

(For imaging bone infectious or inflammatory disease with a bone imaging radiopharmaceutical, see 78300, 78305, 78306)

(For RAST, see 82785, 83518, 86003, 86005)

(For gamma-E immunoglobulin, use 82785)

(For gamma-G immunoglobulin, use 82784)

(For alpha-1 antitrypsin, see 82103, 82104)

(For alpha-1 fetoprotein, see 82105, 82106)

(For amikacin, use 80150)

(For aminophylline, use 80198)

(For amitriptyline, use 80152)

(For amphetamine, chemical quantitative, use 82145)

(For chlordiazepoxide, see code for specific method)

(For chlorpromazine, see phenothiazine, urine 84022)

(For clonazepam, use 80154)

(For cocaine, quantitative, use 82520)

(For diazepam, use 80154)

(For dihydromorphinone, quantitative, use 82649)

(For diphenylhydantoin, use 80185)

(For flucytosine, see code for specific method)

(For gentamicin, use 80170)

(For lactic dehydrogenase, use 83615)

(For lysergic acid diethylamide (LSD), see 80100-80103, 80299)

(For morphine (heroin), see 80100-80103, 83925)

(For phencyclidine (PCP), see 80100-80103, 83992)

(For phenobarbital, see barbiturates 80100-80103, 82205)

(For phenytoin (diphenylthydantoin), use 80185)

(For tobramycin, use 80200)

78810   Tumor imaging, positron emission tomography (PET), metabolic evaluation

78890   Generation of automated data: interactive process involving nuclear physician and/or allied health professional personnel; simple manipulations and interpretation, not to exceed 30 minutes

78891   complex manipulations and interpretation, exceeding 30 minutes

(Use 78890 or 78891 in addition to primary procedure)

(78895 has been deleted)

78990   Provision of diagnostic radiopharmaceutical(s)

78999   Unlisted miscellaneous procedure, diagnostic nuclear medicine

Therapeutic

79000   Radiopharmaceutical therapy, hyper-thyroidism; initial, including evaluation of patient

79001   subsequent, each therapy

(For follow-up visit, see 99211-99215)

79020   Radiopharmaceutical therapy, thyroid suppression (euthyroid cardiac disease), including evaluation of patient

79030   Radiopharmaceutical ablation of gland for thyroid carcinoma

79035   Radiopharmaceutical therapy for metastases of thyroid carcinoma

79100   Radiopharmaceutical therapy, polycythemia vera, chronic leukemia, each treatment

79200   Intracavitary radioactive colloid therapy

79300   Interstitial radioactive colloid therapy

79400   Radiopharmaceutical therapy, nonthyroid, nonhematologic

79420   Intravascular radiopharmaceutical therapy, particulate

79440   Intra-articular radiopharmaceutical therapy

79900   Provision of therapeutic radiopharmaceutical(s)

79999   Unlisted radiopharmaceutical therapeutic procedure

Pathology and Laboratory Guidelines

Items used by all physicians in reporting their services are presented in the **Introduction.** Some of the commonalities are repeated here for the convenience of those physicians referring to this section on **Pathology and Laboratory.** Other definitions and items unique to Pathology and Laboratory are also listed.

Services in Pathology and Laboratory

Services in Pathology and Laboratory are provided by a physician or by technologists under responsible supervision of a physician.

Separate or Multiple Procedures

It is appropriate to designate multiple procedures that are rendered on the same date by separate entries.

Subsection Information

Several of the subheadings or subsections have special needs or instructions unique to that section. Where these are indicated, (eg, "Panel Tests"), special **"Notes"** will be presented preceding those procedural terminology listings referring to that subsection specifically. If there is an "Unlisted Procedure" code number (see section below) for the individual subsection, it will be shown. Those subsections with **"Notes"** are as follows:

Organ or Disease Panels 80048-80090
Drug Testing 80100-80103
Therapeutic Drug Assays 80150-80299
Evocative/Suppression Testing 80400-80440
Consultations
    (Clinical Pathology) 80500-80502
Urinalysis 81000-81099
Chemistry 82000-84999
Molecular Diagnostics 83890-83912
    ►Infectious Agent Detection◄ . .►87470-87999◄
Infectious Agent Antibodies 86602-86804
Microbiology . . . .►87001-87254◄
    ►Infectious Agent Detection◄ . .►87260-87999◄
Anatomic Pathology 88000-88099
Cytopathology . . . .►88104-88199◄
Surgical Pathology 88300-88399

Unlisted Service or Procedure

A service or procedure may be provided that is not listed in this edition of *CPT.* When reporting such a service, the appropriate "Unlisted Procedure" code may be used to indicate the service, identifying it by "Special Report" as discussed below. The "Unlisted Procedures" and accompanying codes for **Pathology and Laboratory** are as follows:

81099	Unlisted urinalysis procedure
84999	Unlisted chemistry procedure
85999	Unlisted hematology and coagulation procedure
86586	Unlisted antigen, each
86849	Unlisted immunology procedure
86999	Unlisted transfusion medicine procedure
87999	Unlisted microbiology procedure
88099	Unlisted necropsy (autopsy) procedure
88199	Unlisted cytopathology procedure
88299	Unlisted cytogenetic study
88399	Unlisted surgical pathology procedure
89399	Unlisted miscellaneous pathology test

Special Report

A service that is rarely provided, unusual, variable, or new may require a special report in determining medical appropriateness of the service. Pertinent information should include an adequate definition or description of the nature, extent, and need for the procedure; and the time, effort, and equipment necessary to provide the service. Additional items which may be included are:

- complexity of symptoms;
- final diagnosis;
- pertinent physical findings;
- diagnostic and therapeutic procedures;
- concurrent problems;
- follow-up care.

► ◄ =New or Revised Text

Notes

Pathology and Laboratory

(80002-80019 have been deleted. To report, see codes under Organ or Disease Oriented Panels)

(80031-80034 have been deleted. To report, see Therapeutic Drug Assays)

(80040 has been deleted. To report, see 80150-80299)

(80042 has been deleted. For serum cidal level, see 87197)

Organ or Disease Oriented Panels

These panels were developed for coding purposes only and should not be interpreted as clinical parameters. The tests listed with each panel identify the defined components of that panel.

These panel components are not intended to limit the performance of other tests. If one performs tests in addition to those specifically indicated for a particular panel, those tests should be reported separately in addition to the panel code.

80048 Basic metabolic panel

This panel must include the following:

Calcium (82310)

Carbon dioxide (82374)

Chloride (82435)

Creatinine (82565)

Glucose (82947)

Potassium (84132)

Sodium (84295)

Urea Nitrogen (BUN) (84520)

(Do not use 80048 in addition to 80053)

(80049 has been deleted. To report, use 80048)

80050 General health panel

This panel must include the following:

Comprehensive metabolic panel (80053)

Hemogram, automated, and manual differential WBC count (CBC) (85022) OR

Hemogram and platelet count, automated, and automated complete differential WBC count (CBC) (85025)

Thyroid stimulating hormone (TSH) (84443)

80051 Electrolyte panel

This panel must include the following:

Carbon dioxide (82374)

Chloride (82435)

Potassium (84132)

Sodium (84295)

(80052 has been deleted. To report, see codes for specific tests)

80053 Comprehensive metabolic panel

This panel must include the following:

Albumin (82040)

Bilirubin, total (82247)

Calcium (82310)

Carbon dioxide (bicarbonate) (82374)

Chloride (82435)

Creatinine (82565)

Glucose (82947)

Phosphatase, alkaline (84075)

Potassium (84132)

Protein, total (84155)

Sodium (84295)

Transferase, alanine amino (ALT) (SGPT) (84460)

Transferase, aspartate amino (AST) (SGOT) (84450)

Urea Nitrogen (BUN) (84520)

(Do not use 80053 in addition to 80048, 80076)

(80054 has been deleted. To report, use 80053)

80055 Obstetric panel

This panel must include the following:

Hemogram, automated, and manual differential WBC count (CBC) (85022) OR

Hemogram and platelet count, automated, and automated complete differential WBC count (CBC) (85025)

Hepatitis B surface antigen (HBsAg) (87340)

Antibody, rubella (86762)

Syphilis test, qualitative (eg, VDRL, RPR, ART) (86592)

Antibody screen, RBC, each serum technique (86850)

Blood typing, ABO (86900) AND

Blood typing, Rh (D) (86901)

(80056 has been deleted. To report, see codes for specific tests)

(80057 has been deleted. To report, see codes for specific tests)

(80058 has been deleted. To report, use 80076)

(80059 has been deleted. To report, use 80074)

(80060 has been deleted. To report, see codes for specific tests)

80061   Lipid panel

This panel must include the following:

Cholesterol, serum, total (82465)

Lipoprotein, direct measurement, high density cholesterol (HDL cholesterol) (83718)

Triglycerides (84478)

(80062 has been deleted. To report, see 80061 and/or codes for specific tests)

(80063 has been deleted. To report, see codes for specific tests)

(80064 has been deleted. To report, see codes for specific tests)

(80065 has been deleted. To report, see codes for specific tests)

(80066 has been deleted. To report, see codes for specific tests)

(80067 has been deleted. To report, see codes for specific tests)

(80068 has been deleted. To report, see codes for specific tests)

80069   Renal function panel

This panel must include the following:

Albumin (82040)

Calcium (82310)

Carbon dioxide (bicarbonate) (82374)

Chloride (82435)

Creatinine (82565)

Glucose (82947)

Phosphorus inorganic (phosphate) (84100)

Potassium (84132)

Sodium (84295)

Urea nitrogen (BUN) (84520)

(80070 has been deleted. To report, use 80091)

(80071 has been deleted. To report, see codes for specific tests)

▶(80072 has been deleted. To report, see 84550, 85651, 86255, 86430)◀

(80073 has been deleted. To report, see codes for specific tests)

80074   Acute hepatitis panel

This panel must include the following:

Hepatitis A antibody (HAAb), IgM antibody (86709)

Hepatitis B core antibody (HbcAb), IgM antibody (86705)

Hepatitis B surface antigen (HbsAg) (87340)

Hepatitis C antibody (86803)

(80075 has been deleted. To report, see codes for specific tests)

80076   Hepatic function panel

This panel must include the following:

Albumin (82040)

Bilirubin, total (82247)

Bilirubin, direct (82248)

Phosphatase, alkaline (84075)

Protein, total (84155)

Transferase, alanine amino (ALT) (SGPT) (84460)

Transferase, aspartate amino (AST) (SGOT) (84450)

(Do not use 80076 in addition to 80053)

(80080 has been deleted. To report PSA, use 84153)

(80082 has been deleted. To report, see codes for specific tests)

(80084 has been deleted. To report, see codes for specific tests)

(80085 has been deleted. To report, see codes for specific tests)

(80086 has been deleted. To report, see codes for specific tests)

(80088 has been deleted. To report, see codes for specific tests)

(80089 has been deleted. To report, see codes for specific tests)

80090   TORCH antibody panel

This panel must include the following tests:

Antibody, cytomegalovirus (CMV) (86644)

Antibody, herpes simplex, non-specific type test (86694)

Antibody, rubella (86762)

Antibody, toxoplasma (86777)

(80091 has been deleted. To report, see codes for specific tests)

(80092 has been deleted. To report, see codes for specific test)

(80099 has been deleted. To report, see codes for specific tests)

Drug Testing

The following list contains examples of drugs or classes of drugs that are commonly assayed by qualitative screen, followed by confirmation with a second method.

Alcohols

Amphetamines

Barbiturates

Benzodiazepines

Cocaine and Metabolites

Methadones

Methaqualones

Opiates

Phencyclidines

Phenothiazines

Propoxyphenes

Tetrahydrocannabinoids

Tricyclic Antidepressants

Confirmed drugs may also be quantitated.

Use 80100 for each multiple drug class chromatographic procedure. Use 80102 for each procedure necessary for confirmation. For chromatography, each combination of stationary and mobile phase is to be counted as one procedure. For example, if detection of three drugs by chromatography requires one stationary phase with three mobile phases, use 80100 three (3) times. However, if multiple drugs can be detected using a single analysis (eg, one stationary phase with one mobile phase), use 80100 only once.

For quantitation of drugs screened, use appropriate code in **Chemistry** section (82000-84999) or **Therapeutic Drug Assay** section (80150-80299).

80100 Drug screen, qualitative; multiple drug classes chromatographic method, each procedure

80101 single drug class method (eg, immunoassay, enzyme assay), each drug class

80102 Drug confirmation, each procedure

80103 Tissue preparation for drug analysis

Therapeutic Drug Assays

The material for examination may be from any source. Examination is quantitative. For nonquantitative testing, see Drug Testing (80100-80103).

80150 Amikacin
80152 Amitriptyline
80154 Benzodiazepines
80156 Carbamazepine; total
80157   free
80158 Cyclosporine
80160 Desipramine
80162 Digoxin
80164 Dipropylacetic acid (valproic acid)
80166 Doxepin
80168 Ethosuximide
80170 Gentamicin
80172 Gold
80173 Haloperidol
80174 Imipramine
80176 Lidocaine
80178 Lithium
80182 Nortriptyline
80184 Phenobarbital
80185 Phenytoin; total
80186   free
80188 Primidone
80190 Procainamide;
80192   with metabolites (eg, n-acetyl procainamide)
80194 Quinidine
80196 Salicylate
80197 Tacrolimus
80198 Theophylline
80200 Tobramycin
80201 Topiramate
80202 Vancomycin
80299 Quantitation of drug, not elsewhere specified

Evocative/Suppression Testing

The following test panels involve the administration of evocative or suppressive agents, and the baseline and subsequent measurement of their effects on chemical constituents. These codes are to be used for the reporting of the laboratory component of the overall testing protocol. For the physician's administration of the evocative or suppressive agents, see 90780-90784; for the supplies and drugs, see 99070. To report physician attendance and monitoring during the testing, use the appropriate evaluation and management code, including the prolonged physician care codes if required. Prolonged physician care codes are not separately reported when evocative/suppression testing involves prolonged infusions reported with 90780 and 90781. In the code descriptors where reference is made to a particular analyte (eg, Cortisol (82533 x 2)) the "x 2" refers to the number of times the test for that particular analyte is performed.

80400   ACTH stimulation panel; for adrenal insufficiency

This panel must include the following:

Cortisol (82533 x 2)

80402   for 21 hydroxylase deficiency

This panel must include the following:

Cortisol (82533 x 2)

17 hydroxyprogesterone (83498 x 2)

80406   for 3 beta-hydroxydehydrogenase deficiency

This panel must include the following:

Cortisol (82533 x 2)

17 hydroxypregnenolone (84143 x 2)

80408   Aldosterone suppression evaluation panel (eg, saline infusion)

This panel must include the following:

Aldosterone (82088 x 2)

Renin (84244 x 2)

80410   Calcitonin stimulation panel (eg, calcium, pentagastrin)

This panel must include the following:

Calcitonin (82308 x 3)

80412   Corticotropic releasing hormone (CRH) stimulation panel

This panel must include the following:

Cortisol (82533 x 6)

Adrenocorticotropic hormone (ACTH) (82024 x 6)

80414   Chorionic gonadotropin stimulation panel; testosterone response

This panel must include the following:

Testosterone (84403 x 2 on three pooled blood samples)

80415   estradiol response

This panel must include the following:

Estradiol (82670 x 2 on three pooled blood samples)

80416   Renal vein renin stimulation panel (eg, captopril)

This panel must include the following:

Renin (84244 x 6)

80417   Peripheral vein renin stimulation panel (eg, captopril)

This panel must include the following:

Renin (84244 x 2)

80418   Combined rapid anterior pituitary evaluation panel

This panel must include the following:

Adrenocorticotropic hormone (ACTH) (82024 x 4)

Luteinizing hormone (LH) (83002 x 4)

Follicle stimulating hormone (FSH) (83001 x 4)

Prolactin (84146 x 4)

Human growth hormone (HGH) (83003 x 4)

Cortisol (82533 x 4)

Thyroid stimulating hormone (TSH) (84443 x 4)

80420   Dexamethasone suppression panel, 48 hour

This panel must include the following:

Free cortisol, urine (82530 x 2)

Cortisol (82533 x 2)

Volume measurement for timed collection (81050 x 2)

(For single dose dexamethasone, use 82533)

80422   Glucagon tolerance panel; for insulinoma

This panel must include the following:

Glucose (82947 x 3)

Insulin (83525 x 3)

80424   for pheochromocytoma

This panel must include the following:

Catecholamines, fractionated (82384 x 2)

80426   Gonadotropin releasing hormone stimulation panel

This panel must include the following:

Follicle stimulating hormone (FSH) (83001 x 4)

Luteinizing hormone (LH) (83002 x 4)

80428   Growth hormone stimulation panel (eg, arginine infusion, I-dopa administration)

This panel must include the following:

Human growth hormone (HGH) (83003 x 4)

80430   Growth hormone suppression panel (glucose administration)

This panel must include the following:

Glucose (82947 x 3)

Human growth hormone (HGH) (83003 x 4)

80432   Insulin-induced C-peptide suppression panel

This panel must include the following:

Insulin (83525)

C-peptide (84681 x 5)

Glucose (82947 x 5)

80434   Insulin tolerance panel; for ACTH insufficiency

This panel must include the following:

Cortisol (82533 x 5)

Glucose (82947 x 5)

80435   for growth hormone deficiency

This panel must include the following:

Glucose (82947 x 5)

Human growth hormone (HGH) (83003 x 5)

80436   Metyrapone panel

This panel must include the following:

Cortisol (82533 x 2)

11 deoxycortisol (82634 x 2)

80438   Thyrotropin releasing hormone (TRH) stimulation panel; one hour

This panel must include the following:

Thyroid stimulating hormone (TSH) (84443 x 3)

80439   two hour

This panel must include the following:

Thyroid stimulating hormone (TSH) (84443 x 4)

80440   for hyperprolactinemia

This panel must include the following:

Prolactin (84146 x 3)

Consultations (Clinical Pathology)

A clinical pathology consultation is a service, including a written report, rendered by the pathologist in response to a request from an attending physician in relation to a test result(s) requiring additional medical interpretive judgment.

Reporting of a test result(s) without medical interpretive judgment is not considered a clinical pathology consultation.

80500   Clinical pathology consultation; limited, without review of patient's history and medical records

80502   comprehensive, for a complex diagnostic problem, with review of patient's history and medical records

(These codes may also be used for pharmacokinetic consultations)

(For consultations involving the examination and evaluation of the patient, see 99241-99275)

Urinalysis

For specific analyses, see appropriate section.

81000   Urinalysis, by dip stick or tablet reagent for bilirubin, glucose, hemoglobin, ketones, leukocytes, nitrite, pH, protein, specific gravity, urobilinogen, any number of these constituents; non-automated, with microscopy

81001   automated, with microscopy

81002   non-automated, without microscopy

81003   automated, without microscopy

(81004 has been deleted. To report, use 81000)

81005   Urinalysis; qualitative or semiquantitative, except immunoassays

(For non-immunoassay reagent strip urinalysis, see 81000, 81002)

(For immunoassay, qualitative or semiquantitative, use 83518)

(81006 has been deleted. To report, use 81099)

(For microalbumin, see 82043, 82044)

81007   bacteriuria screen, except by culture or dipstick

(For culture, see 87086-87088)

(For dipstick, use 81000 or 81002)

(81010, 81011, and 81012 have been deleted)

81015   microscopic only

81020   two or three glass test

81025   Urine pregnancy test, by visual color comparison methods

(81030 has been deleted)

81050   Volume measurement for timed collection, each

81099   Unlisted urinalysis procedure

Chemistry

The material for examination may be from any source unless otherwise specified in the code descriptor. When an analyte is measured in multiple specimens from different sources, or in specimens that are obtained at different times, the analyte is reported separately for each source and for each specimen. The examination is quantitative unless specified. To report an organ or disease oriented panel, see codes 80048-80090.

When a code describes a method where measurement of multiple analytes may require one or several procedures, each procedure is coded separately (eg, 82491-82492, 82541-82544). For example, if two (2) analytes are measured using column chromatography using a single stationary or mobile phase, use 82492. If the same two analytes are measured using different stationary or mobile phase conditions, 82491 would be used twice. If a total of four (4) analytes are measured where two (2) analytes are measured with a single stationary and mobile phase, and the other two (2) analytes are measured using a different stationary and mobile phase, use 82492 twice. If a total of three (3) analytes are measured where two (2) analytes are measured using a single stationary or mobile phase condition, and the third analyte is measured separately using a different stationary or mobile phase procedure, use 82492 once for the (2) analytes measured under the same condition, and use 82491 once for the third analyte measured separately.

Clinical information derived from the results of laboratory data that is mathematically calculated (eg, free thyroxine index (T7)) is considered part of the test procedure and therefore is not a separately reportable service.

82000   Acetaldehyde, blood

82003   Acetaminophen

(82005 has been deleted)

82009   Acetone or other ketone bodies, serum; qualitative

82010   quantitative

(82011 has been deleted. To report, use 80196)

(82012 has been deleted)

82013   Acetylcholinesterase

(Acid, gastric, see gastric acid, 82926, 82928)

(Acid phosphatase, see 84060-84066)

(82015 has been deleted)

82016   Acylcarnitines; qualitative, each specimen

82017   quantitative, each specimen

(For carnitine, use 82379)

82024   Adrenocorticotropic hormone (ACTH)

82030   Adenosine, 5-monophosphate, cyclic (cyclic AMP)

(82035 has been deleted)

82040   Albumin; serum

82042   urine or other source, quantitative, each specimen

82043   urine, microalbumin, quantitative

82044   urine, microalbumin, semiquantitative (eg, reagent strip assay)

(For prealbumin, use 84134)

82055   Alcohol (ethanol); any specimen except breath

(For other volatiles, alcohol, use 84600)

(82060, 82065, 82070 have been deleted. To report, use 82055)

(82072 has been deleted)

82075   breath

(82076, 82078 have been deleted. For ethanol, use 82055; for volatiles, use 84600)

82085   Aldolase

(82086 has been deleted. To report, use 82085)

(82087 has been deleted. To report, use 82088)

82088   Aldosterone

(82089 has been deleted. To report, use 82088)

(82091 has been deleted. To report, use 80408)

(82095 has been deleted. To report, see 80100, 80101, and 80103)

(82096 has been deleted. To report, use code for specific drug and 80103)

(82100 has been deleted. To report, use 80100 and 80101)

(Alkaline phosphatase, see 84075, 84080)

82101   Alkaloids, urine, quantitative

(Alphaketoglutarate, see 82009, 82010)

(Alpha tocopherol (Vitamin E), use 84446)

82103   Alpha-1-antitrypsin; total

82104   phenotype

82105   Alpha-fetoprotein; serum

82106   amniotic fluid

82108   Aluminum

(82112 has been deleted. To report, use 80150)

82120   Amines, vaginal fluid, qualitative

(For combined pH and amines test for vaginitis, use 82120 and 83986)

(82126 has been deleted)

82127   Amino acids; single, qualitative, each specimen

82128   multiple, qualitative, each specimen

(82130 has been deleted. To report, see 82131, 82136, 82139)

82131   single, quantitative, each specimen

(82134 has been deleted)

82135   Aminolevulinic acid, delta (ALA)

82136   Amino acids, 2 to 5 amino acids, quantitative, each specimen

(82137 has been deleted. To report, use 80198)

(82138 has been deleted. To report, use 80152)

82139   Amino acids, 6 or more amino acids, quantitative, each specimen

82140   Ammonia

(82141 has been deleted. To report, use 82140)

(82142 has been deleted)

82143   Amniotic fluid scan (spectrophotometric)

(For L/S ratio, use 83661)

(Amobarbital, see 80100-80103 for qualitative analysis, 82205 for quantitative analysis)

82145   Amphetamine or methamphetamine

(For qualitative analysis, see 80100-80103)

82150   Amylase

82154   Androstanediol glucuronide

(82155 has been deleted)

(82156 has been deleted. To report, use 82150)

82157   Androstenedione

(82159 has been deleted. To report, use 82160)

82160   Androsterone

82163   Angiotensin II

82164   Angiotensin I - converting enzyme (ACE)

(82165 has been deleted)

(Antidiuretic hormone (ADH), use 84588)

(82168 has been deleted. For antihistamines, see code for specific method)

(82170 has been deleted. To report, see 83015, 83018)

(Antimony, use 83015)

(Antitrypsin, alpha-1-, see 82103, 82104)

82172   Apolipoprotein, each

(82173 has been deleted. To report, use 80428)

82175   Arsenic

(For heavy metal screening, use 83015)

82180   Ascorbic acid (Vitamin C), blood

(Aspirin, see acetylsalicylic acid, 80196)

(Atherogenic index, blood, ultracentrifugation, quantitative, use 83717)

82190   Atomic absorption spectroscopy, each analyte

82205   Barbiturates, not elsewhere specified

(For qualitative analysis, see 80100-80103)

(82210 has been deleted. To report, see 80100-80103, 82205)

(82225, 82230 have been deleted. To report, see 83015, 83018)

(82231 has been deleted. To report, use 82232)

82232   Beta-2 microglobulin

(82235, 82236 have been deleted)

(Bicarbonate, use 82374)

82239   Bile acids; total

82240   cholylglycine

(For bile pigments, urine, see 81000-81005)

(82245 has been deleted. To report, see 81000, 81002, 81005)

82247   Bilirubin; total

82248   direct

(82250 has been deleted. To report, see 82247, 82248 as appropriate)

(82251 has been deleted. To report, use 82247 and 82248)

82252   feces, qualitative

(82260 has been deleted. To report, see 81000-81003, 82247, 82248, 82251)

82261   Biotinidase, each specimen

(82265 has been deleted. To report spectrophotometric scan, use 82143)

(82268 has been deleted. To report, see 83015, 83018)

▲ **82270**   Blood, occult, by peroxidase activity (eg, guaiac), qualitative; feces, 1-3 simultaneous determinations

▲ **82273**   other sources

(Blood urea nitrogen (BUN), see 84520, 84525)

(82280, 82285 have been deleted. To report, see code for specific method)

● **82274**   Blood, occult, by fecal hemoglobin determination by immunoassay, qualitative, feces, 1-3 simultaneous determinations

82286   Bradykinin

(82290, 82291 have been deleted. To report, use 84311)

82300   Cadmium

(82305 has been deleted. To report, see 82486, 82491)

82306   Calcifediol (25-OH Vitamin D-3)

82307   Calciferol (Vitamin D)

(For 1,25-Dihydroxyvitamin D, use 82652)

82308   Calcitonin

82310   Calcium; total

(82315, 82320, 82325 have been deleted. To report, use 82310)

82330   ionized

82331   after calcium infusion test

(82335 has been deleted)

82340   urine quantitative, timed specimen

(82345 has been deleted)

▲ **82355**   Calculus; qualitative analysis

82360   quantitative analysis, chemical

82365   infrared spectroscopy

82370   x-ray diffraction

(82372 has been deleted. To report, use 80156)

(Carbamates, see individual listings)

82373   Carbohydrate deficient transferrin

82374   Carbon dioxide (bicarbonate)

(See also 82803)

82375   Carbon monoxide, (carboxyhemoglobin); quantitative

82376   qualitative

82378   Carcinoembryonic antigen (CEA)

82379   Carnitine (total and free), quantitative, each specimen

(For acylcarnitine, see 82016, 82017)

82380   Carotene

82382   Catecholamines; total urine

82383   blood

82384   fractionated

(For urine metabolites, see 83835, 84585)

82387   Cathepsin-D

82390   Ceruloplasmin

82397   Chemiluminescent assay

(82400 has been deleted. To report, see code for specific method)

(82405 has been deleted)

82415   Chloramphenicol

(82418, 82420, 82425 have been deleted. To report, see code for specific method)

82435   Chloride; blood

82436   urine

(82437 has been deleted)

82438   other source

(For sweat collection by iontophoresis, use 89360)

82441   Chlorinated hydrocarbons, screen

(82443 has been deleted. To report, see code for specific method)

(Chlorpromazine, use 84022)

(Cholecalciferol (Vitamin D), use 82307)

82465   Cholesterol, serum or whole blood, total

(For high density lipoprotein (HDL), use 83718)

(82470 has been deleted)

82480   Cholinesterase; serum

82482   RBC

(82484 has been deleted. To report, use 82480 and 82482)

82485   Chondroitin B sulfate, quantitative

(Chorionic gonadotropin, see gonadotropin, 84702, 84703)

82486   Chromatography, qualitative; column (eg, gas liquid or HPLC), analyte not elsewhere specified

82487   paper, 1-dimensional, analyte not elsewhere specified

82488   paper, 2-dimensional, analyte not elsewhere specified

82489   thin layer, analyte not elsewhere specified

(82490 has been deleted)

82491   Chromatography, quantitative, column (eg, gas liquid or HPLC); single analyte not elsewhere specified, single stationary and mobile phase

82492   multiple analytes, single stationary and mobile phase

82495   Chromium

(82505 has been deleted)

82507   Citrate

(82512 has been deleted. To report, use 80154)

⊘=Modifier '-51' Exempt   ►◄=New or Revised Text   ✚=Add-on Code

82520   Cocaine or metabolite

(Cocaine, qualitative analysis, see 80100-80103)

(Codeine, qualitative analysis, see 80100-80103)

(Codeine, quantitative analysis, see 82101)

(Complement, see 86160-86162)

82523   Collagen cross links, any method

82525   Copper

(82526 has been deleted. To report, use 82525)

(Coproporphyrin, see 84119, 84120)

(Corticosteroids, use 83491)

82528   Corticosterone

(82529 has been deleted. To report, use 82533)

82530   Cortisol; free

(82531, 82532 have been deleted)

82533   total

(82534 has been deleted. To report, use 82533)

(82536 has been deleted. To report, see 80400-80406)

(82537 has been deleted. To report, see 80400-80406)

(82538 has been deleted. To report, use 80436)

(82539 has been deleted. To report, use 80420)

(C-peptide, use 84681)

82540   Creatine

82541   Column chromatography/mass spectrometry (eg, GC/MS, or HPLC/MS), analyte not elsewhere specified; qualitative, single stationary and mobile phase

82542   quantitative, single stationary and mobile phase

82543   stable isotope dilution, single analyte, quantitative, single stationary and mobile phase

82544   stable isotope dilution, multiple analytes, quantitative, single stationary and mobile phase

(82545 has been deleted. To report, use 82540)

(82546 has been deleted. To report, see 82540, 82565)

82550   Creatine kinase (CK), (CPK); total

82552   isoenzymes

82553   MB fraction only

82554   isoforms

(82555 has been deleted)

82565   Creatinine; blood

82570   other source

82575   clearance

82585   Cryofibrinogen

82595   Cryoglobulin, qualitative or semi-quantitative (eg, cryocrit)

(For quantitative, cryoglobulin, see 82784, 82785)

(Crystals, pyrophosphate vs. urate, use 89060)

82600   Cyanide

(82601 has been deleted. To report, see 80103, 82600)

(82606 has been deleted)

82607   Cyanocobalamin (Vitamin B-12);

82608   unsaturated binding capacity

(Cyclic AMP, use 82030)

(Cyclic GMP, use 83008)

(Cyclosporine, use 80158)

(82610, 82614 have been deleted)

82615   Cystine and homocystine, urine, qualitative

(82620 has been deleted. For cystine and homocystine, quantitative, use 82130)

(82624 has been deleted)

82626   Dehydroepiandrosterone (DHEA)

82627   Dehydroepiandrosterone-sulfate (DHEA-S)

(82628 has been deleted. To report, see 80100-80103 for qualitative analysis; see 80160 for quantitative analysis)

(Delta-aminolevulinic acid (ALA), use 82135)

82633   Desoxycorticosterone, 11-

82634   Deoxycortisol, 11-

(Dexamethasone suppression test, use 80420)

(82635 has been deleted)

(Diastase, urine, use 82150)

(82636 has been deleted. To report, see 80100-80103, 80154)

82638   Dibucaine number

(82639 has been deleted. To report, use code for specific method)

(Dichloroethane, use 84600)

(Dichloromethane, use 84600)

(Diethylether, use 84600)

(82640, 82641 have been deleted)

(82643 has been deleted. To report, use 80162)

82646   Dihydrocodeinone

(For qualitative analysis, see 80100-80103)

82649   Dihydromorphinone

(For qualitative analysis, see 80100-80103)

82651   Dihydrotestosterone (DHT)

82652	Dihydroxyvitamin D, 1,25-
82654	Dimethadione

(For qualitative analysis, see 80100-80103)

(Diphenylhydantoin, use 80185)

(Dipropylacetic acid, use 80164)

(Dopamine, see 82382-82384)

(82656 has been deleted. To report, use 80166)

(Duodenal contents, see individual enzymes; for intubation and collection, use 89100)

82657 Enzyme activity in blood cells, cultured cells, or tissue, not elsewhere specified; nonradioactive substrate, each specimen

82658 radioactive substrate, each specimen

(82660 has been deleted. To report, see 80100, 80101)

(82662 has been deleted. To report, see 80100-80103)

82664 Electrophoretic technique, not elsewhere specified

(Endocrine receptor assays, see 84233-84235)

82666 Epiandrosterone

(Epinephrine, see 82382-82384)

82668 Erythropoietin

82670 Estradiol

82671 Estrogens; fractionated

82672 total

(82673, 82674, 82676 have been deleted. To report, use 82677)

(Estrogen receptor assay, use 84233)

82677 Estriol

(82678 has been deleted. To report, use 82679)

82679 Estrone

(Ethanol, see 82055 and 82075)

82690 Ethchlorvynol

(82691 has been deleted. To report, use 82690)

(82692 has been deleted. To report, use 80168)

(Ethyl alcohol, see 82055 and 82075)

82693 Ethylene glycol

(82694 has been deleted. To report, use 82696)

82696 Etiocholanolone

(For fractionation of ketosteroids, use 83593)

82705 Fat or lipids, feces; qualitative

82710 quantitative

82715 Fat differential, feces, quantitative

(82720 has been deleted)

82725 Fatty acids, nonesterified

82726 Very long chain fatty acids

(82727 has been deleted. To report ferric chloride test, urine, use 81005)

82728 Ferritin

(Fetal hemoglobin, see hemoglobin 83030, 83033, and 85460)

(Fetoprotein, alpha-1, see 82105, 82106)

(82730 has been deleted. To report fibrinogen, see 85384, 85385)

82731 Fetal fibronectin, cervicovaginal secretions, semi-quantitative

82735 Fluoride

(82740 has been deleted. To report, use 82735)

(82741 has been deleted. To report, see code for specific method)

82742 Flurazepam

(For qualitative analysis, see 80100-80103)

(Foam stability test, use 83662)

(82745 has been deleted)

82746 Folic acid; serum

82747 RBC

(Follicle stimulating hormone (FSH), use 83001)

(82750 has been deleted. To report, see code for specific method)

(82755, 82756 have been deleted)

82757 Fructose, semen

(Fructosamine, use 82985)

(Fructose, TLC screen, use 84375)

82759 Galactokinase, RBC

82760 Galactose

(82763 has been deleted. To report, use 82760 and codes for administration)

(82765 has been deleted. To report, use 82760)

82775 Galactose-1-phosphate uridyl transferase; quantitative

82776 screen

(82780 has been deleted. To report gallium, see code for specific method)

82784 Gammaglobulin; IgA, IgD, IgG, IgM, each

82785 IgE

(For allergen specific IgE, see 86003, 86005)

(82786 has been deleted)

⊘=Modifier '-51' Exempt ► ◄=New or Revised Text ✦=Add-on Code

82787   immunoglobulin subclasses, (IgG1, 2, 3, or 4), each

(Gamma-glutamyltransferase (GGT), use 82977)

(82790, 82791 have been deleted)

(82792 has been deleted. To report, see 82805, 82810)

(82793, 82795 have been deleted)

82800   Gases, blood, pH only

(82801, 82802 have been deleted. To report, use 82803)

82803   Gases, blood, any combination of pH, pCO_2, pO_2, CO_2, HCO_3 (including calculated O_2 saturation);

(Use 82803 for two or more of the above listed analytes)

(82804 has been deleted. To report, use 82803)

82805   with O_2 saturation, by direct measurement, except pulse oximetry

82810   Gases, blood, O_2 saturation only, by direct measurement, except pulse oximetry

(For pulse oximetry, use 94760)

(82812 has been deleted. To report, use 82803)

(82817 has been deleted. To report, use 82803)

82820   Hemoglobin-oxygen affinity (pO_2 for 50% hemoglobin saturation with oxygen)

82926   Gastric acid, free and total, each specimen

(82927 has been deleted. To report, use 82926)

82928   Gastric acid, free or total; each specimen

(82929, 82931, and 82932 have been deleted. To report, use 82928)

82938   Gastrin after secretin stimulation

82941   Gastrin

(Gentamicin, use 80170)

(GGT, use 82977)

(GLC, gas liquid chromatography, use 82486)

(82942 has been deleted)

82943   Glucagon

(82944 has been deleted)

82945   Glucose, body fluid, other than blood

82946   Glucagon tolerance test

82947   Glucose; quantitative, blood (except reagent strip)

82948   blood, reagent strip

(82949 has been deleted)

82950   post glucose dose (includes glucose)

82951   tolerance test (GTT), three specimens (includes glucose)

82952   tolerance test, each additional beyond three specimens

82953   tolbutamide tolerance test

(For insulin tolerance test, see 80434, 80435)

(For leucine tolerance test, use 80428)

(For semiquantitative urine glucose, see 81000, 81002, 81005, 81099)

(82954 has been deleted. To report, use 82947)

82955   Glucose-6-phosphate dehydrogenase (G6PD); quantitative

82960   screen

(82961 has been deleted)

(For glucose tolerance test with medication, use 90784 in addition)

82962   Glucose, blood by glucose monitoring device(s) cleared by the FDA specifically for home use

82963   Glucosidase, beta

82965   Glutamate dehydrogenase

82975   Glutamine (glutamic acid amide)

82977   Glutamyltransferase, gamma (GGT)

82978   Glutathione

82979   Glutathione reductase, RBC

82980   Glutethimide

(Glycohemoglobin, use 83036)

82985   Glycated protein

(82995 has been deleted. To report, use 80172)

(82996-82998 have been deleted. To report, see 84702, 84703)

(Gonadotropin, chorionic, see 84702, 84703)

(83000 has been deleted)

83001   Gonadotropin; follicle stimulating hormone (FSH)

83002   luteinizing hormone (LH)

(For luteinizing releasing factor (LRH), use 83727)

83003   Growth hormone, human (HGH) (somatotropin)

(83004 has been deleted. To report, use 80430)

(For antibody to human growth hormone, use 86277)

(83005 has been deleted)

83008   Guanosine monophosphate (GMP), cyclic

83010   Haptoglobin; quantitative

(83011 has been deleted. To report, use 83010)

83012   phenotypes

▲**83013**   Helicobacter pylori; analysis for urease activity, non-radioactive isotope

83014   drug administration and sample collection

(For H. pylori, stool, use 87338. For H. pylori, liquid scintillation counter, see 78267, 78268. For H. pylori, enzyme immunoassay, use 87339)

83015   Heavy metal (arsenic, barium, beryllium, bismuth, antimony, mercury); screen

83018   quantitative, each

(83019 has been deleted. To report, see 83013, 83014)

83020   Hemoglobin fractionation and quantitation; electrophoresis (eg, A2, S, C, and/or F)

83021   chromatography (eg, A2, S, C, and/or F)

83026   Hemoglobin; by copper sulfate method, non-automated

83030   F (fetal), chemical

83033   F (fetal), qualitative

83036   glycated

(For fecal hemoglobin detection by immunoassay, use ▶82274)◀

(83040 has been deleted. To report, use 83050)

83045   methemoglobin, qualitative

83050   methemoglobin, quantitative

83051   plasma

(83052, 83053 have been deleted. To report, use 85660)

83055   sulfhemoglobin, qualitative

83060   sulfhemoglobin, quantitative

83065   thermolabile

83068   unstable, screen

83069   urine

83070   Hemosiderin; qualitative

83071   quantitative

(Heroin, see 80100-80103)

(HIAA, use 83497)

(High performance liquid chromatography (HPLC), use 82486)

83080   b-Hexosaminidase, each assay

(83086, 83087 have been deleted. To report, use 82128)

83088   Histamine

(Hollander test, use 91052)

83090   Homocystine

(83093, 83095 have been deleted. For homogentisic acid, qualitative urine screen, see 81005. For quantitative assay, see code for specific method)

83150   Homovanillic acid (HVA)

(Hormones, see individual alphabetic listings in **Chemistry** section)

(Hydrogen breath test, use 91065)

(83485, 83486 have been deleted)

83491   Hydroxycorticosteroids, 17- (17-OHCS)

(For cortisol, see 82530, 82533. For deoxycortisol, use 82634)

(83492 has been deleted. To report, use 83491)

(83493 has been deleted)

(83494-83496 have been deleted. To report, use 83491)

83497   Hydroxyindolacetic acid, 5-(HIAA)

(For urine qualitative test, use 81005)

(5-Hydroxytryptamine, use 84260)

83498   Hydroxyprogesterone, 17-d

83499   Hydroxyprogesterone, 20-

83500   Hydroxyproline; free

83505   total

(83510 has been deleted. To report, use 83500 and 83505)

83516   Immunoassay for analyte other than infectious agent antibody or infectious agent antigen, qualitative or semiquantitative; multiple step method

83518   single step method (eg, reagent strip)

83519   Immunoassay, analyte, quantitative; by radiopharmaceutical technique (eg, RIA)

83520   not otherwise specified

(83523 has been deleted. To report, use 80174)

(For immunoassays for antibodies to infectious agent antigens, see analyte and method specific codes in the **Immunology** section)

(For immunoassay of tumor antigen not elsewhere specified, use 86316)

(Immunoglobulins, see 82784, 82785)

(83524 has been deleted)

83525   Insulin; total

(For proinsulin, use 84206)

(83526 has been deleted. To report, see 80434, 80435)

83527   free

83528   Intrinsic factor

(For intrinsic factor antibodies, use 86340)

(83530 has been deleted)

(83533, 83534 have been deleted. To report, use 84999)

83540   Iron

(83545, 83546 have been deleted. To report, use 83540)

83550   Iron binding capacity

(83555, 83565 have been deleted. To report, use 83550)

⊘ =Modifier '-51' Exempt   ▶ ◀=New or Revised Text   ✛=Add-on Code   CPT 2002

83570   Isocitric dehydrogenase (IDH)

(Isonicotinic acid hydrazide, INH, see code for specific method)

(Isopropyl alcohol, use 84600)

(83571 has been deleted. To report, use 83570)

(83576 has been deleted. To report, see code for specific method)

(83578 has been deleted)

83582   Ketogenic steroids, fractionation

(83583, 83584 have been deleted)

(Ketone bodies, for serum, see 82009, 82010; for urine, see 81000-81003)

83586   Ketosteroids, 17- (17-KS); total

(83587 has been deleted. To report, use 83593)

(83588, 83589 have been deleted. To report, use 83586)

(83590 has been deleted)

83593   fractionation

(83596 has been deleted)

(83597 has been deleted)

(83599 has been deleted. To report, use 83586)

(83600 has been deleted. To report, see code for specific method)

83605   Lactate (lactic acid)

(83610 has been deleted. To report, use 83615)

83615   Lactate dehydrogenase (LD), (LDH);

(83620 has been deleted. To report, use 83615)

(83624 has been deleted)

83625   isoenzymes, separation and quantitation

(83626 has been deleted)

(83628 has been deleted. To report, use 83625)

(83629, 83631 have been deleted. To report, use 83615)

83632   Lactogen, human placental (HPL) human chorionic somatomammotropin

83633   Lactose, urine; qualitative

83634   quantitative

(For tolerance, see 82951, 82952)

(For breath hydrogen test for lactase deficiency, use 91065)

(83645 has been deleted. To report, see quantitative code or screening for toxicity)

(83650 has been deleted)

83655   Lead

(83660 has been deleted. To report, use 83655)

83661   Fetal lung maturity assessment; lecithin sphingomyelin (L/S) ratio

83662   foam stability test

83663   fluorescence polarization

83664   lamellar body density

(For phosphatidylglycerol, use 84081)

83670   Leucine aminopeptidase (LAP)

(83675, 83680 have been deleted. To report, use 83670)

(83681 has been deleted. To report, use 80428)

(83685 has been deleted. To report, use 80176)

83690   Lipase

(83700, 83705 have been deleted. For cholesterol, see 82465, 83718-83721. For triglycerides, use 84478)

83715   Lipoprotein, blood; electrophoretic separation and quantitation

83716   high resolution fractionation and quantitation of lipoprotein cholesterols (eg, electrophoresis, nuclear magnetic resonance, ultracentrifugation)

(83717 has been deleted. To report, use 83716)

83718   Lipoprotein, direct measurement; high density cholesterol (HDL cholesterol)

83719   direct measurement, VLDL cholesterol

(83720 has been deleted)

83721   direct measurement, LDL cholesterol

(For fractionation by nuclear magnetic resonance or high resolution electrophoresis, use 83716)

▶(To report direct measurement, intermediate density lipoproteins (remnant lipoproteins), use Category III code 0026T)◀

(Luteinizing hormone (LH), use 83002)

(83725 has been deleted. To report, use 80178)

83727   Luteinizing releasing factor (LRH)

(83728 has been deleted. To report, see 80100-80103, 80299)

(83730 has been deleted)

(For qualitative analysis, see 80100-80103)

(Macroglobulins, alpha-2, use 86329)

83735   Magnesium

(83740, 83750, 83755, 83760, 83765 have been deleted. To report, use 83735)

83775   Malate dehydrogenase

(Maltose tolerance, see 82951, 82952)

(Mammotropin, use 84146)

83785   Manganese

(83790 has been deleted)

(Marijuana, see 80100-80103)

(83795 has been deleted)

(83799 has been deleted. To report, use 83925)

83788   Mass spectrometry and tandem mass spectrometry (MS, MS/MS), analyte not elsewhere specified; qualitative, each specimen

83789   quantitative, each specimen

83805   Meprobamate

(For qualitative analysis, see 80100-80103)

83825   Mercury, quantitative

(83830 has been deleted. To report, use 83825)

(Mercury screen, use 83015)

83835   Metanephrines

(For catecholamines, see 82382-82384)

83840   Methadone

(For methadone qualitative analysis, see 80100-80103)

(Methamphetamine, see 80100-80103, 82145)

(Methanol, use 84600)

(83842 has been deleted. To report, see code for specific method)

(83845 has been deleted. To report, see 80101-80103)

83857   Methemalbumin

(Methemoglobin, see hemoglobin 83045, 83050)

83858   Methsuximide

(Methyl alcohol, use 84600)

(Microalbumin, see 82043 for quantitative, see 82044 for semiquantitative)

(Microglobulin, beta-2, use 82232)

(83859 has been deleted)

(83860-83862 have been deleted. To report, see 80100-80103 for qualitative analysis, 83925 for quantitative analysis)

83864   Mucopolysaccharides, acid; quantitative

(83865 has been deleted. To report, use 83864)

83866   screen

(83870 has been deleted. To report, use 84999)

83872   Mucin, synovial fluid (Ropes test)

▲ **83873**   Myelin basic protein, cerebrospinal fluid

(For oligoclonal bands, use 83916)

83874   Myoglobin

(83875 has been deleted)

(83880 has been deleted. To report, use 83925)

83883   Nephelometry, each analyte not elsewhere specified

83885   Nickel

83887   Nicotine

Codes 83890-83912 are intended for use with molecular diagnostic techniques for analysis of nucleic acids.

Codes 83890-83912 are coded by procedure rather than analyte.

Code separately for each procedure used in an analysis. For example, a procedure requiring isolation of DNA, restriction endonuclease digestion, electrophoresis, and nucleic acid probe amplification would be coded 83890, 83892, 83894, and 83898.

(For microbial identification, see 87797, 87798)

83890   Molecular diagnostics; molecular isolation or extraction

83891   isolation or extraction of highly purified nucleic acid

83892   enzymatic digestion

83893   dot/slot blot production

83894   separation by gel electrophoresis (eg, agarose, polyacrylamide)

(83895 has been deleted)

83896   nucleic acid probe, each

83897   nucleic acid transfer (eg, Southern, Northern)

83898   amplification of patient nucleic acid (eg, PCR, LCR), single primer pair, each primer pair

(83900 has been deleted)

83901   amplification of patient nucleic acid, multiplex, each multiplex reaction

83902   reverse transcription

83903   mutation scanning, by physical properties (eg, single strand conformational polymorphisms (SSCP), heteroduplex, denaturing gradient gel electrophoresis (DGGE), RNA'ase A), single segment, each

83904   mutation identification by sequencing, single segment, each segment

83905   mutation identification by allele specific transcription, single segment, each segment

83906   mutation identification by allele specific translation, single segment, each segment

(83910 has been deleted)

83912   interpretation and report

(83913 has been deleted. To report, use 83898)

83915   Nucleotidase 5-

▲ **83916**   Oligoclonal immune (oligoclonal bands)

(83917 has been deleted)

83918   Organic acids; total, quantitative, each specimen

83919   qualitative, each specimen

(83920 has been deleted. To report, use code for specific method)

83921   Organic acid, single, quantitative

83925   Opiates, (eg, morphine, meperidine)

83930   Osmolality; blood

83935   urine

83937   Osteocalcin (bone g1a protein)

(83938 has been deleted)

83945   Oxalate

(83946 has been deleted. To report, use 80154)

(83947 has been deleted. To report, see 82009, 82010)

(83948 has been deleted. To report, see 80100-80103, 83925)

(83949 has been deleted)

(83965 has been deleted. To report, see code for specific method)

● **83950**   Oncoprotein, HER-2/neu

▶(For tissue, see 88342, 88365)◀

83970   Parathormone (parathyroid hormone)

(83971, 83972 have been deleted. To report, see code for specific method)

(83973 has been deleted. To report, use 84375)

(83974 has been deleted)

(83975, 83985 have been deleted. To report, see code for specific method)

(Pesticide, quantitative, see code for specific method. For screen for chlorinated hydrocarbons, use 82441)

83986   pH, body fluid, except blood

(For blood pH, see 82800, 82803)

83992   Phencyclidine (PCP)

(For qualitative analysis, see 80100-80103)

(Phenobarbital, use 80184)

(83995 has been deleted. To report, see code for specific method)

(84005 has been deleted)

(84021 has been deleted. To report, see 80100, 80101, 84022)

84022   Phenothiazine

(For qualitative analysis, see 80100, 80101)

84030   Phenylalanine (PKU), blood

(Phenylalanine-tyrosine ratio, see 84030, 84510)

(84031 has been deleted)

(84033 has been deleted. To report, see code for specific method)

84035   Phenylketones, qualitative

(84037 has been deleted. To report, use 84035)

(84038 has been deleted. To report, see code for specific method)

(84039, 84040 have been deleted)

(84045 has been deleted. To report, see 80185, 80186)

84060   Phosphatase, acid; total

84061   forensic examination

(84065 has been deleted. To report, use 84066)

84066   prostatic

84075   Phosphatase, alkaline;

84078   heat stable (total not included)

84080   isoenzymes

84081   Phosphatidylglycerol

(84082 has been deleted)

(Phosphates inorganic, use 84100)

(Phosphates, organic, see code for specific method. For cholinesterase, see 82480, 82482)

(84083 has been deleted)

84085   Phosphogluconate, 6-, dehydrogenase, RBC

84087   Phosphohexose isomerase

(84090 has been deleted)

84100   Phosphorus inorganic (phosphate);

84105   urine

(Pituitary gonadotropins, see 83001-83002)

(PKU, see 84030, 84035)

84106   Porphobilinogen, urine; qualitative

84110   quantitative

(84118 has been deleted. To report, use 84120)

84119   Porphyrins, urine; qualitative

84120   quantitation and fractionation

(84121 has been deleted. To report, use 84120)

84126   Porphyrins, feces; quantitative

84127   qualitative

(84128 has been deleted)

(Porphyrin precursors, see 82135, 84106, 84110)

(For protoporphyrin, RBC, see 84202, 84203)

84132 Potassium; serum

84133   urine

84134 Prealbumin

(For microalbumin, see 82043, 82044)

84135 Pregnanediol

(84136 has been deleted. To report, use 84135)

84138 Pregnanetriol

(84139 has been deleted. To report, use 84138)

84140 Pregnenolone

(84141 has been deleted. To report, use 80188)

(84142 has been deleted. To report, see 80190, 80192)

84143 17-hydroxypregnenolone

84144 Progesterone

(Progesterone receptor assay, use 84234)

(For proinsulin, use 84206)

84146 Prolactin

(84147 has been deleted. To report, see 80100-80103)

(84149 has been deleted)

84150 Prostaglandin, each

84152 Prostate specific antigen (PSA); complexed (direct measurement)

84153   total

84154   free

84155 Protein; total, except refractometry

84160   refractometric

84165   electrophoretic fractionation and quantitation

(84170 has been deleted)

(84175 has been deleted. To report, use 84165)

(84176 has been deleted)

(84180 has been deleted. To report, use 81050 and 84155)

84181   Western Blot, with interpretation and report, blood or other body fluid

84182   Western Blot, with interpretation and report, blood or other body fluid, immunological probe for band identification, each

(For Western Blot tissue analysis, use 88371)

(84185 has been deleted)

(84190 has been deleted. To report, use 84165)

(84195 has been deleted)

(84200 has been deleted. To report, use 84165)

(84201 has been deleted. To report, see 80438, 80439)

84202 Protoporphyrin, RBC; quantitative

84203   screen

(84205 has been deleted. To report, use code for specific method)

84206 Proinsulin

(Pseudocholinesterase, use 82480)

84207 Pyridoxal phosphate (Vitamin B-6)

(84208 has been deleted. To report, use 89060)

84210 Pyruvate

84220 Pyruvate kinase

84228 Quinine

(84230 has been deleted. To report, use 80194)

(84231 has been deleted. To report radioimmunoassay not elsewhere specified, use 83519)

(84232 has been deleted)

84233 Receptor assay; estrogen

84234   progesterone

84235   endocrine, other than estrogen or progesterone (specify hormone)

(84236 has been deleted. To report, use 84233 and 84234)

84238   non-endocrine (eg, acetylcholine) (specify receptor)

84244 Renin

(84246 has been deleted)

(84250, 84251 have been deleted. To report, use 84479)

84252 Riboflavin (Vitamin B-2)

(Salicylates, use 80196)

(Secretin test, see 99070, 89100 and appropriate analyses)

84255 Selenium

84260 Serotonin

(For urine metabolites (HIAA), use 83497)

84270 Sex hormone binding globulin (SHBG)

84275 Sialic acid

(Sickle hemoglobin, use 85660)

84285 Silica

84295 Sodium; serum

84300   urine

(Somatomammotropin, use 83632)

(Somatotropin, use 83003)

84305 Somatomedin

84307 Somatostatin

(84310 has been deleted)

⊘ =Modifier '-51' Exempt ▶◀=New or Revised Text ✛ =Add-on Code

84311 Spectrophotometry, analyte not elsewhere specified

84315 Specific gravity (except urine)

(For specific gravity, urine, see 81000-81003)

(84317 has been deleted)

(84318 has been deleted)

(Stone analysis, see 82355-82370)

(84324 has been deleted. To report, see code for specific method)

84375 Sugars, chromatographic, TLC or paper chromatography

84376 Sugars (mono-, di-, and oligosaccharides); single qualitative, each specimen

84377   multiple quantitative, each specimen

84378   single quantitative, each specimen

84379   multiple quantitative, each specimen

(84382 has been deleted)

84392 Sulfate, urine

(Sulfhemoglobin, see hemoglobin, 83055, 83060)

(84395 has been deleted)

(84397 has been deleted)

(T-3, see 84479-84481)

(T-4, see 84436-84439)

(84401 has been deleted)

84402 Testosterone; free

84403   total

(84404 has been deleted)

(84405 has been deleted. To report, use 84403)

(84406 has been deleted. For testosterone binding protein, use sex hormone binding globulin, 84270)

(84407 has been deleted. To report, see code for specific method)

(84408 has been deleted. To report, see 80100-80103, 80299)

(84409, 84410 have been deleted. To report, see code for specific method)

(84420 has been deleted. To report, use 80198)

84425 Thiamine (Vitamin B-1)

84430 Thiocyanate

84432 Thyroglobulin

(Thyroglobulin, antibody, use 86800)

(84434 has been deleted. To report, use 84022)

(Thyrotropin releasing hormone (TRH) test, see 80438, 80439)

(84435 has been deleted. To report, use 84436)

84436 Thyroxine; total

84437   requiring elution (eg, neonatal)

84439   free

(84441 has been deleted. To report, see 84436-84439)

84442 Thyroxine binding globulin (TBG)

84443 Thyroid stimulating hormone (TSH)

(84444 has been deleted. To report, see 80438, 80439)

▲ **84445** Thyroid stimulating immune globulins (TSI)

(Tobramycin, use 80200)

84446 Tocopherol alpha (Vitamin E)

(Tolbutamide tolerance, use 82953)

(84447, 84448 have been deleted. To report, see 80100-80103)

84449 Transcortin (cortisol binding globulin)

84450 Transferase; aspartate amino (AST) (SGOT)

(84455 has been deleted. To report, use 84450)

84460   alanine amino (ALT) (SGPT)

(84465 has been deleted. To report, use 84460)

84466 Transferrin

(Iron binding capacity, use 83550)

(84472 has been deleted. To report, see code for specific method)

(84474 has been deleted. To report, see code for specific method)

(84476 has been deleted. To report, use 84022)

84478 Triglycerides

84479 Thyroid hormone (T3 or T4) uptake or thyroid hormone binding ratio (THBR)

84480 Triiodothyronine T3; total (TT-3)

84481   free

84482   reverse

(84483 has been deleted. To report, see 80100-80103, 80299)

84484 Troponin, quantitative

(For Troponin, qualitative assay, use 84512)

84485 Trypsin; duodenal fluid

84488   feces, qualitative

84490   feces, quantitative, 24-hour collection

84510 Tyrosine

(Urate crystal identification, use 89060)

84512 Troponin, qualitative

(For Troponin, quantitative assay, use 84484)

84520   Urea nitrogen; quantitative

84525   semiquantitative (eg, reagent strip test)

84540   Urea nitrogen, urine

84545   Urea nitrogen, clearance

84550   Uric acid; blood

(84555 has been deleted. To report, use 84550)

84560   other source

(84565, 84570, 84575 have been deleted)

84577   Urobilinogen, feces, quantitative

84578   Urobilinogen, urine; qualitative

84580   quantitative, timed specimen

84583   semiquantitative

(84584 has been deleted)

(Uroporphyrins, use 84120)

(Valproic acid (dipropylacetic acid), use 80164)

84585   Vanillylmandelic acid (VMA), urine

84586   Vasoactive intestinal peptide (VIP)

84588   Vasopressin (antidiuretic hormone, ADH)

(84589 has been deleted. To report, use 85810)

84590   Vitamin A

(84595 has been deleted. To report, use 82380 and 84590)

(Vitamin B-1, use 84425)

(Vitamin B-2, use 84252)

(Vitamin B-6, use 84207)

(Vitamin B-12, use 82607)

(Vitamin B-12, absorption (Schilling), see 78270, 78271)

(Vitamin C, use 82180)

(Vitamin D, see 82306, 82307, 82652)

(Vitamin E, use 84446)

84591   Vitamin, not otherwise specified

84597   Vitamin K

(VMA, use 84585)

84600   Volatiles (eg, acetic anhydride, carbon tetrachloride, dichloroethane, dichloromethane, diethylether, isopropyl alcohol, methanol)

(For acetaldehyde, use 82000)

(84605 has been deleted)

(84610 has been deleted)

(Volume, blood, RISA or Cr-51, see 78110, 78111)

(84613 has been deleted)

(84615 has been deleted. To report, see code for specific method)

84620   Xylose absorption test, blood and/or urine

(For administration, use 99070)

84630   Zinc

(84635 has been deleted. To report, use 84630)

(84645 has been deleted)

(84680 has been deleted. To report, use 82677)

84681   C-peptide

(84695 has been deleted. To report, use 80170)

(84701 has been deleted. To report, see 84702-84703)

84702   Gonadotropin, chorionic (hCG); quantitative

84703   qualitative

(For urine pregnancy test by visual color comparison, use 81025)

(84800 has been deleted. To report, use 84443)

(84810 has been deleted. To report, use 80200)

84830   Ovulation tests, by visual color comparison methods for human luteinizing hormone

84999   Unlisted chemistry procedure

Hematology and Coagulation

(For blood banking procedures, see **Transfusion Medicine**)

(Agglutinins, see **Immunology**)

(Antiplasmin, use 85410)

(Antithrombin III, see 85300, 85301)

(85000 has been deleted. To report, use 85002)

85002   Bleeding time

(85003 has been deleted. To report, use 85999)

(85005 has been deleted)

85007   Blood count; manual differential WBC count (includes RBC morphology and platelet estimation)

85008   manual blood smear examination without differential parameters

(See also 85585)

(For other fluids (eg, CSF), see 89050, 89051)

85009   differential WBC count, buffy coat

(85012 has been deleted)

(Eosinophils, nasal smear, use 89190)

85013   spun microhematocrit

85014   other than spun hematocrit

85018   hemoglobin

(For other hemoglobin determination, see 83020-83069)

(For immunoassay, hemoglobin, fecal, use 86683)

85021   hemogram, automated (RBC, WBC, Hgb, Hct and indices only)

85022   hemogram, automated, and manual differential WBC count (CBC)

85023   hemogram and platelet count, automated, and manual differential WBC count (CBC)

85024   hemogram and platelet count, automated, and automated partial differential WBC count (CBC)

85025   hemogram and platelet count, automated, and automated complete differential WBC count (CBC)

85027   hemogram and platelet count, automated

(85028 has been deleted. To report, see 85023-85025)

(85029, 85030 have been deleted. To report, see 85021-85027)

85031   Blood count; hemogram, manual, complete CBC (RBC, WBC, Hgb, Hct, differential and indices)

85041   red blood cell (RBC) only

(See also 85021-85031, 89050)

85044   reticulocyte count, manual

85045   reticulocyte count, flow cytometry

85046   reticulocytes, hemoglobin concentration

85048   white blood cell (WBC)

(See also 85021-85031)

85060   Blood smear, peripheral, interpretation by physician with written report

▶(85095 has been deleted. To report, use 38220)◀

(85096 has been deleted. For interpretation of smear, use 85097; for cell block interpretation, use 88305)

▲ **85097**   Bone marrow, smear interpretation

(85100 has been deleted. To report, use ▶38220◀ and 85097)

(85101 has been deleted. For aspiration, use ▶38220)◀

(For special stains, see 85540, 88312, 88313)

▶(85102 has been deleted. To report, use 38221)◀

(For bone biopsy, see 20220, 20225, 20240, 20245, 20250, 20251)

(85103, 85105 have been deleted. For bone marrow biopsy interpretation, use 88305)

(85109 has been deleted)

(85120 has been deleted. To report, see 38230-38240)

85130   Chromogenic substrate assay

(85150, 85160, 85165 have been deleted)

(Circulating anti-coagulant screen (mixing studies), see 85611, 85732)

85170   Clot retraction

(85171, 85172 have been deleted)

85175   Clot lysis time, whole blood dilution

(Clotting factor I (fibrinogen), see 85384, 85385)

85210   Clotting; factor II, prothrombin, specific

(See also 85610-85613)

85220   factor V (AcG or proaccelerin), labile factor

85230   factor VII (proconvertin, stable factor)

85240   factor VIII (AHG), one stage

(85242 has been deleted)

85244   factor VIII related antigen

85245   factor VIII, VW factor, ristocetin cofactor

85246   factor VIII, VW factor antigen

85247   factor VIII, von Willebrand factor, multimetric analysis

85250   factor IX (PTC or Christmas)

85260   factor X (Stuart-Prower)

85270   factor XI (PTA)

85280   factor XII (Hageman)

85290   factor XIII (fibrin stabilizing)

85291   factor XIII (fibrin stabilizing), screen solubility

85292   prekallikrein assay (Fletcher factor assay)

85293   high molecular weight kininogen assay (Fitzgerald factor assay)

85300   Clotting inhibitors or anticoagulants; antithrombin III, activity

85301   antithrombin III, antigen assay

85302   protein C, antigen

85303   protein C, activity

85305   protein S, total

85306   protein S, free

85307   Activated Protein C (APC) resistance assay

(85310, 85311 have been deleted)

(85320 has been deleted)

(85330 has been deleted. To report, use 85335)

85335   Factor inhibitor test

85337   Thrombomodulin

(For mixing studies for inhibitors, use 85732)

(85340, 85341 have been deleted)

85345   Coagulation time; Lee and White

85347   activated

85348   other methods

(Differential count, see 85007 et seq)

(Duke bleeding time, use 85002)

(Eosinophils, nasal smear, use 89190)

85360   Euglobulin lysis

(Fetal hemoglobin, see 83030, 83033, 85460)

85362   Fibrin(ogen) degradation (split) products (FDP)(FSP); agglutination slide, semiquantitative

(85363, 85364 have been deleted)

(85365 has been deleted. To report, use 86320)

(Immunoelectrophoresis, use 86320)

85366   paracoagulation

(85367 has been deleted)

(85368 has been deleted. To report, use 85366)

(85369 has been deleted)

85370   quantitative

(85371 has been deleted. To report, see 85384, 85385)

(85372 has been deleted)

(85376, 85377 have been deleted. To report, see 85384, 85385)

85378   Fibrin degradation products, D-dimer; semiquantitative

85379   quantitative

85384   Fibrinogen; activity

85385   antigen

85390   Fibrinolysins or coagulopathy screen, interpretation and report

(85392 has been deleted)

(85395 has been deleted)

(85398 has been deleted)

85400   Fibrinolytic factors and inhibitors; plasmin

85410   alpha-2 antiplasmin

85415   plasminogen activator

85420   plasminogen, except antigenic assay

85421   plasminogen, antigenic assay

(85426 has been deleted. For von Willebrand factor assay, see 85245-85247)

(Fragility, red blood cell, see 85547, 85555-85557)

85441   Heinz bodies; direct

85445   induced, acetyl phenylhydrazine

(Hematocrit (PCV), see 85014, 85021-85031)

(Hemoglobin, see 83020-83068, 85018-85031)

85460   Hemoglobin or RBCs, fetal, for fetomaternal hemorrhage; differential lysis (Kleihauer-Betke)

(See also 83030, 83033)

(Hemogram, see 85021-85031)

(Hemolysins, see 86940, 86941)

85461   rosette

85475   Hemolysin, acid

(See also 86940, 86941)

85520   Heparin assay

85525   Heparin neutralization

85530   Heparin-protamine tolerance test

▶(85535 has been deleted. To report use 85536)◀

85536   Iron stain, peripheral blood

(For iron stains on bone marrow or other tissues with physician evaluation, use 88313)

(85538 has been deleted. For leder stain, esterase, blood or bone marrow, use 88319)

85540   Leukocyte alkaline phosphatase with count

(85544 has been deleted)

85547   Mechanical fragility, RBC

(85548 has been deleted. To report, use 85008)

85549   Muramidase

(Nitroblue tetrazolium dye test, use 86384)

85555   Osmotic fragility, RBC; unincubated

(85556 has been deleted)

85557   incubated

(Packed cell volume, use 85013)

(Partial thromboplastin time, see 85730, 85732)

(Parasites, blood (eg, malaria smears), use 87207)

(Plasmin, use 85400)

(Plasminogen, use 85420)

(Plasminogen activator, use 85415)

(85560 has been deleted. For peroxidase stain, WBC, use 88319)

(85575 has been deleted)

85576   Platelet; aggregation (in vitro), each agent

(85577 has been deleted)

(85580 has been deleted. To report, use 85590)

85585   estimation on smear, only

(See also 85008)

85590   manual count

85595   automated count

85597   Platelet neutralization

85610   Prothrombin time;

85611   substitution, plasma fractions, each

85612   Russell viper venom time (includes venom); undiluted

85613   diluted

(85614 has been deleted)

(85615 has been deleted)

(85618 has been deleted)

(Red blood cell count, see 85021, 85031, 85041)

(85630 has been deleted. To report, see 85021- 85027)

(85632 has been deleted)

85635   Reptilase test

(Reticulocyte count, see 85044, 85045)

(85650 has been deleted)

85651   Sedimentation rate, erythrocyte; non-automated

85652   automated

85660   Sickling of RBC, reduction

(Hemoglobin electrophoresis, use 83020)

(Smears (eg, for parasites, malaria), use 87207)

(85665 has been deleted. For plasminogen activator, use 85415)

(85667 has been deleted)

85670   Thrombin time; plasma

85675   titer

(85700 has been deleted)

85705   Thromboplastin inhibition; tissue

(85710, 85711 have been deleted)

(85720 has been deleted)

(For individual clotting factors, see 85245-85247)

85730   Thromboplastin time, partial (PTT); plasma or whole blood

85732   substitution, plasma fractions, each

85810   Viscosity

(85820 has been deleted. To report, use 85810)

(von Willebrand factor assay, see 85245-85247)

(WBC count, see 85021-85031, 85048, 89050)

85999   Unlisted hematology and coagulation procedure

Immunology

(Acetylcholine receptor antibody, see 86255, 86256)

(Actinomyces, antibodies to, use 86602)

(Adrenal cortex antibodies, see 86255, 86256)

▶(For tuberculosis test, cell mediated immunity measurement of gamma interferon antigen response, use Category III code 0010T)◀

86000   Agglutinins, febrile (eg, Brucella, Francisella, Murine typhus, Q fever, Rocky Mountain spotted fever, scrub typhus), each antigen

(For antibodies to infectious agents, see 86602-86804)

86001   Allergen specific IgG quantitative or semiquantitative, each allergen

(86002 has been deleted)

(Agglutinins and autohemolysins, see 86940, 86941)

86003   Allergen specific IgE; quantitative or semiquantitative, each allergen

(For total quantitative IgE, use 82785)

(86004 has been deleted. To report, see 86940, 86941)

86005   qualitative, multiallergen screen (dipstick, paddle or disk)

(For total qualitative IgE, use 83518)

(Alpha-1 antitrypsin, see 82103, 82104)

(Alpha-1 feto-protein, see 82105, 82106)

(Anti-AChR (acetylcholine receptor) antibody titer, see 86255, 86256)

(86006 has been deleted. To report, see 83519, 86318, 86403)

(86007, 86008, 86009 have been deleted)

(86011 has been deleted. To report, use 86021)

(86012 has been deleted. To report, use 86978)

(86013 has been deleted)

(86014 has been deleted. To report, use 86022)

(86016 has been deleted. To report, use 86850)

(86017 has been deleted. To report, see 86850 and 86901)

(86018 has been deleted)

(86019 has been deleted. To report, use 86860)

(Anticardiolipin antibody, use 86147)

(Anti-DNA, use 86225)

(Anti-deoxyribonuclease titer, use 86215)

86021 Antibody identification; leukocyte antibodies

86022   platelet antibodies

86023   platelet associated immunoglobulin assay

(86024 has been deleted. For RBC antibodies, use 86870)

(86026, 86028 have been deleted)

(86031 has been deleted. To report, use 86880)

(86032 has been deleted. To report, use 86885)

(86033 has been deleted. To report, use 86886)

(86034 has been deleted. To report, see 86880-86886 and 86971)

(86035 has been deleted. To report, use 86970)

86038 Antinuclear antibodies (ANA);

86039   titer

(86045 has been deleted)

(Antistreptococcal antibody, ie, anti-DNAse, use 86215)

(Antistreptokinase titer, use 86590)

86060 Antistreptolysin O; titer

(For antibodies to infectious agents, see 86602-86804)

86063   screen

(For antibodies to infectious agents, see 86602-86804)

(86064 has been deleted. For antitrypsin, alpha-1 use 82103, for phenotyping use 82104)

(86066 has been deleted. To report, use 82104)

(86067 has been deleted. To report, use 82103)

(86068 has been deleted. For blood compatibility test, see 86920-86922)

(Blastomyces, antibodies to, use 86612)

(86069 has been deleted)

(86070 has been deleted. To report, use 86920)

(86072 has been deleted)

(86073 has been deleted. To report, see 86156, 86157, 86904)

(86074 has been deleted)

(86075, 86076 have been deleted)

86077 Blood bank physician services; difficult cross match and/or evaluation of irregular antibody(s), interpretation and written report

86078   investigation of transfusion reaction including suspicion of transmissible disease, interpretation and written report

86079   authorization for deviation from standard blood banking procedures (eg, use of outdated blood, transfusion of Rh incompatible units), with written report

(86080 has been deleted. For blood typing, see 86900-86910)

(86082 has been deleted. To report, see 86900, 86901)

(86083 has been deleted. To report, use 86850 and 86900 or 86901)

(86084 has been deleted. To report, use 86903)

(86085 has been deleted. To report, use 86904)

(86090 has been deleted)

(86095 has been deleted. To report, use 86905)

(86096 has been deleted)

(86100 has been deleted. To report, use 86901)

(86105 has been deleted. To report, use 86906)

(86115 has been deleted)

(86120 has been deleted. To report, use 86905)

(86128 has been deleted. To report, use 86890)

(86129 has been deleted)

(86130 has been deleted. To report, use 86891)

(86131, 86134, 86138 and 86139 have been deleted)

(Brucella, antibodies to, use 86622)

(Candida, antibodies to, use 86628. For skin testing, use 86485)

86140 C-reactive protein;

(Candidiasis, use 86628)

● **86141**   high sensitivity (hsCRP)

86146 Beta 2 Glycoprotein I antibody, each

86147 Cardiolipin (phospholipid) antibody, each Ig class

86148 Anti-phosphatidylserine (phospholipid) antibody

(86149 has been deleted. To report, use 82378)

(86151 has been deleted. To report, use 82378)

86155 Chemotaxis assay, specify method

(Clostridium difficile toxin, use 87230)

(Coccidioides, antibodies to, see 86635. For skin testing, use 86490)

86156 Cold agglutinin; screen

86157   titer

(86158 has been deleted)

(86159 has been deleted. To report, see 86160 and 86161)

86160 Complement; antigen, each component

86161   functional activity, each component

86162   total hemolytic (CH50)

(86163, 86164 have been deleted. To report, see 86160 and 86161)

86171 Complement fixation tests, each antigen

(Coombs test, see 86880-86886)

86185 Counterimmunoelectrophoresis, each antigen

(86201, 86202 have been deleted)

(Cryptococcus, antibodies to, use 86641)

(86209 has been deleted. To report, use 86999)

86215 Deoxyribonuclease, antibody

86225 Deoxyribonucleic acid (DNA) antibody; native or double stranded

(Echinococcus, antibodies to, see code for specific method)

(For HIV antibody tests, see 86701-86703)

86226   single stranded

(Anti D.S., DNA, IFA, eg, using C.Lucilae, see 86255 and 86256)

(86227, 86228 have been deleted. To report, use 86317)

(86229 has been deleted)

86235 Extractable nuclear antigen, antibody to, any method (eg, nRNP, SS-A, SS-B, Sm, RNP, Sc170, J01), each antibody

(86240, 86241 have been deleted)

86243 Fc receptor

(86244 has been deleted. To report fetoprotein, alpha-1, see 82105, 82106)

(86245 has been deleted)

(Filaria, antibodies to, see code for specific method)

86255 Fluorescent noninfectious agent antibody; screen, each antibody

86256   titer, each antibody

(Fluorescent technique for antigen identification in tissue, use 88346; for indirect fluorescence, use 88347)

(86265 has been deleted. To report, use 86930)

(86266 has been deleted. To report, use 86931)

(FTA, see 86781)

(86267 has been deleted. To report, use 86932)

(Gel (agar) diffusion tests, use 86331)

(86272, 86273 have been deleted)

(86274 has been deleted. To report, use 90742)

86277 Growth hormone, human (HGH), antibody

86280 Hemagglutination inhibition test (HAI)

(For rubella, use 86762)

(86281 has been deleted. To report, use 85475)

(86282 has been deleted. To report, use 86940)

(86283 has been deleted. To report, use 86941)

(86285, 86286 have been deleted)

(86287 has been deleted. To report, use 87340)

(86289 has been deleted. To report, use 86704)

(For antibodies to infectious agents, see 86602-86804)

(86290 has been deleted. To report, use 86705)

(86291 has been deleted. To report, use 86706)

(86293 has been deleted. To report, use 87350)

86294 Immunoassay for tumor antigen, qualitative or semiquantitative (eg, bladder tumor antigen)

(86295 has been deleted. To report, use 86707)

(86296 has been deleted. To report, use 86708)

(86297 has been deleted. To report, use 86708)

(86299 has been deleted. To report, use 86709)

86300 Immunoassay for tumor antigen, quantitative; CA 15-3 (27.29)

86301   CA 19-9

(86302 has been deleted. To report, use 86803)

(86303 has been deleted. To report, use 86804)

86304   CA 125

▶(For measurement of serum HER-2/neu oncoprotein, see 83950)◀

(86306 has been deleted. To report, use 87380)

(For hepatitis delta agent, antibody, use 86692)

86308 Heterophile antibodies; screening

(For antibodies to infectious agents, see 86602-86804)

86309   titer

(For antibodies to infectious agents, see 86602-86804)

86310   titers after absorption with beef cells and guinea pig kidney

(Histoplasma, antibodies to, use 86698. For skin testing, use 86510)

(For antibodies to infectious agents, see 86602-86804)

(86311 has been deleted. To report, see 87390, 87391)

(86312 has been deleted. To report, see 86701-86703)

(86313 has been deleted. To report, use 87449)

(86314 has been deleted. To report, use 86689)

(86315 has been deleted. To report, use 87450)

(Human growth hormone antibody, use 86277)

▲=Revised Code   ●=New Code

86316   Immunoassay for tumor antigen; other antigen, quantitative (eg, CA 50, 72-4, 549), each

86317   Immunoassay for infectious agent antibody, quantitative, not otherwise specified

(For immunoassay techniques for antigens, see 83516, 83518, 83519, 83520, 87301-87450, 87810-87899)

(For particle agglutination procedures, use 86403)

86318   Immunoassay for infectious agent antibody, qualitative or semiquantitative, single step method (eg, reagent strip)

(86319 has been deleted. To report immunoassays for drugs, see 80100-80103)

86320   Immunoelectrophoresis; serum

▲ **86325**   other fluids (eg, urine, cerebrospinal fluid) with concentration

86327   crossed (2-dimensional assay)

86329   Immunodiffusion; not elsewhere specified

86331   gel diffusion, qualitative (Ouchterlony), each antigen or antibody

86332   Immune complex assay

(86333 has been deleted. To report, use 86332)

86334   Immunofixation electrophoresis

(86335 has been deleted)

● **86336**   Inhibin A

86337   Insulin antibodies

(86338 has been deleted. To report, use 86337)

86340   Intrinsic factor antibodies

(Leptospira, antibodies to, use 86720)

(Leukoagglutinins, use 86021)

86341   Islet cell antibody

(86342 has been deleted. To report, use 86945)

86343   Leukocyte histamine release test (LHR)

86344   Leukocyte phagocytosis

(86345, 86346, 86347 have been deleted)

(86349 has been deleted. To report, use 86950)

(86351 has been deleted)

86353   Lymphocyte transformation, mitogen (phytomitogen) or antigen induced blastogenesis

(Lymphocytes immunophenotyping, use 88180 for cytometry; see 88342, 88346 for microscopic techniques)

(86357 has been deleted. To report, see 88180, 88342, 88346)

(86358 has been deleted. To report, see 88180, 88342, 88346)

(Malaria antibodies, use 86750)

86359   T cells; total count

86360   absolute CD4 and CD8 count, including ratio

86361   absolute CD4 count

(86365 has been deleted)

86376   Microsomal antibodies (eg, thyroid or liver-kidney), each

(86377 has been deleted. To report, use 86376)

86378   Migration inhibitory factor test (MIF)

(Mitochondrial antibody, liver, see 86255, 86256)

(Mononucleosis, see 86308-86310)

86382   Neutralization test, viral

86384   Nitroblue tetrazolium dye test (NTD)

(Ouchterlony diffusion, use 86331)

(86385, 86386 have been deleted. To report, see 86910, 86911)

(86388, 86389, 86391 have been deleted)

(Platelet antibodies, see 86022, 86023)

(86392, 86393, 86398 have been deleted)

(86402 has been deleted)

86403   Particle agglutination; screen, each antibody

(86404 has been deleted. To report, use 86965)

(86405 has been deleted)

86406   titer, each antibody

(Pregnancy test, see 84702, 84703)

(86410 has been deleted. To report, use 86970)

(86411 has been deleted. To report, use 86971)

(86412 has been deleted. To report, use 86972)

(86415, 86416 have been deleted)

(86417 has been deleted. To report, use 86975)

(86418 has been deleted. To report, use 86976)

(86419 has been deleted. To report, use 86977)

(86420 has been deleted. To report, use 86978)

(86421-86423 have been deleted. To report, see 82785, 83518, 86003, 86005)

(86424, 86425, 86427 have been deleted)

(Rapid plasma reagin test (RPR), see 86592, 86593)

86430   Rheumatoid factor; qualitative

86431   quantitative

(Serologic test for syphilis, see 86592, 86593)

(86450 has been deleted)

(86455 has been deleted. To report, use 86586)

(86460, 86470, 86480 have been deleted)

86485   Skin test; candida

(For antibody, candida, use 86628)

86490   coccidioidomycosis

(86495, 86500 have been deleted)

86510   histoplasmosis

(For histoplasma, antibody, use 86698)

(86520, 86530 have been deleted)

(86540 has been deleted. For mumps antibody, use 86735)

(86550, 86565, 86570 have been deleted)

86580   tuberculosis, intradermal

86585   tuberculosis, tine test

▶(For tuberculosis test, cell mediated immunity measurement of gamma interferon antigen response, use Category III code 0010T)◀

, (For skin tests for allergy, see 95010-95199)

(Smooth muscle antibody, see 86255, 86256)

(Sporothrix, antibodies to, see code for specific method)

86586   unlisted antigen, each

(86587 has been deleted. To report, use 86985)

(86588 has been deleted. To report, see 86403, 87081, 87430, or 87880)

86590   Streptokinase, antibody

(For antibodies to infectious agents, see 86602-86804)

(Streptolysin O antibody, see antistreptolysin O, 86060, 86063)

86592   Syphilis test; qualitative (eg, VDRL, RPR, ART)

(For antibodies to infectious agents, see 86602-86804)

86593   quantitative

(For antibodies to infectious agents, see 86602-86804)

(Tetanus antibody, use 86774)

(Thyroglobulin antibody, use 86800)

(Thyroglobulin, use 84432)

(Thyroid microsomal antibody, use 86376)

(86594 has been deleted. To report, see 86376 and 86800)

(86595 has been deleted)

(86597 has been deleted. To report see 86812-86822)

(86600 has been deleted)

(For toxoplasma antibody, see 86777-86778)

The following codes (86602-86804) are qualitative or semiquantitative immunoassays performed by multiple step methods for the detection of antibodies to infectious agents. For immunoassays by single step method (eg, reagent strips), use code 86318. Procedures for the identification of antibodies should be coded as precisely as possible. For example, an antibody to a virus could be coded with increasing specificity for virus, family, genus, species, or type. In some cases, further precision may be added to codes by specifying the class of immunoglobulin being detected. When multiple tests are done to detect antibodies to organisms classified more precisely than the specificity allowed by available codes, it is appropriate to code each as a separate service. For example, a test for antibody to an enterovirus is coded as 86658. Coxsackie viruses are enteroviruses, but there are no codes for the individual species of enterovirus. If assays are performed for antibodies to coxsackie A and B species, each assay should be separately coded. Similarly, if multiple assays are performed for antibodies of different immunoglobulin classes, each assay should be coded separately.

For the detection of antibodies other than those to infectious agents, see specific antibody (eg, 86021, 86022, 86023, 86376, 86800, 86850-86870) or specific method (eg, 83516, 86255, 86256).

(For infectious agent/antigen detection, see 87260-87899)

86602   Antibody; actinomyces

86603   adenovirus

86606   Aspergillus

86609   bacterium, not elsewhere specified

86611   Bartonella

86612   Blastomyces

86615   Bordetella

86617   Borrelia burgdorferi (Lyme disease) confirmatory test (eg, Western blot or immunoblot)

86618   Borrelia burgdorferi (Lyme disease)

86619   Borrelia (relapsing fever)

86622   Brucella

86625   Campylobacter

86628   Candida

(For skin test, candida, use 86485)

(86630 has been deleted)

86631   Chlamydia

86632   Chlamydia, IgM

(For chlamydia antigen, see 87270, 87320. For fluorescent antibody technique, see 86255, 86256)

86635   Coccidioides

86638   Coxiella Brunetii (Q fever)

86641   Cryptococcus

86644   cytomegalovirus (CMV)

(For TORCH panel, use 80090)

86645	cytomegalovirus (CMV), IgM
86648	Diphtheria

(86650 has been deleted. To report, use 86781)

86651	encephalitis, California (La Crosse)
86652	encephalitis, Eastern equine
86653	encephalitis, St. Louis
86654	encephalitis, Western equine
86658	enterovirus (eg, coxsackie, echo, polio)

(86662 has been deleted. To report, use 86781)

(Trichinella, antibodies to, use 86784)

(Trypanosoma, antibodies to, see code for specific method)

(Tuberculosis, use 86580 for skin testing)

(Viral antibodies, see code for specific method)

86663	Epstein-Barr (EB) virus, early antigen (EA)
86664	Epstein-Barr (EB) virus, nuclear antigen (EBNA)
86665	Epstein-Barr (EB) virus, viral capsid (VCA)
86666	Ehrlichia
86668	Francisella Tularensis
86671	fungus, not elsewhere specified
86674	Giardia Lamblia
86677	Helicobacter pylori

(86681 has been deleted. To report, see 86255, 86256)

86682	helminth, not elsewhere specified

►(86683 has been deleted. To report, use 82274)◄

86684	Hemophilus influenza

(86685 has been deleted. To report, see 86255, 86256)

86687	HTLV-I
86688	HTLV-II
86689	HTLV or HIV antibody, confirmatory test (eg, Western Blot)
86692	hepatitis, delta agent

(For hepatitis delta agent, antigen, use 87380)

86694	herpes simplex, non-specific type test

(For TORCH panel, use 80090)

86695	herpes simplex, type 1
86696	herpes simplex, type 2
86698	histoplasma
86701	HIV-1
86702	HIV-2
86703	HIV-1 and HIV-2, single assay

(For HIV-1 antigen, use 87390)

(For HIV-2 antigen, use 87391)

(For confirmatory test for HIV antibody (eg, Western Blot), use 86689)

86704	Hepatitis B core antibody (HBcAb); total
86705	IgM antibody
86706	Hepatitis B surface antibody (HBsAb)
86707	Hepatitis Be antibody (HBeAb)
86708	Hepatitis A antibody (HAAb); total
86709	IgM antibody
86710	Antibody; influenza virus
86713	Legionella
86717	Leishmania
86720	Leptospira
86723	Listeria monocytogenes
86727	lymphocytic choriomeningitis
86729	Lymphogranuloma Venereum
86732	mucormycosis
86735	mumps
86738	Mycoplasma
86741	Neisseria meningitidis
86744	Nocardia
86747	parvovirus
86750	Plasmodium (malaria)
86753	protozoa, not elsewhere specified
86756	respiratory syncytial virus
86757	Rickettsia
86759	rotavirus
86762	rubella
86765	rubeola
86768	Salmonella
86771	Shigella
86774	tetanus
86777	Toxoplasma
86778	Toxoplasma, IgM
86781	Treponema Pallidum, confirmatory test (eg, FTA-abs)
86784	trichinella
86787	varicella-zoster

⊘ =Modifier '-51' Exempt ►◄=New or Revised Text ✛=Add-on Code

86790	virus, not elsewhere specified
86793	Yersinia
86800	Thyroglobulin antibody
	(For thyroglobulin, use 84432)
86803	Hepatitis C antibody;
86804	confirmatory test (eg, immunoblot)

Tissue Typing

(For pretransplant cross-match, see appropriate code or codes)

86805	Lymphocytotoxicity assay, visual crossmatch; with titration
86806	without titration
86807	Serum screening for cytotoxic percent reactive antibody (PRA); standard method
86808	quick method
	(86810 has been deleted)
86812	HLA typing; A, B, or C (eg, A10, B7, B27), single antigen
86813	A, B, or C, multiple antigens
86816	DR/DQ, single antigen
86817	DR/DQ, multiple antigens
86821	lymphocyte culture, mixed (MLC)
86822	lymphocyte culture, primed (PLC)
86849	Unlisted immunology procedure

Transfusion Medicine

(For apheresis, use 36520)

(For therapeutic phlebotomy, use 99195)

86850	Antibody screen, RBC, each serum technique
86860	Antibody elution (RBC), each elution
86870	Antibody identification, RBC antibodies, each panel for each serum technique
86880	Antihuman globulin test (Coombs test); direct, each antiserum
86885	indirect, qualitative, each antiserum
86886	indirect, titer, each antiserum
86890	Autologous blood or component, collection processing and storage; predeposited
86891	intra- or postoperative salvage
	(For physician services to autologous donors, see 99201-99204)

86900	Blood typing; ABO
86901	Rh (D)
86903	antigen screening for compatible blood unit using reagent serum, per unit screened
86904	antigen screening for compatible unit using patient serum, per unit screened
86905	RBC antigens, other than ABO or Rh (D), each
86906	Rh phenotyping, complete
86910	Blood typing, for paternity testing, per individual; ABO, Rh and MN
86911	each additional antigen system
86915	Bone marrow or peripheral stem cell harvest, modification or treatment to eliminate cell type(s) (eg, T-cells, metastatic carcinoma)
86920	Compatibility test each unit; immediate spin technique
86921	incubation technique
86922	antiglobulin technique
86927	Fresh frozen plasma, thawing, each unit
86930	Frozen blood, preparation for freezing, each unit;
86931	with thawing
86932	with freezing and thawing
86940	Hemolysins and agglutinins; auto, screen, each
86941	incubated
86945	Irradiation of blood product, each unit
86950	Leukocyte transfusion
	(For leukapheresis, use 36520)
86965	Pooling of platelets or other blood products
86970	Pretreatment of RBCs for use in RBC antibody detection, identification, and/or compatibility testing; incubation with chemical agents or drugs, each
86971	incubation with enzymes, each
86972	by density gradient separation
86975	Pretreatment of serum for use in RBC antibody identification; incubation with drugs, each
86976	by dilution
86977	incubation with inhibitors, each
86978	by differential red cell absorption using patient RBCs or RBCs of known phenotype, each absorption
86985	Splitting of blood or blood products, each unit
86999	Unlisted transfusion medicine procedure

Microbiology

Includes bacteriology, mycology, parasitology, and virology.

Presumptive identification of microorganisms is defined as identification by colony morphology, growth on selective media, Gram stains, or up to three tests (eg, catalase, oxidase, indole, urease). Definitive identification of microorganisms is defined as an identification to the genus or species level that requires additional tests (eg, biochemical panels, slide cultures). If additional studies involve molecular probes, chromatography, or immunologic techniques, these should be separately coded in addition to definitive identification codes (87140-87158). For multiple specimens/sites use modifier '-59'. For repeat laboratory tests performed on the same day, use modifier '-91'.

87001 Animal inoculation, small animal; with observation

87003 with observation and dissection

87015 Concentration (any type), for infectious agents

(Do not report 87015 in conjunction with 87177)

87040 Culture, bacterial; blood, with isolation and presumptive identification of isolates (includes anaerobic culture, if appropriate)

▲ **87045** feces, with isolation and preliminary examination (eg, KIA, LIA), Salmonella and Shigella species

87046 stool, additional pathogens, isolation and preliminary examination (eg, Campylobacter, Yersinia, Vibrio, E. coli 0157), each plate

(87060 has been deleted. To report, use 87070 or 87081)

87070 any other source except urine, blood or stool, with isolation and presumptive identification of isolates

(For urine, use 87088)

87071 quantitative, aerobic with isolation and presumptive identification of isolates, any source except urine, blood or stool

(For urine, use 87088)

(87072 has been deleted. To report, use 87076 or 87077)

87073 quantitative, anaerobic with isolation and presumptive identification of isolates, any source except urine, blood or stool

(For definitive identification of isolates, use 87076 or 87077. For typing of isolates see 87140-87158)

87075 any source, anaerobic with isolation and presumptive identification of isolates

87076 anaerobic isolate, additional methods required for definitive identification, each isolate

(For gas liquid chromatography (GLC) or high pressure liquid chromatography (HPLC), use 87143)

87077 aerobic isolate, additional methods required for definitive identification, each isolate

(For gas liquid chromatography (GLC) or high pressure liquid chromatography (HPLC), use 87143)

87081 Culture, presumptive, pathogenic organisms, screening only;

(87082 and 87083 have been deleted. To report, use 87081)

87084 with colony estimation from density chart

(87085 has been deleted. To report, use 87086)

87086 Culture, bacterial; quantitative colony count, urine

(87087 has been deleted. To report, use 87088)

87088 with isolation and presumptive identification of isolates, urine

87101 Culture, fungi (mold or yeast) isolation, with presumptive identification of isolates; skin, hair, or nail

87102 other source (except blood)

87103 blood

87106 Culture, fungi, definitive identification, each organism; yeast

(Use 87106 in addition to codes 87101, 87102, or 87103 when appropriate)

87107 mold

87109 Culture, mycoplasma, any source

87110 Culture, chlamydia, any source

(For immunofluorescence staining of shell vials, use 87140)

87116 Culture, tubercle or other acid-fast bacilli (eg, TB, AFB, mycobacteria) any source, with isolation and presumptive identification of isolates

(87117 has been deleted. For concentration, use 87015)

87118 Culture, mycobacterial, definitive identification, each isolate

(For nucleic acid probe identification, use 87149)

(For GLC or HPLC identification, use 87143)

87140 Culture, typing; immunofluorescent method, each antiserum

87143 gas liquid chromatography (GLC) or high pressure liquid chromatography (HPLC) method

(87145 has been deleted)

87147 immunologic method, other than immunofluoresence (eg, agglutination grouping), per antiserum

87149 identification by nucleic acid probe

(87151 has been deleted. To report, use 87147)

87152 identification by pulse field gel typing

(87155 has been deleted. To report, use 87147)

⊘ =Modifier '-51' Exempt ▶ ◀ =New or Revised Text ✚ =Add-on Code CPT 2002

87158	other methods

(87163 has been deleted. To report, use 87076 or 87077)

87164	Dark field examination, any source (eg, penile, vaginal, oral, skin); includes specimen collection
87166	without collection
87168	Macroscopic examination; arthropod
87169	parasite
87172	Pinworm exam (eg, cellophane tape prep)

(87173 has been deleted)

(87174 has been deleted)

(87175 has been deleted)

87176	Homogenization, tissue, for culture
87177	Ova and parasites, direct smears, concentration and identification

(Do not report 87177 in conjunction with 87015)

(For coccidia or microsporidia exam, use 87207)

(For trichrome, iron hemotoxylin and other special stains, use ▶88313◀)

(For nucleic acid probes in cytologic material, use 88365)

(For molecular diagnostics, see 83890-83898, 87470-87799)

(87178 has been deleted. To report, use 87797)

(87179 has been deleted. To report, use 87798)

87181	Susceptibility studies, antimicrobial agent; agar dilution method, per agent (eg, antibiotic gradient strip)
87184	disk method, per plate (12 or fewer agents)
87185	enzyme detection (eg, beta lactamase), per enzyme
87186	microdilution or agar dilution (minimum inhibitory concentration (MIC) or breakpoint), each multi-antimicrobial, per plate
✛ 87187	microdilution or agar dilution, minimum lethal concentration (MLC), each plate (List separately in addition to code for primary procedure)

(Use 87187 in conjuction with 87186 or 87188)

87188	macrobroth dilution method, each agent
87190	mycobacteria, proportion method, each agent

(For other mycobacterial susceptibility studies, see 87181, 87184, 87186, or 87188)

(87192 has been deleted. For fungal susceptibility studies, see 87181, 87184, 87186, 87187, or 87188)

87197	Serum bactericidal titer (Schlicter test)
● 87198	Cytomegalovirus, direct fluorescent antibody (DFA)
● 87199	Enterovirus, direct fluorescent antibody (DFA)

87205	Smear, primary source with interpretation; Gram or Giemsa stain for bacteria, fungi, or cell types
87206	fluorescent and/or acid fast stain for bacteria, fungi, parasites, viruses or cell types
87207	special stain for inclusion bodies or intracellular parasites (eg, malaria, coccidia, microsporidia, cytomegalovirus, herpes viruses)

(87208 has been deleted)

(For thick smear preparation, use 87015)

(For complex special stains, see 88312, 88313)

(For fat, meat, fibers, nasal eosinophils, and starch, see miscellaneous section)

87210	wet mount for infectious agents (eg, saline, India ink, KOH preps)

(For KOH examination of skin, hair or nails, see 87220)

(87211 has been deleted. To report, use 87177)

87220	Tissue examination by KOH slide of samples from skin, hair, or nails for fungi or ectoparasite ova or mites (eg, scabies)
87230	Toxin or antitoxin assay, tissue culture (eg, Clostridium difficile toxin)
87250	Virus isolation; inoculation of embryonated eggs, or small animal, includes observation and dissection
87252	tissue culture inoculation, observation, and presumptive identification by cytopathic effect
87253	tissue culture, additional studies or definitive identification (eg, hemabsorption, neutralization, immunofluoresence stain), each isolate

(Electron microscopy, use 88348)

(Inclusion bodies in tissue sections, see 88304-88309; in smears, see 87207-87210; in fluids, use 88106)

87254	shell vial, includes identification with immunofluorescence stain, each virus

(Report 87254 in addition to 87252 as appropriate)

These codes are intended for primary source only. For similar studies on culture material, refer to codes 87140-87158. Infectious agents by antigen detection, immunofluorescence microscopy, or nucleic acid probe techniques should be reported as precisely as possible. The most specific code possible should be reported. If there is no specific agent code, the general methodology code (eg, 87299, 87449, 87450, 87797, 87798, 87799, 87899) should be used. For identification of antibodies to many of the listed infectious agents, see 86602-86804. ▶When separate assays are performed for different species or strain(s) of organisms, each assay should be reported separately.◀

87260	Infectious agent antigen detection by immunofluorescent technique; adenovirus
87265	Bordetella pertussis/parapertussis
87270	Chlamydia trachomatis

87272	cryptosporidium/giardia
87273	Herpes simplex virus type 2
87274	Herpes simplex virus type 1
87275	Influenza B virus
87276	influenza A virus
87277	Legionella micdadei
87278	Legionella pneumophila
87279	Parainfluenza virus, each type
87280	respiratory syncytial virus
87281	Pneumocystis carinii
87283	Rubeola
87285	Treponema pallidum
87290	Varicella zoster virus
87299	not otherwise specified, each organism

87300 Infectious agent antigen detection by immunofluorescent technique, polyvalent for multiple organisms, each polyvalent antiserum

(For physician evaluation of infectious disease agents by immunofluorescence, use 88346)

87301 Infectious agent antigen detection by enzyme immunoassay technique, qualitative or semiquantitative, multiple step method; adenovirus enteric types 40/41

87320	Chlamydia trachomatis
87324	Clostridium difficile toxin(s)
87327	Cryptococcus neoformans

(For Cryptococcus latex agglutination, use 86403)

87328	cryptosporidium/giardia
87332	cytomegalovirus
87335	Escherichia coli 0157

(For giardia antigen, use 87328)

87336	Entamoeba histolytica dispar group
87337	Entamoeba histolytica group
87338	Helicobacter pylori, stool
87339	Helicobacter pylori

(For H. pylori, stool, use 87338. For H. pylori, breath and blood by mass spectrometry, see 83013, 83014. For H. pylori, liquid scintillation counter, see 78267, 78268)

87340	hepatitis B surface antigen (HBsAg)
87341	hepatitis B surface antigen (HBsAg) neutralization
87350	hepatitis Be antigen (HBeAg)
87380	hepatitis, delta agent
87385	Histoplasma capsulatum
87390	HIV-1
87391	HIV-2

87400	Influenza, A or B, each
87420	respiratory syncytial virus
87425	rotavirus
87427	Shiga-like toxin
87430	Streptococcus, group A

87449 Infectious agent antigen detection by enzyme immunoassay technique qualitative or semiquantitative; multiple step method, not otherwise specified, each organism

87450 single step method, not otherwise specified, each organism

87451 multiple step method, polyvalent for multiple organisms, each polyvalent antiserum

87470 Infectious agent detection by nucleic acid (DNA or RNA); Bartonella henselae and Bartonella quintana, direct probe technique

87471 Bartonella henselae and Bartonella quintana, amplified probe technique

87472 Bartonella henselae and Bartonella quintana, quantification

87475	Borrelia burgdorferi, direct probe technique
87476	Borrelia burgdorferi, amplified probe technique
87477	Borrelia burgdorferi, quantification
87480	Candida species, direct probe technique
87481	Candida species, amplified probe technique
87482	Candida species, quantification
87485	Chlamydia pneumoniae, direct probe technique
87486	Chlamydia pneumoniae, amplified probe technique
87487	Chlamydia pneumoniae, quantification
87490	Chlamydia trachomatis, direct probe technique
87491	Chlamydia trachomatis, amplified probe technique
87492	Chlamydia trachomatis, quantification
87495	cytomegalovirus, direct probe technique
87496	cytomegalovirus, amplified probe technique
87497	cytomegalovirus, quantification
87510	Gardnerella vaginalis, direct probe technique
87511	Gardnerella vaginalis, amplified probe technique
87512	Gardnerella vaginalis, quantification
87515	hepatitis B virus, direct probe technique
87516	hepatitis B virus, amplified probe technique
87517	hepatitis B virus, quantification
87520	hepatitis C, direct probe technique
87521	hepatitis C, amplified probe technique
87522	hepatitis C, quantification

⊘ =Modifier '-51' Exempt   ▶ ◀ =New or Revised Text   ✚ =Add-on Code   CPT 2002

87525	hepatitis G, direct probe technique
87526	hepatitis G, amplified probe technique
87527	hepatitis G, quantification
87528	Herpes simplex virus, direct probe technique
87529	Herpes simplex virus, amplified probe technique
87530	Herpes simplex virus, quantification
87531	Herpes virus-6, direct probe technique
87532	Herpes virus-6, amplified probe technique
87533	Herpes virus-6, quantification
87534	HIV-1, direct probe technique
87535	HIV-1, amplified probe technique
87536	HIV-1, quantification
87537	HIV-2, direct probe technique
87538	HIV-2, amplified probe technique
87539	HIV-2, quantification
87540	Legionella pneumophila, direct probe technique
87541	Legionella pneumophila, amplified probe technique
87542	Legionella pneumophila, quantification
87550	Mycobacteria species, direct probe technique
87551	Mycobacteria species, amplified probe technique
87552	Mycobacteria species, quantification
87555	Mycobacteria tuberculosis, direct probe technique
87556	Mycobacteria tuberculosis, amplified probe technique
87557	Mycobacteria tuberculosis, quantification
87560	Mycobacteria avium-intracellulare, direct probe technique
87561	Mycobacteria avium-intracellulare, amplified probe technique
87562	Mycobacteria avium-intracellulare, quantification
87580	Mycoplasma pneumoniae, direct probe technique
87581	Mycoplasma pneumoniae, amplified probe technique
87582	Mycoplasma pneumoniae, quantification
87590	Neisseria gonorrhoeae, direct probe technique
87591	Neisseria gonorrhoeae, amplified probe technique
87592	Neisseria gonorrhoeae, quantification
87620	papillomavirus, human, direct probe technique
87621	papillomavirus, human, amplified probe technique
87622	papillomavirus, human, quantification
87650	Streptococcus, group A, direct probe technique
87651	Streptococcus, group A, amplified probe technique
87652	Streptococcus, group A, quantification

87797	Infectious agent detection by nucleic acid (DNA or RNA), not otherwise specified; direct probe technique, each organism
87798	amplified probe technique, each organism
87799	quantification, each organism
87800	Infectious agent detection by nucleic acid (DNA or RNA), multiple organisms; direct probe(s) technique
87801	amplified probe(s) technique
● 87802	Infectious agent antigen detection by immunoassay with direct optical observation; Streptococcus, group B
● 87803	Clostridium difficile toxin A
● 87804	Influenza
87810	Infectious agent detection by immunoassay with direct optical observation; Chlamydia trachomatis
87850	Neisseria gonorrhoeae
87880	Streptococcus, group A
87899	not otherwise specified
87901	Infectious agent genotype analysis by nucleic acid (DNA or RNA); HIV 1, reverse transcriptase and protease
	▶(For infectious agent drug susceptibility phenotype prediction for HIV-1, use Category III code 0023T)◀
● 87902	Hepatitis C virus
▲ 87903	Infectious agent phenotype analysis by nucleic acid (DNA or RNA) with drug resistance tissue culture analysis, HIV 1; first through 10 drugs tested
+ ▲ 87904	each additional 1 through 5 drugs tested (List separately in addition to code for primary procedure)
	(Use 87904 in conjunction with code 87903)
87999	Unlisted microbiology procedure

Anatomic Pathology

Postmortem Examination

Procedures 88000 through 88099 represent physician services only. Use modifier '-90' or 09990 for outside laboratory services.

88000	Necropsy (autopsy), gross examination only; without CNS
88005	with brain
88007	with brain and spinal cord
88012	infant with brain
88014	stillborn or newborn with brain
88016	macerated stillborn
88020	Necropsy (autopsy), gross and microscopic; without CNS
88025	with brain
88027	with brain and spinal cord

88028   infant with brain

88029   stillborn or newborn with brain

88036   Necropsy (autopsy), limited, gross and/or microscopic; regional

88037   single organ

88040   Necropsy (autopsy); forensic examination

88045   coroner's call

88099   Unlisted necropsy (autopsy) procedure

Cytopathology

88104   Cytopathology, fluids, washings or brushings, except cervical or vaginal; smears with interpretation

88106   filter method only with interpretation

88107   smears and filter preparation with interpretation

88108   Cytopathology, concentration technique, smears and interpretation (eg, Saccomanno technique)

(88109 has been deleted. For interpretation of smear, use 88104; for cell block interpretation, use 88305)

(For cervical or vaginal smears, see 88150-88155)

(For gastric intubation with lavage, see 89130-89141, 91055)

(For x-ray localization, use 74340)

88125   Cytopathology, forensic (eg, sperm)

88130   Sex chromatin identification; Barr bodies

88140   peripheral blood smear, polymorphonuclear drumsticks

(For Guard stain, use 88313)

Codes 88141-88155, 88164-88167 are used to report cervical or vaginal screening by various methods and to report physician interpretation services. Use codes 88150-88154 to report Pap smears that are examined using non-Bethesda reporting. Use codes 88164-88167 to report Pap smears that are examined using the Bethesda System of reporting. Use codes 88142-88145 to report specimens collected in fluid medium with automated thin layer preparation that are examined using any system of reporting (Bethesda or non-Bethesda). Within each of these three code families choose the one code that describes the screening method(s) used. Codes 88141 and 88155 should be reported in addition to the screening code chosen when the additional services are provided.

✛ 88141   Cytopathology, cervical or vaginal (any reporting system); requiring interpretation by physician (List separately in addition to code for technical service)

(Use 88141 in conjunction with codes 88142-88154, 88164-88167)

88142   Cytopathology, cervical or vaginal (any reporting system), collected in preservative fluid, automated thin layer preparation; manual screening under physician supervision

88143   with manual screening and rescreening under physician supervision

88144   with manual screening and computer-assisted rescreening under physician supervision

88145   with manual screening and computer-assisted rescreening using cell selection and review under physician supervision

88147   Cytopathology smears, cervical or vaginal; screening by automated system under physician supervision

88148   screening by automated system with manual rescreening under physician supervision

88150   Cytopathology, slides, cervical or vaginal; manual screening under physician supervision

(88151 has been deleted. To report, use 88141)

88152   with manual screening and computer-assisted rescreening under physician supervision

88153   with manual screening and rescreening under physician supervision

88154   with manual screening and computer-assisted rescreening using cell selection and review under physician supervision

✛ 88155   Cytopathology, slides, cervical or vaginal, definitive hormonal evaluation (eg, maturation index, karyopyknotic index, estrogenic index) (List separately in addition to code(s) for other technical and interpretation services)

(Use 88155 in conjunction with 88142-88154, 88164-88167)

(88156 has been deleted. To report, use 88164)

(88157 has been deleted. To report, use 88141)

(88158 has been deleted. To report, use 88166)

88160   Cytopathology, smears, any other source; screening and interpretation

88161   preparation, screening and interpretation

88162   extended study involving over 5 slides and/or multiple stains

(For obtaining specimen, see percutaneous needle biopsy under individual organ in **Surgery**)

(For aerosol collection of sputum, use 89350)

(For special stains, see 88312-88314)

88164   Cytopathology, slides, cervical or vaginal (the Bethesda System); manual screening under physician supervision

88165   with manual screening and rescreening under physician supervision

88166   with manual screening and computer-assisted rescreening under physician supervision

88167	with manual screening and computer-assisted rescreening using cell selection and review under physician supervision

▶(88170 has been deleted. To report, use 10021)◀

▶(88171 has been deleted. To report, use 10022)◀

88172 Cytopathology, evaluation of fine needle aspirate; immediate cytohistologic study to determine adequacy of specimen(s)

88173 interpretation and report

88180 Flow cytometry; each cell surface, cytoplasmic or nuclear marker

88182 cell cycle or DNA analysis

(For tumor morphometry and DNA and ploidy analysis by imaging techniques, use 88358)

88199 Unlisted cytopathology procedure

(For electron microscopy, see 88348, 88349)

Cytogenetic Studies

(For acetylcholinesterase, use 82013)

(For alpha-fetoprotein, serum or amniotic fluid, see 82105, 82106)

▶(For laser microdissection of cells from tissue sample, see 88380)◀

88230 Tissue culture for non-neoplastic disorders; lymphocyte

88233 skin or other solid tissue biopsy

88235 amniotic fluid or chorionic villus cells

88237 Tissue culture for neoplastic disorders; bone marrow, blood cells

88239 solid tumor

88240 Cryopreservation, freezing and storage of cells, each cell line

88241 Thawing and expansion of frozen cells, each aliquot

88245 Chromosome analysis for breakage syndromes; baseline Sister Chromatid Exchange (SCE), 20-25 cells

88248 baseline breakage, score 50-100 cells, count 20 cells, 2 karyotypes (eg, for ataxia telangiectasia, Fanconi anemia, fragile X)

88249 score 100 cells, clastogen stress (eg, diepoxybutane, mitomycin C, ionizing radiation, UV radiation)

(88250 has been deleted. To report, use 88248)

(88260 has been deleted. To report, use 88261)

88261 Chromosome analysis; count 5 cells, 1 karyotype, with banding

88262 count 15-20 cells, 2 karyotypes, with banding

88263 count 45 cells for mosaicism, 2 karyotypes, with banding

88264 analyze 20-25 cells

(88265 has been deleted. To report, use 88262)

88267 Chromosome analysis, amniotic fluid or chorionic villus, count 15 cells, 1 karyotype, with banding

(88268 has been deleted. To report, use 88261)

88269 Chromosome analysis, in situ for amniotic fluid cells, count cells from 6-12 colonies, 1 karyotype, with banding

(88270 has been deleted. To report, use 88261)

88271 Molecular cytogenetics; DNA probe, each (eg, FISH)

88272 chromosomal in situ hybridization, analyze 3-5 cells (eg, for derivatives and markers)

88273 chromosomal in situ hybridization, analyze 10-30 cells (eg, for microdeletions)

88274 interphase in situ hybridization, analyze 25-99 cells

88275 interphase in situ hybridization, analyze 100-300 cells

88280 Chromosome analysis; additional karyotypes, each study

88283 additional specialized banding technique (eg, NOR, C-banding)

88285 additional cells counted, each study

88289 additional high resolution study

88291 Cytogenetics and molecular cytogenetics, interpretation and report

88299 Unlisted cytogenetic study

Surgical Pathology

Services 88300 through 88309 include accession, examination, and reporting. They do not include the services designated in codes 88311 through 88365 and 88399, which are coded in addition when provided.

The unit of service for codes 88300 through 88309 is the specimen.

A specimen is defined as tissue or tissues that is (are) submitted for individual and separate attention, requiring individual examination and pathologic diagnosis. Two or more such specimens from the same patient (eg, separately identified endoscopic biopsies, skin lesions, etc.) are each appropriately assigned an individual code reflective of its proper level of service.

Service code 88300 is used for any specimen that in the opinion of the examining pathologist can be accurately diagnosed without microscopic examination. Service code 88302 is used when gross and microscopic examination is performed on a specimen to confirm identification and the absence of disease. Service codes 88304 through 88309 describe all other specimens requiring gross and microscopic examination, and represent additional ascending levels of physician work. Levels 88302 through 88309 are specifically defined by the assigned specimens.

Any unlisted specimen should be assigned to the code which most closely reflects the physician work involved when compared to other specimens assigned to that code.

88300 **Level I** - Surgical pathology, gross examination only

88302 **Level II** - Surgical pathology, gross and microscopic examination

Appendix, Incidental

Fallopian Tube, Sterilization

Fingers/Toes, Amputation, Traumatic

Foreskin, Newborn

Hernia Sac, Any Location

Hydrocele Sac

Nerve

Skin, Plastic Repair

Sympathetic Ganglion

Testis, Castration

Vaginal Mucosa, Incidental

Vas Deferens, Sterilization

▲ **88304** **Level III** - Surgical pathology, gross and microscopic examination

Abortion, Induced

Abscess

Aneurysm - Arterial/Ventricular

Anus, Tag

Appendix, Other than Incidental

Artery, Atheromatous Plaque

Bartholin's Gland Cyst

Bone Fragment(s), Other than Pathologic Fracture

Bursa/Synovial Cyst

Carpal Tunnel Tissue

Cartilage, Shavings

Cholesteatoma

Colon, Colostomy Stoma

Conjunctiva - Biopsy/Pterygium

Cornea

Diverticulum - Esophagus/Small Intestine

Dupuytren's Contracture Tissue

Femoral Head, Other than Fracture

Fissure/Fistula

Foreskin, Other than Newborn

Gallbladder

Ganglion Cyst

Hematoma

Hemorrhoids

Hydatid of Morgagni

Intervertebral Disc

Joint, Loose Body

Meniscus

Mucocele, Salivary

Neuroma - Morton's/Traumatic

Pilonidal Cyst/Sinus

Polyps, Inflammatory - Nasal/Sinusoidal

Skin - Cyst/Tag/Debridement

Soft Tissue, Debridement

Soft Tissue, Lipoma

Spermatocele

Tendon/Tendon Sheath

Testicular Appendage

Thrombus or Embolus

Tonsil and/or Adenoids

Varicocele

Vas Deferens, Other than Sterilization

Vein, Varicosity

▲ **88305** **Level IV** - Surgical pathology, gross and microscopic examination

Abortion - Spontaneous/Missed

Artery, Biopsy

Bone Marrow, Biopsy

Bone Exostosis

Brain/Meninges, Other than for Tumor Resection

Breast, Biopsy, Not Requiring Microscopic Evaluation of Surgical Margins

Breast, Reduction Mammoplasty

Bronchus, Biopsy

Cell Block, Any Source

Cervix, Biopsy

Colon, Biopsy

Duodenum, Biopsy

Endocervix, Curettings/Biopsy

Endometrium, Curettings/Biopsy

Esophagus, Biopsy

Extremity, Amputation, Traumatic

⊘ = Modifier '-51' Exempt ▶ ◀ = New or Revised Text ✛ = Add-on Code CPT 2002

Fallopian Tube, Biopsy

Fallopian Tube, Ectopic Pregnancy

Femoral Head, Fracture

Fingers/Toes, Amputation, Non-traumatic

Gingiva/Oral Mucosa, Biopsy

Heart Valve

Joint, Resection

Kidney, Biopsy

Larynx, Biopsy

Leiomyoma(s), Uterine Myomectomy - without Uterus

Lip, Biopsy/Wedge Resection

Lung, Transbronchial Biopsy

Lymph Node, Biopsy

Muscle, Biopsy

Nasal Mucosa, Biopsy

Nasopharynx/Oropharynx, Biopsy

Nerve, Biopsy

Odontogenic/Dental Cyst

Omentum, Biopsy

Ovary with or without Tube, Non-neoplastic

Ovary, Biopsy/Wedge Resection

Parathyroid Gland

Peritoneum, Biopsy

Pituitary Tumor

Placenta, Other than Third Trimester

Pleura/Pericardium - Biopsy/Tissue

Polyp, Cervical/Endometrial

Polyp, Colorectal

Polyp, Stomach/Small Intestine

Prostate, Needle Biopsy

Prostate, TUR

Salivary Gland, Biopsy

Sinus, Paranasal Biopsy

Skin, Other than Cyst/Tag/Debridement/Plastic Repair

Small Intestine, Biopsy

Soft Tissue, Other than Tumor/Mass/Lipoma/
Debridement

Spleen

Stomach, Biopsy

Synovium

Testis, Other than Tumor/Biopsy/Castration

Thyroglossal Duct/Brachial Cleft Cyst

Tongue, Biopsy

Tonsil, Biopsy

Trachea, Biopsy

Ureter, Biopsy

Urethra, Biopsy

Urinary Bladder, Biopsy

Uterus, with or without Tubes and Ovaries, for Prolapse

Vagina, Biopsy

Vulva/Labia, Biopsy

88307 **Level V** - Surgical pathology, gross and microscopic examination

Adrenal, Resection

Bone - Biopsy/Curettings

Bone Fragment(s), Pathologic Fracture

Brain, Biopsy

Brain/Meninges, Tumor Resection

Breast, Excision of Lesion, Requiring Microscopic Evaluation of Surgical Margins

Breast, Mastectomy - Partial/Simple

Cervix, Conization

Colon, Segmental Resection, Other than for Tumor

Extremity, Amputation, Non-traumatic

Eye, Enucleation

Kidney, Partial/Total Nephrectomy

Larynx, Partial/Total Resection

Liver, Biopsy - Needle/Wedge

Liver, Partial Resection

Lung, Wedge Biopsy

Lymph Nodes, Regional Resection

Mediastinum, Mass

Myocardium, Biopsy

Odontogenic Tumor

Ovary with or without Tube, Neoplastic

Pancreas, Biopsy

Placenta, Third Trimester

Prostate, Except Radical Resection

Salivary Gland

Sentinel Lymph Node

Small Intestine, Resection, Other than for Tumor

Soft Tissue Mass (except Lipoma) - Biopsy/Simple Excision

Stomach - Subtotal/Total Resection, Other than for Tumor

Testis, Biopsy

Thymus, Tumor

Thyroid, Total/Lobe

Ureter, Resection

Urinary Bladder, TUR

Uterus, with or without Tubes and Ovaries, Other than Neoplastic/Prolapse

88309 **Level VI** - Surgical pathology, gross and microscopic examination

Bone Resection

Breast, Mastectomy - with Regional Lymph Nodes

Colon, Segmental Resection for Tumor

Colon, Total Resection

Esophagus, Partial/Total Resection

Extremity, Disarticulation

Fetus, with Dissection

Larynx, Partial/Total Resection - with Regional Lymph Nodes

Lung - Total/Lobe/Segment Resection

Pancreas, Total/Subtotal Resection

Prostate, Radical Resection

Small Intestine, Resection for Tumor

Soft Tissue Tumor, Extensive Resection

Stomach - Subtotal/Total Resection for Tumor

Testis, Tumor

Tongue/Tonsil - Resection for Tumor

Urinary Bladder, Partial/Total Resection

Uterus, with or without Tubes and Ovaries, Neoplastic

Vulva, Total/Subtotal Resection

►(For fine needle aspiration, see 10021, 10022)◄

►(For evaluation of fine needle aspirate, see 88172-88173)◄

+ **88311** Decalcification procedure (List separately in addition to code for surgical pathology examination)

+ **88312** Special stains (List separately in addition to code for surgical pathology examination); Group I for microorganisms (eg, Gridley, acid fast, methenamine silver), each

+ **88313** Group II, all other, (eg, iron, trichrome), except immunocytochemistry and immunoperoxidase stains, each

(For immunocytochemistry and immunoperoxidase tissue studies, use 88342)

+ **88314** histochemical staining with frozen section(s)

(88316 has been deleted. To report, use 99070)

(88317 has been deleted)

88318 Determinative histochemistry to identify chemical components (eg, copper, zinc)

88319 Determinative histochemistry or cytochemistry to identify enzyme constituents, each

88321 Consultation and report on referred slides prepared elsewhere

88323 Consultation and report on referred material requiring preparation of slides

88325 Consultation, comprehensive, with review of records and specimens, with report on referred material

88329 Pathology consultation during surgery;

88331 first tissue block, with frozen section(s), single specimen

88332 each additional tissue block with frozen section(s)

88342 Immunocytochemistry (including tissue immunoperoxidase), each antibody

(88345 has been deleted. To report, use 88346)

88346 Immunofluorescent study, each antibody; direct method

88347 indirect method

88348 Electron microscopy; diagnostic

88349 scanning

88355 Morphometric analysis; skeletal muscle

88356 nerve

88358 tumor

(When semi-thin plastic-embedded sections are performed in conjunction with morphometric analysis, only the morphometric analysis should be coded; if performed as an independent procedure, see codes 88300-88309 for surgical pathology.)

(88360 has been deleted. To report, use 88399)

88362 Nerve teasing preparations

(For physician interpretation of peripheral blood smear, use 85060)

88365 Tissue in situ hybridization, interpretation and report

(88370 has been deleted. To report, use 88342)

88371 Protein analysis of tissue by Western Blot, with interpretation and report;

88372 immunological probe for band identification, each

● **88380** Microdissection (eg, mechanical, laser capture)

88399 Unlisted surgical pathology procedure

Transcutaneous Procedures

88400 Bilirubin, total, transcutaneous

Other Procedures

(Basal metabolic rate has been deleted. If necessary to report, use 89399)

(89005-89007 have been deleted)

▲ **89050** Cell count, miscellaneous body fluids (eg, cerebrospinal fluid, joint fluid), except blood;

89051   with differential count

89060 Crystal identification by light microscopy with or without polarizing lens analysis, any body fluid (except urine)

(89070, 89080 have been deleted)

89100 Duodenal intubation and aspiration; single specimen (eg, simple bile study or afferent loop culture) plus appropriate test procedure

89105   collection of multiple fractional specimens with pancreatic or gallbladder stimulation, single or double lumen tube

(For radiological localization, use 74340)

(For chemical analyses, see **Chemistry,** this section)

(Electrocardiogram, see 93000-93268)

(Esophagus acid perfusion test (Bernstein), see 91030)

89125 Fat stain, feces, urine, or respiratory secretions

89130 Gastric intubation and aspiration, diagnostic, each specimen, for chemical analyses or cytopathology;

89132   after stimulation

89135 Gastric intubation, aspiration, and fractional collections (eg, gastric secretory study); one hour

89136   two hours

89140   two hours including gastric stimulation (eg, histalog, pentagastrin)

89141   three hours, including gastric stimulation

(For gastric lavage, therapeutic, use 91105)

(For radiologic localization of gastric tube, use 74340)

(For chemical analyses, see 82926, 82928)

(Joint fluid chemistry, see **Chemistry,** this section)

89160 Meat fibers, feces

(89180 has been deleted. To report, use 89190)

89190 Nasal smear for eosinophils

(89205 has been deleted. To report, use 82273)

(Occult blood, feces, use 82270)

(Paternity tests, use 86910)

(89210 has been deleted)

89250 Culture and fertilization of oocyte(s);

89251   with co-culture of embryos

89252 Assisted oocyte fertilization, microtechnique (any method)

89253 Assisted embryo hatching, microtechniques (any method)

89254 Oocyte identification from follicular fluid

89255 Preparation of embryo for transfer (any method)

89256 Preparation of cryopreserved embryos for transfer (includes thaw)

89257 Sperm identification from aspiration (other than seminal fluid)

(For semen analysis, see 89300-89320)

(For sperm identification from testis tissue, use 89264)

89258 Cryopreservation; embryo

89259   sperm

89260 Sperm isolation; simple prep (eg, sperm wash and swim-up) for insemination or diagnosis with semen analysis

89261   complex prep (eg, Percoll gradient, albumin gradient) for insemination or diagnosis with semen analysis

(For semen analysis without sperm wash or swim-up, use 89320)

89264 Sperm identification from testis tissue, fresh or cryopreserved

(For biopsy of testis, see 54500, 54505)

(For sperm identification from aspiration, use 89257)

(For semen analysis, see 89300-89320)

89300 Semen analysis; presence and/or motility of sperm including Huhner test (post coital)

89310   motility and count

89320   complete (volume, count, motility, and differential)

(Skin tests, see 86485-86585 and 95010-95199)

89321 Semen analysis, presence and/or motility of sperm

(89323 has been deleted. To report, use 89325)

89325 Sperm antibodies

(For medicolegal identification of sperm, use 88125)

89329   Sperm evaluation; hamster penetration test

89330   cervical mucus penetration test, with or without spinnbarkeit test

(89345 has been deleted)

89350   Sputum, obtaining specimen, aerosol induced technique (separate procedure)

89355   Starch granules, feces

89360   Sweat collection by iontophoresis

(For chloride and sodium analysis, use 84295)

89365   Water load test

89399   Unlisted miscellaneous pathology test

Medicine Guidelines

In addition to the definitions and commonly used terms presented in the **Introduction,** several other items unique to this section on **Medicine** are defined or identified here.

Multiple Procedures

It is appropriate to designate multiple procedures that are rendered on the same date by separate entries. For example: If individual medical psychotherapy (90841) is rendered in addition to subsequent hospital care (eg, 99231), the psychotherapy would be reported separately from the hospital visit. In this instance, both 99231 and 90841 would be reported.

Add-on Codes

Some of the listed procedures are commonly carried out in addition to the primary procedure performed. All add-on codes found in *CPT* are exempt from the multiple procedure concept. They are exempt from the use of the modifier '-51', as these procedures are not reported as stand-alone codes. These additional or supplemental procedures are designated as "add-on" codes. Add-on codes in *CPT* can be readily identified by specific descriptor nomenclature which includes phrases such as "each additional" or "(List separately in addition to primary procedure)."

Separate Procedures

Some of the procedures or services listed in *CPT* that are commonly carried out as an integral component of a total service or procedure have been identified by the inclusion of the term "separate procedure." The codes designated as "separate procedure" should not be reported in addition to the code for the total procedure or service of which it is considered an integral component.

However, when a procedure or service that is designated as a "separate procedure" is carried out independently or considered to be unrelated or distinct from other procedures/services provided at that time, it may be reported by itself, or in addition to other procedures/services by appending the modifier '-59' to the specific "separate procedure" code to indicate that the procedure is not considered to be a component of another procedure, but is a distinct, independent procedure. This may represent a different session or patient encounter, different procedure or surgery, different site or organ system, separate incision/excision, separate lesion, or separate injury (or area of injury in extensive injuries).

Subsection Information

Several of the subheadings or subsections have special instructions unique to that section. These special instructions will be presented preceding those procedural terminology listings, referring to that subsection specifically. If there is an "Unlisted Procedure" code number (see section below) for the individual subsection, it will also be shown. Those subsections within the **Medicine** section that have special instructions are as follows:

Immune Globulins 90281-90399
Immunization Administration for
    Vaccines/Toxoids 90471-90474
Vaccines, Toxoids 90476-90749
Therapeutic or Diagnostic
    Infusions .90780-90781
Psychiatry 90801-90899
Dialysis 90918-90999
Ophthalmology 92002-92499
Otorhinolaryngology 92502-92599
Echocardiography 93303-93350
Cardiac Catheterization 93501-93556
▶**Intracardiac Electrophysiological**
    Procedures/Studies . . . . .93600-93662◀
Peripheral Arterial Disease
    Rehabilitation 93668
Non-Invasive Vascular
    Diagnostic Studies 93875-93990
Pulmonary 94010-94799
Allergy and Clinical Immunology . . .95004-95199
Neurology and Neuromuscular 95805-95999
Neurostimulators,
    Analysis-Programming 95970-95975
▶**Motion Analysis** . . . . .96000-96004◀
Central Nervous System
    Assessments/Tests 96100-96117
▶**Health and Behavior**
    Assessment/Intervention . . . . .96150-96155◀
Chemotherapy Administration 96400-96549
Dermatological Procedures 96900-96999
Physical Medicine and Rehabilitation
    Modalities 97010-97028
    Constant Attendance 97032-97039
    Therapeutic Procedures 97110-97546
    Active Wound
      Care Management 97601-97602
Osteopathic Manipulative
    Treatment 98925-98929

Chiropractic Manipulative
   Treatment 98940-98943
Special Services, Procedures and
   Reports ....99000-►99091◄
Conscious Sedation 99141-99142
►Home Health
   Procedures/Services ....99500-99539◄
►Home Infusion Procedures ....99551-99569◄

Unlisted Service or Procedure

A service or procedure may be provided that is not listed in this edition of *CPT*. When reporting such a service, the appropriate "Unlisted Procedure" code may be used to indicate the service, identifying it by "Special Report" as discussed on this page. The "Unlisted Procedures" and accompanying codes for **Medicine** are as follows:

90399 Unlisted immune globulin

90749 Unlisted vaccine/toxoid

90799 Unlisted therapeutic, prophylactic or diagnostic injection

90899 Unlisted psychiatric service or procedure

90999 Unlisted dialysis procedure, inpatient or outpatient

91299 Unlisted diagnostic gastroenterology procedure

92499 Unlisted ophthalmological service or procedure

92599 Unlisted otorhinolaryngological service or procedure

93799 Unlisted cardiovascular service or procedure

94799 Unlisted pulmonary service or procedure

95199 Unlisted allergy/clinical immunologic service or procedure

95999 Unlisted neurological or neuromuscular diagnostic procedure

96549 Unlisted chemotherapy procedure

96999 Unlisted special dermatological service or procedure

97039 Unlisted modality (specify type and time if constant attendance)

97139 Unlisted therapeutic procedure (specify)

97799 Unlisted physical medicine/rehabilitation service or procedure

99199 Unlisted special service, procedure or report

► **99539** Unlisted home visit service or procedure◄

Special Report

A service that is rarely provided, unusual, variable, or new may require a special report in determining medical appropriateness of the service. Pertinent information should include an adequate definition or description of the nature, extent, and need for the procedure; and the time, effort, and equipment necessary to provide the service. Additional items which may be included are:

- complexity of symptoms;
- final diagnosis;
- pertinent physical findings;
- diagnostic and therapeutic procedures;
- concurrent problems;
- follow-up care.

Materials Supplied by Physician

Supplies and materials provided by the physician (eg, sterile trays/drugs), over and above those usually included with the ►procedure(s)◄ rendered ►are reported◄ separately. List drugs, trays, supplies, and materials provided. Identify as 99070 ►or specific supply code.◄

Medicine

(90000-90080 have been deleted. To report, see 99201-99215)

(90100-90170 have been deleted. To report, see 99341-99350)

(90200-90220 have been deleted. To report, see 99221-99223)

(90225 has been deleted. To report, use 99431)

(90240-90280 have been deleted. To report, see 99231-99233)

(90282 has been deleted. To report, use 99433)

(90292 has been deleted. To report, use 99238)

(90300-90370 have been deleted. To report, see 99301-99313)

(90400-90470 have been deleted. To report, see 99321-99333)

(90500-90580 have been deleted. To report, see 99281-99288)

(90590 has been deleted. To report, use 99288)

(90600-90630 have been deleted. To report, see 99241-99255)

(90640-90643 have been deleted. To report, see 99241-99245 or 99261-99263)

(90650-90654 have been deleted. To report, see 99271-99275)

(90699 has been deleted. To report, use 99499)

Immune Globulins

Codes 90281-90399 identify the immune globulin product only and must be reported in addition to the administration codes 90780-90784 as appropriate. Immune globulin products listed here include broad-spectrum and anti-infective immune globulins, antitoxins, and various isoantibodies.

⊘ **90281**   Immune globulin (Ig), human, for intramuscular use

⊘ **90283**   Immune globulin (IgIV), human, for intravenous use

⊘ **90287**   Botulinum antitoxin, equine, any route

⊘ **90288**   Botulism immune globulin, human, for intravenous use

⊘ **90291**   Cytomegalovirus immune globulin (CMV-IgIV), human, for intravenous use

⊘ **90296**   Diphtheria antitoxin, equine, any route

⊘ **90371**   Hepatitis B immune globulin (HBIg), human, for intramuscular use

⊘ **90375**   Rabies immune globulin (RIg), human, for intramuscular and/or subcutaneous use

⊘ **90376**   Rabies immune globulin, heat-treated (RIg-HT), human, for intramuscular and/or subcutaneous use

⊘ **90378**   Respiratory syncytial virus immune globulin (RSV-IgIM), for intramuscular use, 50 mg, each

⊘ **90379**   Respiratory syncytial virus immune globulin (RSV-IgIV), human, for intravenous use

⊘ **90384**   Rho(D) immune globulin (RhIg), human, full-dose, for intramuscular use

⊘ **90385**   Rho(D) immune globulin (RhIg), human, mini-dose, for intramuscular use

⊘ **90386**   Rho(D) immune globulin (RhIgIV), human, for intravenous use

⊘ **90389**   Tetanus immune globulin (TIg), human, for intramuscular use

⊘ **90393**   Vaccinia immune globulin, human, for intramuscular use

⊘ **90396**   Varicella-zoster immune globulin, human, for intramuscular use

⊘ **90399**   Unlisted immune globulin

Immunization Administration for Vaccines/Toxoids

Codes 90471-90474 must be reported in addition to the vaccine and toxoid code(s) 90476-90749.

If a significant separately identifiable Evaluation and Management service (eg, office or other outpatient services, preventive medicine services) is performed, the appropriate E/M service code should be reported in addition to the vaccine and toxoid administration codes.

(For allergy testing, see 95004 et seq)

(For skin testing of bacterial, viral, fungal extracts, see 86485-86586)

(For therapeutic or diagnostic injections, see 90782-90799)

▲ **90471**   Immunization administration (includes percutaneous, intradermal, subcutaneous, intramuscular and jet injections); one vaccine (single or combination vaccine/toxoid)

+ **90472**   each additional vaccine (single or combination vaccine/toxoid) (List separately in addition to code for primary procedure)

(Use 90472 in conjunction with code 90471)

▲=Revised Code   ●=New Code

(For administration of immune globulins, use 90780-90784, and see 90281-90399)

(For intravesical administration of BCG vaccine, use 51720, and see 90586)

● **90473** Immunization administration by intranasal or oral route; one vaccine (single or combination vaccine/toxoid)

✛ ● **90474** each additional vaccine (single or combination vaccine/toxoid) (List separately in addition to code for primary procedure)

▶(Use 90474 in conjunction with code 90473)◀

Vaccines, Toxoids

Codes 90476-90748 identify the vaccine product **only.** To report the administration of a vaccine/toxoid, the vaccine/toxoid product codes 90476-90749 must be used in addition to an immunization administration code(s) 90471, 90472. Do not append the modifier '-51' to the vaccine/toxoid product codes 90476-90749.

If a significantly separately identifiable Evaluation and Management service (eg, office or other outpatient services, preventive medicine services) is performed, the appropriate E/M service code should be reported in addition to the vaccine and toxoid administration codes.

To meet the reporting requirements of immunization registries, vaccine distribution programs, and reporting systems (eg, Vaccine Adverse Event Reporting System) the exact vaccine product administered needs to be reported. Multiple codes for a particular vaccine are provided in *CPT* when the schedule (number of doses or timing) differs for two or more products of the same vaccine type (eg, hepatitis A, Hib) or the vaccine product is available in more than one chemical formulation, dosage, or route of administration.

Separate codes are available for combination vaccines (eg, DTP-Hib, DtaP-Hib, HepB-Hib). It is inappropriate to code each component of a combination vaccine separately. If a specific vaccine code is not available, the unlisted procedure code should be reported, until a new code becomes available.

(For immune globulins, see codes 90281-90399, and 90780-90784 for administration of immune globulins)

⊘ **90476** Adenovirus vaccine, type 4, live, for oral use

⊘ **90477** Adenovirus vaccine, type 7, live, for oral use

⊘ **90581** Anthrax vaccine, for subcutaneous use

⊘ **90585** Bacillus Calmette-Guerin vaccine (BCG) for tuberculosis, live, for percutaneous use

⊘ **90586** Bacillus Calmette-Guerin vaccine (BCG) for bladder cancer, live, for intravesical use

(90592 has been deleted)

⊘ **90632** Hepatitis A vaccine, adult dosage, for intramuscular use

⊘ **90633** Hepatitis A vaccine, pediatric/adolescent dosage-2 dose schedule, for intramuscular use

⊘ **90634** Hepatitis A vaccine, pediatric/adolescent dosage-3 dose schedule, for intramuscular use

⊘ **90636** Hepatitis A and hepatitis B vaccine (HepA-HepB), adult dosage, for intramuscular use

⊘ **90645** Hemophilus influenza b vaccine (Hib), HbOC conjugate (4 dose schedule), for intramuscular use

⊘ **90646** Hemophilus influenza b vaccine (Hib), PRP-D conjugate, for booster use only, intramuscular use

⊘ **90647** Hemophilus influenza b vaccine (Hib), PRP-OMP conjugate (3 dose schedule), for intramuscular use

⊘ **90648** Hemophilus influenza b vaccine (Hib), PRP-T conjugate (4 dose schedule), for intramuscular use

⊘ **90657** Influenza virus vaccine, split virus, 6-35 months dosage, for intramuscular or jet injection use

⊘ **90658** Influenza virus vaccine, split virus, 3 years and above dosage, for intramuscular or jet injection use

⊘ **90659** Influenza virus vaccine, whole virus, for intramuscular or jet injection use

⊘ **90660** Influenza virus vaccine, live, for intranasal use

⊘ **90665** Lyme disease vaccine, adult dosage, for intramuscular use

⊘ **90669** Pneumococcal conjugate vaccine, polyvalent, for children under five years, for intramuscular use

⊘ **90675** Rabies vaccine, for intramuscular use

⊘ **90676** Rabies vaccine, for intradermal use

⊘ **90680** Rotavirus vaccine, tetravalent, live, for oral use

⊘ **90690** Typhoid vaccine, live, oral

⊘ **90691** Typhoid vaccine, Vi capsular polysaccharide (ViCPs), for intramuscular use

⊘ **90692** Typhoid vaccine, heat- and phenol-inactivated (H-P), for subcutaneous or intradermal use

⊘ **90693** Typhoid vaccine, acetone-killed, dried (AKD), for subcutaneous or jet injection use (U.S. military)

⊘ **90700** Diphtheria, tetanus toxoids, and acellular pertussis vaccine (DTaP), for intramuscular use

⊘ **90701** Diphtheria, tetanus toxoids, and whole cell pertussis vaccine (DTP), for intramuscular use

⊘ **90702** Diphtheria and tetanus toxoids (DT) adsorbed for use in individuals younger than seven years, for intramuscular use

⊘ **90703** Tetanus toxoid adsorbed, for intramuscular or jet injection use

⊘ **90704** Mumps virus vaccine, live, for subcutaneous or jet injection use

⊘ **90705** Measles virus vaccine, live, for subcutaneous or jet injection use

⊘ **90706**   Rubella virus vaccine, live, for subcutaneous or jet injection use

⊘ **90707**   Measles, mumps and rubella virus vaccine (MMR), live, for subcutaneous or jet injection use

⊘ **90708**   Measles and rubella virus vaccine, live, for subcutaneous or jet injection use

⊘ **90709**   Rubella and mumps virus vaccine, live, for subcutaneous use

⊘ **90710**   Measles, mumps, rubella, and varicella vaccine (MMRV), live, for subcutaneous use

(90711 has been deleted)

⊘ **90712**   Poliovirus vaccine, (any type(s)) (OPV), live, for oral use

⊘ **90713**   Poliovirus vaccine, inactivated, (IPV), for subcutaneous use

(90714 has been deleted. To report, see 90690-90693)

⊘ **90716**   Varicella virus vaccine, live, for subcutaneous use

⊘ **90717**   Yellow fever vaccine, live, for subcutaneous use

⊘ **90718**   Tetanus and diphtheria toxoids (Td) adsorbed for use in individuals seven years or older, for intramuscular or jet injection

⊘ **90719**   Diphtheria toxoid, for intramuscular use

⊘ **90720**   Diphtheria, tetanus toxoids, and whole cell pertussis vaccine and Hemophilus influenza B vaccine (DTP-Hib), for intramuscular use

⊘ **90721**   Diphtheria, tetanus toxoids, and acellular pertussis vaccine and Hemophilus influenza B vaccine (DtaP-Hib), for intramuscular use

(90724 has been deleted. To report, see 90657-90660)

⊘ **90723**   Diphtheria, tetanus toxoids, acellular pertussis vaccine, Hepatitis B, and poliovirus vaccine, inactivated (DtaP-HepB-IPV), for intramuscular use

⊘ **90725**   Cholera vaccine for injectable use

(For oral cholera, use 90592)

(90726 has been deleted. To report, see 90675, 90676)

⊘ **90727**   Plague vaccine, for intramuscular or jet injection use

(90728 has been deleted. To report, see 90585, 90586)

(90730 has been deleted. To report, see 90632-90634)

(90731 has been deleted. To report, see 90744-90747)

⊘ ▲ **90732**   Pneumococcal polysaccharide vaccine, 23-valent, adult or immunosuppressed patient dosage, for use in individuals 2 years or older, for subcutaneous or intramuscular use

⊘ **90733**   Meningococcal polysaccharide vaccine (any group(s)), for subcutaneous or jet injection use

⊘ **90735**   Japanese encephalitis virus vaccine, for subcutaneous use

(90737 has been deleted. To report, see 90645-90648)

(90741 has been deleted. To report, see 90281-90283)

(90742 has been deleted. To report, see 90287-90399)

⊘ **90740**   Hepatitis B vaccine, dialysis or immunosuppressed patient dosage (3 dose schedule), for intramuscular use

⊘ **90743**   Hepatitis B vaccine, adolescent (2 dose schedule), for intramuscular use

⊘ **90744**   Hepatitis B vaccine, pediatric/adolescent dosage (3 dose schedule), for intramuscular use

(90745 has been deleted)

⊘ **90746**   Hepatitis B vaccine, adult dosage, for intramuscular use

⊘ **90747**   Hepatitis B vaccine, dialysis or immunosuppressed patient dosage (4 dose schedule), for intramuscular use

⊘ **90748**   Hepatitis B and Hemophilus influenza b vaccine (HepB-Hib), for intramuscular use

⊘ **90749**   Unlisted vaccine/toxoid

(90750-90754 have been deleted. To report, see 99381-99387)

(90755 has been deleted)

(90757 has been deleted. To report, use 99432)

(90760-90764 have been deleted. To report, see 99391-99397)

(90774 has been deleted. To report, use 96110)

(90778 has been deleted. To report, use 94772)

Therapeutic or Diagnostic Infusions (Excludes Chemotherapy)

These procedures encompass prolonged intravenous injections.

These codes require the presence of the physician during the infusion. These codes are not to be used for intradermal, subcutaneous or intramuscular or routine IV drug injections. For these services, see 90782-90788.

These codes may not be used in addition to prolonged services codes.

▲ **90780**   Intravenous infusion for therapy/diagnosis, administered by physician or under direct supervision of physician; up to one hour

+ **90781**   each additional hour, up to eight (8) hours (List separately in addition to code for primary procedure)

(Use 90781 in conjunction with code 90780)

Therapeutic, Prophylactic or Diagnostic Injections

90782 Therapeutic, prophylactic or diagnostic injection (specify material injected); subcutaneous or intramuscular

 (For administration of vaccines/toxoids, see 90471-90472)

90783 intra-arterial

90784 intravenous

 (90782-90784 do not include injections for allergen immunotherapy. For allergen immunotherapy injections, see 95115-95117)

90788 Intramuscular injection of antibiotic (specify)

 (90790-90796 have been deleted. To report, see 96408-96414, 96420-96425, 96440, 96450, 96530, 96545, 96549)

 (90798 has been deleted. To report, see 90780, 90781, 90784)

90799 Unlisted therapeutic, prophylactic or diagnostic injection

 (For allergy immunizations, see 95004 et seq)

Psychiatry

▶(For repetitive transcranial magnetic stimulation for treatment of clinical depression, use Category III code 0018T)◀

Hospital care by the attending physician in treating a psychiatric inpatient or partial hospitalization may be initial or subsequent in nature (see 99221-99233) and may include exchanges with nursing and ancillary personnel. Hospital care services involve a variety of responsibilities unique to the medical management of inpatients, such as physician hospital orders, interpretation of laboratory or other medical diagnostic studies and observations.

Some patients receive hospital evaluation and management services only and others receive evaluation and management services and other procedures. If other procedures such as electroconvulsive therapy or psychotherapy are rendered in addition to hospital evaluation and management services, these should be listed separately (ie, hospital care service plus electroconvulsive therapy or when psychotherapy is done, an appropriate code defining psychotherapy with medical evaluation and management services). The modifier '-22' may be used to indicate a more extensive service. The modifier '-52' may be used to signify a service that is reduced or less extensive than the usual procedure.

Other evaluation and management services, such as office medical service or other patient encounters, may be described as listed in the section on **Evaluation and Management,** if appropriate.

The evaluation and management services should not be reported separately, when reporting codes 90805, 90807, 90809, 90811, 90813, 90815, 90817, 90819, 90822, 90824, 90827, 90829.

Consultation for psychiatric evaluation of a patient includes examination of a patient and exchange of information with the primary physician and other informants such as nurses or family members, and preparation of a report. These consultation services (99241-99263) are limited to initial or follow-up evaluation and do not involve psychiatric treatment.

Psychiatric Diagnostic or Evaluative Interview Procedures

Psychiatric diagnostic interview examination includes a history, mental status, and a disposition, and may include communication with family or other sources, ordering and medical interpretation of laboratory or other medical diagnostic studies. In certain circumstances other informants will be seen in lieu of the patient.

Interactive psychiatric diagnostic interview examination is typically furnished to children. It involves the use of physical aids and non-verbal communication to overcome barriers to therapeutic interaction between the clinician and a patient who has not yet developed, or has lost, either the expressive language communication skills to explain his/her symptoms and response to treatment, or the receptive communication skills to understand the clinician if he/she were to use ordinary adult language for communication.

90801 Psychiatric diagnostic interview examination

90802 Interactive psychiatric diagnostic interview examination using play equipment, physical devices, language interpreter, or other mechanisms of communication

Psychiatric Therapeutic Procedures

Psychotherapy is the treatment for mental illness and behavioral disturbances in which the clinician establishes a professional contract with the patient and, through definitive therapeutic communication, attempts to alleviate the emotional disturbances, reverse or change maladaptive patterns of behavior, and encourage personality growth and development. The codes for reporting psychotherapy are divided into two broad categories: Interactive Psychotherapy; and Insight Oriented, Behavior Modifying and/or Supportive Psychotherapy.

Interactive psychotherapy is typically furnished to children. It involves the use of physical aids and non-verbal communication to overcome barriers to therapeutic interaction between the clinician and a patient who has not yet developed, or has lost, either the expressive language communication skills to explain his/her symptoms and response to treatment, or the receptive communication skills to understand the clinician if he/she were to use ordinary adult language for communication.

Insight oriented, behavior modifying and/or supportive psychotherapy refers to the development of insight or affective understanding, the use of behavior modification techniques, the use of supportive interactions, the use of cognitive discussion of reality, or any combination of the above to provide therapeutic change.

Some patients receive psychotherapy only and others receive psychotherapy and medical evaluation and management services. These evaluation and management services involve a variety of responsibilities unique to the medical management of psychiatric patients, such as medical diagnostic evaluation (eg, evaluation of comorbid medical conditions, drug interactions, and physical examinations), drug management when indicated, physician orders, interpretation of laboratory or other medical diagnostic studies and observations.

In reporting psychotherapy, the appropriate code is chosen on the basis of the type of psychotherapy (interactive using non-verbal techniques versus insight oriented, behavior modifying and/or supportive using verbal techniques), the place of service (office versus inpatient), the face-to-face time spent with the patient during psychotherapy, and whether evaluation and management services are furnished on the same date of service as psychotherapy.

To report medical evaluation and management services furnished on a day when psychotherapy is not provided, select the appropriate code from the **Evaluation and Management Services Guidelines.**

Office or Other Outpatient Facility

Insight Oriented, Behavior Modifying and/or Supportive Psychotherapy

90804   Individual psychotherapy, insight oriented, behavior modifying and/or supportive, in an office or outpatient facility, approximately 20 to 30 minutes face-to-face with the patient;

90805   with medical evaluation and management services

90806   Individual psychotherapy, insight oriented, behavior modifying and/or supportive, in an office or outpatient facility, approximately 45 to 50 minutes face-to-face with the patient;

90807   with medical evaluation and management services

90808   Individual psychotherapy, insight oriented, behavior modifying and/or supportive, in an office or outpatient facility, approximately 75 to 80 minutes face-to-face with the patient;

90809   with medical evaluation and management services

Interactive Psychotherapy

90810   Individual psychotherapy, interactive, using play equipment, physical devices, language interpreter, or other mechanisms of non-verbal communication, in an office or outpatient facility, approximately 20 to 30 minutes face-to-face with the patient;

90811   with medical evaluation and management services

90812   Individual psychotherapy, interactive, using play equipment, physical devices, language interpreter, or other mechanisms of non-verbal communication, in an office or outpatient facility, approximately 45 to 50 minutes face-to-face with the patient;

90813   with medical evaluation and management services

90814   Individual psychotherapy, interactive, using play equipment, physical devices, language interpreter, or other mechanisms of non-verbal communication, in an office or outpatient facility, approximately 75 to 80 minutes face-to-face with the patient;

90815   with medical evaluation and management services

Inpatient Hospital, Partial Hospital or Residential Care Facility

Insight Oriented, Behavior Modifying and/or Supportive Psychotherapy

90816   Individual psychotherapy, insight oriented, behavior modifying and/or supportive, in an inpatient hospital, partial hospital or residential care setting, approximately 20 to 30 minutes face-to-face with the patient;

90817   with medical evaluation and management services

90818   Individual psychotherapy, insight oriented, behavior modifying and/or supportive, in an inpatient hospital, partial hospital or residential care setting, approximately 45 to 50 minutes face-to-face with the patient;

90819   with medical evaluation and management services

(90820 has been deleted. To report, use 90802)

90821   Individual psychotherapy, insight oriented, behavior modifying and/or supportive, in an inpatient hospital, partial hospital or residential care setting, approximately 75 to 80 minutes face-to-face with the patient;

90822   with medical evaluation and management services

Interactive Psychotherapy

90823   Individual psychotherapy, interactive, using play equipment, physical devices, language interpreter, or other mechanisms of non-verbal communication, in an inpatient hospital, partial hospital or residential care setting, approximately 20 to 30 minutes face-to-face with the patient;

90824   with medical evaluation and management services

(90825 has been deleted. To report, use 90885)

90826   Individual psychotherapy, interactive, using play equipment, physical devices, language interpreter, or other mechanisms of non-verbal communication, in an inpatient hospital, partial hospital or residential care setting, approximately 45 to 50 minutes face-to-face with the patient;

90827   with medical evaluation and management services

90828   Individual psychotherapy, interactive, using play equipment, physical devices, language interpreter, or other mechanisms of non-verbal communication, in an inpatient hospital, partial hospital or residential care setting, approximately 75 to 80 minutes face-to-face with the patient;

90829   with medical evaluation and management services

(90830 has been deleted. To report, use 96100)

(90831 has been deleted. To report, see 99371-99373)

(90835 has been deleted. To report, use 90865)

(90841 has been deleted)

(90842 has been deleted. To report, see 90808, 90809, 90821, 90822)

(90843 has been deleted. To report, see 90804, 90805, 90816, 90817)

(90844 has been deleted. To report, see 90806, 90807, 90818, 90819)

Other Psychotherapy

90845   Psychoanalysis

90846   Family psychotherapy (without the patient present)

90847   Family psychotherapy (conjoint psychotherapy) (with patient present)

(90848 has been deleted. To report, use 90847)

90849   Multiple-family group psychotherapy

90853   Group psychotherapy (other than of a multiple-family group)

(90855 has been deleted. To report, see 90810-90815, and 90823-90829)

90857   Interactive group psychotherapy

Other Psychiatric Services or Procedures

90862   Pharmacologic management, including prescription, use, and review of medication with no more than minimal medical psychotherapy

90865   Narcosynthesis for psychiatric diagnostic and therapeutic purposes (eg, sodium amobarbital (Amytal) interview)

90870   Electroconvulsive therapy (includes necessary monitoring); single seizure

90871   multiple seizures, per day

(90872 has been deleted. To report, use 90899)

90875   Individual psychophysiological therapy incorporating biofeedback training by any modality (face-to-face with the patient), with psychotherapy (eg, insight oriented, behavior modifying or supportive psychotherapy); approximately 20-30 minutes

90876   approximately 45-50 minutes

90880   Hypnotherapy

90882   Environmental intervention for medical management purposes on a psychiatric patient's behalf with agencies, employers, or institutions

90885   Psychiatric evaluation of hospital records, other psychiatric reports, psychometric and/or projective tests, and other accumulated data for medical diagnostic purposes

90887   Interpretation or explanation of results of psychiatric, other medical examinations and procedures, or other accumulated data to family or other responsible persons, or advising them how to assist patient

90889   Preparation of report of patient's psychiatric status, history, treatment, or progress (other than for legal or consultative purposes) for other physicians, agencies, or insurance carriers

90899   Unlisted psychiatric service or procedure

Biofeedback

(For psychophysiological therapy incorporating biofeedback training, see 90875, 90876)

(90900 has been deleted. To report, use 90901)

90901   Biofeedback training by any modality

(90902, 90904, 90906, 90908, 90910 have been deleted. To report, use 90901)

90911   Biofeedback training, perineal muscles, anorectal or urethral sphincter, including EMG and/or manometry

(90915 has been deleted. To report, use 90901)

Dialysis

Codes 90918-90921 are reported ONCE per month to distinguish age-specific services related to the patient's end-stage renal disease (ESRD) performed in an outpatient setting. ESRD related physician services include establishment of a dialyzing cycle, outpatient evaluation and management of the dialysis visits, telephone calls, and patient management during the dialysis, provided during a full month. These codes are not used if a hospitalization occurred during the month.

⊘ =Modifier '-51' Exempt   ▶ ◀=New or Revised Text   ✚ =Add-on Code

Codes 90918-90921 do not include the dialysis treatment (90935, 90937, 90945, 90947) or any non-ESRD related services or other patient care services rendered outside of the dialysis setting during that month.

Evaluation and management services unrelated to ESRD services that cannot be performed during the dialysis session may be reported separately.

Codes 90922-90925 are reported when outpatient ESRD related services are not performed consecutively during an entire full month. Codes 90922-90925 are used to report ESRD related services on a per day basis for the remaining days of that month, preceding and/or following the period of hospitalization.

Example:

A four-year old receiving continuous peritoneal dialysis has sixteen days of daily outpatient care, preceding or following a period of hospitalization.

Report 90923 for each date outpatient care was performed.

For ESRD related services and dialysis procedure(s) performed during period of hospitalization: Report appropriate inpatient Evaluation and Management Service code(s) for the hospitalized period if service(s) is unrelated to ESRD services. Report 90945 or 90947 for each inpatient dialysis procedure.

End Stage Renal Disease Services

90918   End stage renal disease (ESRD) related services per full month; for patients under two years of age to include monitoring for the adequacy of nutrition, assessment of growth and development, and counseling of parents

90919   for patients between two and eleven years of age to include monitoring for the adequacy of nutrition, assessment of growth and development, and counseling of parents

90920   for patients between twelve and nineteen years of age to include monitoring for the adequacy of nutrition, assessment of growth and development, and counseling of parents

90921   for patients twenty years of age and over

90922   End stage renal disease (ESRD) related services (less than full month), per day; for patients under two years of age

90923   for patients between two and eleven years of age

90924   for patients between twelve and nineteen years of age

90925   for patients twenty years of age and over

Hemodialysis

Codes 90935, 90937 are reported to describe the hemodialysis procedure with all evaluation and management services related to the patient's renal disease

on the day of the hemodialysis procedure. These codes are used for inpatient ESRD and non-ESRD procedures or for outpatient non-ESRD dialysis services. Code 90935 is reported if only one evaluation of the patient is required related to that hemodialysis procedure. Code 90937 is reported when patient re-evaluation(s) is required during a hemodialysis procedure. Utilize the modifier '-25' with Evaluation and Management codes for ▶separately identifiable◀ services unrelated to the dialysis procedure or renal failure ▶which◀ cannot be rendered during the dialysis session.

▶(For home visit hemodialysis services performed by a non-physician health care professional, use 99512)◀

(For cannula declotting, see 36831, 36833, 36860, 36861)

(For declotting of implanted vascular access device or catheter by thrombolytic agent, use 36550)

(For collection of blood specimen from a partially or completely implantable venous access device, use 36540)

(For prolonged physician attendance, see 99354-99360)

90935   Hemodialysis procedure with single physician evaluation

90937   Hemodialysis procedure requiring repeated evaluation(s) with or without substantial revision of dialysis prescription

● 90939   Hemodialysis access flow study to determine blood flow in grafts and arteriovenous fistulae by an indicator dilution method, hook-up; transcutaneous measurement and disconnection

90940   measurement and disconnection

(For duplex scan of hemodialysis access, use 93990)

(90941-90944 have been deleted. To report, see 90935-90937)

Miscellaneous Dialysis Procedures

Codes 90945, 90947 describe dialysis procedures other than hemodialysis (eg, peritoneal dialysis, hemofiltration or continuous renal replacement therapies), and all evaluation and management services related to the patient's renal disease on the day of the procedure. Code 90945 is reported if only one evaluation of the patient is required related to that procedure. Code 90947 is reported when patient re-evaluation(s) is required during a procedure. Utilize the modifier '-25' with Evaluation and Management codes for ▶separately identifiable◀ services unrelated to the procedure or the renal failure ▶which◀ cannot be rendered during the dialysis session.

(For insertion of intraperitoneal cannula or catheter, see 49420, 49421)

(For prolonged physician attendance, see 99354-99360)

90945   Dialysis procedure other than hemodialysis (eg, peritoneal dialysis, hemofiltration, or other continuous renal replacement therapies), with single physician evaluation

►(For home infusion of peritoneal dialysis, use 99559)◄

90947 Dialysis procedure other than hemodialysis (eg, peritoneal dialysis, hemofiltration, or other continuous renal replacement therapies) requiring repeated physician evaluations, with or without substantial revision of dialysis prescription

(90951-90958 have been deleted. To report, see 90935, 90937)

(90966-90985 have been deleted. To report, see 90945, 90947)

(90988, 90991 and 90994 have been deleted. To report, see 90918-90921)

90989 Dialysis training, patient, including helper where applicable, any mode, completed course

(90990, 90992 have been deleted. To report, see 90989 and 90993)

90993 Dialysis training, patient, including helper where applicable, any mode, course not completed, per training session

(90995 has been deleted. To report, see 90918-90921)

90997 Hemoperfusion (eg, with activated charcoal or resin)

(90998 has been deleted. To report, use 90922)

90999 Unlisted dialysis procedure, inpatient or outpatient

Gastroenterology

(For duodenal intubation and aspiration, see 89100-89105)

(For gastrointestinal radiologic procedures, see 74210-74363)

(For esophagoscopy procedures, see 43200-43228; upper GI endoscopy 43234-43259; endoscopy, small intestine and stomal 44360-44393; proctosigmoidoscopy 45300-45321; sigmoidoscopy 45330-45339; colonoscopy 45355-45385; anoscopy 46600-46615)

91000 Esophageal intubation and collection of washings for cytology, including preparation of specimens (separate procedure)

91010 Esophageal motility (manometric study of the esophagus and/or gastroesophageal junction) study;

91011   with mecholyl or similar stimulant

91012   with acid perfusion studies

91020 Gastric motility (manometric) studies

91030 Esophagus, acid perfusion (Bernstein) test for esophagitis

91032 Esophagus, acid reflux test, with intraluminal pH electrode for detection of gastroesophageal reflux;

91033   prolonged recording

91052 Gastric analysis test with injection of stimulant of gastric secretion (eg, histamine, insulin, pentagastrin, calcium and secretin)

(For gastric biopsy by capsule, peroral, via tube, one or more specimens, use 43600)

(For gastric laboratory procedures, see also 89130-89141)

91055 Gastric intubation, washings, and preparing slides for cytology (separate procedure)

(For gastric lavage, therapeutic, use 91105)

91060 Gastric saline load test

(For biopsy by capsule, small intestine, per oral, via tube (one or more specimens), use 44100)

91065 Breath hydrogen test (eg, for detection of lactase deficiency)

(91090 has been deleted)

91100 Intestinal bleeding tube, passage, positioning and monitoring

91105 Gastric intubation, and aspiration or lavage for treatment (eg, for ingested poisons)

(For cholangiography, see 47500, 74320)

(For abdominal paracentesis, see 49080, 49081; with instillation of medication, see 96440, 96445)

(For peritoneoscopy, use 49320; with biopsy, use 49321)

(For peritoneoscopy and guided transhepatic cholangiography, use 47560; with biopsy, use 47561)

(For splenoportography, see 38200, 75810)

91122 Anorectal manometry

● **91123** Pulsed irrigation of fecal impaction

Gastric Physiology

91132 Electrogastrography, diagnostic, transcutaneous;

91133   with provocative testing

Other Procedures

91299 Unlisted diagnostic gastroenterology procedure

Ophthalmology

(For surgical procedures, see **Surgery,** Eye and Ocular Adnexa, 65091 et seq)

Definitions

Intermediate ophthalmological services describes an evaluation of a new or existing condition complicated with a new diagnostic or management problem not necessarily relating to the primary diagnosis, including history, general medical observation, external ocular and adnexal examination and other diagnostic procedures as

⊘ =Modifier '-51' Exempt   ► ◄=New or Revised Text   ✚ =Add-on Code   CPT 2002

indicated; may include the use of mydriasis for ophthalmoscopy.

For example:

a. Review of history, external examination, ophthalmoscopy, biomicroscopy for an acute complicated condition (eg, iritis) not requiring comprehensive ophthalmological services.

b. Review of interval history, external examination, ophthalmoscopy, biomicroscopy and tonometry in established patient with known cataract not requiring comprehensive ophthalmological services.

Comprehensive ophthalmological services describes a general evaluation of the complete visual system. The comprehensive services constitute a single service entity but need not be performed at one session. The service includes history, general medical observation, external and ophthalmoscopic examinations, gross visual fields and basic sensorimotor examination. It often includes, as indicated: biomicroscopy, examination with cycloplegia or mydriasis and tonometry. It always includes initiation of diagnostic and treatment programs.

Intermediate and comprehensive ophthalmological services constitute integrated services in which medical decision making cannot be separated from the examining techniques used. Itemization of service components, such as slit lamp examination, keratometry, routine ophthalmoscopy, retinoscopy, tonometry, or motor evaluation is not applicable.

For example:

The comprehensive services required for diagnosis and treatment of a patient with symptoms indicating possible disease of the visual system, such as glaucoma, cataract or retinal disease, or to rule out disease of the visual system, new or established patient.

Initiation of diagnostic and treatment program includes the prescription of medication, and arranging for special ophthalmological diagnostic or treatment services, consultations, laboratory procedures and radiological services.

Special ophthalmological services describes services in which a special evaluation of part of the visual system is made, which goes beyond the services included under general ophthalmological services, or in which special treatment is given. Special ophthalmological services may be reported in addition to the general ophthalmological services or evaluation and management services.

For example:

Fluorescein angioscopy, quantitative visual field examination, refraction or extended color vision examination (such as Nagel's anomaloscope) should be separately reported.

Prescription of lenses, when required, is included in 92015 Determination of refractive state. It includes specification of lens type (monofocal, bifocal, other), lens

power, axis, prism, absorptive factor, impact resistance, and other factors.

Interpretation and report by the physician is an integral part of special ophthalmological services where indicated. Technical procedures (which may or may not be performed by the physician personally) are often part of the service, but should not be mistaken to constitute the service itself.

General Ophthalmological Services

New Patient

▶Solely for the purposes of distinguishing between new and established patients, **professional services** are those face-to-face services rendered by a physician and reported by a specific CPT code(s).◀ A new patient is one who has not received any professional services from the physician or another physician of the same specialty who belongs to the same group practice within the past three years.

92002 Ophthalmological services: medical examination and evaluation with initiation of diagnostic and treatment program; intermediate, new patient

92004 comprehensive, new patient, one or more visits

Established Patient

▶Solely for the purposes of distinguishing between new and established patients, **professional services** are those face-to-face services rendered by a physician and reported by a specific CPT code(s).◀ An established patient is one who has received professional services from the physician or another physician of the same specialty who belongs to the same group practice within the past three years.

92012 Ophthalmological services: medical examination and evaluation, with initiation or continuation of diagnostic and treatment program; intermediate, established patient

92014 comprehensive, established patient, one or more visits

(For surgical procedures, see **Surgery,** Eye and Ocular Adnexa, 65091 et seq)

Special Ophthalmological Services

92015 Determination of refractive state

92018 Ophthalmological examination and evaluation, under general anesthesia, with or without manipulation of globe for passive range of motion or other manipulation to facilitate diagnostic examination; complete

92019 limited

92020 Gonioscopy (separate procedure)

(For gonioscopy under general anesthesia, use 92018)

92060 Sensorimotor examination with multiple measurements of ocular deviation (eg, restrictive or paretic muscle with diplopia) with interpretation and report (separate procedure)

92065 Orthoptic and/or pleoptic training, with continuing medical direction and evaluation

92070 Fitting of contact lens for treatment of disease, including supply of lens

92081 Visual field examination, unilateral or bilateral, with interpretation and report; limited examination (eg, tangent screen, Autoplot, arc perimeter, or single stimulus level automated test, such as Octopus 3 or 7 equivalent)

92082 intermediate examination (eg, at least 2 isopters on Goldmann perimeter, or semiquantitative, automated suprathreshold screening program, Humphrey suprathreshold automatic diagnostic test, Octopus program 33)

92083 extended examination (eg, Goldmann visual fields with at least 3 isopters plotted and static determination within the central 30°, or quantitative, automated threshold perimetry, Octopus program G-1, 32 or 42, Humphrey visual field analyzer full threshold programs 30-2, 24-2, or 30/60-2)

(Gross visual field testing (eg, confrontation testing) is a part of general ophthalmological services and is not reported separately)

92100 Serial tonometry (separate procedure) with multiple measurements of intraocular pressure over an extended time period with interpretation and report, same day (eg, diurnal curve or medical treatment of acute elevation of intraocular pressure)

92120 Tonography with interpretation and report, recording indentation tonometer method or perilimbal suction method

92130 Tonography with water provocation

92135 Scanning computerized ophthalmic diagnostic imaging (eg, scanning laser) with interpretation and report, unilateral

● 92136 Ophthalmic biometry by partial coherence interferometry with intraocular lens power calculation

92140 Provocative tests for glaucoma, with interpretation and report, without tonography

Ophthalmoscopy

Routine ophthalmoscopy is part of general and special ophthalmologic services whenever indicated. It is a non-itemized service and is not reported separately.

92225 Ophthalmoscopy, extended, with retinal drawing (eg, for retinal detachment, melanoma), with interpretation and report; initial

92226 subsequent

92230 Fluorescein angioscopy with interpretation and report

92235 Fluorescein angiography (includes multiframe imaging) with interpretation and report

92240 Indocyanine-green angiography (includes multiframe imaging) with interpretation and report

92250 Fundus photography with interpretation and report

92260 Ophthalmodynamometry

(For ophthalmoscopy under general anesthesia, use 92018)

Other Specialized Services

92265 Needle oculoelectromyography, one or more extraocular muscles, one or both eyes, with interpretation and report

92270 Electro-oculography with interpretation and report

92275 Electroretinography with interpretation and report

(92280 has been deleted. To report visual evoked potential testing of the central nervous system, use 95930)

(For electronystagmography for vestibular function studies, see 92541 et seq)

(For ophthalmic echography (diagnostic ultrasound), see 76511-76529)

92283 Color vision examination, extended, eg, anomaloscope or equivalent

(Color vision testing with pseudoisochromatic plates (such as HRR or Ishihara) is not reported separately. It is included in the appropriate general or ophthalmological service, or 99172)

92284 Dark adaptation examination with interpretation and report

92285 External ocular photography with interpretation and report for documentation of medical progress (eg, close-up photography, slit lamp photography, goniophotography, stereo-photography)

92286 Special anterior segment photography with interpretation and report; with specular endothelial microscopy and cell count

92287 with fluorescein angiography

Contact Lens Services

The prescription of contact lens includes specification of optical and physical characteristics (such as power, size, curvature, flexibility, gas-permeability). It is NOT a part of the general ophthalmological services.

The fitting of contact lens includes instruction and training of the wearer and incidental revision of the lens during the training period.

Follow-up of successfully fitted extended wear lenses is reported as part of a general ophthalmological service (92012 et seq).

$\oslash$ =Modifier '-51' Exempt ▶ ◀=New or Revised Text ✚=Add-on Code CPT 2002

The supply of contact lenses may be reported as part of the service of fitting. It may also be reported separately by using 92391 or 92396 and modifier '-26' for the service of fitting without supply.

> (For therapeutic or surgical use of contact lens, see 68340, 92070)

92310   Prescription of optical and physical characteristics of and fitting of contact lens, with medical supervision of adaptation; corneal lens, both eyes, except for aphakia

> (For prescription and fitting of one eye, add modifier '-52')

92311   corneal lens for aphakia, one eye

92312   corneal lens for aphakia, both eyes

92313   corneoscleral lens

92314   Prescription of optical and physical characteristics of contact lens, with medical supervision of adaptation and direction of fitting by independent technician; corneal lens, both eyes except for aphakia

> (For prescription and fitting of one eye, add modifier '-52')

92315   corneal lens for aphakia, one eye

92316   corneal lens for aphakia, both eyes

92317   corneoscleral lens

92325   Modification of contact lens (separate procedure), with medical supervision of adaptation

92326   Replacement of contact lens

Ocular Prosthetics, Artificial Eye

92330   Prescription, fitting, and supply of ocular prosthesis (artificial eye), with medical supervision of adaptation

> (If supply is not included, use modifier '-26'; to report supply separately, use 92393)

92335   Prescription of ocular prosthesis (artificial eye) and direction of fitting and supply by independent technician, with medical supervision of adaptation

Spectacle Services (Including Prosthesis for Aphakia)

Prescription of lenses, when required, is included in 92015 Determination of refractive state. It includes specification of lens type (monofocal, bifocal, other), lens power, axis, prism, absorptive factor, impact resistance, and other factors.

Fitting of spectacles is a separate service; when provided by the physician, it is reported as indicated by 92340-92371.

Fitting includes measurement of anatomical facial characteristics, the writing of laboratory specifications, and the final adjustment of the spectacles to the visual axes and anatomical topography. Presence of physician is not required.

Supply of materials is a separate service component; it is not part of the service of fitting spectacles.

92340   Fitting of spectacles, except for aphakia; monofocal

92341   bifocal

92342   multifocal, other than bifocal

92352   Fitting of spectacle prosthesis for aphakia; monofocal

92353   multifocal

92354   Fitting of spectacle mounted low vision aid; single element system

92355   telescopic or other compound lens system

92358   Prosthesis service for aphakia, temporary (disposable or loan, including materials)

92370   Repair and refitting spectacles; except for aphakia

92371   spectacle prosthesis for aphakia

Supply of Materials

92390   Supply of spectacles, except prosthesis for aphakia and low vision aids

92391   Supply of contact lenses, except prosthesis for aphakia

> (For supply of contact lenses reported as part of the service of fitting, see 92310-92313)

> (For replacement of contact lens, use 92326)

92392   Supply of low vision aids (A low vision aid is any lens or device used to aid or improve visual function in a person whose vision cannot be normalized by conventional spectacle correction. Includes reading additions up to 4D.)

92393   Supply of ocular prosthesis (artificial eye)

> (For supply reported as part of the service of fitting, use 92330)

92395   Supply of permanent prosthesis for aphakia; spectacles

> (For temporary spectacle correction, use 92358)

92396   contact lenses

> (For supply reported as part of the service of fitting, see 92311, 92312)

> (Use 99070 for the supply of other materials, drugs, trays, etc.)

Other Procedures

92499   Unlisted ophthalmological service or procedure

Special Otorhinolaryngologic Services

Diagnostic or treatment procedures usually included in a comprehensive otorhinolaryngologic evaluation or office visit, are reported as an integrated medical service, using appropriate descriptors from the 99201 series.
Itemization of component procedures (eg, otoscopy, rhinoscopy, tuning fork test) does not apply.

Special otorhinolaryngologic services are those diagnostic and treatment services not usually included in a comprehensive otorhinolaryngologic evaluation or office visit. These services are reported separately, using descriptors from the 92500 series.

All services include medical diagnostic evaluation. Technical procedures (which may or may not be performed by the physician personally) are often part of the service, but should not be mistaken to constitute the service itself.

(For laryngoscopy with stroboscopy, use 31579)

92502 Otolaryngologic examination under general anesthesia

92504 Binocular microscopy (separate diagnostic procedure)

92506 Evaluation of speech, language, voice, communication, auditory processing, and/or aural rehabilitation status

92507 Treatment of speech, language, voice, communication, and/or auditory processing disorder (includes aural rehabilitation); individual

92508 group, two or more individuals

92510 Aural rehabilitation following cochlear implant (includes evaluation of aural rehabilitation status and hearing, therapeutic services) with or without speech processor programming

92511 Nasopharyngoscopy with endoscope (separate procedure)

92512 Nasal function studies (eg, rhinomanometry)

92516 Facial nerve function studies (eg, electroneuronography)

92520 Laryngeal function studies

92525 Evaluation of swallowing and oral function for feeding

92526 Treatment of swallowing dysfunction and/or oral function for feeding

Vestibular Function Tests, With Observation and Evaluation by Physician, Without Electrical Recording

92531 Spontaneous nystagmus, including gaze

▲ **92532** Positional nystagmus test

92533 Caloric vestibular test, each irrigation (binaural, bithermal stimulation constitutes four tests)

▲ **92534** Optokinetic nystagmus test

Vestibular Function Tests, With Recording (eg, ENG, PENG), and Medical Diagnostic Evaluation

92541 Spontaneous nystagmus test, including gaze and fixation nystagmus, with recording

92542 Positional nystagmus test, minimum of 4 positions, with recording

92543 Caloric vestibular test, each irrigation (binaural, bithermal stimulation constitutes four tests), with recording

92544 Optokinetic nystagmus test, bidirectional, foveal or peripheral stimulation, with recording

92545 Oscillating tracking test, with recording

92546 Sinusoidal vertical axis rotational testing

+ **92547** Use of vertical electrodes (List separately in addition to code for primary procedure)

(Use 92547 in conjunction with codes 92541-92546)

(For unlisted vestibular tests, use 92599)

92548 Computerized dynamic posturography

Audiologic Function Tests With Medical Diagnostic Evaluation

The audiometric tests listed below imply the use of calibrated electronic equipment. Other hearing tests (such as whispered voice, tuning fork) are considered part of the general otorhinolaryngologic services and are not reported separately. All descriptors refer to testing both ears. Use the modifier '-52' if a test is applied to one ear instead of to two ears. All descriptors (except 92559) apply to testing of individuals; for testing of groups, use 92559 and specify test(s) used.

(For evaluation of speech, language and/or hearing problems through observation and assessment of performance, use 92506)

92551 Screening test, pure tone, air only

92552 Pure tone audiometry (threshold); air only

92553 air and bone

92555 Speech audiometry threshold;

92556 with speech recognition

92557 Comprehensive audiometry threshold evaluation and speech recognition (92553 and 92556 combined)

(For hearing aid evaluation and selection, see 92590-92595)

92559 Audiometric testing of groups

92560 Bekesy audiometry; screening

92561 diagnostic

92562 Loudness balance test, alternate binaural or monaural

92563   Tone decay test

92564   Short increment sensitivity index (SISI)

92565   Stenger test, pure tone

(92566 has been deleted. To report, use 92567)

92567   Tympanometry (impedance testing)

92568   Acoustic reflex testing

92569   Acoustic reflex decay test

92571   Filtered speech test

92572   Staggered spondaic word test

92573   Lombard test

(92574 has been deleted)

92575   Sensorineural acuity level test

92576   Synthetic sentence identification test

92577   Stenger test, speech

(92578 has been deleted)

92579   Visual reinforcement audiometry (VRA)

(92580 has been deleted)

(92581 has been deleted. To report, use 92585)

92582   Conditioning play audiometry

92583   Select picture audiometry

92584   Electrocochleography

92585   Auditory evoked potentials for evoked response audiometry and/or testing of the central nervous system; comprehensive

92586   limited

92587   Evoked otoacoustic emissions; limited (single stimulus level, either transient or distortion products)

92588   comprehensive or diagnostic evaluation (comparison of transient and/or distortion product otoacoustic emissions at multiple levels and frequencies)

92589   Central auditory function test(s) (specify)

92590   Hearing aid examination and selection; monaural

92591   binaural

92592   Hearing aid check; monaural

92593   binaural

92594   Electroacoustic evaluation for hearing aid; monaural

92595   binaural

92596   Ear protector attenuation measurements

92597   Evaluation for use and/or fitting of voice prosthetic or augmentative/alternative communication device to supplement oral speech

92598   Modification of voice prosthetic or augmentative/alternative communication device to supplement oral speech

Other Procedures

92599   Unlisted otorhinolaryngological service or procedure

Cardiovascular

Therapeutic Services

▶(For non-surgical septal reduction therapy (eg, alcohol ablation), use Category III code 0024T)◄

92950   Cardiopulmonary resuscitation (eg, in cardiac arrest)

(See also critical care services, 99291, 99292)

92953   Temporary transcutaneous pacing

(For physician direction of ambulance or rescue personnel outside the hospital, use 99288)

92960   Cardioversion, elective, electrical conversion of arrhythmia; external

92961   internal (separate procedure)

(Do not report 92961 in addition to codes 93662, 93618-93624, 93631, 93640-93642, 93650-93652, 93741-93744)

92970   Cardioassist-method of circulatory assist; internal

92971   external

(For balloon atrial-septostomy, use 92992)

(For placement of catheters for use in circulatory assist devices such as intra-aortic balloon pump, use 33970)

+ ● **92973**   Percutaneous transluminal coronary thrombectomy (List separately in addition to code for primary procedure)

▶(Use 92973 in conjunction with codes 92980, 92982)◄

+ ● **92974**   Transcatheter placement of radiation delivery device for subsequent coronary intravascular brachytherapy (List separately in addition to code for primary procedure)

▶(Use 92974 in conjunction with codes 92980, 92982, 93508)◄

▶(For intravascular radioelement application, see 77781 - 77784)◄

92975   Thrombolysis, coronary; by intracoronary infusion, including selective coronary angiography

92977   by intravenous infusion

(For thrombolysis of vessels other than coronary, see 37201, 75896)

(For cerebral thrombolysis, use 37195)

+ **92978**   Intravascular ultrasound (coronary vessel or graft) during diagnostic evaluation and/or therapeutic intervention including imaging supervision, interpretation and report; initial vessel (List separately in addition to code for primary procedure)

+ 92979   each additional vessel (List separately in addition to code for primary procedure)

(Use 92979 in conjunction with code 92978)

(Intravascular ultrasound services include all transducer manipulations and repositioning within the specific vessel being examined, both before and after therapeutic intervention (eg, stent placement))

92980   Transcatheter placement of an intracoronary stent(s), percutaneous, with or without other therapeutic intervention, any method; single vessel

+ 92981   each additional vessel (List separately in addition to code for primary procedure)

(Use 92981 in conjunction with code 92980)

(To report additional vessels treated by angioplasty or atherectomy only during the same session, see 92984, 92996)

▶(To report transcatheter placement of radiation delivery device for coronary intravascular brachytherapy, use 92974)◀

▶(For intravascular radioelement application, see 77781-77784)◀

92982   Percutaneous transluminal coronary balloon angioplasty; single vessel

+ 92984   each additional vessel (List separately in addition to code for primary procedure)

(Use 92984 in conjunction with codes 92980, 92982, 92995)

(For stent placement following completion of angioplasty or atherectomy, see 92980, 92981)

▶(To report transcatheter placement of radiation delivery device for coronary intravascular brachytherapy, use 92974)◀

▶(For intravascular radioelement application, see 77781-77784)◀

92986   Percutaneous balloon valvuloplasty; aortic valve

92987   mitral valve

92990   pulmonary valve

92992   Atrial septectomy or septostomy; transvenous method, balloon (eg, Rashkind type) (includes cardiac catheterization)

92993   blade method (Park septostomy) (includes cardiac catheterization)

92995   Percutaneous transluminal coronary atherectomy, by mechanical or other method, with or without balloon angioplasty; single vessel

+ 92996   each additional vessel (List separately in addition to code for primary procedure)

(Use 92996 in conjunction with code(s) 92980, 92982, 92995)

(For stent placement following completion of angioplasty or atherectomy, see 92980, 92981)

(To report additional vessels treated by angioplasty only during the same session, use 92984)

92997   Percutaneous transluminal pulmonary artery balloon angioplasty; single vessel

+ 92998   each additional vessel (List separately in addition to code for primary procedure)

(Use 92998 in conjunction with code 92997)

Cardiography

(For echocardiography, see 93303-93350)

93000   Electrocardiogram, routine ECG with at least 12 leads; with interpretation and report

93005   tracing only, without interpretation and report

93010   interpretation and report only

(For ECG monitoring, see 99354-99360)

93012   Telephonic transmission of post-symptom electrocardiogram rhythm strip(s), per 30 day period of time; tracing only

93014   physician review with interpretation and report only

93015   Cardiovascular stress test using maximal or submaximal treadmill or bicycle exercise, continuous electrocardiographic monitoring, and/or pharmacological stress; with physician supervision, with interpretation and report

93016   physician supervision only, without interpretation and report

93017   tracing only, without interpretation and report

93018   interpretation and report only

93024   Ergonovine provocation test

● **93025**   Microvolt T-wave alternans for assessment of ventricular arrhythmias

93040   Rhythm ECG, one to three leads; with interpretation and report

93041   tracing only without interpretation and report

93042   interpretation and report only

(93045 has been deleted. To report, use 93615)

(93201, 93202, 93204, 93205, 93208, 93209 and 93210 have been deleted. To report, use 93799)

(93220, 93221, 93222 have been deleted. To report, use 93799)

93224   Electrocardiographic monitoring for 24 hours by continuous original ECG waveform recording and storage, with visual superimposition scanning; includes recording, scanning analysis with report, physician review and interpretation

⊘ =Modifier '-51' Exempt   ▶ ◀=New or Revised Text   ✚=Add-on Code   CPT 2002

93225   recording (includes hook-up, recording, and disconnection)

93226   scanning analysis with report

93227   physician review and interpretation

93230   Electrocardiographic monitoring for 24 hours by continuous original ECG waveform recording and storage without superimposition scanning utilizing a device capable of producing a full miniaturized printout; includes recording, microprocessor-based analysis with report, physician review and interpretation

93231   recording (includes hook-up, recording, and disconnection)

93232   microprocessor-based analysis with report

93233   physician review and interpretation

93235   Electrocardiographic monitoring for 24 hours by continuous computerized monitoring and non-continuous recording, and real-time data analysis utilizing a device capable of producing intermittent full-sized waveform tracings, possibly patient activated; includes monitoring and real-time data analysis with report, physician review and interpretation

93236   monitoring and real-time data analysis with report

93237   physician review and interpretation

(93255 has been deleted)

(93258, 93259, 93262, 93263, 93266 have been deleted. To report, see 93224-93237)

93268   Patient demand single or multiple event recording with presymptom memory loop, per 30 day period of time; includes transmission, physician review and interpretation

(93269 has been deleted. To report, use 93268)

93270   recording (includes hook-up, recording, and disconnection)

93271   monitoring, receipt of transmissions, and analysis

93272   physician review and interpretation only

(For postsymptom recording, see 93012, 93014)

(For implanted patient activated cardiac event recording, see 33282, 93727)

(93273-93277 have been deleted. To report, see 93224-93237)

93278   Signal-averaged electrocardiography (SAECG), with or without ECG

(For interpretation and report only, use 93278 with modifier '-26')

(For unlisted cardiographic procedure, use 93799)

(93280 has been deleted. To report, use 76000)

Echocardiography

Echocardiography includes obtaining ultrasonic signals from the heart and great arteries, with two-dimensional image and/or Doppler ultrasonic signal documentation, and interpretation and report. When interpretation is performed separately use modifier '-26'.

(For fetal echocardiography, see 76825-76828)

(93300 has been deleted)

93303   Transthoracic echocardiography for congenital cardiac anomalies; complete

93304   follow-up or limited study

(93305 has been deleted)

93307   Echocardiography, transthoracic, real-time with image documentation (2D) with or without M-mode recording; complete

93308   follow-up or limited study

(93309 has been deleted. To report, see 93307, 93308)

93312   Echocardiography, transesophageal, real time with image documentation (2D) (with or without M-mode recording); including probe placement, image acquisition, interpretation and report

93313   placement of transesophageal probe only

93314   image acquisition, interpretation and report only

93315   Transesophageal echocardiography for congenital cardiac anomalies; including probe placement, image acquisition, interpretation and report

93316   placement of transesophageal probe only

93317   image acquisition, interpretation and report only

93318   Echocardiography, transesophageal (TEE) for monitoring purposes, including probe placement, real time 2-dimensional image acquisition and interpretation leading to ongoing (continuous) assessment of (dynamically changing) cardiac pumping function and to therapeutic measures on an immediate time basis

+ 93320   Doppler echocardiography, pulsed wave and/or continuous wave with spectral display (List separately in addition to codes for echocardiographic imaging); complete

(Use 93320 in conjunction with codes 93303, 93304, 93307, 93308, 93312, 93314, 93315, 93317, 93350)

+ 93321   follow-up or limited study (List separately in addition to codes for echocardiographic imaging)

(Use 93321 in conjunction with codes 93303, 93304, 93307, 93308, 93312, 93314, 93315, 93317, 93950)

+ 93325   Doppler echocardiography color flow velocity mapping (List separately in addition to codes for echocardiography)

(Use 93325 in conjunction with codes 76825, 76826, 76827, 76828, 93303, 93304, 93307, 93308, 93312, 93314, 93315, 93317, 93320, 93321, 93350)

93350 Echocardiography, transthoracic, real-time with image documentation (2D), with or without M-mode recording, during rest and cardiovascular stress test using treadmill, bicycle exercise and/or pharmacologically induced stress, with interpretation and report

(The appropriate stress testing code from the 93015-93018 series should be reported in addition to 93350 to capture the exercise stress portion of the study)

Cardiac Catheterization

Cardiac catheterization is a diagnostic medical procedure which includes introduction, positioning and repositioning of catheter(s), when necessary, recording of intracardiac and intravascular pressure, obtaining blood samples for measurement of blood gases or dilution curves and cardiac output measurements (Fick or other method, with or without rest and exercise and/or studies) with or without electrode catheter placement, final evaluation and report of procedure. When selective injection procedures are performed without a preceding cardiac catheterization, these services should be reported using codes in the Vascular Injection Procedures section, 36011-36015 and 36215-36218.

When coronary artery, arterial coronary conduit or venous bypass graft angiography is performed without concomitant left heart cardiac catheterization, use 93508. Injection procedures 93539, 93540, 93544, and 93545 represent separate identifiable services and may be coded in conjunction with one another in addition to code 93508, as appropriate. To report imaging supervision, interpretation and report in conjunction with code 93508, use code 93556.

Modifier '-51' should not be appended to codes 93501-93533, 93539-93556.

⊘ **93501** Right heart catheterization

(For bundle of His recording, use 93600)

⊘ **93503** Insertion and placement of flow directed catheter (eg, Swan-Ganz) for monitoring purposes

(For subsequent monitoring, see 99356-99357)

⊘ **93505** Endomyocardial biopsy

⊘ **93508** Catheter placement in coronary artery(s), arterial coronary conduit(s), and/or venous coronary bypass graft(s) for coronary angiography without concomitant left heart catheterization

(93508 is to be used only when left heart catheterization 93510, 93511, 93524, 93526 is not performed)

(93508 is to be used only once per procedure)

▶(To report transcatheter placement of radiation delivery device for coronary intravascular brachytherapy, use 92974)◀

▶(For intravascular radioelement application, see 77781-77784)◀

⊘ **93510** Left heart catheterization, retrograde, from the brachial artery, axillary artery or femoral artery; percutaneous

⊘ **93511** by cutdown

⊘ **93514** Left heart catheterization by left ventricular puncture

(93515 has been deleted. To report, use 93524)

⊘ **93524** Combined transseptal and retrograde left heart catheterization

⊘ **93526** Combined right heart catheterization and retrograde left heart catheterization

⊘ **93527** Combined right heart catheterization and transseptal left heart catheterization through intact septum (with or without retrograde left heart catheterization)

⊘ **93528** Combined right heart catheterization with left ventricular puncture (with or without retrograde left heart catheterization)

⊘ **93529** Combined right heart catheterization and left heart catheterization through existing septal opening (with or without retrograde left heart catheterization)

⊘ **93530** Right heart catheterization, for congenital cardiac anomalies

⊘ **93531** Combined right heart catheterization and retrograde left heart catheterization, for congenital cardiac anomalies

⊘ **93532** Combined right heart catheterization and transseptal left heart catheterization through intact septum with or without retrograde left heart catheterization, for congenital cardiac anomalies

⊘ **93533** Combined right heart catheterization and transseptal left heart catheterization through existing septal opening, with or without retrograde left heart catheterization, for congenital cardiac anomalies

(93535 has been deleted. To report, see 33971)

▶(93536 has been deleted. To report, use 33967)◀

(When injection procedures are performed in conjunction with cardiac catheterization, these services do not include introduction of catheters but do include repositioning of catheters when necessary and use of automatic power injectors. Injection procedures 93539-93545 represent separate identifiable services and may be coded in conjunction with one another when appropriate. The technical details of angiography, supervision of filming and processing, interpretation and report are not included. To report imaging supervision, interpretation and report, use 93555 and/or 93556. Modifier '-51' should not be appended to 93539-93556.)

⊘ **93539** Injection procedure during cardiac catheterization; for selective opacification of arterial conduits (eg, internal mammary), whether native or used for bypass

⊘ **93540** for selective opacification of aortocoronary venous bypass grafts, one or more coronary arteries

⊘ **93541** for pulmonary angiography

⊘ **93542** for selective right ventricular or right atrial angiography

⊘ =Modifier '-51' Exempt   ▶ ◀=New or Revised Text   ✚=Add-on Code   CPT 2002

⊘ **93543**   for selective left ventricular or left atrial angiography

⊘ **93544**   for aortography

⊘ **93545**   for selective coronary angiography (injection of radiopaque material may be by hand)

(93546 has been deleted. To report, use 93510 and 93543)

(To report imaging supervision and interpretation, use 93555)

(93547 has been deleted. To report, use 93510, 93543, and 93545)

(To report imaging supervision and interpretation, use 93555 and 93556)

(93548 has been deleted. To report, use 93510, 93543, 93544, 93545)

(To report imaging supervision and interpretation, use 93555 and 93556)

(93549 has been deleted. To report, use 93526, 93527 or 93528; 93543, 93545)

(To report imaging supervision and interpretation, use 93555 and 93556)

(93550 has been deleted. To report, use 93526 or 93527 or 93528; 93540, 93543; and 93545)

(To report imaging supervision and interpretation, use 93555 and 93556)

(93551 has been deleted. To report, use 93539 or 93540)

(93552 has been deleted. To report, use 93510; 93539 or 93540; 93543 and 93545)

(To report imaging supervision and interpretation, use 93555 and 93556)

(93553 has been deleted. To report, use 93510; 93539 or 93540; 93543, 93544, 93545)

(To report imaging supervision and interpretation, use 93555 and 93556)

⊘ **93555**   Imaging supervision, interpretation and report for injection procedure(s) during cardiac catheterization; ventricular and/or atrial angiography

⊘ **93556**   pulmonary angiography, aortography, and/or selective coronary angiography including venous bypass grafts and arterial conduits (whether native or used in bypass)

(Codes 93561 and 93562 are not to be used with cardiac catheterization codes)

93561   Indicator dilution studies such as dye or thermal dilution, including arterial and/or venous catheterization; with cardiac output measurement (separate procedure)

93562   subsequent measurement of cardiac output

(For radioisotope method of cardiac output, see 78472, 78473, or 78481)

(93570 has been deleted. To report, use 92982)

+ **93571**   Intravascular doppler velocity and/or pressure derived coronary flow reserve measurement (coronary vessel or graft) during coronary angiography including pharmacologically induced stress; initial vessel (List separately in addition to code for primary procedure)

+ **93572**   each additional vessel (List separately in addition to code for primary procedure)

(Intravascular distal coronary blood flow velocity measurements include all Doppler transducer manipulations and repositioning within the specific vessel being examined, during coronary angiography or therapeutic intervention (eg, angioplasty))

(For unlisted cardiac catheterization procedure, use 93799)

Intracardiac Electrophysiological Procedures►/Studies◄

►Intracardiac electrophysiologic studies (EPS) are an invasive diagnostic medical procedure which include the insertion and repositioning of electrode catheters, recording of electrograms before and during pacing or programmed stimulation of multiple locations in the heart, analysis of recorded information, and report of the procedure. Electrophysiologic studies are most often performed with two or more electrode catheters. In many circumstances, patients with arrhythmias are evaluated and treated at the same encounter. In this situation, a diagnostic *electrophysiologic study* is performed, induced tachycardia(s) are *mapped*, and on the basis of the diagnostic and mapping information, the tissue is *ablated*. Electrophysiologic study(ies), mapping, and ablation represent distinctly different procedures, requiring individual reporting whether performed on the same or subsequent dates.◄

Definitions

►*Arrhythmia Induction*: In most electrophysiologic studies, an attempt is made to induce arrhythmia(s) from single or multiple sites within the heart. Arrhythmia induction is achieved by performing pacing at different rates, programmed stimulation (introduction of critically timed electrical impulses), and other techniques. Because arrhythmia induction occurs via the same catheter(s) inserted for the electrophysiologic study(ies), catheter insertion and temporary pacemaker codes are not additionally reported. Codes 93600-93603, 93610-93612 and 93618 are used to describe unusual situations where there may be recording, pacing or an attempt at arrhythmia induction from only one site in the heart. Code 93619 describes only evaluation of the sinus node, atrioventricular node and His-Purkinje conduction system, without arrhythmia induction. Codes 93620-93624 and 93640-93642 all include recording, pacing and attempted arrhythmia induction from one or more site(s) in the heart.◄

▶**Mapping**: Mapping is a distinct procedure performed in addition to a diagnostic electrophysiologic procedure and should be separately reported using code 93609 or 93613. When a tachycardia is induced, the site of tachycardia origination or its electrical path through the heart is often defined by mapping. Mapping creates a multidimensional depiction of a tachycardia by recording multiple electrograms obtained sequentially or simultaneously from multiple catheter sites in the heart. Depending upon the technique, certain types of mapping catheters may be repositioned from point-to-point within the heart, allowing sequential recording from the various sites to construct maps. Other types of mapping catheters allow mapping without a point-to-point technique by allowing simultaneous recording from many electrodes on the same catheter and computer-assisted three dimensional reconstruction of the tachycardia activation sequence.◀

▶**Ablation**: Once the part of the heart involved in the tachycardia is localized, the tachycardia may be treated by ablation (the delivery of a radiofrequency energy to the area to selectively destroy cardiac tissue). Ablation procedures (93651-93652) may be performed: independently on a date subsequent to a diagnostic electrophysiologic study and mapping; or, at the time a diagnostic electrophysiologic study, tachycardia(s) induction and mapping is performed. When an electrophysiologic study, mapping, and ablation are performed on the same date, each procedure should be separately reported. In reporting catheter ablation, code 93651 and/or 93652 should be reported once to describe ablation of cardiac arrhythmias, regardless of the number of arrhythmias ablated.◀

Modifier '-51' should not be appended to 93600-93660.

⊘ **93600** Bundle of His recording

⊘ **93602** Intra-atrial recording *

⊘ **93603** Right ventricular recording

(93604, 93606 have been deleted. To report, see 93603, 93609, and ▶93622◀ as appropriate)

(93605 has been deleted. To report, use 93609)

▶(93607 has been deleted. To report, use 93622)◀

(93608 has been deleted. To report, use 93609)

+ ▲ **93609** Intraventricular and/or intra-atrial mapping of tachycardia site(s) with catheter manipulation to record from multiple sites to identify origin of tachycardia (List separately in addition to code for primary procedure)

▶(Use 93609 in conjunction with codes 93620, 93651, 93652)◀

⊘ **93610** Intra-atrial pacing

⊘ **93612** Intraventricular pacing

▶(Do not report 93612 in conjunction with codes 93620-93622)◀

+ ● **93613** Intracardiac electrophysiologic 3-dimensional mapping (List separately in addition to code for primary procedure)

▶(Use 93613 in conjunction with codes 93620, 93651, 93652)◀

(93614 has been deleted)

⊘ **93615** Esophageal recording of atrial electrogram with or without ventricular electrogram(s);

⊘ **93616** with pacing

⊘ **93618** Induction of arrhythmia by electrical pacing

(For intracardiac phonocardiogram, use 93799)

⊘ ▲ **93619** Comprehensive electrophysiologic evaluation with right atrial pacing and recording, right ventricular pacing and recording, His bundle recording, including insertion and repositioning of multiple electrode catheters, without induction or attempted induction of arrhythmia

▶(Do not report 93619 in conjunction with codes 93600, 93602, 93610, 93612, 93618, or 93620-93622)◀

⊘ ▲ **93620** Comprehensive electrophysiologic evaluation with right atrial pacing and recording, right ventricular pacing and recording, His bundle recording, including insertion and repositioning of multiple electrode catheters with induction or attempted induction of arrhythmia;

▶(Do not report 93620 in conjunction with codes 93600, 93602, 93610, 93612, 93618 or 93619)◀

+ ▲ **93621** with left atrial pacing and recording from coronary sinus or left atrium (List separately in addition to code for primary procedure)

▶(Use 93621 in conjunction with code 93620)◀

+ ▲ **93622** with left ventricular pacing and recording (List separately in addition to code for primary procedure)

▶(Use 93622 in conjunction with code 93620)◀

+ **93623** Programmed stimulation and pacing after intravenous drug infusion (List separately in addition to code for primary procedure)

(Use 93623 in conjunction with codes ▶93619,◀ 93620)

⊘ **93624** Electrophysiologic follow-up study with pacing and recording to test effectiveness of therapy, including induction or attempted induction of arrhythmia

(93630 has been deleted. To report, use 93631 and 33261)

⊘ **93631** Intra-operative epicardial and endocardial pacing and mapping to localize the site of tachycardia or zone of slow conduction for surgical correction

⊘ **93640** Electrophysiologic evaluation of single or dual chamber pacing cardioverter-defibrillator leads including defibrillation threshold evaluation (induction of arrhythmia, evaluation of sensing and pacing for arrhythmia termination) at time of initial implantation or replacement;

⊘ **93641** with testing of single or dual chamber pacing cardioverter-defibrillator pulse generator

(For subsequent or periodic electronic analysis and/or reprogramming of single or dual chamber pacing cardioverter-defibrillators, see 93642, 93741-93744)

⊘ **93642**   Electrophysiologic evaluation of single or dual chamber pacing cardioverter-defibrillator (includes defibrillation threshold evaluation, induction of arrhythmia, evaluation of sensing and pacing for arrhythmia termination, and programming or reprogramming of sensing or therapeutic parameters)

⊘ **93650**   Intracardiac catheter ablation of atrioventricular node function, atrioventricular conduction for creation of complete heart block, with or without temporary pacemaker placement

⊘ **93651**   Intracardiac catheter ablation of arrhythmogenic focus; for treatment of supraventricular tachycardia by ablation of fast or slow atrioventricular pathways, accessory atrioventricular connections or other atrial foci, singly or in combination

⊘ **93652**   for treatment of ventricular tachycardia

⊘ **93660**   Evaluation of cardiovascular function with tilt table evaluation, with continuous ECG monitoring and intermittent blood pressure monitoring, with or without pharmacological intervention

(For testing of autonomic nervous system function, see 95921-95923)

+ **93662**   Intracardiac echocardiography during therapeutic/diagnostic intervention, including imaging supervision and interpretation (List separately in addition to code for primary procedure)

(Use 93662 in conjunction with codes 93621, 93622, 93651, or 93652, as appropriate)

(Do not report 92961 in addition to 93662)

Peripheral Arterial Disease Rehabilitation

Peripheral arterial disease (PAD) rehabilitative physical exercise consists of a series of sessions, lasting 45-60 minutes per session, involving use of either a motorized treadmill or a track to permit each patient to achieve symptom-limited claudication. Each session is supervised by an exercise physiologist or nurse. The supervising provider monitors the individual patient's claudication threshold and other cardiovascular limitations for adjustment of workload. During this supervised rehabilitation program, the development of new arrhythmias, symptoms that might suggest angina or the continued inability of the patient to progress to an adequate level of exercise may require physician review and examination of the patient. These physician services would be separately reported with an appropriate level E/M service code.

93668   Peripheral arterial disease (PAD) rehabilitation, per session

Other Vascular Studies

(For arterial cannulization and recording of direct arterial pressure, use 36620)

(For radiographic injection procedures, see 36000-36299)

(For vascular cannulization for hemodialysis, see 36800-36821)

(For chemotherapy for malignant disease, see 96408-96549)

(For penile plethysmography, use 54240)

(93700 has been deleted)

● **93701**   Bioimpedance, thoracic, electrical

(93710 has been deleted)

93720   Plethysmography, total body; with interpretation and report

93721   tracing only, without interpretation and report

93722   interpretation and report only

(For regional plethysmography, see 93875-93931)

93724   Electronic analysis of antitachycardia pacemaker system (includes electrocardiographic recording, programming of device, induction and termination of tachycardia via implanted pacemaker, and interpretation of recordings)

(93725-93730 have been deleted. To report, see 93875-93971)

93727   Electronic analysis of implantable loop recorder (ILR) system (includes retrieval of recorded and stored ECG data, physician review and interpretation of retrieved ECG data and reprogramming)

93731   Electronic analysis of dual-chamber pacemaker system (includes evaluation of programmable parameters at rest and during activity where applicable, using electrocardiographic recording and interpretation of recordings at rest and during exercise, analysis of event markers and device response); without reprogramming

93732   with reprogramming

93733   Electronic analysis of dual chamber internal pacemaker system (may include rate, pulse amplitude and duration, configuration of wave form, and/or testing of sensory function of pacemaker), telephonic analysis

93734   Electronic analysis of single chamber pacemaker system (includes evaluation of programmable parameters at rest and during activity where applicable, using electrocardiographic recording and interpretation of recordings at rest and during exercise, analysis of event markers and device response); without reprogramming

93735   with reprogramming

93736   Electronic analysis of single chamber internal pacemaker system (may include rate, pulse amplitude and duration, configuration of wave form, and/or testing of sensory function of pacemaker), telephonic analysis

▶(93737 has been deleted. To report, use 93741 or 93743)◀

▲=Revised Code   ●=New Code

▶(93738 has been deleted. To report, use 93742 or 93744)◀

93740 Temperature gradient studies

(93750 has been deleted. To report, see 93875-93971)

93741 Electronic analysis of pacing cardioverter-defibrillator (includes interrogation, evaluation of pulse generator status, evaluation of programmable parameters at rest and during activity where applicable, using electrocardiographic recording and interpretation of recordings at rest and during exercise, analysis of event markers and device response); single chamber, without reprogramming

93742 single chamber, with reprogramming

93743 dual chamber, without reprogramming

93744 dual chamber, with reprogramming

93760 Thermogram; cephalic

93762 peripheral

93770 Determination of venous pressure

(For central venous cannulization and pressure measurements, see 36488-36491, 36500)

(93780, 93781 have been deleted)

93784 Ambulatory blood pressure monitoring, utilizing a system such as magnetic tape and/or computer disk, for 24 hours or longer; including recording, scanning analysis, interpretation and report

93786 recording only

93788 scanning analysis with report

93790 physician review with interpretation and report

(93791-93796 have been deleted. To report, see 93731-93736)

Other Procedures

93797 Physician services for outpatient cardiac rehabilitation; without continuous ECG monitoring (per session)

93798 with continuous ECG monitoring (per session)

93799 Unlisted cardiovascular service or procedure

Non-Invasive Vascular Diagnostic Studies

Vascular studies include patient care required to perform the studies, supervision of the studies and interpretation of study results with copies for patient records of hard copy output with analysis of all data, including bidirectional vascular flow or imaging when provided.

The use of a simple hand-held or other Doppler device that does not produce hard copy output, or that produces a record that does not permit analysis of bidirectional vascular flow, is considered to be part of the physical examination of the vascular system and is not separately reported.

Duplex scan describes an ultrasonic scanning procedure with display of both two-dimensional structure and motion with time and Doppler ultrasonic signal documentation with spectral analysis and/or color flow velocity mapping or imaging.

Cerebrovascular Arterial Studies

(93850, 93860 have been deleted. To report, see 93875-93882)

(93870 has been deleted. To report, see 93880 and 93882)

93875 Non-invasive physiologic studies of extracranial arteries, complete bilateral study (eg, periorbital flow direction with arterial compression, ocular pneumoplethysmography, Doppler ultrasound spectral analysis)

93880 Duplex scan of extracranial arteries; complete bilateral study

93882 unilateral or limited study

93886 Transcranial Doppler study of the intracranial arteries; complete study

93888 limited study

Extremity Arterial Studies (Including Digits)

(93890, 93910 have been deleted. To report, see 93922-93931)

(93920, 93921 have been deleted. To report, see 93922-93924)

93922 Non-invasive physiologic studies of upper or lower extremity arteries, single level, bilateral (eg, ankle/brachial indices, Doppler waveform analysis, volume plethysmography, transcutaneous oxygen tension measurement)

93923 Non-invasive physiologic studies of upper or lower extremity arteries, multiple levels or with provocative functional maneuvers, complete bilateral study (eg, segmental blood pressure measurements, segmental Doppler waveform analysis, segmental volume plethysmography, segmental transcutaneous oxygen tension measurements, measurements with postural provocative tests, measurements with reactive hyperemia)

93924 Non-invasive physiologic studies of lower extremity arteries, at rest and following treadmill stress testing, complete bilateral study

93925 Duplex scan of lower extremity arteries or arterial bypass grafts; complete bilateral study

93926 unilateral or limited study

⊘ =Modifier '-51' Exempt   ▶ ◀=New or Revised Text   ✛ =Add-on Code   CPT 2002

93930 Duplex scan of upper extremity arteries or arterial bypass grafts; complete bilateral study

93931   unilateral or limited study

Extremity Venous Studies (Including Digits)

(93950, 93960 have been deleted. To report, see 93965-93971)

93965 Non-invasive physiologic studies of extremity veins, complete bilateral study (eg, Doppler waveform analysis with responses to compression and other maneuvers, phleborheography, impedance plethysmography)

93970 Duplex scan of extremity veins including responses to compression and other maneuvers; complete bilateral study

93971   unilateral or limited study

Visceral and Penile Vascular Studies

93975 Duplex scan of arterial inflow and venous outflow of abdominal, pelvic, scrotal contents and/or retroperitoneal organs; complete study

93976   limited study

93978 Duplex scan of aorta, inferior vena cava, iliac vasculature, or bypass grafts; complete study

93979   unilateral or limited study

93980 Duplex scan of arterial inflow and venous outflow of penile vessels; complete study

93981   follow-up or limited study

Extremity Arterial-Venous Studies

93990 Duplex scan of hemodialysis access (including arterial inflow, body of access and venous outflow)

(For measurement of hemodialysis access flow using indicator dilution methods, use 90940)

Pulmonary

Items 94010-94799 include laboratory procedure(s) and interpretation of test results. If a separate identifiable Evaluation and Management service is performed, the appropriate E/M service code should be reported in addition to 94010-94799.

94010 Spirometry, including graphic record, total and timed vital capacity, expiratory flow rate measurement(s), with or without maximal voluntary ventilation

94014 Patient-initiated spirometric recording per 30-day period of time; includes reinforced education, transmission of spirometric tracing, data capture, analysis of transmitted data, periodic recalibration and physician review and interpretation

94015   recording (includes hook-up, reinforced education, data transmission, data capture, trend analysis, and periodic recalibration)

94016   physician review and interpretation only

94060 Bronchospasm evaluation: spirometry as in 94010, before and after bronchodilator (aerosol or parenteral)

(For prolonged exercise test for bronchospasm with pre- and post-spirometry, use 94620)

94070 Prolonged postexposure evaluation of bronchospasm with multiple spirometric determinations after antigen, cold air, methacholine or other chemical agent, with subsequent spirometrics

94150 Vital capacity, total (separate procedure)

(94160 has been deleted. For vital capacity measurement only, use 94150. For spirometry with timed expiratory volumes, use 94010)

94200 Maximum breathing capacity, maximal voluntary ventilation

94240 Functional residual capacity or residual volume: helium method, nitrogen open circuit method, or other method

94250 Expired gas collection, quantitative, single procedure (separate procedure)

94260 Thoracic gas volume

(For plethysmography, see 93720-93722)

94350 Determination of maldistribution of inspired gas: multiple breath nitrogen washout curve including alveolar nitrogen or helium equilibration time

94360 Determination of resistance to airflow, oscillatory or plethysmographic methods

94370 Determination of airway closing volume, single breath tests

94375 Respiratory flow volume loop

94400 Breathing response to CO_2 (CO_2 response curve)

94450 Breathing response to hypoxia (hypoxia response curve)

94620 Pulmonary stress testing; simple (eg, prolonged exercise test for bronchospasm with pre- and post-spirometry)

94621   complex (including measurements of CO_2 production, O_2 uptake, and electrocardiographic recordings)

94640 Nonpressurized inhalation treatment for acute airway obstruction

94642 Aerosol inhalation of pentamidine for pneumocystis carinii pneumonia treatment or prophylaxis

94650 Intermittent positive pressure breathing (IPPB) treatment, air or oxygen, with or without nebulized medication; initial demonstration and/or evaluation

---

▲=Revised Code   ●=New Code

94651   subsequent

94652   newborn infants

94656   Ventilation assist and management, initiation of pressure or volume preset ventilators for assisted or controlled breathing; first day

94657   subsequent days

94660   Continuous positive airway pressure ventilation (CPAP), initiation and management

94662   Continuous negative pressure ventilation (CNP), initiation and management

94664   Aerosol or vapor inhalations for sputum mobilization, bronchodilation, or sputum induction for diagnostic purposes; initial demonstration and/or evaluation

94665   subsequent

94667   Manipulation chest wall, such as cupping, percussing, and vibration to facilitate lung function; initial demonstration and/or evaluation

94668   subsequent

94680   Oxygen uptake, expired gas analysis; rest and exercise, direct, simple

94681   including CO_2 output, percentage oxygen extracted

94690   rest, indirect (separate procedure)

(94700, 94705, 94710 have been deleted. For analysis of arterial blood gas results, see appropriate Evaluation and Management code. For test procedure, see 82800-82810)

(For single arterial puncture, use 36600)

(94715 has been deleted. To report, use 82820)

▲ **94720**   Carbon monoxide diffusing capacity (eg, single breath, steady state)

94725   Membrane diffusion capacity

▲ **94750**   Pulmonary compliance study (eg, plethysmography, volume and pressure measurements)

94760   Noninvasive ear or pulse oximetry for oxygen saturation; single determination

(For blood gases, see 82803-82810)

94761   multiple determinations (eg, during exercise)

94762   by continuous overnight monitoring (separate procedure)

94770   Carbon dioxide, expired gas determination by infrared analyzer

(For bronchoscopy, see 31622-31656)

(For placement of flow directed catheter, use 93503)

(For venipuncture, use 36410)

(For central venous catheter placement, see 36488-36491)

(For arterial puncture, use 36600)

(For arterial catheterization, use 36620)

(For thoracentesis, use 32000)

(For phlebotomy, therapeutic, use 99195)

(For lung biopsy, needle, use 32405)

(For intubation, orotracheal or nasotracheal, use 31500)

94772   Circadian respiratory pattern recording (pediatric pneumogram), 12 to 24 hour continuous recording, infant

(Separate procedure codes for electromyograms, EEG, ECG, and recordings of respiration are excluded when 94772 is reported)

94799   Unlisted pulmonary service or procedure

Allergy and Clinical Immunology

Definitions

Allergy sensitivity tests describe the performance and evaluation of selective cutaneous and mucous membrane tests in correlation with the history, physical examination, and other observations of the patient. The number of tests performed should be judicious and dependent upon the history, physical findings, and clinical judgment. All patients should not necessarily receive the same tests nor the same number of sensitivity tests.

Immunotherapy (desensitization, hyposensitization) is the parenteral administration of allergenic extracts as antigens at periodic intervals, usually on an increasing dosage scale to a dosage which is maintained as maintenance therapy. Indications for immunotherapy are determined by appropriate diagnostic procedures coordinated with clinical judgment and knowledge of the natural history of allergic diseases.

Other therapy: for medical conferences on the use of mechanical and electronic devices (precipitators, air conditioners, air filters, humidifiers, dehumidifiers), climatotherapy, physical therapy, occupational and recreational therapy, see **Evaluation and Management** section.

Allergy Testing

(95000-95003 have been deleted. To report, use 95004)

95004   Percutaneous tests (scratch, puncture, prick) with allergenic extracts, immediate type reaction, specify number of tests

(95005-95007 have been deleted. To report, use 95010)

95010   Percutaneous tests (scratch, puncture, prick) sequential and incremental, with drugs, biologicals or venoms, immediate type reaction, specify number of tests

(95011 has been deleted. To report, use 95010)

(95014 has been deleted. To report, use 95015)

⊘ =Modifier '-51' Exempt   ▶◀=New or Revised Text   ✦=Add-on Code   CPT 2002

95015   Intracutaneous (intradermal) tests, sequential and incremental, with drugs, biologicals, or venoms, immediate type reaction, specify number of tests

(95016-95018 have been deleted. To report, use 95015)

(95020-95023 have been deleted. To report, use 95024)

95024   Intracutaneous (intradermal) tests with allergenic extracts, immediate type reaction, specify number of tests

95027   Skin end point titration

95028   Intracutaneous (intradermal) tests with allergenic extracts, delayed type reaction, including reading, specify number of tests

(95030-95034 have been deleted. To report, use 95028)

(95040-95043 have been deleted. To report, use 95044)

95044   Patch or application test(s) (specify number of tests)

(95050, 95051 have been deleted. To report, use 95052)

95052   Photo patch test(s) (specify number of tests)

95056   Photo tests

95060   Ophthalmic mucous membrane tests

95065   Direct nasal mucous membrane test

95070   Inhalation bronchial challenge testing (not including necessary pulmonary function tests); with histamine, methacholine, or similar compounds

95071   with antigens or gases, specify

(For pulmonary function tests, see 94060, 94070)

95075   Ingestion challenge test (sequential and incremental ingestion of test items, eg, food, drug or other substance such as metabisulfite)

(95077 has been deleted)

95078   Provocative testing (eg, Rinkel test)

(95080-95082 have been deleted)

(For allergy laboratory tests, see 86000-86999)

(For intravenous therapy for severe or intractable allergic disease, see 90780, 90781, 90784)

(95105 has been deleted. To report, see appropriate E/M code(s))

Allergen Immunotherapy

Codes 95115-95199 include the professional services necessary for allergen immunotherapy. Office visit codes may be used in addition to allergen immunotherapy if other identifiable services are provided at that time.

95115   Professional services for allergen immunotherapy not including provision of allergenic extracts; single injection

95117   two or more injections

95120   Professional services for allergen immunotherapy in prescribing physicians office or institution, including provision of allergenic extract; single injection

95125   two or more injections

95130   single stinging insect venom

95131   two stinging insect venoms

95132   three stinging insect venoms

95133   four stinging insect venoms

95134   five stinging insect venoms

(95135 has been deleted. To report, use 95144)

(95140 has been deleted. To report, use 95144)

▲95144   Professional services for the supervision of preparation and provision of antigens for allergen immunotherapy; single dose vial(s) (specify number of vials)

►(A single dose vial contains a single dose of antigen administered in one injection)◄

▲95145   Professional services for the supervision of preparation and provision of antigens for allergen immunotherapy (specify number of doses); single stinging insect venom

95146   two single stinging insect venoms

95147   three single stinging insect venoms

95148   four single stinging insect venoms

95149   five single stinging insect venoms

(95150, 95155 have been deleted. To report, use 95165)

(95160 has been deleted. To report, see 95145-95149)

▲95165   Professional services for the supervision of preparation and provision of antigens for allergen immunotherapy; single or multiple antigens (specify number of doses)

95170   whole body extract of biting insect or other arthropod (specify number of doses)

►(For allergy immunotherapy reporting, a dose is the amount of antigen(s) administered in a single injection from a multiple dose vial)◄

▲95180   Rapid desensitization procedure, each hour (eg, insulin, penicillin, equine serum)

95199   Unlisted allergy/clinical immunologic service or procedure

(For skin testing of bacterial, viral, fungal extracts, see 95028, 86485-86586)

(For special reports on allergy patients, use 99080)

(For testing procedures such as radioallergosorbent testing (RAST), rat mast cell technique (RMCT), mast cell degranulation test (MCDT), lymphocytic transformation test (LTT), leukocyte histamine release (LHR), migration inhibitory factor test (MIF), transfer factor test (TFT), nitroblue tetrazolium dye test (NTD), see Immunology section in **Pathology** or use 95199)

▶Endocrinology◀

● **95250** Glucose monitoring for up to 72 hours by continuous recording and storage of glucose values from interstitial tissue fluid via a subcutaneous sensor (includes hook-up, calibration, patient initiation and training, recording, disconnection, downloading with printout of data)

▶(Do not report 95250 in conjunction with 99091)◀

▶(To report physician review, interpretation and written report associated with code 95250, see **Evaluation and Management** services codes)◀

Neurology and Neuromuscular Procedures

Neurologic services are typically consultative, and any of the levels of consultation (99241-99263) may be appropriate.

In addition, services and skills outlined under **Evaluation and Management** levels of service appropriate to neurologic illnesses should be coded similarly.

The EEG, ▶autonomic function, and◀ evoked potential services (▶95812◀-95829, 95920-▶95930◀ and 95950-95962) include ▶recording,◀ interpretation ▶by a physician,◀ and report. For interpretation only, use modifier '-26'.

▶(For repetitive transcranial magnetic stimulation for treatment of clinical depression, use Category III code 0018T)◀

▶(Do not report codes 95860-95875 in addition to 96000-96004)◀

Sleep Testing

Sleep studies and polysomnography refer to the continuous and simultaneous monitoring and recording of various physiological and pathophysiological parameters of sleep for 6 or more hours with physician review, interpretation and report. The studies are performed to diagnose a variety of sleep disorders and to evaluate a patient's response to therapies such as nasal continuous positive airway pressure (NCPAP). Polysomnography is distinguished from sleep studies by the inclusion of sleep staging which is defined to include a 1-4 lead electroencephalogram (EEG), an electro-oculogram (EOG), and a submental electromyogram (EMG). Additional parameters of sleep include: 1) ECG; 2) airflow; 3) ventilation and respiratory effort; 4) gas exchange by oximetry, transcutaneous monitoring, or end tidal gas analysis; 5) extremity muscle activity, motor activity-movement; 6) extended EEG monitoring; 7) penile tumescence; 8) gastroesophageal reflux; 9) continuous blood pressure monitoring; 10) snoring; 11) body positions; etc.

▶The sleep services (95805-95811) include recording, interpretation and report. For interpretation only, use modifier '-26'.◀

For a study to be reported as polysomnography, sleep must be recorded and staged.

(Report with a '-52' modifier if less than 6 hours of recording or in other cases of reduced services as appropriate)

(For unattended sleep study, use 95806)

95805 Multiple sleep latency or maintenance of wakefulness testing, recording, analysis and interpretation of physiological measurements of sleep during multiple trials to assess sleepiness

95806 Sleep study, simultaneous recording of ventilation, respiratory effort, ECG or heart rate, and oxygen saturation, unattended by a technologist

95807 Sleep study, simultaneous recording of ventilation, respiratory effort, ECG or heart rate, and oxygen saturation, attended by a technologist

95808 Polysomnography; sleep staging with 1-3 additional parameters of sleep, attended by a technologist

95810 sleep staging with 4 or more additional parameters of sleep, attended by a technologist

95811 sleep staging with 4 or more additional parameters of sleep, with initiation of continuous positive airway pressure therapy or bilevel ventilation, attended by a technologist

95812 Electroencephalogram (EEG) extended monitoring; up to one hour

95813 greater than one hour

95816 Electroencephalogram (EEG) including recording awake and drowsy (including hyperventilation and/or photic stimulation when appropriate)

(For extended EEG monitoring, see 95812, 95813)

(95817 has been deleted. To report, use 95816)

95819 Electroencephalogram (EEG) including recording awake and asleep (including hyperventilation and/or photic stimulation when appropriate)

(For extended EEG monitoring, see 95812, 95813)

(For digital analysis of EEG, use 95957)

(95821 has been deleted. To report, use 95819)

95822 Electroencephalogram (EEG); sleep only

(For extended EEG monitoring, see 95812, 95813)

(95823 has been deleted. To report, use 95954)

95824 cerebral death evaluation only

(95826 has been deleted. To report, use 95829, 95951 or 95956)

95827 all night sleep only

(For ambulatory 24-hour EEG monitoring, use 95950)

⊘ =Modifier '-51' Exempt ▶ ◀=New or Revised Text ✛ =Add-on Code CPT 2002

(For EEG during nonintracranial surgery, use 95955)

(For Wada activation test, use 95958)

(95828 has been deleted. To report, see 95807-95810)

(For recording of circadian respiratory patterns of infants, use 94772)

95829   Electrocorticogram at surgery (separate procedure)

95830   Insertion by physician of sphenoidal electrodes for electroencephalographic (EEG) recording

95831   Muscle testing, manual (separate procedure) with report; extremity (excluding hand) or trunk

95832   hand, with or without comparison with normal side

95833   total evaluation of body, excluding hands

95834   total evaluation of body, including hands

(95842 has been deleted. To report, use 95999)

95851   Range of motion measurements and report (separate procedure); each extremity (excluding hand) or each trunk section (spine)

95852   hand, with or without comparison with normal side

95857   Tensilon test for myasthenia gravis;

95858   with electromyographic recording

95860   Needle electromyography, one extremity with or without related paraspinal areas

95861   Needle electromyography, two extremities with or without related paraspinal areas

►(For dynamic electromyography performed during motion analysis studies, see 96002-96003)◄

95863   Needle electromyography, three extremities with or without related paraspinal areas

95864   Needle electromyography, four extremities with or without related paraspinal areas

95867   Needle electromyography, cranial nerve supplied muscles, unilateral

95868   Needle electromyography, cranial nerve supplied muscles, bilateral

95869   Needle electromyography; thoracic paraspinal muscles

95870   limited study of muscles in one extremity or non-limb (axial) muscles (unilateral or bilateral), other than thoracic paraspinal, cranial nerve supplied muscles, or sphincters

(To report a complete study of the extremities, see 95860-95864)

(For needle electromyography of cranial supplied muscles, see 95867, 95868)

(For anal or urethral sphincter, detrusor, urethra, perineum musculature, see 51785-51792)

(For eye muscles, use 92265)

95872   Needle electromyography using single fiber electrode, with quantitative measurement of jitter, blocking and/or fiber density, any/all sites of each muscle studied

▲ **95875**   Ischemic limb exercise test with serial specimen(s) acquisition for muscle metabolite(s)

(95880 has been deleted. To report, use 96105)

(95881 has been deleted. To report, use 96111)

(95882 has been deleted. To report, use 96115)

(95883 has been deleted. To report, use 96117)

►Nerve Conduction Studies◄

⊘ **95900**   Nerve conduction, amplitude and latency/velocity study, each nerve; motor, without F-wave study

⊘ **95903**   motor, with F-wave study

⊘ ▲ **95904**   sensory

(Report 95900, 95903, and/or 95904 only once when multiple sites on the same nerve are stimulated or recorded)

+ **95920**   Intraoperative neurophysiology testing, per hour (List separately in addition to code for primary procedure)

(Use code 95920 in conjunction with the study performed, 92585, 95822, 95860, 95861, 95867, 95868, 95900, 95904, 95925, 95926, 95927, 95930, 95933, 95934, 95936, 95937)

►(Code 95920 describes ongoing electrophysiologic testing and monitoring performed during surgical procedures. Code 95920 is reported per hour of service, and includes only the ongoing electrophysiologic monitoring time distinct from performance of specific type(s) of baseline electrophysiologic study(ies) (95860, 95861, 95867, 95868, 95900, 95904, 95933, 95934, 95936, 95937) or interpretation of specific type(s) of baseline electrophysiologic study(ies) (92585, 95822, 95925, 95926, 95927, 95930). The time spent performing or interpreting the baseline electrophysiologic study(ies) should not be counted as intraoperative monitoring, but represents separately reportable procedures. Code 95920 should be used once per hour even if multiple electrophysiologic studies are performed. The baseline electrophysiologic study(ies) should be used once per operative session.)◄

95921   Testing of autonomic nervous system function; cardiovagal innervation (parasympathetic function), including two or more of the following: heart rate response to deep breathing with recorded R-R interval, Valsalva ratio, and 30:15 ratio

95922   vasomotor adrenergic innervation (sympathetic adrenergic function), including beat-to-beat blood pressure and R-R interval changes during Valsalva maneuver and at least five minutes of passive tilt

95923   sudomotor, including one or more of the following: quantitative sudomotor axon reflex test (QSART), silastic sweat imprint, thermoregulatory sweat test, and changes in sympathetic skin potential

95925   Short-latency somatosensory evoked potential study, stimulation of any/all peripheral nerves or skin sites, recording from the central nervous system; in upper limbs

95926   in lower limbs

95927   in the trunk or head

(To report a unilateral study, use modifier '-52')

(For visual evoked potentials, use 95930)

(For brainstem evoked response recording, use 92585)

(For auditory evoked potentials, use 92585)

95930   Visual evoked potential (VEP) testing central nervous system, checkerboard or flash

95933   Orbicularis oculi (blink) reflex, by electrodiagnostic testing

95934   H-reflex, amplitude and latency study; record gastrocnemius/soleus muscle

(95935 has been deleted. To report, see 95903, 95934, 95936)

95936   record muscle other than gastrocnemius/soleus muscle

(To report a bilateral study, use modifier '-50')

95937   Neuromuscular junction testing (repetitive stimulation, paired stimuli), each nerve, any one method

95950   Monitoring for identification and lateralization of cerebral seizure focus, electroencephalographic (eg, 8 channel EEG) recording and interpretation, each 24 hours

95951   Monitoring for localization of cerebral seizure focus by cable or radio, 16 or more channel telemetry, combined electroencephalographic (EEG) and video recording and interpretation (eg, for presurgical localization), each 24 hours

(95952 has been deleted. To report, use 95950)

95953   Monitoring for localization of cerebral seizure focus by computerized portable 16 or more channel EEG, electroencephalographic (EEG) recording and interpretation, each 24 hours

95954   Pharmacological or physical activation requiring physician attendance during EEG recording of activation phase (eg, thiopental activation test)

(For digital analysis of EEG, use 95957)

95955   Electroencephalogram (EEG) during nonintracranial surgery (eg, carotid surgery)

95956   Monitoring for localization of cerebral seizure focus by cable or radio, 16 or more channel telemetry, electroencephalographic (EEG) recording and interpretation, each 24 hours

95957   Digital analysis of electroencephalogram (EEG) (eg, for epileptic spike analysis)

95958   Wada activation test for hemispheric function, including electroencephalographic (EEG) monitoring

95961   Functional cortical and subcortical mapping by stimulation and/or recording of electrodes on brain surface, or of depth electrodes, to provoke seizures or identify vital brain structures; initial hour of physician attendance

+ 95962   each additional hour of physician attendance (List separately in addition to code for primary procedure)

(Use 95962 in conjunction with code 95961)

● 95965   Magnetoencephalography (MEG), recording and analysis; for spontaneous brain magnetic activity (eg, epileptic cerebral cortex localization)

● 95966   for evoked magnetic fields, single modality (eg, sensory, motor, language, or visual cortex localization)

+ ● 95967   for evoked magnetic fields, each additional modality (eg, sensory, motor, language, or visual cortex localization) (List separately in addition to code for primary procedure)

▶(Use 95967 in conjunction with code 95966)◀

▶(For electroencephalography performed in addition to magnetoencephalography, see 95812-95827)◀

▶(For somatosensory evoked potentials, auditory evoked potentials, and visual evoked potentials performed in addition to magnetic evoked field responses, see 92585, 95925, 95926, and/or 95930)◀

▶(For computerized tomography performed in addition to magnetoencephalography, see 70450-70470, 70496)◀

▶(For magnetic resonance imaging performed in addition to magnetoencephalography, see 70551-70553)◀

Neurostimulators, Analysis-Programming

A simple neurostimulator pulse generator/transmitter (95970, 95971) is one capable of affecting 3 or fewer of the following: pulse amplitude, pulse duration, pulse frequency, 8 or more electrode contacts, cycling, stimulation train duration, train spacing, number of programs, number of channels, alternating electrode polarities, ▶dose time (stimulation parameters changing in time periods of minutes including dose lockout times),◀ more than 1 clinical feature (eg, rigidity, dyskinesia, tremor). A complex neurostimulator pulse generator/transmitter (95970, 95972, 95973, 95974, 95975) is one capable of affecting more than 3 of the above.

Code 95970 describes subsequent electronic analysis of a previously-implanted simple or complex brain, spinal cord, or peripheral neurostimulator pulse generator system, without reprogramming. Code 95971 describes intraoperative or subsequent electronic analysis of an implanted simple brain, spinal cord, or peripheral (ie, peripheral nerve, autonomic nerve, neuromuscular) neurostimulator pulse generator system, with programming. Codes 95972 and 95973 describe intraoperative (at initial insertion/revision) or subsequent electronic analysis of an implanted complex brain, spinal cord or peripheral (except cranial nerve) neurostimulator pulse generator system, with programming. Codes 95974 and 95975 describe intraoperative (at initial insertion/revision) or subsequent electronic analysis of an implanted complex cranial nerve neurostimulator pulse generator system, with programming.

> (For insertion of neurostimulator pulse generator, see 61885, 63685, 63688, 64590)

> (For revision or removal of neurostimulator pulse generator or receiver, see 61888, 63688, 64595)

> (For implantation of neurostimulator electrodes, see 61850-61875, 63650-63655, 64553-64580. For revision or removal of neurostimulator electrodes, see 61880, 63660, 64585)

95970   Electronic analysis of implanted neurostimulator pulse generator system (eg, rate, pulse amplitude and duration, configuration of wave form, battery status, electrode selectability, output modulation, cycling, impedance and patient compliance measurements); simple or complex brain, spinal cord, or peripheral (ie, cranial nerve, peripheral nerve, autonomic nerve, neuromuscular) neurostimulator pulse generator/transmitter, without reprogramming

95971   simple brain, spinal cord, or peripheral (ie, peripheral nerve, autonomic nerve, neuromuscular) neurostimulator pulse generator/transmitter, with intraoperative or subsequent programming

95972   complex brain, spinal cord, or peripheral (except cranial nerve) neurostimulator pulse generator/transmitter, with intraoperative or subsequent programming, first hour

+ 95973   complex brain, spinal cord, or peripheral (except cranial nerve) neurostimulator pulse generator/transmitter, with intraoperative or subsequent programming, each additional 30 minutes after first hour (List separately in addition to code for primary procedure)

> (Use 95973 in conjunction with code 95972)

95974   complex cranial nerve neurostimulator pulse generator/transmitter, with intraoperative or subsequent programming, with or without nerve interface testing, first hour

95975   complex cranial nerve neurostimulator pulse generator/transmitter, with intraoperative or subsequent programming, each additional 30 minutes after first hour (List separately in addition to code for primary procedure)

> (Use 95975 in conjunction with code 95974)

Other Procedures

95999   Unlisted neurological or neuromuscular diagnostic procedure

►Motion Analysis◄

►Codes 96000-96004 describe services performed as part of a major therapeutic or diagnostic decision making process. Motion analysis is performed in a dedicated motion analysis laboratory (ie, a facility capable of performing videotaping from the front, back and both sides, computerized 3-D kinematics, 3-D kinetics, and dynamic electromyography). Code 96000 may include 3-D kinetics and stride characteristics. Codes 96002-96003 describe dynamic electromyography. Do not report codes 95860-95875 in addition to the motion analysis codes.◄

►Code 96004 should only be reported once regardless of the number of study(ies) reviewed/interpreted.◄

> ►(For performance of needle electromyography procedures, see 95860-95875)◄

> ►(For gait training, use 97116)◄

● **96000**   Comprehensive computer-based motion analysis by video-taping and 3-D kinematics;

● **96001**   with dynamic plantar pressure measurements during walking

● **96002**   Dynamic surface electromyography, during walking or other functional activities, 1-12 muscles

● **96003**   Dynamic fine wire electromyography, during walking or other functional activities, 1 muscle

> ►(Do not report codes 95860-95875 in addition to 96002, 96003)◄

● **96004**   Physician review and interpretation of comprehensive computer based motion analysis, dynamic plantar pressure measurements, dynamic surface electromyography during walking or other functional activities, and dynamic fine wire electromyography, with written report

Central Nervous System Assessments/Tests (eg, Neuro-Cognitive, Mental Status, Speech Testing)

The following codes are used to report the services provided during testing of the cognitive function of the central nervous system. The testing of cognitive processes, visual motor responses, and abstractive abilities is accomplished by the combination of several types of testing procedures. It is expected that the administration of these tests will generate material that will be formulated into a report.

(For development of cognitive skills, see 97532, 97533)

96100 Psychological testing (includes psychodiagnostic assessment of personality, psychopathology, emotionality, intellectual abilities, eg, WAIS-R, Rorschach, MMPI) with interpretation and report, per hour

96105 Assessment of aphasia (includes assessment of expressive and receptive speech and language function, language comprehension, speech production ability, reading, spelling, writing, eg, by Boston Diagnostic Aphasia Examination) with interpretation and report, per hour

96110 Developmental testing; limited (eg, Developmental Screening Test II, Early Language Milestone Screen), with interpretation and report

96111 extended (includes assessment of motor, language, social, adaptive and/or cognitive functioning by standardized developmental instruments, eg, Bayley Scales of Infant Development) with interpretation and report, per hour

96115 Neurobehavioral status exam (clinical assessment of thinking, reasoning and judgment, eg, acquired knowledge, attention, memory, visual spatial abilities, language functions, planning) with interpretation and report, per hour

►(For mini-mental status examination performed by a physician, see **Evaluation and Management** services codes)◄

96117 Neuropsychological testing battery (eg, Halstead-Reitan, Luria, WAIS-R) with interpretation and report, per hour

►Health and Behavior Assessment/Intervention◄

►Health and behavior assessment procedures are used to identify the psychological, behavioral, emotional, cognitive, and social factors important to the prevention, treatment, or management of physical health problems. The focus of the assessment is not on mental health but on the biopsychosocial factors important to physical health problems and treatments.◄

►Health and behavior intervention procedures are used to modify the psychological, behavioral, emotional, cognitive, and social factors identified as important to or directly affecting the patient's physiological functioning, disease status, health, and well being. The focus of the intervention is to improve the patient's health and well being utilizing cognitive, behavioral, social, and/or psychophysiological procedures designed to ameliorate specific disease-related problems.◄

►Codes 96150-96155 describe services associated with an acute or chronic illness (not meeting criteria for psychiatric diagnosis), prevention of a physical illness or disability, and maintenance of health, not meeting criteria

for a psychiatric diagnosis, or representing a preventive medicine service.◄

►For patients that require psychiatric services (90801-90899) as well as health and behavior assessment/intervention (96150-96155), report the predominant service performed. Do not report codes 96150-96155 in addition to codes 90801-90899 on the same date.◄

►**Evaluation and Management** services codes should not be reported on the same day.◄

● **96150** Health and behavior assessment (eg, health-focused clinical interview, behavioral observations, psychophysicological monitoring, health-oriented questionnaires), each 15 minutes face-to-face with the patient; initial assessment

● **96151** re-assessment

● **96152** Health and behavior intervention, each 15 minutes, face-to-face; individual

● **96153** group (2 or more patients)

● **96154** family (with the patient present)

● **96155** family (without the patient present)

►(For health and behavior assessment and/or intervention performed by a physician, see **Evaluation and Management** or **Preventive Medicine** services codes)◄

Chemotherapy Administration

Procedures 96400-96549 are independent of the patient's visit.

If a signficant separately identifiable Evaluation and Management service is performed, the appropriate E/M service code should be reported in addition to 96400-96549.

Either may occur independently on any date of service, or they may occur sequentially on the same day.

Preparation of chemotherapy agent(s) is included in the service for administration of the agent.

Regional (isolation) chemotherapy perfusion should be reported using the codes for arterial infusion ►(96420-96425).◄ Placement of the intra-arterial catheter should be reported using the appropriate code from the **Cardiovascular Surgery** section. ►Placement of arterial and venous cannula(s) for extracorporeal circulation via a membrane oxygenator perfusion pump should be reported using code 36823. Code 36823 includes dose calculation and administration of the chemotherapy agent by injection into the perfusate. Do not report code(s) 96408-96425 in conjunction with code 36823.◄

Report separate codes for each parenteral method of administration employed when chemotherapy is administered by different techniques. Medications (eg, antibiotics, steroidal agents, antiemetics, narcotics, analgesics, biological agents) administered independently or sequentially as supportive management of chemotherapy administration, should be separately reported using 90780-90788, as appropriate.

96400 Chemotherapy administration, subcutaneous or intramuscular, with or without local anesthesia

96405 Chemotherapy administration, intralesional; up to and including 7 lesions

96406 more than 7 lesions

96408 Chemotherapy administration, intravenous; push technique

96410 infusion technique, up to one hour

+ 96412 infusion technique, one to 8 hours, each additional hour (List separately in addition to code for primary procedure)

(Use 96412 in conjunction with code 96410)

96414 infusion technique, initiation of prolonged infusion (more than 8 hours), requiring the use of a portable or implantable pump

(For pump or reservoir refilling, see 96520, 96530)

96420 Chemotherapy administration, intra-arterial; push technique

96422 infusion technique, up to one hour

+ 96423 infusion technique, one to 8 hours, each additional hour (List separately in addition to code for primary procedure)

(Use 96423 in conjunction with code 96422)

(For regional chemotherapy perfusion ▶via membrane oxygenator perfusion pump◀ to an extremity, use 36823)

96425 infusion technique, initiation of prolonged infusion (more than 8 hours), requiring the use of a portable or implantable pump

(For implanted pump or reservoir refilling, see 96520, 96530)

96440 Chemotherapy administration into pleural cavity, requiring and including thoracentesis

96445 Chemotherapy administration into peritoneal cavity, requiring and including peritoneocentesis

▲ 96450 Chemotherapy administration, into CNS (eg, intrathecal), requiring and including spinal puncture

(For intravesical (bladder) chemotherapy administration, use 51720)

(For insertion of subarachnoid catheter and reservoir for infusion of drug, see 62350, 62351, 62360, 62361, 62362; for insertion of intraventricular catheter and reservoir, see 61210, 61215)

(96500-96512 have been deleted. To report, see 96408-96414)

96520 Refilling and maintenance of portable pump

(96524, 96526 have been deleted. To report, see 96420-96425)

96530 Refilling and maintenance of implantable pump or reservoir

(For collection of blood specimen from a partially or completely implantable venous access device, use 36540)

(96535 has been deleted. To report, see 96440, 96445)

(96540 has been deleted. To report, use 96542)

96542 Chemotherapy injection, subarachnoid or intraventricular via subcutaneous reservoir, single or multiple agents

96545 Provision of chemotherapy agent

(For radioactive isotope therapy, see 79000-79999)

96549 Unlisted chemotherapy procedure

Photodynamic Therapy

● 96567 Photodynamic therapy by external application of light to destroy premalignant and/or malignant lesions of the skin and adjacent mucosa (eg, lip) by activation of photosensitive drug(s), each phototherapy exposure session

(96570, 96571 are to be used in addition to bronchoscopy, endoscopy codes)

(To report ocular photodynamic therapy, use 67221)

+ 96570 Photodynamic therapy by endoscopic application of light to ablate abnormal tissue via activation of photosensitive drug(s); first 30 minutes (List separately in addition to code for endoscopy or bronchoscopy procedures of lung and esophagus)

+ 96571 each additional 15 minutes (List separately in addition to code for endoscopy or bronchoscopy procedures of lung and esophagus)

(Use 96570, 96571 in conjunction with codes 31641, 43228 as appropriate)

Special Dermatological Procedures

Dermatologic services are typically consultative, and any of the five levels of consultation (99241-99263) may be appropriate.

In addition, services and skills outlined under **Evaluation and Management** levels of service appropriate to dermatologic illnesses should be coded similarly.

(For intralesional injections, see 11900, 11901)

(For Tzanck smear, use 87207)

96900 Actinotherapy (ultraviolet light)

96902 Microscopic examination of hairs plucked or clipped by the examiner (excluding hair collected by the patient) to determine telogen and anagen counts, or structural hair shaft abnormality

96910 Photochemotherapy; tar and ultraviolet B (Goeckerman treatment) or petrolatum and ultraviolet B

96912   psoralens and ultraviolet A (PUVA)

96913 Photochemotherapy (Goeckerman and/or PUVA) for severe photoresponsive dermatoses requiring at least four to eight hours of care under direct supervision of the physician (includes application of medication and dressings)

96999 Unlisted special dermatological service or procedure

Physical Medicine and Rehabilitation

(For muscle testing, range of joint motion, electromyography, see 95831 et seq)

(For biofeedback training by EMG, use 90901)

(For transcutaneous nerve stimulation (TNS), use 64550)

(97000 has been deleted. To report, see 97010-97039)

97001 Physical therapy evaluation

97002 Physical therapy re-evaluation

97003 Occupational therapy evaluation

97004 Occupational therapy re-evaluation

● **97005** Athletic training evaluation

● **97006** Athletic training re-evaluation

Modalities

Any physical agent applied to produce therapeutic changes to biologic tissue; includes but not limited to thermal, acoustic, light, mechanical, or electric energy.

Supervised

The application of a modality that does not require direct (one-on-one) patient contact by the provider.

97010 Application of a modality to one or more areas; hot or cold packs

97012   traction, mechanical

97014   electrical stimulation (unattended)

(For acupuncture with electrical stimulation, use 97781)

97016   vasopneumatic devices

97018   paraffin bath

97020   microwave

97022   whirlpool

97024   diathermy

97026   infrared

97028   ultraviolet

Constant Attendance

The application of a modality that requires direct (one-on-one) patient contact by the provider.

97032 Application of a modality to one or more areas; electrical stimulation (manual), each 15 minutes

97033   iontophoresis, each 15 minutes

97034   contrast baths, each 15 minutes

97035   ultrasound, each 15 minutes

97036   Hubbard tank, each 15 minutes

97039 Unlisted modality (specify type and time if constant attendance)

Therapeutic Procedures

A manner of effecting change through the application of clinical skills and/or services that attempt to improve function.

Physician or therapist required to have direct (one-on-one) patient contact.

(97100 has been deleted. To report, see 97110-97139)

(97101 has been deleted. To report, see 97110-97139)

97110 Therapeutic procedure, one or more areas, each 15 minutes; therapeutic exercises to develop strength and endurance, range of motion and flexibility

▲ **97112**   neuromuscular reeducation of movement, balance, coordination, kinesthetic sense, posture, and/or proprioception for sitting and/or standing activities

97113   aquatic therapy with therapeutic exercises

(97114 has been deleted. To report, use 97530)

97116   gait training (includes stair climbing)

▶(Use 96000-96003 to report comprehensive gait and motion analysis procedures)◀

(97118 has been deleted. To report, use 97032)

(97120 has been deleted. To report, use 97033)

(97122 has been deleted. To report, use 97140)

97124   massage, including effleurage, petrissage and/or tapotement (stroking, compression, percussion)

(For myofascial release, use 97140)

(97126 has been deleted. To report, use 97034)

(97128 has been deleted. To report, use 97035)

97139 Unlisted therapeutic procedure (specify)

97140   Manual therapy techniques (eg, mobilization/ manipulation, manual lymphatic drainage, manual traction), one or more regions, each 15 minutes

(97145 has been deleted. To report, see 97110-97139)

97150   Therapeutic procedure(s), group (2 or more individuals)

(Report 97150 for each member of group)

(Group therapy procedures involve constant attendance of the physician or therapist, but by definition do not require one-on-one patient contact by the physician or therapist)

(97200, 97201 have been deleted. To report, see 97010-97039, 97110-97139)

(97220, 97221 have been deleted. To report, use 97036)

(97240, 97241 have been deleted. To report, see 97036, 97113)

(97250 has been deleted. To report, use 97140)

(97260, 97261 have been deleted. To report, use 97140)

(97265 has been deleted. To report, use 97140)

(For manipulation under general anesthesia, see appropriate anatomic section in **Musculoskeletal System**)

(For osteopathic manipulative treatment (OMT), see 98925-98929)

(97500, 97501 have been deleted. To report, use 97504)

▲**97504**   Orthotic(s) fitting and training, upper extremity(ies), lower extremity(ies), and/or trunk, each 15 minutes

(Code 97504 should not be reported with 97116)

(For casting and strapping of fracture, injury or dislocation, see 29000, 29590)

97520   Prosthetic training, upper and/or lower extremities, each 15 minutes

(97521 has been deleted. To report, use 97520)

97530   Therapeutic activities, direct (one-on-one) patient contact by the provider (use of dynamic activities to improve functional performance), each 15 minutes

(97531 has been deleted. To report, use 97530)

97532   Development of cognitive skills to improve attention, memory, problem solving, (includes compensatory training), direct (one-on-one) patient contact by the provider, each 15 minutes

97533   Sensory integrative techniques to enhance sensory processing and promote adaptive responses to environmental demands, direct (one-on-one) patient contact by the provider, each 15 minutes

▲**97535**   Self-care/home management training (eg, activities of daily living (ADL) and compensatory training, meal preparation, safety procedures, and instructions in use of assistive technology devices/adaptive equipment) direct one-on-one contact by provider, each 15 minutes

97537   Community/work reintegration training (eg, shopping, transportation, money management, avocational activities and/or work environment/modification analysis, work task analysis), direct one-on-one contact by provider, each 15 minutes

(97540 has been deleted. To report, see 97535, 97537)

(97541 has been deleted. To report, see 97535, 97537)

(For wheelchair management/propulsion training, use 97542)

97542   Wheelchair management/propulsion training, each 15 minutes

97545   Work hardening/conditioning; initial 2 hours

✚**97546**   each additional hour (List separately in addition to code for primary procedure)

(Use 97546 in conjunction with code 97545)

Active Wound Care Management

Active wound care procedures are performed to promote healing, and involve selective and non-selective debridement techniques.

(Do not report 97601, 97602 in addition to 11040-11044)

▲**97601**   Removal of devitalized tissue from wound(s); selective debridement, without anesthesia (eg, high pressure waterjet, sharp selective debridement with scissors, scalpel and tweezers), including topical application(s), wound assessment, and instruction(s) for ongoing care, per session

97602   non-selective debridement, without anesthesia (eg, wet-to-moist dressings, enzymatic, abrasion), including topical application(s), wound assessment, and instruction(s) for ongoing care, per session

Tests and Measurements

(For muscle testing, manual or electrical, joint range of motion, electromyography or nerve velocity determination, see 95831-95904)

(97700, 97701 have been deleted. To report, use 97703)

97703   Checkout for orthotic/prosthetic use, established patient, each 15 minutes

(97720, 97721 have been deleted. To report, use 97750)

(97740, 97741 have been deleted. To report, use 97530)

97750   Physical performance test or measurement (eg, musculoskeletal, functional capacity), with written report, each 15 minutes

(97752 has been deleted. To report, use 97750)

Other Procedures

▶(For extracorporeal shock wave musculoskeletal therapy, use Category III code 0019T)◀

(97770 has been deleted. To report, see 97532, 97533)

97780 Acupuncture, one or more needles; without electrical stimulation

97781 with electrical stimulation

97799 Unlisted physical medicine/rehabilitation service or procedure

(98900-98902 have been deleted. To report, use appropriate category and level of **Evaluation and Management** codes)

(98910-98912 have been deleted. To report, see 99361-99362)

(98920-98922 have been deleted. To report, see 99371-99373)

Medical Nutrition Therapy

97802 Medical nutrition therapy; initial assessment and intervention, individual, face-to-face with the patient, each 15 minutes

97803 re-assessment and intervention, individual, face-to-face with the patient, each 15 minutes

97804 group (2 or more individual(s)), each 30 minutes

(For medical nutrition therapy assessment and/or intervention performed by a physician, see **Evaluation and Management** or **Preventive Medicine** service codes)

Osteopathic Manipulative Treatment

Osteopathic manipulative treatment is a form of manual treatment applied by a physician to eliminate or alleviate somatic dysfunction and related disorders. This treatment may be accomplished by a variety of techniques.

Evaluation and Management services may be reported separately if, using the modifier '-25,' the patient's condition requires a significant separately identifiable E/M service, above and beyond the usual preservice and postservice work associated with the procedure. The E/M service may be caused or prompted by the same symptoms or condition for which the OMT service was provided. As such, different diagnoses are not required for the reporting of the OMT and E/M service on the same date.

Body regions referred to are: head region; cervical region; thoracic region; lumbar region; sacral region; pelvic region; lower extremities; upper extremities; rib cage region; abdomen and viscera region.

98925 Osteopathic manipulative treatment (OMT); one to two body regions involved

98926 three to four body regions involved

98927 five to six body regions involved

98928 seven to eight body regions involved

98929 nine to ten body regions involved

Chiropractic Manipulative Treatment

Chiropractic manipulative treatment (CMT) is a form of manual treatment to influence joint and neurophysiological function. This treatment may be accomplished using a variety of techniques.

The chiropractic manipulative treatment codes include a pre-manipulation patient assessment. Additional Evaluation and Management services may be reported separately using the modifier '-25', if the patient's condition requires a significant separately identifiable E/M service, above and beyond the usual preservice and postservice work associated with the procedure. The E/M service may be caused or prompted by the same symptoms or condition for which the CMT service was provided. As such, different diagnoses are not required for the reporting of the CMT and E/M service on the same date.

For purposes of CMT, the five spinal regions referred to are: cervical region (includes atlanto-occipital joint); thoracic region (includes costovertebral and costotransverse joints); lumbar region; sacral region; and pelvic (sacro-iliac joint) region. The five extraspinal regions referred to are: head (including temporomandibular joint, excluding atlanto-occipital) region; lower extremities; upper extremities; rib cage (excluding costotransverse and costovertebral joints) and abdomen.

98940 Chiropractic manipulative treatment (CMT); spinal, one to two regions

98941 spinal, three to four regions

98942 spinal, five regions

98943 extraspinal, one or more regions

Special Services, Procedures and Reports

The procedures with code numbers 99000 through ▶99091◀ provide the reporting physician with the means of identifying the completion of special reports and services that are an adjunct to the basic services rendered. The specific number assigned indicates the special circumstances under which a basic procedure is performed.

⊘ =Modifier '-51' Exempt　　▶ ◀=New or Revised Text　　✚ =Add-on Code　　CPT 2002

►Code 99091 should be reported no more than once in a 30 day period to include the physician or health care provider time involved with data accession, review and interpretation, modification of care plan as necessary (including communication to patient and/or caregiver), and associated documentation.◄

►If the services described by code 99091 are provided on the same day the patient presents for an E/M service, these services should be considered part of the E/M service and not separately reported.◄

►Do not report 99091 if it occurs within 30 days of care plan oversight services 99374-99380. Do not report 99091 if other more specific CPT codes exist (eg, 93014, 93227, 93233, 93272 for cardiographic services; 95250 for continuous glucose monitoring). Do not report 99091 for transfer and interpretation of data from hospital or clinical laboratory computers.◄

Miscellaneous Services

99000 Handling and/or conveyance of specimen for transfer from the physician's office to a laboratory

99001 Handling and/or conveyance of specimen for transfer from the patient in other than a physician's office to a laboratory (distance may be indicated)

99002 Handling, conveyance, and/or any other service in connection with the implementation of an order involving devices (eg, designing, fitting, packaging, handling, delivery or mailing) when devices such as orthotics, protectives, prosthetics are fabricated by an outside laboratory or shop but which items have been designed, and are to be fitted and adjusted by the attending physician

(For routine collection of venous blood, use 36415)

(99012, 99013, 99014, 99015 have been deleted. To report, see 99371-99373)

99024 Postoperative follow-up visit, included in global service

(As a component of a surgical "package," see **Surgery** guidelines)

99025 Initial (new patient) visit when starred (*) surgical procedure constitutes major service at that visit

99050 Services requested after office hours in addition to basic service

99052 Services requested between 10:00 PM and 8:00 AM in addition to basic service

99054 Services requested on Sundays and holidays in addition to basic service

99056 Services provided at request of patient in a location other than physician's office which are normally provided in the office

99058 Office services provided on an emergency basis

(99062, 99064, 99065 have been deleted. To report, see 99281-99285)

99070 Supplies and materials (except spectacles), provided by the physician over and above those usually included with the office visit or other services rendered (list drugs, trays, supplies, or materials provided)

(For spectacles, see 92390-92395)

99071 Educational supplies, such as books, tapes, and pamphlets, provided by the physician for the patient's education at cost to physician

99075 Medical testimony

99078 Physician educational services rendered to patients in a group setting (eg, prenatal, obesity, or diabetic instructions)

99080 Special reports such as insurance forms, more than the information conveyed in the usual medical communications or standard reporting form

99082 Unusual travel (eg, transportation and escort of patient)

▲ 99090 Analysis of clinical data stored in computers (eg, ECGs, blood pressures, hematologic data)

►(For physician/health care professional collection and interpretation of physiologic data stored/transmitted by patient/caregiver, see 99091)◄

►(Do not report 99090 if other more specific CPT codes exist, eg, 93014, 93227, 93233, 93272 for cardiographic services; 95250 for continuous glucose monitoring, 97750 for musculoskeletal function testing)◄

● 99091 Collection and interpretation of physiologic data (eg, ECG, blood pressure, glucose monitoring) digitally stored and/or transmitted by the patient and/or caregiver to the physician or other qualified health care professional, requiring a minimum of 30 minutes of time

Qualifying Circumstances for Anesthesia

(For explanation of these services, see **Anesthesia** guidelines)

+ 99100 Anesthesia for patient of extreme age, under one year and over seventy (List separately in addition to code for primary anesthesia procedure)

+ 99116 Anesthesia complicated by utilization of total body hypothermia (List separately in addition to code for primary anesthesia procedure)

+ 99135 Anesthesia complicated by utilization of controlled hypotension (List separately in addition to code for primary anesthesia procedure)

+ 99140 Anesthesia complicated by emergency conditions (specify) (List separately in addition to code for primary anesthesia procedure)

(An emergency is defined as existing when delay in treatment of the patient would lead to a significant increase in the threat to life or body part.)

Sedation With or Without Analgesia (Conscious Sedation)

Sedation with or without analgesia (conscious sedation) is used to achieve a medically controlled state of depressed consciousness while maintaining the patient's airway, protective reflexes and ability to respond to stimulation or verbal commands. Conscious sedation includes performance and documentation of pre- and post-sedation evaluations of the patient, administration of the sedation and/or analgesic agent(s), and monitoring of cardiorespiratory function (ie, pulse oximetry, cardiorespiratory monitor, and blood pressure). The use of these codes requires the presence of an independent trained observer to assist the physician in monitoring the patient's level of consciousness and physiological status.

(If the sedation with or without analgesia (conscious sedation) is administered in support of a procedure provided by another physician, see **Anesthesia** section)

⊘ **99141**   Sedation with or without analgesia (conscious sedation); intravenous, intramuscular or inhalation

(94760-94762 may not be reported in addition to 99141)

⊘ **99142**   oral, rectal and/or intranasal

(94760-94762 may not be reported in addition to 99142)

(99150, 99151 have been deleted. To report, see 99354-99360)

Other Services and Procedures

99170   Anogenital examination with colposcopic magnification in childhood for suspected trauma

(For conscious sedation, use 99141, 99142)

99172   Visual function screening, automated or semi-automated bilateral quantitative determination of visual acuity, ocular alignment, color vision by pseudoisochromatic plates, and field of vision (may include all or some screening of the determination(s) for contrast sensitivity, vision under glare)

(This service must employ graduated visual acuity stimuli that allow a quantitative determination of visual acuity (eg, Snellen chart). This service may not be used in addition to a general ophthalmological service or an E/M service)

(Do not report 99172 in conjunction with code 99173)

99173   Screening test of visual acuity, quantitative, bilateral

(The screening test used must employ graduated visual acuity stimuli that allow a quantitative estimate of visual acuity (eg, Snellen chart). Other identifiable services unrelated to this screening test provided at the same time may be reported separately (eg, preventive medicine services). When acuity is measured as part of a general ophthalmological service or of an E/M service of the eye, it is a diagnostic examination and not a screening test.)

(Do not report 99173 in conjunction with code 99172)

99175   Ipecac or similar administration for individual emesis and continued observation until stomach adequately emptied of poison

(For diagnostic intubation, see 82926-82928, 89130-89141)

(For gastric lavage for diagnostic purposes, see 91055)

(99178 has been deleted. To report, use 96110)

(99180 has been deleted. To report, use 99183)

(99182 has been deleted. To report, use 99183)

99183   Physician attendance and supervision of hyperbaric oxygen therapy, per session

(Evaluation and Management services and/or procedures (eg, wound debridement) provided in a hyperbaric oxygen treatment facility in conjunction with a hyperbaric oxygen therapy session should be reported separately)

99185   Hypothermia; regional

99186   total body

99190   Assembly and operation of pump with oxygenator or heat exchanger (with or without ECG and/or pressure monitoring); each hour

99191   3/4 hour

99192   1/2 hour

99195   Phlebotomy, therapeutic (separate procedure)

99199   Unlisted special service, procedure or report

►Home Health Procedures/Services◄

►These codes are used by non-physician health care professionals. Physicians should utilize the home visit codes 99341-99350, and utilize CPT codes other than 99500-99539, for any additional procedure/service provided to a patient living in a residence.◄

►The following codes are used to report services provided in a patient's residence (including assisted living apartments, group homes, non-traditional private homes, custodial care facilities, or schools).◄

►Health care professionals who are authorized to use Evaluation and Management Home Visit codes (99341-99350) may report codes 99500-99539 in addition to codes 99341-99350 if both services are performed. Evaluation and Management services may be reported separately, using the modifier '-25', if the patient's condition requires a significant separately identifiable E/M service, above and beyond the home health service(s)/procedure(s) codes 99500-99539.◄

● **99500**   Home visit for prenatal monitoring and assessment to include fetal heart rate, non-stress test, uterine monitoring, and gestational diabetes monitoring

● **99501**   Home visit for postnatal assessment and follow-up care

● **99502**   Home visit for newborn care and assessment

● **99503**   Home visit for respiratory therapy care (eg, bronchodilator, oxygen therapy, respiratory assessment, apnea evaluation)

● **99504**   Home visit for patients receiving mechanical ventilation

● **99505**   Home visit for stoma care and maintenance including colostomy and cystostomy

● **99506**   Home visit for intramuscular injections

● **99507**   Home visit for care and maintenance of catheter(s) (eg, urinary, drainage, and enteral)

● **99508**   Home visit for polysomnography and sleep studies

● **99509**   Home visit for assistance with activities of daily living and personal care

►(To report self-care/home management training, see 97535)◄

►(To report home medical nutrition assessment and intervention services, see 97802-97804)◄

►(To report home speech therapy services, see 92507-92508)◄

● **99510**   Home visit for individual, family, or marriage counseling

● **99511**   Home visit for fecal impaction management and enema administration

● **99512**   Home visit for hemodialysis, per diem

►(For home infusion of peritoneal dialysis, use 99559)◄

● **99539**   Unlisted home visit service or procedure

►Home Infusion Procedures◄

►Codes 99551-99569 include a home visit by a health care professional and all necessary solutions, equipment, and supplies (except drugs) required to deliver a therapy in a single 24-hour period. All drugs are excluded and should be reported separately. If more than one therapy is given in a 24-hour period, the most complex therapy should be reported first and 99569 should be reported separately for each additional therapy given in that 24-hour period. These codes do not represent self-administration of medications by the patient.◄

● **99551**   Home infusion for pain management (intravenous or subcutaneous), per diem

● **99552**   Home infusion for pain management (epidural or intrathecal), per diem

● **99553**   Home infusion for tocolytic therapy, per diem

● **99554**   Home infusion for hematopoietic hormones (eg, erythropoietin, G-CSF, CM-CSF) or platelets, per diem

● **99555**   Home infusion for chemotherapy, per diem

● **99556**   Home infusion for antibiotics/antifungals/antivirals, per diem

● **99557**   Home infusion of continuous anticoagulant therapy (eg, heparin), per diem

● **99558**   Home infusion of immunotherapy, per diem

● **99559**   Home infusion of peritoneal dialysis, per diem

►(For home visit for hemodialysis, use 99512)◄

● **99560**   Home infusion of enteral nutrition, per diem

● **99561**   Home infusion of hydration therapy, per diem

● **99562**   Home infusion of total parenteral nutrition, per diem

● **99563**   Home administration of aerosolized pentamidine, per diem

● **99564**   Home infusion for anti-hemophilic agents (eg, Factor VIII), per diem

● **99565**   Home infusion of alpha-1-proteinase inhibitor (eg, Prolastin), per diem

● **99566**   Home infusion for uninterrupted, long-term intravenous treatment (eg, epoprostenol), per diem

● **99567**   Home infusion of sympathomimetic agents (eg, dobutamine), per diem

● **99568**   Home infusion of miscellaneous drugs, per diem

+ ● **99569**   Home infusion, each additional therapy given on same day (List separately in addition to code for primary visit)

Notes

Category III Codes

►The following section contains a set of temporary codes for emerging technology, services, and procedures. Category III codes will allow data collection for these services/procedures. Use of unlisted codes does not offer the opportunity for the collection of specific data. If a Category III code is available, this code must be reported instead of a Category I unlisted code. This is an activity that is critically important in the evaluation of health care delivery and the formation of public and private policy. The use of the codes in this section will allow physicians and other qualified health care professionals, insurers, health services researchers, and health policy experts to identify emerging technology, services, and procedures for clinical efficacy, utilization and outcomes.◄

►The inclusion of a service or procedure in this section neither implies nor endorses clinical efficacy, safety or the applicability to clinical practice. The codes in this section do not conform to the usual requirements for CPT Category I codes established by the Editorial Panel. For Category I codes, the Panel requires that the service/procedure be performed by many health care professionals in clinical practice in multiple locations and that FDA approval, as appropriate, has already been received. The nature of emerging technology, services, and procedures is such that these requirements may not be met. For these reasons, temporary codes for emerging technology, services, and procedures have been placed in a separate section of the CPT book and the codes are differentiated from Category I CPT codes by the use of alphanumeric characters.◄

►Services/procedures described in this section make use of alphanumeric characters. These codes have an alpha character as the 5th character in the string, preceded by four digits. The digits are not intended to reflect the placement of the code in the Category I section of CPT nomenclature. Codes in this section may or may not eventually receive a Category I CPT code. In either case, a given Category III code will be archived after five years of its inception unless it is demonstrated that a temporary code is still needed. New codes in this section are released semi-annually via the AMA/CPT internet site, to expedite dissemination for reporting. The full set of temporary codes for emerging technology, services, and procedures are published annually in the CPT book.◄

● **0001T**   Endovascular repair of infrarenal abdominal aortic aneurysm or dissection; modular bifurcated prosthesis (two docking limbs)

● **0002T**   aorto-uni-iliac or aorto-unifemoral prosthesis

►(For radiological supervision and interpretation, use 75952 in conjunction with 0001T-0002T)◄

● **0003T**   Cervicography

►(0004T has been deleted. To report, use 88380)◄

● **0005T**   Transcatheter placement of extracranial cerebrovascular artery stent(s), percutaneous; initial vessel

+ ● **0006T**   each additional vessel (List separately in addition to code for primary procedure)

►(Use 0006T in conjunction with code 0005T)◄

►(For radiological supervision and interpretation, use 0007T)◄

● **0007T**   Transcatheter placement of extracranial cerebrovascular artery stent(s), percutaneous, radiological supervision and interpretation, each vessel

►(For procedure, see 0005T, 0006T)◄

● **0008T**   Upper gastrointestinal endoscopy including esophagus, stomach, and either the duodenum and/or jejunum as appropriate, with suturing of the esophagogastric junction

● **0009T**   Endometrial cryoablation with ultrasonic guidance

● **0010T**   Tuberculosis test, cell mediated immunity measurement of gamma interferon antigen response

● **0012T**   Arthroscopy, knee, surgical, implantation of osteochondral graft(s) for treatment of articular surface defect; autografts

● **0013T**   allografts

● **0014T**   Meniscal transplantation, medial or lateral, knee (any method)

● **0016T**   Destruction of localized lesion of choroid (eg, choroidal neovascularization), transpupillary thermotherapy

● **0017T**   Destruction of macular drusen, photocoagulation

● **0018T**   Delivery of high power, focal magnetic pulses for direct stimulation to cortical neurons

● **0019T**   Extracorporeal shock wave therapy; involving musculoskeletal system

● **0020T**   involving plantar fascia

● **0021T**   Insertion of transcervical or transvaginal fetal oximetry sensor

● **0023T**   Infectious agent drug susceptibility phenotype prediction using genotypic comparison to known genotypic/phenotypic database, HIV 1

● **0024T**   Non-surgical septal reduction therapy (eg, alcohol ablation), for hypertrophic obstructive cardiomyopathy, with coronary arteriograms, with or without temporary pacemaker

● **0025T**   Determination of corneal thickness (eg, pachymetry) with interpretation and report, bilateral

● **0026T**   Lipoprotein, direct measurement, intermediate density lipoproteins (IDL) (remnant lipoproteins)

Notes

Appendix A

Modifiers

This list includes all of the modifiers applicable to *CPT* 2002 codes.

-21 **Prolonged Evaluation and Management Services:** When the face-to-face or floor/unit service(s) provided is prolonged or otherwise greater than that usually required for the highest level of evaluation and management service within a given category, it may be identified by adding modifier '-21' to the evaluation and management code number or by use of the separate five digit modifier code 09921. A report may also be appropriate.

-22 **Unusual Procedural Services:** When the service(s) provided is greater than that usually required for the listed procedure, it may be identified by adding modifier '-22' to the usual procedure number or by use of the separate five digit modifier code 09922. A report may also be appropriate.

-23 **Unusual Anesthesia:** Occasionally, a procedure, which usually requires either no anesthesia or local anesthesia, because of unusual circumstances must be done under general anesthesia. This circumstance may be reported by adding the modifier '-23' to the procedure code of the basic service or by use of the separate five digit modifier code 09923.

-24 **Unrelated Evaluation and Management Service by the Same Physician During a Postoperative Period:** The physician may need to indicate that an evaluation and management service was performed during a postoperative period for a reason(s) unrelated to the original procedure. This circumstance may be reported by adding the modifier '-24' to the appropriate level of E/M service, or the separate five digit modifier 09924 may be used.

-25 **Significant, Separately Identifiable Evaluation and Management Service by the Same Physician on the Same Day of the Procedure or Other Service:** The physician may need to indicate that on the day a procedure or service identified by a CPT code was performed, the patient's condition required a significant, separately identifiable E/M service above and beyond the other service provided or beyond the usual preoperative and postoperative care associated with the procedure that was performed. The E/M service may be prompted by the symptom or condition for which the procedure and/or service was provided. As such, different diagnoses are not required for reporting of the E/M services on the same date. This circumstance may be reported by adding the modifier '-25' to the appropriate level of E/M service, or the separate five digit modifier 09925 may be used. **Note:** This modifier is not used to report an E/M service that resulted in a decision to perform surgery. See modifier '-57.'

-26 **Professional Component:** Certain procedures are a combination of a physician component and a technical component. When the physician component is reported separately, the service may be identified by adding the modifier '-26' to the usual procedure number or the service may be reported by use of the five digit modifier code 09926.

-32 **Mandated Services:** Services related to *mandated* consultation and/or related services (eg, PRO, third party payer, governmental, legislative or regulatory requirement) may be identified by adding the modifier '-32' to the basic procedure or the service may be reported by use of the five digit modifier 09932.

-47 **Anesthesia by Surgeon:** Regional or general anesthesia provided by the surgeon may be reported by adding the modifier '-47' to the basic service or by use of the separate five digit modifier code 09947. (This does not include local anesthesia.) **Note:** Modifier '-47' or 09947 would not be used as a modifier for the anesthesia procedures 00100-01999.

-50 **Bilateral Procedure:** Unless otherwise identified in the listings, bilateral procedures that are performed at the same operative session should be identified by adding the modifier '-50' to the appropriate five digit code or by use of the separate five digit modifier code 09950.

-51 **Multiple Procedures:** When multiple procedures, other than E/M services, are performed at the same session by the same provider, the primary procedure or service may be reported as listed. The additional procedure(s) or service(s) may be identified by appending the modifier '-51' to the additional procedure or service code(s) or by the use of the separate five digit modifier 09951. **Note:** This modifier should not be appended to designated "add-on" codes (see Appendix E).

-52 **Reduced Services:** Under certain circumstances a service or procedure is partially reduced or eliminated at the physician's discretion. Under these circumstances the service provided can be identified by its usual procedure number and the addition of the modifier '-52', signifying that the service is reduced. This provides a means of reporting reduced services without disturbing the identification of the basic service. Modifier code 09952 may be used as an alternative to modifier '-52.' **Note:** For hospital outpatient reporting of a previously scheduled procedure/service that is partially reduced or cancelled as a result of extenuating circumstances or those that threaten the well-being of the patient prior to or after administration of anesthesia, see modifiers '-73' and '-74' (see modifiers approved for ASC hospital outpatient use).

-53 **Discontinued Procedure:** Under certain circumstances, the physician may elect to terminate a surgical or diagnostic procedure. Due to extenuating circumstances or those that threaten the well being of the patient, it may be necessary to indicate that a surgical or diagnostic procedure was started but discontinued. This circumstance may be reported by adding the modifier '-53' to the code reported by the physician for the discontinued procedure or by use of the separate five digit modifier code 09953. **Note:** This modifier is not used to report the elective cancellation of a procedure prior to the patient's anesthesia induction and/or surgical preparation in the operating suite. For outpatient hospital/ambulatory surgery center (ASC) reporting of a previously scheduled procedure/service that is partially reduced or cancelled as a result of extenuating circumstances or those that threaten the well being of the patient prior to or after administration of anesthesia, see modifiers '-73' and '-74' (see modifiers approved for ASC hospital outpatient use).

-54 **Surgical Care Only:** When one physician performs a surgical procedure and another provides preoperative and/or postoperative management, surgical services may be identified by adding the modifier '-54' to the usual procedure number or by use of the separate five digit modifier code 09954.

-55 **Postoperative Management Only:** When one physician performed the postoperative management and another physician performed the surgical procedure, the postoperative component may be identified by adding the modifier '-55' to the usual procedure number or by use of the separate five digit modifier code 09955.

-56 **Preoperative Management Only:** When one physician performed the preoperative care and evaluation and another physician performed the surgical procedure, the preoperative component may be identified by adding the modifier '-56' to the usual procedure number or by use of the separate five digit modifier code 09956.

-57 **Decision for Surgery:** An evaluation and management service that resulted in the initial decision to perform the surgery may be identified by adding the modifier '-57' to the appropriate level of E/M service, or the separate five digit modifier 09957 may be used.

-58 **Staged or Related Procedure or Service by the Same Physician During the Postoperative Period:** The physician may need to indicate that the performance of a procedure or service during the postoperative period was: a) planned prospectively at the time of the original procedure (staged); b) more extensive than the original procedure; or c) for therapy following a diagnostic surgical procedure. This circumstance may be reported by adding the modifier '-58' to the staged or related procedure, or the separate five digit modifier 09958 may be used. **Note:** This modifier is not used to report the treatment of a problem that requires a return to the operating room. See modifier '-78.'

-59 **Distinct Procedural Service:** Under certain circumstances, the physician may need to indicate that a procedure or service was distinct or independent from other services performed on the same day. Modifier '-59' is used to identify procedures/services that are not normally reported together, but are appropriate under the circumstances. This may represent a different session or patient encounter, different procedure or surgery, different site or organ system, separate incision/excision, separate lesion, or separate injury (or area of injury in extensive injuries) not ordinarily encountered or performed on the same day by the same physician. However, when another already established modifier is appropriate it should be used rather than modifier '-59.' Only if no more descriptive modifier is available, and the use of modifier '-59' best explains the circumstances, should modifier '-59' be used. Modifier code 09959 may be used as an alternative to modifier '-59.'

-62 **Two Surgeons:** When two surgeons work together as primary surgeons performing distinct part(s) of a procedure, each surgeon should report his/her distinct operative work by adding the modifier '-62' to the procedure code ▶and any associated add-on code(s) for that procedure as long as both surgeons continue to work together as primary surgeons.◀ Each surgeon should report the co-surgery once using the same procedure code. If additional procedure(s) (including add-on procedure(s), are performed during the same surgical session, separate code(s) may ▶also◀ be reported with the modifier '-62' added. Modifier code 09962 may be used as an alternative to modifier '-62'. **Note:** If a co-surgeon acts as an assistant in the performance of additional procedure(s) during the same surgical session, those services may be reported using separate procedure code(s) with the modifier '-80' or modifier ▶'-82'◀ added, as appropriate.

-66 **Surgical Team:** Under some circumstances, highly complex procedures (requiring the concomitant services of several physicians, often of different specialties, plus other highly skilled, specially trained personnel, various types of complex equipment) are carried out under the "surgical team" concept. Such circumstances may be identified by each participating physician with the addition of the modifier '-66' to the basic procedure number used for reporting services. Modifier code 09966 may be used as an alternative to modifier '-66.'

-76 **Repeat Procedure by Same Physician:** The physician may need to indicate that a procedure or service was repeated subsequent to the original procedure or service. This circumstance may be reported by adding the modifier '-76' to the repeated procedure/service or the separate five digit modifier code 09976 may be used.

-77 **Repeat Procedure by Another Physician:** The physician may need to indicate that a basic procedure or service performed by another physician had to be repeated. This situation may be reported by adding modifier '-77' to the repeated procedure/service or the separate five digit modifier code 09977 may be used.

-78 **Return to the Operating Room for a Related Procedure During the Postoperative Period:** The physician may need to indicate that another procedure was performed during the postoperative period of the initial procedure. When this subsequent procedure is related to the first, and requires the use of the operating room, it may be reported by adding the modifier '-78' to the related procedure, or by using the separate five digit modifier 09978. (For repeat procedures on the same day, see '-76'.)

-79 Unrelated Procedure or Service by the Same Physician During the Postoperative Period: The physician may need to indicate that the performance of a procedure or service during the postoperative period was unrelated to the original procedure. This circumstance may be reported by using the modifier '-79' or by using the separate five digit modifier 09979. (For repeat procedures on the same day, see '-76'.)

-80 Assistant Surgeon: Surgical assistant services may be identified by adding the modifier '-80' to the usual procedure number(s) or by use of the separate five digit modifier code 09980.

-81 Minimum Assistant Surgeon: Minimum surgical assistant services are identified by adding the modifier '-81' to the usual procedure number or by use of the separate five digit modifier code 09981.

-82 Assistant Surgeon (when qualified resident surgeon not available): The unavailability of a qualified resident surgeon is a prerequisite for use of modifier '-82' appended to the usual procedure code number(s) or by use of the separate five digit modifier code 09982.

-90 Reference (Outside) Laboratory: When laboratory procedures are performed by a party other than the treating or reporting physician, the procedure may be identified by adding the modifier '-90' to the usual procedure number or by use of the separate five digit modifier code 09990.

-91 Repeat Clinical Diagnostic Laboratory Test: In the course of patient treatment, it may be necessary to repeat the same laboratory test on the same day to obtain subsequent (multiple) test results. Under these circumstances, the laboratory test performed can be identified by its usual procedure number and the addition of the modifier '-91'. **Note:** This modifier may not be used when tests are rerun to confirm initial results; due to testing problems with specimens or equipment; or for any other reason when a normal, one-time, reportable result is all that is required. This modifier may not be used when other code(s) describe a series of test results (eg, glucose tolerance tests, evocative/suppression testing). This modifier may only be used for laboratory test(s) performed more than once on the same day on the same patient.

-99 Multiple Modifiers: Under certain circumstances two or more modifiers may be necessary to completely delineate a service. In such situations modifier '-99' should be added to the basic procedure, and other applicable modifiers may be listed as part of the description of the service. Modifier code 09999 may be used as an alternative to modifier '-99.'

▶Anesthesia Physical Status Modifiers◀

▶The Physical Status modifiers are consistent with the American Society of Anesthesiologists' ranking of patient physical status, and distinguish various levels of complexity of the anesthesia service provided. All anesthesia services are reported by use of the anesthesia five-digit procedure code (00100-03108) with the appropriate physical status modifier appended.◀

▶Example: 00100-P1

Under certain circumstances, when another established modifier(s) is appropriate, it should be used in addition to the physical status modifier.

Example: 00100-P4-53◀

▶**Physical Status Modifier P1:** A normal healthy patient

Physical Status Modifier P2: A patient with mild systemic disease

Physical Status Modifier P3: A patient with severe systemic disease

Physical Status Modifier P4: A patient with severe systemic disease that is a constant threat to life

Physical Status Modifier P5: A moribund patient who is not expected to survive without the operation

Physical Status Modifier P6: A declared brain-dead patient whose organs are being removed for donor purposes◀

Modifiers Approved for Ambulatory Surgery Center (ASC) Hospital Outpatient Use

CPT Level I Modifiers

-25 Significant, Separately Identifiable Evaluation and Management Service by the Same Physician on the Same Day of the Procedure or Other Service: The physician may need to indicate that on the day a procedure or service identified by a CPT code was performed, the patient's condition required a significant, separately identifiable E/M service above and beyond the other service provided or beyond the usual preoperative and postoperative care associated with the procedure that was performed. The E/M service may be prompted by the symptom or condition for which the procedure and/or service was provided. As such, different diagnoses are not required for reporting of the E/M services on the same date. This circumstance may be reported by adding the modifier '-25' to the appropriate level of E/M service, or the separate five digit modifier 09925 may be used. **Note:** This modifier is not used to report an E/M service that resulted in a decision to perform surgery. See modifier '-57.'

-27 Multiple Outpatient Hospital E/M Encounters on the Same Date: For hospital outpatient reporting purposes, utilization of hospital resources related to separate and distinct E/M encounters performed in multiple outpatient hospital settings on the same date may be reported by adding the modifier '-27' to each appropriate level outpatient and/or emergency department E/M code(s). This modifier provides a means of reporting circumstances involving evaluation and management services provided by physician(s) in more than one (multiple) outpatient hospital setting(s) (eg, hospital emergency department, clinic). **Note:** This modifier is not to be used for physician reporting of multiple E/M services performed by the same physician on the same date. For physician reporting of all outpatient evaluation and management services provided by the same physician on the same date and performed in multiple outpatient setting(s) (eg, hospital emergency department, clinic), see **Evaluation and Management, Emergency Department, or Preventive Medicine Services** codes.

-50 **Bilateral Procedure:** Unless otherwise identified in the listings, bilateral procedures that are performed at the same operative session should be identified by adding the modifier '-50' to the appropriate five digit code or by use of the separate five digit modifier code 09950.

-52 **Reduced Services:** Under certain circumstances a service or procedure is partially reduced or eliminated at the physician's discretion. Under these circumstances the service provided can be identified by its usual procedure number and the addition of the modifier '-52', signifying that the service is reduced. This provides a means of reporting reduced services without disturbing the identification of the basic service. Modifier code 09952 may be used as an alternative to modifier '-52.' **Note:** For hospital outpatient reporting of a previously scheduled procedure/service that is partially reduced or cancelled as a result of extenuating circumstances or those that threaten the well-being of the patient prior to or after administration of anesthesia, see modifiers '-73' and '-74' (see modifiers approved for ASC hospital outpatient use).

-58 **Staged or Related Procedure or Service by the Same Physician During the Postoperative Period:** The physician may need to indicate that the performance of a procedure or service during the postoperative period was: a) planned prospectively at the time of the original procedure (staged); b) more extensive than the original procedure; or c) for therapy following a diagnostic surgical procedure. This circumstance may be reported by adding the modifier '-58' to the staged or related procedure, or the separate five digit modifier 09958 may be used. Note: This modifier is not used to report the treatment of a problem that requires a return to the operating room. See modifier '-78.'

-59 **Distinct Procedural Service:** Under certain circumstances, the physician may need to indicate that a procedure or service was distinct or independent from other services performed on the same day. Modifier '-59' is used to identify procedures/services that are not normally reported together, but are appropriate under the circumstances. This may represent a different session or patient encounter, different procedure or surgery, different site or organ system, separate incision/excision, separate lesion, or separate injury (or area of injury in extensive injuries) not ordinarily encountered or performed on the same day by the same physician. However, when another already established modifier is appropriate it should be used rather than modifier '-59.' Only if no more descriptive modifier is available, and the use of modifier '-59' best explains the circumstances, should modifier '-59' be used. Modifier code 09959 may be used as an alternative to modifier '-59.'

-73 **Discontinued Out-Patient Hospital/Ambulatory Surgery Center (ASC) Procedure Prior to the Administration of Anesthesia:** Due to extenuating circumstances or those that threaten the well being of the patient, the physician may cancel a surgical or diagnostic procedure subsequent to the patient's surgical preparation (including sedation when provided, and being taken to the room where the procedure is to be performed), but prior to the administration of anesthesia (local, regional block(s) or general). Under these circumstances, the intended service that is prepared for but cancelled can be reported by its usual procedure number and the addition of the modifier '-73' or by use of the separate five digit modifier code 09973. **Note:** The elective cancellation of a service prior to the administration of anesthesia and/or surgical preparation of the patient should not be reported. For physician reporting of a discontinued procedure, see modifier '-53.'

-74 **Discontinued Out-Patient Hospital/Ambulatory Surgery Center (ASC) Procedure After Administration of Anesthesia:** Due to extenuating circumstances or those that threaten the well being of the patient, the physician may terminate a surgical or diagnostic procedure after the administration of anesthesia (local, regional block(s), general) or after the procedure was started (incision made, intubation started, scope inserted, etc). Under these circumstances, the procedure started but terminated can be reported by its usual procedure number and the addition of the modifier '-74' or by use of the separate five digit modifier code 09974. **Note:** The elective cancellation of a service prior to the administration of anesthesia and/or surgical preparation of the patient should not be reported. For physician reporting of a discontinued procedure, see modifier '-53.'

-76 **Repeat Procedure by Same Physician:** The physician may need to indicate that a procedure or service was repeated subsequent to the original procedure or service. This circumstance may be reported by adding the modifier '-76' to the repeated procedure/service or the separate five digit modifier code 09976 may be used.

-77 **Repeat Procedure by Another Physician:** The physician may need to indicate that a basic procedure or service performed by another physician had to be repeated. This situation may be reported by adding modifier '-77' to the repeated procedure/service or the separate five digit modifier code 09977 may be used.

-78 **Return to the Operating Room for a Related Procedure During the Postoperative Period:** The physician may need to indicate that another procedure was performed during the postoperative period of the initial procedure. When this subsequent procedure is related to the first, and requires the use of the operating room, it may be reported by adding the modifier '-78' to the related procedure, or by using the separate five digit modifier 09978. (For repeat procedures on the same day, see '-76')

-79 **Unrelated Procedure or Service by the Same Physician During the Postoperative Period:** The physician may need to indicate that the performance of a procedure or service during the postoperative period was unrelated to the original procedure. This circumstance may be reported by using the modifier '-79' or by using the separate five digit modifier 09979. (For repeat procedures on the same day, see '-76'.)

-91 **Repeat Clinical Diagnostic Laboratory Test:** In the course of treatment of the patient, it may be necessary to repeat the same laboratory test on the same day to obtain subsequent (multiple) test results. Under these circumstances, the laboratory test performed can be identified by its usual procedure number and the addition of the modifier '-91'. **Note:** This modifier may not be used when tests are rerun to confirm initial results; due to testing problems with specimens or equipment; or for any other reason when a normal, one-time, reportable result is all that is required. This modifier may not be used when other code(s) describe a series of test results (eg, glucose tolerance tests, evocative/suppression testing). This modifier may only be used for laboratory test(s) performed more than once on the same day on the same patient.

Level II (HCPCS/National) Modifiers

-E1 Upper left, eyelid

-E2 Lower left, eyelid

-E3 Upper right, eyelid

-E4 Lower right, eyelid

-F1 Left hand, second digit

-F2 Left hand, third digit

-F3 Left hand, fourth digit

-F4 Left hand, fifth digit

-F5 Right hand, thumb

-F6 Right hand, second digit

-F7 Right hand, third digit

-F8 Right hand, fourth digit

-F9 Right hand, fifth digit

-FA Left hand, thumb

-LC Left circumflex coronary artery (Hospitals use with codes 92980-92984, 92995, 92996)

-LD Left anterior descending coronary artery (Hospitals use with codes 92980-92984, 92995, 92996)

-LT Left side (used to identify procedures performed on the left side of the body)

-QM Ambulance service provided under arrangement by a provider of services

-QN Ambulance service furnished directly by a provider of services

-RC Right coronary artery (Hospitals use with codes 92980-92982, 92995, 92996)

-RT Right side (used to identify procedures performed on the right side of the body)

-T1 Left foot, second digit

-T2 Left foot, third digit

-T3 Left foot, fourth digit

-T4 Left foot, fifth digit

-T5 Right foot, great toe

-T6 Right foot, second digit

-T7 Right foot, third digit

-T8 Right foot, fourth digit

-T9 Right foot, fifth digit

-TA Left foot, great toe

Appendix B

Summary of Additions, Deletions, and Revisions

This listing is a summary of additions, deletions, and revisions applicable to *CPT 2002* codes.

The notes, introductory paragraphs, and cross-references that have been revised or added to *CPT 2002* are not included in Appendix B, but are identified in the main text of *CPT* with "▶ ◀" symbols.

The descriptors of the codes listed as "grammatical change" have not been substantially altered, but involve placement of the semicolon, or other punctuation, or a similar minor change. These codes will not be identified in *CPT* with a ▲ symbol.

'-22'	Modifier revised
'-60'	Modifier deleted
0001T	Endovascular repair of abdominal aortic aneurysm code added
0002T	Endovascular repair of abdominal aortic aneurysm code added
0003T	Cervicography code added
0004T	Code deleted. To report, use 88380
0005T	Percutaneous extracranial cerebrovascular artery stent code added
0006T	Percutaneous extracranial cerebrovascular artery stent code added
0007T	Percutaneous extracranial cerebrovascular artery stent code added
0008T	Upper GI endoscopy with suture of esophagogastric junction code added
0009T	Endometrial cryoablation code added
0010T	Tuberculosis test, cell mediated immunity code added
0012T	Osteochondral knee autograft code added
0013T	Osteochondral knee allograft code added
0014T	Meniscal transplant of knee code added
0016T	Thermotherapy of choroidal eye lesion code added
0017T	Photocoagulation of macular drusen code added
0018T	Transcranial magnetic stimulation code added
0019T	Extracorporeal shock wave therapy code added
0020T	Extracorporeal shock wave therapy code added
0021T	Fetal oximetry code added
0023T	Phenotype drug test for HIV 1 code added
0024T	Transcatheter cardiac reduction code added
0025T	Ultrasonic pachymetry code added
0026T	Remnant lipoproteins code added
00220	Terminology revised
00560	Terminology revised

00797	Anesthesia for surgery for morbid obesity code added
00850	Code deleted. To report, use 01961
00851	Anesthesia for tubal ligation code added
00855	Code deleted. To report, use 01963
00857	Code deleted. To report, see 01968, 01969
00869	Anesthesia for vasectomy code added
00884	Code deleted. To report, use 01930
00942	Terminology revised
00946	Code deleted. To report, use 01960
00955	Code deleted. To report, use 01967
01214	Terminology revised
01402	Terminology revised
01904	Code deleted. To report, use 01905
01905	Anesthesia for spinal injection/repair code added
01906	Code deleted. To report, use 01905
01908	Code deleted. To report, use 01905
01910	Code deleted. To report, use 01905
01912	Code deleted. To report, use 01905
01914	Code deleted. To report, use 01905
01916	Terminology revised
01918	Code deleted. To report, use 01916
01920	Terminology revised
01921	Code deleted. To report, see 01924-01926
01924	Anesthesia for therapeutic interventional radiology arterial procedure code added
01925	Anesthesia for therapeutic interventional radiology arterial procedure code added
01926	Anesthesia for therapeutic interventional radiology arterial procedure code added
01930	Anesthesia for therapeutic interventional radiology venous procedure code added
01931	Anesthesia for therapeutic interventional radiology venous procedure code added
01932	Anesthesia for therapeutic interventional radiology venous procedure code added
01933	Anesthesia for therapeutic interventional radiology venous procedure code added
01951	Terminology revised
01952	Terminology revised
01960	Anesthesia for vaginal delivery code added
01961	Anesthesia for cesarean delivery code added
01962	Anesthesia for urgent hysterectomy following delivery code added
01963	Anesthesia for cesarean hysterectomy code added
01964	Anesthesia for abortion procedures code added
01967	Neuroaxial labor analgesia/anesthesia code added
01968	Neuroaxial labor analgesia/anesthesia add-on procedure code added

01969	Neuroaxial labor analgesia/anesthesia add-on procedure code added
01995	Terminology revised
10021	Fine needle aspiration code added
10022	Fine needle aspiration code added
11755	Terminology revised
11981	Insertion of drug delivery implant device code added
11982	Removal of drug delivery implant device code added
11983	Removal and reinsertion of drug delivery implant device code added
15732	Terminology revised
15860	Terminology revised
17000	Terminology revised
17004	Terminology revised
17110	Terminology revised
17260	Terminology revised
17270	Terminology revised
17280	Terminology revised
20225	Terminology revised
20526	Carpal tunnel therapeutic injection code added
20550	Terminology revised
20551	Injection, tendon origin/insertion code added
20552	Trigger point injection code added
20553	Trigger point injection code added
21182	Terminology revised
21183	Terminology revised
21184	Terminology revised
21750	Terminology revised
23000	Terminology revised
23350	Terminology revised
24075	Terminology revised
24076	Grammatical change
24300	Manipulation, elbow, under anesthesia code added
24332	Tenolysis of triceps code added
24343	Repair of elbow ligament code added
24344	Repair of elbow ligament code added
24345	Repair of elbow ligament code added
24346	Reconstruct elbow ligament code added
25001	Incision of flexor tendon sheath, wrist code added
25020	Terminology revised
25024	Decompression fasciotomy of forearm/wrist code added
25025	Decompression fasciotomy of forearm/wrist code added
25075	Terminology revised
25076	Grammatical change
25259	Manipulation of wrist under anesthesia code added
25274	Terminology revised

25275	Repair of tendon sheath, forearm/wrist code added
25394	Osteoplasty of carpal bone code added
25405	Terminology revised
25420	Terminology revised
25430	Vascular pedicle graft for carpal bone code added
25431	Repair of nonunion carpal bone code added
25440	Terminology revised
25443	Terminology revised
25520	Terminology revised
25526	Terminology revised
25645	Terminology revised
25651	Percutaneous skeletal fixation of ulnar styloid fracture code added
25652	Open treatment of ulnar styloid fracture code added
25671	Percutaneous skeletal fixation of distal radioulnar dislocation code added
26115	Terminology revised
26116	Terminology revised
26160	Terminology revised
26340	Manipulation of finger joint under anesthesia code added
26350	Terminology revised
26356	Terminology revised
26390	Terminology revised
26392	Terminology revised
26415	Terminology revised
26416	Terminology revised
26426	Terminology revised
26428	Terminology revised
26445	Terminology revised
26510	Terminology revised
26585	Code deleted. To report, use 26587
26587	Terminology revised
26590	Terminology revised
26597	Code deleted. To report, see 11041-11042, 14040-14041, or 15120, 15240)
26607	Terminology revised
26670	Terminology revised
26676	Terminology revised
26685	Terminology revised
26843	Terminology revised
27110	Terminology revised
27130	Terminology revised
27132	Terminology revised
27140	Terminology revised
27185	Terminology revised
27447	Terminology revised
27475	Grammatical change

28104	Terminology revised		35131	Terminology revised
28238	Terminology revised		35141	Terminology revised
28299	Terminology revised		35151	Terminology revised
28737	Terminology revised		35161	Terminology revised
29049	Terminology revised		35646	Terminology revised
29086	Application of finger cast code added		35647	Aortofemoral bypass graft code added
29805	Shoulder arthroscopy code added		35685	Bypass graft patency/vein patch code added
29806	Shoulder arthroscopy code added		35686	Bypass graft patency/AV fistula code added
29807	Shoulder arthroscopy code added		36002	Pseudoaneurysm injection code added
29815	Code deleted. To report, use 29805		36005	Terminology revised
29819	Grammatical change		36400	Terminology revised
29824	Shoulder arthroscopy code added		36819	Terminology revised
29900	Metacarpophalangeal joint arthroscopy code added		36820	Anastomosis, forearm vein transposition code added
29901	Metacarpophalangeal joint arthroscopy code added		36823	Terminology revised
29902	Metacarpophalangeal joint arthroscopy code added		38220	Bone marrow aspiration code added
29909	Code deleted. To report, use 29999		38221	Bone marrow biopsy code added
29999	Unlisted arthroscopy procedure code added		42970	Terminology revised
30117	Terminology revised		43108	Terminology revised
30801	Terminology revised		43113	Terminology revised
30905	Terminology revised		43118	Terminology revised
31238	Terminology revised		43123	Terminology revised
31528	Terminology revised		43227	Terminology revised
31529	Terminology revised		43245	Terminology revised
31641	Terminology revised		43260	Grammatical change
32420	Terminology revised		43264	Terminology revised
32650	Terminology revised		43265	Terminology revised
33250	Terminology revised		43313	Esophagoplasty for congenital defect code added
33406	Terminology revised		43314	Esophagoplasty for congenital defect code added
33413	Terminology revised		43361	Terminology revised
33610	Terminology revised		43847	Terminology revised
33967	Percutaneous insertion of intra-aortic balloon code added		43860	Terminology revised
33975	Terminology revised		44020	Terminology revised
33976	Terminology revised		44110	Terminology revised
33977	Terminology revised		44126	Enterectomy of small intestine for congenital atresia code added
33978	Terminology revised		44127	Enterectomy of small intestine for congenital atresia code added
33979	Insertion of intracorporal ventricular assist device code added		44128	Enterectomy of small intestine for congenital atresia code added
33980	Removal of intracorporal ventricular assist device code added		44160	Terminology revised
35001	Terminology revised		44202	Terminology revised
35005	Terminology revised		44203	Laparoscopic resection of small intestine code added
35021	Terminology revised		44204	Laparoscopic partial colectomy code added
35045	Terminology revised		44205	Laparoscopic partial colectomy code added
35081	Terminology revised		44322	Terminology revised
35091	Terminology revised		44366	Terminology revised
35102	Terminology revised		44378	Terminology revised
35111	Terminology revised		44391	Terminology revised
35121	Terminology revised		44661	Terminology revised

44700	Terminology revised
45136	Excision of ileoanal reservoir code added
45190	Terminology revised
45303	Terminology revised
45317	Terminology revised
45334	Terminology revised
45382	Terminology revised
46020	Placement of anal seton code added
46604	Terminology revised
46614	Terminology revised
46924	Terminology revised
46940	Terminology revised
47370	Laparoscopic radiofrequency ablation of liver tumor code added
47371	Laparoscopic cryosurgical ablation of liver tumor code added
47380	Open radiofrequency ablation of liver tumor code added
47381	Open cryosurgical ablation of liver tumor code added
47382	Percutaneous radiofrequency ablation of liver tumor code added
47554	Terminology revised
48100	Terminology revised
48160	Terminology revised
48500	Terminology revised
48545	Terminology revised
48547	Terminology revised
49220	Terminology revised
49424	Terminology revised
49491	Inguinal hernia repair on preterm infant code added
49492	Inguinal hernia repair on preterm infant code added
49495	Terminology revised
50220	Terminology revised
50810	Terminology revised
50815	Terminology revised
50820	Terminology revised
50825	Terminology revised
50840	Terminology revised
51065	Terminology revised
51590	Terminology revised
51596	Terminology revised
51940	Terminology revised
51960	Terminology revised
52001	Cystourethroscopy with removal of clots code added
52347	Cystourethroscopy with transurethral resection of ejaculatory ducts code added
52510	Terminology revised
53431	Urethroplasty code added
53443	Code deleted. To report, use 53431
53444	Insertion of tandem cuff code added

53445	Terminology revised
53446	Removal of urethral/bladder neck sphincter code added
53447	Terminology revised
53448	Removal/replacement of urethral/bladder neck sphincter code added
53449	Terminology revised
53853	Prostatic water-induced thermotherapy code added
54065	Terminology revised
54162	Lysis of penile circumcision adhesions code added
54163	Repair of incomplete circumcision code added
54164	Frenulotomy of the penis code added
54402	Code deleted. To report, see 54415, 54416
54405	Terminology revised
54406	Removal of penile prosthesis code added
54407	Code deleted. To report, see 54406, 54408, 54410
54408	Repair of penile prosthesis code added
54409	Code deleted. To report, use 54408
54410	Removal/replacement of penile prosthesis code added
54411	Removal/replacement of penile prosthesis code added
54415	Removal of penile prosthesis code added
54416	Removal/replacement of penile prosthesis code added
54417	Removal/replacement of penile prosthesis code added
54510	Code deleted. To report, use 54512
56501	Terminology revised
56515	Terminology revised
57022	Terminology revised
57061	Terminology revised
57065	Terminology revised
57155	Insertion of uterine tandems/vaginal ovoids for clinical brachytherapy code added
57510	Terminology revised
58140	Terminology revised
58275	Terminology revised
58346	Insertion of Heyman capsules for clinical brachytherapy code added
58563	Terminology revised
58611	Terminology revised
58953	Hysterectomy/removal of tubes/ovaries w/radical dissection code added
58954	Hysterectomy/removal of tubes/ovaries w/radical dissection/lymphadenectomy code added
59000	Terminology revised
59001	Therapeutic amniotic fluid reduction code added
60000	Terminology revised
60270	Terminology revised
61026	Terminology revised
61055	Terminology revised

61618	Terminology revised
62100	Terminology revised
62230	Terminology revised
62252	Terminology revised
62256	Terminology revised
62272	Terminology revised
63707	Terminology revised
63709	Terminology revised
64555	Terminology revised
64561	Percutaneous implantation of neurostimulator electrodes code added
64575	Terminology revised
64581	Incision for neurostimulator electrode implant code added
64755	Terminology revised
64820	Terminology revised
64821	Sympathectomy code added
64822	Sympathectomy code added
64823	Sympathectomy code added
65235	Terminology revised
65900	Terminology revised
65920	Terminology revised
65930	Terminology revised
66020	Terminology revised
66982	Terminology revised
67225	Ocular photodynamic therapy code added
67515	Terminology revised
69310	Terminology revised
69990	Terminology revised
74230	Terminology revised
74245	Terminology revised
74249	Terminology revised
74250	Terminology revised
74305	Terminology revised
74327	Terminology revised
74363	Terminology revised
75898	Terminology revised
75989	Terminology revised
76066	Terminology revised
76070	Terminology revised
76078	Terminology revised
76085	Computerized screening mammography code added
76120	Terminology revised
76125	Terminology revised
76355	Terminology revised
76360	Terminology revised
76362	CAT guidance for tissue ablation code added
76370	Terminology revised
76375	Terminology revised
76380	Terminology revised
76394	MRI guidance for tissue ablation code added
76490	US guidance for tissue ablation code added
76536	Terminology revised
76604	Terminology revised
76645	Terminology revised
76700	Terminology revised
76770	Terminology revised
76778	Terminology revised
76800	Terminology revised
76805	Terminology revised
76819	Terminology revised
76830	Terminology revised
76856	Terminology revised
76870	Terminology revised
76880	Terminology revised
76885	Terminology revised
76886	Terminology revised
76936	Grammatical change
77300	Terminology revised
77301	Intensity modulated radiotherapy plan code added
77418	Intensity modulated treatment delivery code added
78195	Terminology revised
78290	Terminology revised
78615	Terminology revised
78650	Terminology revised
80072	Code deleted. To report, see 84550, 85651, 86255, 86430
82270	Terminology revised
82273	Terminology revised
82274	Fecal hemoglobin immunoassay test code added
82355	Terminology revised
83013	Terminology revised
83873	Terminology revised
83916	Terminology revised
83950	Oncoprotein, HER-2/neu code added
84445	Terminology revised
85095	Code deleted. To report, use 38220
85097	Terminology revised
85102	Code deleted. To report, use 38221
85535	Code deleted. To report, use 85536
86140	Grammatical change
86141	High sensitivity C-reactive protein code added
86325	Terminology revised
86336	Inhibin A code added

87045	Terminology revised
87198	Cytomegalovirus antibody (DFA) code added
87199	Enterovirus antibody (DFA) code added
87802	Strep B detection immunoassay detection with optic code added
87803	Clostridium difficile toxin A immunoassay detection with optic code added
87804	Influenza immunoassay detection with optic code added
87902	Hepatitis C genotype analysis code added
87903	Terminology revised
87904	Terminology revised
88170	Code deleted. To report, use 10021
88171	Code deleted. To report, use 10022
88304	Terminology revised
88305	Terminology revised
88380	Microdissection code added
89050	Terminology revised
90471	Terminology revised
90473	Immunization administration code added
90474	Immunization administration code added
90732	Terminology revised
90780	Terminology revised
90939	Hemodialysis access flow study code added
90940	Grammatical change
91123	Pulsed irrigation of fecal impaction code added
92136	Ophthalmic biometry code added
92532	Terminology revised
92534	Terminology revised
92973	Percutaneous coronary thrombectomy code added
92974	Placement of radiation delivery device for coronary brachytherapy code added
93025	Microvolt T-wave assessment code added
93536	Code deleted. To report, use 33967
93607	Code deleted. To report, use 93622
93609	Terminology revised
93613	3-D intracardiac mapping code added
93619	Terminology revised
93620	Terminology revised
93621	Terminology revised
93622	Terminology revised
93701	Thoracic bioimpedance code added
93737	Code deleted. To report, use 93741 or 93743
93738	Code deleted. To report, use 93742 or 93744
94720	Terminology revised
94750	Terminology revised
95144	Terminology revised
95145	Terminology revised

95165	Terminology revised
95180	Terminology revised
95250	Glucose continuous monitoring code added
95875	Terminology revised
95904	Terminology revised
95965	Magnetoencephalography code added
95966	Magnetoencephalography code added
95967	Magnetoencephalography code added
96000	Motion analysis code added
96001	Motion analysis code added
96002	Motion analysis code added
96003	Motion analysis code added
96004	Motion analysis code added
96150	Health/behavior assessment code added
96151	Health/behavior reassessment code added
96152	Health/behavior intervention code added
96153	Health/behavior intervention code added
96154	Health/behavior intervention code added
96155	Health/behavior intervention code added
96450	Terminology revised
96567	Photodynamic therapy of skin code added
97005	Athletic training evaluation code added
97006	Athletic training re-evaluation code added
97112	Terminology revised
97504	Terminology revised
97535	Terminology revised
97601	Terminology revised
99090	Terminology revised
99091	Collection and interpretation of patient transmitted data code added
99289	Patient transport code added
99290	Patient transport code added
99374	Terminology revised
99377	Terminology revised
99379	Terminology revised
99381	Terminology revised
99391	Terminology revised
99500	Home visit for prenatal assessment code added
99501	Home visit for postnatal assessment code added
99502	Home visit for newborn care assessment code added
99503	Home visit for respiratory therapy care code added
99504	Home visit for patients receiving mechanical ventilation code added
99505	Home visit for stoma care code added
99506	Home visit for intramuscular injections code added
99507	Home visit for catheter maintenance code added

99508   Home visit for sleep studies code added

99509   Home visit for assistance with activities of daily living code added

99510   Home visit for individual, family or marriage counseling code added

99511   Home visit for fecal impaction code added

99512   Home visit for hemodialysis code added

99539   Home visit, NOS code added

99551   Home infusion for pain management code added

99552   Home infusion for pain management code added

99553   Home infusion for tocolytic therapy code added

99554   Home infusion for hematopoietic hormones code added

99555   Home infusion for chemotherapy code added

99556   Home infusion for antibiotics/antifungal/antiviral code added

99557   Home infusion for continuous anticoagulant therapy code added

99558   Home infusion of immunotherapy code added

99559   Home infusion of peritoneal dialysis code added

99560   Home infusion of enteral nutrition code added

99561   Home infusion of hydration therapy code added

99562   Home infusion of total parenteral nutrition code added

99563   Home infusion of aerosolized pentamidine code added

99564   Home infusion for anti-hemophilic agents code added

99565   Home infusion of alpha-1 proteinase inhibitor code added

99566   Home infusion for long-term intravenous treatment code added

99567   Home infusion of sympathomimetic agents code added

99568   Home infusion of miscellaneous drugs code added

99569   Home infusion, each additional therapy code added

Appendix C

Update to Short Descriptors

This listing includes changes necessary to update the short descriptors on the *CPT 2002* data file.

The descriptors have been changed to reflect additions, revisions, or deletions to the *CPT 2002* codes, or to enhance or correct the data file.

The descriptors which have been enhanced, but do not necessarily reflect a change to the *CPT 2002* codes, are indicated with an asterisk.

0001T	Add:ENDOVAS REPR ABDO AO ANEURYS
0002T	Add:ENDOVAS REPR ABDO AO ANEURYS
0003T	Add:CERVICOGRAPHY
0004T	Delete
0005T	Add:PERC CATH STENT/BRAIN CV ART
0006T	Add:PERC CATH STENT/BRAIN CV ART
0007T	Add:PERC CATH STENT/BRAIN CV ART
0008T	Add:UPPER GI ENDOSCOPY W/SUTURE
0009T	Add:ENDOMETRIAL CRYOABLATION
0010T	Add:TB TEST, GAMMA INTERFERON
0012T	Add:OSTEOCHONDRAL KNEE AUTOGRAFT
0013T	Add:OSTEOCHONDRAL KNEE ALLOGRAFT
0014T	Add:MENISCAL TRANSPLANT, KNEE
0016T	Add:THERMOTX CHOROID VASC LESION
0017T	Add:PHOTOCOAGULAT MACULAR DRUSEN
0018T	Add:TRANSCRANIAL MAGNETIC STIMUL
0019T	Add:EXTRACORP SHOCK WAVE TX, MS
0020T	Add:EXTRACORP SHOCK WAVE TX, FT
0021T	Add:FETAL OXIMETRY, TRNSVAG/CERV
0023T	Add:PHENOTYPE DRUG TEST, HIV 1
0024T	Add:TRANSCATH CARDIAC REDUCTION
0025T	Add:ULTRASONIC PACHYMETRY
0026T	Add:MEASURE REMNANT LIPOPROTEINS
00797	Add:ANESTH, SURGERY FOR OBESITY
00850	Delete
00851	Add:ANESTH, TUBAL LIGATION
00855	Delete
00857	Delete
00869	Add:ANESTH, VASECTOMY
00884	Delete
00946	Delete
00955	Delete
01214	Revise:ANESTH, HIP ARTHROPLASTY

01402	Revise:ANESTH, KNEE ARTHROPLASTY
01904	Delete
01905	ANES, SPINE INJECT, X-RAY/REPAIR
01906	Delete
01908	Delete
01910	Delete
01912	Delete
01914	Delete
01916	Revise: ANESTH, DX ARTERIOGRAPHY
01918	Delete
01921	Delete
01924	Add:ANES, THER INTERVEN RAD, ART
01925	Add:ANES, THER INTERVEN RAD, CAR
01926	Add:ANES, TX INTERV RAD HRT/CRAN
01930	Add:ANES, THER INTERVEN RAD, VEIN
01931	Add:ANES, THER INTERVEN RAD, TIPS
01932	Add:ANES, TX INTERV RAD, TH VEIN
01933	Add:ANES, TX INTERV RAD, CRAN V
01951	Revise:ANESTH, BURN, LESS 4 PERCENT
01952	Revise:ANESTH, BURN, 4-9 PERCENT
01960	Add:ANESTH, VAGINAL DELIVERY
01961	Add:ANESTH, CS DELIVERY
01962	Add:ANESTH, EMER HYSTERECTOMY
01963	Add:ANESTH, CS HYSTERECTOMY
01964	Add:ANESTH, ABORTION PROCEDURES
01967	Add:ANESTH/ANALG, VAG DELIVERY
01968	Add:ANES/ANALG CS DELIVER ADD-ON
01969	Add:ANESTH/ANALG CS HYST ADD-ON
01995	Revise: REGIONAL ANESTHESIA LIMB
10021	Add:FNA W/O IMAGE
10022	Add:FNA W/IMAGE
11981	Add:INSERT DRUG IMPLANT DEVICE
11982	Add:REMOVE DRUG IMPLANT DEVICE
11983	Add:REMOVE/INSERT DRUG IMPLANT
20526	Add:THER INJECTION, CARPAL TUNNEL
20551	Add:INJECT TENDON ORIGIN/INSERT
20552	Add:INJECT TRIGGER POINT, 1 OR 2
20553	Add:INJECT TRIGGER POINTS, > 3
24300	Add:MANIPULATE ELBOW W/ANESTH
24332	Add:TENOLYSIS, TRICEPS
24343	Add:REPR ELBOW LAT LIGMNT W/TISS
24344	Add:RECONSTRUCT ELBOW LAT LIGMNT
24345	Add:REPR ELBW MED LIGMNT W/TISSU
24346	Add:RECONSTRUCT ELBOW MED LIGMNT
25001	Add:INCISE FLEXOR CARPI RADIALIS
25020	Revise:DECOMPRESS FOREARM 1 SPACE

* 25023	Revise:DECOMPRESS FOREARM 1 SPACE		**38221**	Add:BONE MARROW BIOPSY
25024	Add:DECOMPRESS FOREARM 2 SPACES		**43313**	Add:ESOPHAGOPLASTY CONGENITAL
25025	Add:DECOMPRESS FOREARM 2 SPACES		**43314**	Add:TRACHEO-ESOPHAGOPLASTY CONG
25075	Revise:REMOVE FOREARM LESION SUBCUT		**44020**	Revise:EXPLORE SMALL INTESTINE
25076	Revise: REMOVE FOREARM LESION DEEP		**44110**	Revise:EXCISE INTESTINE LESION(S)
25259	Add:MANIPULATE WRIST W/ANESTHES		**44126**	Add:ENTERECTOMY W/TAPER, CONG
25275	Add:REPAIR FOREARM TENDON SHEATH		**44127**	Add:ENTERECTOMY W/O TAPER, CONG
25394	Add:REPAIR CARPAL BONE, SHORTEN		**44128**	Revise:ENTERECTOMY CONG, ADD-ON
25430	Add:VASC GRAFT INTO CARPAL BONE		**44202**	Revise:LAP RESECT S/INTESTINE SINGL
25431	Add:REPAIR NONUNION CARPAL BONE		**44203**	Add:LAP RESECT S/INTESTINE, ADDL
25651	Add:PIN ULNAR STYLOID FRACTURE		**44204**	Add:LAPARO PARTIAL COLECTOMY
25652	Add:TREAT FRACTURE ULNAR STYLOID		**44205**	Add:LAP COLECTOMY PART W/ILEUM
25671	Add:PIN RADIOULNAR DISLOCATION		**45136**	Add:EXCISE ILEOANAL RESERVOIR
26115	Revise: REMOVE HAND LESION SUBCUT		**46020**	Add:PLACEMENT OF SETON
26116	Revise: REMOVE HAND LESION, DEEP		**47370**	Add:LAPARO ABLATE LIVER TUMOR RF
26340	Add:MANIPULATE FINGER W/ANESTH		**47371**	Add:LAPARO ABLATE LIVER CRYOSURG
26585	Delete		**47380**	Add:OPEN ABLATE LIVER TUMOR RF
26597	Delete		**47381**	Add:OPEN ABLATE LIVER TUMOR CRYO
27130	Revise:TOTAL HIP ARTHROPLASTY		**47382**	Add:PERCUT ABLATE LIVER RF
27132	Revise:TOTAL HIP ARTHROPLASTY		**48100**	Revise: BIOPSY OF PANCREAS, OPEN
27447	Revise:TOTAL KNEE ARTHROPLASTY		**48500**	Revise: SURGERY OF PANCREATIC CYST
29086	Add:APPLY FINGER CAST		**49491**	Add:REPAIR ING HERN PREMIE REDUC
29805	Add:SHOULDER ARTHROSCOPY, DX		**49492**	Add:RPR ING HERN PREMIE, BLOCKED
29806	Add:SHOULDER ARTHROSCOPY/SURGERY		**49495**	Revise:RPR ING HERNIA BABY, REDUC
29807	Add:SHOULDER ARTHROSCOPY/SURGERY		*** 49496**	Revise:RPR ING HERNIA BABY, BLOCKED
29815	Delete		*** 49500**	Revise:RPR ING HERNIA, INIT, REDUCE
29824	Add:SHOULDER ARTHROSCOPY/SURGERY		*** 49501**	Revise:RPR ING HERNIA, INIT BLOCKED
29900	Add:MCP JOINT ARTHROSCOPY, DX		*** 49505**	Revise:RPR I/HERN INIT REDUC > 5 YR
29901	Add:MCP JOINT ARTHROSCOPY, SURG		*** 49507**	Revise:RPR I/HERN INIT BLOCK > 5 YR
29902	Add:MCP JOINT ARTHROSCOPY, SURG		*** 49520**	Revise:REREPAIR ING HERNIA, REDUCE
29909	Delete		*** 49521**	Revise:REREPAIR ING HERNIA, BLOCKED
29999	Add:ARTHROSCOPY OF JOINT		*** 49525**	Revise:REPAIR ING HERNIA, SLIDING
31528	Revise:LARYNGOSCOPY AND DILATION		*** 49550**	Revise:RPR FEM HERNIA, INIT, REDUCE
31529	Revise:LARYNGOSCOPY AND DILATION		*** 49553**	Revise:RPR FEM HERNIA, INIT BLOCKED
33967	Add:INSERT IA PERCUT DEVICE		*** 49555**	Revise:REREPAIR FEM HERNIA, REDUCE
33979	Add:INSERT INTRACORPOREAL DEVICE		*** 49557**	Revise:REREPAIR FEM HERNIA, BLOCKED
33980	Add:REMOVE INTRACORPOREAL DEVICE		*** 49560**	Revise:RPR VENTRAL HERN INIT, REDUC
35647	Add:ARTERY BYPASS GRAFT		*** 49561**	Revise:RPR VENTRAL HERN INIT, BLOCK
35685	Add:BYPASS GRAFT PATENCY/PATCH		*** 49565**	Revise:REREPAIR VENTRL HERN, REDUCE
35686	Add:BYPASS GRAFT/AV FIST PATENCY		*** 49566**	Revise:REREPAIR VENTRL HERN, BLOCK
36002	Add:PSEUDOANEURYSM INJECTION TRT		*** 49570**	Revise:RPR EPIGASTRIC HERN, REDUCE
36005	Revise:INJECTION EXT VENOGRAPHY		*** 49572**	Revise:RPR EPIGASTRIC HERN, BLOCKED
36819	Revise:AV FUSION/UPPR ARM VEIN		*** 49580**	Revise:RPR UMBIL HERN, REDUC < 5 YR
36820	Add:AV FUSION/FOREARM VEIN		*** 49582**	Revise:RPR UMBIL HERN, BLOCK < 5 YR
38220	Add:BONE MARROW ASPIRATION		*** 49585**	Revise:RPR UMBIL HERN, REDUC > 5 YR
			* 49587	Revise:RPR UMBIL HERN, BLOCK > 5 YR

* 49590   Revise:REPAIR SPIGELIAN HERNIA

50220   Revise:REMOVE KIDNEY, OPEN

* 50225   Revise:REMOVE KIDNEY OPEN, COMPLEX

* 50230   Revise:REMOVE KIDNEY OPEN, RADICAL

50815   Revise:URINE SHUNT TO INTESTINE

51065   Revise:REMOVE URETER CALCULUS

52001   Add:CYSTOSCOPY, REMOVAL OF CLOTS

52347   Add:CYSTOSCOPY, RESECT DUCTS

53431   Add:RECONSTUCT URETHRA/BLADDER

53443   Delete

53444   Add:INSERT TANDEM CUFF

53445   Revise:INSERT URO/VES NCK SPHINCTER

53446   Add:REMOVE URO SPHINCTER

53447   Revise:REMOVE/REPLACE UR SPHINCTER

53448   Add:REMOV/REPLC UR SPHINCTR COMP

53449   Revise:REPAIR URO SPHINCTER

53853   Add:PROSTATIC WATER THERMOTHER

54162   Add:LYSIS PENIL CIRCUMCIS LESION

54163   Add:REPAIR OF CIRCUMCISION

54164   Add:FRENULOTOMY OF PENIS

54402   Delete

54405   Revise:INSERT MULTI-COMP PENIS PROS

54406   Add:REMOVE MULTI-COMP PENIS PROS

54407   Delete

54408   Add:REPAIR MULTI-COMP PENIS PROS

54409   Delete

54410   Add:REMOVE/REPLACE PENIS PROSTH

54411   Add:REMV/REPLC PENIS PROS, COMPL

54415   Add:REMOVE SELF-CONTD PENIS PROS

54416   Add:REMV/REPL PENIS CONTAIN PROS

54417   Add:REMV/REPLC PENIS PROS, COMPL

54510   Delete

56501   Revise:DESTROY, VULVA LESIONS, SIMP

56515   Revise:DESTROY VULVA LESION/S COMPL

57022   Revise:I & D, VAGINAL HEMATOMA, PP

* 57023   Revise:I & D VAG HEMATOMA, NON-OB

57061   Revise:DESTROY VAG LESIONS, SIMPLE

57065   Revise:DESTROY VAG LESIONS, COMPLX

57155   Add:INSERT UTERI TANDEMS/OVOIDS

58346   Add:INSERT HEYMAN UTERI CAPSULE

58953   Add:TAH, RAD DISSECT FOR DEBULK

58954   Add:TAH RAD DEBULK/LYMPH REMOVE

59000   Revise:AMNIOCENTESIS, DIAGNOSTIC

59001   Add:AMNIOCENTESIS, THERAPEUTIC

62272   Revise:DRAIN CEREBRO SPINAL FLUID

64561   Add:IMPLANT NEUROELECTRODES

64581   Add:IMPLANT NEUROELECTRODES

64821   Add: REMOVE SYMPATHETIC NERVES

64822   Add:REMOVE SYMPATHETIC NERVES

64823   Add:REMOVE SYMPATHETIC NERVES

67225   Add:EYE PHOTODYNAMIC THER ADD-ON

74230   Revise: CINE/VIDEO X-RAY, THROAT/ESOPH

75898   Revise: FOLLOW-UP ANGIOGRAPHY

76066   Revise:JOINT SURVEY, SINGLE VIEW

76078   Revise:RADIOGRAPHIC ABSORPTIOMETRY

76085   Add:COMPUTER MAMMOGRAM ADD-ON

76120   Revise: CINE/VIDEO X-RAYS

76125   Revise: CINE/VIDEO X-RAYS ADD-ON

76362   Add:CAT SCAN FOR TISSUE ABLATION

76394   Add:MRI FOR TISSUE ABLATION

76490   Add:US FOR TISSUE ABLATION

76536   Revise:US EXAM OF HEAD AND NECK

76604   Revise:US EXAM, CHEST, B-SCAN

76645   Revise:US EXAM, BREAST(S)

76700   Revise:US EXAM, ABDOM, COMPLETE

* 76705   Revise:US EXAM, ABDOM, LIMITED

76770   Revise:US EXAM ABDO BACK WALL, COMP

* 76775   Revise:US EXAM ABDO BACK WALL, LIM

76778   Revise:US EXAM KIDNEY TRANSPLANT

76800   Revise:US EXAM, SPINAL CANAL

76805   Revise:US EXAM, PG UTERUS, COMPL

* 76810   Revise:US EXAM, PG UTERUS, MULT

* 76815   Revise:US EXAM, PG UTERUS LIMIT

* 76816   Revise:US EXAM PG UTERUS REPEAT

* 76818   Revise:FETAL BIOPHY PROFILE W/NST

76819   Revise:FETAL BIOPHYS PROFIL W/O NST

76830   Revise:US EXAM, TRANSVAGINAL

76856   Revise:US EXAM, PELVIC, COMPLETE

* 76857   Revise:US EXAM, PELVIC, LIMITED

76870   Revise:US EXAM, SCROTUM

76880   Revise:US EXAM, EXTREMITY

76885   Revise:US EXAM INFANT HIPS, DYNAMIC

76886   Revise:US EXAM INFANT HIPS, STATIC

77301   Add:RADIOTHERAPY DOSE PLAN, IMRT

77418   Add:RADIATION TX DELIVERY, IMRT

78615   Revise:CEREBRAL VASCULAR FLOW IMAGE

80072   Delete

82274   Add:ASSAY TEST FOR BLOOD, FECAL

82355   Revise:CALCULUS ANALYSIS, QUAL

* 82360   Revise:CALCULUS ASSAY, QUANT

* 82365   Revise:CALCULUS SPECTROSCOPY

83950	Add:ONCOPROTEIN, HER-2/NEU	96151	Add:ASSESS HLTH/BEHAVE, SUBSEQ
85095	Delete	96152	Add:INTERVENE HLTH/BEHAVE, INDIV
85102	Delete	96153	Add:INTERVENE HLTH/BEHAVE, GROUP
85535	Delete	96154	Add:INTERV HLTH/BEHAV, FAM W/PT
86141	Add:C-REACTIVE PROTEIN, HS	96155	Add:INTERV HLTH/BEHAV FAM NO PT
86336	Add:INHIBIN A	99289	Add:PT TRANSPORT, 30-74 MIN
86683	Delete	99290	Add:PT TRANSPORT, ADDL 30 MIN
87045	Revise:FECES CULTURE, BACTERIA	96567	Add:PHOTODYNAMIC TX, SKIN
87198	Add:CYTOMEGALOVIRUS ANTIBODY DFA	97005	Add:ATHLETIC TRAIN EVAL
87199	Add:ENTEROVIRUS ANTIBODY, DFA	97006	Add:ATHLETIC TRAIN REEVAL
87802	Add:STREP B ASSAY W/OPTIC	97601	Revise:WOUND(S) CARE, SELECTIVE
87803	Add:CLOSTRIDIUM TOXIN A W/OPTIC	* 97602	Revise:WOUND(S) CARE NON-SELECT
87804	Add:INFLUENZA ASSAY W/OPTIC	99091	Add:COLLECT/REVIEW DATA FROM PT
87902	Add:GENOTYPE, DNA, HEPATITIS C	99500	Add:HOME VISIT, PRENATAL
88170	Delete	99501	Add:HOME VISIT, POSTNATAL
88171	Delete	99502	Add:HOME VISIT, NB CARE
88380	Add:MICRODISSECTION	99503	Add:HOME VISIT, RESP THERAPY
90473	Add:IMMUNE ADMIN ORAL/NASAL	99504	Add:HOME VISIT MECH VENTILATOR
90474	Add:IMMUNE ADMIN ORAL/NASAL ADDL	99505	Add:HOME VISIT, STOMA CARE
90732	Revise: PNEUMOCOCCAL VACCINE	99506	Add:HOME VISIT, IM INJECTION
90939	Add:HEMODIALYSIS STUDY, TRANSCUT	99507	Add:HOME VISIT, CATH MAINTAIN
91123	Add:IRRIGATE FECAL IMPACTION	99508	Add:HOME VISIT, SLEEP STUDIES
92136	Add:OPHTHALMIC BIOMETRY	99509	Add:HOME VISIT DAY LIFE ACTIVITY
92532	Revise:POSITIONAL NYSTAGMUS TEST	99510	Add:HOME VISIT, SING/M/FAM COUNS
92534	Revise:OPTOKINETIC NYSTAGMUS TEST	99511	Add:HOME VISIT, FECAL/ENEMA MGMT
92973	Add:PERCUT CORONARY THROMBECTOMY	99512	Add:HOME VISIT, HEMODIALYSIS
92974	Add:CATH PLACE, CARDIO BRACHYTX	99539	Add:HOME VISIT, NOS
93025	Add:MICROVOLT T-WAVE ASSESS	99551	Add:HOME INFUS, PAIN MGMT, IV/SC
93536	Delete	99552	Add:HM INFUS PAIN MGMT, EPID/ITH
93607	Delete	99553	Add:HOME INFUSE, TOCOLYTIC TX
93609	Revise:MAP TACHYCARDIA, ADD-ON	99554	Add:HOME INFUS, HORMONE/PLATELET
93613	Add:ELECTROPHYS MAP, 3D, ADD-ON	99555	Add:HOME INFUSE, CHEMOTHERAPY
93701	Add:BIOIMPEDANCE, THORACIC	99556	Add:HOME INFUS, ANTIBIO/FUNG/VIR
93737	Delete	99557	Add:HOME INFUSE, ANTICOAGULANT
93738	Delete	99558	Add:HOME INFUSE, IMMUNOTHERAPY
95250	Add:GLUCOSE MONITORING, CONT	99559	Add:HOME INFUS, PERITON DIALYSIS
95904	Revise:SENSE NERVE CONDUCTION TEST	99560	Add:HOME INFUS, ENTERO NUTRITION
95965	Add:MEG, SPONTANEOUS	99561	Add:HOME INFUSE, HYDRATION TX
95966	Add:MEG, EVOKED, SINGLE	99562	Add:HOME INFUS, PARENT NUTRITION
95967	Add:MEG, EVOKED, EACH ADDL	99563	Add:HOME ADMIN, PENTAMIDINE
96000	Add:MOTION ANALYSIS, VIDEO/3D	99564	Add:HME INFUS, ANTIHEMOPHIL AGNT
96001	Add:MOTION TEST W/FT PRESS MEAS	99565	Add:HOME INFUS, PROTEINASE INHIB
96002	Add:DYNAMIC SURFACE EMG	99566	Add:HOME INFUSE, IV THERAPY
96003	Add:DYNAMIC FINE WIRE EMG	99567	Add:HOME INFUSE, SYMPATH AGENT
96004	Add:PHYS REVIEW OF MOTION TESTS	99568	Add:HOME INFUS, MISC DRUG, DAILY
96150	Add:ASSESS HLTH/BEHAVE, INIT	99569	Add:HOME INFUSE, EACH ADDL TX

Appendix D

Clinical Examples

As described in *CPT 2002*, clinical examples of the CPT codes for Evaluation and Management (E/M) services are intended to be an important element of the coding system. The clinical examples, when used with the E/M descriptors contained in the full text of *CPT*, provide a comprehensive and powerful new tool for physicians to report the services provided to their patients.

The American Medical Association is pleased to provide you with these clinical examples for *CPT 2002*. The clinical examples that are provided in this supplement are limited to Office or Other Outpatient Services, Hospital Inpatient Services, Consultations, Critical Care, Prolonged Services and Care Plan Oversight.

These clinical examples do not encompass the entire scope of medical practice. Inclusion or exclusion of any particular specialty group does not infer any judgment of importance or lack thereof; nor does it limit the applicability of the example to any particular specialty.

Of utmost importance is that these clinical examples are just that: examples. A particular patient encounter, depending on the specific circumstances, must be judged by the services provided by the physician for that particular patient. Simply because the patient's complaints, symptoms, or diagnoses match those of a particular clinical example, does not automatically assign that patient encounter to that particular level of service. The three key components (history, examination, and medical decision making) must be met and documented in the medical record to report a particular level of service.

Office or Other Outpatient Services

New Patient

99201 Initial office visit for a 50-year-old male from out-of-town who needs a prescription refill for a nonsteroidal anti-inflammatory drug. (Anesthesiology)

Initial office visit for a 40-year-old female, new patient, requesting information about local pain clinics. (Anesthesiology/Pain Medicine)

Initial office visit for a 10-year-old girl for determination of visual acuity as part of a summer camp physical (does not include determination of refractive error). (Ophthalmology)

Initial office visit for an out-of-town patient requiring topical refill. (Dermatology)

Initial office visit for a 65-year-old male for reassurance about an isolated seborrheic keratosis on upper back. (Plastic Surgery)

Initial office visit for an out-of-state visitor who needs refill of topical steroid to treat lichen planus. (Dermatology)

Initial office visit for an 86-year-old male, out-of-town visitor, who needs prescription refilled for an anal skin preparation that he forgot. (General Surgery/Colon & Rectal Surgery)

Initial office visit for a transient patient with alveolar osteitis for repacking. (Oral & Maxillofacial Surgery)

Initial office visit for a patient with a pedunculated lesion of the neck which is unsightly. (Dermatology)

Initial office visit for a 10-year-old male, for limited subungual hematoma not requiring drainage. (Internal Medicine)

Initial office visit with an out-of-town visitor who needs a prescription refilled because she forgot her hay fever medication. (Allergy & Immunology/Internal Medicine)

Initial office visit with a 9-month-old female with diaper rash. (Pediatrics)

Initial office visit with a 10-year-old male with severe rash and itching for the past 24 hours, positive history for contact with poison oak 48 hours prior to the visit. (Family Medicine)

Initial office visit with a 5-year-old female to remove sutures from simple wound placed by another physician. (Plastic Surgery)

Initial office visit for a 22-year-old male with a small area of sunburn requiring first aid. (Dermatology/Family Medicine/Internal Medicine)

Initial office visit for the evaluation and management of a contusion of a finger. (Orthopaedic Surgery)

99202 Initial office visit for a 13-year-old patient with comedopapular acne of the face unresponsive to over-the-counter medications. (Family Medicine)

Initial office visit for a patient with a clinically benign lesion or nodule of the lower leg which has been present for many years. (Dermatology)

Initial office visit for a patient with a circumscribed patch of dermatitis of the leg. (Dermatology)

Initial office visit for a patient with papulosquamous eruption of elbows. (Dermatology)

Initial office visit for a 9-year-old patient with erythematous, grouped, vesicular eruption of the lip of three days' duration. (Pediatrics)

Initial office visit for an 18-year-old male referred by an orthodontist for advice regarding removal of four wisdom teeth. (Oral & Maxillofacial Surgery)

Initial office visit for a 14-year-old male, who was referred by his orthodontist, for advice on the exposure of impacted maxillary cuspids. (Oral & Maxillofacial Surgery)

Initial office visit for a patient presenting with itching patches on the wrists and ankles. (Dermatology)

Initial office visit for a 30-year-old male for evaluation and discussion of treatment of rhinophyma. (Plastic Surgery)

Initial office visit for a 16-year-old male with severe cystic acne, new patient. (Dermatology)

Initial office evaluation for gradual hearing loss, 58-year-old male, history and physical examination, with interpretation of complete audiogram, air bone, etc. (Otolaryngology)

Initial evaluation and management of recurrent urinary infection in female. (Internal Medicine)

Initial office visit with a 10-year-old girl with history of chronic otitis media and a draining ear. (Pediatrics)

Initial office visit for a 10-year-old female with acute maxillary sinusitis. (Family Medicine)

Initial office visit for a patient with recurring episodes of herpes simplex who has developed a clustering of vesicles on the upper lip. (Internal Medicine)

Initial office visit for a 25-year-old patient with single season allergic rhinitis. (Allergy & Immunology)

Initial office visit to plan transient dialysis for a 56-year-old stable dialysis patient who has accompanying records. (Nephrology)

99203 Initial office visit for a 76-year-old male with a stasis ulcer of three months' duration. (Dermatology)

Initial office visit for a 30-year-old female with pain in the lateral aspect of the forearm. (Physical Medicine & Rehabilitation)

Initial office visit for a 15-year-old patient with a four-year history of moderate comedopapular acne of the face, chest, and back with early scarring. Discussion of use of systemic medication. (Dermatology)

Initial office visit for a patient with papulosquamous eruption of the elbow with pitting of nails and itchy scalp. (Dermatology)

Initial office visit for a 57-year-old female who complains of painful parotid swelling for one week's duration. (Oral & Maxillofacial Surgery)

Initial office visit for a patient with an ulcerated non-healing lesion or nodule on the tip of the nose. (Dermatology)

Initial office visit for a patient with dermatitis of the antecubital and popliteal fossae. (Dermatology)

Initial office visit for a 22-year-old female with irregular menses. (Family Medicine)

Initial office visit for a 50-year-old female with dyspepsia and nausea. (Family Medicine)

Initial office visit for a 53-year-old laborer with degenerative joint disease of the knee with no prior treatment. (Orthopaedic Surgery)

Initial office visit for a 60-year-old male with Dupuytren's contracture of one hand with multiple digit involvement. (Orthopaedic Surgery)

Initial office visit for a 33-year-old male with painless gross hematuria without cystoscopy. (Internal Medicine)

Initial office visit for a 55-year-old female with chronic blepharitis. There is a history of use of many medications. (Ophthalmology)

Initial office visit for an 18-year-old female with a two-day history of acute conjunctivitis. Extensive history of possible exposures, prior normal ocular history, and medication use is obtained. (Ophthalmology)

Initial office visit for a 14-year-old male with unilateral anterior knee pain. (Physical Medicine & Rehabilitation)

Initial office visit of an adult who presents with symptoms of an upper-respiratory infection that has progressed to unilateral purulent nasal discharge and discomfort in the right maxillary teeth. (Otolaryngology, Head & Neck Surgery)

Initial office visit of a 40-year-old female with symptoms of atopic allergies including eye and sinus congestion, often associated with infections. She would like to be tested for allergies. (Otolaryngology, Head & Neck Surgery)

Initial office visit of a 65-year-old with nasal stuffiness. (Otolaryngology, Head & Neck Surgery)

Initial office visit for initial evaluation of a 48-year-old man with recurrent low back pain radiating to the leg. (General Surgery)

Initial office visit for evaluation, diagnosis and management of painless gross hematuria in a new patient, without cystoscopy. (Internal Medicine)

Initial office visit with couple for counseling concerning voluntary vasectomy for sterility. Spent 30 minutes discussing procedure, risks and benefits, and answering questions. (Urology)

Initial office visit of a 49-year-old male with nasal obstruction. Detailed exam with topical anesthesia. (Plastic Surgery)

Initial office visit for evaluation of a 13-year-old female with progressive scoliosis. (Physical Medicine & Rehabilitation)

Initial office visit for a 21-year-old female desiring counseling and evaluation of initiation of contraception. (Family Practice/Internal Medicine/Obstetrics & Gynecology)

Initial office visit for a 49-year-old male presenting with painless blood per rectum associated with bowel movement. (Colon & Rectal Surgery)

Initial office visit for a 19-year-old football player with three-day-old acute knee injury; now with swelling and pain. (Orthopaedic Surgery)

99204 Initial office visit for a 13-year-old female with progressive scoliosis. (Orthopaedic Surgery)

Initial office visit for a 34-year-old female with primary infertility for evaluation and counseling. (Obstetrics & Gynecology)

Initial office visit for a 6-year-old male with multiple upper respiratory infections. (Allergy & Immunology)

Initial office visit for a patient with generalized dermatitis of 80 percent of the body surface area. (Dermatology)

Initial office visit for an adolescent who was referred by school counselor because of repeated skipping school. (Psychiatry)

Initial office visit for a 50-year-old machinist with a generalized eruption. (Dermatology)

Initial office visit for a 45-year-old female who has been abstinent from alcohol and benzodiazepines for three months but complains of headaches, insomnia, and anxiety. (Psychiatry)

Initial office visit for a 60-year-old male with recent change in bowel habits, weight loss, and abdominal pain. (Abdominal Surgery/General Surgery)

Initial office visit for a 50-year-old male with an aortic aneurysm who is considering surgery. (General Surgery)

Initial office visit for a 17-year-old female with depression. (Internal Medicine)

Initial office visit of a 40-year-old with chronic draining ear, imbalance, and probable cholesteatoma. (Otolaryngology, Head & Neck Surgery)

Initial office visit for initial evaluation of a 63-year-old male with chest pain on exertion. (Cardiology/Internal Medicine)

Initial office visit for evaluation of a 70-year-old patient with recent onset of episodic confusion. (Internal Medicine)

Initial office visit for a 7-year-old female with juvenile diabetes mellitus, new to area, past history of hospitalization times three. (Pediatrics)

Initial office visit of a 50-year-old female with progressive solid food dysphagia. (Gastroenterology)

Initial office visit for a 34-year-old patient with primary infertility, including counseling. (Obstetrics & Gynecology)

Initial office visit for evaluation of a 70-year-old female with polyarthralgia. (Rheumatology)

Initial office visit for a patient with papulosquamous eruption involving 60 percent of the cutaneous surface with joint pain. Combinations of topical and systemic treatments discussed. (Dermatology)

99205 Initial office visit for a patient with disseminated lupus erythematosus with kidney disease, edema, purpura, and scarring lesions on the extremities plus cardiac symptoms. (Dermatology/General Surgery/Internal Medicine)

Initial office visit for a 25-year-old female with systemic lupus erythematosus, fever, seizures, and profound thrombocytopenia. (Rheumatology/Allergy & Immunology)

Initial office visit for an adult with multiple cutaneous blisters, denuded secondarily infected ulcerations, oral lesions, weight loss, and increasing weakness refractory to high dose corticosteroid. Initiation of new immunosuppressive therapy. (Dermatology)

Initial office visit for a 28-year-old male with systemic vasculitis and compromised circulation to the limbs. (Rheumatology)

Initial office visit for a 41-year-old female new to the area requesting rheumatologic care, on disability due to scleroderma and recent hospitalization for malignant hypertension. (Rheumatology)

Initial office visit for a 52-year-old female with acute four extremity weakness and shortness of breath one week post-flu vaccination. (Physical Medicine & Rehabilitation)

Initial office visit for a 60-year-old male with previous back surgery; now presents with back and pelvic pain, two-month history of bilateral progressive calf and thigh tightness and weakness when walking, causing several falls. (Orthopaedic Surgery)

Initial office visit for an adolescent referred from ER after making suicide gesture. (Psychiatry)

Initial office visit for a 49-year-old female with a history of headaches and dependence on opioids. She reports weight loss, progressive headache, and depression. (Psychiatry)

Initial office visit for a 50-year-old female with symptoms of rash, swellings, recurrent arthritic complaints, and diarrhea and lymphadenopathy. Patient has had a 25 lb. weight loss and was recently camping in the Amazon. (Allergy & Immunology)

Initial office visit for a 34-year-old uremic Type I diabetic patient referred for ESRD modality assessment and planning. (Nephrology)

Initial office visit for a 75-year-old female with neck and bilateral shoulder pain, brisk deep tendon reflexes, and stress incontinence. (Physical Medicine & Rehabilitation)

Initial office visit for an 8-year-old male with cerebral palsy and spastic quadriparesis. (Physical Medicine & Rehabilitation)

Initial office visit for a 73-year-old male with known prostate malignancy, who presents with severe back pain and a recent onset of lower extremity weakness. (Physical Medicine & Rehabilitation)

Initial office visit for a 38-year-old male with paranoid delusions and a history of alcohol abuse. (Psychiatry)

Initial office visit for a 12-week-old with bilateral hip dislocations and bilateral club feet. (Orthopaedic Surgery)

Initial office visit for a 29-year-old female with acute orbital congestion, eyelid retraction, and bilateral visual loss from optic neuropathy. (Ophthalmology)

Initial office visit for a 70-year-old diabetic patient with progressive visual field loss, advanced optic disc cupping and neovascularization of retina. (Ophthalmology)

Initial office visit for a newly diagnosed Type I diabetic patient. (Endocrinology)

Initial office evaluation of a 65-year-old female with exertional chest pain, intermittent claudication, syncope and a murmur of aortic stenosis. (Cardiology)

Initial office visit for a 73-year-old male with an unexplained 20 lb. weight loss. (Hematology/Oncology)

Initial office evaluation, patient with systemic lupus erythematosus, fever, seizures and profound thrombocytopenia. (Allergy & Immunology/Internal Medicine/Rheumatology)

Initial office evaluation and management of patient with systemic vasculitis and compromised circulation to the limbs. (Rheumatology)

Initial office visit for a 24-year-old homosexual male who has a fever, a cough, and shortness of breath. (Infectious Disease)

Initial outpatient evaluation of a 69-year-old male with severe chronic obstructive pulmonary disease, congestive heart failure, and hypertension. (Family Medicine)

Initial office visit for a 17-year-old female, who is having school problems and has told a friend she is considering suicide. The patient and her family are consulted in regard to treatment options. (Psychiatry)

Initial office visit for a female with severe hirsutism, amenorrhea, weight loss and a desire to have children. (Endocrinology/Obstetrics & Gynecology)

Initial office visit for a 42-year-old male on hypertensive medication, newly arrived to the area, with diastolic blood pressure of 110, history of recurrent calculi, episodic headaches, intermittent chest pain and orthopnea. (Internal Medicine)

Established Patient

99211 Office visit for an 82-year-old female, established patient, for a monthly B12 injection with documented Vitamin B12 deficiency. (Geriatrics/Internal Medicine/Family Medicine)

Office visit for a 50-year-old male, established patient, for removal of uncomplicated facial sutures. (Plastic Surgery)

Office visit for an established patient who lost prescription for lichen planus. Returned for new copy. (Dermatology)

Office visit for an established patient undergoing orthodontics who complains of a wire which is irritating his/her cheek and asks you to check it. (Oral & Maxillofacial Surgery)

Office visit for a 50-year-old female, established patient, seen for her gold injection by the nurse. (Rheumatology)

Office visit for a 73-year-old female, established patient, with pernicious anemia for weekly B12 injection. (Gastroenterology)

Office visit for an established patient for dressing change on a skin biopsy. (Dermatology)

Office visit for a 19-year-old, established patient, for removal of sutures from a two cm. laceration of forehead, which you placed four days ago in ER. (Plastic Surgery)

Office visit of a 20-year-old female, established patient, who receives an allergy vaccine injection and is observed for a reaction by the nurse. (Otolaryngology, Head & Neck Surgery)

Office visit for a 45-year-old male, established patient, with chronic renal failure for the administration of erythropoietin. (Nephrology)

Office visit for an established patient, a Peace Corps enlistee, who requests documentation that third molars have been removed. (Oral & Maxillofacial Surgery)

Office visit for a 69-year-old female, established patient, for partial removal of antibiotic gauze from an infected wound site. (Plastic Surgery)

Office visit for a 9-year-old, established patient, successfully treated for impetigo, requiring release to return to school. (Dermatology/Pediatrics)

Office visit for an established patient requesting a return-to-work certificate for resolving contact dermatitis. (Dermatology)

Office visit for an established patient who is performing glucose monitoring and wants to check accuracy of machine with lab blood glucose by technician who checks accuracy and function of patient machine. (Endocrinology)

Follow-up office visit for a 65-year-old female with a chronic indwelling percutaneous nephrostomy catheter seen for routine pericatheter skin care and dressing change. (Interventional Radiology)

Outpatient visit with 19-year-old male, established patient, for supervised drug screen. (Addiction Medicine)

Office visit with 12-year-old male, established patient, for cursory check of hematoma one day after venipuncture. (Internal Medicine)

Office visit with 31-year-old female, established patient, for return to work certificate. (Anesthesiology)

Office visit for a 42-year-old, established patient, to read tuberculin test results. (Allergy & Immunology)

Office visit for 14-year-old, established patient, to re-dress an abrasion. (Orthopaedic Surgery)

Office visit for a 45-year-old female, established patient, for a blood pressure check. (Obstetrics & Gynecology)

Office visit for a 23-year-old, established patient, for instruction in use of peak flow meter. (Allergy & Immunology)

Office visit for prescription refill for a 35-year-old female, established patient, with schizophrenia who is stable but has run out of neuroleptic and is scheduled to be seen in a week. (Psychiatry)

99212 Office visit for an 11-year-old, established patient, seen in follow-up for mild comedonal acne of the cheeks on topical desquamating agents. (Dermatology/Family Medicine/Pediatrics)

Office visit for a 10-year-old female, established patient, who has been swimming in a lake, now presents with a one-day history of left ear pain with purulent drainage. (Family Medicine)

Office visit of a child, established patient, with chronic secretory otitis media. (Otolaryngology, Head & Neck Surgery)

Office visit for an established patient seen in follow-up of clearing patch of localized contact dermatitis. (Family Medicine/Dermatology)

Office visit for an established patient returning for evaluation of response to treatment of lichen planus on wrists and ankles. (Dermatology)

Office visit for an established patient with tinea pedis being treated with topical therapy. (Dermatology)

Office visit for an established patient with localized erythematous plaque of psoriasis with topical hydration. (Dermatology)

Office visit for a 50-year-old male, established patient, recently seen for acute neck pain, diagnosis of spondylosis, responding to physical therapy and intermittent cervical traction. Returns for evaluation for return to work. (Neurology)

Office visit for an established patient with recurring episodes of herpes simplex who has developed a clustering of vesicles on the upper lip. (Oral & Maxillofacial Surgery)

Evaluation for a 50-year-old male, established patient, who has experienced a recurrence of knee pain after he discontinued NSAID. (Anesthesiology/Pain Medicine)

Office visit for an established patient with an irritated skin tag for reassurance. (Dermatology)

Office visit for a 40-year-old, established patient, who has experienced a systemic allergic reaction following administration of immunotherapy. The dose must be readjusted. (Allergy & Immunology)

Office visit for a 33-year-old, established patient, for contusion and abrasion of lower extremity. (Orthopaedic Surgery)

Office visit for a 22-year-old male, established patient, one month after I & D of "wrestler's ear." (Plastic Surgery)

Office visit for a 21-year-old, established patient, who is seen in follow-up after antibiotic therapy for acute bacterial tonsillitis. (Otolaryngology, Head & Neck Surgery)

Office visit for a 4-year-old, established patient, with tympanostomy tubes, check-up. (Otolaryngology, Head & Neck Surgery)

Office visit for an established patient who has had needle aspiration of a peritonsillar abscess. (Otolaryngology, Head & Neck Surgery)

Follow-up office examination for evaluation and treatment of acute draining ear in a 5-year-old with tympanotomy tubes. (Otolaryngology, Head & Neck Surgery)

Office visit, established patient, 6-year-old with sore throat and headache. (Family Medicine/Pediatrics)

Office evaluation for possible purulent bacterial conjunctivitis with one- to two-day history of redness and discharge, 16-year-old female, established patient. (Pediatrics/Internal Medicine/Family Medicine)

Office visit with a 65-year-old female, established patient, returns for three-week follow-up for resolving severe ankle sprain. (Orthopaedic Surgery)

Office visit, sore throat, fever and fatigue in a 19-year-old college student, established patient. (Internal Medicine)

Office visit with a 33-year-old female, established patient, recently started on treatment for hemorrhoidal complaints, for re-evaluation. (Colon & Rectal Surgery)

Office visit with a 36-year-old male, established patient, for follow-up on effectiveness of medicine management of oral candidiasis. (Oral & Maxillofacial Surgery)

Office visit for a 27-year-old female, established patient, with complaints of vaginal itching. (Obstetrics & Gynecology)

Office visit for a 65-year-old male, established patient, with eruptions on both arms from poison oak exposure. (Allergy & Immunology/Internal Medicine)

99213   Office visit for an established patient with new lesions of lichen planus in spite of topical therapies. (Dermatology)

Office visit for the quarterly follow-up of a 45-year-old male with stable chronic asthma requiring regular drug therapy. (Allergy & Immunology)

Office visit for a 13-year-old, established patient, with comedopapular acne of the face which has shown poor response to topical medication. Discussion of use of systemic medication. (Dermatology)

Office visit for a 62-year-old female, established patient, for follow-up for stable cirrhosis of the liver. (Internal Medicine/Family Medicine)

Office visit for a 3-year-old, established patient, with atopic dermatitis and food hypersensitivity for quarterly follow-up evaluation. The patient is on topical lotions and steroid creams as well as oral antihistamines. (Allergy & Immunology)

Office visit for an 80-year-old female, established patient, to evaluate medical management of osteoarthritis of the temporomandibular joint. (Rheumatology)

Office visit for a 70-year-old female, established patient, one year post excision of basal cell carcinoma of nose with nasolabial flap. Now presents with new suspicious recurrent lesion and suspicious lesion of the back. (Plastic Surgery)

Office visit for a 68-year-old female, established patient, with polymyalgia rheumatic, maintained on chronic low-dose corticosteroid, with no new complaints. (Rheumatology)

Office visit for a 3-year-old female, established patient, for earache and dyshidrosis of feet. (Pediatrics/Family Medicine)

Office visit for an established patient for 18 months post-operative follow-up of TMJ repair. (Oral & Maxillofacial Surgery)

Office visit for a 45-year-old male, established patient, being re-evaluated for recurrent acute prostatitis. (Urology)

Office visit for a 43-year-old male, established patient, with known reflex sympathetic dystrophy. (Anesthesiology)

Office visit for an established patient with an evenly pigmented superficial nodule of leg which is symptomatic. (Dermatology)

Office visit for an established patient with psoriasis involvement of the elbows, pitting of the nails, and itchy scalp. (Dermatology)

Office visit for a 27-year-old male, established patient, with deep follicular and perifollicular inflammation unable to tolerate systemic antibiotics due to GI upset, requires change of systemic medication. (Dermatology)

Office visit for a 16-year-old male, established patient, who is on medication for exercise-induced bronchospasm. (Allergy & Immunology)

Office visit for a 60-year-old, established patient, with chronic essential hypertension on multiple drug regimen, for blood pressure check. (Family Medicine)

Office visit for a 20-year-old male, established patient, for removal of sutures in hand. (Family Medicine)

Office visit for a 58-year-old female, established patient, with unilateral painful bunion. (Orthopaedic Surgery)

Office visit for a 45-year-old female, established patient, with known osteoarthritis and painful swollen knees. (Rheumatology)

Office visit for a 25-year-old female, established patient, complaining of bleeding and heavy menses. (Obstetrics & Gynecology)

Office visit for a 55-year-old male, established patient, with hypertension managed by a beta blocker/thiazide regime; now experiencing mild fatigue. (Nephrology)

Office visit for a 65-year-old female, established patient, with primary glaucoma for interval determination of intraocular pressure and possible adjustment of medication. (Ophthalmology)

Office visit for a 56-year-old man, established patient, with stable exertional angina who complains of new onset of calf pain while walking. (Cardiology)

Office visit for a 63-year-old female, established patient, with rheumatoid arthritis on auranofin and ibuprofin, seen for routine follow-up visit. (Rheumatology)

Office visit for an established patient with Graves' disease, three months post I-131 therapy, who presents with lassitude and malaise. (Endocrinology)

Office visit for the quarterly follow-up of a 63-year-old male, established patient, with chronic myofascial pain syndrome, effectively managed by doxepin, who presents with new onset urinary hesitancy. (Pain Medicine)

Office visit for the biannual follow-up of an established patient with migraine variant having infrequent, intermittent, moderate to severe headaches with nausea and vomiting, which are sometimes effectively managed by ergotamine tartrate and an antiemetic, but occasionally requiring visits to an emergency department. (Pain Medicine)

Office visit for an established patient after discharge from a pain rehabilitation program to review and adjust medication dosage. (Pain Medicine)

Office visit with 55-year-old male, established patient, for management of hypertension, mild fatigue, on beta blocker/thiazide regimen. (Family Medicine/Internal Medicine)

Outpatient visit with 37-year-old male, established patient, who is three years post total colectomy for chronic ulcerative colitis, presents for increased irritation at his stoma. (General Surgery)

Office visit for a 70-year-old diabetic hypertensive established patient with recent change in insulin requirement. (Internal Medicine/Nephrology)

Office visit with 80-year-old female, established patient, for follow-up osteoporosis, status-post compression fractures. (Rheumatology)

Office visit for an established patient with stable cirrhosis of the liver. (Gastroenterology)

Routine, follow-up office evaluation at a three-month interval for a 77-year-old female, established patient, with nodular small cleaved-cell lymphoma. (Hematology/Oncology)

Quarterly follow-up office visit for a 45-year-old male, established patient, with stable chronic asthma, on steroid and bronchodilator therapy. (Pulmonary Medicine)

Office visit for a 50-year-old female, established patient, with insulin-dependent diabetes mellitus and stable coronary artery disease, for monitoring. (Family Medicine/Internal Medicine)

99214 Office visit for an established patient now presenting with generalized dermatitis of 80 percent of the body surface area. (Dermatology)

Office visit for a 32-year-old female, established patient, with new onset right lower quadrant pain. (Family Medicine)

Office visit for reassessment and reassurance/counseling of a 40-year-old female, established patient, who is experiencing increased symptoms while on a pain management treatment program. (Pain Medicine)

Office visit for a 30-year-old, established patient, under management for intractable low back pain, who now presents with new onset right posterior thigh pain. (Pain Medicine)

Office visit for an established patient with frequent intermittent, moderate to severe headaches requiring beta blocker or tricyclic antidepressant prophylaxis, as well as four symptomatic treatments, but who is still experiencing headaches at a frequency of several times a month that are unresponsive to treatment. (Pain Medicine)

Office visit for an established patient with psoriasis with extensive involvement of scalp, trunk, palms, and soles with joint pain. Combinations of topical and systemic treatments discussed and instituted. (Dermatology)

Office visit for a 55-year-old male, established patient, with increasing night pain, limp, and progressive varus of both knees. (Orthopaedic Surgery)

Follow-up visit for a 15-year-old withdrawn patient with four-year history of papulocystic acne of the face, chest, and back with early scarring and poor response to past treatment. Discussion of use of systemic medication. (Dermatology)

Office visit for a 28-year-old male, established patient, with regional enteritis, diarrhea, and low-grade fever. (Internal Medicine)

Office visit for a 25-year-old female, established patient, following recent arthrogram and MR imaging for TMJ pain. (Oral & Maxillofacial Surgery)

Office visit for a 32-year-old female, established patient, with large obstructing stone in left mid-ureter, to discuss management options including urethroscopy with extraction or ESWL. (Urology)

Evaluation for a 28-year-old male, established patient, with new onset of low back pain. (Anesthesiology/Pain Medicine)

Office visit for a 28-year-old female, established patient, with right lower quadrant abdominal pain, fever, and anorexia. (Internal Medicine/Family Medicine)

Office visit for a 45-year-old male, established patient, four months follow-up of L4-5 diskectomy, with persistent incapacitating low back and leg pain. (Orthopaedic Surgery)

Outpatient visit for a 77-year-old male, established patient, with hypertension, presenting with a three-month history of episodic substernal chest pain on exertion. (Cardiology)

Office visit for a 25-year-old female, established patient, for evaluation of progressive saddle nose deformity of unknown etiology. (Plastic Surgery)

Office visit for a 65-year-old male, established patient, with BPH and severe bladder outlet obstruction, to discuss management options such as TURP. (Urology)

Office visit for an adult diabetic established patient with a past history of recurrent sinusitis who presents with a one-week history of double vision. (Otolaryngology, Head & Neck Surgery)

Office visit for an established patient with lichen planus and 60 percent of the cutaneous surface involved, not responsive to systemic steroids, as well as developing symptoms of progressive heartburn and paranoid ideation. (Dermatology)

Office visit for a 52-year-old male, established patient, with a 12-year history of bipolar disorder responding to lithium carbonate and brief psychotherapy. Psychotherapy and prescription provided. (Psychiatry)

Office visit for a 63-year-old female, established patient, with a history of familial polyposis, status post-colectomy with sphincter sparing procedure, who now presents with rectal bleeding and increase in stooling frequency. (General Surgery)

Office visit for a 68-year-old male, established patient, with the sudden onset of multiple flashes and floaters in the right eye due to a posterior vitreous detachment. (Ophthalmology)

Office visit for a 55-year-old female, established patient, on cyclosporin for treatment of resistant, small vessel vasculitis. (Rheumatology)

Follow-up office visit for a 55-year-old male, two months after iliac angioplasty with new onset of contralateral extremity claudication. (Interventional Radiology)

Office visit for a 68-year-old male, established patient, with stable angina, two months post myocardial infarction, who is not tolerating one of his medications. (Cardiology)

Weekly office visit for 5FU therapy for an ambulatory established patient with metastatic colon cancer and increasing shortness of breath. (Hematology/Oncology)

Follow-up office visit for a 60-year-old male, established patient, whose post-traumatic seizures have disappeared on medication and who now raises the question of stopping the medication (Neurology)

Office evaluation on new onset RLQ pain in a 32-year-old woman, established patient. (Urology/General Surgery/Internal Medicine/Family Medicine)

Office evaluation of 28-year-old, established patient, with regional enteritis, diarrhea and low-grade fever. (Family Medicine/Internal Medicine)

Office visit with 50-year-old female, established patient, diabetic, blood sugar controlled by diet. She now complains of frequency of urination and weight loss, blood sugar of 320 and negative ketones on dipstick. (Internal Medicine)

Follow-up office visit for a 45-year-old, established patient, with rheumatoid arthritis on gold, methotrexate, or immunosuppressive therapy. (Rheumatology)

Office visit for a 60-year-old male, established patient, two years post-removal of intracranial meningioma, now with new headaches and visual disturbance. (Neurosurgery)

Office visit for a 68-year-old female, established patient, for routine review and follow-up of non-insulin dependent diabetes, obesity, hypertension and congestive heart failure. Complains of vision difficulties and admits dietary noncompliance. Patient is counseled concerning diet and current medications adjusted. (Family Medicine)

99215 Office visit for an established patient who developed persistent cough, rectal bleeding, weakness, and diarrhea plus pustular infection on skin. Patient on immunosuppressive therapy. (Dermatology)

Office visit for an established patient with disseminated lupus erythematosus, extensive edema of extremities kidney disease, and weakness requiring monitored course on azathioprene, corticosteroid and complicated by acute depression. (Dermatology/Internal Medicine/Rheumatology)

Office visit for an established patient with progressive dermatomyositis and recent onset of fever, nasal speech, and regurgitation of fluids through the nose. (Dermatology)

Office visit for a 28-year-old female, established patient, who is abstinent from previous cocaine dependence, but reports progressive panic attacks and chest pains. (Psychiatry)

Office visit for an established adolescent patient with history of bipolar disorder treated with lithium; seen on urgent basis at family's request because of severe depressive symptoms. (Psychiatry)

Office visit for an established patient having acute migraine with new onset neurological symptoms and whose headaches are unresponsive to previous attempts at management with a combination of preventive and abortive medication. (Pain Medicine)

Office visit for an established patient with exfoliative lichen planus with daily fever spikes, disorientation, and shortness of breath. (Dermatology)

Office visit for a 25-year-old, established patient, two years post-burn with bilateral ectropion, hypertrophic facial burn scars, near absence of left breast, and burn syndactyly of both hands. Discussion of treatment options following examination. (Plastic Surgery)

Office visit for a 6-year-old, established patient, to review newly diagnosed immune deficiency with recommendations for therapy including IV immunoglobulin and chronic antibiotics. (Allergy & Immunology)

Office visit for a 36-year-old, established patient, three months status post-transplant, with new onset of peripheral edema, increased blood pressure, and progressive fatigue. (Nephrology)

Office visit for an established patient with Kaposi's sarcoma who presents with fever and widespread vesicles. (Dermatology)

Office visit for a 27-year-old female, established patient, with bipolar disorder who was stable on lithium carbonate and monthly supportive psychotherapy but now has developed symptoms of hypomania. (Psychiatry)

Office visit for a 25-year-old male, established patient with a history of schizophrenia who has been seen bi-monthly but is complaining of auditory hallucinations. (Psychiatry)

Office visit for a 62-year-old male, established patient, three years post-op abdominal perineal resection, now with a rising carcinoembryonic antigen, weight loss, and pelvic pain. (Abdominal Surgery)

Office visit for a 42-year-old male, established patient, nine months post-op emergency vena cava shunt for variceal bleeding, now presents with complaints of one episode of "dark" bowel movement, weight gain, tightness in abdomen, whites of eyes seem "yellow" and occasional drowsiness after eating hamburgers. (Abdominal Surgery)

Office visit for a 68-year-old male, established patient, with biopsy-proven rectal carcinoma, for evaluation and discussion of treatment options. (General Surgery)

Office visit for a 60-year-old, established patient, with diabetic nephropathy with increasing edema and dyspnea. (Endocrinology)

Office visit with 30-year-old male, established patient for three-month history of fatigue, weight loss, intermittent fever, and presenting with diffuse adenopathy and splenomegaly. (Family Medicine)

Office visit for restaging of an established patient with new lymphadenopathy one year post-therapy for lymphoma. (Hematology/Oncology)

Office visit for evaluation of recent onset syncopal attacks in a 70-year-old woman, established patient. (Internal Medicine)

Follow-up visit, 40-year-old mother of three, established patient, with acute rheumatoid arthritis, anatomical Stage 3, ARA function Class 3 rheumatoid arthritis, and deteriorating function. (Rheumatology)

Office evaluation and discussion of treatment options for a 68-year-old male, established patient, with a biopsy-proven rectal carcinoma. (General Surgery)

Follow-up office visit for a 65-year-old male, established patient, with a fever of recent onset while on outpatient antibiotic therapy for endocarditis. (Infectious Disease)

Office visit for a 75-year-old, established patient, with ALS (amyotrophic lateral sclerosis), who is no longer able to swallow. (Neurology)

Office visit for a 70-year-old female, established patient, with diabetes mellitus and hypertension, presenting with a two-month history of increasing confusion, agitation and short-term memory loss. (Family Medicine/Internal Medicine)

Hospital Inpatient Services

Initial Hospital Care

New or Established Patient

99221 Initial hospital visit following admission for a 42-year-old male for observation following an uncomplicated mandible fracture. (Plastic Surgery/Oral & Maxillofacial Surgery)

Initial hospital visit for a 40-year-old patient with a thrombosed synthetic arteriovenous conduit. (Nephrology)

Initial hospital visit for a healthy 24-year-old male with an acute onset of low back pain following a lifting injury. (Internal Medicine/Anesthesiology/Pain Medicine)

Initial hospital visit for a 69-year-old female with controlled hypertension, scheduled for surgery. (Internal Medicine/Cardiology)

Initial hospital visit for a 24-year-old healthy female with benign tumor of palate. (Oral & Maxillofacial Surgery)

Initial hospital visit for a 14-year-old female with infectious mononucleosis and dehydration. (Internal Medicine)

Initial hospital visit for a 62-year-old female with stable rheumatoid arthritis, admitted for total joint replacement. (Rheumatology)

Initial hospital visit for a 12-year-old patient with a laceration of the upper eyelid, involving the lid margin and superior canaliculus, admitted prior to surgery for IV antibiotic therapy. (Plastic Surgery)

Initial hospital visit for a 69-year-old female with controlled hypertension, scheduled for surgery. (Cardiology)

Hospital admission, examination, and initiation of treatment program for a 67-year-old male with uncomplicated pneumonia who requires IV antibiotic therapy. (Internal Medicine)

Hospital admission for an 18-month-old with 10 percent dehydration. (Pediatrics)

Hospital admission for a 12-year-old with a laceration of the upper eyelid involving the lid margin and superior canaliculus, admitted prior to surgery for IV antibiotic therapy. (Ophthalmology)

Hospital admission for a 32-year-old female with severe flank pain, hematuria and presumed diagnosis of ureteral calculus as determined by Emergency Department physician. (Urology)

Initial hospital visit for a patient with several large venous stasis ulcers not responding to outpatient therapy. (Dermatology)

Initial hospital visit for 21-year-old pregnant patient (nine weeks gestation) with hyperemesis gravidarum. (Obstetrics & Gynecology)

Initial hospital visit for a 73-year-old female with acute pyelonephritis who is otherwise generally healthy. (Geriatrics)

Initial hospital visit for 62-year-old patient with cellulitis of the foot requiring bedrest and intravenous antibiotics. (Orthopaedic Surgery)

99222 Initial hospital visit for a 50-year-old patient with lower quadrant abdominal pain and increased temperature, but without septic picture. (General Surgery/Abdominal Surgery/Colon & Rectal Surgery)

Initial hospital visit for airway management, due to a benign laryngeal mass. (Otolaryngology, Head & Neck Surgery)

Initial hospital visit for a 66-year-old female with an L-2 vertebral compression fracture with acute onset of paralytic ileus; seen in the office two days previously. (Orthopaedic Surgery)

Initial hospital visit and evaluation of a 15-year-old male admitted with peritonsillar abscess or cellulitis requiring intravenous antibiotic therapy. (Otolaryngology, Head & Neck Surgery)

Initial hospital visit for a 42-year-old male with vertebral compression fracture following a motor vehicle accident. (Orthopaedic Surgery)

Initial hospital visit for a patient with generalized atopic dermatitis and secondary infection. (Dermatology)

Initial hospital visit for a 3-year-old patient with high temperature, limp, and painful hip motion of 18 hours' duration. (Pediatrics/Orthopaedic Surgery)

Initial hospital visit for a young adult, presenting with an acute asthma attack unresponsive to outpatient therapy. (Allergy & Immunology)

Initial hospital visit for an 18-year-old male who has suppurative sialoadenitis and dehydration. (Oral & Maxillofacial Surgery)

Initial hospital visit for a 65-year-old female for acute onset of thrombotic cerebrovascular accident with contralateral paralysis and aphasia. (Neurology)

Initial hospital visit for a 50-year-old male chronic paraplegic patient with pain and spasm below the lesion. (Anesthesiology)

Partial hospital admission for an adolescent patient from chaotic blended family, transferred from inpatient setting, for continued treatment to control symptomatic expressions of hostility and depression. (Psychiatry)

Initial hospital visit for a 15-year-old male with acute status asthmaticus, unresponsive to outpatient therapy. (Internal Medicine)

Initial hospital visit for a 61-year-old male with history of previous myocardial infarction, who now complains of chest pain. (Internal Medicine)

Initial hospital visit of a 15-year-old on medications for a sore throat over the last two weeks. The sore throat has worsened and now has dysphagia. The exam shows large necrotic tonsils with an adequate airway and small palpable nodes. The initial mono test was negative. (Otolaryngology, Head & Neck Surgery)

Initial hospital evaluation of a 23-year-old allergy patient admitted with eyelid edema and pain on fifth day of oral antibiotic therapy. (Otolaryngology, Head & Neck Surgery)

Hospital admission, young adult patient, failed previous therapy and now presents in acute asthmatic attack. (Family Medicine/Allergy & Immunology)

Hospital admission of a 62-year-old smoker, established patient, with bronchitis in acute respiratory distress. (Internal Medicine/Pulmonary Medicine)

Hospital admission, examination, and initiation of a treatment program for a 65-year-old female with new onset of right-sided paralysis and aphasia. (Neurology)

Hospital admission for a 50-year-old with left lower quadrant abdominal pain and increased temperature, but without septic picture. (General Surgery)

Hospital admission, examination, and initiation of treatment program for a 66-year-old chronic hemodialysis patient with fever and a new pulmonary infiltrate. (Nephrology)

Hospital admission for an 8-year-old febrile patient with chronic sinusitis and severe headache, unresponsive to oral antibiotics. (Allergy & Immunology)

Hospital admission for a 40-year-old male with submaxillary cellulitis and trismus from infected lower molar. (Oral & Maxillofacial Surgery)

99223 Initial hospital visit for a 45-year-old female, who has a history of rheumatic fever as a child and now has anemia, fever, and congestive heart failure. (Cardiology)

Initial hospital visit for a 50-year-old male with acute chest pain and diagnostic electrocardiographic changes of an acute anterior myocardial infarction. (Cardiology/Family Medicine/Internal Medicine)

Initial hospital visit of a 75-year-old with progressive stridor and dysphagia with history of cancer of the larynx treated by radiation therapy in the past. Exam shows a large recurrent tumor of the glottis with a mass in the neck. (Otolaryngology, Head & Neck Surgery)

Initial hospital visit for a 70-year-old male admitted with chest pain, complete heart block, and congestive heart failure. (Cardiology)

Initial hospital visit for an 82-year-old male who presents with syncope, chest pain, and ventricular arrhythmias. (Cardiology)

Initial hospital visit for a 75-year-old male with history of arteriosclerotic coronary vascular disease, who is severely dehydrated, disoriented, and experiencing auditory hallucinations. (Psychiatry)

Initial hospital visit for a 70-year-old male with alcohol and sedative-hypnotic dependence, admitted by family for severe withdrawal, hypertension, and diabetes mellitus. (Psychiatry)

Initial hospital visit for a persistently suicidal latency-aged child whose parents have requested admission to provide safety during evaluation, but are anxious about separation from her. (Psychiatry)

Initial psychiatric visit for an adolescent patient without previous psychiatric history, who was transferred from the medical ICU after a significant overdose. (Psychiatry)

Initial hospital visit for a 35-year-old female with severe systemic lupus erythematosus on corticosteroid and cyclophosphamide, with new onset of fever, chills, rash, and chest pain. (Rheumatology)

Initial hospital visit for a 52-year-old male with known rheumatic heart disease who presents with anasarca, hypertension, and history of alcohol abuse. (Cardiology)

Initial hospital visit for a 55-year-old female with a history of congenital heart disease; now presents with cyanosis. (Cardiology)

Initial hospital visit for a psychotic, hostile, violently combative adolescent, involuntarily committed, for seclusion and restraint in order to provide for safety on unit. (Psychiatry)

Initial hospital visit for a now subdued and sullen teenage male with six-month history of declining school performance, increasing self-endangerment, and resistance of parental expectations, including running away past weekend after physical fight with father. (Psychiatry)

Initial partial hospital admission for a 17-year-old female with history of borderline mental retardation who has developed auditory hallucinations. Parents are known to abuse alcohol, and Child Protective Services is investigating allegations of sexual abuse of a younger sibling. (Psychiatry)

Initial hospital visit of a 67-year old male admitted with a large neck mass, dysphagia, and history of myocardial infarction three months before. (Otolaryngology, Head & Neck Surgery)

Initial hospital visit for a patient with suspected cerebrospinal fluid rhinorrhea which developed two weeks after head injury. (Otolaryngology, Head & Neck Surgery)

Initial hospital visit for a 25-year-old female with history of poly-substance abuse and psychiatric disorder. The patient appears to be psychotic with markedly elevated vital signs. (Psychiatry)

Initial hospital visit for a 70-year-old male with cutaneous T-cell lymphoma who has developed fever and lymphadenopathy. (Internal Medicine)

Initial hospital visit for a 62-year-old female with known coronary artery disease, for evaluation of increasing edema, dyspnea on exertion, confusion, and sudden onset of fever with productive cough. (Internal Medicine)

Initial hospital visit for a 3-year-old female with 36-hour history of sore throat and high fever; now with sudden onset of lethargy, irritability, photophobia, and nuchal rigidity. (Pediatrics)

Initial hospital visit for a 26-year-old female for evaluation of severe facial fractures (LeFort's II/III). (Plastic Surgery)

Initial hospital visit for a 55-year-old female for bilateral mandibular fractures resulting in flail mandible and airway obstruction. (Plastic Surgery)

Initial hospital visit for a 71-year-old patient with a red painful eye four days following uncomplicated cataract surgery due to endophthalmitis. (Ophthalmology)

Initial hospital visit for a 45-year-old patient involved in a motor vehicle accident who suffered a perforating corneoscleral laceration with loss of vision. (Ophthalmology)

Initial hospital visit for a 58-year-old male who has Ludwig's angina and progressive airway compromise. (Oral & Maxillofacial Surgery)

Initial hospital visit for a patient with generalized systemic sclerosis, receiving immunosuppressive therapy because of recent onset of cough, fever, and inability to swallow. (Dermatology)

Initial hospital visit for an 82-year-old male who presents with syncope, chest pain, and ventricular arrhythmias. (Cardiology)

Initial hospital visit for a 62-year-old male with history of previous myocardial infarction, comes in with recurrent, sustained ventricular tachycardia. (Cardiology)

Initial hospital visit for a chronic dialysis patient with infected PTFE fistula, septicemia, and shock. (Nephrology)

Initial hospital visit for a 1-year-old male, victim of child abuse, with central nervous system depression, skull fracture, and retinal hemorrhage. (Family Medicine/Neurology)

Initial hospital visit for a 25-year-old female with recent C4-5 quadriplegia, admitted for rehabilitation. (Physical Medicine & Rehabilitation)

Initial hospital visit for an 18-year-old male, post-traumatic brain injury with multiple impairment. (Physical Medicine & Rehabilitation)

Initial partial hospital admission for 16-year-old male, sullen and subdued, with six-month history of declining school performance, increasing self-endangerment, and resistance to parental expectations. (Psychiatry)

Initial hospital visit for a 16-year-old primigravida at 32 weeks gestation with severe hypertension (200/110), thrombocytopenia, and headache. (Obstetrics & Gynecology)

Initial hospital visit for a 49-year-old male with cirrhosis of liver with hematemesis, hepatic encephalopathy, and fever. (Gastroenterology)

Initial hospital visit for a 55-year-old female in chronic pain who has attempted suicide. (Psychiatry)

Initial hospital visit for a 70-year-old male, with multiple organ system disease, admitted with history of being aneuric and septic for 24 hours prior to admission. (Urology)

Initial hospital visit for a 3-year-old female with 36-hour history of sore throat and high fever, now with sudden onset of lethargy, irritability, photophobia, and nuchal rigidity. (Internal Medicine)

Initial hospital visit for a 78-year-old male, transfers from nursing home with dysuria and pyuria, increasing confusion, and high fever. (Internal Medicine)

Initial hospital visit for a 1-day-old male with cyanosis, respiratory distress, and tachypnea. (Cardiology)

Initial hospital visit for a 3-year-old female with recurrent tachycardia and syncope. (Cardiology)

Initial hospital visit for a thyrotoxic patient who presents with fever, atrial fibrillation, and delirium. (Endocrinology)

Initial hospital visit for a 50-year-old Type I diabetic who presents with diabetic ketoacidosis with fever and obtundation. (Endocrinology)

Initial hospital visit for a 40-year-old female with anatomical stage 3, ARA functional class 3 rheumatoid arthritis on methotrexate, corticosteroid, and nonsteroidal anti-inflammatory drugs. Patient presents with severe arthritis flare, new oral ulcers, abdominal pain, and leukopenia. (Rheumatology)

Initial hospital exam of a pediatric patient with high fever and proptosis. (Otolaryngology, Head & Neck Surgery)

Initial hospital visit for a 25-year-old patient admitted for the first time to the rehab unit, with recent C-4-5 quadriplegia. (Physical Medicine & Rehabilitation)

Hospital admission, examination, and initiation of treatment program for a previously unknown 58-year-old male who presents with acute chest pain (Cardiology)

Hospital admission, examination, and initiation of induction chemotherapy for a 42-year-old patient with newly diagnosed acute myelogenous leukemia. (Hematology/Oncology)

Hospital admission following a motor vehicle accident of a 24-year-old male with fracture dislocation of C5-6; neurologically intact. (Neurosurgery)

Hospital admission for a 78-year-old female with left lower lobe pneumonia and a history of coronary artery disease, congestive heart failure, osteoarthritis and gout. (Family Medicine)

Hospital admission, examination, and initiation of treatment program for a 65-year-old immunosuppressed male with confusion, fever, and a headache. (Infectious Disease)

Hospital admission for a 9-year-old with vomiting, dehydration, fever, tachypnea and an admitting diagnosis of diabetic ketoacidosis. (Pediatrics)

Initial hospital visit for a 65-year-old male who presents with acute myocardial infarction, oliguria, hypotension, and altered state of consciousness. (Cardiology)

Initial hospital visit for a hostile/resistant adolescent patient who is severely depressed and involved in poly-substance abuse. Patient is experiencing significant conflict in his chaotic family situation and was suspended from school following an attack on a teacher with a baseball bat. (Psychiatry)

Initial hospital visit for 89-year-old female with fulminant hepatic failure and encephalopathy. (Gastroenterology)

Initial hospital visit for a 42-year-old female with rapidly progressing scleroderma, malignant hypertension, digital infarcts, and oligurea. (Rheumatology)

Subsequent Hospital Care

99231 Subsequent hospital visit for a 65-year-old female, post-open reduction and internal fixation of a fracture. (Physical Medicine & Rehabilitation)

Subsequent hospital visit for a 33-year-old patient with pelvic pain who is responding to pain medication and observation. (Obstetrics & Gynecology)

Subsequent hospital visit for a 21-year-old female with hyperemesis who has responded well to intravenous fluids. (Obstetrics & Gynecology)

Subsequent hospital visit to re-evaluate post-op pain and titrate patient-controlled analgesia for a 27-year-old female. (Anesthesiology)

Follow-up hospital visit for a 35-year-old female, status post-epidural analgesia. (Anesthesiology/Pain Medicine)

Subsequent hospital visit for a 56-year-old male, post-gastrectomy, for maintenance of analgesia using an intravenous dilaudid infusion. (Anesthesiology)

Subsequent hospital visit for a 4-year-old on day three receiving medication for uncomplicated pneumonia. (Allergy & Immunology)

Subsequent hospital visit for a 30-year-old female with urticaria which has stabilized with medication. (Allergy & Immunology)

Subsequent hospital visit for a 76-year-old male with venous stasis ulcers. (Dermatology)

Subsequent hospital visit for a 24-year-old female with otitis externa, seen two days before in consultation, now to have otic wick removal. (Otolaryngology, Head & Neck Surgery)

Subsequent hospital visit for a 27-year-old with acute labyrinthitis. (Otolaryngology, Head & Neck Surgery)

Subsequent hospital visit for a 10-year-old male admitted for lobar pneumonia with vomiting and dehydration; is becoming afebrile and tolerating oral fluids. (Family Medicine/Pediatrics)

Subsequent hospital visit for a 62-year-old patient with resolving cellulitis of the foot. (Orthopaedic Surgery)

Subsequent hospital visit for a 25-year-old male admitted for supra-ventricular tachycardia and converted on medical therapy. (Cardiology)

Subsequent hospital visit for a 27-year-old male two days after open reduction and internal fixation for malar complex fracture. (Plastic Surgery)

Subsequent hospital visit for a 76-year-old male with venous stasis ulcers. (Geriatrics)

Subsequent hospital visit for a 67-year-old female admitted three days ago with bleeding gastric ulcer; now stable. (Gastroenterology)

Subsequent hospital visit for stable 33-year-old male, status post-lower gastrointestinal bleeding. (General Surgery/Gastroenterology)

Subsequent hospital visit for a 29-year-old auto mechanic with effort thrombosis of left upper extremity. (General Surgery)

Subsequent hospital visit for a 14-year-old female in middle phase of inpatient treatment, who is now behaviorally stable and making satisfactory progress in treatment. (Psychiatry)

Subsequent hospital visit for an 18-year-old male with uncomplicated asthma who is clinically stable. (Allergy & Immunology)

Subsequent hospital visit for a 55-year-old male with rheumatoid arthritis, two days following an uncomplicated total joint replacement. (Rheumatology)

Subsequent hospital visit for a 60-year-old dialysis patient with an access infection, now afebrile on antibiotic. (Nephrology)

Subsequent hospital visit for a 36-year-old female with stable post-rhinoplasty epistaxis. (Plastic Surgery)

Subsequent hospital visit for a 66-year-old female with L-2 vertebral compression fracture with resolving ileus. (Orthopaedic Surgery)

Subsequent hospital visit for a patient with peritonsillar abscess. (Otolaryngology, Head & Neck Surgery)

Subsequent hospital visit for an 18-year-old female responding to intravenous antibiotic therapy for ear or sinus infection. (Otolaryngology, Head & Neck Surgery)

Subsequent hospital visit for a 70-year-old male admitted with congestive heart failure who has responded to therapy. (Cardiology)

Follow-up hospital visit for a 32-year-old female with left ureteral calculus; being followed in anticipation of spontaneous passage. (Urology)

Subsequent hospital visit for a 4-year-old female, admitted for acute gastroenteritis and dehydration, requiring IV hydration; now stable. (Family Medicine)

Subsequent hospital visit for a 50-year-old Type II diabetic who is clinically stable and without complications requiring regulation of a single dose of insulin daily. (Endocrinology)

Subsequent hospital visit to reassesses the status of a 65-year-old patient post-open reduction and internal fixation of hip fracture, on the rehab unit. (Physical Medicine & Rehabilitation)

Subsequent hospital visit for a 78-year-old male with cholangiocarcinoma managed by biliary drainage. (Interventional Radiology)

Subsequent hospital visit for a 50-year-old male with uncomplicated myocardial infarction who is clinically stable and without chest pain. (Family Medicine/Cardiology/Internal Medicine)

Subsequent hospital visit for a stable 72-year-old lung cancer patient undergoing a five-day course of infusion chemotherapy. (Hematology/Oncology)

Subsequent hospital visit, two days post admission for a 65-year-old male with a CVA (cerebral vascular accident) and left hemiparesis, who is clinically stable. (Neurology/Physical Medicine and Rehabilitation)

Subsequent hospital visit for now stable, 33-year-old male, status post lower gastrointestinal bleeding. (General Surgery)

Subsequent visit on third day of hospitalization for a 60-year-old female recovering from an uncomplicated pneumonia. (Infectious Disease/Internal Medicine/Pulmonary Medicine)

Subsequent hospital visit for a 3-year-old patient in traction for a congenital dislocation of the hip. (Orthopaedic Surgery)

Subsequent hospital visit for a 4-year-old female, admitted for acute gastroenteritis and dehydration, requiring IV hydration; now stable. (Family Medicine/Internal Medicine)

Subsequent hospital visit for 50-year-old female with resolving uncomplicated acute pancreatitis. (Gastroenterology)

99232 Subsequent hospital visit for a patient with venous stasis ulcers who developed fever and red streaks adjacent to the ulcer. (Dermatology/Internal Medicine/Family Medicine)

Subsequent hospital visit for a 66-year-old male for dressing changes and observation. Patient has had a myocutaneous flap to close a pharyngeal fistula and now has a low-grade fever. (Plastic Surgery)

Subsequent hospital visit for a 54-year-old female admitted for myocardial infarction, but who is now having frequent premature ventricular contractions. (Internal Medicine)

Subsequent hospital visit for an 80-year-old patient with a pelvic rim fracture, inability to walk, and severe pain; now 36 hours post-injury, experiencing urinary retention. (Orthopaedic Surgery)

Subsequent hospital visit for a 17-year-old female with fever, pharyngitis, and airway obstruction, who after 48 hours develops a maculopapular rash. (Pediatrics/Family Medicine)

Follow-up hospital visit for a 32-year-old patient admitted the previous day for corneal ulcer. (Dermatology)

Follow-up visit for a 67-year-old male with congestive heart failure who has responded to antibiotics and diuretics, and has now developed a monoarthropathy. (Internal Medicine)

Follow-up hospital visit for a 58-year-old male receiving continuous opioids who is experiencing severe nausea and vomiting. (Pain Medicine)

Subsequent hospital visit for a patient after an auto accident who is slow to respond to ambulation training. (Physical Medicine & Rehabilitation)

Subsequent hospital visit for a 14-year-old with unstable bronchial asthma complicated by pneumonia. (Allergy & Immunology)

Subsequent hospital visit for a 50-year-old diabetic, hypertensive male with back pain not responding to conservative inpatient management with continued radiation of pain to the lower left extremity. (Orthopaedic Surgery)

Subsequent hospital visit for a 37-year-old female on day five of antibiotics for bacterial endocarditis, who still has low-grade fever.

Subsequent hospital visit for a 54-year-old patient, post MI (myocardial infarction), who is out of the CCU (coronary care unit) but is now having frequent premature ventricular contractions on telemetry. (Cardiology/Internal Medicine)

Subsequent hospital visit for a patient with neutropenia, a fever responding to antibiotics, and continued slow gastrointestinal bleeding on platelet support. (Hematology/Oncology)

Subsequent hospital visit for a 50-year-old male admitted two days ago for sub-acute renal allograft rejection. (Nephrology)

Subsequent hospital visit for a 35-year-old drug addict, not responding to initial antibiotic therapy for pyelonephritis. (Urology)

Subsequent hospital visit of an 81-year-old male with abdominal distention, nausea, and vomiting. (General Surgery)

Subsequent hospital care for a 62-year-old female with congestive heart failure, who remains dyspneic and febrile. (Internal Medicine)

Subsequent hospital visit for a 73-year-old female with recently diagnosed lung cancer, who complains of unsteady gait. (Pulmonary Medicine)

Subsequent hospital visit for a 20-month-old male with bacterial meningitis treated one week with antibiotic therapy; has now developed a temperature of 101.0. (Pediatrics)

Subsequent hospital visit for 13-year-old male admitted with left lower quadrant abdominal pain and fever, not responding to therapy. (General Surgery)

Subsequent hospital visit for a 65-year-old male with hemiplegia and painful paretic shoulder. (Physical Medicine & Rehabilitation)

99233 Subsequent hospital visit for a 38-year-old male, quadriplegic with acute autonomic hyperreflexia, who is not responsive to initial care. (Physical Medicine & Rehabilitation)

Follow-up hospital visit for a teenage female who continues to experience severely disruptive, violent and life-threatening symptoms in a complicated multi-system illness. Family/social circumstances also a contributing factor. (Psychiatry)

Subsequent hospital visit for a 42-year-old female with progressive systemic sclerosis (scleroderma), renal failure on dialysis, congestive heart failure, cardiac arrhythmias, and digital ulcers. (Allergy & Immunology)

Subsequent hospital visit for a 50-year-old diabetic, hypertensive male with nonresponding back pain and radiating pain to the lower left extremity, who develops chest pain, cough, and bloody sputum. (Orthopaedic Surgery)

Subsequent hospital visit for a 64-year-old female, status post-abdominal aortic aneurysm resection, with non-responsive coagulopathy, who has now developed lower GI bleeding. (Abdominal Surgery/Colon & Rectal Surgery/General Surgery)

Follow-up hospital care of a patient with pansinusitis infection complicated by a brain abscess and asthma; no response to current treatment. (Otolaryngology, Head & Neck Surgery)

Subsequent hospital visit for a patient with a laryngeal neoplasm who develops airway compromise, suspected metastasis. (Otolaryngology, Head & Neck Surgery)

Subsequent hospital visit for a 49-year-old male with significant rectal bleeding, etiology undetermined, not responding to treatment. (Abdominal Surgery/General Surgery/Colon & Rectal Surgery)

Subsequent hospital visit for a 50-year-old male, post-aortocoronary bypass surgery; now develops hypotension and oliguria. (Cardiology)

Subsequent hospital visit for an adolescent patient who is violent, unsafe, and noncompliant, with multiple expectations for participation in treatment plan and behavior on the treatment unit. (Psychiatry)

Subsequent hospital visit for an 18-year-old male being treated for presumed PCP psychosis. Patient is still moderately symptomatic with auditory hallucinations and is insisting on signing out against medical advice. (Psychiatry)

Subsequent hospital visit for an 8-year-old female with caustic ingestion, who now has fever, dyspnea, and dropping hemoglobin. (Gastroenterology)

Follow-up hospital visit for a chronic renal failure patient on dialysis who develops chest pain and shortness of breath and a new onset pericardial friction rub. (Nephrology)

Subsequent hospital visit for a 44-year-old patient with electrical burns to the left arm with ascending infection. (Orthopaedic Surgery)

Subsequent hospital visit for a patient with systemic sclerosis who has aspirated and is short of breath. (Dermatology)

Subsequent hospital visit for a 65-year-old female, status post-op resection of abdominal aortic aneurysm, with suspected ischemic bowel. (General Surgery)

Subsequent hospital visit for a 50-year-old male, post-aortocoronary bypass surgery, now develops hypotension and oliguria. (Cardiology)

Subsequent hospital visit for a 65-year-old male, following an acute myocardial infarction, who complains of shortness of breath and new chest pain. (Cardiology)

Subsequent hospital visit for a 65-year-old female with rheumatoid arthritis (stage 3, class 3) admitted for urosepsis. On the third hospital day, chest pain, dyspnea and fever develop. (Rheumatology)

Follow-up hospital care of a pediatric case with stridor, laryngomalcia, established tracheostomy, complicated by multiple medical problems in PICU. (Otolaryngology, Head & Neck Surgery)

Subsequent hospital visit for a 60-year-old female, four days post uncomplicated inferior myocardial infarction who has developed severe chest pain, dyspnea, diaphoresis and nausea. (Family Medicine)

Subsequent hospital visit for a patient with AML (acute myelogenous leukemia), fever, elevated white count and uric acid undergoing induction chemotherapy. (Hematology/Oncology)

Subsequent hospital visit for a 38-year-old quadriplegic male with acute autonomic hyperreflexia, who is not responsive to initial care. (Physical Medicine & Rehabilitation)

Subsequent hospital visit for a 65-year-old female post-op resection of abdominal aortic aneurysm, with suspected ischemic bowel. (General Surgery)

Subsequent hospital visit for a 60-year-old female with persistent leukocytosis and a fever seven days after a sigmoid colon resection for carcinoma. (Infectious Disease)

Subsequent hospital visit for a chronic renal failure patient on dialysis, who develops chest pain, shortness of breath and new onset of pericardial friction rub. (Nephrology)

Subsequent hospital visit for a 65-year-old male with acute myocardial infarction who now demonstrates complete heart block and congestive heart failure. (Cardiology)

Subsequent hospital visit for a 25-year-old female with hypertension and systemic lupus erythmatosus, admitted for fever and respiratory distress. On the third hospital day, the patient presented with purpuric skin lesions and acute renal failure. (Allergy & Immunology)

Subsequent hospital visit for a 55-year-old male with severe chronic obstructive pulmonary disease and bronchospasm; initially admitted for acute respiratory distress requiring ventilatory support in the ICU. The patient was stabilized, extubated and transferred to the floor, but has now developed acute fever, dyspnea, left lower lobe rhonchi and laboratory evidence of carbon dioxide retention and hypoxemia. (Family Medicine/Internal Medicine)

Subsequent hospital visit for 46-year-old female, known liver cirrhosis patient, with recent upper gastrointestinal hemorrhage from varices; now with worsening ascites and encephalopathy. (Gastroenterology)

Subsequent hospital visit for 62-year-old female admitted with acute subarachnoid hemorrhage, negative cerebral arteriogram, increased lethargy and hemiparesis with fever. (Neurosurgery)

Consultations

Office or Other Outpatient Consultations

New or Established Patient

99241   Initial office consultation for a 40-year-old female in pain from blister on lip following a cold. (Oral & Maxillofacial Surgery)

Initial office consultation for a 62-year-old construction worker with olecranon bursitis. (Orthopaedic Surgery)

Office consultation with 25-year-old postpartum female with severe symptomatic hemorrhoids. (Colon & Rectal Surgery)

Office consultation with 58-year-old male, referred for follow-up of creatinine level and evaluation of obstructive uropathy, relieved two months ago. (Nephrology)

Office consultation for 30-year-old female tennis player with sprain or contusion of the forearm. (Orthopaedic Surgery)

Office consultation for a 45-year-old male, requested by his internist, with asymptomatic torus palatinus requiring no further treatment. (Oral & Maxillofacial Surgery)

99242   Initial office consultation for a 20-year-old male with acute upper respiratory tract symptoms. (Allergy & Immunology)

Initial office consultation for a 29-year-old soccer player with painful proximal thigh/groin injury. (Orthopaedic Surgery)

Initial office consultation for a 66-year-old female with wrist and hand pain, numbness of finger tips, suspected median nerve compression by carpal tunnel syndrome. (Plastic Surgery)

Initial office consultation for a patient with a solitary lesion of discoid lupus erythematosus on left cheek to rule out malignancy of self-induced lesion. (Dermatology)

Office consultation for management of systolic hypertension in a 70-year-old male scheduled for elective prostate resection. (Geriatrics)

Office consultation with 27-year-old female, with old amputation, for evaluation of existing above-knee prosthesis. (Physical Medicine & Rehabilitation)

Office consultation with 66-year-old female with wrist and hand pain, and finger numbness, secondary to suspected carpal tunnel syndrome. (Orthopaedic Surgery)

Office consultation for 61-year-old female, recently on antibiotic therapy, now with diarrhea and leukocytosis. (Abdominal Surgery)

Office consultation for a patient with papulosquamous eruption of elbow with pitting of nails and itchy scalp. (Dermatology)

Office consultation for a 30-year-old female with single season allergic rhinitis. (Allergy & Immunology)

99243   Initial office consultation for a 60-year-old male with avascular necrosis of the left femoral head with increasing pain. (Orthopaedic Surgery)

Office consultation for a 31-year-old woman complaining of palpitations and chest pains. Her internist had described a mild systolic click. (Cardiology)

Office consultation for a 65-year-old female with persistent bronchitis. (Infectious Disease)

Office consultation for a 65-year-old man with chronic low-back pain radiating to the leg. (Neurosurgery)

Office consultation for 23-year-old female with Crohn's disease not responding to therapy. (Abdominal Surgery/Colon & Rectal Surgery)

Office consultation for 25-year-old patient with symptomatic knee pain and swelling, with torn anterior cruciate ligament and/or torn meniscus. (Orthopaedic Surgery)

Office consultation for a 67-year-old patient with osteoporosis and mandibular atrophy with regard to reconstructive alternatives. (Oral & Maxillofacial Surgery)

Office consultation for 39-year-old patient referred at a perimenopausal age for irregular menses and menopausal symptoms. (Obstetrics & Gynecology)

99244   Initial office consultation for a 28-year-old male, HIV+, with a recent change in visual acuity. (Ophthalmology)

Initial office consultation for a 15-year-old male with failing grades, suspected drug abuse. (Pediatrics)

Initial office consultation for a 36-year-old factory worker, status four months post-occupational low back injury and requires management of intractable low back pain. (Pain Medicine)

Initial office consultation for a 45-year-old female with a history of chronic arthralgia of TMJ and associated myalgia and sudden progressive symptomatology over last two to three months. (Oral & Maxillofacial Surgery)

Initial office consultation for evaluation of a 70-year-old male with appetite loss and diminished energy. (Psychiatry)

Initial office consultation for an elementary school-aged patient, referred by pediatrician, with multiple systematic complaints and recent onset of behavioral discontrol. (Psychiatry)

Initial office consultation for a 23-year-old female with developmental facial skeletal anomaly and subsequent abnormal relationship of jaw(s) to cranial base. (Oral & Maxillofacial Surgery)

Initial office consultation for a 45-year-old myopic patient with a one-week history of floaters and a partial retinal detachment. (Ophthalmology)

Initial office consultation for a 65-year-old female with moderate dementia, mild unsteadiness, back pain fatigue on ambulation, intermittent urinary incontinence. (Neurosurgery)

Initial office consultation for a 33-year-old female referred by endocrinologist with amenorrhea and galactorrhea, for evaluation of pituitary tumor. (Neurosurgery)

Initial office consultation for a 34-year-old male with new onset nephrotic syndrome. (Nephrology)

Initial office consultation for a 39-year-old female with intractable chest wall pain secondary to metastatic breast cancer. (Anesthesiology/Pain Medicine)

Initial office consultation for a patient with multiple giant tumors of jaws. (Oral & Maxillofacial Surgery)

Initial office consultation for a patient with a failed total hip replacement with loosening and pain upon walking. (Orthopaedic Surgery)

Initial office consultation for a 60-year-old female with three-year history of intermittent tic-like unilateral facial pain; now constant pain for six weeks without relief by adequate carbamazepine dosage. (Neurosurgery)

Initial office consultation for a 45-year-old male heavy construction worker with prior lumbar disk surgery two years earlier; now gradually recurring low back and unilateral leg pain for three months, unable to work for two weeks. (Neurosurgery)

Initial office consultation of a patient who presents with a 30-year history of smoking and right neck mass. (Otolaryngology, Head & Neck Surgery)

Office consultation with 38-year-old female, with inflammatory bowel disease, who now presents with right lower quadrant pain and suspected intra-abdominal abscess. (General Surgery/Colon & Rectal Surgery)

Office consultation with 72-year-old male with esophageal carcinoma, symptoms of dysphagia and reflux. (Thoracic Surgery)

Office consultation for discussion of treatment options for a 40-year-old female with a two-centimeter adenocarcinoma of the breast. (Radiation Oncology)

Office consultation for young patient referred by pediatrician because of patient's short attention span, easy distractibility and hyperactivity. (Psychiatry)

Office consultation for 66-year-old female, history of colon resection for adenocarcinoma six years earlier, now with severe mid-back pain; x-rays showing osteoporosis and multiple vertebral compression fractures. (Neurosurgery)

Office consultation for a patient with chronic pelvic inflammatory disease who now has left lower quadrant pain with a palpable pelvic mass. (Obstetrics & Gynecology)

Office consultation for a patient with long-standing psoriasis with acute onset of erythroderma, pustular lesions, chills and fever. Combinations of topical and systemic treatments discussed and instituted. (Dermatology)

99245 Initial office consultation for a 35-year-old multiple-trauma male patient with complex pelvic fractures, for evaluation and formulation of management plan. (Orthopaedic Surgery)

Initial emergency room consultation for 10-year-old male in status epilepticus, recent closed head injury, information about medication not available. (Neurosurgery)

Initial emergency room consultation for a 23-year-old patient with severe abdominal pain, guarding, febrile, and unstable vital signs. (Obstetrics & Gynecology)

Office consultation for a 67-year-old female longstanding uncontrolled diabetic who presents with retinopathy, nephropathy, and a foot ulcer. (Endocrinology)

Office consultation for a 37-year-old male for initial evaluation and management of Cushing's disease. (Endocrinology)

Office consultation for a 60-year-old male who presents with thyrotoxicosis, exophthalmos, frequent premature ventricular contractions and congestive heart failure. (Endocrinology)

Initial office consultation for a 36-year-old patient, one year status post occupational herniated cervical disk treated by laminectomy, requiring management of multiple sites of intractable pain, depression, and narcotic dependence. (Pain Medicine)

Office consultation for a 58-year-old man with a history of MI and CHF who complains of the recent onset of rest angina and shortness of breath. The patient has a systolic blood pressure of 90mmHG and is in Class IV heart failure. (Cardiology)

Emergency room consultation for a 1-year-old with a three-day history of fever with increasing respiratory distress who is thought to have cardiac tamponade by the ER physician. (Cardiology)

Office consultation in the emergency room for a 25-year-old male with severe, acute, closed head injury. (Neurosurgery)

Office consultation for a 23-year-old female with Stage II A Hodgkins disease with positive supraclavicular and mediastinal nodes. (Radiation Oncology)

Office consultation for a 27-year-old juvenile diabetic patient with severe diabetic retinopathy, gastric atony, nephrotic syndrome and progressive renal failure, now with a serum creatinine of 2.7, and a blood pressure of 170/114. (Nephrology)

Office consultation for independent medical evaluation of a patient with a history of complicated low back and neck problems with previous multiple failed back surgeries. (Orthopaedic Surgery)

Office consultation for an adolescent referred by pediatrician for recent onset of violent and self-injurious behavior. (Psychiatry)

Office consultation for a 6-year-old male for evaluation of severe muscle and joint pain and a diffuse rash. Well until four-six weeks earlier, when he developed arthralgia, myalgias, and a fever of 102 for one week. (Rheumatology)

Initial Inpatient Consultations

New or Established Patient

99251 Initial hospital consultation for a 27-year-old female with fractured incisor post-intubation. (Oral & Maxillofacial Surgery)

Initial hospital consultation for an orthopaedic patient on IV antibiotics who has developed an apparent candida infection of the oral cavity. (Oral & Maxillofacial Surgery)

Initial inpatient consultation for a 30-year-old female complaining of vaginal itching, post orthopaedic surgery. (Obstetrics & Gynecology)

Initial inpatient consultation for a 36-year-old male on orthopaedic service with complaint of localized dental pain. (Oral & Maxillofacial Surgery)

99252 Initial hospital consultation for a 45-year-old male, previously abstinent alcoholic, who relapsed and was admitted for management of gastritis. The patient readily accepts the need for further treatment. (Addiction Medicine)

Initial hospital consultation for a 35-year-old dialysis patient with episodic oral ulcerations. (Oral & Maxillofacial Surgery)

Initial inpatient preoperative consultation for a 43-year-old woman with cholecystitis and well-controlled hypertension. (Cardiology)

Initial inpatient consultation for recommendation of antibiotic prophylaxis for a patient with a synthetic heart valve who will undergo urologic surgery. (Internal Medicine)

Initial inpatient consultation for possible drug induced skin eruption in 50-year-old male. (Dermatology)

Preoperative inpatient consultation for evaluation of hypertension in a 60-year-old male who will undergo a cholecystectomy. Patient had a normal annual check-up in your office four months ago. (Internal Medicine)

Initial inpatient consultation for 66-year-old patient with wrist and hand pain and finger numbness, secondary to carpal tunnel syndrome. (Orthopaedic Surgery/Plastic Surgery)

Initial inpatient consultation for a 66-year-old male smoker referred for pain management immediately status post-biliary tract surgery done via sub-costal incision. (Anesthesiology/Pain Medicine)

99253 Initial hospital consultation for a 50-year-old female with incapacitating knee pain due to generalized rheumatoid arthritis. (Orthopaedic Surgery)

Initial hospital consultation for a 60-year-old male with avascular necrosis of the left femoral heel with increasing pain. (Orthopaedic Surgery)

Initial hospital consultation for a 45-year-old female with compound mandibular fracture and concurrent head, abdominal and/or orthopaedic injuries. (Oral & Maxillofacial Surgery)

Initial hospital consultation for a 22-year-old female, paraplegic, to evaluate wrist and hand pain. (Orthopaedic Surgery)

Initial hospital consultation for a 40-year-old male with 10-day history of incapacitating unilateral sciatica, unable to walk now, not improved by bed rest. (Neurosurgery)

Initial hospital consultation, requested by pediatrician, for treatment recommendations for a patient admitted with persistent inability to walk following soft tissue injury to ankle. (Physiatry)

Initial hospital consultation for a 27-year-old previously healthy male who vomited during IV sedation and may have aspirated gastric contents. (Anesthesiology)

Initial hospital consultation for a 33-year-old female, post-abdominal surgery, who now has a fever. (Internal Medicine)

Initial inpatient consultation for a 57-year-old male, post lower endoscopy, for evaluation of abdominal pain and fever. (General Surgery)

Initial inpatient consultation for rehabilitation of a 73-year-old female one week after surgical management of a hip fracture. (Physical Medicine & Rehabilitation)

Initial inpatient consultation for diagnosis/management of fever following abdominal surgery. (Internal Medicine)

Initial inpatient consultation for a 35-year-old female with a fever and pulmonary infiltrate following cesarean section. (Pulmonary Medicine)

Initial inpatient consultation for a 42-year-old non-diabetic patient, post-op cholecystectomy, now with an acute urinary tract infection. (Nephrology)

Initial inpatient consultation for 53-year-old female with moderate uncomplicated pancreatitis. (Gastroenterology)

Initial inpatient consultation for 45-year-old patient with chronic neck pain with radicular pain of the left arm. (Orthopaedic Surgery)

Initial inpatient consultation for 8-year-old patient with new onset of seizures who has a normal examination and previous history. (Neurology)

99254 Initial hospital consultation for a 15-year-old patient with painless swelling of proximal humerus with lytic lesion by x-ray. (Orthopaedic Surgery)

Initial hospital consultation for evaluation of a 29-year-old female with a diffusely positive medical review of systems and history of multiple surgeries. (Psychiatry)

Initial hospital consultation for a 70-year-old diabetic female with gangrene of the foot. (Orthopaedic Surgery)

Initial inpatient consultation for a 47-year-old female with progressive pulmonary infiltrate, hypoxemia, and diminished urine output. (Anesthesiology)

Initial hospital consultation for a 13-month-old with spasmodic cough, respiratory distress, and fever. (Allergy & Immunology)

Initial hospital consultation for a patient with failed total hip replacement with loosening and pain upon walking. (Orthopaedic Surgery)

Initial hospital consultation for a 62-year-old female with metastatic breast cancer to the femoral neck and thoracic vertebra. (Orthopaedic Surgery)

Initial hospital consultation for a 39-year-old female with nephrolithiasis requiring extensive opioid analgesics, whose vital signs are now elevated. She initially denied any drug use, but today gives history of multiple substance abuse, including opioids and prior treatment for a personality disorder. (Psychiatry)

Initial hospital consultation for a 70-year-old female without previous psychiatric history, who is now experiencing nocturnal confusion and visual hallucinations following hip replacement surgery. (Psychiatry)

Initial inpatient consultation for evaluation of a 63-year-old in the ICU with diabetes and chronic renal failure who develops acute respiratory distress syndrome 36 hours after a mitral valve replacement. (Anesthesiology)

Initial inpatient consultation for a 66-year-old female with enlarged supraclavicular lymph nodes, found on biopsy to be malignant. (Hematology/Oncology)

Initial inpatient consultation for a 43-year-old female for evaluation of sudden painful visual loss, optic neuritis and episodic paresthesia. (Ophthalmology)

Initial inpatient consultation for evaluation of a 71-year-old male with hyponatremia (serum sodium 114) who was admitted to the hospital with pneumonia. (Nephrology)

Initial inpatient consultation for a 72-year-old male with emergency admission for possible bowel obstruction. (Internal Medicine/General Surgery)

Initial inpatient consultation for a 35-year-old female with fever, swollen joints, and rash of one-week duration. (Rheumatology)

99255 Initial inpatient consultation for a 76-year-old female with massive, life-threatening gastrointestinal hemorrhage and chest pain. (Gastroenterology)

Initial inpatient consultation for a 75-year-old female, admitted to intensive care with acute respiratory distress syndrome, who is hypersensitive, has a moderate metabolic acidosis, and a rising serum creatinine. (Nephrology)

Initial hospital consultation for patient with a history of complicated low back pain and neck problems with previous multiple failed back surgeries. (Orthopaedic Surgery/Neurosurgery)

Initial hospital consultation for a 66-year-old female, two days post-abdominal aneurysm repair, with oliguria and hypertension of one-day duration. (Nephrology/Internal Medicine)

Initial hospital consultation for a patient with shotgun wound to face with massive facial trauma and airway obstruction. (Oral & Maxillofacial Surgery)

Initial hospital consultation for patient with severe pancreatitis complicated by respiratory insufficiency, acute renal failure, and abscess formation. (General Surgery/Colon & Rectal Surgery)

Initial hospital consultation for a 35-year-old multiple-trauma male patient with complex pelvic fractures to evaluate and formulate management plan. (Orthopaedic Surgery)

Initial inpatient consultation for adolescent patient with fractured femur and pelvis who pulled out IVs and disconnected traction in attempt to elope from hospital. (Psychiatry)

Initial hospital consultation for a 16-year-old primigravida at 32 weeks gestation requested by a family practitioner for evaluation of severe hypertension, thrombocytopenia, and headache. (Obstetrics & Gynecology)

Initial hospital consultation for a 58-year-old insulin-dependent diabetic with multiple antibiotic allergies, now with multiple fascial plane abscesses and airway obstruction. (Oral & Maxillofacial Surgery)

Initial inpatient consultation for a 55-year-old male with known cirrhosis and ascites, now with jaundice, encephalopathy, and massive hematemesis. (Gastroenterology)

Initial hospital consultation for a 25-year-old male, seen in emergency room with severe, closed head injury. (Neurosurgery)

Initial hospital consultation for a 2-day-old male with single ventricle physiology and subaortic obstruction. Family counseling following evaluation for multiple, staged surgical procedures. (Thoracic Surgery)

Initial hospital consultation for a 45-year-old male admitted with subarachnoid hemorrhage and intracranial aneurysm on angiogram. (Neurosurgery)

Initial inpatient consultation for myxedematous patient who is hypoventilating and obtunded. (Endocrinology)

Initial hospital consultation for a 45-year-old patient with widely metastatic lung carcinoma, intractable back pain, and a history that includes substance dependence, NSAID allergy, and two prior laminectomies with fusion for low back pain. (Pain Medicine)

Initial hospital consultation for evaluation of treatment options in a 50-year-old patient with cirrhosis, known peptic ulcer disease, hypotension, encephalopathy, and massive acute upper gastrointestinal bleeding which cannot be localized by endoscopy. (Interventional Radiology)

Initial inpatient consultation in the ICU for a 70-year-old male who experienced a cardiac arrest during surgery and was resuscitated. (Cardiology)

Initial inpatient consultation for a patient with severe pancreatitis complicated by respiratory insufficiency, acute renal failure and abscess formation. (Gastroenterology)

Initial inpatient consultation for a 70-year-old cirrhotic male admitted with ascites, jaundice, encephalopathy, and massive hematemesis. (Gastroenterology)

Initial inpatient consultation in the ICU for a 51-year-old patient who is on a ventilator and has a fever two weeks after a renal transplantation. (Infectious Disease)

Initial inpatient consultation for evaluation and formulation of plan for management of multiple trauma patient with complex pelvic fracture, 35-year-old male. (General Surgery/Orthopaedic Surgery)

Initial inpatient consultation for a 50-year-old male with a history of previous myocardial infarction, now with acute pulmonary edema and hypotension. (Cardiology)

Initial inpatient consultation for 45-year-old male with recent, acute subarachnoid hemorrhage, hesitant speech, mildly confused, drowsy. High risk group for HIV+ status. (Neurosurgery)

Initial inpatient consultation for 36-year-old female referred by her internist to evaluate a patient being followed for abdominal pain and fever. The patient has developed diffuse abdominal pain, guarding, rigidity and increased fever. (Obstetrics & Gynecology)

Follow-up Inpatient Consultations

Established Patient

99261   Follow-up consultation for a 78-year-old female nursing home resident for evaluation of medical management of pruritus ani. (Colon & Rectal Surgery/Geriatrics/General Surgery)

Follow-up hospital consultation on first post-op day for a 64-year-old male who has undergone uneventful CABG. (Anesthesiology)

Follow-up inpatient consultation for a 67-year-old female admitted several days ago for bleeding ulcer; now stable. (Gastroenterology)

Follow-up hospital consultation for a 35-year-old female with history of mitral valve prolapse. (Cardiology)

Follow-up inpatient consultation to complete initial consultation for dental pain after review of radiographs. (Oral & Maxillofacial Surgery)

Follow-up inpatient consultation for evaluation of response to therapy for moniliasis. (Oral & Maxillofacial Surgery)

Follow-up inpatient consultation for a 22-year-old female with recurrent aphthous ulcers. (Oral & Maxillofacial Surgery)

Follow-up hospital consultation for a 37-year-old female to complete review of previously unavailable studies. (Therapeutic Radiology & Oncology)

Follow-up consultation for a highly functional 75-year-old female with urinary incontinence to review preliminary results of diagnostic evaluation. (Geriatrics)

Follow-up inpatient consultation for a 1-week-old premature female with patent ductus arteriosus. The murmur has disappeared. (Cardiology)

Follow-up hospital consultation to review the results of an audiogram. (Otolaryngology, Head & Neck Surgery)

Follow-up inpatient consultation with 35-year-old female with pulmonary embolism post-op cesarean section, now stable, for assessment of response to anticoagulation and recommended adjustment of heparin dose. (Pulmonary Medicine)

Follow-up inpatient consultation for a 74-year-old male whose postoperative facial paralysis after a cholecystectomy is now resolving. (Neurology)

Follow-up inpatient consultation with 67-year-old female, established patient, for review of diagnostic studies ordered at time of first contact. (Internal Medicine)

Follow-up inpatient consultation for 78-year-old female nursing home resident for evaluation of medical management of pruritis ani. (General Surgery/Colon & Rectal Surgery)

Follow-up inpatient consultation for a 36-year-old female two days after spontaneous passage of 3mm stone. (Urology)

Follow-up inpatient consultation for a 94-year-old male nursing home resident for re-evaluation of hemorrhoids following conservative therapy. (Colon & Rectal Surgery/General Surgery/Geriatrics)

Follow-up inpatient consultation for a 50-year-old male, asymptomatic with borderline ECG abnormality, needs preoperative opinion after a thallium exercise perfusion scan. (Cardiology)

99262   Follow-up inpatient consultation for a 6-year-old female, established patient, with endocarditis and changing heart murmur. (Cardiology)

Follow-up inpatient consultation on a 2-year-old male, one day postoperative ventricular septal defect closure with signs of tachycardia. (Cardiology)

Follow-up inpatient consultation for a 63-year-old man, established patient, with moderately severe pulmonary insufficiency, 10 days postoperative coronary artery bypass for unstable angina. Patient has developed severe dyspnea, fever, and a new exudative right pleural effusion. (Cardiology)

Follow-up inpatient consultation for a 67-year-old woman with lung cancer and syndrome of inappropriate secretion of antidiuretic hormone (SIADH) who has had a seizure following intravenous saline. (Endocrinology)

Follow-up inpatient consultation for a 22-year-old female, established patient, with steroid-dependent systemic lupus erythematosus, arthritis, and glomerulonephritis. Patient is re-evaluated for loss of consciousness and chest pain. (Rheumatology)

Follow-up inpatient consultation for a 75-year-old diabetic with fever, chills, a gangrenous heel ulcer, rhonchi, and dyspnea who appears lethargic and tachypneic. (Endocrinology)

Follow-up inpatient consultation for a 30-year-old, established patient, with intractable neck and low back pain, who is excessively sedated after institution of methadone therapy. (Pain Medicine)

Follow-up inpatient consultation for a 65-year-old man with a history of hypertension and MI who is five days post uncomplicated GI procedure with an unremarkable postoperative recovery. He has just been resuscitated from a cardiopulmonary arrest. (Cardiology)

Follow-up inpatient consultation with 72-year-old female, established patient with bullous pemphigoid on combined oral therapy steroids and immunosuppressive to evaluate progress of cutaneous care orders and adjustment of oral/parenteral therapy dosages. (Dermatology)

Follow-up inpatient consultation for a 71-year-old male who has developed a maculopapular skin rash while on antibiotics recommended for an uncomplicated pneumonia. (Infectious Disease)

Follow-up inpatient consultation with 68-year-old, incapacitated male with spinal stenosis and failure to respond to bedrest, analgesics, and PT. (Neurosurgery)

Follow-up inpatient consultation with 51-year-old male for evaluation and determination of the etiology of postoperative hyponatremia following TURP. (Family Medicine)

Follow-up inpatient consultation for re-evaluation of a stroke patient, and development of plan for initial rehabilitation services. (Neurology)

Follow-up inpatient consultation with 45-year-old male, established patient for discussion of CT scan which demonstrates a cavernous hemangioma. (Ophthalmology)

Follow-up inpatient consultation for an asymptomatic 35-year-old Type I diabetic patient with hyperkalemic, hyperchloremia acidosis, to review lab results. (Nephrology)

Follow-up inpatient consultation for an elderly male with a perioperative myocardial infarction requiring adjustment of vasoactive medications. (Anesthesiology)

99263   Follow-up hospital consultation of an AIDS patient admitted with a sore throat who now has enlarging neck mass. (Otolaryngology, Head & Neck Surgery)

Follow-up hospital consultation of a pansinusitis patient with sudden onset of proptosis. (Otolaryngology, Head & Neck Surgery)

Follow-up inpatient consultation for a 53-year-old man with known angina who develops crescendo angina post cholecystectomy. (Cardiology)

Follow-up inpatient consultation with 72-year-old male established patient admitted for management of alcohol withdrawal, now confused and febrile. (Addiction Medicine)

Follow-up inpatient consultation for an HIV+ patient with an increasing fever following 10 days of antibiotic therapy for pneumocystis carinii pneumonia. (Infectious Disease)

Follow-up inpatient consultation with 58-year-old diabetic female, with bacterial endocarditis, continued fever after two weeks of intravenous antibiotic therapy, and new onset ventricular ectopia. (Cardiology)

Follow-up inpatient consultation for a 90-year-old female with urinary incontinence who has a complicated medical history requiring reassessment of multiple medical problems, recommendations for placement, further recommendation for management of incontinence and reevaluation of cognitive status because of competency issues. (Geriatrics/Psychiatry)

Follow-up inpatient consultation for 42-year-old male with persistent gastrointestinal bleeding, etiology undetermined, not responding to conservative therapy of transfusions. (General Surgery/Colon & Rectal Surgery)

Follow-up inpatient consultation for a 62-year-old female with steroid-dependent asthma, diabetes mellitus, thyrotoxicosis, abdominal pain and possible vasculitis. (Rheumatology)

Follow-up inpatient consultation for a 62-year-old male, status post-op acute small bowel obstruction; now with acute renal failure. (Family Medicine)

Emergency Department Services

New or Established Patient

99281   Emergency department visit for a patient for removal of sutures from a well-healed, uncomplicated laceration. (Emergency Medicine)

Emergency department visit for a patient for tetanus toxoid immunization. (Emergency Medicine)

Emergency department visit for a patient with several uncomplicated insect bites. (Emergency Medicine)

99282   Emergency department visit for a 20-year-old student who presents with a painful sunburn with blister formation on the back. (Emergency Medicine)

Emergency department visit for a child presenting with impetigo localized to the face. (Emergency Medicine)

Emergency department visit for a patient with a minor traumatic injury of an extremity with localized pain, swelling, and bruising. (Emergency Medicine)

Emergency department visit for an otherwise healthy patient whose chief complaint is a red, swollen cystic lesion on his/her back. (Emergency Medicine)

Emergency department visit for a patient presenting with a rash on both legs after exposure to poison ivy. (Emergency Medicine)

Emergency department visit for a young adult patient with infected sclera and purulent discharge from both eyes without pain, visual disturbance or history of foreign body in either eye. (Emergency Medicine)

99283 Emergency department visit for a sexually active female complaining of vaginal discharge who is afebrile and denies experiencing abdominal or back pain. (Emergency Medicine)

Emergency department visit for a well-appearing 8-year-old who has a fever, diarrhea and abdominal cramps, is tolerating oral fluids and is not vomiting. (Emergency Medicine)

Emergency department visit for a patient with an inversion ankle injury, who is unable to bear weight on the injured foot and ankle. (Emergency Medicine)

Emergency department visit for a patient who has a complaint of acute pain associated with a suspected foreign body in the painful eye. (Emergency Medicine)

Emergency department visit for a healthy, young adult patient who sustained a blunt head injury with local swelling and bruising without subsequent confusion, loss of consciousness or memory deficit. (Emergency Medicine)

99284 Emergency department visit for a 4-year-old who fell off a bike sustaining a head injury with brief loss of consciousness. (Emergency Medicine)

Emergency department visit for an elderly female who has fallen and is now complaining of pain in her right hip and is unable to walk. (Emergency Medicine)

Emergency department visit for a patient with flank pain and hematuria. (Emergency Medicine)

Emergency department visit for a female presenting with lower abdominal pain and a vaginal discharge. (Emergency Medicine)

99285 Emergency department visit for a patient with a complicated overdose requiring aggressive management to prevent side effects from the ingested materials. (Emergency Medicine)

Emergency department visit for a patient with a new onset of rapid heart rate requiring IV drugs. (Emergency Medicine)

Emergency department visit for a patient exhibiting active, upper gastrointestinal bleeding. (Emergency Medicine)

Emergency department visit for a previously healthy young adult patient who is injured in an automobile accident and is brought to the emergency department immobilized and has symptoms compatible with intra-abdominal injuries or multiple extremity injuries. (Emergency Medicine)

Emergency department visit for a patient with an acute onset of chest pain compatible with symptoms of cardiac ischemia and/or pulmonary embolus. (Emergency Medicine)

Emergency department visit for a patient who presents with a sudden onset of "the worst headache of her life," and complains of a stiff neck, nausea, and inability to concentrate. (Emergency Medicine)

Emergency department visit for a patient with a new onset of a cerebral vascular accident. (Emergency Medicine)

Emergency department visit for acute febrile illness in an adult, associated with shortness of breath and an altered level of alertness. (Emergency Medicine)

Critical Care Services

99291 First hour of critical care of a 65-year-old man with septic shock following relief of ureteral obstruction caused by a stone.

First hour of critical care of a 15-year-old with acute respiratory failure from asthma.

First hour of critical care of a 45-year-old who sustained a liver laceration, cerebral hematoma, flailed chest, and pulmonary contusion after being struck by an automobile.

First hour of critical care of a 65-year-old woman who, following a hysterectomy, suffered a cardiac arrest associated with a pulmonary embolus.

First hour of critical care of a 6-month-old with hypovolemic shock secondary to diarrhea and dehydration.

First hour of critical care of a 3-year-old with respiratory failure secondary to pneumocystis carinii pneumonia.

Comprehensive Nursing Facility Assessments

New or Established Patient

99301 Annual nursing facility history and physical and MDS/RAI evaluation for a two-year nursing facility resident who is an 84-year-old female with multiple chronic health problems, including: stable controlled hypertension, chronic constipation, osteoarthritis, and moderated stable dementia.

Nursing facility visit for an assessment of a resident with non-insulin dependent diabetes, stable angina, and chronic obstructive pulmonary disease (COPD) one year after previous MDS/RAI.

99302 Nursing facility visit one year after previous MDS/RAI to assess an 80-year-old woman with Parkinson's disease, chronic hypertension, and degenerative arthritis. Visit reveals Stage II decubitus.

Nursing facility assessment of a 28-year-old diabetic, male resident with a new Stage IV pressure ulcer on his left lateral malleolus that is unresponsive to treatment, thus triggering the need for a new MDS/RAI and new medical plan of care.

Nursing facility assessment of an 88-year-old male resident with a permanent change in status following a new cerebral vascular accident (CVA) that has triggered the need for a new MDS/RAI and medical plan of care.

Nursing facility visit and assessment to take over the primary care of a 75-year-old diabetic, previously stable, who was on oral hypoglycemic agents, but who now requires initiation of insulin therapy, a new MDS/RAI, and medical plan of care.

Nursing facility visit and assessment for an 81-year-old female resident with dementia who under structured guidance and intensive nutritional support has regained significant levels of function in three activities of daily living and is now able to feed and dress herself and ambulate with appliance and who now thus requires a new MDS/RAI and medical plan of care.

99303 Initial nursing facility assessment (MDS/RAI and medical plan of care) of a 72-year-old insulin dependent diabetic amputee with hearing and visual impairments and possible dementia seen in the office the day before and judged to require nursing facility care.

Sub-acute nursing facility assessment of a previously independently living 90-year-old male who suffered a recent cerebral vascular accident (CVA) and is transferred to the hospital sub-acute rehabilitation unit for further rehabilitation supportive services.

Initial nursing facility visit to evaluate a 72-year-old woman found confused and wandering, admitted by Adult Protective Services without a qualifying hospital stay or inpatient diagnostic work. The patient lives alone and has no relatives or significant others in the community.

Nursing facility assessment and creation of medical plan of care upon readmission to the nursing facility of an 82-year-old male who was previously discharged. The patient has just been discharged from the hospital where he had been treated for an acute gastric ulcer bleed associated with transient delirium. The patient returns to the nursing facility debilitated, protein depleted, and with a Stage III coccygeal decubitus.

Subsequent Nursing Facility Care

New or Established Patient

99311 Scheduled follow-up visit for a known 70-year-old stable paraplegic with no status change noted during visit.

Scheduled monthly nursing home visit with a patient who has mild senile dementia, Alzheimers' type, with no change in status, stable hypertension, and who is ambulating with a walker one year past stroke.

Follow-up in skilled nursing facility with a 70-year-old patient following a 10-day treatment of a cellulitis of the foot.

99312 Scheduled follow-up visit to a resident with controlled dementia, hypertension, and diabetes. During visit, patient seems to exhibit flu symptoms.

Scheduled nursing facility visit with an afebrile demented resident who also has a mild cough, requiring no change in the medical plan of care.

Subsequent visit in a skilled nursing facility with a patient who is six months post stroke and now has a fever and mild cough.

Scheduled nursing facility visit for an 84-year-old male with chronic renal insufficiency, on digitalis and diuretics, requiring adjustment of medications and revision of medical plan of care.

Nursing facility visit of a resident with multiple chronic health problems who is six months post stroke and now has a fever and mild cough, to evaluate for possible pneumonia. Requires the development of a new medical plan of care, but not a revised MDS/RAI.

99313 Follow-up nursing facility visit to evaluate the reason for frequent falls by a 90-year-old ataxic resident, and to determine possible need for change in medications and medical care plan.

Re-admission of a 75-year-old man with stroke who was hospitalized with pneumonia for his illness and who returns to the nursing facility with no permanent change in status from his condition prior to hospitalization; no new MDS/RAI is required.

Nursing facility visit with a diabetic resident who has developed Stage II decubitus ulcers with cellulitis, requiring a revision in the medical plan of care.

Nursing facility visit to develop a new plan of care for an amputee with atherosclerosis obliterans who has refused to eat for three days and has developed decreased urinary output.

Nursing facility visit for a 78-year-old resident with chronic atrial fibrillation and a history of heart failure to evaluate an acute confusional state and to revise the medical plan of care.

Unscheduled nursing facility visit for evaluation of a patient with fever and obtundation who is determined not to require hospital admission or new MDS, but who does require workup and revision of medical plan of care.

Prolonged Services

Prolonged Physician Service With Direct (Face-to-Face) Patient Contact

Office or Other Outpatient

99354/ 99355 A 20-year-old female with history of asthma presents with acute bronchospasm and moderate respiratory distress. Initial evaluation shows respiratory rate 30, labored breathing and wheezing heard in all lung fields. Office treatment is initiated which includes intermittent bronchial dilation and subcutaneous epinephrine. Requires intermittent physician face-to-face time with patient over a period of two-three hours. (Family Medicine/Internal Medicine)

Inpatient

99356 A 34-year-old primigravida presents to hospital in early labor. Admission history and physical reveals severe preeclampsia. Physician supervises management of preeclampsia, IV magnesium initiation and maintenance, labor augmentation with pitocin, and close maternal-fetal monitoring. Physician face-to-face involvement includes 40 minutes of continuous bedside care until the patient is stable, then is intermittent over several hours until the delivery. (Family Medicine/Internal Medicine/Obstetrics & Gynecology)

Prolonged Physician Service Without Direct Patient (Face-to-Face) Contact

99358/ 99359 A 65-year-old new patient with multiple problems is seen and evaluated. After the visit, the physician requires extensive time to talk with the patient's daughter, to review complex, detailed medical records transferred from previous physicians and to complete a comprehensive treatment plan. This plan also requires the physician to personally initiate and coordinate the care plan with a local home health agency and a dietician. (Family Medicine/Internal Medicine)

Physician Standby Services

99360 A 24-year-old patient is admitted to OB unit attempting VBAC. Fetal monitoring shows increasing fetal distress. Patient's blood pressure is rising and labor progressing slowly. A primary care physician is requested by the OB/GYN to standby in the unit for possible cesarean delivery and neonatal resuscitation. (Family Medicine/Internal Medicine)

Care Plan Oversight Services

99375 First month of care plan oversight for terminal care of a 58-year-old woman with advanced intraabdominal ovarian cancer. Care plan includes home oxygen, diuretics IV for edema and ascites control and pain control management involving IV morphine infusion when progressive ileus occurred. Physician phone contacts with nurse, family, and MSW. Discussion with MSW concerning plans to withdraw supportive measures per patient wishes. Documentation includes review and modification of care plan and certifications from nursing, MSW, pharmacy, and DME. (Family Medicine/Internal Medicine)

Appendix E

Summary of CPT Add-on Codes

This listing is a summary of CPT add-on codes for *CPT 2002*. The codes listed below are identified in *CPT 2002* with a **+** symbol.

0006T	22522	38747	64472	88313	99359
01953	22585	43635	64476	88314	99569
01968	22614	44015	64480	90472	
01969	22632	44121	64484	90474	
11001	26125	44128	64623	90781	
11101	26861	44139	64627	92547	
11201	26863	44203	64727	92973	
11732	27358	44955	64778	92974	
11922	27692	47001	64783	92978	
13102	32501	47550	64787	92979	
13122	33141	48400	64832	92981	
13133	33530	49568	64837	92984	
13153	33572	49905	64859	92996	
15001	33924	56606	64872	92998	
15101	33961	58611	64874	93320	
15121	34808	59525	64876	93321	
15201	34813	60512	64901	93325	
15221	34826	61609	64902	93571	
15241	35390	61610	67225	93572	
15261	35400	61611	67320	93609	
15343	35500	61612	67331	93613	
15351	35681	61795	67332	93621	
15401	35682	63035	67334	93622	
15787	35683	63043	67335	93623	
16036	35685	63044	67340	93662	
17003	35686	63048	69990	95920	
19001	35700	63057	74301	95962	
19126	36218	63066	75774	95967	
19291	36248	63076	75946	95973	
19295	37206	63078	75964	96412	
22103	37208	63082	75968	96423	
22116	37250	63086	75993	96570	
22216	37251	63088	75996	96571	
22226	38102	63091	76085	97546	
22328	38746	63308	76125	99100	
			78020	99116	
			78478	99135	
			78480	99140	
			78496	99290	
			87187	99292	
			87904	99354	
			88141	99355	
			88155	99356	
			88311	99357	
			88312	99358	

Appendix F

Summary of CPT Codes Exempt from Modifier '-51'

This listing is a summary of CPT codes that are exempt from the use of modifier '-51' but have NOT been designated as CPT add-on procedures/services. The codes listed below are identified in *CPT 2002* with a ⊘ symbol.

17004	31500	90385	90702	93533
17304	32000	90386	90703	93539
17305	32002	90389	90704	93540
17306	32020	90393	90705	93541
17307	33517	90396	90706	93542
17310	33518	90399	90707	93543
20660	33519	90476	90708	93544
20690	33521	90477	90709	93545
20692	33522	90581	90710	93555
20900	33523	90585	90712	93556
20902	35600	90586	90713	93600
20910	36488	90632	90716	93602
20912	36489	90633	90717	93603
20920	36490	90634	90718	93610
20922	36491	90636	90719	93612
20924	36620	90645	90720	93615
20926	36660	90646	90721	93616
20930	38792	90647	90723	93618
20931	44500	90648	90725	93619
20936	61107	90657	90727	93620
20937	61210	90658	90732	93624
20938	62284	90659	90733	93631
20974	90281	90660	90735	93640
20975	90283	90665	90740	93641
22840	90287	90669	90743	93642
22841	90288	90675	90744	93650
22842	90291	90676	90746	93651
22843	90296	90680	90747	93652
22844	90371	90690	90748	93660
22845	90375	90691	90749	95900
22846	90376	90692	93501	95903
22847	90378	90693	93503	95904
22848	90379	90700	93505	99141
22851	90384	90701	93508	99142
			93510	
			93511	
			93514	
			93524	
			93526	
			93527	
			93528	
			93529	
			93530	
			93531	
			93532	

Index

Instructions for the Use of the CPT Index

Main Terms

The index is organized by main terms. Each main term can stand alone, or be followed by up to three modifying terms. There are four primary classes of main entries:

1. Procedure or service.
   For example: Endoscopy; Anastomosis; Splint

2. Organ or other anatomic site.
   For example: Tibia; Colon; Salivary Gland

3. Condition.
   For example: Abscess; Entropion; Tetralogy of Fallot

4. Synonyms, Eponyms and Abbreviations.
   For example: EEG; Bricker Operation; Clagett Procedure

Modifying Terms

A main term may be followed by a series of up to three indented terms that modify the main term. When modifying terms appear, one should review the list, as these subterms do have an effect on the selection of the appropriate code for the procedure.

Code Ranges

Whenever more than one code applies to a given index entry, a code range is listed. If several non-sequential codes apply, they will be separated by a comma. For example:

Esophagus
      Reconstruction 43300, 43310, 43113

If two or more sequential codes apply, they will be separated by a hyphen. For example:

Debridement
      Burns 01951-01953, 16010-16030

Conventions

As a space saving convention, certain words infer some meaning. This convention is primarily used when a procedure or service is listed as a subterm. For example:

Knee
      Incision (of)

In this example, the word in parentheses (of) does not appear in the index, but it is inferred. As another example:

Pancreas
      Anesthesia (for procedures on)

In this example, as there is no such entity as pancreas anesthesia, the words in parentheses are inferred. That is, anesthesia for procedures on the pancreas.

The alphabetic index is NOT a substitute for the main text of *CPT*. Even if only one code appears, the user must refer to the main text to ensure that the code selection is accurate.

A

A-II
See Angiotensin II

Abbe-Estlander Procedure
See Reconstruction; Repair, Cleft Lip

Abdomen
Abdominal Wall
    Repair
        Hernia 49491-49496, 49501, 49507,
                  49521, 49590
    Tumor
        Excision 22900
        Unlisted Services and Procedures 22999
Abscess
    Incision and Drainage 49020, 49040
        Open 49040
        Percutaneous 49021
Angiography 74175, 75635
Artery
    Ligation 37617
Biopsy 49000
Bypass Graft 35907
Cannula/Catheter
    Removal 49422
CAT Scan 74150-74175, 75635
Celiotomy
    for Staging 49220
Cyst
    Destruction/Excision 49200-49201
Drainage
    Fluid 49080-49081
Ectopic Pregnancy 59130
Endometrioma
    Destruction/Excision 49200-49201
Exploration 49000-49002
    Blood Vessel 35840
    Staging 58960
Incision 49000
    Staging 58960
Incision and Drainage
    Pancreatitis 48000
Injection
    Air 49400
    Contrast Material 49400
Insertion
    Catheter 49420-49421
    Venous Shunt 49425
Intraperitoneal
    Catheter Removal 49422
    Shunt
        Ligation 49428
        Removal 49429
Laparotomy
    Staging 49220
Magnetic Resonance Imaging
(MRI) 74181-74183
Needle Biopsy
    Mass 49180
Peritoneocentesis 49080-49081
Radical Resection 51597

Repair
    Blood Vessel 35221
        with Other Graft 35281
        with Vein Graft 35251
    Hernia 49491-49525, 49560-49587
    Suture 49900
Revision
    Venous Shunt 49426
Suture 49900
Tumor
    Destruction/Excision 49200-49201
Ultrasound 76700-76705
Unlisted Services and Procedures 49999
Wound Exploration
    Penetrating 20102
X-Ray 74000-74022

Abdominal Aorta
See Aorta, Abdominal

Abdominal Aortic Aneurysm
See Aorta, Abdominal, Aneurysm

Abdominal Deliveries
See Cesarean Delivery

Abdominal Hysterectomy
See Hysterectomy, Abdominal

Abdominal Lymphangiogram
See Lymphangiography, Abdomen

Abdominal Paracentesis
See Abdomen, Drainage

Abdominal Radiographies
See Abdomen, X-Ray

Abdominal Wall
Surgery 22999
Tumor
    Excision 22900

Abdominohysterectomy
See Hysterectomy, Abdominal

Abdominopelvic Amputation
See Amputation, Interpelviabdominal

Abdominoplasty 15831

Ablation
Anal
    Polyp 46615
    Tumor 46615
CAT Scan Guidance 76362
Colon
    Tumor 45339
Endometrial 0009T, 58353, 58563
Endometrium
    Ultrasound Guidance 0009T
Heart
    Arrhythmogenic Focus 93650-93652
        See Cardiology; Diagnostic, Intracardiac
        Pacing and Mapping
Liver
    Tumor 47380-47383
        Laparoscopic 47370-47371
Magnetic Resonance Guidance 76394
Prostate 55873

Renal Cyst 50541
Turbinate Mucosa 30801-30802
Ultrasound Guidance 76490

Abortion
See Obstetrical Care
Incomplete 59812
Induced
    by Dilation and Curettage 59840
    by Dilation and Evacuation 59841
    by Saline 59850-59851
    by Vaginal Suppositories 59855-59856
    with Hysterectomy ...59100, 59852, 59857
Missed
    First Trimester 59820
    Second Trimester 59821
Septic 59830
Spontaneous 59812
Therapeutic
    by Saline 59850
        with Dilation and Curettage 59851
        with Hysterectomy 59852

Abrasion
Skin
    Chemical Peel 15788-15793
    Dermabrasion 15780-15783
    Lesion 15786-15787
    Salabrasion 15810-15811

Abscess
Abdomen 49040-49041
    Incision and Drainage
        Open 49040
        Percutaneous 49021
Anal
    Incision and Drainage 46045-46050
Ankle 27603
Appendix
    Incision and Drainage 44900
        Open 44900
        Percutaneous 44901
Arm, Lower 25028
    Excision 25145
    Incision and Drainage 25035
Arm, Upper
    Incision and Drainage 23930-23935
Auditory Canal, External 69020
Bartholin's Gland
    Incision and Drainage 56420
Bladder
    Incision and Drainage 51080
Brain
    Drainage 61150-61151
    Excision 61514, 61522
    Incision and Drainage 61320-61321
Breast
    Incision and Drainage 19020
Carpals
    Incision, Deep 25035
Clavicle
    Sequestrectomy 23170
Drainage
    with X-Ray 75989
Ear, External
    Complicated 69005
    Simple 69000

Elbow
    Incision and Drainage 23930-23935
Epididymis
    Incision and Drainage 54700
Excision
    Olecranon Process 24138
    Radius 24136
    Ulna 24138
Eyelid
    Incision and Drainage 67700
Facial Bones
    Excision 21026
Finger 26010-26011
    Incision and Drainage 26034
Foot
    Incision 28005
Gums
    Incision and Drainage 41800
Hand
    Incision and Drainage 26034
Hematoma
    Incision and Drainage 27603
Hip
    Incision and Drainage 26990-26992
Humeral Head 23174
Humerus
    Excision 24134
    Incision and Drainage 23935
Kidney
    Incision and Drainage 50020
       Open 50020
       Percutaneous 50021
Leg, Lower
    Incision and Drainage 27603
Liver 47010
    Drainage
       Open 47010
       Injection 47015
       Repair 47300
Localization
    Nuclear Medicine 78806-78807
Lung
    Percutaneous Drainage 32200-32201
Lymphocele Drainage 49062
Lymph Node
    Incision and Drainage 38300-38305
Mandible
    Excision 21025
Mouth
    Incision and Drainage 40800-40801,
        41005-41009, 41015-41018
Nasal Septum
    Incision and Drainage 30020
Neck
    Incision and Drainage 21501-21502
Ovarian
    Incision and Drainage 58820-58822
      Abdominal Approach 58822
      Vaginal Approach 58820
Ovary
    Drainage
       Percutaneous 58823
Palate
    Incision and Drainage 42000
Paraurethral Gland
    Incision and Drainage 53060
Parotid Gland Drainage 42300-42305

Pelvic
    Drainage
       Percutaneous 58823
Pelvis
    Incision and Drainage ...26990-26992, 45000
Pericolic
    Drainage
       Percutaneous 58823
Perineum
    Incision and Drainage 56405
Perirenal or Renal
    Drainage 50020-50021
       Percutaneous 50021
Peritoneum
    Incision and Drainage
       Open 49020
       Percutaneous 49021
Prostate
    Incision and Drainage 55720-55725
    Transurethral Drainage 52700
Radius
    Incision, Deep 25035
Rectum
    Incision and Drainage 45005-45020,
         46040, 46060
Retroperitoneal 49060-49061
    Drainage
       Open 49060
       Percutaneous 49061
Salivary Gland
    Drainage 42300-42320
Scapula
    Sequestrectomy 23172
Scrotum
    Incision and Drainage 54700, 55100
Shoulder
    Drainage 23030
Skene's Gland
    Incision and Drainage 53060
Skin
    Incision and Drainage 10060-10061
    Puncture Aspiration 10160
Soft Tissue
    Incision 20000-20005
Subdiaphragmatic 49040-49041
Sublingual Gland
    Drainage 42310-42320
Submaxillary Gland
    Drainage 42310-42320
Subphrenic 49040-49041
Testis
    Incision and Drainage 54700
Thoracostomy 32020
Thorax
    Incision and Drainage 21501-21502
Throat
    Incision and Drainage 42700-42725
Tongue
    Incision and Drainage 41000-41006
Tonsil
    Incision and Drainage 42700
Ulna
    Incision, Deep 25035
Urethra
    Incision and Drainage 53040
Uvula
    Incision and Drainage 42000

Vagina
    Incision and Drainage 57010
Vulva
    Incision and Drainage 56405
Wrist
    Excision 25145
    Incision and Drainage 25028, 25035
X-Ray 76080

Abscess, Nasal
See Nose, Abscess

Abscess, Parotid Gland
See Parotid Gland, Abscess

Absorptiometry
Dual Energy
    Bone 76075
      Appendicular 76076
      Axial Skeleton 76075
Dual Photon
    Bone 78351
Radiographic
    Photodensity 76078
Single Photon
    Bone 78350

Absorption Spectrophotometry, Atomic
See Atomic Absorption Spectroscopy

Accessory, Toes
See Polydactyly, Toes

Accessory Nerve, Spinal
See Nerves, Spinal Accessory

ACE
See Angiotensin Converting Enzyme

Acetabuloplasty 27120-27122

Acetabulum
Fracture
    Closed Treatment 27220-27222
    Open Treatment 27226-27228
    without Manipulation 27220
    with Manipulation 27222
Reconstruction 27120
    with Resection, Femoral Head 27122
Tumor
    Excision 27076

Acetaldehyde
Blood 82000

Acetaminophen
Urine 82003

Acetic Anhydrides 84600

Acetone
Blood or Urine 82009-82010

Acetone Body 82009-82010

Acetylcholinesterase
Blood or Urine 82013

AcG
See Clotting Factor

Achilles Tendon
Incision 27605-27606
Lengthening 27612
Repair 27650-27654

Achillotomy
See Tenotomy, Achilles Tendon

Acid
Gastric 82926-82928

Acid, Adenylic
See Adenosine Monophosphate (AMP)

Acid, Aminolevulinic
See Aminolevulinic Acid (ALA)

Acid, Ascorbic
See Ascorbic Acid

Acid, Deoxyribonucleic
See Deoxyribonucleic Acid

Acid, Folic
See Folic Acid

Acid, Glycocholic
See Cholylglycine

Acid, Lactic
See Lactic Acid

Acid, N-Acetylneuraminic
See Sialic Acid

Acid, Phenylethylbarbituric
See Phenobarbital

Acid, Uric
See Uric Acid

Acidity /Alkalinity
See pH

Acids, Amino
See Amino Acids

Acids, Bile
See Bile Acids

Acids, Fatty
See Fatty Acid

Acids, Guanylic
See Guanosine Monophosphate

Acids, N-Acetylneuraminic
See Sialic Acid

Acid Diethylamide, Lysergic
See Lysergic Acid Diethylamide

Acid Fast Bacilli (AFB)
Culture 87116

Acid Fast Bacillus Culture
See Culture, Acid Fast Bacilli

Acid Fast Stain 88312

Acid Perfusion Test
Esophagus 91012, 91030

Acid Phosphatase 84060-84066

Acid Probes, Nucleic
See Nucleic Acid Probe

Acid Reflux Test
Esophagus 91032-91033

Acne Surgery
Incision and Drainage
　Abscess 10060-10061
　Comedones 10040
　Cyst 10040
　Milia, Multiple 10040
　Pustules 10040

Acne Treatment
Abrasion 15786-15787
Chemical Peel 15788-15793
Cryotherapy 17340
Dermabrasion 15780-15783
Exfoliation
　Chemical 17360
Salabrasion 15810-15811

Acoustic Evoked Brain Stem Potential
See Evoked Potential, Auditory Brainstem

Acoustic Neuroma
See Brain, Tumor, Excision; Brainstem; Mesencephalon; Skull Base Surgery

Acromioclavicular Joint
Arthrocentesis 20605
Arthrotomy 23044
　with Biopsy 23101
Dislocation 23540-23552
　Open Treatment 23550-23552
X-Ray 73050

Acromion
Excision
　Shoulder 23130

Acromionectomy
Partial 23130

Acromioplasty 23415-23420
Partial 23130

ACTH
See Adrenocorticotropic Hormone (ACTH)

ACTH Releasing Factor
See Corticotropic Releasing Hormone (CRH)

Actinomyces
Antibody 86602

Actinomycosis 86000

Actinomycotic Infection
See Actinomycosis

Actinotherapy 96900
See Dermatology

Activated Factor X
See Thrombokinase

Activated Partial Thromboplastin Time
See Thromboplastin, Partial, Time

Activation, Lymphocyte
See Blastogenesis

Activities of Daily Living
See Physical Medicine/Therapy/Occupational Therapy

Activity, Glomerular Procoagulant
See Thromboplastin

Acupuncture
One or More Needles
　Electrical Stimulation 97781
　without Electric Stimulation 97780

Acute Poliomyelitis
See Polio

Acylcarnitines 82016-82017

Adamantinoma, Pituitary
See Craniopharyngioma

Addam Operation
See Dupuytren's Contracture

Adductor Tenotomy of Hip
See Tenotomy, Hip, Adductor

Adenoidectomy 42820-42821, 42830-42836

Adenoids
Excision 42830-42836
　with Tonsils 42820-42821
Unlisted Services and Procedures 42999

Adenoma
Pancreas
　Excision 48120
Thyroid Gland Excision 60200

Adenosine 3'5' Monophosphate
See Cyclic AMP

Adenosine Diphosphate
Blood 82030

Adenosine Monophosphate (AMP)
Blood 82030

Adenovirus
Antibody 86603
Antigen Detection
　Enzyme Immunoassay 87301
　Immunofluorescence 87260

Adenovirus Vaccine
See Vaccines

Adenylic Acid
See Adenosine Monophosphate (AMP)

ADH
See Antidiuretic Hormone

Adhesions
Epidural 62263
Eye
　Corneovitreal 65880
　Incision
　　Anterior Segment 65860-65870
　　Posterior Segment 65875

Intermarginal
    Construction 67880
        Transposition of Tarsal Plate 67882
Intestinal
    Enterolysis 44005
        Laparoscopic 44200
Intrauterine
    Lysis 58559
Labial
    Lysis 56441
Lungs
    Lysis 32124
Pelvic
    Lysis 58660, 58662, 58740
Penile
    Lysis
        Post-circumcision 54162
Preputial
    Lysis 54450

Adipectomy
See Lipectomy

ADL
See Activities of Daily Living

Administration
Immunization
    Each Additional Vaccine/Toxoid 90472,
                         90474
    One Vaccine/Toxoid 90471, 90473

ADP
See Adenosine Diphosphate

ADP Phosphocreatine Phosphotransferase
See CPK

Adrenalectomy 60540
Anesthesia 00866
Laparoscopic 50545

Adrenalin
See Catecholamines
Blood 82383
Urine 82384

Adrenaline-Noradrenaline
Testing 82382-82384

Adrenal Cortex Hormone
See Corticosteroids

Adrenal Gland
Biopsy 60540-60545
Excision
    Laparoscopy 60650
    Retroperitoneal Tumor 60545
Exploration 60540-60545
Nuclear Medicine
    Imaging 78075

Adrenal Medulla
See Medulla

Adrenocorticotropic Hormone (ACTH) 80400-80406,
                     80412, 80418, 82024
Blood or Urine 82024
Stimulation Panel 80400-80406

Adrenogenital Syndrome .56805, 57335

Adult T Cell Leukemia Lymphoma Virus I
See HTLV I

Advanced Life Support
See Emergency Department Services
Physician Direction 99288

Advancement
Tendon
      Foot 28238

Advancement Flap
See Skin, Adjacent Tissue Transfer

Aerosol Inhalation
See Pulmonology, Therapeutic
Pentamidine 94642, 99563

AFB
See Acid Fast Bacilli (AFB)

Afferent Nerve
See Sensory Nerve

AFP
See Alpha-Fetoprotein

After Hours Medical Services 99050-99054

Agents, Anticoagulant
See Clotting Inhibitors

Agglutinin
Cold 86156-86157
Febrile 86000

Aggregation
Platelet 85576

AHG
See Clotting Factor

AICD (Pacing Cardioverter-Defibrillator)
See Defibrillator, Heart; Pacemaker, Heart

Aid, Hearing
See Hearing Aid

AIDS Antibodies
See Antibody, HIV

AIDS Virus
See HIV-1

Akin Operation
See Bunion Repair

ALA
See Aminolevulinic Acid (ALA)

Alanine 2 Oxoglutarate Aminotransferase
See Transaminase, Glutamic Pyruvic

Alanine Amino (ALT) 84460

Alanine Transaminase
See Transaminase, Glutamic Pyruvic

Albarran Test
See Water Load Test

Albumin
Serum 82040
Urine 82042

Alcohol
Breath 82075
Ethyl
    Blood 82055
    Urine 82055
Ethylene Glycol 82693

Alcohol, Isopropyl
See Isopropyl Alcohol

Alcohol, Methyl
See Methanol

Alcohol Dehydrogenase
See Antidiuretic Hormone

Aldolase
Blood 82085

Aldosterone
Blood 82088
Suppression Evaluation 80408
Urine 82088

Alimentary Canal
See Gastrointestinal Tract

Alkaline Phosphatase 84075-84080
Leukocyte 85540
WBC 85540

Alkaloids
See Specific Drug
Urine 82101

Allergen Bronchial Provocation Tests
See Allergy Tests; Bronchial Challenge Test

Allergen Challenge, Endobronchial
See Bronchial Challenge Test

Allergen Immunotherapy
Allergen
    Prescription/Supply/Injection ..95120-95125
    with Extract Supply 95144
        Injection 95115-95117
Antigens 95144
IgE 86003-86005
IgG 86001
Insect Venom
    Prescription/Supply 95145-95149
    Prescription/Supply/Injection ..95130-95134
Prescription/Supply 95165
    Insect, Whole Body 95170
Rapid Desensitization 95180

Allergy Services/Procedures
See Office and/or Other Outpatient Services;
Allergen and Immunotherapy
Education and Counseling 99201-99215
Unlisted Services and Procedures 95199

Allergy Tests
Challenge Test
    Bronchial 95070-95071
    Ingestion 95075
Eye Allergy 95060
Food Allergy 95075
Intradermal
    Allergen Extract 95024, 95028
    Biologicals 95015
    Drugs 95015
    Venoms 95015
Nasal Mucous Membrane Test 95065
Nose Allergy 95065
Patch
    Application Tests 95044
    Photo Patch 95052
Photosensitivity 95056
Provocative Testing 95078
Skin Tests
    Allergen Extract 95004
    Biologicals 95010
    Drugs 95010
    End Point Titration 95027
    Venoms 95010

Allogeneic Transplantation
See Homograft

Allograft
Aortic Valve 33406, 33413
Bone
    Structural 20931
Lung Transplant 32850
Skin 15350-15351
Spine Surgery
    Morselized 20930
    Structural 20931

Alloplastic Dressing
Burns 15000-15001

Allotransplantation
Intestines 44135-44136
Renal 50360-50365
    Removal 50370

Almen Test
See Blood, Feces

Alpha-1 Antitrypsin 82103-82104,
                                     99565

Alpha-2 Antiplasmin 85410

Alpha-Fetoprotein
Amniotic Fluid 82106
Serum 82105

Alphatocopherol 84446

ALT
See Transaminase, Glutamic Pyruvic

Altemeier Procedure
See Anus; Rectum, Prolapse, Excision

Aluminum
Blood 82108

Alveola
Fracture
    Closed Treatment 21421
    Open Treatment 21422-21423

Alveolar Cleft
Ungrafted Bilateral 21147
Ungrafted Unilateral 21146

Alveolar Nerve
Avulsion 64738
Incision 64738
Transection 64738

Alveolar Ridge
Fracture
    Closed Treatment 21440
    Open Treatment 21445

Alveolectomy 41830

Alveoloplasty 41874

Alveolus
Excision 41830

Amide, Procaine
See Procainamide

Amikacin
Assay 80150

Amine
Vaginal Fluid 82120

Aminolevulinic Acid (ALA)
Blood or Urine 82135

Aminotransferase
See Transaminase

Aminotransferase, Alanine
See Transaminase, Glutamic Pyruvic

Aminotransferase, Aspartate
See Transaminase, Glutamic Oxaloacetic

Amino Acids 82127-82139

Amitriptyline
Assay 80152

Ammonia
Blood 82140
Urine 82140

Amniocenteses
See Amniocentesis

Amniocentesis 59000
See Chromosome Analysis
Induced Abortion 59850
    with Dilation and Curettage 59851
    with Dilation and Evacuation 59851
    with Hysterectomy 59852
with Amniotic Fluid Reduction 59001

Amnion
Amniocentesis 59000
    with Amniotic Fluid Reduction 59001

Amniotic Fluid
Alpha-Fetoprotein 82106
Scan 82143
Testing 83661, 83663-83664

Amniotic Membrane
See Amnion

Amobarbital 82205

AMP
See Adenosine Monophosphate (AMP)

AMP, Cyclic
See Cyclic AMP

Amphetamine
Blood or Urine 82145

Amputation
See Radical Resection; Replantation
Ankle 27888
Arm, Lower 25900-25905, 25915
    Revision 25907-25909
Arm, Upper 24900-24920
    and Shoulder 23900-23921
    Revision 24925-24930
    with Implant 24931-24935
Cervix
    Total 57530
Ear
    Partial 69110
    Total 69120
Finger 26910-26952
Foot 28800-28805
Hand at Metacarpal 25927
    at Wrist 25920
        Revision 25922
    Revision 25924, 25929-25931
Interpelviabdominal 27290
Interthoracoscapular 23900
Leg, Lower 27598, 27880-27882
    Revision 27884-27886
Leg, Upper 27590-27592
    at Hip 27290-27295
    Revision 27594-27596
Metacarpal 26910
Metatarsal 28810
Penis
    Partial 54120
    Radical 54130-54135
    Total 54125
Thumb 26910-26952
Toe 28810-28825
Tuft of Distal Phalanx 11752
Upper Extremity 24940
    Cineplasty 24940

Amputation, Nose
See Resection, Nose

Amputation through Hand
See Hand, Amputation

Amylase
Blood 82150
Urine 82150

ANA
See Antinuclear Antibodies (ANA)

Anabolic Steroid
See Androstenedione

Analgesia 99141-99142
See Anesthesia; Sedation

Analgesic Cutaneous Electrostimulation
See Application, Neurostimulation

Analysis
Computer Data 99090
Electroencephalogram
   Digital 95957
Electronic
   Drug Infusion Pump 62367-62368
   Pacing Cardioverter-
   Defibrillator 93741-93744
     See Pacemaker, Heart
   Pulse Generator 95970-95971
Physiologic Data, Remote 99091
Protein
   Tissue
     Western Blot 88372
Semen
   Sperm Isolation 89260-89261

Analysis, Spectrum
See Spectrophotometry

Anal Abscess
See Abscess, Anal

Anal Bleeding
See Anus, Hemorrhage

Anal Fistula
See Fistula, Anal

Anal Fistulectomy
See Excision, Fistula, Anal

Anal Fistulotomy
See Fistulotomy, Anal

Anal Sphincter
Dilation 45905
Incision 46080

Anal Ulceration
See Anus, Fissure

Anaspadias
See Epispadias

Anastomosis
Arteriovenous Fistula
   Direct 36821
   with Bypass Graft 35686
   with Graft 36825-36830, 36832
Artery
   to Aorta 33606
   to Artery
     Cranial 61711
Bile Duct
   to Bile Duct 47800
   to Intestines 47760, 47780
Bile Duct to Gastrointestinal 47785
Broncho-Bronchial 32486
Caval to Mesenteric 37160
Colorectal 44620

Epididymis
   to Vas Deferens
     Bilateral 54901
     Unilateral 54900
Excision
   Trachea 31780-31781
Fallopian Tube 58750
Gallbladder to Intestines 47720-47740
Hepatic Duct to Intestines 47765, 47802
Ileo-Anal 45113
Intestines
   Colo-anal 45119
   Cystectomy 51590
   Enterocystoplasty 51960
   Resection
     Laparoscopic 44202-44205
Intestine to Intestine 44130
Jejunum 43825
Microvascular
   Free Transfer
     Jejunum 43496
Nerve
   Facial to Hypoglossal 64868
   Facial to Phrenic 64870
Oviduct 58750
Pancreas to Intestines 48180, 48520-48540
Portocaval 37140
Pulmonary 33606
Renoportal 37145
Splenorenal 37180-37181
Stomach 43825
   to Duodenum 43810, 43855
   Revision 43850
   to Jejunum 43820, 43860-43865
Tubotubal 58750
Ureter
   to Bladder 50780-50785
   to Colon 50810-50815
   Removal 50830
   to Intestine 50800, 50820-50825
   Removal 50830
   to Kidney 50727-50750
   to Ureter 50727, 50760-50770
Vein
   Saphenopopliteal 34530
Vein to Vein 37140-37160

Anastomosis, Aorta-Pulmonary Artery
See Aorta, Anastomosis, to Pulmonary Artery

Anastomosis, Bladder, to Intestine
See Enterocystoplasty

Anastomosis, Hepatic Duct
See Hepatic Duct, Anastomosis

Anastomosis of Lacrimal Sac to Conjunctival Sac
See Conjunctivorhinostomy

Anastomosis of Pancreas
See Pancreas, Anastomosis

Anderson Tibial Lengthening 27715
See Ankle; Tibia, Osteoplasty, Lengthening

Androstanediol Glucuronide ...82154

Androstanolone
See Dihydrotestosterone

Androstenedione
Blood or Urine 82157

Androstenolone
See Dehydroepiandrosterone

Androsterone
Blood or Urine 82160

Anesthesia
See Analgesia
Abbe-Estlander Procedure 00102
Abdomen
   Abdominal Wall 00700-00730,
               00800-00802, 00820-00832
     Halsted Repair 00750-00756
     Blood Vessels 00770, 00880-00882
     Endoscopy 00740, 00810
     Extraperitoneal ..00860-00862, 00866-00870
     Hernia Repair 00830-00832
     Halsted Repair 00750-00756
     Intraperitoneal ..00790-00797, 00840-00842
Abdominoperineal Resection 00844
Abortion
   Induced 01964
Achilles Tendon Repair 01472
Acromioclavicular Joint 01620
Adrenalectomy 00866
Amniocentesis 00842
Aneurysm
   Axillary-Brachial 01652
   Knee 01444
   Popliteal Artery 01444
Angiography 01920
Ankle 00400, 01462-01522
Anorectal Procedure 00902
Anus 00902
Arm
   Lower 00400, 01810-01860
   Upper 00400, 01710-01782
Arrhythmias 00410
Arteriography 01916
Arteriovenous Fistula 01432
Arthroplasty
   Hip 01214-01215
   Knee 01402
Arthroscopic Procedures
   Ankle 01464
   Elbow 01732
   Hip 01202
   Knee 01382
   Shoulder 01622
Auditory Canal, External
   Removal Foreign Body 69205
Axilla 00400, 01610-01682
Back Skin 00300
Batch-Spittler-McFaddin Operation 01404
Biopsy 00100
   Liver 00702
Bladder 00870, 00912
Brain 00210-00218, 00220-00222
Breast 00402-00406
Bronchi 00542
   Intrathoracic Repair of Trauma 00548

Bronchoscopy 00520
Burns
    Debridement and/or
      Excision 01951-01953
    Dressings and/or
      Debridement 16010-16015
Burr Hole 00214
Bypass Graft
    Leg, Lower 01500
    Leg, Upper 01270
    Shoulder, Axillary 01654-01656
Cardiac Catheterization 01920
Cast
    Knee 01420
Cast Application
    Forearm, Wrist and Hand 01860
    Leg 01490
    Pelvis 01130
    Shoulder 01680-01682
Central Venous Circulation 00532
Cervical Cerclage 00948
Cervix 00948
Cesarean Delivery 01961, 01963
Chemonucleolysis 00634
Chest 00400-00410, 00470-00474,
          00522-00530, 00540-00550
Chest Skin 00400
Childbirth
    Cesarean Delivery 01961, 01963,
             01968-01969
    Vaginal Delivery 01960, 01967
Clavicle 00450-00454
Cleft Lip Repair 00102
Cleft Palate Repair 00172
Colpectomy 00942
Colporrhaphy 00942
Colpotomy 00942
Corneal Transplant 00144
Cranioplasty 00215
Culdoscopy 00950
Cystectomy 00864
Cystolithotomy 00870
Cystourethroscopy
    Local 52265
    Spinal 52260
Decortication 00542
Defibrillator 00534, 00560
Diaphragm 00540
Disarticulation
    Hip 01212
    Knee 01404
    Shoulder 01634
Diskography 01905
Dressing Change 15852
Drug Administration
    Epidural or Subarachnoid 01996
Ear 00120-00126
Elbow 00400, 01710-01782
Electrocoagulation
    Intracranial Nerve 00222
Electroconvulsive Therapy 00104
Embolectomy
    Arm, Upper 01772
    Femoral 01274
    Femoral Artery 01274
    Forearm, Wrist and Hand 01842
    Leg, Lower 01502

Endoscopy
    Gastrointestinal 00740
    Intestines 00810
    Uterus 00952
    Vagina 00950
Esophagus 00320, 00500
External Fixation System
    Adjustment/Revision 20693
    Removal 20694
Eye 00140-00148
    Cornea 00144
    Iridectomy 00147
    Iris 00147
Eyelid 00103
Facial Bones 00190-00192
Fallopian Tube
    Ligation 00851
Femoral Artery
    Ligation 01272
Femur 01220-01234, 01340-01360
Fibula 01390-01392
Foot 00400, 01462-01522
Forearm 00400, 01810-01860
Fowler-Stephens Orchiopexy 00930
Gastrocnemius Recession 01474
Gastrointestinal Endoscopy 00740
Genitalia
    Female 00940-00952, 01960-01969
    Male 00920-00938
Great Vessels of Chest 00560-00563
Hand 00400, 01810-01860
Harrington Rod Technique 00670
Head 00222, 00300
    Muscles 00300
    Nerves 00300
Heart 00560-00580
    Coronary Artery Bypass Grafting 00566
    Electrophysiology/Ablation 00537
    Transplant 00580
Hepatectomy
    Partial 00792
Hernia Repair
    Abdomen
      Lower 00830-00832
      Upper 00750-00752, 00756
Hip 01200-01215
Humerus 01620, 01730, 01740-01744, 01758
Hysterectomy 01962
    Cesarean 01963, 01969
    Radical 00846
    Vaginal 00944
Hysterosalpingography 00952
Hysteroscopy 00952
Induced Abortion 01964
Inferior Vena Cava Ligation 00882
Integumentary System
    Anterior Trunk 00400
    Arm, Upper 00400
    Axilla 00400
    Elbow 00400
    Extremity 00400
    Forearm 00400
    Hand 00400
    Head 00300
    Knee 00400
    Leg, Lower 00400
    Leg, Upper 00400
    Neck 00300

Perineum 00400
Popliteal Area 00400
Posterior Pelvis 00300
Posterior Trunk 00300
Shoulder 00400
Wrist 00400
Intestines
    Endoscopy 00810
Intracranial Procedures 00210-00218,
             00220-00222
Intraoral Procedures 00170-00176
Intrathoracic Procedures
    Bronchi 00548
    Trachea 00548
Intrathoracic System 00500-00580
Iridectomy 00147
Keen Operation 00604
Kidney 00862, 00868, 00872-00873
Knee 00400, 01320-01444
Knee Skin 00400
Laminectomy 00604
Laparoscopy 00790-00792, 00840
Larynx 00320
Leg
    Lower 00400, 01462-01522
    Upper 01200-01274
Lens 00142
Leriche Operation 00622
Life Support for Organ Donor 01990
Ligation
    Fallopian Tube 00851
Lithotripsy 00872-00873
Liver 00702, 00796
    Transplant 00796
Liver Hemorrhage 00792
Local
    Intravenous 01995
Lumbar Puncture 00635
Lungs 00522, 00540-00548
    Transplant 00580
Lymphadenectomy 00934-00936
Lymphatic System 00320
Mammoplasty 00402
Marcellation Operation 00944
Mediastinoscopy 00528
Mediastinum 00528, 00540
Mouth 00170-00172
Myelography 01905
Myringotomy 69421
Neck 00300-00352
Nephrectomy 00862
Neuraxial
    Cesarean Delivery 01968-01969
    Labor 01967-01969
    Vaginal Delivery 01967
Neurectomy 01180-01190
Nose 00160-00164
    Removal
      Foreign Body 30310
Omphalocele 00754
Ophthalmoscopy 00148
Orchiectomy 00926-00928
Orchiopexy 00930
    Torek Procedure 00930
Organ Harvesting
    Brain-Dead Patient 01990
Osteoplasty
    Tibia/Fibula 01484

Osteotomy
   Humerus .01742
   Tibia/Fibula 01484
Other Procedures 01990-01999
Otoscopy 00124
Pacemaker Insertion 00530
Pacing Cardioverter/Defibrillator 00534
Pancreas 00794
Pancreatectomy 00794
Panniculectomy 00802
Patella 01390-01392
Pectus Excavatum 00474
Pelvic Exenteration 00848
Pelvis 00400, 00865, 01112-01190
   Amputation 01140
   Bone 01120
   Bone Marrow 01112
   Examination 57400
   Extraperitoneal 00864
   Intraperitoneal 00844-00848
   Skin 00300, 00400
Penis 00932-00938
Pericardial Sac 00560-00563
Perineum 00904-00908
Pharynx 00174-00176
Phleborrhaphy
   Arm, Upper 01782
   Forearm, Wrist and Hand 01852
Pleura 00540
   Needle Biopsy 00522
Pleurectomy .00544
Pneumocentesis 00524
Popliteal Area 00400, 01320, 01430-01444
Prognathism .00192
Prostate 00865, 00908, 00914
Prostatectomy
   Perineal .00908
   Radical 00865
   Walsh Modified Radical 00865
Radiological Procedures 01905-01922
   Arterial
      Therapeutic 01924-01926
   Venous/Lymphatic
      Therapeutic 01930-01933
Renal Procedures 00862
Repair of Skull 00215
Replacement
   Ankle 01486
   Elbow 01760
   Hip 01212-01215
   Knee 01402
   Shoulder .01638
   Wrist 01832
Restriction
   Gastric
      for Obesity 00797
Retropharyngeal Tumor Excision 00174
Rib Resection 00470-00474
Sacroiliac Joint 01160-01170, 27096
Salivary Glands 00100
Scheie Procedure 00147
Sedation
   Analgesia 99141-99142
Seminal Vesicles 00922
Shoulder 00400, 00450-00454, 01610-01682
   Dislocation
      Closed Treatment 23655

Shunt
   Spinal Fluid 00220
Sinuses
   Accessory 00160-00164
Skull 00190
Skull Fracture
   Elevation 00215
Special Circumstances
   Emergency 99140
   Extreme Age 99100
   Hypotension 99135
   Hypothermia 99116
Spinal Instrumentation 00670
Spine and Spinal Cord 00600-00670
   Cervical 00600-00604, 00670
   Injection 62310-62319
   Lumbar 00630-00670
   Thoracic 00620-00622, 00670
   Vascular .00670
Sternoclavicular Joint 01620
Sternum 00550
Stomach
   Restriction
      for Obesity 00797
Strayer Procedure 01474
Subdural Taps 00212
Suture Removal 15850-15851
Sympathectomy
   Lumbar .00632
   Thoracolumbar 00622
Symphysis Pubis 01160-01170
Tenodesis 01716
Tenoplasty 01714
Tenotomy 01712
Testis 00924-00930
Thoracoplasty 00472
Thoracoscopy 00528, 00540
Thoracotomy .00540
Thorax 00400-00474
Thromboendarterectomy 01442
Thyroid 00320-00322
Tibia 01390-01392, 01484
Trachea 00320, 00542
Transplantation
   Cornea 00144
   Heart 00580
   Kidney 00868
   Liver 00796, 01990
   Lungs 00580
   Organ Harvesting 01990
Transurethral Procedures 00910-00918
Tubal Ligation 00851
Tuffier Vaginal Hysterectomy 00944
TURP 00914
Tympanostomy 69436
Tympanotomy 00126
Unlisted Services and Procedures 01999
Urethra 00910, 00918-00920, 00942
Urethrocystoscopy 00910
Urinary Bladder 00864, 00870, 00912
Urinary Tract 00860
Uterus 00952
Vagina 00940-00942, 00950
   Dilation .57400
   Removal
      Foreign Body 57415
Vaginal Delivery 01960
Vascular Access 00532

Vascular Shunt 01844
Vascular Surgery
   Abdomen, Lower 00880-00882
   Abdomen, Upper 00770
   Arm, Lower 01840-01852
   Arm, Upper 01770-01782
   Brain 00216
   Elbow 01770-01782
   Hand 01840-01852
   Knee 01430-01444
   Leg, Lower 01500-01522
   Leg, Upper 01260-01274
   Neck 00350-00352
   Shoulder 01650-01670
   Wrist 01840-01852
Vasectomy 00869
Vas Deferens
   Excision .00869
Venography .01916
Ventriculography 00214, 01920
Vertebral Process
   Fracture/Dislocation
      Closed Treatment 22315
Vertebroplasty 01905
Vitrectomy 00145
Vitreoretinal Surgery 00145
Vitreous Body 00145
Vulva 00906
Vulvectomy .00906
Wertheim Operation 00846
Wrist 00400, 01810-01860

Anesthesia Local

See Anesthesia, Local

Aneurysm, Aorta, Abdominal

See Aorta, Abdominal, Aneurysm

Aneurysm, Basilar Artery

See Artery, Basilar, Aneurysm

Aneurysm Artery, Femoral

See Artery, Femoral, Aneurysm

Aneurysm Artery, Radial

See Artery, Radial, Aneurysm

Aneurysm Artery, Renal

See Artery, Renal, Aneurysm

Aneurysm Repair

Abdominal Aorta 0001T-0002T, 34800-34804,
   34825-34832, 35081-35103, 75952-75953
Axillary Artery 35011-35013
Basilar Artery 61698, 61702
Brachial Artery 35011-35013
Carotid Artery 35001-35002,
   61613, 61697, 61700, 61703
Celiac Artery 35121-35122
Femoral Artery 35141-35142
Hepatic Artery 35121-35122
Iliac Artery 35131-35132
Innominate Artery 35021-35022
Intracranial Artery 61705-61708
Mesenteric Artery 35121-35122
Other Artery 35161-35162
Popliteal Artery 35151-35152
Radial Artery 35045
Renal Artery 35121-35122
Splenic Artery 35111-35112

Subclavian Artery . . .35001-35002, 35021-35022
Thoracoabdominal Aorta 33877
Ulnar Artery 35045
Vascular Malformation or Carotid-Cavernous
Fistula 61710
Vertebral Artery 61698, 61702

Angel Dust
See Phencyclidine

Angiocardiographies
See Heart, Angiography

Angiography
See Aortography
Abdomen 74175, 74185, 75635, 75726
Abdominal Aorta 75635, 75952-75953
Adrenal 75731-75733
Aorta
    Injection 93544
Arm Artery 73206, 75710-75716
Arteriovenous Shunt 75790
Brachial Artery 75658
Brain 70496
Carotid Artery 75660-75671
    Cervical
        Bilateral .75680
        Unilateral 75676
Chest .71275, 71555
Coronary Artery 93556
    Flow Velocity Measurement During
    Angiography 93571-93572
Coronary Bypass 93556
Endovascular Repair 75952-75953
Extremity, Lower 73725
Extremity, Upper 73225
Fluorescein 92235
Head 70496, 70544-70546
    Artery 75650
Heart Vessels
    Injection 93545
Indocyanine-green 92240
Left Heart
    Injection 93543
Leg Artery 73706, 75635, 75710-75716
Lung
    Injection 93541
        See Cardiac Catheterization, Injection
Mammary Artery 75756
    See Aortography
Neck 70498, 70547-70549
    Artery 75650
Nuclear Medicine 78445
Other Artery 75774
Pelvic Artery 72198, 75736
Pelvis 72191
Pulmonary 75741-75746
Renal Artery 75722-75724
Right Heart
    Injection 93542
Spinal Artery 75705
Spinal Canal 72159
Thorax 71275
Transcatheter Therapy
    Embolization 75894, 75898
    Infusion 75894, 75898
Vertebral 75685

Angioma
See Lesion, Skin

Angioplasties, Coronary Balloon
See Percutaneous Transluminal Angioplasty

Angioplasty
Aorta
    Intraoperative 35452
    Percutaneous 35472
Axillary Artery
    Intraoperative 35458
Brachiocephalic Artery
    Intraoperative 35458
    Percutaneous 35475
Coronary Artery
    Percutaneous Transluminal 92982-92984
Femoral Artery
    Intraoperative 35456
    Percutaneous 35474
Iliac Artery
    Intraoperative 35454
    Percutaneous 35473
Percutaneous Transluminal
Angioplasty 92982-92984
    See Angioplasty; Percutaneous, Transluminal
Popliteal Artery
    Intraoperative 35456
    Percutaneous 35474
Pulmonary Artery
    Percutaneous Transluminal 92997-92998
Renal Artery
    Intraoperative 35450
    Percutaneous 35471
Subclavian Artery
    Intraoperative 35458
Tibioperoneal Artery
    Intraoperative 35459
    Percutaneous 35470
Transluminal
    Arterial 75962-75968
    Venous 75978
Venous
    Intraoperative 35460
    Percutaneous 35476
Visceral Artery
    Intraoperative 35450
    Percutaneous 35471

Angioscopy
Non-Coronary Vessels 35400

**Angiotensin Converting Enzyme
(ACE)** 82164

Angiotensin Forming Enzyme
See Renin

Angiotensin I 84244
Riboflavin 84252

Angiotensin II
Blood or Urine .82163

Angle Deformity
Reconstruction
    Toe 28313

Anhydride, Carbonic
See Carbon Dioxide

Anhydrides, Acetic
See Acetic Anhydrides

Animal Inoculation 87001-87003,
87250

Ankle
See Fibula; Leg, Lower; Tibia; Tibiofibular Joint
Abscess
    Incision and Drainage 27603
Amputation 27888
Arthrocentesis .20605
Arthrodesis 27870
Arthrography 73615
Arthroplasty 27700-27703
Arthroscopy
    Surgical 29891-29898
Arthrotomy 27610-27612, 27620-27626
Biopsy 27613-27614, 27620
Bursa
    Incision and Drainage 27604
Disarticulation .27889
Dislocation
    Closed Treatment 27840-27842
    Open Treatment 27846-27848
Exploration 27610, 27620
Fracture
    Lateral 27786-27814
    Medial 27760-27766, 27808-27814
    Trimalleolar 27816-27823
Fusion 27870
Hematoma
    Incision and Drainage 27603
Incision 27607
Injection
    Radiologic 27648
Lesion
    Excision 27630
Magnetic Resonance Imaging
(MRI) 73721-73723
Manipulation 27860
Removal
    Foreign Body 27610, 27620
    Implant 27704
    Loose Body .27620
Repair
    Achilles Tendon 27650-27654
    Ligament 27695-27698
    Tendon 27612, 27680-27687
Strapping 29540
Synovium
    Excision 27625-27626
Tenotomy 27605-27606
Tumor
    Excision 27615-27619
Unlisted Services and Procedures 27899
X-Ray 73600-73610
    with Contrast 73615

Ankylosis (Surgical)
See Arthrodesis

Anogenital Region
See Perineum

Anoplasty
Stricture 46700-46705

Anorectal Myectomy
See Myomectomy, Anorectal

Anorectal Procedure
Biofeedback 90911

Anorectovaginoplasty 46744-46746

Anoscopy
Ablation
    Polyp 46615
    Tumor 46615
Biopsy 46606
Dilation 46604
Exploration 46600
Hemorrhage 46614
Removal
    Foreign Body 46608
    Polyp 46610-46612
    Tumor 46610-46612

Antebrachium
See Forearm

Antecedent, Plasma Thromboplastin
See Plasma Thromboplastin, Antecedent

Antepartum Care
Cesarean Delivery 59510
    Previous 59610, 59618
Vaginal Delivery 59425-59426

Anterior Ramus of Thoracic Nerve
See Intercostal Nerve

Anthrax Vaccine
See Vaccines

Anthrogon
See Follicle Stimulating Hormone (FSH)

Anti-Human Globulin Consumption Test
See Coombs Test

Anti-Phospholipid Antibody
See Antibody, Phospholipid

Antiactivator, Plasmin
See Alpha-2 Antiplasmin

Antibiotic Administration
Home Infusion Procedures 99556
Injection 90788

Antibiotic Sensitivity 87181-87184, 87188
Enzyme Detection 87185
Minimum Bactericidal Concentration 87187
Minimum Inhibitory Concentration 87186

Antibodies, Thyroid-Stimulating
See Immunoglobulin, Thyroid Stimulating

Antibodies, Viral
See Viral Antibodies

Antibody
See Antibody Identification; Microsomal Antibody
Actinomyces 86602
Adenovirus 86603
Antinuclear 86038-86039
Antiphosphatidylserine (Phospholipid) 86148
Antistreptolysin O 86060-86063
Aspergillus 86606

Bacterium 86609
Bartonella 86611
Beta 2 Glycoprotein I 86146
Blastomyces 86612
Blood Crossmatch 86920-86922
Bordetella 86615
Borrelia 86618-86619
Brucella 86622
Campylobacter 86625
Candida 86628
Cardiolipin 86147
Chlamydia 86631-86632
Coccidioides 86635
Coxiella Burnetii 86638
Cryptococcus 86641
Cytomegalovirus 86644-86645
Cytotoxic Screen 86807-86808
Deoxyribonuclease 86215
Deoxyribonucleic Acid (DNA) 86225-86226
Diphtheria 86648
Ehrlichia 86666
Encephalitis 86651-86654
Enterovirus 86658
Epstein-Barr Virus 86663-86665
Fluorescent 86255-86256
Francisella Tularensis 86668
Fungus 86671
Giardia Lamblia 86674
Growth Hormone 86277
Helicobacter Pylori 86677
Helminth 86682
Hemoglobin, Fecal 86683
Hemophilus Influenza 86684
Hepatitis
    Delta Agent 86692
Hepatitis A 86708-86709
Hepatitis B
    Core 86704
    IgM 86705
    Surface 86706
Hepatitis Be 86707
Hepatitis C 86803-86804
Herpes Simplex 86694-86696
Heterophile 86308-86310
Histoplasma 86698
HIV 86689, 86701-86703
HIV-1 ....86701, 86703
HIV-2 86702-86703
HTLV-I 86687, 86689
HTLV-II 86688
Influenza Virus 86710
Insulin 86337
Intrinsic Factor 86340
Islet Cell 86341
Legionella 86713
Leishmania 86717
Leptospira 86720
Listeria Monocytogenes 86723
Lyme Disease 86617
Lymphocytic Choriomeningitis 86727
Lymphogranuloma Venereum 86729
Microsomal 86376
Mucormycosis 86732
Mumps 86735
Mycoplasma 86738
Neisseria Meningitidis 86741
Nocardia 86744
Nuclear Antigen 86235

Other Virus 86790
Panel 80090
Parvovirus 86747
Phospholipid 86147
Plasmodium 86750
Platelet 86022-86023
Protozoa 86753
Red Blood Cell 86850-86870
Respiratory Syncytial Virus 86756
Rickettsia 86757
Rotavirus 86759
Rubella 86762
Rubeola 86765
Salmonella 86768
Shigella 86771
Sperm 89325
Streptokinase 86590
Tetanus 86774
Thyroglobulin 86800
Toxoplasma 86777-86778
Treponema Pallidum 86781
Trichinella 86784
Varicella-Zoster 86787
White Blood Cell 86021
Yersinia 86793

Antibody Identification
Leukocyte Antibodies 86021
Platelet 86022-86023
Red Blood Cell
    Pretreatment 86970-86972
Serum
    Pretreatment 86975-86978

Antibody Neutralization Test
See Neutralization Test

Antibody Receptor
See FC Receptor

Anticoagulant
See Clotting Inhibitors

Antidiabetic Hormone
See Glucagon

Antidiuretic Hormone 84588

Antidiuretic Hormone Measurement
See Vasopressin

AntiDNA Autoantibody
See Antinuclear Antibodies (ANA)

Antigen
Allergen Immunotherapy 95144
Carcinoembryonic 82378
Prostate Specific 84152-84153

Antigen, Australia
See Hepatitis Antigen, B Surface

Antigen, CD4
See CD4

Antigen, CD8
See CD8

Antigens, CD142
See Thromboplastin

Antigens, CD143
See Angiotensin Converting Enzyme (ACE)

Antigens, E
See Hepatitis Antigen, Be

Antigens, Hepatitis
See Hepatitis Antigen

Antigens, Hepatitis B
See Hepatitis Antigen, B

Antigen Bronchial Provocation Tests
See Bronchial Challenge Test

Antigen Detection
Direct Fluorescence . . .87198-87199, 87265-87272,
        87276, 87278, 87280, 87285-87290
  Bordetella 87265
  Chlamydia Trachomatis 87270
  Cryptosporidium/Giardia 87272
  Cytomegalovirus 87198
  Enterovirus .87199
  Influenza A .87276
  Legionella Pneumophila 87278
  Not Otherwise Specified 87299
  Respiratory Syncytial Virus 87280
  Treponema Pallidum 87285
  Varicella-Zoster 87290
Enzyme Immunoassay
  Adenovirus .87301
  Chlamydia Trachomatis 87320
  Clostridium Difficile 87324
  Cryptococcus Neoformans 87327
  Cryptosporidium/Giardia 87328
  Cytomegalovirus 87332
  Entamoeba Histolytica Dispar Group . .87336
  Entamoeba Histolytica Group 87337
  Escherichia coli 0157 87335
  Helicobacter Pylori 87338-87339
  Hepatitis Be Antigen (HBeAg) 87350
  Hepatitis B Surface Antigen (HBsAg) . .87340
  Hepatitis B Surface Antigen (HBsAg)
  Neutralization 87341
  Hepatitis Delta Agent 87380
  Histoplasma capsulatum 87385
  HIV-1 87390
  HIV-2 87391
  Influenza A .87400
  Influenza B .87400
  Multiple Step Method 87301-87449
    Polyvalent 87451
  Not Otherwise Specified 87449, 87451
  Respiratory Syncytial Virus 87420
  Rotavirus 87425
  Shigella-like Toxin 87427
  Single Step Method 87450
  Streptococcus, Group A 87430
Immunofluorescence 87260, 87273-87275,
    87277, 87279, 87281-87283, 87299-87300
  Adenovirus .87260
  Herpes Simplex 87273-87274
  Influenza B .87275
  Legionella Micdadei 87277
  Not Otherwise Specified 87299
  Parainfluenza Virus 87279
  Pneumocystis Carinii 87281
  Polyvalent 87300
  Rubeola 87283

Antihemophilic Factor B
See Christmas Factor

Antihemophilic Factor C
See Plasma Thromboplastin, Antecedent

Antihemophilic Globulin (AHG) 85240

Antihuman Globulin 86880-86886

Antimony 83015

Antinuclear Antibodies (ANA) 86038-86039

Antiplasmin, Alpha-2 85410

Antiprotease, Alpha 1
See Alpha-1 Antitrypsin

Antistreptococcal Antibody 86215

Antistreptokinase Titer 86590

Antistreptolysin O 86060-86063

Antithrombin III 85300-85301

Antithrombin VI
See Fibrin Degradation Products

Antitoxin Assay 87230

Antiviral Antibody
See Viral Antibodies

Anti Australia Antigens
See Antibody, Hepatitis B

Anti D Immunoglobulin
See Immune Globulins, Rho (D)

Antrostomy
Sinus
  Maxillary 31256-31267

Antrotomy
Sinus
  Maxillary 31020-31032
Transmastoid 69501

Antrum of Highmore
See Sinus, Maxillary

Antrum Puncture
Sinus
  Maxillary 31000
  Sphenoid 31002

Anus
See Hemorrhoids; Rectum
Ablation 46615
Abscess
  Incision and Drainage 46045-46050
Biofeedback 90911
Biopsy
  Endoscopy 46606
Crypt
  Excision 46210-46211
Dilation
  Endoscopy 46604

Endoscopy
  Biopsy 46606
  Dilation .46604
  Exploration 46600
  Hemorrhage 46614
  Removal
    Foreign Body 46608
    Polyp 46610, 46612
    Tumor 46610, 46612
Excision
  Tag 46220, 46230
Exploration
  Endoscopy 46600
Fissure
  Destruction 46940-46942
  Excision .46200
Fistula
  Excision 46270-46285
Hemorrhage
  Endoscopic Control 46614
Hemorrhoids
  Clot Excision 46320
  Destruction 46934-46936
  Excision 46250-46262
  Injection 46500
  Ligation 46221, 46945-46946
  Suture 46945-46946
Imperforated
  Repair 46715-46742
Incision
  Septum .46070
Lesion
  Destruction 46900-46917, 46924
  Excision 45108, 46922
Manometry 91122
Placement
  Seton 46020
Reconstruction 46742
  Congenital Absence 46730-46740
  Sphincter 46750-46751, 46760-46762
  with Graft 46753
  with Implant 46762
Removal
  Foreign Body 46608
  Seton 46030
  Suture 46754
  Wire 46754
Repair
  Anovaginal Fistula 46715-46716
  Cloacal Anomaly 46748
  Stricture 46700-46705
Sphincter
  Electromyography 51784-51785
  Needle 51785
Unlisted Services and Procedures 46999

Aorta
Abdominal
  Aneurysm 0001T-0002T, 34800-34804,
    34825-34832, 35081-35103, 75952-75953
  Thromboendarterectomy 35331
Anastomosis
  to Pulmonary Artery 33606
Angiogram
  Radiologic Injection 93544
  See Cardiac Catheterization, Injection
Angioplasty 35452
Aortography 75600-75630

Balloon 33967, 33970
Catheterization
     Catheter 36200
     Intracatheter/Needle 36160
Circulation Assist 33967, 33970
Conduit to Heart 33404
Excision
     Coarctation 33840-33851
Insertion
     Balloon Device 33967
     Graft 33330-33335
     Intracatheter/Needle 36160
Removal
     Balloon Assist Device 33968, 33971
Repair 33320-33322, 33802-33803
     Coarctation 33840-33851
     Graft 33860-33877
     Hypoplastic or Interrupted Aortic Arch
        without Cardiopulmonary Bypass . . .33852
        with Cardiopulmonary Bypass 33853
     Sinus of Valsalva 33702-33720
Suspension 33800
Suture 33320-33322
Valve
     Incision 33415
     Repair 33400-33403
        Left Ventricle 33414
        Supravalvular Stenosis 33417
     Replacement 33405-33413
X-Ray with Contrast 75600-75630

Aorta-Pulmonary ART Transposition
See Transposition, Great Arteries

Aortic Sinus
See Sinus of Valsalva

Aortic Stenosis
Repair 33415
     Supravalvular 33417

Aortic Valve
See Heart, Aortic Valve

Aortic Valve Replacement
See Replacement, Aortic Valve

Aortocoronary Bypass
See Coronary Artery Bypass Graft (CABG)

Aortocoronary Bypass for Heart Revascularization
See Artery, Coronary, Bypass

Aortography 75600-75605, 75630, 93544
See Angiography
Serial 75625
with Iliofemoral Artery 75630

Aortoiliac
Embolectomy 34151-34201
Thrombectomy 34151-34201

Aortopexy 33800

Aortoplasty
Supravalvular Stenosis 33417

AP
See Voiding Pressure Studies

Apert-Gallais Syndrome
See Adrenogenital Syndrome

Aphasia Testing 96105
See Neurology, Diagnostic

Apheresis
Therapeutic 36520-36521

Apical-Aortic Conduit 33404

Apicectomy
with Mastoidectomy 69605
     Petrous 69530

Apoaminotransferase, Aspartate
See Transaminase, Glutamic Oxaloacetic

Apolipoprotein
Blood or Urine 82172

Appendectomy 44950-44960
Laparoscopic .44970

Appendiceal Abscess
See Abscess, Appendix

Appendico-Vesicostomy
Cutaneous 50845

Appendix
Abscess
     Incision and Drainage
        Open .44900
        Percutaneous 44901
Excision 44950-44960

Application
Allergy Tests .95044
Bone Fixation Device
     Multiplane 20692
     Uniplane .20690
Caliper 20660
Cranial Tongs 20660
Fixation Device
     Shoulder .23700
Halo
     Cranial 20661
        Thin Skull Osteology 20664
     Femoral .20663
     Maxillofacial Fixation 21100
     Pelvic 20662
Interdental Fixation Device 21110
Neurostimulation 64550
Radioelement 77761-77778
     Surface .77789
     with Ultrasound 76965
Stereotactic Frame 20660

Application of External Fixation Device
See Fixation Device, Application, External

APPT
See Thromboplastin, Partial, Time

APTT
See Thromboplastin, Partial, Time

Aquatic Therapy
See Physical Medicine/Therapy/Occupational Therapy

Aqueous Shunt
to Extraocular Reservoir 66180
     Revision .66185

Arch, Zygomatic
See Zygomatic Arch

Arm
See Radius; Ulna; Wrist
Lower
     Abscess .25028
     Amputation 24900-24920, 25900-25905, 25915
        Cineplasty 24940
        Revision 25907-25909
     Angiography 73206
     Artery
        Ligation 37618
     Biopsy 25065-25066
     Bursa
        Incision and Drainage 25031
     Bypass Graft 35903
     Cast 29075
     CAT Scan 73200-73206
     Decompression 25020-25025
     Exploration
        Blood Vessel 35860
     Fasciotomy 24495, 25020-25025
     Hematoma 25028
     Lesion, Tendon Sheath
        Excision 25110
     Magnetic Resonance Imaging
     (MRI) 73218-73220, 73223
     Reconstruction
        Ulna .25337
     Removal
        Foreign Body 25248
     Repair
        Blood Vessel with Other Graft 35266
        Blood Vessel with Vein Graft 35236
        Decompression 24495
        Muscle 25260-25263, 25270
            Secondary 25265
        Secondary
            Muscle 25272-25274
            Tendon 25272-25274
        Tendon 25260-25263, 25270, 25280-25295, 25310-25316
            Secondary 25265
        Tendon Sheath 25275
     Replantation 20805
     Splint 29125-29126
     Tenotomy 25290
     Tumor
        Excision 25075-25077
     Ultrasound 76880
     Unlisted Services and Procedures 25999
     X-Ray 73090
        with Upper Arm 73092
Removal
     Foreign Body
        Forearm or Wrist 25248
Repair
     Muscle .24341
     Tendon .24341

Upper
  Abscess
    Incision and Drainage 23930
      See Elbow; Humerus
  Amputation 23900-23921, 24900-24920
    Cineplasty 24940
    Revision 24925-24930
    with Implant 24931-24935
  Anesthesia 00400, 01710-01782
  Angiography 73206
  Artery
    Ligation 37618
  Biopsy 24065-24066
  Bypass Graft 35903
  Cast 29065
  CAT Scan 73200-73206
  Exploration
    Blood Vessel 35860
  Hematoma
    Incision and Drainage 23930
  Magnetic Resonance Imaging
  (MRI) 73218-73220, 73223
  Muscle Revision 24330-24331
  Removal
    Cast 29705
    Foreign Body 24200-24201
  Repair
    Blood Vessel with Other Graft 35266
    Blood Vessel with Vein Graft 35236
    Muscle Transfer 24301, 24320
    Tendon 24332
    Tendon Lengthening 24305
    Tendon Revision 24320
    Tendon Transfer 24301
    Tenotomy 24310
  Replantation 20802
  Splint 29105
  Tumor
    Excision 24075-24077
  Ultrasound 76880
  Unlisted Services and Procedures 24999
  Wound Exploration
    Penetrating 20103
X-Ray
  with Lower Arm
    Infant 73092

Arnold-Chiari Malformation Repair
See Decompression, Skull

Arrest, Epiphyseal
See Epiphyseal Arrest

Arrhythmogenic Focus
Heart
  Catheter Ablation 93650-93652
  Destruction 33250-33251, 33261

Arsenic 83015
Blood or Urine 82175

ART
See Syphilis Test

Arterial Catheterization
See Cannulation, Arterial

Arterial Dilatation, Transluminal
See Angioplasty, Transluminal

Arterial Grafting for Coronary Artery Bypass
See Bypass Graft, Coronary Artery, Arterial

Arterial Pressure
See Blood Pressure

Arterial Puncture 36600

Arteriography, Aorta
See Aortography

Arteriosus, Ductus
See Ductus Arteriosus

Arteriosus, Truncus
See Truncus Arteriosus

Arteriotomy
See Incision, Artery; Transection, Artery

Arteriovenous Anastomosis 36819-36820

Arteriovenous Fistula
Cannulization
  Vein 36815
Repair
  Abdomen 35182
    Acquired or Traumatic 35189
  Head 35180
    Acquired or Traumatic 35188
  Lower Extremity 35184
    Acquired or Traumatic 35190
  Neck 35180
    Acquired or Traumatic 35188
  Thorax 35182
    Acquired or Traumatic 35189
  Upper Extremity 35184
    Acquired or Traumatic 35190
Revision
  Hemodialysis Graft or Fistula
    without Thrombectomy 36832
    with Thrombectomy 36833
Thrombectomy
  Dialysis Graft
    without Revision 36831
  Graft 36870

Arteriovenous Malformation
Cranial
  Repair 61680-61692, 61705-61708
Spinal
  Excision 63250-63252
  Injection 62294
  Repair 63250-63252

Arteriovenous Shunt
Angiography 75790
Catheterization 36145

Artery
Abdomen
  Angiography 75726
  Catheterization 36245-36248
  Ligation 37617
Adrenal
  Angiography 75731-75733
Anastomosis
  Cranial 61711

Angioplasty 75962-75968
Aorta
  Angioplasty 35452
  Atherectomy 35481, 35491
Aortoiliac
  Embolectomy 34151-34201
  Thrombectomy 34151-34201
Aortoiliofemoral 35363
Arm
  Angiography 75710-75716
  Harvest of Artery for Coronary Artery
    Bypass Graft 35600
Atherectomy
  Open 35480-35485
  Percutaneous 35490-35495
Axillary
  Aneurysm 35011-35013
  Angioplasty 35458
  Bypass Graft 35516-35521, 35533,
         35616-35623, 35650, 35654
  Embolectomy 34101
  Thrombectomy 34101
  Thromboendarterectomy 35321
Basilar
  Aneurysm 61698, 61702
Biopsy
  Transcatheter 75970
Brachial
  Aneurysm 35011-35013
  Angiography 75658
  Catheterization 36120
  Embolectomy 34101
  Exploration 24495
  Thrombectomy 34101
  Thromboendarterectomy 35321
Brachiocephalic
  Angioplasty 35458
  Atherectomy 35484, 35494
  Catheterization 36215-36218
Bypass Graft
  with Composite Graft 35681-35683
Cannulization
  for Extra Corporeal Circulation 36823
  to Vein 36810-36815
Carotid
  Aneurysm 35001-35002, 61697-61705
    Vascular Malformation or Carotid
    Cavernous Fistula 61710
  Angiography 75660-75680
  Bypass Graft 35501-35509, 35526,
         35601-35606, 35626, 35642
  Catheterization 36100
  Decompression ..61590-61591, 61595-61596
  Embolectomy 34001
  Exploration 35701
  Ligation 37600-37606, 61611-61612
  Thrombectomy 34001
  Thromboendarterectomy 35301, 35390
  Transection 61611-61612
Celiac
  Aneurysm 35121-35122
  Bypass Graft 35531, 35631
  Embolectomy 34151
  Thrombectomy 34151
  Thromboendarterectomy 35341

Chest
  Ligation 37616
Coronary
  Angiography 93556
  Atherectomy 92995-92996
  Bypass 33517-33519
    Arterial 33533-33536
    Bypass Venous Graft 33510-33516
    Graft 33503-33505
    Ligation 33502
    Repair 33500-33506
  Thrombectomy
    Percutaneous 92973
Digital
  Sympathectomy 64820
Ethmoidal
  Ligation 30915
Extracranial
  Vascular Studies
    Non-Invasive, Physiologic 93875
Extra Corporeal Circulation
  for Regional Chemotherapy
  of Extremity .36823
Extremities
  Vascular Studies 93922-93923
Extremity
  Bypass graft revision 35879-35881
  Catheterization 36140
  Ligation 37618
Femoral
  Aneurysm 35141-35142
  Angioplasty .35456
  Atherectomy 35483, 35493
  Bypass Graft 35521, 35533, 35546,
    35551-35558, 35566, 35621, 35646-35647,
    35651-35661, 35666, 35700
  Bypass In-Situ 35582-35585
  Embolectomy 34201
  Exploration .35721
  Exposure 34812-34813
  Thrombectomy 34201
  Thromboendarterectomy 35371-35381
Great Vessel
  Repair 33770-33781
Head
  Angiography 75650
Hepatic
  Aneurysm 35121-35122
Iliac
  Aneurysm 35131-35132
  Angioplasty .35454
  Atherectomy 35482, 35492
  Bypass Graft . . .35541, 35563, 35641, 35663
  Embolectomy 34151-34201
  Exposure 34820
  Occulsion Device 34808
  Thrombectomy 34151-34201
  Thromboendarterectomy 35351,
    35361-35363
Iliofemoral
  Bypass Graft 35548-35549, 35565, 35665
  Thromboendarterectomy 35355, 35363
  X-Ray with Contrast 75630
Innominate
  Aneurysm 35021-35022
  Embolectomy 34001-34101
  Thrombectomy 34001-34101
  Thromboendarterectomy 35311

Leg
  Angiography 75710-75716
  Catheterization 36245-36248
Mammary
  Angiography 75756
Maxillary
  Ligation 30920
Mesenteric
  Aneurysm 35121-35122
  Bypass Graft 35531, 35631
  Embolectomy 34151
  Thrombectomy 34151
  Thromboendarterectomy 35341
Neck
  Angiography 75650
  Ligation 37615
Nose
  Incision 30915-30920
Other Angiography 75774
Other Artery
  Aneurysm 35161-35162
  Exploration .35761
  Occlusive Disease 35161
Pelvic
  Angiography 75736
  Catheterization 36245-36248
Peripheral Arterial Rehabilitation 93668
Peroneal
  Bypass Graft 35566-35571, 35666-35671
  Bypass In-Situ 35585-35587
  Embolectomy 34203
  Thrombectomy 34203
  Thromboendarterectomy 35381
Popliteal
  Aneurysm 35151-35152
  Angioplasty .35456
  Atherectomy 35483, 35493
  Bypass Graft . . .35551-35556, 35571, 35623,
    35651, 35656, 35671, 35700
  Bypass In-Situ 35582-35583, 35587
  Embolectomy 34203
  Exploration .35741
  Thrombectomy 34203
  Thromboendarterectomy 35381
Pulmonary
  Anastomosis 33606
  Angiography 75741-75746
  Repair 33690
Radial
  Aneurysm 35045
  Embolectomy 34111
  Sympathectomy 64821
  Thrombectomy 34111
Rehabilitation 93668
Reimplantation
  Carotid 35691, 35694-35695
  Subclavian 35693-35695
  Vertebral 35691-35693
Renal
  Aneurysm 35121-35122
  Angiography 75722-75724
  Angioplasty .35450
  Atherectomy 35480, 35490
  Bypass Graft 35536, 35560, 35631-35636
  Embolectomy 34151
  Thrombectomy 34151
  Thromboendarterectomy 35341

Repair
  Aneurysm 36834, 61697-61708
  Angioplasty 75962-75968
Revision
  Hemodialysis Graft or Fistula
    without Thrombectomy 36832
    with Thrombectomy 36833
Spine
  Angiography 75705
Splenic
  Aneurysm 35111-35112
  Bypass Graft 35536, 35636
Subclavian
  Aneurysm 35001-35002, 35021-35022
  Angioplasty .35458
  Bypass Graft 35506-35507, 35511-35516,
    35526, 35606-35616, 35626, 35645
  Embolectomy 34001-34101
  Thrombectomy 34001-34101
  Thromboendarterectomy 35301-35311
  Unlisted Services and Procedures 37799
Superficial Palmar Arch
  Sympathectomy 64823
Temporal
  Biopsy 37609
  Ligation 37609
Thoracic
  Catheterization 36215-36218
Thrombectomy
  Hemodialysis Graft or Fistula 36831
  Other than Hemodialysis Graft
  or Fistula 35875, 36870
Tibial
  Bypass Graft 35566-35571,
    35623, 35666-35671
  Bypass In-Situ 35585-35587
  Embolectomy 34203
  Thrombectomy 34203
  Thromboendarterectomy 35381
Tibioperoneal
  Angioplasty 35459, 35470
  Atherectomy 35485, 35495
Transcatheter Therapy
  with Angiography 75894-75898
Transposition
  Carotid 35691, 35694-35695
  Subclavian 35693-35695
  Vertebral 35691-35693
Ulnar
  Aneurysm 35045
  Embolectomy 34111
  Sympathectomy 64822
  Thrombectomy 34111
Unlisted Services and Procedures 37799
Vertebral
  Aneurysm 35005, 61698, 61702
  Angiography 75685
  Bypass Graft 35508, 35515, 35642-35645
  Catheterization 36100
  Decompression 61597
  Thromboendarterectomy 35301
Visceral
  Angioplasty .35450
  Atherectomy 35480, 35490

Artery Catheterization, Pulmonary
See Catheterization, Pulmonary Artery

Arthrectomy
Elbow 24155

Arthrocentesis
Intermediate Joint 20605
Large Joint 20610
Small Joint 20600

Arthrodeses
See Arthrodesis

Arthrodesis
Ankle 27870
Carpometacarpal Joint
    Hand .26843-26844
    Thumb 26841-26842
Cervical Anterior
    with Discectomy 22554
Elbow 24800-24802
Finger Joint 26852
    Interphalangeal 26860-26863
    Metacarpophalangeal 26850
Foot Joint 28730-28735, 28740
    Pantalar 28705
    Subtalar 28725
    Triple 28715
    with Advancement 28737
    with Lengthening 28737
Hand Joint 26843-26844
Hip Joint 27284-27286
Intercarpal Joint 25820
    with Autograft 25825
Interphalangeal Joint 26860-26863
    Great Toe 28755
        with Tendon Transfer 28760
Knee 27580
Metacarpophalangeal Joint 26850-26852
Metatarsophalangeal Joint
    Great Toe 28750
Pubic Symphysis 27282
Radioulnar Joint
    with Resection of Ulna 25830
Sacroiliac Joint .27280
Shoulder
    See Shoulder, Arthrodesis
Shoulder Joint .23800
    with Autogenous Graft 23802
Talus
    Pantalar 28705
    Subtalar 28725
    Triple 28715
Tarsal Joint 28730-28735, 28740
    with Advancement 28737
    with Lengthening 28737
Tarsometatarsal Joint 28730-28735, 28740
Thumb Joint 26841-26842
Tibiofibular Joint 27871
Vertebra
    Additional Interspace
        Anterior/Anterolateral Approach 22585
        Posterior .22632
    Cervical
        Anterior/Anterolateral Approach 22548
        Posterior/Posterolateral and/or Lateral
        Traverse Process 22590-22600
    Lumbar
        Anterior/Anterolateral Approach 22558
        Posterior/Interbody 22630
        Posterior/Posterolateral and/or Lateral
        Transverse Process 22612

Spinal Deformity
    Anterior Approach 22808-22812
    Posterior Approach 22800-22804
Spinal Fusion
    Exploration 22830
Thoracic
    Anterior/Anterolateral Approach 22556
    Posterior/Posterolateral and/or Lateral
    Traverse Process 22610
Vertebrae
    Posterior .22614
Wrist 25800
    with Graft .25810
    with Sliding Graft 25805

Arthrography
Ankle 73615
    Injection 27648
Elbow 73085
    Injection 24220
Hip 73525
    Injection 27093, 27095
Knee 73580
    Injection 27370
Sacroiliac Joint .73542
    Injection 27096
Shoulder 73040
    Injection 23350
Temporomandibular Joint (TMJ) . . .70328-70332
    Injection 21116
Wrist 73115
    Injection 25246

Arthroplasties, Knee Replacement
See Prosthesis, Knee

Arthroplasty
Ankle 27700-27703
Elbow 24360
    Total Replacement 24363
    with Implant 24361-24362
Hip 27132
    Partial Replacement 27125
    Revision 27134-27138
    Total Replacement 27130
Interphalangeal Joint 26535-26536
Knee 27437-27443, 27446-27447
    Revision 27486-27487
    with Prosthesis 27438, 27445
Metacarpophalangeal Joint 26530-26531
Radius 24365
    with Implant 24366
Reconstruction
    Prosthesis
        Hip 27125
Shoulder Joint
    with Implant 23470-23472
Temporomandibular Joint 21240-21243
Wrist 25447
    Carpal 25443
    Lunate 25444
    Navicular 25443
    Radius 25441
    Revision 25449
    Total Replacement 25446
    Trapezium .25445
    Ulna 25442
    with Implant 25441-25445
Wrist (Pseudarthrosis Type) 25332

Arthroplasty, Hip, Total
See Hip, Total Replacement

Arthroplasty, Shoulder
See Repair, Shoulder

Arthropods
Examination 87168

Arthroscopy
Diagnostic
    Elbow 29830
    Hip 29860
    Knee 29870
    Metacarpophalangeal Joint 29900
    Shoulder 29805
    Temporomandibular Joint 29800
    Wrist 29840
Surgical
    Ankle 29891-29898
    Elbow 29834-29838
    Hip .29861-29863
    Knee 29871-29889
        Cartilage Allograft 0013T
        Cartilage Autograft 0012T
    Metacarpophalangeal Joint 29901-29902
    Shoulder 29806-29826
    Temporomandibular Joint 29804
    Wrist 29843-29848
Unlisted Services and Procedures 29999

Arthroscopy of Ankle
See Ankle, Arthroscopy

Arthrotomy
Acromioclavicular Joint 23044
Ankle 27610-27612, 27620
Ankle Joint 27625-27626
Carpometacarpal Joint 26070
    with Biopsy, Synovium
        with Synovial Biopsy 26100
Elbow 24000
    Capsular Release 24006
    with Joint Exploration 24101
    with Synovectomy 24102
    with Synovial Biopsy 24100
Finger Joint 26075
    Interphalangeal
        with Synovial Biopsy 26110
    Metacarpophalangeal
        with Biopsy, Synovium 26105
Glenohumeral Joint 23040
Hip 27033
    for Infection
        with Drainage 27030
    with Synovectomy 27054
Interphalangeal Joint 26080, 26110
    Toe .28024, 28054
Intertarsal Joint 28020, 28050
Knee 27310, 27330-27335, 27403
Metacarpophalangeal Joint . . .26075, 26105
Metatarsophalangeal Joint 28022, 28052
Shoulder 23044, 23105-23107
Shoulder Joint 23100-23101
    Exploration and/or Removal of Loose or
    Foreign Body 23107
Sternoclavicular Joint 23044
Tarsometatarsal Joint 28020, 28050

Temporomandibular Joint 21010
with Biopsy
    Acromioclavicular Joint 23101
    Glenohumeral Joint 23100
    Hip Joint 27052
    Knee Joint 27330
    Sacroiliac Joint
      Hip Joint .27050
    Sternoclavicular Joint 23101
with Synovectomy
    Glenohumeral Joint 23105
    Sternoclavicular Joint 23106
Wrist 25040, 25100-25107

Arthrotomy for Removal of Prosthesis of Ankle
See Ankle, Removal, Implant

Arthrotomy for Removal of Prosthesis of Hip
See Hip, Removal, Prosthesis

Arthrotomy for Removal of Prosthesis of Wrist
See Prosthesis, Wrist, Removal

Articular Ligament
See Ligament

Artificial Abortion
See Abortion

Artificial Cardiac Pacemaker
See Heart, Pacemaker

Artificial Eye
See Prosthesis

Artificial Genitourinary Sphincter
See Prosthesis, Urethral Sphincter

Artificial Insemination 58976
See In Vitro Fertilization
Intra-Cervical 58321
Intra-Uterine 58322
Sperm Washing 58323

Artificial Knee Joints
See Prosthesis, Knee

Artificial Penis
See Penile Prosthesis

Artificial Pneumothorax
See Pneumothorax, Therapeutic

Arytenoid
Excision
    Endoscopic 31560-31561

Arytenoidectomy 31400
Endoscopic 31560

Arytenoidopexy 31400

Arytenoid Cartilage
Excision 31400
Repair 31400

Ascorbic Acid
Blood 82180

Aspartate Aminotransferase
See Transaminase, Glutamic Oxaloacetic

Aspergillus
Antibody 86606

Aspiration
See Puncture Aspiration
Bladder .51000-51010
Bone Marrow .38220
Brain Lesion
    Stereotactic 61750-61751
Bronchi
    Endoscopy 31645-31646
Bursa 20600-20610
Catheter
    Nasotracheal 31720
    Tracheobronchial 31725
Cyst
    Bone 20615
    Kidney 50390
    Pelvis 50390
    Spinal Cord 62268
    Thyroid 60001
Duodenal 89100-89105
Ganglion Cyst 20600-20605
Hydrocele
    Tunica Vaginalis 55000
Joint 20600-20610
Laryngoscopy
    Direct 31515
Lens Material .66840
Liver 47015
Lung 32420
Nucleus of Disk
    Lumbar 62287
Orbital Contents 67415
Pelvis
    Endoscopy 49322
Pericardium 33010-33011
Pleural Cavity 32000-32002
Puncture
    Cyst
      Breast 19000-19001
Spinal Cord
    Stereotaxis 63615
Syrinx
    Spinal Cord 62268
Thyroid 60001
Trachea
    Nasotracheal 31720
    Puncture 31612
Tunica Vaginalis
    Hydrocele .55000
Vitreous 67015

Aspiration, Chest
See Thoracentesis

Aspiration, Lung Puncture
See Pneumocentesis

Aspiration, Nail
See Evacuation, Hematoma, Subungual

Aspiration, Spinal Puncture
See Spinal Tap

Aspiration Lipectomies
See Liposuction

Aspiration of Bone Marrow from Donor for Transplant
See Bone Marrow, Harvesting

Assay, Very Long Chain Fatty Acids
See Fatty Acid, Very Long Chain

Assay Tobramycin
See Tobramycin

Assisted Circulation
See Circulation Assist

AST
See Transaminase, Glutamic Oxaloacetic

Astragalectomy 28130

Astragalus
See Talus

Asymmetry, Face
See Hemifacial Microsomia

Ataxia Telangiectasia
Chromosome Analysis 88248

Ataxy, Telangiectasia
See Ataxia Telangiectasia

Atherectomies, Coronary
See Artery, Coronary, Atherectomy

Atherectomy
See X-Ray, Artery
Open
    Aorta 35481
    Brachiocephalic 35484
    Femoral 35483
    Iliac 35482
    Popliteal 35483
    Renal 35480
    Tibioperoneal 35485
    Visceral 35480
Percutaneous
    Aorta 35491
    Brachiocephalic 35494
    Coronary 92995-92996
      See Artery, Coronary
    Femoral 35493
    Iliac 35492
    Popliteal 35493
    Renal 35490
    Tibioperoneal 35495
    Visceral 35490
X-Ray
    Peripheral Artery 75992-75993
    Renal Artery 75994
    Visceral Artery 75995-75996

ATLV
See HTLV I

ATLV Antibodies
See Antibody, HTLV-I

Atomic Absorption Spectroscopy 82190

ATP Creatine Phosphotransferase
See CPK

Atresia, Choanal
See Choanal Atresia

Atresia, Congenital
Auditory Canal, External
Reconstruction .69320

Atria
Reconstruction 33253

Atrial Electrogram
See Cardiology, Diagnostic
Esophageal Recording 93615-93616

Atrial Fibrillation
See Fibrillation, Atrial

Atrioseptopexy
See Heart, Repair, Atrial Septum

Atrioseptoplasty
See Heart, Repair, Atrial Septum

Attachment
See Fixation

Atticotomy 69631, 69635

Audiologic Function Tests
See Ear, Nose and Throat; Hearing Evaluation
Acoustic Reflex 92568
Acoustic Reflex Decay 92569
Audiometry
　Bekesy 92560-92561
　Comprehensive 92557
　Conditioning Play 92582
　Groups 92559
　Pure Tone 92552-92553
　Select Picture 92583
　Speech 92555-92556
　Visual Reinforcement 92579
Central Auditory Function 92589
Electrocochleography 92584
Evoked Otoacoustic Emission 92587-92588
Filtered Speech .92571
Lombard Test 92573
Loudness Balance 92562
Screening 92551
Sensorineural Acuity 92575
Short Increment Sensitivity Index 92564
Staggered Spondaic Word Test 92572
Stenger Test 92565, 92577
Synthetic Sentence Test 92576
Tone Decay 92563

Audiometry
Bekesy 92560-92561
Brainstem Evoked Response 92585-92586
Comprehensive 92557
Conditioning Play 92582
Groups 92559
　See Ear, Nose and Throat
Pure Tone 92552-92553
Select Picture 92583
Speech .92555-92556
Tympanometry 92567

Auditory Brain Stem Evoked Response
See Evoked Potential, Auditory Brainstem

Auditory Canal
Decompression 61591
External
　Abscess
　　Incision and Drainage 69020
　Biopsy 69105
　Lesion
　　Excision 69140-69155
　Reconstruction
　　for Congenital Atresia 69320
　　for Stenosis 69310
　Removal
　　Cerumen .69210
　　Ear Wax 69210
　　Foreign Body 69200-69205
Internal
　Decompression 69960

Auditory Canal Atresia, External
See Atresia, Congenital, Auditory Canal, External

Auditory Evoked Otoacoustic Emission 92587-92588

Auditory Evoked Potentials 92585-92586
See Audiologic Function Tests

Auditory Labyrinth
See Ear, Inner

Auditory Meatus
X-Ray 70134

Auditory Tube
See Eustachian Tube

Augmentation
Chin 21120, 21123
Malar 21270
Mandibular Body
　with Bone Graft 21127
　with Prosthesis 21125
Osteoplasty
　Facial Bones .21208

Augmentation Mammoplasty
See Breast, Augmentation

Augmented Histamine Test 91052
See Gastric Analysis Test

Aural Rehabilitation 92510

Auricle (Heart)
See Atria

Auricular Fibrillation
See Fibrillation, Atrial

Auricular Prosthesis 21086

Australia Antigen
See Hepatitis Antigen, B Surface

Autograft
Bone
　Local 20936
　Morselized 20937
　Structural 20938

for Spine Surgery
　Local 20936
　Morselized 20937
　Structural 20938

Autologous Blood Transfusion
See Autotransfusion

Autologous Transplantation
See Autograft

Automated Data
Nuclear Medicine 78890-78891

Autonomic Nervous System Function
See Neurology, Diagnostic; Neurophysiologic Testing

Autoprothrombin C
See Thrombokinase

Autoprothrombin I
See Proconvertin

Autoprothrombin II
See Christmas Factor

Autoprothrombin III
See Stuart-Prower Factor

Autopsy
Coroner's Exam .88045
Forensic Exam 88040
Gross and Micro Exam 88020-88029
Gross Exam 88000-88016
Organ 88037
Regional 88036
Unlisted Services and Procedures 88099

Autotransfusion
Blood 86890-86891

Autotransplant
See Autograft

Autotransplantation
Renal 50380

Avulsion
Nails 11730-11732
Nerve 64732-64772

AV Fistula
See Arteriovenous Fistula

AV Shunt
See Arteriovenous Shunt

Axillary Arteries
See Artery, Axillary

Axillary Nerve
Injection
　Anesthetic 64417

Axis, Dens
See Odontoid Process

A Vitamin
See Vitamin, A

B

B-DNA
See Deoxyribonucleic Acid

b-Hexosaminidase 83080

B1 Vitamin
See Thiamine

B6 Vitamin
See Vitamin, B-6

Babcock Operation
See Ligation, Vein, Saphenous

Bacillus Calmette Guerin Vaccine
See BCG Vaccine

Back/Flank
Biopsy 21920-21925
Repair
    Hernia .49540
Strapping .29220
Tumor
    Excision 21930
    Radical Resection 21935
Wound Exploration
    Penetrating 20102

Backbone
See Spine
Bacterial Endotoxins 87176

Bacteria Culture
Additional Methods 87077
Anaerobic 87073-87076
Blood 87040
Feces 87045-87046
Other Source 87070-87073
Screening 87081
Urine .87086-87088

Bactericidal Titer, Serum 87197

Bacterium
Antibody .86609

BAER
See Evoked Potential, Auditory Brainstem

Baker's Cyst 27345

Baker Tube
Intestine Decompression 44021

Balanoplasty
See Penis, Repair

Baldy-Webster Operation
See Uterus, Repair, Suspension

Balkan Grippe
See Q Fever

Balloon Angioplasties, Coronary
See Percutaneous Transluminal Angioplasty

Balloon Angioplasty
See Angioplasty

Balloon Assisted Device
Aorta 33967-33974, 93727

Band, Pulmonary Artery
See Banding, Artery, Pulmonary

Banding
Artery
    Fistula 37607
    Pulmonary 33690

Bank, Blood
See Blood Banking

Bankart Procedure
See Capsulorrhaphy, Anterior

Barany Caloric Test
See Caloric Vestibular Test

Barbiturates
Blood or Urine 82205

Bardenheurer Operation
See Ligation, Artery, Chest

Barium 83015

Barium Enema 74270-74280

Barker Operation
See Talus, Excision

Barr Bodies 88130

Barr Procedure
See Tendon, Transfer, Leg, Lower

Bartholin's Gland
Abscess
    Incision and Drainage 56420
Cyst
    Repair 56440
Excision .56740
Marsupialization 56440

Bartonella
Antibody .86611

Bartonella Detection 87470-87472

Basic Life Services 99450

Basic Proteins, Myelin
See Myelin Basic Protein

Basilar Arteries
See Artery, Basilar

Batch-Spittler-McFaddin Operation
See Disarticulation, Knee

BCG Vaccine
See Vaccines

Bed Sores
See Debridement; Pressure Ulcer (Decubitus);
Skin Graft and Flap

Bekesy Audiometry
See Audiometry, Bekesy

Belsey IV Procedure
See Fundoplasty

Bender-Gestalt Test 96100

Benedict Test for Urea
See Urinalysis, Qualitative

Benign Cystic Mucinous Tumor
See Ganglion

**Benign Neoplasm of Cranial
Nerves**
See Cranial Nerve

Bennett Fracture
See Phalanx; Thumb, Fracture

Bennett Procedure
See Repair, Leg, Upper, Muscle; Revision

Benzidine Test
See Blood, Feces

Benzodiazepine
Assay 80154

Benzoyl Cholinesterase
See Cholinesterase

Bernstein Test
See Acid Perfusion Test, Esophagus

Beryllium .83015

Beta-2-Microglobulin
Blood 82232
Urine 82232

Beta-hydroxydehydrogenase . .80406

Beta 2 Glycoprotein I Antibody . .86146

Beta Glucosidase 82963

Beta Hypophamine
See Antidiuretic Hormone

Beta Lipoproteins
See Lipoprotein, LDL

Beta Test .96100
See Psychiatric Diagnosis

Bethesda System 88164-88167

Be Antigens, Hepatitis
See Hepatitis Antigen, Be

Bicarbonate 82374

Biceps Tendon
Insertion .24342

Bichloride, Methylene
See Dichloromethane

Bicuspid Valve
See Mitral Valve

Bifrontal Craniotomy 61557

**Bilaminate Skin
Substitute/Neodermis**
See Tissue
Repair
    See Tissue, Culture
        Repair; Tissue, Culture, Skin Grafts

Bile Acids 82239
Blood 82240

Bile Duct
See Gallbladder
Anastomosis
    Cyst 47716
    with Intestines 47760, 47780-47785
Biopsy
    Endoscopy 47553
Catheterization 75982
Change Catheter Tube 75984
Cyst
    Excision 47715
    Repair 47716
Destruction
    Calculi (Stone) 43265
Dilation
    Endoscopy 43271, 47555-47556
Drainage
    Transhepatic 75980
Endoscopy
    Biopsy 47553
    Destruction
        Calculi (Stone) 43265
        Tumor 43272
    Dilation 43271, 47555-47556
    Exploration 47552
    Intraoperative 47550
    Removal
        Calculi (Stone) 43264, 47554
        Foreign Body 43269
        Stent 43269
    Specimen Collection 43260
    Sphincterotomy 43262
    Sphincter Pressure 43263
    Tube Placement 43267-43268
Exploration
    Atresia 47700
    Endoscopy 47552
Incision
    Sphincter 43262, 47460
Incision and Drainage 47420-47425
Insertion
    Catheter 47510, 47525, 75982
        Revision 47530
    Stent 47511, 47801
Nuclear Medicine
    Imaging .78223
Reconstruction
    Anastomosis 47800
Removal
    Calculi (Stone) 43264, 47420-47425
        Percutaneous 47630
    Foreign Body 43269
    Stent 43269
Repair 47701
    Cyst 47716
    Gastrointestinal Tract 47785
    with Intestines 47760, 47780
Tube Placement
    Nasobiliary 43267
    Stent 43268
Tumor
    Destruction 43271
    Excision 47711-47712
Unlisted Services and Procedures 47999

X-Ray
    Guide Dilation 74360
    with Contrast 74300-74320
        Calculus Removal 74327
    Guide Catheter 74328, 74330

Bile Duct, Common, Cystic Dilatation
See Cyst, Choledochal

Bilirubin
Blood 82247-82248
Feces 82252
Total
    Direct 82247-82248
    Transcutaneous 88400

Billroth I or II
See Gastrectomy, Partial

Bilobectomy 32482

Bimone
See Testosterone

Binding Globulin, Testosterone-Estradiol
See Globulin, Sex Hormone Binding

Binet-Simon Test 96100

Binet Test 96100

Binocular Microscopy 92504

Biofeedback
See Training, Biofeedback
Anorectal 90911
Psychiatric Treatment 90875-90876

Biofeedback Training
See Training, Biofeedback

Bioimpedance
Thorax 93701

Biological Skin Grafts
See Allograft, Skin

Biometry
Eye 76516-76519, 92136

Biopsies, Needle
See Needle Biopsy

Biopsy
See Brush Biopsy; Needle Biopsy
Abdomen 49000
Adrenal Gland 60540-60545
Anal
    Endoscopy 46606
Ankle 27613-27614, 27620
Arm, Lower 25065-25066
Arm, Upper 24065-24066
Artery
    Temporal 37609
Auditory Canal, External 69105
Back/Flank 21920-21925
Bile Duct
    Endoscopy 47553
Bladder 52354
    Cystourethroscope 52204
    Cystourethroscopy 52224, 52250

Blood Vessel
    Transcatheter 75970
Bone 20220-20245
Bone Marrow 38221
Brain 61140
    Stereotactic 61750-61751
Brainstem 61575-61576
Breast 19100-19103
    Stereotactic Localization 76095
Bronchi
    Catheterization 31717
    Endoscopic 31625-31629
Brush
    Bronchi .31717
    Renal Pelvis 52007
    Ureter 52007
    with Cystourethroscopy 52204
Carpometacarpal Joint
    Synovium 26100
Cervix 57500, 57520
Chorionic Villus 59015
Colon 44025, 44100
    Endoscopy 44389, 45380
    Multiple
        with Colostomy, Cecostomy 44322
Colon-Sigmoid
    Endoscopy 45305, 45331
Conjunctiva 68100
Cornea 65410
Duodenum 44010
Ear
    External .69100
Elbow 24065-24066, 24101
    Synovium 24100
Endometrium 58100, 58558
Epididymis 54800-54820
Esophagus
    Endoscopy 43202
Eyelid 67810
Eye Muscle 67350
Forearm
    Soft Tissue 25065-25066
Gallbladder
    Endoscopy 43261
Gastrointestinal, Upper
    Endoscopy 43239
Hand Joint
    Synovium 26100
Heart 93505
Hip 27040-27041
    Joint 27052
Hypopharynx 42802
Ileum
    Endoscopy 44382
Interphalangeal Joint
    Finger 26110
    Toe 28054
Intertarsal Joint
    Toe 28050
Intestines, Small 44020, 44100
    Endoscopy 44361, 44377
Kidney 50200-50205, 52354
    Endoscopic 50555-50559, 50574-50578
Knee 27323-27324
    Synovium 27330
Knee Joint
    Synovium 27330
Lacrimal Gland 68510

Lacrimal Sac .68525
Larynx
    Endoscopy 31510, 31576
Leg
    Lower 27613-27614
    Upper 27323-27324
Lip 40490
Liver 47000-47001, 47100
    Percutaneous 00702
Lung
    Needle 32405
    Thoracotomy 32095-32100
Lymph Nodes 38500-38530
    Injection Procedure
      for Identification of Sentinel Node . .38792
    Laparoscopic 38570-38572
    Needle 38505
    Open 38500, 38510-38530
      Superficial 38500
Mediastinum .39400
    Needle 32405
Metacarpophalangeal Joint 26105
Metatarsophalangeal Joint 28052
Mouth 40808, 41108
Muscle 20200-20206
Nail 11755
Nasopharynx 42804-42806
Neck 21550
Nerve 64795
Nose
    Endoscopic 31237
    Intranasal .30100
Orbit 61332
    Exploration 67400, 67450
    Fine Needle Aspiration 67415
Oropharynx 42800
Ovary 58900
Palate 42100
Pancreas 48100
Pelvis 27040-27041
Penis 54100
    Deep Structures 54105
Percutaneous Needle
    Spinal Cord 62269
Perineum 56605-56606
Peritoneum
    Endoscopic 47561
Pharynx 42800-42806
Pleura
    Needle 32400-32402
    Thoracotomy 32095-32100
Pleural
    Open 32402
Prostate 55700-55705
Rectum 45100
Retroperitoneal Area 49010
Sacroiliac Joint 27050
Salivary Gland 42405
Shoulder
    Deep 23066
    Soft Tissue 23065
Shoulder Joint 23100-23101
Sinus
    Sphenoid 31050-31051
Skin Lesion 11100-11101
Spinal Cord 63275-63290
    Percutaneous 62269
    Stereotaxis 63615

Stomach 43600-43605
Tarsometatarsal Joint
    Synovial 28050
Testis 54500-54505
Thorax 21550
Throat 42800-42806
Tongue 41100-41105
Transcatheter 37200
Ureter 52354
    Endoscopic 50955-50959, 50974-50978
Urethra 52204, 52354, 53200
Uterus
    Endometrial 58100
    Endoscopic 58558
Uvula 42100
Vagina 57100-57105
    Endocervical 57454
Vertebral Body 20250-20251
Vulva 56605-56606
with Arthrotomy
    Acromioclavicular Joint 23101
    Glenohumeral Joint 23100
    Sternoclavicular Joint 23101
with Cystourethroscopy 52354
Wrist 25065-25066, 25100-25101

Biopsy, Skin
See Skin, Biopsy

Biopsy, Vein
See Vein, Biopsy

Biostatistics
See Biometry

Biosterol
See Vitamin, A

Biotinidase .82261

Birthing Room
Newborn Care 99431

Bischof Procedure
See Laminectomy, Surgical

Bismuth 83015

Bizzozero's Corpuscle/Cell
See Blood, Platelet

Bladder
Abscess
    Incision and Drainage 51080
Anastomosis .51960
Aspiration 51000-51010
Biopsy 52204
Catheterization 51045
Change Tube 51705-51710
Creation
    Stoma 51980
Cyst
    Urachal
      Excision 51500
Destruction
    Endoscopic 52214-52224, 52354
Dilation
    Ureter 52260-52265, 52341-52342,
                     52344-52345

Diverticulum
    Excision 51525
    Incision 52305
    Resection .52305
Endoscopy 52000
    Biopsy 52204, 52354
    Catheterization 52005, 52010
    Destruction 52214-52224, 52400
    Dilation 52260-52265
    Diverticulum 52305
    Evacuation
      Clot 52001
    Excision
      Tumor 52234-52240, 52355
    Exploration 52351
    Injection 52283
    Lithotripsy .52353
    Radiotracer 52250
    Removal
      Calculus 52310-52315, 52352
      Foreign Body 52310-52315
    Sphincter Surgery 52277
    Tumor
      Excision 52355
    Ureter Surgery 52290-52300
    Urethral Syndrome 52285
    with Urethrotomy 52270-52276
Excision
    Partial 51550-51565
    Total 51570, 51580, 51590-51597
      with Nodes 51575, 51585, 51595
    Transurethral 52640
    Tumor 52234-52240
Incision
    Catheter 51045
    with Destruction 51020-51030
    with Radiotracer 51020
Incision and Drainage 51040
Injection
    Radiologic 51600-51610
Insertion
    Stent 51045, 52334
Instillation
    Drugs 51720
Irrigation 51700
Lesion
    Destruction 51030
Neck
    Endoscopy
      Injection of Implant Material 51715
    Excision 51520
Nuclear Medicine
    Residual Study 78730
Radiotracer 52250
Reconstruction
    and Urethra 51800-51820
    with Intestines 51960
Removal
    Calculus 51050, 52310-52315
    Foreign Body 52310-52315
    Urethral Stent 52310-52315
Repair
    Diverticulum 52305
    Exstrophy .51940
    Fistula 44660-44661,
            45800-45805, 51880-51925
    Neck 51845
    Wound 51860-51865

Resection 52500
Sphincter Surgery 52277
Suspension 51990
Suture
　　Fistula 44660-44661,
　　　　　　45800-45805, 51880-51925
　　Wound 51860-51865
Tumor
　　Excision 51530
Unlisted Services and Procedures 53899
Urethrocystography 74450-74455
Urethrotomy 52270-52276
Urinary Incontinence Procedures
　　Laparoscopy 51990-51992
X-Ray 74430
　　with Contrast 74450-74455

**Bladder Voiding Pressure
Studies** 51795

**Blalock-Hanlon
Procedure** 33735-33737
See Septostomy, Atrial

Blalock-Taussig Procedure
See Shunt, Great Vessel

Blastocyst Implantation
See Implantation

Blastocyst Transfer
See Embryo Transfer

Blastogenesis 86353

Blastomyces
Antibody 86612

Blastomycosis, European
See Cryptococcus

Blast Cells
See Stem Cell

Blast Transformation
See Blastogenesis

Bleeding
See Hemorrhage

Bleeding, Anal
See Anus, Hemorrhage

Bleeding, Uterine
See Hemorrhage, Uterus

Bleeding Disorder
See Coagulopathy

Bleeding Time 85002

Bleeding Tube
Passage and Placement 91100

Bleeding Vaginal
See Hemorrhage, Vagina

Blepharoplasty 15820-15823
See Canthoplasty
Anesthesia 00103
Ectropion
　　Excision Tarsal Wedge 67916
　　Extensive 67917

Entropion 67923-67924
　　Excision Tarsal Wedge 67923
　　Extensive 67924

Blepharoptosis
Repair 67901-67909
　　Frontalis Muscle Technique 67901
　　　　with Fascial Sling 67902
　　Superior Rectus Technique with
　　　　Fascial Sling 67906
　　Tarso Levator Resection/Advancement
　　　　External Approach 67904
　　　　Internal Approach 67903

Blepharorrhaphy
See Tarsorrhaphy

Blepharospasm
Chemodenervation 64612

Blepharotomy 67700

Blister
See Bulla

Blom-Singer Prosthesis 31611

Blood
Bleeding Time 85002
Collection, for Autotransfusion
　　Intraoperative 86891
　　Preoperative 86890
Feces 82270
　　by Hemoglobin Immunoassay 82274
Gastric Contents 82273
Harvesting of Stem Cells 38231
Hemoglobin Concentration 85046
Nuclear Medicine
　　Flow Imaging 78445
　　Plasma Iron 78160
　　Red Cell 78140
　　Red Cell Survival 78130-78135
Osmolality 83930
Other Source 82273
Plasma
　　Exchange 36520-36521
Platelet
　　Aggregation 85576
　　Automated Count 85595
　　Count 85585
　　Manual Count 85590
Stem Cell
　　Transplantation 38240-38241
　　　　Cryopreservation 88240
　　　　Modification 86915
　　　　Thawing 88241
Transfusion 36430
　　Exchange 36455
　　　　Newborn 36450
　　Fetal 36460
　　Push
　　　　Infant 36440
Unlisted Services and Procedures 85999
Urine 83491
Viscosity 85810

Blood, Occult
See Occult Blood

Blood Banking
Frozen Blood Preparation 86930-86932
Frozen Plasma Preparation 86927
Physician Services 86077-86079

Blood Cell
CD4 and CD8
　　Including Ratio 86360
Enzyme Activity 82657
Exchange 36520-36521
Sedimentation Rate
　　Automated 85652
　　Manual 85651
Stem 38231

Blood Cell, Red
See Red Blood Cell (RBC)

Blood Cell, White
See Leukocyte

Blood Cell Count 85014
Differential WBC Count 85007, 85009
Hemoglobin 85018
Hemogram
　　Added Indices 85021-85027
　　Automated 85021-85027
　　Manual 85031
Manual Blood Smear 85008
Microhematocrit 85013
Other 85014
Red Blood Cells 85041
Reticulocyte 85044-85045
T-Cells 86359-86361
White Blood Cells 85048

Blood Cell Count, Red
See Red Blood Cell (RBC), Count

Blood Cell Count, White
See White Blood Cell, Count

Blood Clot
Clotting Factor 85250-85293
Clotting Factor Test 85210-85244
Clotting Inhibitors ...85300-85302, 85305, 85307
Clot Lysis Time 85175
Clot Retraction 85170
Coagulation Time 85345-85348

Blood Coagulation Defect
See Coagulopathy

Blood Coagulation Disorders
See Clot

Blood Coagulation Factor
See Clotting Factor

Blood Coagulation Factor I
See Fibrinogen

Blood Coagulation Factor II
See Prothrombin

Blood Coagulation Factor III
See Thromboplastin

Blood Coagulation Factor IV
See Calcium

Blood Coagulation Factor IX
See Christmas Factor

Blood Coagulation Factor VII
See Proconvertin

Blood Coagulation Factor VIII
See Clotting Factor

Blood Coagulation Factor X
See Stuart-Prower Factor

Blood Coagulation Factor X, Activated
See Thrombokinase

Blood Coagulation Factor XI
See Plasma Thromboplastin, Antecedent

Blood Coagulation Factor XIII
See Fibrin Stabilizing Factor

Blood Coagulation Test
See Coagulation

Blood Component Removal
See Apheresis

Blood Count, Complete
See Complete Blood Count (CBC)

Blood Flow Check, Graft 15860, 90939-90940

Blood Gases
CO2 82803
HCO3 82803
O2 Saturation 82805-82810
pCO2 82803
pH 82800-82803
pO2 82803

Blood Letting
See Phlebotomy

Blood Lipoprotein
See Lipoprotein

Blood Pool Imaging 78472-78473, 78481-78483, 78494-78496

Blood Pressure
Monitoring, 24 Hour 93784-93790
Venous 93770

Blood Products
Irradiation 86945
Pooling 86965
Splitting 86985

Blood Sample
Fetal 59030

Blood Serum
See Serum

Blood Smear 85060

Blood Syndrome
Chromosome Analysis 88245-88248

Blood Tests
Nuclear Medicine
Iron, Chelatable 78172
Iron Absorption 78162
Iron Utilization 78170
Plasma Volume 78110-78111

Platelet Survival 78190-78191
Red Cell Volume 78120-78121
Whole Blood Volume 78122
Panels
Electrolyte 80051
General Health Panel 80050
Hepatic Function 80076
Hepatitis, Acute 80074
Lipid Panel 80061
Metabolic
Basic 80048
Comprehensive 80053
Obstetric Panel 80055
Renal Function 80069
Volume Determination 78122

Blood Transfusion, Autologous
See Autotransfusion

Blood Typing
ABO Only 86900
Antigen Screen 86903-86904
Crossmatch 86920-86922
Other RBC Antigens 86905
Paternity Testing 86910-86911
Rh (D) 86901
Rh Phenotype 86906

Blood Urea Nitrogen 84520-84525

Blood Vessels
See Artery; Vein
Angioscopy
Non-Coronary 35400
Excision
Arteriovenous Malformation ...63250-63252
Exploration
Abdomen 35840
Chest 35820
Extremity 35860
Neck 35800
Great
Suture 33320-33322
Harvest
Upper Extremity Artery 35600
Upper Extremity Vein 35500
Kidney
Repair 50100
Repair
Abdomen
See Aneurysm Repair; Fistula, Repair
with Composite Graft 35681-35683
with Other Graft 35281
with Vein Graft 35251
Aneurysm 61705-61708
Arteriovenous Malformation ..61680-61692,
61705-61710, 63250-63252
Chest
with Composite Graft 35681-35683
with Other Graft 35271-35276
with Vein Graft 35241-35246
Direct 35201-35226
Finger 35207
Graft Defect 35870
Hand 35207
Lower Extremity 35226
with Composite Graft 35681-35683
with Other Graft 35281
with Vein Graft 35251

Neck
with Composite Graft 35681-35683
with Other Graft 35261
with Vein Graft 35231
Upper Extremity 35206
with Composite Graft ...35681-35683
with Other Graft 35266
with Vein Graft 35236
Shunt Creation
Direct 36821
Thomas Shunt 36835
with Bypass Graft 35686
with Graft 36825-36830
Shunt Revision
with Graft 36832

Bloom Syndrome
Chromosome Analysis 88245

Blotting, Western
See Western Blot

Blot Test, Ink
See Inkblot Test

Blow-Out Fracture
Orbital Floor 21385-21395

Blue, Dome Cyst
See Breast, Cyst

BMT
See Bone Marrow, Transplantation

Boarding Home Care 99321-99333

Bodies, Acetone
See Acetone Body

Bodies, Barr
See Barr Bodies

Bodies, Carotid
See Carotid Body

Bodies, Ciliary
See Ciliary Body

Bodies, Heinz
See Heinz Bodies

Bodies, Inclusion
See Inclusion Bodies

Bodies, Ketone
See Ketone Body

Body Cast
Halo 29000
Removal 29700, 29710-29715
Repair 29720
Risser Jacket 29010-29015
Turnbuckle Jacket 29020-29025
Upper Body and Head 29040
Upper Body and Legs 29046
Upper Body and One Leg 29044
Upper Body Only 29035

Body Fluid
Crystal Identification 89060

Body of Vertebra
See Vertebral Body

Body Section
X-Ray 76100
   Motion 76101-76102

Body System, Neurologic
See Nervous System

Boil
See Furuncle

Boil, Vulva
See Abscess, Vulva

Bone
See Specific Bone
Biopsy 20220-20245
CAT Scan
   Density Study 76070
Cyst
   Drainage 20615
   Injection 20615
Dual Energy X-Ray
Absorptiometry 76075-76076
Excision
   Epyphyseal Bar 20150
   Facial Bones 21026
   Mandible 21025
Fixation
   Caliper 20660
   Cranial Tong .20660
   Halo 20661-20663, 21100
   Interdental 21110
   Multiplane 20692
   Pin/Wire 20650
   Skeletal
      Humeral Epicondyle
         Percutaneous 24566
      Stereotactic Frame 20660
      Uniplane 20690
Insertion
   Needle 36680
   Osseointegrated Implant
      for External Speech Processor/Cochlear
      Stimulator 69714-69718
Nuclear Medicine
   Density Study 78350-78351
   Imaging 78300-78320
   SPECT 78320
   Unlisted Services and Procedures 78399
Protein 83937
Removal
   Fixation Device 20670-20680
Replacement
   Osseointegrated Implant
      for External Speech Processor/Cochlear
      Stimulator 69717-69718
X-Ray
   Age Study 76020
   Dual Energy Absorptiometry . . .76075-76076
   Length Study 76040
   Osseous Survey 76061-76065

Bone, Carpal
See Carpal Bone

Bone, Cheek
See Cheekbone

Bone, Facial
See Facial Bone

Bone, Hyoid
See Hyoid Bone

Bone, Metatarsal
See Metatarsal

Bone, Nasal
See Nasal Bone

Bone, Navicular
See Navicular

Bone, Scan
See Bone, Nuclear Medicine; Nuclear Medicine
Imaging

Bone, Semilunar
See Lunate

Bone, Sesamoid
See Sesamoid Bone

Bone, Tarsal
See Ankle Bone

Bone, Temporal
See Temporal Bone

Bone 4-Carboxyglutamic Protein
See Osteocalcin

**Bone Conduction Hearing Device,
Electromagnetic**
Implantation/Replacement 69710
Removal/Repair .69711

Bone Density Study
Appendicular Skeleton 76076
Axial Skeleton 76075
Ultrasound 76977

Bone Graft
Augmentation
   Mandibular Body 21127
Femur 27170
Fracture
   Orbit 21408
Harvesting 20900-20902
Malar Area 21210
Mandible 21215
Mandibular Ramus 21194
Maxilla 21210
Microvascular Anastomosis
   Fibula 20955
   Other 20962
Nasal Area 21210
Nasomaxillary Complex Fracture 21348
Open Treatment
   Craniofacial Separation 21436
Osteocutaneous Flap 20969-20973
Reconstruction
   Mandibular Rami 21194
   Midface 21145-21160
Spine Surgery
   Allograft
      Morselized 20930
      Structural 20931
   Autograft
      Local 20936
      Morselized 20937
      Structural 20938
Vascular Pedicle 25430

Bone Healing
Electrical Stimulation
   Invasive 20975
   Noninvasive .20974
Ultrasound Stimulation 20979

Bone Infection
See Osteomyelitis

Bone Marrow
Aspiration 38220
Harvesting 38230
Magnetic Resonance Imaging (MRI) 76400
Needle Biopsy .38221
Nuclear Medicine
   Imaging 78102-78104
Smear 85097
T-Cell
   Depletion 86915
Transplantation 38240-38241
Trocar Biopsy 38221

Bone Plate
Mandible 21244

Bone Scan
See Bone, Nuclear Medicine; Nuclear Medicine

Bone Spur
See Exostosis

Bone Wedge Reversal
Osteotomy 21122

Bordetella
Antibody 86615
Antigen Detection
   Direct Fluorescence 87265

Borrelia
Antibody 86618-86619

Borrelia burgdorferi ab
See Antibody, Lyme Disease

Borreliosis, Lyme
See Lyme Disease

Borthen Operation
See Iridotasis

Bost Fusion
See Arthrodesis, Wrist

Bosworth Operation
See Acromioclavicular Joint, Dislocation;
Arthrodesis, Vertebrae; Fasciotomy, Elbow

Bottle Type Procedure 55060

Botulinum Toxin
See Chemodenervation

Boutonniere Deformity 26426-26428

Bowel
See Intestine

Bowleg Repair 27455-27457

Boyce Operation
See Nephrotomy

Boyd Hip Disarticulation
See Amputation, Leg, Upper; Radical Resection;
Replantation

Brace
See Cast
for Leg Cast 29358

Brachial Arteries
See Artery, Brachial

Brachial Plexus
Decompression 64713
Injection
    Anesthetic 64415
Neuroplasty 64713
Release 64713
Repair/Suture 64861

Brachiocephalic Artery
See Artery, Brachiocephalic

Brachycephaly 21175

Brachytherapy 77761-77778, 77789
Dose Plan 77326-77328
Remote Afterloading
    1-4 Positions .77781
    5-8 Positions .77782
    9-12 Positions 77783
    Over 12 Positions 77784
    Over 4 Positions 77781-77784
Unlisted Services and Procedures 77799

Bradykinin
Blood or Urine 82286

Brain
See Brainstem; Mesencephalon; Skull Base
Surgery
Abscess
    Drainage 61150-61151
    Excision 61514, 61522
    Incision and Drainage 61320-61321
Anesthesia 00210-00218, 00220-00222
Angiography 70496
Biopsy 61140
    Stereotactic 61750-61751
Catheter
    Irrigation 62194, 62225
    Replacement 62194, 62225
CAT Scan 70450-70470, 70496
Cisternography 70015
Computer Assisted
    Surgery 61795
Cortex
    Magnetic Stimulation 0018T
Craniopharyngioma
    Excision 61545
Cyst
    Drainage 61150-61151
    Excision 61516, 61524
Epileptogenic Focus
    Excision 61534, 61536
Excision
    Choroid Plexus 61544
    Hemisphere 61542-61543
    Other Lobe 61539
    Temporal Lobe 61538

Exploration
    Infratentorial .61305
    Supratentorial 61304
Hematoma
    Drainage 61154
    Incision and Drainage 61312-61315
Implantation
    Electrode 61850-61875
    Pulse Generator 61885-61886
    Receiver 61885-61886
Incision
    Corpus Callosum 61541
    Frontal Lobe .61490
    Mesencephalic Tract 61480
Insertion
    Catheter 61210
    Electrode 61531-61533, 61850-61875
    Pulse Generator 61885-61886
    Receiver 61885-61886
    Reservoir 61210-61215
Lesion
    Aspiration Stereotactic 61750-61751
    Excision 61534, 61536,
              61600-61608, 61615-61616
Magnetic Resonance Imaging
(MRI) 70551-70553
Meningioma
    Excision 61512, 61519
Myelography 70010
Nuclear Medicine
    Blood Flow 78610-78615
    Cerebrospinal Fluid 78630-78650
    Imaging 78600-78607
        Vascular Flow 78610
Positron Emission Tomography 78608-78609
Removal
    Electrode 61535, 61880
    Foreign Body 61570
    Pulse Generator 61888
    Receiver 61888
    Shunt .62256-62258
Repair
    Dura 61618
    Wound 61571
Shunt
    Creation 62180-62192, 62200-62223
    Removal 62256-62258
    Replacement 62194, 62225-62230,
                  62256-62258
    Reprogramming 62252
Skull
    Transcochlear Approach 61596
    Transcondylar Approach 61597
    Transpetrosal Approach 61598
    Transtemporal Approach 61595
Skull Base
    Craniofacial Approach 61580-61585
    Infratemporal Approach 61590-61591
    Orbitocranial Zygomatic Approach 61592
Stereotactic
    Aspiration 61750-61751
    Biopsy 61750-61751
    Create Lesion . . .61720-61735, 61790-61791
    Localization for Placement
    Therapy Fields 61770
    Radiation Treatment 77432
    Radiosurgery 61793

    Surgery 61795
    Trigeminal Tract 61791
Tumor
    Excision 61510, 61518, 61520-61521,
                 61526-61530, 61545
X-Ray
    with Contrast 70010-70015

Brainstem
See Brain
Biopsy 61575-61576
Decompression 61575-61576
Evoked Potentials 92585-92586
Lesion
    Excision 61575-61576

Brain Coverings
See Meninges

Brain Death
Determination 95824

Brain Stem
See Brainstem

Brain Stem Auditory Evoked Potential
See Evoked Potential, Auditory Brainstem

Brain Surface Electrode
Stimulation 95961-95962

Brain Tumor, Acoustic Neuroma
See Brain, Tumor, Excision

Brain Tumor, Craniopharyngioma
See Craniopharyngioma

Brain Tumor, Meningioma
See Meningioma

Brain Ventriculography
See Ventriculography

Branchial Cleft
Cyst
    Excision 42810-42815

Branchioma
See Branchial Cleft, Cyst

Breast
Abscess
    Incision and Drainage 19020
Augmentation 19324-19325
Biopsy 19100-19103
Cyst
    Puncture Aspiration 19000-19001
Excision
    Biopsy 19100-19103
    Capsules 19371
    Chest Wall Tumor 19260-19272
    Cyst 19120
    Lactiferous Duct Fistula 19112
    Lesion 19120-19126
        by Needle Localization 19125-19126
    Mastectomy 19140-19240
    Nipple Exploration 19110
Exploration 19020

Implants
     Insertion 19340-19342
     Preparation of Moulage 19396
     Removal 19328-19330
     Supply 19396
Incision
     Capsules 19370
Injection
     Radiologic 19030
Magnetic Resonance Imaging
(MRI) 76093-76094
Mammoplasty
     Augmentation 19324-19325
     Reduction 19318
Mastopexy 19316
Metallic Localization Clip Placement 19295
Needle Biopsy 19100
Needle Wire Placement 19290-19291
Periprosthetic Capsulectomy 19371
Periprosthetic Capsulotomy 19370
Reconstruction 19357-19369
     Augmentation 19324-19325
     Mammoplasty 19318-19325
     Nipple 19350-19355
       Areola 19350
     Revision 19380
     with Free Flap 19364
     with Latissimus Dorsi Flap 19361
     with Other Techniques 19366
     with Tissue Expander 19357
     with Transverse Rectus Abdominis
     Myocutaneous Flap 19367-19369
Reduction 19318
Removal
     Capsules 19371
     Modified Radical 19240
     Partial 19140-19162
     Radical 19200-19220
     Simple, Complete 19180
     Subcutaneous 19182
Repair
     Suspension 19316
Stereotactic Localization 76095
Ultrasound 76645
Unlisted Services and Procedures 19499
X-Ray 76090-76092
     Localization Nodule 76096
     with Computer-aided Detection 76085

Breathing, Inspiratory Positive-Pressure
See Intermittent Positive Pressure Breathing
(IPPB)

Breath Odor Alcohol
See Alcohol, Breath

Breath Test
Alcohol, Ethyl 82075
Helicobacter Pylori ...78267-78268, 83013-83014
Hydrogen 91065

Bricker Procedure
Intestines Anastomosis 50820

Bristow Procedure
See Capsulorrhaphy, Anterior

Brock Operation
See Valvotomy, Pulmonary Valve

Broken, Nose
See Fracture, Nasal Bone

Bronchi
Aspiration
     Endoscopic 31645-31646
Biopsy
     Endoscopic 31625-31629
Catheterization
     Insertion 31710
     with Bronchial Brush Biopsy 31717
Endoscopy
     Aspiration 31645-31646
     Biopsy 31625-31629
     Destruction
       Tumor 31641
     Dilation 31630-31631
     Excision
       Lesion 31640
     Exploration 31622
     Foreign Body Removal 31635
     Fracture 31630
     Injection 31656
     Lesion 31640-31641
     Stenosis 31641
     Tumor 31640-31641
Exploration
     Endoscopic 31622
Fracture
     Endoscopy 31630
Injection
     X-Ray 31656, 31715
Instillation
     Contrast Material 31708
Needle Biopsy 31629
Reconstruction 31770
     Graft Repair 31770
     Stenosis 31775
Removal
     Foreign Body 31635
Repair
     Fistula 32815
Stenosis
     Endoscopic Treatment 31641
Tumor
     Excision 31640
Unlisted Services and Procedures 31899
X-Ray
     with Contrast 71040-71060

Bronchial Allergen Challenge
See Bronchial Challenge Test

Bronchial Alveolar Lavage 31624

Bronchial Brushings/Protected Brushing 31623

Bronchial Brush Biopsy
with Catheterization 31717

Bronchial Challenge Test
See Allergy Tests
with Antigens, Gases 95070
with Chemicals 95071

Bronchial Provocation Tests
See Bronchial Challenge Test

Bronchioalveolar Lavage
See Lung, Lavage

Broncho-Bronchial Anastomosis 32486

Bronchoalveolar Lavage
See Lung, Lavage

Bronchography 71040-71060
Catheterization 31710
Injection
     Transtracheal 31715
Instillation
     Contrast Material 31708
Segmental
     Injection 31656

Bronchoplasty 32501
See Reconstruction, Bronchi
Excision Stenosis and Anastomosis 31775
Graft Repair 31770

Bronchopneumonia, Hiberno-Vernal
See Q Fever

Bronchopulmonary Lavage
See Lung, Lavage

Bronchoscopy
Alveolar Lavage 31624
Aspiration 31645-31646
Biopsy 31625-31629
Brushing/Protected Brushing 31623
Catheter Placement
     Intracavitary Radioelement 31643
Dilation 31630-31631
Exploration 31622
Fracture 31630
Injection 31656
Needle Biopsy 31629
Removal
     Foreign Body 31635
     Tumor 31640-31641
Stenosis 31641
Stent Placement 31631
X-Ray Contrast 31656

Bronchospasm Evaluation
See Pulmonology, Diagnostic, Spirometry

Bronkodyl
See Theophylline

Brow Pyrosis
Repair 67900

Brucella 86000
Antibody 86622

Bruise
See Hematoma

Brunschwig Operation 58240
See Hip; Pelvis, Exenteration

Brush Biopsy
See Biopsy; Needle Biopsy
Bronchi 31717

Brush Border ab
See Antibody, Heterophile

Bucca
See Cheek

Buccal Mucosa
See Mouth, Mucosa

Bulbourethral Gland
Excision 53250

Bulla
Incision and Drainage
   Puncture Aspiration 10160
Lung
   Excision-Plication 32141
     Endoscopic 32655

BUN
See Blood Urea Nitrogen; Urea Nitrogen

Bunion Repair 28296-28299
Chevron Procedure 28296
Concentric Procedure 28296
Joplin Procedure 28294
Keller Procedure 28292
Lapidus Procedure 28297
Mayo Procedure 28292
McBride Procedure 28292
Mitchell Procedure 28296
Silver Procedure 28290
with Implant 28293

Burgess Amputation
See Disarticulation, Ankle

Burhenne Procedure
See Bile Duct, Removal, Calculi (Stone);
Gallbladder

Burkitt Herpesvirus
See Epstein-Barr Virus

Burns
Allograft 15350-15351
Debridement 01951-01953,
         15000-15001, 16010-16030
Dressings 16010-16030
Escharotomy 16035-16036
Excision 01951-01953, 15000-15001
Initial Treatment 16000
Tissue Culture Skin Grafts 15100-15121,
             15342-15343
Xenograft 15400-15401

Burrow's Operation
See Skin, Adjacent Tissue Transfer

Burr Hole
Anesthesia 00214
Skull
   Biopsy Brain 61140
   Catheterization 61210

Drainage
   Abscess 61150-61151
   Cyst 61150-61151
   Hematoma 61154-61156
Exploration
   Infratentorial 61253
   Supratentorial 61250
for Implant of Neurostimulator
   Array 61862
   Injection, Contrast Media 61120
Insertion
   Catheter 61210
   Reservoir 61210

Bursa
Ankle 27604
Arm, Lower 25031
Elbow
   Excision 24105
   Incision and Drainage 23931
Femur
   Excision 27062
Foot
   Incision and Drainage 28001
Hip
   Incision and Drainage 26991
Injection 20600-20610
Ischial
   Excision 27060
Joint
   Aspiration 20600-20610
   Drainage 20600-20610
   Injection 20600-20610
Knee
   Excision 27340
Leg, Lower 27604
Palm
   Incision and Drainage 26025-26030
Pelvis
   Incision and Drainage 26991
Shoulder
   Drainage 23031
Wrist 25031
   Excision 25115-25116

Bursectomy
See Excision, Bursa

Bursitis, Radiohumeral
See Tennis Elbow

Bursocentesis
See Aspiration, Bursa

Button
Nasal Septal Prosthesis
   Insertion 30220

Butyrylcholine Esterase
See Cholinesterase

Bypass, Cardiopulmonary
See Cardiopulmonary Bypass

Bypass Graft
Axillary Artery 35516-35521, 35533,
        35616-35623, 35650, 35654
Carotid Artery 35501-35509, 35526,
        35601-35606, 35626, 35642
Celiac Artery 35531, 35631

Coronary Artery
   Angiography 93556
   Arterial 33533-33536
   Venous Graft 33510-33516
Excision
   Abdomen 35907
   Extremity 35903
   Neck 35901
   Thorax 35905
Femoral Artery 35521, 35533, 35546,
    35551-35558, 35566, 35621, 35646-35647,
      35651-35661, 35666, 35700
Harvest
   Upper Extremity Vein 35500
Iliac Artery 35541, 35563, 35641, 35663
Iliofemoral Artery ..35548-35549, 35565, 35665
Mesenteric Artery 35531, 35631
Peroneal Artery 35566-35571, 35666-35671
Placement
   Vein Patch 35685
Popliteal Artery 35551-35558, 35571, 35623,
      35651, 35656, 35671, 35700
Renal Artery 35536, 35560, 35631-35636
Reoperation 35700
Repair
   Abdomen 35907
   Extremity 35903
   Lower Extremity
     with Composite Graft 35681-35683
   Neck 35901
   Thorax 35905
Revascularization
   Extremity 35903
   Neck 35901
   Thorax 35905
Revision
   Lower Extremity
     with Angioplasty 35879
     with Vein Interposition 35881
Secondary Repair 35870
Splenic Artery 35536, 35636
Subclavian Artery ..35506-35507, 35511-35516,
    35526, 35606-35616, 35626, 35645
Thrombectomy
   Other than Hemodialysis Graft
   or Fistula 35875-35876
Tibial Artery ..35566-35571, 35623, 35666-35671
Vertebral Artery 35508, 35515, 35642-35645
with Composite Graft 35681

Bypass In-Situ
Femoral Artery 35582-35585
Peroneal Artery 35585-35587
Popliteal Artery 35582-35583, 35587
Tibial Artery 35585-35587

B 12, Vitamin
See Cyanocobalamin

B Antibodies, Hepatitis
See Antibody, Hepatitis B

B Antigens, Hepatitis
See Hepatitis Antigen, B

B Complex Vitamins
B-12 Absorption 78270-78272

C

C-13
Urease Activity 83013-83014
Urea Breath Test 83013-83014

C-14
Urease Activity 83013-83014
Urea Breath Test 78267-78268

C-Peptide 80432, 84681

C-Reactive Protein 86140-86141

C-Section
See Cesarean Delivery

CABG
See Coronary Artery Bypass Graft (CABG)

Cadmium
Urine 82300

Calcaneal Spur
See Heel Spur

Calcaneus
Craterization 28120
Cyst
　　Excision 28100-28103
Diaphysectomy 28120
Excision 28118-28120
Fracture
　　Open Treatment 28415-28420
　　Percutaneous Fixation 28406
　　without Manipulation 28400
　　with Manipulation 28405-28406
Repair
　　Osteotomy 28300
Saucerization 28120
Tumor
　　Excision 27647, 28100-28103
X-Ray 73650

Calcareous Deposits
Subdeltoid
　　Removal 23000

Calcifediol
Blood or Urine 82306

Calcifediol Assay
See Calciferol

Calciferol
Blood or Urine 82307

Calcification
See Calcium, Deposits

Calciol
See Vitamin, D-3

Calcitonin
Blood or Urine 82308
Stimulation Panel 80410

Calcium
Blood
　　Infusion Test 82331
Deposits
　　See Removal, Calculi (Stone); Removal,
　　Foreign Bodies
Ionized 82330
Total 82310
Urine 82340

Calcium-Binding Protein, Vitamin K-Dependent
See Osteocalcin

Calcium-Pentagastrin Stimulation 80410

Calculus
Analysis 82355-82370
Destruction
　　Bile Duct 43265
　　Pancreatic Duct 43265
Removal
　　Bile Duct 43264, 47554, 74327
　　Bladder 51050, 52310-52318, 52352
　　Kidney ..50060-50081, 50130, 50561, 50580,
　　　　　　　　　　　　　　　　52352
　　Pancreatic Duct 43264
　　Ureter ..50610-50630, 50961, 50980, 51060-
　　　　　　　51065, 52320-52325, 52352
　　Urethra 52310-52315, 52352

Calculus of Kidney
See Calculus, Removal, Kidney

Caldwell-Luc Procedure
See Sinus, Maxillary; Sinusotomy; Sternum,
Fracture
Orbital Floor Blowout Fracture 21385
Sinusotomy 31030-31032

Caliper
Application/Removal 20660

Callander Knee Disarticulation
See Disarticulation, Knee

Callosum, Corpus
See Corpus Callosum

Calmette Guerin Bacillus Vaccine
See BCG Vaccine

Caloric Vestibular Test 92533

Calycoplasty 50405

Camey Enterocystoplasty 50825

CAMP
See Cyclic AMP

Campbell Procedure 27422

Campylobacter
Antibody 86625

Campylobacter Pylori
See Helicobacter Pylori

Canal, Ear
See Auditory Canal

Canal, Semicircular
See Semicircular Canal

Canaloplasty 69631, 69635

Candida
Antibody 86628
Skin Test 86485

Cannulation 36821
Arterial 36620-36625
Sinus
　　Maxillary 31000
　　Sphenoid 31002
Thoracic Duct 38794

Cannulation, Renoportal
See Anastomosis, Renoportal

Cannulization
See Catheterization
Arteriovenous 36145, 36810-36815
Declotting 36550, 36860-36861
ECMO 36822
External
　　Declotting 36860-36861
Vas Deferens 55200
Vein to Vein 36800

Canthocystostomy
See Conjunctivorhinostomy

Canthopexy
Lateral 21282
Medial 21280

Canthoplasty 67950

Canthorrhaphy 67880-67882

Canthotomy 67715

Canthus
Reconstruction 67950

Cap, Cervical
See Cervical Cap

Capsule
See Capsulodesis
Elbow
　　Arthrotomy 24006
　　Excision 24006
Foot 28264
Interphalangeal Joint
　　Excision 26525
　　Incision 26525
Knee 27435
Metacarpophalangeal Joint
　　Excision 26520
　　Incision 26520
Metatarsophalangeal Joint
　　Release 28289
Shoulder
　　Incision 23020
Wrist
　　Excision 25320

Capsulectomy
Breast
　　Periprosthetic 19371

Capsulodesis
Metacarpophalangeal Joint 26516-26518

Capsulorrhaphy
Anterior 23450-23462
Multi-Directional Instability 23466
Posterior 23465
Wrist 25320

Capsulotomy
Breast
    Periprosthetic 19370
Foot 28260-28262
Hip
    with Release, Flexor Muscles 27036
Interphalangeal Joint 28272
Knee 27435
Metacarpophalangeal Joint 26520
Metatarsophalangeal Joint 28270
Toe 28270-28272
Wrist 25085

Captopril .80416-80417

Carbamazepine
Assay 80156-80157

Carbazepin
See Carbamazepine

Carbinol
See Methanol

Carbohydrate Deficient
Transferrin 82373

Carbon Dioxide
Blood or Urine 82374

Carbon Monoxide
Blood 82375-82376

Carbon Tetrachloride 84600

Carboxycathepsin
See Angiotensin Converting Enzyme (ACE)

Carboxyhemoglobin 82375-82376

Carbuncle
Incision and Drainage 10060-10061

Carcinoembryonal Antigen
See Antigen, Carcinoembryonic

Carcinoembryonic Antigen 82378

Cardiac
See Coronary

Cardiac Arrhythmia, Tachycardia
See Tachycardia

Cardiac Atria
See Atria

Cardiac Catheterization
Combined Left and Right Heart 93526-93529
Combined Right and Retrograde Left
    Congenital Cardiac Anomalies 93531
Combined Right and Transseptal Left
    Congenital Cardiac Anomalies . .93532-93533
for Biopsy 93505

for Dilution Studies 93561-93562
Imaging 93555-93556
Injection 93539-93545
    See Catheterization, Cardiac
Left Heart .93510-93524
Pacemaker 33210
Right
    Congenital Cardiac Anomalies 93530
Right Heart 93501-93503

Cardiac Electroversion
See Cardioversion

Cardiac Event Recorder
Implantation 33282
Removal 33284

Cardiac Magnetic Resonance
Imaging (CMRI)
Complete Study .75554
Limited Study 75555
Morphology 75553
Velocity Flow Mapping 75556

Cardiac Massage
Thoracotomy 32160

Cardiac Muscle
See Myocardium

Cardiac Neoplasm
See Heart, Tumor

Cardiac Output
Indicator Dilution 93561-93562

Cardiac Pacemaker
See Heart, Pacemaker

Cardiac Rehabilitation 93797-93798

Cardiac Septal Defect
See Septal Defect

Cardiac Transplantation
See Heart, Transplantation

Cardiectomy
Donor 33930, 33940

Cardioassist 92970-92971

Cardiolipin Antibody 86147

Cardiology
See Electrocardiography
Diagnostic
    Atrial Electrogram
      Esophageal Recording 93615-93616
    Cardio-Defibrillator
      Evaluation and Testing 93640-93642,
                       93741-93744
    Echocardiography
      Doppler 93303-93321, 93662
      Intracardiac 93662
      Transesophageal 93318
      Transthoracic 93303-93317, 93350
    Electrocardiogram
      Evaluation 93000, 93010, 93014
      Microvolt T-wave Alternans 93025
      Monitoring 93224-93237
      Patient-Demand 93268-93272

      Rhythm 93040-93042
      Tracing 93005
      Transmission 93012
    Ergonovine Provocation Test 93024
    Implantable Loop Recorder System . . .93727
    Intracardiac Pacing and Mapping 93631
      3-D Mapping 93613
      Follow-up Study 93624
      Stimulation and Pacing 93623
    Intracardiac Pacing and Recording
      Arrhythmia Induction 93618-93620
      Bundle of His 93600
      Comprehensive 93619-93622
      Intra-Atrial 93602, 93610
      Right Ventricle 93603
      Tachycardia Sites 93609
      Ventricular 93612
    Intravascular Ultrasound 92978-92979
    Pacemaker Testing 93642
      Antitachycardia System 93724
      Dual Chamber 93731-93733
      Leads 93641
      Single Chamber 93734-93736
    Perfusion Imaging 78460-78461
      See Nuclear Medicine
    Stress Tests
      Cardiovascular 93015-93018
      Drug Induced 93024
      Multiple Gated Acquisition
      (MUGA) .78473
    Tilt Table Evaluation 93660
Therapeutic
    Cardioassist 92970-92971
    Cardioversion 92960-92961
    Intravascular Ultrasound 92978-92979
    Pacing
      Transcutaneous, Temporary 92953
    Thrombolysis 92975-92977
    Thrombolysis, Coronary 92977
    Valvuloplasty
      Percutaneous 92986-92990

Cardiomyotomy
See Esophagomyotomy

Cardioplasty 43320

Cardiopulmonary Bypass
See Heart; Lung, Transplantation

Cardiopulmonary
Resuscitation 92950

Cardiotomy 33310-33315

Cardiovascular Stress Test
See Exercise Stress Tests

Cardioversion 92960-92961

Care, Custodial
See Nursing Facility Services

Care, Intensive
See Intensive Care

Care, Neonatal Intensive
See Intensive Care, Neonatal

Care, Self
See Self Care

Care Plan Oversight Services
See Physician Services

Carneous Mole
See Abortion

Carnitine 82379

Carotene 82380

Caroticum, Glomus
See Carotid Body

Carotid Artery
Aneurysm Repair
    Vascular Malformation or Carotid-Cavernous
    Fistula 61710
Excision 60605
Ligation 37600-37606
Transection
    with Skull Base Surgery 61609

Carotid Body
Lesion
    Carotid Artery 60605
    Excision 60600

Carpals
Incision and Drainage 25035

Carpal Bone
See Wrist
Arthroplasty
    with Implant 25443
Cyst
    Excision 25130-25136
Dislocation
    Closed Treatment 25690
    Open Treatment 25695
Excision 25210-25215
    Partial 25145
Fracture
    Closed Treatment 25622, 25630
    Open Treatment 25628, 25645
    without Manipulation 25630
    with Manipulation 25624, 25635
Incision and Drainage 26034
Insertion
    Vascular Pedicle 25430
Osteoplasty 25394
Repair 25431-25440
Sequestrectomy 25145
Tumor
    Excision 25130-25136

Carpal Tunnel
Injection
    Therapeutic 20526

Carpal Tunnel Syndrome
Decompression 64721

Carpectomy 25210-25215

Carpometacarpal Joint
Arthrodesis
    Hand 26843-26844
    Thumb 26841-26842
Arthrotomy 26070
Biopsy
    Synovium 26100

Dislocation
    Closed Treatment 26670
        with Manipulation 26675-26676
    Open Treatment 26685-26686
Exploration 26070
Fusion
    Hand 26843-26844
    Thumb 26841-26842
Removal
    Foreign Body 26070
Repair 25447
Synovectomy 26130

Cartilage, Arytenoid
See Arytenoid

Cartilage, Ear
See Ear Cartilage

Cartilage Graft
Ear to Face 21235
Harvesting 20910-20912
Rib to Face 21230

Cartilaginous Exostoses
See Exostosis

Case Management
Services 99361-99373
Team Conferences 99361-99373
Telephone Calls 99361-99373

Cast
See Brace; Splint
Body
    Risser Jacket 29010-29015
Body Cast
    Halo 29000
    Turnbuckle Jacket 29020-29025
    Upper Body and Head 29040
    Upper Body and Legs 29046
    Upper Body and One Leg 29044
    Upper Body Only 29035
Clubfoot 29450
Cylinder 29365
Finger 29086
Hand 29085
Hip 29305-29325
Leg
    Rigid Total Contact 29445
Long Arm 29065
Long Leg 29345-29355, 29365, 29450
Long Leg Brace 29358
Patellar Tendon Bearing (PTB) 29435
Removal 29700-29715
Repair 29720
Short Arm 29075
Short Leg 29405-29435, 29450
Shoulder 29049-29058
Walking 29355, 29425
    Revision 29440
Wedging 29740-29750
Windowing 29730
Wrist 29085

Casting
Unlisted Services and Procedures 29799

Castration
See Orchiectomy

Castration, Female
See Oophorectomy

Cataract
Excision 66830
Incision 66820-66821
    Laser 66821
    Stab Incision 66820
Removal/Extraction
    Extracapsular 66982, 66984
    Intracapsular 66983

Catecholamines 80424, 82382-82384,
                      99567
Blood 82383
Urine 82382

Cathepsin-D 82387

Catheter
See Cannulization; Venipuncture
Aspiration
    Nasotracheal 31720
    Tracheobronchial 31725
Declotting 36550
Exchange
    Arterial 37209, 75900
    Peritoneal 49423
Irrigation 99507
    Bladder 51700
Placement
    Bronchus
        for Intracavitary Radioelement
        Application 31643
Removal
    Peritoneum 49422
    Spinal Cord 62355

Catheterization
Abdomen 49420-49421
Abdominal Artery 36245-36248
Aorta 36160-36215
Arterial
    Cutdown 36625
    Intracatheter/Needle 36100-36140
    Percutaneous 36620
Arteriovenous Shunt 36145
Bile Duct 47530
    Change 47525
    Percutaneous 47510
Bladder 51010, 51045
Brachiocephalic Artery 36215-36218
Brain 61210
    Replacement 62194, 62225
Bronchography 31710
Cardiac
    Combined Left and Right
        Heart 93526-93529
    Combined Right and Retrograde Left
        for Congenital Cardiac Anomalies ...93531
    Combined Right and Transseptal Left
        for Congenital Cardiac
        Anomalies 93532-93533
    Flow Directed 93503
    for Biopsy 93505
    for Dilution Studies 93561-93562
    Imaging 93555-93556
    Injection 93539-93545
    Left Heart 93510-93524

Pacemaker 33210
Right Heart 36013, 93501
   for Congenital Cardiac Anomalies . . .93530
Cerebral Artery .36215
Cystourethroscopy
   Ejaculatory Duct 52010
   Ureteral 52005
Ear, Middle 69405
Eustachian Tube 69405
Fallopian Tube 58345, 74742
Intracardiac
   Ablation 93650-93652
Jejunum
   for Enteral .44015
Kidney
   Drainage 50392
   with Ureter 50393
Legs .36245-36248
Nasotracheal 31720
Newborn
   Umbilical Vein 36510
Pelvic Artery 36245-36248
Placement
   Arterial Coronary Conduit
     without Concomitant Left Heart
      Catheterization 93508
   Coronary Artery
     without Concomitant Left Heart
      Catheterization 93508
   Venous Coronary Bypass Graft
     without Concomitant Left Heart
      Catheterization 93508
Portal Vein 36481
Pulmonary Artery 36013-36015
Radioelement Application 55859
Removal
   Fractured Catheter 75961
Salivary Duct .42660
Skull 61107
Spinal Cord 62350-62351
Thoracic Artery 36215-36218
Tracheobronchi 31725
Transglottic 31700
Umbilical Artery 36660
Umbilical Vein 36510
Ureter
   Endoscopic 50553, 50572, 50953, 50972,
                    52005
   Injection 50394, 50684
   Manometric Studies 50396, 50686
Urethra 53670-53675
Uterus
   Radiology .58340
Vena Cava 36010
Venous
   Central Line 36488-36491
   First Order 36011
   Intracatheter/Needle 36000
   Organ Blood 36500
   Second Order 36012
   Umbilical Vein 36510
Ventricular 61020-61026, 61210-61215

CAT Scan

Bone
   Density Study 76070
Drainage 75989
Follow-up Study 76380

Guidance
   Localization 76355
   Needle Biopsy 76360
   Radiation Therapy 76370
   Tissue Ablation 76362
   Vertebroplasty 76013
Other Planes .76375
without and with Contrast
   Abdomen 74170-74175, 75635
   Arm 73202-73206
   Brain 70470, 70496
   Chest 71275
   Ear 70482
   Face 70488
   Head 70470, 70496
   Leg 73702-73706, 75635
   Maxilla 70488
   Neck 70492, 70498
   Orbit 70482
   Pelvis 72191, 72194
   Sella Turcica 70482
   Spine
     Cervical 72127
     Lumbar 72133
     Thoracic 72130
   Thorax 71270-71275
without Contrast 70450
   Abdomen .74150
   Arm 73200
   Brain 70450
   Ear 70480
   Face 70486
   Head 70450
   Leg 73700
   Maxilla 70486
   Neck 70490
   Orbit 70480
   Pelvis 72192
   Sella Turcica 70480
   Spine
     Cervical 72125
     Lumbar 72131
     Thoracic 72128
   Thorax 71250
with Contrast 70460
   Abdomen .74160
   Arm 73201
   Brain 70460
   Ear 70481
   Face 70487
   Head 70460
   Leg 73701
   Maxilla 70487
   Neck 70491
   Orbit 70481
   Pelvis 72193
   Sella Turcica 70481
   Spine
     Cervical 72126
     Lumbar 72132
     Thoracic 72129
   Thorax 71260

CAT Scan, Radionuclide

See Emission Computerized Tomography

Cauda Equina

See Spinal Cord
Decompression 63005-63011, 63017,
          63047-63057, 63087-63091
Exploration 63005-63011, 63017

Cauterization

Anal Fissure 46940-46942
Cervix 57522
   Cryocautery 57511
   Electro or Thermal 57510
   Laser Ablation 57513
Chemical
   Granulation Tissue 17250
Everted Punctum 68705
Nasopharyngeal Hemorrhage 42970
Nose
   Hemorrhage 30901-30906
Skin Lesion 11055-11057, 17000-17004
Skin Tags 11200-11201
Turbinate Mucosa 30801-30802

Cavernitides, Fibrous

See Peyronie Disease

Cavernosography

Corpora 54230

Cavernosometry

                          .54231

Cavities, Pleural

See Pleural Cavity

Cavus Foot Correction 28309

CBC

See Blood Cell Count; Complete Blood Count
(CBC)

CCL4

See Carbon Tetrachloride

CCU Visit

See Critical Care Services

CD142 Antigens

See Thromboplastin

CD143 Antigens

See Angiotensin Converting Enzyme (ACE)

CD4 86360

CD8 86360

CEA

See Carcinoembryonic Antigen

Cecil Repair

See Urethroplasty

Cecostomy 44300

Celiac Plexus

Destruction .64680
Injection
   Anesthetic 64530
   Neurolytic 64680

Celiac Trunk Artery

See Artery, Celiac

Celioscopy

See Endoscopy, Peritoneum

Celiotomy 49000
Abdomen
   for Staging 49220

Cell, Blood
See Blood Cell

Cell, Islet
See Islet Cell

Cell, Mother
See Stem Cell

Cell-Stimulating Hormone, Interstitial
See Luteinizing Hormone (LH)

Cellobiase
See Beta Glucosidase

Cellular Inclusion
See Inclusion Bodies

Cell Count
Body Fluid 89050-89051

Central Shunt 33764

Central Venous Catheter Placement
Cutdown
   Child/Adult 36491
   Infant 36490
Percutaneous
   Child/Adult 36489
   Infant 36488
Repositioning 36493

Cephalic Version
of Fetus
   External 59412

Cephalocele
See Encephalocele

Cephalogram, Orthodontic
See Orthodontic Cephalogram

Cerclage
Cervix 57700
   Abdominal 59325
   Removal Under Anesthesia 59871
   Vaginal 59320

Cerebellopontine Angle Tumor
See Brain, Tumor, Excision; Brainstem; Mesencephalon; Skull Base Surgery

Cerebral Cortex Decortication
See Decortication

Cerebral Death
See Brain Death

Cerebral Hernia
See Encephalocele

Cerebral Thermography
See Thermogram, Cephalic

Cerebral Ventriculographies
See Ventriculography

Cerebrose
See Galactose

Cerebrospinal Fluid 86325
Nuclear Imaging 78630-78650

Cerebrospinal Fluid Leak 63744
Brain
   Repair 61618-61619, 62100
Nasal/Sinus Endoscopy
   Repair 31290-31291
Spinal Cord
   Repair 63707-63709

Cerebrospinal Fluid Shunt 63740, 63746
Creation 62180-62192, 62200-62223
Irrigation 62194
Removal 62256-62258
Replacement 62194, 62225-62230
Reprogramming 62252

Ceruloplasmin 82390

Cerumen
Removal 69210

Cervical Cap 57170

Cervical Lymphadenectomy 38720-38724

Cervical Mucus Penetration Test 89330

Cervical Plexus
Injection
   Anesthetic 64413

Cervical Pregnancy 59140

Cervical Puncture 61050-61055

Cervical Smears 88141-88155, 88164-88167
See Cytopathology

Cervical Spine
See Vertebra, Cervical

Cervical Sympathectomy
See Sympathectomy, Cervical

Cervicectomy 57530

Cervicography 0003T

Cervicoplasty 15819

Cervicothoracic Ganglia
See Stellate Ganglion

Cervix
See Cytopathology
Amputation
   Total 57530
Biopsy 57500, 57520
Cauterization 57522
   Cryocautery 57511
   Electro or Thermal 57510
   Laser Ablation 57513
Cerclage 57700
   Abdominal 59325
   Removal Under Anesthesia 59871
   Vaginal 59320
Cervicography 0003T

Conization 57520-57522
Curettage
   Endocervical 57454, 57505
Dilation
   Canal 57800
   Stump 57820
Dilation and Curettage 57820
Ectopic Pregnancy 59140
Excision
   Electrode .57460
   Radical 57531
   Stump
      Abdominal Approach 57540-57545
      Vaginal Approach 57550-57556
   Total 57530
Insertion
   Dilation 59200
   Laminaria .59200
   Prostaglandin 59200
   Sensor, Fetal Oximetry 0021T
Repair
   Cerclage .57700
      Abdominal 59325
      Suture 57720
      Vaginal 59320
Unlisted Services and Procedures 58999

Cesarean Delivery
Antepartum Care 59610, 59618
Delivery
   after Attempted Vaginal Delivery 59618
      Delivery Only 59620
      Postpartum Care 59622
      Routine Care 59610, 59618
Delivery Only 59514
Postpartum Care 59515
Routine Care 59510
Tubal Ligation at Time of 58611
with Hysterectomy 59525

CGMP
See Cyclic GMP

Chalazion
Excision 67805
   Multiple
      Different Lids 67805
      Same Lid 67801
   Single 67800
   Under Anesthesia 67808

Challenge Tests
Bronchial Ingestion 95070-95075

Chambers Procedure 28300

Change
Catheter
   Bile Duct .75984
Fetal Position
   by Manipulation 59412
Tube or Stent
   Endoscopic
      Bile or Pancreatic Duct 43269

Change, Gastrostomy Tube
See Gastrostomy Tube, Change of

Change of, Dressing
See Dressings, Change

Cheek

Bone
 Fracture
  Closed Treatment with
   Manipulation 21355
  Open Treatment 21360-21366
  Reconstruction 21270
Fascia Graft 15840
Muscle Graft 15841-15845
Muscle Transfer 15845

Cheilectomy

Metatarsophalangeal Joint Release 28289

Cheiloplasty

See Lip, Repair

Cheiloschisis

See Cleft Lip

Cheilotomy

See Incision, Lip

Chemical Cauterization

Granulation Tissue 17250

Chemical Exfoliation 17360

Chemical Peel 15788-15793

Chemiluminescent Assay 82397

Chemistry Tests

Clinical
 Unlisted Services and Procedures 84999

Chemocauterization

Corneal Epithelium 65435
 with Chelating Agent 65436

Chemodenervation

Cervical Spinal Muscle 64613
Extraocular Muscle 67345
Extremity Muscle 64614
Facial Muscle 64612
Trunk Muscle 64614

Chemonucleolysis 62292

Chemosurgery

Mohs Technique 17304-17310
Skin Lesion 17004, 17110, 17270, 17280

Chemotaxis Assay 86155

Chemotherapy

Arterial Catheterization 36640
Bladder Instillation 51720
CNS 96450
Extracorporeal Circulation
 Extremity 36823
Home Infusion Procedures 99555
Intra-Arterial 96420-96425
Intralesional 96405-96406
Intramuscular 96400
Intravenous 96408-96414
Peritoneal Cavity 96445
Pleural Cavity 96440
Pump Services
 Implantable 96530
 Portable 96520
Reservoir Filling .96542

Subcutaneous 96400
Supply of Agent .96545
Unlisted Services and Procedures 96549

Chest

See Mediastinum; Thorax
Angiography 71275
Artery
 Ligation 37616
CAT Scan 71250-71275
Exploration
 Blood Vessel 35820
Magnetic Resonance Imaging
(MRI) 71550-71552
Repair
 Blood Vessel 35211-35216
  with Other Graft 35271-35276
  with Vein Graft 35241-35246
Ultrasound 76604
Wound Exploration
 Penetrating .20101
X-Ray 71010-71035
 Complete (four Views)
  with Fluoroscopy 71034
 Insertion Pacemaker 71090
 Partial (Two Views)
  with Fluoroscopy 71023
 Stereo 71015
 with Fluoroscopy 71090

Chest, Funnel

See Pectus Excavatum

Chest Cavity

Bypass Graft 35905
Endoscopy
 Exploration 32601-32606
 Surgical 32650-32665

Chest Wall

See Pulmonology, Therapeutic
Manipulation 94667-94668
Reconstruction 49905
 Trauma 32820
Repair 32905
 Closure 32810
 Fistula 32906
Tumor
 Excision 19260-19272
Unlisted Services and Procedures 32999

Chest Wall Fistula

See Fistula, Chest Wall

Chevron Procedure 28296

Chiari Osteotomy of the Pelvis

See Osteotomy, Pelvis

Chicken Pox Vaccine 90716

Child Procedure

See Excision, Pancreas, Partial

Chin

Repair
 Augmentation 21120
 Osteotomy 21121-21123

Chinidin

See Quinidine

Chiropractic Manipulation

See Manipulation, Chiropractic

Chiropractic Treatment

Spinal
 Extraspinal 98940-98943

Chlamydia

Antibody .86631-86632
Antigen Detection
 Direct Fluorescence 87270
 Enzyme Immunoassay 87320
Culture 87110

Chloramphenicol 82415

Chloride

Blood 82435
Other Source 82438
Spinal Fluid 82438
Urine 82436

Chloride, Methylene

See Dichloromethane

Chlorinated Hydrocarbons 82441

Chlorohydrocarbon

See Chlorinated Hydrocarbons

Chlorpromazine 84022

Choanal Atresia

Repair 30540-30545

Cholangiography

Injection .47500-47505
Intraoperative 74300-74301
Percutaneous 74320
 with Laparoscopy 47560-47561
Postoperative 74305
Repair
 with Bile Duct Exploration 47700
 with Cholecystectomy . .47563, 47605, 47620

Cholangiopancreatography 43260

See Bile Duct; Pancreatic Duct
Repair
 See Bile Duct; Pancreatic Duct
  with Biopsy 43261
  with Surgery 43262-43267, 43269

Cholangiostomy

See Hepaticostomy

Cholangiotomy

See Hepaticostomy

Cholecalciferol

See Vitamin, D-3

Cholecystectomy 47562-47564,

47600-47620
Any Method 47562-47564
 with Cholangiography . .47563, 47605, 47620
 with Exploration Common
 Duct .47564, 47610

Cholecystenterostomy 47570,

47720-47741

Cholecystography 74290-74291

Cholecystotomy 47480, 48001
Percutaneous 47490

Choledochoplasty
See Bile Duct, Repair

Choledochoscopy 47550

Choledochostomy 47420-47425

Choledochotomy 47420-47425

Choledochus, Cyst
See Cyst, Choledochal

Cholera Vaccine
Injectable 90725

Cholesterol
Measurement 83721
Serum 82465
Testing 83718-83719

Cholinesterase
Blood 82480-82482

Choline Esterase I
See Acetylcholinesterase

Choline Esterase II
See Cholinesterase

Cholylglycine
Blood 82240

Chondroitin Sulfate 82485

Chondromalacia Patella
Repair 27418

Chondropathia Patellae
See Chondromalacia Patella

Chondrosteoma
See Exostosis

Chopart Procedure 28800-28805
See Amputation, Foot; Radical Resection;
Replantation

Chordotomies
See Cordotomy

Chorioangioma
See Lesion, Skin

Choriogonadotropin
See Chorionic Gonadotropin

Choriomeningitides, Lymphocytic
See Lymphocytic Choriomeningitis

Chorionic Gonadotropin 80414,
84702-84703
Stimulation 80414-80415

Chorionic Growth Hormone
See Lactogen, Human Placental

Chorionic Tumor
See Hydatidiform Mole

Chorionic Villi
See Biopsy, Chorionic Villus

Chorionic Villus
Biopsy 59015

Choroid
Destruction
Lesion 0016T, 67220-67225

Choroid Plexus
Excision 61544

Christmas Factor 85250, 99564

Chromaffinoma, Medullary
See Pheochromocytoma

Chromatin, Sex
See Barr Bodies

Chromatography
Column/Mass Spectrometry 82541-82544
Gas Liquid or HPLC 82486, 82491-82492
Paper 82487-82488
Thin-Layer 82489

Chromium 82495

Chromogenic Substrate Assay .85130

Chromosome Analysis
See Amniocentesis
Added Study 88280-88289
Amniotic Fluid 88267-88269
Culture 88235
Biopsy Culture
Tissue 88233
Bone Marrow Culture 88237
Chorionic Villus 88267
15-20 Cells 88262
20-25 Cells 88264
45 Cells 88263
5 Cells 88261
Culture 88235
for Breakage Syndromes 88245-88249
Fragile-X 88248
Lymphocyte Culture 88230
Skin Culture
Tissue 88233
Tissue Culture 88239
Unlisted Services and Procedures 88299

Chromotubation 58350
Oviduct 58350

Chronic Erection
See Priapism

Chronic Interstitial Cystitides
See Cystitis, Interstitial

Ciliary Body
Cyst
Destruction
Cryotherapy 66720
Cyclodialysis 66740
Cyclophotocoagulation 66710
Diathermy 66700
Nonexcisional 66770
Lesion
Destruction 66770
Repair 66680

Cimino Type Procedure 36821

Cinefluorographies
See Cineradiography

Cineplasty
Arm, Lower or Upper 24940

Cineradiography
Esophagus 74230
Pharynx 70371, 74230
Speech Evaluation 70371
Swallowing Evaluation 74230
Unlisted Services and Procedures ..76120-76125

Circulation, Extracorporeal
See Extracorporeal Circulation

Circulation Assist
Aortic 33967, 33970
Balloon 33967, 33970
External 33960-33961

Circulatory Assist
See Circulation Assist

Circumcision
Repair 54163
Surgical Excision 54161
Newborn 54160
with Clamp or Other Device 54152
Newborn 54150

Cisternal Puncture 61050-61055

Cisternography 70015
Nuclear 78630

Citrate
Blood or Urine 82507

Clagett Procedure
See Chest Wall, Repair, Closure

Clavicle
Craterization 23180
Cyst
Excision 23140
with Allograft 23146
with Autograft 23145
Diaphysectomy 23180
Dislocation
Acromioclavicular Joint
Closed Treatment 23540-23545
Open Treatment 23550-23552
Sternoclavicular Joint
Closed Treatment 23520-23525
Open Treatment 23530-23532
without Manipulation 23540
Excision 23170
Partial 23120, 23180
Total 23125
Fracture
Closed Treatment
without Manipulation 23500
with Manipulation 23505
Open Treatment 23515
Pinning, Wiring 23490
Prophylactic Treatment 23490
Repair Osteotomy 23480-23485
Saucerization 23180
Sequestrectomy 23170

Tumor
Excision 23140, 23146, 23200
    with Autograft 23145
    Radical Resection 23200
X-Ray 73000

Clavicula
See Clavicle

Claviculectomy
Partial 23120
Total 23125

Claw Finger Repair 26499

Cleft, Branchial
See Branchial Cleft

Cleft Cyst, Branchial
See Branchial Cleft, Cyst

Cleft Foot
Reconstruction 28360

Cleft Hand
Repair 26580

Cleft Lip
Repair 40700-40761
Rhinoplasty 30460-30462

Cleft Palate
Repair 42200-42225
Rhinoplasty 30460-30462

Clinical Act of Insertion
See Insertion

Clinical Chemistry Test
See Chemistry Tests, Clinical

Clinical Pathology
See Pathology, Clinical

Clitoroplasty
Intersex State 56805

Closed [Transurethral] Biopsy of Bladder
See Biopsy, Bladder, Cystourethroscopy

Clostridial Tetanus
See Tetanus

Clostridium Botulinum Toxin
See Chemodenervation

Clostridium Difficile
Antigen Detection
    Enzyme Immunoassay 87324
by Immunoassay
    with Direct Optical Observation 87803

Clostridium Tetani ab
See Antibody, Tetanus

Closure 12001-13160
Anal Fistula 46288
Atrioventricular Valve 33600
Cystostomy 51880
Enterostomy 44625-44626
Lacrimal Fistula 68770

Lacrimal Punctum
    Plug 68761
    Thermocauterization, Ligation or Laser
    Surgery 68760
Rectovaginal Fistula 57300-57308
Semilunar Valve 33602
Septal Defect 33615
Sternotomy 21750
Ventricular Tunnel 33722

Closure, Atrial Septal Defect
See Heart, Repair, Atrial Septum

Closure, Cranial Sutures, Premature
See Craniosynostosis

Closure, Fistula, Vesicouterine
See Fistula, Vesicouterine, Closure

Closure, Meningocele Spinal
See Meningocele Repair

Closure, Vagina
See Vagina, Closure

Closure of Esophagostomy
See Esophagostomy, Closure

Closure of Gastrostomy
See Gastrostomy, Closure

Clot 34401-34490, 35875-35876, 50230
See Thrombectomy; Thromboendarterectomy

Clotting Disorder
See Coagulopathy

Clotting Factor 85210-85293

Clotting Inhibitors 85300-85305,
85307, 99557

Clotting Operation
See Excision, Nail Fold

Clotting Test
Protein C 85303, 85307
Protein S 85306

Clotting Time
See Coagulation Time

Clot Lysis Time 85175

Clot Retraction 85170

Clubfoot Cast 29450
Wedging 29750

CMG
See Cystometrogram

CMRI
See Cardiac Magnetic Resonance Imaging

CMV
See Cytomegalovirus

CNPB
See Continuous Negative Pressure Breathing (CNPB); Pulmonology, Therapeutic

Co-Factor I, Heparin
See Antithrombin III

CO2
See Carbon Dioxide

Coagulation
Unlisted Services and Procedures 85999

Coagulation, Blood
See Blood Clot

Coagulation, Light
See Photocoagulation

Coagulation Defect
See Coagulopathy

Coagulation Factor
See Clotting Factor

Coagulation Factor I
See Fibrinogen

Coagulation Factor II
See Prothrombin

Coagulation Factor III
See Thromboplastin

Coagulation Factor IV
See Calcium

Coagulation Factor IX
See Christmas Factor

Coagulation Factor VII
See Proconvertin

Coagulation Factor VIII
See Clotting Factor

Coagulation Factor X
See Stuart-Prower Factor

Coagulation Factor Xa
See Thrombokinase

Coagulation Factor XI
See Plasma Thromboplastin, Antecedent

Coagulation Factor XII
See Hageman Factor

Coagulation Factor XIII
See Fibrin Stabilizing Factor

Coagulation Time 85345-85348

Coagulin
See Thromboplastin

Coagulopathy 85390
Assay 85130

Cocaine
Blood or Urine 82520
Screen 82486

Coccidioides
Antibody 86635

Coccidioidin Test
See Streptokinase, Antibody

Coccidioidomycosis
Skin Test 86490

Coccygeal Spine Fracture
See Coccyx, Fracture

Coccygectomy 15920-15922, 27080

Coccyx
Excision 27080
Fracture
    Closed Treatment 27200
    Open Treatment 27202
Tumor
    Excision 49215
X-Ray 72220

Cochlear Device
Insertion 69930

Codeine
Alkaloid Screening 82101

Codeine Screen 82486

Cofactor Protein S
See Protein S

Coffey Operation
See Uterus, Repair, Suspension

Cognitive Function Tests 96115
See Neurology, Diagnostic

Cognitive Skills
Development 97532
See Physical Medicine/Therapy/Occupational
Therapy

Cold Agglutinin 86156-86157

Cold Pack Treatment 97010

Cold Preservation
See Cryopreservation

Cold Therapies
See Cryotherapy

Colectomy
Partial 44140
    with Anastomosis 44140
      Laparoscopic 44204
    with Coloproctostomy 44145-44146
    with Colostomy 44141-44144
    with Ileocolostomy
      Laparoscopic 44205
    with Ileostomy 44144
    with Ileum Removal 44160
    with Transcanal Approach 44147
Total
    with Anastomosis 44152
    with Complete Proctectomy 45121
    with Ileal Reservoir 44153
    with Ileostomy 44150-44151
    with Proctectomy 44155-44156

Collagen Cross Links 82523

Collagen Injection 11950-11954

Collar Bone
See Clavicle

Collateral Ligament
Ankle
    Repair 27695-27698
Interphalangeal Joint 26545
Knee Joint
    Repair 27409
Knee Repair 27405
Metacarpophalangeal Joint 26540-26542
Repair
    Ankle 27695-27698

Collection and Processing
Autologous Blood
    Harvesting of Stem Cells 38231
    Intraoperative 86891
    Preoperative 86890
Specimen
    Venous Blood 36415, 36540
Washings
    Esophagus 91000
    Stomach 91055

Colles Fracture 25600-25620

Colles Fracture Reversed
See Smith Fracture

Collins Syndrome, Treacher
See Treacher-Collins Syndrome

Collis Procedure
See Gastroplasty with Esophagogastric
Fundoplasty

Colon
See Colon-Sigmoid
Biopsy 44025, 44100, 44322
    Endoscopic 44389, 45380
Colostomy
    Revision 44340-44346
Colotomy 44322
    Colostomy 44320
Destruction
    Lesion 44393, 45383
    Tumor 44393, 45383
Endoscopy
    Biopsy 44389, 45380
    Destruction
      Lesion 44393
      Tumor 44393, 45383
    Exploration 44388, 45378
    Hemorrhage 44391, 45382
    Placement
      Stent 45387
    Removal
      Foreign Body 44390, 45379
      Polyp 44392, 45384-45385
      Tumor 45384-45385
    Specimen Collection 45380
    via Colotomy 45355
    via Stoma 44388-44397
Excision
    Partial 44140-44147, 44160
      Laparoscopic 44204-44205
    Total 44150-44156
Exploration 44025
    Endoscopy 44388, 45378
Hemorrhage
    Endoscopic Control 44391, 45382
Hernia 44050

Incision
    Creation
      Stoma 44320-44322
    Exploration 44025
    Revision
      Stoma 44340-44346
Lesion
    Destruction 45383
    Excision 44110-44111
Lysis
    Adhesions 44005
Obstruction 44025-44050
Reconstruction
    Bladder from 50810
Removal
    Foreign Body 44025, 44390, 45379
    Polyp 44392
Repair
    Diverticula 44605
    Fistula 44650-44661
    Hernia 44050
    Malrotation 44055
    Obstruction 44050
    Ulcer 44605
    Volvulus 44050
    Wound 44605
Stoma Closure 44620-44625
Suture
    Diverticula 44605
    Fistula 44650-44661
    Plication 44680
    Stoma 44620-44625
    Ulcer 44605
    Wound 44605
Tumor
    Destruction 45383
Unlisted Services and Procedures 44799
X-Ray with Contrast
    Barium Enema 74270-74280

Colon-Sigmoid
See Colon
Biopsy
    Endoscopy 45331
Endoscopy
    Ablation
      Polyp 45339
      Tumor 45339
    Biopsy 45331
    Exploration 45330
    Hemorrhage 45334
    Needle Biopsy 45342
    Placement
      Stent 45327, 45345
    Removal
      Foreign Body 45332
      Polyp 45333, 45338
      Tumor 45333, 45338
    Ultrasound 45341-45342
    Volvulus 45337
Exploration
    Endoscopy 45330
Hemorrhage
    Endoscopy 45334
Needle Biopsy
    Endoscopy 45342
Removal
    Foreign Body 45332

Repair
  Volvulus
    Endoscopy 45337
Ultrasound
  Endoscopy 45341-45342

Colonna Procedure
See Acetabulum, Reconstruction

Colonoscopy
Biopsy 45380
Collection Specimen 45380
    via Colotomy 45355
Destruction
    Lesion 45383
    Tumor 45383
Hemorrhage Control 45382
Placement
    Stent 45387
Removal
    Foreign Body 45379
    Polyp 45384-45385
    Tumor 45384-45385
via Stoma 44388-44390
    Biopsy 44389
    Destruction
        of Lesion 44393
        of Tumor 44393
    Exploration 44388
    Hemorrhage 44391
    Placement
        Stent 44397
    Removal
        Foreign Body 44390
        Polyp 44392, 44394
        Tumor 44392, 44394

Colorrhaphy 44604

Color Vision Examination 92283

Colostomy 44320, 45563
Abdominal
    Establishment 50810
Home Visit 99505
Intestine, Large
    with Suture 44605
Perineal
    Establishment 50810
Revision 44340
    Paracolostomy Hernia 44345-44346

Colotomy 44025

Colpectomy
Partial 57106
Total 57110
with Hysterectomy 58275-58280
    with Repair of Enterocele 58280

Colpo-Urethrocystopexy 58152,
                                    58267
Marshall-Marchetti-Krantz Procedure 58152,
                                    58267
Pereyra Procedure 58267

Colpoceliocentesis
See Colpocentesis

Colpocentesis 57020

Colpocleisis 57120

Colpocleisis Complete
See Vagina, Closure

Colpohysterectomies
See Excision, Uterus, Vaginal

Colpoperineorrhaphy 57210

Colpopexy 57280

Colpoplasty
See Repair, Vagina

Colporrhaphy
Anterior 57240, 57289
Anteroposterior 57260-57265
    with Enterocele Repair 57265
Nonobstetrical 57200
Posterior 57250

Colposcopy
Biopsy 57454
Exploration 57452
Loop Electrode Excision 57460
Perineum 99170

Colpotomy
Drainage
    Abscess 57010
    Exploration 57000

Colprosterone
See Progesterone

Columna Vertebralis
See Spine

Column Chromatography/Mass
Spectrometry 82541-82544

Combined Heart-Lung
Transplantation
See Transplantation, Heart-Lung

Combined Right and Left Heart
Cardiac Catheterization
See Cardiac Catheterization, Combined Left and Right Heart

Comedones
Removal 10040

Commissurotomy
Right Ventricle 33476-33478

Common Sensory Nerve
Repair/Suture 64834

Common Truncus
See Truncus Arteriosus

Community/Work Reintegration
Training 97537
    See Physical Medicine/Therapy/Occupational
    Therapy

Compatibility Test
Blood 86920

Complement
Antigen 86160
Fixation Test 86171

Functional Activity 86161
Hemolytic
    Total 86162
Total 86162

Complete Blood Count
(CBC) 85022-85025
See Blood Cell Count
Manual 85031

Complete Colectomy
See Colectomy, Total

Complete Pneumonectomy
See Pneumonectomy, Completion

Complete Transposition of Great
Vessels
See Transposition, Great Arteries

Complex, Factor IX
See Christmas Factor

Complex, Vitamin B
See B Complex Vitamins

Component Removal, Blood
See Apheresis

Composite Graft 15760-15770,
                                35681-35683

Compound B
See Corticosterone

Compound F
See Cortisol

Compression, Nerve, Median
See Carpal Tunnel Syndrome

Computed Axial Tomography (CAT)
See CAT Scan; Specific Anatomic Site

Computed Tomographic
Scintigraphy
See Emission Computerized Tomography

Computer-aided Detection
Mammography
    Screening 76085

Computerized Emission
Tomography
See Emission Computerized Tomography

Computer Data Analysis 99090

Concentration, Hydrogen-Ion
See pH

Concentration, Minimum Inhibitory
See Minimum Inhibitory Concentration

Concentration of Specimen 87015

Concentric Procedure 28296

Conchae Nasale
See Nasal Turbinate

Concha Bullosa Resection
with Nasal/Sinus Endoscopy 31240

Conduction, Nerve
See Nerve Conduction

Conduit, Ileal
See Ileal Conduit

Condyle
Humerus
    Fracture
        Closed Treatment 24576-24577
        Open Treatment 24579
        Percutaneous 24582
Metatarsal
    Excision 28288
Phalanges
    Toe
        Excision .28126

Condyle, Mandibular
See Mandibular Condyle

Condylectomy
Temporomandibular Joint 21050
with Skull Base Surgery 61596-61597

Condyloma
Destruction .54050-54065

Conference
Medical
    with Interdisciplinary Team 99361-99373

Confirmation
Drug 80102

Confirmatory Consultations
See Consultations
New or Established Patient 99271-99275

Congenital Arteriovenous Malformation
See Arteriovenous Malformation

Congenital Elevation of Scapula
See Sprengel's Deformity

Congenital Heart Septum Defect
See Septal Defect

Congenital Kidney Abnormality
Nephrolithotomy .50070
Pyeloplasty 50405
Pyelotomy 50135

Congenital Laryngocele
See Laryngocele

Congenital Vascular Anomaly
See Vascular Malformation

Conisation
See Cervix, Conization

Conization
Cervix 57520-57522

Conjoint Psychotherapy 90847
See Psychiatric Treatment, Family

Conjunctiva
Biopsy 68100
Cyst
    Incision and Drainage 68020
Fistulize for Drainage
    without Tube 68745
    with Tube 68750
Insertion Stent 68750
Lesion
    Destruction 68135
    Excision 68110-68130
        Over 1 cm 68115
        with Adjacent Sclera 68130
Reconstruction 68320-68335
    Symblepharon
        with Graft 68335
    with Flap
        Bridge or Partial 68360
        Total 68362
Repair
    Symblepharon
        Division 68340
        without Graft 68330
        with Graft 68335
    Wound
        Direct Closure 65270
        Mobilization and Rearrangement . . .65272-65273
Unlisted Services and Procedures 68399

Conjunctivo-Tarso-Muller Resection 67908

Conjunctivocystorhinostomy
See Conjunctivorhinostomy

Conjunctivodacryocystostomy
See Conjunctivorhinostomy

Conjunctivoplasty 68320-68330
Reconstruction Cul de Sac
    with Extensive Rearrangement 68326
    with Graft 68326
        Buccal Mucous Membrane 68328
with Extensive Rearrangement 68320
with Graft 68320
    Buccal Mucous Membrane 68325

Conjunctivorhinostomy
without Tube .68745
with Tube 68750

Conscious Sedation
See Sedation

Construction
Finger
    Toe to Hand Transfer 26551-26556
Neobladder 51596
Vagina
    without Graft 57291
    with Graft 57292

Consultation
See Second Opinion; Third Opinion
Clinical Pathology 80500-80502
Confirmatory 99271-99275
    New or Established Patient 99271-99275
Follow-up Inpatient
    Established Patient 99261-99263
Initial Inpatient 99251-99255
    New or Established Patient 99251-99255
Office and/or Other Outpatient 99241-99245
    New or Established Patient . . .99241-99245
Psychiatric, with Family 90887
Radiation Therapy
    Radiation Physics 77336-77370
Surgical Pathology 88321-88325
    Intraoperation 88329-88332
X-Ray 76140

Consumption Test, Antiglobulin
See Coombs Test

Contact Lens Services
Fittings and Prescription 92070, 92310-92313
Modification 92325
Prescription 92314-92317
Replacement 92326
Supply 92391, 92396

Continuous Negative Pressure Breathing (CNPB) 94662

Continuous Positive Airway Pressure (CPAP) 94660
See Pulmonology, Therapeutic

Contouring
Silicone Injections 11950-11954
Tumor
    Facial Bone 21029

Contraception
Cervical Cap
    Fitting 57170
Diaphragm
    Fitting 57170
Intrauterine Device (IUD)
    See Insertion, Intrauterine Device (IUD);
    Intrauterine Device (IUD); Removal,
    Intrauterine Device (IUD)
    Insertion 58300
    Removal 58301

Contraceptive Capsules, Implantable
Insertion 11975
Removal 11976
    with Reinsertion 11977

Contraceptive Device, Intrauterine
See Intrauterine Device (IUD)

Contracture
Elbow
    Release
        with Radical Resection of Capsule . .24149
Palm
    Release 26121-26125
Thumb
    Release 26508

Contracture of Palmar Fascia
See Dupuytren's Contracture

Contralateral Ligament
Repair
    Knee 27405

Contrast Aortogram
See Aortography

Contrast Bath Therapy 97034
See Physical Medicine/Therapy/Occupational Therapy

Contrast Material
Injection
    via Peritoneal Catheter 49424
Instillation
    Bronchography 31708
    Laryngography 31708

Contrast Phlebogram
See Venography

Contusion
See Hematoma

Converting Enzyme, Angiotensin
See Angiotensin Converting Enzyme (ACE)

Coombs Test 86880

Copper 82525

Coprobilinogen
Feces 84577

Coproporphyrin 84120

Coracoacromial Ligament Release 23415

Coracoid Process Transfer 23462

Cord, Spermatic
See Spermatic Cord

Cord, Spinal
See Spinal Cord

Cord, Vocal
See Vocal Cords

Cordectomy 31300

Cordocenteses
See Cordocentesis

Cordocentesis 59012

Cordotomy 63194-63199

Corectomy
See Excision, Iris

Coreoplasty 66762

Cornea
Biopsy 65410
Curettage 65435-65436
    with Chelating Agent 65436
Epithelium
    Excision 65435-65436
        with Chelating Agent 65436
Lesion
    Destruction 65450
    Excision 65400
        without Graft 65420
        with Graft 65426
Prosthesis 65770

Pterygium
    Excision 65420
Puncture 65600
Relaxing Incisions 65772-65775
Repair
    Astigmatism 65772-65775
    Wedge Resection 65775
    with Glue 65286
    Wound
        Nonperforating 65275
        Perforating 65280-65285
        Tissue Glue 65286
Reshape
    Epikeratoplasty 65765
    Keratomileusis 65760
    Keratoprosthesis 65767
Scraping
    Smear 65430
Tattoo 65600
Transplantation
    Autograft or Homograft
        Lamellar 65710
        Penetrating 65730-65755
    for Aphakia 65750

Coronary
Atherectomy
    Percutaneous 92995-92996
Thrombectomy
    Percutaneous 92973

Coronary Angioplasty, Transluminal Balloon
See Percutaneous Transluminal Angioplasty

Coronary Artery
Insertion
    Stent 92980-92981
Ligation 33502
Placement
    Radiation Delivery Device 92974
Repair 33500-33506

Coronary Artery Bypass Graft (CABG) 33503-33505, 33510-33516
Arterial 33533-33536
Arterial-Venous 33517-33523
Harvest
    Upper Extremity Artery 35600
Reoperation 33530
Venous 33510-33516

Coronary Endarterectomy 33572

Coroner's Exam 88045

Coronoidectomy
Temporomandibular Joint 21070

Corpora Cavernosa
Corpus Spongiosum Shunt 54430
Glans Penis Fistulization 54435
Injection 54235
Irrigation
    Priapism 54220
Saphenous Vein Shunt 54420
X-Ray with Contrast 74445

Corpora Cavernosa, Plastic Induration
See Peyronie Disease

Corpora Cavernosography 74445

Corpus Callosum
Transection 61541

Corpus Vertebrae (Vertebrale)
See Vertebral Body

Correction of Cleft Palate
See Cleft Palate, Repair

Correction of Lid Retraction
See Repair, Eyelid, Retraction

Correction of Malrotation of Duodenum
See Ladd Procedure

Correction of Syndactyly
See Syndactyly, Repair

Correction of Ureteropelvic Junction
See Pyeloplasty

Cortex Decortication, Cerebral
See Decortication

Cortical Mapping
Transection
    by Electric Stimulation 95961-95962

Corticoids
See Corticosteroids

Corticoliberin
See Corticotropic Releasing Hormone (CRH)

Corticosteroids
Blood 83491
Urine 83491

Corticosteroid Binding Globulin
See Transcortin

Corticosteroid Binding Protein
See Transcortin

Corticosterone
Blood or Urine 82528

Corticotropic Releasing Hormone (CRH) 80412

Cortisol 80400-80406, 80418-80420,
                      80436, 82530
Stimulation 80412
Total 82533

Cortisol Binding Globulin 84449

Costectomy
See Resection, Ribs

Costen Syndrome
See Temporomandibular Joint (TMJ)

Costotransversectomy 21610

Cothromboplastin
See Proconvertin

Cotte Operation 58400-58410
See Repair, Uterus, Suspension; Revision

Cotton Procedure
Bohler Procedure 28405

Counseling
See Preventive Medicine

**Counseling and/or Risk Factor
Reduction Intervention - Preventive
Medicine, Individual Counseling**
See Preventive Medicine, Counseling and/or Risk
Factor Reduction Intervention, Individual
Counseling

Count, Blood Cell
See Blood Cell Count

Count, Blood Platelet
See Blood, Platelet, Count

Count, Cell
See Cell Count

Count, Complete Blood
See Complete Blood Count (CBC)

Count, Erythrocyte
See Red Blood Cell (RBC), Count

Count, Leukocyte
See White Blood Cell, Count

Count, Reticulocyte
See Reticulocyte, Count

**Counterimmuno-
electrophoresis** 86185

Counters, Cell
See Cell Count

Countershock, Electric
See Cardioversion

Coventry Tibial Wedge Osteotomy
See Osteotomy, Tibia

Cowper's Gland
Excision 53250

Coxa
See Hip

Coxiella Burnetii
Antibody 86638

Coxsackie
Antibody 86658

CPAP
See Continuous Positive Airway Pressure

CPK
Blood 82550-82552

**CPR (Cardiopulmonary
Resuscitation)** 92950

Cranial Bone
Halo
   Thin Skull Osteology 20664
Reconstruction
   Extracranial 21181-21184
Tumor
   Excision 61563-61564

Cranial Halo .20661

Cranial Nerve
See Specific Nerve
Avulsion 64732-64760, 64771
Decompression 61458, 64716
Implantation
   Electrode 64553, 64573
Incision 64732-64752, 64760, 65771
Injection
   Anesthetic 64400-64408, 64412
   Neurolytic 64600-64610
Insertion
   Electrode 64553, 64573
Neuroplasty .64716
Release 64716
Repair
   Suture, with or without Graft . . .64864-64865
Section 61460
Transection 64732-64760, 64771
Transposition 64716

Cranial Nerve II
See Optic Nerve

Cranial Nerve V
See Trigeminal Nerve

Cranial Nerve VII
See Facial Nerve

Cranial Nerve X
See Vagus Nerve

Cranial Nerve XI
See Accessory Nerve

Cranial Nerve XII
See Hypoglossal Nerve

Cranial Tongs
Application/Removal 20660
Removal 20665

Craniectomy 61501
See Craniotomy
Decompression 61343
Exploratory 61304-61305
Extensive, for Multiple Suture
Craniosynostosis 61558-61559
for Electrode 61860-61875
Release Stenosis 61550-61552
Surgical 61312-61321,
                  61440-61480, 61500-61522

Craniofacial Procedures
Unlisted Services and Procedures 21299

Craniofacial Separation
Closed Treatment 21431
Open Treatment 21432-21436
Wire Fixation 21431

Craniomegalic Skull
Reduction 62115-62117

Craniopharyngioma
Excision 61545

Cranioplasty 62120
Encephalocele Repair 62120
for Defect 62140-62141, 62145
with Autograft 62146-62147
with Bone Graft 62146-62147

Craniostenosis
See Craniosynostosis

Craniosynostosis
Bifrontal Craniotomy 61557
Extensive Craniectomy 61558-61559

Craniotomy
See Burr Hole; Craniectomy; Drill Hole; Puncture
Bifrontal 61557
Exploratory 61304-61305
for Craniosynostosis 61556-61557
for Encephalocele 62121
for Implant of Neurostimulators 61850-61875
Frontal 61556
Parietal 61556
Surgery 61312-61321, 61440, 61490, 61546,
         61570-61571, 61582-61583, 61590, 61592,
                                  61760, 62120
with Bone Flap 61510-61516, 61526-61530,
                              61533-61545

Cranium
See Skull

Craterization
Calcaneus 28120
Clavicle 23180
Femur 27070-27071, 27360
Fibula 27360, 27641
Hip 27070
Humerus 23184, 24140
Ileum 27070
Metacarpal 26230
Metatarsal 28122
Olecranon Process 24147
Phalanges
   Finger 26235-26236
   Toe 28124
Pubis 27070
Radius 24145, 25151
Scapula 23182
Talus 28120
Tarsal 28122
Tibia 27360, 27640
Ulna 24147, 25150

Creatine 82553-82554
Blood or Urine 82540

Creatine Kinase
Total 82550

Creatine Phosphokinase
Blood 82552
Total 82550

Creatinine
Blood 82565
Clearance 82575
Other Source .82570
Urine .82570-82575

Creation

Arteriovenous
    Fistula/Autogenous Graft 36825
Colonic Reservoir 45119
Complete Heart Block 93650
Defect 40720
Ileal Reservoir 44153, 45113
Lesion 61790, 63600
Mucofistula 44144
Pericardial Window 32659
Recipient Site 15000
Shunt
    Cerebrospinal Fluid 62200
    Subarachnoid
        Lumbar-Peritoneal 63740
    Subarachnoid-Subdural 62190
    Ventriculo 62220
Sigmoid Bladder 50810
Speech Prosthesis 31611
Stoma
    Bladder 51980
    Kidney 50395
    Renal Pelvis 50395
    Tympanic Membrane 69433-69436
    Ureter 50860
Ventral Hernia 39503

CRF
See Corticotropic Releasing Hormone (CRH)

CRH
See Corticotropic Releasing Hormone (CRH)

Cricoid Cartilage Split
Larynx 31587

Cricothyroid Membrane
Incision 31605

Cristobalite
See Silica

Critical Care Services 99289-99292
See Emergency Department Services; Prolonged Attendance
Evaluation and Management 99291-99292
Gastric Intubation 91105
Interfacility Transport 99289-99290
Ipecac Administration for Poison 99175
Neonatal
    Initial 99295
    Intensive Care 99295-99297
    Subsequent 99296-99297

Crossmatch 86920-86922

Crossmatching, Tissue
See Tissue Typing

Cross Finger Flap 15574

Cruciate Ligament
Arthroscopic Repair 29888-29889
Repair 27407-27409
Knee
    with Collateral Ligament 27409

Cryoablation
See Cryosurgery

Cryofibrinogen 82585

Cryofixation
See Cryopreservation

Cryoglobulin 82595

Cryopreservation
Cells 88240-88241
Embryo 89258
Freezing and Storage 88240
Sperm 89259

Cryosurgery 17000-17286, 47371, 47381
See Destruction
Labyrinthotomy 69801
Lesion
    Mouth 40820
    Penis 54056, 54065
    Vagina 57061-57065
    Vulva 56501-56515

Cryotherapy
Acne 17340
Destruction
    Ciliary Body 66720
Lesion
    Cornea 65450
    Retina 67208, 67227
Retinal Detachment
    Prophylaxis 67141
    Repair 67101
Trichiasis
    Correction 67825

Cryptectomy 46210-46211

Cryptococcus
Antibody 86641
Antigen Detection
    Enzyme Immunoassay 87327

Cryptococcus Neoformans
Antigen Detection
    Enzyme Immunoassay 87327

Cryptorchism
See Testis, Undescended

Cryptosporidium
Antigen Detection
    Direct Fluorescence 87272
    Enzyme Immunoassay 87328

Crystal Identification
Any Body Fluid 89060

CSF
See Cerebrospinal Fluid Leak

CT Scan
See CAT Scan

Cuff, Rotator
See Rotator Cuff

Culdocentesis
See Colpocentesis

Culture
Acid Fast Bacilli 87116
Amniotic Fluid
    Chromosome Analysis 88235

Bacteria
    Additional Methods 87077
    Anaerobic 87073-87076
    Blood 87040
    Feces 87045-87046
    Other 87070-87073
    Screening 87081
    Urine 87086-87088
Bone Marrow
    Chromosome Analysis 88237
Chlamydia 87110
Chorionic Villus
    Chromosome Analysis 88235
Fertilized Oocyte
    for In Vitro Fertilization
        Co-Culture of Embryo 89251
Fertilized Oocytes
    for In Vitro Fertilization 89250
Fungus
    Blood 87103
    Identification 87106
    Other 87102
    Skin 87101
Lymphocyte
    Chromosome Analysis 88230
Mold 87107
Mycobacteria 87116-87118
Mycoplasma 87109
Oocyte
    Co-Culture of Embryo 89250-89251
Pathogen
    by Kit 87084
Skin
    Chromosome Analysis 88233
Tissue
    Toxin/Antitoxin 87230
    Virus 87252-87253
Tubercle Bacilli 87116
Typing 87140-87158
Unlisted Services and Procedures 87999
Yeast 87106

Curettage
See Dilation and Curettage
Cervix
    Endocervical 57454, 57505
Cornea 65435-65436
    Chelating Agent 65436
Hydatidiform Mole 59870
Postpartum 59160

Curettage, Uterus
See Uterus, Curettage

Curettage and Dilatation
See Dilation and Curettage

Curettement
Skin Lesion 11055-11057, 17004, 17110,
                       17270, 17280

Curietherapy
See Brachytherapy

Custodial Care
See Domiciliary Services; Nursing Facility Services

Cutaneolipectomy
See Lipectomy

Cutaneous-Vesicostomy
See Vesicostomy, Cutaneous

Cutaneous Electrostimulation, Analgesic
See Application, Neurostimulation

Cutaneous Tag
See Skin, Tags

Cutaneous Tissue
See Integumentary System

CVS
See Biopsy, Chorionic Villus

Cyanacobalamin
See Cyanocobalamin

Cyanide
Blood 82600
Tissue 82600

Cyanocobalamin 82607-82608

Cyclic AMP 82030

Cyclic GMP 83008

Cyclic Somatostatin
See Somatostatin

Cyclocryotherapy
See Cryotherapy, Destruction, Ciliary Body

Cyclodialysis
Destruction
    Ciliary Body 66740

Cyclophotocoagulation
Destruction
    Ciliary Body 66710

Cyclosporine
Assay 80158

Cyst
Abdomen
    Destruction/Excision 49200-49201
Ankle
    Capsule 27630
    Tendon Sheath 27630
Bartholin's Gland Excision 56740
    See Bartholin's Gland, Cyst
    Repair 56440
Bile Duct 47715-47716
Bladder
    Excision 51500
Bone
    Drainage 20615
    Injection 20615
Brain
    Drainage 61150-61151, 61156
    Excision 61516, 61524
Branchial Cleft
    Excision 42810-42815
Breast
    Incision and Drainage 19020
    Puncture Aspiration 19000-19001

Calcaneus 28100-28103
Carpal 25130-25136
Choledochal 47715-47716
Ciliary Body
    Destruction 66770
Clavicle
    Excision 23140-23146
Conjunctiva 68020
Dermoid
    Nose
        Excision 30124-30125
Drainage
    Contrast Injection 49424
        with X-Ray 76080
Excision
    Clavicle 23140
        with Allograft 23146
        with Autograft 23145
    Femur 27355-27358
    Ganglion
        See Ganglion
    Humerus
        with Allograft 23156
        with Autograft 23155
    Hydatid
        See Echinococcosis
    Lymphatic
        See Lymphocele
    Mediastinum 32662
    Olecranon Process
        with Allograft 24126
        with Autograft 24125
    Pericardial 32661
    Pilonidal 11770-11772
    Radius
        with Allograft 24126
        with Autograft 24125
    Scapula 23140
        with Allograft 23146
        with Autograft 23145
    Ulna
        with Allograft 24126
        with Autograft 24125
Facial Bones
    Excision 21030
Femur 27065-27067
Fibula 27635-27638
Gums
    Incision and Drainage 41800
Hip 27065-27067
Humerus
    Excision 23150-23156, 24110
        with Allograft 24116
        with Autograft 24115
Ileum 27065-27067
Incision and Drainage 10060-10061
    Pilonidal 10080-10081
Iris
    Destruction 66770
Kidney
    Ablation 50541
    Aspiration 50390
    Excision 50280-50290
    Injection 50390
    X-Ray 74470

Knee
    Baker's 27345
    Excision 27347
Leg, Lower
    Capsule 27630
    Tendon Sheath 27630
Liver 47010
    Drainage 47010
        Open 47010
    Repair 47300
Lung
    Incision and Drainage 32200
    Removal 32140
Lymph Node
    Axillary/Cervical
        Excision 38550-38555
Mandible
    Excision 21040-21041
Mediastinal
    Excision 39200
Metacarpal 26200-26205
Metatarsal 28104-28107
Mouth 41005-41009, 41015-41018
    Incision and Drainage 40800-40801
Mullerian Duct
    Excision 55680
Nose
    Excision 30124-30125
Olecranon 24120
Ovarian
    Excision 58925
    Incision and Drainage 58800-58805
Pancreas 48500
    Anastomosis 48520-48540
    Excision 48120
Pelvis
    Aspiration 50390
    Injection 50390
Pericardial
    Excision 33050
Phalanges
    Finger 26210-26215
    Toe 28108
Pilonidal
    Excision 11770-11772
    Incision and Drainage 10080-10081
Pubis 27065-27067
Radius 24120, 25120-25126
Rathke's Pouch
    See Craniopharingioma
Removal
    Skin 10040
Retroperitoneal
    Destruction/Excision 49200-49201
Salivary Gland Creation
    Destruction/Excision
        Fistula 42325-42326
        Drainage 42409
        Excision 42408
Scapula
    Excision 23140-23146
Seminal Vesicle
    Excision 55680
Skin
    Puncture Aspiration 10160

Spinal Cord
 Aspiration 62268
  Incision and Drainage 63172-63173
Sublingual Gland Drainage 42409
 Excision 42408
Talus 28100-28103
Tarsal 28104-28107
Thyroglossal Duct
 Excision 60280-60281
 Incision and Drainage 60000
Thyroid Gland Aspiration 60001
 Excision 60200
 Injection 60001
Tibia 27635-27638
Tongue 41000-41006, 41015
Ulna 24120, 25120-25126
Urachal
 Bladder
  Excision 51500
Vaginal
 Excision 57135
Wrist 25130-25136
 Excision 25111-25112

Cystatins, Kininogen
See Kininogen

Cystectomy
Complete 51570
 with Bilateral Pelvic
 Lymphadenectomy 51575, 51585, 51595
 with Continent Diversion 51596
 with Ureteroileal Conduit 51590
 with Ureterosigmoidostomy 51580
Ovarian 58925
 Laparoscopic 58661
Partial
 Complicated 51555
 Reimplantation of Ureters 51565
 Simple 51550

Cystic Hygroma
See Hygroma

Cystine
Urine 82615

Cystitis
Interstitial 52260-52265

Cystography 74430
Injection 52281
 Radiologic 51600

Cystolithotomy 51050

Cystometrogram 51725-51726

Cystoplasty 51800

Cystorrhaphy 51860-51865

Cystoscopy 52000

Cystoscopy, with Biopsy
See Biopsy, Bladder, Cystourethroscopy

Cystostomy
Change Tube 51705-51710
Closure 51880
Home Visit 99505
with Fulguration 51020
with Insertion Radioactive Material 51020
with Urethrectomy
 Female 53210
 Male 53215

Cystotomy
Excision
 Bladder Diverticulum 51525
 Bladder Tumor 51530
 Repair of Ureterocele 51535
 Vesical Neck 51520
Repair Ureterocele 51535
with Calculus Basket Extraction 51065
with Destruction Intravesical Lesion 51030
with Drainage 51040
with Fulguration 51020
with Insertion
 Radioactive Material 51020
 Ureteral Catheter 51045
with Removal Calculus 51050, 51065

Cystourethrogram, Retrograde
See Urethrocystography, Retrograde

Cystourethropexy
See Vesicourethropexy

Cystourethroplasty 51800-51820

Cystourethroscopy 52000, 52351,
       52601, 52647-52648
Biopsy 52204, 52354
 Brush 52007
Calibration and/or Dilation Urethral Stricture or
Stenosis 52281
Catheterization
 Ejaculatory Duct 52010
 Ureteral 52005
Destruction
 Lesion 52400
Dilation
 Bladder 52260-52265
 Intra-Renal Stricture 52343, 52346
 Ureter 52341-52342, 52344-52345
 Urethra 52281
Evacuation
 Clot 52001
Female Urethral Syndrome 52285
Incision
 Ejaculatory Duct 52347
Injection of Implant Material 52327
Insertion
 Indwelling Ureteral Stent 50947, 52332
 Radioactive Substance 52250
 Ureteral Guide Wire 52334
 Urethral Stent 52282
Lithotripsy 52353
Manipulation of Ureteral Calculus 52330
Meatotomy
 Ureteral 52290-52305

Removal
 Calculus . .52310-52315, 52320-52325, 52352
 Foreign Body 52310-52315
 Urethral Stent 52310-52315
Resection
 Ejaculatory Duct 52347
 External Sphincter 52277
 Tumor 52355
Urethral Syndrome 52285
Vasectomy
 Transurethral 52347
Vasotomy
 Transurethral 52347
with Direct Vision Internal Urethrotomy ..52276
with Ejaculatory Duct Catheterization 52010
with Fulguration 52214, 52354
 Lesion 52224
 Tumor 52234-52240
with Internal Urethrotomy
 Female 52270
 Male 52275
with Steroid Injection 52283
with Ureteral Catheterization 52005
with Ureteral Meatotomy 52290-52305

Cyst Ovary
See Ovary, Cyst

Cytochrome Reductase, Lactic
See Lactic Dehydrogenase

Cytogenetic Study
Molecular
 DNA Probe 88271-88275, 88291
Unlisted Services and Procedures 88299

Cytomegalovirus
Antibody 86644-86645
Antigen Detection
 Direct Fluorescence 87198
 Enzyme Immunoassay 87332
 Nucleic Acid 87495-87497

Cytometries, Flow
See Flow Cytometry

Cytopathology
Cervical or Vaginal
 Requiring Interpretation by Physician ..88141
 Thin Layer Prep 88142-88145
Concentration Technique 88108
 See Saccomonno Technique
Evaluation 88172
Fluids, Washings, Brushings 88104-88108
Forensic 88125
Other Source 88160-88162
Smears
 Cervical or Vaginal 88141-88155, 88164-
          88167
Unlisted Services and Procedures 88199

Cytoscopy
See Bladder, Endoscopy

Cytosol Aminopeptidase
See Leucine Aminopeptidase

Cytotoxic Screen
Lymphocyte 86805-86806
Percent Reactive Antibody (PRA) . . .86807-86808
Serum Antibodies 86807-86808

C Vitamin
See Ascorbic Acid

D

D-Xylose Absorption Test 84620

Dacryoadenectomy
Partial 68505
Total 68500

Dacryocystectomy 68520

Dacryocystogram
See Dacryocystography

Dacryocystography 68850, 70170
Nuclear Imaging .78660

Dacryocystorhinostomy 68720
Total
    with Nasal/Sinus Endoscopy 31239

Dacryocystostomies
See Dacryocystotomy

Dacryocystotomy 68420

Daily Living Activities
See Activities of Daily Living

Damus-Kaye-Stansel Procedure
See Anastomosis, Pulmonary

Dana Operation
See Rhizotomy

Dandy Operation
See Ventriculocisternostomy

Darkroom Test
See Glaucoma, Provocative Test

Dark Adaptation Examination . .92284

Dark Field Examination . . .87164-87166

Darrach Procedure
See Excision, Ulna, Partial

Day Test
See Blood, Feces

Death, Brain
See Brain Death

Debridement
Brain 62010
Burns 01951-01953, 16010-16030
Mastoid Cavity
    Complex 69222
    Simple 69220
Metatarsophalangeal Joint 28289

Nails 11720-11721
Nose
    Endoscopic 31237
Pancreatic Tissue 48005
Skin
    Eczematous 11000-11001
    Full Thickness 11041
    Infected 11000-11001
    Partial Thickness 11040
    Subcutaneous Tissue 11042-11044
    with Open Fracture and/or
    Dislocation 11010-11012
Sternum 21627
Wound
    Non-Selective 97602
    Selective 97601

Debulking Procedure
Ovary/Pelvis 58952-58954

Decompression
See Section
Arm, Lower 24495, 25020-25025
Auditory Canal, Internal 69960
Brainstem 61575-61576
Cauda Equina 63011, 63017, 63047-63048,
                     63056-63057, 63087-63091
Cranial Nerve 61458
Esophagogastric Varices 37181
Facial Nerve 61590
    Intratemporal
        Lateral to Geniculate Ganglion 69720,
                          69740
        Medial to Geniculate Ganglion 69725,
                          69745
    Total 69955
Finger 26035
Gasserian Ganglion
    Sensory Root 61450
Hand 26035-26037
Intestines
    Small 44021
Jejunostomy
    Laparoscopic .44201
Leg
    Fasciotomy 27600-27602
Nerve 64702-64727
    Root 63020-63091
Nucleus of Disk
    Lumbar 62287
Optic Nerve 67570
Orbit 61330
    Removal of Bone 67414, 67445
Skull 61340-61345
Spinal Cord 63001-63017, 63045-63091
    Cauda Equina 63005
Tarsal Tunnel Release 28035
Volvulus 45321, 45337
with Nasal/Sinus Endoscopy
    Optic Nerve 31294
    Orbit Wall 31292-31293
Wrist 25020-25025

Decortication
Lung
    Endoscopic 32651-32652
    Partial 32225
    Total 32220
    with Parietal Pleurectomy 32320

Decubiti
See Pressure Ulcer (Decubitus)

Decubitus Ulcers
See Debridement; Pressure Ulcer (Decubitus);
Skin Graft and Flap

Deetjeen's Body
See Blood, Platelet

Defect, Coagulation
See Coagulopathy

Defect, Heart Septal
See Septal Defect

Defect, Septal Closure, Atrial
See Heart, Repair, Atrial Septum

Deferens, Ductus
See Vas Deferens

Defibrillation
See Cardioversion

Defibrillator, Heart
See Pacemaker, Heart
Evaluation and Testing 93640-93642
Insertion Single/Dual Chamber
    Electrodes 33216-33217, 33245-33249
    Pulse Generator 33240, 33246
Removal Single/Dual Chamber
    Electrodes 33243-33244
    Pulse Generator 33241
Repair 33218-33220
Revise Pocket Chest 33223

Deformity, Boutonniere
See Boutonniere Deformity

Deformity, Sprengel's
See Sprengel's Deformity

Degenerative, Articular Cartilage, Patella
See Chondromalacia Patella

Degradation Products, Fibrin
See Fibrin Degradation Products

Dehydroepiandrosterone 82626

Dehydroepiandrosterone Sulfate 82627

Dehydrogenase, 6-Phosphogluconate
See Phosphogluconate-6, Dehydrogenase

Dehydrogenase, Alcohol
See Antidiuretic Hormone

Dehydrogenase, Glucose-6-Phosphate
See Glucose-6-Phosphate, Dehydrogenase

Dehydrogenase, Glutamate
See Glutamate Dehydrogenase

Dehydrogenase, Isocitrate
See Isocitric Dehydrogenase

Dehydrogenase, Lactate
See Lactic Dehydrogenase

Dehydrogenase, Malate
See Malate Dehydrogenase

Dehydroisoandrosterone Sulfate
See Dehydroepiandrosterone Sulfate

Delay of Flap
Skin Graft 15600-15630

Deligation
Ureter 50940

Deliveries, Abdominal
See Cesarean Delivery

Delivery
See Cesarean Delivery; Vaginal Delivery

Delorme Operation
See Pericardiectomy

Denervation
Hip
    Femoral 27035
    Obturator 27035
    Sciatic 27035

Denervation, Sympathetic
See Excision, Nerve, Sympathetic

Denis-Browne Splint 29590

Dens Axis
See Odontoid Process

Denver-Krupin Procedure 66180

Denver Developmental Screening Test 96100

Denver Krupic Procedure
See Aqueous Shunt, to Extraocular Reservoir

Denver Shunt
Patency Test 78291

Deoxycorticosterone
See Desoxycorticosterone

Deoxycortisol 80436, 82634

Deoxyephedrine
See Methamphetamine

Deoxyribonuclease
Antibody 86215

Deoxyribonuclease I
See DNAse

Deoxyribonucleic Acid
Antibody 86225-86226

Depilation
See Removal, Hair

Depletion
T-Cell 86915

Deposit Calcium
See Calcium, Deposits

Depth Electrode
Insertion 61760

Derma-Fat-Fascia Graft 15770

Dermabrasion 15780-15783

Dermatology
Actinotherapy .96900
Examination of Hair
    Microscopic 96902
Ultraviolet A Treatment 96912
Ultraviolet B Treatment 96910-96913
Ultraviolet Light Treatment 96900-96913
Unlisted Services and Procedures 96999

Dermatoplasty
Septal 30620

Dermoid
See Cyst, Dermoid

Derrick-Burnet Disease
See Q Fever

Descending Abdominal Aorta
See Aorta, Abdominal

Desipramine
Assay 80160

Desmotomy
See Ligament, Release

Desoxycorticosterone 82633

Desoxycortone
See Desoxycorticosterone

Desoxyephedrine
See Methamphetamine

Desoxynorephedrin
See Amphetamine

Desoxyphenobarbital
See Primidone

Desquamation
See Exfoliation

Destruction
Acne 17340-17360
    Cryotherapy 17340
Arrhythmogenic Focus
    Heart 33250-33251, 33261
Bladder 51020, 52214-52224, 52354
Calculus
    Bile Duct 43265
    Kidney 50590
    Pancreatic Duct 43265
Chemical Cauterization
    Granulation Tissue 17250
Ciliary Body
    Cryotherapy 66720
    Cyclodialysis 66740
    Cyclophotocoagulation 66710
    Diathermy 66700
Cyst
    Abdomen 49200-49201
    Ciliary Body 66770
    Iris 66770
    Retroperitoneal 49200-49201
Endometriomas
    Abdomen 49200-49201
    Retroperitoneal 49200-49201

Fissure
    Anal 46940-46942
Hemorrhoids 46934-46936
Kidney 52354
    Endoscopic 50557, 50576
Lesion
    Anal 46900-46917, 46924
    Bladder 51030
    Choroid 0016T, 67220-67225
    Ciliary Body 66770
    Colon 45383
    Conjunctiva 68135
    Cornea 65450
    Eyelid 67850
    Facial 17000-17004, 17280-17286
    Gastrointestinal, Upper 43258
    Gums 41850
    Intestines
        Large 44393
        Small 44369
    Iris 66770
    Mouth 40820
    Nose
        Intranasal 30117-30118
    Palate 42160
    Penis
        Cryosurgery 54056
        Electrodesiccation 54055
        Extensive 54065
        Laser Surgery 54057
        Simple 54050-54060
        Surgical Excision 54060
    Pharynx 42808
    Prostate 45320
        Thermotherapy 53850-53853
            Microwave 53850
            Radio Frequency 53852
    Rectum 45320
    Retina
        Cryotherapy, Diathermy 67208, 67227
        Photocoagulation 0017T, 67210, 67228
        Radiation by Implantation
        of Source 67218
    Skin
        Benign 17000-17250
        Malignant 17260-17286, 96567
        Premalignant 96567
    Spinal Cord 62280-62282
    Ureter 52341-52342, 52344-52345
    Urethra 52400, 53265
    Uvula 42160
    Vagina
        Extensive 57065
        Simple .57061
    Vascular, Cutaneous 17106-17108
    Vulva
        Extensive 56515
        Simple .56501
Molluscum Contagiosum 17110
Muscle Endplate
    Cervical Spine 64613
    Extraocular .67345
    Extremity 64614
    Facial 64612
    Trunk 64614
Nerve 64600-64680
    Laryngeal, Recurrent 31595

Polyp
    Aural 69540
    Nose .30110-30115
    Urethra 53260
Prostate 55873
Prostate Tissue
    Transurethral
      Thermotherapy 53850-53853
Sinus
    Frontal 31080-31085
Skene's Gland .53270
Skin Lesion
    Benign 17000-17004
      Fifteen or More Lesions 17004
      Two - Fourteen Lesions 17003
    Malignant 17260-17286
      by Photodynamic Therapy 96567
    Premalignant 17000-17004
      by Photodynamic Therapy 96567
      Fifteen or More Lesions 17004
      Two - Fourteen Lesions 17003
Tonsil
    Lingual 42870
Tumor
    Abdomen 49200-49201
    Bile Duct 43272
    Chemosurgery 17304-17310
    Colon 45383
    Intestines
      Large 44393
      Small 44369
    Pancreatic Duct 43272
    Rectum 45190, 46937-46938
    Retroperitoneal 49200-49201
    Urethra 53220
Tumor or Polyp
    Rectum 45320
Turbinate Mucosa 30801-30802
Ureter 52354
    Endoscopic 50957-50959, 50976-50978
Urethra 52214-52224, 52354
    Prolapse 53275
Warts
    Flat 17110-17111
with Cystourethroscopy 52354

Determination, Blood Pressure
See Blood Pressure

Developmental Testing . . .96110-96111

Device
Iliac Artery Occulsion Device
    Insertion 34808
Venous Access
    Collection of Blood Specimen 36540
    Insertion 36533
    Removal 36535
    Revision 36534

Device, Intrauterine
See Intrauterine Device (IUD)

Device, Orthotic
See Orthotics

Device Handling 99002

DEXA
See Dual Energy X-Ray Absorptiometry (DEXA)

Dexamethasone
Suppression Test 80420

de Quervain's Disease
Treatment 25000

DHA Sulfate
See Dehydroepiandrosterone Sulfate

DHEA
See Dehydroepiandrosterone

DHEA Sulfate
See Dehydroepiandrosterone Sulfate

DHT
See Dihydrotestosterone

Diagnosis, Psychiatric
See Psychiatric Diagnosis

Diagnostic Amniocentesis
See Amniocentesis

Diagnostic Aspiration of Anterior Chamber of Eye
See Eye, Paracentesis, Anterior Chamber, with Diagnostic Aspiration of Aqueous

Diagnostic Radiologic Examination
See Radiology, Diagnostic

Diagnostic Skin and Sensitization Tests
See Allergy Tests

Diagnostic Ultrasound
See Echography

Diagnostic Ultrasound of Heart
See Echocardiography

Dialyses, Peritoneal
See Dialysis, Peritoneal

Dialysis
Arteriovenous Fistula
    Revision
      without Thrombectomy 36832
Arteriovenous Shunt 36145
    Revision
      with Thrombectomy 36833
    Thrombectomy 36831
End Stage Renal Disease 90918-90925
Hemodialysis 90935-90937
    Blood Flow Study 90939-90940
Hemoperfusion 90997
Patient Training
    Completed Course 90989
    Per Session 90993
Peritoneal 90945-90947, 99559
Unlisted Services and Procedures 90999

Dialysis, Extracorporeal
See Hemodialysis

Diaphragm
Repair
    for Eventration 39545
    Hernia 39502-39541
    Laceration .39501

Resection 39560-39561
Unlisted Procedures 39599
Vagina
    Fitting 57170

Diaphragm Contraception
See Contraception, Diaphragm

Diaphysectomy
Calcaneus 28120
Clavicle 23180
Femur 27360
Fibula 27360, 27641
Humerus 23184, 24140
Metacarpal 26230
Metatarsal 28122
Olecranon Process 24147
Phalanges
    Finger 26235-26236
    Toe 28124
Radius 24145, 25151
Scapula 23182
Talus 28120
Tarsal 28122
Tibia 27360, 27640
Ulna 24147, 25150

Diastase
See Amylase

Diastasis
See Separation

Diathermy 97024
See Physical Medicine/Therapy/Occupational Therapy
Destruction
    Ciliary Body 66700
Lesion
    Retina 67208, 67227
Retinal Detachment
    Prophylaxis 67141
    Repair 67101

Diathermy, Surgical
See Electrocautery

Dibucaine Number 82638

Dichloride, Methylene
See Dichloromethane

Dichlorides, Ethylene
See Dichloroethane

Dichloroethane 84600

Dichloromethane 84600

Diethylamide, Lysergic Acid
See Lysergic Acid Diethylamide

Diethylether 84600

Differential Count
See White Blood Cell Count

Differentiation Reversal Factor
See Prothrombin

Diffusion Test, Gel
See Immunodiffusion

Digestive Tract
See Gastrointestinal Tract

Digit
See Finger; Toe
Replantation 20816-20822

Digital Artery Sympathectomy 64820

Digital Slit-Beam Radiograph
See Scanogram

Digits
Pinch Graft 15050

Digoxin
Assay 80162

Dihydrocodeinone 82646

Dihydrocodeinone Screen 82486

Dihydroepitestosterone
See Dihydrotestosterone

Dihydrohydroxycodeinone
See Oxycodinone

Dihydromorphinone 82486, 82649

Dihydrotestosterone 82651

Dihydroxyethanes
See Ethylene Glycol

Dihydroxyvitamin D 82652

Dilatation, Transluminal Arterial
See Angioplasty, Transluminal

Dilation
See Dilation and Curettage
Anal
    Endoscopy 46604
    Sphincter 45905
Bile Duct
    Endoscopy 43271, 47555-47556
    Stricture 74363
Bladder
    Cystourethroscopy 52260-52265
Bronchi
    Endoscopy 31630
Cervix
    Canal 57800
    Stump 57820
Esophagus 43450-43458
    Balloon 43249
    Endoscopy 0008T, 43220-43228,
      43234-43239, 43241, 43243-43249, 43256
    Surgical 43510
Intestines, Small
    Endoscopy 44370
Kidney 50395
    Intra-Renal Stricture 52343, 52346
Lacrimal Punctum 68801
Larynx
    Endoscopy 31528-31529
Pancreatic Duct
    Endoscopy 43271
Rectum
    Endoscopy 45303
    Sphincter 45910

Salivary Duct 42650-42660
Trachea
    Endoscopy 31630-31631
Ureter 50395, 52341-52342, 52344-52345
    Endoscopy 50553, 50572, 50953, 50972
Urethra 52260-52265
    General 53665
    Suppository and/or
    Instillation 53660-53661
Urethral
    Stenosis 52281
    Stricture 52281, 53600-53621
Vagina.............................57400

Dilation and Curettage 59840
See Curettage; Dilation
Cervix 57800-57820
Corpus Uteri 58120
Hysteroscopy 58558
Postpartum 59160
with Amniotic Injections 59851
with Vaginal Suppositories 59856

Dilation and Evacuation 59841
with Amniotic Injections 59851

Dimethadione 82654

Dioxide, Carbon
See Carbon Dioxide

Dioxide, Silicon
See Silica

Dipeptidyl Peptidase A
See Angiotensin Converting Enzyme (ACE)

Diphenylhydantoin
See Phenytoin

Diphosphate, Adenosine
See Adenosine Diphosphate

Diphtheria
See Vaccines
Antibody 86648

Dipropylacetic Acid
Assay 80164

Direct Pedicle Flap
Formation 15570-15576

Disability Evaluation Services
Basic Life and/or Disability Evaluation 99450
Work-Related or Medical
Disability Evaluation 99455-99456

Disarticulation
Ankle 27889
Hip 27295
Knee 27598
Wrist 25920, 25924
    Revision 25922

Disarticulation of Shoulder
See Shoulder, Disarticulation

Disc, Intervertebral
See Intervertebral Disk

Discectomies
See Diskectomy

Discectomies, Percutaneous
See Diskectomy, Percutaneous

Discharge, Body Substance
See Drainage

Discharge Services
See Hospital Services
Hospital 99238-99239
Nursing Facility 99315-99316
Observation Care 99234-99236

Discission
Cataract
    Laser Surgery 66821
    Stab Incision 66820
Vitreous Strands 67030

Discography
See Diskography

Discolysis
See Chemonucleolysis

Disease
Durand-Nicolas-Favre
    See Lymphogranuloma Venereum
Erb-Goldflam
    See Myasthenia Gravis
Heine-Medin
    See Polio
Hydatid
    See Echinococcosis
Lyme
    See Lyme Disease
Ormond
    See Retroperitoneal Fibrosis
Peyronie
    See Peyronie Disease
Posada-Wernicke
    See Coccidioidomycosis

Disease/Organ Panel
See Organ/Disease Panel

Diskectomy 63075-63078
Additional Segment 22226
Arthrodesis
    Additional Interspace 22585
    Cervical 22554
    Lumbar 22558, 22630
    Thoracic 22556
Cervical...........................22220
Lumbar 22224, 22630
Percutaneous 62287
Thoracic 22222

Diskography
Cervical Disk 72285
Injection 62290-62291
Lumbar Disk 72295
Thoracic 72285

Disk Chemolyses, Intervertebral
See Chemonucleolysis

Dislocated Elbow
See Dislocation, Elbow

Dislocated Hip
See Dislocation, Hip Joint

Dislocated Jaw
See Dislocation, Temporomandibular Joint

Dislocated Joint
See Dislocation

Dislocated Shoulder
See Dislocation, Shoulder

Dislocation
Acromioclavicular Joint
    Open Treatment 23550-23552
Ankle
    Closed Treatment 27840-27842
    Open Treatment 27846-27848
Carpal
    Closed Treatment 25690
    Open Treatment 25695
Carpometacarpal Joint 26670
    Closed Treatment
      with Manipulation 26675-26676
    Open Treatment 26685-26686
    Percutaneous Fixation 26676
Clavicle
    Closed Treatment 23540-23545
    Open Treatment 23550-23552
    without Manipulation 23540
    with Manipulation 23545
Closed Treatment
    Carpometacarpal Joint 26670-26675
    Metacarpophalangeal 26700-26706
    Thumb 26641
Elbow
    Closed Treatment 24600-24605, 24640
    Open Treatment 24615
Hip Joint
    Closed Treatment 27250-27252, 27265-27266
    Congenital 27256-27259
    Open Treatment . .27253-27254, 27258-27259
    without Trauma 27265-27266
Interphalangeal Joint
    Closed Treatment 26770-26775
    Open Treatment 26785
    Percutaneous Fixation 26776
    Toe
      Closed Treatment 28660-28665
      Open Treatment 28675
      Percutaneous Fixation 26770-26776, 28666
    with Manipulation 26770
Knee 27560-27562
    Closed Treatment 27550-27752
    Open Treatment 27556-27558, 27566
    Recurrent 27420-27424
Lunate
    Closed Treatment 25690
    Open Treatment 25695
    with Manipulation 25690, 26670-26676,
                          26700-26706
Metacarpophalangeal Joint
    Closed Treatment 26700-26706
    Open Treatment 26715
Metatarsophalangeal Joint
    Closed Treatment 28630-28635
    Open Treatment 28645
    Percutaneous Fixation 28636
Open Treatment 26685-26686

Patella
    Closed Treatment 27560-27562
    Open Treatment 27566
    Recurrent 27420-27424
Pelvic Ring
    Closed Treatment 27193-27194
    Open Treatment 27217-27218
    Percutaneous Fixation 27216
    without Manipulation 27193-27194
Percutaneous Fixation
    Metacarpophalangeal 26705
Peroneal Tendons 27675-27676
Radio-Ulnar Joint 25520-25526
Radius
    Closed Treatment 24640
    with Fracture
      Closed Treatment 24620
      Open Treatment 24635
Shoulder
    Closed Treatment
      with Manipulation 23650-23655
    Open Treatment with Surgical or
    Anatomical Neck Fracture 23660
      Closed Treatment with Manipulation 23675
      Open Treatment 23680
    with Greater Tuberosity Fracture
      Closed Treatment 23665
      Open Treatment 23670
Skin
    Debridement 11010-11012
Sternoclavicular Joint
    Closed Treatment
      without Manipulation 23520
      with Manipulation 23525
    Open Treatment 23530-23532
Talotarsal Joint
    Closed Treatment 28570-28575
    Open Treatment 28546
    Percutaneous Fixation 28576
Tarsal
    Closed Treatment 28540-28545
    Open Treatment 28555
    Percutaneous Fixation 28546
Tarsometatarsal Joint
    Closed Treatment 28600-28605
    Open Treatment 28615
    Percutaneous Fixation 28606
Temporomandibular Joint
    Closed Treatment 21480-21485
    Open Treatment 21490
Thumb
    Closed Treatment 26641-26645
    Open Treatment 26665
    Percutaneous Fixation 26650
    with Fracture 26645
      Open Treatment 26665
      Percutaneous Fixation 26650-26665
    with Manipulation 26641-26650
Tibiofibular Joint
    Closed Treatment 27830-27831
    Open Treatment 27832
Vertebra
    Additional Segment
      Open Treatment 22328
    Cervical
      Open Treatment 22326

    Closed Treatment 22305
      without Manipulation 22310
      with Manipulation, Casting
      and/or Bracing 22315
    Lumbar
      Open Treatment 22325
    Thoracic
      Open Treatment 22327
Wrist
    Closed Treatment 25660, 25675, 25680
    Intercarpal 25660
      Open Treatment 25670
    Open Treatment 25670, 25685
    Percutaneous Fixation 25671
    Radiocarpal 25660
      Open Treatment 25670
    Radioulnar
      Closed Treatment 25675
      Open Treatment 25676
      Percutaneous Fixation 25671
    with Fracture
      Closed Treatment 25680
      Open Treatment 25685
    with Manipulation 25660, 25675, 25680

Dislocation, Radiocarpal Joint
See Radiocarpal Joint, Dislocation

Disorder
Blood Coagulation
    See Coagulopathy
Penis
    See Penis
Retinal
    See Retina

Displacement Therapy
Nose 30210

Dissection
Hygroma, Cystic
    Axillary/Cervical 38550-38555
Lymph Nodes .38542

Dissection, Neck, Radical
See Radical Neck Dissection

Distention
See Dilation

Diverticula, Meckel's
See Diverticulum, Meckel's

Diverticulectomy 44800
Esophagus 43130-43135

Diverticulectomy, Meckel's
See Meckel's Diverticulum, Excision

Diverticulum
Bladder
    See Bladder, Diverticulum
Meckel's
    Excision 44800
Repair
    Urethra 53400-53405

Division
Muscle
    Foot 28250
Plantar Fascia
    Foot 28250

Division, Isthmus, Horseshoe Kidney
See Symphysiotomy, Horseshoe Kidney

Division, Scalenus Anticus Muscle
See Muscle Division, Scalenus Anticus

Dl-Amphetamine
See Amphetamine

DMO
See Dimethadione

DNA
Antibody 86225-86226

DNAse
Antibody 86215

DNA Endonuclease
See DNAse

DNA Probe
See Cytogenetics Studies; Nucleic Acid Probe

Domiciliary Services
See Nursing Facility Services
Discharge Services 99315-99316
Established Patient 99331-99333
New Patient 99321-99323

Donor Procedures
Heart/Lung Excision 33930
Heart Excision 33940

Dopamine
See Catecholamines
Blood 82383-82384
Urine 82382, 82384

Doppler Echocardiography 76827-
76828, 93307-93308, 93320-93350
Extracranial 93875
Intracardiac 93662
Transesophageal 93318
Transthoracic 93303-93317

Doppler Scan
Arterial Studies, Extremities 93922-93924
Extremities 93965
Intracranial Arteries 93886-93888

Dorsal Vertebra
See Vertebra, Thoracic

Dose Plan
See Dosimetry

Dosimetry
Radiation Therapy 77300, 77331
Brachytherapy 77326-77328
Intensity Modulation 77301
Teletherapy 77305-77321

Double-Stranded DNA
See Deoxyribonucleic Acid

Doxepin
Assay 80166

DPH
See Phenytoin

Drainage
See Excision; Incision; Incision and Drainage
Abdomen
Abdomen Fluid 49080-49081
Abscess
Appendix 44900-44901
Percutaneous 44901
Brain 61150-61151
Eyelid 67700
Liver 47010-47011
Ovary
Percutaneous 58823
Pelvic
Percutaneous 58823
Pericolic
Percutaneous 58823
Perirenal or Renal 50020-50021
Percutaneous 50021
Prostate 52700
Retroperitoneal 49060-49061
Percutaneous 49061
Subdiaphragmatic or
Subphrenic 49040-49041
Percutaneous 49040-49041
with X-Ray 75989
Bile Duct
Transhepatic .75980
Brain Fluid 61070
Bursa 20600-20610
Cerebrospinal Fluid 61000-61020, 61050,
61070, 62272
Cervical Fluid 61050
Cisternal Fluid .61050
Cyst
Bone 20615
Brain 61150-61151
Breast 19000-19001
Ganglion 20600
Liver 47010-47011
Percutaneous 47011
Salivary Gland 42409
Sublingual Gland 42409
with Fistula 42325-42326
Extraperitoneal Lymphocele
Laparoscopic 49323
Open 49062
Eye
Anterior Chamber Paracentesis
with Diagnostic Aspiration of
Aqueous .65800
with Therapeutic Release of
Aqueous .65805
Removal Blood 65815
Removal of Vitreous and/or Discission
Anterior Hyaloid Membrane 65810
Ganglion Cyst 20600-20605
Hematoma
Brain 61154-61156
Vagina 57022-57023
Hematoma, Subungual 11740
Joint 20600-20610
Liver
Abscess or Cyst 47010-47011
Percutaneous 47011
Lymphocele
Endoscopic 49323
Onychia 10060-10061
Orbit 67405, 67440

Pancreas
See Anastomosis, Pancreas to Intestines
Pseudocyst 48510-48511
Percutaneous 48511
Paronychia 10060-10061
Pericardial Sac .32659
Pericardium
See Aspiration, Pericardium
Pseudocyst
Gastrointestinal, Upper
Transmural Endoscopic 43240
Pancreas 48510
Open 48510
Percutaneous 48511
Puncture
Chest 32000-32002
Skin 10040-10180
Spinal Cord
Cerebrospinal Fluid 62272
Subdural Fluid 61000-61001
Urethra
Extravasation 53080-53085
Ventricular Fluid 61020

Drainage Implant, Glaucoma
See Aqueous Shunt

Dressings
Burns 16010-16030
Change
Anesthesia 15852

DREZ Procedure
See Incision, Spinal Cord; Incision and Drainage

Drill Hole
Skull
Catheter 61107
Drain Hematoma 61108
Exploration 61105
Implant Electrode 61850, 61862

Drinking Test for Glaucoma
See Glaucoma, Provocative Test

Drug
See Drug Assay; Specific Drug
Analysis
Tissue Preparation 80103
Confirmation 80102
Infusion 62360-62362

Drugs, Anticoagulant
See Clotting Inhibitors

Drug Assay
Amikacin 80150
Amitriptyline 80152
Benzodiazepine 80154
Carbamazepine 80156-80157
Cyclosporine 80158
Desipramine 80160
Digoxin 80162
Dipropylacetic Acid 80164
Doxepin 80166
Ethosuximide 80168
Gentamicin 80170
Gold 80172
Haloperidol 80173
Imipramine 80174

Lidocaine 80176
Lithium 80178
Nortriptyline .80182
Phenobarbital .80184
Phenytoin 80185-80186
Primidone 80188
Procainamide 80190-80192
Quantitative
    Other 80299
Quinidine 80194
Salicylate 80196
Tacrolimus 80197
Theophylline .80198
Tobramycin 80200
Topiramate 80201
Vancomycin .80202

Drug Delivery Implant
Insertion 11981
Removal 11982-11983
    with Reinsertion 11983

Drug Instillation
See Instillation, Drugs

Drug Management
Psychiatric 90862

Drug Screen 80100-80101, 82486

DST
See Dexamethasone, Suppression Test

DTaP-HepB-IPV Immunization
. 90723

DTaP Immunization 90721

DTP Immunization 90701, 90720

DT Shots 90702

Dual Energy X-Ray Absorptiometry
(DEXA) 76075
Appendicular 76076
Axial Skeleton 76075

Dual Photon Absorptiometry
See Absorptiometry, Dual Photon

Duct, Bile
See Bile Duct

Duct, Hepatic
See Hepatic Duct

Duct, Nasolacrimal
See Nasolacrimal Duct

Duct, Omphalomesenteric
See Omphalomesenteric Duct

Duct, Pancreatic
See Pancreatic Duct

Duct, Salivary
See Salivary Duct

Duct, Stensen's
See Parotid Duct

Duct, Thoracic
See Thoracic Duct

Ductogram, Mammary
See Galactogram

Ductus Arteriosus
Repair .33820-33824

Ductus Deferens
See Vas Deferens

Duhamel Procedure
See Proctectomy, Total

Dunn Operation
See Arthrodesis, Foot Joint

Duodenotomy 44010

Duodenum
Biopsy 44010
Exclusion 48547
Exploration .44010
Incision 44010
Removal
    Foreign Body 44010
X-Ray 74260

Duplex Scan
See Vascular Studies
Arterial Studies
    Aorta 93978-93979
    Extracranial 93880-93882
    Lower Extremity 93925-93926
    Penile 93980-93981
    Upper Extremity 93930-93931
    Visceral 93975-93979
Hemodialysis Access 93990
Venous Studies
    Extremity 93970-93971
    Penile 93980-93981

Dupuy-Dutemp Operation
See Reconstruction, Eyelid; Revision

Dupuytren's
Contracture 26040-26045

Durand-Nicolas-Favre Disease
See Lymphogranuloma Venereum

Dust, Angel
See Phencyclidine

Duvries Operation
See Tenoplasty

Dwyer Procedure
See Osteotomy, Calcaneus

Dynamometry
See Osteotomy, Calcaneus
Venous Studies
    See Osteotomy, Calcaneus
    with Ophthalmoscopy 92260

D & C Yellow No. 7
See Fluorescein

D 2, Vitamin
See Calciferol

D and C
See Dilation and Curettage

D and E
See Dilation and Evacuation

D Galactose
See Galactose

D Glucose
See Glucose

D Vitamin
See Vitamin, D

E

E1
See Estrone

E2
See Estradiol

E3
See Estriol

Ear
Collection of Blood 36415
Drum 69420-69421, 69433-69436,
                                 69450, 69610-69620
    See Tympanic Membrane
External
    Abscess Incision and Drainage
        Complicated 69005
        Simple 69000
    Biopsy 69100
    Excision
        Partial 69110
        Total .69120
    Hematoma
        Incision and Drainage 69000-69005
    Reconstruction 69300
    Unlisted Services and Procedures 69399
Inner
    CAT Scan 70480-70482
    Excision
        Labyrinth 69905-69910
    Exploration
        Endolymphatic Sac 69805-69806
    Incision 69820
        Labyrinth 69801-69802
        Semicircular Canal 69840
    Insertion
        Cochlear Device 69930
    Semicircular Canal 69820
    Unlisted Services and Procedures 69949
Middle
    Catheterization 69405
    CAT Scan 70480-70482
    Exploration 69440
    Inflation
        without Catheterization 69401
        with Catheterization 69400
    Insertion
        Baffle 69410
        Catheter 69405

Lesion
  Excision 69540
Reconstruction
  Tympanoplasty without
  Mastoidectomy 69631-69633
  Tympanoplasty with Antrotomy or
  Mastoidotomy 69635-69637
  Tympanoplasty with
  Mastoidectomy 69641-69646
Removal
  Ventilating Tube 69424
Repair
  Oval Window 69666
  Round Window 69667
Revision
  Stapes 69662
Tumor
  Excision 69550-69554
Unlisted Services and Procedures 69799
Outer
  CAT Scan 70480-70482

Ear, Nose, and Throat

See Hearing Aid Services; Otorhinolaryngology, Diagnostic
Audiologic Function Tests
  Acoustic Reflex 92568
  Acoustic Reflex Decay 92569
  Audiometry
    Bekesy 92560-92561
    Comprehensive 92557
    Conditioning Play 92582
    Evoked Response 92585-92586
    Groups 92559
    Pure Tone 92552-92553
    Select Picture 92583
    Speech 92555-92556
  Brainstem Evoked Response . .92585-92586
  Central Auditory Function 92589
  Ear Protector Evaluation 92596
  Electrocochleography 92584
  Filtered Speech 92571
  Hearing Aid Evaluation 92590-92595
  Lombard Test 92573
  Loudness Balance 92562
  Screening Test 92551
  Sensorineural Acuity 92575
  Short Increment Sensitivity
  Index (SISI) 92564
  Staggered Spondaic Word Test 92572
  Stenger Test 92565, 92577
  Synthetic Sentence Test 92576
  Tone Decay .92563
  Tympanometry 92567
Audiometry
  Evoked Otoacoustic Emissions . .92587-92588
  Visual Reinforcement 92579
Binocular Microscopy 92504
Facial Nerve Function Study 92516
Hearing, Language and Speech
Evaluation 92506
Laryngeal Function Study 92520
Nasal Function Study 92512
Nasopharyngoscopy 92511
Vestibular Function Tests
  Additional Electrodes 92547
  Caloric Tests 92533, 92543

Nystagmus
  Optokinetic 92534, 92544
  Positional 92532, 92542
  Spontaneous 92531, 92541
Posturography .92548
Torsion Swing Test 92546
Tracking Tests .92545

Ear Canal

See Auditory Canal

Ear Cartilage

Graft
  to Face 21235

Ear Lobes

Pierce 69090

Ear Protector Attenuation 92596

See Hearing Aid Services

Ear Wax

See Cerumen

Ebstein Anomaly Repair 33468

ECG

See Electrocardiogram

Echinococcosis 86171, 86280

Echocardiography

Cardiac 93320-93350
  Intracardiac 93662
  Transesophageal 93318
  Transthoracic 93303-93317
Doppler 93303-93317, 93320-93321, 93662
Fetal Heart 76825-76826
  Doppler
    Complete 76827
    Follow-up or Repeat Study 76828
  for Congenital Anomalies
    Transesophageal 93315-93317
    Transthoracic 93303-93304
Intracardiac 93662
Transesophageal 93318
  for Congenital Anomalies 93315-93317
Transthoracic 93303-93318, 93350
  for Congenital Anomalies 93303-93304

Echoencephalography 76506

Echography

Abdomen .76700-76705
Arm 76880
Breast 76645
Cardiac 93303-93317, 93320-93321,
                       93350, 93662
  Guidance 76932
Chest 76604
Extracranial Arteries 93880-93882
Eyes 76511-76529
Follow-up 76970
Head 76536
Heart
  Imaging Guidance 76932
Hip
  Infant 76885-76886
Intracranial Arteries 93886-93888
Intraoperative 76986

Kidney
  Transplant .76778
Leg 76880
Neck 76536
Pelvis 76856-76857
Placement Therapy Fields 76950
Pregnant Uterus 76805-76816
Prostate 76872-76873
Retroperitoneal 76770-76775
Scrotum 76870
Spine 76800
Transrectal 76872-76873
Transvaginal .76830
Unlisted Services and Procedures 76999
Vagina 76830

Echotomography

See Echography

ECMO

See Extracorporeal Membrane Oxygenation

ECS

See Emission Computerized Tomography

ECSF (Erythrocyte Colony Stimulating Factor)

See Erythropoietin

ECT

See Emission Computerized Tomography

Ectasia

See Dilation

Ectopic Pregnancy

See Obstetrical Care
Abdominal 59130
Cervix 59140
Interstitial
  Partial Resection Uterus 59136
  Total Hysterectomy 59135
Laparoscopy .59150
  with Salpingectomy and/or
  Oophorectomy 59151
Tubal 59121
  with Salpingectomy and/or
  Oophorectomy 59120

Ectropion

Repair
  Blepharoplasty
    Excision Tarsal Wedge 67916
    Extensive .67917
    Suture 67914
    Thermocauterization 67915

Education Services

Group 99078

Education Supplies 99071

EEG

See Electroencephalography (EEG)

Egg

See Ova

Ehrlichia

Antibody 86666

EKG
See Electrocardiogram

Elbow
See Humerus; Radius; Ulna
Abscess
   Incision and Drainage 23930, 23935
Anesthesia 00400, 01710-01782
Arthrectomy 24155
Arthrocentesis 20605
Arthrodesis 24800-24802
Arthroplasty 24360
   Total Replacement 24363
   with Implant 24361-24362
Arthroscopy
   Diagnostic .29830
   Surgical 29834-29838
Arthrotomy 24000
   Capsular Release 24006
   with Joint Exploration 24101
   with Synovectomy 24102
   with Synovial Biopsy 24101
Biopsy 24065-24066, 24101
Bursa
   Incision and Drainage 23931
Dislocation
   Closed Treatment 24600-24605, 24640
   Open Treatment 24615
   Subluxate 24640
Excision 24155
   Bursa 24105
   Synovium 24102
Exploration 24000, 24101
Fracture
   Monteggia 24620-24635
   Open Treatment 24586-24587
Hematoma
   Incision and Drainage 23930
Implant
   Removal 24164
Incision and Drainage 24000
Injection
   Arthrography
     Radiologic 24220
Magnetic Resonance Imaging (MRI) 73221
Manipulation 24300
Radical Resection
   Capsule, Soft Tissue and Bone
     with Contracture Release 24149
Removal
   Foreign Body 24000, 24101, 24200-24201
   Implant 24160
   Loose Body .24101
Repair
   Epicondylitis 24350
   Fasciotomy 24350-24356
   Flexorplasty 24330
   Hemiepiphyseal Arrest 24470
   Ligament 24343-24346
   Muscle 24341
   Muscle Transfer 24301
   Tendon 24340-24342
     Lengthening 24305
     Transfer .24301
   Tennis Elbow 24350-24356
Steindler Advancement 24330
Strapping 29260

Tumor
   Excision 24075-24077
Unlisted Services and Procedures 24999
X-Ray 73070-73080
   with Contrast 73085

Elbow, Golfer
See Tennis Elbow

Elbows, Tennis
See Tennis Elbow

Electrical Stimulation
Bone Healing
   Invasive 20975
   Noninvasive 20974
Brain Surface 95961-95962
Physical Therapy
   Attended, Manual 97032
   Unattended 97014

Electric Countershock
See Cardioversion

Electric Stimulation
See Electrical Stimulation

Electric Stimulation, Transcutaneous
See Application, Neurostimulation

Electro-Hydraulic Procedure 52325

Electro-oculography 92270

Electroanalgesia
See Application, Neurostimulation

Electrocardiography
24 Hour Monitoring 93224-93237
Evaluation 93000, 93010, 93014
Patient-Demand Recording
   Transmission and Evaluation 93270
Patient-Demand Transmission and Evaluation
   Interpretation 93272
   Monitoring .93271
Rhythm
   Evaluation .93042
   Microvolt T-wave Alternans 93025
   Tracing 93041
   Tracing and Evaluation 93040
Signal Averaged 93278
Transmission 93012

Electrocautery 17000-17286
See Destruction

Electrochemistry
See Electrolysis

Electroconvulsive Therapy 90870-90871

Electrocorticogram
Intraoperative 95829

Electrode, Depth
See Depth Electrode

Electrodesiccation 17000-17286
Lesion
   Penis 54055

Electroejaculation 55870

Electroencephalography (EEG) 95816
Brain Death 95824
Digital Analysis 95957
Electrode Placement 95830
Intraoperative .95955
Monitoring . . .95812-95813, 95950-95953, 95956
   with Drug Activation 95954
   with Physical Activation 95954
   with WADA Activation 95958
Sleep 95822, 95827
Standard 95819

Electrogastrography 91132-91133

Electrogram, Atrial
Esophageal Recording 93615-93616

Electrolysis 17380

Electromyographs
See Electromyography, Needle

Electromyography
Anorectal with Biofeedback 90911
Fine Wire
   Dynamic 96004
Needle
   Extremities 95861-95864
   Extremity 95860
   Face and Neck Muscles 95867-95868
   Limited Study 95869
   Ocular 92265
   Other than Thoracic Paraspinal 95870
   Single Fiber Electrode 95872
   Thoracic Paraspinal Muscles 95869
Sphincter Muscles
   Anus 51784-51785
     Needle .51785
   Urethra 51784-51785
     Needle .51785
Surface
   Dynamic 96002-96004

Electronic Analysis
Drug Infusion Pump 62367-62368
Implantable Loop Recorder System 93727
Neurostimulator Pulse Generator . . .95970-95975
Pacing Cardioverter-Defibrillator . . .93741-93744

Electron Microscopy 88348-88349

Electrophoresis
Counterimmuno- 86185
Immuno- 86320-86327
Unlisted Services and Procedures 82664

Electrophysiology Procedure 93600-93660

Electroretinogram
See Electroretinography

Electroretinography 92275

Electrostimulation, Analgesic Cutaneous
See Application, Neurostimulation

Electrosurgery
Trichiasis
    Correction .... .67825

Electroversion, Cardiac
See Cardioversion

Elevation, Scapula, Congenital
See Sprengel's Deformity

Elliot Operation
See Excision, Lesion, Sclera

Eloesser Procedure
See Thoracostomy, Empyema

Eloesser Thoracoplasty
See Thoracoplasty

Embolectomy
Aortoiliac Artery 34151-34201
Axillary Artery .... .34101
Brachial Artery .... .34101
Carotid Artery .... .34001
Celiac Artery .... .34151
Femoral .... .34201
Iliac 34151-34201
Innominate Artery 34001-34101
Mesentery Artery .... .34151
Peroneal Artery .... .34203
Popliteal Artery .... .34203
Pulmonary Artery 33910-33916
Radial Artery .... .34111
Renal Artery .... .34151
Subclavian Artery 34001-34101
Tibial Artery .... .34203
Ulnar Artery .... .34111

Embryo
Cryopreservation .... .89258
Cryopreserved
    Preparation
        Transfer .... .89256
Culture
    with Culture
        Fertilized Oocyte .... .89251
Hatching
    Assisted
        Microtechnique .... .89253
Preparation
    for Transfer .... .89255

Embryonated Eggs
Inoculation .... .87250

Embryo /Fetus Monitoring
See Monitoring, Fetal

Embryo Implantation
See Implantation

Embryo Transfer
In Vitro Fertilization 58974-58976
    Intrafallopian Transfer .... .58976
    Intrauterine Transfer .... .58974

Emergency Department Services 99281-99288
See Critical Care; Emergency Department
Services
Anesthesia .... .99140
Physician Direction of Advanced
Life Support .... .99288

Emesis Induction .... .99175

EMG
See Electromyography, Needle

Emission-Computed Tomography, Single-Photon
See SPECT

Emission Computerized Tomography .... .78607

EMI Scan
See CAT Scan

Emmet Operation
See Vagina, Repair, Obstetric

Empyema
Closure
    Chest Wall .... .32810
Thoracostomy 32020-32036

Empyema, Lung
See Abscess, Thorax

Empyemectomy .... .32540

Encephalitis
Antibody 86651-86654

Encephalitis Virus Vaccine ... .90735

Encephalocele
Repair .... .62120
    Craniotomy .... .62121

Encephalon
See Brain

End-Expiratory Pressure, Positive
See Pressure Breathing, Positive

Endarterectomy
Coronary Artery .... .33572
Pulmonary .... .33916

Endemic Flea-Borne Typhus
See Murine Typhus

Endobronchial Challenge Tests
See Bronchial Challenge Test

Endocavitary Fulguration
See Electrocautery

Endocrine, Pancreas
See Islet Cell

Endocrine System
Unlisted Services and Procedures . .60699, 78099

Endolymphatic Sac
Exploration
    without Shunt .... .69805
    with Shunt .... .69806

Endometrial Ablation ..... .0009T, 58353
Exploration
    via Hysteroscopy .... .58563

Endometrioma
Abdomen
    Destruction/Excision 49200-49201
Retroperitoneal
    Destruction/Excision 49200-49201

Endometriosis, Adhesive
See Adhesions, Intrauterine

Endometrium
Biopsy .... .58100, 58558

Endonuclease, DNA
See DNAse

Endoscopic Retrograde Cannulation of Pancreatic Duct (ERCP)
See Cholangiopancreatography

Endoscopies, Pleural
See Thoracoscopy

Endoscopy
See Arthroscopy; Thoracoscopy
Adrenal Gland
    Biopsy .... .60650
    Excision .... .60650
Anus
    Biopsy .... .46606
    Dilation .... .46604
    Exploration .... .46600
    Hemorrhage .... .46614
    Removal
        Foreign Body .... .46608
        Polyp .... .46610, 46612
        Tumor .... .46610, 46612
Bile Duct
    Biopsy .... .47553
    Destruction
        Calculi (Stone) .... .43265
        Tumor .... .43272
    Dilation .... .43271, 47555-47556
    Exploration .... .47552
    Intraoperative .... .47550
    Percutaneous 47552-47555
    Removal
        Calculi (Stone) .... .43264, 47554
        Foreign Body .... .43269
        Stent .... .43269
    Specimen Collection .... .43260
    Sphincterotomy .... .43262
    Sphincter Pressure .... .43263
    Tube Placement 43267-43268
Bladder .... .52000
    Biopsy .... .52204, 52354
    Catheterization .... .52005, 52010
    Destruction .... .52354
        Lesion .... .52400
    Evacuation
        Clot .... .52001
    Excision
        Tumor .... .52355
    Exploration .... .52351
    Lithotripsy .... .52353

Removal
　Calculus 52352
　Urethral Stent 52282
Bladder Neck
　Injection of Implant Material 51715
Bronchi
　Aspiration 31645-31646
　Biopsy 31625-31629
　Destruction
　　Lesion 31641
　　Tumor 31641
　Dilation 31630-31631
　Exploration 31622
　Injection 31656
　Lesion
　　Destruction 31641
　Needle Biopsy 31629
　Placement
　　Stent 31631
　　Stenosis 31641
　Tumor
　　Destruction 31641
Chest Cavity
　Exploration 32601-32606
　Surgical 32650-32665
Colon
　Biopsy 44389, 45380
　Destruction
　　Lesion 44393, 45383
　　Tumor 44393, 45383
　Exploration 45378
　Hemorrhage 44391, 45382
　Placement
　　Stent 45387
　Removal
　　Foreign Body 44390, 45379
　　Polyp 44392, 45384-45385
　　Tumor 44392, 45384-45385
　Specimen Collection 45380
　via Colotomy 45355
　via Stoma 44388-44393, 44397
Colon-Sigmoid
　Ablation
　　Polyp 45339
　　Tumor 45339
　Biopsy 45331
　Exploration 45330
　Hemorrhage 45334
　Needle Biopsy 45342
　Placement
　　Stent 45327, 45345
　Removal
　　Foreign Body 45332
　　Polyp 45333, 45338
　　Tumor 45333, 45338
　Specimen Collection 45331
　Ultrasound 45341-45342
　Volvulus 45337
Esophagus
　Biopsy 43202
　Dilation 43220-43226
　Exploration 43200
　Hemorrhage 43227
　Injection 43204
　Insertion Stent 43219
　Needle Biopsy 43232

Removal
　Foreign Body 43215
　Polyp 43216-43217, 43228
　Tumor 43216, 43228
　Ultrasound 43231-43232
　Vein Ligation 43205
Foot
　Plantar Fasciotomy 29893
Gastrointestinal
　Upper
　　Biopsy 43239
　　Catheterization 43241
　　Destruction of Lesion 43258
　　Dilation 43245, 43248-43249
　　Drainage of Pseudocyst 43240
　　Exploration 43234-43235
　　Foreign Body 43247
　　Hemorrhage 43255
　　Inject Varices 43243
　　Needle Biopsy 43242
　　Removal 43247, 43250-43251
　　Stent Placement 43256
　　Suturing 0008T
　　Tube Placement 43246
　　Ultrasound 43242, 43259, 76975
　　Vein Ligation 43244
Ileum
　via Stoma 44383
Intestines, Small
　Biopsy 44361, 44377
　Destruction
　　Lesion 44369
　　Tumor 44369
　Diagnostic 44376
　Exploration 44360
　Hemorrhage 44366, 44378
　Insertion
　　Stent 44370, 44379
　　Tube 44379
　Pelvic Pouch 44385-44386
　Removal
　　Foreign Body 44363
　　Lesion 44365
　　Polyp 44364-44365
　Tube Placement 44372
　Tube Revision 44373
　via Stoma 44380-44383
　Tumor 44364-44365
Kidney
　Biopsy 50555, 50574-50578, 52354
　Catheterization 50553, 50572
　Destruction 50557, 50576, 52354
　Dilation of Ureter 50553
　Excision
　　Tumor 52355
　Exploration 52351
　Lithotripsy 52353
　Radioactive Substance 50559, 50578
　Removal
　　Calculus 50561, 50580, 52352
　　Foreign Body 50561, 50580
　via Incision 50570-50580
　via Stoma 50551-50561
Larynx
　Biopsy 31510, 31535-31536
　Direct 31515-31571
　Exploration 31505, 31520-31526, 31575

Fiberoptic 31575-31579
Indirect 31505-31513
Operative 31530-31561
Removal
　Foreign Body 31530-31531
　Lesion 31511
　　　　　See Endoscopic
Mediastinoscopy
　Biopsy 39400
　Exploration 39400
Nose
　Diagnostic 31231-31235
　Surgical 31237-31294
　Unlisted Services and Procedures 31299
Pancreatic Duct
　Destruction
　　Calculi (Stone) 43265
　　Tumor 43272
　Dilation 43271
　Removal
　　Calculi (Stone) 43264
　　Foreign Body 43269
　　Stent 43269
　Specimen Collection 43260
　Sphincterotomy 43262
　Sphincter Pressure 43263
　Tube Placement 43267-43268
Pelvis
　Aspiration 49322
　Destruction of Lesion 58662
　Lysis of Adhesions 58660
　Oviduct Surgery 58670-58671
　Removal of Adnexal Structures 58661
Peritoneum
　Biopsy 47561
　Drainage
　　Lymphocele 49323, 54690
　　Radiologic 47560
Rectum
　Biopsy 45305
　Destruction
　　Tumor 45320
　Dilation 45303
　Exploration 45300
　Hemorrhage 45317
　Removal
　　Foreign Body 45307
　　Polyp 45308-45315
　　Tumor 45308-45315
　Volvulus 45321
Spleen
　Removal 38120
Testis
　Removal 54690
Trachea
　Dilation 31630-31631
　via Tracheostomy 31615
Ureter
　Biopsy . . .50955-50959, 50974-50978, 52354
　Catheterize 50953, 50972
　Destruction 50957-50959,
　　　　　　　　　　　　　50976-50978, 52354
　Excision
　　Tumor 52355
　Exploration 52351
　Injection of Implant Material 52327
　Lithotripsy 52353

Manipulation of Ureteral Calculus 52330
Placement
    Stent 50947
Radioactive Substance 50959, 50978
Removal
    Calculus 50961, 50980, 52352
    Foreign Body 50961, 50980
Resection 52355
via Incision 50970-50980
via Stoma 50951-50961
Ureteral
Biopsy 52007
Catheterization 52005
Urethra 52000
Biopsy 52204, 52354
Catheterization 52010
Destruction .52354
    Lesion 52400
Evacuation
    Clot 52001
Excision
    Tumor 52355
Exploration 52351
Incision
    Ejaculatory Duct 52347
    Injection of Implant Material 51715
    Lithotripsy .52353
Removal
    Calculus 52352
Resection
    Ejaculatory Duct 52347
Vasectomy 52347
Vasotomy 52347
Uterus
Anesthesia 00952
Hysteroscopy
    Diagnostic .58555
    with Division/Resection Intrauterine
    Septum 58560
    with Lysis of Intrauterine
    Adhesions .58559
Removal
    Endometrial 58563
    Impacted Foreign Body 58562
    Leiomyomata 58561
    Surgical with Biopsy 58558
Vagina
Anesthesia 00950
Biopsy 57454
Exploration 57452

Endosteal Implant
Reconstruction
Mandible 21248-21249
Maxilla 21248-21249

Endothelioma, Dural
See Meningioma

Endotoxin
Bacteria 87176

Endotracheal Intubation
See Insertion, Endotracheal Tube

Endotracheal Tube
Intubation 31500

Endovascular Repair 0001T-0002T,
34800-34804, 34825-34826
Angiography 75952-75953

End Stage Renal Disease
Services 90918-90925

Enema
Home Visit for Fecal Impaction 99511
Intussusception 74283
Therapeutic
    for Intussusception 74283

Energies, Electromagnetic
See Irradiation

ENT
See Ear, Nose, and Throat; Otorhinolaryngology,
Diagnostic
Therapeutic
    See Otorhinolaryngology

Entamoeba Histolytica
Antigen Detection
    Enzyme Immunoassay 87336-87337

Enterectomy 44120-44121,
44126-44128, 44202
Donor 44132-44133
with Enterostomy 44125

Enterocele
Repair 57556
    Hysterectomy
      with Colpectomy 58280

Enterocystoplasty 51960
Camey 50825

Enteroenterostomy
See Anastomosis, Intestines

Enterolysis 44005
Laparoscopic .44200

Enteropancreatostomy
See Anastomosis, Pancreas to Intestines

Enterorrhaphy 44602-44603, 44615

Enterostomy 44300
Closure 44625-44626
with Enterectomy
    Intestine, Small 44125

Enterotomy 44615

Enterovirus
Antibody 86658
Antigen Detection
    Direct Fluorescence 87199

Entropion
Repair 67921-67924
    Blepharoplasty
      Excision Tarsal Wedge 67923
    Suture 67921
    Thermocauterization 67922

Enucleation
Eye
    without Implant 65101
    with Implant 65103
      Muscles Attached 65105
Pleural 32540

Enucleation, Cyst, Ovarian
See Cystectomy, Ovarian

Environmental Intervention
for Psychiatric Patients 90882

Enzyme, Angiotensin-Forming
See Renin

Enzyme, Angiotensin Converting
See Angiotensin Converting Enzyme (ACE)

Enzyme Activity 82657
Radioactive Substrate 82658

EOG
See Electro-oculography

Eosinocyte
See Eosinophils

Eosinophils
Nasal Smear 89190

Epiandrosterone 82666

Epicondylitides, Lateral Humeral
See Tennis Elbow

Epicondylitis, Radiohumeral
See Tennis Elbow

Epidemic Parotitis
See Mumps

Epididymectomy
Bilateral 54861
Unilateral 54860

Epididymis
Abscess
    Incision and Drainage 54700
Anastomosis
    to Vas Deferens
      Bilateral .54901
      Unilateral 54900
Biopsy 54800-54820
Epididymography 74440
Excision
    Bilateral 54861
    Unilateral 54860
Exploration
    Biopsy 54820
Hematoma
    Incision and Drainage 54700
Lesion
    Excision
      Local 54830
      Spermatocele 54840
Needle Biopsy 54800
Spermatocele
    Excision 54840
Unlisted Services and Procedures 55899
X-Ray with Contrast 74440

Epididymograms 55300

Epididymography 74440

Epididymoplasty
See Repair, Epididymis

Epididymovasostomy
Bilateral 54901
Unilateral 54900

Epidural
Electrode
   Insertion .61531
   Removal 61535
Injection 62281-62282, 62310-62319,
                     64479-64484
Lysis 62263

Epidural Anesthesia
See Anesthesia, Epidural

Epidurography 72275

Epigastric
Hernia Repair 49572

Epiglottidectomy 31420

Epiglottis
Excision 31420

Epikeratoplasty 65767

Epilation
See Removal, Hair

Epinephrine
See Catecholamines
Blood .82383-82384
Urine 82384

Epiphyseal Arrest
Femur 20150, 27185, 27475, 27479-27485, 27742
Fibula 20150, 27477-27485, 27730-27742
Radius 20150, 25450-25455
Tibia . .20150, 27477-27485, 27730, 27734-27742
Ulna 20150, 25450-25455

Epiphyseal Separation
Radius
   Closed Treatment 25600
   Open Treatment 25620

Epiphysiodesis
See Epiphyseal Arrest

Epiphysis
See Bone; Specific Bone

Epiploectomy 49255

Episiotomy 59300

Epispadias
Penis
   Reconstruction 54385
Repair 54380-54390
   with Exstrophy of Bladder 54390
   with Incontinence 54380-54390

Epistaxis 30901-30906
with Nasal/Sinus Endoscopy 31238

EPO
See Erythropoietin

Epstein-Barr Virus
Antibody .86663-86665

Equina, Cauda
See Cauda Equina

ERCP
See Bile Duct; Cholangiopancreatography;
Pancreatic Duct

ERG
See Electroretinography

Ergocalciferol
See Calciferol

Ergocalciferols
See Calciferol

Ergonovine Provocation Test . . .93024

Erythrocyte
See Red Blood Cell (RBC)

Erythrocyte ab
See Antibody, Red Blood Cell

Erythrocyte Count
See Red Blood Cell (RBC), Count

Erythropoietin 82668, 99554

Escharotomy
Burns .16035-16036

Escherichia coli 0157
Antigen Detection
   Enzyme Immunoassay 87335

ESD
See Endoscopy, Gastrointestinal, Upper

Esophageal Acid Infusion Test
See Acid Perfusion Test

Esophageal Polyp
See Polyp, Esophagus

Esophageal Tumor
See Tumor, Esophagus

Esophageal Varices
Ligation 43205, 43400
Transection/Repair 43401

Esophagectomy
Partial 43116-43124
Total 43107-43113, 43124

Esophagoenterostomy
with Total Gastrectomy 43620

Esophagogastroduodenoscopies
See Endoscopy, Gastrointestinal, Upper

Esophagogastromyotomy
See Esophagomyotomy

Esophagogastrostomy 43320

Esophagojejunostomy . . .43340-43341

Esophagomyotomy . .32665, 43330-43331

Esophagorrhaphy
See Esophagus, Suture

Esophagoscopies
See Endoscopy, Esophagus

Esophagostomy 43350-43352
Closure 43420-43425

Esophagotomy 43020, 43045

Esophagotracheal Fistula
See Fistula, Tracheoesophageal

Esophagus
Acid Perfusion Test 91030
Acid Reflux Tests 91032-91033
Biopsy
   Endoscopy 43202
Cineradiography 74230
Dilation 43450-43458
   Endoscopic 43220-43226, 43248-43249
   Surgical .43510
Endoscopy
   Biopsy 43202
   Dilation 43220-43226
   Exploration 43200
   Hemorrhage 43227
   Injection .43204
   Insertion Stent 43219
   Needle Biopsy 43232
   Removal
      Foreign Body 43215
      Polyp 43216-43217, 43228
      Tumor 43216, 43228
   Ultrasound 43231-43232
   Vein Ligation 43205
Excision
   Diverticula 43130-43135
   Partial 43116-43124
   Total 43107-43113, 43124
Exploration
   Endoscopy 43200
Hemorrhage .43227
Incision 43020, 43045
   Muscle 43030
Injection
   Sclerosing Agent 43204
Insertion
   Stent 43219
   Tamponade 43460
   Tube 43510
Intubation with Specimen Collection 91000
Lesion
   Excision 43100-43101
Ligation 43405
Motility Study 78258, 91010-91012
Needle Biopsy
   Endoscopy 43232
Nuclear Medicine
   Imaging (Motility) 78258
   Reflux Study 78262
Reconstruction 43300, 43310, 43313
   Creation
      Stoma 43350-43352
      Esophagostomy 43350
      Fistula 43305, 43312, 43314
      Gastrointestinal 43360-43361

Removal
    Foreign Bodies . .43020, 43045, 43215, 74235
    Lesion 43216
    Polyp 43216-43217, 43228
Repair 43300, 43310, 43313
    Esophagogastric Fundoplasty . .43324-43325
        Laparoscopic 43280
    Esophagogastrostomy 43320
    Esophagojejunostomy 43340-43341
    Fistula . . .43305, 43312, 43314, 43420-43425
    Muscle 43330-43331
    Pre-existing Perforation 43405
    Varices 43401
    Wound 43410-43415
Suture 43405
    Wound 43410-43415
Ultrasound
    Endoscopy 43231-43232
Unlisted Services and Procedures . .43289, 43499
Vein
    Ligation 43205, 43400
Video 74230
X-Ray 74220

Esophagus, Varix
See Esophageal Varices

Esophagus Neoplasm
See Tumor, Esophagus

Established Patient
Confirmatory Consultations 99271-99275
Domiciliary or Rest Home Visit 99331-99333
Emergency Department Services . .99281-99285
Home Services 99347-99350
Hospital Inpatient Services 99221-99239
Hospital Observation Services 99217-99220
Initial Inpatient Consultations 99251-99255
Office and/or Other Outpatient
Consultations 99241-99245
Office Visit 99211-99215
Outpatient Visit 99211-99215

Establishment
Colostomy
    Abdominal 50810
    Perineal .50810

Estes Operation
See Ovary, Transposition

Estlander Procedure 40525

Estradiol 82670
Response 80414

Estriol
Blood or Urine 82677

Estrogen
Blood or Urine 82671-82672
Receptor 84233

Estrone
Blood or Urine 82679

Ethanediols
See Ethylene Glycol

Ethanol
Blood 82055
Breath 82075
Urine 82055

Ethchlorovynol
See Ethchlorvynol

Ethchlorvinol
See Ethchlorvynol

Ethchlorvynol
Blood 82690
Urine 82690

Ethmoid
Fracture
    with Fixation 21340

Ethmoid, Sinus
See Sinus, Ethmoid

Ethmoidectomy 31200-31205
Endoscopic 31254-31255
Skull Base Surgery 61580-61581
with Nasal/Sinus Endoscopy 31254-31255

Ethosuccimid
See Ethosuximide

Ethosuximide 80168
Assay 80168

Ethylene Dichlorides
See Dichloroethane

Ethylene Glycol 82693

Ethylmethylsuccimide
See Ethosuximide

Ethyl Alcohol
See Ethanol

Etiocholanalone Measurement
See Etiocholanolone

Etiocholanolone 82696

ETOH
See Alcohol, Ethyl

Euglobulin Lysis 85360

European Blastomycosis
See Cryptococcus

Eustachian Tube
Catheterization 69405
Inflation
    Myringotomy 69420
        Anesthesia 69421
    without Catheterization 69401
    with Catheterization 69400
Insertion
    Catheter .69405

Eutelegenesis
See Artificial Insemination

Evacuation
Cervical Pregnancy 59140
Hematoma
    Brain 61312-61315
    Subungual 11740
Hydatidiform Mole 59870

Evaluation and Management
Athletic Training
    Evaluation 97005
    Re-evaluation 97006
Basic Life and/or Disability
Evaluation Services 99450
Care Plan Oversight Services 99374-99380
    Home Health Agency Care 99374
    Hospice 99377-99378
    Nursing Facility 99379-99380
Case Management Services 99361-99373
Consultation 99241-99275
Critical Care 99291-99292
    Interfacility Transport 99289-99290
Domiciliary or Rest Home 99321-99333
Emergency Department 99281-99288
Health Behavior
    Assessment 96150
    Family Intervention 96154-96155
    Group Intervention 96153
    Individual Intervention 96152
    Re-assessment 96151
Home Services 99341-99350
Hospital 99221-99233
    Discharge 99238-99239
Hospital Services
    Observation Care 99217-99220
Insurance Exam 99455-99456
Medical
    with Individual Psychotherapy
        Hospital or Residential Care 90817,
            90819, 90822, 90824, 90827, 90829
        Office or Outpatient . .90805, 90807, 90809
    with Individual Psychotherapy, Interactive
        Office or Outpatient . .90811, 90813, 90815
Neonatal Intensive Care 99295-99297
Newborn Care 99431-99440
Nursing Facility 99301-99313
    See Nursing Facility Services
Occupation Therapy Evaluation 97003
    Re-evaluation 97004
Office and Other Outpatient 99201-99215
Physical Therapy Evaluation 97001
    Re-evaluation 97002
Physician Standby Services 99360
Preventive Services 99381-99429
Prolonged Services 99356-99357
Psychiatric
    Records or Reports 90885
Psychiatric Residential Treatment
Facility Care 99301-99313
Unlisted Services and Procedures 99499
Work-Related and/or Medical Disability
Evaluation .99450

Evaluation Studies, Drug, Pre-Clinical
See Drug Screen

Evisceration
Ocular Contents
    without Implant 65091
    with Implant 65093

Evisceration, Pelvic
See Exenteration, Pelvis

Evocative/Suppression
Test 80400-80440
Stimulation Panel 80410

Evoked Potential
See Audiologic Function Tests
Auditory Brainstem 92585-92586
Somatosensory Testing 95925-95927
Visual, CNS 95930

Evoked Potential, Auditory
See Auditory Evoked Potentials

Ewart Procedure
See Palate, Reconstruction, Lengthening

Excavatum, Pectus
See Pectus Excavatum

Exchange
Arterial Catheter 37209, 75900
Drainage Catheter
    Under Radiologic Guidance 49423
Intraocular Lens 66986

Exchange Transfusion
See Blood, Transfusion, Exchange

Excision
See Debridement; Destruction
Abscess
    Brain 61514, 61522
    Olecranon Process 24138
    Radius 24136
    Ulna 24138
Acromion
    Shoulder .23130
Adenoids 42830-42836
Adenoma
    Thyroid Gland 60200
Adrenal Gland 60540
    Laparoscopic 60650
    with Excision Retroperitoneal Tumor . .60545
Alveolus 41830
Anal Crypt 46210-46211
Anal Fissure .46200
Anal Tag 46220, 46230
Aorta
    Coarctation 33840-33851
Appendix 44950-44960
Arteriovenous Malformation
    Spinal 63250-63252
Arytenoid Cartilage 31400
    Endoscopic 31560-31561
Atrial Septum 33735-33737
Bartholin's Gland 56740
Bladder
    Diverticulum 51525
    Neck 51520
    Partial 51550-51565
    Total 51570, 51580, 51590-51597
      with Nodes 51575, 51585, 51595

    Transurethral 52640
    Tumor 51530
Bladder Neck Contracture
    Postoperative 52640
Bone
    Facial 21026
    Mandible .21025
    Postoperative
      Femur .20150
      Fibula .20150
      Radius .20150
      Tibia 20150
      Ulna 20150
Bone Abscess
    Facial 21026
    Mandible .21025
Brain
    Hemisphere 61542-61543
    Other Lobe 61539
    Temporal Lobe 61538
Brain Lobe
    See Lobectomy, Brain
Breast
    Biopsy 19100-19103
    Chest Wall Tumor 19260-19272
    Cyst 19120-19126
    Lactiferous Duct Fistula 19112
    Lesion 19120-19126
      by Needle Localization 19125-19126
    Mastectomy 19140-19240
    Nipple Exploration 19110
Bulbourethral Gland 53250
Bullae
    Lung 32141
    Endoscopic 32655
Burns 01951-01953, 15000-15001
Bursa
    Elbow 24105
    Femur 27062
    Ischial 27060
    Knee 27340
    Wrist 25115-25116
Bypass Graft 35901-35907
Calcaneus 28118-28120
Calculi (Stone)
    Parotid Gland 42330, 42340
    Salivary Gland 42330-42340
    Sublingual Gland 42330
    Submandibular Gland 42330-42335
Carotid Artery 60605
Carpal 25145, 25210-25215
Cartilage
    Knee Joint 27332-27333
    Shoulder Joint 23101
    Temporomandibular Joint 21060
    Wrist 25107
Caruncle
    Urethra 53265
Cataract
    Secondary 66830
Cervix
    Electrode .57460
    Radical 57531
    Stump
      Abdominal Approach 57540-57545
      Vaginal Approach 57550-57556
    Total 57530

Chalazion
    Multiple
      Different Lids 67805
      Same Lid 67801
    Single 67800
    with Anesthesia 67808
Chest Wall
    Tumor 19260-19272
Choroid Plexus 61544
Clavicle
    Partial 23120, 23180
    Sequestrectomy 23170
    Total 23125
    Tumor
      Radical Resection 23200
Coccyx 27080
Colon
    Excision
      Partial 44140-44147, 44160
        with Anastomosis 44140
      Total 44150-44156
    Laparoscopic
      with Anastomosis 44204
      with Ileocolostomy 44205
Condyle
    Temporomandibular Joint 21050
Constricting Ring
    Finger 26596
Cornea
    Epithelium 65435
      with Chelating Agent 65436
    Scraping .65430
Coronoidectomy 21070
Cowper's Gland 53250
Cranial Bone
    Tumor 61563-61564
Cyst
    See Ganglion Cyst
    Bile Duct .47715
    Bladder 51500
    Brain 61516, 61524
    Branchial 42810-42815
    Calcaneus 28100-28103
    Carpal 25130-25136
    Clavicle .23140
      with Allograft 23146
      with Autograft 23145
    Facial Bone 21030
    Femur 27065-27067, 27355-27358
    Fibula 27635-27638
    Finger 26160
    Foot 28090
    Hand 26160
    Hip 27065-27067
    Humerus 23150, 24110
      with Allograft 23156, 24116
      with Autograft 23155, 24115
    Ileum 27065-27067
    Kidney 50280-50290
    Knee 27345-27347
    Lung 32140
    Mandible 21040-21041
    Mediastinal 39200
    Mediastinum 32662
    Metacarpal 26200-26205
    Metatarsal 28104-28107
    Mullerian Duct 55680
    Nose 30124-30125
    Olecranon 24120

Olecranon Process
  with Allograft 24126
  with Autograft 24125
Ovarian 58925
  See Cystectomy, Ovarian
Pericardial 33050
  Endoscopic 32661
Phalanges 26210-26215
  Toe 28108
Pilonidal 11770-11772
Pubis 27066-27067
Radius 24120, 25120-25126
  with Allograft 24126
  with Autograft 24125
Salivary Gland 42408
Scapula 23140
  with Allograft 23146
  with Autograft 23145
Seminal Vesicle 55680
Sublingual Gland 42408
Talus 28100-28103
Tarsal 28104-28107
Thyroglossal Duct 60280-60281
Thyroid Gland 60200
Tibia 27635-27638
Toe 28092
Ulna 24120, 25120-25126
  with Allograft 24126
  with Autograft 24125
Urachal
  Bladder 51500
Vaginal 57135
Destruction of the Vestibule of the Mouth
  See Mouth, Vestibule of, Excision, Destruction
Diverticulum, Meckel's
  See Meckel's Diverticulum, Excision
Ear, External
  Partial 69110
  Total 69120
Elbow Joint .24155
Electrode 57522
Embolectomy/Thrombectomy
  Aortoiliac Artery 34151-34201
  Axillary Artery 34101
  Brachial Artery 34101
  Carotid Artery 34001
  Celiac Artery 34151
  Femoral Artery 34201
  Iliac Artery 34151-34201
  Innominate Artery 34001-34101
  Mesentery Artery 34151
  Peroneal Artery 34203
  Popliteal Artery 34203
  Radial Artery 34111
  Renal Artery 34151
  Subclavian Artery 34001-34101
  Tibial Artery 34203
  Ulnar Artery 34111
Embolism
  Pulmonary Artery 33910-33916
Empyema
  Lung 32540
  Pleural 32540
Epididymis
  Bilateral .54861
  Unilateral 54860
Epiglottis 31420

Esophagus
  Diverticula 43130-43135
  Partial 43116-43124
  Total 43107-43113, 43124
Eye
  See Enucleation, Eye
Fallopian Tube
  Salpingectomy 58700
  Salpingo-Oophorectomy 58720
Fascia
  See Fasciectomy
Femur 27360
  Partial 27070-27071
Fibula 27360, 27455-27457, 27641
Fistula
  Anal 46270-46285
Foot
  Fasciectomy 28060
  Radical 28060-28062
Gallbladder 47600-47620
  Cholecystectomy 47562-47564
  with Cholangiography 47563
  with Exploration Common Duct 47564
Ganglion Cyst
  Knee 27347
  Wrist 25111-25112
Gingiva 41820
Gums 41820
  Alveolus .41830
  Operculum 41821
Heart
  Donor 33940
Heart/Lung
  Donor 33930
Hemangioma 11400-11446
Hemorrhoids 46221, 46250
  Clot 46320
  Complex 46260-46262
  Simple 46255
  with Fissurectomy 46257-46258
Hip
  Partial 27070-27071
Humeral Head
  Resection 23195
  Sequestrectomy 23174
Humerus 23184, 23220-23222, 24134, 24140,
                                          24150-24151
Hydrocele
  Spermatic Cord 55500
  Tunica Vaginalis 55040-55041
    Bilateral 55041
    Unilateral 55040
Hygroma, Cystic
  Axillary/Cervical 38550-38555
Hymenotomy 56700
  See Hymen, Excision
Ileum
  Ileoanal Reservoir 45136
  Partial 27070-27071
Inner Ear
  See Ear, Inner, Excision
Interphalangeal Joint
  Toe 28160
Intervertebral Disk
  Decompression 63075-63078
  Hemilaminectomy 63040, 63043-63044
  Herniated 63020-63044, 63055-63066

Intestine
  Laparoscopic
    with Anastomosis 44202-44203
Intestines
  Donor 44132-44133
Intestines, Small 44120-44128
Iris
  Iridectomy
    Optical .66635
    Peripheral 66625
    Sector .66630
    with Corneoscleral or
    Corneal Section 66600
    with Cyclectomy 66605
Kidney
  Donor 50300-50320, 50547
  Partial 50240
  Recipient 50340
  Transplantation 50370
  with Ureters 50220-50236
Kneecap 27350
Labyrinth
  Transcanal 69905
  with Mastoidectomy 69910
Lacrimal Gland
  Partial 68505
  Total 68500
Lacrimal Sac 68520
Larynx
  Partial 31367-31382
  Total 31360-31365
  with Pharynx 31390-31395
Lesion
  Anal 45108, 46922
  Ankle 27630
    Arthroscopic 29891
  Auditory Canal, External
    Exostosis 69140
    Radical without Neck Dissection 69150
    Radical with Neck Dissection 69155
    Soft Tissue 69145
  Bladder .52224
  Brain 61534, 61536
  Brainstem 61575-61576
  Carotid Body 60600-60605
  Colon 44110-44111
  Conjunctiva 68110-68130
    Over 1 cm 68115
    with Adjacent Sclera 68130
  Cornea .65400
    without Graft 65420
  Ear, Middle 69540
  Epididymis
    Local 54830
    Spermatocele 54840
  Esophagus 43100-43101
  Eye 65900
  Eyelid
    Multiple, Different Lids 67805
    Multiple, Same Lid 67801
    Single .67800
    Under Anesthesia 67808
    without Closure 67840
  Femur 27062
  Finger 26160
  Foot 28080, 28090
  Gums 41822-41828
  Hand 26160

Intestines 44110
    Small 43250, 44111
Intraspinal 63265-63273
Knee 27347
Leg, Lower 27630
Meniscus 27347
Mesentery .44820
Mouth 40810-40816, 41116
Nerve 64774-64792
Neuroma .64778
Nose
    Intranasal 30117-30118
Orbit 61333
    Lateral Approach 67420
    Removal 67412
Palate 42104-42120
Pancreas .48120
Penis 54060
    Surgical Excision Penile
        Plaque 54110-54112
Pharynx 42808
Rectum 45108
Sclera 66130
Skin
    Benign 11400-11471
    Malignant 11600-11646
Skull 61500, 61615-61616
Spermatic Cord 55520
Spinal Cord 63300-63308
Stomach .43611
Talus
    Arthroscopic 29891
Testis 54512
Tibia
    Arthroscopic 29891
Toe 28092
Tongue 41110-41114
Urethra 52224, 53265
Uterus 59100
    Leiomyomata 58140, 58551, 58561
Uvula 42104-42107
Wrist Tendon 25110
Lesion, Arthroscopic
    Ankle 29891
    Talus 29891
    Tibia 29891
Lesion, Tendon Sheath
    Arm, Lower 25110
Lip 40500-40530
    Frenum .40819
Liver
    Extensive 47122
    Lobectomy 47125-47130
    Partial 47120, 47125-47130, 47134
    Total 47133
Lung
    Bronchus Resection 32486
    Bullae
        Endoscopic 32655
    Chest Resection 32520-32525
    Completion 32488
    Emphysematous 32491
    Lobe 32480-32482
    Segment 32484
    Total 32440-32445
    Wedge Resection 32500
        Endoscopic 32657

Lung/Heart
    Donor .33930
Lymph Nodes 38500, 38510-38530
    Abdominal 38747
    Inguinofemoral 38760-38765
    Limited, for Staging
        Para-Aortic 38562
        Pelvic 38562
        Retroperitoneal 38564
    Pelvic .38770
    Radical
        Axillary 38740-38745
        Cervical 38720-38724
        Suprahyoid 38700
    Retroperitoneal Transabdominal . . .38780
    Thoracic 38746
Mandibular
    Exostosis 21031
Mastoid
    Complete 69502
    Radical 69511
        Modified 69505
        Petrous Apicectomy 69530
    Simple 69501
Maxilla
    Exostosis 21032
Maxillary Torus Palatinus 21032
Meningioma
    Brain 61512, 61519
Meniscectomy
    Temporomandibular Joint 21060
Metacarpal 26230
Metatarsal 28110-28114, 28122, 28140
    Condyle 28288
Mouth
    Frenum 40819
Mucosa
    Gums .41828
    Mouth 40818
Nails 11750-11752
Nail Fold .11765
Nerve
    Foot 28030
    Leg, Upper 27315-27320
    Sympathetic 64802-64818
Neurofibroma 64788-64790
Neurolemmoma 64788-64792
Neuroma 64774-64786
Nose
    Dermoid Cyst
        Complex 30125
        Simple 30124
    Polyp 30110-30115
    Rhinectomy 30150-30160
    Skin 30120
    Submucous Resection
        Nasal Septum 30520
        Turbinate 30140
    Turbinate 30130-30140
Odontoid Process 22548
Olecranon Process 24147
Omentum .49255
Ovary 58720
    Partial
        Oophorectomy 58940
        Ovarian Malignancy 58943
        Peritoneal Malignancy 58943

Tubal Malignancy 58943
    Wedge Resection 58920
    Total 58940-58943
Oviduct 58720
Palate 42120, 42145
Pancreas
    Ampulla of Vater 48148
    Duct 48148
    Partial 48140-48146, 48150,
                                    48153-48154, 48160
    Peripancreatic Tissue 48005
    Total 48155-48160
Parathyroid Gland 60500-60502
Parotid Gland 42340
    Partial 42410-42415
    Total 42420-42426
Patella 27350
    See Patellectomy
Penile Adhesions
    Post-circumcision 54162
Penis
    Frenulum 54164
    Partial .54120
    Prepuce 54150-54161, 54163
    Radical 54130-54135
    Total 54125
Pericardium 33030-33031
    Endoscopic 32659
Petrous Temporal
    Apex 69530
Phalanges
    Finger 26235-26236
    Toe 28124-28126, 28150-28160
Pharynx 42145
    Partial .42890
    Resection 42892-42894
    with Larynx 31390-31395
Pituitary Gland 61546-61548
Pleura 32310-32320
    Endoscopic 32656
Polyp
    Intestines 43250
    Nose
        Extensive 30115
        Simple 30110
    Sinus .31032
    Urethra 53260
Pressure Ulcers 15920-15999
    See Skin Graft and Flap
Prostate
    Abdominoperineal 45119
    Partial 55801, 55821-55831
    Perineal 55801-55815
    Radical 55810-55815, 55840-55845
    Regrowth 52630
    Residual Obstructive Tissue 52620
    Retropubic 55831-55845
    Suprapubic 55821
    Transurethral 52601, 52612-52614
Pterygium
    with Graft 65426
Pubis
    Partial 27070-27071
Radical Synovium Wrist 25115-25116
Radius 24130, 24136, 24145,
                                    24152-24153, 25145
    Styloid Process 25230

Rectum
  Partial 45111, 45113-45116, 45123
  Prolapse 45130-45135
  Stricture 45150
  Total 45119-45120
  with Colon .45121
Redundant Skin of Eyelid
  See Blepharoplasty
Ribs 21600-21616, 32900
Scapula
  Ostectomy 23190
  Partial 23182
  Sequestrectomy 23172
  Tumor
    Radical Resection 23210
Sclera 66160
Scrotum 55150
Semilunar Cartilage of Knee
  See Knee, Meniscectomy
Seminal Vesicle 55650
Sesamoid Bone
  Foot 28315
Sinus
  Ethmoid 31200-31205
  Maxillary 31225-31230
Skene's Gland 53270
Skin
  Excess 15831-15839
  Lesion
    Benign 11400-11471
    Malignant 11600-11646
  Nose 30120
Skin Graft
  Preparation of Site 15000
Skull 61501
Spermatic Veins 55530-55540
  Abdominal Approach 55535
  Hernia Repair 55540
Spleen 38100-38102
  Laparoscopic 38120
Stapes
  without Foreign Material 69660
  with Footplate Drill Out 69661
Sternum 21620, 21630-21632
Stomach
  Partial 43631-43639
  Total 43620-43622
Sublingual Gland 42450
Submandibular Gland 42440, 42508
Sweat Glands
  Axillary 11450-11451
  Inguinal 11462-11463
  Perianal 11470-11471
  Perineal 11470-11471
  Umbilical 11470-11471
Synovium
  Ankle 27625-27626
  Carpometacarpal Joint 26130
  Elbow 24102
  Hip Joint 27054
  Interphalangeal Joint 26140
  Intertarsal Joint 28070
  Knee Joint 27334-27335
  Metacarpophalangeal Joint 26135
  Metatarsophalangeal Joint 28072
  Shoulder 23105-23106
  Tarsometatarsal Joint 28070
  Wrist 25105, 25118-25119

Talus 28120, 28130
Tarsal 28116, 28122
Temporal, Petrous
  Apex 69530
Temporal Bone 69535
Tendon
  Finger 26180, 26390, 26415
  Hand 26390, 26415
  Palm 26170
Tendon Sheath
  Finger 26145
  Foot 28086-28088
  Palm 26145
  Wrist 25115-25116
Testis
  Laparoscopic 54690
  Partial 54522
  Radical 54530-54535
  Simple 54520
  Tumor 54530-54535
Thrombectomy
  Axillary Vein 34490
  Bypass Graft 35875-35876
  Femoropopliteal Vein 34401-34451
  Iliac Vein 34401-34451
  Subclavian Vein 34471-34490
  Vena Cava 34401-34451
Thromboendarterectomy
  Aorta, Abdominal 35331
  Aortoiliofemoral 35363
  Axillary Artery 35321
  Brachial Artery 35321
  Carotid Artery 35301, 35390
  Celiac Artery 35341
  Femoral Artery 35371-35381
  Iliac 35361-35363
  Iliac Artery 35351
  Iliofemoral Artery 35355, 35363
  Innominate Artery 35311
  Mesenteric Artery 35341
  Peroneal Artery 35381
  Popliteal Artery 35381
  Renal Artery 35341
  Subclavian Artery 35301-35311
  Tibial Artery 35381
  Vertebral Artery 35301
Thymus Gland 60521
Thyroid Gland for Malignancy
  Partial 60210-60225
  Removal All Thyroid Tissue 60260
  Secondary 60260
  Total 60240
    Cervical Approach 60271
    Limited Neck Dissection 60252
    Radical Neck Dissection 60254
    Sternal Split/Transthoracic
    Approach 60270
Tibia 27360, 27640
Tongue
  Complete 41140-41155
  Frenum .41115
  Partial 41120-41135
  with Mouth Resection 41150-41153
  with Radical Neck 41135, 41145-41155
Tonsils 42825-42826
  Lingual .42870
  Radical 42842-42845

Tag 42860
  with Adenoids 42820-42821
Torus Mandibularis 21031
Trachea
  Stenosis 31780-31781
Transcervical Approach 60520
Tricuspid Valve 33460
Tumor
  Abdominal Wall 22900
  Acetabulum 27076
  Ankle 27615-27619
  Arm, Lower 25075-25077
  Arm, Upper 24075-24077
  Back/Flank 21930
  Bile Duct 47711-47712
  Bladder 51530, 52234-52240, 52355
  Brain 61510, 61518, 61520-61521,
                    61526-61530, 61545
  Bronchi .31640
  Calcaneus 27647, 28100-28103
  Carpal 25130-25136
  Clavicle .23140
    with Allograft 23146
    with Autograft 23145
  Ear, Middle
    Extended 69554
    Transcanal 69550
    Transmastoid 69552
  Elbow 24075-24077
  Esophagus
    Endoscopic Ablation 43228
  Facial Bones 21029-21030, 21034
  Facial Tissue 21015
  Femur . . .27065-27067, 27355-27358, 27365
  Fibula 27635-27638, 27646
  Finger 26115-26117
  Foot 28043-28046
  Gums 41825-41827
  Hand 26115-26117
  Heart 33120-33130
  Hip 27047-27049, 27065-27067
    Radical 27075-27076
  Humerus 23150, 23220-23222,
                    24110-24115
    with Allograft 23156, 24116
    with Autograft 23155, 24116
  Ileum 27065-27067
  Innominate 27077
  Intestines
    Small .43250
  Ischial 27078-27079
  Kidney .52355
  Knee 27327-27329, 27365
  Lacrimal Gland
    Frontal Approach 68540
    Involving Osteotomy 68550
  Larynx 31300
    Endoscopic 31540-31541, 31578
  Leg, Lower 27615-27619
  Leg, Upper 27327-27329
  Mandible 21040-21045
  Mediastinal 39220
  Mediastinum 32662
  Metacarpal 26200-26205
    Radical 26250-26255
  Metatarsal 28104-28107, 28173
  Neck 21555-21557

Olecranon Process 24120
    with Allograft 24126
    with Autograft 24125
Parotid Gland 42410-42426
Pelvis 27047-27049
Pericardial 33050
Pericardium 32661
Phalanges 26210-26215, 26260-26262
    Toe 26215, 28108, 28175
Pituitary Gland 61546-61548
Presacral 49215
Pubis 27065-27067
Radius ...24120-24125, 25120-25126, 25170
Rectum 45160-45170
Sacrococcygeal 49215
Scapula 23140
    with Allograft 23146
    with Autograft 23145
Shoulder 23075-23077
Skull 61500
Spermatocele
    See Spermatocele, Excision
Spinal Cord 63275-63290
Spleen, Total
    See Splenectomy, Total
Sternum 21630
Stomach 43610
Talus 27647, 28100-28103
Tarsal 28104-28107, 28171
Thorax 21555-21557
Thyroid 60200
Tibia 27635-27638, 27645-27646
Trachea
    Cervical 31785
    Thoracic 31786
Ulna 24120-24125, 25120-25126, 25170
Ureter 52355
Urethra 52234-52240, 52355, 53220
Uterus
    Abdominal Approach 58140
    Vaginal Approach 58145
Vagina 57135
Vertebra, Lumbar 22102
Vertebra, Thoracic 22101
Wrist 25075-25077
Turbinate 30130-30140
Tympanic Nerve 69676
Ulcer
    Stomach 43610
Ulna 24147, 25145
    Complete 25240
    Partial 25150-25151, 25240
Umbilicus 49250
Ureter
    See Ureterectomy
Ureterocele 51535
Urethra
    Diverticulum 53230-53235
    Prolapse 53275
    Total
        Female 53210
        Male 53215
Uterus
    Laparoscopic 58550
    Partial 58180
    Radical 58210, 58285
    Total 58150-58152, 58200

Vaginal 58260-58270, 58550
    Removal Tubes and/or
    Ovaries 58262-58263
    with Colpectomy 58275-58280
    with Colpo-Urethrocystopexy 58267
    with Repair of Enterocele 58270
Uvula 42140-42145
Vagina
    Closure 57120
    Complete
        with Removal of Paravaginal
        Tissue 57111
        with Removal of Paravaginal Tissue with
        Lymphadenectomy 57112
        with Removal of Vaginal Wall 57110
    Partial
        with Removal of Paravaginal Tissue .57107
        with Removal of Paravaginal Tissue with
        Lymphadenectomy 57109
        with Removal of Vaginal Wall 57106
    Septum 57130
    Total 57110
    with Hysterectomy 58275-58280
    Repair of Enterocele 58280
Varicocele
    Spermatic Cord 55530-55540
        Abdominal Approach 55535
        Hernia Repair 55540
Vascular Malformation
    Finger 26115
    Hand 26115
Vas Deferens 55250
Vertebra
    Additional Segment 22103, 22116
    Cervical 22110
        for Tumor 22100, 22110
    Lumbar 22102
        for Tumor 22114
    Thoracic 22112
        for Tumor 22101
Vertebral Body
    Decompression 63081-63091
    Lesion 63300-63308
Vitreous 67039
    Total
        Pars Plana Approach 67036
        with Epiretinal Membrane
        Stripping 67038
        with Retinal Surgery 67038
Vulva
    Radical
        Complete 56633-56640
        Partial 56630-56632
    Simple
        Complete 56625
        Partial 56620

Exclusion
Duodenum 48547
Small Intestine 44700

Exenteration
Eye
    Removal Orbital Contents 65110
    Therapeutic Removal of Bone 65112
    with Muscle or Myocutaneous Flap ..65114
Pelvis 45126, 58240

Exercise Stress Tests 93015-93018

Exercise Test
See Electromyography, Needle
Ischemic Limb 95875

Exercise Therapy 97110-97113
See Physical Medicine/Therapy/Occupational Therapy

Exfoliation
Chemical 17360

Exocrine, Pancreas
See Pancreas

Exomphalos
See Omphalocele

Exostectomy 28288, 28290

Exostoses
See Exostosis

Exostoses, Cartilaginous
See Exostosis

Exostosis
Excision 69140

Expander, Skin, Inflatable
See Tissue, Expander

Expired Gas Analysis 94680-94690, 94770

See Pulmonology, Diagnostic

Exploration
Abdomen 49000-49002
    Penetrating Wound 20102
    Staging 58960
Adrenal Gland 60540-60545
Anal
    Endoscopy 46600
Ankle 27610, 27620
Arm, Lower 25248
Artery
    Brachial 24495
    Carotid 35701
    Femoral 35721
    Other 35761
    Popliteal 35741
Back
    Penetrating Wound 20102
Bile Duct
    Atresia 47700
    Endoscopy 47552-47553
Blood Vessel
    Abdomen 35840
    Chest 35820
    Extremity 35860
    Neck 35800
Brain
    Infratentorial 61305
    Supratentorial 61304
    via Burr Hole
        Infratentorial 61253
        Supratentorial 61250
Breast 19020
Bronchi
    Endoscopy 31622

Bronchoscopy 31622
Cauda Equina 63005-63011, 63017
Chest
  Penetrating Wound 20101
Colon
  Endoscopic 44388, 45378
Colon-Sigmoid
  Endoscopic 45330
Common Bile Duct
  with Cholecystectomy 47610
Duodenum 44010
Ear, Inner
  Endolymphatic Sac
    without Shunt 69805
    with Shunt 69806
Ear, Middle 69440
Elbow 24000, 24101
Epididymis 54820
Esophagus
  Endoscopy 43200
Extremity
  Penetrating Wound 20103
Finger Joint 26075-26080
Flank
  Penetrating Wound 20102
Gallbladder 47480
Gastrointestinal Tract, Upper
  Endoscopy 43234-43235
Hand Joint 26070
Heart 33310-33315
Hepatic Duct 47400
Hip 27033
Interphalangeal Joint
  Toe 28024
Intertarsal Joint .28020
Intestines, Small
  Endoscopy 44360
  Enterotomy 44020
Kidney 50010, 50045, 50120
Knee 27310, 27331
Lacrimal Duct 68810
  Canaliculi 68840
  with Anesthesia 68811
  with Insertion Tube or Stent 68815
Larynx 31320
  Endoscopy 31505, 31520-31526, 31575
Liver
  Wound 47361-47362
Mediastinum 39000-39010
Metatarsophalangeal Joint 28022
Nasolacrimal Duct 68810
  with Anesthesia 68811
  with Insertion Tube or Stent 68815
Neck
  Lymph Nodes 38542
  Penetrating Wound 20100
Nipple 19110
Nose
  Endoscopy 31231-31235
Orbit 61332-61334
  with/without Biopsy 67450
  without Bone Flap 67400
Parathyroid Gland 60500-60505
Pelvis 49320
Prostate 55860
  with Nodes 55862-55865

Rectum
  Endoscopic 45300
  Injury 45562-45563
Retroperitoneal Area 49010
Scrotum 55110
Shoulder Joint 23040-23044, 23107
Sinus
  Frontal 31070-31075
  Maxillary 31020-31030
Skull 61105
Spinal Cord 63001-63011,
                    63015-63017, 63040-63044
Spine Fusion 22830
Stomach 43500
Tarsometatarsal Joint 28020
Testis
  Undescended 54550-54560
Toe Joint 28024
Ureter 50600
Vagina 57000
  Endocervical .57452
Wrist 25101, 25248
  Joint 25040

Exploration, Larynx by Incision
See Laryngotomy, Diagnostic

Exploratory Laparotomy
See Abdomen, Exploration

Expression
Lesion
  Conjunctiva 68040

Exteriorization, Small Intestine
See Enterostomy

External Auditory Canal
See Auditory Canal

External Cephalic Version 59412

External Ear
See Ear, External

External Extoses
See Exostosis

External Fixation
Adjustment/Revision 20693
Application 20690-20692
Mandibular Fracture
  Open Treatment 21454
  Percutaneous Treatment 21452
Removal 20694

Extirpation, Lacrimal Sac
See Dacryocystectomy

Extracorporeal Circulation 33960-33961
for Regional Chemotherapy
  Extremity 36823

Extracorporeal Dialyses
See Hemodialysis

Extracorporeal Membrane Oxygenation
Cannulization 36822

Extracorporeal Photochemotherapies
See Photopheresis

Extracorporeal Shock Wave Therapy
See Lithotripsy
Musculoskeletal 0019T
Plantar Fascia 0020T

Extraction
Lens
  Extracapsular 66940
  Intracapsular 66920
    for Dislocated Lens 66930

Extraction, Cataract
See Cataract, Excision

Extradural Anesthesia
See Anesthesia, Epidural

Extradural Injection
See Epidural, Injection

Extraocular Muscle
See Eye Muscles

Extrauterine Pregnancy
See Ectopic Pregnancy

Extravasation Blood
See Hemorrhage

Extremity
Lower
  Harvest of Vein for Bypass Graft 35500
    Revision 35879-35881
Upper
  Harvest of Artery for Coronary Artery
    Bypass Graft 35600
  Harvest of Vein for Bypass Graft 35500
  Repair
    Blood Vessel 35206
Wound Exploration
  Penetrating Wound 20103

Eye
See Ciliary Body; Cornea; Iris; Lens; Retina; Sclera; Vitreous
Biometry 76516-76519, 92136
Drainage
  Anterior Chamber
    Discission of Anterior Hyaloid
      Membrane 65810
    with Diagnostic Aspiration of
      Aqueous .65800
    with Removal of Blood 65815
    with Removal of Vitreous and/or with
      Therapeutic Release of Aqueous 65805
Goniotomy 65820
Incision
  Adhesions
    Anterior Synechiae 65860, 65870
    Corneovitreal Adhesions 65880
    Goniosynechiae 65865
    Posterior Synechiae 65875
  Anterior Chamber 65820
  Trabeculae 65850

Injection
    Air 66020
    Medication 66030
Insertion
    Implantation
      Drug Delivery System 67027
      Foreign Material for
      Reinforcement 65155
      Muscles, Not Attached 65135
      Muscles Attached 65140
      Reinsertion 65150
      Scleral Shell 65130
Interferometry
    Biometry 92136
Lesion
    Excision 65900
Nerve
    Destruction 67345
Paracentesis
    Anterior Chamber
      Removal of Blood 65815
      Removal or Vitreous and/or Discission
      Anterior Hyaloid Membrane 65810
      with Diagnostic Aspiration of
      Aqueous 65800
      with Therapeutic Release of
      Aqueous 65805
Radial Keratotomy 65771
Removal
    Blood Clot 65930
    Bone 65112
    Foreign Body
      Conjunctival Embedded 65210
      Conjunctival Superficial 65205
      Corneal without Slit Lamp 65220
      Corneal with Slit Lamp 65222
      Intraocular 65235-65265
    Implant 65175
      Anterior Segment 65920
      Muscles, Not Attached 65103
      Posterior Segment 67120-67121
Repair
    Conjunctiva
      by Mobilization and Rearrangement
      without Hospitalization 65272
      by Mobilization and Rearrangement with
      Hospitalization 65273
      Direct Closure 65270
    Cornea
      Nonperforating 65275
      Perforating 65280-65285
    Muscles 65290
    Sclera
      Anterior Segment 66250
      without Graft 66220
      with Graft 66225
      with Tissue Glue 65286
    Trabeculae 65855
    Wound
      by Mobilization and
      Rearrangement 65272-65273
      Direct Closure 65270
Shunt, Aqueous
    to Extraocular Reservoir 66180
Ultrasound 76511-76513
    Biometry 76516-76519
    Foreign Body 76529

Unlisted Services and Procedures
    Anterior Segment 66999
    Posterior Segment 67299
with Muscle or Myocutaneous Flap 65114
    Muscles Attached 65105
    Ocular Contents
      without Implant 65091
      with Implant 65093
    Orbital Contents 65110
      without Implant 65101
X-Ray 70030

Eyebrow
Repair
    Ptosis 67900

Eyeglasses
See Spectacle Services

Eyelashes
Repair Trichiasis
    Epilation
      by Forceps Only 67820
      by Other than Forceps 67825
    Incision of Lid Margin 67830
      with Free Mucous Membrane
      Graft 67835

Eyelid
Abscess
    Incision and Drainage 67700
Biopsy 67810
Blepharoplasty 15820-15823
Chalazion
    Excision 67805
      Multiple 67801-67805
      Single 67800
      with Anesthesia 67808
Closure by Suture 67875
Incision
    Canthus 67715
    Sutures 67710
Injection
    Subconjunctival 68200
Lesion
    Destruction 67850
    Excision
      Multiple 67801-67805
      Single 67800
      without Closure 67840
      with Anesthesia 67808
Reconstruction
    Canthus 67950
    Total 67973-67975
    Total Eyelid
      Lower 67973-67975
      Second Stage 67975
      Upper 67974
    Transfer of Tarsoconjunctival Flap from
    Opposing Eyelid 67971
Removal
    Foreign Body 67938
Repair 21280-21282
    Blepharoptosis
      Conjunctivo-Tarso-Muller's
      Muscle-Levator Resection 67908
      Frontalis Muscle Technique ..67901-67904
      Reduction Overcorrection of Ptosis ..67909
      Superior Rectus Technique with Fascial
      Sling 67906

Ectropion
    Blepharoplasty 67914
    Suture 67914
Entropion
    Blepharoplasty 67923-67924
    Suture 67921
    Thermocauterization 67922
Excisional 67961
    over One-Fourth of Lid Margin 67966
Lashes
    Epilation, by Forceps Only 67820
    Epilation, by Other than Forceps 67825
    Lid Margin 67830-67835
Wound
    Full Thickness 67935
    Partial Thickness 67930
Repair with Graft
    Retraction 67911
Skin Graft
    Full Thickness 67961
    Split 67961
Suture 67880
    with Transposition of Tarsal Plate 67882
Tissue Transfer, Adjacent 67961
Unlisted Services and Procedures 67999

Eyelid Ptoses
See Blepharoptosis

Eye Allergy Test 95060
See Allergy Tests

Eye Evisceration
See Evisceration, Ocular Contents

Eye Exam
Established Patient 92012-92014
New Patient 92002-92004
with Anesthesia 92018-92019

Eye Exercises
Training 92065

Eye Muscles
Biopsy 67350
Repair
    Strabismus
      Adjustable Sutures 67335
      Exploration and/or Repair Detached
      Extraocular Muscle 67340
      One Vertical Muscle............67314
      on Patient with Previous Surgery ...67331
      Posterior Fixation Suture 67334
      Recession or Resection 67311-67312
      Release of Scar Tissue without Detaching
      Extraocular Muscle 67343
      Two or More Vertical Muscles 67316
      with Scarring Extraocular Muscles ..67332
      with Superior Oblique Muscle 67318
Transposition 67320
Unlisted Services and Procedures 67399

Eye Prosthesis
See Prosthesis

Eye Socket
See Orbit; Orbital Contents; Orbital Floor;
Periorbital Region

E Antigens
See Hepatitis Antigen, Be

E B Virus
See Epstein-Barr Virus

E Vitamin
See Tocopherol

F

Face
CAT Scan 70486-70488
Lesion
    Destruction 17000-17004, 17280-17286
Magnetic Resonance Imaging
(MRI) 70540-70543
Tumor Resection 21015

Face Lift 15824-15828

Facial Asymmetries
See Hemifacial Microsomia

Facial Bone
See Mandible; Maxilla
Tumor
    Excision 21034

Facial Bones
Abscess
    Excision 21026
Reconstruction
    Secondary 21275
Repair 21208-21209
Tumor
    Excision 21029-21030
    Resection
        Radical 21015
X-Ray 70140-70150

Facial Nerve
Anastomosis
    to Hypoglossal 64868
    to Phrenic Nerve 64870
    to Spinal Accessory 64866
Avulsion 64742
Decompression 61590, 61596
    Intratemporal
        Lateral to Geniculate
        Ganglion 69720, 69740
        Medial to Geniculate
        Ganglion 69725, 69745
        Total 69955
Function Study 92516
Incision 64742
Injection
    Anesthetic 64402
Mobilization 61590
Repair
    Lateral to Geniculate Ganglion 69740
    Medial to Geniculate Ganglion 69745
Repair/Suture
    with or without Graft 64864-64865
Suture
    Lateral to Geniculate Ganglion 69740
    Medial to Geniculate Ganglion 69745
Transection 64742

Facial Nerve Paralysis
Graft 15840-15845
Repair 15840-15845

Facial Prosthesis
Impression 21088

Facial Rhytidectomy
See Face Lift

Factor, ACTH-Releasing
See Corticotropic Releasing Hormone (CRH)

Factor, Antinuclear
See Antinuclear Antibodies (ANA)

Factor, Blood Coagulation
See Clotting Factor

Factor, Fitzgerald
See Fitzgerald Factor

Factor, Fletcher
See Fletcher Factor

Factor, Hyperglycemic-Glycogenolytic
See Glucagon

Factor, Intrinsic
See Intrinsic Factor

Factor, Sulfation
See Somatomedin

Factor I
See Fibrinogen

Factor II
See Prothrombin

Factor III
See Thromboplastin

Factor Inhibitor Test 85335

Factor IV
See Calcium

Factor IX
See Christmas Factor

Factor Rheumatoid
See Rheumatoid Factor

Factor VII
See Proconvertin

Factor VIII
See Clotting Factor

Factor X
See Stuart-Prower Factor

Factor X, Activated
See Thrombokinase

Factor Xa Inhibitor
See Antithrombin III

Factor XI
See Plasma Thromboplastin, Antecedent

Factor XII
See Hageman Factor

Factor XIII
See Fibrin Stabilizing Factor

Fallopian Tube
Anastomosis 58750
Catheterization 58345, 74742
Destruction
    Endoscopy 58670
Ectopic Pregnancy 59121
    with Salpingectomy and/or
    Oophorectomy 59120
Excision 58700-58720
Ligation 58600-58611
Lysis
    Adhesions 58740
Occlusion 58615
    Endoscopy 58671
Repair 58752
    Anastomosis 58750
    Create Stoma 58770
Tumor
    Resection 58950, 58952-58954
Unlisted Services and Procedures 58999
X-Ray 74742

Fallopian Tube Pregnancy
See Ectopic Pregnancy, Tubal

Fallot, Tetralogy of
See Tetralogy of Fallot

Family Psychotherapy
See Psychotherapy, Family

Fanconi Anemia
Chromosome Analysis 88248

Farnsworth-Munsell Color Test
See Color Vision Examination

Farr Test
See Gammaglobulin, Blood

Fasanella-Servat Procedure ...67908

Fascial Defect
Repair 50728

Fascial Graft
Free
    Microvascular Anastomosis 15758
Open Treatment
    Sternoclavicular Dislocation 23532

Fascia Graft 15840

Fascia Lata Graft
Harvesting 20920-20922

Fasciectomy
Foot 28060
    Radical 28060-28062
Palm 26121-26125

Fasciocutaneous Flaps ...15732-15738

Fasciotomy
Arm, Lower 24495, 25020-25025
Elbow 24350-24356
Foot 28008
Hand Decompression 26037
Hip 27025

Knee 27305, 27496-27499
Leg, Lower 27600-27602, 27892-27894
Leg, Upper . . .27305, 27496-27499, 27892-27894
Palm 26040-26045
Plantar
    Endoscopic 29893
Thigh 27025
Toe 28008
Wrist 25020-25025

FAST
See Allergen Immunotherapy

Fat
Feces 82705-82715
Removal
    Lipectomy 15876-15879

Fatty Acid
Blood 82725
Very Long Chain .82726

Fat Stain
Feces 89125
Respiratory Secretions 89125
Sputum 89125
Urine 89125

Favre-Durand Disease
See Lymphogranuloma Venereum

FC Receptor .86243

FDP
See Fibrin Degradation Products

Feedback, Psychophysiologic
See Biofeedback; Training, Biofeedback

Female Castration
See Oophorectomy

Female Gonad
See Ovary

Femoral Arteries
See Artery, Femoral

Femoral Stem Prosthesis
See Arthroplasty, Hip

Femoral Vein
See Vein, Femoral

Femur
See Hip; Knee; Leg, Upper
Abscess
    Incision 27303
Bursa
    Excision 27062
Craterization 27070, 27360
Cyst
    Excision 27065-27067, 27355-27358
Diaphysectomy .27360
Drainage 27303
Excision 27070, 27360
    Epiphyseal Bar 20150
Fracture
    Closed Treatment 27501-27503
    Distal 27508, 27510, 27514
    Distal, Medial or Lateral Condyle 27509
    Epiphysis 27516-27519

Intertrochanteric
    Closed Treatment 27238
    Open Treatment 27244
    with Implant 27245
    with Manipulation 27240
Neck
    Closed Treatment 27230-27232
    Open Treatment 27236
    Percutaneous Fixation 27235
Open Treatment 27244-27245,
             27506-27507, 27511-27513
Percutaneous Fixation 27509
Pertrochanteric
    Closed Treatment 27238
    Open Treatment 27244
    with Implant 27245
    with Manipulation 27240
Shaft 27500, 27502, 27506-27507
Subtrochanteric
    Closed Treatment 27238
    Open Treatment 27244
    with Implant 27245
    with Manipulation 27240
Supracondylar 27501-27503, 27509,
                        27511-27513
Transcondylar 27501-27503, 27509,
                        27511-27513
Trochanteric
    Closed Treatment 27246
    Open Treatment 27248
    without Manipulation 27501
    with Manipulation 27503
Halo 20663
Lesion
    Excision 27062
Osteoplasty
    Lengthening 27466-27468
    Shortening 27465, 27468
Osteotomy
    without Fixation 27448
Prophylactic Treatment 27187, 27495
Realignment 27454
Reconstruction .27468
    at Knee 27442-27443, 27446
    Lengthening 27466-27468
    Shortening 27465, 27468
Repair 27470-27472
    Epiphysis 27181, 27475, 27742
      Arrest 27185
    Muscle Transfer 27110
    Osteotomy 27140, 27151-27156,
             27161-27165, 27450-27454
    with Graft 27170
Saucerization 27070, 27360
Tumor
    Excision . .27065-27067, 27355-27358, 27365
X-Ray 73550

Fenestration, Pericardium
See Pericardiostomy

Fenestration Procedure
Semicircular Canal 69820
    Revision 69840
Tracheostomy .31610

Fern Test 87210
See Smear and Stain, Wet Mount

Ferric Chloride
Urine 81005

Ferrihemoglobin
See Methemoglobin

Ferritin
Blood or Urine .82728

Ferroxidase
See Ceruloplasmin

Fertility Control
See Contraception

Fertility Test
Semen Analysis 89300-89321
Sperm Analysis
    Cervical Mucus Penetration Test 89330
    Hamster Penetration 89329

Fertilization
Assisted
    Oocyte
        Microtechnique 89252
Oocyte
    with Co-Culture of Embryo 89250-89251
Oocytes (Eggs)
    In Vitro 89250

Fertilization in Vitro
See In Vitro Fertilization

Fetal Biophysical Profile .76818-76819

Fetal Contraction Stress Test . .59020

Fetal Hemoglobin 85461

Fetal Lung Maturity Assessment;
Lecithin Sphingomyelin Ratio . .83661

Fetal Monitoring
See Monitoring, Fetal

Fetal Non-Stress Test 59025
Ultrasound 76818

Fetal Testing
Amniotic Fluid
    Lung Maturity 83661, 83663-83664
Heart .76825-76826
    Doppler
        Complete 76827
        Follow-up or Repeat Study 76828
Hemoglobin 83030-83033, 85460
Ultrasound 76805-76816, 76819
    Heart 76825

Fetuin
See Alpha-Fetoprotein

Fever, Australian Q
See Q Fever

Fever, Japanese River
See Scrub Typhus

Fibrillation
Atrial 33253

Fibrillation, Heart
See Heart, Fibrillation

Fibrinase
See Plasmin

Fibrinogen 85384-85385

Fibrinolysin
See Plasmin

Fibrinolysins 85390

Fibrinolysis
Alpha-2 Antiplasmin 85410
Plasmin 85400
Plasminogen 85420-85421
Plasminogen Activator 85415

**Fibrin Degradation
Products** 85362-85379

Fibrin Deposit
Removal 32150

**Fibrin Stabilizing
Factor** 85290-85291

Fibroadenoma
Excision 19120-19126

Fibroblastoma, Arachnoidal
See Meningioma

Fibrocutaneous Tags 11200-11201

Fibromatosis, Dupuytren's
See Dupuytren's Contracture

Fibromatosis, Penile
See Peyronie Disease

Fibromyoma
See Leiomyomata

Fibronectin, Fetal 82731

Fibrosis, Penile
See Peyronie Disease

Fibrosis, Retroperitoneal
See Retroperitoneal Fibrosis

Fibrous Cavernitides
See Peyronie Disease

Fibrous Dysplasia 21029,
21181-21184

Fibula
See Ankle; Knee; Tibia
Bone Graft with Microvascular
Anastomosis 20955
Craterization 27360, 27641
Cyst
    Excision 27635-27638
Diaphysectomy 27360, 27641
Excision 27360, 27641
    Epiphyseal Bar 20150
Fracture
    Malleolus 27786-27814
    Shaft 27780-27784
Incision 27607
Osteoplasty
    Lengthening 27715

Repair
    Epiphysis 27477-27485, 27730-27742
    Osteotomy 27707-27712
Saucerization 27360, 27641
Tumor
    Excision 27635-27638, 27646
    X-Ray 73590

Figure of Eight Cast 29049

Filariasis 86280

Filtering Operation
See Incision, Sclera, Fistulization; Incision and Drainage

Filtration Implant, Glaucoma
See Aqueous Shunt

Fimbrioplasty 58760
Laparoscopic 58672

Fine Needle Aspiration ...10021-10022
Evaluation 88172-88173

Finger
See Phalanx, Finger
Abscess
    Bone
        Incision and Drainage 26034
    Incision and Drainage 26010-26011
Amputation 26951-26952
    with Exploration or Removal 26910
Arthrocentesis 20600
Arthrodesis
    Interphalangeal Joint 26860-26863
    Metacarpophalangeal Joint 26850-26852
Bone
    Incision and Drainage 26034
Cast 29086
Collection of Blood 36415
Decompression 26035
Excision
    Constricting Ring 26596
    Tendon 26180, 26390, 26415
Insertion
    Tendon Graft 26392
Magnetic Resonance Imaging (MRI) 73221
Reconstruction
    Extra Digit 26587
    Toe to Hand Transfer 26551-26556
Removal
    Implantation 26320
    Tube 26392, 26416
Repair
    Blood Vessel 35207
    Claw Finger 26499
    Extra Digit 26587
    Macrodactylia 26590
    Tendon
        Extensor 26415-26434,
                        26445-26449, 26460
        Flexor 26356-26358,
                        26440-26442, 26455
    Volar Plate 26548
    Web Finger 26560-26562
Replantation 20816-20822
Reposition 26555
Sesamoidectomy 26185

Splint 29130-29131
Strapping 29280
Tendon Sheath
    Excision 26145
    Incision 26055
    Incision and Drainage 26020
Tenotomy 26060, 26460
    Flexor 26455
Tumor
    Excision 26115-26117
Unlisted Services and Procedures 26989
X-Ray 73140

Finger Flap
Tissue Transfer 14350

Finger Joint
See Intercarpal Joint

Finney Operation
See Gastroduodenostomy

Fishberg Concentration Test
See Water Load Test

Fissurectomy 46200

Fissurectomy, Anal
See Anus, Fissure, Excision

Fissure in Ano
See Anus, Fissure

Fistula
Anal
    Repair 46288
Autogenous Graft 36825
Bronchi
    Repair 32815
Carotid-Cavernous
    Repair 61710
Chest Wall
    Repair 32906
Conjunctiva
    without Tube 68745
    with Tube or Stent 68750
Enterovesical
    Closure 44660-44661
Kidney 50520-50526
Lacrimal Gland Closure 68770
    Dacryocystorhinostomy 68720
Nose
    Repair 30580-30600
Oval Window 69666
Postauricular 69700
Rectovaginal
    Abdominal Approach 57305
    Transperineal Approach 57308
    with Concomitant Colostomy 57307
Round Window 69667
Sclera
    Iridencleisis or Iridotasis 66165
    Sclerectomy with Punch or Scissors
    with Iridectomy 66160
    Thermocauterization with Iridectomy ..66155
    Trabeculectomy ab Externo in
    Absence Previous Surgery 66170
    Trabeculectomy ab Externo with
    Scarring 66172
    Trephination with Iridectomy 66150

Suture
    Kidney 50520-50526
    Ureter 50920-50930
Trachea 31755
Tracheoesophageal
    Repair 43305, 43312, 43314
    Speech Prosthesis 31611
Ureter 50920-50930
Urethra 53400-53405
Urethrovaginal 57310
    with Bulbocavernosus Transplant 57311
Vesicouterine
    Closure 51920-51925
Vesicovaginal
    Closure 51900
    Transvesical and Vaginal Approach . . .57330
    Vaginal Approach 57320
X-Ray 76080

Fistula Arteriovenous
See Arteriovenous Fistula

Fistulectomy
Anal 46060, 46270-46285
    See Hemorrhoids

Fistulization
Conjunction
    to Nasal Cavity 68745
Esophagus 43350-43352
Intestines 44300-44346
Lacrimal Sac
    to Nasal Cavity 68720
Penis 54435
Pharynx 42955
Repair Salivary Cyst
    Sublingual 42325-42326
Tracheopharyngeal 31755

Fistulization, Interatrial
See Septostomy, Atrial

Fistulotomy
Anal .46270, 46280

Fitting
Cervical Cap 57170
Contact Lens 92070, 92310-92313
    See Contact Lens Services
Diaphragm 57170
Low Vision Aid 92354-92355
    See Spectacle Services
Ocular Prosthesis 92330
Spectacles 92340-92342
Spectacle Prosthesis 92352-92353

Fitzgerald Factor 85293

Fixation
Interdental
    without Fracture 21497

Fixation, External
See External Fixation

Fixation, Kidney
See Nephropexy

Fixation, Rectum
See Proctopexy

Fixation, Tongue
See Tongue, Fixation

Fixation (Device)
See Application; Bone, Fixation; Spinal
Instrumentation
Application
    External 20690-20692
Pelvic
    Insertion 22848
Removal
    External 20694
    Internal 20670-20680
Sacrospinous Ligament
    Vaginal Prolapse 57282
Shoulder 23700
Skeletal
    Humeral Epycondyle
        Percutaneous 24566
Spinal
    Insertion 22841-22847
    Prosthetic .22851
    Reinsertion 22849

Fixation Test, Complement
See Complement, Fixation Test

Flank
See Back/Flank

Flap
See Skin Graft and Flap
Free
    Breast Reconstruction 19364
Grafts 15574-15650, 15842
Latissimus Dorsi
    Breast Reconstruction 19361
Omentum
    Free
        with Microvascular Anastomosis . . .49906
Transverse Rectus Abdominis Myocutaneous
    Breast Reconstruction 19367-19369

Flatfoot Correction 28735

Flea Typhus
See Murine Typhus

Fletcher Factor 85292

Flow-Volume Loop
See Pulmonology, Diagnostic
Pulmonary 94375

Flow Cytometry 88180-88182

Fluid, Amniotic
See Amniotic Fluid

Fluid, Body
See Body Fluid

Fluid, Cerebrospinal
See Cerebrospinal Fluid

Fluid Collection
Incision and Drainage
    Skin 10140

Fluorescein
Angiography, Ocular 92287
Intravenous Injection
    Vascular Flow Check, Graft 15860

Fluorescein Angiography
See Angiography, Fluorescein

Fluoride
Blood 82735
Urine 82735

Fluoroscopy
Bile Duct
    Calculus Removal 74327
    Guide Catheter 74328, 74330
Chest 31628
    Complete (Four Views) 71034
    Partial (Two Views) 71023
Drain Abscess 75989
GI Tract
    Guide Intubation 74340
Hourly 76000-76001
Introduction
    GI Tube 74340
Larynx 70370
Needle Biopsy 76003
Pancreatic Duct
    Guide Catheter 74329-74330
Pharynx 70370
Renal
    Guide Catheter 74475
Spine/Paraspinous
    Guide Catheter/Needle 76005
Ureter
    Guide Catheter 74480
Vertebra
    Osteoplasty 76012

Flurazepam
Blood or Urine 82742

Flush Aortogram 75722-75724

Flu Vaccines 90645-90660

FNA
See Fine Needle Aspiration

Foam Stability Test 83662

Fold, Vocal
See Vocal Cords

Foley Operation Pyeloplasty
See Pyeloplasty

Foley Y-Pyeloplasty 50400-50405

Folic Acid 82747
Blood 82746

**Follicle Stimulating Hormone
(FSH)** 80418, 80426, 83001

Folliculin
See Estrone

Follitropin
See Follicle Stimulating Hormone (FSH)

Follow-up Inpatient Consultations
See Consultation, Follow-up Inpatient

Follow-up Services
See Hospital Services; Office and/or Other Outpatient Services
Inpatient Consultations 99261-99263
Post-Op 99024

Fontan Procedure
See Repair, Heart, Anomaly; Revision

Food Allergy Test 95075
See Allergy Tests

Foot
See Metatarsal; Tarsal
Amputation 28800-28805
Bursa
    Incision and Drainage 28001
Capsulotomy 28260-28264
Cast 29450
Fasciectomy 28060
    Radical .28060-28062
Fasciotomy 28008
    Endoscopic 29893
Incision .28002-28005
Joint
    See Talotarsal Joint; Tarsometatarsal Joint
    Magnetic Resonance Imaging
    (MRI) 73721-73723
Lesion
    Excision 28080, 28090
Magnetic Resonance Imaging
(MRI) 73718-73720
Nerve
    Excision 28030
    Incision 28035
Neuroma
    Excision 28080
Reconstruction
    Cleft Foot 28360
Removal
    Foreign Body 28190-28193
Repair
    Muscle 28250
    Tendon 28200-28230, 28234-28238
Replantation 20838
Sesamoid
    Excision 28315
Splint 29590
Strapping 29590
Suture
    Tendon 28200-28210
Tendon Sheath
    Excision 28086-28088
Tenotomy 28230, 28234
Tumor
    Excision 28043-28046
Unlisted Services and Procedures 28899
X-Ray 73620-73630

Foot Abscess
See Abscess, Foot

Foot Navicular Bone
See Navicular

Forearm 20805
See Arm, Lower

Forehead
Reconstruction 21179-21180, 21182-21184
    Midface 21159-21160
Reduction 21137-21139

Forehead and Orbital Rim
Reconstruction 21172-21180

Foreign Body Removal
Pharynx 42809
Shoulder 23331

Forensic Exam 88040
Cytopathology .88125
Phosphatase, Acid 84061

Foreskin of Penis
See Penis, Prepuce

Formycin Diphosphate
See Fibrin Degradation Products

Fowler-Stephens Orchiopexy
See Orchiopexy

Fowler-Stephens Procedure . . .54650

Fox Operation
See Entropion, Repair

Fraction, Factor IX
See Christmas Factor

Fracture
Acetabulum
    Closed Treatment 27220-27222
    Open Treatment 27226-27228
    without Manipulation 27220
    with Manipulation 27222
Alveola
    Closed Treatment 21421
    Open Treatment 21422-21423
Alveolar Ridge
    Closed Treatment 21440
    Open Treatment 21445
Ankle
    Closed Treatment 27816-27818
    Lateral 27786-27814
    Medial 27760-27766, 27808-27814
    Open Treatment 27822-27823
    Trimalleolar 27816-27823
    without Manipulation 27816
    with Manipulation 27818
Ankle Bone
    Medial 27760-27762
Bennett's
    See Thumb, Fracture
Bronchi
    Endoscopy 31630
Calcaneus
    Closed Treatment 28400-28405
    Open Treatment 28415-28420
    Percutaneous Fixation 28436
    without Manipulation 28400
    with Manipulation 28405-28406

Carpal
    Closed Treatment
        without Manipulation 25622, 25630
        with Manipulation 25624, 25635
    Open Treatment 25628, 25645
Carpal Scaphoid
    Closed Treatment 25622
Cheekbone
    Open Treatment 21360-21366
    with Manipulation 21355
Clavicle
    Closed Treatment
        without Manipulation 23500
        with Manipulation 23505
    Open Treatment 23515
Closed Treatment 27520
Coccyx
    Closed Treatment 27200
    Open Treatment 27202
Colles
    See Colles Fracture
Colles-Reversed
    See Smith Fracture
Elbow
    Monteggia
        Closed Treatment 24620
        Open Treatment 24635
    Open Treatment 24586-24587
Femur
    Closed Treatment 27230, 27238-27240,
        27246, 27500-27503, 27508, 27510,
        27516-27517
    with Manipulation 27232
    Distal 27508, 27510, 27514
    Epiphysis 27516-27519
    Intertrochanteric
        Closed Treatment 27238
        Open Treatment 27244
        with Implant 27245
        with Manipulation 27240
    Neck
        Closed Treatment 27230
        Open Treatment 27236
        Percutaneous Fixation 27235
        with Manipulation 27232
    Open Treatment 27244-27245, 27248,
        27506-27507, 27511-27514, 27519
    Percutaneous Fixation 27235, 27509
    Pertrochanteric
        Closed Treatment 27238
        Open Treatment 27244-27245
        with Manipulation 27240
    Shaft 27500, 27502, 27506-27507
    Subtrochanteric
        Closed Treatment 27238
        Open Treatment 27244-27245
        with Manipulation 27240
    Supracondylar 27501-27503, 27509,
        27511-27513
    Transcondylar 27501-27503, 27509,
        27511-27513
    Trochanteric
        Closed Treatment 27246
        Open Treatment 27248
    without Manipulation 27230, 27238,
        27246, 27500-27501, 27508,
        27516-27517, 27520
    with Manipulation 27232, 27502-27503,
        27510

Fibula
    Closed Treatment 27780-27781,
            27786-27788, 27808-27810
    Malleolus 27786-27814
    Open Treatment 27784, 27792, 27814
    Shaft 27780-27786, 27808
    without Manipulation 27780-27781
    with Manipulation 27788, 27810
Frontal Sinus
    Open Treatment 21343-21344
Great Toe
    Closed Treatment 28490
    without Manipulation 28490
Heel
    Open Treatment 28415-28420
    without Manipulation 28400
    with Manipulation 28405-28406
Humerus
    Closed Treatment 24500-24505
       without Manipulation 23600
       with Manipulation 23605
    Condyle
       Closed Treatment 24576-24577
       Open Treatment 24579
       Percutaneous 24582
    Epicondyle
       Closed Treatment 24560-24565
       Open Treatment 24575
       Skeletal Fixation
         Percutaneous 24566
    Greater Tuberosity Fracture
       Closed Treatment without
       Manipulation 23620
       Closed Treatment with
       Manipulation 23625
       Open Treatment 23630
    Open Treatment 23615-23616
    Shaft 24500-24505
       Open Treatment 24515-24516
    Supracondylar
       Closed Treatment 24530-24535
       Open Treatment 24545-24546
       Percutaneous Fixation 24538
    Transcondylar
       Closed Treatment 24530-24535
       Open Treatment 24545-24546
       Percutaneous Fixation 24538
    with Dislocation
       Closed Treatment 23665
       Open Treatment 23670
    with Shoulder Dislocation
       Closed Treatment 23675
       Open Treatment 23680
Hyoid Bone
    Closed Treatment
       Manipulation 21494
       without Manipulation 21493
    Open Treatment 21495
Ilium
    Open Treatment 27215, 27218
    Percutaneous Fixation 27216
Knee 27520
    Arthroscopic Treatment 29850-29851
    Open Treatment 27524

Larynx
    Closed Treatment
       without Manipulation 31585
       with Manipulation 31586
    Open Treatment 31584
Malar Area
    Open Treatment 21360-21366
    with Bone Graft 21366
    with Manipulation 21355
Mandible
    Closed Treatment
       Interdental Fixation 21453
       without Manipulation 21450
       with Manipulation 21451
    Open Treatment 21454-21470
       External Fixation 21454
       without Interdental Fixation 21461
       with Interdental Fixation 21462
    Percutaneous Treatment 21452
Maxilla
    Closed Treatment 21421
    Open Treatment 21422-21423
Metacarpal
    Closed Treatment 26600-26605
       with Fixation 26607
    Open Treatment 26615
    Percutaneous Fixation 26608
    without Manipulation 26600
    with Manipulation 26605-26607
Metatarsal
    Closed Treatment 28470-28475
    Open Treatment 28485
    Percutaneous Fixation 28476
    without Manipulation 28450, 28470
    with Manipulation 28475-28476
Monteggia
    See Fracture, Ulna; Monteggia Fracture
Nasal Bone
    Closed Treatment 21310-21320
    Open Treatment 21325-21335
    without Manipulation 21310
    with Manipulation 21315-21320
Nasal Septum
    Closed Treatment 21337
    Open Treatment 21336
Nasal Turbinate
    Therapeutic 30930
Nasoethmoid
    Open Treatment 21338-21339
    Percutaneous Treatment 21340
    with Fixation 21340
Nasomaxillary
    Closed Treatment 21345
    Open Treatment 21346-21348
    with Bone Grafting 21348
    with Fixation 21345-21347
Navicular
    Closed Treatment 25622
    Open Treatment 25628
    with Manipulation 25624
Odontoid
    Open Treatment
       without Graft 22318
       with Graft 22319
Orbit
    Closed Treatment
       without Manipulation 21400
       with Manipulation 21401

    Open Treatment 21406-21408
    Blowout Fracture 21385-21395
Orbital Floor
    Blow Out 21385-21395
Palate
    Closed Treatment 21421
    Open Treatment 21422-21423
Patella
    Closed Treatment
       without Manipulation 27520
    Open Treatment 27524
Pelvic Ring
    Closed Treatment 27193-27194
    Open Treatment
       Anterior 27217
       Posterior 27218
    Percutaneous Fixation 27216
    without Manipulation 27193-27194
Phalanges
    Articular
       Closed Treatment 26740
       Open Treatment 26746
       with Manipulation 26742
    Closed Treatment 26742, 28510
       Articular 26740
       Distal .26750
       with Manipulation 26755
    Distal 26755-26756
       Closed Treatment 26750
       Open Treatment 26765
       Percutaneous Fixation 26756
    Finger/Thumb
       Closed Treatment 26720-26725
       Shaft 26720, 26727
       with Manipulation 26725-26727
    Great Toe 28490
       Closed Treatment 28495
       Open Treatment 28505
       Percutaneous Fixation 28496
       with Manipulation 28495-28496
    Open Treatment 26735, 26746
       Distal .26765
    Shaft
       Closed Treatment 26725
       Open Treatment 26735
       Percutaneous Fixation 26727
    Toe
       Closed Treatment 28515
       Open Treatment 28525
       without Manipulation 28510
       with Manipulation 28515
    without Manipulation 26740, 26750
    with Manipulation 26742, 26755
Radius
    Closed Treatment 25560-25565
    Colles 25600-25605
    Distal 25600-25611
       Open Treatment 25620
       Smith 25600-25620
    Head/Neck
       Closed Treatment 24650-24655
       Open Treatment 24665-24666
    Open Treatment 25515, 25620
    Percutaneous Fixation 25611
    Shaft 25500, 25525-25526
       Closed Treatment 25500-25505, 25520
       Open Treatment 25515, 25525-25526,
                   25574

without Manipulation 25560, 25600
with Manipulation 25565, 25605
with Ulna 25560-25565
    Open Treatment 25575
Rib
    Closed Treatment 21800
    External Fixation 21810
    Open Treatment 21805
Scaphoid
    Closed Treatment 25622
    Open Treatment 25628
    with Dislocation
        Closed Treatment 25680
        Open Treatment 25685
    with Manipulation 25624
Scapula
    Closed Treatment
        without Manipulation 23570
        with Manipulation 23575
    Open Treatment 23585
Sesamoid
    Closed Treatment 28530
    Foot 28530-28531
    Open Treatment 28531
Skin
    Debridement 11010-11012
Skull 62000-62010
    Closed Treatment 21300
Sternum
    Closed Treatment 21820
    Open Treatment 21825
Talus
    Closed Treatment 28430-28435
    Open Treatment 28445
    without Manipulation 28430
    with Manipulation 28435-28436
Tarsal
    Open Treatment 28465
    Percutaneous Fixation 28456
    with Manipulation 28455-28456
Thumb
    with Dislocation 26645-26650
        Open Treatment 26665
Tibia
    Arthroscopic Treatment 29855-29856
    Closed Treatment 27530-27532, 27538,
                    27750-27752, 27760-27762,
                    27808-27810, 27824-27825
    Distal 27824-27828
    Intercondylar 27538-27540
    Malleolus 27760-27766, 27808-27814
    Open Treatment 27535-27536, 27540,
       27758-27759, 27766, 27814, 27826-27828
    Percutaneous Fixation 27756
    Plateau 27530-27536, 29855-29856
    Shaft 27750-27759
    without Manipulation 27530, 27750,
                   27760-27762, 27808, 27825
    with Manipulation 27752, 27760-27762,
                              27810
Trachea
    Endoscopy 31630
Ulna
    See Elbow; Humerus; Radius
    Closed Treatment 25560-25565
    Olecranon
        Closed Treatment 24670-24675
        Open Treatment 24685

Open Treatment 25574-25575
Shaft
    Closed Treatment 25530-25535
    Open Treatment 25545, 25574
Styloid Process
    Closed Treatment 25650
    Open Treatment 25652
    Percutaneous Fixation 25651
    without Manipulation 25530, 25560
    with Dislocation
        Closed Treatment 24620
        Monteggia 24620-24635
        Open Treatment 24635
    with Manipulation 25535, 25565
    with Radius 25560-25565
        Open Treatment 25575
Vertebra
    Additional Segment
        Open Treatment 22328
    Cervical
        Open Treatment 22326
    Closed Treatment
        without Manipulation 22310
        with Manipulation, Casting and/or
        Bracing 22315
    Lumbar
        Open Treatment 22325
    Posterior
        Open Treatment 22325-22327
    Thoracic
        Open Treatment 22327
    with Shoulder Dislocation
        Closed Treatment 23675
        Open Treatment 23680
Vertebral Process
    Closed Treatment 22305
Wrist
    with Dislocation
        Closed Treatment 25680
        Open Treatment 25685
Zygomatic Arch
    Open Treatment 21356-21366
    with Manipulation 21355

Fragile-X
Chromosome Analysis 88248

Fragility
Red Blood Cell
    Mechanical 85547
    Osmotic 85555-85557

Frames, Stereotactic
See Stereotactic Frame

Francisella 86000
Antibody 86668

Fredet-Ramstedt Procedure 43520

Free E3
See Estriol

Free Skin Graft
See Skin, Grafts, Free

Free T4
See Thyroxine, Free

Frei Disease
See Lymphogranuloma Venereum

Frenectomy 40819, 41115

Frenectomy, Lingual
See Excision, Tongue, Frenum

Frenotomy 40806, 41010

Frenulectomy 40819

Frenuloplasty 41520

Frenum
Lip
    Incision 40806
       See Lip

Frenumectomy 40819

Frickman Operation
See Proctopexy

Frontal Craniotomy 61556

Frontal Sinus
See Sinus, Frontal

Frontal Sinusotomy
See Exploration, Sinus, Frontal

Frost Suture 67875

**Frozen Blood
Preparation** 86930-86932

Fructose 84375
Semen 82757

Fruit Sugar
See Fructose

FSF 85290-85291

FSH
See Follicle Stimulating Hormone (FSH)

FSP
See Fibrin Degradation Products

FT-4 84439

Fulguration
See Destruction
Bladder 51020
Cystourethroscopy with 52214
    Lesion 52224
    Tumor 52234-52240
Ureter 50957-50959, 50976-50978
Ureterocele
    Ectopic 52301
    Orthotopic 52300

Fulguration, Endocavitary
See Electrocautery

Full Thickness Graft 15200-15261

Function, Study, Nasal
See Nasal Function Study

Functional Ability
See Activities of Daily Living

Function Test, Lung
See Pulmonology, Diagnostic

Function Test, Vestibular
See Vestibular Function Tests

Fundoplasty
Esophagogastric 43324-43325
    Laparoscopic .43280
    with Gastroplasty 43326

Fundoplication
See Fundoplasty, Esophagogastric

Fungus
Antibody 86671
Culture
    Blood 87103
    Identification 87106
    Other 87102
    Skin 87101
Tissue Exam 87220

Funnel Chest
See Pectus Excavatum

Furuncle
Incision and Drainage 10060-10061

Furuncle, Vulva
See Abscess, Vulva

Fusion
See Arthrodesis
Pleural Cavity 32005
Thumb
    in Opposition 26820

Fusion, Epiphyseal-Diaphyseal
See Epiphyseal Arrest

Fusion, Joint
See Arthrodesis

Fusion, Joint, Ankle
See Ankle, Arthrodesis

Fusion, Joint, Interphalangeal, Finger
See Arthrodesis, Finger Joint, Interphalangeal

G

Gago Procedure
See Repair, Tricuspid Valve; Revision

Gait Training .97116
See Physical Medicine/Therapy/Occupational Therapy

Galactogram 76086-76088
Injection 19030

Galactokinase
Blood 82759

Galactose
Blood 82760
Urine 82760

Galactose-1-Phosphate
Uridyl Transferase 82775-82776

Gallbladder
See Bile Duct
Anastomosis
    with Intestines 47720-47741
Excision 47562-47564, 47600-47620
Exploration 47480
Incision 47490
Incision and Drainage 47480
Nuclear Medicine
    Imaging 78223
Removal
    Calculi (Stone) 47480
Repair
    with Gastroenterostomy 47741
    with Intestines 47720-47740
Unlisted Services and Procedures 47999
X-Ray with Contrast 74290-74291

Gall Bladder
See Gallbladder

Galvanocautery
See Electrocautery

Galvanoionization
See Iontophoresis

Gamete Intrafallopian Transfer
See GIFT

Gamete Transfer
In Vitro Fertilization 58976

Gammacorten
See Dexamethasone

Gammaglobulin
Blood 82784-82787

Gamma Camera Imaging
See Nuclear Medicine

Gamma Glutamyl Transferase 82977

Gamma Seminoprotein
See Antigen, Prostate Specific

Gamulin Rh
See Immune Globulins, Rho (D)

Ganglia, Trigeminal
See Gasserian Ganglion

Ganglion
See Gasserian Ganglion
Cyst
    Drainage 20600-20605
    Injection 20550, 20600-20605
    Wrist
      Excision 25111-25112
Injection
    Anesthetic 64505, 64510

Ganglion, Gasser's
See Gasserian Ganglion

Ganglion Cervicothoracicum
See Stellate Ganglion

Ganglion Pterygogpalatinum
See Sphenopalatine Ganglion

Gardnerella Vaginalis Detection 87510-87512

Gardner Operation
See Meningocele Repair

Gasserian Ganglion
Sensory Root
    Decompression 61450
    Section 61450
Stereotactic 61790

Gasser Ganglion
See Gasserian Ganglion

Gastrectomy
Partial .43631-43639
    with Gastrojejunostomy 43632
Total 43621-43622
    with Esophagoenterostomy 43620
with Gastroduodenostomy 43631

Gastric Acid 82926-82928

Gastric Analysis Test 91052

Gastric Intubation . . .89130-89141, 91105

Gastric Lavage, Therapeutic . . .91105

Gastric Tests
Manometry 91020

Gastric Ulcer Disease
See Stomach, Ulcer

Gastrin 82938-82941

Gastrocnemius Recession
Leg, Lower 27687

Gastroduodenostomy 43810, 43850-43855

Gastroenterology, Diagnostic
Breath Hydrogen Test 91065
Esophagus Tests
    Acid Perfusion 91030
    Acid Reflux 91032-91033
    Intubation with Specimen Collection . .91000
    Motility Study 91010-91012
Gastric Tests
    Manometry .91020
Intestine
    Bleeding Tube 91100
Manometry 91020
Rectum/Anus
    Manometry .91122
Stomach
    Intubation with Specimen Prep 91055
    Saline Load Test 91060
    Stimulation of Secretion 91052
Unlisted Services and Procedures 91299

Gastroenterostomy
for Obesity 43846

Gastrointestinal, Upper

Biopsy
    Endoscopy 43239
Dilation
    Endoscopy 43245
    Esophagus 43248
Endoscopy
    Catheterization 43241
    Destruction
      Lesion 43258
    Dilation 43245
    Drainage
      Pseudocyst 43240
    Exploration 43234-43235
    Hemorrhage .43255
    Inject Varices 43243
    Needle Biopsy 43242
    Removal
      Foreign Body 43247
      Lesion 43251
      Polyp 43251
      Tumor 43251
    Stent Placement 43256
    Suturing
      Esophagogastric junction 0008T
    Tube Placement 43246
    Ultrasound 43242, 76975
Exploration
    Endoscopy 43234-43235
Hemorrhage
    Endoscopic Control 43255
Injection
    Varices 43243
Lesion
    Destruction .43258
Ligation of Vein 43244
Needle Biopsy
    Endoscopy .43242
Removal
    Foreign Body 43247
    Lesion 43250
    Polyp 43250-43251
    Tumor 43250
Tube Placement
    Endoscopy .43246
Ultrasound
    Endoscopy 43242, 43259

Gastrointestinal Endoscopies

See Endoscopy, Gastrointestinal

Gastrointestinal Exam

Nuclear Medicine
    Blood Loss Study 78278
    Protein Loss Study 78282
    Shunt Testing 78291
    Unlisted Services and Procedures 78299

Gastrointestinal Tract

Reconstruction 43360-43361
Upper
    Dilation 43249
    X-Ray 74240-74245
      Guide Dilator 74360
      Guide Intubation 74340-74350
      with Contrast 74246-74249

Gastrojejunostomy 43860-43865

without Vagotomy 43820
with Duodenal Exclusion 48547
with Partial Gastrectomy 43632
with Vagotomy 43825

Gastroplasty

Revision
    for Obesity .43848

Gastroplasty with Esophagogastric Fundoplasty 43326, 43842-43843

Gastrorrhaphy 43840

Gastroschises

See Gastroschisis

Gastroschisis 49605

Gastrostomy

Closure 43870
Laparoscopic
    Temporary 43653
Temporary 43830
    Laparoscopic 43653
    Neonatal 43831
with Pancreatic Drain 48001
with Pyloroplasty 43640
with Vagotomy 43640

Gastrostomy Tube

Change of 43760
Directed Placement
    Endoscopic 43246
Insertion
    Percutaneous 43750
Percutaneous .43750
Repositioning .43761

Gastrotomy 43500-43501, 43510

GDH

See Glutamate Dehydrogenase

Gel Diffusion 86331

Gel Diffusion Test

See Immunodiffusion

Gene Product

See Protein

Genioplasty 21120-21123

Augmentation 21120, 21123
Osteotomy 21121-21123

Genitourinary Sphincter, Artificial

See Prosthesis, Urethral Sphincter

Genotype Analysis

by Nucleic Acid
    Infectious Agent
      Hepatitis C Virus 87902
      HIV-1 Protease/Reverse
      Transcriptase 87901

Gentamicin 80170

Assay 80170

Gentamycin Level

See Gentamicin

Gentiobiase

See Beta Glucosidase

Genus: Human Cytomegalovirus Group

See Cytomegalovirus

German Measles

See Rubella

Gestational Trophoblastic Tumor

See Hydatidiform Mole

GGT

See Gamma Glutamyl Transferase

Giardia Lamblia

Antibody 86674

Gibbons Stent 52332

GIF

See Somatostatin

GIFT 89250

Gillies Approach

Fracture
    Zygomatic Arch 21356

Gill Operation 63012

Gingiva

See Gums

Gingiva, Abcess

See Abscess
Fracture
    See Abscess, Gums; Gums
    Zygomatic Arch
      See Abscess, Gums; Gums, Abscess

Gingivectomy 41820

Gingivoplasty 41872

Girdlestone Laminectomy

See Laminectomy

Girdlestone Procedure

See Acetabulum, Reconstruction

GI Tract

See Gastrointestinal Tract

Gland

See Specific Gland

Gland, Adrenal

See Adrenal Gland

Gland, Bartholin's

See Bartholin's Gland

Gland, Bulbourethral

See Bulbourethral Gland

Gland, Lacrimal

See Lacrimal Gland

Gland, Mammary

See Breast

Gland, Parathyroid

See Parathyroid Gland

Gland, Parotid
See Parotid Gland

Gland, Pituitary
See Pituitary Gland

Gland, Salivary
See Salivary Glands

Gland, Sublingual
See Sublingual Gland

Gland, Sweat
See Sweat Glands

Gland, Thymus
See Thymus Gland

Gland, Thyroid
See Thyroid Gland

Glasses
See Spectacle Services

Glaucoma
Fistulization of Sclera 66150
Provocative Test 92140

Glaucoma Drainage Implant
See Aqueous Shunt

Gla Protein (Bone)
See Osteocalcin

Glenn Procedure 33766-33767

Glenohumeral Joint
Arthrotomy 23040
    with Biopsy .23100
    with Synovectomy 23105
Exploration 23107
Removal
    Foreign or Loose Body 23107

Glenoid Fossa
Reconstruction 21255

GLN
See Glutamine

Globulin
Antihuman .86880-86886
Immune 90281-90399
Sex Hormone Binding 84270

Globulin, Corticosteroid-Binding
See Transcortin

Globulin, Rh Immune
See Immune Globulins, Rho (D)

Globulin, Thyroxine-Binding
See Thyroxine Binding Globulin

Glomerular Procoagulant Activity
See Thromboplastin

Glomus Caroticum
See Carotid Body

Glossectomies
See Excision, Tongue

Glossopexy
See Tongue, Fixation

Glossorrhaphy
See Suture, Tongue

Glucagon 82943
Tolerance Panel 80422-80424
Tolerance Test 82946

Glucose . .80422-80424, 80430-80435, 95250
Blood Test 82947-82950, 82962
Body Fluid 82945
Interstitial Fluid
    Continuous Monitoring 95250
Tolerance Test 82951-82952
    with Tolbutamide 82953

Glucose-6-Phosphate
Dehydrogenase 82955-82960

Glucose Phosphate Isomerase
See Phosphohexose Isomerase

Glucose Phosphate Isomerase Measurement
See Phosphohexose Isomerase

Glucosidase .82963

Glucuronide Androstanediol . . .82154

Glue
Cornea Wound 65286
Sclera Wound 65286

Glukagon
See Glucagon

Glutamate Dehydrogenase
Blood 82965

Glutamate Pyruvate Transaminase
See Transaminase, Glutamic Pyruvic

Glutamic Alanine Transaminase
See Transaminase, Glutamic Pyruvic

Glutamic Aspartic Transaminase
See Transaminase, Glutamic Oxaloacetic

Glutamic Dehydrogenase
See Glutamate Dehydrogenase

Glutamine 82975

Glutamyltransferase, Gamma 82977

Glutathione .82978

Glutathione Reductase 82979

Glutethimide 82980

Glycanhydrolase, N-Acetylmuramide
See Lysozyme

Glycated Hemoglobins
See Glycohemoglobin

Glycated Protein 82985

Glycerol, Phosphatidyl
See Phosphatidylglycerol

Glycerol Phosphoglycerides
See Phosphatidylglycerol

Glycerophosphatase
See Alkaline Phosphatase

Glycinate, Theophylline Sodium
See Theophylline

Glycocholic Acid
See Cholylglycine

Glycohemoglobin 83036

Glycol, Ethylene
See Ethylene Glycol

Glycols, Ethylene
See Ethylene Glycol

Glycosaminoglycan
See Mucopolysaccharides

GMP
See Guanosine Monophosphate

GMP, Cyclic
See Cyclic GMP

Goeckerman Treatment 96910-96913

Gol-Vernet Operation
See Pyelotomy, Exploration

Gold
Assay 80172

Goldwaite Procedure 27422

Golfer's Elbow
See Tennis Elbow

Gonadectomy, Female
See Oophorectomy

Gonadectomy, Male
See Excision, Testis

Gonadotropin
Chorionic .84702-84703
FSH 83001
ICSH 83002
LH 83002

Gonadotropin Panel 80426

Gonioscopy .92020

Goniotomy 65820

Gonococcus
See Neisseria Gonorrhoeae

Goodenough Harris Drawing Test 96100

GOTT
See Transaminase, Glutamic Oxaloacetic

GPUT
See Galactose-1-Phosphate, Uridyl Transferase

Graft

See Bone Graft; Bypass Graft
Anal 46753
Aorta 33840-33851, 33860-33877
Artery
    Coronary 33503-33505
Bone
    See Bone Marrow, Transplantation
    Harvesting 20900-20902
    Microvascular Anastomosis 20955-20962
    Osteocutaneous Flap with Microvascular
    Anastomosis 20969-20973
    Vascular Pedicle 25430
Bone and Skin 20969-20973
Cartilage
    Ear to Face 21235
    Harvesting 20910-20912
        See Cartilage Graft
    Rib to Face 21230
Cornea
    with Lesion Excision 65426
Cornea Transplant
    in Aphakia 65750
    in Pseudophakia 65755
    Lamellar 65710
    Penetrating 65730
Dura
    Spinal Cord 63710
Facial Nerve Paralysis 15840-15845
Fascia
    Cheek 15840
Fascia Lata
    Harvesting 20920-20922
Gum Mucosa 41870
Heart
    See Heart, Transplantation
Heart Lung
    See Transplantation, Heart-Lung
Kidney
    See Kidney, Transplantation
Liver
    See Liver, Transplantation
Lung
    See Lung, Transplantation
Muscle
    Cheek 15841-15845
Nail Bed
    Reconstruction 11762
Nerve 64885-64907
Oral Mucosa 40818
Organ
    See Transplantation
Pancreas
    See Pancreas, Transplantation
Skin
    Biological
        See Allograft, Skin
    Blood Flow Check, Graft 15860
        See Skin Graft and Flap
    Vascular Flow Check, Graft 15860
Tendon
    Finger 26392
    Hand 26392
    Harvesting 20924
Tissue
    Harvesting 20926
Vein
    Cross-Over 34520

Grain Alcohol

See Alcohol, Ethyl

Granulation Tissue

Cauterization, Chemical 17250

Gravi, Myasthenia

See Myasthenia Gravis

Gravities, Specific

See Specific Gravity

Greater Tuberosity Fracture

with Shoulder Dislocation
    Closed Treatment 23665
    Open Treatment 23670

Greater Vestibular Gland

See Bartholin's Gland

Great Toe

Free Osteocutaneous Flap with
Microvascular Anastomosis 20973

Great Vessels

Shunt
    Aorta to Pulmonary Artery
        Ascending 33755
        Descending 33762
    Central 33764
    Subclavian to Pulmonary Artery 33750
    Vena Cava to Pulmonary
    Artery 33766-33767
Unlisted Services and Procedures 33999

Great Vessels Transposition

See Transposition, Great Arteries

Green Operation

See Scapulopexy

Gridley Stain 88312

Grippe, Balkan

See Q Fever

Gritti Operation

See Amputation, Leg, Upper; Radical Resection;
Replantation

Groin Area

Repair
    Hernia 49550-49557

Grouping, Blood

See Blood Typing

Group Health Education 99078

Growth Factors, Insulin-Like

See Somatomedin

Growth Hormone 83003

Human 80418, 80428-80430, 86277

Growth Hormone Release Inhibiting Factor

See Somatostatin

GTT

See Hydatidiform Mole

Guaiac Test

See Blood, Feces

Guanosine Monophosphate 83008

Guanosine Monophosphate, Cyclic

See Cyclic GMP

Guanylic Acids

See Guanosine Monophosphate

Guard Stain 88313

Gullet

See Esophagus

Gums

Abscess
    Incision and Drainage 41800
Alveolus
    Excision 41830
Cyst
    Incision and Drainage 41800
Excision
    Gingiva 41820
    Operculum 41821
Graft
    Mucosa 41870
Hematoma
    Incision and Drainage 41800
Lesion
    Destruction 41850
    Excision 41822-41828
Mucosa
    Excision 41828
Reconstruction
    Alveolus 41874
    Gingiva 41872
Removal
    Foreign Body 41805
Tumor
    Excision 41825-41827
Unlisted Services and Procedures 41899

Gunning-Lieben Test

See Acetone, Blood or Urine

Guthrie Test 84030

H

H-Reflex Study 95934-95936

HAAb

See Antibody, Hepatitis

HAA (Hepatitis Associated Antigen)

See Hepatitis Antigen, B Surface

Haemoglobin F

See Fetal Hemoglobin

Haemorrhage

See Hemorrhage

Haemorrhage Rectum

See Hemorrhage, Rectum

Hageman Factor 85280

Hair
Electrolysis 17380
KOH Examination 87220
Microscopic Evaluation 96902
Transplant
    Punch Graft 15775-15776
    Strip Graft 15220-15221

Hair Removal
See Removal, Hair

HAI Test
See Hemagglutination Inhibition Test

Hallux
See Great Toe

Halo
Body Cast 29000
Cranial 20661
    for Thin Skull Osteology 20664
Femur 20663
Maxillofacial 21100
Pelvic 20662
Removal 20665

Haloperidol
Assay 80173

Halsted Mastectomy
See Mastectomy, Radical

Halsted Repair
See Hernia, Repair, Inguinal

Hammertoe Repair 28285-28286

Hamster Penetration Test 89329

Ham Test
See Hemolysins

Hand
See Carpometacarpal Joint; Intercarpal Joint
Amputation
    at Metacarpal 25927
    at Wrist 25920
      Revision 25922
    Revision 25924, 25929-25931
Arthrodesis
    Carpometacarpal Joint 26843-26844
    Intercarpal Joint 25820-25825
Bone
    Incision and Drainage 26034
Cast 29085
Decompression 26035-26037
Fracture
    Metacarpal 26600
Insertion
    Tendon Graft 26392
Magnetic Resonance Imaging
(MRI) 73218-73223
Reconstruction
    Tendon Pulley 26500-26504
Removal
    Implantation 26320
    Tube/Rod 26390-26392, 26416

Repair
    Blood Vessel 35207
    Cleft Hand 26580
    Muscle 26591-26593
    Tendon
      Extensor 26410-26416, 26426-26428,
                  26433-26437
      Flexor 26350-26358, 26440
      Profundus 26370-26373
Replantation 20808
Strapping 29280
Tendon
    Excision 26390
    Extensor 26415
Tenotomy 26450, 26460
Tumor
    Excision 26115-26117
Unlisted Services and Procedures 26989
X-Ray 73120-73130

Hand(s) Dupuytrens Contracture(s)
See Dupuytren's Contracture

Handling
Device 99002
Radioelement 77790
Specimen 99000-99001

Hand Abscess
See Abscess, Hand

Hand Phalange
See Finger, Bone

Hanganutziu Deicher Antibodies
See Antibody, Heterophile

Haptoglobin 83010-83012

Hard Palate
See Palate

Harelip Operation
See Cleft Lip, Repair

Harii Procedure 25430

Harrington Rod
Insertion 22840
Removal 22850

Hartmann Procedure 44143

Harvesting
Bone Graft 20900-20902
Bone Marrow 38230
Cartilage Graft 20910-20912
Eggs
    In Vitro Fertilization 58970
Fascia Lata Graft 20920-20922
Intestines 44132-44133
Kidney 50300-50320, 50547
Liver 47133-47134
Stem Cell 38231
Tendon Graft 20924
Tissue Grafts 20926
Upper Extremity Artery
    for Coronary Artery Bypass Graft 35600
Upper Extremity Vein
    for Bypass Graft 35500

Hauser Procedure 27420

Hayem's Elementary Corpuscle
See Blood, Platelet

Haygroves Procedure
See Reconstruction, Acetabulum; Revision

HBcAb
See Antibody, Hepatitis

HBeAb
See Antibody, Hepatitis

HBeAg
See Hepatitis Antigen, Be

HBsAb
See Antibody, Hepatitis

HBsAg (Hepatitis B Surface Antigen)
See Hepatitis Antigen, B Surface

HCG
See Chorionic Gonadotropin

HCO3
See Bicarbonate

HCV Antibodies
See Antibody, Hepatitis C

HDL
See Lipoprotein

Head
Angiography 70496, 70544-70546
CAT Scan 70450-70470, 70496
Excision 21015-21070
Fracture and/or Dislocation 21300-21497
Incision 21010
Introduction or Removal 21076-21116
Lipectomy, Suction Assisted 15876
Magnetic Resonance Angiography
(MRA) 70544-70546
Nerve
    Graft 64885-64886
Other Procedures 21299, 21499
Repair/Revision and/or
Reconstruction 21120-21296
Ultrasound Exam 76506, 76536
Unlisted Services and Procedures 21499
X-Ray 70350

Headbrace
Application 21100
Application/Removal 20661

Head Rings, Stereotactic
See Stereotactic Frame

Heaf Test
See TB Test

Health Behavior
See Evaluation and Management, Health Behavior

Health Risk Assessment Instrument
See Preventive Medicine

Hearing Aid

Bone Conduction
Implantation 69710
Removal 69711
Repair 69711
Replacement 69710

Hearing Aid Check 92592-92593

Hearing Aid Services

Electroacoustic Test 92594-92595
Examination 92590-92591

Hearing Evaluation 92510

Hearing Tests

See Audiologic Function Tests; Hearing
Evaluation

Hearing Therapy 92507-92510

Heart

Ablation
Ventricular Septum
Non-surgical 0024T
Angiography
Injection 93542-93543
See Cardiac Catheterization; Injection
Aortic Arch
without Cardiopulmonary Bypass 33852
with Cardiopulmonary Bypass 33853
Aortic Valve
Repair
Left Ventricle 33414
Replacement 33405-33413
Arrhythmogenic Focus
Catheter Ablation 93650-93652
Destruction 33250-33251, 33261
Atria
See Atria
Biopsy 93505
Imaging Guidance 76932
Ultrasound
Imaging Guidance 76932
Blood Vessel
Repair 33320-33322
Cardiac Output Measurements 93561-93562
Cardiac Rehabilitation 93797-93798
Cardioassist 92970-92971
Cardiopulmonary Bypass
with Lung Transplant 32852, 32854
Catheterization 93501, 93510-93533
Combined Right and Retrograde Left
for Congenital Cardiac Anomalies . . .93531
Combined Right and Transseptal Left
for Congenital Cardiac
Anomalies 93532-93533
Flow Directed 93503
Right
for Congenital Cardiac Anomalies . . .93530
See Catheterization, Cardiac
Closure
Septal Defect 33615
Valve
Atrioventricular 33600
Semilunar 33602
Commissurotomy
Right Ventricle 33476-33478
Destruction
Arrhythmogenic Focus 33250, 33261

Electrical Recording
3-D Mapping 93613
Atria 93602
Atrial Electrogram, Esophageal
(or Trans-esophageal) 93615-93616
Bundle of His 93600
Comprehensive 93619-93622
Right Ventricle 93603
Tachycardia Sites 93609
Electroconversion 92960-92961
Electrophysiologic Follow-up Study 93624
Excision
Donor 33930, 33940
Tricuspid Valve 33460
Fibrillation
Atrial 33253
Great Vessels
See Great Vessels
Heart-Lung Bypass
See Cardiopulmonary Bypass
Heart-Lung Transplantation
See Transplantation, Heart-Lung
Implantation
Ventricular Assist Device 33976
Intracorporeal 33979
Incision
Atrial 33253
Exploration 33310-33315
Injection
Radiologic 93542-93543
See Cardiac Catheterization, Injection
Insertion
Balloon Device 33973
Defibrillator 33246
Electrode 33210-33211, 33216-33217
Pacemaker 33200-33208
Catheter .33210
Pulse Generator 33212-33213
Ventricular Assist Device 33975
Intraoperative Pacing and Mapping 93631
Ligation
Fistula 37607
Magnetic Resonance Imaging
(MRI) 75552-75553
Mitral Valve
See Mitral Valve
Muscle
See Myocardium
Myocardium
Imaging 78466-78469
Perfusion Study 78460-78465
Nuclear Medicine
Blood Flow Study 78414
Blood Pool Imaging 78472-78473,
78481-78483, 78494-78496
Myocardial Imaging 78466-78469
Myocardial Perfusion 78460-78465
Shunt Detection 78428
Unlisted Services and Procedures 78499
Open Chest Massage 32160
Output
See Cardiac Output
Pacemaker
Conversion .33214
Insertion 33200-33208
Pulse Generator 33212-33213
Removal 33233-33237

Replacement 33206-33208
Catheter 33210
Upgrade 33214
Pacing
Arrhythmia Induction 93618
Atria 93610
Transcutaneous
Temporary 92953
Ventricular .93612
Pacing Cardioverter-Defibrillator
Evaluation and Testing 93640-93642,
93740-93744
Insertion Single/Dual Chamber
Electrodes 33216-33217, 33245-33249
Pulse Generator 33240, 33246
Positron Emission Tomography (PET) 78459
Perfusion Study 78491-78492
Pulmonary Valve
See Pulmonary Valve
Rate Increase
See Tachycardia
Reconstruction
Atrial Septum 33735-33737
Vena Cava .34502
Reduction
Ventricular Septum
Non-surgical 0024T
Removal
Balloon Device 33974
Electrode 33238
Ventricular Assist Device 33977-33978
Intracorporeal 33980
Removal Single/Dual Chamber
Electrodes 33243-33244
Pulse Generator 33241
Repair 33218-33220
Repair
Anomaly 33615-33617
Aortic Sinus 33702-33722
Atrial Septum 33253, 33641, 33647
Atrioventricular Canal 33660-33665
Complete 33670
Prosthetic Valve 33670
Atrioventricular Valve 33660-33665
Cor Triatriatum 33732
Electrode 33218
Infundibular 33476-33478
Mitral Valve 33420-33430
Myocardium 33542
Outflow Tract 33476-33478
Postinfarction 33542-33545
Prosthetic Valve Dysfunction 33496
Septal Defect 33608-33610, 33660,
33813-33814
Sinus of Valsalva 33702-33722
Sinus Venosus 33645
Tetralogy of Fallot 33692-33697, 33924
Tricuspid Valve 33463-33468
Ventricle 33611-33612
Obstruction 33619
Ventricular Septum 33545, 33647,
33681-33688, 33692-33697
Ventricular Tunnel 33722
Wound 33300-33305
Replacement
Electrode 33210-33211, 33217
Mitral Valve 33430
Tricuspid Valve 33465

Repositioning
　　Electrode 33216-33217
　　Tricuspid Valve 33468
Resuscitation 92950
Septal Defect
　　See Septal Defect
Stimulation and Pacing 93623
Transplantation 33935, 33945
Tricuspid Valve
　　See Tricuspid Valve
Tumor
　　Excision 33120-33130
Unlisted Services and Procedures 33999
Ventriculography
　　See Ventriculography
Ventriculomyectomy 33416
Wound
　　Repair 33300-33305

Heart Vessels
Angioplasty
　　Percutaneous 92982-92984
　　　See Angioplasty; Percutaneous
　　　Transluminal Angioplasty
Insertion
　　Graft 33330-33335
Thrombolysis 92975-92977
Valvuloplasty
　　See Valvuloplasty
　　Percutaneous 92986-92990

Heat Unstable Haemoglobin
See Hemoglobin, Thermolabile

Heavy Lipoproteins
See Lipoprotein

Heavy Metal 83015-83018

Heel
See Calcaneus
Collection of Blood 36415
X-Ray 73650

Heel Bone
See Calcaneus

Heel Fracture
See Calcaneus, Fracture

Heel Spur
Excision 28119

Heine-Medin Disease
See Polio

Heine Operation
See Cyclodialysis

Heinz Bodies 85441-85445

Helicobacter Pylori
Antibody 86677
Antigen Detection
　　Enzyme Immunoassay 87338-87339
Breath Test 78267-78268, 83013-83014
Stool 87338
Urease Activity 83013-83014

Heller Operation
See Esophagomyotomy

Heller Procedure 32665, 43330-43331

Helminth
Antibody 86682

**Hemagglutination Inhibition
Test** 86280

Hemangioma
See Lesion, Skin; Tumor

Hemapheresis
See Apheresis

Hematochezia
See Blood, Feces

Hematologic Test
See Blood Tests

Hematology
Unlisted Services and Procedures 85999

Hematoma
Ankle 27603
Arm, Lower 25028
Arm, Upper
　　Incision and Drainage 23930
Brain
　　Drainage 61154-61156
　　Evacuation 61312-61315
　　Incision and Drainage 61312-61315
Drain 61108
Ear, External
　　Complicated 69005
　　Simple 69000
Elbow
　　Incision and Drainage 23930
Epididymis
　　Incision and Drainage 54700
Gums
　　Incision and Drainage 41800
Hip 26990
Incision and Drainage
　　Neck 21501-21502
　　Skin 10140
　　Thorax 21501-21502
Knee 27301
Leg, Lower 27603
Leg, Upper 27301
Mouth 41005-41009, 41015-41018
　　Incision and Drainage 40800-40801
Nasal Septum
　　Incision and Drainage 30020
Nose
　　Incision and Drainage 30000-30020
Pelvis 26990
Scrotum
　　Incision and Drainage 54700
Shoulder
　　Drainage 23030
Skin
　　Puncture Aspiration 10160
Subdural 61108
Subungual
　　Evacuation 11740
Testis
　　Incision and Drainage 54700
Tongue 41000-41006, 41015

Vagina
　　Incision and Drainage 57022-57023
Wrist 25028

**Hematopoietic Stem Cell
Transplantation**
See Stem Cell, Transplantation

Hematopoietin
See Erythropoietin

Hematuria
See Blood, Urine

Hemic System
Unlisted Procedure 38999

Hemiepiphyseal Arrest
Elbow 24470

Hemifacial Microsomia
Reconstruction
　　Mandibular Condyle 21247

Hemilaminectomy 63020-63044

Hemilaryngectomy 31370-31382

Hemipelvectomies
See Amputation, Interpelviabdominal

Hemiphalangectomy
Toe 28160

Hemispherectomy
Partial 61543
Total 61542

Hemocytoblast
See Stem Cell

Hemodialyses
See Hemodialysis

Hemodialysis 90935-90937, 99512
Blood Flow Study 90939-90940
Duplex Scan of Access 93990

Hemofiltration 90945-90947

Hemoglobin 83036
Analysis
　　O2 Affinity 82820
Antibody
　　Fecal 86683
Carboxyhemoglobin 82375-82376
Chromatography 83021
Concentration 85046
Electrophoresis 83020
Fetal 83030-83033, 85460-85461
Fractionation and Quantitation 83020
Methemoglobin 83045-83050
Non-Automated 83026
Plasma 83051
Sulfhemoglobin 83055-83060
Thermolabile 83065-83068
Urine 83069

Hemoglobin, Glycosylated
See Glycohemoglobin

Hemoglobin F
Fetal
- Chemical .... .83030
- Qualitative .... .83033

Hemogram
Added Indices 85021-85027
Automated 85021-85027
Manual .... .85031

Hemolysins .... .85475
with Agglutinins 86940-86941

Hemolytic Complement
See Complement, Hemolytic

Hemolytic Complement, Total
See Complement, Hemolytic, Total

Hemoperfusion .... .90997

Hemophil
See Clotting Factor

Hemophilus Influenza
Antibody .... .86684

Hemorrhage
Abdomen .... .49002
Anal
- Endoscopic Control .... .46614
Bladder
- Postoperative .... .52606
Chest Cavity
- Endoscopic Control .... .32654
Colon
- Endoscopic Control .... .44391, 45382
Colon-Sigmoid
- Endoscopic Control .... .45334
Esophagus
- Endoscopic Control .... .43227
Gastrointestinal, Upper
- Endoscopic Control .... .43255
Intestines, Small
- Endoscopic Control .... .44366, 44378
Liver
- Control .... .47350
Lung .... .32110
Nasal
- Cauterization 30901-30906
- Endoscopic Control .... .31238
Nasopharynx 42970-42972
Oropharynx 42960-42962
Rectum
- Endoscopic Control .... .45317
Throat 42960-42962
Uterus
- Postpartum .... .59160
Vagina .... .57180

Hemorrhoidectomy
Complex .... .46260
- with Fissurectomy 46261-46262
External Complete .... .46250
Ligature .... .46221
Simple .... .46255
- with Fissurectomy 46257-46258

Hemorrhoids
Destruction 46934-46936
Incision
- External .... .46083
Injection
- Sclerosing Solution .... .46500
Ligation 46945-46946
Suture 46945-46946

Hemosiderin 83070-83071

Hemothorax
Thoracostomy .... .32020

Heparin .... .85520
See Clotting Inhibitors
Neutralization .... .85525
Protamine Tolerance Test .... .85530

Heparin Cofactor I
See Antithrombin III

Hepatectomy
Extensive .... .47122
Left Lobe .... .47125
Partial
- Donor .... .47134
- Lobe .... .47120
Right Lobe .... .47130
Total
- Donor .... .47133

Hepaticodochotomy
See Hepaticostomy

Hepaticoenterostomy .... .47802

Hepaticostomy .... .47400

Hepaticotomy .... .47400

Hepatic Abscess
See Abscess, Liver

Hepatic Arteries
See Artery, Hepatic

Hepatic Artery Aneurysm
See Artery, Hepatic, Aneurysm

Hepatic Duct
Anastomosis
- with Intestines .... .47765, 47802
Exploration .... .47400
Incision and Drainage .... .47400
Nuclear Medicine
- Imaging .... .78223
Removal
- Calculi (Stone) .... .47400
Repair
- with Intestines .... .47765, 47802
Unlisted Services and Procedures .... .47999

Hepatic Haemorrhage
See Hemorrhage, Liver

Hepatic Portal Vein
See Vein, Hepatic Portal

Hepatic Portoenterostomies
See Hepaticoenterostomy

Hepatic Transplantation
See Liver, Transplantation

Hepatitis Antibody
A 86708-86709
B
- Be .... .86707
- B Core 86704-86705
- B Surface .... .86706
C 86803-86804
Delta Agent .... .86692
IgG .... .86704, 86708
IgM 86704-86705, 86708-86709

Hepatitis Antigen
B 87515-87517
Be .... .87350
B Surface 87340-87341
C 87520-87522
Delta Agent .... .87380
G 87525-87527

Hepatitis A and Hepatitis B ... .90636

Hepatitis A Vaccine
Adolescent/Pediatric
- 2 Dose Schedule .... .90633
- 3 Dose Schedule .... .90634
Adult Dosage .... .90632

Hepatitis B and Hib .... .90748

Hepatitis B Vaccine
Dosage
- Adolescent .... .90743
- Adult .... .90746
- Immunosuppressed .... .90740, 90747
- Pediatric/Adolescent .... .90744

Hepatitis B Virus E Antibody
See Antibody, Hepatitis

Hepatitis B Virus Surface ab
See Antibody, Hepatitis B, Surface

Hepatorrhaphy
See Liver, Repair

Hepatotomy
Abscess 47010-47011
- Percutaneous .... .47011
Cyst 47010-47011
- Percutaneous .... .47011

Hernia
Repair
- Abdominal .... .49590
  - Incisional .... .49560
  - Recurrent .... .49565
- Diaphragmatic 39502-39541
- Epigastric .... .49570
  - Incarcerated .... .49572
- Femoral .... .49550
  - Incarcerated .... .49553
  - Recurrent .... .49555
  - Recurrent Incarcerated .... .49557
- Incisional
  - Incarcerated .... .49561

Inguinal 49491, 49495-49500, 49505
  Incarcerated 49492, 49496, 49501,
                                          49507, 49521
  Laparoscopic 49650-49651
  Recurrent 49520
  Sliding .49525
  Strangulated 49492
Lumbar 49540
Lung 32800
Orchiopexy 54640
Recurrent Incisional
  Incarcerated 49566
Umbilicus 49580, 49585
  Incarcerated 49582, 49587
with Spermatic Cord 55540
Spigelian 49590

Hernia, Cerebral
See Encephalocele

Hernia, Rectovaginal
See Rectocele

Hernia, Umbilical
See Omphalocele

Heroin, Alkaloid Screening 82101

Heroin Screen 82486

Herpesvirus 4 (Gamma), Human
See Epstein-Barr Virus

Herpes Simplex
Antibody 86696
Antigen Detection
  Immunofluorescence 87273-87274
  Nucleic Acid 87528-87530

Herpes Smear 87207
Herpes Virus-6 Detection 87531-87533

Herpes Virus-6
Detection 87531-87533

Herpetic Vesicle
Destruction 54050-54065

Heteroantibodies
See Antibody, Heterophile

Heterograft
Skin 15400

Heterologous Transplant
See Xenograft

Heterologous Transplantation
See Heterograft

Heterophile Antibody 86308-86310

Heterotropia
See Strabismus

Hexadecadrol
See Dexamethasone

Hexosephosphate Isomerase
See Phosphohexose Isomerase

Hex B
See b-Hexosaminidase

Heyman Procedure 27179, 28264

HGB
See Hemoglobin, Concentration

HGH
See Growth Hormone, Human

Hg Factor
See Glucagon

HHV-4
See Epstein-Barr Virus

HIAA
See Hydroxyindolacetic Acid, Urine

Hibb Operation
See Spinal Cord; Spine, Fusion; Vertebra;
Vertebral Body; Vertebral Process

Hib Vaccine
4 Dose Schedule
  HbOC 90645
  PRP-T 90648
PRP-D
  Booster .90646
PRP-OMP
  3 Dose Schedule 90647

Hickmann Catheterization
See Cannulization; Catheterization, Venous,
Central Line; Venipuncture

Hidradenitis
See Sweat Gland
Excision 11450-11471
Suppurative
  Incision and Drainage 10060-10061

Highly Selective Vagotomy
See Vagotomy, Highly Selective

Highmore Antrum
See Sinus, Maxillary

High Density Lipoprotein
See Lipoprotein

High Molecular Weight Kininogen
See Fitzgerald Factor

Hill Procedure 43324
Laparoscopic 43280

Hinton Positive
See RPR

Hip
See Femur; Pelvis
Abscess
  Incision and Drainage 26990
Arthrocentesis 20610
Arthrodesis 27284-27286
Arthrography 73525
Arthroplasty 27130-27132
Arthroscopy 29860-29863
Arthrotomy 27030-27033
Biopsy 27040-27041
Bone
  Drainage 26992
Bursa
  Incision and Drainage 26991

Capsulectomy
  with Release, Flexor Muscles 27036
Cast 29305-29325
Craterization 27070
Cyst
  Excision 27065-27067
Denervation 27035
Echography
  Infant 76885-76886
Endoprosthesis
  See Prosthesis, Hip
Excision 27070
Exploration 27033
Fasciotomy 27025
Fusion 27284-27286
Hematoma
  Incision and Drainage 26990
Injection
  Radiologic 27093-27096
Reconstruction
  Total Replacement 27130
Removal
  Cast 29710
  Foreign Body 27033, 27086-27087
    Arthroscopic 29861
  Loose Body
    Arthroscopic 29861
  Prosthesis 27090-27091
Repair
  Muscle Transfer 27100-27105, 27111
  Osteotomy 27146-27156
  Tendon .27097
Saucerization 27070
Stem Prostheses
  See Arthroplasty, Hip
Strapping 29520
Tenotomy
  Abductor Tendon 27006
  Adductor Tendon 27000-27003
  Iliopsoas 27005
Total Replacement 27130-27132
Tumor
  Excision 27047-27049, 27065-27067
    Radical 27075-27076
Ultrasound
  Infant 76885-76886
X-Ray 73500-73520, 73540
  Intraoperative 73530
  with Contrast 73525

Hip Joint
Arthroplasty 27132
  Revision 27134-27138
Arthrotomy 27052
Biopsy 27052
Capsulotomy
  with Release, Flexor Muscles 27036
Dislocation 27250-27252
  Congenital 27256-27259
  Open Treatment 27253-27254
  without Trauma 27265-27266
Manipulation 27275
Reconstruction
  Revision 27134-27138
Synovium
  Excision .27054
    Arthroscopic 29863
Total Replacement 27132

Hip Stem Prostheses
See Arthroplasty, Hip

Histamine 83088

Histamine Release Test 86343

Histochemistry 88318-88319

Histocompatibility Testing
See Tissue Typing

Histoplasma
Antibody 86698
Antigen 87385

Histoplasma capsulatum
Antigen Detection
    Enzyme Immunoassay 87385

Histoplasmin Test
See Histoplasmosis, Skin Test

Histoplasmoses
See Histoplasmosis

Histoplasmosis
Skin Test 86510

History and Physical
See Evaluation and Management, Office and/or
Other Outpatient Services
Pelvic Exam 57410

HIV
Antibody 86701-86703
    Confirmation Test 86689

HIV-1
Antigen Detection
    Enzyme Immunoassay 87390

HIV-2
Antigen Detection
    Enzyme Immunoassay 87391

HK3 Kallikrein
See Antigen, Prostate Specific

HLA Typing 86812-86817

HMRK
See Fitzgerald Factor

HMW Kininogen
See Fitzgerald Factor

Hoffman Apparatus 20690

Hofmeister Operation
See Gastrectomy, Total

Holographic Imaging 76375

Holten Test
See Creatinine, Urine, Clearance

Home Services
Activities of Daily Living 99509
Catheter Care 99507
Enema Administration 99511
Established Patient 99347-99350
Hemodialysis 99512

Home Infusion Procedures 99550-99560,
                     99562, 99564-99569
Individual or Family Counseling 99510
Inhalation Therapy 99563
Intramuscular Injections 99506
Mechanical Ventilation 99504
Newborn Care 99502
New Patient 99341-99345
Postnatal Assessment 99501
Prenatal Monitoring 99500
Respiratory Therapy 99503
Sleep Studies 99508
Stoma Care 99505
Unlisted Services and Procedures 99539

Home Visit
See House Calls

Homocystine 83090
Urine 82615

Homogenization, Tissue 87176

Homograft
Skin 15350

Homologous Grafts
See Graft

Homologous Transplantation
See Homograft

Homovanillic Acid
Urine 83150

Hormone, Adrenocorticotrophic
See Adrenocorticotropic Hormone (ACTH)

Hormone, Corticotropin-Releasing
See Corticotropic Releasing Hormone (CRH)

Hormone, Growth
See Growth Hormone

Hormone, Human Growth
See Growth Hormone, Human

Hormone, Interstitial Cell-Stimulating
See Luteinizing Hormone (LH)

Hormone, Parathyroid
See Parathormone

Hormone, Pituitary Lactogenic
See Prolactin

Hormone, Placental Lactogen
See Lactogen, Human Placental

Hormone, Somatotropin Release-Inhibiting
See Somatostatin

Hormone, Thyroid-Stimulating
See Thyroid Stimulating Hormone (TSH)

Hormone-Binding Globulin, Sex
See Globulin, Sex Hormone Binding

Hormones, Adrenal Cortex
See Corticosteroids

Hormones, Antidiuretic
See Antidiuretic Hormone

Hormone Assay
ACTH 82024
Aldosterone
    Blood or Urine 82088
Androstenedione
    Blood or Urine 82157
Androsterone
    Blood or Urine 82160
Angiotensin II 82163
Corticosterone 82528
Cortisol
    Total 82533
Dehydroepiandrosterone 82626
Dihydroelestosterone 82651
Dihydrotestosterone 82651
Epiandrosterone 82666
Estradiol 82670
Estriol 82677
Estrogen 82671-82672
Estrone 82679
Follicle Stimulating Hormone 83001
Growth Hormone 83003
Hydroxyprogesterone 83498-83499
Luteinizing Hormone 83002
Somatotropin 83003
Testosterone 84403
Vasopressin 84588

Hormone Pellet Implantation 11980

Hospital Discharge Services
See Discharge Services, Hospital

Hospital Services
Inpatient Services 99238-99239
    Discharge Services 99238-99239
    Initial Care
        New or Established Patient ..99221-99233
    Initial Hospital Care 99221-99223
    Newborn 99431-99433
    Prolonged Services 99356-99357
    Subsequent Hospital Care 99231-99233
Observation
    Discharge Services 99234-99236
    Initial Care 99218-99220
        New or Established Patient ..99218-99220
Same Day Admission
    Discharge Services 99234-99236
Subsequent Newborn Care 99433

Hot Pack Treatment 97010
See Physical Medicine and Rehabilitation

House Calls 99341-99350

Howard Test
See Cystourethroscopy, Catheterization, Ureter

HPL
See Lactogen, Human Placental

HTLV-IV
See HIV-2

HTLV I
Antibody
　　Confirmatory Test 86689
　　Detection 86687

HTLV II
Antibody 86688

HTLV III
See HIV

HTLV III Antibodies
See Antibody, HIV

Hubbard Tank Therapy 97036
See Physical Medicine/Therapy/Occupational
Therapy

Hue Test 92283

Huggin Operation
See Orchiectomy, Simple

Huhner Test 89300-89320

Human Chorionic Gonadotropin
See Chorionic Gonadotropin

Human Chorionic Somatomammotropin
See Lactogen, Human Placental

Human Cytomegalovirus Group
See Cytomegalovirus

Human Growth Hormone (HGH) 80418, 80428-80430

Human Herpes Virus 4
See Epstein-Barr Virus

Human Immunodeficiency Virus
See HIV

Human Immunodeficiency Virus 1
See HIV-1

Human Immunodeficiency Virus 2
See HIV-2

Human Papillomavirus Detection 87620-87622

Human Placental Lactogen
See Lactogen, Human Placental

Human T Cell Leukemia Virus I
See HTLV I

Human T Cell Leukemia Virus II
See HTLV II

Human T Cell Leukemia Virus II Antibodies
See Antibody, HTLV-II

Human T Cell Leukemia Virus I Antibodies
See Antibody, HTLV-I

Humeral Epicondylitides, Lateral
See Tennis Elbow

Humeral Fracture
See Fracture, Humerus

Humerus
See Arm, Upper; Shoulder
Abscess
　　Incision and Drainage 23935
Craterization 23184, 24140
Cyst
　　Excision 23150, 24110
　　　with Allograft 23156, 24116
　　　with Autograft 23155, 24115
Diaphysectomy 23184, 24140
Excision 23174, 23184, 23195, 24134, 24140,
　　　　　　　　　　　　　　24150-24151
Fracture
　　Closed Treatment 24500-24505
　　　without Manipulation 23600
　　　with Manipulation 23605
　　Condyle
　　　Closed Treatment 24576-24577
　　　Open Treatment 24579
　　　Percutaneous Fixation 24582
　　Epicondyle
　　　Closed Treatment 24560-24565
　　　Open Treatment 24575
　　　Skeletal Fixation
　　　　Percutaneous 24566
　　Greater Tuberosity Fracture
　　　Closed Treatment without
　　　Manipulation 23620
　　　Closed Treatment with
　　　Manipulation 23625
　　　Open Treatment 23630
　　Open Treatment 23615-23616
　　Shaft 24500-24505
　　　Open Treatment 24515-24516
　　Supracondylar
　　　Closed Treatment 24530-24535
　　　Open Treatment 24545-24546
　　　Percutaneous Fixation 24538
　　Transcondylar
　　　Closed Treatment 24530-24535
　　　Open Treatment 24545-24546
　　　Percutaneous Fixation 24538
　　with Dislocation 23665-23670
Osteomyelitis 24134
Pinning, Wiring 23491, 24498
Prophylactic Treatment 23491, 24498
Radical Resection 23220-23222
Repair 24430
　　Nonunion, Malunion 24430-24435
　　Osteoplasty 24420
　　Osteotomy 24400-24410
　　with Graft 24435
Resection Head 23195
Saucerization 23184, 24140
Sequestrectomy 23174, 24134
Tumor
　　Excision 23150, 23220-23222, 24110
　　　with Allograft 23156, 24116
　　　with Autograft 23155, 24115
X-Ray 73060

Hummelshein Operation
See Strabismus, Repair

Humor Shunt, Aqueous
See Aqueous Shunt

HVA
See Homovanillic Acid

Hybridization Probes, DNA
See Nucleic Acid Probe

Hydatidiform Mole
Evacuation and Curettage 59870
Excision 59100

Hydatid Disease
See Echinococcosis

Hydatid Mole
See Hydatidiform Mole

Hydrocarbons, Chlorinated
See Chlorinated Hydrocarbons

Hydrocele
Aspiration 55000
Excision
　　Bilateral
　　　Tunica Vaginalis 55041
　　Unilateral
　　　Spermatic Cord 55500
　　　Tunica Vaginalis 55040
Repair 55060

Hydrocele, Tunica Vaginalis
See Tunica Vaginalis, Hydrocele

Hydrochloric Acid, Gastric
See Acid, Gastric

Hydrochloride, Vancomycin
See Vancomycin

Hydrocodon
See Dihydrocodeinone

Hydrogen Ion Concentration
See pH

Hydrolase, Acetylcholine
See Acetylcholinesterase

Hydrolase, Triacylglycerol
See Lipase

Hydrolases, Phosphoric Monoester
See Phosphatase

Hydrotherapy (Hubbard Tank) 97036
See Physical Medicine/Therapy/Occupational
Therapy

Hydrotubation 58350

Hydroxyacetanilide
See Acetaminophen

Hydroxycorticosteroid 83491

Hydroxyindolacetic Acid 83497
Urine 83497

Hydroxypregnenolone 80406, 84143

Hydroxyprogesterone ...80402-80406,
　　　　　　　　　　　　　83498-83499

Hydroxyproline 83500-83505

Hydroxytyramine
See Dopamine

Hygroma
Cystic
    Axillary/Cervical
        Excision 38550-38555

Hymen
Excision 56700
Incision 56720

Hymenal Ring
Revision 56700

Hymenectomy 56700

Hymenotomy 56720

Hyoid Bone
Fracture
    Closed Treatment
        without Manipulation 21493
        with Manipulation 21494
    Open Treatment 21495

Hyperbaric Oxygen Pressurization 99183

Hypercycloidal X-Ray 76101-76102

Hyperdactylies
See Supernumerary Digit

Hyperglycemic Glycogenolytic Factor
See Glucagon

Hypertelorism of Orbit
See Orbital Hypertelorism

Hyperthermia Therapy
See Thermotherapy

Hyperthermia Treatment ..77600-77620

Hypnotherapy 90880

Hypodermis
See Subcutaneous Tissue

Hypoglossal-Facial Anastomosis
See Anastomosis, Nerve, Facial to Hypoglossal

Hypoglossal Nerve
Anastomosis
    to Facial Nerve 64868

Hypopharynges
See Hypopharynx

Hypopharynx
Biopsy 42802

Hypophysectomy 61546-61548

Hypophysis
See Pituitary Gland

Hypopyrexia
See Hypothermia

Hypospadias
Repair 54300, 54352
    Complications 54340-54348
    First Stage 54304
        Proximal Penile or Penoscrotal 54332

One Stage
    Meatal Advancement 54322
    Perineal 54336
Urethroplasty
    Local Skin Flaps 54324
    Local Skin Flaps, Skin Graft Patch
    and/or Island Flap 54328
    Local Skin Flaps and Mobilization of
    Urethra 54326
    Urethroplasty for Second Stage .54308-54316
        Free Skin Graft 54316
    Urethroplasty for Third Stage 54318

Hypothermia 99185-99186

Hysterectomy
Abdominal
    Radical 58210
    Resection of Ovarian Malignancy ...58951,
                  58953-58954
    Supracervical 58180
    Total 58150, 58200
        with Colpo-Urethrocystopexy 58152
        with Partial Vaginectomy 58200
Cesarean
    after Cesarean Delivery 59525
    with Closure of Vesicouterine Fistula ..51925
Removal
    Lesion 59100
Vaginal 58260-58270, 58550
    Laparoscopic 58550
    Radical 58285
    Removal Tubes/Ovaries 58262-58263
        Repair of Enterocele 58263
    with Colpectomy 58275-58280
    with Colpo-Urethrocystopexy 58267

Hysterolysis
See Lysis, Adhesions, Uterus

Hysteroplasty 58540

Hysterorrhaphy 58520, 59350

Hysterosalpingography 74740
Catheterization 58345
Injection Procedure 58340

Hysterosalpingostomy
See Implantation, Tubouterine

Hysteroscopy
Ablation
    Endometrial 58563
Diagnostic 58555
Lysis
    Adhesions 58559
Removal
    Impacted Foreign Body 58562
    Leiomyomata 58561
Resection
    of Intrauterine Septum 58560
Surgical with Biopsy 58558
Unlisted Services and Procedures 58579

Hysterosonography 76831
See Ultrasound

Hysterotomy 59100
See Ligation, Uterus
Induced Abortion
    with Amniotic Injections 59852
    with Vaginal Suppositories 59857

Hysterotrachelectomy
See Amputation, Cervix

H Flu
See Hemophilus Influenza

I

I, Angiotensin
See Angiotensin I

I, Coagulation Factor
See Fibrinogen

I, Heparin Co-Factor
See Antithrombin III

ICCE
See Extraction, Lens, Intracapsular

Ichthyosis, Sex Linked
See Syphilis Test

ICSH
See Luteinizing Hormone (LH)

Identification
Oocyte
    from Follicular Fluid 89254
Sperm
    from Aspiration 89257
    from Tissue 89264

IDH
See Isocitric Dehydrogenase, Blood

IG
See Immune Globulins

IgE 86003-86005

IgG 86001

II, Coagulation Factor
See Prothrombin

II, Cranial Nerve
See Optic Nerve

Ileal Conduit
Visualization 50690

Ileoscopy
via Stoma 44383

Ileostomy 44310, 45136
Continent (Kock Procedure) 44316
Revision 44312-44314

Iliac Arteries
See Artery, Iliac

Iliac Crest
Free Osteocutaneous Flap with Microvascular
Anastomosis 20970

Iliohypogastric Nerve
Injection
    Anesthetic 64425

Ilioinguinal Nerve
Injection
    Anesthetic 64425

Ilium
Craterization 27070
Cyst
    Excision 27065-27067
Excision 27070
Fracture
    Open Treatment 27215, 27218
Saucerization 27070
Tumor
    Excision 27065-27067

Ilizarov Procedure
Monticelli Type 20692
    See Application, Bone Fixation Device

Imaging
See Vascular Studies

Imaging, Gamma Camera
See Nuclear Medicine

Imaging, Magnetic Resonance
See Magnetic Resonance Imaging (MRI)

Imaging, Ultrasonic
See Echography

Imbrication
Diaphragm 39545

Imidobenzyle
See Imipramine

Imipramine
Assay 80174

Immune Complex Assay 86332

Immune Globulins
Antitoxin
    Botulinum 90287
    Diphtheria 90296
Botulism 90288
Cytomegalovirus 90291
Hepatitis B 90371
Human 90281-90283
Rabies 90375-90376
Respiratory Syncytial Virus 90378-90379
Rho (D) 90384-90386
Tetanus 90389
Unlisted Immune Globulin 90399
Vaccinia 90393
Varicella-Zoster 90396

Immune Globulin Administration 90780-90784

Immune Globulin E
See IgE

Immunization, Mumps
See Mumps, Immunization

Immunization Administration
Each Additional Vaccine/Toxoid 90472, 90474
One Vaccine/Toxoid 90471, 90473

Immunoassay
Analyte 83519-83520
Infectious Agent 86317-86318, 87449-87451
Nonantibody 83516-83519
Tumor Antigen 86294, 86316
    CA 125 86304
    CA 15-3 86300
    CA 19-9 86301

Immunoblotting, Western
See Western Blot

Immunochemical, Lysozyme (Muramidase)
See Lysozyme

Immunocytochemistry 88342

Immunodeficiency Virus, Human
See HIV

Immunodeficiency Virus Type 1, Human
See HIV-1

Immunodeficiency Virus Type 2, Human
See HIV-2

Immunodiffusion 86329-86331

Immunoelectrophoresis 86320-86327, 86334

Immunofixation Electrophoresis 86334

Immunofluorescent Study 88346-88347

Immunogen
See Antigen

Immunoglobulin 82787
Platelet Associated 86023
Thyroid Stimulating 84445

Immunoglobulin E
See IgE

Immunoglobulin Receptor Assay 86243

Immunologic Skin Test
See Skin, Tests

Immunology
Unlisted Services and Procedures ..86849, 99558

Immunotherapies, Allergen
See Allergen Immunotherapy

Impedance Testing 92567
See Audiologic Function Tests

Imperfectly Descended Testis
See Testis, Undescended

Implant, Breast
See Breast, Implants

Implant, Glaucoma Drainage
See Aqueous Shunt

Implant, Orbital
See Orbital Implant

Implant, Penile
See Penile Prosthesis

Implant, Penile Prosthesis, Inflatable
See Penile Prosthesis, Insertion, Inflatable

Implant, Subperiosteal
See Subperiosteal Implant

Implant, Ureters into, Bladder
See Anastomosis, Ureter, to Bladder

Implantation
Bone
    for External Speech Processor/Cochlear
      Stimulator 69714-69718
Cardiac Event Recorder 33282
Contraceptive Capsules 11975, 11977
Drug Delivery Device 11981, 11983
Electrode
    Brain 61850-61875
    Nerve 64553-64581
    Spinal Cord 63650-63655
Eye
    Anterior Segment 65920
    Aqueous Shunt to Extraocular Placement or
      Replacement of Pegs 65125
    Posterior Segment
      Extraocular 67120
      Intraocular 67121
    Reservoir 66180
    Vitreous
      Drug Delivery System 67027
Hearing Aid Hormone Pellet(s)
    Bone Conduction 69710
Hip Prosthesis
    See Arthroplasty, Hip
Hormone Pellet 11980
Intraocular Lens
    See Insertion, Intraocular Lens
Joint
    See Arthroplasty
Mesh
    Hernia Repair 49568
Nerve
    into Bone 64787
    into Muscle 64787
Neurostimulators
    Pulse Generator 61885
    Receiver 61886
Pulse Generator
    Brain 61885-61886
    Spinal Cord Electrode Array 63685
Receiver
    Brain 61885-61886
    Spinal Cord 63685
Removal 20670-20680
    Elbow 24164
    Radius 24164

Reservoir Vascular Access Device
    Declotting .... .36550
Tubouterine .... .58752
Ventricular Assist Device .... .33976
    Intracorporeal .... .33979

Implant Removal
See Specific Anatomical Site

Impression, Maxillofacial
Auricular Prosthesis .... .21086
Definitive Obturator Prosthesis .... .21080
Facial Prosthesis .... .21088
Interim Obturator .... .21079
Mandibular Resection Prosthesis .... .21081
Nasal Prosthesis .... .21087
Oral Surgical Splint .... .21085
Orbital Prosthesis .... .21077
Palatal Augmentation Prosthesis .... .21082
Palatal Lift Prosthesis .... .21083
Speech Aid Prosthesis .... .21084
Surgical Obturator .... .21076

IM Injection
See Injection, Intramuscular

Incision
See Incision and Drainage
Abdomen .... .49000
    Exploration .... .58960
Abscess
    Soft Tissue 20000-20005
Accessory Nerve .... .63191
Anal
    Fistula .... .46270, 46280
    Septum .... .46070
    Sphincter .... .46080
Ankle .... .27607
    Tendon 27605-27606
Anus
    See Anus, Incision
Aortic Valve
    for Stenosis .... .33415
Artery
    Nose 30915-30920
Atrial Septum 33735-33737
Bile Duct
    Sphincter .... .43262, 47460
Bladder
    Catheterization .... .51045
    with Destruction 51020-51030
    with Radiotracer .... .51020
Bladder Diverticulum .... .52305
Breast
    Capsules .... .19370
Burn Scab 16035-16036
Cataract
    Secondary
       Laser Surgery .... .66821
       Stab Incision Technique .... .66820
Chest
    Biopsy 32095-32100
Colon
    Exploration .... .44025
    Stoma
       Creation 44320-44322
       Revision 44340-44346
Cornea
    for Astigmatism .... .65772

Corpus Callosum .... .61541
Cricothyroid Membrane .... .31605
Dentate Ligament 63180-63182
Duodenum .... .44010
Ear, Inner
    Labyrinth
       with Mastoidectomy .... .69802
       with or without Cryosurgery .... .69801
Elbow .... .24000
Esophagus .... .43020, 43045
    Muscle .... .43030
Exploration
    Kidney .... .50010
Eye
    Adhesions .... .65880
       Anterior Segment 65860-65865
       Anterior Synechiae .... .65870
       Corneovitreal .... .65880
       Posterior .... .65875
    Anterior Chamber .... .65820
    Trabeculae .... .65850
Eyelid
    Canthus .... .67715
    Sutures .... .67710
Femoral Artery
    Exposure 34812-34813
Fibula .... .27607
Finger
    Decompression .... .26035
    Tendon .... .26060, 26455-26460
    Tendon Sheath .... .26055
Foot .... .28005
    Capsule 28260-28264
    Fasciotomy .... .28008
    for Infection 28002-28003
    Tendon .... .28230, 28234
Frontal Lobe .... .61490
Gallbladder .... .47490
Hand Decompression 26035-26037
    Tendon .... .26450, 26460
Heart
    Exploration 33310-33315
Hemorrhoids
    External .... .46083
Hepatic Ducts
    See Hepaticostomy
Hip
    Denervation .... .27035
    Exploration .... .27033
    Fasciotomy .... .27025
    Joint Capsule
       for Flexor Release .... .27036
    Tendon
       Abductor .... .27006
       Adductor 27000-27003
       Iliopsoas .... .27005
Hymen
    See Hymen, Incision
Hymenotomy .... .56720
Iliac Artery
    Exposure .... .34820
Intercarpal Joint
    Dislocation .... .25670
Interphalangeal Joint
    Capsule .... .26525
Intestines, Small .... .44010
    Biopsy .... .44020

Creation
    Pouch .... .44316
    Stoma 44300-44310, 44314
Decompression .... .44021
Exploration .... .44020
Incision .... .44020
Removal
    Foreign Body .... .44020
Revision
    Stoma .... .44312
Intestines (Except Rectum)
    See Enterotomy
Iris 66500-66505
Kidney .... .50010, 50045
Knee
    Capsule .... .27435
    Exploration .... .27310
    Fasciotomy .... .27305
    Removal of Foreign Body .... .27310
Lacrimal Punctum .... .68440
Lacrimal Sac
    See Dacryocystotomy
Larynx 31300-31320
Leg, Lower
    Fasciotomy 27600-27602
Leg, Upper
    Fasciotomy .... .27305
    Tenotomy 27306-27307, 27390-27392
Lip
    Frenum .... .40806
Liver
    See Hepatotomy
Lung
    Biopsy 32095-32100
    Decortication
       Partial .... .32225
       Total .... .32220
Lymphatic Channels .... .38308
Mastoid
    See Mastoidotomy
Medullary Tract .... .61470
Mesencephalic Tract .... .61480
Metacarpophalangeal Joint
    Capsule .... .26520
Mitral Valve 33420-33422
Muscle
    See Myotomy
Nerve 64400-64560, 64565-64580,
           64585-64772
    Foot .... .28035
    Root 63185-63190
    Sacral .... .64581
    Vagus 43640-43641
Nose
    See Rhinotomy
Orbit
    See Orbitotomy
Palm
    Fasciotomy 26040-26045
Pancreas
    Sphincter .... .43262
Penis
    Prepuce 54000-54001
    Newborn .... .54000
Pericardium
    with Clot Removal .... .33020
    with Foreign Body Removal .... .33020
    with Tube .... .33015

Pharynx
    Stoma 42955
Pleura
    Biopsy 32095-32100
Pleural Cavity
    Empyema 32035-32036
    Pneumothorax 32020
Prostate
    Exposure
       Bilateral Pelvic Lymphadenectomy ..55865
       Insertion Radioactive Substance 55860
       Lymph Node Biopsy 55862
       Transurethral 52450
Pterygomaxillary Fossa 31040
Pulmonary Valve 33470-33474
Pyloric Sphincter 43520
Retina
    Encircling Material 67115
Sclera
    Fistulization
       Iridencleisis or Iridotasis 66165
       Sclerectomy with Punch or Scissors
       with Iridectomy 66160
       Thermocauterization with
       Iridectomy 66155
       Trabeculectomy ab Externo in Absence
       Previous Surgery 66170
       Trephination with Iridectomy 66150
Semicircular Canal
    Fenestration 69820
    Revision 69840
Seminal Vesicle 55600-55605
    Complicated 55605
Shoulder
    Bone 23035
    Capsular Contracture Release 23020
    Removal
       Calcareous Deposits 23000
    Tenomyotomy 23405-23406
Shoulder Joint 23040-23044
Sinus
    Frontal 31070-31087
    Maxillary 31020-31032
       Endoscopic 31256-31267
       Multiple 31090
    Sphenoid
       Sinusotomy 31050-31051
Skin 10040-10180
Skull
    Suture 61550-61552
Spinal Cord 63200
    Tract 63170, 63194-63199
Stomach
    Creation
       Stoma 43830-43832
    Exploration 43500
    Pyloric Sphincter 43520
Synovectomy 26140
Temporomandibular Joint 21010
Tendon
    Arm, Upper 24310
Thigh
    Fasciotomy 27025
Thorax
    Empyema 32035-32036
    Pneumothorax 32020

Thyroid Gland
    See Thyrotomy
Tibia 27607
Toe
    Capsule 28270-28272
    Fasciotomy 28008
    Tendon 28232-28234
    Tenotomy 28010-28011
Tongue
    Frenum 41010
Trachea
    Emergency 31603-31605
    Planned 31600-31601
    with Flaps 31610
Tympanic Membrane 69420
    with Anesthesia 69421
Ureter 50600
Ureterocele 51535
Urethra 53000-53010
    Meatus 53020-53025
Uterus
    Remove Lesion 59100
Vagina
    Exploration 57000
Vas Deferens 55200
    for X-Ray 55300
Vestibule of the Mouth
    See Mouth, Vestibule of, Incision
Vitreous Strands
    Laser Surgery 67031
    Pars Plana Approach 67030
Wrist 25100-25105
    Capsule 25085
    Decompression 25020-25025
    Tendon Sheath 25000-25001

Incisional Hernia Repair

See Hernia, Repair, Incisional

Incision and Drainage

See Drainage; Incision
Abdomen
    Fluid 49080-49081
    Pancreatitis 48000
Abscess
    Abdomen 49020, 49040
       Open 49040
       Percutaneous 49021
    Anal 46045-46050
    Ankle 27603
    Appendix 44900
       Open 44900
       Percutaneous 44901
    Arm, Lower 25028
    Arm, Upper 23930-23931
    Auditory Canal, External 69020
    Bartholin's Gland 56420
    Bladder 51080
    Brain 61320-61321
    Breast 19020
    Ear, External
       Complicated 69005
       Simple 69000
    Elbow 23930
    Epididymis 54700
    Eyelid 67700
    Finger 26010-26011
    Gums 41800
    Hip 26990

Kidney 50020
    Open 50020
    Percutaneous 50021
Knee 27301
Leg, Lower 27603
Leg, Upper 27301
Liver 47010
    Open 47010
    Percutaneous 47011
Lung 32200
    Percutaneous 32201
Lymph Node 38300-38305
Mouth 40800-40801, 41005-41009,
                   41015-41018
Nasal Septum 30020
Neck 21501-21502
Nose 30000-30020
Ovary 58820-58822
    Abdominal Approach 58822
Palate 42000
Paraurethral Gland 53060
Parotid Gland 42300-42305
Pelvis 26990, 45000
Perineum 56405
Peritoneum 49020
    Percutaneous 49021
Prostate 55720-55725
Rectum ..45005-45020, 46040, 46050-46060
Retroperitoneal 49060
    Open 49060
Salivary Gland 42300-42320
Scrotum 54700, 55100
Skene's Gland 53060
Skin 10060-10061
Subdiaphragmatic
    Percutaneous 49040-49041
Sublingual Gland 42310-42320
Submaxillary Gland 42310-42320
Subphrenic
    Percutaneous 49040-49041
Testis 54700
Thorax 21501-21502
Throat 42700-42725
Tongue 41000-41006, 41015
Tonsil 42700
Urethra 53040
Uvula 42000
Vagina 57010
Vulva 56405
Wrist 25028
Ankle 27610
Bile Duct 47420-47425
Bladder 51040
Bulla
    Skin
       Puncture Aspiration 10160
Bursa
    Ankle 27604
    Arm, Lower 25031
    Elbow 23931
    Foot 28001
    Hip 26991
    Knee 27301
    Leg, Lower 27604
    Leg, Upper 27301
    Palm 26025-26030
    Pelvis 26991
    Wrist 25031

Carbuncle
  Skin 10060-10061
Carpals 25035, 26034
Comedones
  Skin 10040
Cyst
  Conjunctiva 68020
  Gums 41800
  Liver
    Open .47010
    Percutaneous 47011
  Lung 32200
    Percutaneous 32201
  Mouth 40800-40801, 41005-41009,
                    41015-41018
  Ovarian 58800-58805
  Skin 10040-10061
    Pilonidal 10080-10081
    Puncture Aspiration 10160
  Spinal Cord 63172-63173
  Thyroid Gland 60000
  Tongue 41000-41006, 41015, 60000
Elbow
  Abscess .23935
  Arthrotomy .24000
Femur 27303
Fluid Collection
  Skin 10140
Foreign Body
  Skin .10120-10121
Furuncle 10060-10061
Gallbladder .47480
Hematoma
  Ankle 27603
  Arm, Lower 25028
  Arm, Upper 23930
  Brain 61312-61315
  Ear, External
    Complicated 69005
    Simple .69000
  Elbow 23930
  Epididymis 54700
  Gums 41800
  Hip 26990
  Knee 27301
  Leg, Lower 27603
  Leg, Upper 27301
  Mouth 40800-40801, 41005-41009,
                    41015-41018
  Nasal Septum 30020
  Neck 21501-21502
  Nose 30000-30020
  Pelvis 26990
  Scrotum 54700
  Skin 10140
    Puncture Aspiration 10160
  Skull 61312-61315
  Testis 54700
  Thorax 21501-21502
  Tongue 41000-41006, 41015
  Vagina 57022-57023
  Wrist 25028
Hepatic Duct 47400
Hip
  Bone 26992, 27030
Humerus
  Abscess .23935

Interphalangeal Joint
  Toe 28024
Intertarsal Joint 28020
Kidney 50040, 50125
Knee 27303, 27310
Lacrimal Gland 68400
Lacrimal Sac 68420
Liver
  Abscess or Cyst 47010-47011
    Percutaneous 47011
Mediastinum 39000-39010
Metatarsophalangeal Joint 28022
Milia, Multiple 10040
Onychia 10060-10061
Orbit 67405, 67440
Paronychia 10060-10061
Pelvic
  Bone 26992
Penis 54015
Pericardium 33025
Phalanges
  Finger 26034
Pilonidal Cyst 10080-10081
Pustules
  Skin 10040
Radius 25035
Seroma
  Skin 10140
Shoulder
  Abscess .23030
  Arthrotomy
    Acromioclavicular Joint 23044
    Sternoclavicular Joint 23044
  Bursa 23031
  Hematoma 23030
Shoulder Joint
  Arthrotomy
    Glenohumeral Joint 23040
Tarsometatarsal Joint 28020
Tendon Sheath
  Finger 26020
  Palm 26020
Thorax
  Deep 21510
Toe 28024
Ulna 25035
Ureter 50600
Vagina 57020
Wound Infection
  Skin 10180
Wrist 25028, 25040

Inclusion Bodies
Fluid 88106
Smear 87207-87210

Incomplete Abortion
See Abortion, Incomplete

**Indicator Dilution
Studies** 93561-93562

Induced Abortion
See Abortion

Induced Hyperthermia
See Thermotherapy

Induced Hypothermia
See Hypothermia

Induratio Penis Plastica
See Peyronie Disease

Infant, Newborn, Intensive Care
See Intensive Care, Neonatal

Infantile Paralysis
See Polio

Infection
Immunoassay 86317-86318
Rapid Test 86403-86406

Infection, Actinomyces
See Actinomycosis

Infection, Bone
See Osteomyelitis

Infection, Filarioidea
See Filariasis

Infection, Postoperative Wound
See Postoperative Wound Infection

Infection, Wound
See Wound, Infection

Infectious Agent
Antigen Detection
  Direct Fluorescence . . .87198-87199, 87265-
      87272, 87276, 87278, 87280, 87285-87290
    Bordetella 87265
    Chlamydia Trachomatis 87270
    Cryptosporidium/Giardia 87272
    Cytomegalovirus 87198
    Enterovirus 87199
    Influenza A 87276
    Legionella Pneumophila 87278
    Respiratory Syncytial Virus . . .87280
    Treponema Pallidum 87285
    Varicella-Zoster 87290
  Enzyme Immunoassay
    Adenovirus 87301
    Chlamydia Trachomatis 87320
    Clostridium Difficile 87324
    Cryptococcus Neoformans 87327
    Cryptosporidium/Giardia 87328
    Cytomegalovirus 87332
    Entamoeba Histolytica Dispar
      Group 87336
    Entamoeba Histolytica Group 87337
    Escherichia coli 0157 87335
    Helicobacter Pylori 87338-87339
    Hepatitis, Delta Agent 87380
    Hepatitis Be Antigen (HBeAg) 87350
    Hepatitis B Surface Antigen
    (HBsAg) .87340
    Hepatitis B Surface Antigen (HBsAg)
    Neutralization 87341
    Histoplasma capsulatum 87385
    HIV-1 87390
    HIV-2 87391
    Influenza A 87400
    Influenza B 87400
    Multiple Step Method 87301-87449,
                       87451
      See specific agent
    Not Otherwise Specified 87449, 87451
    Respiratory Syncytial Virus 87420
    Rotavirus 87425

Shiga-like Toxin 87427
Single Step Method 87450
Streptococcus, Group A 87430
Immunofluorescence . . .87260, 87273-87275,
   87277, 87279, 87281-87283, 87299-87300
   Adenovirus .87260
   Herpes Simplex 87273-87274
   Influenza B 87275
   Legionella Micdadei 87277
   Not Otherwise Specified 87299
   Parainfluenza Virus 87279
   Pneumocystis Carinii 87281
   Polyvalent 87300
   Rubeola .87283
Concentration 87015
Detection
   by Immunoassay with Direct Optical
   Observation 87802-87899
      Chlamydia Trachomatis 87810
      Clostridium difficile 87803
      Influenza 87804
      Neisseria gonorrheae 87850
      Not Otherwise Specified 87899
      Streptococcus, Group A 87880
      Streptococcus, Group B 87802
   by Nucleic Acid
      Bartonella henselae 87470-87472
      Bartonella quintana 87470-87472
      Borrelia burgdorferi 87475-87477
      Candida species 87480-87482
      Chlamydia pneumoniae . . .87485-87487
      Chlamydia Trachomatis 87490-87492
      Cytomegalovirus 87495-87497
      Gardnerella Vaginalis 87510-87512
      Hepatitis B Virus 87515-87517
      Hepatitis C 87520-87522
      Hepatitis G 87525-87527
      Herpes Simplex Virus 87528-87530
      Herpes Virus-6 87531-87533
      HIV-1 87534-87536
      HIV-2 87537-87539
      Legionella Pneumophila 87540-87542
      Multiple Organisms 87800-87801
      Mycobacteria
      avium-intracellulare 87560-87562
      Mycobacteria species 87550-87552
      Mycobacteria tuberculosis . . .87555-87557
      Mycoplasma pneumoniae . . .87580-87582
      Neisseria gonorrheae 87590-87592
      Not Otherwise Specified 87797-87799
      Papillomavirus, Human 87620-87622
      Streptococcus, Group A 87650-87652
   Genotype Analysis
      by Nucleic acid
         Hepatitis C Virus 87902
         HIV-1 Protease/Reverse
         Transcriptase 87901
   Phenotype Analysis
      by Nucleic acid
         HIV-1 Drug Resistance 87903-87904
   Phenotype Prediction
      by Genetic Database
         HIV-1 Drug Resistance 0023T

Infectious Mononucleosis Virus
See Epstein-Barr Virus

Inflammatory Process
Localization
   Nuclear Medicine 78805-78807

Inflation
Ear, Middle
   Eustachian Tube
      without Catheterization 69401
      with Catheterization 69400
Eustachian Tube
   Myringotomy 69420
   Anesthesia 69424

Influenza A
Antigen Detection
   Direct Fluorescence 87276
   Enzyme Immunoassay 87400

Influenza B
Antigen Detection
   Enzyme Immunoassay 87400
   Immunofluorescence 87275

Influenza Vaccine
See Vaccines

Influenza Virus
Antibody 86710
by Immunoassay
   with Direct Optical Observation 87804

Infraorbital Nerve
Avulsion 64734
Incision 64734
Transection 64734

Infrared Light Treatment 97026
See Physical Medicine/Therapy/Occupational
Therapy

Infratentorial Craniectomy 61520-61521

Infusion
Cerebral
   Intravenous
      for Thrombolysis 37195
Intraosseous .36680
Radioelement 77750
Transcatheter Therapy 37201-37202

Infusion Pump
Electronic Analysis
   Spinal Cord 62367-62368
Insertion
   Intra-arterial 36260
Intraarterial
   Removal 36262
   Revision 36261
Intravenous
   Insertion 36530
   Removal 36532
   Revision 36531
Maintenance 96520-96530
   See Chemotherapy, Pump Services
Spinal Cord 62361-62362
Ventricular Catheter 61215

Infusion Therapy 62350-62351,
                                          62360-62362
See Injection, Chemotherapy
Arterial Catheterization 36640
Chemotherapy 96410-96414, 96422-96425
Home Infusion Procedures 99550-99562,
                                          99564-99569
Intravenous 90780-90781
Pain 62360-62362, 62367-62368
Transcatheter Therapy 75896

Ingestion Challenge Test 95075
See Allergy Tests

Inguinal Hernia Repair
See Hernia, Repair, Inguinal

INH
See Drug Assay

Inhalation
Pentamidine 94642, 99563

Inhalation Provocation Tests
See Bronchial Challenge Test

Inhalation Treatment 94640,
                                    94664-94665, 99503
See Pulmonology, Therapeutic

Inhibin A 86336

Inhibition, Fertilization
See Contraception

Inhibition Test, Hemagglutination
See Hemagglutination Inhibition Test

Inhibitor, Alpha 1-Protease
See Alpha-1 Antitrypsin

Inhibitor, Alpha 2-Plasmin
See Alpha-2 Antiplasmin

Inhibitory Concentration, Minimum
See Minimum Inhibitory Concentration

Initial Inpatient Consultations
See Consultation, Initial Inpatient

Injection
See Allergen Immunotherapy; Infusion
Abdomen
   Air 49400
   Contrast Material 49400
Angiography
   Pulmonary 75746
Ankle
   Radial 27648
Antibiotic
   See Antibiotic Administration
Antigen (Allergen) 95115-95125
Aorta (Aortography)
   Radiologic .93544
Bladder
   Radiologic 51600-51610
Brain Canal 61070
Bronchography
   Segmental .31656
Bursa 20600-20610
Cardiac Catheterization 93539-93545

Carpal Tunnel
    Therapeutic 20526
Chemotherapy 96400-96450, 96542
Cistern
    Medication or Other 61055
Contrast
    via Catheter 49424
Corpora Cavernosa 54235
Cyst
    Bone 20615
    Kidney 50390
    Pelvis 50390
    Thyroid 60001
Elbow
    Arthrography
      Radiologic 24220
Epidural
    See Epidural, Injection
Esophageal Varices
    Endoscopy 43243
Esophagus
    Sclerosing Agent 43204
Extremity
    Pseudoaneurysm 36002
Eye
    Air 66020
    Medication 66030
Eyelid
    Subconjunctival 68200
Ganglion
    Anesthetic 64505, 64510
Ganglion Cyst 20550, 20600-20605
Gastric Secretion Stimulant 91052
Gastric Varices
    Endoscopy 43243
Heart Vessels
    Cardiac Catheterization 93539-93545
      See Catheterization, Cardiac
    Radiologic 93545
Hemorrhoids
    Sclerosing Solution 46500
Hip
    Radiologic 27093-27095
Insect Venom 95130-95134
Intervertebral Disk
    Chemonucleolysis Agent 62292
    Radiological 62290-62291
Intraamniotic 59852
Intraarterial
    Diagnostic 90783
    Therapeutic 90783
Intradermal
    for Tattooing 11920-11922
Intralesional
    Skin 11900-11901
Intramuscular
    Antibiotic 90788
    Diagnostic 90782
    Therapeutic 90782, 99506
Intravenous
    Diagnostic 90784
    Therapeutic 90784
    Vascular Flow Check, Graft 15860
Joint 20600-20610
Kidney
    Radiologic 50394
Knee
    Radiologic 27370

Lacrimal Gland
    Radiologic 68850
Left Heart
    Radiologic 93543
Lesion
    Skin 11900-11901
Ligament 20550
Liver 47015
    Radiologic 47500-47505
Mammary Ductogram/Galactogram 19030
Muscle Endplate
    Cervical Spine 64613
    Extremity 64614
    Facial 64612
    Trunk 64614
Nerve
    Anesthetic 64400-64530
    Neurolytic Agent 64600-64680
Orbit
    Retrobulbar
      Alcohol 67505
      Medication 67500
    Tenon's Capsule 67515
Pancreatography 48400
Paravertebral Facet Joint/Nerve ..64470-64476
Penis
    for Erection 54235
    Peyronie Disease 54200
      with Surgical Exposure of Plaque ...54205
    Radiology 54230
    Vasoactive Drugs 54231
Peritoneal Cavity Air
    See Pneumoperitoneum
Radiologic
    Breast 19030
Rectum
    Sclerosing Solution 45520
Right Heart
    See Cardiac Catheterization, Injection
    Radiologic 93542
Sacroiliac Joint
    for Arthrography 27096
Salivary Duct 42660
Salivary Gland
    Radiologic 42550
Sclerosing Agent
    Esophagus 43204
    Intravenous 36470-36471
Sentinel Node Identification 38792
Shoulder
    Arthrography
      Radiologic 23350
Shunt
    Peritoneal
      Venous 49427
Sinus Tract 20500
    Diagnostic 20501
Spider Veins
    Telangiectasia 36468-36469
Spinal Artery 62294
Spinal Cord
    Anesthetic 62310-62319
    Blood 62273
    Neurolytic Agent 62280-62282
    Other 62310-62311
    Radiological 62284

Steroids
    Urethral Stricture 52283
Subcutaneous
    Diagnostic 90782
    Silicone 11950-11954
    Therapeutic 90782
Temporomandibular Joint
    Arthrography 21116
Tendon Origin, Insertion 20551
Tendon Sheath 20550
Therapeutic
    Extremity Pseudoaneurysm 36002
    Lung 32960
    Thyroid 60001
    Turbinate 30200
Thoracic Cavity
    See Pleurodesis, Chemical
Trachea 31612
    Puncture 31612
Transtracheal
    Bronchography 31715
Trigger Point(s)
    One or Two Muscle Groups 20552
    Two or More Muscle Groups 20553
Turbinate 30200
Unlisted Services and Procedures 90799
Ureter
    Radiologic 50684
Venography 36005
Ventricle
    Dye 61120
    Medication or Other 61026
Vitreous 67028
    Fluid Substitute 67025
Vocal Cords
    Therapeutic 31513, 31570-31571
Wrist
    Carpal Tunnel
      Therapeutic 20526
    Radiologic 25246

Inkblot Test 96100

Inner Ear
See Ear, Inner

Innominate
Tumor
    Excision 27077

Innominate Arteries
See Artery, Brachiocephalic

Inorganic Sulfates
See Sulfate

Insemination
Artificial 58321-58322

Insertion
See Implantation; Intubation; Transplantation
Baffle
    Ear, Middle 69410
Balloon
    Intra-Aortic 33967, 33973
Breast
    Implants 19340-19342

Cannula
   Arteriovenous 36810-36815
   ECMO 36822
   Extra Corporeal Circulation
     for Regional Chemotherapy
     of Extremity 36823
   Thoracic Duct 38794
   Vein to Vein 36800
Catheter
   Abdomen 49420-49421
   Abdominal Artery 36245-36248
   Aorta 36200
   Bile Duct 47525-47530, 75982
     Percutaneous 47510
   Bladder 51045
   Brachiocephalic Artery 36215-36218
   Brain 61210, 61770
   Bronchi 31710, 31717
   Bronchus
     for Intracavitary Radioelement
     Application 31643
   Cardiac
     See Catheterization, Cardiac
     Flow Directed 93503
   Ear, Middle 69405
   Eustachian Tube 69405
   Gastrointestinal, Upper 43241
   Jejunum 44015
   Kidney 50392
   Lower Extremity Artery 36245-36248
   Nasotracheal 31720
   Pelvic Artery 36245-36248
   Portal Vein 36481
   Prostate 55859
   Pulmonary Artery 36013-36015
   Right Heart 36013
   Skull 61107
   Spinal Cord 62350-62351
   Suprapubic 51010
   Thoracic Artery 36215-36218
   Trachea 31700
   Tracheobronchial 31725
   Ureter via Kidney 50393
   Urethra 53670-53675
   Vein 36489, 36491
   Vena Cava 36010
   Venous 36011-36012, 36400-36425,
                36500-36510
     Child/Adult 36489, 36491
     Infant 36488
Cervical Dilation 59200
Cochlear Device 69930
Contraceptive Capsules 11975, 11977
Drug Delivery Implant 11981, 11983
Electrode
   Brain 61531-61533, 61760, 61850-61875
   Heart 33210-33211, 33216-33217
   Nerve 64553-64581
   Sphenoidal 95830
   Spinal Cord 63650-63655
Endotracheal Tube 31500
Gastrostomy Tube
   Laparoscopic 43653
   Percutaneous 43750
Graft
   Aorta 33330-33335
   Heart Vessel 33330-33335

Guide
   Kidney Pelvis 50395
Guide Wire
   Endoscopy 43248
   Esophagoscopy 43248
     with Dilation 43226
Heyman Capsule
   Uterus
     for Brachytherapy 58346
Iliac Artery
   Occlusion Device 34808
Implant
   Bone
     for External Speech Processor/Cochlear
     Stimulator 69714-69718
Infusion Pump
   Intraarterial 36260
   Intravenous 36530
   Spinal Cord 62361-62362
Intracatheter/Needle
   Aorta 36160
   Arteriovenous Shunt 36145
   Intraarterial 36100-36140
   Intravenous 36000
   Kidney 50392
Intraocular Lens 66983
   Manual or Mechanical
   Technique 66982, 66984
   Not Associated with Concurrent Cataract
   Removal .66985
Intrauterine Device (IUD) 58300
IVC Filter 75940
Jejunostomy Tube
   Endoscopy 44372
Keel
   Laryngoplasty 31580
Laminaria 59200
Nasobiliary Tube
   Endoscopy 43267
Nasopancreatic Tube
   Endoscopy 43267
Needle
   Bone 36680
   Intraosseous 36680
   Prostate 55859
Needle Wire
   Trachea 31730
Neurostimulator
   Pulse Generator 64590
   Receiver .64590
Nose
   Septal Prosthesis 30220
Obturator
   Larynx 31527
Ocular Implant
   in Scleral Shell 65130
   Muscles, Not Attached 65135
   Muscles Attached 65140
   with/without Conjunctival Graft 65150
   with Foreign Material 65155
Orbital Transplant 67550
Oviduct
   Chromotubation 58350
   Hydrotubation 58350
Ovoid
   Vagina
     for Brachytherapy 57155

Pacemaker
   Fluoroscopy/Radiography 71090
   Heart 33200-33208, 33212-33213
Pacing Cardio-Defibrillator
   Electrodes 33245-33246
   Leads 33216-33220, 33243-33245
   Pulse Generator only 33240-33241
Packing
   Vagina 57180
Penile Prosthesis, Inflatable
   See Penile Prosthesis, Insertion, Inflatable
Pessary
   Vagina 57160
Pin
   Skeletal Traction 20650
Probe
   Brain 61770
Prostaglandin 59200
Prostate
   Radioactive Substance 55860
Prosthesis
   Knee 27438, 27445
   Nasal Septal 30220
   Palate 42281
   Penis
     Inflatable 54401-54405
     Noninflatable 54400
   Speech 31611
   Testis 54660
   Urethral Sphincter 53444-53445
Pulse Generator
   Brain 61885-61886
   Heart 33212-33213
   Spinal Cord 63685
Radioactive Material
   Bladder 51020
   Cystourethroscopy 52250
   Kidney 50559, 50578
   Ureteral Endoscopic 50978
   Urethral Endoscopic 50959
Receiver
   Brain 61885-61886
   Spinal Cord 63685
Reservoir
   Brain 61210-61215
   Spinal Cord 62360
Sensor, Fetal Oximetry
   Cervix 0021T
   Vagina 0021T
Shunt 36835
   Abdomen
     Vein 49425
     Venous .49426
Spinal Instrument 22849
   Spinous Process 22841
Spinal Instrumentation
   Anterior 22845-22847
   Internal Spinal Fixation 22841
   Pelvic Fixation 22848
   Posterior Nonsegmental
     Harrington Rod Technique 22840
   Posterior Segmental 22842-22844
   Prosthetic Device 22851
Stent
   Bile Duct 43268, 47801
     Percutaneous 47511
   Bladder 51045
   Conjunctiva 68750

Coronary 92980-92981
Esophagus 43219
Gastrointestinal, Upper 43256
Ileum 44383
Indwelling 50605
Lacrimal Duct 68815
Pancreatic Duct 43268
Small Intestines 44370, 44379
Ureteral 50947, 52332
Ureter via Kidney 50393
Urethral 52282
Tamponade
Esophagus 43460
Tandem
Uterus
for Brachytherapy 57155
Tendon Graft
Finger 26392
Hand 26392
Testicular Prosthesis
See Prosthesis, Testicular, Insertion
Tissue Expanders
Skin .11960-11971
Tube
Bile Duct 43268
Esophagus 43510
Gastrointestinal, Upper 43241
Ileum 44383
Kidney 50398
Pancreatic Duct 43268
Small Intestines 44379
Trachea 31730
Ureter 50688
Ureteral Guide Wire 52334
Vascular Pedicle
Carpal Bone .25430
Venous Access Device 36533
Ventilating Tube 69433
Ventricular Assist Device 33975
Wire
Skeletal Traction 20650

Inspiratory Positive Pressure Breathing
See Intermittent Positive Pressure Breathing (IPPB)

Instillation
Contrast Material
Bronchography 31708
Laryngography 31708
Drugs
Bladder 51720

Instillation, Bladder
See Bladder, Instillation

Instrumentation
See Application; Bone, Fixation; Spinal Instrumentation
Spinal
Insertion 22840-22848, 22851
Reinsertion 22849
Removal 22850, 22852-22855

Insufflation, Eustachian Tube
See Eustachian Tube, Inflation

Insulin 80422, 80432-80435
Antibody 86337
Blood 83525
Free 83527

Insulin C-Peptide Measurement
See C-Peptide

Insulin Like Growth Factors
See Somatomedin

Insurance
Basic Life and/or Disability
Evaluation Services 99450
Examination 99450-99456

Integumentary System
Biopsy 11100-11101
Breast
Excision 19100-19272
Incision 19000-19030
Metallic Localization Clip Placement . .19295
Preoperative Placement of Needle
Localization 19290-19291
Reconstruction 19316-19396
Repair 19316-19396
Unlisted Services and Procedures 19499
Burns . .15000-15001, 15100-15121, 15342-15401
Debridement 11000-11044
Destruction
See Dermatology
Actinotherapy 96900
Benign or Premalignant Lesion 17000-17250
by Photodynamic Therapy 96567
Chemical Exfoliation 17360
Cryotherapy 17340
Electrolysis Epilation 17380
Malignant Lesion 17260-17286
by Photodynamic Therapy 96567
Mohs Micrographic Surgery . .17304-17310
Unlisted Services and Procedures 17999
Drainage 10040-10180
Excision
Benign Lesion 11400-11471
Debridement 11000-11044
Malignant Lesion 11600-11646
Incision 10040-10180
Introduction 11900-11977
Drug Delivery Implant 11981, 11983
Nails .11720-11765
Paring 11055-11057
Pressure Ulcers 15920-15999
Removal
Drug Delivery Implant 11982-11983
Repair
Adjacent Tissue
Transfer/Rearrangement 14000-14350
Complex 13100-13160
Flaps
Other 15740-15776
Free Skin Grafts 15000-15400
Intermediate 12031-12057
Other Procedures 15780-15879
Simple 12001-12021
Skin and/or Deep Tissue 15570-15738
Shaving of Epidermal or
Dermal Lesion 11300-11313
Skin Tags
Removal 11200-11201

Integumentum Commune
See Integumentary System

Intelligence Test 96100

Intensive Care
Neonatal
Initial Care .99295
Subsequent Care 99296-99297

Intercarpal Joint
Arthrodesis 25820-25825
Dislocation
Closed Treatment 25660
Repair 25447

Intercostal Nerve
Destruction 64620
Injection
Anesthetic 64420-64421
Neurolytic .64620

Interdental Fixation
Device
Application .21110
Mandibular Fracture
Closed Treatment 21453
Open Treatment 21462
without Fracture 21497

Interdental Papilla
See Gums

Interdental Wire Fixation
Closed Treatment
Craniofacial Separation 21431

Interferometry
Eye
Biometry 92136

Intermediate Care Facilities (ICFs)
See Nursing Facility Services

Intermediate Care Facility Visits .99301-99313

Intermittent Positive Pressure Breathing (IPPB) 94650-94652
See Continuous Negative Pressure Breathing (CNPB); Continuous Positive Airway Pressure (CPAP)

Internal Breast Prostheses
See Breast, Implants

Internal Ear
See Ear, Inner

Internal Rigid Fixation
Reconstruction
Mandibular Rami 21196

Interphalangeal Joint
Arthrodesis 26860-26863
Arthroplasty 26535-26536
Arthrotomy 26080, 28054
Biopsy
Synovium 26110
Capsule
Excision 26525
Incision 26525

Dislocation
 Closed Treatment 26770
 Open Treatment 26785
 Percutaneous Fixation 26776
 with Manipulation 26340
Exploration 26080
Fracture
 Closed Treatment 26740
 Open Treatment 26746
 with Manipulation 26742
Fusion 26860-26863
Great Toe
 Arthrodesis 28755
 with Tendon Transfer 28760
 Fusion 28755
 with Tendon Transfer 28760
Removal of Foreign Body 26080
Repair
 Collateral Ligament 26545
 Volar Plate 26548
Synovectomy 26140
Toe 28272
 Arthrotomy.....................28024
 Dislocation 28660-28665, 28675
 Percutaneous Fixation 28666
 Excision 28160
 Exploration 28024
 Removal
 Foreign Body 28024
 Loose Body 28024
 Synovial
 Biopsy 28054

Interruption
Vein
 Femoral 37650
 Iliac 37660
 Vena Cava 37620

Intersex State
Clitoroplasty 56805
Vaginoplasty 57335

Intersex Surgery
Female to Male 55980
Male to Female 55970

Interstitial Cell Stimulating Hormone
See Luteinizing Hormone (LH)

Interstitial Cystitides, Chronic
See Cystitis, Interstitial

Interstitial Cystitis
See Cystitis, Interstitial

Interstitial Fluid Pressure
Monitoring 20950

Interstitual Cell Stimulating Hormone
See Luteinizing Hormone (LH)

Intertarsal Joint
Arthrotomy..............28020, 28050
Exploration 28020
Removal
 Foreign Body 28020
 Loose Body 28020

Synovial
 Biopsy 28050
 Excision 28070

Interthoracoscapular Amputation
See Amputation, Interthoracoscapular

Intertrochanteric Femur Fracture
See Femur, Fracture, Intertrochanteric

Intervertebral Chemonucleolysis
See Chemonucleolysis

Intervertebral Disk
Diskography
 Cervical 72285
 Lumbar 72295
 Thoracic 72285
Excision
 Decompression 63075-63078
 Herniated 63020-63044, 63055-63066
Injection
 Chemonucleolysis Agent 62292
 X-Ray 62290-62291

Intestinal Anastomosis
See Anastomosis, Intestines

Intestinal Invagination
See Intussusception

Intestinal Peptide, Vasoactive
See Vasoactive Intestinal Peptide

Intestine
Biopsy 44100
Lesion
 Excision 44110-44111

Intestines
Allotransplantation 44135-44136
Anastomosis 44625-44626
Bleeding Tube 91100
Closure
 Enterostomy
 Large or Small 44625-44626
 Stoma 44620-44625
Excision
 Donor 44132-44133
Exclusion 44700
Laparoscopic Resection
 with Anastomosis 44202-44203
Lysis of Adhesions
 Laparoscopic 44200
Nuclear Medicine
 Imaging 78290
Reconstruction
 Bladder 50820
 Colonic Reservoir 45119
Repair
 Diverticula 44605
 Obstruction 44615
 Ulcer 44605
 Wound 44605
Suture
 Diverticula 44605
 Stoma 44620-44625
 Ulcer 44605
 Wound 44605
Transplantation
 Donor Enterectomy 44132-44133

Intestines, Large
See Anus; Cecum; Colon; Rectum

Intestines, Small
Anastomosis 44130
Biopsy 44020
 Endoscopy 44361
Catheterization
 Jejunum 44015
Decompression 44021
Destruction
 Lesion 44369
 Tumor 44369
Endoscopy 44364
 Biopsy 44361, 44377
 Control of Bleeding 44366, 44378
 via Stoma 44382
 Destruction
 Lesion 44369
 Tumor 44369
 Diagnostic 44376
 Exploration 44360
 Hemorrhage 44366
 Insertion
 Stent 44370, 44379
 Tube 44379
 Pelvic Pouch 44385-44386
 Removal
 Foreign Body 44363
 Lesion 44365
 Polyp 44364-44365
 Tumor 44364-44365
 Tube Placement 44372
 Tube Revision 44373
 via Stoma 44380
Enterostomy 44300
Excision 44120-44128
 Partial with Anastomosis 44140
Exclusion 44700
Exploration 44020
Gastrostomy Tube 44373
Hemorrhage 44378
Hemorrhage Control 44366
Ileostomy 44310-44314, 45136
 Continent 44316
Incision 44020
 Creation
 Pouch 44316
 Stoma 44300-44310, 44314
 Decompression 44021
 Exploration 44020
 Revision
 Stoma 44312
 Stoma Closure 44620-44626
Insertion
 Catheter 44015
 Jejunostomy Tube 44372
Jejunostomy 44310
 Laparoscopic 44201
Lysis
 Adhesions 44005
Removal
 Foreign Body 44020, 44363
Repair
 Diverticula 44602-44603
 Enterocele
 Abdominal Approach 57270
 Vaginal Approach 57268

Fistula 44640-44661
Hernia 44050
Malrotation 44055
Obstruction 44050
Ulcer 44602-44603
Volvulus 44050
Wound 44602-44603
Revision
Jejunostomy Tube 44373
Specimen Collection 89100-89105
Suture
Diverticula 44602-44603
Fistula 44640-44661
Plication 44680
Ulcer 44602-44603
Wound 44602-44603
Unlisted Services and Procedures 44799
X-Ray 74245, 74249-74251
Guide Intubation 74355

Intestinovesical Fistula
See Fistula, Enterovesical

Intimectomy
See Endarterectomy

Intra-Abdominal Voiding Pressure Studies 51797

Intra-Osseous Infusion
See Infusion, Intraosseous

Intracapsular Extraction of Lens
See Extraction, Lens, Intracapsular

Intracardiac Echocardiography 93662

Intracranial
Biopsy 61140
Microdissection 69990

Intracranial Arterial Perfusion
Thrombolysis 61624

Intracranial Neoplasm, Acoustic Neuroma
See Brain, Tumor, Excision

Intracranial Neoplasm, Craniopharyngioma
See Craniopharyngioma

Intracranial Neoplasm, Meningioma
See Meningioma

Intrafallopian Transfer, Gamete
See GIFT

Intraluminal Angioplasty
See Angioplasty

Intramuscular Injection
See Injection, Intramuscular

Intraocular Lens
Exchange 66986
Insertion 66983
Manual or Mechanical
Technique 66982, 66984
Not Associated with Concurrent Cataract
Removal 66985

Intratracheal Intubation
See Insertion, Endotracheal Tube

Intrauterine Contraceptive Device
See Intrauterine Device (IUD)

Intrauterine Device (IUD)
Insertion 58300
Removal 58301

Intrauterine Synechiae
See Adhesions, Intrauterine

Intravascular Stent
See Transcatheter, Placement, Intravascular Stents
X-Ray 75960

Intravascular Ultrasound
Intraoperative 37250-37251

Intravenous Injection
See Injection, Intravenous

Intravenous Pyelogram
See Urography, Intravenous

Intravenous Therapy 90780-90781, 99566
See Injection, Chemotherapy
Pain Management 90783-90784

Intravesical Instillation
See Bladder, Instillation

Intravitreal Injection
Pharmacologic Agent 67028

Intra Arterial Injections
See Injection, Intraarterial

Intrinsic Factor 83528
Antibody 86340

Introduction
Breast
Metallic Localization Clip Placement . .19295
Preoperative Placement, Needle 19290-19291
Contraceptive Capsules
Implantable 11975-11977
Drug Delivery Implant 11981, 11983
Gastrointestinal Tube 44500
with Fluoroscopic Guidance 74340
Tissue Expanders
Skin 11960-11971

Intubation
See Insertion
Endotracheal Tube 31500
Eustachian Tube
See Catheterization, Eustachian Tube
Gastric 89130-89141, 91105
Specimen Collection
Esophagus 91000
Stomach 91055

Intubation Tube
See Endotracheal Tube

Intussusception
Barium Enema 74283
Reduction
Laparotomy 44050

Invagination, Intestinal
See Intussusception

Inversion, Nipple
See Nipples, Inverted

In Vivo NMR Spectroscopy
See Magnetic Resonance Spectroscopy

Iodide Test
See Nuclear Medicine, Thyroid, Uptake

Iodine Test
See Starch Granules, Feces

Ionization, Medical
See Iontophoresis

Iontophoreses
See Iontophoresis

Iontophoresis 97033
See Physical Medicine and Rehabilitation

IP
See Allergen Immunotherapy

Ipecac Administration 99175

IPPB
See Intermittent Positive Pressure Breathing; Pulmonology, Therapeutic

Iridectomy
by Laser Surgery 66761
Peripheral for Glaucoma 66625
with Corneoscleral or Corneal Section 66600
with Sclerectomy with Punch or Scissors . .66160
with Thermocauterization 66155
with Transfixion as for Iris Bombe 66605
with Trephination 66150

Iridencleisis 66165

Iridodialysis 66680

Iridoplasty 66762

Iridotasis 66165

Iridotomy
by Laser Surgery 66761
by Stab Incision 66500
Excision
Optical 66635
Peripheral 66625
with Corneoscleral or Corneal
Section 66600
with Cyclectomy 66605
Incision
Stab 66500
with Transfixion as for Iris Bombe 66505
Optical 66635
Peripheral 66625
Sector 66630

Iris
Cyst
Destruction 66770
Excision
Iridectomy
Optical 66635
Peripheral 66625

Sector 66630
with Corneoscleral or
Corneal Section 66600
with Cyclectomy 66605
Incision
Iridotomy
Stab .66500
with Transfixion as for Iris Bombe . . .66505
Lesion
Destruction 66770
Repair
with Ciliary Body 66680
Suture 66682
Revision
Laser Surgery 66761
Photocoagulation 66762
Suture
with Ciliary Body 66682

Iron 83540
Absorption 78162
Chelatable
Total Body Iron 78172
Turnover Rate 78160
Utilization 78170

Iron Binding Capacity 83550

Iron Hematoxylin Stain 88312

Iron Stain 85536, 88313

Irradiation
Blood Products 86945

Irrigation
Bladder 51700
Catheter
Brain 62194, 62225
Corpora Cavernosa
Priapism .54220
Penis
Priapism .54220
Peritoneal
See Peritoneal Lavage
Rectum
for Fecal Impaction 91123
Shunt
Spinal Cord 63744
Sinus
Maxillary 31000
Sphenoid 31002
Vagina 57150

Irving Sterilization
See Ligation, Fallopian Tube, Oviduct

Ischial
Bursa
Excision .27060
Tumor
Excision 27078-27079

Ischiectomy 15941

Islands of Langerhans
See Islet Cell

Island Pedicle Flaps 15740

Islet Cell
Antibody 86341

Isocitrate Dehydrogenase
See Isocitric Dehydrogenase

Isocitric Dehydrogenase
Blood 83570

Isolation
Sperm 89260-89261

Isomerase, Glucose 6 Phosphate
See Phosphohexose Isomerase

Isopropanol
See Isopropyl Alcohol

Isopropyl Alcohol 84600

Isthmusectomy
Thyroid Gland 60210-60225

IUD
See Intrauterine Device (IUD)

IV
See Injection, Chemotherapy; Intravenous
Therapy

IV, Coagulation Factor
See Calcium

IVC Filter
Placement 75940

IVF
See Artificial Insemination; In Vitro Fertilization

Ivy Bleeding Time 85002

IV Infusion Therapy
See Allergen Immunotherapy; Chemotherapy;
Infusion; Injection, Chemotherapy

IV Injection
See Injection, Intravenous

IX Complex, Factor
See Christmas Factor

I Antibodies, HTLV
See Antibody, HTLV-I

J

Jaboulay Operation
See Gastroduodenostomy

**Jaboulay Operation
Gastroduodenostomy**
See Gastroduodenostomy

Jannetta Procedure
See Decompression, Cranial Nerve; Section

Japanese, River Fever
See Scrub Typhus

Jatene Type 33770-33781

Jaws
Muscle Reduction 21295-21296
X-Ray
for Orthodontics 70355

Jaw Joint
See Facial Bones; Mandible; Maxilla

Jejunostomy
Catheterization 44015
Insertion
Catheter .44015
Laparoscopic 44201
Non-Tube .44310
with Pancreatic Drain 48001

Jejunum
Creation
Stoma
Laparoscopic 44201
Transfer
with Microvascular Anastomosis
Free .43496

Johannsen Procedure 53400

Johanson Operation
See Reconstruction, Urethra

Joint
See Specific Joint
Acromioclavicular
See Acromioclavicular Joint
Arthrocentesis 20600-20610
Aspiration 20600-20610
Dislocation
See Dislocation
Drainage 20600-20610
Finger
See Intercarpal Joint
Fixation (Surgical)
See Arthrodesis
Foot
See Foot, Joint
Hip
See Hip Joint
Injection 20600-20610
Intertarsal
See Intertarsal Joint
Knee
See Knee Joint
Ligament
See Ligament
Metacarpophalangeal
See Metacarpophalangeal Joint
Metatarsophalangeal
See Metatarsophalangeal Joint
Nuclear Medicine
Imaging 78300, 78315
Radiology
Stress Views 76006
Sacroiliac
See Sacroiliac Joint
Shoulder
See Glenohumeral Joint
Sternoclavicular
See Sternoclavicular Joint
Survey 76066

Temporomandibular
  See Temporomandibular Joint (TMJ)
  Dislocation Temporomandibular
    See Dislocation, Temporomandibular Joint
  Implant
    See Prosthesis, Temporomandibular Joint
Wrist
  See Radiocarpal Joint

Joint Syndrome, Temporomandibular
See Temporomandibular Joint (TMJ)

Jones and Cantarow Test
See Blood Urea Nitrogen; Urea Nitrogen, Clearance

Jones Procedure 28760

Joplin Procedure 28294

Jugal Bone
See Cheekbone

Jugular Vein
See Vein, Jugular

K

K-Wire Fixation
Tongue 41500

Kader Operation
See Incision, Stomach, Creation, Stoma; Incision and Drainage

Kala Azar Smear 87207

Kallidin I /Kallidin 9
See Bradykinin

Kallikreinogen
See Fletcher Factor

Kallikrein HK3
See Antigen, Prostate Specific

Kasai Procedure 47701

Kedani Fever
See Scrub Typhus

Keel
Insertion/Removal
  Laryngoplasty 31580

Keen Operation
See Laminectomy

Kelikian Procedure 28280

Keller Procedure 28292

Kelly Urethral Plication 57220

Keratectomy
Partial
  for Lesion 65400

Keratomileusis 65760

Keratophakia 65765

Keratoplasty
Lamellar 65710
Penetrating 65730
  in Aphakia 65750
  in Pseudophakia 65755

Keratoprosthesis 65770

Keratotomy
Radial 65771

Ketogenic Steroids 83582

Ketone Body
Acetone 82009-82010

Ketosteroids 83586-83593

Kidner Procedure 28238

Kidney
Abscess
  Incision and Drainage 50020
    Open 50020
    Percutaneous 50021
Anesthesia 00862
Biopsy 50200-50205
  Endoscopic 50555-50559
Catheterization
  Endoscopic 50572
Cyst
  Ablation 50541
  Aspiration 50390
  Excision 50280-50290
  Injection 50390
  X-Ray 74470
Destruction
  Calculus 50590
  Endoscopic 50557, 50576
Dilation 50395
Endoscopy
  Biopsy 50555, 50574-50578, 52354
  Catheterization 50553, 50572
  Destruction 50557, 50576, 52354
  Dilation
    Intra-Renal Stricture 52343, 52346
    Ureter 50553
  Excision
    Tumor 52355
  Exploration 52351
  Lithotripsy 52353
  Radioactive Substance 50578
  Radiotracer 50559
  Removal
    Calculus 50561, 50580, 52352
    Foreign Body 50561, 50580
  via Incision 50570-50580
  via Stoma 50551-50561
Excision
  Donor 50300-50320, 50547
  Partial 50240
  Recipient 50340
  Transplantation 50370
  with Ureters 50220-50236
Exploration 50010, 50045, 50120
Incision 50010, 50045
Incision and Drainage 50040, 50125

Injection
  Radiologic 50394
Insertion
  Catheter 50392-50393
  Guide 50395
  Intracatheter 50392
  Stent 50393
  Tube 50398
Lithotripsy 50590
Manometry
  Pressure 50396
Needle Biopsy 50200
Nuclear Medicine
  Blood Flow 78715
  Function Study 78725
  Imaging 78700-78710
  Unlisted Services and Procedures 78799
Removal
  Calculus 50060-50081, 50130, 50561
  Foreign Body 50561, 50580
Repair
  Blood Vessels 50100
  Fistula 50520-50526
  Horseshoe Kidney 50540
  Renal Pelvis 50400-50405
  Wound 50500
Solitary 50405
Suture
  Fistula 50520-50526
  Horseshoe Kidney 50540
Transplantation
  Donor 00862
  Donor Nephrectomy 50300-50320, 50547
  Implantation of Graft 50360
  Recipient Nephrectomy 50340, 50365
  Reimplantation Kidney 50380
  Removal Transplant Renal Autograft . 50370
Ultrasound 76770-76778
X-Ray with Contrast
  Guide Catheter 74475

Kidney Stone
See Calculus, Removal, Kidney

Killian Operation
See Sinusotomy, Frontal

Kinase, Creatine
See CPK

Kineplasty
See Cineplasty

Kinetic Therapy 97530
See Physical Medicine/Therapy/Occupational Therapy

Kininase A
See Angiotensin Converting Enzyme (ACE)

Kininogen 85293

Kininogen, High Molecular Weight
See Fitzgerald Factor

Kleihauer-Betke Test 85460

Kloramfenikol
See Chloramphenicol

Knee
See Femur; Fibula; Patella; Tibia
Abscess 27301
Arthrocentesis 20610
Arthrodesis 27580
Arthroplasty 27440-27445, 27447
 Revision 27486-27487
Arthroscopy
 Diagnostic 29870
 Surgical 0012T-0013T, 29871-29889
Arthrotomy 27310, 27330-27335, 27403
Biopsy 27323-27324, 27330-27331
 Synovium 27330
Bone
 Drainage 27303
Bursa 27301
 Excision 27340
Cyst
 Excision 27345-27347
Disarticulation 27598
Dislocation 27550-27552, 27560-27562
 Open Treatment 27556-27558, 27566
Drainage 27310
Excision
 Cartilage 27332-27333
 Ganglion 27347
 Lesion 27347
 Synovial Lung 27334-27335
Exploration 27310, 27331
Fasciotomy 27305, 27496-27499
Fracture 27520-27524
 Arthroscopic Treatment 29850-29851
Fusion 27580
Hematoma 27301
Incision
 Capsule 27435
Injection
 X-Ray 27370
Magnetic Resonance Imaging
(MRI) 73721-73723
Manipulation 27570
Meniscectomy 27332-27333
Reconstruction 27437-27438
 Ligament 27427-27429
 with Prosthesis 27445
Removal
 Foreign Body 27310, 27331, 27372
 Loose Body 27331
 Prosthesis 27488
Repair
 Ligament 27405-27409
 Collateral 27405
 Collateral and Cruciate 27409
 Cruciate 27407-27409
 Meniscus 27403
 Tendon 27380-27381
Replacement 27447
Retinacular
 Release 27425
Strapping 29530
Suture
 Tendon 27380-27381
Transplantation
 Meniscus 0014T
Tumor
 Excision 27327-27329, 27365
Unlisted Services and Procedures 27599

X-Ray 73560-73564
 Arthrography 73580
 Bilateral 73565
X-Ray with Contrast
 Arthrography 73580

Kneecap
Excision 27350
Repair
 Instability 27420-27424

Knee Joint
Arthroplasty 27446

Knee Prosthesis
See Prosthesis, Knee

Knock-Knee Repair 27455-27457

Kocher Operation 23650-23680
See Clavicle; Scapula; Shoulder, Dislocation,
Closed Treatment

Kocher Pylorectomy
See Gastrectomy, Partial

Kock Pouch 44316
Formation 50825

Kock Procedure 44316

KOH
See Hair, Nails, Tissue, Examination for Fungi

Kraske Procedure 45116

Krause Operation
See Gasserian Ganglion, Sensory Root,
Decompression

Kroenlein Procedure 67420

Krukenberg Procedure 25915

Kuhlmann Test 96100

Kuhnt-Szymanowski
Procedure 67917

Kyphectomy
More than Two Segments 22819
Up to Two Segments 22818

L

L-Alanine
See Aminolevulinic Acid (ALA)

L-Leucylnaphthylamidase
See Leucine Aminopeptidase

L/S Ratio
Amniotic Fluid 83661

Labial Adhesions
Lysis 56441

Labyrinth
See Ear, Inner

Labyrinthectomy 69905
with Mastoidectomy 69910
with Skull Base Surgery 61596

Labyrinthotomy
with/without Cryosurgery 69801
with Mastoidectomy 69802

Laceration Repair
See Specific Site

Lacrimal Duct
Canaliculi
 Repair 68700
Exploration 68810
 Canaliculi 68840
 Stent 68815
 with Anesthesia 68811
Insertion
 Stent 68815
Removal
 Dacryolith 68530
 Foreign Body 68530
X-Ray with Contrast 70170

Lacrimal Gland
Biopsy 68510
Close Fistula 68770
Excision
 Partial 68505
 Total 68500
Fistulization 68720
Incision and Drainage 68400
Injection
 X-Ray 68850
Nuclear Medicine
 Tear Flow 78660
Removal
 Dacryolith 68530
 Foreign Body 68530
Repair
 Fistula 68770
Tumor
 Excision
 without Closure 68540
 with Osteotomy 68550

Lacrimal Punctum
Closure
 by Plug 68761
 by Thermocauterization, Ligation or Laser
 Surgery 68760
Dilation 68801
Incision 68440
Repair 68705

Lacrimal Sac
Biopsy 68525
Excision 68520
Incision and Drainage 68420

Lacrimal System
Unlisted Services and Procedures 68899

Lactase Deficiency Breath
Test 91065

Lactate 83605

Lactate Dehydrogenase
See Lactic Dehydrogenase

Lactic Acid 83605

Lactic Acid Measurement
See Lactate

Lactic Cytochrome Reductase
See Lactic Dehydrogenase

Lactic Dehydrogenase 83615-83625

Lactiferous Duct
Excision 19112
Exploration 19110

Lactogen, Human Placental 83632

Lactogenic Hormone
See Prolactin

Lactose
Urine 83633-83634

Ladd Procedure 44055

Laki Lorand Factor
See Fibrin Stabilizing Factor

Lamblia Intestinalis
See Giardia Lamblia

Lambrinudi Operation
See Arthrodesis, Foot Joint

Lamellar Keratoplasties
See Keratoplasty, Lamellar

Laminaria
Insertion 59200

Laminectomy .. 62351, 63001, 63005-63011,
          63015-63044, 63180-63200, 63265-63655
Lumbar 22630, 63012
Surgical 63170-63172
with Facetectomy 63045-63048

Langerhans Islands
See Islet Cell

Language Evaluation 92506

Language Therapy 92507-92508

LAP
See Leucine Aminopeptidase

Laparoscopic Appendectomy
See Appendectomy, Laparoscopic

Laparoscopic Biopsy of Ovary
See Biopsy, Ovary, Laparoscopic

Laparoscopy
Adrenalectomy 50545
Adrenal Gland
     Biopsy 60650
     Excision 60650
Appendectomy 44970
Aspiration 49322
Biopsy 47561, 49321
     Lymph Nodes 38570
Cholangiography 47560-47561
Cholecystectomy 47562-47564
Cholecystenterostomy 47570

Destruction
     Lesion 58662
Diagnostic 49320
Drainage
     Extraperitoneal Lymphocele 49323
Ectopic Pregnancy 59150
     with Salpingectomy and/or
     Oophorectomy 59151
Enterolysis 44200
Esophagogastric Fundoplasty 43280
Fimbrioplasty 58672
Gastrostomy
     Temporary 43653
Hernia Repair
     Initial 49650
     Recurrent 49651
Incontinence Repair 51990-51992
In Vitro Fertilization 58976
     Retrieve Oocyte 58970
     Transfer Embryo 58974
     Transfer Gamete 58976
Jejunostomy 44201
Ligation
     Veins, Spermatic 55550
Liver
     Ablation
          Tumor 47370-47371
Lymphadenectomy 38571-38589
Lysis of Adhesions 58660
Lysis of Intestinal Adhesions 44200
Nephrectomy 50545-50548
Orchiectomy 54690
Orchiopexy 54692
Oviduct Surgery 58670-58671, 58679
Pelvis 49320
Pyeloplasty 50544
Removal
     Fallopian Tube 58661
     Leiomyomata 58551
     Ovaries 58661
     Spleen 38120
     Testis 54690
Resection
     Intestines
          with Anastomosis 44202-44203
Salpingostomy 58673
Splenectomy 38120-38129
Surgical 38570-38572, 43651-43653, 44200-
          44205, 44970, 47370-47371, 49321-49323,
          49650-49651, 50541, 50545, 50945-50948,
          51990-51992, 54690-54692, 55550
     with Guided Transhepatic
          Cholangiography 47560-47561
Unlisted Services and Procedures 38129,
                    38589, 43289, 43659, 44209,
          44979, 47379, 47579, 49329, 49659,
               50549, 50949, 54699, 55559,
                    58578-58579, 58679, 59898
Ureterolithotomy 50945
Ureteroneocystostomy 50947-50948
Urethral Suspension 51990
Vaginal Hysterectomy 58550
Vagus Nerves
     Transection 43651-43652
with X-Ray 47560

Laparotomy
Exploration 47015, 49000-49002, 58960
for Staging 49220
Hemorrhage Control 49002
Second Look 58960
Staging 58960
with Biopsy 49000

Laparotomy, Exploratory
See Abdomen, Exploration

Lapidus Procedure 28297

Large Bowel
See Anus; Cecum; Rectum

Laroyenne Operation
See Vagina, Abscess, Incision and Drainage

Laryngeal Function Study 92520

Laryngectomy 31360-31382
Partial 31367-31382
Subtotal 31367-31368

Laryngocele
Removal 31300

Laryngofissure 31300

Laryngography 70373
Instillation
     Contrast Material 31708

Laryngopharyngectomy
See Excision, Larynx, with Pharynx

Laryngopharynx
See Hypopharynx

Laryngoplasty
Burns 31588
Cricoid Split 31587
Laryngeal Stenosis 31582
Laryngeal Web 31580
Open Reduction of Fracture 31584

Laryngoscopy
Diagnostic 31505
Direct 31515-31571
Exploration 31505, 31520-31526, 31575
Fiberoptic 31575-31579
     with Stroboscopy 31579
Indirect 31505-31513
Newborn 31520
Operative 31530-31561

Laryngotomy 31300
Diagnostic 31320
Total 31360-31368

Larynx
Aspiration
     Endoscopy 31515
Biopsy
     Endoscopy 31510, 31535-31536, 31576
Dilation
     Endoscopic 31528-31529
Endoscopy
     Direct 31515-31571
     Exploration 31505, 31520-31526, 31575

Fiberoptic 31575-31579
　with Stroboscopy 31579
Indirect 31505-31513
Operative 31530-31561
Excision
　Lesion 31512, 31578
　Partial 31367-31382
　Total 31360-31365
　with Pharynx 31390-31395
Exploration
　Endoscopic 31505, 31520-31526, 31575
Fracture
　Closed Treatment
　　without Manipulation 31585
　　with Manipulation 31586
　Open Treatment 31584
Insertion
　Obturator 31527
Nerve
　Destruction 31595
Reconstruction
　Burns .31588
　Cricoid Split 31587
　Other .31588
　Stenosis 31582
　Web 31580
Removal
　Foreign Body
　　Endoscopic . . .31511, 31530-31531, 31577
　Lesion
　　Endoscopic 31512, 31578
Repair
　Reinnervation Neuromuscular
　Pedicle 31590
Stroboscopy 31579
Tumor
　Excision 31300
　Endoscopic 31540-31541
Unlisted Services and Procedures 31599
Vocal Cord(s)
　Injection 31513, 31570-31571
X-Ray 70370
　with Contrast 70373

Laser Surgery
Anal 46917
Lesion
　Mouth .40820
　Nose 30117-30118
　Penis .54057

Laser Treatment 17000-17286
See Destruction

Lateral Epicondylitis
See Tennis Elbow

Latex Fixation 86403-86406

LATS
See Thyrotropin Releasing Hormone (TRH)

Latzko Operation
See Repair, Vagina, Fistula; Revision

LAV
See HIV

LAV-2
See HIV-2

Lavage, Bronchioalveolar
See Lung, Lavage

Lavage, Peritoneal
See Peritoneal Lavage

Lav Antibodies
See Antibody, HIV

LCM
See Lymphocytic Choriomeningitis

LD
See Lactic Dehydrogenase

LDH 83615-83625

LDL
See Lipoprotein, LDL

Lead .83655

Leadbetter Procedure 53431

Lecithin-Sphingomyelin
Ratio .83661

Lecithinase C
See Tissue Typing

LEEP Procedure 57460

Lee and White Test 85345

LeFort III Procedure
Craniofacial Separation 21431-21436
Midface Reconstruction 21154-21159

LeFort II Procedure
Midface Reconstruction 21150-21151
Nasomaxillary Complex Fracture . . .21345-21348

LeFort I Procedure
Midface Reconstruction 21141-21147, 21155,
　　　　　　　　　　　　　　　　　　　　　21160
Palatal or Maxillary Fracture 21421-21423

LeFort Procedure
Vagina .57120

Left Atrioventricular Valve
See Mitral Valve

Left Heart Cardiac Catheterization
See Cardiac Catheterization, Left Heart

Leg
Cast
　Rigid Total Contact 29445
Lower
　See Ankle; Fibula; Knee; Tibia
　Abscess
　　Incision and Drainage 27603
　Amputation 27598, 27880-27882
　　Revision 27884-27886
　Angiography 73706
　Artery
　　Ligation 37618
　Biopsy 27613-27614
　Bursa
　　Incision and Drainage 27604
　Bypass Graft 35903
　Cast 29405-29435, 29450

CAT Scan 73700-73706
Decompression 27600-27602
Exploration
　Blood Vessel 35860
Fasciotomy 27600-27602, 27892-27894
Hematoma
　Incision and Drainage 27603
Lesion
　Excision 27630
Magnetic Resonance Imaging
(MRI) 73718-73720
Repair
　Blood Vessel 35226
　Blood Vessel with Other Graft 35286
　Blood Vessel with Vein Graft 35256
　Fascia .27656
　Tendon 27658-27692
　Splint .29515
　Strapping 29580
　Suture
　　Tendon 27658-27665
Tumor
　Excision 27615-27619
Ultrasound 76880
Unlisted Services and Procedures 27899
Unna Boot 29580
X-Ray 73592
Upper
See Femur
　Abscess 27301
　Amputation 27590-27592
　　at Hip 27290-27295
　　Revision 27594-27596
　Angiography 73706, 75635
　Artery
　　Ligation 37618
　Biopsy 27323-27324
　Bursa .27301
　Bypass Graft 35903
　Cast 29345-29355, 29365, 29450
　Cast Brace 29358
　CAT Scan 73700-73706, 75635
　Exploration
　　Blood Vessel 35860
　Fasciotomy 27305, 27496-27499,
　　　　　　　　　　　　　　　　　27892-27894
　Halo Application 20663
　Hematoma 27301
　Magnetic Resonance Imaging
　(MRI) 73718-73720
　Neurectomy 27315-27320
　Removal
　　Cast .29705
　　Foreign Body 27372
　Repair
　　Blood Vessel with Other Graft 35286
　　Blood Vessel with Vein Graft 35256
　　Muscle 27385-27386, 27400, 27430
　　Tendon 27393-27400
　Splint .29505
　Strapping 29580
　Suture
　　Muscle 27385-27386
　Tenotomy 27306-27307, 27390-27392
　Tumor
　　Excision 27327-27329
　Ultrasound 76880
　Unlisted Services and Procedures 27599

Unna Boot 29580
X-Ray 73592
Wound Exploration
Penetrating 20103

Legionella
Antibody 86713
Antigen 87277-87278, 87540-87542

Legionella Micdadei
Antigen Detection
Immunofluorescence 87277

Legionella Pneumophila
Antigen Detection
Direct Fluorescence 87278

Leg Length Measurement X-Ray
See Scanogram

Leiomyomata
Removal 58140, 58551, 58561

Leishmania
Antibody 86717

Lengthening, Tendon
See Tendon, Lengthening

Lens
Extracapsular 66940
Intracapsular 66920
Dislocated 66930
Intraocular
Exchange 66986
Reposition 66825
Prosthesis
Insertion 66983
Manual or Mechanical
Technique 66982, 66984
Not Associated with Concurrent Cataract
Removal 66985
Removal
Lens Material
Aspiration Technique 66840
Extracapsular 66940
Intracapsular 66920-66930
Pars Plana Approach 66852
Phacofragmentation Technique 66850

Lens Material
Aspiration Technique 66840
Pars Plana Approach 66852
Phacofragmentation Technique 66850

Leptomeningioma
See Meningioma

Leptospira
Antibody 86720

Leriche Operation 64809
See Sympathectomy, Thoracolumbar

Lesion
See Tumor
Anal
Destruction 46900-46917, 46924
Excision 45108, 46922
Ankle
Tendon Sheath 27630

Arm, Lower
Tendon Sheath
Excision 25110
Auditory Canal, External
Excision
Exostosis 69140
Radical without Neck Dissection 69150
Radical with Neck Dissection 69155
Soft Tissue 69145
Bladder
Destruction 51030
Brain
Excision 61534, 61536,
61600-61608, 61615-61616
Radiation Treatment 77432
Brainstem
Excision 61575-61576
Breast
Excision 19120-19126
Carotid Body
Excision 60600-60605
Chemotherapy 96405-96406
Destruction 67220-67225
Choroid
Destruction 0016T
Ciliary Body
Destruction 66770
Colon
Destruction 44393, 45383
Excision 44110-44111
Conjunctiva
Destruction 68135
Excision 68110-68130
Over 1 cm 68115
with Adjacent Sclera 68130
Expression 68040
Cornea
Destruction 65450
Excision 65400
of Pterygium 65420-65426
Destruction
Ureter 52341-52342, 52344-52345
Ear, Middle
Excision 69540
Epididymis
Excision 54830
Esophagus
Ablation 43228
Excision 43100-43101
Removal 43216
Excision 59100
Bladder 52224
Urethra 52224, 53265
Eye
Excision 65900
Eyelid
Destruction 67850
Excision
Multiple, Different Lids 67805
Multiple, Same Lid 67801
Single 67800
Under Anesthesia 67808
without Closure 67840
Facial
Destruction 17000-17004, 17280-17286
Femur
Excision 27062

Finger
Tendon Sheath 26160
Foot
Excision 28080, 28090
Gums
Destruction 41850
Excision 41822-41828
Hand Tendon Sheath 26160
Intestines
Excision 44110
Intestines, Small
Destruction 44369
Excision 44111
Iris
Destruction 66770
Leg, Lower
Tendon Sheath 27630
Lymph Node
Incision and Drainage 38300-38305
Mesentery
Excision 44820
Mouth
Destruction 40820
Excision 40810-40816, 41116
Vestibule
Destruction 40820
Repair 40830
Nerve
Excision 64774-64792
Nose
Intranasal
External Approach 30118
Internal Approach 30117
Orbit
Excision 61333, 67412
Palate
Destruction 42160
Excision 42104-42120
Pancreas
Excision 48120
Pelvis
Destruction 58662
Penis
Destruction
Cryosurgery 54056
Electrodesiccation 54055
Extensive 54065
Laser Surgery 54057
Simple 54050-54060
Surgical Excision 54060
Excision 54060
Penile Plaque 54110-54112
Pharynx
Destruction 42808
Excision 42808
Rectum
Excision 45108
Removal
Larynx 31512, 31578
Resection 52354
Retina
Destruction
Extensive 67227-67228
Localized 0017T, 67208-67210
Radiation by Implantation of Source ...67218
Sclera
Excision 66130

Skin
- Abrasion 15786-15787
- Biopsy 11100-11101
- Destruction
  - Benign 17000-17250
  - Malignant 17260-17286
    - by Photodynamic Therapy 96567
- Excision
  - Benign 11400-11471
  - Malignant 11600-11646
- Injection 11900-11901
- Paring or Curettement 11055-11057
- Shaving 11300-11313

Skin Tags
- Removal 11200-11201

Skull
- Excision . .61500, 61600-61608, 61615-61616

Spermatic Cord
- Excision 55520

Spinal Cord
- Destruction 62280-62282
- Excision 63265-63273

Stomach
- Excision 43611

Testis
- Excision 54512

Toe
- Excision 28092

Tongue
- Excision 41110-41114

Uvula
- Destruction 42145
- Excision 42104-42107

Vagina
- Destruction 57061-57065

Vulva
- Destruction
  - Extensive .56515
  - Simple 56501

Wrist Tendon
- Excision 25110

Lesion of Sciatic Nerve
See Sciatic Nerve, Lesion

Leucine Aminopeptidase 83670

Leukemia Lymphoma Virus I, Adult T Cell
See HTLV I

Leukemia Lymphoma Virus II Antibodies, Human T Cell
See Antibody, HTLV-II

Leukemia Lymphoma Virus I Antibodies, Human T Cell
See Antibody, HTLV-I

Leukemia Virus II, Hairy Cell Associated, Human T Cell
See HTLV II

Leukoagglutinins 86021

Leukocyte
See White Blood Cell
- Alkaline Phosphatase 85540
- Antibody 86021

- Histamine Release Test 86343
- Phagocytosis 86344
- Transfusion 86950

Leukocyte Count
See White Blood Cell, Count

Leu 2 Antigens
See CD8

Levarterenol
See Noradrenalin

Levator Muscle Rep
See Blepharoptosis, Repair

LeVeen Shunt
- Insertion 49425
- Patency Test 78291
- Revision 49426

Levulose
See Fructose

LGV
See Lymphogranuloma Venereum

LH
See Luteinizing Hormone (LH)

LHR
See Leukocyte Histamine Release Test

Lidocaine
- Assay 80176

Lid Suture
See Blepharoptosis, Repair

Lift, Face
See Face Lift

Ligament
See Specific Site
Collateral
- Repair
  - Knee
    - with Cruciate Ligament 27409
Dentate
- Incision 63180-63182
- Section 63180-63182
Injection 20550
Release
- Coracoacromial 23415
- Transverse Carpal 29848
Repair
- Elbow 24343-24346
- Knee Joint 27405-27409

Ligation
Artery
- Abdomen 37617
- Carotid 37600-37606
- Chest 37616
- Coronary 33502
- Coronary Artery 33502
- Ethmoidal 30915
- Extremity 37618
- Fistula 37607
- Maxillary 30920
- Neck 37615
- Temporal 37609

- Esophageal Varices 43204, 43400
Fallopian Tube
- Oviduct 58600-58611, 58670
Gastroesophageal 43405
Hemorrhoids 46945-46946
Oviducts 59100
Salivary Duct 42665
Shunt
- Aorta
  - Pulmonary 33924
- Peritoneal
  - Venous 49428
Thoracic Duct .38380
- Abdominal Approach 38382
- Thoracic Approach 38381
Vas Deferens .55450
Vein
- Esophagus 43205, 43244, 43400
- Femoral 37650
- Gastric 43244
- Iliac 37660
- Jugular, Internal 37565
- Perforate 37760
- Saphenous 37700-37735, 37780
- Secondary 37785
- Vena Cava 37620

Ligature Strangulation
- Skin Tags 11200-11201

Light Coagulation
See Photocoagulation

Light Scattering Measurement
See Nephelometry

Light Therapy, UV
See Actinotherapy

Limb
See Extremity

Limited Lymphadenectomy for Staging
See Lymphadenectomy, Limited, for Staging

Limited Neck Dissection
- with Thyroidectomy 60252

Limited Resection Mastectomies
See Breast, Excision, Lesion

Lindholm Operation
See Tenoplasty

Lingual Bone
See Hyoid Bone

Lingual Frenectomy
See Excision, Tongue, Frenum

Lingual Nerve
- Avulsion 64740
- Incision 64740
- Transection 64740

Lingual Tonsil
See Tonsils, Lingual

Linton Procedure 37760

Lip
Biopsy 40490
Excision 40500-40530
    Frenum .40819
Incision
    Frenum .40806
Reconstruction 40525-40527
Repair 40650-40654
    Cleft Lip 40700-40761
    Fistula .42260
Unlisted Services and Procedures 40799

Lip, Cleft
See Cleft Lip

Lipase 83690

Lipectomies, Aspiration
See Liposuction

Lipectomy 15831-15839
Suction Assisted 15876-15879

Lipids
Feces 82705-82710

Lipo-Lutin
See Progesterone

Lipolysis, Aspiration
See Liposuction

Lipophosphodiesterase I
See Tissue Typing

Lipoprotein
Blood 83715-83719
LDL 83716, 83721

Lipoprotein, Alpha
See Lipoprotein

Lipoprotein, Pre-Beta
See Lipoprotein, Blood

Liposuction 15876-15879

Lisfranc Operation
See Amputation, Foot; Radical Resection;
Replantation

Listeria Monocytogenes
Antibody 86723

Lithium
Assay 80178

Litholapaxy 52317-52318

Lithotripsy
See Extracorporeal Shock Wave Therapy
Bile Duct Calculi (Stone)
    Endoscopy 43265
Bladder 52353
Kidney 50590, 52353
Pancreatic Duct Calculi (Stone)
    Endoscopy 43265
Ureter 52353
Urethra 52353
with Cystourethroscopy 52353

Lithotrity
See Litholapaxy

Liver
See Hepatic Duct
Ablation
    Tumor 47380-47383
    Laparoscopic 47370-47371
Abscess
    Aspiration 47015
    Incision and Drainage
        Open 47010
        Percutaneous 47011
    Injection 47015
Aspiration .47015
Biopsy 47100
Cyst
    Aspiration 47015
    Incision and Drainage
        Open 47010
        Percutaneous 47011
Excision
    Extensive 47122
    Partial 47120, 47125-47130, 47134
    Total .47133
Injection .47015
    Radiologic 47505
    X-Ray .47500
Lobectomy 47125-47130
    Partial .47120
Needle Biopsy 47000-47001
Nuclear Medicine
    Function Study 78220
    Imaging 78201-78216
    Vascular Flow 78206
Repair
    Abscess 47300
    Cyst 47300
    Wound 47350-47362
Suture
    Wound 47350-47362
Transplantation 47135-47136
Trisegmentectomy 47122
Unlisted Services and Procedures . .47379, 47399

Living Activities, Daily
See Activities of Daily Living

Lobectomy
Brain 61539
Contralateral Subtotal
    Thyroid Gland 60212, 60225
Liver 47120-47130
Lung 32480-32482
    Sleeve 32486
Parotid Gland 42410-42415
Segmental .32663
Sleeve 32486
Temporal Lobe 61538
Thyroid Gland Partial 60210-60212
    Total 60220-60225
Total 32663

Lobotomy
Frontal 61490

Localization of Nodule
Radiographic
    Breast .76096

Local Excision Mastectomies
See Breast, Excision, Lesion

Local Excision of Lesion or Tissue of Femur
See Excision, Lesion, Femur

Log Hydrogen Ion Concentration
See pH

Lombard Test
See Audiologic Function Test

Longmire Operation
See Anastomosis, Hepatic Duct to Intestines

Long Acting Thyroid Stimulator
See Thyrotropin Releasing Hormone (TRH)

Long Term Care Facility Visits
See Nursing Facility Services

Loopogram
See Urography, Antegrade

Loose Body
Removal
    Ankle 27620
    Carpometacarpal Joint 26070
    Elbow .24101
    Interphalangeal Joint 28020
        Toe 28024
    Knee Joint 27331
    Metatarsophalangeal Joint 28022
    Tarsometatarsal Joint 28020
    Toe 28022
    Wrist .25101

Lord Procedure
See Anal Sphincter, Dilation

Louis Bar Syndrome
See Ataxia Telangiectasia

Lower Extremities
See Extremity, Lower

Lower GI Series
See Barium Enema

Low Density Lipoprotein
See Lipoprotein, LDL

Low Vision Aids
See Spectacle Services
Fitting 92354-92355
Supply 92392

LRH
See Luteinizing Releasing Factor

LSD
See Lysergic Acid Diethylamide

LTH
See Prolactin

Lumbar
See Spine
Aspiration, Disk
    Percutaneous 62287

Lumbar Plexus
Decompression 64714
Neuroplasty .64714
Release 64714
Repair/Suture 64862

Lumbar Puncture
See Spinal Tap

Lumbar Spine Fracture
See Fracture, Vertebra, Lumbar

Lumbar Sympathectomy
See Sympathectomy, Lumbar

Lumbar Vertebra
See Vertebra, Lumbar

Lumen Dilation 74360

Lumpectomies
See Breast, Excision, Lesion

Lunate
Arthroplasty
    with Implant 25444
Dislocation
    Closed Treatment 25690
    Open Treatment 25695

Lung
Abscess
    Incision and Drainage
        Open 32200
        Percutaneous 32200-32201
Aspiration 32420
Biopsy 32095-32100
Bullae
    Excision 32141
        Endoscopic 32655
Cyst
    Incision and Drainage
        Open 32200
    Removal 32140
Decortication
    Endoscopic 32651-32652
    Partial 32225
    Total 32220
    with Parietal Pleurectomy 32320
Empyema
    Excision 32540
Excision
    Bronchus Resection 32486
    Chest Resection 32520-32525
    Completion 32488
    Donor 33930
    Emphysematous 32491
    Lobe 32480-32482
    Segment 32484
    Total 32440-32445
    Wedge Resection 32500
        Endoscopic 32657
Foreign Body
    Removal 32151
Hemorrhage 32110
Lavage
    Bronchial 31624
    Total 32997
Lysis
    Adhesions 32124
Needle Biopsy 32405
Nuclear Medicine
    Imaging, Perfusion 78580-78585
    Imaging, Ventilation 78586-78594
    Unlisted Services and Procedures 78599

Pneumocentesis 32420
Pneumolysis 32940
Pneumothorax 32960
Puncture 32420
Removal
    Bronchoplasty 32501
    Completion Pneumonectomy 32488
    Extrapleural 32445
    Single Lobe 32480
    Single Segment 32484
    Sleeve Lobectomy 32486
    Sleeve Pneumonectomy 32442
    Total Pneumonectomy 32440-32445
    Two Lobes 32482
    Volume Reduction 32491
    Wedge Resection 32500
Repair
    Hernia 32800
Segmentectomy 32484
Tear
    Repair 32110
Thoracotomy
    Biopsy 32095-32100
    Cardiac Massage 32160
    for Post-Op Complications 32120
    Removal
        Bullae 32141
        Cyst 32140
        Intrapleural Foreign Body 32150
        Intrapulmonary Foreign Body 32151
    Repair 32110
    with Excision-Plication of Bullae 32141
    with Open Intrapleural
        Pneumonolysis 32124
Transplantation 32851-32854, 33935
Unlisted Services and Procedures 32999

Lung Function Tests
See Pulmonology, Diagnostic

Lung Volume Reduction
Emphysematous 32491

Lupus Anticoagulant Assay 85705

Lupus Band Test
See Immunofluorescent Study

Luteinizing Hormone (LH) 80418,
                              80426, 83002

Luteinizing Releasing Factor ...83727

Lutenizing Hormone
See Luteinizing Hormone (LH)

Luteotropic Hormone
See Prolactin

Luteotropin
See Prolactin

Luteotropin, Placental
See Lactogen, Human Placental

Lyme Disease 86617-86618

Lyme Disease ab
See Antibody, Lyme Disease

Lyme Disease Vaccine
See Vaccination

Lymph Duct
Injection 38790

Lymph Nodes
Abscess
    Incision and Drainage 38300-38305
Biopsy 38500, 38510-38530, 38570
    Needle 38505
Dissection 38542
Excision 38500, 38510-38530
    Abdominal 38747
    Inguinofemoral 38760-38765
    Laparoscopic 38571-38572
    Limited, for Staging
        Para-Aortic 38562
        Pelvic 38562
        Retroperitoneal 38564
    Pelvic 38770
    Radical
        Axillary 38740-38745
        Cervical 38720-38724
        Suprahyoid 38720-38724
    Retroperitoneal Transabdominal 38780
    Thoracic 38746
Exploration 38542
Hygroma, Cystic
    Axillary/Cervical
        Excision 38550-38555
Nuclear Medicine
    Imaging 78195
Removal
    Abdominal 38747
    Inguinofemoral 38760-38765
    Pelvic 38770
    Retroperitoneal Transabdominal 38780
    Thoracic 38746

Lymph Vessels
Abdomen
    Lymphangiography 75805-75807
Arm
    Lymphangiography 75801-75803
Leg
    Lymphangiography 75801-75803
Nuclear Medicine
    Imaging 78195
Pelvis
    Lymphangiography 75805-75807

Lymphadenectomy
Abdominal 38747
Bilateral Inguinofemoral ..54130, 56632, 56637
Bilateral Pelvic 51575, 51585, 51595, 54135,
                         55845, 55865
    Total 38571-38572, 57531, 58210
Diaphragmatic Assessment 58960
Gastric 38747
Inguinofemoral 38760-38765
Inguinofemoral, Iliac and Pelvic 56640
Injection
    Sentinel Node 38792
Limited, for Staging
    Para-Aortic 38562
    Pelvic 38562
    Retroperitoneal 38564
Limited Para-Aortic, Resection of Ovarian
    Malignancy 58951, 58954
Limited Pelvic 55842, 55862, 58954
Mediastinal 21632

Peripancreatic .... .38747
Portal .... .38747
Radical
  Axillary 38740-38745
  Cervical 38720-38724
  Pelvic 54135, 55845
  Suprahyoid .... .38700
Regional .... .50230
Retroperitoneal Transabdominal .... .38780
Thoracic .... .38746
Unilateral Inguinofemoral .... .56631, 56634

Lymphadenitis
Incision and Drainage 38300-38305

Lymphadenopathy Associated Antibodies
See Antibody, HIV

Lymphadenopathy Associated Virus
See HIV

Lymphangiogram, Abdominal
See Lymphangiography, Abdomen

Lymphangiography
Abdomen 75805-75807
Arm 75801-75803
Injection .... .38790
Leg 75801-75803
Pelvis 75805-75807

Lymphangioma, Cystic
See Hygroma

Lymphangiotomy .... .38308

Lymphatics
See Specific Procedure

Lymphatic Channels
Incision .... .38308

Lymphatic Cyst
See Lymphocele

Lymphatic System
Unlisted Procedure .... .38999

Lymphoblast Transformation
See Blastogenesis

Lymphocele
Drainage
  Laparoscopic .... .49323
Extraperitoneal
  Open Drainage .... .49062

Lymphocoele
See Lymphocele

Lymphocyte
Culture 86821-86822
Toxicity Assay 86805-86806
Transformation .... .86353

Lymphocyte, Thymus-Dependent
See T-Cells

Lymphocytes, CD4
See CD4

Lymphocytes, CD8
See CD8

Lymphocytic Choriomeningitis
Antibody .... .86727

Lymphocytotoxicity 86805-86806

Lymphogranuloma Venereum
Antibody .... .86729

Lymphoma Virus, Burkitt
See Epstein-Barr Virus

Lynch Procedure .... .31075

Lysergic Acid Diethylamide ..80102-
80103, 80299

Lysergide
See Lysergic Acid Diethylamide

Lysis
Adhesions
  Epidural .... .62263
  Fallopian Tube .... .58740
  Foreskin .... .54450
  Intestinal .... .44005
  Labial .... .56441
  Lung .... .32124
  Nose .... .30560
  Ovary .... .58740
  Oviduct .... .58740
  Penile
    Post-circumcision .... .54162
  Ureter 50715-50725
  Uterus .... .58559
Euglobulin .... .85360
Labial
  Adhesions .... .56441
Nose
  Intranasal Synechia .... .30560

Lysozyme .... .85549

L Ascorbic Acid
See Ascorbic Acid

L Aspartate 2 Oxoglutarate Aminotransferase
See Transaminase, Glutamic Oxaloacetic

L Glutamine
See Glutamine

M

MacEwen Operation
See Hernia, Repair, Inguinal

Machado Test
See Complement, Fixation Test

MacLean-De Wesselow Test
See Blood Urea Nitrogen; Urea Nitrogen, Clearance

Macrodactylia
Repair .... .26590

Madlener Operation
See Tubal Ligation

Magnesium .... .83735

Magnetic Resonance Angiography (MRA)
Abdomen .... .74185
Arm .... .73225
Chest .... .71555
Head 70544-70546
Leg .... .73725
Neck 70547-70549
Pelvis .... .72198
Spine .... .72159

Magnetic Resonance Imaging (MRI)
Abdomen 74181-74183
Ankle 73721-73723
Arm 73218-73220, 73223
Bone Marrow Study .... .76400
Brain 70551-70553
Breast 76093-76094
Chest 71550-71552
Elbow .... .73221
Face 70540-70543
Finger Joint .... .73221
Foot 73718-73719
Foot Joints 73721-73723
Guidance
  Needle Placement .... .76393
  Tissue Ablation .... .76394
Hand 73218-73220, 73223
Heart .... .75552
  Complete Study .... .75554
  Flow Mapping .... .75556
  Limited Study .... .75555
  Morphology .... .75553
Joint
  Lower Extremity 73721-73723
  Upper Extremity 73221-73223
Knee 73721-73723
Leg 73718-73720
Neck 70540-70543
Orbit 70540-70543
Pelvis 72195-72197
Radiology
  Diagnostic
    Procedures .... .76499
Spectroscopy .... .76390
Spine
  Cervical 72141-72142, 72156-72158
  Lumbar 72148-72158
  Thoracic 72146-72147, 72156-72158
Temporomandibular Joint (TMJ) .... .70336
Toe 73721-73723
Wrist .... .73221

Magnetic Resonance Spectroscopy .... .76390

Magnetic Stimulation
Brain Cortex .... .0018T

Magnetoencephalography (MEG) 95965-95967

Magnet Operation
See Ciliary Body; Cornea; Eye, Removal, Foreign Body; Iris; Lens; Retina; Sclera; Vitreous

Magnuson Procedure 23450

Magpi Operation 54322

Magpi Procedure
See Hypospadias, Repair

Major Vestibular Gland
See Bartholin's Gland

Malar Area
Augmentation 21270
Bone Graft 21210
Fracture
　　Open Treatment 21360-21366
　　with Bone Graft 21366
　　with Manipulation 21355
Reconstruction 21270

Malar Bone
See Cheekbone

Malaria Antibody 86750

Malaria Smear 87207

Malate Dehydrogenase 83775

Maldescent, Testis
See Testis, Undescended

Male Circumcision
See Circumcision

Malformation, Arteriovenous
See Arteriovenous Malformation

Malic Dehydrogenase
See Malate Dehydrogenase

Malleolus
See Ankle; Fibula; Leg, Lower; Tibia; Tibiofibular Joint
Metatarsophalangeal Joint 27889

Mallet Finger Repair 26432

Maltose
Tolerance Test 82951-82952

Malunion Repair
Femur
　　without Graft 27470
　　with Graft 27472
Metatarsal 28322
Tarsal Joint 28320

Mammalian Oviduct
See Fallopian Tube

Mammaplasties
See Breast, Reconstruction

Mammary Abscess
See Abscess, Breast

Mammary Arteries
See Artery, Mammary

Mammary Duct
X-Ray with Contrast 76086-76088

Mammary Ductogram
Injection 19030

Mammary Stimulating Hormone
See Prolactin

Mammilliplasty
See Nipples, Reconstruction

Mammogram
Breast
　　Localization Nodule 76096

Mammography 76090-76092
Screening 76092
　　with Computer-aided Detection 76085

Mammoplasty
Augmentation 19324-19325
Reduction 19318

Mammotomy
See Mastotomy

Mammotropic Hormone, Pituitary
See Prolactin

Mammotropic Hormone, Placental
See Lactogen, Human Placental

Mammotropin
See Prolactin

Mandible
See Facial Bones; Maxilla; Temporomandibular Joint (TMJ)
Abscess
　　Excision 21025
Bone Graft 21215
Fracture
　　Closed Treatment
　　　　without Manipulation 21450
　　　　with Interdental Fixation 21453
　　　　with Manipulation 21451
　　Open Treatment 21454-21470
　　　　External Fixation 21454
　　　　without Interdental Fixation 21461
　　　　with Interdental Fixation 21462
　　Percutaneous Treatment 21452
Osteotomy 21198-21199
Reconstruction
　　with Implant 21244-21246, 21248-21249
Removal
　　Foreign Body 41806
Torus Mandibularis
　　Excision 21031
Tumor
　　Excision 21040-21045
X-Ray 70100-70110

Mandibular Body
Augmentation
　　with Bone Graft 21127
　　with Prosthesis 21125

Mandibular Condyle
Fracture
　　Open Treatment 21465
Reconstruction 21247

Mandibular Condylectomy
See Condylectomy

Mandibular Fracture
See Fracture, Mandible

Mandibular Rami
Reconstruction
　　without Bone Graft 21193
　　without Internal Rigid Fixation 21195
　　with Bone Graft 21194
　　with Internal Rigid Fixation 21196

Mandibular Resection Prosthesis 21081

Mandibular Staple Bone Plate
Reconstruction
　　Mandible 21244

Manganese 83785

Manipulation
Chest Wall 94667-94668
Chiropractic 98940-98943
Dislocation and/or Fracture 25535
　　Acetabulum 27222
　　Acromioclavicular 23545
　　Ankle 27810, 27818, 27860
　　Carpometacarpal 26670-26676
　　Clavicular 23505
　　Elbow 24300, 24640
　　Femoral 27232, 27502, 27510, 27517
　　　　Pertrochanteric 27240
　　Fibula 27781, 27788
　　Finger 26725-26727, 26742, 26755
　　Greater Tuberosity
　　　　Humeral 23625
　　Hand 26670-26676
　　Heel 28405-28406
　　Hip 27257
　　Hip Socket 27222
　　Humeral 23605, 24505, 24535, 24577
　　　　Epicondyle 24565
　　Hyoid 21494
　　Intercarpal 25660
　　Interphalangeal Joint ...26340, 26770-26776
　　Larynx 31586
　　Lunate 25690
　　Malar Area 21355
　　Mandibular 21451
　　Metacarpal 26605-26607
　　Metacarpophalangeal 26700-26706,
　　　　　　　　　　　　　　　　　　26742
　　Metacarpophalangeal Joint 26340
　　Metatarsal 28475-28476
　　Nasal Bone 21315-21320
　　Orbit 21401
　　Phalangeal Shaft 26727
　　　　Distal, Finger or Thumb 26755
　　　　Phalanges, Finger/Thumb 26725
　　Phalanges
　　　　Finger 26742, 26755, 26770-26776
　　　　Finger/Thumb 26727

Great Toe 28495-28496
Toes 28515
Radial 24655, 25565
Radial Shaft 25505
Radiocarpal 25660
Radioulnar 25675
Scapular 23575
Shoulder 23650-23655
with Greater Tuberosity 23665
Shoulder Dislocation
Sternoclavicular 23525
with Surgical or Anatomical Neck . . .23675
Talus 28435-28436
Tarsal 28455-28456
Thumb 26641-26650
Tibial 27532, 27752
Trans-Scaphoperilunar 25680
Ulnar 24675, 25535, 25565
Vertebral .22315
Wrist . . .25259, 25624, 25635, 25660, 25675,
25680, 25690
Foreskin 54450
Globe .92018-92019
Hip 27275
Interphalangeal Joint, Proximal 26742
Knee 27570
Osteopathic 98925-98929
Shoulder
Application of Fixation Apparatus 23700
Spine
Anesthesia 22505
Tibial, Distal .27762

Manometric Studies
Kidney
Pressure .50396
Rectum/Anus 91122
Ureter
Pressure .50686
Ureterostomy 50686

Manometry
Rectum 90911

Mantoux Test
See TB Test, Skin Test

Manual Therapy 97140

Maquet Procedure 27418

Marcellation Operation
See Hysterectomy, Vaginal

Marrow, Bone
See Bone Marrow

Marshall-Marchetti-Krantz
Procedure 51840-51841, 58152, 58267

Marsupialization 10040
Bartholin's Gland Cyst 56440
Cyst
Sublingual Salivary 42409
Liver
Cyst or Abscess 47300
Pancreatic Cyst 48500
Urethral Diverticulum 53240

Massage
Cardiac 32160
Therapy 97124
See Physical Medicine/Therapy/Occupational
Therapy

Masseter Muscle/Bone
Reduction 21295-21296

Mass Spectrometry and Tandem
Mass Spectrometry
Analyte
Qualitative 83788
Quantitative 83789

Mastectomy
Gynecomastia 19140
Modified Radical 19240
Partial 19160-19162
Radical 19200-19220
Simple, Complete 19180
Subcutaneous 19182

Mastectomy, Halsted
See Mastectomy, Radical

Mastoid
Excision
Complete .69502
Radical 69511
Modified 69505
Petrous Apicectomy 69530
Simple .69501
Obliteration 69670
Repair
by Excision 69601-69603
Fistula 69700
with Apicectomy 69605
with Tympanoplasty 69604

Mastoidectomy
Osseointegrated Implant
for External Speech Processor/Cochlear
Stimulator 69715, 69718
with Apicectomy 69605
with Skull Base Surgery 61590, 61597
Decompression 61595
Facial Nerve 61595
with Tympanoplasty 69604, 69641-69646
Cochlear Device Implantation 69930
Complete 69502
Revision 69601
Ossicular Chain Reconstruction 69605
Radical .69511
Modified 69505
Revision 69602-69603
Simple .69501
with Labyrinthectomy 69910
with Labyrinthotomy 69802
with Petrous Apicectomy 69530

Mastoidotomy 69635-69637
with Tympanoplasty 69635
Ossicular Chain Reconstruction 69636
and Synthetic Prosthesis 69636

Mastoids
Polytomography 76101-76102
X-Ray 70120-70130

Mastoid Cavity
Debridement 69220-69222

Mastopexy 19316

Mastotomy 19020

Maternity Care
See Abortion; Cesarean Delivery; Ectopic
Pregnancy; Obstetrical Care

Maternity Care and
Delivery 59612-59622, 59898

Maxilla
See Facial Bones; Mandible
Bone Graft .21210
CAT Scan 70486-70488
Excision 21032
Fracture
Closed Treatment 21345, 21421
Open Treatment . .21346-21348, 21422-21423
with Fixation 21345-21347
Osteotomy .21206
Reconstruction
with Implant 21245-21246, 21248-21249

Maxillary Arteries
See Artery, Maxillary

Maxillary Sinus
See Sinus, Maxillary

Maxillary Torus Palatinus
Tumor Excision 21032

Maxillectomy 31225-31230

Maxillofacial Fixation
Application
Halo Type Appliance 21100

Maxillofacial Impressions
Auricular Prosthesis 21086
Definitive Obturator Prosthesis 21080
Facial Prosthesis 21088
Interim Obturator Prosthesis 21079
Mandibular Resection Prosthesis 21081
Nasal Prosthesis 21087
Oral Surgical Splint 21085
Orbital Prosthesis 21077
Palatal Augmentation Prosthesis 21082
Palatal Lift Prosthesis 21083
Speech Aid Prosthesis 21084
Surgical Obturator Prosthesis 21076

Maxillofacial Procedures
Unlisted Services and Procedures 21299

Maxillofacial
Prosthetics 21076-21089
Unlisted Services and Procedures 21089

Maydl Operation 45563, 50810
See Colostomy

Mayo Hernia Repair
See Hernia, Repair, Umbilicus

Mayo Operation
See Varicose Vein, Removal

Mayo Procedure 28292

MBC
See Minimum Bactericidal Concentration

McBride Procedure 28292

McBurney Operation
See Hernia, Repair, Inguinal

McCannel Procedure 66682

McDonald Operation
See Repair, Cervix, Cerclage, Abdominal; Revision

McIndoe Procedure
See Vagina, Construction

McKissock Surgery
See Breast, Reduction

McVay Operation
See Hernia, Repair, Inguinal

Measles, German
See Rubella

Measles Uncomplicated
See Rubeola

Measles Vaccine
See Vaccines

Meatoplasty 69310

Meatotomy 53020-53025
Contact Laser Vaporization with/without
   Transurethral Resection of Prostate . . .52648
   with Cystourethroscopy 52281
Infant 53025
Non-Contact Laser Coagulation Prostate . .52647
Transurethral Electrosurgical Resection
   Prostate .52601
Ureter 52290
Ureteral
   Cystourethroscopy 52290-52305

Meat Fibers
Feces 89160

Meckel's Diverticulum
Excision 44800
Unlisted Services and Procedures 44899

Median Nerve
Decompression 64721
Neuroplasty 64721
Release 64721
Repair/Suture
   Motor 64835
Transposition .64721

Median Nerve Compression
See Carpal Tunnel Syndrome

Mediastinal Cyst
See Cyst, Mediastinal

Mediastinoscopy 39400

Mediastinotomy
Cervical Approach 39000
Transthoracic Approach 39010

Mediastinum
See Chest; Thorax
Cyst
   Excision 32662, 39200
Endoscopy
   Biopsy 39400
   Exploration 39400
Exploration 39000-39010
Incision and Drainage 39000-39010
Needle Biopsy 32405
Removal
   Foreign Body 39000-39010
Tumor
   Excision 32662, 39220
Unlisted Procedures 39499

**Medical Disability Evaluation
Services** 99455-99456

Medical Testimony 99075

Medicine, Preventive
See Preventive Medicine

Medicine, Pulmonary
See Pulmonology

Medulla
Tractotomy 61470

Medullary Tract
Incision 61470
Section 61470

Meibomian Cyst
See Chalazion

Membrane, Mucous
See Mucosa

Membrane, Tympanic
See Ear, Drum

**Membrane Oxygenation,
Extracorporeal**
See Extracorporeal Membrane Oxygenation

Meninges
Tumor
   Excision 61512, 61519

Meningioma
Excision 61512, 61519
Tumor
   Excision 61512, 61519

Meningitis, Lymphocytic Benign
See Lymphocytic Choriomeningitis

Meningocele Repair 63700-63702

Meningococcal
See Vaccines

Meningococcal Vaccine
See Vaccines

Meningococcus
See Neisseria Meningitidis

Meningomyelocele
See Myelomeningocele

Meniscectomy
Knee Joint 27332-27333
Temporomandibular Joint 21060

Meniscus
Knee
   Excision 27332-27333
   Repair 27403
   Transplantation 0014T

Mental Nerve
Avulsion 64736
Incision 64736
Transection .64736

Meprobamate 83805

Mercury 83015, 83825

Merskey Test
See Fibrin Degradation Products

Mesencephalic Tract
Incision 61480
Section 61480

Mesencephalon
Tractotomy .61480

Mesenteric Arteries
See Artery, Mesenteric

Mesentery
Lesion
   Excision .44820
Repair 44850
Suture 44850
Unlisted Services and Procedures 44899

Metabisulfite Test
See Red Blood Cell (RBC), Sickling

Metabolite 82520

Metacarpal
Amputation .26910
Craterization .26230
Cyst
   Excision 26200-26205
Diaphysectomy 26230
Excision 26230
   Radical
      for Tumor 26250-26255
Fracture
   Closed Treatment 26605
      with Fixation 26607
   Open Treatment 26615
   Percutaneous Fixation 26608
   without Manipulation 26600
   with Manipulation 26605-26607
Ostectomy
   Radical
      for Tumor 26250-26255
Repair
   Lengthening 26568
   Nonunion 26546
   Osteotomy 26565
Saucerization 26230
Tumor
   Excision 26200-26205

Metacarpophalangeal Joint

Arthrodesis 26850-26852
Arthroplasty 26530-26531
Arthroscopy
    Diagnostic 29900
    Surgical 29901-29902
Arthrotomy 26075
Biopsy
    Synovium 26105
Capsule
    Excision 26520
    Incision 26520
Capsulodesis 26516-26518
Dislocation
    Closed Treatment 26700
    Open Treatment 26715
    Percutaneous Fixation 26705-26706
    with Manipulation 26340
Exploration 26075
Fracture
    Closed Treatment 26740
    Open Treatment 26746
    with Manipulation 26742
Fusion 26516-26518, 26850-26852
Removal of Foreign Body 26075
Repair
    Collateral Ligament 26540-26542
Synovectomy 26135

Metadrenaline
See Metanephrines

Metals, Heavy
See Heavy Metal

Metamfetamine
See Methamphetamine

Metanephrines 83835

Metatarsal
See Foot
Amputation 28810
Condyle
    Excision 28288
Craterization 28122
Cyst
    Excision 28104-28107
Diaphysectomy 28122
Excision 28110-28114, 28122, 28140
Fracture
    Closed Treatment
        without Manipulation 28470
        with Manipulation 28475-28476
    Open Treatment 28485
    Percutaneous Fixation 28476
Free Osteocutaneous Flap with Microvascular
Anastomosis 20972
Repair 28322
    Lengthening 28306-28307
    Osteotomy 28306-28309
Saucerization 28122
Tumor
    Excision 28104-28107, 28173

Metatarsectomy 28140

Metatarsophalangeal Joint

Arthrotomy 28022, 28052
Cheilectomy 28289
Dislocation 28630-28635, 28645
    Percutaneous Fixation 28636
Exploration 28022
Great Toe
    Arthrodesis 28750
    Fusion 28750
Removal
    of Foreign Body 28022
    of Loose Body 28022
Repair
    Hallux Rigidus 28289
Synovial
    Biopsy 28052
    Excision 28072
Toe 28270

Methadone 83840

Methaemoglobin
See Methemoglobin

Methamphetamine
Blood or Urine 82145

Methanol 84600

Methbipyranone
See Metyrapone

Methemalbumin 83857

Methemoglobin 83045-83050

Methenamine Silver Stain 88312

Methopyrapone
See Metyrapone

Methoxyhydroxymandelic Acid
See Vanillylmandelic Acid

Methsuximide 83858

Methylamphetamine
See Methamphetamine

Methylene Bichloride
See Dichloromethane

Methylfluorprednisolone
See Dexamethasone

Methylmorphine
See Codeine

Methyl Alcohol
See Methanol

Metroplasty
See Hysteroplasty

Metyrapone 80436

MIC
See Minimum Inhibitory Concentration

Micro-Ophthalmia
Orbit Reconstruction 21256

Microalbumin
Urine 82043-82044

Microbiology 0023T, 87001-87999

Microdissection 88380

Microfluorometries, Flow
See Flow Cytometry

Microglobulin, Beta 2
Blood 82232
Urine 82232

Micrographic Surgery
Mohs Technique 17304-17310

Micrographic Surgery, Moh
See Mohs Micrographic Surgery

Micropigmentation
Correction 11920-11922

Microscope, Surgical
See Operating Microscope

Microscopic Evaluation
Hair 96902

Microscopies, Electron
See Electron Microscopy

Microscopy
Ear Exam 92504

Microsomal Antibody 86376

Microsomia, Hemifacial
See Hemifacial Microsomia

Microsurgery
Operating Microscope 69990

Microvascular Anastomosis
Bone Graft
    Fibula 20955
    Other 20962
Fascial Flap, Free 15758
Muscle Flap, Free 15756
Osteocutaneous Flap with 20969-20973
Skin Flap, Free 15757

Microvite A
See Vitamin, A

Microwave Therapy 97020
See Physical Medicine/Therapy/Occupational
Therapy

Midbrain
See Brain; Brainstem; Mesencephalon; Skull
Base Surgery

Midcarpal Medioccipital Joint
Arthrotomy 25040

Middle Ear
See Ear, Middle

Midface
Reconstruction
    Forehead Advancement 21159-21160
    without Bone Graft 21141-21143
    with Bone Graft 21145-21160, 21188

Migration Inhibitory Factor (MIF) 86378

Mile Operation
See Colectomy, Total, with Proctectomy

Milia, Multiple
Removal 10040

Miller-Abbott Intubation 44500, 74340

Miller Procedure 28737

Minerva Cast 29035
Removal 29710

Minimum Inhibitory Concentration 87186

Minimum Lethal Concentration 87187

Minnesota Multiphasic Personality Inventory
See MMPI

Miscarriage
Incomplete Abortion 59812
Missed Abortion
    First Trimester 59820
    Second Trimester 59821
Septic Abortion 59830

Missed Abortion
See Abortion

Mitchell Procedure 28296

Mitogen Blastogenesis 86353

Mitral Valve
Incision 33420-33422
Repair 33420-33427
    Incision 33420-33422
Replacement 33430

Mitrofanoff Operation 50845
See Appendico-Vesicostomy

Miyagawanella
See Chlamydia

MMPI 96100

MMR Shots 90707
See Vaccines

Mobilization
Splenic Flexure 44139
Stapes 69650

Modified Radical Mastectomy
See Mastectomy, Modified Radical

Mohs Micrographic Surgery 17304-17310

Molar Pregnancy
See Hydatidiform Mole

Mold
Culture 87107

Mole, Carneous
See Abortion

Mole, Hydatid
See Hydatidiform Mole

Molecular Cytogenetics 88271-88275
Interpretation and Report 88291

Molecular Diagnostics ...83890-83898
Amplification 83898-83901
Dot/Slot Production 83893
Enzymatic Digestion 83892
Extraction 83890-83891
Interpretation 83912
Molecular Isolation (Extraction) 83890
Mutation Identification 83904-83906
Mutation Scanning 83903
Nucleic Acid Probe 83896
Nucleic Acid Transfer 83897
Polymerase Reaction Chain 83898
Reverse Transcription 83902
Separation 83894

Molecular Oxygen Saturation
See Oxygen Saturation

Molluscum Contagiosum
Destruction 17110-17111, 54050-54065

Molteno Procedure 66180

Monilia
See Candida

Monitoring
Blood Pressure, 24 Hour 93784-93790
Electrocardiogram 93224-93237
    See Electrocardiography
Electroencephalogram 95812-95813,
                              95950-95953, 95956
    with Drug Activation 95954
    with Physical Activation 95954
    with WADA Activation 95958
Fetal
    During Labor 59050-59051, 99500
        Interpretation Only 59051
Glucose
    Interstitial Fluid 95250
Interstitial Fluid Pressure 20950
Seizure 61531, 61760

Monitoring, Sleep
See Polysomnography

Monoethylene Glycol
See Ethylene Glycol

Mononucleosis Virus, Infectious
See Epstein-Barr Virus

Monophosphate, Adenosine
See Adenosine Monophosphate (AMP)

Monophosphate, Adenosine Cyclic
See Cyclic AMP

Monophosphate, Guanosine
See Guanosine Monophosphate

Monophosphate, Guanosine Cyclic
See Cyclic GMP

Monospot Test
See Rapid Test for Infection

Monoxide, Carbon
See Carbon Monoxide

Monteggia Fracture 24620-24635

Monticelli Procedure
See Application, Bone Fixation Device

Morbilli
See Rubeola

Morphine Methyl Ether
See Codeine

Morphometric Analysis
Nerve 88356
Skeletal Muscle 88355
Tumor 88358

Morton's Neuroma
Excision 28080

Moschcowitz Operation
See Repair, Hernia, Femoral; Revision

Mosenthal Test
See Urinalysis, Routine

Mother Cell
See Stem Cell

Motility Study
Esophagus 91010-91012

Motion Analysis
by Video and 3-D Kinematics 96000, 96004
Computer-based 96000, 96004

Mouth
Abscess
    Incision and Drainage 40800-40801,
                              41005-41009, 41015-41018
Biopsy 40808, 41108
Cyst
    Incision and Drainage 40800-40801,
                              41005-41009, 41015-41018
Excision
    Frenum 40819
Hematoma
    Incision and Drainage 40800-40801,
                              41005-41009, 41015-41018
Lesion
    Destruction 40820
    Excision 40810-40816, 41116
    Vestibule of
        Destruction 40820
        Repair 40830
Mucosa
    Excision 40818
Reconstruction 40840-40845
Removal
    Foreign Body 40804-40805
Repair
    Laceration 40830-40831
Unlisted Services and Procedures ..40899, 41599

Vestibule of
Excision
Destruction 40808-40820
Incision 40800-40806
Other Procedures 40899
Removal
Foreign Body 40804
Repair 40830-40845

Move
See Transfer
Finger 26555
Toe Joint 26556
Toe to Hand 26551-26554

Moynihan Test
See Gastrointestinal Tract, X-Ray, with Contrast

MPD Syndrome
See Temporomandibular Joint (TMJ)

MPR
See Multifetal Pregnancy Reduction

MRA
See Magnetic Resonance Angiography

MRI
See Magnetic Resonance Imaging (MRI)

MR Spectroscopy
See Magnetic Resonance Spectroscopy

MSLT
See Multiple Sleep Latency Testing (MSLT)

Mucin
Synovial Fluid 83872

Mucocele
Sinusotomy
Frontal 31075

Mucopolysaccharides 83864-83866

Mucormycoses
See Mucormycosis

Mucormycosis
Antibody 86732

Mucosa
Ectopic Gastric Imaging 78290
Excision of Lesion
Alveolar, Hyperplastic 41828
Vestibule of Mouth 40810-40818
via Esophagoscopy 43228
via Small Intestinal Endoscopy 44369
via Upper GI Endoscopy 43258
Periodontal Grafting 41870
Urethra, Mucosal Advancement 53450
Vaginal Biopsy 57100-57105

Mucosa, Buccal
See Mouth, Mucosa

Mucous Cyst
Antibody
Hand or Finger 26160

Mucous Membrane
See Mouth, Mucosa
Cutaneous
Biopsy 11100-11101

Excision, Benign Lesion 11440-11446
Layer Closure, Wounds 12051-12057
Simple Repair, Wounds 12011-12018
Excision
Sphenoid Sinus 31288
Lid Margin
Correction of Trichiasis 67835
Nasal Test 95065
Ophthalmic Test 95060
Rectum
Proctoplasty for Prolapse 45505

Mucus Cyst
See Mucous Cyst

MUGA (Multiple Gated Acquisition) 78472-78478, 78483

Muller Procedure
See Sleep Study

Multifetal Pregnancy Reduction 59866

Multiple Sleep Latency Testing (MSLT) 95805

Multiple Valve Procedures
See Valvuloplasty

Mumford Operation
See Claviculectomy, Partial

Mumford Procedure 29824

Mumps
Antibody 86735
Immunization 90704, 90707, 90709-90710
Vaccine 90704
MMR 90707
MMRV 90710
Rubella and Mumps 90709

Muramidase 85549

Murine Typhus 86000

Muscle
See Specific Muscle
Abdomen
See Abdominal Wall
Biopsy 20200-20206
Heart
See Myocardium
Neck
See Neck Muscle
Removal
Foreign Body 20520-20525
Repair
Forearm 25260-25274
Wrist 25260-25274
Revision
Arm, Upper 24330-24331
Transfer
Arm, Upper 24301, 24320
Elbow 24301
Femur 27110
Hip 27100-27105, 27111
Shoulder 23395-23397, 24301, 24320

Muscle, Oculomotor
See Eye Muscles

Muscles
Repair
Extraocular 65290

Muscle Compartment Syndrome
Detection 20950

Muscle Denervation
See Denervation

Muscle Division
Scalenus Anticus 21700-21705
Sternocleidomastoid 21720-21725

Muscle Flaps 15732-15738
Free 15756

Muscle Grafts 15841-15845

Muscle Testing
Dynamometry, Eye 92260
Extraocular Multiple Muscles 92265
Manual 95831-95834

Musculo-Skeletal System
See Musculoskeletal System

Musculoplasty
See Muscle, Repair

Musculoskeletal System
Unlisted Services and Procedures 20999,
24999, 25999, 26989, 27299, 27599, 27899
Unlisted Services and Procedures, Head ...21499

Musculotendinous (Rotator) Cuff
Repair 23410-23412

Mustard Procedure
See Repair, Great Arteries; Revision

Myasthenia Gravis
Tensilon Test 95857-95858

Myasthenic, Gravis
See Myasthenia Gravis

Mycobacteria
Culture 87116
Identification 87118
Detection 87550-87562
Sensitivity Studies 87190

Mycoplasma
Antibody 86738
Culture 87109
Detection 87580-87582

Mycota
See Fungus

Myectomy, Anorectal
See Myomectomy, Anorectal

Myelencephalon
See Medulla

Myelin Basic Protein
Cerebrospinal Fluid 83873

Myelography
Brain 70010
Spine
    Cervical 72240
    Lumbosacral 72265
    Thoracic 72255
    Total 72270

Myelomeningocele
Repair 63704-63706

Myelotomy 63170

Myocardial
Perfusion Imaging ...78460-78465, 78478-78480
   See Nuclear Medicine
Positron Emission Tomography (PET) 78459

Myocardial Imaging 78466-78469
Positron Emission Tomography
    Perfusion Study 78491-78492
Repair
    Postinfarction 33542

Myocutaneous Flaps 15732-15738

Myofascial Pain Dysfunction Syndrome
See Temporomandibular Joint (TMJ)

Myofibroma
See Leiomyomata

Myoglobin 83874

Myomectomy
Anorectal 45108
Uterus 58140-58145

Myoplasty
See Muscle, Repair

Myotomy
Esophagus 43030

Myringoplasty 69620

Myringostomy
See Myringotomy

Myringotomy 69420-69421

Myxoid Cyst
See Ganglion

N

N. Meningitidis
See Neisseria Meningitidis

Naffziger Operation
See Decompression, Orbit; Section

Nagel Test
See Color Vision Examination

Nails
Avulsion 11730-11732
Biopsy 11755
Debridement 11720-11721
Evacuation
    Hematoma, Subungual 11740
Excision 11750-11752
  Cyst
    Pilonidal 11770-11772
KOH Examination 87220
Removal 11730-11732, 11750-11752
Trimming 11719

Nail Bed
Reconstruction 11762
Repair 11760

Nail Fold
Excision
    Wedge 11765

Nail Plate Separation
See Onychia

Narcosynthesis
Diagnostic and Therapeutic 90865

Nasal Abscess
See Nose, Abscess

Nasal Area
Bone Graft 21210

Nasal Bleeding
See Epistaxis

Nasal Bone
Fracture
    Closed Treatment 21310-21320
    Open Treatment 21325-21335
    without Manipulation 21310
    with Manipulation 21315-21320
X-Ray 70160

Nasal Deformity
Repair 40700-40761

Nasal Function Study 92512

Nasal Polyp
See Nose, Polyp

Nasal Prosthesis
Impression 21087

Nasal Septum
Abscess
    Incision and Drainage 30020
Fracture
    Closed Treatment 21337
    Open Treatment 21336
Hematoma
    Incision and Drainage 30020
Repair 30630
Submucous Resection 30520

Nasal Sinuses
See Sinus; Sinuses

Nasal Smear
Eosinophils 89190

Nasal Turbinate
Fracture
    Therapeutic 30930

Nasoethmoid Complex
Fracture
    Open Treatment 21338-21339
    Percutaneous Treatment 21340
Reconstruction 21182-21184

Nasogastric Tube
Placement 43752

Nasolacrimal Duct
Exploration 68810
    with Anesthesia 68811
Insertion
    Stent 68815
X-Ray
    with Contrast 70170

Nasomaxillary
Fracture
    Closed Treatment 21345
    Open Treatment 21346-21348
    with Bone Grafting 21348

Nasopharynges
See Nasopharynx

Nasopharyngoscopy 92511

Nasopharynx
See Pharynx
Biopsy 42804-42806
Hemorrhage 42970-42972
Unlisted Services and Procedures 42999

Natural Ostium
Sinus
    Maxillary 31000
    Sphenoid 31002

Navicular
Arthroplasty
    with Implant 25443
Fracture
    Closed Treatment 25622
    Open Treatment 25628
    with Manipulation 25624
Repair 25440

Neck
Angiography 70498, 70547-70549
Artery
    Ligation 37615
Biopsy 21550
Bypass Graft 35901
CAT Scan 70490-70492, 70498
Dissection, Radical
    See Radical Neck Dissection
Exploration
    Blood Vessel 35800
    Lymph Nodes 38542
Incision and Drainage
    Abscess 21501-21502
    Hematoma 21501-21502
Lipectomy, Suction Assisted 15876
Magnetic Resonance Angiography
(MRA) 70547-70549

Magnetic Resonance Imaging
(MRI) 70540-70543
Nerve
    Graft 64885-64886
Repair
    Blood Vessel 35201
      with Other Graft 35261
      with Vein Graft 35231
Skin
    Revision 15819
Tumor
    Excision 21555-21556
    Excision/Resection 21557
Ultrasound Exam 76536
Unlisted Services and Procedures,
Surgery 21899
Urinary Bladder
   See Bladder, Neck
Wound Exploration
    Penetrating 20100
X-Ray 70360

Neck Muscle
Division
    Scalenus Anticus 21700-21705
    Sternocleidomastoid 21720-21725

Necropsy
Coroner's Exam 88045
Forensic Exam 88040
Gross and Micro Exam 88020-88029
Gross Exam 88000-88016
Organ 88037
Regional 88036
Unlisted Services and Procedures 88099

Needle Biopsy
See Biopsy
Abdomen Mass 49180
Bone 20220-20225
Bone Marrow 38221
Breast 19100
CAT Scan Guidance 76360
Colon-Sigmoid
    Endoscopy 45342
Epididymis 54800
Esophagus
    Endoscopy 43232
Fluoroscopic Guidance 76003
Gastrointestinal, Upper
    Endoscopy 43242
Kidney 50200
Liver 47000-47001
Lung 32405
Lymph Nodes 38505
Mediastinum 32405
Muscle 20206
Pancreas 48102
Pleura 32400
Prostate 55700
Retroperitoneal Mass 49180
Salivary Gland 42400
Spinal Cord 62269
Testis 54500
Thyroid Gland 60100
Transbronchial 31629

Needle Localization
Breast
    Placement 19290-19291
    with Lesion Excision 19125-19126
Magnetic Resonance Guidance 76393

Needle Manometer Technique 20950

Needle Wire
Introduction
    Trachea 31730
Placement
    Breast 19290-19291

Neer Procedure 23470

Neisseria gonorrheae 87590-87592,
                            87850

Neisseria Meningitidis
Antibody 86741

Neobladder
Construction 51596

Neonatal Intensive Care
See Newborn Care
Initial 99295
Subsequent 99296-99298

Neoplasm
Cancer Photoradiation Therapy
   See Photochemotherapy
Cardiac
   See Heart, Tumor
Colon
   See Colon, Tumor
Esophageal
   See Tumor, Esophagus
Spinal Cord
   See Spinal Cord, Neoplasm
Unspecified Nature of Brain
   See Brain, Tumor

Neoplastic Growth
See Tumor

Nephelometry 83883

Nephrectomy
Donor 50300-50320, 50547
Laparoscopic 50545-50548
Partial 50240
Recipient 50340
with Ureters 50220-50236, 50546, 50548

Nephrolith
See Calculus, Removal, Kidney

Nephrolithotomy 50060-50075

Nephropexy 50400-50405

Nephroplasty
See Kidney, Repair

Nephropyeloplasty
See Pyeloplasty

Nephrorrhaphy 50500

Nephroscopy
See Endoscopy, Kidney

Nephrostogram 50394

Nephrostolithotomy
Percutaneous 50080-50081

Nephrostomy 50040
Change Tube 50398
Endoscopic 50570
Percutaneous 52334
with Drainage 50040
X-Ray with Contrast
    Guide Dilation 74485

Nephrostomy Tract
Establishment 50395

Nephrotomogram
See Nephrotomography

Nephrotomography 74415

Nephrotomy 50040-50045
with Exploration 50045

Nerve
Cranial
   See Cranial Nerve
Facial
   See Facial Nerve
Intercostal
   See Intercostal Nerve
Lingual
   See Lingual Nerve
Median
   See Median Nerve
Obturator
   See Obturator Nerve
Peripheral
   See Peripheral Nerve
Phrenic
   See Phrenic Nerve
Sciatic
   See Sciatic Nerve
Spinal
   See Spinal Nerve
Tibial
   See Tibial Nerve
Ulnar
   See Ulnar Nerve
Vestibular
   See Vestibular Nerve

Nerves
Anastomosis
    Facial to Hypoglossal 64868
    Facial to Phrenic 64870
    Facial to Spinal Accessory 64866
Avulsion 64732-64772
Biopsy 64795
Decompression 64702-64727
Destruction 64600-64680
    Laryngeal, Recurrent 31595
Foot
    Excision 28030
    Incision 28035
Graft 64885-64907

Implantation
  Electrode 64553-64581
    to Bone 64787
    to Muscle .64787
Incision 43640-43641, 64732-64772
Injection
  Anesthetic 64400-64530
  Neurolytic Agent 64600-64680
Insertion
  Electrode 64553-64581
Lesion
  Excision 64774-64792
Neurofibroma
  Excision 64788-64792
Neurolemmoma
  Excision 64788-64792
Neurolytic
  Internal 64727
Neuroma
  Excision 64774-64786
Neuroplasty 64702-64721
Removal
  Electrode .64585
Repair
  Graft 64885-64907
  Microdissection 69990
  Suture 64831-64876
Spinal Accessory
  Incision 63191
  Section 63191
Suture 64831-64876
Sympathectomy
  Excision 64802-64818
Transection 43640-43641, 64732-64772
Transposition 64718-64721
Unlisted Services and Procedures 64999

Nerve Conduction
Motor Nerve 95900-95903
Sensory Nerve or Mixed 95904

Nerve II, Cranial
See Optic Nerve

Nerve Root
See Cauda Equina; Spinal Cord
Decompression 63020-63091
Incision 63185-63190
Section 63185-63190

Nerve Stimulation, Transcutaneous
See Application, Neurostimulation

Nerve Teasing 88362

Nerve V, Cranial
See Trigeminal Nerve

Nerve VII, Cranial
See Facial Nerve

Nerve X, Cranial
See Vagus Nerve

Nerve XI, Cranial
See Accessory Nerve

Nerve XII, Cranial
See Hypoglossal Nerve

Nervous System
Nuclear Medicine
  Unlisted Services and Procedures 78699

Nesidioblast
See Islet Cell

Neural Conduction
See Nerve Conduction

Neural Ganglion
See Ganglion

Neurectomy
Foot 28030
Gastrocnemius 27320
Hamstring Muscle 27315
Leg, Upper 27315-27320
Popliteal 27320
Tympanic 69676

Neurofibroma
Cutaneous Nerve
  Excision .64788
Extensive
  Excision .64792
Peripheral Nerve
  Excision .64790

Neurolemmoma
Cutaneous Nerve
  Excision .64788
Extensive
  Excision .64792
Peripheral Nerve
  Excision .64790

Neurologic System
See Nervous System

Neurology
Diagnostic
  Anal Sphincter 51785
  Autonomic Nervous Function
    Heart Rate Response 95921-95923
    Pseudomotor Response 95921-95923
    Sympathetic Function 95921-95923
  Brain Cortex Magnetic Stimulation 0018T
  Brain Surface Electrode
  Stimulation 95961-95962
  Electrocorticogram
    Intraoperative 95829
  Electroencephalogram (EEG) . . .95812-95827,
                          95955
    Brain Death 95824
    Electrode Placement 95830
    Intraoperative 95955
    Monitoring . . .95812-95813, 95950-95953,
                          95956
    Physical or Drug Activation 95954
    Sleep 95822, 95827
    Standard 95819
    WADA Activation 95958
  Electroencephalography (EEG)
    Digital Analysis 95957
  Electromyography
    See Electromyography
    Fine Wire
      Dynamic 96004

  Ischemic Limb Exercise Test 95875
  Needle 51785, 95860-95872
  Surface
    Dynamic 96002-96004
  Higher Cerebral Function
    Aphasia Test 96105
    Cognitive Function Tests 96115
    Developmental Tests 96110-96111
  Magnetoencephalography
  (MEG) 95965-95967
  Motion Analysis
    by Video and 3-D Kinematics .96000, 96004
    Computer-based 96000, 96004
  Muscle Testing
    Manual 95831-95834
  Nerve Conduction
    Motor Nerve 95900-95903
    Sensory Nerve or Mixed 95904
  Neuromuscular Junction Tests 95937
  Neurophysiological Testing
    Intraoperative 95920
  Neuropsychological Testing 96117
  Plantar Pressure Measurements
    Dynamic 96001, 96004
  Polysomnography 95808-95811
  Range of Motion 95851-95852
  Reflex
    H-Reflex 95933-95934
  Reflex Test
    Blink Reflex 95933
  Sleep Study 95807-95810
  Somatosensory Testing 95925-95927
  Tensilon Test 95857-95858
  Unlisted Services and Procedures 95999
  Urethral Sphincter 51785
  Visual Evoked Potential, CNS 95930

Neurolysis
Nerve .64704-64708
  Internal .64727

Neuroma
Acoustic
  See Brain, Tumor, Excision
Cutaneous Nerve
  Excision .64774
Digital Nerve
  Excision 64776-64778
Excision 64774
Foot
  Excision .28080
Foot Nerve
  Excision 64782-64783
Hand Nerve
  Excision 64782-64783
Interdigital
  See Morton's Neuroma
Peripheral Nerve
  Excision .64784
Sciatic Nerve
  Excision .64786

Neuromuscular Junction Tests 95937

Neuromuscular Pedicle
Reinnervation
  Larynx 31590

Neuromuscular Reeducation 97112
See Physical Medicine/Therapy/Occupational
Therapy
Intraoperative, Per Hour 95920

Neurophysiologic Testing
Autonomic Nervous Function
    Heart Rate Response 95921-95923
    Pseudomotor Response 95921-95923
    Sympathetic Function 95921-95923
Intraoperative, Per Hour 95920

Neuroplasty 64712
Cranial Nerve 64716
Digital Nerve 64702-64704
Peripheral Nerve 64708-64714, 64718-64721

Neuropsychological Testing ...96117

Neurorrhaphy 64831-64876
Peripheral Nerve
    with Graft 64885-64907

Neurostimulation
Application 64550

Neurostimulators
Analysis 95970-95975
Insertion
    Pulse Generator 64590
    Receiver 64590
Removal
    Pulse Generator 64595
    Receiver 64595

Neurotomy, Sympathetic
See Gasserian Ganglion, Sensory Root,
Decompression

Neurovascular Pedicle Flaps 15750

Neutralization Test
Virus 86382

Newborn Care 99431-99440, 99502
Attendance at Delivery 99436
Birthing Room 99431
Blood Transfusion 36450
    See Neonatal Intensive Care
Circumcision
    Clamp or Other Device 54150
    Surgical Excision 54160
History and Examination 99431, 99435
Intermittent Positive Pressure Breathing
(IPPB) 94652
Laryngoscopy 31520
Normal 99431-99433
Prepuce Slitting 54000
Preventive
    Office 99432
Resuscitation 99440
Standby for Cesarean Delivery 99360
Subsequent Hospital Care 99433
Umbilical Artery Catheterization 36660

New Patient
Confirmatory Consultations 99271-99275
Domiciliary or Rest Home Visit 99321-99323
Emergency Department Services ...99281-99288

Home Services 99341-99345
Hospital Inpatient Services 99221-99239
Hospital Observation Services 99217-99220
Initial Inpatient Consultations ...99251-99255
Initial Office Visit 99201-99205
    See Evaluation and Management; Office and
    Other Outpatient
Office and/or Other Outpatient
Consultations 99241-99245

Nickel 83885

Nicolas-Durand-Favre Disease
See Lymphogranuloma Venereum

Nicotine 83887

Nidation
See Implantation

Nipples
See Breast
Inverted 19355
Reconstruction 19350

Nissen Operation
See Fundoplasty, Esophagogastric

Nissen Procedure 43324
Laparoscopic 43280

Nitrate Reduction Test
See Urinalysis

Nitroblue Tetrazolium Dye Test 86384

Nitrogen, Blood Urea
See Blood Urea Nitrogen

NMR Imaging
See Magnetic Resonance Imaging (MRI)

NMR Spectroscopies
See Magnetic Resonance Spectroscopy

Noble Procedure
See Repair; Suture

Nocardia
Antibody 86744

Nocturnal Penile Rigidity Test 54250

Nocturnal Penile Tumescence Test 54250

Node, Lymph
See Lymph Nodes

Nodes
See Lymph Nodes

Node Dissection, Lymph
See Dissection, Lymph Nodes

Non-Invasive Vascular Imaging
See Vascular Studies

Non-Office Medical Services ..99056

Non-Stress Test, Fetal 59025

Nonunion Repair
Femur
    without Graft 27470
    with Graft 27472
Metatarsal 28322
Tarsal Joint 28320

Noradrenalin
Blood 82383-82384
Urine 82384

Norchlorimipramine
See Imipramine

Norepinephrine
See Catecholamines
Blood 82383-82384
Urine 82384

Nortriptyline
Assay 80182

Norwood Procedure 33611-33612, 33619
See Repair, Heart, Ventricle; Revision

Nose
Abscess
    Incision and Drainage 30000-30020
Artery
    Incision 30915-30920
Biopsy
    Intranasal 30100
Dermoid Cyst
    Excision
        Complex 30125
        Simple 30124
Displacement Therapy 30210
Endoscopy
    Diagnostic 31231-31235
    Surgical 31237-31294
Excision
    Rhinectomy 30150-30160
Fracture
    Closed Treatment 21345
    Open Treatment 21325-21336,
        21338-21339, 21346-21347
    Percutaneous Treatment 21340
    with Fixation 21330, 21340, 21345-21347
Hematoma
    Incision and Drainage 30000-30020
Hemorrhage
    Cauterization 30901-30906
Insertion
    Septal Prosthesis 30220
Intranasal
    Lesion
        External Approach 30118
        Internal Approach 30117
Lysis of Adhesions 30560
Polyp
    Excision
        Extensive 30115
        Simple 30110
Reconstruction
    Cleft Lip/Cleft Palate 30460-30462
    Dermatoplasty 30620
    Primary 30400-30420
    Secondary 30430-30450
    Septum 30520

Removal
　Foreign Body .30300
　　Anesthesia 30310
　　Lateral Rhinotomy 30320
Repair
　Adhesions .30560
　Cleft Lip 40700-40761
　Fistula 30580-30600, 42260
　Rhinophyma 30120
　Septum 30540-30545, 30630
　Synechia 30560
　Vestibular Stenosis 30465
Skin
　Excision 30120
　Surgical Planing 30120
Submucous Resection Turbinate
　Excision 30140
Turbinate
　Excision 30130-30140
　Fracture 30930
　Injection 30200
Turbinate Mucosa
　Cauterization 30801-30802
Unlisted Services and Procedures 30999

Nose Bleed 30901-30906
See Hemorrhage, Nasal

No Man's Land
Tendon Repair 26356-26358

NTD 86384
See Nitroblue Tetrazolium Dye Test

Nuclear Antigen
Antibody 86235

Nuclear Imaging
See Nuclear Medicine

Nuclear Magnetic Resonance Imaging
See Magnetic Resonance Imaging (MRI)

Nuclear Magnetic Resonance Spectroscopy
See Magnetic Resonance Spectroscopy

Nuclear Medicine
Adrenal Gland Imaging 78075
Automated Data 78890-78891
Bile Duct
　Imaging 78223
Bladder
　Residual Study 78730
Blood
　Bone
　　Density Study 78350-78351
　　Imaging 78300-78320
　　SPECT 78320
　　Ultrasound 76977
　　Unlisted Services and Procedures . . .78399
　Flow Imaging 78445
　Iron
　　Absorption 78162
　　Chelatable 78172
　　Plasma 78160
　　Red Cells 78140
　　Utilization 78170

Platelet Survival 78190-78191
Red Cells 78120-78121
Red Cell Survival 78130-78135
Unlisted Services and Procedures 78199
Whole Blood Volume 78122
Bone Marrow
　Imaging 78102-78104
Brain
　Blood Flow 78610-78615
　Cerebrospinal Fluid 78630-78650
　Imaging 78600-78609
　　Vascular Flow 78610
Endocrine System
　Unlisted Services and Procedures 78099
Esophagus
　Imaging (Motility) 78258
　Reflux Study 78262
Gallbladder
　Imaging .78223
Gastric Mucosa
　Imaging .78261
Gastrointestinal
　Blood Loss Study 78278
　Protein Loss Study 78282
　Shunt Testing 78291
　Unlisted Services and Procedures 78299
Genitourinary System
　Unlisted Services and Procedures 78799
Heart
　Blood Flow 78414
　Blood Pool Imaging 78472-78473, 78481-
　　　　　　　　　　　78483, 78494-78496
　Myocardial Imaging 78459, 78466-78469
　Myocardial Perfusion 78460-78465,
　　　　　　　　　　　　　　78478-78480
　Shunt Detection 78428
　Unlisted Services and Procedures 78499
Hepatic Duct
　Imaging .78223
Inflammatory Process 78805-78807
Intestines
　Imaging .78290
Kidney
　Blood Flow 78715
　Function Study 78725
　Imaging 78700-78707, 78710
Lacrimal Gland Tear Flow 78660
Liver
　Function Study 78220
　Imaging 78201-78216
　Vascular Flow 78206
Lung
　Imaging Perfusion 78580-78585
　Imaging Ventilation 78586-78594
　Unlisted Services and Procedures 78599
Lymphatics 78195
　Unlisted Services and Procedures 78199
Lymph Nodes .78195
Musculoskeletal System
　Unlisted Services and Procedures 78399
Nervous System
　Unlisted Services and Procedures 78699
Parathyroid Gland Imaging 78070
Pulmonary Perfusion Imaging 78588
Salivary Gland Function Study 78232
　Imaging 78230-78231

Spleen
　Imaging 78185, 78215-78216
　Unlisted Services and Procedures 78199
Stomach
　Blood Loss Study 78278
　Emptying Study 78264
　Protein Loss Study 78282
　Reflux Study 78262
　Vitamin B-12 Absorption 78270-78272
Supply Radionuclide 78990, 79900
Supply Radiopharmaceutical 78990
Testes
　Imaging 78760-78761
Therapeutic
　Heart 79440
　Intravascular 79420
　Leukemia 79100
　Other 79400
　Polycythemia Vera 79100
　Thyroid 79000-79035, 79200-79300
　Unlisted Services and Procedures 79999
Thyroid
　Imaging .78010
　Imaging for Metastases 78015-78018
　Imaging with Flow 78011
　Imaging with Uptake 78006
　Metastases Uptake 78020
　Uptake 78000-78003
Tumor Imaging
　Positron Emission Tomography (PET) . .78810
Tumor Localization 78800-78803
Unlisted Services and Procedures 78999
Urea Breath Test 78267-78268
Ureter
　Reflux Study 78740
Vein
　Thrombosis Imaging 78455-78458

Nucleases, DNA
See DNAse

Nucleic Acid Probe 83896
Amplified Probe Detection
　Infectious Agent
　　Bartonella henselae 87471
　　Bartonella quintana 87471
　　Borrelia burgdorferi 87476
　　Candida species 87481
　　Chlamydia pneumoniae 87486
　　Chlamydia Trachomatis 87491
　　Cytomegalovirus 87496
　　Gardnerella Vaginalis 87511
　　Hepatitis B Virus 87516
　　Hepatitis C 87521
　　Hepatitis G 87526
　　Herpes Simplex Virus 87529
　　Herpes Virus-6 87532
　　HIV-1 87535
　　HIV-2 87538
　　Legionella Pneumophila 87541
　　Multiple Organisms 87801
　　Mycobacteria avium-intracellulare . .87561
　　Mycobacteria species 87551
　　Mycobacteria tuberculosis 87556
　　Mycoplasma pneumoniae 87581
　　Neisseria gonorrheae 87591
　　Not Otherwise Specified 87798, 87801
　　Papillomavirus, Human 87621
　　Streptococcus, Group A 87651

Direct Probe Detection
   Infectious Agent
      Bartonella henselae 87470
      Bartonella quintana 87470
      Borrelia burgdorferi 87475
      Candida species 87480
      Chlamydia pneumoniae 87485
      Chlamydia Trachomatis 87490
      Cytomegalovirus 87495
      Gardnerella Vaginalis 87510
      Hepatitis B Virus 87515
      Hepatitis C 87520
      Hepatitis G 87525
      Herpes Simplex Virus 87528
      Herpes Virus-6 87531
      HIV-1 87534
      HIV-2 87537
      Legionella Pneumophila 87540
      Multiple Organisms 87800
      Mycobacteria avium-intracellulare . .87560
      Mycobacteria species 87550
      Mycobacteria tuberculosis 87555
      Mycoplasma pneumoniae 87580
      Neisseria gonorrheae 87590
      Not Otherwise Specified 87797
      Papillomavirus, Human 87620
      Streptococcus, Group A 87650
Genotype Analysis
   Infectious Agent
      Hepatitis C Virus 87902
      HIV-1 87901
In Situ Hybridization 88365
Phenotype Analysis
   Infectious Agent
      HIV-1 Drug Resistance 87903-87904
Quantification
   Infectious Agent
      Bartonella henselae 87472
      Bartonella quintana 87472
      Borrelia burgdorferi 87477
      Candida species 87482
      Chlamydia pneumoniae 87487
      Chlamydia Trachomatis 87492
      Cytomegalovirus 87497
      Gardnerella Vaginalis 87512
      Hepatitis B Virus 87517
      Hepatitis C 87522
      Hepatitis G 87527
      Herpes Simplex Virus 87530
      Herpes Virus-6 87533
      HIV-1 87536
      HIV-2 87539
      Legionella Pneumophila 87542
      Mycobacteria avium-intracellulare . .87562
      Mycobacteria species 87552
      Mycobacteria tuberculosis 87557
      Mycoplasma pneumoniae 87582
      Neisseria gonorrheae 87592
      Not Otherwise Specified 87799
      Papillomavirus, Human 87622
      Streptococcus, Group A 87652

Nucleolysis, Intervertebral Disk
See Chemonucleolysis

Nucleotidase .83915

Nursemaid Elbow 24640

Nursing Facility Discharge Services
See Discharge Services, Nursing Facility

Nursing Facility Services
Care Plan Oversight Services 99379-99380
Comprehensive Assessments
   New or Established Patient 99301-99303
Discharge Services 99315-99316
Subsequent Care
   New or Established Patient 99311-99313
     See Domiciliary Services

Nutrition Therapy
Enteral 99560-99561
Group 97804
Initial Assessment 97802
Reassessment 97803
Total Parenteral .99562

Nystagmus Tests
See Vestibular Function Tests
Optokinetic 92534, 92544
Positional 92532, 92542
Spontaneous 92531, 92541

O

O2 Saturation
See Oxygen Saturation

Ober-Yount Procedure 27025
See Fasciotomy, Hip

Obliteration
Mastoid 69670

Obliteration, Total Excision of Vagina
See Excision, Vagina, Complete

Obliteration, Vaginal Vault
See Vagina, Closure

Oblongata, Medulla
See Medulla

Observation 99234-99236
See Evaluation and Management; Hospital Services

Obstetrical Care
Abortion
   Induced
      by Amniocentesis Injection . .59850-59852
       See Abortion; Cesarean Delivery;
       Ectopic Pregnancy
      by Dilation and Curettage 59840
      by Dilation and Evaluation 59841
   Missed
      First Trimester 59820
      Second Trimester 59821
   Spontaneous 59812
   Therapeutic 59840-59852
Antepartum Care 59425-59426

Cesarean Delivery 59618-59622
   Only 59514
   Postpartum Care 59515
   Routine 59510
   with Hysterectomy 59525
Curettage
   Hydatidiform Mole 59870
Evacuation
   Hydatidiform Mole 59870
External Cephalic Version 59412
Miscarriage
   Surgical Completion 59812-59821
Placenta Delivery 59414
Postpartum Care 59430, 59514
Septic Abortion .59830
Total (Global) 59400, 59610, 59618
Unlisted Services and Procedures . .59898-59899
Vaginal
   after Cesarean 59610-59614
Vaginal Delivery 59409-59410
   Delivery after Cesarean 59610-59614

Obstruction
See Occlusion

Obstruction Colon
See Colon, Obstruction

Obturator Nerve
Avulsion .64763-64766
Incision 64763-64766
Transection 64763-64766

Obturator Prosthesis 21076
Definitive 21080
Insertion
   Larynx 31527
   Interim 21079

Occipital Nerve, Greater
Avulsion 64744
Incision 64744
Injection
   Anesthetic .64405
Transection 64744

Occlusion
Fallopian Tube
   Oviduct 58615
Penis
   Vein 37790

Occlusive Disease of Artery
See Repair, Artery; Revision

Occult Blood 82270
   by Hemoglobin Immunoassay 82274

Occupational Therapy
Evaluation 97003-97004

Ocular Implant 65175
See Orbital Implant
Insertion
   in Scleral Shell 65130
   Muscles, Not Attached 65135
   Muscles Attached 65140
Modification 65125
Reinsertion 65150
   with Foreign Material 65155
Removal 65175

Ocular Muscle
See Eye Muscles

Ocular Orbit
See Orbit

Ocular Prostheses
See Prosthesis, Ocular

Oculomotor Muscle
See Eye Muscles

Oddi Sphincter
See Sphincter of Oddi

Odontoid Dislocation
Open Treatment/Reduction 22318
    with Grafting .22319

Odontoid Fracture
Open Treatment/Reduction 22318
    with Grafting .22319

Odontoid Process
Excision 22548

Oesophageal Neoplasm
See Tumor, Esophagus

Oesophageal Varices
See Esophageal Varices

Oesophagus
See Esophagus

Oestradiol
See Estradiol

Office and/or Other Outpatient Services
See History and Physical
Consultation
    Confirmatory Consultations 99271-99275
Established Patient 99211-99215
New Patient 99201-99205
Normal Newborn 99432
Office Visit
    Established Patient 99211-99215
    New Patient 99201-99205
Outpatient Visit
    Established Patient 99211-99215
    New Patient 99201-99205
    Prolonged Services 99354-99355
with Surgical Procedure 99025

Office Medical Services
After Hours 99050-99054
Emergency Care 99058

Office or Other Outpatient Consultations
See Consultation, Office and/or Other Outpatient

Olecranon
See Elbow; Humerus; Radius; Ulna
Bursa
    Arthrocentesis 20605
Cyst
    Excision 24125-24126
Tumor
    Cyst 24120
    Excision 24125-24126

Olecranon Process
Craterization 24147
Diaphysectomy .24147
Excision 24147
    Abscess 24138
Fracture
    See Elbow; Humerus; Radius
        Closed Treatment 24670-24675
        Open Treatment 24685
Osteomyelitis 24138, 24147
Saucerization 24147
Sequestrectomy 24138

Oligoclonal Immunoglobulins .83916

Omentectomy 49255, 58950-58954
Laparotomy 58960
Oophorectomy 58943
Resection Ovarian Malignancy 58950-58954
Resection Peritoneal Malignancy . . .58950-58954
Resection Tubal Malignancy 58950-58954

Omentum
Excision 49255, 58950-58954
Flap 49905
    Free
        with Microvascular Anastomosis . . .49906
Unlisted Services and Procedures 49999

Omphalectomy 49250

Omphalocele
Repair .49600-49611

Omphalomesenteric Duct
Excision 44800

Omphalomesenteric Duct, Persistent
See Diverticulum, Meckel's

Oncoprotein
HER-2/neu 83950

One Stage Prothrombin Time .85610-85611
See Prothrombin Time

Onychectomy
See Excision, Nails

Onychia
Drainage 10060-10061

Oocyte
Assisted Fertilization
    Microtechnique 89252
Culture
    for In Vitro Fertilization 89250
Identification
    Follicular Fluid 89254
Retrieval
    for In Vitro Fertilization 58970

Oophorectomy 58262-58263, 58661,
                    58940-58943
Ectopic Pregnancy
    Laparoscopic Treatment 59120
    Surgical Treatment 59120

Oophorectomy, Partial
See Excision, Ovary, Partial

Oophorocystectomy
See Cystectomy, Ovarian

Open Biopsy, Adrenal Gland
See Adrenal Gland, Biopsy

Operating Microscope 69990

Operation
Blalock-Hanlon
    See Septostomy, Atrial
Blalock-Taussig Subclavian-Pulmonary
Anastomosis
    See Pulmonary Artery, Shunt, Subclavian
Borthen
    See Iridotasis
Dana
    See Rhizotomy
Dunn
    See Arthrodesis, Foot Joint
Duvries
    See Tenoplasty
Estes
    See Ovary, Transposition
Foley Pyeloplasty
    See Pyeloplasty
Fontan
    See Repair, Heart, Anomaly
Fox
    See Fox Operation
Gardner
    See Meningocele Repair
Green
    See Scapulopexy
Harelip
    See Cleft Lip, Repair
Heine
    See Cyclodialysis
Heller
    See Esophagomyotomy
Iris, Inclusion
    See Iridencleisis
Jaboulay Gastroduodenostomy
    See Gastroduodenostomy
Johanson
    See Reconstruction, Urethra
Keller
    See Keller Procedure
Krause
    See Gasserian Ganglion, Sensory Root,
    Decompression
Kuhnt-Szymanowski
    See Ectropion, Repair, Blepharoplasty
Mumford
    See Claviculectomy, Partial
Nissen
    See Fundoplasty, Esophagogastric
Peet
    See Nerves, Sympathectomy, Excision
Ramstedt
    See Pyloromyotomy
Richardson Hysterectomy
    See Hysterectomy, Abdominal, Total
Schanz
    See Femur, Osteotomy

Schlatter Total Gastrectomy
　See Excision, Stomach, Total
Smithwick
　See Excision, Nerve, Sympathetic
Winiwarter Cholecystoenterostomy
　See Anastomosis, Gallbladder to Intestines

Operation Microscopes
See Operating Microscope

Operculectomy 41821

Operculum
See Gums

Ophthalmic Mucous Membrane
Test 95060
See Allergy Tests

Ophthalmology
Unlisted Services and Procedures 92499
　See Ophthalmology, Diagnostic

Ophthalmology, Diagnostic
Color Vision Exam 92283
Computerized Scanning 92135
Computerized Screening 99172
Dark Adaptation 92284
Electro-oculography 92270
Electromyography, Needle 92265
Electroretinography 92275
Eye Exam
　　Established Patient 92012-92014
　　New Patient 92002-92004
　　with Anesthesia 92018-92019
Glaucoma Provocative Test 92140
Gonioscopy 92020
Ocular Photography
　　External 92285
　　Internal 92286-92287
Ophthalmoscopy 92225-92226
　　with Dynamometry 92260
　　with Fluorescein Angiography 92235
　　with Fluorescein Angioscopy 92230
　　with Fundus Photography 92250
　　with Indocyanine-green Angiography . 92240
Refractive Determination 92015
Sensorimotor Exam 92060
Tonography 92120
　　with Provocation 92130
Tonometry
　　Serial 92100
Visual Acuity Screen 99172-99173
Visual Field Exam 92081-92083
Visual Function Screen 99172

Ophthalmoscopy 92225-92226
See Ophthalmology, Diagnostic

Opiates 83925

Opinion, Second
See Confirmatory Consultations

Optic Nerve
Decompression 67570
　　with Nasal/Sinus Endoscopy 31294

Optokinetic Nystagmus Test
See Nystagmus Tests, Optokinetic

Oral Lactose Tolerance
Test 82951-82953
See Glucose, Tolerance Test

Oral Mucosa
See Mouth, Mucosa

Oral Surgical Splint 21085

Orbit
See Orbital Contents; Orbital Floor; Periorbital
Region
Biopsy 61332
　　Exploration 67450
　　Fine Needle Aspiration or Orbital
　　Contents 67415
　　Orbitotomy without Bone Flap 67400
CAT Scan 70480-70482
Decompression 61330
　　Bone Removal 67414, 67445
Exploration 61332, 67400, 67450
　　Lesion
　　　Excision 61333
Fracture
　　Closed Treatment
　　　without Manipulation 21400
　　　with Manipulation 21401
　　Open Treatment 21406-21408
　　　Blowout Fracture 21385-21395
Incision and Drainage 67405, 67440
Injection
　　Retrobulbar 67500-67505
　　Tenon's Capsule 67515
Insertion
　　Implant 67550
Lesion
　　Excision 67412, 67420
Magnetic Resonance Imaging
(MRI) 70540-70543
Removal
　　Decompression 67445
　　Exploration 61334
　　Foreign Body 61334, 67413, 67430
　　Implant 67560
Sella Turcica 70482
Unlisted Services and Procedures 67599
X-Ray 70190-70200

Orbital Contents
Aspiration 67415

Orbital Floor
See Orbit; Periorbital Region
Fracture
　　Blow Out 21385-21395

Orbital Hypertelorism
Osteotomy
　　Periorbital 21260-21263

Orbital Implant
See Ocular Implant
Insertion 67550
Removal 67560

Orbital Prosthesis 21077

Orbital Rims
Reconstruction 21182-21184

Orbital Rim and Forehead
Reconstruction 21172-21180

Orbital Transplant 67560

Orbital Walls
Reconstruction 21182-21184

Orbitocraniofacial Reconstruction
Secondary 21275

Orbitotomy
without Bone Flap
　　for Exploration 67400
　　with Drainage Only 67405
　　with Removal Lesion 67412
with Bone Flap
　　for Exploration 67450
　　Lateral Approach 67420
　　with Drainage 67440
　　with Removal Foreign Body 67430
　　with Removal of Bone for
　　Decompression 67445
with Removal Foreign Body 67413
with Removal of Bone for Decompression .67414

Orbit Area
Reconstruction
　　Secondary 21275

Orbit Wall
Decompression
　　with Nasal/Sinus Endoscopy ...31292-31293

Orchidectomies
See Excision, Testis

Orchidopexy
See Orchiopexy

Orchidoplasty
See Repair, Testis

Orchiectomy
Laparoscopic 54690
Partial 54522
Radical
　　Abdominal Exploration 54535
　　Inguinal Approach 54530
Simple 54520

Orchiopexy
Abdominal Approach 54650
Inguinal Approach 54640
Intra-Abdominal Testis 54692

Orchioplasty
See Repair, Testis

Organic Acids 83918-83921

Organ Grafting
See Transplantation

Organ or Disease-Oriented Panel
Electrolyte 80051
General Health Panel 80050
Hepatic Function Panel 80076
Hepatitis Panel 80074
Lipid Panel 80061
Metabolic
　　Basic 80048
　　Comprehensive 80053

Obstetric Panel 80055
Renal Function 80069
TORCH Antibody Panel 80090

Organ System, Neurologic
See Nervous System

Ormond Disease
See Retroperitoneal Fibrosis

Orogastric Tube
Placement 43752

Oropharynx
Biopsy 42800

Orthodontic Cephalogram 70350

Orthomyxoviridae
See Influenza Virus

Orthomyxovirus
See Influenza Virus

Orthopantogram 70355

Orthopedic Cast
See Cast

Orthoptic Training 92065

Orthoroentgenogram 76040

Orthosis
See Orthotics

Orthotics
Check-Out 97703
Fitting and Training 97504

Osmolality
Blood 83930
Urine 83935

Osseous Survey 76061-76065

Osseous Tissue
See Bone

Ossicles
Excision
   Stapes
      without Foreign Material 69660-69661
      with Footplate Drill Out 69661
Reconstruction
   Ossicular Chain
      Tympanoplasty without
      Mastoidectomy 69632-69633
      Tympanoplasty with Antrotomy or
      Mastoidotomy 69636-69637
      Tympanoplasty with
      Mastoidectomy 69642, 69644, 69646
Release
   Stapes 69650
Replacement
   with Prosthesis 69633, 69637

Ostectomy
Metacarpal 26250-26255
Metatarsal 28288
Phalanges
   Finger .26260-26262

Pressure Ulcer
   Ischial 15941, 15945
   Sacral 15933, 15935, 15937
   Trochanteric 15951, 15953, 15958
Scapula 23190
Sternum 21620

Osteocalcin 83937

Osteocartilaginous Exostoses
See Exostosis

Osteochondroma
See Exostosis

Osteocutaneous Flap
with Microvascular Anastomosis . . .20969-20973

Osteoma
Sinusotomy
   Frontal 31075

Osteomyelitis 20000-20005
Elbow
   Incision and Drainage 23935
Excision
   Clavicle 23180
   Facial 21026
   Humerus, Proximal 23184
   Mandible 21025
   Scapula 23182
Femur/Knee
   Incision and Drainage 27303
Finger
   Incision 26034
Hand Incision 26034
Hip
   Incision, Deep 26992
Humerus 24134
   Incision and Drainage 23935
Incision
   Foot 28005
   Shoulder 23035
   Thorax 21510
Olecranon Process 24138, 24147
Pelvis
   Incision, Deep 26992
Radius .24136, 24145
Sequestrectomy
   Clavicle 23170
   Humeral Head 23174
   Scapula 23172
   Skull 61501

**Osteopathic
Manipulation** 98925-98929

Osteoplasty
Carpal Bone 25394
Facial Bones
   Augmentation 21208
   Reduction 21209
Femoral Neck 27179
Femur 27179
   Lengthening 27466-27468
   Shortening 27465, 27468
Fibula
   Lengthening 27715
Humerus 24420

Metacarpal 26568
Phalanges, Finger 26568
Radius .25390-25393
Tibia
   Lengthening 27715
Ulna 25390-25393
Vertebra 76012-76013
   Lumbar 22521-22522
   Thoracic 22520-22522

Osteotomy
Calcaneus 28300
Chin 21121-21123
Clavicle 23480-23485
Femur 27140, 27151
   Femoral Neck 27161
   for Slipped Epiphysis 27181
   without Fixation 27448-27450
   with Fixation .27165
   with Open Reduction of Hip 27156
   with Realignment 27454
Fibula 27707-27712
Hip 27146-27151
   Femoral
      with Open Reduction 27156
      Femur 27151
Humerus 24400-24410
Mandible 21198-21199
Maxilla 21206
Metacarpal 26565
Metatarsal 28306-28309
Orbit Reconstruction 21256
Pelvis 27158
Periorbital
   Orbital Hypertelorism 21260-21263
   Osteotomy with Graft 21267-21268
Phalanges
   Finger 26567
   Toe 28299, 28310-28312
Radius
   and Ulna 25365, 25375
   Distal Third 25350
   Middle or Proximal Third 25355
   Multiple 25370
Skull Base 61582-61585, 61592
Spine
   Anterior 22220-22226
   Posterior
      Posterolateral 22210-22214
Talus 28302
Tarsal 28304-28305
Tibia 27455-27457, 27705, 27709-27712
Ulna 25360
   and Radius 25365, 25375
   Multiple 25370
Vertebra
   Additional Segment
      Anterior Approach 22226
      Posterior/Posterolateral Approach . .22216
   Cervical
      Anterior Approach 22220
      Posterior/Posterolateral Approach . .22210
   Lumbar
      Anterior Approach 22224
      Posterior/Posterolateral Approach . .22214

Thoracic
   Anterior Approach 22222
   Posterior/Posterolateral Approach ..22212
with Graft
  Reconstruction
   Periorbital Region 21267-21268

Os Calcis Fracture
See Calcaneus, Fracture

Otolaryngology
Diagnostic
  Exam Under Anesthesia 92502

Otomy
See Incision

Otoplasty 69300

Otorhinolaryngology
Unlisted Services and Procedures 92599

Ouchterlony Immunodiffusion 86331

Outer Ear
See Ear, Outer

Outpatient Visit
See History and Physical; Office and/or Other Outpatient Services

Output, Cardiac
See Cardiac Output

Ova
Smear 87177

Oval Window
Repair Fistula 69666

Oval Window Fistula
See Fistula, Oval Window

Ovarian Cyst
See Cyst, Ovarian; Ovary, Cyst

Ovarian Vein Syndrome
Ureterolysis 50722

Ovariectomies
See Oophorectomy

Ovariolysis 58740

Ovary
Abscess
  Incision and Drainage 58820-58822
   Abdominal Approach 58822
Biopsy 58900
Cyst
  Incision and Drainage 58800-58805
Excision 58662, 58720
  Cyst 58925
  Partial
   Oophorectomy 58661, 58940
   Ovarian Malignancy 58943
   Peritoneal Malignancy 58943
   Tubal Malignancy 58943
   Wedge Resection 58920
  Total 58940-58943
Laparoscopy 58660-58662, 58679

Lysis
  Adhesions 58660, 58740
Radical Resection 58950-58952
Transposition 58825
Tumor
  Resection 58950-58954
Unlisted Services and Procedures ..58679, 58999
Wedge Resection 58920

Oviduct
Anastomosis 58750
Chromotubation 58350
Ectopic Pregnancy 59120-59121
Excision 58700-58720
Fulguration
  Laparoscopic 58670
Hysterosalpingography 74740
Laparoscopy 58679
Ligation 58600-58611
Lysis
  Adhesions 58740
Occlusion 58615
  Laparoscopic 58671
Repair 58752
  Anastomosis 58750
  Create Stoma 58770
Unlisted Services and Procedures ..58679, 58999
X-Ray with Contrast 74740

Ovocyte
See Oocyte

Ovulation Tests 84830

Ovum Implantation
See Implantation

Ovum Transfer Surgery
See GIFT

Oxalate 83945

Oxidase, Ceruloplasmin
See Ceruloplasmin

Oxidoreductase, Alcohol-Nad+
See Antidiuretic Hormone

Oximetry (Noninvasive)
See Pulmonology, Diagnostic
Blood O2 Saturation
  Ear or Pulse 94760-94762

Oxoisomerase
See Phosphohexose Isomerase

Oxosteroids
See Ketosteroids

Oxycodinone 80102-80103, 83925

Oxygenation, Extracorporeal Membrane
See Extracorporeal Membrane Oxygenation

Oxygen Saturation 82805-82810

Oxyproline
See Hydroxyproline

Oxytocin Stress Test, Fetal 59020

P-Acetamidophenol
See Acetaminophen

Pacemaker, Heart
See Defibrillator, Heart
Conversion 33214
Electronic Analysis 93641-93642
  Antitachycardia System 93724
  Dual Chamber 93731-93732
  Single Chamber 93734-93735
Insertion 33200-33208
  Electrode 33210-33211, 33216-33217
  Pulse Generator Only 33212-33213
Removal 33233-33237
  via Thoracotomy 33236-33237
Repair
  Electrode 33218-33220
Replacement
  Catheter 33210
  Electrode 33210-33211, 33217
  Insertion 33200-33208
  Pulse Generator 33212-33213
Revise Pocket
  Chest 33222
Telephonic Analysis 93733, 93736
Upgrade 33214

Packing
Nasal Hemorrhage 30901-30906

Pain Management 99551
See Injection, Chemotherapy
Epidural/Intrathecal 62351, 62360-62362,
              99552
Intravenous Therapy 90783-90784

Palatal Augmentation Prosthesis 21082

Palatal Lift Prosthesis 21083

Palate
Abscess
  Incision and Drainage 42000
Biopsy 42100
Excision 42120, 42145
Fracture
  Closed Treatment 21421
  Open Treatment 21422-21423
Lesion
  Destruction 42160
  Excision 42104-42120
Prosthesis 42280-42281
Reconstruction
  Lengthening 42226-42227
Repair
  Cleft Palate 42200-42225
  Laceration 42180-42182
  Vomer Flap 42235
Unlisted Services and Procedures 42299

Palate, Cleft
See Cleft Palate

Palatoplasty 42200-42225

Palatoschisis
See Cleft Palate

Palm
Bursa
   Incision and Drainage 26025-26030
Fasciectomy 26121-26125
Fasciotomy 26040-26045
Tendon
   Excision 26170
Tendon Sheath
   Excision 26145
   Incision and Drainage 26020

Palsy, Seventh Nerve
See Facial Nerve Paralysis

Pancreas
Anastomosis
   to Intestines 48180
   with Intestines 48520-48540
Anesthesia 00794
Biopsy 48100
Cyst
   Anastomosis 48520-48540
   Repair 48500
Debridement
   Peripancreatic Tissue 48005
Excision
   Ampulla of Vater 48148
   Duct 48148
   Partial . . .48140-48146, 48150, 48153-48154,
                  48160
   Peripancreatic Tissue 48005
   Total 48155-48160
Lesion
   Excision .48120
Needle Biopsy 48102
Placement
   Drainage .48001
Pseudocyst
   Drainage
      Open .48510
      Percutaneous 48511
Removal
   Calculi (Stone) 48020
Removal Transplanted Allograft 48556
Repair
   Cyst 48500
Suture 48545
Transplantation 48160, 48550-48556
Unlisted Services and Procedures 48999
X-Ray with Contrast 74300-74305
   Injection Procedure 48400

Pancreas, Endocrine Only
See Islet Cell

Pancreatectomy
Partial 48140-48146, 48150-48154, 48160
Total 48155-48160
with Transplantation 48160

Pancreaticojejunostomy 48180

Pancreatic DNAse
See DNAse

Pancreatic Duct
Destruction
   Calculi (Stone) 43265
Dilation
   Endoscopy 43271
Endoscopy
   Collection
      Specimen 43260
   Destruction
      Calculi (Stone) 43265
      Tumor 43272
   Dilation .43271
   Removal
      Calculi (Stone) 43264
      Foreign Body 43269
      Stent 43269
   Sphincterotomy 43262
   Sphincter Pressure 43263
   Tube Placement 43267-43268
Incision
   Sphincter 43262
Removal
   Calculi (Stone) 43264
   Foreign Body 43269
   Stent .43269
Tube Placement
   Nasopancreatic 43267
   Stent .43268
Tumor
   Destruction 43272
X-Ray with Contrast
   Guide Catheter 74329-74330

Pancreatic Islet Cell AB
See Antibody, Islet Cell

Pancreatography
Injection Procedure 48400
Intraoperative 74300-74301
Postoperative 74305

Pancreatojejunostomies
See Pancreaticojejunostomy

Pancreatorrhaphy 48545

Pancreatotomy
See Incision, Pancreas

Pancreozymin-Secretin Test . . .82938

Panel
See Organ or Disease Oriented Panel

Panniculectomy
See Lipectomy

Paper, Chromatography
See Chromatography, Paper

Paper Chromatographies
See Chromatography, Paper

Papilla, Interdental
See Gums

Papillectomy 46220

Papilloma
Destruction 54050-54065

PAPP D
See Lactogen, Human Placental

Pap Smears 88141-88155,
                  88164-88167

Para-Tyrosine
See Tyrosine

Paracentesis 49080
Eye
   Anterior Chamber
      with Diagnostic Aspiration of
         Aqueous 65800
      with Removal of Blood 65815
      with Removal Vitreous and/or Discission
        of Anterior Hyaloid Membrane 65810
      with Therapeutic Release of
        Aqueous 65805

Paracentesis, Abdominal
See Abdomen, Drainage

Paracentesis, Thoracic
See Thoracentesis

Paracervical Nerve
Injection
   Anesthetic 64435

Paraffin Bath Therapy 97018
See Physical Medicine/Therapy/Occupational
Therapy

Paraganglioma, Medullary
See Pheochromocytoma

Parainfluenza Virus
Antigen Detection
   Immunofluorescence 87279

Paralysis, Facial Nerve
See Facial Nerve Paralysis

Paralysis, Infantile
See Polio

Paranasal Sinuses
See Sinus; Sinuses

Parasites
Blood 87207
Examination 87169
Smear 87177

Parasitic Worms
See Helminth

Parathormone 83970

Parathyrin
See Parathormone

Parathyroidectomy 60500-60505

**Parathyroid
Autotransplantation** 60512

Parathyroid Gland
Autotransplant 60512
Excision 60500-60502
Exploration 60500-60505
Nuclear Medicine
   Imaging 78070

Parathyroid Hormone 83970

Parathyroid Hormone Measurement
See Parathormone

Parathyroid Transplantation
See Transplantation, Parathyroid

Paraurethral Gland
Abscess
　　Incision and Drainage 53060

Paravertebral Nerve
Destruction 64622-64627
Injection
　　Anesthetic 64470-64484
　　Neurolytic 64622-64627

Parietal Cell Vagotomies
See Vagotomy, Highly Selective

Parietal Craniotomy 61556

Paring
Skin Lesion
　　Benign Hyperkeratotic
　　　　More than Four Lesions 11057
　　　　Single Lesion 11055
　　　　Two to Four Lesions 11056

Paronychia
Incision and Drainage 10060-10061

Parotid Duct
Diversion .42507-42510
Reconstruction 42507-42510

Parotid Gland
Abscess
　　Incision and Drainage 42300-42305
Calculi (Stone)
　　Excision 42330, 42340
Excision
　　Partial 42410-42415
　　Total .42420-42426
Tumor
　　Excision 42410-42426

Parotitides, Epidemic
See Mumps

Pars Abdominalis Aortae
See Aorta, Abdominal

Partial Colectomy
See Colectomy, Partial

Partial Cystectomy
See Cystectomy, Partial

Partial Esophagectomy
See Esophagectomy, Partial

Partial Gastrectomy
See Excision, Stomach, Partial

Partial Glossectomy
See Excision, Tongue, Partial

Partial Hepatectomy
See Excision, Liver, Partial

Partial Mastectomies
See Breast, Excision, Lesion

Partial Nephrectomy
See Excision, Kidney, Partial

Partial Pancreatectomy
See Pancreatectomy, Partial

Partial Splenectomy
See Splenectomy, Partial

Partial Thromboplastin Time
See Thromboplastin, Partial, Time

Partial Ureterectomy
See Ureterectomy, Partial

Particle Agglutination 86403-86406

Parvovirus
Antibody 86747

Patch
Allergy Tests 95044
　　See Allergy Tests

Patella
See Knee
Dislocation 27560-27566
Excision 27350
　　with Reconstruction 27424
Fracture 27520-27524
Reconstruction 27437-27438
Repair
　　Chondromalacia 27418
　　Instability 27420-27424

Patella, Chondromalacia
See Chondromalacia Patella

Patellar Tendon Bearing (PTB) Cast .29435

Patellectomy
with Reconstruction 27424

Paternity Testing 86910-86911

Patey's Operation
See Mastectomy, Radical

Pathologic Dilatation
See Dilation

Pathology
Clinical
　　Consultation 80500-80502
Surgical 88355
　　Consultation 88321-88325
　　　　Intraoperative 88329-88332
　　Decalcification Procedure 88311
　　Electron Microscopy 88348-88349
　　Gross and Micro Exam
　　　　Level II 88302
　　　　Level III .88304
　　　　Level IV .88305
　　　　Level V .88307
　　　　Level VI .88309
　　Gross Exam
　　　　Level I 88300
　　Histochemistry 88318-88319

Immunocytochemistry 88342
Immunofluorescent Study 88346-88347
Morphometry
　　Nerve 88356
　　Skeletal Muscle 88355
　　Tumor 88358
Nerve Teasing 88362
Special Stain 88312-88314
Staining 88312-88314
Tissue Hybridization 88365
Unlisted Services and
　　Procedures 88399, 89399

Patterson's Test
See Blood Urea Nitrogen

Paul-Bunnell Test
See Antibody; Antibody Identification;
Microsomal Antibody

PBG
See Porphobilinogen

PCP
See Phencyclidine

PCR
See Polymerase Chain Reaction

Peans' Operation
See Amputation, Leg, Upper, at Hip; Radical
Resection; Replantation

Pectoral Cavity
See Chest Cavity

Pectus Carinatum
Reconstructive Repair 21740

Pectus Excavatum
Reconstructive Repair 21740

Pedicle Fixation
Insertion .22842-22844

Pedicle Flap
Formation 15570-15576
Island 15740
Neurovascular .15750
Transfer 15650

PEEP
See Pressure Breathing, Positive

Peet Operation
See Nerves, Sympathectomy, Excision

Pelvi-Ureteroplasty
See Pyeloplasty

Pelvic Adhesions
See Adhesions, Pelvic

Pelvic Exam 57410

Pelvic Exenteration 51597

Pelvic Fixation
Insertion 22848

Pelvic Lymphadenectomy 58240

Pelvimetry 74710

Pelviolithotomy 50130

Pelvis
See Hip
Abscess
     Incision and Drainage 26990, 45000
Angiography 72191
Biopsy 27040-27041
Bone
     Drainage 26992
Brace Application 20662
Bursa
     Incision and Drainage 26991
CAT Scan 72191-72194
Cyst
     Aspiration 50390
     Injection 50390
Destruction
     Lesion 58662
Endoscopy
     Destruction of Lesion 58662
     Lysis of Adhesions 58660
     Oviduct Surgery 58670-58671
Exclusion
     Small Intestine 44700
Exenteration 45126, 58240
Halo 20662
Hematoma
     Incision and Drainage 26990
Lysis
     Adhesions 58660
Magnetic Resonance Angiography 72198
Magnetic Resonance Imaging
(MRI) 72195-72197
Removal
     Foreign Body 27086-27087
Repair
     Osteotomy 27158
     Tendon 27098
Ring
     Dislocation 27193-27194, 27216-27218
     Fracture 27216-27218
        Closed Treatment 27193-27194
Tumor
     Excision 27047-27049
Ultrasound 76856-76857
Unlisted Services and Procedures for Hips and
Hip Joint 27299
X-Ray 72170-72190, 73540
     Manometry 74710

Pemberton Osteotomy of Pelvis
See Osteotomy, Pelvis

Penectomy
See Amputation, Penis

Penetrating Keratoplasties
See Keratoplasty, Penetrating

Penile Induration
See Peyronie Disease

Penile Prosthesis
Insertion
     Inflatable 54401-54405
     Noninflatable 54400
Removal
     Inflatable 54406, 54410-54417
     Semi-Rigid 54415-54417

Repair
     Inflatable 54408
Replacement
     Inflatable 54410-54411, 54416-54417
     Semi-Rigid 54416-54417

Penile Rigidity Test 54250

Penile Tumescence Test 54250

Penis
Amputation
     Partial 54120
     Radical 54130-54135
     Total 54125
Biopsy 54100-54105
Circumcision
     Repair 54163
     Surgical Excision
        Newborn 54160
        with Clamp or Other Device 54152
        Newborn 54150
Excision
     Partial 54120
     Prepuce 54150-54161, 54163
     Total 54125-54135
Frenulum
     Excision 54164
Incision
     Prepuce 54000-54001
Incision and Drainage 54015
Injection
     for Erection 54235
     Peyronie Disease 54200
        Surgical Exposure Plague 54205
     Vasoactive Drugs 54231
     X-Ray 54230
Insertion
     Prosthesis
        Inflatable 54401-54405
        Noninflatable 54400
Irrigation
     Priapism 54220
Lesion
     Destruction
        Cryosurgery 54056
        Electrodesiccation 54055
        Extensive 54065
        Laser Surgery 54057
        Simple 54050-54060
        Surgical Excision 54060
     Excision 54060
        Penile Plaque 54110-54112
Nocturnal Penile Tumescence Test 54250
Occlusion
     Vein 37790
Plaque
     Excision 54110-54112
Plethysmography 54240
Prepuce
     Stretch 54450
Reconstruction
     Angulation 54360
     Chordee 54300-54304, 54328
     Complications 54340-54348
     Epispadias 54380-54390
     Hypospadias 54328-54352
     Injury 54440

Removal
     Foreign Body 54115
     Prosthesis
        Inflatable 54406, 54410-54417
        Semi-Rigid 54415-54417
Repair
     Fistulization 54435
     Priapism with Shunt 54420-54430
     Prosthesis
        Inflatable 54408
Replacement
     Prosthesis
        Inflatable 54410-54411, 54416-54417
        Semi-Rigid 54416-54417
Revascularization 37788
Rigidity Test 54250
Test Erection 54250
Unlisted Services and Procedures 55899
Venous Studies 93980-93981

Penis Adhesions
Lysis
     Post-circumcision 54162

Penis Prostheses
See Penile Prosthesis

Pentagastrin Test
See Gastric Analysis Test

Pentamidine
See Inhalation Treatment

Peptidase P
See Angiotensin Converting Enzyme (ACE)

Peptidase S
See Leucine Aminopeptidase

Peptide, Connecting
See C-Peptide

Peptide, Vasoactive Intestinal
See Vasoactive Intestinal Peptide

Peptidyl Dipeptidase A
See Angiotensin Converting Enzyme (ACE)

**Percutaneous Abdominal
Paracentesis**
See Abdomen, Drainage

Percutaneous Atherectomies
See Artery, Atherectomy

**Percutaneous Biopsy,
Gallbladder/Bile Ducts**
See Bile Duct, Biopsy

Percutaneous Discectomies
See Diskectomy, Percutaneous

**Percutaneous Electric Nerve
Stimulation**
See Application, Neurostimulation

**Percutaneous Lumbar
Diskectomy** 62287
See Aspiration, Nucleus of Disk, Lumbar;
Puncture Aspiration

Percutaneous Lysis .... .62263

Percutaneous Nephrostomies
See Nephrostomy, Percutaneous

Percutaneous Transluminal Angioplasty
Artery
    Aortic .... .35472
    Brachiocephalic .... .35475
    Coronary 92982-92984
    Femoral-Popliteal .... .35474
    Iliac .... .35473
    Pulmonary 92997-92998
    Renal .... .35471
    Tibioperoneal .... .35470
    Visceral .... .35471
Venous .... .35476

Percutaneous Transluminal Coronary Angioplasty
See Percutaneous Transluminal Angioplasty

Pereyra Procedure ...... .51845, 57289,
    58267

Performance Test .... .96100
See Physical Medicine/Therapy/Occupational Therapy
Physical Therapy .... .97750

Perfusion
Myocardial 78460-78465, 78478-78480
    Imaging 78466-78469
Positron Emission Tomography (PET)
    Myocardial Imaging 78491-78492

Perfusion, Intracranial Arterial
Thrombolysis .... .61624

Perfusion Pump
See Infusion Pump

Pericardectomies
See Excision, Pericardium

Pericardial Cyst
See Cyst, Pericardial

Pericardial Sac
Drainage .... .32659

Pericardial Window
for Drainage .... .33025

Pericardial Window Technic
See Pericardiostomy

Pericardiectomy
Complete 33030-33031
Subtotal 33030-33031
Total
    Endoscopic .... .32660

Pericardiocentesis 33010-33011
Ultrasound Guidance .... .76930

Pericardiostomy
Tube .... .33015

Pericardiotomy
Removal
    Clot .... .33020
    Foreign Body .... .33020

Pericardium
Cyst
    Excision .... .32661, 33050
Excision .... .32659, 33030-33031
Incision
    Removal
        Clot .... .33020
        Foreign Body .... .33020
    with Tube .... .33015
Incision and Drainage .... .33025
Puncture Aspiration 33010-33011
Removal
    Clot
        Endoscopic .... .32658
    Foreign Body
        Endoscopic .... .32658
Tumor
    Excision .... .32661, 33050

Peridural Anesthesia
See Anesthesia, Epidural

Peridural Injection
See Epidural, Injection

Perineal Prostatectomy
See Prostatectomy, Perineal

Perineoplasty .... .56810

Perineorrhaphy
Repair
    Rectocele .... .57250

Perineum
Abscess
    Incision and Drainage .... .56405
Colposcopy .... .99170
Removal
    Prosthesis .... .53442
Repair .... .56810
X-Ray with Contrast .... .74775

Perionychia
See Paronychia

Periorbital Region
Reconstruction
    Osteotomy with Graft 21267-21268
Repair-Osteotomy 21260-21263

Peripheral Artery Disease (PAD) Rehabilitation .... .93668

Peripheral Nerve
Repair/Suture
    Major .... .64856, 64859

Periprosthetic Capsulectomy
Breast .... .19371

Peristaltic Pumps
See Infusion Pump

Peritoneal Dialysis 90945-90947

Peritoneal Free Air
See Pneumoperitoneum

Peritoneal Lavage .... .49080

Peritoneocentesis 49080-49081

Peritoneoscopy
See Endoscopy, Peritoneum

Peritoneum
Abscess
    Incision and Drainage .... .49020
        Percutaneous .... .49021
Chemotherapy Administration .... .96445
    See Chemotherapy
Endoscopy
    Biopsy .... .47561
    Drainage
        Lymphocele .... .49323
        X-Ray .... .47560
Exchange
    Drainage Catheter .... .49423
Injection
    Contrast
        via Catheter .... .49424
Ligation
    Shunt .... .49428
Removal
    Cannula/Catheter .... .49422
    Foreign Body .... .49085
    Shunt .... .49429
Tumor
    Resection 58950-58954
Unlisted Services and Procedures .... .49999
Venous Shunt
    Injection .... .49427
X-Ray .... .74190

Persistent, Omphalomesenteric Duct
See Diverticulum, Meckel's

Persistent Truncus Arteriosus
See Truncus Arteriosus

Personal Care
See Self Care

Pessary
Insertion .... .57160

Pesticides
Chlorinated Hydrocarbons .... .82441

PET
See Positron Emission Tomography

Petrous Temporal
Excision
    Apex.......................... .69530

Peyronie Disease
Injection .... .54200
Surgical Exposure .... .54205
with Graft 54110-54112

pH
See Blood
Other Fluid .... .83986
Urine .... .83986

Phacoemulsification
Removal
    Extracapsular Cataract 66982, 66984
    Secondary Membranous Cataract 66850

Phagocytosis
White Blood Cells 86344

Phalangectomy
Toe 28150
    Partial 28160

Phalanges (Hand)
See Finger, Bone

Phalanx, Finger
Craterization 26235-26236
Cyst
    Excision 26210-26215
Diaphysectomy 26235-26236
Excision 26235-26236
    Radical
      for Tumor 26260-26262
Fracture
    Articular
      Closed Treatment 26740
      Open Treatment 26746
      with Manipulation 26742
    Distal 26755-26756
      Closed Treatment 26750
      Open Treatment 26765
      Percutaneous Fixation 26756
    Open Treatment 26735
      Distal 26765
    Shaft 26720-26727
      Open Treatment 26735
Incision and Drainage 26034
Ostectomy
    Radical
      for Tumor 26260-26262
Repair
    Lengthening 26568
    Nonunion 26546
    Osteotomy 26567
Saucerization 26235-26236
Thumb
    Fracture
      Shaft 26720-26727
Tumor
    Excision 26210-26215

Phalanx, Great Toe
See Phalanx, Toe
Fracture 28490
    Open Treatment 28505
    with Manipulation 28495-28496
    Percutaneous Fixation 28496
    without Manipulation 28490

Phalanx, Toe
Condyle
    Excision 28126
Craterization 28124
Cyst
    Excision 28108
Diaphysectomy 28124
Excision 28124, 28150-28160

Fracture
    Open Treatment 28525
    without Manipulation 28510
    with Manipulation 28515
Repair
    Osteotomy 28310-28312
Saucerization 28124
Tumor
    Excision 28108, 28175

Pharmaceutic Preparations
See Drug

Pharmacotherapies
See Chemotherapy

Pharyngeal Tonsil
See Adenoids

Pharyngectomy
Partial 42890

Pharyngolaryngectomy ...31390-31395

Pharyngoplasty 42950

Pharyngorrhaphy
See Suture, Pharynx

Pharyngostomy 42955

Pharyngotomy
See Incision, Pharynx

Pharyngotympanic Tube
See Eustachian Tube

Pharynx
See Nasopharynx; Throat
Biopsy 42800-42806
Cineradiography 70371, 74230
Creation
    Stoma 42955
Excision 42145
    Partial 42890
    Resection 42892-42894
    with Larynx 31390-31395
Hemorrhage 42960-42962
Lesion
    Destruction 42808
    Excision 42808
Reconstruction 42950
Removal
    Foreign Body 42809
Repair
    with Esophagus 42953
Unlisted Services and Procedures 42999
Video Study 70371, 74230
X-Ray 70370, 74210

Phencyclidine 83992

Phenobarbital 82205
Assay 80184

Phenothiazine 84022

Phenotype Analysis
by Nucleic acid
    Infectious Agent
      HIV-1 Drug Resistance 87903-87904

Phenotype Prediction
by Genetic Database
    HIV-1
      Drug Resistance 0023T

Phenylalanine 84030

Phenylalanine-Tyrosine
Ratio 84030

Phenylketones 84035

Phenylketonuria
See Phenylalanine

Phenytoin
Assay 80185-80186

Pheochromocytoma 80424

Pheresis
See Apheresis

Phlebectasia
See Varicose Vein

Phlebographies
See Venography

Phleborrhaphy
See Suture, Vein

Phlebotomy
Therapeutic 99195

Phoria
See Strabismus

Phosphatase
Alkaline 84075, 84080
    Blood 84078
Forensic Examination 84061

Phosphatase Acid 84060
Blood 84066

Phosphate, Pyridoxal
See Pyridoxal Phosphate

Phosphatidylcholine
Cholinephosphohydrolase
See Tissue Typing

Phosphatidylglycerol 84081

Phosphatidyl Glycerol
See Phosphatidylglycerol

Phosphocreatine
Phosphotransferase, ADP
See CPK

Phosphogluconate-6
Dehydrogenase 84085

Phosphoglycerides, Glycerol
See Phosphatidylglycerol

Phosphohexose Isomerase 84087

Phosphohydrolases
See Phosphatase

Phosphokinase, Creatine
See CPK

Phospholipase C
See Tissue Typing

Phospholipid Antibody 86147

Phosphomonoesterase
See Phosphatase

Phosphoric Monoester Hydrolases
See Phosphatase

Phosphorus 84100
Urine 84105

Phosphotransferase, ADP Phosphocreatine
See CPK

Photochemotherapies, Extracorporeal
See Photopheresis

Photochemotherapy 96910-96913
See Dermatology
Endoscopic Light 96570-96571

Photocoagulation
Endolaser Panretinal
    Vitrectomy 67040
Focal Endolaser
    Vitrectomy 67040
Iridoplasty 66762
Lesion
    Cornea 65450
    Retina 0017T, 67210, 67227-67228
Retinal Detachment
    Prophylaxis 67145
    Repair 67105

Photodensity
Radiographic
    Absorptiometry 76078

Photodynamic Therapy
External 96567

Photography, Ocular
See Ophthalmosocpy, Diagnostic

Photopheresis
Extracorporeal 36522

Photophoresis
See Actinotherapy; Photochemotherapy

Photoradiation Therapies
See Actinotherapy

Photosensitivity Testing 95056
See Allergy Tests

Phototherapies
See Actinotherapy

Phototherapy, Ultraviolet
See Actinotherapy

Photo Patch
Allergy Test 95052
    See Allergy Tests

Phrenic Nerve
Anastomosis
    to Facial Nerve 64870
Avulsion 64746
Incision 64746
Injection
    Anesthetic 64410
Transection 64746

Physical Medicine/Therapy/Occupational Therapy
See Neurology, Diagnostic
Activities of Daily Living 97535, 99509
Aquatic Therapy
    with Exercises 97113
Athletic Training
    Evaluation 97005
    Re-evaluation 97006
Check-Out
    Orthotic/Prosthetic 97703
Cognitive Skills Development 97532
Community/Work Reintegration 97537
Evaluation 97001-97002
Kinetic Therapy 97530
Manual Therapy 97140
Modalities
    Contrast Baths 97034
    Diathermy Treatment 97024
    Electric Simulation
        Unattended 97014
    Electric Stimulation
        Attended, Manual 97032
    Hot or Cold Pack 97010
    Hydrotherapy (Hubbard Tank) 97036
    Infrared Light Treatment 97026
    Iontophoresis 97033
    Microwave Therapy 97020
    Paraffin Bath 97018
    Traction 97012
    Ultrasound 97035
    Ultraviolet Light 97028
    Unlisted Services and Procedures 97039
    Vasopneumatic Device 97016
    Whirlpool Therapy 97022
Orthotics Training 97504
Osteopathic Manipulation 98925-98929
Procedures
    Aquatic Therapy 97113
    Gait Training 97116
    Group Therapeutic 97150
    Massage Therapy 97124
    Neuromuscular Reeducation 97112
    Physical Performance Test 97750
    Therapeutic Exercises 97110
    Traction Therapy 97140
    Work Hardening 97545-97546
Prosthetic Training 97520
Sensory Integration 97533
Therapeutic Activities 97530
Unlisted Services and Procedures ..97139, 97799
Wheelchair Management/Propulsion 97542
Work Reintegration 97537

Physical Therapy
See Physical Medicine/Therapy/Occupational Therapy

Physician Services
Care Plan Oversight Services 99374-99380
    Home Health Agency Care 99374
    Hospice 99377-99378
    Nursing Facility 99379-99380
Direction, Advanced Life Support 99288
Prolonged
    without Direct Patient Contact .99358-99359
    with Direct Patient Contact ...99354-99357
        Outpatient/Office 99354-99355
    with Direct Patient Services
        Inpatient 99356-99357
Standby 99360
Supervision, Care Plan Oversight
Services 99374-99380

Pierce Ears 69090

Piercing of Ear Lobe
See Ear Lobes, Pierce

Piles
See Hemorrhoids

Pilonidal Cyst
Excision 11770-11772
Incision and Drainage 10080-10081

Pin
See Wire
Insertion/Removal
    Skeletal Traction 20650
Prophylactic Treatment
    Femur 27187
    Humerus 24498
    Shoulder 23490-23491

Pinch Graft 15050

Pinna
See Ear, External

Pinworms
Examination 87172

Pirogoff Procedure 27888

Pituitary Epidermoid Tumor
See Craniopharyngioma

Pituitary Gland
Excision 61546-61548
Tumor
    Excision 61546-61548

Pituitary Growth Hormone
See Growth Hormone

Pituitary Lactogenic Hormone
See Prolactin

Pituitectomy
See Excision, Pituitary Gland

PKU
See Phenylalanine

Placement
Catheter
  Bile Duct 75982
  Bronchus
    for Intracavitary Radioelement
      Application 31643
      See Catheterization
Catheter, Cardiac 93503
  See Catheterization, Cardiac
Colonic Stent 44397, 45327, 45345, 45387
Drainage
  Pancreas 48001
IVC Filter 75940
Jejunostomy Tube
  Endoscopic .44372
Metallic Localization Clip
  Breast 19295
Nasogastric Tube 43752
Needle
  Bone 36680
Needle Wire
  Breast 19290-19291
Orogastric Tube 43752
Radiation Delivery Device
  Intracoronary Artery 92974
Seton
  Anal 46020
Tracheal Stent .31631
Ureteral Stent .50947

Placenta
Delivery 59414

Placental Lactogen
See Lactogen, Human Placental

Placental Villi
See Chorionic Villus

Plagiocephaly 21175

Plague Vaccine 90727

Planing
Nose
  Skin 30120

Plantar Digital Nerve
Decompression 64726

Plantar Pressure Measurements
Dynamic 96001, 96004

Plasma
Frozen Preparation 86927

Plasma Prokallikrein
See Fletcher Factor

Plasma Test
Volume Determination 78110-78111

Plasma Thromboplastin
Antecedent 85270, 99564
Component 85250

Plasmin 85400

Plasminogen 85420-85421

Plasmin Antiactivator
See Alpha-2 Antiplasmin

Plasmodium
Antibody 86750

Plastic Repair of Mouth
See Mouth, Repair

Plate, Bone
See Bone Plate

Platelet
Aggregation 85576
Antibody 86022-86023
Automated Count 85595
Count 85585
Manual Count 85590
Neutralization 85597

Platelet Cofactor I
See Clotting Factor

Platelet Test
Survival Test 78190-78191

Platysmal Flap 15825

PLC
See Tissue Typing

Pleoptic Training 92065

Plethysmography
See Vascular Studies
Extremities 93922-93923
  Veins 93965
Penis 54240
Total Body 93720-93722

Pleura
Biopsy 32095-32100, 32400-32402
Decortication 32320
Empyema
  Excision 32540
Excision 32310-32320
  Endoscopic 32656
Foreign Body
  Removal 32150-32151
Needle Biopsy 32400
Removal
  Foreign Body 32653
Repair 32215
Thoracotomy 32095-32100
Unlisted Services and Procedures 32999

Pleural Cavity
Aspiration 32000-32002
Chemotherapy Administration 96440
  See Chemotherapy
Fusion 32005
Incision
  Empyema 32035-32036
  Pneumothorax 32020
Puncture and Drainage 32000-32002
Thoracostomy 32035-32036

Pleural Endoscopies
See Thoracoscopy

Pleural Scarification
for Repeat Pneumothorax 32215

Pleural Tap
See Thoracentesis

Pleurectomy
Anesthesia 00544
Parietal 32310-32320
  Endoscopic 32656

Pleuritis, Purulent
See Abscess, Thorax

Pleurocentesis
See Thoracentesis

Pleurodesis
Chemical 32005
Endoscopic .32650

Pleurosclerosis
See Pleurodesis

Pleurosclerosis, Chemical
See Pleurodesis, Chemical

Plexectomy, Choroid
See Choroid Plexus, Excision

Plexus, Choroid
See Choroid Plexus

Plexus Brachialis
See Brachial Plexus

Plexus Cervicalis
See Cervical Plexus

Plexus Coeliacus
See Celiac Plexus

Plexus Lumbalis
See Lumbar Plexus

PLGN
See Plasminogen

Plication, Sphincter, Urinary Bladder
See Bladder, Repair, Neck

Pneumocentesis
Lung 32420

Pneumocisternogram
See Cisternography

Pneumococcal Vaccine
See Vaccines

Pneumocystis Carinii
Antigen Detection
  Immunofluorescence 87281

Pneumogastric Nerve
See Vagus Nerve

Pneumogram
Pediatric 94772

Pneumolysis 32940

Pneumonectomy 32440-32500
Completion .32488
Donor 32850, 33930
Sleeve 32442
Total .32440-32445

Pneumonology
See Pulmonology

Pneumonolysis .... .32940
Intrapleural .... .32652
Open Intrapleural .... .32124

Pneumonostomy 32200-32201

Pneumonotomy
See Incision, Lung

Pneumoperitoneum .... .49400

Pneumoplethysmography
Ocular .... .93875

Pneumothorax
Chemical Pleurodesis .... .32005
Pleural Scarification for Repeat .... .32215
Therapeutic
    Injection Intrapleural Air .... .32960
Thoracentesis with Tube Insertion ...... .32002

Polio
Antibody .... .86658
Vaccine 90712-90713

Poliovirus Vaccine, Inactivated
See Vaccines

Pollicization
Digit .... .26550

Polya Gastrectomy
See Gastrectomy, Partial

Polydactylism
See Supernumerary Digit

Polydactylous Digit
Reconstruction .... .26587
Repair .... .26587

Polydactyly, Toes .... .28344

Polymerase Chain Reaction ... .83898

Polyp
Antrochoanal
    Removal .... .31032
Esophagus
    Ablation .... .43228
Nose
    Excision
        Endoscopic 31237-31240
        Extensive .... .30115
        Simple .... .30110
    Sphenoid Sinus
        Removal .... .31051
    Urethra
        Excision .... .53260

Polypectomy
Nose
    Endoscopic .... .31237
Uterus .... .58558

Polypeptide, Vasoactive Intestinal
See Vasoactive Intestinal Peptide

Polysomnography 95808-95811, 99508

Polyuria Test
See Water Load Test

Pomeroy's Operation
See Tubal Ligation

Pooling
Blood Products .... .86965

Popliteal Arteries
See Artery, Popliteal

Popliteal Synovial Cyst
See Baker's Cyst

Poradenitistras
See Lymphogranuloma Venereum

Porphobilinogen
Urine 84106-84110

Porphyrins
Feces 84126-84127
Urine 84119-84120

Porphyrin Precursors .... .82135

PORP (Partial Ossicular Replacement Prosthesis) ...... .69633, 69637

Portal Vein
See Vein, Hepatic Portal

Porter-Silber Test
See Corticosteroid, Blood

Portoenterostomies, Hepatic
See Hepaticoenterostomy

Portoenterostomy .... .47701

Port Film .... .77417

Posadas-Wernicke Disease
See Coccidioidomycosis

Positional Nystagmus Test
See Nystagmus Tests, Positional

Positive-Pressure Breathing, Inspiratory
See Intermittent Positive Pressure Breathing (IPPB)

Positive End Expiratory Pressure
See Pressure Breathing, Positive

Positron Emission Tomography (PET)
Brain 78608-78609
Heart .... .78459
Myocardial Imaging
    Perfusion Study 78491-78492
Tumor .... .78810

Post-Op Visit .... .99024

Postauricular Fistula
See Fistula, Postauricular

Postcaval Ureter
See Retrocaval Ureter

Postmortem
See Autopsy

Postoperative Wound Infection
Incision and Drainage .... .10180

Postop Vas Reconstruction
See Vasovasorrhaphy

Postpartum Care
Cesarean Delivery .... .59515
    after Attempted Vaginal Delivery ..... .59622
    Previous .... .59610, 59614-59618, 59622
Vaginal Delivery .... .59430
    after Previous Cesarean Delivery ..... .59614

Potassium .... .84132
Urine .... .84133

Potential, Auditory Evoked
See Auditory Evoked Potentials

Potential, Evoked
See Evoked Potential

Potts-Smith Procedure .... .33762

Pouch, Kock
See Kock Pouch

PPP
See Fibrin Degradation Products

PRA
See Cytotoxic Screen

Prealbumin .... .84134

Prebeta Lipoproteins
See Lipoprotein, Blood

Pregl's Test
See Cystourethroscopy, Catheterization, Urethral

Pregnancy
Abortion
    Induced 59855-59857
        by Amniocentesis Injection .. .59850-59852
        by Dilation and Curettage .... .59840
        by Dilation and Evaluation .... .59841
        Septic .... .59830
    Therapeutic
        by Dilation and Curettage .... .59851
        by Hysterectomy .... .59852
        by Saline .... .59850
Cesarean Delivery 59618-59622
    Only .... .59514
    Postpartum Care 59514-59515
    Routine Care .... .59510
    Vaginal Birth After 59610-59614
    with Hysterectomy .... .59525
Ectopic
    Abdominal .... .59130
    Cervix .... .59140
    Interstitial
        Partial Resection Uterus .... .59136
        Total Hysterectomy .... .59135
    Laparoscopy
        without Salpingectomy and/or
            Oophorectomy .... .59150
        with Salpingectomy and/or
            Oophorectomy .... .59151

Tubal .... .59121
  with Salpingectomy and/or
  Oophorectomy .... .59120
Miscarriage
  Surgical Completion
    Any Trimester .... .59812
    First Trimester .... .59820
    Second Trimester .... .59821
Molar
  See Hydatidiform Mole
Multifetal Reduction .... .59866
Placenta Delivery .... .59414
Vaginal Delivery 59409-59410
  after Cesarean Delivery 59610-59614
  Antepartum Care 59425-59426
  Postpartum Care .... .59430
  Total Obstetrical Care ..59400, 59610, 59618

Pregnancy Test 84702-84703
Urinalysis .... .81025

Pregnanediol .... .84135

Pregnanetriol .... .84138

Pregnenolone .... .84140

Prekallikrein
See Fletcher Factor

Prekallikrein Factor .... .85292

Premature, Closure, Cranial Suture
See Craniosynostosis

Prenatal Testing
Amniocentesis .... .59000
  with Amniotic Fluid Reduction ...... .59001
Chorionic Villus Sampling .... .59015
Cordocentesis .... .59012
Fetal Blood Sample .... .59030
Fetal Monitoring .... .59050
  Interpretation Only .... .59051
Non-Stress Test, Fetal .... .59025, 99500
Oxytocin Stress Test .... .59020
Stress Test
  Oxytocin .... .59020
Ultrasound 76805-76816
  Fetal Biophysical Profile 76818-76819
  Fetal Heart .... .76825

Prentiss Operation
See Orchiopexy, Inguinal Approach

Preparation
for Transfer
  Embryo .... .89255
  Cryopreserved .... .89256

Presacral Sympathectomy
See Sympathectomy, Presacral

Prescription
Contact Lens 92310-92317
  See Contact Lens Services
Ocular Prosthesis 92330-92335
  See Prosthesis, Ocular

Pressure, Blood
See Blood Pressure

Pressure, Venous
See Blood Pressure, Venous

Pressure Breathing
See Pulmonology, Therapeutic
Negative
  Continuous (CNP) .... .94662
Positive
  Continuous (CPAP) .... .94660
  Intermittent (IPPB) 94650-94652

Pressure Measurement of Sphincter of Oddi
See Sphincter of Oddi, Pressure Measurement

Pressure Ulcers
Excision 15920-15999

Pressure Ulcer (Decubitus)
See Debridement; Skin Graft and Flap
Excision
  Unlisted Services and Procedures ..... .15999

Pretreatment
Red Blood Cell
  Antibody Identification 86970-86972
Serum
  Antibody Identification 86975-86978

Prevention & Control
See Prophylaxis

Preventive Medicine 99381-99397
See Immunization; Newborn Care, Normal; Office and/or Other Outpatient Services; Prophylactic Treatment
Administration/Interpretation of Health Risk
Assessment .... .99420
Counseling and/or Risk Factor Reduction
Intervention 99401-99429
  Group Counseling 99411-99412
  Individual Counseling 99401-99404
Established Patient 99382-99397
Newborn Care .... .99432
New Patient 99381-99387
Respiratory Pattern Recording .... .94772
Unlisted Services and Procedures .... .99429

Priapism
Repair
  Fistulization .... .54435
  with Shunt 54420-54430

Primidone
Assay .... .80188

PRL
See Prolactin

Pro-Insulin C Peptide
See C-Peptide

Proalbumin
See Prealbumin

Probes, DNA
See Nucleic Acid Probe

Probes, Nucleic Acid
See Nucleic Acid Probe

Procainamide
Assay 80190-80192

Procedure, Fontan
See Repair, Heart, Anomaly

Procedure, Maxillofacial
See Maxillofacial Procedures

Process, Odontoid
See Odontoid Process

Procidentia
Rectum
  Excision 45130-45135
  Repair .... .45900

Procoagulant Activity, Glomerular
See Thromboplastin

Proconvertin .... .85230

Proctectasis
See Dilation, Rectum

Proctectomy
Partial .... .45111, 45113-45116, 45123
Total .... .45110, 45112, 45119-45120
  with Colon .... .45121

Proctocele
See Rectocele

Proctopexy 45540-45541
with Sigmoid Excision .... .45550

Proctoplasty 45500-45505

Proctorrhaphy
See Rectum, Suture

Proctoscopies
See Anoscopy

Proctosigmoidoscopy
Ablation
  Polyp or Lesion .... .45320
Biopsy .... .45305
Destruction
  Tumor .... .45320
Dilation .... .45303
Exploration .... .45300
Hemorrhage Control .... .45317
Placement
  Stent .... .45327
Removal
  Foreign Body .... .45307
  Polyp 45308-45315
  Tumor .... .45315
Volvulus Repair .... .45321

Products, Gene
See Protein

Proetz Therapy
Nose .... .30210

Profibrinolysin
See Plasminogen

Progenitor Cell
See Stem Cell

Progesterone 84144

Progesterone Receptors 84234

Progestin Receptors
See Progesterone Receptors

Proinsulin 84206

Projective Test 96100

Prokallikrein
See Fletcher Factor

Prokallikrein, Plasma
See Fletcher Factor

Prokinogenase
See Fletcher Factor

Prolactin 80418, 80440, 84146

Prolapse
See Procidentia

Prolapse, Rectal
See Procidentia, Rectum

Prolastin
See Alpha-1 Antitrypsin

Prolonged Services 99354-99357,
99360
without Direct Patient Contact 99358-99359

Prophylactic Treatment
See Preventive Medicine
Femur 27495
    Pinning 27187
Humerus
    Pinning, Wiring 24498
Radius 25490, 25492
    Nailing 25490, 25492
    Pinning 25490, 25492
    Plating 25490, 25492
    Wiring 25490, 25492
Shoulder
    Clavicle 23490
    Humerus 23491
Tibia 27745
Ulna 25491-25492
    Nailing 25491-25492
    Pinning 25491-25492
    Plating 25491-25492
    Wiring 25491-25492

Prophylaxis
Retina
    Detachment
        Cryotherapy, Diathermy 67141
        Photocoagulation 67145

Prostaglandin 84150
Insertion 59200

Prostanoids
See Prostaglandin

Prostate
Ablation
    Cryosurgery 55873

Abscess
    Drainage 52700
    Incision and Drainage 55720-55725
Biopsy 55700-55705
Brachytherapy
    Needle Insertion 55859
Coagulation
    Laser 52647
Destruction
    Cryosurgery 55873
    Thermotherapy 53850-53853
        Microwave 53850
        Radio Frequency 53852
Excision
    Partial 55801, 55821-55831
    Perineal 55801-55815
    Radical 55810-55815, 55840-55845
    Retropubic 55831-55845
    Suprapubic 55821
    Transurethral 52601, 52612-52614
Exploration
    Exposure 55860
    with Nodes 55862-55865
Incision
    Exposure 55860-55865
    Transurethral 52450
Insertion
    Radioactive Substance 55860
Needle Biopsy .55700
Thermotherapy
    Transurethral 53850-53853
Ultrasound 76872-76873
Unlisted Services and Procedures 55899
    Urinary System 53899
Urethra
    Transurethral Balloon Dilation 52510
Vaporization
    Laser 52648

Prostatectomy 52601
Perineal
    Partial 55801
    Radical 55810-55815
Retropubic
    Partial 55831
    Radical 55840-55845
Suprapubic
    Partial 55821
Transurethral 52612-52614

**Prostate Specific
Antigen** 84152-84154

Prostatic Abscess
See Abscess, Prostate

Prostatotomy 55720-55725

Prosthesis
Augmentation
    Mandibular Body 21125
Auricular 21086
Breast
    Insertion 19340-19342
    Removal 19328-19330
    Supply 19396
Check-Out 97703
    See Physical Medicine/Therapy/Occupational
Therapy

Cornea 65770
Facial 21088
Hernia
    Mesh 49568
Hip
    Removal 27090-27091
Intestines 44700
Knee
    Insertion 27438, 27445
Lens
    Insertion 66982-66985
    Manual or Mechanical
    Technique 66982-66984
    Not Associated with Concurrent Cataract
    Removal 66985
Mandibular Resection 21081
Nasal 21087
Nasal Septum
    Insertion 30220
Obturator 21076
    Definitive 21080
    Interim 21079
Ocular 21077, 65770, 66982-66985,
                92330-92335, 92358, 92393
    Fitting and Prescription 92330
    Loan 92358
    Prescription 92335
    Supply 92393
Orbital 21077
    Partial or Total 69633, 69637
Ossicle Reconstruction
    Chain 69633
Palatal Augmentation 21082
Palatal Lift 21083
Palate .42280-42281
Penile
    Insertion 54400-54405
    Removal 54406, 54410-54417
    Repair 54408
    Replacement 54410-54411, 54416-54417
Perineum
    Removal 53442
Skull Plate
    Removal 62142
    Replacement 62143
Spectacle
    Fitting 92352-92353
    Repair 92371
Speech Aid 21084
Spinal
    Insertion 22851
Synthetic 69633, 69637
Temporomandibular Joint
    Arthroplasty 21243
Testicular
    Insertion 54660
Training 97520
Urethral Sphincter
    Insertion 53444-53445
    Removal 53446-53447
    Repair 53449
    Replacement 53448
Wrist
    Removal 25250-25251

Protease F
See Plasmin

Protein

C-Reactive	.86140-86141
Glycated	.82985
Myelin Basic	.83873
Osteocalcin	.83937
Prealbumin	.84134
Serum	.84160-84165
Total	.84155
Western Blot	.84181-84182, 88372

Protein Analysis, Tissue

Western Blot	.88371

Protein Blotting
See Western Blot

Protein C Activator 85337

Protein C Antigen 85302

Protein C Assay 85303

Protein C Resistance Assay 85307

Protein S

Assay	.85306
Total	.85305

Prothrombase
See Thrombokinase

Prothrombin 85210

Prothrombinase
See Thromboplastin

Prothrombin Time 85610-85611

Prothrombokinase 85230

Protime
See Prothrombin Time

Proton Treatment Delivery

Complex	.77525
Intermediate	.77523
Simple	.77520-77522

Protoporphyrin 84202-84203

Protozoa

Antibody	.86753

Provitamin A
See Vitamin, A

Provocation Test

for Allergies	.95078
See Allergy Tests	
for Glaucoma	.92140

Provocation Tonography 92130

Prower Factor
See Stuart-Prower Factor

PSA
See Prostate Specific Antigen

Pseudocyst, Pancreas
See Pancreas, Pseudocyst

PSG
See Polysomnography

Psoriasis Treatment 96910-96913
See Dermatology; Photochemotherapy

Psychiatric Diagnosis

Evaluation of Records or Reports	.90885
Interventional Evaluation	
Interactive	.90802
Interview and Evaluation	.90801-90802
Psychological Testing	.96100
Unlisted Services and Procedures	.90899

Psychiatric Treatment
See Psychotherapy

Biofeedback Training	.90875-90876
Consultation with Family	.90887
Drug Management	.90862
Electroconvulsive Therapy	.90870-90871
Environmental Intervention	.90882
Family	.90846-90849, 99510
Group	.90853-90857
Hypnotherapy	.90880
Individual	
Insight-Oriented	
Home Visit	.99510
Hospital or Residential Care	.90816-90822
Office or Outpatient	.90804-90809
Interactive	
Home Visit	.99510
Hospital or Residential Care	.90823-90829
Office or Outpatient	.90810-90815
Narcosynthesis Analysis	.90865
Psychoanalysis	.90845
Report Preparation	.90889
Residential	
Facility Care	.90816-90829
Unlisted Services and Procedures	.90899

Psychoanalysis 90845

Psychophysiologic Feedback
See Biofeedback

Psychotherapy

Family	.90846-90849, 99510
Group	.90853-90857
Insight-Oriented	
Hospital or Residential Care	.90816-90822
Office or Outpatient	.90804-90809
Interactive	
Hospital or Residential Care	.90823-90829
Office or Outpatient	.90810-90815

PTA 85270

PTA (Factor XI)
See Clotting Factor

PTC Factor 85250

PTCA
See Percutaneous Transluminal Angioplasty

Pteroylglutamic Acid
See Folic Acid

Pterygium

Excision	.65420
with Graft	.65426

Pterygomaxillary Fossa

Incision	.31040

Pterygopalatine Ganglion
See Sphenopalatine Ganglion

PTH
See Parathormone

Ptosis
See Blepharoptosis; Procidentia

PTT
See Thromboplastin, Partial, Time

Ptyalectasis
See Dilation, Salivary Duct

Pubic Symphysis 27282

Pubis

Craterization	.27070
Cyst	
Excision	.27065-27067
Excision	.27070
Saucerization	.27070
Tumor	
Excision	.27065-27067

Pudendal Nerve

Avulsion	.64761
Destruction	.64630
Incision	.64761
Injection	
Anesthetic	.64430
Neurolytic	.64630
Transection	.64761

Puestow Procedure 48180

Pulled Elbow
See Nursemaid Elbow

Pulmonary Artery 33690

Catheterization	
See Catheterization, Pulmonary Artery	
Embolism	.33910-33916
Excision	.33910-33916
Percutaneous Transluminal	
Angioplasty	.92997-92998
Reimplantation	.33788
Repair	.33690, 33917-33920
Reimplantation	.33788
Shunt	
from Aorta	.33755-33762, 33924
from Vena Cava	.33766-33767
Subclavian	.33750
Transection	.33922

Pulmonary Function Test
See Pulmonology, Diagnostic

Pulmonary Haemorrhage
See Hemorrhage, Lung

Pulmonary Perfusion Imaging

Nuclear Medicine	.78588

Pulmonary Valve

Incision	.33470-33474
Repair	.33470-33474
Replacement	.33475

Pulmonary Vein
Repair 33730

Pulmonology
Diagnostic
   Airway Closing Volume 94370
   Bronchodilation 94664-94665
   Carbon Dioxide Response Curve 94400
   Carbon Monoxide Diffusion Capacity . .94720
   Expired Gas Analysis 94250
     CO2 94770
     O2 and CO2 94681
     O2 Update, Direct 94680
     O2 Uptake, Indirect 94690
   Flow-Volume Loop 94375
   Functional Residual Capacity 94240
   Function Study 78596
   Hemoglobin O2 Affinity 82820
   Hypoxia Response Curve 94450
   Maldistribution of Inspired Air 94350
   Maximum Breathing Capacity 94200
   Maximum Voluntary Ventilation 94200
   Membrane Compliance 94750
   Membrane Diffusion Capacity 94725
   Nitrogen Washout Curve 94350
   Oximetry
     Ear or Pulse 94760-94762
   Resistance to Airflow 94360
   Spirometry 94010-94070
     Evaluation 94010-94070
     Patient Initiated with
     Bronchospasm 94014-94016
   Sputum Mobilization with
     Inhalants 94664-94665
   Stress Test 94621
   Stress Test, Pulmonary 94620
   Thoracic Gas Volume 94260
Therapeutic
   Expired Gas Analysis 94250
   Inhalation
     Pentamidine 94642, 99563
   Inhalation Treatment . . .94640, 94664-94665,
                     99503
   Manipulation of Chest Wall 94667-94668
   Pressure Ventilation
     Negative CNPB 94662
     Positive CPAP 94660
     Positive IPPB 94650-94652
   Unlisted Services and Procedures 94799
   Ventilation Assist 94656-94657, 99504
Unlisted Services and Procedures 94799

Pulse Generator
Electronic Analysis 95970-95971
Heart
   Insertion/Replacement 33212-33213

Pulse Rate Increased
See Tachycardia

Pump
See Chemotherapy, Pump Services; Infusion
Pump

Pump, Infusion
See Infusion Pump

Pump Services
Oxygenator/Heat Exchanger 99190-99192

Pump Stomach for Poison 91105

Punch Graft 15775-15776

Puncture
Artery 36600
Chest
   Drainage 32000-32002
Cisternal
   See Cisternal Puncture
Lumbar
   See Spinal Tap
Lung 32420
Pericardium 33010-33011
Pleural Cavity
   Drainage 32000-32002
Skull
   Drain Fluid 61000-61020
     Cistern 61050
   Inject Cistern 61055
   Inject Ventricle 61026
   Shunt
     Drain Fluid 61070
     Injection .61070
Spinal Cord
   Diagnostic .62270
   Drain Fluid .62272
   Lumbar 62270
Tracheal
   Aspiration and/or Injection 31612

Puncture Aspiration
Abscess
   Skin 10160
Bulla 10160
Cyst
   Breast 19000-19001
   Skin 10160
Hematoma 10160

Puncturing
See Puncture

Pure-Tone Audiometry
See Audiometry, Pure Tone

Pustules
Removal 10040

Putti-Platt Procedure 23450

PUVA
See Dermatology; Photochemotherapy;
Ultraviolet Light Therapy

Pyelogram
See Urography, Intravenous; Urography,
Retrograde

Pyelography 74400, 74425
Injection 50394

Pyelolithotomy 50130
Anatrophic 50075
Coagulum 50130

Pyeloplasty 50400-50405, 50544
Repair
   Horseshoe Kidney 50540
Secondary 50405

Pyeloscopy
with Cystourethroscopy 52351
   Biopsy 52354
   Destruction 52354
   Lithotripsy .52353
   Removal
     Calculus 52352
   Tumor Excision 52355

Pyelostogram 50394

Pyelostolithotomy
Percutaneous 50080-50081

Pyelostomy 50125, 50400-50405
Change Tube 50398

Pyelotomy
Complicated 50135
Endoscopic 50570
Exploration 50120
with Drainage .50125
with Removal Calculus 50130

Pyeloureterogram
Antegrade 50394

Pyeloureteroplasty
See Pyeloplasty

Pyloric Sphincter
Incision 43520
Reconstruction .43800

Pyloromyotomy 43520
with Gastrectomy 43639

Pyloroplasty 43800
with Gastrectomy 43639
with Vagotomy .43640

Pyothorax
See Abscess, Thorax

Pyridoxal Phosphate 84207

Pyrophosphate, Adenosine
See Adenosine Diphosphate

Pyrophosphorylase, Udp Galactose
See Galactose-1-Phosphate, Uridyl Transferase

Pyruvate 84210-84220

P & P
See Proconvertin

P B Antibodies
See Antibody, Heterophile

Q

Quadriceps Repair 27430

Quick Test
See Prothrombin Time

Quinidine
Assay 80194

Quinine 84228

Q Fever 86000, 86638

Q Fever ab
See Antibody, Coxiella Burnetii

R

Rabies Vaccine
See Vaccines

Rachicentesis
See Spinal Tap

Radial Arteries
See Artery, Radial

Radial Head, Subluxation
See Nursemaid Elbow

Radial Keratotomy 65771

Radiation
See Irradiation

Radiation, X
See X-Ray

Radiation Physics
Consultation 77336-77370
Unlisted Services and Procedures 77399

Radiation Therapy 77280-77295
CAT Scan Guidance 76370
Consultation
    Radiation Physics 77336-77370
Dose Plan 77300, 77305-77331
    Brachytherapy 77326-77328
    Intensity Modulation 77301
    Teletherapy 77305-77321
Field Set-up 77280-77295
Planning 77261-77263, 77299
Special 77470
Stereotactic 77432
Treatment Delivery
    Intensity Modulation 77418
    Proton Beam 77520-77525
    Single .77402-77406
    Superficial 77401
    Three or More Areas 77412-77416
    Two Areas 77407-77411
    Weekly 77427

Treatment Device 77332-77334
Treatment Management
    One or Two Fractions Only 77431
    Unlisted Services and Procedures 77499
    Weekly 77427

Radical Excision of Lymph Nodes
See Excision, Lymph Nodes, Radical

Radical Mastectomies, Modified
See Mastectomy, Modified Radical

Radical Neck Dissection
Laryngectomy 31365-31368
Pharyngolaryngectomy 31390-31395
with Auditory Canal Surgery 69155
with Thyroidectomy 60254
with Tongue Excision 41135, 41145,
                                    41153-41155

Radical Resection
See Resection, Radical
Abdomen 51597
Acetabulum 27076
Ankle 27615
Arm, Lower 25077
Calcaneus 27647
Elbow
    Capsule, Soft Tissue, Bone
        with Contracture Release 24149
Face 21015
Fibula 27646
Finger 26117
Foot 28046
Forearm 25077
Hand 26115
Hip
    Soft Tissue .27049
    Tumor or Infection 27075-27076
Humerus 23220-23222
Innominate 27077
Ischial .27078-27079
Knee 27329
Leg
    Lower 27615
    Upper 27329
Metacarpal 26250-26255
Metatarsal 28173
Mouth
    with Tongue Excision 41150, 41155
Ovarian Tumor
    Bilateral Salpingo-Oophorectomy-
    Omentectomy 58950-58954
    with Radical Dissection for
    Debulking 58952-58954
    with Total Abdominal Hysterectomy . .58951,
                                    58953-58954
Pelvis
    Soft Tissue .27049
Peritoneal Tumor
    Bilateral Salpingo-Oophorectomy-
    Omentectomy 58952-58954
    with Radical Dissection for
    Debulking 58952-58954
Phalanges
    Finger 26260-26262
    Toe 28175
Radius 25170
Scalp 21015

Scapula 23210
Shoulder 23077
Sternum 21630-21632
Talus
    Tumor 27647
Tarsal 28171
Tibia 27645
Tonsil .42842-42845
Tumor
    Back/Flank .21935
    Femur 27365
    Knee 27329, 27365
    Leg, Upper .27329
    Neck 21557
    Thorax 21557
Ulna 25170
Wrist 25077

Radical Vaginal Hysterectomy
See Hysterectomy, Vaginal, Radical

Radical Vulvectomy
See Vulvectomy, Radical

Radio-Cobalt B12 Schilling Test
See Vitamin, B12, Absorption Study

**Radioactive Colloid
Therapy** 79200-79300

Radioactive Substance
Insertion
    Kidney 50578
    Prostate 55860
    Ureteral Endoscopic 50978
    Urethral Endoscopic 50959

Radiocarpal Joint
Arthrotomy 25040
Dislocation
    Closed Treatment 25660

Radiocinematographies
See Cineradiography

Radioelement
Application 77761-77778
    Surface 77789
    with Ultrasound 76965
Handling 77790
Infusion 77750

Radioelement Substance
Catheterization 55859
Catheter Placement
    Bronchus 31643

Radiography
See Radiology, Diagnostic; X-Ray

Radioimmunosorbent Test
See Gammaglobulin, Blood

Radioisotope Brachytherapy
See Brachytherapy

Radioisotope Scan
See Nuclear Medicine

Radiological Marker
Preoperative Placement
    Excision of Breast Lesion 19125-19126

Radiology

Diagnostic
    Unlisted Services and Procedures 76499
Examination 70030
    Stress Views 76006
Therapeutic
    See Specific Procedure
    Field Set-up 77280-77290
    Planning 77261-77263, 77299
    Port Film 77417

Radionuclide CAT Scan
See Emission Computerized Tomography

Radionuclide Imaging
See Nuclear Medicine

Radionuclide Therapy
Intra-articular 79440
Intravascular 79420
Leukemia 79100
Other 79400
Polycythemia Vera 79100
Thyroid Gland 79000-79035
Unlisted Services and Procedures 79999

Radionuclide Tomography, Single-Photon Emission-Computed
See SPECT

Radiopharmaceutical Therapy
Heart 79440
Intravascular 79420
Leukemia 79100
Other 79400
Polycythemia Vera 79100
Thyroid Gland 79020-79035
Unlisted Services and Procedures 79999

Radiotherapeutic
See Radiation Therapy

Radiotherapies
See Irradiation

Radiotherapy, Surface
See Application, Radioelement, Surface

Radioulnar Joint
Arthrodesis
    with Resection of Ulna 25830
Dislocation
    Closed Treatment 25675
    Open Treatment 25676
    Percutaneous Fixation 25671

Radius
See Arm, Lower; Elbow; Ulna
Arthroplasty 24365
    with Implant 24366, 25441
Craterization 24145, 25151
Cyst
    Excision 24125-24126, 25120-25126
Diaphysectomy 24145, 25151
Dislocation
    Partial 24640
    Subluxate 24640
    with Fracture
        Closed Treatment 24620
        Open Treatment 24635

Excision 24130, 24136, 24145, 24152-24153
    Epiphyseal Bar 20150
    Partial 25145
    Styloid Process 25230
Fracture 25605
    Closed Treatment 25500-25505, 25520,
                   25600-25605
    without Manipulation 25600
    with Manipulation 25605
    Distal 25600-25611
        Open Treatment 25620
    Head/Neck
        Closed Treatment 24650-24655
        Open Treatment 24665-24666
    Open Treatment 25515, 25525-25526,
                   25574
    Percutaneous Fixation 25611
    Shaft 25500-25526
        Open Treatment 25574
    with Ulna 25560-25565
        Open Treatment 25575
Implant
    Removal 24164
Incision and Drainage 25035
Osteomyelitis 24136, 24145
Osteoplasty 25390-25393
Prophylactic Treatment 25490, 25492
Repair
    Epiphyseal Arrest 25450-25455
    Epiphyseal Separation
        Closed 25600
        Closed with Manipulation 25605
        Open Treatment 25620
        Percutaneous Fixation 25611
    Malunion or Nonunion 25400, 25415
    Osteotomy 25350-25355, 25370-25375
        and Ulna 25365
    with Graft 25405, 25420-25426
Saucerization 24145, 25151
Sequestrectomy 24136, 25145
Tumor
    Cyst 24120
    Excision ..24125-24126, 25120-25126, 25170

Ramstedt Operation
See Pyloromyotomy

Ramus Anterior, Nervus Thoracicus
See Intercostal Nerve

Range of Motion Test
Extremities or Trunk 95851
Eye 92018-92019
Hand 95852

Rapid Heart Rate
See Tachycardia

Rapid Plasma Reagin Test 86592-86593

Rapid Test for Infection 86308, 86403-86406
Monospot Test 86308

Rapoport Test 52005

Raskind Procedure 33735-33737

Rathke Pouch Tumor
See Craniopharyngioma

Rat Typhus
See Murine Typhus

Rays, Roentgen
See X-Ray

Raz Procedure 51845
See Repair, Bladder, Neck

RBC
See Red Blood Cell (RBC)

RBC ab
See Antibody, Red Blood Cell

Reaction
Lip
    without Reconstruction 40530

Reaction, Polymerase Chain
See Polymerase Chain Reaction

Realignment
Femur
    with Osteotomy 27454
Knee
    Extensor 27422

Receptor
See CD4; Estrogen, Receptor; FC Receptor; Progesterone Receptors

Receptor Assay
Hormone 84233-84235
Non Hormone 84238

Recession
Gastrocnemius
    Leg, Lower 27687

Reconstruction
See Revision
Acetabulum 27120-27122
Anal
    Congenital Absence 46730-46740
    Fistula 46742
    Graft 46753
    Sphincter 46750-46751, 46760-46762
    with Implant 46762
Ankle 27700-27703
Apical-Aortic Conduit 33404
Atrial 33253
Auditory Canal, External 69310-69320
Bile Duct
    Anastomosis 47800
Bladder
    and Urethra 51800-51820
    from Colon 50810
    from Intestines 50820, 51960
Breast 19357-19369
    Augmentation 19324-19325
    Mammoplasty 19318-19325
    Nipple 19350-19355
    Revision 19380
    Transverse Rectus Abdominis Myocutaneous
        Flap 19367-19369
    with Free Flap 19364
    with Latissimus Dorsi Flap 19361
    with Other Techniques 19366
    with Tissue Expander 19357

Bronchi 32501
   Graft Repair 31770
   Stenosis 31775
Canthus 67950
Carpal 25443
Carpal Bone 25394, 25430
Cheekbone 21270
Chest Wall
   Omental Flap 49905
   Trauma 32820
Cleft Palate 42200-42225
Conduit
   Apical-Aortic 33404
Conjunctiva 68320-68335
   with Flap
      Bridge or Partial 68360
      Total 68362
Cranial Bone
   Extracranial 21181-21184
Ear, Middle
   Tympanoplasty without
   Mastoidectomy 69631
      with Ossicular Chain
      Reconstruction 69632-69633
   Tympanoplasty with Antrotomy or
   Mastoidotomy
      with Ossicular Chain
      Reconstruction 69636-69637
   Tympanoplasty with Mastoidectomy . .69641
      Radical or Complete 69644-69645
      with Intact or Reconstructed
      Wall 69643-69644
      with Ossicular Chain
      Reconstruction 69642
Elbow 24360
   Total Replacement 24363
   with Implant 24361-24362
Esophagus 43300, 43310, 43313
   Creation
      Stoma 43350-43352
   Esophagostomy 43350
   Fistula 43305, 43312, 43314
   Gastrointestinal 43360-43361
Eyelid
   Canthus 67950
   Second Stage 67975
   Total 67973-67975
   Total Eyelid
      Lower, One Stage 67973
      Upper, One State 67974
   Transfer Tarsoconjunctival Flap from
   Opposing Eyelid 67971
Facial Bones
   Secondary 21275
Fallopian Tube
   See Repair
Femur
   Lengthening 27466-27468
   Shortening 27465, 27468
Fibula
   Lengthening 27715
Finger
   Polydactylous 26587
Foot
   Cleft 28360
Forehead 21172-21180, 21182-21184
Glenoid Fossa 21255

Gums
   Alveolus 41874
   Gingiva 41872
Hand
   Tendon Pulley 26500-26504
   Toe to Finger Transfer 26551-26556
Heart
   Atrial 33253
   Atrial Septum 33735-33737
   Pulmonary Artery Shunt 33924
   Vena Cava 34502
Hip
   Replacement 27130-27132
   Secondary 27134-27138
Hip Joint
   with Prosthesis 27125
Interphalangeal Joint 26535-26536
   Collateral Ligament 26545
Intestines, Small
   Anastomosis 44130
Knee 27437-27438
   Femur 27442-27443, 27446
   Ligament 27427-27429
   Replacement 27447
   Revision 27486-27487
   Tibia 27440-27443, 27446
   with Prosthesis 27438, 27445
Kneecap
   Instability 27420-27424
Larynx
   Burns 31588
   Cricoid Split 31587
   Other 31588
   Stenosis 31582
   Web 31580
Lip 40525-40527, 40761
Lunate 25444
Malar Augmentation
   Prosthetic Material 21270
   with Bone Graft 21210
Mandible
   with Implant . . .21244-21246, 21248-21249
Mandibular Condyle 21247
Mandibular Rami
   without Bone Graft 21193
   without Internal Rigid Fixation 21195
   with Bone Graft 21194
   with Internal Rigid Fixation 21196
Maxilla
   with Implant . . .21245-21246, 21248-21249
Metacarpophalangeal Joint 26530-26531
Midface
   Forehead Advancement 21159-21160
   without Bone Graft 21141-21143
   with Bone Graft 21145-21160, 21188
Mouth 40840-40845
Nail Bed 11762
Nasoethmoid Complex 21182-21184
Navicular 25443
Nose
   Cleft Lip/Cleft Palate 30460-30462
   Dermatoplasty 30620
   Primary 30400-30420
   Secondary 30430-30450
   Septum 30520
Orbit 21256
Orbital Rim 21172-21180

Orbital Rims 21182-21184
Orbital Walls 21182-21184
Orbitocraniofacial
   Secondary Revision 21275
Orbit Area
   Secondary 21275
Orbit with Bone Grafting 21182-21184
Oviduct
   Fimbrioplasty 58760
Palate
   Cleft Palate 42200-42225
   Lengthening 42226-42227
Parotid Duct
   Diversion 42507-42510
Patella 27437-27438
   Instability 27420-27424
Penis
   Angulation 54360
   Chordee 54300-54304
   Complications 54340-54348
   Epispadias 54380-54390
   Hypospadias 54332, 54352
      One Stage Distal with
      Urethroplasty 54324-54328
      One Stage Perineal 54336
Periorbital Region
   Osteotomy with Graft 21267-21268
Pharynx 42950
Pyloric Sphincter 43800
Radius 24365, 25390-25393, 25441
   Arthroplasty
      with Implant 24366
Shoulder Joint
   with Implant 23470-23472
Skull 21172-21180
   Defect 62140-62141, 62145
Sternum 21740
Stomach
   for Obesity 43846-43848
   Gastric Bypass 43846
   Roux-En-Y 43846
   with Duodenum 43810, 43850-43855,
                            43865
   with Jejunum 43820-43825, 43860
Superior-Lateral Orbital Rim
and Forehead 21172-21175
Supraorbital Rim and Forehead 21179-21180
Symblepharon 68335
Temporomandibular Joint
   Arthroplasty 21240-21243
Throat 42950
Thumb
   from Finger 26550
   Opponensplasty 26490-26496
Tibia
   Lengthening 27715
   Tubercle 27418
Toe
   Angle Deformity 28313
   Extra Toes 28344
   Hammertoe 28285-28286
   Macrodactyly 28340-28341
   Polydactylous 26587
   Syndactyly 28345
   Webbed Toe 28345
Tongue
   Frenum 41520

Trachea
Carina 31766
Cervical 31750
Fistula 31755
Intrathoracic 31760
Trapezium 25445
Tympanic Membrane 69620
Ulna 25390-25393, 25442
Radioulnar .25337
Ureter 50700
with Intestines 50840
Urethra 53410-53440, 53445
Complications 54340-54348
Hypospadias
One Stage Distal with Meatal
Advancement 54322
One Stage Distal with
Urethroplasty 54324-54328
Suture to Bladder 51840-51841
Urethroplasty for Second
Stage 54308-54316
Urethroplasty for Third Stage 54318
Uterus 58540
Vas Deferens
See Vasovasorrhaphy
Vena Cava 34502
with Resection 37799
Wound Repair 13100-13160
Wrist 25332
Capsulectomy 25320
Capsulorrhaphy 25320
Realign 25335
Zygomatic Arch 21255

Rectal Bleeding
See Hemorrhage, Rectum

Rectal Prolapse
See Procidentia, Rectum

Rectal Sphincter
Dilation 45910

Rectocele
Repair 45560

Rectopexy
See Proctopexy

Rectoplasty
See Proctoplasty

Rectorrhaphy
See Rectum, Suture

Rectovaginal Fistula
See Fistula, Rectovaginal

Rectovaginal Hernia
See Rectocele

Rectum
See Anus
Abscess
Incision and Drainage 45005-45020,
46040, 46060
Biopsy 45100
Dilation
Endoscopy .45303

Endoscopy
Destruction
Tumor 45320
Dilation 45303
Exploration .45300
Hemorrhage 45317
Removal
Foreign Body 45307
Polyp 45308-45315
Tumor 45308-45315
Volvulus .45321
Excision
Partial 45111, 45113-45116, 45123
Total 45110, 45112, 45119-45120
with Colon 45121
Exploration
Endoscopic 45300
Hemorrhage
Endoscopic 45317
Injection
Sclerosing Solution 45520
Lesion
Excision 45108
Manometry .91122
Prolapse
Excision 45130-45135
Pulsed Irrigation
Fecal Impaction 91123
Removal
Fecal Impaction 45915
by Pulsed Irrigation 91123
Foreign Body 45307, 45915
Repair
Fistula 45800-45825
Injury 45562-45563
Prolapse 45505-45541, 45900
Rectocele .45560
Stenosis 45500
with Sigmoid Excision 45550
Stricture
Excision 45150
Suture
Fistula 45800-45825
Prolapse 45540-45541
Tumor
Destruction 45190, 45320, 46937-46938
Excision 45160-45170
Unlisted Services and Procedures 45999

Reductase, Glutathione
See Glutathione Reductase

Reductase, Lactic Cytochrome
See Lactic Dehydrogenase

Reduction
Forehead 21137-21139
Lung Volume 32491
Mammoplasty .19318
Masseter Muscle/Bone 21295-21296
Osteoplasty
Facial Bones 21209
Pregnancy
Multifetal .59866
Skull
Craniomegalic 62115-62117
Ventricular Septum
Non-surgical 0024T

Red Blood Cell (RBC)
Antibody 86850-86870
Pretreatment 86970-86972
Count 85041
Fragility
Mechanical 85547
Osmotic 85555-85557
Hematocrit 85014
Iron Utilization 78170
Morphology .85007
Platelet Estimation 85007
Sedimentation Rate
Automated 85652
Manual 85651
Sequestration 78140
Sickling 85660
Survival Test 78130-78135
Volume Determination 78120-78121

Red Blood Cell ab
See Antibody, Red Blood Cell

Reflex Test
Blink Reflex 95933
H-Reflex 95934-95936

Reflux Study 78262

Refraction .92015

Rehabilitation
Artery
Occlusive Disease 93668
Aural 92510
Cardiac 93797-93798

Rehabilitative
See Rehabilitation

Rehfuss Test
See Gastroenterology, Diagnostic, Stomach

Reichstein's Substance S
See Deoxycortisol

Reimplantation
Arteries
Carotid 35691, 35694-35695
Subclavian 35693-35695
Vertebral 35691-35693
Kidney 50380
Ovary 58825
Pulmonary Artery 33788
Ureter, to Bladder 50780-50785
Ureters 51565

Reinnervation
Larynx
Neuromuscular Pedicle 31590

Reinsch Test 83015

Reinsertion
Drug Delivery Implant 11983
Implantable Contraceptive Capsules 11977
Spinal Fixation Device 22849

Relative Density
See Specific Gravity

Release

Carpal Tunnel 64721
Elbow Contracture
    with Radical Release of Capsule 24149
Flexor Muscles
    Hip 27036
Muscle
    Knee 27422
Nerve .64702-64726
    Neurolytic 64727
Retina
    Encircling Material 67115
Spinal Cord 63200
Stapes 69650
Tarsal Tunnel 28035
Tendon 24332, 25295

Release-Inhibiting Hormone, Somatotropin

See Somatostatin

Removal

Balloon
    Intra-Aortic 33974
Balloon Assist Device
    Intra-Aortic 33968, 33971
Blood Clot
    Eye 65930
Blood Component
    Apheresis 36520-36521
Breast
    Capsules .19371
    Implants 19328-19330
    Modified Radical 19240
    Partial 19140-19162
    Radical 19200-19220
    Simple, Complete 19180
    Subcutaneous 19182
Calcareous Deposits
    Subdeltoid 23000
Calculi (Stone)
    Bile Duct 43264, 47420-47425
        Percutaneous 47554, 47630
    Bladder 51050, 52310-52318, 52352
    Gallbladder 47480
    Hepatic Duct 47400
    Kidney 50060-50081, 50130, 50561,
               50580, 52352
    Pancreas .48020
    Pancreatic Duct 43264
    Salivary Gland 42330-42340
    Ureter 50610-50630, 50961, 50980,
        51060-51065, 52320-52330, 52352
    Urethra 52310-52315, 52352
Cardiac Event Recorder 33284
Cast .29700-29715
Cataract
    with Replacement
        Extracapsular 66982, 66984
        Intracapsular 66983
        Not Associated with Concurrent 66983
Catheter
    Fractured .75961
    Peritoneum 49422
    Spinal Cord 62355
Cerclage
    Cervix 59871

Cerumen
    Auditory Canal, External 69210
Clot
    Pericardium 33020
        Endoscopic 32658
Comedones .10040
Contraceptive Capsules 11976-11977
Cranial Tongs 20665
Cyst 10040
Dacryolith
    Lacrimal Duct 68530
    Lacrimal Gland 68530
Defibrillator
    Heart 33244
        Pulse Generator Only 33241
        via Thoracotomy 33243
Drug Delivery Implant 11982-11983
Ear Wax
    Auditory Canal, External 69210
Electrode
    Brain 61535, 61880
    Heart 33238
    Nerve 64585
    Spinal Cord 63660
Embolus
    See Embolectomy
External Fixation System 20694
Eye
    Bone 67414, 67445
    Ocular Contents
        without Implant 65091
        with Implant 65093
    Orbital Contents Only 65110
    without Implant 65101
    with Bone 65112
    with Implant
        Muscles, Not Attached 65103
        Muscles Attached 65105
    with Muscle or Myocutaneous Flap . . .65114
Fallopian Tube
    Laparoscopy 58661
Fat
    Lipectomy 15876-15879
Fecal Impaction
    Rectum 45915
Fibrin Deposit 32150
Fixation Device 20670-20680
Foreign Bodies 65205-65265
    Anal 46608
    Ankle Joint 27610, 27620
    Arm
        Lower 25248
        Upper 24200-24201
    Auditory Canal, External 69200
        with Anesthesia 69205
    Bile Duct .43269
    Bladder 52310-52315
    Brain 61570
    Bronchi .31635
    Colon 44025, 44390, 45379
    Colon-Sigmoid 45332
    Conjunctival Embedded 65210
    Cornea
        without Slit Lamp 65220
        with Slit Lamp 65222
    Duodenum 44010
    Elbow 24000, 24101, 24200-24201

Esophagus 43020, 43045, 43215, 74235
External Eye .65205
Eyelid 67938
Finger 26075-26080
Foot .28190-28193
Gastrointestinal, Upper 43247
Gum 41805
Hand 26070
Hip 27033, 27086-27087
Hysteroscopy 58562
Interphalangeal Joint
    Toe 28024
Intertarsal Joint 28020
Intestines, Small 44020, 44363
Intraocular 65235
Kidney 50561, 50580
Knee Joint 27310, 27331, 27372
Lacrimal Duct 68530
Lacrimal Gland 68530
Larynx 31511, 31530-31531, 31577
Leg, Upper 27372
Lung 32151
Mandible 41806
Mediastinum 39000-39010
Metatarsophalangeal Joint 28022
Mouth 40804-40805
Muscle 20520-20525
Nose 30300
    Anesthesia 30310
    Lateral Rhinotomy 30320
Orbit 61334, 67413, 67430
    without Bone Flap 67413
    with Bone Flap 67430
Pancreatic Duct 43269
Patella
    See Patellectomy
Pelvis 27086-27087
Penile Tissue 54115
Penis 54115
Pericardium .33020
    Endoscopic 32658
Peritoneum .49085
Pharynx 42809
Pleura 32150-32151
    Endoscopic 32653
Posterior Segment
    Magnetic Extraction 65260
    Nonmagnetic Extraction 65265
Rectum 45307, 45915
Scrotum 55120
Shoulder 23040-23044
    Complicated 23332
    Deep 23331
    Subcutaneous 23330
Skin
    with Debridement 11010-11012
Stomach 43500
Subcutaneous Tissue 10120-10121
    with Debridement 11010-11012
Tarsometatarsal Joint 28020
Tendon Sheath 20520-20525
Toe 28022
Ureter 50961, 50980
Urethra 52310-52315
Uterus 58562
Vagina 57415
Wrist 25040, 25101, 25248

Foreign Body
  Elbow 24101
Hair
  Electrolysis 17380
Halo 20665
Hearing Aid
  Bone Conduction 69711
Hematoma
  Brain 61312-61315
Implantation 20670-20680
  Ankle 27704
  Contraceptive Capsules 11976-11977
  Elbow 24160
  Eye 67120-67121
  Finger 26320
  Hand 26320
  Radius 24164
  Wrist 25449
Infusion Pump
  Intraarterial 36262
  Intravenous 36532
  Spinal Cord 62365
Intra-Aortic Balloon 33974
  Assist Device 33968, 33971
Intrauterine Device (IUD) 58301
Keel
  Laryngoplasty 31580
Lacrimal Gland
  Partial 68505
  Total 68500
Lacrimal Sac
  Excision/(Optional) 68520
Laryngocele 31300
Leiomyomata 58551, 58561
Lens 66920-66940
Lens Material 66840-66852
Lesion
  Conjunctiva 68040
  Larynx 31512, 31578
Loose Body
  Ankle 27620
  Carpometacarpal Joint 26070
  Elbow 24101
  Interphalangeal Joint
    Toe 28024
  Intertarsal Joint 28020
  Knee Joint 27331
  Metatarsophalangeal Joint 28022
  Tarsometatarsal Joint 28020
  Toe 28022
  Wrist 25101
Lung
  Bronchoplasty 32501
  Completion Pneumonectomy 32488
  Cyst 32140
  Extrapleural 32445
  Single Lobe 32480
  Single Segment 32484
  Sleeve Lobectomy 32486
  Sleeve Pneumonectomy 32442
  Total Pneumonectomy 32440-32445
  Two Lobes 32482
  Volume Reduction 32491
  Wedge Resection 32500
Lymph Nodes
  Abdominal 38747
  Inguinofemoral 38760-38765
  Pelvic 38770

Retroperitoneal
  Transabdominal 38780
  Thoracic 38746
Mammary Implant 19328-19330
Mastoid
  Air Cells 69670
Milia, Multiple 10040
Nails 11730-11732, 11750-11752
Neurostimulators
  Pulse Generator 64595
  Receiver 64595
Ocular Implant 65175, 65920
Orbital Implant 67560
Ovaries
  Laparoscopy 58661
Pacemaker
  Heart 33233-33237
Patella, Complete 27424
Plate
  Skull 62142
Polyp
  Anal 46610, 46612
  Antrochoanal 31032
  Colon 44392, 45385
  Colon-Sigmoid 45333
  Endoscopy 44364-44365, 44394
  Esophagus 43217, 43250
  Gastrointestinal, Upper 43250-43251
  Rectum 45315
  Sphenoid Sinus 31051
Prosthesis
  Abdomen 49606
  Hip 27090-27091
  Knee 27488
  Penis 54406, 54410-54417
  Perineum 53442
  Skull 62142
  Urethral Sphincter 53446-53447
  Wrist 25250-25251
Pulse Generator
  Brain 61888
  Spinal Cord 63688
Pustules 10040
Receiver
  Brain 61888
  Spinal Cord 63688
Reservoir
  Spinal Cord 62365
Seton
  Anal 46030
Shoulder Joint
  Foreign or Loose Body 23107
Shunt
  Brain 62256-62258
  Heart 33924
  Peritoneum 49429
  Spinal Cord 63746
Skin Tags 11200-11201
Sling
  Vagina 57287
Spinal Instrumentation
  Anterior 22855
  Posterior Nonsegmental
    Harrington Rod 22850
  Posterior Segmental 22852
Stent
  Bile Duct 43269
  Pancreatic Duct 43269

Suture
  Anal 46754
  Anesthesia 15850-15851
Thrombus
  See Thrombectomy
Tissue Expanders
  Skin 11971
Transplant Kidney 50370
Tube
  Ear, Middle 69424
  Finger 26392, 26416
  Hand 26392, 26416
Tumor
  Temporal Bone 69970
Ureter
  Ligature 50940
Urethral Stent
  Bladder 52310-52315
  Urethra 52310-52315
Vein
  Perforation 37760
  Saphenous 37720-37735, 37780
  Secondary 37785
Venous Access Device 36535
Ventilating Tube
  Ear, Middle 69424
Ventricular Assist Device 33977-33978
  Intracorporeal 33980
Vitreous
  Anterior Approach 67005-67010
Wire
  Anal 46754

Renal Abscess
See Abscess, Kidney

Renal Arteries
See Artery, Renal

Renal Autotransplantation
See Autotransplantation, Renal

Renal Calculus
See Calculus, Removal, Kidney

Renal Cyst
See Cyst, Kidney

Renal Dialyses
See Hemodialysis

Renal Disease Services
See Dialysis

Renal Transplantation
See Kidney, Transplantation

Renin 80408, 80416, 84244
Peripheral Vein 80417

Renin-Converting Enzyme 82164

Reoperation
Carotid
  Thromboendarterectomy 35390
Coronary Artery Bypass
  Valve Procedure 33530
Distal Vessel Bypass 35700

Repair

See Revision
Abdomen 49900
    Hernia 49491-49525, 49565, 49570,
                      49582-49590
    Omphalocele 49600-49611
    Suture 49900
Abdominal Wall 15831
Anal
    Anomaly 46744-46748
    Fistula 46288, 46715-46716
    Stricture 46700-46705
Anastomosis
    Cyst 47716
Aneurysm
    Aorta 0001T-0002T, 33877, 34800-34804,
           34825-34832, 75952-75953
    Arteriovenous 36834
    Intracranial Artery 61697-61708
Ankle
    Ligament 27695-27698
    Tendon ...27612, 27650-27654, 27680-27687
Aorta 33320-33322, 33802-33803
    Coarctation 33840-33851
    Graft 33860-33877
    Sinus of Valsalva 33702-33720
Aortic Arch
    without Cardiopulmonary Bypass 33852
    with Cardiopulmonary Bypass 33853
Aortic Valve 33400-33403
    Obstruction
        Outflow Tract 33414
        Septic Hypertrophy 33416
        Stenosis 33415
Arm
    Lower 25260-25263, 25270
        Fasciotomy 24495
        Secondary 25265, 25272-25274
        Tendon 25290
        Tendon Sheath 25275
        Muscle 24341
        Tendon 24332, 24341, 25280, 25295,
                 25310-25316
    Upper
        Muscle Revision 24330-24331
        Muscle Transfer 24301, 24320
        Tendon Lengthening 24305
        Tendon Revision 24320
        Tendon Transfer 24301
        Tenotomy 24310
Arteriovenous Aneurysm 36834
Arteriovenous Fistula
    Abdomen 35182
        Acquired or Traumatic 35189
    Head 35180
        Acquired or Traumatic 35188
    Lower Extremity 35184
        Acquired or Traumatic 35190
    Neck 35180
        Acquired or Traumatic 35188
    Thorax 35182
        Acquired or Traumatic 35189
    Upper Extremity 35184
        Acquired or Traumatic 35190
Arteriovenous Malformation
    Intracranial 61680-61692
    Intracranial Artery 61705-61708

Spinal Artery 62294
Spinal Cord 63250-63252
Artery
    Angioplasty 75962-75968
    Aorta 35452, 35472
    Axillary 35458
    Brachiocephalic 35458, 35475
    Bypass Graft 35501-35571, 35601-35683,
              35691-35700
    Bypass In-Situ 35582-35587
    Bypass Venous Graft 33510-33516
    Femoral 35456, 35474
    Iliac 35454, 35473
    Occlusive Disease 35001, 35005-35021,
          35045-35081, 35091, 35102, 35111,
          35121, 35131, 35141, 35151, 35161
    Popliteal 35456, 35474
    Pulmonary 33690
    Renal 35450
    Renal or Visceral 35471
    Subclavian 35458
    Thromboendarterectomy 35301-35321,
              35341-35390
    Tibioperoneal 35459, 35470
    Viscera 35450, 35471
Arytenoid Cartilage 31400
Atrial Fibrillation 33253
Bile Duct 47701
    Cyst 47716
    with Intestines 47760, 47780-47785
    Wound 47900
Bladder
    Exstrophy 51940
    Fistula 44660-44661, 45800-45805,
              51880-51925
    Neck 51845
    Resection 52500
    Wound 51860-51865
Blepharoptosis
    Frontalis Muscle Technique
    with Fascial Sling 67902
Blood Vessel
    Abdomen 35221
        with Other Graft 35281
        with Vein Graft 35251
    Chest 35211-35216
        with Other Graft 35271-35276
        with Vein Graft 35241-35246
    Finger 35207
    Graft Defect 35870
    Hand 35207
    Kidney 50100
    Lower Extremity 35226
        with Other Graft 35286
        with Vein Graft 35256
    Neck 35201
        with Other Graft 35261
        with Vein Graft 35231
    Upper Extremity 35206
        with Other Graft 35266
        with Vein Graft 35236
Body Cast 29720
Brain
    Wound 61571
Breast
    Suspension 19316

Bronchi
    Fistula 32815
Brow Pyrosis 67900
Bunion 28290-28299
Bypass Graft 35901-35907
    Fistula 35870
Calcaneus
    Osteotomy 28300
Cannula 36860-36861
Carpal 25440
Carpal Bone 25431
Cervix
    Cerclage 57700
        Abdominal 59320-59325
    Suture 57720
Chest Wall 32905
    Closure 32810
    Fistula 32906
Chin
    Augmentation 21120, 21123
    Osteotomy 21121-21123
Clavicle
    Osteotomy 23480-23485
Cleft Hand 26580
Cleft Lip 40525-40527, 40700-40761
    Nasal Deformity 40700-40701,
              40720-40761
Cleft Palate
    See Cleft Palate Repair
Colon
    Fistula 44650-44661
    Hernia 44050
    Malrotation 44055
    Obstruction 44050
Cornea
    See Cornea, Repair
Coronary Chamber Fistula 33500-33501
Cyst
    Bartholin's Gland 56440
    Liver 47300
    Repair 47716
Diaphragm
    for Eventration 39545
    Hernia 39502-39541
    Laceration 39501
Ductus Arteriosus 33820-33824
Ear, Middle
    Oval Window Fistula 69666
    Round Window Fistula 69667
Elbow
    Fasciotomy 24350-24356
    Hemiepiphyseal Arrest 24470
    Ligament 24343-24346
    Muscle 24341
    Muscle Transfer 24301
    Tendon 24340-24342
        Each 24341
    Tendon Lengthening 24305
    Tendon Transfer 24301
    Tennis Elbow 24350-24356
Encephalocele 62121
Enterocele
    Hysterectomy 58270
Epididymis 54900-54901
Epispadias 54380-54390
Esophagus 43300, 43310, 43313
    Esophagogastrostomy 43320
    Esophagojejunostomy 43340-43341

Fistula . . .43305, 43312, 43314, 43420-43425
Fundoplasty 43324-43325
Muscle 43330-43331
Pre-existing Perforation 43405
Varices 43401
Wound 43410-43415
Eye
  Ciliary Body 66680
    Suture 66682
  Conjunctiva 65270-65273
    Wound 65270-65273
  Cornea 65275
    Astigmatism 65772-65775
    with Glue 65286
    Wound 65275-65285
  Fistula
    Lacrimal Gland 68770
  Iris
    Suture 66682
    with Ciliary Body 66680
  Lacrimal Duct
    Canaliculi 68700
  Lacrimal Punctum 68705
  Retina
    Detachment 67101-67112
  Sclera
    Reinforcement 67250-67255
    Staphyloma 66220-66225
    with Glue 65286
    with Graft 66225
    Wound 65286, 66250
  Strabismus
    Chemodenervation 67345
  Symblepharon
    Division 68340
    without Graft 68330
    with Graft 68335
  Trabeculae 65855
Eyebrow
  Ptosis 67900
Eyelashes
  Epilation
    by Forceps .67820
    by Other than Forceps 67825
  Incision of Lid Margin 67830
    with Free Mucous Membrane
    Graft 67835
Eyelid 21280-21282
  Ectropion
    Blepharoplasty 67916-67917
    Suture 67914
    Thermocauterization 67915
  Entropion
    Blepharoplasty 67923-67924
    Suture 67921-67924
    Thermocauterization 67922
  Excisional 67961-67966
  Ptosis
    Conjunctivo-Tarso-Muller's
    Muscle-Levator Resection 67908
    Frontalis Muscle Technique . .67901-67902
    Levator Resection 67903-67904
    Reduction of Overcorrection 67909
    Superior Rectus Technique 67906
  Retraction 67911
  Wound
    Suture 67930-67935

Eye Muscles
  Strabismus
    Adjustable Sutures 67335
    One Horizontal Muscle 67311
    One Vertical Muscle 67314
    Posterior Fixation Suture
    Technique 67334-67335
    Previous Surgery, Not Involving
    Extraocular Muscles 67331
    Release Extensive Scar Tissue 67343
    Superior Oblique Muscle 67318
    Two Horizontal Muscles 67312
    Two or More Vertical Muscles 67316
  Wound
    Extraocular Muscle 65290
Facial Bones 21208-21209
Facial Nerve
  Paralysis 15840-15845
  Suture
    Intratemporal, Lateral to Geniculate
    Ganglion 69740
    Intratemporal, Medial to Geniculate
    Ganglion 69745
Fallopian Tube .58752
  Anastomosis .58750
  Create Stoma 58770
Fascial Defect .50728
Femur 27470-27472
  Epiphysis 27475-27485, 27742
    Arrest 27185
    by Pinning .27176
    by Traction .27175
    Open Treatment 27177-27178
    Osteoplasty 27179
    Osteotomy .27181
  Muscle Transfer 27110
  Osteotomy 27140, 27151, 27450-27454
    Femoral Neck 27161
    with Fixation 27165
    with Open Reduction 27156
    with Graft .27170
Fibula
  Epiphysis 27477-27485, 27730-27742
  Osteotomy 27707-27712
Finger
  Claw Finger .26499
  Macrodactylia 26590
  Polydactylous 26587
  Syndactyly 26560-26562
  Tendon
    Extensor 26415-26434, 26445-26449
    Flexor 26356-26358, 26440-26442
    Joint Stabilization 26474
    PIP Joint 26471
  Toe Transfer 26551-26556
  Trigger 26055
  Volar Plate 26548
  Web Finger 26560-26562
Fistula
  Carotid-Cavernous 61710
  Mastoid 69700
  Rectovaginal 57308
Foot
  Fascia 28250
  Muscle 28250
  Tendon 28200-28226, 28238

Gallbladder
  with Gastroenterostomy 47741
  with Intestines 47720-47740
Great Arteries 33770-33781
Great Vessel 33320-33322
Hallux Valgus 28290-28299
Hamstring 27097
Hand
  Cleft Hand 26580
  Muscle 26591-26593
  Tendon
    Extensor 26410-26416, 26426-26428,
                       26433-26437
    Flexor 26350-26358, 26440
    Profundus 26370-26373
Hearing Aid
  Bone Conduction 69711
Heart
  Anomaly 33600-33617
  Aortic Sinus 33702-33722
  Atrial 33253
  Atrioventricular Canal 33660-33665
    Complete 33670
  Atrioventricular Valve 33660-33665
  Blood Vessel 33320-33322
  Cor Triatriatum 33732
  Fibrillation .33253
  Infundibular 33476-33478
  Mitral Valve 33420-33427
  Myocardium 33542
  Outflow Tract 33476-33478
  Postinfarction 33542-33545
  Prosthetic Valve 33670, 33852-33853
  Prosthetic Valve Dysfunction 33496
  Pulmonary Artery Shunt 33924
  Pulmonary Valve 33470-33474
  Septal Defect 33545, 33608-33610,
              33681-33688, 33692-33697
    Atrial and Ventricular 33647
    Atrium 33641
  Sinus of Valsalva 33702-33722
  Sinus Venosus 33645
  Tetralogy of Fallot 33692-33697
  Tricuspid Valve 33465
  Ventricle 33611-33612
    Obstruction 33619
  Ventricular Tunnel 33722
  Wound 33300-33305
Hepatic Duct
  with Intestines 47765, 47802
Hernia 50728
  Abdomen 49565, 49590
    Incisional 49560
  Epigastric 49570
    Incarcerated 49572
  Femoral 49550
    Incarcerated 49553
    Recurrent .49555
    Recurrent Incarcerated 49557
    Reducible Recurrent 49555
  Incisional
    Incarcerated 49561
    Recurrent Incarcerated 49566
  Inguinal 49491-49521
    Initial 49650
    Recurrent .49651
    Sliding 49525

Intestinal 44025-44050
Lumbar 49540
Lung 32800
Orchiopexy 54640
Reducible 49565, 49570
  Femoral 49550
  Incisional 49560
  Inguinal 49500, 49505
  Recurrent 49520
  Sliding 49525
  Spigelian 49590
  Umbilical 49580, 49585
    Incarcerated 49582, 49587
    Reducible 49580
  with Spermatic Cord 54640
Hip
  Muscle Transfer 27100-27105, 27111
  Osteotomy 27146-27156
  Tendon 27097
Humerus 24420-24430
  Osteotomy 24400-24410
  with Graft 24435
Ileostomy
  See Ileostomy, Repair
Interphalangeal Joint
  Volar Plate 26548
Intestine
  Large
    Ulcer 44605
    Wound 44605
Intestines
  Enterocele
    Abdominal Approach 57270
    Vaginal Approach 57268
  Large
    Closure Enterostomy 44620-44626
    Diverticula 44605
    Obstruction 44615
Intestines, Small
  Closure Enterostomy 44620-44626
  Diverticula 44602-44603
  Fistula 44640-44661
  Hernia 44050
  Malrotation 44055
  Obstruction 44025-44050
  Ulcer 44602-44603
  Wound 44602-44603
Introitus
  Vagina 56800
Iris, Ciliary Body 66680
Jejunum
  Free Transfer
    with Microvascular Anastomosis ...43496
Kidney
  Fistula 50520-50526
  Horseshoe 50540
  Renal Pelvis 50400-50405
  Wound 50500
Knee
  Cartilage 27403
  Instability 27420
  Ligament 27405-27409
    Collateral 27405
    Collateral and Cruciate 27409
    Cruciate 27407-27409
  Meniscus 27403
  Tendon 27380-27381

Larynx
  Fracture 31584-31586
  Reinnervation
    Neuromuscular Pedicle 31590
Leg
  Lower
    Fascia 27656
    Tendon 27658-27692
  Upper
    Muscle 27385-27386, 27400, 27430
    Tendon 27393-27400
Ligament
  See Ligament, Repair
Lip 40650-40654
  Cleft Lip 40700-40761
  Fistula 42260
Liver
  Abscess 47300
  Cyst 47300
  Wound 47350-47361
Lung
  Hernia 32800
  Pneumolysis 32940
  Tear 32110
Mastoidectomy
  Complete 69601
  Modified Radical 69602
  Radical 69603
  with Apicectomy 69605
  with Tympanoplasty 69604
Maxilla
  Osteotomy 21206
Mesentery 44850
Metacarpal
  Lengthening 26568
  Nonunion 26546
  Osteotomy 26565
Metacarpophalangeal Joint
  Capsulodesis 26516-26518
  Collateral Ligament 26540-26542
  Fusion 26516-26518
Metatarsal 28322
  Osteotomy 28306-28309
Microsurgery 69990
Mitral Valve 33420-33427
Mouth
  Laceration 40830-40831
  Vestibule of 40830-40845
Musculotendinous Cuff 23410-23412
Nail Bed 11760
Nasal Deformity
  Cleft Lip 40700-40761
Nasal Septum 30630
Navicular 25440
Neck Muscles
  Scalenus Anticus 21700-21705
  Sternocleidomastoid ...21720-21725
Nerve 64876
  Graft 64885-64907
  Microrepair 69990
  Suture 64831-64876
Nose
  Adhesions 30560
  Fistula 30580-30600, 42260
  Rhinophyma 30120
  Septum 30540-30545, 30630
  Synechia 30560
  Vestibular Stenosis 30465

Omphalocele 49600-49611
Osteotomy
  Femoral Neck 27161
  Radius
    and Ulna 25365
  Ulna
    and Radius 25365
  Vertebra
    Additional Segment ...22216, 22226
    Cervical 22210, 22220
    Lumbar 22214, 22224
    Thoracic 22212, 22222
Oviduct 58752
  Create Stoma 58770
Pacemaker
  Heart
    Electrode 33218-33220
Palate
  Laceration 42180-42182
  Vomer Flap 42235
Pancreas
  Cyst 48500
  Pseudocyst 48510-48511
    Percutaneous 48511
Paravaginal Defect 57284
Pectus Carinatum 21740
Pectus Excavatum 21740
Pelvis
  Osteotomy 27158
  Tendon 27098
Penis
  Fistulization 54435
  Injury 54440
  Priapism 54420-54435
  Shunt 54420-54430
Perineum 56810
Periorbital Region
  Osteotomy 21260-21263
Phalanx
  Finger
    Lengthening 26568
    Osteotomy 26567
    Nonunion 26546
  Toe
    Osteotomy 28310-28312
Pharynx
  with Esophagus 42953
Pleura 32215
Prosthesis
  Penis 54408
Pulmonary Artery 33917-33920
  Reimplantation 33788
Pulmonary Valve 33470-33474
Quadriceps
  See Quadriceps, Repair
Radius
  Epiphyseal 25450-25455
  Malunion or Nonunion ...25400, 25415
  Osteotomy 25350-25355, 25370-25375
  with Graft 25405, 25420-25426
Rectocele
  See Rectocele, Repair
Rectovaginal Fistula 57308
Rectum
  Fistula 45800-45825
  Injury 45562-45563
  Prolapse 45505-45541, 45900

Rectocele 45560
Stenosis .45500
with Sigmoid Excision 45550
Retinal Detachment with Diathermy
See Diathermy, Retinal Detachment, Repair
Rotator Cuff
See Rotator Cuff, Repair
Salivary Duct 42500-42505
Fistula .42600
Scapula
Fixation .23400
Scapulopexy 23400
Sclera
See Sclera, Repair
Scrotum 55175-55180
Septal Defect 33813-33814
Shoulder
Capsule 23450-23466
Cuff .23410-23412
Ligament Release 23415
Muscle Transfer 23395-23397
Musculotendinous Rotator
Cuff .23415-23420
Tendon 23410-23412, 23430-23440
Tenomyotomy 23405-23406
Simple, Integumentary System
See Integumentary System, Repair, Simple
Sinus
Ethmoid
Cerebrospinal Fluid Leak 31290
Sphenoid
Cerebrospinal Fluid Leak 31291
Sinus of Valsalva 33702-33722
Skin
Wound
Complex 13100-13160
Intermediate 12031-12057
Simple 12020-12021
Skull
Cerebrospinal Fluid Leak 62100
Encephalocele 62120
Spica Cast 29720
Spinal Cord 63700
Cerebrospinal Fluid Leak 63707-63709
Meningocele 63700-63702
Myelomeningocele 63704-63706
Spinal Meningocele
See Meningocele, Repair
Spine
Osteotomy 22210-22226
Spleen 38115
Stomach
Esophagogastrostomy 43320
Fistula 43880
Fundoplasty 43324-43325
Laceration 43501-43502
Stoma 43870
Ulcer 43501
Talus
Osteotomy 28302
Tarsal 28320
Osteotomy 28304-28305
Testis
Injury 54670
Suspension 54620-54640
Torsion 54600

Throat
Pharyngoesophageal 42953
Wound .42900
Thumb
Muscle 26508
Tendon .26510
Tibia 27720-27725
Epiphysis 27477-27485, 27730-27742
Osteotomy 27455-27457, 27705,
27709-27712
Pseudoarthrosis 27727
Toe
Bunion 28290-28299
Muscle .28240
Tendon .28240
Webbing 28280, 28345
Toes
Macrodactylia 26590
Polydactylous 26587
Tongue .41250-41252
Fixation .41500
Laceration 41250-41252
Mechanical 41500
Suture .41510
Trachea
Fistula 31755
without Plastic Repair 31820
with Plastic Repair 31825
Stenosis 31780-31781
Stoma 31613-31614
Scar .31830
without Plastic Repair 31820
with Plastic Repair 31825
Wound
Cervical 31800
Intrathoracic 31805
Tricuspid Valve 33463-33465
Truncus Arteriosus
Rastelli Type 33786
Tunica Vaginalis
Hydrocele 55060
Tympanic Membrane 69450, 69610
Ulna
Epiphyseal 25450-25455
Malunion or Nonunion 25400, 25415
Osteotomy 25360, 25370-25375,
25425-25426
with Graft 25405, 25420
Umbilicus
Omphalocele 49600-49611
Ureter
Anastomosis 50740-50825
Continent Diversion 50825
Deligation 50940
Fistula 50920-50930
Lysis Adhesions 50715-50725
Suture .50900
Urinary Undiversion 50830
Ureterocele .51535
Urethra
Artificial Sphincter 53449
Diverticulum 53240, 53400-53405
Fistula . . .45820-45825, 53400-53405, 53520
Stoma .53520
Stricture 53400-53405
Urethrocele 57230
Wound 53502-53515

Urethral Sphincter 57220
Urinary Incontinence 53431-53440, 57284
Uterus
Fistula 51920-51925
Rupture 58520, 59350
Suspension 58400-58410
Vagina
Anterior
See Colporrhaphy, Anterior
Cystocele 57240, 57260
Enterocele 57265
Fistula 46715-46716, 51900
Rectovaginal 57300-57307
Transvesical and Vaginal Approach . .57330
Urethrovaginal 57310-57311
Vesicovaginal 57320-57330
Hysterectomy 58267
Incontinence 57284, 57288
Pereyra Procedure 57289
Postpartum 59300
Prolapse 57282-57284
Rectocele 57250-57260
Suspension 57280, 57284
Wound 57200-57210
Vaginal Wall Prolapse
See Colporrhaphy
Vas Deferens
Suture .55400
Vein
Angioplasty 35460, 35476, 75978
Femoral 34501
Graft 34520
Pulmonary 33730
Transposition 34510
Vulva
Postpartum 59300
Wound
Complex 13100-13160
Intermediate 12031-12057
Simple 12001-12021
Wound Dehiscence
Complex 13160
Simple 12020-12021
Wrist 25260-25263, 25270, 25447
Bone 25440
Carpal Bone 25431
Cartilage 25107
Removal
Implant 25449
Secondary 25265, 25272-25274
Tendon 25280-25316
Tendon Sheath 25275
Total Replacement 25446

Repeat Surgeries
See Reoperation

Replacement
Aortic Valve 33405-33413
Arthroplasties, Hip
See Arthroplasty, Hip
Cerebrospinal Fluid Shunt . . .62194, 62225-62230
Contact Lens
See Contact Lens Services
Elbow
Total 24363
Electrode
Heart 33210-33211, 33216-33217

Eye
  Drug Delivery System 67121
Gastrostomy Tube 43760
Hearing Aid
  Bone Conduction 69710
Hip 27130-27132
  Revision 27134-27138
Implant
  Bone
    for External Speech Processor/Cochlear
    Stimulator 69717-69718
Knee
  Total 27447
Mitral Valve 33430
Nephrostomy Tube
  See Nephrostomy, Change Tube
Nerve 64726
Ossicles
  with Prosthesis 69633, 69637
Ossicular Replacement
  See TORP (Total Ossicular Replacement
  Prosthesis)
Pacemaker 33206-33208
  Catheter 33210
  Electrode 33210-33211, 33216-33217
Pacing Cardioverter-Defibrillator
  Leads 33243-33244
  Pulse Generator Only 33241
Penile
  Prosthesis 54410-54411, 54416-54417
Prosthesis
  Skull 62143
  Urethral Sphincter 53448
Pulmonary Valve 33475
Skull Plate 62143
Spinal Cord
  Reservoir 62360
Tissue Expanders
  Skin 11970
Total Replacement
  See Hip, Total Replacement
Tricuspid Valve 33465
Ureter
  with Intestines 50840

Replantation
Arm, Upper 20802
Digit 20816-20822
Foot 20838
Forearm 20805
Hand 20808
Thumb 20824-20827

Report Preparation
Extended, Medical 99080
Psychiatric 90889

Reposition
Toe to Hand 26551-26556

Repositioning
Central Venous Catheter 36493
Electrode
  Heart 33216-33217
Gastrostomy Tube 43761
Heart
  Defibrillator
    Leads 33216, 33249

Intraocular Lens 66825
Tricuspid Valve 33468

Reprogramming
Shunt
  Brain 62252

Reptilase Test 85635

Reptilase Time
See Thrombin Time

Resection
Aortic Valve
  Stenosis 33415
Bladder Diverticulum 52305
Bladder Neck
  Transurethral 52500
Brain Lobe
  See Lobectomy, Brain
Diaphragm 39560-39561
Endaural
  See Ear, Inner, Excision
Humeral Head 23195
Intestines, Small
  Laparoscopic 44202-44203
Lung 32520-32525
Mouth
  with Tongue Excision 41153
Myocardium
  Aneurysm .33542
  Septal Defect 33545
Nasal Septum Submucous
  See Nasal Septum, Submucous Resection
Nose
  Septum 30520
Ovary, Wedge
  See Overy, Wedge Resection
Palate 42120
Phalangeal Head
  Toe 28153
Prostate Transurethral
  See Prostatectomy, Transurethral
Radical
  Arm, Upper 24077
  Elbow 24077
    with Contracture Release 24149
  Foot 28046
  Humerus 24150-24151
  Radius 24152-24153
  Tumor
    Ankle 27615
    Calcaneus or Talus 27647
    Clavicle 23200
    Femur .27365
    Fibula .27646
    Humerus 23220
    Humerus with Autograft 23221
    Humerus with Prosthetic
    Replacement 23222
    Knee 27329, 27365
    Leg, Lower 27615
    Leg, Upper 27329
    Metatarsal 28173
    Phalanx, Toe 28175
    Scapula 23210
    Tarsal .28171
    Tibia 27645
  Ribs 32900

Synovial Membrane
  See Synovectomy
Temporal Bone 69535
Ulna
  Arthrosedis
    Radioulnar Joint 25830
Ureterocele
  Ectopic 52301
  Orthotopic 52300
Vena Cava
  with Reconstruction 37799

Resonance Spectroscopy,
Magnetic
See Magnetic Resonance Spectroscopy

Respiration, Positive-Pressure
See Pressure Breathing, Positive

Respiratory Pattern Recording
Preventive
  Infant 94772

Respiratory Syncytial Virus
Antibody 86756
Antigen Detection
  Direct Fluorescence 87280
  Enzyme Immunoassay 87420

Respiratory Syncytial Virus
Immune Globulin
See Immune Globulins
Antigen Detection
  See Immune Globulins, Respiratory Syncytial
  Virus

Response, Auditory Evoked
See Auditory Evoked Potentials

Rest Home Visit
See Domiciliary Services

Resuscitation
Cardiac
  See Cardiac Massage
Cardio-Pulmonary
  See Cardio-Pulmonary Resuscitation
Newborn 99440

Reticulocyte
Count 85044-85045

Retina
Incision
  Encircling Material 67115
Lesion
  Extensive
    Destruction 67227-67228
  Localized
    Destruction 0017T, 67208-67218
Repair
  Detachment
    by Scleral Buckling 67112
    Cryotherapy or Diathermy 67101
    Injection of Air 67110
    Photocoagulation 67105
    Scleral Dissection 67107
    with Vitrectomy 67108, 67112
  Prophylaxis
    Detachment 67141-67145

Retinopathy
  Destruction
    Cryotherapy, Diathermy .... .67227
    Photocoagulation .... .67228

Retinacular
Knee
  Release .... .27425

Retinopathy
Destruction
  Cryotherapy, Diathermy .... .67227
  Photocoagulation .... .67228

Retraction, Clot
See Clot Retraction

Retrieval
Transcatheter Foreign Body .... .37203

Retrocaval Ureter
Ureterolysis .... .50725

Retrograde Cholangiopancreatographies, Endoscopic
See Cholangiopancreatography

Retrograde Cystourethrogram
See Urethrocystography, Retrograde

Retrograde Pyelogram
See Urography, Retrograde

Retroperitoneal Area
Abscess
  Incision and Drainage
    Open .... .49060
    Percutaneous .... .49061
Biopsy .... .49010
Cyst
  Destruction/Excision 49200-49201
Endometriomas
  Destruction/Excision 49200-49201
Exploration .... .49010
Needle Biopsy
  Mass .... .49180
Tumor
  Destruction/Excision 49200-49201

Retroperitoneal Fibrosis
Ureterolysis .... .50715

Retropubic Prostatectomies
See Prostatectomy, Retropubic

Revascularization
Penis .... .37788
Transmyocardial 33140-33141

Reversal, Vasectomy
See Vasovasorrhaphy

Reverse T3
See Triiodothyronine, Reverse

Reverse Triiodothyronine
See Triiodothyronine, Reverse

Revision
See Reconstruction
Aorta .... .33404
Atrial .... .33253

Blepharoplasty 15820-15823
Bronchus .... .32501
Bypass Graft
  Vein Patch .... .35685
Cervicoplasty .... .15819
Colostomy
  See Colostomy, Revision
Cornea
  Prosthesis .... .65770
  Reshaping
    Epikeratoplasty .... .65767
    Keratomileusis .... .65760
    Keratophakia .... .65765
Defibrillator Site
  Chest .... .33223
Ear, Middle .... .69662
External Fixation System .... .20693
Eye
  Aqueous Shunt .... .66185
Gastrostomy Tube .... .44373
Hip Replacement
  See Replacement, Hip, Revision
Hymenal Ring .... .56700
Ileostomy
  See Ileostomy, Revision
Infusion Pump
  Intraarterial .... .36261
  Intravenous .... .36531
Iris
  Iridoplasty .... .66762
  Iridotomy .... .66761
Jejunostomy Tube .... .44373
Lower Extremity Arterial Bypass 35879-35881
Pacemaker Site
  Chest .... .33222
Rhytidectomy 15824-15829
Semicircular Canal
  Fenestration .... .69840
Stapedectomy
  See Stapedectomy, Revsion
Stomach
  for Obesity .... .43848
Tracheostomy
  Scar .... .31830
Urinary-Cutaneous Anastomosis 50727-50728
Vagina
  Sling
    Stress Incontinence .... .57287
Venous Access Device .... .36534
Ventricle
  Ventriculomyectomy .... .33416
  Ventriculomyotomy .... .33416

Rh (D)
See Blood Typing

Rh Immune Globulin
See Immune Globulins, Rho (D)

Rheumatoid Factor 86430-86431

Rhinectomy
Partial .... .30150
Total .... .30160

Rhinomanometry .... .92512

Rhinopharynx
See Nasopharynx

Rhinophyma
Repair .... .30120

Rhinoplasty
Cleft Lip/Cleft Palate 30460-30462
Primary 30400-30420
Secondary 30430-30450

Rhinoscopy
See Endoscopy, Nose

Rhinotomy
Lateral .... .30118, 30320

Rhizotomy 63185-63190

Rho Variant Du .... .86905

Rhytidectomy 15824-15829

Rhytidoplasties
See Face Lift

Rib
Excision 21600-21616, 32900
Fracture
  Closed Treatment .... .21800
  External Fixation .... .21810
  Open Treatment .... .21805
Graft
  to Face .... .21230
Resection .... .32900
X-Ray 71100-71111

Riboflavin .... .84252

Richardson Operation Hysterectomy
See Hysterectomy, Abdominal, Total

Richardson Procedure .... .53460

Rickettsia
Antibody .... .86757

Ridell Operation
See Sinusotomy, Frontal

Ridge, Alveolar
See Alveolar Ridge

Right Atrioventricular Valve
See Tricuspid Valve

Right Heart Cardiac Catheterization
See Cardiac Catheterization, Right Heart

Ripstein Operation
See Proctopexy

Risk Factor Reduction Intervention
See Preventive Medicine

Risser Jacket 29010-29015
Removal .... .29710

Rocky Mountain Spotted Fever .... .86000

Roentgenographic
See X-Ray

Roentgenography
See Radiology, Diagnostic

Roentgen Rays
See X-Ray

Ropes Test 83872

Rorschach Test 96100

Ross Procedure 33413

Rotation Flap
See Skin, Adjacent Tissue Transfer

Rotator Cuff
Repair 23410-23420

Rotavirus
Antibody 86759
Antigen Detection
   Enzyme Immunoassay 87425

Rotavirus Vaccine 90680

Round Window
Repair Fistula 69667

Round Window Fistula
See Fistula, Round Window

Roux-En-Y Procedure 43621,
   43633-43634, 43846, 47740-47741,
   47780-47785, 48540

RPR 86592-86593

RSV
See Immune Globulins; Respiratory Syncytial
Virus

RT3
See Triiodothyronine, Reverse

Rubbing Alcohol
See Isopropyl Alcohol

Rubella
Antibody 86762
Vaccine 90706, 90709

Rubella/Mumps
See Vaccines

Rubella HI Test
See Hemagglutination Inhibition Test

Rubeola
Antibody 86765
Antigen Detection
   Immunofluorescence 87283

Rubeolla
See Rubeola

**Russell Viper Venom
Time** 85612-85613

S

Sac, Endolymphatic
See Endolymphatic Sac

Saccomanno Technique 88108

Sacral Nerve
Implantation
   Electrode 64561, 64581
Insertion
   Electrode 64561, 64581

Sacroiliac Joint
Arthrodesis 27280
Arthrotomy 27050
Biopsy 27050
Dislocation
   Open Treatment 27218
Fusion 27280
Injection for Arthrography 27096
X-Ray 72200-72202, 73542

Sacrum
Tumor
   Excision 49215
X-Ray 72220

Sahli Test
See Gastroenterology, Diagnostic, Stomach

Salabrasion 15810-15811

Salicylate
Assay 80196

Saline-Solution Abortion
See Abortion, Induced, by Saline

Saline Load Test 91060

Salivary Duct
Catheterization 42660
Dilation 42650-42660
Ligation 42665
Repair 42500-42505
   Fistula 42600

Salivary Glands
Abscess
   Incision and Drainage 42310-42320
Biopsy 42405
Calculi (Stone)
   Excision 42330-42340
Cyst
   Creation
      Fistula 42325-42326
   Drainage 42409
   Excision 42408
Injection
   X-Ray 42550
Needle Biopsy 42400
Nuclear Medicine
   Function Study 78232
   Imaging 78230-78231
Parotid
   Abscess 42300-42305

Unlisted Services and Procedures 42699
X-Ray 70380-70390
   with Contrast 70390

Salivary Gland Virus
See Cytomegalovirus

Salmonella
Antibody 86768

Salpingectomy 58262-58263, 58661,
   58700
Ectopic Pregnancy
   Laparoscopic Treatment 59151
   Surgical Treatment 59120
Oophorectomy 58943

Salpingo-Oophorectomy 58720
Resection Ovarian Malignancy 58950-58954
Resection Peritoneal Malignancy ... 58950-58954
Resection Tubal Malignancy 58950-58954

Salpingohysterostomy
See Implantation, Tubouterine

Salpingolysis 58740

Salpingoneostomy 58673, 58770

Salpingoplasty
See Fallopian Tube, Repair

Salpingostomy 58673, 58770
Laparoscopic 58673

Salter Osteotomy of the Pelvis
See Osteotomy, Pelvis

Sampling
See Biopsy; Brush Biopsy; Needle Biopsy

Sang-Park Procedure 33735-33737

Sao Paulo Typhus
See Rocky Mountain Spotted Fever

Saucerization
Calcaneus 28120
Clavicle 23180
Femur 27070, 27360
Fibula 27360, 27641
Hip 27070
Humerus 23184, 24140
Ileum 27070
Metacarpal 26230
Metatarsal 28122
Olecranon Process 24147
Phalanges
   Finger 26235-26236
   Toe 28124
Pubis 27070
Radius 24145, 25151
Scapula 23182
Talus 28120
Tarsal 28122
Tibia 27360, 27640
Ulna 24147, 25150

Saundby Test
See Blood, Feces

Scabies
See Tissue, Examination for Ectoparasites

Scalenotomy
See Muscle Division, Scalenus Anticus

Scalenus Anticus
Division 21700-21705

Scaling
See Exfoliation

Scalp
Tumor Resection
    Radical 21015

Scalp Blood Sampling 59030

Scan
See Specific Site, Nuclear Medicine
Abdomen
    See Abdomen, C.A.T. Scan
C.A.T.
    See C.A.T. Scan
MRI
    See Magnetic Resonance Imaging
PET
    See Positron Emission Tomography
Radionuclide
    See Emission Computerized Tomography

Scanning, Radioisotope
See Nuclear Medicine

Scanogram 76040

Scaphoid
Fracture
    Closed Treatment 25622
    Open Treatment 25628
    with Manipulation 25624

Scapula
Craterization 23182
Cyst
    Excision 23140
    with Allograft 23146
    with Autograft 23145
Diaphysectomy 23182
Excision 23172, 23190
    Partial 23182
Fracture
    Closed Treatment
      without Manipulation 23570
      with Manipulation 23575
    Open Treatment 23585
Ostectomy 23190
Repair
    Fixation 23400
    Scapulopexy 23400
Saucerization 23182
Sequestrectomy 23172
Tumor
    Excision 23140, 23210
    with Allograft 23146
    with Autograft 23145
    Radical Resection 23210
X-Ray 73010

Scapulopexy 23400

Scarification
Pleural 32215

Scarification of Pleura
See Pleurodesis

Schanz Operation
See Femur, Osteotomy

Schauta Operation
See Hysterectomy, Vaginal, Radical

Schede Procedure 32905-32906

Scheie Procedure
See Iridectomy

Schilling Test 78270
See Vitamin B-12 Absorption Study

Schlatter Operation Total Gastrectomy
See Excision, Stomach, Total

Schlicter Test 87197
See Bactericidal Titer, Serum

Schocket Procedure 66180
See Aqueous Shunt

Schonbein Test
See Blood, Feces

Schuchard Procedure
Osteotomy
    Maxilla 21206

Schwannoma, Acoustic
See Brain, Tumor, Excision

Sciatic Nerve
Decompression 64712
Injection
    Anesthetic 64445
Lesion
    Excision 64786
Neuroma
    Excision 64786
Neuroplasty 64712
Release 64712
Repair/Suture 64858

Scintigraphy
See Nuclear Medicine
Computed Tomographic
    See Emission Computerized Tomography

Scissoring
Skin Tags 11200-11201

Sclera
Excision
    Sclerectomy with Punch or Scissors ...66160
Fistulization
    Iridencleisis or Iridotasis 66165
    Sclerectomy with Punch or Scissors with
    Iridectomy 66160
    Thermocauterization with Iridectomy ..66155

Trabeculectomy ab Externo in Absence of
    Previous Surgery 66170
Trephination with Iridectomy 66150
Incision
    Fistulization
      Iridencleisis or Iridotasis 66165
      Sclerectomy with Punch or Scissors with
      Iridectomy 66160
      Thermocauterization
      with Iridectomy 66155
      Trabeculectomy ab Externo in Absence of
      Previous Surgery 66170
      Trephination with Iridectomy 66150
Lesion
    Excision 66130
Repair
    Reinforcement
      without Graft 67250
      with Graft 67255
    Staphyloma
      without Graft 66220
      with Graft 66225
    with Glue 65286
    Wound
      Operative 66250
      Tissue Glue 65286

Scleral Buckling Operation
See Retina, Repair, Detachment

Scleral Ectasia
See Staphyloma, Sclera

Sclerectomy 66160

Sclerotherapy
Venous 36468-36471

Sclerotomy
See Incision, Sclera

Screening, Drug
See Drug Screen

Scribner Cannulization 36810

Scrotal Varices
See Varicocele

Scrotoplasty 55175-55180

Scrotum
Abscess
    Incision and Drainage 54700, 55100
Excision 55150
Exploration 55110
Hematoma
    Incision and Drainage 54700
Removal
    Foreign Body 55120
Repair 55175-55180
Ultrasound 76870
Unlisted Services and Procedures 55899

Scrub Typhus 86000

Second Look Surgery
See Reoperation

Second Opinion
See Confirmatory Consultations

Section
See Decompression
Cesarean
  See Cesarean Delivery
Cranial Nerve 61460
  Spinal Access .63191
Dentate Ligament 63180-63182
Gasserian Ganglion
  Sensory Root .61450
Medullary Tract .61470
Mesencephalic Tract 61480
Nerve Root 63185-63190
Spinal Accessory Nerve 63191
Spinal Cord Tract 63194-63199
Tentorium Cerebelli 61440
Vestibular Nerve
  Transcranial Approach 69950
  Translabyrinthine Approach 69915

Sedation
with or without Analgesia 99141-99142

Seddon-Brookes Procedure . . .24320

Sedimentation Rate
Blood Cell
  Automated 85652
  Manual 85651

Segmentectomy
Lung 32484

Seidlitz Powder Test
See X-Ray, with Contrast

Selenium .84255

Self Care
See Physical Medicine/Therapy/Occupational
Therapy
Training 97535, 99509

Sella Turcica
CAT Scan 70480-70482
X-Ray 70240

Semenogelase
See Antigen, Prostate Specific

Semen Analysis 89300-89321
Sperm Analysis
  Antibodies 89325
with Sperm Isolation 89260-89261

Semicircular Canal
Incision
  Fenestration 69820
  Revised 69840

Semilunar
Bone
  See Lunate
Ganglion
  See Gasserian Ganglion

Seminal Vesicle
Cyst
  Excision 55680
Excision 55650
Incision .55600-55605

Mullerian Duct
  Excision 55680
Unlisted Services and Procedures 55899

Seminal Vesicles
Vesiculography 74440
X-Ray with Contrast 74440

Seminin
See Antigen, Prostate Specific

Semiquantitative 81005

Sengstaaken Tamponade
Esophagus 43460

Senning Procedure 33774-33777
See Repair, Great Arteries; Revision

Senning Type 33774-33777

Sensitivity Study
Antibiotic
  Agar 87181
  Disc 87184
  Enzyme Detection 87185
  Macrobroth 87188
  MIC 87186
  Microtiter 87186
  MLC 87187
  Mycobacteria .87190
Antiviral Drugs
  HIV-1
    Tissue Culture 87904

Sensor, Fetal Oximetry
Insertion
  Cervix 0021T
  Vagina 0021T

Sensorimotor Exam 92060

Sensory Nerve
Common
  Repair/Suture 64834

Sentinel Node
Injection Procedure 38792

Separation
Craniofacial
  Closed Treatment 21431
  Open Treatment 21432-21436

Septal Defect
Repair 33813-33814

Septectomy
Atrial 33735-33737
  Balloon (Rashkind Type) 92992
  Blade Method (Park) 92993
Closed
  See Septostomy, Atrial
Submucous Nasal
  See Nasal Septum, Submucous Resection

Septic Abortion
See Abortion, Septic

Septoplasty 30520

Septostomy
Atrial 33735-33737
  Balloon (Rashkind Type) 92992
  Blade Method (Park) 92993

Septum, Nasal
See Nasal Septum

Sequestrectomy
Carpal 25145
Clavicle 23170
Humeral Head 23174
Humerus 24134
Olecranon Process 24138
Radius 24136, 25145
Scapula 23172
Skull 61501
Ulna 24138, 25145

Serialography
Aorta 75625

Serodiagnosis, Syphilis
See Serologic Test for Syphilis

**Serologic Test for
Syphilis** 86592-86593

Seroma
Incision and Drainage
  Skin 10140

Serotonin .84260

Serum
Albumin
  See Albumin, Serum
Antibody Identification
  Pretreatment 86975-86978
CPK
  See Creatine Kinase, Total
Serum Immune Globulin 90281-90283

Sesamoidectomy
Toe 28315

Sesamoid Bone
Excision 28315
Finger
  Excision 26185
Foot
  Fracture 28530-28531
Thumb
  Excision 26185

Severing of Blepharorrhaphy
See Tarsorrhaphy, Severing

Sever Procedure
See Contracture, Palm, Release

Sex-Linked Ichthyoses
See Syphilis Test

Sex Change Operation
Female to Male .55980
Male to Female .55970

Sex Chromatin
See Barr Bodies

Sex Chromatin Identification 88130-88140

Sex Hormone Binding Globulin 84270

SGOT 84450

SGPT 84460

Shaving
Skin Lesion 11300-11313

SHBG
See Sex Hormone Binding Globulin

Shelf Procedure
See Osteotomy, Hip

Shiga-like Toxin
Antigen Detection
    Enzyme Immunoassay 87427

Shigella
Antibody 86771

Shirodkar Operation
See Repair, Cervix, Cerclage, Abdominal

Shock Wave, Ultrasonic
See Ultrasound

Shock Wave Lithotripsy 50590

Shock Wave (Extracorporeal) Therapy 0019T-0020T

Shop Typhus of Malaya
See Murine Typhus

Shoulder
See Clavicle; Scapula
Abscess
    Drainage 23030
Amputation 23900-23921
Arthrocentesis 20610
Arthrodesis 23800
    with Autogenous Graft 23802
Arthrography
    Injection
        Radiologic 23350
Arthroscopy
    Diagnostic 29805
    Surgical 29806-29826
Arthrotomy
    with Removal Loose or Foreign Body ..23107
Biopsy
    Deep 23066
    Soft Tissue 23065
Blade
    See Scapula
Bone
    Excision
        Acromion 23130
        Clavicle 23120-23125
    Incision 23035
    Tumor
        Excision 23140-23146
Bursa
    Drainage 23031
Capsular Contracture Release 23020

Cast
    Figure Eight 29049
    Removal 29710
    Spica 29055
    Velpeau 29058
Disarticulation 23920-23921
Dislocation
    Closed Treatment
        with Manipulation 23650-23655
    Exploration 23107
    Hematoma
        Drainage 23030
    Manipulation
        Application of Fixation Apparatus 23700
    Prophylactic Treatment 23490-23491
    Radical Resection 23077
    Removal
        Calcareous Deposits 23000
        Cast 29710
        Foreign Body
            Complicated 23332
            Deep 23331
            Subcutaneous 23330
        Foreign or Loose Body 23107
    Repair
        Capsule 23450-23466
        Ligament Release 23415
        Muscle Transfer 23395-23397
        Rotator Cuff 23410-23420
        Tendon 23410-23412, 23430-23440
        Tenomyotomy 23405-23406
    Strapping 29240
    Surgery
        Unlisted Services and Procedures 23929
    Tumor
        Excision 23075-23077
    Unlisted Services and Procedures 23929
    X-Ray 73020-73030
    X-Ray with Contrast 73040

Shoulder Joint
See Clavicle; Scapula
Arthroplasty
    with Implant 23470-23472
Arthrotomy
    with Biopsy 23100-23101
    with Synovectomy 23105-23106
Dislocation
    Open Treatment 23660
    with Greater Tuberosity Fracture
        Closed Treatment 23665
        Open Treatment 23670
    with Surgical or Anatomical Neck Fracture
        Closed Treatment with
            Manipulation 23675
        Open Treatment 23680
Excision
    Torn Cartilage 23101
Exploration 23040-23044
Incision and Drainage 23040-23044
Removal
    Foreign Body 23040-23044
X-Ray 73050

Shunt(s)
Aqueous
    to Extraocular Reservoir 66180
        Revision 66185
Arteriovenous
    See Arteriovenous Shunt
Brain
    Creation 62180-62223
    Removal 62256-62258
    Replacement ...62194, 62225-62230, 62258
    Reprogramming 62252
Cerebrospinal Fluid
    See Cerebrospinal Fluid Shunt
Creation
    Arteriovenous
        Direct 36821
        ECMO 36822
        Thomas Shunt 36835
        Transposition 36820
        with Bypass Graft 35686
        with Graft 36825-36830
    Cerebrospinal Fluid 62200
    Thomas Shunt 36835
Great Vessel
    Aorta
        Pulmonary 33924
    Aorta to Pulmonary Artery
        Ascending 33755
        Descending 33762
    Central 33764
    Subclavian Pulmonary Artery 33750
    Vena Cava to Pulmonary Artery .33766-33767
Intra-atrial 33735-33737
LeVeen
    See LeVeen Shunt
Nonvascular
    X-Ray 75809
Peritoneal
    Venous
        Injection 49427
        Ligation 49428
        Removal 49429
        X-Ray 75809
Pulmonary Artery
    See Pulmonary Artery, Shunt
Revision
    Arteriovenous 36832
Spinal Cord
    Creation 63740-63741
    Irrigation 63744
    Removal 63746
    Replacement 63744
Superior Mesenteric-Caval
    See Anastomosis, Caval to Mesenteric
Ureter to Colon 50815
Ventriculocisternal with Valve
    See Ventriculocisternostomy

Shuntogram 75809

Sialic Acid 84275

Sialodochoplasty 42500-42505

Sialogram
See Sialography

Sialography 70390

Sickling
Electrophoresis 83020

Siderocytes 85536

Siderophilin
See Transferrin

Sigmoid
See Colon-Sigmoid

Sigmoidoscopy
Ablation
　Polyp 45339
　Tumor 45339
Biopsy 45331
Collection
　Specimen 45331
Exploration 45330
Hemorrhage Control 45334
Needle Biopsy 45342
Placement
　Stent 45345
Removal
　Foreign Body 45332
　Polyp 45333, 45338
　Tumor 45333, 45338
Repair
　Volvulus 45337
Ultrasound 45341-45342

Sigmoid Bladder
Cystectomy 51590

Signal-Averaged Electrocardiography
See Electrocardiogram

Silica 84285

Silicone
Contouring Injections 11950-11954

Silicon Dioxide
See Silica

Silver Operation
See Keller Procedure

Silver Procedure 28290

Simple Mastectomies
See Mastectomy

Single Photon Absorptiometry
See Absorptiometry, Single Photon

Single Photon Emission Computed Tomography
See SPECT

Sinu, Sphenoid
See Sinuses, Sphenoid

Sinus
Ethmoidectomy
　Excision 31254
Pilonidal
　See Cyst, Pilonidal

Sinusectomy, Ethmoid
See Ethmoidectomy

Sinuses
Ethmoid
　Excision 31200-31205
　with Nasal/Sinus
　　Endoscopy 31254-31255
　Repair of Cerebrospinal Leak 31290
Frontal
　Destruction 31080-31085
　Exploration 31070-31075
　　with Nasal/Sinus Endoscopy 31276
　Fracture
　　Open Treatment 21343-21344
　Incision 31070-31087
　Injection 20500
　　Diagnostic 20501
Maxillary
　Antrostomy 31256-31267
　Excision 31225-31230
　Exploration 31020-31032
　　with Nasal/Sinus Endoscopy 31233
　Incision 31020-31032, 31256-31267
　Irrigation 31000
　Skull Base 61581
　Surgery 61581
Multiple
　Incision 31090
Paranasal
　Incision 31090
Sphenoid
　Biopsy 31050-31051
　Exploration 31050-31051
　　with Nasal/Sinus Endoscopy 31235
　Incision 31050-31051
　　with Nasal/Sinus Endoscopy .31287-31288
　Irrigation 31002
　Repair of Cerebrospinal Leak 31291
　Sinusotomy 31050-31051
　Skull Base Surgery 61580-61581
Unlisted Services and Procedures 31299
X-Ray 70210-70220

Sinusoidal Rotational Testing
See Ear, Nose and Throat

Sinusoscopy
Sinus
　Maxillary 31233
　Sphenoid 31235

Sinusotomy
See Sinus, Multiple
Combined 31090
Frontal Sinus
　Exploratory 31070-31075
　Nonobliterative 31086-31087
　Obliterative 31080-31085
Maxillary 31020-31032
Multiple
　Paranasal 31090
Sphenoid Sinus 31050-31051

Sinus of Valsalva
Repair 33702-33722

Sinus Venosus
Repair 33645

SISI Test 92564

Sistrunk Operation
See Cyst, Thyroid Gland, Excision

Size Reduction, Breast
See Breast, Reduction

Skeletal Fixation
Humeral Epicondyle
　Percutaneous 24566

Skeletal Traction
Insertion/Removal
　Pin/Wire 20650

Skene's Gland
Abscess
　Incision and Drainage 53060
Destruction 53270
Excision 53270

Skilled Nursing Facilities (SNFs)
See Nursing Facility Services

Skin
Abrasion 15786-15787
　Chemical Peel 15788-15793
　Dermabrasion 15780-15783
　Salabrasion 15810-15811
Abscess
　See Abscess, Skin
Adjacent Tissue Transfer 14000-14350
Allografts
　See Allograft, Skin
Biopsy 11100-11101
Chemical Exfoliation 17360
Cyst
　See Cyst, Skin
Debridement 11000-11044
　Eczematous 11000-11001
　Full Thickness 11041
　Infected 11000-11001
　Partial Thickness 11040
　Subcutaneous Tissue 11042-11044
　with Open Fracture and/or
　　Dislocation 11010-11012
Decubitus Ulcer(s)
　See Pressure Ulcer (Decubitus)
Desquamation
　See Exfoliation
Destruction
　Benign Lesions
　　Fifteen or More Lesions 17004
　　First Lesion 17000
　　Two - Fourteen Lesions 17003
　　Flat Warts 17110-17111
　　Lesions 17106-17108
　　Malignant Lesions 17260-17286
　　by Photodynamic Therapy 96567
　Premalignant Lesions
　　by Photodynamic Therapy 96567
　　Fifteen or More Lesions 17004
　　First Lesion 17000
　　Two - Fourteen Lesions 17003
Excision
　Debridement 11000-11044
　Excess Skin 15831-15839
　Hemangioma 11400-11446

Lesion
   Benign 11400-11446
   Malignant 11600-11646
Expanders
  See Tissue, Expander
Fasciocutaneous Flaps 15732-15738
Grafts
   Free 15000-15400, 15757
Homografts
  See Homograft, Skin
Incision and Drainage 10040-10180
  See Incision, Skin
Lesion
  See Lesion; Tumor
  Verrucous
    See Warts
Muscle Flaps 15732-15738
Myocutaneous Flaps 15732-15738
Nose
  Surgical Planing 30120
Paring 11055-11057
Removal
  Skin Tags 11200-11201
Revision
  Blepharoplasty 15820-15823
  Cervicoplasty 15819
  Rhytidectomy 15824-15829
Shaving .11300-11313
Tags
  Removal 11200-11201
Tests
  See Allergy Tests
  Candida .86485
  Coccidioidomycosis 86490
  Histoplasmosis 86510
  Other Antigen 86586
  Tuberculosis 86580-86585
Unlisted Services and Procedures 17999
Wound Repair
  Complex 13100-13160
  Intermediate 12031-12057
  Simple 12001-12021

Skin Graft and Flap

Allograft 15350-15351
Composite Graft 15760-15770
Cross Finger Flap 15574
Delay 15600-15630
Delay of Flap 15600-15630
Derma-Fat-Fascia 15770
Fascial
  Free 15758
Fasciocutaneous 15732-15738
Formation 15570-15576
Free
  Microvascular Anastomosis 15756-15758
Free Skin Graft
  Full Thickness 15200-15261
Island Pedicle Flap 15740
Muscle 15732-15738, 15842
  Free 15756
Myocutaneous 15732-15738
Pedicle Flap
  Formation 15570-15576
  Island 15740
  Neurovascular 15750
  Transfer .15650

Pinch Graft .15050
Platysmal 15825
Punch Graft 15775-15776
Punch Graft for Hair Transplant 15775-15776
Recipient Site Preparation 15000-15001
Skin
  Free 15757
Split Graft 15100-15121
Superficial Musculoaponeurotic System . . .15829
Tissue-Cultured 15100-15121, 15342-15343
Tissue Transfer 14000-14350
Transfer 15650
Vascular Flow Check 15860
Xenograft 15400-15401

Skull

Burr Hole
  Biopsy Brain 61140
  Drainage
   Abscess 61150-61151
   Cyst 61150-61151
   Hematoma 61154-61156
  Exploration
   Infratentorial 61253
   Supratentorial 61250
  Insertion
   Catheter 61210
   EEG Electrode 61210
   Reservoir 61210
  Intracranial
   Biopsy 61140
  with Injection 61120
Decompression 61340-61345
  Orbit 61330
Drill Hole
  Catheter 61107
  Drainage Hematoma 61108
  Exploration 61105
Excision 61501
Exploration
  Drill Hole 61105
Fracture 62000-62010
  Closed Treatment 21300
Hematoma
  Drainage 61108
Incision
  Suture 61550-61552
Insertion
  Catheter 61107
Lesion
  Excision . .61500, 61600-61608, 61615-61616
Orbit
  Biopsy 61332
  Excision
   Lesion 61333
  Exploration 61332-61334
  Removal Foreign Body 61334
Puncture
  Cervical 61050
  Cisternal 61050
  Drain Fluid 61070
  Injection 61070
  Subdural 61000-61001
  Ventricular Fluid 61020
Reconstruction 21172-21180
  Defect 62140-62141, 62145
Reduction
  Craniomegalic 62115-62117

Removal
  Plate 62142
  Prosthesis 62142
Repair
  Cerebrospinal Fluid Leak 62100
  Encephalocele 62120
Replacement
  Plate 62143
  Prosthesis 62143
Tumor
  Excision 61500
X-Ray 70250-70260

Skull Base Surgery

Anterior Cranial Foss
  Bicoronal Approach 61586
Anterior Cranial Fossa
  Craniofacial Approach 61580-61583
  Extradural 61600-61601
  LeFort I Osteotomy Approach 61586
  Orbitocranial Approach 61584-61585
  Transzygomatic Approach 61586
Carotid Aneurysm 61613
Carotid Artery 61610
  Transection/Ligation 61609-61612
Craniotomy 62121
Dura
  Repair of Cerebrospinal Fluid
   Leak 61618-61619
Middle Cranial Fossa
  Extradural 61605, 61607
  Infratemporal Approach 61590-61591
  Intradural 61606, 61608
Orbitocranial Zygomatic Approach 61592
Posterior Cranial Fossa
  Extradural 61615
  Intradural 61616
  Transcondylar Approach 61596-61597
  Transpetrosal Approach 61598
  Transtemporal Approach 61595

Sleep Study 95806-95807

Sliding Inlay Graft, Tibia
See Ankle; Tibia, Repair

Sling Operation
Stress Incontinence 51992, 57287
Vagina 57287-57288

Small Bowel
See Intestines, Small
Neoplasm
  See Tumor, Intestines, Small

SMAS Flap 15829

Smear
Cervical
  See Cervical Smears
Papanicolaou
  See Pap Smears

Smear and Stain
See Cytopathology, Smears
Cornea 65430
Fluorescent .87206
Gram or Giesma 87205
Intracellular Parasites 87207

Ova
    Parasites 87177
Wet Mount 87210

Smith-Robinson Operation
See Arthrodesis, Vertebra

Smithwick Operation
See Excision, Nerve, Sympathetic

Smith Fracture 25600-25620

SO4
See Sulfate

Soave Procedure 45120

Sodium 84295
Urine 84300

Sodium Glycinate, Theophylline
See Theophylline

Sofield Procedure 24410

Soft Tissue
See Tissue, Soft

Solar Plexus
See Celiac Plexus

Solitary Cyst
See Bone, Cyst

Somatomammotropin, Chorionic 83632

Somatomedin 84305

Somatosensory Testing
Lower Limbs 95926
Trunk or Head 95927
Upper Limbs 95925

Somatostatin 84307

Somatotropin 83003

Somatotropin Release Inhibiting Hormone
See Somatostatin

Somatropin
See Growth Hormone, Human

Somnographies
See Polysomnography

Somophyllin T
See Theophylline

Sonography
See Echography

Sore, Bed
See Pressure Ulcer (Decubitus)

Spasm Eyelid
See Blepharospasm

Special Services
After Hours Medical Services 99050-99054
Analysis
    Remote Physiologic Data 99091
Computer Data Analysis 99090

Device Handling 99002
Emergency Care In Office 99058
Group Education 99078
Hyperbaric Oxygen 99183
Hypothermia 99185-99186
Medical Testimony 99075
Non-Office Medical Services 99056
Office Visit with Surgery 99025
Phlebotomy 99199
Post-Op Visit 99024
Pump Services 99190-99192
Reports and Forms
    Medical, Extended 99080
    Psychiatric 90889
Specimen Handling 99000-99001
Supply of Materials 99070
    Educational 99071
Unlisted Services and Procedures 99199
Unusual Travel 99082

Specific Gravity
Body Fluid 84315

Specimen Collection
Intestines 89100-89105
Stomach 89130-89141

Specimen Concentration 87015

Specimen Handling 99000-99001

SPECT 78607
See Emission Computerized Tomography
Abscess Localization 78807
Bone 78320
Cerebrospinal Fluid 78647
Heart
    Multiple 78465
    Single 78464
Kidney 78710
Liver 78205
Tumor Localization 78803

Spectacle Services
Fitting
    Low Vision Aid 92354-92355
    Spectacles 92340-92342
    Spectacle Prosthesis 92352-92353
Repair 92370-92371
Supply
    Low Vision Aids 92392
    Spectacles 92390
    Spectacle Prosthesis 92395

Spectrometry
Mass
    Analyte
        Qualitative 83788
        Quantitative 83789

Spectrophotometry 84311
Atomic Absorption
    See Atomic Absorption Spectroscopy

Spectroscopy
Atomic Absorption 82190
Magnetic Resonance 76390

Spectrum Analyses
See Spectrophotometry

Speech Evaluation 92506
Cine 70371
for Prosthesis 92597
Video 70371

Speech Prosthesis 21084, 92598
Creation 31611
Evaluation for Speech 92597
Insertion 31611

Speech Therapy 92507-92508

Spermatic Cord
Hydrocele
    Excision 55500
Laparoscopy 55559
Lesion
    Excision 55520
Repair
    Veins 55530-55540
        Abdominal Approach 55535
        with Hernia Repair 55540
Varicocele
    Excision 55530-55540

Spermatic Veins
Excision 55530-55540
Ligation 55550

Spermatocele
Excision 54840

Spermatocystectomy
See Spermatocele, Excision

Sperm Analysis
Antibodies 89325
Cervical Mucus Penetration Test 89330
Cryopreservation 89259
Hamster Penetration Test 89329
Identification
    Aspiration 89257
    from Testis Tissue 89264
Isolation 89260-89261

Sperm Evaluation, Cervical Mucus Penetration Test
See Huhner Test

Sperm Washing 58323

Sphenoidotomy
Excision
    with Nasal/Sinus Endoscopy ...31287-31288

Sphenoid Sinus
See Sinuses, Sphenoid

Sphenopalatine Ganglion
Injection
    Anesthetic 64505

Sphincter
See Specific Sphincter
Anal
    See Anal Sphincter
Artificial Genitourinary
    See Prosthesis, Urethral Sphincter
Pyloric
    See Pyloric Sphincter

Sphincteroplasty

Anal 46750-46751, 46760-46761
   with Implant 46762
Bile Duct 47460
Bladder Neck
   See Bladder, Repair, Neck

Sphincterotomy 52277

Anal 46080
Bile Duct 47460

Sphincter of Oddi

Pressure Measurement
   Endoscopy 43263

Spica Cast

Hip 29305-29325
Repair 29720
Shoulder 29055

Spinal Accessory Nerve

Anastomosis
   to Facial Nerve 64866
Incision 63191
Injection
   Anesthetic 64412
Section 63191

Spinal Column

See Spine

Spinal Cord

See Cauda Equina; Nerve Root
Biopsy 63275-63290
Cyst
   Aspiration 62268
   Incision and Drainage 63172-63173
Decompression 63001-63091
Drain Fluid 62272
Exploration 63001-63044
Graft
   Dura 63710
Implantation
   Electrode 63650-63655
   Pulse Generator 63685
   Receiver 63685
Incision 63200
   Dentate Ligament 63180-63182
   Tract 63170, 63194-63199
Injection
   Anesthetic 62310-62319
   Blood 62273
   CAT Scan 62284
   Neurolytic Agent 62280-62282
   Other 62310-62311
   X-Ray 62284
Insertion
   Electrode 63650-63655
   Pulse Generator 63685
   Receiver 63685
Lesion
   Destruction 62280-62282
   Excision 63265-63273, 63300-63308
Needle Biopsy 62269
Neoplasm
   Excision 63275-63290
Puncture (Tap)
   Diagnostic 62270
   Drain Fluid 62272
   Lumbar 62270

Release 63200
Removal
   Catheter 62355
   Electrode 63660
   Pulse Generator 63688
   Pump 62365
   Receiver 63688
   Reservoir 62365
Repair
   Cerebrospinal Fluid Leak 63707-63709
   Meningocele 63700-63702
   Myelomeningocele 63704-63706
Section
   Dentate Ligament 63180-63182
   Tract 63194-63199
Shunt
   Create 63740-63741
   Irrigation 63744
   Removal 63746
   Replacement 63744
Stereotaxis
   Aspiration 63615
   Biopsy 63615
   Creation Lesion 63600
   Excision Lesion 63615
   Stimulation 63610
Syrinx
   Aspiration 62268
Tumor
   Excision 63275-63290

Spinal Cord Neoplasms

See Spinal Cord
Tumor
   See Spinal Cord, Tumor; Tumor
   Excision
      See Spinal Cord, Tumor; Tumor, Spinal
      Cord

Spinal Fluid

See Cerebrospinal Fluid

Spinal Fracture

See Fracture, Vertebra

Spinal Instrumentation

Anterior 22845-22847
   Removal 22855
Internal Fixation 22841
Pelvic Fixation 22848
Posterior Nonsegmental
   Harrington Rod Technique 22840
   Removal 22850
Posterior Segmental 22842-22844
   Removal 22852
Prosthetic Device 22851
Reinsertion of Spinal Fixation Device 22849

Spinal Manipulation

See Manipulation, Chiropractic

Spinal Nerve

Avulsion 64772
Transection 64772

Spinal Tap

See Cervical Puncture; Cisternal Puncture;
Subdural Tap; Ventricular Puncture
Drainage Fluid 62272
Lumbar 62270

Spine

See Spinal Cord; Vertebra; Vertebral Body;
Vertebral Process
Allograft
   Morselized 20930
   Structural 20931
Autograft
   Local 20936
   Morselized 20937
   Structural 20938
Biopsy 20250-20251
CAT Scan
   Cervical 72125-72127
   Lumbar 72131-72133
   Thoracic 72128-72130
Fixation 22842
Fusion
   Anterior 22808-22812
   Anterior Approach 22548-22585, 22812
   Exploration 22830
   Posterior Approach 22590-22802
Insertion
   Instrumentation 22840-22848, 22851
Kyphectomy 22818-22819
Magnetic Resonance Angiography 72159
Magnetic Resonance Imaging
   Cervical 72141-72142, 72156-72158
   Lumbar 72148-72158
   Thoracic 72146-72147, 72156-72158
Manipulation
   Anesthesia 22505
Myelography
   Cervical 72240
   Lumbosacral 72265
   Thoracic 72255
   Total 72270
Reinsertion
   Instrumentation 22849
Removal
   Instrumentation 22850, 22852-22855
Repair, Osteotomy
   Anterior 22220-22226
   Posterior 22210-22214
   Posterolateral 22216
Ultrasound 76800
Unlisted Services and Procedures,
Surgery 22899
X-Ray 72020, 72090
   Cervical 72040-72052
   Lumbosacral 72100-72120
   Standing 72069
   Thoracic 72070-72074
   Thoracolumbar 72080
   Total 72010
   with Contrast
      Cervical 72240
      Lumbosacral 72265
      Thoracic 72255
      Total 72270

Spine Chemotherapy

Administration 96450
   See Chemotherapy

Spirometry 94010-94070

See Pulmonology, Diagnostic
Patient Initiated 94014-94016

Splanchnicectomy
See Nerves, Sympathectomy, Excision

Spleen
Excision .38100-38102
        Laparoscopic 38120
Injection
        Radiologic .38200
Nuclear Medicine
        Imaging 78185, 78215-78216
Repair 38115

Splenectomy
Laparoscopic 38120
Partial 38101
Partial with Repair, Ruptured Spleen 38115
Total 38100
        En bloc 38102

Splenoplasty
See Repair, Spleen

Splenoportography 75810
Injection Procedures 38200

Splenorrhaphy 38115

Splint
See Casting; Strapping
Arm
        Long 29105
        Short 29125-29126
Finger 29130-29131
Foot 29590
Leg
        Long 29505
        Short 29515
Oral Surgical 21085
Ureteral
        See Ureteral Splinting

Splitting
Blood Products .86985

Split Grafts 15100-15121

Split Renal Function Test
See Cystourethroscopy, Catheterization, Ureteral

Spontaneous Abortion
See Abortion

Sprengel's Deformity 23400

Spring Water Cyst
See Cyst, Pericardial

Spur, Bone
See Exostosis
Calcaneal
        See Heel Spur

Sputum Analysis 89350

SRIH
See Somatostatin

Ssabanejew-Frank Operation
See Incision, Stomach, Creation, Stoma; Incision
and Drainage

Stabilizing Factor, Fibrin
See Fibrin Stabilizing Factor

Stable Factor 85230

Stallard Procedure
See Conjunctivorhinostomy

Stamey Procedure 51845
See Repair, Bladder, Neck

Standby Services
Physician 99360

Stanford-Binet Test
See Psychiatric Diagnosis

Stanftan
See Binet Test

Stapedectomy
Revision 69662
without Foreign Material 69660
with Footplate Drill Out 69661

Stapedotomy
Revision 69662
without Foreign Material 69660
with Footplate Drill Out 69661

Stapes
Excision
        without Foreign Material 69660
        with Footplate Drill Out 69661
Mobilization
        See Mobilization, Stapes
Release 69650
Revision 69662

Staphyloma
Sclera
        Repair
                without Graft 66220
                with Graft 66225

Starch Granules
Feces 89355

State Operation
See Proctectomy

Statistics /Biometry
See Biometry

Steindler Stripping 28250

Stellate Ganglion
Injection
        Anesthetic 64510

Stem, Brain
See Brainstem

Stem Cell
Cryopreservation 88240
Harvesting 38231
Modification or Treatment 86915
Thawing 88241
Transplantation 38240-38241

Stenger Test 92565, 92577
See Audiologic Function Test; Ear, Nose and
Throat

Stenosis
Aortic
        See Aortic Stenosis
Bronchi 31641
        Reconstruction 31775
Excision
        Trachea 31780-31781
Laryngoplasty .31582
Reconstruction
        Auditory Canal, External 69310
Repair
        Trachea 31780-31781
Tracheal
        See Trachea Stenosis
Urethral
        See Urethral Stenosis

Stensen Duct
See Parotid Duct

Stent
Indwelling
        Insertion
                Ureter 50605
Placement
        Bronchoscopy 31631
        Colonoscopy 45387
                via Stoma 44397
        Endoscopy
                Gastrointestinal, Upper 43256
        Enteroscopy 44370
        Proctosigmoidoscopy 45327
        Sigmoidoscopy 45345
        Ureteroneocystomy 50947-50948
Urethra
        Insertion .52282

Stent, Intravascular
See Transcatheter, Placement, Intravascular
Stents

Stents, Tracheal
See Tracheal Stent

Stereotactic Frame
Application/Removal 20660

Stereotaxis
Aspiration
        Brain Lesion 61750
                with CAT Scan and/or MRI 61751
        Spinal Cord 63615
Biopsy
        Aspiration
                Brain Lesion 61750
        Brain 61750
                with CAT Scan and/or MRI 61751
        Breast 76095
        Spinal Cord 63615
CAT Scan
        Aspiration 61751
        Biopsy 61751
Computer Assisted
        Brain Surgery 61795
Creation Lesion
        Brain
                Deep 61720-61735
                Percutaneous 61790

Gasserian Ganglion 61790
Spinal Cord 63600
Trigeminal Tract 61791
Excision Lesion
Brain 61750
Spinal Cord 63615
Focus Beam
Radiosurgery 61793
Localization
Brain 61770
Radiation Therapy 77432
Stimulation
Spinal Cord 63610

Sterile Coverings
See Dressings

Sternal Fracture
See Fracture, Sternum

Sternoclavicular Joint
Arthrotomy 23044
with Biopsy 23101
with Synovectomy 23106
Dislocation
Closed Treatment
without Manipulation 23520
with Manipulation 23525
Open Treatment 23530-23532
with Fascial Graft 23532

Sternocleidomastoid
Division 21720-21725

Sternotomy
Closure 21750

Sternum
Debridement 21627
Excision 21620, 21630-21632
Fracture
Closed Treatment 21820
Open Treatment 21825
Ostectomy 21620
Radical Resection 21630-21632
Reconstruction 21740-21750
X-Ray 71120-71130

Steroid-Binding Protein, Sex
See Globulin, Sex Hormone Binding

Steroids
Anabolic
See Androstenedione
Injection
Urethral Stricture 52283
Ketogenic
Urine 83582

STH (Somatotropic Hormone)
See Growth Hormone

Stimulating Antibody, Thyroid
See Immunoglobulin, Thyroid Stimulating

Stimulation
Electric
See Electrical Stimulation
Lymphocyte
See Blastogenesis

Spinal Cord
Stereotaxis 63610
Transcutaneous Electric
See Application, Neurostimulation

Stimulator, Long-Acting Thyroid
See Thyrotropin Releasing Hormone (TRH)

Stimulators, Cardiac
See Heart, Pacemaker

Stimulus Evoked Response 51792

Stoffel Operation
See Rhizotomy

Stoma
Creation
Bladder 51980
Kidney 50551-50561
Stomach
Neonatal 43831
Temporary 43830-43831
Ureter 50860
Ureter
Endoscopy via 50951-50961

Stomach
Anastomosis
with Duodenum 43810, 43850-43855
with Jejunum . . .43820-43825, 43860-43865
Biopsy 43600-43605
Creation
Stoma
Temporary 43830-43831
Temporary Stoma
Laparoscopic 43653
Electrogastrography 91132-91133
Excision
Partial 43631-43639
Total 43620-43622
Exploration 43500
Gastric Bypass 43846
Revision 43848
Incision 43830-43832
Exploration 43500
Pyloric Sphincter 43520
Removal
Foreign Body 43500
Intubation with Specimen Prep 91055
Nuclear Medicine
Blood Loss Study 78278
Emptying Study 78264
Imaging .78261
Protein Loss Study 78282
Reflux Study 78262
Vitamin B-12 Absorption 78270-78272
Reconstruction
for Obesity 43842-43847
Roux-En-Y 43846
Removal
Foreign Body 43500
Repair 48547
Fistula 43880
Fundoplasty 43324-43325
Laparoscopic 43280
Laceration 43501-43502
Stoma 43870
Ulcer 43501

Saline Load Test 91060
Specimen Collection 89130-89141
Stimulation of Secretion 91052
Suture
Fistula 43880
for Obesity 43842-43843
Stoma 43870
Ulcer 43840
Wound 43840
Tumor
Excision 43610-43611
Ulcer
Excision .43610
Unlisted Services and Procedures . .43659, 43999

Stomatoplasty
See Mouth, Repair

Stone, Kidney
See Calculus, Removal, Kidney

Stookey-Scarff Procedure
See Ventriculocisternostomy

Stool Blood
See Blood, Feces

Strabismus
Chemodenervation 67345
Repair
Adjustable Sutures 67335
Extraocular Muscles 67340
One Horizontal Muscle 67311
One Vertical Muscle 67314
Posterior Fixation Suture
Technique 67334-67335
Previous Surgery, Not Involving Extraocular
Muscles .67331
Release Extensive Scar Tissue 67343
Superior Oblique Muscle 67318
Transposition 67320
Two Horizontal Muscles 67312
Two or More Vertical Muscles 67316

Strapping
See Cast; Splint
Ankle 29540
Back 29220
Chest 29200
Elbow 29260
Finger 29280
Foot 29590
Hand 29280
Hip 29520
Knee 29530
Shoulder 29240
Thorax 29200
Toes 29550
Unlisted Services and Procedures 29799
Unna Boot 29580
Wrist 29260

Strassman Procedure 58540

Strayer Procedure
Leg, Lower .27687

Streptococcus, Group A
Antigen Detection
    Enzyme Immunoassay 87430
    Nucleic Acid 87650-87652
Direct Optical Observation 87880

Streptococcus, Group B
by Immunoassay
    with Direct Optical Observation 87802

Streptococcus pneumoniae Vaccine
See Vaccines

Streptokinase, Antibody 86590

Stress Tests
Cardiovascular 93015-93024
Multiple Gated Acquisition
(MUGA) 78472-78473
Myocardial Perfusion Imaging 78460-78465
Pulmonary .94620-94621
    See Pulmonology, Diagnostic

Stricture
Repair
    Urethra 53400-53405
Urethra
    See Urethral Stenosis

Strictureplasty
Intestines 44615

Stroboscopy
Larynx 31579

STS .86592-86593
See Syphilis Test

Stuart-Power Factor 85260

Study, Color Vision
See Color Vision Examination

Sturmdorf Procedure 57520

Styloidectomy
Radial 25230

Styloid Process
Radial
    Excision 25230

Stypven Time
See Russell Viper Venom Time

Subacromial Bursa
Arthrocentesis 20610

Subclavian Arteries
See Artery, Subclavian

Subcutaneous Injection
See Injection, Subcutaneous

Subcutaneous Mastectomies
See Mastectomy, Subcutaneous

Subcutaneous Tissue
Excision .15831-15839

Subdiaphragmatic Abscess
See Abscess, Subdiaphragmatic

Subdural Electrode
Insertion .61531-61533
Removal 61535

Subdural Hematonia
See Hematoma, Subdural

Subdural Puncture 61105-61108

Subdural Tap 61000-61001

Sublingual Gland
Abscess
    Incision and Drainage 42310-42320
Calculi (Stone)
    Excision 42330
Cyst
    Drainage 42409
    Excision 42408
Excision 42450

Subluxation
Elbow 24640

Submandibular Gland
Calculi (Stone)
    Excision 42330-42335
Excision 42440

Submaxillary Gland
Abscess
    Incision and Drainage 42310-42320

Submucous Resection of Nasal Septum
See Nasal Septum, Submucous Resection

Subperiosteal Implant
Reconstruction
    Mandible 21245-21246
    Maxilla 21245-21246

Subphrenic Abscess
See Abscess, Subdiaphragmatic

Substance S, Reichstein's
See Deoxycortisol

Subtrochanteric Fracture
See Femur, Fracture, Subtrochanteric

Sucrose Hemolysis Test
See Red Blood Cell (RBC), Fragility, Osmotic

Suction Lipectomies
See Liposuction

Sudiferous Gland
See Sweat Glands

Sugars 84375-84379

Sugar Water Test
See Red Blood Cell (RBC), Fragility, Osmotic

Sugiura Procedure
See Esophagus, Repair, Varices

Sulfate
Chondroitin
    See Chondroitin Sulfate

DHA
    See Dehydroepiandrosterone Sulfate
Urine 84392

Sulfation Factor
See Somatomedin

Sulphates
See Sulfate

Sumatran Mite Fever
See Scrub Typhus

Superficial Musculoaponeurotic System (SMAS) Flap
Rhytidectomy 15829

Supernumerary Digit
Reconstruction .26587
Repair 26587

Supply
Chemotherapeutic Agent 96545
    See Chemotherapy
Contact Lenses 92391, 92396
Educational Materials 99071
Low Vision Aids 92392
    See Spectacle Services
Materials 99070
Ocular Prosthesis 92393
Prosthesis
    Breast 19396
Radionuclide 78990
Radionuclide Therapy 79900
Radiopharmaceutical 78990
Radiopharmaceutical Therapy 79900
Spectacles 92390
Spectacle Prosthesis 92395

Suppositories, Vaginal
See Pessary

Suppression 80400-80408

Suppression/Testing
See Evocative/Suppression Test

Suppressor T Lymphocyte Marker
See CD8

Suppurative Hidradenitides
See Hidradenitis, Suppurative

Suprahyoid
Lymphadenectomy 38700

Supraorbital Nerve
Avulsion 64732
Incision 64732
Transection 64732

Supraorbital Rim and Forehead
Reconstruction 21179-21180

Suprapubic Prostatectomies
See Prostatectomy, Suprapubic

Suprarenal
Gland
    See Adrenal Gland

Vein
  See Vein, Adrenal

Suprascapular Nerve
Injection
  Anesthetic 64418

Suprasellar Cyst
See Craniopharyngioma

Surface CD4 Receptor
See CD4

Surface Radiotherapy
See Application, Radioelement, Surface

Surgeries
Breast-Conserving
  See Breast, Excision, Lesion
Conventional
  See Celiotomy
Laser
  See Laser Surgery
Mohs
  See Mohs Micrographic Surgery
Repeat
  See Reoperation

Surgical
Avulsion
  See Avulsion
Cataract Removal
  See Cataract, Excision
Collapse Therapy; Thoracoplasty
  See Thoracoplasty
Diathermy
  See Electrocautery
Galvanism
  See Electrolysis
Incision
  See Incision
Microscopes
  See Operating Microscope
Pathology
  See Pathology, Surgical
Planing
  Nose
    Skin 30120
Pneumoperitoneum
  See Pneumoperitoneum
Removal, Eye
  See Enucleation, Eye
Revision
  See Reoperation
Services
  Post-Op Visit 99024

Surveillance
See Monitoring

Suspension
Aorta 33800
Kidney
  See Nephropexy
Vagina
  See Colpopexy

Suture
See Repair
Abdomen 49900

Aorta 33320-33322
Bile Duct
  Wound 47900
Bladder
  Fistulization 44660-44661, 45800-45805,
                                51880-51925
    Vesicouterine 51920-51925
    Vesicovaginal 51900
    Wound 51860-51865
Cervix 57720
Colon
  Diverticula 44604-44605
  Fistula 44650-44661
  Plication 44680
  Stoma 44620-44625
  Ulcer 44604-44605
  Wound 44604-44605
Esophagus
  Wound 43410-43415
Eyelid 67880
  Closure of 67875
  with Transposition of Tarsal Plate 67882
  Wound
    Full Thickness 67935
    Partial Thickness 67930
Facial Nerve
  Intratemporal
    Lateral to Geniculate Ganglion 69740
    Medial to Geniculate Ganglion 69745
Foot
  Tendon 28200-28210
Gastroesophageal 0008T, 43405
Great Vessel 33320-33322
Hemorrhoids 46945-46946
Hepatic Duct
  See Hepatic Duct, Repair
Intestine
  Large
    Diverticula 44605
    Ulcer 44605
    Wound 44605
Intestines
  Large
    Diverticula 44604
    Ulcer 44604
    Wound 44604
  Small
    Diverticula 44602-44603
    Fistula 44640-44661
    Plication 44680
    Ulcer 44602-44603
    Wound 44602-44603
    Stoma 44620-44625
Iris
  with Ciliary Body 66682
Kidney
  Fistula 50520-50526
  Horseshoe 50540
  Wound 50500
Leg, Lower
  Tendon 27658-27665
Leg, Upper
  Muscle 27385-27386
Liver
  Wound 47350-47361
Mesentery 44850
Nerve 64831-64876

Pancreas 48545
Pharynx
  Wound 42900
Rectum
  Fistula 45800-45825
  Prolapse 45540-45541
Removal
  Anesthesia 15850-15851
Spleen
  See Splenorrhapy
Stomach
  Fistula 43880
  Laceration 43501-43502
  Stoma 43870
  Ulcer 43501, 43840
  Wound 43840
Tendon
  Foot 28200-28210
  Knee 27380-27381
Testis
  Injury 54670
  Suspension 54620-54640
Thoracic Duct
  Abdominal Approach 38382
  Cervical Approach 38380
  Thoracic Approach 38381
Throat
  Wound 42900
Tongue
  to Lip 41510
Trachea
  Fistula
    without Plastic Repair 31820
    with Plastic Repair 31825
  Stoma
    without Plastic Repair 31820
    with Plastic Repair 31825
  Wound
    Cervical 31800
    Intrathoracic 31805
Ulcer 44604-44605
Ureter 50900
  Deligation 50940
  Fistula 50920-50930
Urethra
  Fistula 45820-45825, 53520
  Stoma 53520
  to Bladder 51840-51841
  Wound 53502-53515
Uterus
  Fistula 51920-51925
  Rupture 58520, 59350
  Suspension 58400-58410
Vagina
  Cystocele 57240, 57260
  Enterocele 57265
  Fistula
    Rectovaginal 57300-57307
    Transvesical and Vaginal Approach ..57330
    Urethrovaginal 57310-57311
    Vesicovaginal 51900, 57320-57330
  Rectocele 57250-57260
  Suspension 57280
  Wound 57200-57210
Vas Deferens 55400

Vein
   Femoral 37650
   Iliac 37660
   Vena Cava .37620
Wound 44604-44605

Swallowing
Evaluation 92525-92526
Cine 74230
Treatment 92526
Video 74230

Swanson Procedure 28309

Sweat Collection
Iontophoresis .89360

Sweat Glands
Excision
   Axillary 11450-11451
   Inguinal 11462-11463
   Perianal 11470-11471
   Perineal 11470-11471
   Umbilical 11470-11471

Sweat Test 82435
See Chloride, Blood

Swenson Procedure 45120

Syme Procedure 27888

Sympathectomy
Artery
   Digital 64820
   Radial 64821
   Superficial Palmar Arch 64823
   Ulnar 64822
Cervical 64802
Cervicothoracic 64804
Digital Artery
   with Magnification 64820
Lumbar 64818
Presacral 58410
Thoracic 32664
Thoracolumbar 64809
with Rib Excision 21616

Sympathetic Nerve
Excision 64802-64818
Injection
   Anesthetic 64508, 64520-64530

Sympathins
See Catecholamines

Symphysiotomy
Horseshoe Kidney 50540

Symphysis, Pubic
See Pubic Symphysis

Syncytial Virus, Respiratory
See Respiratory Syncytial Virus

Syndactylism, Toes
See Webbed, Toe

Syndactyly
Repair 26560-26562

Syndesmotomy
See Ligament, Release

Syndrome
Adrenogenital
   See Adrenogenital Syndrome
Ataxia-Telangiectasia
   See Ataxia Telangiectasia
Bloom
   See Bloom Syndrome
Carpal Tunnel
   See Carpal Tunnel Syndrome
Costen's
   See Temporomandibular Joint (TMJ)
Erb -Goldflam
   See Myasthenia Gravis
Ovarian Vein
   See Ovarian Vein Syndrome
Synechiae, Intrauterine
   See Adhesions, Intrauterine
Treacher Collins
   See Treacher-Collins Syndrome
Urethral
   See Urethral Syndrome

Syngesterone
See Progesterone

Synostosis (Cranial)
See Craniosynostosis

Synovectomy
Arthrotomy with
   Glenohumeral Joint 23105
   Sternoclavicular Joint 23106
Elbow 24102
Excision
   Carpometacarpal Joint 26130
   Finger Joint 26135-26140
   Hip Joint .27054
   Interphalangeal Joint 26140
   Metacarpophalangeal Joint 26135
   Palm 26145
Wrist 25105, 25118-25119
   Radical 25115-25116

Synovial
Bursa
   See Bursa
Cyst
   See Ganglion
Membrane
   See Synovium
Popliteal Space
   See Baker's Cyst

Synovium
Biopsy
   Carpometacarpal Joint 26100
   Interphalangeal Joint 26110
   Knee Joint 27330
   Metacarpophalangeal Joint
      with Synovial Biopsy 26105

Syphilis ab
See Antibody, Treponema Pallidum

Syphilis Test 86592-86593

Syrinx
Spinal Cord
   Aspiration 62268

System
Endocrine
   See Endocrine System
Hemic
   See Hemic System
Lymphatic
   See Lymphatic System
Musculoskeletal
   See Musculoskeletal System
Nervous
   See Nervous System

T

T-3
See Triiodothyronine

T-4 . . . . .84436-84439, 86360

T-7 Index
See Thyroxine, Total

T-8
See CD8; T-Cells, Ratio

T-Cells
CD4
   Absolute .86361
Count 86359
Depletion 86915
Ratio 86360

T-Cell T8 Antigens
See CD8

T-Phyl
See Theophylline

T3 Free
See Triiodothyronine, Free

T4 Molecule
See CD4

T4 Total
See Thyroxine, Total

Taarnhoj Procedure
See Decompression, Gasserian Ganglion, Sensory Root; Section

Tachycardia
Heart
   Recording .93609

Tacrolimus
Drug Assay 80197

Tag, Skin
See Skin, Tags

Tail Bone
Excision 27080
Fracture 27200-27202

Takeuchi Procedure 33505

Talectomy
See Astragalectomy

Talotarsal Joint
Dislocation 28570-28575, 28585
    Percutaneous Fixation 28576

Talus
Arthrodesis
    Pantalar 28705
    Subtalar 28725
    Triple 28715
Arthroscopy
    Surgical 29891-29892
Craterization 28120
Cyst
    Excision 28100-28103
Diaphysectomy 28120
Excision 28120, 28130
Fracture
    Open Treatment 28445
    Percutaneous Fixation 28436
    without Manipulation 28430
    with Manipulation 28435-28436
Repair
    Osteochondritis Dissecans 29892
    Osteotomy 28302
Saucerization 28120
Tumor
    Excision 27647, 28100-28103

Tap
Cisternal
    See Cisternal Puncture
Lumbar Diagnostic
    See Spinal Tap

Tarsal
Fracture
    Percutaneous Fixation 28456

Tarsal Bone
See Ankle Bone

Tarsal Joint
See Foot
Arthrodesis 28730-28735, 28740
    with Advancement 28737
    with Lengthening 28737
Craterization 28122
Cyst
    Excision 28104-28107
Diaphysectomy 28122
Dislocation 28540-28545, 28555
    Percutaneous Fixation 28545-28546
Excision 28116, 28122
Fracture
    Open Treatment 28465
    without Manipulation 28450
    with Manipulation 28455-28456
Fusion 28730-28735, 28740
    with Advancement 28737
    with Lengthening 28737
Repair 28320
    Osteotomy 28304-28305
Saucerization 28122
Tumor
    Excision 28104-28107, 28171

Tarsal Strip Procedure 67917

Tarsal Tunnel Release 28035

Tarsometatarsal Joint
Arthrodesis 28730-28735, 28740
Arthrotomy 28020, 28050
Dislocation 28600-28605, 28615
    Percutaneous Fixation 28606
Exploration 28020
Fusion 28730-28735, 28740
Removal
    Foreign Body 28020
    Loose Body 28020
Synovial
    Biopsy 28050
    Excision 28070

Tarsorrhaphy 67875
Median 67880
Severing 67710
    with Transposition of Tarsal Plate 67882

Tattoo
Cornea 65600
Skin 11920-11922

TBG
See Thyroxine Binding Globulin

TBS
See Bethesda System

TB Test
Antigen Response 0010T
Skin Test 86580-86585

TCT
See Thrombin Time

Td Shots
See Tetanus Immunization; Vaccines

Team Conference
Case Management Services 99361-99373

Tear Duct
See Lacrimal Duct

Tear Gland
See Lacrimal Gland

Technique
Pericardial Window
    See Pericardiostomy
Projective
    See Projective Test

Teeth
X-Ray 70300-70320

Telangiectasia
Chromosome Analysis 88248
Injection 36468

Telangiectasia, Cerebello-Oculocutaneous
See Ataxia Telangiectasia

Telephone
Case Management Services 99361-99373
Pacemaker Analysis 93733, 93736
Transmission of ECG 93012

Teletherapy
Dose Plan 77305-77321

Temperature Gradient Studies 93740

Temporal, Petrous
Excision
    Apex 69530

Temporal Arteries
See Artery, Temporal

Temporal Bone
Electromagnetic Bone Conduction Hearing Device
    Implantation/Replacement 69710
    Removal/Repair 69711
Excision 69535
Resection 69535
Tumor
    Removal 69970
Unlisted Services and Procedures 69979

Temporomandibular Joint (TMJ)
Arthrocentesis 20605
Arthrography 70328-70332
    Injection 21116
Arthroplasty 21240-21243
Arthroscopy
    Diagnostic 29800
    Surgical 29804
Arthrotomy 21010
Cartilage
    Excision 21060
Condylectomy 21050
Coronoidectomy 21070
Dislocation
    Closed Treatment 21480-21485
    Open Treatment 21490
Injection
    Radiologic 21116
Magnetic Resonance Imaging (MRI) 70336
Meniscectomy 21060
Prostheses
    See Prosthesis, Temporomandibular Joint
Reconstruction
    See Reconstruction, Temporomandibular Joint
X-Ray with Contrast 70328-70332

Tenago Procedure 53431

Tendinosuture
See Suture, Tendon

Tendon
Achilles
    See Achilles Tendon
Arm, Upper
    Revision 24320
Finger
    Excision 26180
Forearm
    Repair 25260-25274
Graft
    Harvesting 20924
Insertion
    Biceps Tendon 24342

Lengthening
  Ankle 27685-27686
  Arm, Upper 24305
  Elbow 24305
  Finger 26476, 26478
  Forearm 25280
  Hand 26476, 26478
  Leg, Lower 27685-27686
  Leg, Upper 27393-27395
  Toe 28240
  Wrist 25280
Palm
  Excision 26170
Release
  Arm, Lower .25295
  Arm, Upper .24332
  Wrist 25295
Shortening
  Ankle 27685-27686
  Finger 26477, 26479
  Hand 26477, 26479
  Leg, Lower 27685-27686
Transfer
  Arm, Lower 25310-25312, 25316
  Arm, Upper .24301
  Elbow 24301
  Finger 26497-26498
  Hand 26480-26489
  Leg, Lower 27690-27692
  Leg, Upper .27400
  Pelvis 27098
  Thumb 26490-26492, 26510
  Wrist 25310-25312, 25316
Transplant
  Leg, Upper 27396-27397
Wrist
  Repair 25260-25274

Tendon Origin
Insertion
  Injection 20551

Tendon Pulley Reconstruction of Hand
See Hand, Reconstruction, Tendon Pulley

Tendon Sheath
Arm
  Lower
    Repair 25275
Finger
  Incision 26055
  Incision and Drainage 26020
  Lesion 26160
Foot
  Excision 28086-28088
Hand Lesion 26160
Injection 20550
Palm
  Incision and Drainage 26020
Removal
  Foreign Body 20520-20525
Wrist
  Excision, Radical 25115-25116
  Incision 25000-25001
  Repair 25275

Tenectomy, Tendon Sheath
See Excision, Lesion, Tendon Sheath

Tennis Elbow
Repair 24350-24356

Tenodesis
Biceps Tendon
  at Elbow 24340
    Shoulder 23430
Finger 26471-26474
Wrist .25300-25301

Tenolysis
Ankle .27680-27681
Arm, Lower 25295
Arm, Upper 24332
Finger
  Extensor 26445-26449
  Flexor 26440-26442
Foot 28220-28226
Hand Extensor 26445-26449
  Flexor 26440-26442
Leg, Lower 27680-27681
Wrist 25295

Tenomyotomy
Shoulder 23405-23406

Tenon's Capsule
Injection 67515

Tenoplasty
Anesthesia 01714

Tenorrhaphy
See Suture, Tendon

Tenosuspension
See Tenodesis

Tenosuture
See Suture, Tendon

Tenotomy
Achilles Tendon 27605-27606
Ankle .27605-27606
Arm, Lower 25290
Arm, Upper 24310
Finger 26060, 26455-26460
Foot 28230, 28234
Hand .26450, 26460
Hip
  Iliopsoas Tendon 27005
Hip, Abductor 27006
Hip, Adductor 27000-27003
Leg, Upper 27306-27307, 27390-27392
Toe 28010-28011, 28232-28234, 28240
Wrist 25290

TENS
See Application, Neurostimulation; Physical Medicine/Therapy/Occupational Therapy

Tensilon Test 95857-95858

Tension, Ocular
See Glaucoma

Tentorium Cerebelli
Section 61440

Terman-Merrill Test 96100

Termination, Pregnancy
See Abortion

Test
Antiglobulin
  See Coombs Test
Aphasia
  See Aphasia Testing
Bender Visual-Motor Gestalt
  See Bender-Gestalt Test
Binet
  See Binet Test
Blood
  See Blood Tests
Blood Coagulation
  See Coagulation
Breath
  See Breath Test
Cervical Mucus Penetration
  See Cervical Mucus Penetration Test
Clinical Chemistry
  See Chemistry Tests, Clinical
Complement Fixation
  See Complement, Fixation Test
Exercise
  See Exercise Stress Tests
Fern
  See Smear and Stain, Wet Mount
Fetal, Nonstress
  See Fetal Non-Stress Test
Function, Vestibular
  See Vestibular Function Tests
Gel Diffusion
  See Immunodiffusion
Glucose Tolerance
  See Glucose, Tolerance Test
Hearing
  See Audiologic Function Tests
Hemagglutination Inhibition
  See Hemagglutination Inhibition Test
Ink Blot
  See Inkblot Test
Intelligence
  See Intelligence Test
Lung Function
  See Pulmonology, Diagnostic
Neutralization
  See Neutralization Test
Papanicolaou
  See Pap Smears
Pregnancy
  See Pregnancy Test
Quick
  See Prothrombin Time
Radioimmunosorbent
  See Gammaglobulin, Blood
Rorschach
  See Rorschach Test
Schilling
  See Schilling Test
Skin
  See Skin, Tests
Stanford-Binet
  See Psychiatric Diagnosis
Tuberculin
  See Skin, Tests, Tuberculosis

Tester, Color Vision
See Color Vision Examination

Testes
Nuclear Medicine
   Imaging 78760-78761
Undescended
   See Testis, Undescended

Testicular Vein
See Spermatic Veins

Testimony, Medical 99075

Testing, Histocompatibility
See Tissue Typing

Testing, Neurophysiologic
Intraoperative 95920

Testing, Neuropsychological . .96117

Testing, Range of Motion
See Range of Motion Test

Testis
Abscess
   Incision and Drainage 54700
Biopsy 54500-54505
Excision
   Laparoscopic 54690
   Partial 54522
   Radical 54530-54535
   Simple 54520
Hematoma
   Incision and Drainage 54700
Insertion
   Prosthesis 54660
Lesion
   Excision .54512
Needle Biopsy 54500
Repair
   Injury 54670
   Suspension 54620-54640
   Torsion 54600
Suture
   Injury 54670
   Suspension 54620-54640
Transplantation
   to Thigh .54680
Tumor
   Excision 54530-54535
Undescended
   Exploration 54550-54560
Unlisted Services and Procedures . .54699, 55899

Testosterone 84402
Response 80414
   Stimulation 80414-80415
Total 84403

Testosterone Estradiol Binding Globulin
See Globulin, Sex Hormone Binding

Test Tube Fertilization
See In Vitro Fertilization

Tetanus 86280
Antibody 86774
Immunoglobulin 90389
Vaccine 90703

Tetrachloride, Carbon
See Carbon Tetrachloride

Tetralogy of Fallot . . .33692-33697, 33924

Thal-Nissen Procedure 43325

Thawing and Expansion
of Frozen Cell 88241

THBR
See Thyroid Hormone Binding Ratio

Theleplasty
See Nipples, Reconstruction

Theophylline
Assay 80198

Therapeutic
Abortion
   See Abortion, Therapeutic
Apheresis
   See Apheresis, Therapeutic
Drug Assay
   See Drug Assay
Mobilization
   See Mobilization
Photopheresis
   See Photopheresis
Radiology
   See Radiology, Therapeutic

Therapies
Cold
   See Cryotherapy
Exercise
   See Exercise Therapy
Family
   See Psychotherapy, Family
Language
   See Language Therapy
Milieu
   See Environmental Intervention
Occupational
   See Occupational Therapy
Photodynamic
   See Photochemotherapy
Photoradiation
   See Actinotherapy
Physical
   See Physical Medicine/Therapy/Occupational Therapy
Speech
   See Speech Therapy
Tocolytic
   See Tocolysis
Ultraviolet
   See Actinotherapy

Therapy
Desensitization
   See Allergen Immunotherapy
Hemodialysis
   See Hemodialysis
Hot Pack
   See Hot Pack Treatment
Radiation
   See Irradiation
Speech
   See Speech Therapy

Thermocauterization
Ectropion
   Repair 67922
Lesion
   Cornea 65450

Thermocoagulation
See Electrocautery

Thermogram
Cephalic 93760
Peripheral 93762

Thermographies
See Thermogram

Thermography, Cerebral
See Thermogram, Cephalic

Thermotherapy
Prostate 53850-53853
   Microwave 53850
   Radiofrequency 53852

Thiamine .84425

Thiersch Operation 15050
See Pinch Graft

Thiersch Procedure 46753

Thigh
Fasciotomy 27025
   See Femur; Leg, Upper

Thin Layer Chromatographies
See Chromatography, Thin-Layer

Thiocyanate 84430

Third Disease
See Rubella

Third Opinion
See Confirmatory Consultations

Thompson Procedure 27430

Thompson Test
See Smear and Stain, Routine

Thoracectomy
See Thoracoplasty

Thoracentesis 32000-32002

Thoracic
Anterior Ramus
   See Intercostal Nerve
Arteries
   See Artery, Thoracic
Cavity
   See Chest Cavity
Duct
   See Lymphatics
   Cannulation 38794
   Ligation 38380
      Abdominal Approach 38382
      Thoracic Approach 38381
   Suture
      Abdominal Approach 38382
      Cervical Approach 38380
      Thoracic Approach 38381

Empyema
   See Abscess, Thorax
Surgery
   Video-Assisted
      See Thoracoscopy
Vertebra
   See Vertebra, Thoracic
Wall
   See Chest Wall

Thoracocentesis
See Thoracentesis

Thoracoplasty 32905
with Closure Bronchopleural Fistula 32906

Thoracoscopy
Diagnostic 32601-32606
   without Biopsy 32601, 32603, 32605
   with Biopsy 32602, 32604, 32606
Surgical 32650-32665
   with Control Traumatic Hemorrhage ... 32654
   with Creation Pericardial Window 32659
   with Esophagomyotomy 32665
   with Excision-Plication of Bullae 32655
   with Excision Mediastinal Cyst, Tumor
   and/or Mass 32662
   with Excision Pericardial Cyst, Tumor
   and/or Mass 32661
   with Lobectomy 32663
   with Parietal Pleurectomy 32656
   with Partial Pulmonary Decortication .. 32651
   with Pleurodesis 32650
   with Removal Intrapleural Foreign
   Body 32653
   with Removal of Clot/Foreign Body ... 32658
   with Thoracic Sympathectomy 32664
   with Total Pericardiectomy 32660
   with Total Pulmonary Decortication ... 32652
   with Wedge Resection of Lung 32657

Thoracostomy
Empyema 32035-32036
Tube, with/without Water Seal 32020

Thoracotomy
Cardiac Massage 32160
for Pacing Cardioverter-Defibrillator
   Pads 33245-33246
for Post-Op Complications 32120
Hemorrhage 32110
Removal
   Bullae 32141
   Cyst 32140
   Defibrillator 33243
   Electrodes 33238
   Foreign Body
      Intrapleural 32150
      Intrapulmonary 32151
   Pacemaker 33236-33237
      with Biopsy 32095-32100
      with Excision-Plication of Bullae 32141
      with Lung Repair 32110
      with Open Intrapleural
      Pneumolysis 32124
Transmyocardial Laser
Revascularization 33140-33141

Thorax
See Chest; Chest Cavity; Mediastinum
Angiography 71275
Bioimpedance 93701
Biopsy 21550
CAT Scan 71250-71275
Incision
   Empyema 32035-32036
   Pneumothorax 32020
Incision and Drainage
   Abscess 21501-21502
   Deep 21510
   Hematoma 21501-21502
Strapping 29200
Tumor
   Excision 21555-21556
   Excision/Resection 21557
Unlisted Services and Procedures,
Surgery 21899

Three-Day Measles
See Rubella

Three Glass Test
See Urinalysis, Glass Test

Throat
See Pharynx
Abscess
   Incision and Drainage 42700-42725
Biopsy 42800-42806
Hemorrhage 42960-42962
Reconstruction 42950
Removal
   Foreign Body 42809
Repair
   Pharyngoesophageal 42953
   Wound 42900
Suture
   Wound 42900
Unlisted Services and Procedures 42999

Thrombectomy
See Thromboendarterectomy
Aortoiliac Artery 34151-34201
Arteriovenous Fistula
   Graft 36870
Axillary Artery 34101
Axillary Vein 34490
Brachial Artery 34101
Bypass Graft
   Other than Hemodialysis Graft or
   Fistula 35875-35876
Carotid Artery 34001
Celiac Artery 34151
Dialysis Graft
   without Revision 36831
Femoral 34201
Femoropopliteal Vein 34421-34451
Iliac 34151-34201
Iliac Vein 34401-34451
Innominate Artery 34001-34101
Mesentery Artery 34151
Percutaneous
   Coronary Artery 92973
Peroneal Artery 34203
Popliteal Artery 34203
Radial Artery 34111
Renal Artery 34151

Subclavian Artery 34001-34101
Subclavian Vein 34471-34490
Tibial Artery 34203
Ulnar Artery 34111
Vena Cava 34401-34451
Vena Caval 50230

Thrombin Inhibitor I
See Antithrombin III

Thrombin Time 85670-85675

Thrombocyte (Platelet)
See Blood, Platelet

Thrombocyte ab
See Antibody, Platelet

Thromboendarterectomy
See Thrombectomy
Aorta, Abdominal 35331
Aortoiliofemoral Artery 35363
Axillary Artery 35321
Brachial Artery 35321
Carotid Artery 35301, 35390
Celiac Artery 35341
Femoral Artery 35371-35381
Iliac Artery 35351, 35361-35363
Iliofemoral Artery 35355, 35363
Innominate Artery 35311
Mesenteric Artery 35341
Peroneal Artery 35381
Popliteal Artery 35381
Renal Artery 35341
Subclavian Artery 35301-35311
Tibial Artery 35381
Vertebral Artery 35301

Thrombokinase 85260

Thrombolysin
See Plasmin

Thrombolysis
Catheter Exchange
   Arterial 37209, 75900
Cerebral
   Intravenous Infusion 37195
Coronary Vessels 92975-92977
Cranial Vessels 37195

Thrombolysis Biopsy Intracranial
Arterial Perfusion 61624

Thrombolysis Intracranial 65205
See Ciliary Body; Cornea; Eye, Removal, Foreign
Body; Iris; Lens; Retina; Sclera; Vitreous

Thrombomodulin 85337

Thromboplastin
Inhibition 85705
Inhibition Test 85347
Partial Time 85730-85732

Thromboplastinogen
See Clotting Factor

Thromboplastinogen B
See Christmas Factor

Thromboplastin Antecedent, Plasma
See Plasma Thromboplastin, Antecedent

Thumb
See Phalanx
Amputation 26910-26952
Arthrodesis
   Carpometacarpal Joint 26841-26842
Dislocation
   with Fracture 26645-26650
      Open Treatment 26665
   with Manipulation 26641
Fracture
   with Dislocation 26645-26650
      Open Treatment 26665
Fusion
   in Opposition 26820
Reconstruction
   from Finger 26550
   Opponensplasty 26490-26496
Repair
   Muscle 26508
   Muscle Transfer 26494
   Tendon Transfer 26510
Replantation 20824-20827
Sesamoidectomy 26185
Unlisted Services and Procedures 26989

Thymectomy 60520-60521
Sternal Split/Transthoracic
Approach 60521-60522
Transcervical Approach 60520

Thymotaxin
See Beta-2-Microglobulin

Thymus Gland 60520
Excision 60520-60521

Thyramine
See Amphetamine

Thyrocalcitonin
See Calcitonin

Thyroglobulin 84432
Antibody 86800

Thyroglossal Duct
Cyst
   Excision 60280-60281

Thyroidectomy
Partial 60210-60225
Secondary 60260
Total 60240, 60271
   Cervical Approach 60271
   for Malignancy
      Limited Neck Dissection 60252
      Radical Neck Dissection 60254
      Removal All Thyroid Tissue 60260
      Sternal Split/Transthoracic Approach .. 60270

Thyroid Gland
Cyst
   Aspiration 60001
   Excision 60200
   Incision and Drainage 60000
   Injection 60001

Excision
   for Malignancy
      Limited Neck Dissection 60252
      Radical Neck Dissection 60254
   Partial 60210-60225
   Secondary 60260
   Total 60240, 60271
      Cervical Approach 60271
      Removal All Thyroid Tissue 60260
      Sternal Split/Transthoracic
      Approach 60270
      Transcervical Approach 60520
Metastatic Cancer
   Nuclear Imaging 78015-78018
Needle Biopsy 60100
Nuclear Medicine
   Imaging 78010
   Imaging for Metastases 78015-78018
   Imaging with Flow 78011
   Imaging with Uptake 78006-78007
   Metastases Uptake 78020
   Uptake 78000-78003
Radionuclide Therapy
   Ablation 79030
   Hyperthyroidism 79000-79001
   Metastases 79035
   Suppression 79020
Radiopharmaceutical Therapy
   Ablation 79030
   Metastases 79035
   Suppression 79020
Tumor
   Excision 60200

Thyroid Hormone Binding Ratio 84479

Thyroid Hormone Uptake 84479

Thyroid Stimulating Hormone (TSH) 80418, 80438-80440, 84443

Thyroid Stimulating Hormone Receptor ab
See Thyrotropin Releasing Hormone (TRH)

Thyroid Stimulating Immune Globulins 84445

Thyroid Stimulator, Long Acting
See Thyrotropin Releasing Hormone (TRH)

Thyroid Suppression Test
See Nuclear Medicine, Thyroid, Uptake

Thyrolingual Cyst
See Cyst, Thyroglossal Duct

Thyrotomy 31300

Thyrotropin Receptor ab
See Thyrotropin Releasing Hormone (TRH)

Thyrotropin Releasing Hormone (TRH) 80438-80439

Thyroxine
Free 84439
Neonatal 84437
Total 84436
True 84436

Thyroxine Binding Globulin ... 84442

Tibia
See Ankle
Arthroscopy Surgical 29891-29892
Craterization 27360, 27640
Cyst
   Excision 27635-27638
Diaphysectomy 27360, 27640
Excision 27360, 27640
   Epiphyseal Bar 20150
Fracture
   Arthroscopic Treatment 29855-29856
      Plafond 29892
   Closed Treatment 27824-27825
   Distal 27824-27828
   Intercondylar 27538-27540
   Malleolus 27760-27766, 27808-27814
   Open Treatment 27535-27536,
           27758-27759, 27826-27828
   Plateau 29855-29856
      Closed Treatment 27530-27536
   Shaft 27752-27759
   without Manipulation 27824
   with Manipulation 27825
Incision 27607
Osteoplasty
   Lengthening 27715
Prophylactic Treatment 27745
Reconstruction 27418
   at Knee 27440-27443, 27446
Repair 27720-27725
   Epiphysis 27477-27485, 27730-27742
   Osteochondritis Dissecans
      Arthroscopy 29892
   Osteotomy 27455-27457, 27705,
              27709-27712
   Pseudoarthrosis 27727
Saucerization 27360, 27640
Tumor
   Excision 27635-27638, 27645
X-Ray 73590

Tibial
Arteries
   See Artery, Tibial
Nerve
   Repair/Suture
      Posterior 64840

Tibiofibular Joint
Arthrodesis 27871
Dislocation 27830-27832
Disruption
   Open Treatment 27829
Fusion 27871

TIG
See Immune Globulins, Tetanus

Time
Bleeding
   See Bleeding Time
Prothrombin
   See Prothrombin Time
Reptilase
   See Thrombin Time

Tissue

Culture
  Chromosome Analysis 88230-88239
  Homogenization 87176
  Non-neoplastic Disorder 88230, 88237
  Skin Grafts 15100-15121, 15342-15343
  Solid Tumor .88239
  Toxin/Antitoxin 87230
  Virus .87252-87253
Enzyme Activity 82657
Examination for Ectoparasites 87220
Examination for Fungi 87220
Expander
  Breast Reconstruction with 19357
  Insertion
    Skin 11960
  Removal
    Skin 11971
  Replacement
    Skin 11970
Grafts
  Harvesting 20926
Granulation
  See Granulation Tissue
Homogenization 87176
Hybridization In Situ 88365
Mucosal
  See Mucosa
Preparation
  Drug Analysis 80103
Soft
  Abscess 20000-20005
Transfer
  Adjacent
    Eyelids 67961
    Skin 14000-14350
  Facial Muscles 15845
  Finger Flap .14350
  Toe Flap 14350
Typing
  HLA Antibodies 86812-86817
  Lymphocyte Culture 86821-86822

Tissue Factor

See Thromboplastin

TLC

See Chromatography, Thin-Layer
Screen 84375

TMJ

See Temporomandibular Joint (TMJ)
Prostheses
  See Prosthesis, Temporomandibular Joint

Tobramycin

Assay 80200

Tocolysis 59412, 99553

External Cephalic Version 59412

Tocopherol .84446

Toe

See Interphalangeal Joint, Toe;
Metatarsophalangeal Joint; Phalanx
Amputation 28810-28825
Capsulotomy 28270-28272
Fasciotomy 28008

Fracture
  See Fracture, Phalanges, Toe
Lesion
  Excision 28092
Reconstruction
  Angle Deformity 28313
  Extra Toes .28344
  Hammertoe 28285-28286
  Macrodactyly 28340-28341
  Syndactyly .28345
  Webbed Toe 28345
Repair
  Bunion 28290-28299
  Muscle 28240
  Tendon 28232-28234, 28240
  Webbed 28280
  Webbed Toe 28345
Tenotomy 28010-28011, 28232-28234
Unlisted Services and Procedures 28899

Toes

Arthrocentesis .20600
Dislocation
  See Specific Joint
Magnetic Resonance Imaging
(MRI) 73721-73723
Reconstruction
  Extra Digit .26587
Repair
  Extra Digit .26587
  Macrodactylia 26590
Reposition to Hand 26551-26556
Strapping 29550
X-Ray 73660

Toe Flap

Tissue Transfer 14350

Tolbutamide Tolerance Test . . .82953

Tolerance Test

Glucagon 82946
Glucose 82951-82952
  with Tolbutamide 82953
Heparin-Protamine 85530
Insulin 80434-80435
Maltose 82951-82952
Tolbutamide 82953

Tomodensitometries

See CAT Scan

Tomographic Scintigraphy, Computed

See Emission Computerized Tomography

Tomographic SPECT

Myocardial Imaging 78469

Tomographies, Computed X-Ray

See CAT Scan

Tomography, Computerized Axial

Abdomen
  See Abdomen, CAT Scan
Head
  See Head, CAT Scan

Tomography, Emission Computed

See Positron Emission Tomography
Single Photon
  See SPECT

Tompkins Metroplasty 58540

See Uterus, Reconstruction

Tongue

Abscess
  Incision and Drainage . .41000-41006, 41015
Biopsy 41100-41105
Cyst
  Incision and Drainage 41000-41006,
                                      41015, 60000
Excision
  Complete 41140-41155
  Frenum 41115
  Partial 41120-41135
  with Mouth Resection 41150-41153
  with Radical Neck 41135, 41145,
                                      41153-41155
Fixation 41500
Hematoma
  Incision and Drainage . .41000-41006, 41015
Incision
  Frenum 41010
Lesion
  Excision 41110-41114
Reconstruction
  Frenum 41520
Repair
  See Repair, Tongue
  Laceration 41250-41252
  Suture 41510
Suture 41510
Unlisted Services and Procedures 41599

Tonography .92120

with Provocation 92130

Tonometry, Serial 92100

Tonsil, Pharyngeal

See Adenoids

Tonsillectomy 42820-42826

Tonsils

Abscess
  Incision and Drainage 42700
Excision 42825-42826
  Lingual 42870
  Radical 42842-42845
  Tag 42860
  with Adenoids 42820-42821
Lingual
  Destruction 42870
Unlisted Services and Procedures 42999

Topiramate

Assay 80201

TORCH Antibody Panel 80090

Torek Procedure

See Orchiopexy

Torkildsen Procedure 62180

TORP (Total Ossicular Replacement Prosthesis) 69633, 69637

Torsion Swing Test 92546

Torula
See Cryptococcus

Torus Mandibularis
Tumor Excision 21031

Total
Abdominal Hysterectomy
   See Hysterectomy, Abdominal, Total
Bilirubin Level
   See Bilirubin, Total
Catecholamines
   See Catecholamines, Urine
Cystectomy
   See Bladder, Excision, Total
Dacryoadenectomy
   See Dacryoadenectomy, Total
Elbow Replacement
   See Replacement, Elbow, Total
Esophagectomy
   See Esophagectomy, Total
Gastrectomy
   See Excision, Stomach, Total
Hemolytic Complement
   See Complement, Hemolytic, Total
Hip Arthroplasty
   See Hip, Total Replacement
Knee Arthroplasty
   See Prosthesis, Knee
Mastectomies
   See Mastectomy
Ostectomy of Patella
   See Patellectomy
Splenectomy
   See Splenectomy, Total

Touroff Operation 37615
See Ligation, Artery, Neck

Toxicology Screen 80100-80103

Toxin, Botulinum
See Chemodenervation

Toxin Assay 87230

Toxoplasma
Antibody 86777-86778

Trabeculectomies
See Trabeculoplasty

Trabeculectomy ab Externo
in Absence of Previous Surgery 66170
with Scarring Previous Surgery 66172

Trabeculoplasty
by Laser Surgery 65855

Trabeculotomy ab Externo
Eye 65850

Trachea
Aspiration 31720
   Catheter 31720-31725
Catheterization 31700
Dilation 31630-31631

Endoscopy
   via Tracheostomy 31615
Excision
   Stenosis 31780-31781
Fistula
   without Plastic Repair 31820
   with Plastic Repair 31825
Fracture
   Endoscopy 31630
Incision
   Emergency 31603-31605
   Planned 31600-31601
   with Flaps 31610
Instillation
   Contrast Material 31708
Introduction
   Needle Wire 31730
Puncture
   Aspiration and/or Injection 31612
Reconstruction
   Carina 31766
   Cervical 31750
   Fistula 31755
   Intrathoracic 31760
Repair
   Cervical 31750
   Fistula 31755
   Intrathoracic 31760
   Stoma 31613-31614
Revision
   Stoma
      Scars 31830
Scar
   Revision 31830
Stenosis
   Excision 31780-31781
   Repair 31780-31781
Stoma
   Repair
      without Plastic Repair 31820
      with Plastic Repair 31825
   Revision
      Scars 31830
Tumor
   Excision
      Cervical 31785
      Thoracic 31786
Unlisted Services and Procedures
   Bronchi 31899
Wound
   Suture
      Cervical 31800
      Intrathoracic 31805

Tracheal
Stent
   Placement 31631
Tubes
   See Endotracheal Tube

Trachelectomy 57530
Radical 57531

Tracheloplasty
See Cervicoplasty

Trachelorrhaphy 57720

Tracheo-Esophageal Fistula
See Fistula, Tracheoesophageal

Tracheobronchoscopy
through Tracheostomy 31615

Tracheoplasty
Cervical 31750
Intrathoracic 31760
Tracheopharyngeal Fistulization 31755

Tracheostoma
Revision 31613-31614

Tracheostomy
Emergency 31603-31605
Planned 31600-31601
Revision
   Scar 31830
Surgical Closure
   without Plastic Repair 31820
   with Plastic Repair 31825
Tracheobronchoscopy through 31615
with Flaps 31610

Tracheotomy
Tube Change 31502

Tracking Tests (Ocular) 92545
See Ear, Nose and Throat

Tract, Urinary
See Urinary Tract

Traction Therapy
See Physical Medicine/Therapy/Occupational Therapy
Manual 97140
Mechanical 97012

Tractotomy
Medulla 61470
Mesencephalon 61480

Training
Activities of Daily Living 97535, 99509
Biofeedback 90901-90911
Cognitive Skills 97532
Community/Work Reintegration 97537
Home Management 97535, 99509
Orthoptic/Pleoptic 92065
Orthotics 97504
Prosthetics 97520
Self Care 97535, 99509
Sensory Integration 97533
Walking (Physical Therapy) 97116
Wheelchair Management/Propulsion 97542

TRAM Flap
Breast Reconstruction 19367-19369

Trans-Scaphoperilunar
Fracture/Dislocation
   Closed Treatment 25680
   Open Treatment 25685

Transaminase
Glutamic Oxaloacetic 84450
Glutamic Pyruvic 84460

Transcatheter
Biopsy 37200
Embolization
   Percutaneous 37204
   Cranial 61624-61626

Occlusion
    Percutaneous 37204
        Cranial 61624-61626
Placement
    Intravascular Stents 0005T-0007T,
                        37205-37208
Therapy
    Embolization 75894
    Infusion 37201-37202, 75896-75898
    Perfusion
        Cranial 61624-61626
    Retrieval 75961

Transcatheter Foreign Body
Retrieval 37203

Transcortin 84449

Transcutaneous Electric Nerve Stimulation
See Application, Neurostimulation

Transdermal Electrostimulation
See Application, Neurostimulation

Transection
Artery
    Carotid 61610, 61612
Blood Vessel
    Kidney 50100
Carotid
    with Skull Base Surgery 61609
Nerve 64732-64772
    Vagus 43640-43641
Pulmonary Artery 33922

Transesophageal
Doppler Echocardiography 93312-93318

Transfer
Blastocyst
    See Embryo Transfer
Gamete Intrafallopian
    See GIFT
Jejunum
    with Microvascular Anastomosis
        Free 43496
Preparation
    Embryo 89255
        Cryopreserved 89256
Surgical
    See Transposition
Tendon
    See Tendon, Transfer
Toe to Hand 26551-26556

Transferase
Aspartate Amino 84450
Glutamic Oxaloacetic 84450

Transferrin 84466

Transformation
Lymphocyte 86353

Transfusion
Blood 36430
    Exchange 36450-36455
    Fetal 36460
    Push
        Infant 36440

Blood Parts
    Exchange 36520-36521
Unlisted Services and Procedures 86999
White Blood Cells 86950

Transfusion of, Blood, Autologous
See Autotransfusion

Transluminal
Angioplasty
    Arterial 75962-75968
Atherectomies
    See Artery, Atherectomy
Coronary Balloon Dilatation
    See Percutaneous Transluminal Angioplasty

Transmyocardial Laser Revascularization 33140-33141

Transosteal Bone Plate
Reconstruction
    Mandible 21244

Transpeptidase, Gamma-Glutamyl
See Gamma Glutamyl Transferase

Transplant
See Graft
Bone
    See Bone Graft
Hair
    See Hair, Transplant

Transplantation
See Graft
Allogenic
    See Homograft
Autologous
    See Autograft
Bone Marrow 38240-38241
Cartilage
    Allograft
        Knee 0013T
    Autograft
        Knee 0012T
        Knee 0014T
Cornea
    Autograft/Homograft
        Lamellar 65710
        Penetrating 65730-65755
        for Aphakia 65750
Hair
    Punch Graft 15775-15776
    Strip 15220-15221
Heart 33945
Heart-Lung 33935
Heterologous
    See Heterograft
Intestines
    Allotransplantation 44135-44136
    Donor Enterectomy 44132-44133
Liver 47135
    Heterotopic 47136
Lung
    Anesthesia 00580
    Donor Pneumonectomy 32850
    Double, without Cardiopulmonary
        Bypass 32853
    Double, with Cardiopulmonary
        Bypass 32854

    Single, without Cardiopulmonary
        Bypass 32851
    Single, with Cardiopulmonary
        Bypass 32852
Muscle
    See Muscle Flaps
Pancreas 48160, 48550-48556
Parathyroid 60512
Renal
    Allotransplantation 50360
        with Recipient Nephrectomy 50365
    Autotransplantation 50380
    Donor Nephrectomy 50300-50320, 50547
    Recipient Nephrectomy 50340
    Removal Transplanted Renal Allograft .50370
Skin
    See Dermatology
Stem Cells 38240-38241
    Harvesting 38231
Testis
    to Thigh 54680
Tissue, Harvesting
    See Graft, Tissue, Harvesting

Transpleural Thoracoscopy
See Thoracoscopy

Transposition
Arteries
    Carotid 35691, 35694-35695
    Subclavian 35693-35695
    Vertebral 35691-35693
Cranial Nerve 64716
Eye Muscles 67320
Great Arteries
    Repair 33770-33781
Nerve 64718-64721
Ovary 58825
Peripheral Nerve
    Major 64856
Vein Valve 34510

Transthoracic Echocardiography
See Echocardiography

Transthyretin
See Prealbumin

Transureteroureterostomy 50770

Transurethral Balloon Dilation
Prostatic Urethra 52510

Transurethral Fulguration
Postoperative Bleeding 52606

Transurethral Procedure
See Specific Procedure
Prostate
    Incision 52450
    Resection 52612-52614
    Thermotherapy 53850-53853
        Microwave 53850
        Radiofrequency 53852

Trapezium
Arthroplasty
    with Implant 25445

Travel, Unusual 99082

Treacher-Collins Syndrome
Midface Reconstruction 21150-21151

Treatment, Tocolytic
See Tocolysis

Trendelenburg Operation
See Varicose Vein, Removal, Secondary Varicosity

Trephine Procedure
Sinusotomy
    Frontal 31070

Treponema Pallidum
Antibody
    Confirmation Test 86781
Antigen Detection
    Direct Fluorescence 87285

TRH
See Thyrotropin Releasing Hormone (TRH)

Triacylglycerol
See Triglycerides

Triacylglycerol Hydrolase
See Lipase

Tributyrinase
See Lipase

Trichiasis
Repair 67825
    Epilation, by Forceps 67820
    Epilation, by Other than Forceps 67825
    Incision of Lid Margin 67830
       with Free Mucous Membrane Graft .67835

Trichina
See Trichinella

Trichinella
Antibody 86784
Trichogram 96902

Trichrome Stain 88313

Tricuspid Valve
Excision 33460
Repair 33463-33465
Replacement 33465
Repositioning 33468

Tridymite
See Silica

Trigeminal Ganglia
See Gasserian Ganglion

Trigeminal Nerve
Destruction 64600-64610
Injection
    Anesthetic 64400
    Neurolytic 64600-64610

Trigeminal Tract
Stereotactic
    Create Lesion 61791

Trigger Finger Repair 26055

Trigger Point
Injection
    One or Two Muscle Groups 20552
    Two or More Muscle Groups 20553

Triglyceridase
See Lipase

Triglycerides 84478

Triglyceride Lipase
See Lipase

Trigonocephaly 21175

Triiodothyronine
Free 84481
Reverse 84482
Total 84480
True 84480

Triolean Hydrolase
See Lipase

Trioxopurine
See Uric Acid

Tripcellim
See Trypsin

Trisegmentectomy 47122

Trocar Biopsy
Bone Marrow 38221

Trochanteric Femur Fracture
See Femur, Fracture, Trochanteric

Trophoblastic Tumor GTT
See Hydatidiform Mole

Troponin 84484
Qualitative 84512
Quantitative 84484

Truncal Vagotomies
See Vagotomy, Truncal

Truncus Arteriosus
Repair 33786

Truncus Brachiocephalicus
See Artery, Brachiocephalic

Trunk, Brachiocephalic
See Artery, Brachiocephalic

Trypanosomiases
See Trypanosomiasis

Trypanosomiasis 86171, 86280

Trypsin
Duodenum 84485
Feces 84488-84490

**Trypsin Inhibitor, Alpha
1-Antitrypsin**
See Alpha-1 Antitrypsin

Trypure
See Trypsin

Tsalicylate Intoxication
See Salicylate

TSH
See Thyroid Stimulating Hormone

TSI
See Thyroid Stimulating Immunoglobulin

Tsutsugamushi Disease
See Scrub Typhus

TT
See Thrombin Time

TT-3
See Triiodothyronine, True

TT-4
See Thyroxine, True

Tubal Embryo Stage Transfer
See Embryo Transfer

Tubal Ligation 58600
Laparoscopic 58670
with Cesarean Delivery 58611

Tubal Occlusion
See Fallopian Tube
with Cesarean Delivery
    See Fallopian Tube, Occlusion; Occlusion
    Create Lesion
        See Fallopian Tube, Occlusion; Occlusion,
        Fallopian Tube

Tubal Pregnancy 59121
with Salpingectomy and/or
Oophorectomy .59120

Tuba Auditoria (Auditiva)
See Eustachian Tube

Tube Change
Tracheotomy 31502

Tube, Fallopian
See Fallopian Tube

Tube Placement
Endoscopic
    Bile Duct, Pancreatic Duct 43268
    Nasobiliary, Nasopancreatic
       for Drainage 43267
Gastrostomy Tube 43750
Nasogastric Tube 43752
Orogastric Tube 43752

Tubectomy
See Excision, Fallopian Tube

Tubed Pedicle Flap
Formation 15570-15576

Tubercleplasty
Tibia
    Anterior 27418

Tubercle Bacilli
Culture 87116

Tuberculin Test
See Skin, Tests, Tuberculosis

Tuberculosis
Antigen Response Test 0010T
Culture 87116
Skin Test 86580-86585

Tuberculosis Vaccine
(BCG) 90585-90586

Tubes
Endotracheal
　　See Endotracheal Tube
Gastrostomy
　　See Gastrostomy Tube

Tudor 'Rabbit Ear'
See Urethra, Repair

Tuffier Vaginal Hysterectomy
See Hysterectomy, Vaginal

Tumor
See Craniopharyngioma
See Lesion
Abdomen
　　Destruction/Excision 49200-49201
Abdominal Wall
　　Excision 22900
Acetabulum
　　Excision 27076
Ankle 27615-27619
Arm, Lower 25075-25077
Arm, Upper
　　Excision 24075-24077
Back/Flank
　　Excision 21930
　　Radical Resection 21935
Bile Duct
　　Destruction 43272
　　Extrahepatic....................47711
　　Intrahepatic 47712
Bladder 52234-52240
　　Excision 51530, 52355
Brain 61510
　　Excision 61518, 61520-61521,
　　　　　　　　　　　61526-61530, 61545
Breast
　　Excision 19120-19126
Bronchi
　　Excision 31640
Calcaneus 28100-28103
　　Excision 27647
Carpal 25130-25136
Chest Wall
　　Excision 19260-19272
Clavicle
　　Excision 23140, 23200
　　　with Allograft 23146
　　　with Autograft 23145
Coccyx 49215
Colon
　　Destruction 44393, 45383
Cranial Bone
　　Reconstruction 21181-21184
Destruction
　　Chemosurgery 17304-17310
　　Urethra.......................53220
Ear, Middle
　　Extended 69554
　　Transcanal 69550
　　Transmastoid 69552

Elbow
　　Excision 24075-24077
Esophagus
　　Ablation 43228
Excision
　　Femur 27355-27358
Facial Bone 21029-21030, 21034
Fallopian Tube
　　Resection 58950, 58952-58954
Femoral 27355-27358
Femur 27065-27067
　　Excision 27365
Fibroid
　　See Leiomyomata
Fibula 27635-27638
　　Excision 27646
Finger
　　Excision 26115-26117
Foot 28043-28046
Forearm
　　Radical Resection 25077
Gums
　　Excision 41825-41827
Hand
　　Excision 26115-26117
Heart
　　Excision 33120-33130
Hip 27047-27049, 27065-27067
　　Excision 27075-27076
Humerus
　　Excision 23150, 23220-23222, 24110
　　　with Allograft 23156, 24116
　　　with Autograft 23155, 24115
Ileum 27065-27067
Immunoassay for Antigen 86294, 86316
　　CA 125 86304
　　CA 15-3 86300
　　CA 19-9 86301
Innominate
　　Excision 27077
Intestines, Small
　　Destruction 44369
Ischial
　　Excision 27078-27079
Kidney
　　Excision 52355
Knee
　　Excision 27327-27329, 27365
Lacrimal Gland
　　Excision
　　　Frontal Approach 68540
　　　with Osteotomy 68550
Larynx
　　Excision 31300
　　　Endoscopic 31540-31541, 31578
　　　Incision 31300
Leg, Lower 27615-27619
Leg, Upper
　　Excision 27327-27329
Localization
　　Nuclear Medicine 78800-78803
Mandible 21040-21045
Maxillary Torus Palatinus 21032
Mediastinal
　　Excision 39220
Mediastinum 32662
Meningioma 61512
　　Excision 61519

Metacarpal 26200-26205, 26250-26255
Metatarsal 28104-28107
　　Excision 28173
Neck
　　Excision 21555-21556
　　Radical Resection 21557
Olecranon
　　Excision 24120
Olecranon Process
　　with Allograft
　　　Excision 24126
　　with Autograft
　　　Excision 24125
Ovary
　　Resection 58950-58954
Pancreatic Duct
　　Destruction 43272
Parotid Gland
　　Excision 42410-42426
Pelvis 27047-27049
Pericardial
　　Endoscopic 32661
　　Excision 33050
Peritoneum
　　Resection 58950, 58952-58954
Phalanges
　　Finger 26210-26215, 26260-26262
　　Toe 28108
　　Excision 28175
Pituitary Gland
　　Excision 61546-61548
Positron Emission Tomography (PET) 78810
Pubis 27065-27067
Radiation Therapy 77295
Radius 25120-25126, 25170
　　Excision 24120
　　with Allograft
　　　Excision 24126
　　with Autograft
　　　Excision 24125
Rectum
　　Destruction 45190, 45320, 46937-46938
　　Excision 45160-45170
Resection
　　Face 21015
　　Scalp 21015
　　with Cystourethroscopy 52355
Retroperitoneal
　　Destruction/Excision 49200-49201
Sacrum 49215
Scapula
　　Excision 23140, 23210
　　　with Allograft 23146
　　　with Autograft 23145
Shoulder
　　Excision 23075-23077
Skull
　　Excision 61500
Soft Tissue
　　Elbow
　　　Excision 24075
　　Finger
　　　Excision 26115
　　Forearm
　　　Radical Resection 25077
　　Hand
　　　Excision 26115

Wrist
    Excision 25075
    Radical Resection 25077
Spinal Cord
    Excision 63275-63290
Stomach
    Excision 43610-43611
Talus 28100-28103
    Excision 27647
Tarsal 28104-28107
    Excision 28171
Temporal Bone
    Removal 69970
Testis
    Excision 54530-54535
Thorax
    Excision 21555-21556
    Radical Resection 21557
Thyroid
    Excision 60200
Tibia 27365-27638
    Excision 27645
Torus Mandibularis 21031
Trachea
    Excision
        Cervical 31785
        Thoracic 31786
Ulna 25120-25126, 25170
    Excision 24120
    with Allograft
        Excision 24126
    with Autograft
        Excision 24125
Ureter
    Excision 52355
Urethra 52234-52240, 53220
    Excision 52355
Uterus
    Excision 58140-58145
Vagina
    Excision 57135
Vertebra
    Additional Segment
        Excision 22116
    Cervical
        Excision 22100
    Lumbar 22102
    Thoracic
        Excision 22101
Wrist 25075-25077, 25135-25136
    Radical Resection 25077

Tunica Vaginalis
Hydrocele
    Aspiration 55000
    Excision 55040-55041
    Repair 55060

Turbinate
Excision 30130-30140
Fracture
    Therapeutic 30930
Injection 30200
Submucous Resection
    Nose Excision 30140

Turbinate Mucosa
Cauterization 30801-30802

Turcica, Sella
See Sella Turcica

Turnbuckle Jacket 29020-29025
Removal 29715

TURP
See Prostatectomy, Transurethral

Tylectomy
See Breast, Excision, Lesion

Tylenol
Urine 82003

Tympanic Membrane
Create Stoma 69433-69436
Incision 69420-69421
Reconstruction 69620
Repair 69450, 69610

Tympanic Nerve
Excision 69676

Tympanolysis 69450

Tympanometry 92567
See Audiologic Function Tests

Tympanoplasty
See Myringoplasty
Radical or Complete 69645
    with Ossicular Chain Reconstruction .. 69646
without Mastoidectomy 69631
    with Ossicular Chain Reconstruction .. 69632
        and Synthetic Prosthesis 69633
with Antrotomy or Mastoidotomy 69635
    with Ossicular Chain Reconstruction .. 69636
        and Synthetic Prosthesis 69637
with Mastoidectomy 69641
    with Intact or Reconstructed Wall 69643
        and Ossicular Chain Reconstruction .. 69644
    with Ossicular Chain Reconstruction .. 69642

Tympanostomy 69433-69436

Tympanotomy
See Myringotomy

Typhoid Vaccine 90690-90693
AKD 90693
Oral 90690
Polysaccharide 90691

Typhus
Endemic
    See Murine Typhus
Mite-Borne
    See Scrub Typhus
Sao Paulo
    See Rocky Mountain Spotted Fever
Tropical
    See Scrub Typhus

Typing, Blood
See Blood Typing

Typing, HLA
See HLA Typing

Typing, Tissue
See Tissue Typing

Tyrosine 84510

Tzank Smear 87207

T Cell Leukemia Virus I, Human
See HTLV I

T Cell Leukemia Virus II, Human
See HTLV II

**T Cell Leukemia Virus II
Antibodies, Human**
See Antibody, HTLV-II

**T Cell Leukemia Virus I Antibodies,
Adult**
See Antibody, HTLV-I

**T Lymphotropic Virus Type III
Antibodies, Human**
See Antibody, HIV

U

Uchida Procedure
See Tubal Ligation

UDP Galactose Pyrophosphorylase
See Galactose-1-Phosphate, Uridyl Transferase

UFR
See Uroflowmetry

Ulcer
Anal
    See Anus, Fissure
Decubitus
    See Debridement; Pressure Ulcer (Decubitus);
    Skin Graft and Flap
Pinch Graft 15050
Pressure 15920-15999
Stomach
    Excision 43610

Ulcerative, Cystitis
See Cystitis, Interstitial

Ulna
See Arm, Lower; Elbow; Humerus; Radius
Arthrodesis
    Radioulnar Joint
        with Resection 25830
Arthroplasty
    with Implant 25442
Centralization or Wrist 25335
Craterization 24147, 25150-25151
Cyst
    Excision 24125-24126, 25120-25126
Diaphysectomy 24147, 25150-25151
Excision 24147
    Abscess 24138
    Complete 25240
    Epiphyseal Bar 20150
    Partial 25145-25151, 25240

Fracture
    Closed Treatment 25530-25535
    Olecranon 24670-24675
        Open Treatment 24685
    Open Treatment 25545
    Shaft 25530-25545
        Open Treatment 25574
    Styloid
        Closed Treatment 25650
        Open Treatment 25652
        Percutaneous Fixation 25651
    without Manipulation 25530
    with Dislocation
        Closed Treatment 24620
        Open Treatment 24635
    with Manipulation 25535
    with Radius 25560-25565
        Open Treatment 25575
Incision and Drainage 25035
Osteoplasty 25390-25393
Prophylactic Treatment 25491-25492
Reconstruction
    Radioulnar 25337
Repair
    Epiphyseal Arrest 25450-25455
    Malunion or Nonunion 25400, 25415
    Osteotomy 25360, 25370-25375
        and Radius 25365
    with Graft 25405, 25420-25426
Saucerization 24147, 25150-25151
Sequestrectomy 24138, 25145
Tumor
    Cyst 24120
    Excision . .24125-24126, 25120-25126, 25170

Ulnar Arteries
See Artery, Ulnar

Ulnar Nerve
Decompression 64718
Neuroplasty 64718-64719
Reconstruction 64718-64719
Release 64718-64719
Repair/Suture
    Motor 64836
Transposition 64718-64719

Ultrasonic
See Ultrasound

Ultrasonic Cardiography
See Echocardiography

Ultrasonic Procedure 52325

Ultrasonography
See Echography

Ultrasound
See Echocardiography; Echography
Abdomen .76700-76705
Arm 76880
Bone Density Study 76977
Breast 76645
Chest 76604
Colon-Sigmoid
    Endoscopic 45341-45342
Drainage
    Abscess 75989

Echoencephalography
    See Echoencephalography
Esophagus
    Endoscopy 43231-43232
Eye 76511-76513
    Arteries 93875
    Biometry 76516-76519
    Foreign Body 76529
Fetus 76818-76819
Follow-up 76970
for Physical Therapy 97035
Gastrointestinal 76975
Gastrointestinal, Upper
    Endoscopic 43242, 43259
Guidance
    Amniocentesis 59001, 76946
    Arteriovenous Fistulae 76936
    Chorionic Villus Sampling 76945
    Cryosurgery 55873
    Endometrial Ablation 0009T
    Fetal Cordocentesis 76941
    Fetal Transfusion 76941
    Heart Biopsy 76932
    Needle Biopsy . .43232, 43242, 45342, 76942
    Ova Retrieval 76948
    Pericardiocentesis 76930
    Pseudoaneurysm 76936
    Radiation Therapy 76950
    Radioelement 76965
    Radiofrequency Ablation 47383
    Thoracentesis 76942
    Tissue Ablation 76490
Head .76506, 76536
Heart
    Fetal 76825
Hips
    Infant 76885-76886
Hysterosonography 76831
Intraoperative 76986
Intravascular
    Intraoperative 37250-37251
Kidney .76770, 76778
Leg 76880
Neck 76536
Non-Coronary
    Intravascular 75945-75946
Pelvis .76856-76857
Pregnant Uterus 76805-76816
Prostate 76872-76873
Rectal .76872-76873
Retroperitoneal 76770-76775
Scrotum 76870
Spine 76800
Stimulation to Aid Bone Healing 20979
Unlisted Services and Procedures 76999
Vagina 76830

Ultraviolet Light Therapy
Dermatology
    Ultraviolet A 96912
    Ultraviolet B 96910
for Dermatology 96900
for Physical Medicine 97028

Umbilectomy 49250

Umbilical
Hernia
    See Omphalocele
Vein Catheterization
    See Catheterization, Umbilical Vein

Umbilicus
Excision 49250
Repair
    Hernia 49580-49587
    Omphalocele 49600-49611

Undescended Testicle
See Testis, Undescended

Unfertilized Egg
See Ova

Unguis
See Nails

Unilateral Simple Mastectomy
See Mastectomy

Unlisted Services and Procedures 99499, 99539
Abdomen 22999, 49329, 49999
Allergy/Immunology 95199
Anal 46999
Anesthesia 01999
Arm 25999
Arthroscopy 29999
Autopsy 88099
Bile Duct 47999
Brachytherapy 77799
Breast 19499
Bronchi 31899
Cardiac 33999
Cardiovascular Studies 93799
Casting 29799
Cervix 58999
Chemistry Procedure 84999
Chemotherapy 96549
Chest 32999
Coagulation .85999
Colon 44799
Conjunctiva Surgery 68399
Craniofacial .21299
Cytogenetic Study 88299
Cytopathology 88199
Dermatology .96999
Dialysis 90999
Diaphragm 39599
Ear
    External 69399
    Inner 69949
    Middle 69799
Endocrine System 60699
Epididymis 55899
Esophagus 43289, 43499
Evaluation and Management Services 99499
Eyelid 67999
Eye Muscle 67399
Eye Surgery
    Anterior Segment 66999
    Posterior Segment 67299
Forearm 25999
Gallbladder 47999

Gastroenterology Test 91299
Gum 41899
Hand 26989
Hemic System 38999
Hepatic Duct 47999
Hip Joint 27299
Home Services 99539
Hysteroscopy 58579
Immunization 90749
Immunology 86849
Injection 90799
Injection of Medication 90799
Intestine 44209, 44799
Kidney 49659
Lacrimal System 68899
Laparoscopy 38129, 38589, 43289, 43659,
　　　　44209, 44979, 47379, 47579, 49329,
　　　　49659, 50549, 50949, 54699, 55559, 58578,
　　　　　　　　58679, 59898, 60659
Larynx 31599
Lip 40799
Liver 47379, 47399
Lungs 32999
Lymphatic System 38999
Maxillofacial 21299
Maxillofacial Prosthetics 21089
Meckel's Diverticulum 44899
Mediastinum 39499
Mesentery Surgery 44899
Microbiology 87999
Mouth 40899, 41599
Musculoskeletal 25999, 26989
Musculoskeletal Surgery
　　Abdominal Wall 22999
　　Neck 21899
　　Spine 22899
　　Thorax 21899
Musculoskeletal System 20999
　　Ankle 27899
　　Arm, Upper 24999
　　Elbow 24999
　　Head 21499
　　Knee 27599
　　Leg, Lower 27899
　　Leg, Upper 27599
Necropsy 88099
Nervous System Surgery 64999
Neurology/Neuromuscular Testing 95999
Nose 30999
Nuclear Medicine 78999
　　Blood 78199
　　Bone 78399
　　Endocrine System 78099
　　Genitourinary System 78799
　　Heart 78499
　　Hematopoietic System 78199
　　Lymphatic System 78199
　　Musculoskeletal System 78399
　　Nervous System 78699
　　Therapeutic 79999
Obstetrical Care 59898-59899
Omentum 49329, 49999
Ophthalmology 92499
Orbit 67599
Otorhinolaryngology 92599
Ovary 58679, 58999

Oviduct 58679, 58999
Palate 42299
Pancreas Surgery 48999
Pathology 89399
Pelvis 27299
Penis 55899
Peritoneum 49329, 49999
Pharynx 42999
Physical Therapy 97039, 97139, 97799
Pleura 32999
Pressure Ulcer 15999
Preventive Medicine 99429
Prostate 55899
Psychiatric 90899
Pulmonology 94799
Radiation Physics 77399
Radiation Therapy 77499
　　Planning 77299
Radiology, Diagnostic 76499
Radionuclide Therapy 79999
Radiopharmaceutical Therapy 79999
Rectum 45999
Salivary Gland 42699
Scrotum 55899
Seminal Vesicle 55899
Shoulder Surgery 23929
Sinuses 31299
Skin 17999
Special Services and Reports 99199
Spine 22899
Stomach 43659, 43999
Strapping 29799
Surgical Pathology 88399
Temporal Bone 69979
Testis 54699, 55899
Throat 42999
Tongue 41599
Tonsil/Adenoid 42999
Trachea 31899
Transfusion 86999
Ultrasound 76999
Ureter 50949
Urinary System 53899
Uterus 58578-58579, 58999
Uvula 42299
Vagina 58999
Vascular 37799
Vascular Injection 36299
Vascular Studies 93799
Vas Deferens 55899
Wrist 25999

Unna Paste Boot 29580
Removal 29700

UPP
See Urethra Pressure Profile

Upper
Digestive System Endoscopy
　　See Endoscopy, Gastrointestinal, Upper
Extremity
　　See Arm, Upper; Elbow; Humerus
Gastrointestinal Bleeding
　　See Gastrointestinal, Upper, Hemorrhage
Gastrointestinal Endoscopy, Biopsy
　　See Biopsy

　　See Biopsy, Gastrointestinal, Upper
　　and Radius
　　　　See Biopsy, Gastrointestinal, Upper
　　　　Endoscopy; Endoscopy
　　　　See Biopsy, Gastrointestinal, Upper
　　　　Endoscopy; Endoscopy, Gastrointestinal
GI Tract
　　See Gastrointestinal Tract, Upper

Urachal Cyst
See Cyst, Urachal

Urea Breath Test 78267-78268, 83014

Urea Nitrogen
See Blood Urea Nitrogen
Clearance 84545
Quantitative 84520
Semiquantitative 84525
Urine 84540

Urea Nitrogen, Blood
See Blood Urea Nitrogen

Urecholine Supersensitivity Test
See Cystometrogram

Ureter
Anastomosis
　　to Bladder 50780-50785
　　to Colon 50810-50815
　　to Intestine 50800, 50820-50825
　　to Kidney 50740-50750
　　to Ureter 50760-50770
Biopsy 50955-50959, 50974-50978, 52007
Catheterization 52005
Continent Diversion 50825
Creation
　　Stoma 50860
Destruction
　　Endoscopic 50957-50959, 50976-50978
Dilation 52341-52342, 52344-52345
　　Endoscopic 50553, 50572, 50953, 50972
Endoscopy
　　Biopsy ...50955-50959, 50974-50978, 52007,
　　　　　　　　　　52354
　　Catheterization 50953, 50972, 52005
　　Destruction 50957-50959, 50976-50978,
　　　　　　　　　　52354
　　Dilation 52341-52342, 52344-52345
　　Excision
　　　　Tumor 52355
　　Exploration 52351
　　Injection of Implant Material 52327
　　Insertion
　　　　Stent 50947, 52332-52334
　　Lithotripsy 52353
　　Manipulation of Ureteral Calculus 52330
　　Radioactive Substance 50959, 50978
　　Removal
　　　　Calculus 50961, 50980,
　　　　　　　　　　52320-52325, 52352
　　　　Foreign Body 50961, 50980
　　Resection 52355
　　via Incision 50970-50980
　　via Stoma 50951-50961
Exploration 50600
Incision and Drainage 50600

Injection
  Radiologic 50684, 50690
Insertion
  Catheter 50393
  Stent 50393, 50947, 52332-52334
  Tube 50688
Lesion
  Destruction 52354
Lithotripsy 52353
Lysis
  Adhesions 50715-50725
Manometric Studies
  Pressure 50686
Meatotomy 52290
Nuclear Medicine
  Reflux Study 78740
Postcaval
  See Retrocaval Ureter
Reconstruction 50700
  with Intestines 50840
Reflux Study 78740
Reimplantation 51565
Removal
  Anastomosis 50830
  Calculus 50610-50630, 50961,
      51060-51065, 52320-52325
  Foreign Body 50961
Repair 50900
  Anastomosis 50740-50825
  Continent Diversion 50825
  Deligation 50940
  Fistula 50920-50930
  Lysis Adhesions 50715-50725
  Ureterocele 51535
    Ectopic 52301
    Orthotopic 52300
  Urinary Undiversion 50830
Replacement
  with Intestines 50840
Resection 52355
Revision
  Anastomosis 50727-50728
Suture 50900
  Deligation 50940
  Fistula 50920-50930
Tube
  Change 50688
  Insertion 50688
Tumor Resection 52355
Unlisted Services and Procedures ..50949, 53899
X-Ray with Contrast
  Guide Catheter 74480
  Guide Dilation 74485

Ureteral
Catheterization
  See Catheterization, Ureter
Guide Wire Insertion 52334
Meatotomy
  See Meatotomy, Ureteral
Splinting 50400-50405
Stent Insertion 52332

Ureterectomy 50650-50660
Partial 50220, 50546
Total 50548

Ureterocalycostomy 50750

Ureterocele
Excision 51535
Fulguration
  Ectopic 52301
  Orthotopic 52300
Incision 51535
Repair 51535
Resection
  Ectopic 52301
  Orthotopic 52300

Ureterocolon Conduit 50815

Ureteroenterostomy 50800
Revision 50830

Ureterography
Injection Procedure 50684

Ureteroileal Conduit 50820
Cystectomy 51590
Removal 50830

Ureterolithotomy 50610-50630
Laparoscopy 50945
Transvesical 51060

Ureterolysis
for Ovarian Vein Syndrome 50722
for Retrocaval Ureter 50725
for Retroperitoneal Fibrosis 50715

Ureteroneocystostomy ..50780-50785,
        50830, 51565
Laparoscopic 50947-50948

Ureteroplasty 50700

Ureteropyelography 50951, 52005
Injection Procedure 50684, 50690

Ureteropyelostomy 50740

Ureteroscopy
Dilation
  Intra-Renal Stricture 52346
  Ureter 52344-52345
Third Stage with Cystourethroscopy 52351
  Biopsy 52354
  Destruction 52354
  Lithotripsy 52353
  Removal
    Calculus 52352
  Tumor Excision 52355

Ureterosigmoidostomy 50810
Revision 50830

Ureterostomy 50860, 50951
Injection Procedure 50684
Manometric Studies 50686

Ureterostomy Tube
Change 50688

Ureterotomy 50600
Insertion Indwelling Stent 50605

Ureteroureterostomy 50760-50770,
        50830

Urethra
Abscess
  Incision and Drainage 53040
Artificial Sphincter
  Repair 53449
Biopsy 52204, 53200
Destruction 52214-52224
Dilation 52260-52265, 53600-53621
  General 53665
  Suppository and/or
    Instillation 53660-53661
Diverticulum
  See Urethral Diverticulum
Drainage
  Extravasation 53080-53085
Endoscopy 52000
  Biopsy 52204, 52354
  Catheterization 52010
  Destruction 52354, 52400
  Evacuation
    Clot 52001
  Excision
    Tumor 52355
  Exploration 52351
  Incision
    Ejaculatory Duct 52347
  Injection of Implant Material 51715
  Lithotripsy 52353
  Removal
    Calculus 52352
  Resection
    Ejaculatory Duct 52347
  Vasectomy 52347
  Vasotomy 52347
Excision
  Diverticulum 53230-53235
  Total
    Female 53210
    Male 53215
Incision 53000-53010
  Meatus 53020-53025
Incision and Drainage 53060
Insertion
  Catheter 53670-53675
  Stent 52282
Lesion
  Destruction 53265
  Excision 53260
Paraurethral Gland
  Incision and Drainage 53060
Polyp
  Destruction 53260
  Excision 53260
Pressure Profile 51772
Prolapse
  Destruction 53275
  Excision 53275
  Repair 53275
Prostate
  Transurethral Balloon Dilation 52510
Radiotracer 52250
Reconstruction 53410-53440, 53445
  and Bladder 51800-51820
  Complications 54340-54348

Hypospadias
  One Stage 54322-54328
  Second Stage 54308-54316
  Third Stage 54318
  Meatus 53450-53460
Removal
  Calculus 52310-52315
  Foreign Body 52310-52315
  Urethral Stent 52310-52315
Repair
  Diverticulum 53240, 53400-53405
  Fistula ...45820-45825, 53400-53405, 53520
  Sphincter 57220
  Stricture 53400-53405
  Urethrocele 57230
  Wound 53502-53515
Skene's Gland
  Incision and Drainage 53060
Sphincter 52277
  Electromyography 51784-51785
    Needle 51785
  Insertion
    Prosthesis 53444
  Reconstruction 53445
  Removal
    Prosthesis 53446-53447
  Repair
    Prosthesis 53449
  Replacement
    Prosthesis 53448
Suture
  Fistula 45820-45825, 53520
  to Bladder 51840-51841
  Wound 53502-53515
Tumor
  Destruction 53220
  Excision 53220
Unlisted Services and Procedures 53899
Urethrocystography 74450-74455
Urethrotomy 52270-52276
X-Ray with Contrast 74450-74455

Urethral
Diverticulum
  Marsupialization 53240
Meatus, Dorsal
  See Epispadias
Sphincter
  Biofeedback Training 90911
  Insertion
    Prosthesis 53444
  Removal
    Prosthesis 53446-53447
  Replacement
    Prosthesis 53448
Stenosis
  Dilation 52281
Stent
  Insertion 52282
  Removal
    Bladder 52310-52315
    Urethra 52310-52315
Stricture
  Dilation 52281, 53600-53621
  Injection
    Steroids 52283
Syndrome
  Cystourethroscopy 52285

Urethrectomy
Total
  Female 53210
  Male 53215

Urethrocele
See Urethra, Prolapse

Urethrocystography 74450-74455
Contrast and/or Chain 51605
Retrograde 51610
Voiding 51600

Urethrocystopexy
See Vesicourethropexy

Urethromeatoplasty 53450-53460

Urethropexy 51840-51841

Urethroplasty 46744-46746
First Stage 53400
One Stage
  Hypospadias 54322-54328
Reconstruction
  Female Urethra 53430
  Male Anterior Urethra 53410
  Prostatic/Membranous Urethra
    First Stage 53420
    One Stage 53415
    Second Stage 53425
Second Stage 53405
  Hypospadias 54308-54316
Third Stage
  Hypospadias 54318

Urethrorrhaphy 53502-53515

Urethroscopy
See Endoscopy, Urethra

Urethrostomy 53000-53010

Urethrotomy 53000-53010
Direct Vision
  with Cystourethroscopy 52276
Internal 52601, 52647-52648
with Cystourethroscopy
  Female 52270
  Male 52275

Uric Acid
Blood 84550
Other Source 84560
Urine 84560

Uridyltransferase, Galactose-1-Phosphate
See Galactose-1-Phosphate, Uridyl Transferase

Uridylyltransferase, Galactosephosphate
See Galactose-1-Phosphate, Uridyl Transferase

Urinalysis 81000-81099
Automated 81001, 81003
Glass Test 81020
Microalbumin 82043-82044
Microscopic 81015
Pregnancy Test 81025

Qualitative 81005
Routine 81002
Screen 81007
Semiquantitative 81005
Unlisted Services and Procedures 81099
Volume Measurement 81050
without Microscopy 81002

Urinary Bladder
See Bladder

Urinary Catheter Irrigation
See Irrigation, Catheter

Urinary Concentration Test
See Water Load Test

Urinary Sphincter, Artificial
See Prosthesis, Urethral Sphincter

Urinary Tract
X-Ray with Contrast 74400-74425

Urine
Albumin
  See Albumin, Urine
Blood
  See Blood, Urine
Colony Count 87086
Pregnancy Test 81025
Tests 81001

Urobilinogen
Feces 84577
Urine 84578-84583

Urodynamic Tests
Cystometrogram 51725-51726
Electromyography Studies
  Needle 51785
Stimulus Evoked Response 51792
Urethra Pressure Profile 51772
Uroflowmetry 51736-51741
Voiding Pressure Studies
  Bladder 51795
  Intra-Abdominal 51797

Uroflowmetry 51736-51741

Urography
Antegrade 74425
Infusion 74410-74415
Intravenous 74400-74415
Retrograde 74420

Uroporphyrin 84120

Urothromboplastin
See Thromboplastin

Uterine
Adhesion
  See Adhesions, Intrauterine
Cervix
  See Cervix
Endoscopies
  See Endoscopy, Uterus
Haemorrhage
  See Hemorrhage, Uterus

Uterus

Ablation
    Endometrium 0009T, 58353
Biopsy
    Endometrium 58100
    Endoscopic 58558
Catheterization
    X-Ray 58340
Chromotubation 58350
Curettage
    Postpartum 59160
Dilation and Curettage 58120
    Postpartum 59160
Ectopic Pregnancy
    Interstitial
        Partial Resection Uterus 59136
        Total Hysterectomy 59135
Endoscopy
    Endometrial Ablation 58563
    Exploration 58555
    Surgery 58558-58563
    Treatment 58558-58563
Excision
    Laparoscopic 58550
    Partial 58180
    Radical 58210, 58285
    Removal of Tubes and/or
    Ovaries 58262-58263
    Total ... 58150-58152, 58200, 58953-58954
    Vaginal 58260-58270, 58550
        with Colpectomy 58275-58280
        with Colpo-Urethrocystopexy ... 58267
        with Repair of Enterocele 58270
Hemorrhage
    Postpartum 59160
Hydatidiform Mole
    Excision 59100
Hydrotubation 58350
Hysterosalpingography 74740
Hysterosonography 76831
Incision
    Remove Lesion 59100
Insertion
    Heyman Capsule
        for Brachytherapy 58346
    Intrauterine Device (IUD) 58300
    Tandem
        for Brachytherapy 57155
Laparoscopy 58578
Lesion
    Excision 58551, 59100
Reconstruction 58540
Removal
    Intrauterine Device (IUD) 58301
Repair
    Fistula 51920-51925
    Rupture 58520, 59350
    Suspension 58400
        with Presacral Sympathectomy 58410
Suture
    Rupture 59350
Tumor
    Excision
        Abdominal Approach 58140
        Vaginal Approach 58145
Unlisted Services and Procedures .. 58578, 58999
X-Ray with Contrast 74740

UTP Hexose 1 Phosphate Uridylyltransferase
See Galactose-1-Phosphate, Uridyl Transferase

Uvula

Abscess
    Incision and Drainage 42000
Biopsy 42100
Excision 42140-42145
Lesion
    Destruction 42145
    Excision 42104-42107
Unlisted Services and Procedures 42299

Uvulectomy 42140

UV Light Therapy
See Actinotherapy

V

V, Cranial Nerve
See Trigeminal Nerve

V-Y Operation, Bladder, Neck
See Bladder, Repair, Neck

V-Y Plasty
See Skin, Adjacent Tissue Transfer

Vaccination
See Allergen Immunotherapy; Immunization; Vaccines

Vaccines

Adenovirus 90476-90477
Anthrax 90581
Chicken Pox 90716
Cholera
    Injectable 90725
Diphtheria, Tetanus, Acellular Pertussis,
Hepatitis B, and Inactivated Poliovirus
(DTaP-HepB-IPV) 90723
Diphtheria, Tetanus, Acellular
Pertussis (DTaP) 90700
Diphtheria, Tetanus, Acellular Pertussis and
Hemophilus Influenza B (Hib) (DTaP-Hib) ... 90721
Diphtheria, Tetanus, Whole Cell Pertussis
(DTP) 90701
Diphtheria, Tetanus, Whole Cell Pertussis and
Hemophilus Influenza B (Hib) (DTP-Hib) 90720
Diphtheria, Tetanus (DT) 90702
Diphtheria Toxoid 90719
Encephalitis, Japanese 90735
Hemophilus Influenza b 90645-90648
Hepatitis A 90632-90634
Hepatitis A and Hepatitis B 90636
Hepatitis B 90740-90747
Hepatitis B and Hemophilus Influenza B
(HepB-Hib) 90748
Influenza 90657-90660
Lyme Disease 90665
Measles 90705
Measles, Mumps, Rubella and Varicella
(MMRV) 90710

Measles, Mumps and Rubella (MMR) 90707
Measles and Rubella 90708
Meningococcal 90733
Mumps 90704
Plague 90727
Pneumococcal 90669, 90732
Poliovirus, Inactivated
    Subcutaneous 90713
Poliovirus, Live
    Oral 90712
Rabies 90675-90676
Rotavirus 90680
Rubella 90706
Rubella and Mumps 90709
Tetanus and Diphtheria 90718
Tetanus Toxoid 90703
Tuberculosis (BCG) 90585-90586
Typhoid 90690-90693
Unlisted Vaccine/Toxoid 90749
Varicella (Chicken Pox) 90716
Yellow Fever 90717

Vagina

Abscess
    Incision and Drainage 57010
Amines Test 82120
Biopsy
    Endocervical 57454
    Extensive 57105
    Simple 57100
Closure 57120
Construction
    without Graft 57291
    with Graft 57292
Cyst
    Excision 57135
Dilation 57400
Endocervical
    Biopsy 57454
    Exploration 57452
Excision
    Closure 57120
    Complete
        with Removal of Paravaginal Tissue . 57111
        with Removal of Paravaginal Tissue with
        Lymphadenectomy 57112
        with Removal of Vaginal Wall 57110
    Partial
        with Removal of Paravaginal Tissue . 57107
        with Removal of Paravaginal Tissue with
        Lymphadenectomy 57109
        with Removal of Vaginal Wall 57106
    Total 57110
    with Hysterectomy 58275-58280
    with Repair of Enterocele 58280
Exploration
    Endocervical 57452
    Incision 57000
Hematoma
    Incision and Drainage 57022-57023
Hemorrhage 57180
Hysterectomy 58550
Incision and Drainage 57020
Insertion
    Ovoid
        for Brachytherapy 57155
    Packing for Bleeding 57180

Pessary 57160
Sensor, Fetal Oximetry 0021T
Irrigation 57150
Lesion
Destruction 57061-57065
Extensive 57065
Simple 57061
Prolapse
Sacrospinous Ligament Fixation 57282
Removal
Foreign Body 57415
Sling
Stress Incontinence 57287
Repair 56800
Cystocele 57240, 57260
Combined Anteroposterior . .57260-57265
Posterior .57240
Enterocele 57265
Fistula 51900
Rectovaginal 57300-57308
Transvesical and Vaginal Approach . .57330
Urethrovaginal 57310-57311
Vesicovaginal 51900, 57320-57330
Hysterectomy 58267
Incontinence 57284, 57288
Obstetric .59300
Paravaginal Defect 57284
Pereyra Procedure 57289
Prolapse 57282-57284
Rectocele
Combined Anteroposterior . . .57260-57265
Posterior .57250
Suspension 57280
Urethral Sphincter 57220
Wound 57200-57210
Colpoperineorrhaphy 57210
Colporrhaphy 57200
Revision
Sling
Stress Incontinence 57287
Septum
Excision 57130
Suspension 57280
Suture
Cystocele 57240, 57260
Enterocele 57265
Fistula 51900, 57300-57330
Rectocele 57250-57260
Wound 57200-57210
Tumor
Excision 57135
Ultrasound 76830
Unlisted Services and Procedures 58999
X-Ray with Contrast 74775

Vaginal Delivery 59400, 59610-59614
after Previous Cesarean Delivery . . .59610-59612
Attempted 59618-59622
Antepartum Care 59400
Cesarean Delivery after Attempted 59618
Delivery Only 59620
Postpartum Care 59622
Delivery after Previous
Vaginal Delivery Only
Postpartum Care 59614
Delivery Only .59409
External Cephalic Version 59412

Placenta 59414
Postpartum Care 59410
Routine Care .59400

Vaginal Smear
See Pap Smears

Vaginal Suppositories
Induced Abortion 59855
with Dilation and Curettage 59856
with Hysterectomy 59857

Vaginectomy
See Colpectomy

Vaginoplasty
Intersex State 57335

Vaginorrhaphy
See Colporrhaphy

Vaginoscopy
Biopsy 57454
Exploration .57452

Vaginotomy
See Colpotomy

Vagotomy
Abdominal 64760
Highly Selective 43641
Parietal Cell 43641, 64755
Selective 43640
Transthoracic 64752
Truncal 43640
with Gastroduodenostomy Revision,
Reconstruction 43855
with Gastrojejunostomy Revision,
Reconstruction 43865
with Partial Distal Gastrectomy 43635

Vagus Nerve
Avulsion
Abdominal 64760
Selective 64755
Thoracic .64752
Incision 43640-43641
Abdominal 64760
Selective 64755
Thoracic .64752
Injection
Anesthetic 64408
Transection 43640-43641
Abdominal 64760
Selective 43652, 64755
Thoracic .64752
Truncal 43651

Valentine's Test
See Urinalysis, Glass Test

Valproic Acid
See Dipropylacetic Acid

Valproic Acid Measurement
See Dipropylacetic Acid

Valsalva Sinus
See Sinus of Valsalva

**Valva Atrioventricularis Sinistra
(Valva Mitralis)**
See Mitral Valve

Valve
Aortic
See Heart, Aortic Valve
Bicuspid
See Mitral Valve
Mitral
See Mitral Valve
Pulmonary
See Pulmonary Valve
Tricuspid
See Tricuspid Valve

Valvectomy
Tricuspid Valve 33460

Valve Stenoses, Aortic
See Aortic Stenosis

Valvotomy
Mitral Valve 33420-33422
Pulmonary Valve 33470-33474
Reoperation .33530

Valvuloplasty
Aortic Valve 33400-33403
Femoral Vein 34501
Mitral Valve 33425-33427
Percutaneous Balloon
Aortic Valve 92986
Mitral Valve 92987
Pulmonary Valve 92990
Prosthetic Valve 33496
Reoperation .33530
Tricuspid Valve 33463-33465

Vancomycin
Assay 80202

Vanillylmandelic Acid
Urine 84585

Vanilmandelic Acid
See Vanillylmandelic Acid

Van Deen Test
See Blood, Feces

Van Den Bergh Test
See Bilirubin, Blood

Varicella-Zoster
Antibody 86787
Antigen Detection
Direct Fluorescence 87290

Varicella (Chicken Pox)
See Vaccines

Varices Esophageal
See Esophageal Varices

Varicocele
Spermatic Cord
Excision 55530-55540

Varicose Vein

Removal 37720-37730, 37780-37785
Secondary Varicosity 37785
with Tissue Excision 37735-37760

Vascular Flow Check, Graft 15860

Vascular Injection

Unlisted Services and Procedures 36299

Vascular Lesion

Cranial
　　Excision 61600-61608, 61615-61616
Cutaneous
　　Destruction 17106-17108

Vascular Malformation

Cerebral
　　Repair 61710
Finger
　　Excision 26115
Hand
　　Excision 26115

Vascular Procedure

Brachytherapy
　　Intracoronary Artery 92974
Intravascular Ultrasound
　　Coronary Vessels 92978-92979
Stent
　　Intracoronary 92980-92981

Vascular Procedures

Angioscopy
　　Non-Coronary Vessels 35400
Intravascular Ultrasound
　　Non-Coronary Vessels 75945-75946
Thrombolysis
　　Coronary Vessels 92975-92977
　　Cranial Vessels 37195

Vascular Rehabilitation

See Peripheral Artery Disease Rehabilitation
(PAD)

Vascular Studies

See Doppler Scan, Duplex, Plethysmography
Angioscopy
　　Non-Coronary Vessels 35400
Aorta 93978-93979
Arterial Studies (Non-Invasive)
　　Extracranial 93875-93882
　　Extremities 93922-93924
　　Intracranial 93886-93888
　　Lower Extremity 93925-93926
Artery Studies
　　Upper Extremity 93930-93931
Blood Pressure Monitoring, 24 Hour 93784-93790
Cardiac Catheterization
　　Imaging 93555-93556
Hemodialysis Access 93990
Kidney
　　Multiple Study
　　　with Pharmacological Intervention . .78709
　　Single Study
　　　with Pharmacological Intervention . .78708
Penile Vessels 93980-93981
Plethysmography
　　Total Body 93720-93722

Temperature Gradient 93740
Thermogram
　　Cephalic 93760
　　Peripheral .93762
Unlisted Services and Procedures 93799
Venous Studies
　　Extremity 93965-93971
　　Venous Pressure 93770
Visceral Studies 93975-93979

Vascular Surgery

Arm, Upper
　　Anesthesia 01770-01782
Elbow
　　Anesthesia 01770-01782
Unlisted Services and Procedures 37799

Vasectomy 55250

Contact Laser Vaporization with/without
Transurethral Resection
　　of Prostate .52648
Non-Contact Laser Coagulation
of Prostate 52647
Reversal
　　See Vasovasorrhaphy
Transurethral
　　Cystourethroscopic 52347
Transurethral Electrosurgical Resection of
Prostate 52601, 52648

Vasoactive Drugs

Injection
　　Penis 54231

Vasoactive Intestinal
Peptide 84586

Vasogram

See Vasography

Vasography 74440

Vasointestinal Peptide

See Vasoactive Intestinal Peptide

Vasopneumatic Device
Therapy .97016

See Physical Medicine/Therapy/Occupational
Therapy

Vasopressin 84588

Vasotomy 55200, 55300

Transurethral
　　Cystourethroscopic 52347

Vasovasorrhaphy 55400

Vasovasostomy 55400

Vas Deferens

Anastomosis
　　to Epididymis 54900-54901
Excision 55250
Incision 55200
　　for X-Ray 55300
Ligation 55450
Repair
　　Suture 55400
Unlisted Services and Procedures 55899
Vasography 74440
X-Ray with Contrast 74440

VATS

See Thoracoscopy

VDRL 86592-86593

Vein

Adrenal
　　Venography 75840-75842
Anastomosis
　　Caval to Mesenteric 37160
　　Portocaval .37140
　　Reniportal .37145
　　Saphenopopliteal 34530
　　Splenorenal 37180-37181
　　to Vein 37140-37160
Angioplasty 75978
　　Transluminal 35460
Arm
　　Harvest of Vein for Bypass Graft 35500
　　Venography 75820-75822
Axillary
　　Thrombectomy 34490
Biopsy
　　Transcatheter 75970
Cannulization
　　to Artery 36810-36815
　　to Vein 36800
Catheterization
　　Cutdown 36490-36491
　　Organ Blood 36500
　　Percutaneous 36488-36489
　　Umbilical 36510
External Cannula
　　Declotting 36860-36861
Femoral
　　Repair 34501
Femoropopliteal
　　Thrombectomy 34421-34451
Hepatic Portal
　　Splenoportography 75810
　　Venography 75885-75887
Iliac
　　Thrombectomy 34401-34451
Injection
　　Sclerosing Agent 36468-36471
Insertion
　　IVC Filter 75940
Interrupt
　　Femoral 37650
　　Iliac 37660
　　Vena Cava .37620
Jugular
　　Venography .75860
Leg
　　Venography 75820-75822
Ligation
　　Esophagus .43205
　　Jugular 37565
　　Perforation .37760
　　Saphenous 37700-37735, 37780
　　Secondary .37785
Liver
　　Venography 75889-75891
Neck
　　Venography .75860
Nuclear Medicine
　　Thrombosis Imaging 78455-78458
Orbit
　　Venography .75880

Placement
   IVC Filter 75940
Portal
   Catheterization 36481
Pulmonary
   Repair 33730
Removal
   Saphenous 37720-37735, 37780
   Secondary 37785
Renal
   Venography 75831-75833
Repair
   Aneurysm 36834
   Angioplasty 75978
   Graft 34520
Sampling
   Venography 75893
Sinus
   Venography 75870
Skull
   Venography 75870-75872
Spermatic
   Excision 55530-55540
   Ligation 55550
Splenic
   Splenoportography 75810
Stripping
   Saphenous 37720-37735
Subclavian
   Thrombectomy 34471-34490
Thrombectomy
   Other than Hemodialysis Graft
   or Fistula 35875-35876
Unlisted Services and Procedures 37799
Valve Transposition 34510
Varicose
   See Varicose Vein
Vena Cava
   Thrombectomy 34401-34451
   Venography 75825-75827

Velpeau Cast 29058

Vena Cava
Catheterization 36010
Reconstruction 34502
Resection with Reconstruction 37799

Vena Caval
Thrombectomy 50230

Venereal Disease Research Laboratory
See VDRL

Venesection
See Phlebotomy

Venipuncture
See Cannulation; Catheterization
Child/Adult
   Cutdown 36425
   Percutaneous 36410
Infant
   Cutdown 36420
   Percutaneous 36400-36406
Routine 36415

Venography
Adrenal 75840-75842
Arm 75820-75822
Epidural 75872
Hepatic Portal 75885-75887
Injection 36005
Jugular 75860
Leg 75820-75822
Liver 75889-75891
Neck 75860
Nuclear Medicine 78445, 78457-78458
Orbit 75880
Renal 75831-75833
Sagittal Sinus 75870
Vena Cava 75825-75827
Venous Sampling 75893

Venorrhaphy
See Suture, Vein

Venotomy
See Phlebotomy

Venous Access Port
Insertion 36533
Removal 36535
Revision 36534

Venous Blood Pressure
See Blood Pressure, Venous

Venovenostomy
See Anastomosis, Vein

Ventilating Tube
Insertion 69433
Removal 69424

Ventilation Assist ...94656-94657, 99504
See Pulmonology, Therapeutic

Ventricular Puncture 61020-61026,
61105-61120

Ventriculocisternostomy 62180,
62200-62201

Ventriculography
Anesthesia
   Brain 00214
   Cardiac 01920
Nuclear Imaging 78635

Ventriculomyectomy 33416

Ventriculomyotomy 33416

Vermiform Appendix
See Appendix

Vermilionectomy 40500

Verruca(e)
See Warts

Verruca Plana
See Warts, Flat

Version, Cephalic
See Cephalic Version

Vertebra
See Spinal Cord; Spine; Vertebral Body; Vertebral Process
Additional Segment
   Excision 22103, 22116
Arthrodesis
   Exploration 22830
   Posterior 22590-22802
   Spinal Deformity
      Anterior Approach 22808-22812
      Posterior Approach 22800-22804
Cervical
   Excision
      for Tumor 22100, 22110
   Fracture 23675-23680
Fracture/Dislocation
   Additional Segment
      Open Treatment 22328
   Cervical
      Open Treatment 22326
   Lumbar
      Open Treatment 22325
   Thoracic
      Open Treatment 22327
Kyphectomy 22818-22819
Lumbar
   Excision
      for Tumor 22102, 22114
Osteoplasty
   CAT Scan 76013
   Fluoroscopy 76012
   Lumbar 22521-22522
   Thoracic 22520-22522
Osteotomy
   Additional Segment
      Anterior Approach 22226
      Posterior/Posterolateral Approach ..22216
   Cervical
      Anterior Approach 22220
      Posterior/Posterolateral Approach ..22210
   Lumbar
      Anterior Approach 22224
      Posterior/Posterolateral Approach ..22214
   Thoracic
      Anterior Approach 22222
      Posterior/Posterolateral Approach ..22212
Thoracic
   Excision
      for Tumor 22101, 22112

Vertebrae
Arthrodesis
   Anterior 22548-22585
   Spinal Deformity 22818-22819

Vertebral
Arteries
   See Artery, Vertebral
Body
   Biopsy 20250-20251
   Excision
      Decompression 63081-63091
      Lesion 63300-63308
      with Skull Base Surgery 61597
   Fracture/Dislocation
      Closed Treatment 22305
         without Manipulation 22310
      Kyphectomy 22818-22819

Column
   See Spine
Corpectomy .63081-63308
Fracture
   See Fracture, Vertebra
Process
   Fracture/Dislocation
      Closed Treatment
         with Manipulation, Casting and/or
           Bracing .22315

Very Low Density Lipoprotein
See Lipoprotein, Blood

Vesication
See Bulla

Vesicle, Seminal
See Seminal Vesicle

Vesico-Psoas Hitch 50785

Vesicostomy
Cutaneous 51980

Vesicourethropexy 51840-51841

Vesicovaginal Fistula
See Fistula, Vesicovaginal

Vesiculectomy 55650

Vesiculogram, Seminal
See Vesiculography

Vesiculography 55300, 74440

Vesiculotomy 55600-55605
Complicated 55605

Vessel, Blood
See Blood Vessels

Vessels Transposition, Great
See Transposition, Great Arteries

Vestibular Function Tests
See Ear, Nose and Throat
Additional Electrodes 92547
Caloric Test 92533
Caloric Vestibular Tests 92543
Nystagmus
   Optokinetic 92534, 92544
   Positional 92532, 92542
   Spontaneous 92531, 92541
Posturography 92548
Sinusoidal Rotational Testing 92546
Torsion Swing Test 92546
Tracking Test 92545

Vestibular Nerve
Section
   Transcranial Approach 69950
   Translabyrinthine Approach 69915

Vestibule of Mouth
See Mouth, Vestibule of

Vestibuloplasty 40840-40845

Vidal Procedure
See Varicocele, Spermatic Cord, Excision

Video
Esophagus 74230
Pharynx 70371, 74230
Speech Evaluation 70371
Swallowing Evaluation 74230

**Video-Assisted Thoracoscopic
Surgery**
See Thoracoscopy

Videoradiography
Unlisted Services and Procedures . .76120-76125

VII, Coagulation Factor
See Proconvertin

VII, Cranial Nerve
See Facial Nerve

VIII, Coagulation Factor
See Clotting Factor

Villus, Chorionic
See Chorionic Villus

Villusectomy
See Synovectomy

VIP
See Vasoactive Intestinal Peptide

Viral Antibodies 86280

Viral Warts
See Warts

Virus
AIDS
   See HIV-1
Burkitt Lymphoma
   See Epstein-Barr Virus
Human Immunodeficiency
   See HIV
Influenza
   See Influenza Virus
Respiratory Syncytial
   See Respiratory Syncytial Virus
Salivary Gland
   See Cytomegalovirus

Virus Identification
Immunofluorescence 87254

Virus Isolation 87250-87254

Visceral Larval Migrans 86280

Viscosities, Blood
See Blood, Viscosity

Visit, Home
See House Calls

Visualization
Ileal Conduit 50690

Visual Acuity Screen 99172-99173

Visual Field Exam 92081-92083

Visual Function Screen 99172

**Visual Reinforcement
Audiometry** 92579
See Audiologic Function Tests

Vital Capacity Measurement . . .94150

Vitamin 84591
A 84590
B-1 84425
B-12 .82607-82608
   Absorption Study 78270-78272
B-2 84252
B-6 84207
B-6 Measurement
   See Pyridoxal Phosphate
BC
   See Folic Acid
B Complex
   See B Complex Vitamins
C 82180
D 82307, 82652
D, 25-Hydroxy Measurement
   See Calcifediol
D-2
   See Calciferol
D-3 82306
E 84446
K 84597
K-Dependent Protein S
   See Protein S
K Dependent Bone Protein
   See Osteocalcin

Vitelline Duct
See Omphalomesenteric Duct

Vitrectomy
Anterior Approach
   Partial 67005
Pars Plana Approach 67036
Subtotal 67010
with Endolaser Panretinal
   Photocoagulation 67040
with Epiretinal Membrane Stripping 67038
with Focal Endolaser Photocoagulation 67039
with Implantation or Replacement
   Drug Delivery System 67027

Vitreous
Aspiration 67015
Excision
   Pars Planta Approach 67036
   with Epiretinal Membrane Stripping . . .67038
   with Focal Endolaser
      Photocoagulation 67039
Implantation
   Drug Delivery System 67027
Incision
   Strands 67030-67031
Injection
   Fluid Substitute 67025
   Pharmacologic Agent 67028
Removal
   Anterior Approach 67005
   Subtotal 67010
Replacement
   Drug Delivery System 67027

Strands
　　Discission 67030
　　Severing 67031
Subtotal 67010

VLDL
See Lipoprotein, Blood

VMA
See Vanillylmandelic Acid

Vocal Cords
Injection
　　Endoscopy 31513
　　　Therapeutic 31570-31571

Voice Box
See Larynx

Voice Button 31611

Voiding Pressure Studies
Abdominal 51797
Bladder 51795

Volatiles 84600

Volhard's Test
See Water Load Test

Volkman Contracture 25315-25316

Volume Reduction, Lung
See Lung Volume Reduction

Von Kraske Proctectomy
See Proctectomy, Partial

VP
See Voiding Pressure Studies

Vulva
Abscess
　　Incision and Drainage 56405
Excision
　　Complete 56625, 56633-56640
　　Partial 56620, 56630-56632
　　Radical 56630-56631, 56633-56640
　　　Complete 56633-56640
　　　Partial 56630-56632
　　Simple
　　　Complete 56625
　　　Partial 56620
Lesion
　　Destruction 56501-56515
Perineum
　　Biopsy 56605-56606
　　Incision and Drainage 56405
Repair
　　Obstetric 59300

Vulvectomy
Complete 56625, 56633-56640
Partial 56620, 56630-56632
Radical 56630-56631, 56633-56640
　　Complete
　　　with Bilateral Inguinofemoral
　　　Lymphadenectomy 56637
　　　with Inguinofemoral, Iliac, and Pelvic
　　　Lymphadenectomy 56640
　　　with Unilateral Inguinofemoral
　　　Lymphadenectomy 56634

Partial
　　with Bilateral Inguinofemoral
　　Lymphadenectomy 56632
　　with Unilateral Inguinofemoral
　　Lymphadenectomy 56631
Simple
　　Complete 56625
　　Partial 56620

VZIG
See Immune Globulins, Varicella-Zoster

V Flap Procedure
One Stage Distal Hypospadias Repair 54322

W

W-Plasty
See Skin, Adjacent Tissue Transfer

WADA Activation Test 95958
See Electroencephalography

WAIS-R 96100

Waldius Procedure 27445

Wall, Abdominal
See Abdominal Wall

**Walsh Modified Radical
Prostatectomy**
See Prostatectomy

Warts
Flat
　　Destruction 17110-17111

Washing
Sperm 58323

Wasserman Test
See Syphilis Test

Wassmund Procedure
Osteotomy
　　Maxilla 21206

Waterston Procedure 33755

Water Load Test 89365

Water Wart
See Molluscum Contagiosum

**Watson-Jones
Procedure** 27695-27698

Wave, Ultrasonic Shock
See Ultrasound

WBC
See White Blood Cell

Webbed
Toe
　　Repair 28280

Wedge Excision
Osteotomy 21122

Wedge Resection
Ovary 58920

Well-Baby Care 99381, 99391, 99432

Wellness Behavior
See Evaluation and Management, Health
Behavior

Wernicke-Posadas Disease
See Coccidioidomycosis

Westergren Test
See Sedimentation Rate, Blood Cell

Western Blot
HIV 86689
Protein 84181-84182
Tissue Analysis 88371-88372

**Wheelchair
Management/Propulsion**
See Physical Medicine/Therapy/Occupational
Therapy
Training 97542

Wheeler Knife Procedure
See Discission, Cataract

Wheeler Procedure
See Blepharoplasty, Entropion
Blepharoplasty 67924
Discission Secondary Membranous
Cataract 66820

Whipple Procedure 48150

Whirlpool Therapy 97022
See Physical Medicine/Therapy/Occupational
Therapy

Whitemead Operation
See Hemorrhoidectomy, Complex

White Blood Cell
Alkaline Phosphatase 85540
Antibody 86021
Count 85048
Differential 85007, 85009
Histamine Release Test 86343
Phagocytosis 86344
Transfusion
　　See Leukocyte, Transfusion

Whitman Astragalectomy
See Talus, Excision

Whitman Procedure 27120

Wick Catheter Technique 20950

Widal Serum Test
See Agglutinin, Febrile

Window
Oval
　　See Oval Window
Round
　　See Round Window

Window Technic, Pericardial
See Pericardiostomy

Windpipe
See Trachea

Winiwarter Operation
See Anastomosis, Gallbladder to Intestines

Winter Procedure 54435

Wintrobe Test
See Sedimentation Rate, Blood Cell

Wire
See Pin
Insertion/Removal
   Skeletal Traction 20650
Interdental
   without Fracture 21497

Wiring
Prophylactic Treatment
   Humerus 24498

Wirsung Duct
See Pancreatic Duct

Witzel Operation 43500, 43520,
                 43830-43832
See Incision, Stomach, Creation, Stoma; Incision
and Drainage

Womb
See Uterus

Wood Alcohol
See Methanol

Work Hardening 97545-97546
See Physical Medicine/Therapy/Occupational
Therapy

**Work Related Evaluation
Services** 99455-99456

Worm
See Helminth

Wound
Debridement
   Non-Selective 97602
   Selective 97601
Dehiscence
   Repair 12020-12021, 13160
Exploration
   Penetrating
      Abdomen/Flank/Back 20102
      Chest 20101
      Extremity 20103
      Neck 20100
      Penetrating Trauma 20100-20103
Infection
   Incision and Drainage
      Postoperative 10180
Repair
   Complex 13100-13160
   Intermediate 12031-12057
   Simple 12001-12021
   Urethra 53502-53515

Suture
   Bladder 51860-51865
   Kidney 50500
   Trachea
      Cervical 31800
      Intrathoracic 31805
   Urethra 53502-53515
Vagina
   Repair 57200-57210

Wrist
See Arm, Lower; Carpal Bone
Abscess 25028
Arthrocentesis 20605
Arthrodesis .25800
   with Graft 25810
   with Sliding Graft 25805
Arthrography 73115
Arthroplasty 25332, 25443, 25447
   Revision .25449
   Total Replacement 25446
   with Implant 25441-25442, 25444-25445
Arthroscopy
   Diagnostic 29840
   Surgical 29843-29848
Arthrotomy 25040, 25100-25105
   for Repair 25107
Biopsy 25065-25066, 25100-25101
Bursa
   Excision 25115-25116
   Incision and Drainage 25031
Capsule
   Incision .25085
Cast 29085
Cyst 25130-25136
Decompression 25020-25025
Disarticulation 25920
   Reamputation 25924
   Revision .25922
Dislocation
   Closed Treatment 25660
   Intercarpal 25660
      Open Treatment 25670
   Open Treatment 25670, 25676
   Percutaneous Fixation 25671
   Radiocarpal 25660
      Open Treatment 25670
   Radioulnar
      Closed Treatment 25675
      Percutaneous Fixation 25671
   with Fracture
      Closed Treatment 25680
      Open Treatment 25685
      with Manipulation 25259, 25660, 25675
Excision
   Carpal 25210-25215
   Cartilage 25107
Exploration 25040, 25101
Fasciotomy 25020-25025
Fracture .25645
   Closed Treatment 25622, 25630
   Open Treatment 25628
   with Dislocation 25680-25685
   with Manipulation 25259, 25624, 25635
Ganglion Cyst
   Excision 25111-25112
Hematoma .25028

Incision 25040, 25100-25105
   Tendon Sheath 25000-25001
Injection
   Carpal Tunnel
      Therapeutic 20526
      X-Ray .25246
Joint
   See Radiocarpal Joint
Lesion, Tendon Sheath
   Excision .25110
Magnetic Resonance Imaging (MRI) 73221
Reconstruction
   Capsulectomy 25320
   Capsulorrhaphy 25320
   Carpal Bone 25394, 25430
   Realign .25335
Removal
   Foreign Body 25040, 25101, 25248
   Implant .25449
   Loose Body 25101
   Prosthesis 25250-25251
Repair 25447
   Bone 25440
   Carpal Bone 25431
   Muscle 25260, 25270
      Secondary 25263-25265, 25272-25274
   Tendon 25260, 25270, 25280-25316
      Secondary 25263-25265, 25272-25274
   Tendon Sheath 25275
Strapping .29260
Synovium
   Excision 25105, 25115-25119
Tendon Sheath
   Excision 25115-25116
Tenodesis 25300-25301
Tenotomy .25290
Tumor 25130-25136
   Excision 25075-25077
Unlisted Services and Procedures 25999
X-Ray .73100-73110
   with Contrast 73115

X

X, Coagulation Factor
See Stuart-Prower Factor

X, Cranial Nerve
See Vagus Nerve

X-Linked Ichthyoses
See Syphilis Test

X-Ray
Abdomen 74000-74022
Abscess 76080
Acromioclavicular Joint 73050
Ankle .73600-73610
Arm, Lower .73090
Arm, Upper .73092
Artery
   Atherectomy 75992-75996
Auditory Meatus 70134

Bile Duct
    Guide Dilation .74360
Body Section 76100
    Motion 76101-76102
Bone
    Age Study 76020
    Dual Energy Absorptiometry . . .76075-76076
    Length Study 76040
    Osseous Survey 76061-76065
    Ultrasound 76977
Breast 76090-76092
    Localization Nodule 76096
    with Computer-aided Detection 76085
Calcaneus 73650
Chest 71010-71035
    Complete (Four Views)
        with Fluoroscopy 71034
    Insert Pacemaker 71090
    Partial (Two Views)
        with Fluoroscopy 71023
    Stereo 71015
    with Fluoroscopy 71090
Clavicle 73000
Coccyx 72220
Consultation 76140
Duodenum 74260
Elbow 73070-73080
Esophagus 74220
Eye 70030
Facial Bones 70140-70150
Fallopian Tube 74742
Femur 73550
Fibula 73590
Finger 73140
Fistula 76080
Foot 73620-73630
Gastrointestinal Tract 74240-74245
    Guide Dilation 74360
    Guide Intubation 74340-74350
Hand 73120-73130
Head 70350
Heel 73650
Hip 73500-73520, 73540
    Intraoperative 73530
Humerus 73060
Intestines, Small 74245, 74249-74251
    Guide Intubation 74355
Intravascular Stent 75960
Jaws 70355
Joint
    Stress Views .76006
Knee 73560-73564, 73580
    Bilateral 73565
Larynx 70370
Leg 73592
Lumen Dilator 74360
Mandible 70100-70110
Mastoids 70120-70130
Nasal Bone 70160
Neck 70360
Nose to Rectum
    Foreign Body .76010
Orbit 70190-70200
Pelvis 72170-72190, 73540
    Manometry 74710
Peritoneum 74190
Pharynx 70370, 74210

Ribs 71100-71111
Sacroiliac Joint 72200-72202, 73542
Sacrum 72220
Salivary Gland 70380
Scapula 73010
Sella Turcica 70240
Shoulder 73020-73030, 73050
Sinuses .70210-70220
Sinus Tract 76080
Skull 70250-70260
Specimen/Surgical 76098
Spine 72020, 72090
    Cervical 72040-72052
    Lumbosacral 72100-72120
    Thoracic 72070-72074
    Thoracolumbar 72080
    Total 72010
Standing
    Spine 72069
Sternum 71120-71130
Teeth 70300-70320
Tibia 73590
Toe 73660
Total Body
    Foreign Body .76010
Unlisted Services and Procedures . .76120-76125
with Contrast
    Ankle 73615
    Aorta 75600-75630, 75952-75953
    Artery
        Abdominal 75726
        Additional Vessels 75774
        Adrenal 75731-75733
        Arm 75710-75716
        Arteriovenous Shunt 75790
        Brachial .75658
        Carotid 75660-75680
        Coronary 93556
        Coronary Bypass 93556
        Head and Neck 75650
        Leg 75710-75716
        Mammary 75756
        Pelvic 75736
        Pulmonary 75741-75746
        Renal 75722-75724
        Spine 75705
        Transcatheter Therapy 75894-75898
        Vertebral 75685
    Bile Duct 74300-74320
        Calculus Removal 74327
        Catheterization 75982-75984
        Drainage 75980-75982
        Guide Catheter 74328, 74330
    Bladder 74430, 74450-74455
    Brain 70010-70015
    Bronchi 71040-71060
    Colon
        Barium Enema 74270-74280
    Corpora Cavernosa 74445
    Elbow 73085
    Epididymis 74440
    Gallbladder 74290-74291
    Gastrointestinal Tract 74246-74249
    Hip 73525
    Iliofemoral Artery 75630

Intervertebral Disk
    Cervical 72285
    Lumbar 72295
    Thoracic 72285
Joint
    Stress Views .76006
Kidney
    Cyst 74470
    Guide Catheter 74475
Knee 73560-73564, 73580
Lacrimal Duct 70170
Larynx 70373
Lymph Vessel
    Abdomen 75805-75807
    Arm .75801-75803
    Leg .75801-75803
Mammary Duct 76086-76088
Nasolacrimal Duct 70170
    Guide Dilation 74485
Oviduct 74740
Pancreas 74300-74305
Pancreatic Duct
    Guide Catheter 74329-74330
Perineum 74775
Peritoneum 74190
Salivary Gland 70390
Seminal Vesicles 74440
Shoulder 73040
Spine
    Cervical 72240
    Lumbosacral .72265
    Thoracic 72255
    Total 72270
Subtraction Method 76350
Temporomandibular Joint
(TMJ) 70328-70332
Ureter
    Guide Catheter 74480
    Guide Dilation 74485
Urethra .74450-74455
Urinary Tract 74400-74425
Uterus 74740
Vas Deferens 74440
Vein
    Adrenal 75840-75842
    Arm .75820-75822
    Hepatic Portal 75810, 75885-75887
    Jugular 75860
    Leg .75820-75822
    Liver 75889-75891
    Neck 75860
    Orbit 75880
    Renal 75831-75833
    Sampling 75893
    Sinus 75870
    Skull 75870-75872
    Splenic 75810
    Vena Cava 75825-75827
Wrist 73115
Wrist 73100-73110

X-Ray Tomography, Computed
See CAT Scan

Xa, Coagulation Factor
See Thrombokinase

Xenoantibodies
See Antibody, Heterophile

Xenograft 15400-15401

Xenografts, Skin
See Heterograft, Skin

Xenotransplantation
See Heterograft

Xerography
See Xeroradiography

Xeroradiography 76150

XI, Coagulation Factor
See Plasma Thromboplastin, Antecedent

XI, Cranial Nerve
See Accessory Nerve

XII, Coagulation Factor
See Hageman Factor

XII, Cranial Nerve
See Hypoglossal Nerve

XIII, Coagulation Factor
See Fibrin Stabilizing Factor

Xylose Absorption Test
Blood 84620
Urine 84620

Zygoma
See Cheekbone

Zygomatic Arch
Fracture
    Open Treatment 21356-21366
    with Manipulation 21355

Y

Yeast
Culture 87106

Yellow Fever Vaccine 90717

Yersinia
Antibody 86793

Z

Ziegler Procedure
Discission Secondary Membranous
Cataract 66820

Zinc 84630

Zinc Manganese Leucine Aminopeptidase
See Leucine Aminopeptidase

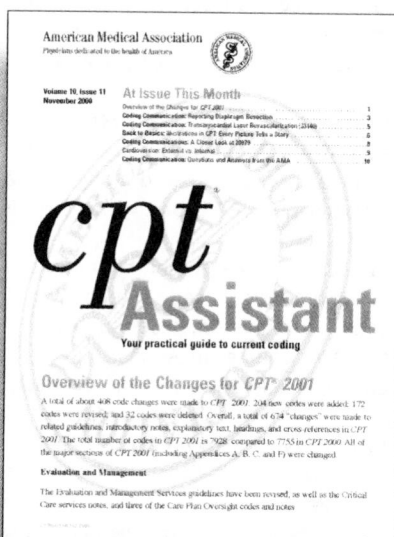

Comprehensive Coding Resources . . .
From the Publisher of CPT®

The American Medical Association, the source of CPT codes, offers so many ways to help health care professionals code more accurately and efficiently. Whether you are new to CPT coding or are a veteran coder, stay up-to-date with the CPT references that simplify the coding process.

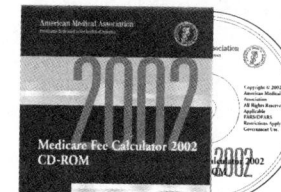

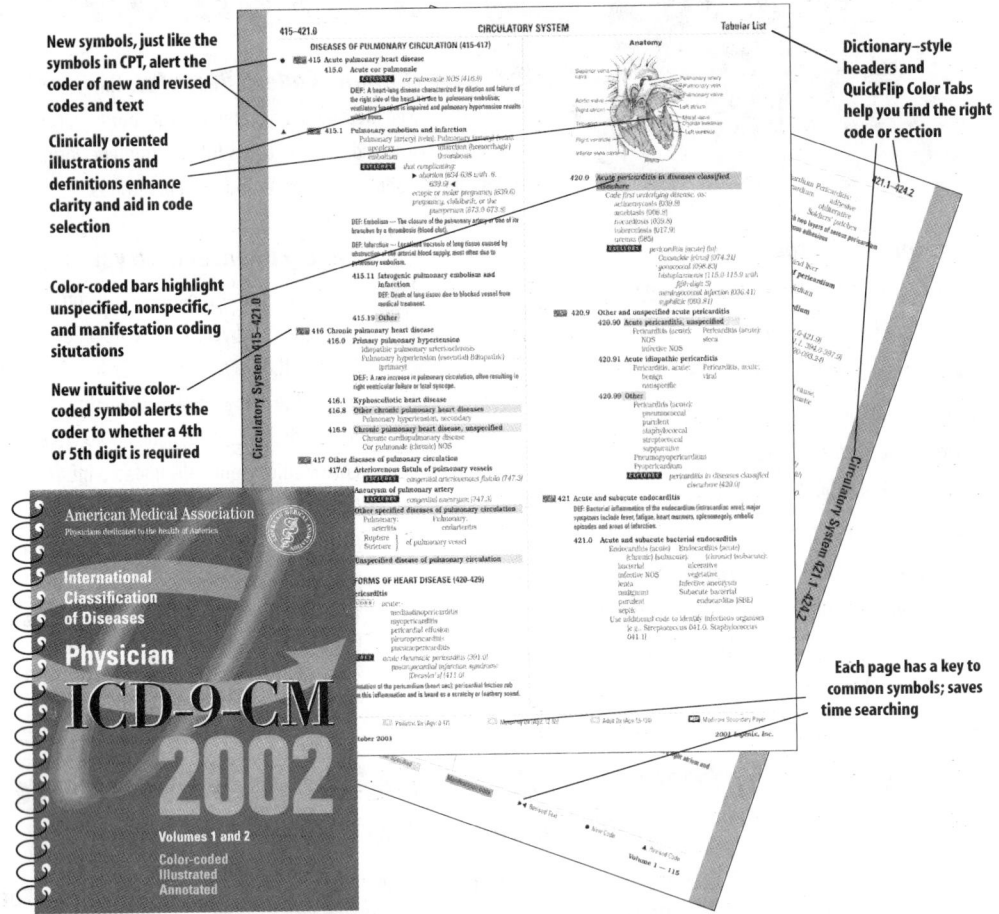